Management of Strategy

CONCEPTS AND CASES

Michael A. Hitt
Texas A&M University

Robert E. Hoskisson
Arizona State University

R. Duane Ireland
Texas A&M University

THOMSON
™
SOUTH-WESTERN

D1556346

Australia · Brazil · Canada · Mexico · Singapore · Spain · United Kingdom · United States

THOMSON

SOUTH-WESTERN

Management of Strategy: Concepts and Cases
Michael A. Hitt, Robert E. Hoskisson, and R. Duane Ireland

VP/Editorial Director:
Jack W. Calhoun

VP/Editor-in-Chief:
Melissa Acuña

Executive Editor:
John Szilagyi

Sr. Developmental Editor:
Mardell Glinski Schultz

Sr. Marketing Manager:
Kimberly Kanakes

Sr. Production Project Manager:
Cliff Kallemeyn

Technology Project Editor:
Kristen Meere

Art Director:
Tippy McIntosh

Sr. Manufacturing Coordinator:
Doug Wilke

Production House:
Lachina Publishing Services

Printer:
China Translation & Printing Services, Ltd.

Cover Image:
© Getty Images

Library of Congress Control Number:
2005911294

For more information about our products, contact us at:

Thomson Learning Academic Resource Center

1-800-423-0563

Thomson Higher Education
5191 Natorp Boulevard
Mason, OH 45040
USA

To all of my current and former students. I am blessed to have the opportunity to teach and learn from you; there is a little piece of each of you in this book.

—Michael A. Hitt

To my dear wife, Kathy, who has been my greatest friend and support through life, and I hope will remain so into the eternities.

—Robert E. Hoskisson

To Jackson Blair Funkhouser, my wonderful new grandson. My hopes for you are that you will always smile, that you will open your heart to those who love you, that you will keep the fire burning, and that you will never forget to dream, baby, dream. I love you, Jackson.

—R. Duane Ireland

Brief
Contents

CHAPTER 5   *The Competitive Nature of Strategy 130*

CHAPTER 6   *Strategy at the Corporate Level 158*

CHAPTER 7   *Acquisitions and Mergers 188*

Part 3 Strategic Actions: Strategy Implementation 288

Part 4   Cases

Case Title	Energy/ Manufacturing	Service	Consumer Goods	Food/Retail	
9Live		X			
Bank One		X			
China on the I-Way					
CQUAY Technologies					
Dell in China	X				
General Motors Defense	X				
Louis V. Gerstner Jr.	X				
Humana Inc.		X			
L'Oréal's Business Strategy			X		
Lucchetti				X	
Lufthansa		X			
MapQuest		X			
Marks and Spencer				X	
Mass Retailing in Asia		X		X	
News Corp. in 2005					
ONGC's Growth Strategy	X				
Tata Steel	X				
Viacom					
Wal-Mart Stores Inc.		X		X	
Whole Foods Market				X	

High Technology	Media/ Entertainment/ Communication	International Perspective	Social/ Ethical Issues	Industry Perspective	Chapters
	X	X	X	X	2, 13
			X	X	1, 12
X		X			1, 2
X		X			3, 7, 9
X		X			5, 8
					5, 6, 9
X					1, 6, 11
			X	X	1, 12
		X			4, 13
		X			6, 8
		X			6, 9, 10, 12
X				X	3, 9, 13
		X			10, 12
		X		X	3, 5, 8
	X				3, 7
					2, 3, 6, 10
		X	X		1, 6, 12
	X				10, 12
		X			4, 8
					2, 3, 4

Our goal in writing this international edition of this book is to present a new up-to-date standard for explaining the strategic management process. To reach this goal, we present you with an intellectually rich yet thoroughly practical analysis of strategic management.

With each edition, we are challenged and invigorated by the goal of establishing a new standard for presenting strategic management knowledge in a readable style. We carefully study the most recent academic research to ensure that the strategic management content presented is highly current and relevant for organizations. In addition, we continuously read articles appearing in many different business publications (e.g., *Wall Street Journal, Business Week, Fortune, Barron's,* and *Fast Company,* to name just a few) to identify valuable examples of how actual companies use the strategic management process. Many of the hundreds of companies we discuss in the book will be quite familiar to you, but some new and different companies are also included. In particular, we use examples of companies from across the world to demonstrate how globalized business has become in the 21st century. To maximize your opportunities to learn as you read and think about how actual companies are using the relevant strategic management tools, techniques, and concepts (based in the most current research), we emphasize a lively and user-friendly writing style.

There are several *characteristics* of this international edition of our book that are intended to enhance your learning opportunities:

- This book presents you with the most comprehensive and thorough coverage of strategic management that is available in the market.
- The research used in this book is drawn from the "classics" as well as the most recent contributions to the strategic management literature. The historically significant (or classical) research provides the foundation for much of what is known about strategic management, while the most recent contributions reveal insights about how to effectively use strategic management in the complex, global business environment in which most firms operate and try to outperform their competitors. Our book also presents you with many examples of how firms use the strategic management tools, techniques, and concepts developed by leading researchers. Indeed, this book is strongly application oriented and presents readers with more examples and applications of strategic management concepts, techniques, and tools than all other strategic management texts. In this edition, for example, we examine more than 600 companies to describe the use of strategic management tools, techniques, or concepts. Collectively, no other strategic management book presents you with the *combination* of useful and insightful *research* and *applications* in a wide variety of organizations as is available in this text.
- We carefully *integrate* two of the most popular and well-known theoretical concepts in the strategic management field: industrial-organization economics and the resource-based view of the firm. Other texts emphasize usually one of these two theories (at the cost of explaining the other one to describe strategic management). However, such an approach is incomplete; research and practical experience indicate that both theories play a major role in understanding the linkage between strategic management and organizational success. No other book integrates these two theoretical perspectives effectively to explain the strategic management process and its application in all types of organizations.
- We use the ideas of prominent scholars (e.g., Richard Bettis, Alfred Chandler, Kathy Eisenhardt, Sumantra Ghoshal, Don Hambrick, Gary Hamel, Rosabeth Kanter, Rita McGrath, Michael Porter, C. K. Prahalad, Richard Rumelt, Ken Smith, David Teece, Oliver Williamson, and numerous others) to shape the discussion of *what* strategic management is. We describe the practices of prominent executives and practitioners (e.g., Carlos Gutierrez, Reed Hastings, Jeffrey Immelt, Steven Jobs,

Herb Kelleher, Anne Mulcahy, Meg Whitman, and many others) to help us describe *how* strategic management is used in many different types of organizations.

- We (authors of this book) are also active scholars. We conduct research on different strategic management topics. Our interest in doing so is to contribute to the strategic management literature and to better understand how to effectively apply strategic management tools, techniques, and concepts to increase organizational performance. Thus, our own research is integrated in the appropriate chapters along with the research of other scholars.

In addition to our book's *characteristics,* as listed above, there are some specific *features* of this international edition that we want to highlight for you:

- **New Opening Cases and Strategic Focus Segments.** We continue our tradition of providing all-new Opening Cases and Strategic Focus segments. In addition, new company-specific examples are included in each chapter. Through all of these venues, we present readers with a wealth of examples of how actual organizations, most of which compete internationally as well as in their home markets, use the strategic management process to increase their ability to compete and achieve higher performance.
- **An Exceptional Balance** between current research and applications of it in actual (and mostly widely recognized) organizations. The content has not only the best research documentation but also the largest amount of effective firm examples to help active learners understand the different types of strategies that organizations use to achieve their vision and mission.
- **All New Cases** with an effective mix of organizations headquartered or based in the United States and a number of other countries. Many of the cases have enhanced financial analyses as part of the Case Notes available to instructors. These timely cases present active learners with opportunities to apply the strategic management process and understand organizational conditions and contexts and to make appropriate recommendations to effectively deal with critical concerns.
- **Lively, Concise Writing Style** to hold readers' attention and to increase their interest in strategic management.
- **Continuing, Updated Coverage** of vital strategic management topics such as competitive rivalry and dynamics, strategic alliances, mergers and acquisitions, international strategies, corporate governance, and ethics. Also, we continue to be the only book in the market with a separate chapter devoted to strategic entrepreneurship.
- **Full four-color** format to enhance readability by attracting and maintaining readers' interests.

To maintain current and up-to-date content, several new concepts are explored in this international edition. New content is provided in Chapter 2 on the concept of complementors. Complementors are a network of companies that sell goods or services that "complement" the focal firm's own good or service. For example, a range of complements is necessary to sell automobiles, including financial services to arrange credit, luxury options including stereo equipment, extended warranties, etc. These complementary products often facilitate a focal firm's ability to sell its products to the consumer.

In Chapter 7, we emphasize how cross-border acquisitions are used to implement firms' strategies and influence their performance. Examples include the Lenovo Group's acquisition of the PC assets of IBM and CNOOC's failed acquisition of Unocal Corporation. Both Lenovo and CNOOC are Chinese companies. We also emphasize the restructuring of large diversified business groups such as the Tata Group in India.

One of the interesting ideas newly introduced in Chapter 8 dealing with international strategy is the effect that recent changes in intellectual property right laws have in both India and China. Multinational firms based in other countries have called for stronger laws to protect their intellectual property in those countries. Interestingly, many of India and China's companies are beginning to emphasize innovation instead of imitating other multinationals' products; therefore, these companies welcome stronger patent protections for intellectual property that they develop.

In Chapter 10, we examine the current impact on firms of the Sarbanes-Oxley (SOX) Act enacted by the U.S. Congress. Although the legal changes were strongly desired by the market, they have increased the intensity of corporate governance mechanisms and have been costly to firms while simultaneously making the strategic management process more risk averse and conservative.

New structures used by transnational firms are described in Chapter 11. Two alternative structures are illustrated as we discover new ways that firms are implementing this emerging strategy to compete globally. The new strategy and structure combinations are illustrated in changes at Unilever Corporation, exemplifying the evolution in structural design.

In Chapter 12, "Leadership," the discussion of managing the firm's resource portfolio has been further enriched with particular focus on the development and use of human capital and social capital.

Supplements

INSTRUCTORS

Instructor Case Notes (Available for download at http://aise.swlearning.com) Prepared by six exceptional case note writers: R. Apana, University of Cincinnati; Charles Byles, Virginia Commonwealth University; Joyce Claterbos, University of Kansas; Tammy Ferguson, University of Louisiana, Lafayette; Marta White, Georgia State University; and Paul Mallette, Colorado State University. All new case notes provide details about the 20 cases found in the second part of the main text. The case notes writers provide consistent and thorough support for instructors, following the method espoused by the author team for preparing an effective case analysis. The case notes for this international edition have been written in great detail and include questions and answers throughout along with industry and company background and resolutions wherever possible.

Instructor's Resource Manual (Available for download at http://aise .swlearning.com) Prepared by Leslie E. Palich, Baylor University. The Instructor's Resource Manual, organized around each chapter's knowledge objectives, includes ideas about how to approach each chapter and how to reinforce essential principles with extra examples. The support product includes lecture outlines, chapter review questions with detailed answers, experiential exercises with instructions, and additional assignments.

Certified Test Bank (Available for download at http://aise.swlearning.com) Prepared by Janelle Dozier and verified for accuracy by Amyn Rehman Dhamani. Thoroughly revised and enhanced, test bank questions are linked to each chapter's knowledge objectives and are ranked by difficulty and question type. We provide an ample number of application questions throughout and we have also retained scenario-based questions as a means of adding in-depth problem-solving questions. With this edition, we introduce the concept of certification, whereby another qualified academic has proofread and verified the accuracy of the test bank questions and answers.

PowerPoint (Available for download at http://aise.swlearning.com) Prepared by Charlie Cook, University of West Alabama. An all-new PowerPoint presentation, created for this international edition, provides support for lectures emphasizing key concepts, key terms, and instructive graphics. Slides can also be used by students as an aid to note-taking.

WebTutor™ WebTutor is used by an entire class under the direction of the instructor and is particularly convenient for distance learning courses. It provides Web-based learning resources to students as well as powerful communication and other course management tools, including course calendar, chat, and e-mail for instructors. WebTutor is available on WebCT (0-324-43110-4) and Blackboard (0-324-43111-2). See http://webtutor.thomsonlearning.com for more information.

Resource Integration Guide (**Available for download at http://aise .swlearning.com**) When you start with a new—or even familiar—text, the amount of supplemental material can seem overwhelming. Identifying each element of a supplement package and piecing together the parts that fit your particular needs can be time-consuming. After all, you may use only a small fraction of the resources available to help you plan, deliver, and evaluate your class. We have created a resource guide to help you and your students extract the full value from the text and its wide range of exceptional supplements. The RIG organizes the book's resources and provides planning suggestions to help you conduct your class, create assignments, and evaluate your students' mastery of the subject. Whatever your teaching style or circumstance, there are planning suggestions to meet your needs. The broad range of techniques provided in the guide helps you increase your repertoire as a teaching expert and enrich your students' learning and understanding. We hope this map and its suggestions enable you to discover new and exciting ways to teach your course.

Acknowledgments

We express our appreciation for the excellent support received from our editorial and production team at South-Western. We especially wish to thank John Szilagyi, our editor, Mardell Glinski Schultz, our senior developmental editor, Kimberly Kanakes, our senior marketing manager, and Cliff Kallemeyn, our production editor. We are grateful for their dedication, commitment, and outstanding contributions to development and publication of this book and its package of support materials.

We are very indebted to the reviewers of earlier editions in preparation for this current edition:

Lowell Busenitz, University of Oklahoma
Radha Chaganti, Rider University
Joyce A. Claterbos, University of Kansas
Harry Domicone, California Lutheran University
Ranjan Karri, Bryant University
Hema Krishnan, Xavier University
Joe Mahoney, University of Illinois at Urbana-Champaign
Paul Mallette, Colorado State University

Ralph W. Parrish, University of Central Oklahoma
Phillip Phan, Rensselaer Polytech Institute
Katsuhiko Shimizu, University of Texas, San Antonio
Marta Szabo White, Georgia State University
Eric Wiseman, University of Colorado, Boulder

Finally, we are very appreciative of the following people for the time and care that went into the preparation of the supplements to accompany this edition:

R. Apana, University of Cincinnati

Charles Byles, Virginia Commonwealth University

Joyce Claterbos, University of Kansas

Charlie Cook, University of West Alabama

Janelle Dozier

Tammy Ferguson, University of Louisiana, Lafayette

Les Palich, Baylor University

Amyn Rehman Dhamani

Marta White, Georgia State University

Paul Mallette, Colorado State University

Michael A. Hitt · **Robert E. Hoskisson** · **R. Duane Ireland**

Michael A. Hitt

Michael A. Hitt is a Distinguished Professor and holds the Joseph Foster Chair in Business Leadership and the C. W. and Dorothy Conn Chair in New Ventures at Texas A&M University. He received his Ph.D. from the University of Colorado. He has coauthored or coedited 25 books and 130 journal articles.

Some of his books are: *Downscoping: How to Tame the Diversified Firm* (Oxford University Press, 1994); *Mergers and Acquisitions: A Guide to Creating Value for Stakeholders* (Oxford University Press, 2001); *Competing for Advantage* (South-Western College Publishing, 2004); and *Understanding Business Strategy* (South-Western College Publishing, 2006). He is coeditor of several recent books: *Managing Strategically in an Interconnected World* (1998); *New Managerial Mindsets: Organizational Transformation and Strategy Implementation* (1998); *Dynamic Strategic Resources: Development, Diffusion and Integration* (1999); *Winning Strategies in a Deconstructing World* (John Wiley & Sons, 2000); *Handbook of Strategic Management* (2001); *Strategic Entrepreneurship: Creating a New Integrated Mindset* (2002); *Creating Value: Winners in the New Business Environment* (Blackwell Publishers, 2002); *Managing Knowledge for Sustained Competitive Advantage* (Jossey Bass, 2003); and *Great Minds in Management: The Process of Theory Development* (Oxford University Press, 2005). He has served on the editorial review boards of multiple journals, including the *Academy of Management Journal, Academy of Management Executive, Journal of Applied Psychology, Journal of Management, Journal of World Business,* and *Journal of Applied Behavioral Sciences.* Furthermore, he has served as Consulting Editor and Editor of the *Academy of Management Journal.* He is President-Elect of the Strategic Management Society and is a Past President of the Academy of Management.

He is a Fellow in the Academy of Management and in the Strategic Management Society. He received an honorary doctorate from the Universidad Carlos III de Madrid and is an Honorary Professor and Honorary Dean at Xi'an Jiao Tong University. He has received several awards for his scholarly research and he received the Irwin Outstanding Educator Award and the Distinguished Service Award from the Academy of Management.

Robert E. Hoskisson

Robert E. Hoskisson holds the W. P. Carey Chair in the Department of Management at the W. P. Carey School of Business at Arizona State University. He received his Ph.D. from the University of California–Irvine. His research topics focus on international diversification, privatization and cooperative strategy, product diversification, corporate governance, and acquisitions and divestitures. He teaches courses in corporate and international strategic management, cooperative strategy, and strategy consulting, among others. Professor Hoskisson has served on several editorial boards for such publications as the *Academy of Management Journal* (including Consulting Editor and Guest Editor of a special issue), *Strategic Management Journal, Journal of Management* (including Associate Editor), and *Organization Science.* He has coauthored several books, including *Understanding Business Strategy: Concepts and Cases* (South-Western/Thomson Learning); *Strategic Management: Competitiveness and Globalization,* 6th Edition (South-Western/Thomson Learning); *Competing for Advantage* (South-Western/Thomson Learning); and *Downscoping: How to Tame the Diversified Firm* (Oxford University Press). Professor Hoskisson's research has appeared in more than 90 publications, including the *Academy of Management Journal, Academy of Management Review, Strategic Management Journal, Organization Science, Journal of Management, Journal of Management Studies, Academy of Management Executive,* and *California Management*

Review. He is a Fellow of the Academy of Management and a charter member of the Academy of Management Journal's Hall of Fame. He also served for three years as a Representative-at-Large on the Board of Governors of the Academy of Management. He is currently on the Board of Directors of the Strategic Management Society and is a member of the Academy of International Business.

R. Duane Ireland

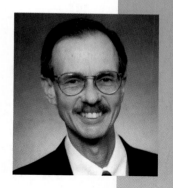

R. Duane Ireland holds the Foreman R. and Ruby S. Bennett Chair in Business in the Mays Business School, Texas A&M University. He also serves as the head of the management department in the Mays School. He teaches strategic management courses at all levels (undergraduate, masters, doctoral, and executive). His research, which focuses on diversification, innovation, corporate entrepreneurship, and strategic entrepreneurship, has been published in a number of journals, including *Academy of Management Journal, Academy of Management Review, Academy of Management Executive, Administrative Science Quarterly, Strategic Management Journal, Journal of Management, Human Relations,* and *Journal of Management Studies,* among others. His recently published books include *Understanding Business Strategy, Concepts and Cases* (South-Western College Publishing, 2006), *Entrepreneurship: Successfully Launching New Ventures* (Prentice-Hall, 2006), and *Competing for Advantage* (South-Western College Publishing, 2004). He is coeditor of *The Blackwell Entrepreneurship Encyclopedia* (Blackwell Publishers, 2005) and *Strategic Entrepreneurship: Creating a New Mindset* (Blackwell Publishers, 2001). He is serving or has served as a member of the editorial review boards for a number of journals, including *Academy of Management Journal, Academy of Management Review, Academy of Management Executive, Journal of Management, Journal of Business Venturing, Entrepreneurship Theory and Practice, Journal of Business Strategy,* and *European Management Journal,* among others. Currently, he is an associate editor for *Academy of Management Journal.* He has coedited special issues of *Academy of Management Review, Academy of Management Executive, Journal of Business Venturing, Strategic Management Journal,* and *Journal of High Technology and Engineering Management.* He received awards for the best article published in *Academy of Management Executive* (1999) and *Academy of Management Journal* (2000). In 2001, his coauthored article published in *Academy of Management Executive* won the Best Journal Article in Corporate Entrepreneurship Award from the U.S. Association for Small Business & Entrepreneurship (USASBE). He is a Fellow of the Academy of Management. He recently completed a three-year term as a Representative-at-Large member of the Academy of Management's Board of Governors. He is a Research Fellow in the National Entrepreneurship Consortium. He received the 1999 Award for Outstanding Intellectual Contributions to Competitiveness Research from the American Society for Competitiveness and the USASBE Scholar in Corporate Entrepreneurship Award (2004) from USASBE.

Management
of Strategy

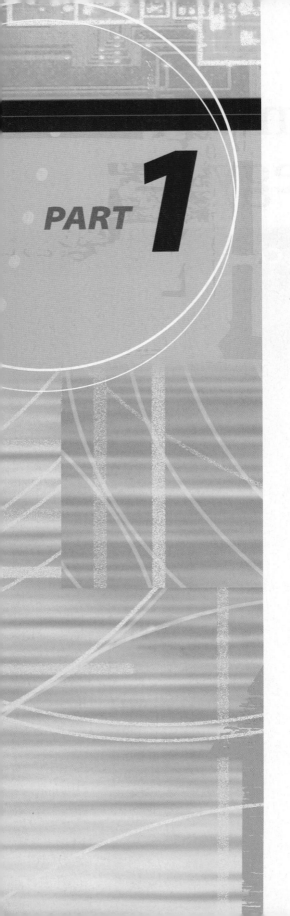

PART **1**

STRATEGIC MANAGEMENT INPUTS

Strategic Management

KNOWLEDGE OBJECTIVES

Studying this chapter should provide you with the strategic management knowledge needed to:

1. Define strategic competitiveness, strategy, competitive advantage, above-average returns, and the strategic management process.

2. Describe the 21st-century competitive landscape and explain how globalization and technological changes shape it.

3. Use the industrial organization (I/O) model to explain how firms can earn above-average returns.

4. Use the resource-based model to explain how firms can earn above-average returns.

5. Describe vision and mission and discuss their value.

6. Define stakeholders and describe their ability to influence organizations.

7. Describe the work of strategic leaders.

8. Explain the strategic management process.

© JOE POLIMENI/GENERAL MOTORS/HANDOUT/REUTERS/CORBIS

One possible strategy GM could use to improve its performance would be to produce a smaller number of models but focus more on design and engineering.

General Motors: How Bright Is the Future?

Declining market share, cost disadvantages relative to some competitors, increasing competition from firms in emerging economies such as China, a downgrade of its debt, and continuing increases in the costs of its health care programs. These are some of the most serious issues facing General Motors (GM).

When thinking about today's GM in terms of the issues it faces, one might wonder if it can get much worse. If nothing else, the status of this huge firm (with global sales of $193 billion in 2004) shows that "no company is too big to fail, or at last shrink dramatically. Not even mighty GM." How did GM get itself into so much trouble? What can this huge company do to reverse its fortunes?

Just how serious is the situation facing GM? To answer this question, consider the following facts. In mid-2005, GM was cash-flow negative, meaning that the firm was consuming more cash than it was earning by selling cars. Some analysts concluded that GM was "saddled with a $1,600-per-vehicle handicap in so-called legacy costs, mostly retiree health and pension benefits." Between the spring of 2000 and roughly the middle of 2005, GM lost 74 percent of its market value. In light of the firm's more recent performance in the design, manufacture, distribution, and service of cars and trucks, some argue that "GM has effectively become a finance company that actually loses money making cars." Others suggest that "it's easy to view [GM] as a huge medical and pension provider with a side business in manufacturing." Perhaps shockingly, given GM's historical prominence in the global economy, in 2005 a few analysts were suggesting that bankruptcy was a viable option for GM. In spite of these difficulties, that same year billionaire investor Kirk Kerkorian boosted his stake in GM to roughly 9 percent. To gain a return on his investment, Kerkorian might challenge GM's board of directors to "sell off noncore assets, cut costs, or restructure the bloated auto business far faster than current management appears inclined to do."

To reverse its fortunes and significantly improve its performance (actions and outcomes with the potential to satisfy Kerkorian as well as the firm's other investors), it seems that GM needs to act quickly and boldly. When we think about influences on GM's performance and as well as corrective actions the firm could take, we should remember that conditions in GM's external environment are outside its direct control. Raw materials costs, for example, were increasing dramatically across the globe in 2005. Because of these increases, GM anticipated spending at least another $500 million to purchase steel products needed to produce its cars and trucks. However, there are actions GM could take to influence its performance.

Perhaps the most basic set of actions GM could take would be to "make cars people actually want to buy." This seems harsh, and perhaps it is to a degree. On the other hand, the past several decades are ones in which GM made design and engineering compromises so its plants could continue to keep up production volume. Perhaps GM would be better served by focusing on a smaller number of products. Rather than producing what some see as "me-too nameplates" (e.g., the differences across the Pontiac, Buick, and Chevrolet nameplates are not easily identified), GM could benefit from presenting consumers with a smaller number of car and truck models, but ones that have interesting designs and high-quality engineering.

The following statistics are interesting in terms of focus. At the time GM offered 89 nameplates across eight brands in North America, Toyota was offering 26 nameplates across three brands. Among other positive outcomes, focusing on a smaller number of brands and nameplates increases the likelihood that products will be distinctive and allows for marketing campaigns to be crisply targeted to precisely identified customer groups. To sharpen its product focus, GM eliminated the Oldsmobile brand a few years ago. Some analysts think that Pontiac, Buick, and Saab should also be shut down. In addition, closing at least five of its assembly plants and producing roughly 4 million cars per year for the North American market instead of the current 5.1 million are other possible courses of action for the firm to pursue. Although needed, taking actions such as these will be difficult, in that GM is a large bureaucratic firm in which there seems to be a fair amount of opposition to the possibility of initiating significant changes. On the other hand, can GM afford not to change how it competes?

Sources: B. Bremner & K. Kerwin, 2005, Here come Chinese cars, *Business Week,* June 6, 34–37; D. Welch, 2005, GM: Flirting with the nuclear option, *Business Week,* July 4, 39–40; D. Welch & D. Beucke, 2005, Why GM's plan won't work, *Business Week,* May 9, 85–93; D. Welch & N. Byrnes, 2005, GM is losing traction, *Business Week,* February 7, 74–76; D. Welch, R. Grover, & E. Thornton, 2005, Just what GM needs, *Business Week,* May 16, 36–37; A. Taylor, III, 2005, GM's new crop: Hot or not? *Business Week,* June 27, 32; 2005, How to keep GM off the disassembly line, *Business Week,* May 9, 116.

As we see from the Opening Case, GM is having difficulty achieving the levels of success desired by people who have a stake in the firm's performance. However, the firm does have the potential to be successful. The posting of record first-half sales in China at mid-year 2005, coupled with the expectation of more than 20 percent growth for the full year, is an example of what GM can do.[1] Nonetheless, given the facts presented in the Opening Case, it is likely that stockholders, employees, suppliers, customers, local communities, and others affected by GM's performance are not fully satisfied with the firm's current accomplishments. Because of this, we can suggest that that GM's strategies aren't as effective as perhaps could be the case. In Chapter 2, you will learn more about how the external environment is affecting GM.

In the final analysis, though, we can be confident in believing that those leading GM want their firm to be highly competitive (something we call a condition of *strategic competitiveness*) and want it to earn profits in the form of *above-average returns*. These are important outcomes firms seek to accomplish when using the strategic management process (see Figure 1.1). The strategic management process is fully explained in this book. We introduce you to this process in the next few paragraphs.

Strategic competitiveness is achieved when a firm successfully formulates and implements a value-creating strategy. A **strategy** is an integrated and coordinated set of commitments and actions designed to exploit core competencies and gain a competitive advantage. When choosing a strategy, firms make choices among competing alternatives. In this sense, the chosen strategy indicates what the firm intends to do as well as what it does not intend to do. Sony Corp., for example, unveiled a new strategy in September 2005 that was intended to restore the firm's ability to earn above-average returns. Changes in the manufacture and distribution of televisions and in its portable music players' products are examples of issues Sony addressed when altering its strategy. Comments by Howard Stringer, Sony's new CEO, demonstrate that choices were being made: "We cannot fight battles on every front. We have to make choices . . . and decide what the company's priorities ought to be."[2]

A firm has a **competitive advantage** when it implements a strategy competitors are unable to duplicate or find too costly to try to imitate.[3] An organization can be confi-

FIGURE 1.1 The Strategic Management Process

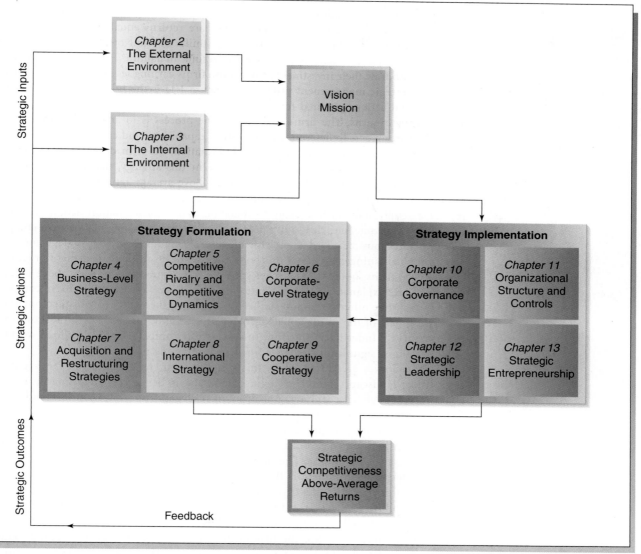

dent that its strategy has resulted in one or more useful competitive advantages only after competitors' efforts to duplicate its strategy have ceased or failed. In addition, firms must understand that no competitive advantage is permanent.[4] The speed with which competitors are able to acquire the skills needed to duplicate the benefits of a firm's value-creating strategy determines how long the competitive advantage will last.[5]

Above-average returns are returns in excess of what an investor expects to earn from other investments with a similar amount of risk. **Risk** is an investor's uncertainty about the economic gains or losses that will result from a particular investment.[6] Returns are often measured in terms of accounting figures, such as return on assets, return on equity, or return on sales. Alternatively, returns can be measured on the basis of stock market returns, such as monthly returns (the end-of-the-period stock price minus the beginning stock price, divided by the beginning stock price, yielding a percentage return). In smaller new venture firms, performance is sometimes measured in terms of the amount and speed of growth (e.g., in annual sales) rather than more traditional profitability measures[7] (the reason for this is that new ventures require time to earn acceptable returns on investors' investments).[8] Understanding how to exploit a competitive advantage is important for firms that seek to earn above-average returns.[9] Firms without a competitive advantage or that are not competing in an attractive industry earn, at best, average returns. **Average returns** are returns equal to those an investor expects to earn from other investments with a similar amount of risk. In the long run, an inability to earn at least average returns results in failure. Failure occurs because investors withdraw their investments from those firms earning less-than-average returns.

The **strategic management process** (see Figure 1.1) is the full set of commitments, decisions, and actions required for a firm to achieve strategic competitiveness and earn above-average returns. The firm's first step in the process is to analyze its external and internal environments to determine its resources, capabilities, and core competencies—the sources of its "strategic inputs." With this information, the firm develops its vision and mission and formulates its strategy. To implement this strategy, the firm takes actions toward achieving strategic competitiveness and above-average returns. The summary of the sequence of activities is as follows: Effective strategic actions that take place in the context of carefully integrated strategy formulation and implementation actions result in desired strategic outcomes. It is a dynamic process, as ever-changing markets and competitive structures must be coordinated with a firm's continuously evolving strategic inputs.[10]

In the remaining chapters of this book, we use the strategic management process to explain what firms should do to achieve strategic competitiveness and earn above-average returns. These explanations demonstrate why some firms consistently achieve competitive success while others fail to do so.[11] As you will see, the reality of global competition is a critical part of the strategic management process and significantly influences firms' performances.[12] Indeed, learning how to successfully compete in the globalized world is one of the most significant challenge for firms competing in the 21st century.[13]

Several topics are discussed in this chapter. First, we describe the 21st-century competitive landscape. This challenging landscape is being created primarily by the emergence of a global economy, globalization resulting from that economy, and rapid technological changes. Next, we examine two models that firms use to gather the information and knowledge required to choose their strategies and decide how to implement them. The insights gained from these models also serve as the foundation for forming the firm's vision and mission. The first model (industrial organization or I/O) suggests that the external environment is the primary determinant of a firm's strategic actions. The key to this model is identifying and competing successfully in an attractive (i.e., profitable) industry.[14] The second model (resource based) suggests that a firm's unique resources and capabilities are the critical link to strategic competitiveness.[15] Thus, the first model is concerned with the firm's external environment while the second model focuses on the firm's internal environment. After discussing vision and mission, direction setting statements influencing the choice and use of organizational strategies, we describe the stakeholders that organizations serve. The degree to which stakeholders' needs can be met directly increases when firms achieve strategic competitiveness and earn above-average returns. Closing the chapter are introductions to strategic leaders and the elements of the strategic management process.

The 21st-Century Competitive Landscape

The fundamental nature of competition in many of the world's industries is changing.[16] The pace of this change is relentless and is increasing. Even determining the boundaries of an industry has become challenging. Consider, for example, how advances in interactive computer networks and telecommunications have blurred the boundaries of the entertainment industry. Today, networks such as ABC, CBS, Fox, NBC, and HBO compete not only among themselves, but also with AT&T, Microsoft, Sony, and others. Partnerships among firms in different segments of the entertainment industry further blur industry boundaries. For example, MSNBC is co-owned by NBC (which itself is owned by General Electric) and Microsoft.[17] With full-motion video and sound rapidly making their way to mobile devices, cellular telephones are also competitors for customers' entertainment expenditures. Wireless companies, for example, are partnering with the music industry to introduce music-playing capabilities into mobile phones.[18] Entertainment giant Walt Disney Company is selling wireless-phone plans to children.[19] That Disney videos can be streamed through phones is yet another example of the difficulty of determining industry boundaries.

Walt Disney company sells wireless-phone plans to children.

Other characteristics of the 21st-century competitive landscape are noteworthy as well. Conventional sources of competitive advantage such as economies of scale and huge advertising budgets are not as effective as they once were. Moreover, the traditional managerial mind-set is unlikely to lead a firm to strategic competitiveness. Managers must adopt a new mind-set that values flexibility, speed, innovation, integration, and the challenges that evolve from constantly changing conditions. The conditions of the competitive landscape result in a perilous business world, one where the investments required to compete on a global scale are enormous and the consequences of failure are severe.[20] Developing and implementing strategy remains an important element of success in this environment. It allows for strategic actions to be planned and to emerge when the environmental conditions are appropriate. It also helps to coordinate the strategies developed by business units in which the responsibility to compete in specific markets is decentralized.[21]

Hypercompetition is a term often used to capture the realities of the 21st-century competitive landscape. Under conditions of hypercompetition, "assumptions of market stability are replaced by notions of inherent instability and change."[22] Hypercompetition results from the dynamics of strategic maneuvering among global and innovative combatants. It is a condition of rapidly escalating competition based on price-quality positioning, competition to create new know-how and establish first-mover advantage, and competition to protect or invade established product or geographic markets.[23] In a hypercompetitive market, firms often aggressively challenge their competitors in the hopes of improving their competitive position and ultimately their performance.[24]

Several factors create hypercompetitive environments and influence the nature of the 21st-century competitive landscape. The two primary drivers are the emergence of a global economy and technology, specifically rapid technological change.

The Global Economy

A **global economy** is one in which goods, services, people, skills, and ideas move freely across geographic borders. Relatively unfettered by artificial constraints, such as tariffs, the global economy significantly expands and complicates a firm's competitive environment.[25]

Interesting opportunities and challenges are associated with the emergence of the global economy.[26] For example, Europe, instead of the United States, is now the world's largest single market, with 700 million potential customers. The European Union and

GE is moving boldly into China and other emerging markets.

the other Western European countries also have a gross domestic product that is over 35 percent higher than the GDP of the United States.[27] China's economy is now larger than Canada's, causing an analyst to suggest, "It's hard to talk meaningfully about the world economy any more without China being included."[28] One indicator of the rapid rise in the capabilities of China's economy is the fact that from roughly 1986 to 2005, China lifted "some 400 million of its 1.3 billion people out of grinding $1-a-day poverty."[29] India, the world's largest democracy, has an economy that also is growing rapidly and now ranks as the world's fourth largest.[30] By 2050, the United States, China, India, Japan, Britain, France, Germany, and South Korea are expected to be the world's largest economies. Russia and Italy are two economies projected to decline in size and influence between 2005 and 2050.[31]

The statistics detailing the nature of the global economy reflect the realities of a hypercompetitive business environment and challenge individual firms to think seriously about the markets in which they will compete. Consider the case of General Electric (GE). Although headquartered in the United States, GE expects that as much as 60 percent of its revenue growth between 2005 and 2015 will be generated by competing in rapidly developing economies (e.g., China and India). The decision to count on revenue growth in developing countries instead of in developed countries such as the United States and European nations seems quite reasonable in the global economy. In fact, according to an analyst, what GE is doing is not by choice but by necessity: "Developing countries are where the fastest growth is occurring and more sustainable growth."[32] Based on its analyses of world markets and their potential, GE estimates that by 2024, China will be the world's largest consumer of electricity and will be the world's largest consumer and consumer-finance market (business areas in which GE competes). GE is making strategic decisions today such as investing significantly in China and India in order to improve its competitive position in what the firm believes are becoming vital sources of revenue and profitability. Similarly, FedEx estimates that in no more than 10 years, the firm will generate the bulk of its revenue growth from business activities outside the United States, not from its domestic operations. Brazil and India are two markets in which the firm is now making significant investments in anticipation of revenue growth possibilities.[33]

The March of Globalization

Globalization is the increasing economic interdependence among countries and their organizations as reflected in the flow of goods and services, financial capital, and knowledge across country borders.[34] Globalization is a product of a larger number of firms competing against one another in an increasing number of global economies.

In globalized markets and industries, financial capital might be obtained in one national market and used to buy raw materials in another one. Manufacturing equipment bought from a third national market can then be used to produce products that are sold in yet a fourth market. Thus, globalization increases the range of opportunities for companies competing in the 21st-century competitive landscape.[35]

Wal-Mart, for instance, is trying to achieve boundaryless retailing with global pricing, sourcing, and logistics. Through boundaryless retailing, the firm seeks to make the movement of goods and the use of pricing strategies as seamless among all of its international operations as historically has been the case among its domestic stores. The firm is pursuing this type of retailing on an evolutionary basis. For example, most of Wal-Mart's original international investments were in Canada and Mexico, because it was easier for the firm to rehearse or apply its global practices in countries that are geographically close to its home base, the United States. Based on what it has learned, the firm has now expanded into Europe, South America, and Asia. Today, Wal-Mart is the world's largest retailer (with over 3,600 total units). Internationally, Wal-Mart now employs over 330,000 people in its more than 1,500 international units.[36] Globalization makes it increasingly difficult to think of firms headquartered in various economies throughout the world as domestic-only companies. Consider the following facts about three U.S.-based organizations: On an annual basis, Wal-Mart continues to increase the percent of its total revenue that is coming from its international operations. Approximately 47 percent of operating income in 2004 was generated by McDonald's international operations.[37] And as we just explained, GE expects more than 60 percent of its growth in sales revenue in the foreseeable future to come from operations in emerging markets. The challenge to companies experiencing globalization to the degree of these three firms is to understand the need for culturally sensitive decisions when using the strategic management process and to anticipate ever-increasing complexity in their operations as goods, services, people, and so forth move freely across geographic borders and throughout different economic markets.

Globalization also affects the design, production, distribution, and servicing of goods and services. In many instances, for example, globalization results in higher-quality goods and services. Global competitor Toyota Motor Company provides an example of how this happens. Because Toyota initially emphasized product reliability and superior customer service, the company's products are in high demand across the globe. Because of the demand for its products, Toyota's competitive actions have forced its global competitors to make reliability and service improvements in their operations.[38] Indeed, almost any car or truck purchased today from virtually any manufacturer is of higher quality and is supported by better service than was the case before Toyota began successfully competing throughout the global economy.

Overall, it is important for firms to understand that globalization has led to higher levels of performance standards in many competitive dimensions, including those of quality, cost, productivity, product introduction time, and operational efficiency. In addition to firms competing in the global economy, these standards affect firms competing on a domestic-only basis. The reason for this is that customers will purchase from a global competitor rather than a domestic firm when the global company's good or service is superior. Because workers now flow rather freely among global economies, and because employees are a key source of competitive advantage, firms must understand that increasingly, "the best people will come from . . . anywhere."[39] Overall, firms must learn how to deal with the reality that in the 21st-century competitive landscape, only companies capable of meeting, if not exceeding, global standards typically have the capability to earn above-average returns.[40]

As we have explained, globalization creates opportunities (such as those being pursued by Toyota, Wal-Mart, McDonald's and GE, among many other firms). However, globalization is not risk free. Collectively, the risks of participating outside of a firm's domestic country in the global economy are labeled a "liability of foreignness."[41]

One risk of entering the global market is that typically a fair amount of time is required for firms to learn how to compete in markets that are new to them. A firm's performance can suffer until this knowledge is either developed locally or transferred from the home market to the newly established global location.[42] Additionally, a firm's

Woodforest National Bank has focused on attracting Latino customers.

performance may suffer with substantial amounts of globalization. In this instance, firms may overdiversify internationally beyond their ability to manage these diversified operations.[43] The result of overdiversification can have strong negative effects on a firm's overall performance.[44]

Thus, entry into international markets, even for firms with substantial experience in the global economy such as Toyota, McDonald's, and GE, requires proper use of the strategic management process. In this regard, firms should choose to enter more international markets only when there is a viable opportunity for them to do so and when they have the competitive advantages required to be successful in those markets.

It is also important to note that while global markets are attractive strategic options for some companies, they are not the only source of strategic competitiveness. In fact, for most companies, even for those capable of competing successfully in global markets, it is critical to remain committed to and strategically competitive in the domestic market.[45] And, domestic markets can be testing grounds for possibly entering an international market at some point in the future. For example, some banks operating in Texas recently recognized the attractiveness of Latinos as a distinct customer group. One reason this group is attractive is that fewer than 50 percent of Latinos living in Texas have bank accounts. To attract Latinos, banks took actions such as redesigning their interiors to resemble haciendas, reduced fees on money transfers to Mexico, and started sponsoring community events that are important to the target population. If these efforts prove successful, at some point these banks may, assuming that regulations permit such actions, use the skills gained locally as the foundation for entering an international market such as Mexico.[46]

Technology and Technological Changes

There are three categories of trends and conditions—technology diffusion and disruptive technologies, the information age, and increasing knowledge intensity—through which technology is significantly altering the nature of competition and contributing to unstable competitive environments as a result of doing so.

Technology Diffusion and Disruptive Technologies

The rate of technology diffusion—the speed at which new technologies become available and are used—has increased substantially over the last 15 to 20 years. Consider the following rates of technology diffusion:

> It took the telephone 35 years to get into 25 percent of all homes in the United States. It took TV 26 years. It took radio 22 years. It took PCs 16 years. It took the Internet 7 years.[47]

Perpetual innovation is a term used to describe how rapidly and consistently new, information-intensive technologies replace older ones. The shorter product life cycles resulting from these rapid diffusions of new technologies place a competitive premium on being able to quickly introduce new, innovative goods and services into the marketplace.[48] In fact, when products become somewhat indistinguishable because of the widespread and rapid diffusion of technologies, speed to market with innovative products may be the primary source of competitive advantage (see Chapter 5).[49] Indeed,

© BOB DAEMMRICH/PHOTOEDIT

some argue that increasingly, the global economy is driven by or revolves around constant innovations. Not surprisingly, such innovations must be derived from an understanding of global standards and global expectations in terms of product functionality.[50]

Another indicator of rapid technology diffusion is that it now may take only 12 to 18 months for firms to gather information about their competitors' research and development and product decisions.[51] In the global economy, competitors can sometimes imitate a firm's successful competitive actions within a few days. Once a source of competitive advantage, the protection firms previously possessed through their patents has been stifled by the current rate of technological diffusion. Today, patents may be an effective way of protecting proprietary technology in a small number of industries such as pharmaceuticals. Indeed, many firms competing in the electronics industry often do not apply for patents to prevent competitors from gaining access to the technological knowledge included in the patent application.

Disruptive technologies—technologies that destroy the value of an existing technology and create new markets[52]—surface frequently in today's competitive markets. Think of the new markets created by the technologies underlying the development of products such as iPods, PDAs, WiFi, and the browser.[53] Products such as these are thought by some to represent radical or breakthrough innovations[54] (we talk more about radical innovations in Chapter 13). A disruptive or radical technology can create what is essentially a new industry or can harm industry incumbents. Some incumbents, though, are able to adapt based on their superior resources, experience, and ability to gain access to the new technology through multiple sources (e.g., alliances, acquisitions, and ongoing internal basic research).[55] When a disruptive technology creates a new industry, competitors follow. As explained in the Strategic Focus, Amazon.com's launching created a new industry by making use of a disruptive technology we know as the Internet.

In addition to making innovative use of the Internet to create Amazon.com, Jeff Bezos also uses core competence in technology to study information about its customers. These efforts result in opportunities to understand individual customers' needs and then target goods and services to satisfy those needs. Clearly, Amazon understands the importance of information and knowledge (topics we discuss next) as competitive weapons for use in the 21st-century competitive landscape.

The Information Age

Dramatic changes in information technology have occurred in recent years. Personal computers, cellular phones, artificial intelligence, virtual reality, and massive databases (e.g., Lexis/Nexis) are a few examples of how information is used differently as a result of technological developments. An important outcome of these changes is that the ability to effectively and efficiently access and use information has become an important source of competitive advantage in virtually all industries.[56]

Both the pace of change in information technology and its diffusion will continue to increase. For instance, the number of personal computers in use in the United States is expected to reach 278 million by 2010. The declining costs of information technologies and the increased accessibility to them are also evident in the 21st-century competitive landscape. The global proliferation of relatively inexpensive computing power and its linkage on a global scale via computer networks combine to increase the speed and diffusion of information technologies. Thus, the competitive potential of information technologies is now available to companies of all sizes throughout the world, not only to large firms in Europe, Japan, and North America.

As noted in the Strategic Focus on Amazon, the Internet is another technological innovation contributing to hypercompetition. Available to an increasing number of people throughout the world, the Internet provides an infrastructure that allows the delivery of information to computers in any location. Access to significant quantities of relatively inexpensive information yields strategic opportunities for a number of companies

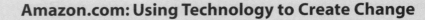

Amazon.com: Using Technology to Create Change

Jeff Bezos, Amazon.com's CEO, founded his company in his basement in 1994. Bezos's innovative concept was to use the still-emerging technology called the Internet to establish an online company selling books. Initially, Bezos intended to sell only books using what became Amazon's proprietary Internet-based software. In fact, Bezos's vision for Amazon was for the firm to be "Earth's biggest bookstore." Because of its growth and expansion, Amazon's vision today is to offer the "Earth's Biggest Selection."

Amazon officially went "live" on July 16, 1995. The first book the firm sold was *Fluid Concepts & Creative Analogies: Computer Models of the Fundamental Mechanisms of Thought*. At the time of Amazon's launching, a large number of business analysts and certainly competitors in the book business (e.g., Barnes & Noble) seriously doubted that consumers would respond favorably to an opportunity to purchase books on the Internet from an unknown start-up venture. However, the skeptics were clearly wrong. Amazon has grown rapidly, establishing its one millionth customer account in 1997, the year the firm went public. The firm now has over 47 million customers. Sales revenue in 2004 was close to $7 billion. Revenue was expected to climb to over $8.5 billion by year-end 2005. Amazon is at the top of *Internet Retailer*'s annual top 400 list, and well ahead of second place Dell Inc. in terms of online business-to-consumer sales.

In the eyes of many, Amazon has become the first successful online retailing marketplace in the United States and probably in the world (given the firm's continuing expansion into international markets). In fact, international sales (from non-North American markets) now account for close to 50 percent of Amazon's sales revenue. Bezos has said that Amazon will continue to devote efforts to increasing the rate of expansion into international markets. The firm sells items around the globe that are grouped into 31 product categories. Apparel, electronics, toys, baby items, banjo cases, kitchen and housewares, travel services, and jewelry are but a few of the products available from Amazon. Because the firm uses "online [instead of physical] shelf space," the goods and services it can add to its offerings are virtually endless in number and variety.

A vast selection of goods and services, a brand name known by many throughout the world, a site that is simple to understand and navigate, and a reputation for reliability are Amazon's competitive advantages. Technological innovations are the source of these advantages. From its inception, Amazon has invested large sums of money in technology to develop an infrastructure that allows it to offer customers a reliable and easy-to-navigate way to buy its products. Consistent with the characteristics of a rapidly changing, unstable environment, Amazon constantly develops new technologies that allow it to improve its offerings to customers. In addition, technology is the source of Amazon's expansion into new areas such as its Web-search service. Through its A9 unit, Amazon offers searches for users to locate restaurants, museums, and other places in particular areas. But Amazon competes with others in this business area including Microsoft, Yahoo!, and Google.

What does the future hold for Amazon? Although it now has competitors that didn't exist at the time of its launching, some analysts think that "Amazon is always one step ahead" of those firms. Bezos believes that the firm's continuing investments in technology will allow it to innovate in ways that prevent competitors from duplicating its competitive advantages.

Sources: J. Kaufman, 2005, A novel heroine: Harriet Klausner, online book reviewer, *Wall Street Journal Online*, www.wsj.com, March 29; M. Mangalindan, 2005, Amazon.com unit launches search for local areas, *Wall Street Journal Online*, www.wsj.com, January 27; J. B. Stewart, 2005, Common sense: Internet big four hold prospects for greater growth, *Wall Street Journal Online*, www.wjs.com, May 4; 2005, Internet: Amazon.com to cut number of merchants, *New York Times Online*, www.nytimes.com, May 12; 2005, Amazon.com, *Standard & Poor's Stock Report*, www.standardandpoors.com, July 2; 2005, At 10 years, Amazon's top challenge: Itself, *Dallas Morning News Online*, www.dallasnews.com, July 4.

in global markets. Virtually all retailers, such as Abercrombie & Fitch, Gap, and Benetton, use the Internet to provide abundant shopping privileges to customers in multiple locations. As a distribution channel, the Internet's popularity is growing in the United States. In mid-2005, for example, over 3 percent of all retail sales (excluding car dealers and gas stations) were accounted for by the Internet.[57] The exploding use of the Internet in China (94 million users in mid-2005, second only to the United States) is creating opportunities for U.S. Internet companies (Google, Yahoo!, and eBay). In fact, the huge potential for these firms caused an analyst to suggest that Internet companies without a major stake in China would experience less growth and a greater possibility of poor long-term performance as a result.[58]

Increasing Knowledge Intensity

Knowledge (information, intelligence, and expertise) is the basis of technology and its application. In the 21st-century competitive landscape, knowledge is a critical organizational resource and is increasingly a valuable source of competitive advantage.[59] Indeed, starting in the 1980s, the basis of competition began shifting from hard assets to intangible resources. For example, "Wal-Mart transformed retailing through its proprietary approach to supply chain management and its information-rich relationships with customers and suppliers."[60] Relationships are an example of an intangible resource.

Knowledge is gained through experience, observation, and inference and is an intangible resource (tangible and intangible resources are fully described in Chapter 3). The value of intangible resources, including knowledge, is growing as a proportion of total shareholder value.[61] The probability of achieving strategic competitiveness in the 21st-century competitive landscape is enhanced for the firm that realizes that its survival depends on the ability to capture intelligence, transform it into usable knowledge, and diffuse it rapidly throughout the company.[62] Therefore, firms must develop (e.g., through training programs) and acquire (e.g., by hiring educated and experienced employees) knowledge, integrate it into the organization to create capabilities, and then apply it to gain a competitive advantage.[63] In addition, firms must build routines that facilitate the diffusion of local knowledge throughout the organization for use everywhere it has value.[64] Firms are better able to do these things when they have strategic flexibility.

Strategic flexibility is a set of capabilities used to respond to various demands and opportunities existing in a dynamic and uncertain competitive environment. Thus, strategic flexibility involves coping with uncertainty and its accompanying risks.[65] Firms should try to develop strategic flexibility in all areas of their operations. However, those working within firms to develop strategic flexibility should understand that this is not an easy task, largely because of inertia that can build up over time.[66]

To be strategically flexible on a continuing basis and to gain the competitive benefits of such flexibility, a firm has to develop the capacity to learn. In the words of John Browne, CEO of British Petroleum: "In order to generate extraordinary value for shareholders, a company has to learn better than its competitors and apply that knowledge throughout its businesses faster and more widely than they do."[67] Continuous learning provides the firm with new and up-to-date sets of skills, which allow it to adapt to its environment as it encounters changes.[68] Firms capable of rapidly and broadly applying what they have learned have strategic flexibility and the resulting capacity to change in ways that will increase the probability of being able to successfully deal with uncertain, hypercompetitive environments. As we discuss in the Strategic Focus, some firms must change dramatically to remain competitive or to again become competitive.

Will the changes being sought at Kodak and Albertsons lead to improved firm performance? Time will provide the answer to this question as it has in part in the Albertsons case. What we do know is that being prepared to consistently engage in change improves the likelihood of a firm achieving above-average returns across time.

Organizational Change: Be Ready, Because It Can't Be Avoided!

In the 21st-century competitive landscape, some argue that competition is about change—being able to change effectively, quickly, and in ways competitors will find difficult to imitate. Through change, organizations have opportunities to grow and to learn. In a continuous cycle, new learning resulting from one change is the foundation for a new cycle of growth and future change. Without change and the resulting learning that pushes this continuous, reinforcing cycle, the likelihood of organizational decline and eventual death greatly increases. Being able to rapidly and successfully change is increasingly an irreplaceable dimension of being able to earn above-average returns in the global economy.

In spite of its importance, change is difficult, for individuals and organizations. If we think of individuals, it may surprise us to learn that roughly 90 percent of heart-bypass patients do not change their lifestyles—even at the risk of dying. The difficulty individuals experience trying to change their behavior suggests the challenge of achieving change in an organization, which, after all, is a collection of what are often change-resistance people! Nonetheless, there are interesting cases about organizational change, two of which we discuss next.

Antonio M. Perez is the new CEO of Eastman Kodak Co. During his previous time at Hewlett-Packard, Perez was "obsessed with creating a new (product) category every two years." Creating new product categories this rapidly and frequently is a function of learning and constant change. In hiring Perez, Kodak's board of directors believed he had the skills to help Kodak introduce new digital products and gain the knowledge required to continue changing frequently and significantly.

Lawrence R. Johnston, a former GE executive, is now Albertsons Inc.'s CEO. In addition to traditional grocery store competitors, Albertsons (as well as other national chains such as Safeway and Kroger) faces a serious threat from Wal-Mart. In fact, estimates are that Wal-Mart will generate over $162 billion in "super-market types of sales" by the end of 2007. This projected amount exceeds the combined annual revenue of Kroger, Albertsons, and Safeway. Knowing that his firm can't compete against Wal-Mart on the basis of price and greater operational efficiencies, Johnston is relying on technology to introduce significant changes at Albertsons as a means of competition. The goal is to change shopping within Albertsons' stores so customers will describe their experience as "quick and easy." To do this, hand-held scanners are available to shoppers in some locations. The scanners are linked to a company database and a global-positioning-satellite system. The scanners will keep tabs of products the consumer has selected as well as direct her or him to the quickest route to take in a store to find a requested item. At the exit, the scanners charge the purchased items to a credit card, allowing the shopper to avoid waiting in a checkout line. A technology-intensive shopping experience such as this will cause major changes in established work patterns among the firm's employees.

What can organizations do to improve their ability to change? One thing to recognize is that there are no shortcuts. Helping a firm learn how to change is hard work—work requiring dedicated efforts on the parts of many. To help firms learn how to effectively and consistently engage in change, research suggests that strategic leaders (whom we talk about more later in this chapter and in full detail in Chapter 12) should engage in a number of actions including the following: (1) phrasing the need for change in ways that appeal to employees' emotions as well as their cognitions, (2) casting the need for change as providing positive outcomes, (3) developing a story to describe the needed changes that is simple, straightforward,

© TIM WIMBORNE/REUTERS/CORBIS

Albertsons is using technology as a competitive strategy.

and appealing, and (4) continuously developing and describing stories about the firm's success with different change efforts. While these actions won't lead to organizational change without disruption and some trepidation on the part of some employees, they do facilitate efforts to improve the chance of success when engaging in organizational change efforts.

Interestingly, if these efforts fail to stimulate change, a firm often has to do something drastic. In September 2005, Albertsons suggested that it was willing to be acquired by the highest bidder. While private equity firms were the most interested initially, one analyst speculated that European discount grocers and competitors to Wal-Mart might be interested: "Britain's Tesco, Belgian retailer Delhaize Group and France's Carrefour were among the likely candidates." Because Albertsons is number two in market share, it would allow these foreign competitors a significant entry opportunity in the United States market. If extensive change does not take place when needed, competitive realities will force changes as illustrated by the Albertsons example.

Sources: 2005, Albertson sale draws bidders, *Los Angeles Times*, www.latimes.com, September 19; A. Deutschman, 2005, Making change, *Fast Company*, May, 52–62; M. Arndt, A. Carter, & C. Arnst, 2005, Needed: More bite to fight fat, *Business Week*, January 31, 36; J. A. Bryne, 2005, The case for change, *Fast Company*, April, 12; J. A. Bryne, 2005, Great work if you can get it, *Fast Company*, April, 14; S. Holmes, 2005, The Jack Welch of the meat aisle, *Business Week*, January 24, 60–61; W. C. Symonds & P. Burrows, 2005, A digital warrior for Kodak, *Business Week*, May 23, 42.

Next, we describe two models firms use to generate the information they need to form their vision and mission and then to select and decide how to implement one or more strategies.

The I/O Model of Above-Average Returns

From the 1960s through the 1980s, the external environment was thought to be the primary determinant of strategies that firms selected to be successful.[69] The industrial organization (I/O) model of above-average returns explains the external environment's dominant influence on a firm's strategic actions. The model specifies that the industry in which a company chooses to compete has a stronger influence on performance than do the choices managers make inside their organizations.[70] The firm's performance is believed to be determined primarily by a range of industry properties, including economies of scale, barriers to market entry, diversification, product differentiation, and the degree of concentration of firms in the industry.[71] These industry characteristics are examined in Chapter 2.

Grounded in economics, the I/O model has four underlying assumptions. First, the external environment is assumed to impose pressures and constraints that determine the strategies that would result in above-average returns. Second, most firms competing within an industry or within a certain segment of that industry are assumed to control similar strategically relevant resources and to pursue similar strategies in light of those resources. Third, resources used to implement strategies are assumed to be highly mobile across firms, so any resource differences that might develop between firms will be short-lived. Fourth, organizational decision makers are assumed to be rational and committed to acting in the firm's best interests, as shown by their profit-maximizing behaviors.[72] The I/O model challenges firms to locate the most attractive industry in which to compete. Because most firms are assumed to have similar valuable resources that are mobile across companies, their performance generally can be increased only when they operate in the industry with the highest profit potential and learn how to use their resources to implement the strategy required by the industry's structural characteristics.[73]

The five forces model of competition is an analytical tool used to help firms with this task. The model (explained in Chapter 2) encompasses several variables and tries to capture the complexity of competition. The five forces model suggests that an industry's profitability (i.e., its rate of return on invested capital relative to its cost of capital) is a function of interactions among five forces: suppliers, buyers, competitive rivalry among firms currently in the industry, product substitutes, and potential entrants to the industry.[74] Firms can use this tool to understand an industry's profit potential and the strategy necessary to establish a defensible competitive position, given the industry's structural characteristics. Typically, the model suggests that firms can earn above-average returns by manufacturing standardized products or producing standardized services at costs below those of competitors (a cost leadership strategy) or by manufacturing differentiated products for which customers are willing to pay a price premium (a differentiation strategy). The cost leadership and product differentiation strategies are fully described in Chapter 4.

As shown in Figure 1.2, the I/O model suggests that above-average returns are earned when firms implement the strategy dictated by the characteristics of the general,

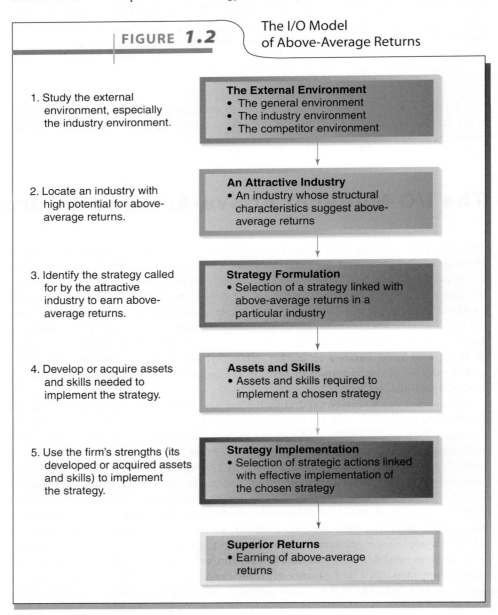

FIGURE 1.2 The I/O Model of Above-Average Returns

1. Study the external environment, especially the industry environment.

The External Environment
- The general environment
- The industry environment
- The competitor environment

2. Locate an industry with high potential for above-average returns.

An Attractive Industry
- An industry whose structural characteristics suggest above-average returns

3. Identify the strategy called for by the attractive industry to earn above-average returns.

Strategy Formulation
- Selection of a strategy linked with above-average returns in a particular industry

4. Develop or acquire assets and skills needed to implement the strategy.

Assets and Skills
- Assets and skills required to implement a chosen strategy

5. Use the firm's strengths (its developed or acquired assets and skills) to implement the strategy.

Strategy Implementation
- Selection of strategic actions linked with effective implementation of the chosen strategy

Superior Returns
- Earning of above-average returns

industry, and competitor environments (environments that are discussed in Chapter 2). Companies that develop or acquire the internal skills needed to implement strategies required by the external environment are likely to succeed, while those that do not are likely to fail. Hence, this model suggests that returns are determined primarily by external characteristics rather than by the firm's unique internal resources and capabilities.

Research findings support the I/O model, in that approximately 20 percent of a firm's profitability can be explained by the industry in which it chooses to compete. This research also shows, however, that 36 percent of the variance in profitability could be attributed to the firm's characteristics and actions.[75] This suggests that both the environment and the firm's characteristics play a role in determining the firm's specific level of profitability. Thus, there is likely a reciprocal relationship between the environment and the firm's strategy, thereby affecting the firm's performance.[76]

As you can see, the I/O model considers a firm's strategy to be a set of commitments, actions, and decisions that are formed in response to the characteristics of the industry in which the firm has decided to compete. The resource-based model, discussed next, takes a different view of the major influences on strategy formulation and implementation.

The Resource-Based Model of Above-Average Returns

The resource-based model assumes that each organization is a collection of unique resources and capabilities. The *uniqueness* of its resources and capabilities is the basis for a firm's strategy and its ability to earn above-average returns.

Resources are inputs into a firm's production process, such as capital equipment, the skills of individual employees, patents, finances, and talented managers. In general, a firm's resources are classified into three categories: physical, human, and organizational capital. Described fully in Chapter 3, resources are either tangible or intangible in nature.

Individual resources alone may not yield a competitive advantage.[77] In fact, resources have a greater likelihood of being a source of competitive advantage when they are formed into a capability. A **capability** is the capacity for a set of resources to perform a task or an activity in an integrative manner. Capabilities evolve over time and must be managed dynamically in pursuit of above-average returns.[78] **Core competencies** are resources and capabilities that serve as a source of competitive advantage for a firm over its rivals. Core competencies are often visible in the form of organizational functions. For example, marketing is a core competence for Philip Morris, a division of the Altria Group, Inc. This means that Philip Morris has used its resources to form marketing-related capabilities that in turn allow the firm to market its products in ways that are superior to how competitors market their products.

According to the resource-based model, differences in firms' performances across time are due primarily to their unique resources and capabilities rather than to the industry's structural characteristics. This model also assumes that firms acquire different resources and develop unique capabilities based on how they combine and use the resources; that resources and certainly capabilities are not highly mobile across firms; and that the differences in resources and capabilities are the basis of competitive advantage.[79] Through continued use, capabilities become stronger and more difficult for competitors to understand and imitate. As a source of competitive advantage, a capability "should be neither so simple that it is highly imitable, nor so complex that it defies internal steering and control."[80]

The resource-based model of superior returns is shown in Figure 1.3. As you will see, the resource-based model suggests that the strategy the firm chooses should allow it to use its competitive advantages in an attractive industry (the I/O model is used to identify an attractive industry).

Not all of a firm's resources and capabilities have the potential to be the basis for competitive advantage. This potential is realized when resources and capabilities are valuable, rare, costly to imitate, and nonsubstitutable.[81] Resources are *valuable* when they allow a firm to take advantage of opportunities or neutralize threats in its external environment. They are *rare* when possessed by few, if any, current and potential competitors. Resources are *costly to imitate* when other firms either cannot obtain them or are at a cost disadvantage in obtaining them compared with the firm that already possesses them. And they are *nonsubstitutable* when they have no structural equivalents.

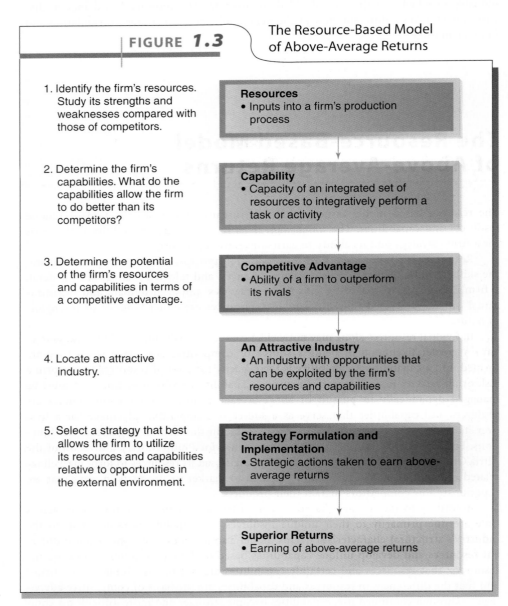

FIGURE **1.3** The Resource-Based Model of Above-Average Returns

1. Identify the firm's resources. Study its strengths and weaknesses compared with those of competitors.

Resources
- Inputs into a firm's production process

2. Determine the firm's capabilities. What do the capabilities allow the firm to do better than its competitors?

Capability
- Capacity of an integrated set of resources to integratively perform a task or activity

3. Determine the potential of the firm's resources and capabilities in terms of a competitive advantage.

Competitive Advantage
- Ability of a firm to outperform its rivals

4. Locate an attractive industry.

An Attractive Industry
- An industry with opportunities that can be exploited by the firm's resources and capabilities

5. Select a strategy that best allows the firm to utilize its resources and capabilities relative to opportunities in the external environment.

Strategy Formulation and Implementation
- Strategic actions taken to earn above-average returns

Superior Returns
- Earning of above-average returns

Many resources can either be imitated or substituted over time. Therefore, it is difficult to achieve and sustain a competitive advantage based on resources alone.[82] When these four criteria are met, however, resources and capabilities become core competencies.

As noted previously, research shows that both the industry environment and a firm's internal assets affect that firm's performance over time.[83] Thus, to form a vision and mission, and subsequently to select one or more strategies and to determine how to implement them, firms use both the I/O and the resource-based models.[84] In fact, these models complement each other in that one (I/O) focuses outside the firm while the other (resource-based) focuses inside the firm. In Chapter 2 we describe how firms use the I/O model, and in Chapter 3 we discuss how firms use the resource-based model. Successful strategy formulation and implementation actions result only when the firm properly uses both models. Next, we discuss the forming of the firm's vision and mission—actions taken after the firm understands the realities of its external (Chapter 2) and internal (Chapter 3) environments.

Vision and Mission

After studying the external environment and the internal environment, the firm has the information it needs to form a vision and a mission (see Figure 1.1). Stakeholders (those who affect or are affected by a firm's performance, as discussed later in the chapter) learn a great deal about a firm by studying its vision and mission. Indeed, a key purpose of vision and mission statements is to inform stakeholders of what the firm is, what it seeks to accomplish, and who it seeks to serve.

Vision

Vision is a picture of what the firm wants to be and, in broad terms, what it wants to ultimately achieve.[85] Thus, a vision statement articulates the ideal description of an organization and gives shape to its intended future. In other words, a vision statement points the firm in the direction of where it would eventually like to be in the years to come. Vision is "big picture" thinking with passion that helps people *feel* what they are supposed to be doing.[86] People feel what they are to do when their firm's vision is simple, positive, and emotional.[87] A vision stretches and challenges people and evokes emotions and dreams. Imagine the dreams evoked and the emotions felt when employees learn that as part of the firm's vision, the new CEO of LG Electronics says, "We must be a great company with great people."[88]

It is also important to note that vision statements reflect a firm's values and aspirations and are intended to capture the heart and mind of each employee and, hopefully, many of its other stakeholders. A firm's vision tends to be enduring while its mission can change in light of changing environmental conditions. A vision statement tends to be relatively short and concise, making it easily remembered. Examples of vision statements include the following:

Our vision is to be the world's best quick service restaurant (McDonald's)

To make the automobile accessible to every American (Ford Motor Company's vision when established by Henry Ford)

As a firm's most important and prominent strategic leader, the CEO is responsible for working with others to form the firm's vision. It is important for the CEO to do this because, in the words of Dan Rosensweig, chief operating officer (COO) for Yahoo!, "With a clear vision and strong leadership, you can make almost anything happen."[89]

Experience shows that the most effective vision statement results when the CEO involves a host of people (e.g., other top-level managers, employees working in different parts of the organization, suppliers, and customers) to develop it. In addition, to help the firm reach its desired future state, a vision statement should be clearly tied to the conditions in the firm's external and internal environments and it must be achievable. Moreover, the decisions and actions of those involved with developing the vision, especially the CEO and the other top-level managers, must be consistent with that vision. In fact, there is nothing worse than for the firm's top-level strategic leaders' actions to be inconsistent with the vision. At McDonald's, for example, a failure to openly provide employees with what they need to quickly and effectively serve customers would be a recipe for disaster.

Mission

The vision is the foundation for the firm's mission. A **mission** specifies the business or businesses in which the firm intends to compete and the customers it intends to serve.[90] As we will learn in Chapter 4, today's customers tend to be quite demanding when it comes to their expectations for product variety and quality.[91]

The firm's mission is more concrete than its vision. However, like the vision, a mission should establish a firm's individuality and should be inspiring and relevant to all stakeholders.[92] Together, vision and mission provide the foundation the firm needs to choose and implement one or more strategies. The probability of forming an effective mission increases when employees have a strong sense of the ethical standards that will guide their behaviors as they work to help the firm reach its vision.[93] Thus, business ethics are a vital part of the firm's discussions to decide what it wants to become (its vision) as well as who it intends to serve and how it desires to serve those individuals and groups (its mission).[94]

As with the vision, the final responsibility for forming the firm's mission rests with the CEO, though the CEO and other top-level managers tend to involve a larger number of people in forming the mission. The main reason for this is that mission deals more directly with product markets and customers. Compared with the CEO and other top-level managers, middle- and first-level managers and other employees have more direct contact with customers and the markets in which they are served. Examples of mission statements include the following:

> *Be the best employer for our people in each community around the world and deliver operational excellence to our customers in each of our restaurants (McDonald's)*

> *Our mission is to be recognized by our customers as the leader in applications engineering. We always focus on the activities customers desire; we are highly motivated and strive to advance our technical knowledge in the areas of material, part design and fabrication technology (LNP, a GE Plastics Company)*

Notice how the McDonald's mission statement flows from its vision of being the world's best quick service restaurant. LNP's mission statement describes the business areas (material, part design, and fabrication technology) in which the firm intends to compete.

While reading the vision and mission statements presented above, you likely recognized that the earning of above-average returns (sometimes called profit maximization) was not mentioned in any of them. The reasons for this are that all firms want to earn above-average returns (meaning that this intention does not differentiate the firm from its rivals) and that desired financial outcomes result from properly serving certain customers while trying to achieving the firm's intended future. In other words, above-average returns are the fruits of the firm's efforts to achieve its vision and mission. In fact, research has shown that having an effectively formed vision and mission has a positive effect on performance as measured by growth in sales, profits, employment, and net worth.[95] In turn, positive firm performance increases the firm's ability to satisfy the interests of its stakeholders (whom we discuss next). The flip side of the coin also seems to be true—namely, the firm without an appropriately formed vision and mission is more likely to fail than the firm that has properly formed vision and mission statements.[96]

Stakeholders

Every organization involves a system of primary stakeholder groups with whom it establishes and manages relationships.[97] **Stakeholders** are the individuals and groups who can affect, and are affected by, the strategic outcomes achieved and who have enforceable claims on a firm's performance.[98] Claims on a firm's performance are enforced through the stakeholders' ability to withhold participation essential to the organization's survival, competitiveness, and profitability.[99] Stakeholders continue to support an organization when its performance meets or exceeds their expectations.[100] Also, recent research suggests that firms effectively managing stakeholder relationships outperform those that do not. Stakeholder relationships can therefore be managed to be a source of competitive advantage.[101]

Although organizations have dependency relationships with their stakeholders, they are not equally dependent on all stakeholders at all times;[102] as a consequence, not every stakeholder has the same level of influence. The more critical and valued a stakeholder's participation, the greater a firm's dependency on it. Greater dependence, in turn, gives the stakeholder more potential influence over a firm's commitments, decisions, and actions. Managers must find ways to either accommodate or insulate the organization from the demands of stakeholders controlling critical resources.[103]

Classifications of Stakeholders

The parties involved with a firm's operations can be separated into at least three groups.[104] As shown in Figure 1.4, these groups are the capital market stakeholders (shareholders and the major suppliers of a firm's capital), the product market stakeholders (the firm's primary customers, suppliers, host communities, and unions representing the workforce), and the organizational stakeholders (all of a firm's employees, including both nonmanagerial and managerial personnel).

Each stakeholder group expects those making strategic decisions in a firm to provide the leadership through which its valued objectives will be reached.[105] The objectives of the various stakeholder groups often differ from one another, sometimes placing those involved with the strategic management process in situations where trade-offs have to be made. The most obvious stakeholders, at least in U.S. organizations, are *shareholders*—individuals and groups who have invested capital in a firm in the expectation of earning a positive return on their investments. These stakeholders' rights are grounded in laws governing private property and private enterprise.

Shareholders want the return on their investment (and, hence, their wealth) to be maximized. Maximization of returns sometimes is accomplished at the expense of investing in a firm's future. Gains achieved by reducing investment in research and

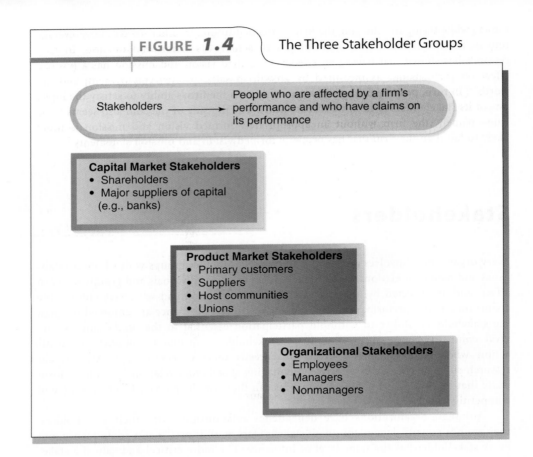

FIGURE **1.4** The Three Stakeholder Groups

Stakeholders ⟶ People who are affected by a firm's performance and who have claims on its performance

Capital Market Stakeholders
- Shareholders
- Major suppliers of capital (e.g., banks)

Product Market Stakeholders
- Primary customers
- Suppliers
- Host communities
- Unions

Organizational Stakeholders
- Employees
- Managers
- Nonmanagers

development, for example, could be returned to shareholders, thereby increasing the short-term return on their investments. However, this short-term enhancement of shareholders' wealth can negatively affect the firm's future competitive ability, and sophisticated shareholders with diversified portfolios may sell their interests if a firm fails to invest in its future. Those making strategic decisions are responsible for a firm's survival in both the short and the long term. Accordingly, it is not in the interests of any stakeholders for investments in the company to be unduly minimized.

In contrast to shareholders, another group of stakeholders—the firm's customers—prefers that investors receive a minimum return on their investments. Customers could have their interests maximized when the quality and reliability of a firm's products are improved, but without a price increase. High returns to customers might come at the expense of lower returns negotiated with capital market shareholders.

Because of potential conflicts, each firm is challenged to manage its stakeholders. First, a firm must carefully identify all important stakeholders. Second, it must prioritize them, in case it cannot satisfy all of them. Power is the most critical criterion in prioritizing stakeholders. Other criteria might include the urgency of satisfying each particular stakeholder group and the degree of importance of each to the firm.[106]

When the firm earns above-average returns, the challenge of effectively managing stakeholder relationships is lessened substantially. With the capability and flexibility provided by above-average returns, a firm can more easily satisfy multiple stakeholders simultaneously. When the firm is earning only average returns, it is unable to maximize the interests of all stakeholders. The objective then becomes one of at least minimally satisfying each stakeholder. Trade-off decisions are made in light of how important the support of each stakeholder group is to the firm. For example, environmental groups may be very important to firms in the energy industry but less important to professional service firms.[107] A firm earning below-average returns does not have the capacity to minimally satisfy all stakeholders. The managerial challenge in this case is to make trade-offs that minimize the amount of support lost from stakeholders. Societal values also influence the general weightings allocated among the three stakeholder groups shown in Figure 1.4. Although all three groups are served by firms in the major industrialized nations, the priorities in their service vary because of cultural differences. Next, we provide more details about each of the three major stakeholder groups.

Capital Market Stakeholders

Shareholders and lenders both expect a firm to preserve and enhance the wealth they have entrusted to it. The returns they expect are commensurate with the degree of risk accepted with those investments (that is, lower returns are expected with low-risk investments, and higher returns are expected with high-risk investments). Dissatisfied lenders may impose stricter covenants on subsequent borrowing of capital. Dissatisfied shareholders may reflect their concerns through several means, including selling their stock.

When a firm is aware of potential or actual dissatisfactions among capital market stakeholders, it may respond to their concerns. The firm's response to stakeholders who are dissatisfied is affected by the nature of its dependency relationship with them (which, as noted earlier, is also influenced by a society's values). The greater and more significant the dependency relationship is, the more direct and significant the firm's response becomes. Given GM's situation, as explained in the Opening Case, it is reasonable to expect that GM's CEO and top-level managers are thinking seriously about what should be done to improve the firm's financial performance in order to satisfy its capital market stakeholders.

Product Market Stakeholders

Some might think that product market stakeholders (customers, suppliers, host communities, and unions) share few common interests. However, all four groups can benefit as firms engage in competitive battles. For example, depending on product and industry characteristics, marketplace competition may result in lower product prices being charged to a firm's customers and higher prices being paid to its suppliers (the firm might be willing to pay higher supplier prices to ensure delivery of the types of goods and services that are linked with its competitive success).

As is noted in Chapter 4, customers, as stakeholders, demand reliable products at the lowest possible prices. Suppliers seek loyal customers who are willing to pay the highest sustainable prices for the goods and services they receive. Host communities want companies willing to be long-term employers and providers of tax revenues without placing excessive demands on public support services. Union officials are interested in secure jobs, under highly desirable working conditions, for employees they represent. Thus, product market stakeholders are generally satisfied when a firm's profit margin reflects at least a balance between the returns to capital market stakeholders (i.e., the returns lenders and shareholders will accept and still retain their interests in the firm) and the returns in which they share.

Organizational Stakeholders

Employees—the firm's organizational stakeholders—expect the firm to provide a dynamic, stimulating, and rewarding work environment. As employees, we are usually satisfied working for a company that is growing and actively developing our skills, especially those skills required to be effective team members and to meet or exceed global work standards. Workers who learn how to use new knowledge productively are critical to organizational success. In a collective sense, the education and skills of a firm's workforce are competitive weapons affecting strategy implementation and firm performance.[108] As suggested by the following statement, strategic leaders are ultimately responsible for serving the needs of organizational stakeholders on a day-to-day basis: "[T]he job of [strategic] leadership is to fully utilize human potential, to create organizations in which people can grow and learn while still achieving a common objective, to nurture the human spirit."[109]

Strategic Leaders

Strategic leaders are people located in different parts of the firm using the strategic management process to help the firm reach its vision and mission. Regardless of their location in the firm, successful strategic leaders are decisive and committed to nurturing those around them[110] and are committed to helping the firm create value for customers and returns for shareholders and other stakeholders.[111]

When identifying strategic leaders, most of us tend to think of chief executive officers (CEOs) and other top-level managers. Clearly, these people are strategic leaders. And, in the final analysis, CEOs are responsible for making certain their firm effectively uses the strategic management process. Indeed, the pressure on CEOs to do this is stronger than ever.[112] However, there are many other people in today's organizations who help choose a firm's strategy and then determine actions to be taken to successfully implement it.[113] The main reason for this is that the realities of 21st-century competition that we discussed earlier in this chapter (e.g., the global economy, globalization, rapid technological change, and the increasing importance of knowledge and people as sources of competitive advantage) are creating a need for those "closest to the action" to be the ones making decisions and determining the actions to be taken.[114] In fact, the most effective CEOs and top-level managers understand how to delegate strategic responsibilities to people throughout the firm who influence the use of organizational resources.[115]

Southwest Airlines has built a unique corporate culture.

Organizational culture also affects strategic leaders and their work. In turn, strategic leaders' decisions and actions shape a firm's culture. **Organizational culture** refers to the complex set of ideologies, symbols, and core values that are shared throughout the firm and that influence how the firm conducts business. It is the social energy that drives—or fails to drive—the organization. For example, highly successful Southwest Airlines is known for having a unique and valuable culture. Its culture encourages employees to work hard but also to have fun while doing so. Moreover, its culture entails respect for others—employees and customers alike. The firm also places a premium on service, as suggested by its commitment to provide POS (Positively Outrageous Service) to each customer. Wal-Mart claims that its continuing success is largely attributable to its culture.[116]

THANH NGUYEN/BLOOMBERG NEWS/LANDOV

Some organizational cultures are a source of disadvantage. Analysts talking about Boeing Co.'s culture suggested that the firm's "dysfunctional corporate culture needs an overhaul, and execs must restore source relations with the Pentagon and Congress." In addition, some allege that Boeing has a "toxic political climate."[117] New CEO W. James McNerney, formerly CEO of 3M, will no doubt take actions to try to correct the dysfunctional aspects of Boeing's culture. It is important for strategic leaders to understand, however, that whether the firm's culture is functional or dysfunctional, their work takes place within the context of that culture. There is a continuing reciprocal relationship between organizational culture and strategic leaders' work, in that the culture shapes how they work while their work helps shape what is an ever-evolving organizational culture.

The Work of Effective Strategic Leaders

Perhaps not surprisingly, hard work, thorough analyses, a willingness to be brutally honest, a penchant for wanting the firm and its people to accomplish more, and common sense are prerequisites to an individual's success as a strategic leader.[118] In addition, strategic leaders must be able to "think seriously and deeply . . . about the purposes of the organizations they head or functions they perform, about the strategies, tactics, technologies, systems, and people necessary to attain these purposes and about the important questions that always need to be asked."[119] Additionally, effective strategic leaders work to set an ethical tone in their firms. The CEO and chairman of Deere & Company speaks plainly about this issue: "We have a slogan around here. No smoke, no mirrors, no tricks: just right down the middle of the field. That's John Deere." The actions suggested by this position helped Deere & Company to earn a rank of sixth on *Business Ethics Magazine*'s 2004 "100 Best Corporate Citizens" list.[120]

Strategic leaders, regardless of their location in the organization, often work long hours, and the work is filled with ambiguous decision situations for which effective solutions are not easily determined.[121] However, the opportunities afforded by this work are appealing and offer exciting chances to dream and to act.[122] The following words, given as advice to the late Time Warner chairman and co-CEO Steven J. Ross by his father, describe the opportunities in a strategic leader's work:

> There are three categories of people—the person who goes into the office, puts his feet up on his desk, and dreams for 12 hours; the person who arrives at 5 A.M. and works for 16 hours, never once stopping to dream; and the person who puts his feet up, dreams for one hour, then does something about those dreams.[123]

The organizational term used for a dream that challenges and energizes a company is vision (discussed earlier in this chapter). Strategic leaders have opportunities to dream and to act, and the most effective ones provide a vision as the foundation for the firm's mission and subsequent choice and use of one or more strategies.

Predicting Outcomes of Strategic Decisions: Profit Pools

Strategic leaders attempt to predict the outcomes of their decisions before taking efforts to

Deere & Company has a strong commitment to ethical practices.

implement them. This is difficult to do, in that many decisions that are a part of the strategic management process are concerned with an uncertain future and the firm's place in that future.[124]

Mapping an industry's profit pool is something strategic leaders can do to anticipate the possible outcomes of different decisions and to focus on growth in profits rather than strictly growth in revenues. A **profit pool** entails the total profits earned in an industry at all points along the value chain (value chain is explained in Chapter 3 and further discussed in Chapter 4).[125] Analyzing the profit pool in the industry may help a firm see something others are unable to see by helping it understand the primary sources of profits in an industry. There are four steps to identifying profit pools: (1) define the pool's boundaries, (2) estimate the pool's overall size, (3) estimate the size of the value-chain activity in the pool, and (4) reconcile the calculations.[126]

Let's think about how General Motors might map the automobile industry's profit pools. First, GM would need to define the industry's boundaries and second, estimate their size. As discussed in the Opening Case, these boundaries would include markets across the globe while the size of many of these markets, especially markets in emerging economies, continues to expand rapidly. GM would then be prepared to estimate the amount of profit potential in each part of the value chain (step 3). Are product design and product quality more important sources of potential profits than distribution channels and marketing campaigns? These are the types of issues to be considered with the third step of actions used to map an industry's profit pool. GM would then have the information and insights needed to identify the strategies to use to be successful where the largest profit pools are located in the value chain.[127] As this brief discussion shows, profit pools are a tool to use to help the firm's strategic leaders recognize the actions to take to increase the likelihood of increasing profits.

The Strategic Management Process

As suggested by Figure 1.1, the strategic management process is a rational approach firms use to achieve strategic competitiveness and earn above-average returns. Figure 1.1 also outlines the topics we examine in this book to present the strategic management process to you.

There are three parts to this book. In Part 1, we describe what firms do to analyze their external environment (Chapter 2) and internal environment (Chapter 3). These analyses are completed to identify marketplace opportunities and threats in the external environment (Chapter 2) and to decide how to use the resources, capabilities, and core competencies in the firm's internal environment to pursue opportunities and overcome threats (Chapter 3). With knowledge about its external and internal environments, the firm forms its vision and mission.

The firm's strategic inputs (see Figure 1.1) provide the foundation for choosing one or more strategies and deciding how to implement them. As suggested in Figure 1.1 by the horizontal arrow linking the two types of strategic actions, formulation and implementation must be simultaneously integrated if the firm is to successfully use the strategic management process. Integration happens as decision makers think about implementation issues when choosing strategies and as they think about possible changes to the firm's strategies while implementing a currently chosen strategy.

In Part 2 of this book, we discuss the different strategies firms may choose to use. First, we examine business-level strategies (Chapter 4). A business-level strategy describes a firm's actions designed to exploit its competitive advantage over rivals. A company competing in a single product market (e.g., a locally owned grocery store operating in only one location) has but one business-level strategy. As you will learn though, a diversified firm competing in multiple product markets (e.g., General Electric) forms a business-level strategy for each of its businesses. In Chapter 5, we describe the actions and reactions that occur among firms while using their strategies in marketplace competitions. As we will see, competitors respond to and try to anticipate each other's actions. The dynamics of competition affect the strategies firms choose to use as well as how they try to implement the chosen strategies.[128]

For the diversified firm, corporate-level strategy (Chapter 6) is concerned with determining the businesses in which the company intends to compete as well as how resources, capabilities, and core competencies are to be allocated among the different businesses. Other topics vital to strategy formulation, particularly in the diversified corporation, include acquiring other companies and, as appropriate, restructuring the firm's portfolio of businesses (Chapter 7) and selecting an international strategy (Chapter 8). With cooperative strategies (Chapter 9), firms form a partnership to share their resources and capabilities in order to develop a competitive advantage. Cooperative strategies are becoming increasingly important as firms try to find ways to compete in the global economy's array of different markets.[129] For example, Microsoft, the world's largest software company, and Toshiba, the world's third-largest maker of notebook PCs, have formed a joint venture to combine some of their resources and capabilities in order to develop software for notebook computers and other mobile devices.[130]

To examine actions taken to implement strategies, we consider several topics in Part 3 of the book. First, we examine the different mechanisms used to govern firms (Chapter 10). With demands for improved corporate governance being voiced today by many stakeholders,[131] organizations are challenged to learn how to simultaneously satisfy their stakeholders' different interests. Finally, the organizational structure and actions needed to control a firm's operations (Chapter 11), the patterns of strategic leadership appropriate for today's firms and competitive environments (Chapter 12), and strategic entrepreneurship (Chapter 13) as a path to continuous innovation are addressed.

Before closing this introductory chapter, it is important to emphasize that primarily because they are related to how a firm interacts with its stakeholders, almost all strategic management process decisions have ethical dimensions.[132] Organizational ethics are revealed by an organization's culture; that is to say, a firm's decisions are a product of the core values that are shared by most or all of a company's managers and employees. Especially in the turbulent and often ambiguous 21st-century competitive landscape, those making decisions that are part of the strategic management process are challenged to recognize that their decisions affect capital market, product market, and organizational stakeholders differently and to evaluate the ethical implications of their decisions on virtually a daily basis.[133] Decision makers failing to recognize these realities accept the risk of putting their firm at a competitive disadvantage when it comes to consistently engaging in ethical business practices.[134]

As you will discover, the strategic management process examined in this book calls for disciplined approaches to the development of competitive advantage. These approaches provide the pathway through which firms will be able to achieve strategic competitiveness and earn above-average returns in the 21st century. Mastery of this strategic management process will effectively serve you, our readers and the organizations for which you will choose to work.

- Firms use the strategic management process to achieve strategic competitiveness and earn above-average returns. Strategic competitiveness is achieved when a firm has developed and learned how to implement a value-creating strategy. Above-average returns (in excess of what investors expect to earn from other investments with similar levels of risk) provide the foundation a firm needs to simultaneously satisfy all of its stakeholders.

- The fundamental nature of competition is different in the 21st-century competitive landscape. As a result, those making strategic decisions must adopt a different mind-set, one that allows them to learn how to compete in highly turbulent and chaotic environments that produce disorder and a great deal of uncertainty. The globalization of industries and their markets and rapid and significant technological changes are the two primary factors contributing to the turbulence of the 21st-century competitive landscape.

- Firms use two major models to help them form their vision and mission and then choose one or more strategies to use in the pursuit of strategic competitiveness and above-average returns. The core assumption of the I/O model is that the firm's external environment has more of an influence on the choice of strategies than do the firm's internal resources, capabilities, and core competencies. Thus, the I/O model is used to understand the effects an industry's characteristics can have on a firm when deciding what strategy or strategies to use to compete against rivals. The logic supporting the I/O model suggests that above-average returns are earned when the firm locates an attractive industry and successfully implements the strategy dictated by that industry's characteristics. The core assumption of the resource-based model is that the firm's unique resources, capabilities, and core competencies have more of an influence on selecting and using strategies than does the firm's external environment. Above-average returns are earned when the firm uses its valuable, rare, costly-to-imitate, and nonsubstitutable resources and capabilities to compete against its rivals in one or more industries. Evidence indicates that both models yield insights that are linked to successfully selecting and using strategies. Thus, firms want to use their unique resources, capabilities, and core competencies as the foundation for one or more strategies that will allow them to compete in industries they understand.

- Vision and mission are formed in light of the information and insights gained from studying a firm's internal and external environments. Vision is a picture of what the firm wants to be and, in broad terms, what it wants to ultimately achieve. Flowing from the vision, the mission specifies the business or businesses in which the firm intends to compete and the customers it intends to serve. Vision and mission provide direction to the firm and signals important descriptive information to stakeholders.

- Stakeholders are those who can affect, and are affected by, a firm's strategic outcomes. Because a firm is dependent on the continuing support of stakeholders (shareholders, customers, suppliers, employees, host communities, etc.), they have enforceable claims on the company's performance. When earning above-average returns, a firm has the resources it needs to at least minimally simultaneously satisfy the interests of all stakeholders. However, when earning only average returns, different stakeholder groups must be carefully managed in order to retain their support. A firm earning below-average returns must minimize the amount of support it loses from dissatisfied stakeholders.

- Strategic leaders are people located in different parts of the firm using the strategic management process to help the firm reach its vision and mission. In the final analysis, though, CEOs are responsible for making certain that their firms properly use the strategic management process. Today, the effectiveness of the strategic management process increases when it is grounded in ethical intentions and behaviors. The strategic leader's work demands decision trade-offs, often among attractive alternatives. It is important for all strategic leaders, and especially the CEO and other members of the top-management team, to work hard, conduct thorough analyses of situations, be brutally and consistently honest, and ask the right questions of the right people at the right time.

- Strategic leaders must predict the potential outcomes of their strategic decisions. To do so, they must first calculate profit pools in their industry that are linked to value chain activities. In so doing, they are less likely to formulate and implement ineffective strategies.

1. E. Chan, 2005, GM posts record China H1, closes in on VW, *Reuters*, www.reuters.com, July 6.
2. N. Layne, 2005, Sony to unveil new strategy in September, *Reuters*, www.reuters.com, June 22.
3. J. B. Barney & T. B. Mackey, 2005, Testing resource-based theory, In D. J. Ketchen Jr. & D. D. Bergh (eds.), *Research Methodology in Strategy and Management* (2nd ed.), London: Elsevier, 1–13; D. G. Sirmon, M. A. Hitt, & R. D. Ireland, 2007, Managing firm resources in dynamic environments to create value: Looking inside the black box, *Academy of Management Review*, in press.
4. D. Lei & J. W. Slocum, 2005, Strategic and organizational requirements for competitive advantage, *Academy of Management Executive*, 19(1): 31–45; T. J. Douglas & J. A. Ryman, 2003, Understanding competitive advantage in the general hospital industry: Evaluating strategic competencies, *Strategic Management Journal*, 24: 333–347.
5. K. Shimizu & M. A. Hitt, 2004, Strategic flexibility: Organizational preparedness to reverse ineffective strategic decisions, *Academy of Management Executive*, 18(4): 44–59; D. J. Teece, G. Pisano, & A. Shuen, 1997, Dynamic capabilities and strategic management, *Strategic Management Journal*, 18: 509–533.
6. P. Shrivastava, 1995, Ecocentric management for a risk society, *Academy of Management Review*, 20: 119.
7. F. Delmar, P. Davidsson, & W. B. Gartner, 2003, Arriving at a high-growth firm, *Journal of Business Venturing*, 18: 189–216.
8. T. Bates, 2005, Analysis of young, small firms that have closed: Delineating successful from unsuccessful closures, *Journal of Business Venturing*, 20: 343–358.
9. A. M. McGahan & M. E. Porter, 2003, The emergence and sustainability of abnormal profits, *Strategic Organization*, 1: 79–108; T. C. Powell, 2001, Competitive advantage: Logical and philosophical considerations, *Strategic Management Journal*, 22: 875–888.
10. R. D. Ireland & C. C. Miller, 2004, Decision-making and firm success, *Academy of Management Executive*, 18(4): 8–12.
11. P. Nutt, 2004, Expanding the search for alternatives during strategic decision-making, *Academy of Management Executive*, 18(4): 13–28; S. Dutta, M. J. Zbaracki, & M. Bergen, 2003, Pricing process as a capability: A resource-based perspective, *Strategic Management Journal*, 24: 615–630.
12. S. Tallman & K. Fladmoe-Lindquist, 2002, Internationalization, globalization, and capability-based strategy, *California Management Review*, 45(1): 116–135; M. A. Hitt, R. D. Ireland, S. M. Camp, & D. L. Sexton, 2001, Strategic entrepreneurship: Entrepreneurial strategies for wealth creation, *Strategic Management Journal*, 22 (Special Issue): 479–491; S. A. Zahra, R. D. Ireland, & M. A. Hitt, 2000, International expansion by new venture firms: International diversity, mode of market entry, technological learning and performance, *Academy of Management Journal*, 43: 925–950.
13. R. Kirkland, 2005, Will the U.S. be flattened by a flatter world? *Fortune*, June 27, 47–48.
14. A. Nair & S. Kotha, 2001, Does group membership matter? Evidence from the Japanese steel industry, *Strategic Management Journal*, 22: 221–235; A. M. McGahan & M. E. Porter, 1997, How much does industry matter, really? *Strategic Management Journal*, 18 (Special Issue): 15–30.
15. D. G. Sirmon & M. A. Hitt, 2003, Managing resources: Linking unique resources, management and wealth creation in family firms, *Entrepreneurship Theory and Practice*, 27(4): 339–358; J. B. Barney, 2001, Is the resource-based "view" a useful perspective for strategic management research? Yes, *Academy of Management Review*, 26: 41–56.
16. M. A. Hitt, B. W. Keats, & S. M. DeMarie, 1998, Navigating in the new competitive landscape: Building competitive advantage and strategic flexibility in the 21st century, *Academy of Management Executive*, 12(4): 22–42; R. A. Bettis & M. A. Hitt, 1995, The new competitive landscape, *Strategic Management Journal*, 16 (Special Issue): 7–19.
17. 2005, NBC could combine network and cable news—*NY Post*, www.reuters.com, June 30.
18. B. Alptert, 2005, Apple's iPod faces threat, *Bryan-College Station Eagle*, July 3, E5.
19. C. Harrison, 2005, Is it Goofy to give your child a phone? *Dallas Morning News*, July 7, D1, D3.
20. G. Probst & S. Raisch, 2005, Organizational crisis: The logic of failure, *Academy of Management Executive*, 19(1): 90–105; M. A. Hitt & V. Pisano, 2003, The cross-border merger and acquisition strategy, *Management Research*, 1: 133–144.
21. R. M. Grant, 2003, Strategic planning in a turbulent environment: Evidence from the oil majors, *Strategic Management Journal*, 24: 491–517.
22. G. McNamara, P. M. Vaaler, & C. Devers. 2003. Same as it ever was: The search for evidence of increasing hypercompetition, *Strategic Management Journal*, 24: 261–278.
23. R. A. D'Aveni, 1995, Coping with hypercompetition: Utilizing the new 7S's framework, *Academy of Management Executive*, 9(3): 46.
24. R. A. D'Aveni, 2004, Corporate spheres of influence, *MIT Sloan Management Review*, 45(4): 38–46; W. J. Ferrier, 2001, Navigating the competitive landscape: The drivers and consequences of competitive aggressiveness, *Academy of Management Journal*, 44: 858–877.
25. S.-J. Chang & S. Park, 2005, Types of firms generating network externalities and MNCs' co-location decisions, *Strategic Management Journal*, 26: 595–615; S. C. Voelpel, M. Dous, & T. H. Davenport, 2005, Five steps to creating a global knowledge-sharing systems: Siemens/ShareNet, *Academy of Management Executive*, 19(2): 9–23.
26. R. Belderbos & L. Sleuwaegen, 2005, Competitive drivers and international plant configuration strategies: A product-level test, *Strategic Management Journal*, 26: 577–593.
27. 2005, Organisation for Economic Co-operation and Development, *OCED Statistical Profile of the United States—2005*, www.oced.org; S. Koudsi & L. A. Costa, 1998, America vs. the new Europe: By the numbers, *Fortune*, December 21, 149–156.
28. T. Raum, 2005, Awakening economic powerhouses eye G8, *Washington Post Online*, www.washingtonpost.com, July 3.
29. Kirkland, Will the U.S. be flattened by a flatter world? 47.
30. A. Virmani, 2005, India a giant economy? Yes, by 2035! Rediff.com, www.rediff.com, January 21.
31. Raum, Awakening economic powerhouses.
32. K. Kranhold, 2005, GE pins hopes on emerging markets, *Wall Street Journal Online*, www.wsj.com, March 2.
33. 2005, Delivering the goods at FedEx, *Business Week*, June 13, 60–62.
34. P. Williamson & M. Zeng, 2004, Strategies for competing in a changed China, *MIT Sloan Management Review*, 45(4): 85–91; V. Govindarajan & A. K. Gupta, 2001, *The Quest for Global Dominance*, San Francisco: Jossey-Bass.
35. T. Khanna, K. G. Palepu, & J. Sinha, 2005, Strategies that fir emerging markets, *Harvard Business Review*, 83(6): 63–76.
36. 2005, Wal-Mart at a glance, www.walmart.com, July 3.
37. 2005, McDonald's Corporation, *Standard and Poor's Stock Report*, www.standardandpoors.com, July 2.
38. P. Barwise & S. Meehan, 2004, Don't be unique, be better, *MIT Sloan Management Review*, 45(4): 23–26.
39. M. A. Prospero, 2005, The march of war, *Fast Company*, May, 14.
40. G. Fink & N. Holden, 2005, The global transfer of management knowledge, *Academy of Management Executive*, 19(2): 5–8; M. Subramaniam & N. Venkataraman, 2001, Determinants of transnational new product devel-

opment capability: Testing the influence of transferring and deploying tacit overseas knowledge, *Strategic Management Journal*, 22: 359–378.

41. S. Zaheer & E. Mosakowski, 1997, The dynamics of the liability of foreignness: A global study of survival in financial services, *Strategic Management Journal*, 18: 439–464.

42. R. C. May, S. M. Puffer, & D. J. McCarthy, 2005, Transferring management knowledge to Russia: A culturally based approach, *Academy of Management Executive*, 19(2): 24–35.

43. M. A. Hitt, R. E. Hoskisson, & H. Kim, 1997, International diversification: Effects on innovation and firm performance in product-diversified firms, *Academy of Management Journal*, 40: 767–798.

44. D'Aveni, Coping with hypercompetition, 46.

45. G. Hamel, 2001, Revolution vs. evolution: You need both, *Harvard Business Review*, 79(5): 150–156.

46. D. Solis, 2005, Accent on trust, *Dallas Morning News*, July 3, D1, D6.

47. K. H. Hammonds, 2001, What is the state of the new economy? *Fast Company*, September, 101–104.

48. L. Yu, 2005, Does knowledge sharing pay off? *MIT Sloan Management Review*, 46(3): 5.

49. L. Valikangas & M. Gibbert, 2005, Boundary-setting strategies for escaping innovation traps, *MIT Sloan Management Review*, 46(3): 58–65; K. M. Eisenhardt, 1999, Strategy as strategic decision making, *Sloan Management Review*, 40(3): 65–72.

50. J. Santos, Y. Doz, & P. Williamson, 2004, Is your innovation process global? *MIT Sloan Management Review*, 45(4): 31–37.

51. C. W. L. Hill, 1997, Establishing a standard: Competitive strategy and technological standards in winner-take-all industries, *Academy of Management Executive*, 11(2): 7–25.

52. C. Gilbert, 2003, The disruptive opportunity, *MIT Sloan Management Review*, 44(4): 27–32; C. M. Christiansen, 1997, *The Innovator's Dilemma*, Boston: Harvard Business School Press.

53. P. Magnusson, 2005, Globalization is great—sort of, *Business Week*, April 25, 25.

54. R. Adner, 2002, When are technologies disruptive? A demand-based view of the emergence of competition, *Strategic Management Journal*, 23: 667–688; G. Ahuja & C. M. Lampert, 2001, Entrepreneurship in the large corporation: A longitudinal study of how established firms create breakthrough inventions, *Strategic Management Journal*, 22 (Special Issue): 521–543.

55. C. L. Nichols-Nixon & C. Y. Woo, 2003, Technology sourcing and output of established firms in a regime of encompassing technological change, *Strategic Management Journal*, 24: 651–666; C. W. L. Hill & F. T. Rothaermel, 2003, The performance of incumbent firms in the face of radical technological innovation, *Academy of Management Review*, 28: 257–274.

56. G. Ferguson, S. Mathur, & B. Shah, 2005, Evolving from information to insight, *MIT Sloan Management Review*, 46(2): 51–58.

57. J. Weber & A. Therese, 2005, How the Net is remaking the mall, *Business Week*, May 9, 60–61.

58. B. Einhorn, B. Elgin, R. D. Hof, & T. Mullaney, 2005, The great Internet race, *Business Week*, June 13, 54–56.

59. A. C. Inkpen & E. W. K. Tsang, 2005, Social capital, networks, and knowledge transfer, *Academy of Management Review*, 30: 146–165; A. S. DeNisi, M. A. Hitt, & S. E. Jackson, 2003, The knowledge-based approach to sustainable competitive advantage, in S. E. Jackson, M. A. Hitt, & A. S. DeNisi (eds.), *Managing Knowledge for Sustained Competitive Advantage*, San Francisco: Jossey-Bass, 3–33.

60. M. Gottfredson, R. Puryear, & S. Phillips, 2005, Strategic sourcing: From periphery to the core, *Harvard Business Review*, 83(2): 132–139.

61. K. G. Smith, C. J. Collins, & K. D. Clark, 2005, Existing knowledge, knowledge creation capability, and the rate of new product introduction in high-technology firms, *Academy of Management Journal*, 48: 346–357; S. K. McEvily & B. Chakravarthy, 2002, The persistence of knowledge-based advantage: An empirical test for product performance and technological knowledge, *Strategic Management Journal*, 23: 285–305.

62. S. K. Ethirau, P. Kale, M. S. Krishnan, & J. V. Singh, 2005, Where do capabilities come from and how do they matter? *Strategic Management Journal*, 26: 25–45; L. Rosenkopf & A. Nerkar, 2001, Beyond local search: Boundary-spanning, exploration, and impact on the optical disk industry, *Strategic Management Journal*, 22: 287–306.

63. Sirmon, Hitt, & Ireland, Managing firm's resources.

64. K. Asakawa & M. Lehrer, 2003, Managing local knowledge assets globally: The role of regional innovation relays, *Journal of World Business*, 38: 31–42.

65. R. E. Hoskisson, M. A. Hitt, & R. D. Ireland, 2004, *Competing for Advantage*, Cincinnati: Thomson South-Western; K. R. Harrigan, 2001, Strategic flexibility in old and new economies, in M. A. Hitt, R. E. Freeman, & J. S. Harrison (eds.), *Handbook of Strategic Management*, Oxford, UK: Blackwell Publishers, 97–123.

66. Shimizu & Hitt, Strategic flexibility, 45.

67. L. Gratton & S. Ghoshal, 2005, Beyond best practice, *MIT Sloan Management Review*, 46(3): 49–55.

68. K. Uhlenbruck, K. E. Meyer, & M. A. Hitt, 2003, Organizational transformation in transition economies: Resource-based and organizational learning perspectives, *Journal of Management Studies*, 40: 257–282.

69. R. E. Hoskisson, M. A. Hitt, W. P. Wan, & D. Yiu, 1999, Swings of a pendulum: Theory and research in strategic management, *Journal of Management*, 25: 417–456.

70. E. H. Bowman & C. E. Helfat, 2001, Does corporate strategy matter? *Strategic Management Journal*, 22: 1–23.

71. J. Shamsie, 2003, The context of dominance: An industry-driven framework for exploiting reputation, *Strategic Management Journal*, 24: 199–215; A. Seth & H. Thomas, 1994, Theories of the firm: Implications for strategy research, *Journal of Management Studies*, 31: 165–191.

72. Seth & Thomas, 169–173.

73. L. F. Feldman, C. G. Brush, & T. Manolova, 2005, Co-alignment in the resource-performance relationship: Strategy as mediator, *Journal of Business Venturing*, 20: 359–383.

74. M. E. Porter, 1985, *Competitive Advantage*, New York: Free Press; M. E. Porter, 1980, *Competitive Strategy*, New York: Free Press.

75. A. M. McGahan, 1999, Competition, strategy and business performance, *California Management Review*, 41(3): 74–101; McGahan & Porter, How much does industry matter, really?

76. R. Henderson & W. Mitchell, 1997, The interactions of organizational and competitive influences on strategy and performance, *Strategic Management Journal* 18 (Special Issue): 5–14; C. Oliver, 1997, Sustainable competitive advantage: Combining institutional and resource-based views, *Strategic Management Journal*, 18: 697–713; J. L. Stimpert & I. M. Duhaime, 1997, Seeing the big picture: The influence of industry, diversification, and business strategy on performance, *Academy of Management Journal*, 40: 560–583.

77. B.-S. Teng & J. L. Cummings, 2002, Trade-offs in managing resources and capabilities, *Academy of Management Executive*, 16(2): 81–91; R. L. Priem & J. E. Butler, 2001, Is the resource-based "view" a useful perspective for strategic management research? *Academy of Management Review*, 26: 22–40.

78. M. Blyler & R. W. Coff, 2003, Dynamic capabilities, social capital, and rent appropriation: Ties that split pies, *Strategic Management Journal*, 24: 677–686.

79. P. Bansal, 2005, Evolving sustainability: A longitudinal study of corporate sustainable development, *Strategic Management Journal*, 26: 197–218.

80. P. J. H. Schoemaker & R. Amit, 1994, Investment in strategic assets: Industry and firm-level perspectives, in P. Shrivastava, A. Huff, & J. Dutton (eds.), *Advances in Strategic Management*, Greenwich, CT: JAI Press, 9.

81. D. M. DeCarolis, 2003, Competencies and imitability in the pharmaceutical industry: An analysis of their relationship with firm performance, *Journal of Management*, 29: 27–50; Barney, Is the resource-based "view" a useful perspective for strategic management research? Yes.

82. C. Zott, 2003, Dynamic capabilities and the emergence of intraindustry differential firm performance: Insights from a simulation study, *Strategic Management Journal*, 24: 97–125.

83. G. Hawawini, V. Subramanian, & P. Verdin, 2003, Is performance driven by industry- or firm-specific factors? A new look at the evidence, *Strategic Management Journal*, 24: 1–16.

84. M. Makhija, 2003, Comparing the resource-based and market-based views of the firm: Empirical evidence from Czech privatization, *Strategic Management Journal,* 24: 433–451; T. J. Douglas & J. A. Ryman, 2003, Understanding competitive advantage in the general hospital industry: Evaluating strategic competencies, *Strategic Management Journal,* 24: 333–347.

85. R. D. Ireland, R. E. Hoskisson, & M. A. Hitt. 2006, *Understanding Business Strategy,* Cincinnati: Thomson South-Western, 32–34.

86. 2005, The CEO's secret handbook, *Business 2.0,* July, 69–76.

87. A. Deutschman, 2005, Making change, *Fast Company,* May, 53–62.

88. M. Ihlwan, C. Edwards, & R. Crockett, 2005, Korea's LG may be the next Samsung, *Business Week,* January 24, 54–55.

89. P. B. Brown, 2005, What I know now, *Fast Company,* February, 96.

90. R. D. Ireland & M. A. Hitt, 1992, Mission statements: Importance, challenge, and recommendations for development, *Business Horizons,* 35(3): 34–42.

91. V. Postrel, 2005, So many choices, *Dallas Morning News,* June 26, P1, P5.

92. W. J. Duncan, 1999, *Management: Ideas and Actions,* New York: Oxford University Press, 122–125.

93. P. Martin, 1999, Lessons in humility, *Financial Times,* June 22, 18.

94. J. A. Pearce & J. P. Doh, 2005, The high impact of collaborative social initiatives, *MIT Sloan Management Review,* 46(3): 30–39.

95. I. R. Baum, E. A. Locke, & S. A. Kirkpatrick, 1998, A longitudinal study of the relation of vision and vision communication to venture growth in entrepreneurial firms, *Journal of Applied Psychology,* 83: 43–54.

96. J. Humphreys, 2004, The vision thing, *MIT Sloan Management Review,* 45(4): 96.

97. P. A. Argenti, R. A. Howell, & K. A. Beck, 2005, The strategic communication imperative, *MIT Sloan Management Review,* 46(3): 83–89; J. Frooman, 1999, Stakeholder influence strategies, *Academy of Management Review,* 24: 191–205.

98. T. M. Jones & A. C. Wicks, 1999, Convergent stakeholder theory, *Academy of Management Review,* 24: 206–221; R. E. Freeman, 1984, *Strategic Management: A Stakeholder Approach,* Boston: Pitman, 53–54.

99. G. Donaldson & J. W. Lorsch, 1983, *Decision Making at the Top: The Shaping of Strategic Direction,* New York: Basic Books, 37–40.

100. S. Sharma & I. Henriques, 2005, Stakeholder influences on sustainability practices in the Canadian Forest products industry, *Strategic Management Journal,* 26: 159–180.

101. A. J. Hillman & G. D. Keim, 2001, Shareholder value, stakeholder management, and social issues: What's the bottom line? *Strategic Management Journal,* 22: 125–139.

102. J. M. Stevens, H. K. Steensma, D. A. Harrison, & P. L. Cochran, 2005, Symbolic or substantive document? The influence of ethics codes on financial executives' decisions, *Strategic Management Journal,* 26: 181–195.

103. R. E. Freeman & J. McVea, 2001, A stakeholder approach to strategic management, in M. A. Hitt, R. E. Freeman, & J. S. Harrison (eds.), *Handbook of Strategic Management,* Oxford, UK: Blackwell Publishers, 189–207.

104. Ibid.

105. C. Caldwell & R. Karri, 2005, Organizational governance and ethical systems: A convenantal approach to building trust, *Journal of Business Ethics,* 58: 249–267; A. McWilliams & D. Siegel, 2001, Corporate social responsibility: A theory of the firm perspective, *Academy of Management Review,* 26: 117–127.

106. C. Hardy, T. B. Lawrence, & D. Grant, 2005, Discourse and collaboration: The role of conversations and collective identity, *Academy of Management Review,* 30: 58–77; R. K. Mitchell, B. R. Agle, & D. J. Wood, 1997, Toward a theory of stakeholder identification and salience: Defining the principle of who and what really count, *Academy of Management Review,* 22: 853–886.

107. S. Maitlis, 2005, The social process of organizational sensemaking, *Academy of Management Journal,* 48: 21–49.

108. T. M. Gardner, 2005, Interfirm competition for human resources: Evidence from the software industry, *Academy of Management Journal,* 48: 237–256.

109. J. A. Byrne, 2005, Working for the boss from hell, *Fast Company,* July, 14.

110. D. Brady & D. Kiley, 2005, Short on sizzle, and losing steam, *Business Week,* April 25, 44.

111. E. T. Prince, 2005, The fiscal behavior of CEOs, *MIT Sloan Management Review,* 46(3): 23–26.

112. D. Brady & J. Weber, 2005, *Business Week,* April 25, 88–96.

113. A. Priestland & T. R. Hanig, 2005, Developing first-level managers, *Harvard Business Review,* 83(6): 113–120.

114. R. T. Pascale & J. Sternin, 2005, Your company's secret change agent, *Harvard Business Review,* 83(5): 72–81.

115. 2005, Jim Collins on tough calls, *Fortune,* June 27, 89–94.

116. 2005, About Wal-Mart, www.walmart.com, July 3.

117. S. Holmes & D. Brady, 2005, Boeing's struggle to find a pilot, *Business Week,* May 23, 44.

118. D. Rooke & W. R. Tolbert, 2005, Seven transformations of leadership, *Harvard Business Review,* 83(4): 66–76.

119. T. Leavitt, 1991, *Thinking about Management,* New York: Free Press, 9.

120. 2005, 100 Best Corporate citizens for 2004, *Business Ethics Magazine,* www.business-ethics.com, June 27.

121. D. C. Hambrick, S. Finkelstein, & A. C. Mooney, 2005, Executive job demands: New insights for explaining strategic decisions and leader behaviors, *Academy of Management Review,* 30: 472–491; J. Brett & L. K. Stroh, 2003, Working 61 plus hours a week: Why do managers do it? *Journal of Applied Psychology,* 88: 67–78.

122. J. A. Byrne, 2005, Great work if you can get it, *Fast Company,* April, 14.

123. M. Loeb, 1993, Steven J. Ross, 1927–1992, *Fortune,* January 25, 4.

124. Collins, Jim Collins on tough calls.

125. O. Gadiesh & J. L. Gilbert, 1998, Profit pools: A fresh look at strategy, *Harvard Business Review,* 76(3): 139–147.

126. O. Gadiesh & J. L. Gilbert, 1998, How to map your industry's profit pool, *Harvard Business Review,* 76(3): 149–162.

127. M. J. Epstein & R. A. Westbrook, 2001, Linking actions to profits in strategic decision making, *Sloan Management Review,* 42(3): 39–49.

128. D. J. Ketchen, C. C. Snow, & V. L. Street, 2004, Improving firm performance by matching strategic decision-making processes to competitive dynamics, *Academy of Management Executive,* 18(4): 29–43.

129. P. Evans & B. Wolf, 2005, Collaboration rules, *Harvard Business Review,* 83(7): 96–104.

130. 2005, Microsoft, Toshiba to develop electronics, *Reuters,* www.reuters .com, June 27.

131. Pearce & Doh, The high impact of collaborative social initiatives, 30–39.

132. J. R. Ehrenfeld, 2005, The roots of sustainability, *MIT Sloan Management Review,* 46(2): 23–25; L. K. Trevino & G. R. Weaver, 2003, *Managing Ethics in Business Organizations,* Stanford, CA: Stanford University Press.

133. J. R. Ehrenfeld, 2005, The roots of sustainability, *MIT Sloan Management Review,* 46(2): 23–25.

134. 2005, Corporate citizenship on the rise, *Business Week,* May 9, S1–S7.

Chapter 2

Analysis of the External Environment

KNOWLEDGE OBJECTIVES

Studying this chapter should provide you with the strategic management knowledge needed to:

1. Explain the importance of analyzing and understanding the firm's external environment.

2. Define and describe the general environment and the industry environment.

3. Discuss the four activities of the external environmental analysis process.

4. Name and describe the general environment's six segments.

5. Identify the five competitive forces and explain how they determine an industry's profit potential.

6. Define strategic groups and describe their influence on the firm.

7. Describe what firms need to know about their competitors and different methods (including ethical standards) used to collect intelligence about them.

Many U.S. airlines have filed bankruptcy in recent years.

KEN CEDENO/BLOOMBERG NEWS/LANDOV

United Airlines, which filed for bankruptcy protection in 2002, and U.S. Airways, which filed in 2004, continued to operate under bankruptcy protection in 2005. This was the second time for U.S. Airways to be in bankruptcy since 2002. Delta and Northwest filed for bankruptcy in late 2005 as fuel prices increased after Hurricane Katrina. American Airlines' AMR Corp. is the only legacy carrier (those that existed before the 1978 deregulation of the airline industry) that has been able to avoid bankruptcy. Minor airlines are faring no better: Hawaiian Airlines emerged from bankruptcy in June 2005, and discount airline AirTran Airways (ATA) continued in bankruptcy in 2005. Airlines in general have been struggling to deal with increased costs and reduced airline travel because of a number of environmental events that have been affecting the industry at large.

Since the terrorist attacks of September 11, 2001, the entire industry has seen a downturn in overall revenues due to decreased worldwide traffic. Similarly, because oil prices have increased substantially, airlines' fuel costs have increased as well. However, airlines have not been able to raise prices due to the overcapacity in the industry. Furthermore, airlines, especially older legacy carriers such as United, Delta, American, and U.S. Air, have unionized workforces with seniority. As such, labor costs have been difficult to reduce. Accordingly, new discount entrants have made the legacy carriers' cost structure seem imposing. In fact, United Airlines proposed to do away with its defined benefit pension system. The United Benefits Guarantee Corporation, a federal agency that underwrites pension plans, has agreed to a settlement with United Airlines for $6.6 billion. This will represent a loss to the workers of United, whose pensions are underfunded by $9.8 billion. Although United and U.S. Air have won significant concessions from their employees, especially pilots, their financial struggles continue. Delta and Northwest expect to reduce their pension cost in bankruptcy as well.

To deal with the changes in industry competition, United has also created its own "low cost" airline, Ted. Similarly, Delta created Song. In response, the discount carriers have learned approaches from the legacy carriers. ATA and Southwest have created a code-sharing alliance that coordinates their reservation systems and flight schedules. As such, Southwest is now able to offer service to such ATA markets as Boston, New York City, Newark, Washington, D.C., San Francisco, and Honolulu, among others. The code-sharing arrangement allows Southwest to expand into a new market, Pittsburgh, and increase the number of its gates at Chicago Midway. This will put added pressure on traditional airlines such as US Airways, American, and United. Although a proposed merger between U.S. Airways and American West Airlines may slightly reduce over-capacity, it is not likely to significantly decrease the cutthroat competition.

The legacy carriers' international routes have been profitable, but discount carriers are entering this market from faraway places, creating more competition globally as well. The Emirates Group, an airline headquartered in Dubai, United Arab Emirates, has been growing passenger traffic 25 percent per year over the past 20 years. As other carriers have been cutting back service to the Middle East because of increased travel risk, the Emirates Group has increased traffic through its hub in Dubai, putting pressure on other airlines such as the recently merged Qantas-Air

New Zealand. Although legacy carriers can pursue routes over the Atlantic, European airlines are far more dependent on transatlantic travel than U.S. carriers are. Accordingly, European carriers are likely to fight U.S. carriers' attempts to expand their North Atlantic routes, as these routes represent the largest profit contributor for European airlines.

As the above points suggest, events in the external environment and in the industry environment have been crucial in the recent difficulties experienced by U.S. airlines. Airlines have been battered by decreased travel due to terrorist threats, significantly increased fuel costs, labor disputes due to downsizing, and industry overcapacity. This has increased the competitive rivalry in the industry. New discount airlines have prompted further competitive actions by legacy carriers with the creation of their own "low cost" labels. Discount international airlines also present threats for legacy carriers. Large suppliers of capital (such as GE Capital) are powerful relative to the airlines and are needed to help them buy or lease new planes. Unions and fuel suppliers have eroded profits for airlines, significantly threatening their survival. Because consumers incur no significant costs in switching from one airline to another (except for frequent flyer loyalty programs), buyers' power is strong. Although substitute products exist such as the automobile and mass transit, when flying long distances the speed of air travel makes such alternative travel less appealing and unrealistic in most instances. Although Southwest Airlines has continued to make a profit relative to the legacy carriers, even its profits have been squeezed by new entrants such as JetBlue into the discount segment space. Events in the external environment have had the most significant influence on airlines' ability to make a profit, even for those in the discount market segment.

Sources: M. A. Hofmann, 2005, PBCG's liability for United pension totals $6.6 billion, *Business Insurance,* April 25, 1–2; D. Michaels, 2005, From tiny Dubais, an airline with global ambition takes off, *Wall Street Journal,* January 11, A1, A15; B. J. Racanelli, 2004, Coming: Not-so-friendly skies over the Atlantic, *Barron's,* November 8, MW10; M. Sunnucks, 2005, Southwest/ATA deal puts more pressure on America West, *The Phoenix Business Journal,* January 21, 1, 58; M. Trottman, 2005, Merged airlines' CEO relishes big challenges, *Wall Street Journal,* May 23, B1,B4; W. Zellner & B. Grow, 2005, Waiting for the first bird to die, *Business Week,* January 24, 38.

As the Opening Case on the airlines industry attests and as research suggests, the external environment affects firm growth and profitability.[1] Major political events such as the war in Iraq, the strength of separate nations' economies at different times, and the emergence of new technologies are a few examples of conditions in the external environment that affect firms in the United States and throughout the world. External environmental conditions such as these create threats to and opportunities for firms that, in turn, have major effects on their strategic actions.[2]

Regardless of the industry, the external environment is critical to a firm's survival and success. This chapter focuses on what firms do to analyze and understand the external environment. As the discussion of the airlines industry shows, the external environment influences the firm's strategic options as well as the decisions made in light of them. The firm's understanding of the external environment is matched with knowledge about its internal environment (discussed in the next chapter) to form its vision, to develop its mission, and to take actions that result in strategic competitiveness and above-average returns (see Figure 1.1).

As noted in Chapter 1, the environmental conditions in the current global economy differ from those previously faced by firms. Technological changes and the continuing growth of information gathering and processing capabilities demand more timely and effective competitive actions and responses.[3] The rapid sociological changes occurring in many countries affect labor practices and the nature of products demanded by increasingly diverse consumers. Governmental policies and laws also affect where and how firms may choose to compete.[4] Deregulation and local government changes, such as those in the global airlines industry, affect not only the general competitive environment but also the strategic decisions made by companies competing globally. To achieve strategic competitiveness and thrive, firms must be aware of and understand the different dimensions of the external environment.

Firms understand the external environment by acquiring information about competitors, customers, and other stakeholders to build their own base of knowledge and capabilities.[5] On the basis of the new information, firms may take actions to build new capabilities and buffer themselves against environmental effects or to build relationships with stakeholders in their environment.[6] In order to take successful action, they must effectively analyze the external environment.

The General, Industry, and Competitor Environments

An integrated understanding of the external and internal environments is essential for firms to understand the present and predict the future.[7] As shown in Figure 2.1, a firm's external environment is divided into three major areas: the general, industry, and competitor environments.

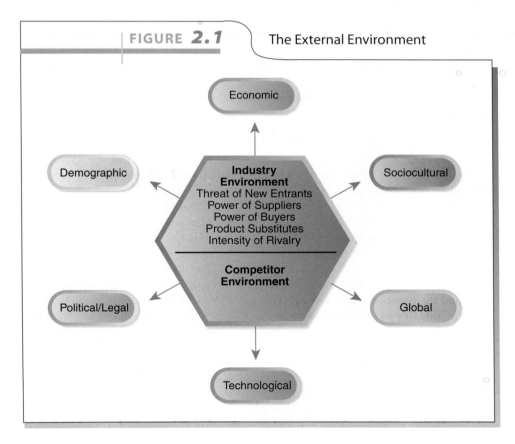

| FIGURE **2.1** | The External Environment

Economic

Demographic

Sociocultural

Industry Environment
Threat of New Entrants
Power of Suppliers
Power of Buyers
Product Substitutes
Intensity of Rivalry

Competitor Environment

Political/Legal

Global

Technological

Demographic Segment	• Population size • Age structure • Geographic distribution	• Ethnic mix • Income distribution
Economic Segment	• Inflation rates • Interest rates • Trade deficits or surpluses • Budget deficits or surpluses	• Personal savings rate • Business savings rates • Gross domestic product
Political/Legal Segment	• Antitrust laws • Taxation laws • Deregulation philosophies	• Labor training laws • Educational philosophies and policies
Sociocultural Segment	• Women in the workforce • Workforce diversity • Attitudes about the quality of work life	• Concerns about the environment • Shifts in work and career preferences • Shifts in preferences regarding product and service characteristics
Technological Segment	• Product innovations • Applications of knowledge	• Focus of private and government-supported R&D expenditures • New communication technologies
Global Segment	• Important political events • Critical global markets	• Newly industrialized countries • Different cultural and institutional attributes

The **general environment** is composed of dimensions in the broader society that influence an industry and the firms within it.[8] We group these dimensions into six environmental *segments:* demographic, economic, political/legal, sociocultural, technological, and global. Examples of *elements* analyzed in each of these segments are shown in Table 2.1.

Firms cannot directly control the general environment's segments and elements. Accordingly, successful companies gather the information required to understand each segment and its implications for the selection and implementation of the appropriate strategies. For example, most firms have little individual effect on the U.S. economy, although that economy has a major effect on their ability to operate and even survive. Thus, companies around the globe were challenged to understand the effects of this economy's decline on their current and future strategies. Certainly, this is the case for firms in the airline industry as explained in the Opening Case. And there are legitimate differences of opinion regarding the particular strategies that should be followed in reaction to the economic changes. Analysts argue that airlines should be merging to reduce capacity and control costs while others are expanding code-sharing agreements to expand their market reach, as Southwest and ATA did in the discount segment.

The **industry environment** is the set of factors that directly influences a firm and its competitive actions and competitive responses: the threat of new entrants, the power of suppliers, the power of buyers, the threat of product substitutes, and the intensity of rivalry among competitors. In total, the interactions among these five factors determine an industry's profit potential. The challenge is to locate a position within an industry where a firm can favorably influence those factors or where it can successfully defend against their influence. In fact, positioning is a major issue for airlines, as discussed in the Opening Case. Airlines face substantial competitive rivalry, and the legacy carriers such as United Airlines face new entry threats from discount airlines start-ups such as JetBlue. The greater a firm's capacity to favorably influence its industry environment, the greater the likelihood that the firm will earn above-average returns.

How companies gather and interpret information about their competitors is called *competitor analysis*. Understanding the firm's competitor environment complements the insights provided by studying the general and industry environments. Understanding its competitor environment may be critical to the survival of United and other struggling airlines.

Analysis of the general environment is focused on the future; analysis of the industry environment is focused on the factors and conditions influencing a firm's profitability within its industry; and analysis of competitors is focused on predicting the dynamics of competitors' actions, responses, and intentions. In combination, the results of the three analyses the firm uses to understand its external environment influence its vision, mission, and strategic actions. Although we discuss each analysis separately, performance improves when the firm integrates the insights provided by analyses of the general environment, the industry environment, and the competitor environment.

External Environmental Analysis

Most firms face external environments that are highly turbulent, complex, and global—conditions that make interpreting them increasingly difficult.[9] To cope with what are often ambiguous and incomplete environmental data and to increase their understanding of the general environment, firms engage in a process called external environmental analysis. The continuous process includes four activities: scanning, monitoring, forecasting, and assessing (see Table 2.2). Those analyzing the external environment should understand that completing this analysis is a difficult, yet significant, activity.[10]

An important objective of studying the general environment is identifying opportunities and threats. An **opportunity** is a condition in the general environment that, if exploited, helps a company achieve strategic competitiveness. For example, in 2004 there were 1.5 billion cell phone uses and 690 million cell phones sold, which was six times the number of PCs and laptops sold. Many large entertainment companies, telephone companies, and a large number of start-ups are looking at the opportunity to move to a cell phone platform that will allow digital video and music to stream more easily on these small devices. In the United States currently there are 182 million cell

Components of the External Environmental Analysis	TABLE 2.2
Scanning	• Identifying early signals of environmental changes and trends
Monitoring	• Detecting meaning through ongoing observations of environmental changes and trends
Forecasting	• Developing projections of anticipated outcomes based on monitored changes and trends
Assessing	• Determining the timing and importance of environmental changes and trends for firms' strategies and their management

phone users, which represents approximately a two thirds penetration ratio. These users spent $4 billion on digital data services. But this is just scratching the surface of this opportunity, because such services accounted for only 4 percent of cellular revenues.[11]

A **threat** is a condition in the general environment that may hinder a company's efforts to achieve strategic competitiveness.[12] The once revered firm Polaroid can attest to the seriousness of external threats. Polaroid was a leader in its industry and considered one of the top 50 firms in the United States. When its competitors developed photographic equipment using digital technology, Polaroid was unprepared and never responded effectively. It filed for bankruptcy in 2001. In 2002, the former Polaroid Corp. was sold to Bank One's OEP Imaging unit, which promptly changed its own name to Polaroid Corp. Jacques Nasser, a former CEO at Ford, took over as CEO and found that the brand had continued life. Nasser used the brand in a partnership with Petters Group to put the Polaroid name on "TVs and DVDs made in Asian factories and sell them through Wal-Mart and Target."[13] Even though Polaroid went public again in 2004 and was sold to Petters Group in early 2005, it was still a much reduced version of its original business. As these examples indicate, opportunities suggest competitive *possibilities,* while threats are potential *constraints.*

Several sources can be used to analyze the general environment, including a wide variety of printed materials (such as trade publications, newspapers, business publications, and the results of academic research and public polls), trade shows and suppliers, customers, and employees of public-sector organizations. People in "boundary spanning" positions can obtain much information. Salespersons, purchasing managers, public relations directors, and customer service representatives, each of whom interacts with external constituents, are examples of individuals in boundary-spanning positions. Expatriates in multinational corporations can act as significant boundary spanners as they act in and return from their foreign assignments.[14]

Scanning

Scanning entails the study of all segments in the general environment. Through scanning, firms identify early signals of potential changes in the general environment and detect changes that are already under way.[15] When scanning, the firm often deals with ambiguous, incomplete, or unconnected data and information. Environmental scanning is critically important for firms competing in highly volatile environments.[16] In addition, scanning activities must be aligned with the organizational context; a scanning system designed for a volatile environment is inappropriate for a firm in a stable environment.[17]

Many firms use special software to help them identify events that are taking place in the environment and announced in public sources. For example, news event detection procedures use information-based systems to categorize text and reduce the trade-off between an important missed event and false alarm rates.[18] The Internet provides multiple opportunities for scanning. For example, Amazon.com, similar to many Internet companies, records significant information about individuals visiting its Web site, particularly if a purchase is made. Amazon then welcomes these customers by name when they visit the Web site again. The firm even sends messages to them about specials and new products similar to those purchased in previous visits.

Additionally, many Web sites and advertisers on the Internet use "cookies" to obtain information from those who visit their sites. These files are saved to the visitors' hard drives, allowing customers to connect more quickly to a firm's Web site, but also allowing the firm to solicit a variety of information about them. Because cookies are often placed without customers' knowledge, their use can be a questionable practice. Although computer cookies have been a boon to online advertisers, they have brought a significant threat of computer viruses, hacking ability, spyware, spam, and other difficulties to computer users. The U.S. Congress is considering legislation that would ban spyware-enabling cookies.[19]

Monitoring

When *monitoring*, analysts observe environmental changes to see if an important trend is emerging from among those spotted by scanning.[20] Critical to successful monitoring is the firm's ability to detect meaning in different environmental events and trends. For example, the size of the middle class of African Americans continues to grow in the United States. With increasing wealth, this group of citizens is more aggressively pursuing investment options.[21] Companies in the financial planning sector could monitor this change in the economic segment to determine the degree to which a competitively important trend is emerging. By monitoring trends, firms can be prepared to introduce new goods and services at the appropriate time to take advantage of the opportunities identified trends provide.[22]

Effective monitoring requires the firm to identify important stakeholders. Because the importance of different stakeholders can vary over a firm's life cycle, careful attention must be given to the firm's needs and its stakeholder groups across time.[23] Scanning and monitoring are particularly important when a firm competes in an industry with high technological uncertainty.[24] Scanning and monitoring not only can provide the firm with information, they also serve as a means of importing new knowledge about markets and about how to successfully commercialize new technologies that the firm has developed.[25]

Forecasting

Scanning and monitoring are concerned with events and trends in the general environment at a point in time. When *forecasting*, analysts develop feasible projections of what might happen, and how quickly, as a result of the changes and trends detected through scanning and monitoring.[26] For example, analysts might forecast the time that will be required for a new technology to reach the marketplace, the length of time before different corporate training procedures are required to deal with anticipated changes in the composition of the workforce, or how much time will elapse before changes in governmental taxation policies affect consumers' purchasing patterns.

Forecasting events and outcomes accurately is challenging. Alcas Corporation is a direct marketing company that features Cutco Cutlery. Cutco Cutlery is in an alliance with Vector Marketing, another firm that is closely held by Alcas. Cutco produces an assortment of knives and cutting utensils and has a well-known brand. However, in 2001 it had a difficult forecasting problem. The company had forecasted a 25 percent increase in sales, but sales actually increased 47 percent. Although generally positive, this created a shortage and Cutco Cutlery did not have the capacity to fill orders in its usual timely fashion. Normal delivery of two to three weeks eventually was pushed to five or six weeks. This was an important problem because the company had built its reputation on quick delivery as a way to differentiate the value it provides to consumers.[27] Forecasting is important in order to adjust sales appropriately to meet demand.

Assessing

The objective of *assessing* is to determine the timing and significance of the effects of environmental changes and trends on the strategic management of the firm.[28] Through

Media producers, cell phone producers, and cell phone service operators are seeking to make money from "cell vision."

scanning, monitoring, and forecasting, analysts are able to understand the general environment. Going a step further, the intent of assessment is to specify the implications of that understanding for the organization. Without assessment, the firm is left with data that may be interesting but are of unknown competitive relevance. Despite the importance of studying the environment, evidence suggests that only a relatively small percentage of firms use formal processes to collect and disseminate such information. Even if formal assessment is inadequate, the appropriate interpretation of that information is important. "Research found that how accurate senior executives are about their competitive environments is indeed less important for strategy and corresponding organizational changes than the way in which they interpret information about their environments."[29] Thus, although gathering and organizing information is important, investing money in the appropriate interpretation of that intelligence may be equally important. Accordingly, after information has been gathered, assessing whether a trend in the environment represents an opportunity or a threat is extremely important.

Assessing is also important in making sure the strategy is right. As noted earlier, the next big opportunity for cell phone companies seems to be "cell vision," the ability to receive video on a cell phone. A lot of companies, including media producers such as Disney, cell phone producers such as Motorola, and cell phone service operators such as Sprint, are seeking to make money off this new trend. The critical issue is assessing the right positioning and gauging whether U.S. consumers are ready for this service. Will the cell phone substitute for Apple's iPod music player, a laptop, or a BlackBerry phone/organizer/browser? Will the emphasis be on entertainment or games, or will there be more practical uses such as receiving weather forecasts, making presentations, or even watching movies? Getting the strategy right will depend on the accuracy of the assessment.[30]

Segments of the General Environment

The general environment is composed of segments that are external to the firm (see Table 2.1). Although the degree of impact varies, these environmental segments affect each industry and its firms. The challenge to the firm is to scan, monitor, forecast, and assess those elements in each segment that are of the greatest importance. These efforts should result in recognition of environmental changes, trends, opportunities, and threats. Opportunities are then matched with a firm's core competencies (the matching process is discussed further in Chapter 3).

The Demographic Segment

The **demographic segment** is concerned with a population's size, age structure, geographic distribution, ethnic mix, and income distribution.[31] Often demographic segments are analyzed on a global basis because of their potential effects across countries' borders and because many firms compete in global markets.

Population Size

Before the end of 2005, the world's population is expected to be slightly less than 6.5 billion, up from 6.1 billion in 2000. Combined, China and India accounted for one-third of the 6.1 billion. Experts speculate that the population might stabilize at 10 billion after 2200 if the deceleration in the rate of increase in the world's head count continues. By 2050, India (with over 1.5 billion people projected) and China (with just under 1.5 billion people projected) are expected to be the most populous countries.[32] Interestingly, only slightly over one billion people live in developed countries whereas over five billion live in developing countries.

Observing demographic changes in populations highlights the importance of this environmental segment. For example, it is projected that by 2006, 20 percent of Japan's citizens will be at least 65, while the United States and China will not reach this level until 2036. In Japan this is up 10 percent from just 20 years ago. Government officials hope that by encouraging the employees to work longer through incentives for improved retirement—71 percent of Japanese ages 60 to 64 continue to work—will counteract lower birthrates enough to prevent a significant decline in the overall work-force. Without older citizens' increasing willingness to work longer, Japan would likely experience cost overruns in its pension system. Like Japan, Italy will reach 20 percent over 65 in 2006 and Germany will reach it in 2009. However, workers in these two countries tend to retire at an earlier age than the Japanese. Their policy makers have encouraged this in order to reduce the unemployment rate. But with workers retiring earlier than the Japanese, these countries are looking at higher expenses in their pension systems and a significant loss of skilled labor that may affect productivity rates.[33] Interestingly, the United States has a higher birthrate and significant immigration, placing it in a better position than Japan and other European nations.

Age Structure

As noted above, in Japan and other countries, the world's population is rapidly aging. In North America and Europe, millions of baby boomers are approaching retirement. However, even in developing countries with large numbers of people under the age of 35, birth rates have been declining sharply. In China, for example, by 2040 there will be 400 million people over the age of 60. The 90 million baby boomers in North America are fueling the current economy because they seem to continue to spend as they age. They are also thus expected to fuel growth in the financial planning sector as they inherit $1 trillion over the next 15 years and rush to save more before retirement. However, the future surrounding baby boomers is clouded in at least two areas. One problem is the significant increase in health-care costs. For instance, Canadian health care, which has strong government subsidies, is predicted to consume 40 percent of all government tax revenues by 2040. The other problem is that as the number of retired baby boomers swells, the number of workers paying Social Security and other taxes will decrease significantly. This will leave governments in North America and Europe facing significant choices; it seems that governments will have to raise the retirement age (as have the Japanese through incentives to stay in the work force), cut benefits, raise taxes and/or run significant budget deficits.[34]

Although emerging economy populations are aging as well, they still have a significantly younger large labor force. The consumer products being produced so cheaply in China and being exported to the United States are helping North American consumers to contain inflation. However, the basic prices of commodities such as copper, oil, and gas have been rising as China increases its productivity and seeks to maintain employment levels of its large population. As the workforce in the West ages and education levels rise in emerging economies, the United States and Canada will be accepting large numbers of immigrant workers. At the same time, Western firms are outsourcing work to such countries as India, which has a growing high-tech sector. India produced 70,000 high tech jobs in 2004.[35] As can be seen, changes in the age structure have significant impacts on firms in an economy.

Geographic Distribution

For decades, the U.S. population has been shifting from the north and east to the west and south. Similarly, the trend of relocating from metropolitan to nonmetropolitan areas continues. These trends are changing local and state governments' tax bases. In turn, business firms' decisions regarding location are influenced by the degree of support that different taxing agencies offer as well as the rates at which these agencies tax businesses.

The geographic distribution of populations throughout the world is also affected by the capabilities resulting from advances in communications technology. Through computer technologies, for example, people can remain in their homes, communicating with others in remote locations to complete their work.

Ethnic Mix

The ethnic mix of countries' populations continues to change. Within the United States, the ethnicity of states and their cities varies significantly. For firms, the challenge is to be sensitive to these changes. The Hispanic market in the United States has been changing significantly. CSI TV, the 24-hour cable channel for young Latinos, was launched in February 2004 and now has 10 million viewers. Its motto is "Speak English. Live Latin." Firms need to focus on marketing not only to the broader Hispanic market but also to those who want to be integrated and "don't want to be segregated."[36] This latter market segment wants to see their own lives being portrayed on television, rather than those of Anglos. They want to shop at the same stores and have a similar lifestyle. Men's Wearhouse learned this by the failure of its Eddie Rodriguez clothing stores, which targeted Latino men; all six stores were scheduled to be closed by the end of 2005. Consumers simply said "no" to the concept because they wanted to be integrated. Hispanic Americans between the ages of 14 and 34 want to be spoken to in English but stay true to their Latino identity. The Latino spending power is important for large consumer sectors such as grocery stores, movie studios, financial services, and clothing stores among others. Overall, the Hispanic market is $636 billion in size.[37] Through careful study, companies can develop and market products that satisfy the unique needs of different ethnic groups.

CSI TV appeals to a changing Hispanic market.

Changes in the ethnic mix also affect a workforce's composition and cooperation.[38] In the United States, for example, the population and labor force will continue to diversify, as immigration accounts for a sizable part of growth. Projections are that the combined Latino and Asian population shares will increase to 34 percent of the total U.S. population by 2050.[39] Interestingly, much of this immigrant workforce is bypassing high-cost coastal cities and settling in smaller rural towns. Many of these workers are in low-wage, labor-intensive industries like construction, food service, lodging, and landscaping.[40] For this reason, if border security is tightened, these industries will likely face labor shortages.

San Francisco, Oakland, San Jose, and the extensive suburbs around these three large cities have a unique ethnic mix: 11 percent of the residents are Asian, while 18 percent are of Hispanic origin. Such an ethnic mix has created a challenge to develop programs to fit this variety for the television stations in this large market. If a TV station receives one or two percentage points increase in listeners, it can become a top-rated station because of the close competition. Accordingly, they must devote programming to meeting the requirements of the different ethnic and eclectic audiences. Also the population is highly educated, thanks to the proximity of Silicon Valley and universities such as Stanford and University of California, Berkeley. An educated but diverse population increases the difficulty in meeting the programming requirements of all the different ethnic market segments as well as meeting the needs of this latter segment.[41]

Income Distribution

Understanding how income is distributed within and across populations informs firms of different groups' purchasing power and discretionary income. Studies of income distributions suggest that although living standards have improved over time, variations exist within and between nations.[42] Of interest to firms are the average incomes of households and individuals. For instance, the increase in dual-career couples has had a notable effect on average incomes. Although real income has been declining in general, the household income of dual-career couples has increased. These figures yield strategically relevant information for firms. For instance, research indicates that whether an employee is part of a dual-career couple can strongly influence the willingness of the employee to accept an international assignment.[43]

The Economic Segment

The health of a nation's economy affects individual firms and industries. Because of this, companies study the economic environment to identify changes, trends, and their strategic implications.

The **economic environment** refers to the nature and direction of the economy in which a firm competes or may compete.[44] Because nations are interconnected as a result of the global economy, firms must scan, monitor, forecast, and assess the health of economies outside their host nation. For example, many nations throughout the world are affected by the U.S. economy.

The U.S. economy declined into a recession in 2001 that extended into 2002. In order to stimulate the economy, interest rates in the United States were cut to near record lows in 2003, equaling the rates in 1958.[45] Largely due to the low interest rates, the economy grew substantially in 2004 and 2005. Global trade was likewise stimulated. For example, the National Institute Economic Review predicted the following: "Global growth prospects remain robust, with world GDP rising by 4.3 percent in 2005 and 4.2 percent in 2006."[46] However, if oil prices continue to remain at high levels, it will dampen global output growth. Globalization and opening of new markets such as China contributed to this phenomenal growth. While bilateral trade can enrich the economies of the countries involved, it also makes each country more vulnerable to negative events.

For instance, research indicates that the risks associated with the war in Iraq contributed to the decline in U.S. interest rates and the decline in treasury yields as well as lower equity prices. Furthermore, the war led to a fall in the dollar and a rise in oil prices. These factors were especially influenced by the three months leading up to the arrival of Coalition forces in Baghdad.[47] Although the war in Iraq was threatening to the U.S. economy, it has also provided the prospect that a more pluralistic Iraq will lead to pressures in the region to increase political and economic liberalization. The region's stock exchanges responded; in 2004 Arab stock markets were up 75.9 percent.[48] It will be interesting to see how the region responds to further democratic reforms such as possible changes in an independent Palestine and Lebanon, each of which held elections in 2005.

As our discussion of the economic segment suggests, economic issues are intertwined closely with the realities of the external environment's political/legal segment.

The Political/Legal Segment

The **political/legal segment** is the arena in which organizations and interest groups compete for attention, resources, and a voice in overseeing the body of laws and regulations guiding the interactions among nations.[49] Essentially, this segment represents how organizations try to influence government and how governments influence them. As the politics of regulations change, for example, this segment influences the nature of competition through changing the rules (for other examples of political/legal elements, see Table 2.1).

For example, when new regulations are adopted based on new laws (e.g., the Sarbanes-Oxley law dealing with corporate governance—see Chapter 10 for more information)—they often affect the competitive actions taken by firms (their actions are regulated). An example is the recent global trend toward privatization of government-owned or -regulated firms. The transformation from state-owned to private firms has substantial implications for the competitive landscapes in countries and industries.[50]

Firms must carefully analyze a new political administration's business-related policies and philosophies. Antitrust laws, taxation laws, industries chosen for deregulation, labor training laws, and the degree of commitment to educational institutions are areas in which an administration's policies can affect the operations and profitability of industries and individual firms. Often, firms develop a political strategy to influence governmental policies and actions that might affect them. The effects of global governmental policies on a firm's competitive position increase the importance of forming an effective political strategy.[51]

Business firms across the globe today confront an interesting array of political/legal questions and issues. For example, the debate continues over trade policies. Some believe that a nation should erect trade barriers to protect its companies' products. However, as countries continue to join the World Trade Organization (WTO), more countries seem to believe that free trade across nations serves the best interests of individual countries and their citizens. A Geneva-based organization, the WTO establishes rules for global trade. For instance, after joining the World Trade Organization, China recently ended a 40-year-old global textile-quota system regulating its exports. Earlier, to ease the problems created for other countries China had voluntarily enacted transition tariffs. When the quota system expired in early 2005, Chinese textiles flooded global markets, threatening domestic textile industries. Several countries responded by imposing even higher tariffs to level the playing field.[52]

The regulations related to pharmaceuticals and telecommunications, along with the approval or disapproval of major acquisitions, shows the power of government entities. This power also suggests how important it is for firms to have a political strategy. Alternatively, the Food and Drug Administration (FDA) was criticized in 2003 for being too slow to act. External critics with knowledge of agency operations expressed concerns that the FDA was limiting enforcement actions to avoid potential litigation.[53] However, problems with Cox-2 pain inhibitors such as Merck's Vioxx (a prescribed pain medication) have caused a backlash such that the pendulum is swinging back; the FDA has suggested that advertising for prescription drugs such as Vioxx is not appropriate. Agencies such as the FDA are continually being swayed one way or another by external critics either from the consumer side or from the drug industry side.[54] The regulations are too few for some and too many for others. Regardless, regulations tend to vary with different presidential administrations, and firms must cope with these variances.

The Sociocultural Segment

The **sociocultural segment** is concerned with a society's attitudes and cultural values. Because attitudes and values form the cornerstone of a society, they often drive demographic, economic, political/legal, and technological conditions and changes.

Sociocultural segments differ across countries. For example, in the United States, 13.1 percent of the nation's GDP is spent on health care. This is the highest percentage of any country in the world. Germany allocates 10.4 percent of GDP to health care, while in Switzerland the percentage is 10.2. Interestingly, the U.S. rate of citizens' access to health care is below that of these and other countries.[55]

The reverse is true for retirement planning. A study in 15 countries indicated that retirement planning in the United States starts earlier than in other countries. "Americans are involved in retirement issues to a greater extent than other countries, particularly in western Europe where the Social Security and pensions systems provide a much higher percentage of income in retirement."[56] U.S. residents start planning for retirement in their 30s, while those in Portugal, Spain, Italy, and Japan start in their 40s and 50s. Attitudes regarding saving for retirement also affect a nation's economic and political/legal segments.

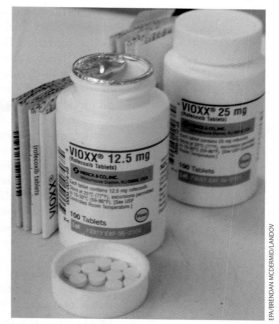

Agencies such as the FDA are continually being swayed one way or another by external critics from the consumer side and from the drug industry side.

A significant trend in many countries is increased workforce diversity. As noted earlier, the composition of the U.S. workforce is changing such that Caucasians will be in the minority in a few years. Effective management of a culturally diverse workforce can produce a competitive advantage. For example, heterogeneous work teams have been shown to produce more effective strategic analyses, more creativity and innovation, and higher-quality decisions than homogeneous work teams.[57] However, evidence also suggests that diverse work teams are difficult to manage and achieve integration. As such, not all diverse work teams are able to achieve these positive outcomes.[58]

As the labor force has increased, it has also become more diverse as significantly more women and minorities from a variety of cultures have entered the labor force. In 1993, the total U.S. workforce was slightly below 130 million, but in 2005, it was slightly over 148 million.[59] An increasing number of women are also starting and managing their own businesses. Using data from the U.S. Census bureau, the Center for Women's Business Research states: "As of 2004, there are an estimated 10.6 million 50 percent or more women-owned privately held firms in the United States, accounting for nearly half (47.7 percent) of all privately held firms in the country."[60] The number of new businesses started by women continues to increase, and thus women own a larger percentage of the total number of businesses.[61]

The growing gender, ethnic, and cultural diversity in the workforce creates challenges and opportunities,[62] including combining the best of both men's and women's traditional leadership styles. Although diversity in the workforce has the potential to add improved performance, research indicates there are important conditions requiring management of diversity initiatives in order to reap these organizational benefits. Human resource practitioners are trained to successfully manage diversity issues to enhance positive outcomes.[63]

Another manifestation of changing attitudes toward work is the continuing growth of contingency workers (part-time, temporary, and contract employees) throughout the global economy. This trend is significant in several parts of the world, including Canada, Japan, Latin America, Western Europe, and the United States. The fastest growing group of contingency workers is in the technical and professional area. Contributing to this growth are corporate restructurings and downsizings in poor economic conditions along with a breakdown of lifetime employment practices (e.g., in Japan).

The continued growth of suburban communities in the United States and abroad is another major sociocultural trend. The increasing number of people living in the suburbs has a number of effects. For example, longer commute times to urban businesses increase pressure for better transportation systems and superhighway systems (e.g., outer beltways to serve the suburban communities). Suburban growth also has an effect on the number of electronic telecommuters, which is expected to increase rapidly in the 21st century. Beyond suburbs lie what the U.S. Census Bureau calls "micropolitan" areas. These areas are often 100 or more miles from a large city and have 10,000 to 49,999 people. They offer rural-like living with many of the larger city amenities such as strip malls and chain restaurants like Starbucks, Chili's, Long John Silver's, and Arby's, but housing and labor costs are much cheaper.[64] Following this growth, some businesses are locating in the suburbs closer to their employees. This work-style option is feasible because of changes in the technological segment, including the Internet's rapid growth and evolution.[65]

The Technological Segment

Pervasive and diversified in scope, technological changes affect many parts of societies. These effects occur primarily through new products, processes, and materials. The **technological segment** includes the institutions and activities involved with creating new knowledge and translating that knowledge into new outputs, products, processes, and materials.

Given the rapid pace of technological change, it is vital for firms to thoroughly study the technological segment.[66] The importance of these efforts is suggested by the finding that early adopters of new technology often achieve higher market shares and earn higher returns. Thus, executives must verify that their firm is continuously scanning the external environment to identify potential substitutes for technologies that are in current use, as well as to spot newly emerging technologies from which their firm could derive competitive advantage.[67]

However, not only is forecasting more difficult in this day and age, but a company that misses its forecast is often disciplined by the market with a reduction in stock price. For example, DreamWorks Animation, a division of DreamWorks SKG, based its forecast of *Shrek 2* DVD sales in part on the historically long sales life of animated DVDs. But today, because of increased competition (more firms are releasing an increasing number of DVDs) and limited shelf space, DVD titles have a much shorter retail life. When retailers started returning millions of unsold copies, DreamWorks' earnings fell short of analysts' forecasts by 25 percent and its stock price tumbled. Misjudging how much a title will sell can have a substantial effect on the bottom line of small studios such as DreamWorks Animation, which releases only two films a year.[68] In contrast, studios that produce many films each year are shielded from the effects of a short life in one film.

Internet technology is playing an increasingly important role in global commerce. For example, Internet pharmacies have facilitated senior U.S. citizens' access to cheaper drugs in Canada, where U.S. citizens can save as much as 80 percent on drug costs. Legislation was passed in the United States in 2003 to ensure that U.S. citizens could continue to access drugs from Canada. As a result, the number of Canadian Internet pharmacies grew sharply in 2003.[69]

While the Internet was a significant technological advance providing substantial power to companies utilizing its potential, wireless communication technology is predicted to be the next critical technological opportunity. By 2003, handheld devices and other wireless communications equipment were being used to access a variety of network-based services. The use of handheld computers with wireless network connectivity, Web-enabled mobile phone handsets, and other emerging platforms (e.g., consumer Internet-access devices) is expected to increase substantially, soon becoming the dominant form of communication and commerce.[70]

Clearly, the Internet and wireless forms of communications are important technological developments for many reasons. One reason for their importance, however, is that they facilitate the diffusion of other technology and knowledge critical for achieving and maintaining a competitive advantage.[71] Companies must stay current with technologies as they evolve, but also must be prepared to act quickly to embrace important new disruptive technologies shortly after they are introduced.[72] Certainly on a global scale, the technological opportunities and threats in the general environment have an effect on whether firms obtain new technology from external sources (such as by licensing and acquisition) or develop it internally.

The Global Segment

The **global segment** includes relevant new global markets, existing markets that are changing, important international political events, and critical cultural and institutional characteristics of global markets.[73] Globalization of business markets creates both opportunities and challenges for firms.[74] For example, firms can identify and enter valuable new global markets.[75] In addition to contemplating opportunities, firms should recognize potential competitive threats in these markets. China presents many opportunities and some threats for international firms.[76] Creating additional opportunities is China's 2001 admission to the World Trade Organization. As mentioned earlier, the low cost of Chinese products threatens many firms in the textile industry. For instance, buyers of textile products such as Marks & Spencer in the United Kingdom and others throughout the world cannot ignore China's comparative advantages, even with tariffs in place. Its average labor costs are 90 percent lower than those in the United States and Italy. Furthermore, their manufacturers are more efficient than garment manufacturers in other low-cost countries such as India or Vietnam. The WTO member countries can restrict Chinese imports until 2008 if they can show that local markets are disrupted. However, even with quotas a number of firms such as Wal-Mart and hotel chains such as Hilton and Radisson are looking to increase their sourcing from Chinese firms because of the significant cost advantage.[77]

Exemplifying the globalization trend is the increasing amount of global outsourcing. For example, Bank of America began major reductions of its back office operations staff (approximately 3,700), outsourcing many of the jobs to Indian businesses. Accenture outsourced the jobs of 5,000 accounting, software, and back office employees to the Philippines. General Electric has outsourced 20,000 jobs to companies in India for a variety of technical tasks.[78] However, recent research suggests that there is a trade-off between flexibility and efficiency if all work in a particular function or product is outsourced. Custom work to fill special orders, for example, is more efficiently done through domestic manufacturing; outsourcing standard products to an offshore facility needs to save at least 15 percent to be justified. Even in the textile industry, where much outsourcing is done for efficiency reasons, many order adjustments or special orders require flexibility and cannot be readily handled by low-cost offshore producers.[79]

Moving into international markets extends a firm's reach and potential. Toyota receives almost 50 percent of its total sales revenue from outside Japan, its home country. Over 60 percent of McDonald's sales revenues and almost 98 percent of Nokia's sales revenues are from outside their home countries.[80] Firms can also increase the opportunity to sell innovations by entering international markets. The larger total market increases the probability that the firm will earn a return on its innovations. Certainly, firms entering new markets can diffuse new knowledge they have created and learn from the new markets as well.[81]

Firms should recognize the different sociocultural and institutional attributes of global markets. Companies competing in South Korea, for example, must understand the value placed on hierarchical order, formality, and self-control, as well as on duty rather than rights. Furthermore, Korean ideology emphasizes communitarianism, a characteristic of many Asian countries. Korea's approach differs from those of Japan and China, however, in that it focuses on *inhwa,* or harmony. Inhwa is based on a respect of hierarchical relationships and obedience to authority. Alternatively, the approach in China stresses *guanxi*—personal relationships or good connections—while in Japan, the focus is on *wa,* or group harmony and social cohesion.[82] The institutional context of China suggests a major emphasis on centralized planning by the government. The Chinese government provides incentives to firms to develop alliances with foreign firms having sophisticated technology in hopes of building knowledge and introducing new technologies to the Chinese markets over time.[83]

Firms based in other countries that compete in these markets can learn from them. For example, the cultural characteristics above suggest the value of relationships. In particular, guanxi emphasizes the importance of social capital when one is doing business in China.[84] Although social capital is important for success in most markets around the world,[85] problems can arise from its strict ethic of reciprocity and obligation. It can divide, for example, loyalties of sales and procurement people who are in networks outside the company. Sales and procurement people need to have their loyalties focused on the company with whom they are employed.[86] Global markets offer firms more opportunities to obtain the resources needed for success. For example, the Kuwait Investment Authority is the second largest shareholder of DaimlerChrysler. Alternatively, globalization can be threatening. In particular, companies in emerging market countries may be vulnerable to larger, more resource-rich, and more effective competitors from developed markets.

Additionally, there are risks in global markets. A decade ago, Argentina's market was full of promise, but in 2001, Argentina experienced a financial crisis that placed it on the brink of bankruptcy forcing it to default on more than $80 billion in public debt. In 2005 Argentina was still struggling to complete the restructuring of its debt. The original bonds will be discounted by 70 percent, although 24 percent of the bondholders refused to participate. While Argentina has enjoyed strong growth since the recession it experienced in 2002, future growth will be difficult to attain because competition for capital around the world is heating up and it will be difficult for Argentina to overcome its reputation for failure to pay its debts.[87]

A key objective of analyzing the general environment is identifying anticipated changes and trends among external elements. With a focus on the future, the analysis of the general environment allows firms to identify opportunities and threats. As noted in the Opening Case, there have been and continue to be a number of threats to airlines from the general environment.

Global markets offer firms more opportunities to obtain the resources needed for success. The Kuwait Investment Authority is the second largest shareholder of DaimlerChrysler.

Perhaps the biggest threat comes from the continuing threat in the economy and global environment; the industry badly needs an economic recovery to increase the demand for air travel. As a result, it is necessary to have a top management team with the experience, knowledge, and sensitivity required to effectively analyze this segment of the environment.[88] Also critical to a firm's future operations is an understanding of its industry environment and its competitors; these issues are considered next.

Industry Environment Analysis

An **industry** is a group of firms producing products that are close substitutes. In the course of competition, these firms influence one another. Typically, industries include a rich mix of competitive strategies that companies use in pursuing strategic competitiveness and above-average returns. In part, these strategies are chosen because of the influence of an industry's characteristics.[89] The Strategic Focus on the global competitive nature of the automobile industry illustrates the difficulties that firms are having with the competitive forces in an industry.

As illustrated in the Strategic Focus on the global auto industry, compared with the general environment, the industry environment often has a more direct effect on the firm's strategic competitiveness and above-average returns.[90] The intensity of industry competition and an industry's profit potential are functions of five forces of competition: the threats posed by new entrants, the power of suppliers, the power of buyers, product substitutes, and the intensity of rivalry among competitors (see Figure 2.2).

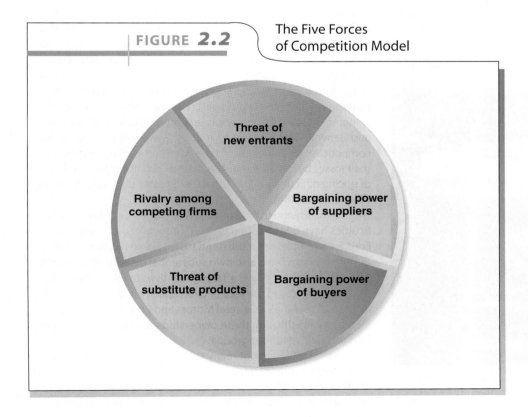

FIGURE **2.2** The Five Forces of Competition Model

Threat of new entrants

Rivalry among competing firms

Bargaining power of suppliers

Threat of substitute products

Bargaining power of buyers

The Nature of the Competitive Forces in the Global Automobile Industry

The global auto industry is becoming more competitive for domestic competitors in the United States and elsewhere because of the globalizing nature of the automobile industry. General Motors' market share in North America dropped to 25.2 percent during the first quarter of 2005 from 26.3 percent a year earlier. At the end of 2004, Ford and Chrysler held 18.3 and 13 percent, respectively, while Toyota, Honda, and Nissan had increased their share to 12.2, 8.2, and 5.8 percent, respectively. Two of the more recent entrants, Korean automakers Kia and Hyundai, have made inroads in the U.S. market as well. However, the next hopeful entrants are to be found in China, for example, Shanghai Automotive Industry Corp. (SAIC).

As a result of this increased foreign competition, in the first quarter of 2005, General Motors experienced an operating loss of $839 million. GM's annual earnings in 2004 were $1.21 billion. Restructuring charges for its European operations and a buyout program for white-collar employees brought GM's total first-quarter 2005 loss to $1.1 billion.

In regard to potential new entrants, SAIC produced over 600,000 vehicles in joint ventures with Volkswagen and General Motors in China. Currently SAIC does not produce any vehicles under its own brand name, but because China has a large growing market for automobiles and the government requires joint ventures, SAIC will have a significant role to play in the global automobile industry. An article in *Fortune* indicates that SAIC for now needs its partners before it can enter with its own products outside of China. "Despite being a longtime maker of commercial vehicles and components, it lacks the capital to develop a full line of autos, the technology to make them powerful, safe and up-to-date and the brand name needed to lure customers." These are just some of the significant barriers to entry in the world auto industry.

Because General Motors has been having difficulties along with Ford financially (Ford also experienced a loss in the first quarter of 2005), they have pushed these difficulties backward to their suppliers by requiring suppliers to reduce their costs. Delphi (with 185,000 employees) is struggling as the number one automotive parts supplier for General Motors. Similarly, Visteon, which has 70,000 employees, has said that it may not be able to cover its debt payments and is seeking a restructuring deal with its former parent Ford. Both Delphi and Visteon were formerly part of General Motors and Ford, respectively. Both Ford and General Motors still have strong ownership positions in their former auto parts divisions, which they kept after spinning off these businesses as separate companies. While Ford and General Motors have demanded lower prices because of their competitive difficulties, these auto parts companies have increased their losses beyond the requests by their dominant buyers because of pricing difficulties in the face of rising costs such as for steel and other commodities.

Similarly, much of General Motors' and Ford's inventory difficulties have been pushed forward onto rental car companies. Ford, for example, has a substantial ownership position in Hertz rental cars. Both firms also own substantial dealership networks through which they have offered incentives to lower their substantial inventory in the face of overcapacity in the global auto industry. Accordingly, General Motors and Ford have significant market power through these ownership arrangements in regard to significant customer groups.

While there are not many substitutes for autos, with increasing gas prices many individuals might turn to mass transit or other forms of transportation if available. However, bicycles are not much of a substitute given the fast-moving pace of transportation these days.

Shanghai Automotive Industry Corp. produced over 600,000 vehicles in joint ventures with Volkswagen and General Motors in China in 2004.

Finally, competition in the global automobile industry, as noted in the opening paragraph, is very intense. The primary reason for *global* competition is that the economies of scale necessary to produce automobiles and especially high-value-added parts such as engines and transmissions often requires companies to expand beyond their national borders. Also, when there is a downturn in one country, the immediate reaction is to seek to sell in another country. Although China, for instance, has had the hottest market as far as growth and in regard to future expectations, as sales have dampened in the short term in China, firms such as DaimlerChrysler have considered manufacturing vehicles there for export to other markets such as Europe and the United States because manufacturing costs are low in China relative to the rest of the world.

Although firms such as Toyota have continued to make money in a difficult environment, even they are experiencing a downturn of profits due to the highly competitive environment. However, Toyota continues to make inroads as do Honda and Nissan in the U.S. market, which has caused severe problems for both Ford and General Motors. Recently, however, DaimlerChrysler has been doing well in the United States, especially with its Chrysler products, although the Mercedes brand had difficulties at the beginning of 2005. These trends are illustrative of the nature of Porter's five forces, discussed in this chapter.

Sources: 2005, China hopes to be next nation to make major inroads in U.S. car market, *USA Today,* April 25, B4; N. E. Boudette, Power play: Chrysler's storied hemi motor helps it escape Detroit's gloom, *Wall Street Journal,* June 17, A1, A10; J. Fox, 2005, A CEO puts his job on the line, *Fortune,* May 2, 17–21; L. Hawkins, 2005, GM shifts to a loss of $1.1 billion, *Wall Street Journal,* April 20, A3, A6; J. Sapsford, 2005, Nissan to sell China vans made in the U.S., *Wall Street Journal,* March 17, A14; D. Welch, D. Beucke, K. Kerwin, M. Arndt, B. Hindo, E. Thornton, D. Kiley, & I. Rowley, 2005, Why GM's plan won't work . . . and the ugly road ahead, *Business Week,* May 9, 84–92; J. B. White & J. S. Lublin, 2005, Visteon, Delphi seek to revamp, as woes mount, *Wall Street Journal,* A3, A4; A. Taylor, III, 2004, Shanghai Auto wants to be the world's next great car company, *Fortune,* October 4, 103–109.

The five forces model of competition expands the arena for competitive analysis. Historically, when studying the competitive environment, firms concentrated on companies with which they competed directly. However, firms must search more broadly to identify current and potential competitors by identifying potential customers as well as the firms serving them. Competing for the same customers and thus being influenced by how customers value location and firm capabilities in their decisions is referred to as the market microstructure.[91] Understanding this area is particularly important, because in recent years industry boundaries have become blurred. For example, telecommunications companies now compete with cable broadcasters, software manufacturers provide personal financial services, airlines sell mutual funds, and automakers sell insurance and provide financing.[92] In addition to the focus on customers rather than on specific industry boundaries to define markets, geographic boundaries are also relevant. Research suggests that different geographic markets for the same product can have considerably different competitive conditions.[93]

The five forces model recognizes that suppliers can become a firm's competitors (by integrating forward), as can buyers (by integrating backward). Several firms have integrated forward in the pharmaceutical industry by acquiring distributors or wholesalers. In addition, firms choosing to enter a new market and those producing products that are adequate substitutes for existing products can become a company's competitors.

Threat of New Entrants

Identifying new entrants is important because they can threaten the market share of existing competitors.[94] One reason new entrants pose such a threat is that they bring additional production capacity. Unless the demand for a good or service is increasing, additional capacity holds consumers' costs down, resulting in less revenue and lower returns for competing firms. Often, new entrants have a keen interest in gaining a large market share. As a result, new competitors may force existing firms to be more effective and efficient and to learn how to compete on new dimensions (for example, using an Internet-based distribution channel).

The likelihood that firms will enter an industry is a function of two factors: barriers to entry and the retaliation expected from current industry participants. Entry barriers make it difficult for new firms to enter an industry and often place them at a competitive disadvantage even when they are able to enter. As such, high entry barriers increase the returns for existing firms in the industry and may allow some firms to dominate the industry.[95] Interestingly, though the airline industry has high entry barriers (e.g., substantial capital costs), new firms have entered in recent years, among them AirTran Airways (ATA) and JetBlue. As the Opening Case indicates, both entrants are creating competitive challenges for the major airlines, especially with the economic problems in the early 21st century. Both firms compete in the low-cost segments, where consumer demand has increased, making the major high-cost legacy airlines less competitive and more vulnerable to these newer airlines' competitive actions.

Barriers to Entry

Existing competitors try to develop barriers to entry. For example, cable firms are entering the phone service business. Accordingly, local firm services such as SBC Communications are developing a bundling strategy to prevent customer turnover. They offer high-speed Internet services, satellite television, and wireless services in a single package that could cost $100 per month. In doing this they are creating switching costs for their customers to prevent defections to alternative substitute-product cable providers (see the Strategic Focus on cable companies).[96] Potential entrants such as the cable firms seek markets in which the entry barriers are relatively insignificant. An absence of entry barriers increases the probability that a new entrant can operate profitably. There are several kinds of potentially significant entry barriers.

Economies of Scale. *Economies of scale* are derived from incremental efficiency improvements through experience as a firm gets larger. Therefore, as the quantity of a product produced during a given period increases, the cost of manufacturing each unit declines. Economies of scale can be developed in most business functions, such as marketing, manufacturing, research and development, and purchasing.[97] Increasing economies of scale enhances a firm's flexibility. For example, a firm may choose to reduce its price and capture a greater share of the market. Alternatively, it may keep its price constant to increase profits. In so doing, it likely will increase its free cash flow, which is helpful in times of recession.

New entrants face a dilemma when confronting current competitors' scale economies. Small-scale entry places them at a cost disadvantage. Alternatively, large-scale entry, in which the new entrant manufactures large volumes of a product to gain economies of scale, risks strong competitive retaliation. This is the situation faced by potential new entrants from China. Although Chinese firms have significant capacity to produce cars and parts, as suggested in the Strategic Focus on the global auto industry, they do not have the brand recognition necessary to challenge larger global auto firms.

GETTY IMAGES

In 2004 many cable companies' stock prices fell relative to the S&P 500 as investors saw video satellite rivals Direct TV and Echostar (Dish Network) pick up former cable TV subscribers.

Some competitive conditions reduce the ability of economies of scale to create an entry barrier. Many companies now customize their products for large numbers of small customer groups. Customized products are not manufactured in the volumes necessary to achieve economies of scale. Customization is made possible by new flexible manufacturing systems (this point is discussed further in Chapter 4). In fact, the new manufacturing technology facilitated by advanced information systems has allowed the development of mass customization in an increasing number of industries. While customization is not appropriate for all products, mass customization is becoming increasingly common in manufacturing products.[98] In fact, online ordering has enhanced the ability of customers to obtain customized products. They are often referred to as "markets of one."[99] Companies manufacturing customized products learn how to respond quickly to customers' desires rather than develop scale economies.

Product Differentiation.   Over time, customers may come to believe that a firm's product is unique. This belief can result from the firm's service to the customer, effective advertising campaigns, or being the first to market a good or service. Companies such as Coca-Cola, PepsiCo, and the world's automobile manufacturers spend a great deal of money on advertising to convince potential customers of their products' distinctiveness. Customers valuing a product's uniqueness tend to become loyal to both the product and the company producing it. Typically, new entrants must allocate many resources over time to overcome existing customer loyalties. To combat the perception of uniqueness, new entrants frequently offer products at lower prices. This decision, however, may result in lower profits or even losses.

Capital Requirements.   Competing in a new industry requires a firm to have resources to invest. In addition to physical facilities, capital is needed for inventories, marketing activities, and other critical business functions. Even when competing in a new industry is attractive, the capital required for successful market entry may not be available to pursue an apparent market opportunity. For example, defense industries would be very difficult to enter because of the substantial resource investments required to be competitive. In addition, because of the high knowledge requirements of the defense industry, a firm might enter the defense industry through the acquisition of an existing firm. For example, through a series of acquisitions and joint ventures with local players, the French defense contractor Thales SA entered the markets of Britain, the Netherlands, Australia, South Africa, South Korea, and Singapore.[100] But it had access to the capital necessary to do it.

Switching Costs.   Switching costs are the one-time costs customers incur when they buy from a different supplier. The costs of buying new ancillary equipment and of retraining employees, and even the psychic costs of ending a relationship, may be incurred in switching to a new supplier. In some cases, switching costs are low, such as when the consumer switches to a different soft drink. Switching costs can vary as a function of time. For example, in terms of credit hours toward graduation, the cost to a student to transfer from one university to another as a freshman is much lower than it is when the student is entering the senior year. Occasionally, a decision made by manufacturers to produce a new, innovative product creates high switching costs for the final consumer. Customer loyalty programs, such as airlines' frequent flier miles, are intended to increase the customer's switching costs.

 If switching costs are high, a new entrant must offer either a substantially lower price or a much better product to attract buyers. Usually, the more established the relationship between parties, the greater is the cost incurred to switch to an alternative offering.

Access to Distribution Channels. Over time, industry participants typically develop effective means of distributing products. Once a relationship with its distributors has been developed, a firm will nurture it to create switching costs for the distributors.

Access to distribution channels can be a strong entry barrier for new entrants, particularly in consumer nondurable goods industries (for example, in grocery stores where shelf space is limited) and in international markets. New entrants have to persuade distributors to carry their products, either in addition to or in place of those currently distributed. Price breaks and cooperative advertising allowances may be used for this purpose; however, those practices reduce the new entrant's profit potential.

Cost Disadvantages Independent of Scale. Sometimes, established competitors have cost advantages that new entrants cannot duplicate. Proprietary product technology, favorable access to raw materials, desirable locations, and government subsidies are examples. Successful competition requires new entrants to reduce the strategic relevance of these factors. Delivering purchases directly to the buyer can counter the advantage of a desirable location; new food establishments in an undesirable location often follow this practice. Similarly, automobile dealerships located in unattractive areas (perhaps in a city's downtown area) can provide superior service (such as picking up the car to be serviced and then delivering it to the customer) to overcome a competitor's location advantage.

Government Policy. Through licensing and permit requirements, governments can also control entry into an industry. Liquor retailing, radio and TV broadcasting, banking, and trucking are examples of industries in which government decisions and actions affect entry possibilities. Also, governments often restrict entry into some industries because of the need to provide quality service or the need to protect jobs. Alternatively, deregulation of industries, exemplified by the airline industry (see the Opening Case) and utilities in the United States, allows more firms to enter.[101] Some of the most publicized government actions are those involving antitrust. For example, the U.S. and European Union governments pursued an antitrust case against Microsoft. The final settlement in the United States involved a relatively small penalty for the company. However, the EU judgments were more severe.[102]

Expected Retaliation

Firms seeking to enter an industry also anticipate the reactions of firms in the industry. An expectation of swift and vigorous competitive responses reduces the likelihood of entry. Vigorous retaliation can be expected when the existing firm has a major stake in the industry (for example, it has fixed assets with few, if any, alternative uses), when it has substantial resources, and when industry growth is slow or constrained. For example, any firm attempting to enter the auto industry at the current time can expect significant retaliation from existing competitors due to the overcapacity.

Locating market niches not being served by incumbents allows the new entrant to avoid entry barriers. Small entrepreneurial firms are generally best suited for identifying and serving neglected market segments. When Honda first entered the U.S. market, it concentrated on small-engine motorcycles, a market that firms such as Harley-Davidson ignored. By targeting this neglected niche, Honda avoided competition. After consolidating its position, Honda used its strength to attack rivals by introducing larger motorcycles and competing in the broader market. Competitive actions and competitive responses between firms such as Honda and Harley-Davidson are discussed fully in Chapter 5.

Bargaining Power of Suppliers

Increasing prices and reducing the quality of their products are potential means used by suppliers to exert power over firms competing within an industry. If a firm is unable to recover cost increases by its suppliers through its own pricing structure, its profitability is reduced by its suppliers' actions. A supplier group is powerful when

- It is dominated by a few large companies and is more concentrated than the industry to which it sells.
- Satisfactory substitute products are not available to industry firms.
- Industry firms are not a significant customer for the supplier group.
- Suppliers' goods are critical to buyers' marketplace success.
- The effectiveness of suppliers' products has created high switching costs for industry firms.
- It poses a credible threat to integrate forward into the buyers' industry. Credibility is enhanced when suppliers have substantial resources and provide a highly differentiated product.

The airline industry is an example of an industry in which suppliers' bargaining power is changing. Though the number of suppliers is low, the demand for the major aircraft is also relatively low. Boeing and Airbus strongly compete for most orders of major aircraft.[103] However, the shift in airline strategy to short-haul flights and low costs has enhanced the fortunes of other aircraft manufacturers who make smaller and more efficient aircraft.

Bargaining Power of Buyers

Firms seek to maximize the return on their invested capital. Alternatively, buyers (customers of an industry or a firm) want to buy products at the lowest possible price—the point at which the industry earns the lowest acceptable rate of return on its invested capital. To reduce their costs, buyers bargain for higher quality, greater levels of service, and lower prices. These outcomes are achieved by encouraging competitive battles among the industry's firms. Customers (buyer groups) are powerful when

- They purchase a large portion of an industry's total output.
- The sales of the product being purchased account for a significant portion of the seller's annual revenues.
- They could switch to another product at little, if any, cost.
- The industry's products are undifferentiated or standardized, and the buyers pose a credible threat if they were to integrate backward into the sellers' industry.

Armed with greater amounts of information about the manufacturer's costs and the power of the Internet as a shopping and distribution alternative, consumers appear to be increasing their bargaining power in many industries. One reason for this shift is that individual buyers incur virtually zero switching costs when they decide to purchase from one manufacturer rather than another or from one dealer as opposed to a second or third one. These realities are also forcing airlines to change their strategies. There is very little differentiation in air travel, and the switching costs are very low. As consolidation occurs in the phone business through the acquisition of AT&T and MCI (see the Strategic Focus on the phone versus cable companies), it is expected that business customers will have less leverage to secure discounts given that there are fewer service providers.[104]

Threat of Substitute Products

Substitute products are goods or services from outside a given industry that perform similar or the same functions as a product that the industry produces. For example, as a sugar substitute, NutraSweet places an upper limit on sugar manufacturers' prices— NutraSweet and sugar perform the same function, though with different characteristics.

Other product substitutes include e-mail and fax machines instead of overnight deliveries, plastic containers rather than glass jars, and tea instead of coffee. Newspaper firms have experienced a circulation decline gradually over a number of years, accelerating to a 1 to 3 percent loss in the six months ending in March of 2005. The declines are due to substitute outlets for news including Internet sources, cable television news channels, and e-mail and cell phone alerts.[105] These products are increasingly popular, especially among younger people, and as product substitutes they have significant potential to continue to reduce overall newspaper circulation sales.

In general, product substitutes present a strong threat to a firm when customers face few, if any, switching costs and when the substitute product's price is lower or its quality and performance capabilities are equal to or greater than those of the competing product. Differentiating a product along dimensions that customers value (such as price, quality, service after the sale, and location) reduces a substitute's attractiveness. As the Strategic Focus illustrates, local phone server companies have lost significant subscriber base to cable companies offering phone services. Similarly, cable companies have lost TV subscriber base to satellite TV operators. Each company has been using a bundling approach to increase switching costs to forestall these substitutions.

Intensity of Rivalry among Competitors

Because an industry's firms are mutually dependent, actions taken by one company usually invite competitive responses. In many industries, firms actively compete against one another. Competitive rivalry intensifies when a firm is challenged by a competitor's actions or when a company recognizes an opportunity to improve its market position.

Firms within industries are rarely homogeneous; they differ in resources and capabilities and seek to differentiate themselves from competitors.[106] Typically, firms seek to differentiate their products from competitors' offerings in ways that customers value and in which the firms have a competitive advantage. Visible dimensions on which rivalry is based include price, quality, and innovation.

As explained in the Opening Case, the rivalry between competitors, such as United, US Airways, American, and other major airlines, is intense. The competitive rivalry is also intense in the automobile industry, as described in the Strategic Focus. In fact, the rivalry is so intense that both General Motors and Ford have experienced significantly lower earnings due to price cuts, which, in turn, have led to their debt ratings being lowered below investment grade or to "junk" levels.[107]

As suggested by the Opening Case and the Strategic Focus on the automobile industry, various factors influence the intensity of rivalry between or among competitors. Next, we discuss the most prominent factors that experience shows to affect the intensity of firms' rivalries.

Numerous or Equally Balanced Competitors

Intense rivalries are common in industries with many companies. With multiple competitors, it is common for a few firms to believe that they can act without eliciting a response. However, evidence suggests that other firms generally are aware of competitors' actions, often choosing to respond to them. At the other extreme, industries with only a few firms of equivalent size and power also tend to have strong rivalries. The large and often similar-sized resource bases of these firms permit vigorous actions and responses. The competitive battles between Airbus and Boeing exemplify intense rivalry between relatively equivalent competitors.[108]

Slow Industry Growth

When a market is growing, firms try to effectively use resources to serve an expanding customer base. Growing markets reduce the pressure to take customers from competitors.

Satellite TV Service Substitutes for Digital Cable Service, Which Substitutes for Local Telephone Service

Many cable companies are offering a bundle of services including digital TV, broadband Internet service, and local and long distance phone service. This bundling approach has worked particularly well for large cable companies such as Comcast, Time Warner, and Cox. However, in 2004 many of these cable companies' stock prices fell relative to the S&P 500 as investors saw video satellite rivals Direct TV and Echostar (Dish Network) pick up former cable TV subscribers. In early 2004 the largest cable operators, holding about 88 percent of cable's 64 million subscribers, lost 338,000 more video buyers compared to 2003 levels. Meanwhile, Direct TV grew by 409,000 subscribers to a total of 13 million, while Echostar's Dish Network added 340,000 subscribers, reaching a total of 10.1 million. Cable subscribers were substituting satellite video products for the cable product.

Similarly, local Bell phone service providers have been losing large numbers of customers to cable service providers' digital telephone service. Local phone companies have been downsizing their employee base not only because of cable companies but also because of wireless phone service becoming available through competitors.

To combat the substitution from both cable companies and wireless companies, phone companies have been creating strategic alliances with satellite companies to offer TV service and have similarly been making deals either to ally or buy wireless service opportunities to prevent further erosion in their dominant business. In addition, local phone service companies have added long distance services. Often this has taken place through acquisition. AT&T was purchased by SBC Communication, while Verizon outbid Quest in a battle to acquire MCI.

Additionally, phone companies have been laying significant amounts of fiber-optic cable, which is capable of providing video feed. However, the companies need a large subscriber base in order to reduce the costs of offering video content. The problem with this strategy is that the available subscriber base is largely encumbered, with 80 percent of the homes already subscribed to satellite. Thus, the question is whether phone companies will be able to compete as a significant late entrant in offering video content services. As a short-term alternative, some phone companies now sell satellite TV service through collaborative ventures, such as Verizon with Direct TV. Similarly, SBC has a deal with Echostar to sell Dish Network services through its customer billing services.

To make matters worse, the costs of offering phone service over the Internet are significantly cheaper than the costs of initiating service to a hard-wired phone service customer (either cable or phone lines). In mid-2005, EarthLink announced it would offer phone service with a new Internet-based technology that allows customers to use traditional phone equipment to make calls. Other Internet-based phone services to this point, based on voice over Internet protocol (VoIP), have required customers to connect phones directly to a computer or router, meaning phone service is not available during a power outage. Substitutions to both cable and phone companies will likely continue through this technology unless they cannibalize their own offerings and move to VoIP as well. Besides costly investment of fiber optics for video service, another disadvantage for phone service companies is significant union contracts with which cable companies and other new entrants in phone service over the Internet are not as yet encumbered.

Sources: P. Grant, 2005, Comcast plans major rollout of phone service over cable, *Wall Street Journal,* January 10, B1, B5; P. Grant, 2005, Comcast aims to dial up profit—and growth, *Wall Street Journal,* January 11, C1, C5; T. Lowry & S. E. Ante, 2005, Verizon's video vision, *Business Week,* May 2, 77; S. N. Mehta, 2005, SBC can't resist a blast from its past, *Fortune,* February 21, 30–31; S. N. Mehta, 2005, Verizon's CEO makes the call, *Fortune,* March 7, 26; D. Searcey, 2005, Earthlink to offer Internet calling on regular phones, *Wall Street Journal,* June 6, B7; K. Brown & A. Latour, 2004, Phone industry faces upheaval as ways of calling change fast, *Wall Street Journal,* August 25, A1, A8; J. Drucker, D. K. Berman, & P. Grant, 2004, Showdown of the giants: Cable titans discuss offering cellular services, intensifying foray into telecom's turf, *Wall Street Journal,* November 8, B1, B4; A. Latour, 2004, Showdown of the giants: Verizon, SBC saddle up to compete head to head with cable and TV service, *Wall Street Journal,* November 8, B1, B2; D. Leiberman, 2004, Cable companies' subscriber base sinks, while satellite firms soar, *USA Today,* August 11, B3; S. Young & A. Latour, 2004, Get ready for a new cell phone service—with an old name, *Wall Street Journal,* May 6, B1, B2.

However, rivalry in no-growth or slow-growth markets becomes more intense as firms battle to increase their market shares by attracting competitors' customers.

Typically, battles to protect market shares are fierce. Certainly, this has been the case in the airline industry. The instability in the market that results from these competitive engagements reduces profitability for all airlines throughout the industry. As the Opening Case notes, reduced profitability is one of the reasons that two major U.S.-based airlines have declared bankruptcy and others on a global basis have experienced major net losses since 2000.

High Fixed Costs or High Storage Costs

When fixed costs account for a large part of total costs, companies try to maximize the use of their productive capacity. Doing so allows the firm to spread costs across a larger volume of output. However, when many firms attempt to maximize their productive capacity, excess capacity is created on an industry-wide basis. To then reduce inventories, individual companies typically cut the price of their product and offer rebates and other special discounts to customers. However, these practices, common in the automobile manufacturing industry, often intensify competition. The pattern of excess capacity at the industry level followed by intense rivalry at the firm level is observed frequently in industries with high storage costs. Perishable products, for example, lose their value rapidly with the passage of time. As their inventories grow, producers of perishable goods often use pricing strategies to sell products quickly.

Lack of Differentiation or Low Switching Costs

When buyers find a differentiated product that satisfies their needs, they frequently purchase the product loyally over time. Industries with many companies that have successfully differentiated their products have less rivalry, resulting in lower competition for individual firms. Firms that develop and sustain a differentiated product that cannot be easily imitated by competitors often earn higher returns.[109] However, when buyers view products as commodities (that is, as products with few differentiated features or capabilities), rivalry intensifies. In these instances, buyers' purchasing decisions are based primarily on price and, to a lesser degree, service. Personal computers are becoming a commodity. Thus, the competition among Dell, HP, and other computer manufacturers is expected to be strong.

The effect of switching costs is identical to the effect of differentiated products. The lower the buyers' switching costs, the easier it is for competitors to attract buyers through pricing and service offerings. High switching costs at least partially insulate the firm from rivals' efforts to attract customers. Interestingly, the switching costs—such as pilot and mechanic training—are high in aircraft purchases, yet the rivalry between Boeing and Airbus remains intense because the stakes for both are extremely high.

High Strategic Stakes

Competitive rivalry is likely to be high when it is important for several of the competitors to perform well in the market. For example, although it is diversified and is a market leader in other businesses, Samsung has targeted market leadership in the consumer electronics market and is doing quite well. This market is quite important to Sony and other major competitors, such as Hitachi, Matsushita, NEC, and Mitsubishi. There is substantial rivalry in this market, and it is likely to continue over the next few years.

High strategic stakes can also exist in terms of geographic locations. For example, Japanese automobile manufacturers are committed to a significant presence in the U.S. marketplace. A key reason for this is that the United States is the world's largest single market for auto manufacturers' products. Because of the stakes involved in this country for Japanese and U.S. manufacturers, rivalry among firms in the U.S. and the global automobile industry is highly intense. It should be noted that while proximity tends to promote greater rivalry, physically proximate competition has potentially positive benefits as well. For example, when competitors are located near each other, it is easier for suppliers to serve them, and competitors can develop economies of scale that lead to lower production costs. Additionally, communications with key industry stakeholders such as suppliers are facilitated and more efficient when they are close to the firm.[110] However, this can work against suppliers who have a close relationship with their customers. As the Strategic Focus on the global auto industry reports, two automotive suppliers that are dominated by their key buyers have been forced to lower their prices, causing them to incur significant losses.

High Exit Barriers

Sometimes companies continue competing in an industry even though the returns on their invested capital are low or negative. Firms making this choice likely face high exit barriers, which include economic, strategic, and emotional factors causing companies to remain in an industry when the profitability of doing so is questionable. Exit barriers are especially high in the airline industry. Common exit barriers are

- Specialized assets (assets with values linked to a particular business or location).
- Fixed costs of exit (such as labor agreements).
- Strategic interrelationships (relationships of mutual dependence, such as those between one business and other parts of a company's operations, including shared facilities and access to financial markets).
- Emotional barriers (aversion to economically justified business decisions because of fear for one's own career, loyalty to employees, and so forth).
- Government and social restrictions (more common outside the United States, these restrictions often are based on government concerns for job losses and regional economic effects).

Interpreting Industry Analyses

Effective industry analyses are products of careful study and interpretation of data and information from multiple sources. A wealth of industry-specific data is available to be analyzed. Because of globalization, international markets and rivalries must be included in the firm's analyses. In fact, research shows that in some industries, international variables are more important than domestic ones as determinants of strategic competitiveness. Furthermore, because of the development of global markets, a country's borders no longer restrict industry structures. In fact, movement into international markets enhances the chances of success for new ventures as well as more established firms.[111]

Following study of the five forces of competition, the firm can develop the insights required to determine an industry's attractiveness in terms of the firm's potential to earn adequate or superior returns on its invested capital. In general, the stronger competitive forces are, the lower is the profit potential for an industry's firms. An unattractive industry has low entry barriers, suppliers and buyers with strong bargaining positions, strong competitive threats from product substitutes, and intense rivalry among competitors. These industry characteristics make it very difficult for firms to achieve strategic competitiveness and earn above-average returns. Alternatively, an attractive industry has high entry barriers, suppliers and buyers with little bargaining power, few competitive threats from product substitutes, and relatively moderate rivalry.[112] Next, we turn to strategic groups operating within industries.

Strategic Groups

A set of firms emphasizing similar strategic dimensions to use a similar strategy is called a **strategic group**.[113] The competition between firms within a strategic group is greater than the competition between a member of a strategic group and companies outside that strategic group. Another way of saying this is that intra-strategic group competition is more intense than is inter-strategic group competition. In fact, there is more heterogeneity in the performance of firms within strategic groups than across the groups. The performance leaders within groups are able to follow strategies similar to those of other firms in the group and yet maintain strategic distinctiveness to gain and sustain a competitive advantage.[114]

The extent of technological leadership, product quality, pricing policies, distribution channels, and customer service are examples of strategic dimensions that firms in a strategic group may treat similarly. Patterns of competition within strategic groups may be described this way: "Organizations in a strategic group occupy similar positions in the market, offer similar goods to similar customers, and may also make similar choices about production technology and other organizational features."[115] Thus, membership in a particular strategic group defines the essential characteristics of the firm's strategy.[116]

The notion of strategic groups can be useful for analyzing an industry's competitive structure. Such analyses can be helpful in diagnosing competition, positioning, and the profitability of firms within an industry.[117] High mobility barriers, high rivalry, and low resources among the firms within an industry will limit the formation of strategic groups.[118] However, research suggests that after strategic groups are formed, their membership remains relatively stable over time, making analysis easier and more useful.[119]

Using strategic groups to understand an industry's competitive structure requires the firm to plot companies' competitive actions and competitive responses along strategic dimensions such as pricing decisions, product quality, distribution channels, and so forth. Doing this shows the firm how certain companies are competing similarly in terms of how they use similar strategic dimensions. For example, there are unique radio markets because consumers prefer different music formats and programming (news radio, talk radio, and so forth). Typically, a radio format is created through choices made regarding music or nonmusic style, scheduling, and announcer style.[120] It is estimated that approximately 30 different radio formats exist, suggesting that there are many strategic groups in this industry. The strategies within each of the 30 groups are similar, while the strategies across the total set of strategic groups are dissimilar. As a result, Clear Channel Communications often owns several stations in a large city, but each uses a different format. Therefore, Clear Channel likely has stations operating in most or all of the 30 strategic groups in this industry. Additionally, a new strategic group has been added as the satellite radio companies XM and Sirius have formed an intense rivalry in trying to attract corporate customers such as auto manufacturers and rental car companies as well as individual subscribers.[121] Satellite radio could be considered a substitute because it is technologically different from terrestrial radio, but the satellite companies, each with more than 100 different channels, offer the same types of music formats and programming that traditional stations do. Although satellite companies obtain most of their revenue from subscriptions, they are similar to terrestrial radio in that some advertising is done on talk, news, and sports channels. Firms could increase their understanding of competition in the commercial radio industry by plotting companies' actions and responses in terms of important strategic dimensions, such as those we have mentioned. With the addition of satellite radio, the competition among different strategic groups is likely to increase.

Strategic groups have several implications. First, because firms within a group offer similar products to the same customers, the competitive rivalry among them can be intense. The more intense the rivalry, the greater the threat to each firm's profitability. Second, the strengths of the five industry forces (the threats posed by new entrants, the power of suppliers, the power of buyers, product substitutes, and the intensity of rivalry among competitors) differ across strategic groups. Third, the closer the strategic groups are in terms of their strategies, the greater is the likelihood of rivalry between the groups.

Having a thorough understanding of primary competitors helps a firm formulate and implement an appropriate strategy. Clearly XM and Sirius are in a strategic group and compete directly against each other. XM has been successful in its focus on new technology, while Sirius has focused on signing innovative and exclusive content. Volkswagen tried to break out of its strategic group of companies selling mid-priced autos. But it was unsuccessful in entering the strategic group of firms with similar strategies selling premium autos (e.g., Mercedes-Benz, BMW). Because of these efforts, VW has lost market share in its primary markets.[122]

Competitor Analysis

The competitor environment is the final part of the external environment requiring study. Competitor analysis focuses on each company against which a firm directly competes. For example, XM and Sirius satellite radio, Home Depot and Lowe's, and Boeing and Airbus should be keenly interested in understanding each other's objectives, strategies, assumptions, and capabilities. Furthermore, intense rivalry creates a strong need to understand competitors.[123] In a competitor analysis, the firm seeks to understand

- What drives the competitor, as shown by its *future objectives.*
- What the competitor is doing and can do, as revealed by its *current strategy.*
- What the competitor believes about the industry, as shown by its *assumptions.*
- What the competitor's capabilities are, as shown by its *strengths* and *weaknesses.*[124]

Information about these four dimensions helps the firm prepare an anticipated response profile for each competitor (see Figure 2.3). The results of an effective competitor analysis help a firm understand, interpret, and predict its competitors' actions and responses. Understanding the actions of competitors clearly contributes to the firm's ability to compete successfully within the industry.[125] Interestingly, research suggests that analyzing possible reactions to competitive moves is not often carried out by executives.[126] This suggests that those firms that do work at such analyses can obtain a competitive advantage over firms that do not.

Critical to an effective competitor analysis is gathering data and information that can help the firm understand its competitors' intentions and the strategic implications resulting from them.[127] Useful data and information combine to form **competitor intelligence:** the set of data and information the firm gathers to better understand and better anticipate competitors' objectives, strategies, assumptions, and capabilities. In competitor analysis, the firm should gather intelligence not only about its competitors, but also regarding public policies in countries around the world. Such intelligence facilitates an understanding of the strategic posture of foreign competitors.

FIGURE **2.3** Competitor Analysis Components

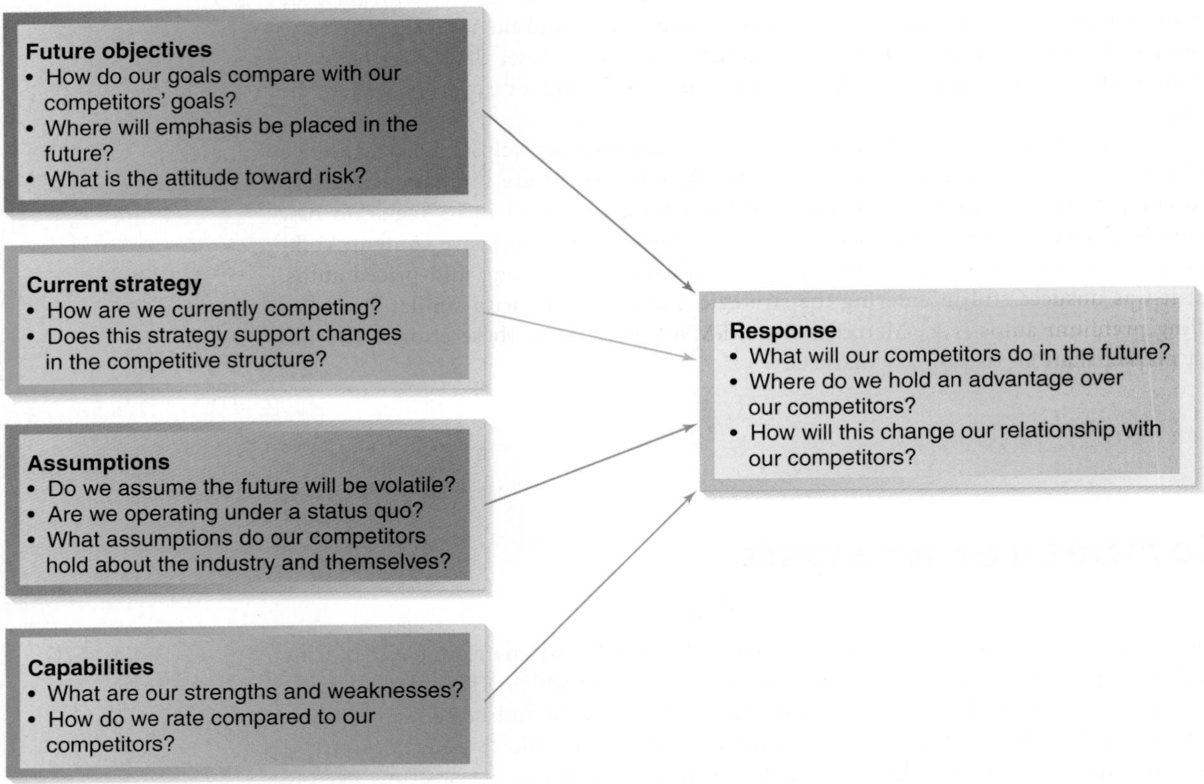

Future objectives
- How do our goals compare with our competitors' goals?
- Where will emphasis be placed in the future?
- What is the attitude toward risk?

Current strategy
- How are we currently competing?
- Does this strategy support changes in the competitive structure?

Assumptions
- Do we assume the future will be volatile?
- Are we operating under a status quo?
- What assumptions do our competitors hold about the industry and themselves?

Capabilities
- What are our strengths and weaknesses?
- How do we rate compared to our competitors?

Response
- What will our competitors do in the future?
- Where do we hold an advantage over our competitors?
- How will this change our relationship with our competitors?

Through effective competitive and public policy intelligence, the firm gains the insights needed to create a competitive advantage and to increase the quality of the strategic decisions it makes when deciding how to compete against its rivals. Microsoft has been analyzing its competitor Google for ways to overcome and dominate the search engine business as it did in the browser contest with Netscape. *Fortune* magazine reported that Bill Gates, Microsoft's founder, in December 2003 was doing his own competitive intelligence on Google by browsing Google's Web site when he came across a help-wanted page: "Why, he wondered, were the qualifications for so many of them identical to Microsoft job specs? Google was a web search business, yet here on the screen were postings for engineers with backgrounds that had nothing to do with search and everything to do with Microsoft's core business-people trained in things like operating-system design, compiler optimization, and distributed-systems architecture. Gates wondered whether Microsoft might be facing much more than a war in search. An e-mail he sent to a handful of execs that day said, in effect, 'We have to watch these guys. It looks like they are building something to compete with us.'"[128]

Microsoft has found Google to be a formidable competitor. The company could not damage Google through a price war as it did Netscape because Google's software is generally offered for free. There is not a way to lure online advertisers because advertisers pay by how many times users click on an ad and on the number of keywords clicked in a search. Thus, ad revenue is set by customer election, not by Google. Also, you cannot expect success by bundling the search engine with the operating system as Microsoft also did in competition with Netscape because Google "works from a Treo, a BlackBerry, a cell phone, a television, an Apple, or a Linux computer—any device with some kind of keyboard and Internet access." As a former Microsoft executive puts it, Microsoft "has to play Google's game to compete with Google."[129]

As the above analysis of Google suggests, one must also pay attention to the complementors of a firm's products and strategy.[130] **Complementors** are the network of companies that sells complementary goods or services or are compatible with the focal firm's own product or service. This could also include suppliers and buyers who have a strong "network" relationship with the focal firm. A strong network of complementors can solidify a competitive advantage, as it has in Google's case because of the number of Internet access products with which it functions smoothly. If a complementor's good or service adds value to the sale of the focal firm's good or service it is likely to create value for the focal firm. For example, there is a range of complements necessary to sell automobiles, including financial services to arrange credit, luxury options including stereo equipment, and extended warranties.

Ethical Considerations

Firms should follow generally accepted ethical practices in gathering competitor intelligence. Industry associations often develop lists of these practices that firms can adopt. Practices considered both legal and ethical include (1) obtaining publicly available information (such as court records, competitors' help-wanted advertisements, annual reports, financial reports of publicly held corporations, and Uniform Commercial Code filings), and (2) attending trade fairs and shows to obtain competitors' brochures, view their exhibits, and listen to discussions about their products.

In contrast, certain practices (including blackmail, trespassing, eavesdropping, and stealing drawings, samples, or documents) are widely viewed as unethical and often are illegal. To protect themselves from digital fraud or theft by competitors that break into their employees' PCs, some companies buy insurance to protect against PC hacking.[131]

Some competitor intelligence practices may be legal, but a firm must decide whether they are also ethical, given the image it desires as a corporate citizen. Especially with electronic transmissions, the line between legal and ethical practices can be difficult to determine. For example, a firm may develop Web site addresses that are very similar to those of its competitors and thus occasionally receive e-mail transmissions that were intended for those competitors. The practice is an example of the challenges companies face when deciding how to gather intelligence about competitors while simultaneously determining what to do to prevent competitors from learning too much about them.

Open discussions of intelligence-gathering techniques can help a firm to ensure that employees, customers, suppliers, and even potential competitors understand its convictions to follow ethical practices for gathering competitor intelligence. An appropriate guideline for competitor intelligence practices is to respect the principles of common morality and the right of competitors not to reveal certain information about their products, operations, and strategic intentions.[132]

- The firm's external environment is challenging and complex. Because of the external environment's effect on performance, the firm must develop the skills required to identify opportunities and threats existing in that environment.

- The external environment has three major parts: (1) the general environment (elements in the broader society that affect industries and their firms), (2) the industry environment (factors that influence a firm, its competitive actions and responses, and the industry's profit potential), and (3) the competitor environment (in which the firm analyzes each major competitor's future objectives, current strategies, assumptions, and capabilities).

- The external environmental analysis process has four steps: scanning, monitoring, forecasting, and assessing. Through environmental analyses, the firm identifies opportunities and threats.

- The general environment has six segments: demographic, economic, political/legal, sociocultural, technological, and global. For each segment, the firm wants to determine the strategic relevance of environmental changes and trends.

- Compared with the general environment, the industry environment has a more direct effect on the firm's strategic actions. The five forces model of competition includes the threat of entry, the power of suppliers, the power of buyers, product substitutes, and the intensity of rivalry among competitors. By studying these forces, the firm finds a position in an industry where it can influence the forces in its favor or where it can buffer itself from the power of the forces in order to increase its ability to earn above-average returns.

- Industries are populated with different strategic groups. A strategic group is a collection of firms that follow similar strategies along similar dimensions. Competitive rivalry is greater within a strategic group than it is between strategic groups.

- Competitor analysis informs the firm about the future objectives, current strategies, assumptions, and capabilities of the companies with whom it competes directly. It should also examine complementors that sustain a competitor's strategy.

- Different techniques are used to create competitor intelligence: the set of data, information, and knowledge that allows the firm to better understand its competitors and thereby predict their likely strategic and tactical actions. Firms should use only legal and ethical practices to gather intelligence. The Internet enhances firms' capabilities to gather insights about competitors and their strategic intentions.

1. C. Williams & W. Mitchell, 2004, Focusing firm evolution: The impact of information infrastructure on market entry by U.S. telecommunications companies, 1984–1998, *Management Science,* 5: 1561–1575; D. J. Ketchen Jr. & T. B. Palmer, 1999, Strategic responses to poor organizational performance: A test of competing perspectives, *Journal of Management,* 25: 683–706.

2. J. Tan, 2005, Venturing in turbulent water: A historical perspective of economic reform and entrepreneurial transformation, *Journal of Business Venturing,* 20: 689–704; J. T. Eckhardt & S. A. Shane, 2003, Opportunities and entrepreneurship, *Journal of Management,* 29: 333–349; P. Chattopadhyay, W. H. Glick, & G. P. Huber, 2001, Organizational actions in response to threats and opportunities, *Academy of Management Journal,* 44: 937–955.

3. J. Gimeno, R. E. Hoskisson, B. D. Beal, & W. P. Wan, 2005, Explaining the clustering of international expansion moves: A critical test in the U.S. telecommunications industry, *Academy of Management Journal,* 48: 297–319; C. M. Grimm, H. Lee, & K. G. Smith, 2005, *Strategy as Action: Competitive Dynamics and Competitive Advantages,* New York: Oxford University Press.

4. S. Rangan & A. Drummond, 2004, Explaining outcomes in competition among foreign multinationals in a focal host market, *Strategic Management Journal,* 25: 285–293; J. M. Mezias, 2002, Identifying liabilities of foreignness and strategies to minimize their effects: The case of labor lawsuit judgments in the United States, *Strategic Management Journal,* 23: 229–244.

5. K. G. Smith, C. J. Collins, & K. D. Clark, 2005, Existing knowledge, knowledge creation capability, and the rate of new product introduction in high-technology firms, *Academy of Management Journal,* 48: 346–357.

6. R. M. Grant, 2003, Strategic planning in a turbulent environment: Evidence from the oil majors, *Strategic Management Journal,* 24: 491–517.

7. M. Song, C. Droge, S. Hanvanich, & R. Calantone, 2005, Marketing and technology resource complementarity: An analysis of their interaction effect in two environmental contexts, *Strategic Management Journal,* 26: 259–276; D. M. De Carolis, 2003, Competencies and imitability in the

pharmaceutical industry: An analysis of their relationship with firm performance, *Journal of Management,* 29: 27–50.

8. L. Fahey, 1999, *Competitors,* New York: John Wiley & Sons; B. A. Walters & R. L. Priem, 1999, Business strategy and CEO intelligence acquisition, *Competitive Intelligence Review,* 10(2): 15–22.

9. R. D. Ireland & M. A. Hitt, 1999, Achieving and maintaining strategic competitiveness in the 21st century: The role of strategic leadership, *Academy of Management Executive,* 13(1): 43–57; M. A. Hitt, B. W. Keats, & S. M. DeMarie, 1998, Navigating in the new competitive landscape: Building strategic flexibility and competitive advantage in the 21st century, *Academy of Management Executive,* 12(4): 22–42.

10. L. Välikangas & M. Gibbert, 2005, Boundary-setting strategies for escaping innovation traps, *MIT Sloan Management Review,* 46(3): 58–65; Q. Nguyen & H. Mintzberg, 2003, The rhythm of change, *MIT Sloan Management Review,* 44(4): 79–84.

11. E. Brown, 2005, Coming soon to a tiny screen near you, *Forbes,* May 23, 64–78.

12. G. Panagiotou, 2003, Bring SWOT into focus, *Business Strategy Review,* 14(2): 8–10.

13. P. Lattman, 2005, Rebound, *Forbes,* March 28, 58.

14. K. Y. Au & J. Fukuda, 2002, Boundary spanning behaviors of expatriates, *Journal of World Business,* 37(4): 285–296; L. Rosenkopf & A. Nerkar, 2001, Beyond local search: Boundary-spanning exploration, and impact in the optical disk industry, *Strategic Management Journal,* 22: 287–306.

15. K. M. Patton & T. M. McKenna, 2005, Scanning for competitive intelligence, *Competitive Intelligence Magazine,* 8(2): 24–26; D. F. Kuratko, R. D. Ireland, & J. S. Hornsby, 2001, Improving firm performance through entrepreneurial actions: Acordia's corporate entrepreneurship strategy, *Academy of Management Executive,* 15(4): 60–71.

16. K. M. Eisenhardt, 2002, Has strategy changed? *MIT Sloan Management Review,* 43(2): 88–91; I. Goll & A. M. A. Rasheed, 1997, Rational decision-making and firm performance: The moderating role of environment, *Strategic Management Journal,* 18: 583–591.

17. J. R. Hough & M. A. White, 2004, Scanning actions and environmental dynamism: Gathering information for strategic decision making, *Management Decision,* 42: 781–793; V. K. Garg, B. A. Walters, & R. L. Priem, 2003, Chief executive scanning emphases, environmental dynamism, and manufacturing firm performance, *Strategic Management Journal,* 24: 725–744.

18. C.-P. Wei & Y.-H. Lee, 2004, Event detection from online news documents for supporting environmental scanning, *Decision Support Systems,* 36: 385–401.

19. R. Goldsborough, 2005, The benefits and fear of cookie technology, *Tech Directions,* May, 9.

20. Fahey, *Competitors,* 71–73.

21. P. Yip, 1999, The road to wealth, *Dallas Morning News,* August 2, D1, D3.

22. F. Dahlsten, 2003, Avoiding the customer satisfaction rut, *MIT Sloan Management Review,* 44(4): 73–77; Y. Luo & S. H. Park, 2001, Strategic alignment and performance of market-seeking MNCs in China, *Strategic Management Journal,* 22: 141–155.

23. K. Buysse & A. Verbke, 2003, Proactive strategies: A stakeholder management perspective, *Strategic Management Journal,* 24: 453–470; I. M. Jawahar & G. L. McLaughlin, 2001, Toward a prescriptive stakeholder theory: An organizational life cycle approach, *Academy of Management Review,* 26: 397–414.

24. M. L. Perry, S. Sengupta, & R. Krapfel, 2004, Effectiveness of horizontal strategic alliances in technologically uncertain environments: Are trust and commitment enough, *Journal of Business Research,* 9: 951–956; M. Song & M. M. Montoya-Weiss, 2001, The effect of perceived technological uncertainty on Japanese new product development, *Academy of Management Journal,* 44: 61–80.

25. M. H. Zack, 2003, Rethinking the knowledge-based organization, *MIT Sloan Management Review,* 44(4): 67–71; H. Yli-Renko, E. Autio, & H. J. Sapienza, 2001, Social capital, knowledge acquisition, and knowledge exploitation in young technologically based firms, *Strategic Management Journal,* 22 (Special Issue): 587–613.

26. Fahey, *Competitors.*

27. K. Schelfhaudt & V. Crittenden, 2005, Growing pains for Alcas Corporation, *Journal of Business Research,* 58: 999–1002.

28. Fahey, *Competitors,* 75–77.

29. K. M. Sutcliffe & K. Weber, 2003, The high cost of accurate knowledge, *Harvard Business Review,* 81(5): 74–82.

30. Brown, Coming soon to a tiny screen near you.

31. L. Fahey & V. K. Narayanan, 1986, *Macroenvironmental Analysis for Strategic Management,* St. Paul, MN: West Publishing Company, 58.

32. 2004, World Population Prospects: 2004 Revision www.un.org/esa/population/unpop.htm, 1999, Six billion . . . and counting, *Time,* October 4, 16.

33. S. Moffett, 2005, Fast-aging Japan keeps its elders on the job longer, *Wall Street Journal,* June 15, A1, A8.

34. T. Fennell, 2005, The next 50 years, www.camagazine.com, April.

35. Ibid.

36. J. Ordonez, 2005, 'Speak English. Live Latin,' *Newsweek,* May 30, 30.

37. Ibid.

38. J. A. Chatman & S. E. Spataro, 2005, Using self-categorization theory to understand relational demography-based variations in people's responsiveness to organizational culture, *Academy of Management Journal,* 48: 321–331.

39. 2001, Millennium in motion; 1999, U.S. Department of Labor, Demographic change and the future workforce, *Futurework,* www.dol.gov, November 8.

40. J. Millman, 2005, Low-wage U.S. jobs get "Mexicanized," but there's a price, *Wall Street Journal,* May 2, A2.

41. A. Romano, 2004, Bay area battlefield, *Broadcasting and Cable,* November 15, 15.

42. E. S. Rubenstein, 1999, Inequality, *Forbes,* November 1, 158–160.

43. R. Konopaske, C. Robie, & J. M. Ivancevich, 2005, A preliminary model of spouse influence on managerial global assignment willingness, *International Journal of Human Resource Management,* 16: 405–426.

44. Fahey & Narayanan, *Macroenvironmental Analysis,* 105.

45. G. Ip, 2003, Federal Reserve maintains interest-rate target at 1%, *Wall Street Journal Online,* www.wsj.com, August 13.

46. 2005, At a glance . . . the world economy, *National Institute Economic Review,* April, 2.

47. R. Rigobon & B. Sack, 2005, The effects of war risk on U.S. financial markets, *Journal of Banking and Finance,* 29: 1769–1789.

48. S. Reed, N. Sandor, & R. Brady, 2005, One giant step for Iraq, smaller steps also, *Business Week,* February 14, 56.

49. J.-P. Bonardi, A. J. Hillman, & G. D. Keim, 2005, The attractiveness of political markets: Implications for firm strategy, *Academy of Management Review,* 30: 397–413; G. Keim, 2001, Business and public policy: Competing in the political marketplace, in M. A. Hitt, R. E. Freeman, and J. S. Harrison (eds.), *Handbook of Strategic Management,* Oxford, UK: Blackwell Publishers, 583–601.

50. I. P. Mahmood & C. Rufin, 2005, Governments' dilemma: The role of government in imitation and innovation, *Academy of Management Review,* 30: 338–360; J. O. De Castro & K. Uhlenbruck, 2003, The transformation into entrepreneurial firms, *Management Research,* 1: 171–184.

51. M. D. Lord, 2003, Constituency building as the foundation for corporate political strategy, *Academy of Management Executive,* 17(1): 112–124; D. A. Schuler, K. Rehbein, & R. D. Cramer, 2003, Pursuing strategic advantage through political means: A multivariate approach, *Academy of Management Journal,* 45: 659–672; A. J. Hillman & M. A. Hitt, 1999, Corporate political strategy formulation: A model of approach, participation, and strategy decisions, *Academy of Management Review,* 24: 825–842.

52. C. Hutzler, 2005, Beijing rescinds textile duties, slams U.S., EU on import limits, *Wall Street Journal,* May 31, A3.

53. M. Peterson, 2003, Who's minding the drugstore? *New York Times,* www.nytimes.com, June 29.

54. A. Barrett, 2005, Will drug makers back off the hard sell? *Business Week,* March 7, 44.

55. 2003, U.S. spends the most on healthcare but dollars do not equal health, Medica Portal, www4.medica.de; J. MacIntyre, 1999, Figuratively speaking, *Across the Board,* May 11.

56. C. Debaise, 2005, U. S. workers start early on retirement savings, *Wall Street Journal,* January 20, D2.

57. D. M. Schweiger, T. Atamer, & R. Calori, 2003, Transnational project teams and networks: Making the multinational organization more effective, *Journal of World Business,* 38: 127–140; G. Dessler, 1999, How to earn your employees' commitment, *Academy of Management Executive,* 13(2): 58–67.

58. L. H. Pelled, K. M. Eisenhardt, & K. R. Xin, 1999, Exploring the black box: An analysis of work group diversity, conflict, and performance, *Administrative Science Quarterly,* 44: 1–28.

59. 2005, U.S. Department of Labor, Bureau of Labor Statistics data, www.bls.gov, April.

60. 2004, Center for women's business research, www.womensbusiness research.org, May.

61. J. Raymond, 2001, Defining women: Does the Census Bureau undercount female entrepreneurs? *Business Week Small Biz,* May 21, 12.

62. C. A. Bartlett & S. Ghoshal, 2002, Building competitive advantage through people, *MIT Sloan Management Review,* 43(2): 33–41.

63. M. E. A. Jayne & R. L. Dipboye, 2004, Leveraging diversity to improve business performance: Research findings and recommendations for organizations, *Human Resource Management,* 43: 409–425.

64. M. J. McCarthy, 2004, New outposts: Granbury, Texas, isn't a rural town: it's a 'micropolis'; census bureau adopts term for main street America, and marketers take note; beans, ribs and Starbucks, *Wall Street Journal,* June 3, A1.

65. T. Fleming, 2003, Benefits of taking the superhighway to work, *Canadian HR Reporter,* 16(11): G7.

66. A. L. Porter & S. W. Cunningham, 2004, *Tech mining: Exploiting new technologies for competitive advantage,* Hoboken, N.J.: Wiley.

67. C. W. L. Hill & F. T. Rothaermel, 2003, The performance of incumbent firms in the face of radical technological innovation, *Academy of Management Review,* 28: 257–274; A. Afuah, 2002, Mapping technological capabilities into product markets and competitive advantage: The case of cholesterol drugs, *Strategic Management Journal,* 23: 171–179.

68. M. Marr, 2005, How DreamWorks misjudged DVD sales of its monster hit, *Wall Street Journal,* May 31, A1, A9.

69. J. Baglole, 2003, Canada's southern drug drain, *Wall Street Journal Online,* www.wsj.com, March 31.

70. N. Wingfield, 2003, Anytime, anywhere: The number of Wi-Fi spots is set to explode, bringing the wireless technology to the rest of us, *Wall Street Journal,* March 31, R6, R12.

71. A. Andal-Ancion, P. A. Cartwright, & G. S. Yip, 2003, The digital transformation of traditional businesses, *MIT Sloan Management Review,* 44(4): 34–41; M. A. Hitt, R. D. Ireland, & H. Lee, 2000, Technological learning, knowledge management, firm growth and performance, *Journal of Technology and Engineering Management,* 17: 231–246.

72. Y. Y. Kor & J. T. Mahoney, 2005, How dynamics, management, and governance of resource deployments influence firm-level performance, *Strategic Management Journal,* 26: 489–497; C. Nichols-Nixon & C. Y. Woo, 2003, Technology sourcing and output of established firms in a regime of encompassing technological change, *Strategic Management Journal,* 24: 651–666.

73. W. P. Wan, 2005, Country resource environments, firm capabilities, and corporate diversification strategies, *Journal of Management Studies,* 42: 161–182; M. Wright, I. Filatotchev, R. E. Hoskisson, & M. W. Peng, 2005, Strategy research in emerging economies: Challenging the conventional wisdom, *Journal of Management Studies,* 42: 1–30; W. P. Wan & R. E. Hoskisson, 2003, Home country environments, corporate diversification strategies and firm performance, *Academy of Management Journal,* 46: 27–45.

74. F. Vermeulen & H. Barkema, 2002, Pace, rhythm, and scope: Process dependence in building a multinational corporation, *Strategic Management Journal,* 23: 637–653.

75. J. Lu & P. Beamish, 2004, International diversification and firm performance: The S-curve hypothesis, *Academy of Management Journal,* 47: 598–609; L. Tihanyi, R. A. Johnson, R. E. Hoskisson, & M. A. Hitt, 2003, Institutional ownership differences, and international diversification: The effects of boards of directors and technological opportunity, *Academy of Management Journal,* 46: 195–211.

76. G. D. Bruton & D. Ahlstrom, 2002, An institutional view of China's venture capital industry: Explaining the differences between China and the West, *Journal of Business Venturing,* 18: 233–259.

77. M. Fong, 2005, Unphased by barriers, retailers flock to China for clothes, *Wall Street Journal,* May 27, B1, B2.

78. P. Engardio, A. Bernstein, & M. Kripalani, 2003, Is your job next? *Business Week,* February 3, 50–60.

79. K. Cattani, E. Dahan, & G. Schmidt, 2005, Offshoring versus "Spackling," *MIT Sloan Management Review,* 46(3): 6–7.

80. R. D. Ireland, M. A. Hitt, S. M. Camp, & D. L. Sexton, 2001, Integrating entrepreneurship and strategic management actions to create firm wealth, *Academy of Management Executive,* 15(1): 49–63.

81. Z. Emden, A. Yaprak, & S. T. Cavusgil, 2005, Learning from experience in international alliances: Antecedents and firm performance implications, *Journal of Business Research,* 58: 883–892; M. Subramaniam & N. Venkataraman, 2001, Determinants of transnational new product development capability: Testing the influence of transferring and deploying tacit overseas knowledge, *Strategic Management Journal,* 22: 359–378.

82. G. D. Bruton, D. Ahlstrom, & J. C. Wan, 2003, Turnaround in East Asian firms: Evidence from ethnic overseas Chinese communities, *Strategic Management Journal,* 24: 519–540; S. H. Park & Y. Luo, 2001, Guanxi and organizational dynamics: Organizational networking in Chinese firms, *Strategic Management Journal,* 22: 455–477; M. A. Hitt, M. T. Dacin, B. B. Tyler, & D. Park, 1997, Understanding the differences in Korean and U.S. executives' strategic orientations, *Strategic Management Journal,* 18: 159–167.

83. M. A. Hitt, D. Ahlstrom, M. T. Dacin, E. Levitas, & L. Svobodina, 2004, The institutional effects on strategic alliance partner selection: China versus Russia, *Organization Science,* 15: 173–185.

84. Park & Luo, Guanxi and organizational dynamics.

85. M. A. Hitt, H. Lee, & E. Yucel, 2002, The importance of social capital to the management of multinational enterprises: Relational capital among Asian and Western firms, *Asia Pacific Journal of Management,* 19: 353–372.

86. W. R. Banhonacker, 2004, When good guanxi turns bad, *Harvard Business Review,* 82(4): 18–21.

87. M. A. O'Grady, 2005, Americas: After the haircut, Argentina readies the shave, *Wall Street Journal,* May 27, A13.

88. C. A. Bartlett & S. Ghoshal, 2003, What is a global manager? *Harvard Business Review,* 81(8): 101–108; M. A. Carpenter & J. W. Fredrickson, 2001, Top management teams, global strategic posture and the moderating role of uncertainty, *Academy of Management Journal,* 44: 533–545.

89. V. K. Narayanan & L. Fahey, 2005, The relevance of the institutional underpinnings of Porter's five forces framework to emerging economies: An epistemological analysis, *Journal of Management Studies,* 42: 207–223; N. Argyres & A. M. McGahan, 2002, An interview with Michael Porter, *Academy of Management Executive,* 16(2): 43–52; Y. E. Spanos & S. Lioukas, 2001, An examination into the causal logic of rent generation: Contrasting Porter's competitive strategy framework and the resource-based perspective, *Strategic Management Journal,* 22: 907–934.

90. G. Hawawini, V. Subramanian, & P. Verdin, 2003, Is performance driven by industry or firm-specific factors? A new look at the evidence, *Strategic Management Journal,* 24: 1–16.

91. S. Zaheer & A. Zaheer, 2001, Market microstructure in a global b2b network, *Strategic Management Journal,* 22: 859–873.

92. Hitt, Ricart, Costa, & Nixon, The new frontier.

93. Gimeno, Hoskisson, Beal, & Wan, Explaining the clustering of international expansion moves; C. Garcia-Pont & N. Nohria, 2002, Local versus global mimetism: The dynamics of alliance formation in the automobile industry, *Strategic Management Journal,* 23: 307–321.

94. E. D. Jaffe, I. D. Nebenzahl, & I. Schorr, 2005, Strategic options of home country firms faced with MNC entry, *Long Range Planning,* 38(2): 183–196.

95. J. Shamsie, 2003, The context of dominance: An industry-driven framework for exploiting reputation, *Strategic Management Journal,*

24: 199–215; K. C. Robinson & P. P. McDougall, 2001, Entry barriers and new venture performance: A comparison of universal and contingency approaches, *Strategic Management Journal,* 22 (Special Issue): 659–685.

96. A. Latour, 2005, To meet the threat from cable, SBC rushes to offer TV services, *Wall Street Journal,* February 16, A1, A10.

97. R. Makadok, 1999, Interfirm differences in scale economies and the evolution of market shares, *Strategic Management Journal,* 20: 935–952.

98. B. J. Pine II, 2004, Mass customization: The new imperative, *Strategic Direction,* January, 2–3.

99. F. Keenan, S. Holmes, J. Greene, & R. O. Crockett, 2002, A mass market of one, *Business Week,* December 2, 68–72.

100. D. Michaels, 2003, World business (a special report); victory at sea: How did a French company capture several British naval contracts? Think 'multidomestic', *Wall Street Journal Europe,* September 26, R5.

101. G. Walker, T. L. Madsen, & G. Carini, 2002, How does institutional change affect heterogeneity among firms? *Strategic Management Journal,* 23: 89–104.

102. A. Reinhardt, 2005, The man who said no to Microsoft, *Business Week,* May 31, 49; 2002, The long shadow of big blue, *The Economist,* November 9, 63–64.

103. J. L. Lunsford & D. Michaels, 2005, New orders: After four years in the rear, Boeing is set to jet past Airbus, *Wall Street Journal,* June 10, A1.

104. J. Drucker & C. Rhoads, 2005, Phone consolidation may cost corporate clients clout, *Wall Street Journal,* May 4, B1, B3.

105. J. Angwin & J. T. Hallinan, 2005, Newspaper circulation continues to decline, forcing tough decisions, *Wall Street Journal,* May 2, A1, A6.

106. S. Dutta, O. Narasimhan, & S. Rajiv, 2005, Conceptualizing and measuring capabilities: Methodology and empirical application, *Strategic Management Journal,* 26: 277–285; A. M. Knott, 2003, Persistent heterogeneity and sustainable innovation, *Strategic Management Journal,* 24: 687–705; T. Noda & D. J. Collies, 2001, The evolution of intraindustry firm heterogeneity: Insights from a process study, *Academy of Management Journal,* 44: 897–925.

107. C. Richard, 2005, Small investors rethink auto bonds; Sector starts to recover after GM, Ford downgrades take toll on retail holders, *Wall Street Journal,* June 15, D3.

108. Lunsford & Michaels, New orders: After four years in the rear, Boeing is set to jet past Airbus; C. Matlack & S. Holmes, 2002, Look out, Boeing: Airbus is grabbing market share, but can it make money this way? *Business Week,* October 28, 50–51.

109. D. M. De Carolis, 2003, Competencies and imitability in the pharmaceutical industry: An analysis of their relationship with firm performance, *Journal of Management,* 29: 27–50; D. L. Deephouse, 1999, To be different, or to be the same? It's a question (and theory) of strategic balance, *Strategic Management Journal,* 20: 147–166.

110. W. Chung & A. Kalnins, 2001, Agglomeration effects and performance: Test of the Texas lodging industry, *Strategic Management Journal,* 22: 969–988.

111. K. D. Brouthers, L. E. Brouthers, & S. Werner, 2003, Transaction cost-enhanced entry mode choices and firm performance, *Strategic Management Journal,* 24: 1239–1248.

112. M. E. Porter, 1980, *Competitive Strategy,* New York: Free Press.

113. M. S. Hunt, 1972, Competition in the major home appliance industry, 1960–1970 (doctoral dissertation, Harvard University); Porter, *Competitive Strategy,* 129.

114. G. McNamara, D. L. Deephouse, & R. A. Luce, 2003, Competitive positioning within and across a strategic group structure: The performance of core, secondary, and solitary firms, *Strategic Management Journal,* 24: 161–181.

115. H. R. Greve, 1999, Managerial cognition and the mimetic adoption of market positions: What you see is what you do, *Strategic Management Journal,* 19: 967–988.

116. M. W. Peng, J. Tan, & T. W. Tong, 2004, Ownership types and strategic groups in an emerging economy, *Journal of Management Studies,* 41: 1105–1129; R. K. Reger & A. S. Huff, 1993, Strategic groups: A cognitive perspective, *Strategic Management Journal,* 14: 103–123.

117. M. Peteraf & M. Shanley, 1997, Getting to know you: A theory of strategic group identity, *Strategic Management Journal,* 18 (Special Issue): 165–186.

118. J. Lee, K. Lee, & S. Rho, 2002, An evolutionary perspective on strategic group emergence: A genetic algorithm-based model, *Strategic Management Journal,* 23: 727–746.

119. J. A. Zuniga-Vicente, J. M. de la Fuente Sabate, & I. S. Gonzalez. 2004, Dynamics of the strategic group membership-performance linkage in rapidly changing environments, *Journal of Business Research,* 57: 1378–1390; J. D. Osborne, C. I. Stubbart, & A. Ramaprasad, 2001, Strategic groups and competitive enactment: A study of dynamic relationships between mental models and performance, *Strategic Management Journal,* 22: 435–454.

120. Greve, Managerial cognition, 972–973.

121. S. McBride, 2005, Battle stations: Two upstarts vie for dominance in satellite radio, *Wall Street Journal,* March 30, A1, A9.

122. V. J. Racanelli, 2005, Turnaround ahead at VW, *Barron's,* May 16, 26–27.

123. Gimeno, Hoskisson, Beal, & Wan, Explaining the clustering of international expansion moves.

124. Porter, *Competitive Strategy,* 49.

125. G. McNamara, R. A. Luce, & G. H. Tompson, 2002, Examining the effect of complexity in strategic group knowledge structures on firm performance, *Strategic Management Journal,* 23: 153–170.

126. D. B. Montgomery, M. C. Moore, & J. E. Urbany, 2005, Reasoning about competitive reactions: Evidence from executives, *Marketing Science,* 24: 138–149.

127. P. M. Norman, R. D. Ireland, K. W. Artz, & M. A. Hitt, 2000, Acquiring and using competitive intelligence in entrepreneurial teams, paper presented at the Academy of Management, Toronto, Canada.

128. F. Vogelstein & P. Lewis, 2005, Search and destroy, *Fortune,* May 2, 73–79.

129. Ibid.

130. A. Afuah, 2000, How much do your co-opetitors' capabilities matter in the face of technological change? *Strategic Management Journal,* 21: 387-A; Brandenburger & B. Nalebuff, 1996, *Co-opetition,* New York: Currency Doubleday.

131. V. Drucker, 1999, Is your computer a sitting duck during a deal? *Mergers & Acquisitions,* July/August, 25–28.

132. A. Crane, 2005, In the company of spies: When competitive intelligence gathering becomes industrial espionage, *Business Horizons,* 48(3): 233–240.

Analysis of the Internal Environment

Studying this chapter should provide you with the strategic management knowledge needed to:

1. Explain the need for firms to study and understand their internal environment.

2. Define value and discuss its importance.

3. Describe the differences between tangible and intangible resources.

4. Define capabilities and discuss how they are developed.

5. Describe four criteria used to determine whether resources and capabilities are core competencies.

6. Explain how value chain analysis is used to identify and evaluate resources and capabilities.

7. Define outsourcing and discuss the reasons for its use.

8. Discuss the importance of identifying internal strengths and weaknesses.

All the comforts of home

ASSOCIATED PRESS, AP

PetsHotel offers innovative services such as temperature controlled rooms for dogs and cats with daily special treats, 24-hour care, and a veterinarian on call.

The Capability to Innovate: A Critical Source of Competitive Advantage

According to the final report on the National Innovation Initiative issued by the U.S. Council on Competitiveness, innovation is the most important factor in determining a company's success in the 21st century. While many firms have become highly efficient in the past 25 years, they must become highly innovative in the next 25 years and beyond to develop sustainable competitive advantages. The world is becoming more interconnected and competitive because of increasing globalization. The competitive landscape is becoming more level across countries as even firms in some emerging markets are now global competitors. Certainly, firms from China and India and some from Russia are competing effectively in global markets. China has almost four times as many engineering graduates as does the United States and receives more foreign direct investment. Sweden, Finland, Japan, and South Korea invest more in research and development as a share of GDP than does the United States. Fourteen of the 25 most competitive information technology companies are located in Asia. Almost 50 percent of the patents filed in the United States come from foreign-owned firms and foreign-born inventors. Some analysts predict that Brazil, China, India, and Russia will be major players in the global economy of the next 50 years.

The enhanced competition has made innovation increasingly important in all types of markets. Incremental improvements in products and processes are no longer enough to sustain a competitive advantage in many industries. For example, PetsMart has been a market leader largely because it continues to offer consumers greater value than competitors through innovative services. In addition to its extensive product lines, the company provides such services for pets as grooming, training, and boarding. The pet-styling salons have been popular with customers, and the newer PetsHotel offers temperature controlled rooms for dogs and cats with daily special treats, 24-hour care, and a veterinarian on call. "Doggie day camps" are being pilot-tested. Top managers at PetsMart expect services to grow to 20 percent of total revenues over the next few years.

Because of the need to innovate in order to remain competitive, Nokia reorganized its business operations into four platforms: mobile phones, multimedia, networks, and enterprise solutions. Executives judged these as growth businesses and wanted them to receive greater emphasis and autonomy to innovate. A global-strategy board reviews the new product ideas proposed to ensure that they match the vision of the company, but the business areas are given significant flexibility to serve their customers with new product offerings. Each division is expected to act as a new product incubator and to obtain insights from customers to ensure that the new products are well received in the market. These actions are intended to help the firm gain or sustain a competitive advantage. Nokia has major competition in Motorola and Microsoft, forcing it to become more innovative or lose market share.

Innovative capabilities have become critical in order for companies to remain competitive. The changes at Nokia are designed to enrich its innovative capabilities. Many firms are reshaping their business models and cultures in addition to the changes in structure exemplified by those made by Nokia.

Sources: M. Elliott, 2005, Small world, big stakes, *Time,* June 27, 30-34; M. Souers, 2005, PetsMart's animal attractions, *Business Week Online,* www.businessweek.com, May 3; M. Kazmierczak, J. James & W. T. Archey, 2005, Losing the competitive advantage: The challenge for science and technology in the United States, Report by the American Electronics Association, February; 2004, *Innovate America,* National Innovation Initiative Report, Council on competitiveness, December; M.A. Prospero, 2004, Innovation awards, *Fast Company,* www.fastcompany.com, December.

As discussed in the first two chapters, several factors in the global economy, including the rapid development of the Internet's capabilities[1] and of globalization in general have made it increasingly difficult for firms to develop a competitive advantage that can be sustained for any period of time.[2] In these instances, firms try to create sustained advantages, but, as suggested in the Opening Case (see Chapter 1 for an explanation of competitive advantage), they are unlikely to do so unless they continually produce innovative products.[3] PetsMart has used innovative services to sustain its competitive advantage in the pet goods and services industry. Nokia has implemented changes to improve its innovative capabilities in order to better compete with the likes of Motorola and Microsoft. Other companies such as Procter & Gamble, General Electric (GE), and Johnson & Johnson have been changing their cultures and their business models in order to enhance their innovation output to remain highly competitive in the current environment.[4] Firms must have not only the correct structure, as Nokia has, but also the appropriate resources to build innovative capabilities. The probability of developing a sustainable competitive advantage increases when firms use their own unique resources, capabilities, and core competencies on which to base and implement their strategies.[5]

Competitive advantages and the differences they create in firm performance are often strongly related to the resources firms hold and how they are managed.[6] "Resources are the foundation for strategy and unique bundles of resources generate competitive advantages leading to wealth creation."[7] To identify and successfully use their resources over time, those leading firms need to think constantly about how to manage them to increase the value for customers.[8] As this chapter shows, firms achieve strategic competitiveness and earn above-average returns when their unique core competencies are effectively acquired, bundled, and leveraged to take advantage of opportunities in the external environment.[9]

People are an especially critical resource for producing innovation and gaining a competitive advantage.[10] Even if they are not as critical in some industries, they are necessary for the development and implementation of firms' strategies.[11] In fact, because of the importance of talented employees, a global labor market now exists. As Richard Florida argues, "[W]herever talent goes, innovation, creativity, and economic growth are sure to follow."[12]

In time, the benefits of any firm's value-creating strategy can be duplicated by its competitors. In other words, all competitive advantages have a limited life.[13] The question of duplication is not *if* it will happen, but *when*. In general, the sustainability of a competitive advantage is a function of three factors: (1) the rate of core competence obsolescence because of environmental changes, (2) the availability of substitutes for the core competence, and (3) the imitability of the core competence.[14]

The challenge in all firms is to effectively manage current core competencies while simultaneously developing new ones.[15] Only when firms develop a continuous stream of capabilities that contribute to competitive advantages do they achieve strategic competitiveness, earn above-average returns, and remain ahead of competitors (see Chapter 5).

In Chapter 2, we examined general, industry, and competitor environments. Armed with this knowledge about the realities and conditions of their external environment, firms have a better understanding of marketplace opportunities and the characteristics of the competitive environment in which they exist. In this chapter, we focus on the firm itself. By analyzing its internal environment, a firm determines what it *can do*—that is, the actions permitted by its unique resources, capabilities, and core competencies. As discussed in Chapter 1, core competencies are a firm's source of competitive advantage. The magnitude of that competitive advantage is a function primarily of the uniqueness of the firm's core competencies.[16] Matching what a firm *can do* with what it *might do* (a function of opportunities and threats in the external environment) allows the firm to develop vision, pursue its mission, and select and implement its strategies.

We begin this chapter with a discussion of the nature of a firm's internal environment analysis. We then discuss the roles of resources and capabilities in developing core competencies, which are the sources of the firm's competitive advantages. Included in this discussion are the techniques firms can use to identify and evaluate resources and capabilities and the criteria for selecting core competencies from among them. Resources and capabilities are not inherently valuable, but they create value when the firm can use them to perform certain activities that result in a competitive advantage. Accordingly, we also discuss in this chapter the value chain concept and examine four criteria to evaluate core competencies that establish competitive advantage.[17] The chapter closes with cautionary comments about the need for firms to prevent their core competencies from becoming core rigidities. The existence of core rigidities indicates that the firm is too anchored to its past, which prevents it from continuously developing new competitive advantages.

The Nature of Internal Environmental Analysis

The Context of Internal Analysis

In the global economy, traditional factors such as labor costs, access to financial resources and raw materials, and protected or regulated markets continue to be sources of competitive advantage, but to a lesser degree.[18] One important reason for this decline is that the advantages created by these more traditional sources can be overcome by competitors through an international strategy (discussed in Chapter 8) and by the flow of resources throughout the global economy. The need to identify additional and perhaps new sources of competitive advantage highlights the importance of understanding the firm's resources and capabilities.

Increasingly, those analyzing their firm's internal environment should use a global mind-set. A **global mind-set** is the ability to study an internal environment in ways that are not dependent on the assumptions of a single country, culture, or context.[19] Those with a global mind-set recognize that their firms must possess resources and capabilities that allow understanding of and appropriate responses to competitive situations that are influenced by country-specific factors and unique societal cultures.

Finally, analysis of the firm's internal environment requires that evaluators examine the firm's portfolio of resources and the *bundles* of heterogeneous resources and capabilities managers have created.[20] This perspective suggests that individual firms possess at least some resources and capabilities that other companies do not—at least not in the same combination. Resources are the source of capabilities, some of which lead to the development of a firm's core competencies or its competitive advantages.[21] Understanding how to *leverage* the firm's unique bundle of resources and capabilities is a key outcome decision makers seek when analyzing the internal environment. Figure 3.1 illustrates the relationships among resources, capabilities, and core competencies and shows how firms use them to create strategic competitiveness. Before examining these topics in depth, we describe value and how firms use their resources, capabilities, and core competencies to create it.

Creating Value

By exploiting their core competencies or competitive advantages to at least meet if not exceed the demanding standards of global competition, firms create value for customers.[22]

FIGURE **3.1**

Components of Internal Analysis Leading to Competitive Advantage and Strategic Competitiveness

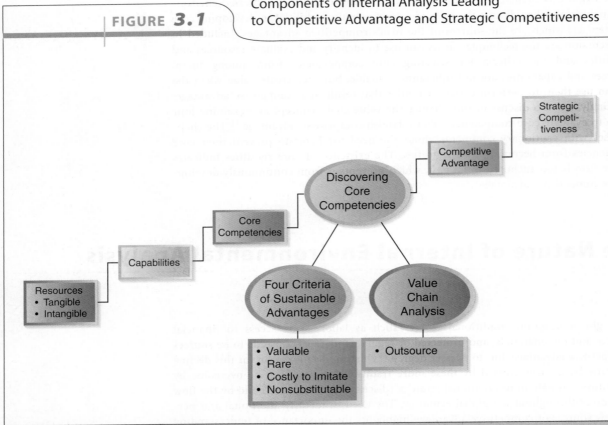

Value is measured by a product's performance characteristics and by its attributes for which customers are willing to pay. Firms must provide value to customers that is superior to the value provided by competitors in order to create a competitive advantage.[23] Evidence suggests that increasingly, customers perceive higher value in global rather than domestic-only brands.[24] Firms create value by innovatively bundling and leveraging their resources and capabilities.[25] Firms unable to creatively bundle and leverage their resources and capabilities in ways that create value for customers suffer performance declines.

Ultimately, creating value for customers is the source of above-average returns for a firm. What the firm intends regarding value creation affects its choice of business-level strategy (see Chapter 4) and its organizational structure (see Chapter 11).[26] In Chapter 4's discussion of business-level strategies, we note that value is created by a product's low cost, by its highly differentiated features, or by a combination of low cost and high differentiation, compared with competitors' offerings. A business-level strategy is effective only when its use is grounded in exploiting the firm's current core competencies. Thus, successful firms continuously examine the effectiveness of current and future core competencies.[27]

At one time, the strategic management process was concerned largely with understanding the characteristics of the industry in which the firm competed and, in light of those characteristics, determining how the firm should position itself relative to competitors. This emphasis on industry characteristics and competitive strategy underestimated the role of the firm's resources and capabilities in developing competitive advantage. In fact, core competencies, in combination with product-market positions, are the firm's most important sources of competitive advantage.[28] The core competencies of a firm, in addition to results of analyses of its general, industry, and competitor environments, should drive its selection of strategies. Both the resources held by the firm and its context are important in the formulation of strategy.[29] As Clayton Christensen noted, "Successful strategists need to cultivate a deep understanding of the processes of competition and progress and of the factors that undergird each advantage. Only thus will they be able to see when old advantages are poised to disappear and how new advantages can be built in their stead."[30] By emphasizing core competencies when formulating strategies, companies learn to compete primarily on the basis of firm-specific differences, but they must be very aware of how things are changing in the external environment as well.

The Challenge of Internal Analysis

The strategic decisions managers make in terms of the firm's resources, capabilities, and core competencies are nonroutine,[31] have ethical implications,[32] and significantly influence the firm's ability to earn above-average returns.[33] Making these decisions—identifying, developing, deploying, and protecting resources, capabilities, and core competencies—may appear to be relatively easy. However, this task is as challenging and difficult as any other with which managers are involved; moreover, it is increasingly internationalized.[34] Some believe that the pressure on managers to pursue only decisions that help the firm meet the quarterly earnings expected by market analysts makes it difficult to analyze the firm's internal resources accurately.[35] Identifying the firm's core competencies is essential before important strategic decisions can be made, including those related to entering or exiting markets, investing in new technologies, building new or additional manufacturing capacity, or forming strategic partnerships.

The challenge and difficulty of making effective decisions are implied by preliminary evidence suggesting that one-half of organizational decisions fail.[36] Sometimes, mistakes are made as the firm analyzes its internal environment. Managers might, for example, identify capabilities as core competencies that do not create a competitive advantage. When a mistake occurs, decision makers must have the confidence to admit it and take corrective actions.[37] A firm can still grow through well-intended errors—the learning generated by making and correcting mistakes can be important to the creation of new competitive advantages.[38] Moreover, firms can learn from the failure resulting from a mistake—that is, what *not* to do when seeking competitive advantage.[39]

To facilitate developing and using core competencies, managers must have courage, self-confidence, integrity, the capacity to deal with uncertainty and complexity, and a willingness to hold people accountable for their work and to be held accountable themselves. Thus, difficult managerial decisions concerning resources, capabilities, and core competencies are characterized by three conditions: uncertainty, complexity, and intraorganizational conflicts (see Figure 3.2).[40]

Managers face *uncertainty* in terms of new proprietary technologies, rapidly changing economic and political trends, transformations in societal values, and shifts in customer demands.[41] Environmental uncertainty increases the *complexity* and range of issues to examine when studying the internal environment.[42] Biases about how to cope with uncertainty affect decisions about the resources and capabilities that will become the foundation of the firm's competitive advantage. Finally, *intraorganizational conflict* surfaces when decisions are made about the core competencies to nurture as well as how to nurture them.

In making decisions affected by these three conditions, judgment is required. *Judgment* is the capability of making successful decisions when no obviously correct model or rule is available or when relevant data are unreliable or incomplete. In this type of

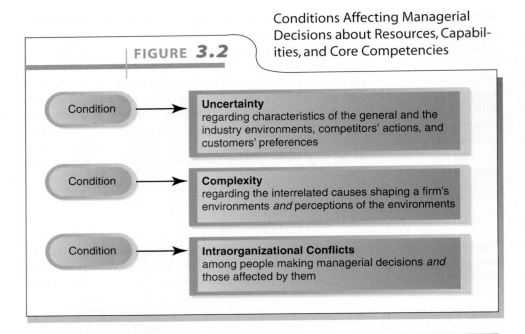

FIGURE **3.2**

| Condition | → | **Uncertainty** regarding characteristics of the general and the industry environments, competitors' actions, and customers' preferences |

| Condition | → | **Complexity** regarding the interrelated causes shaping a firm's environments *and* perceptions of the environments |

| Condition | → | **Intraorganizational Conflicts** among people making managerial decisions *and* those affected by them |

Source: Adapted from R. Amit & P. J. H. Schoemaker, 1993, Strategic assets and organizational rent, *Strategic Management Journal*, 14: 33.

situation, decision makers must be aware of possible cognitive biases. Overconfidence, for example, can often lower value when a correct decision is not obvious, such as making a judgment as to whether an internal resource is a strength or a weakness.[43]

When exercising judgment, decision makers often take intelligent risks. In the current competitive landscape, executive judgment can be a particularly important source of competitive advantage. One reason is that, over time, effective judgment allows a firm to build a strong reputation and retain the loyalty of stakeholders whose support is linked to above-average returns.[44]

Significant changes in the value-creating potential of a firm's resources and capabilities can occur in a rapidly changing global economy. Because these changes affect a company's power and social structure, inertia or resistance to change may surface. Even though these reactions may happen, decision makers should not deny the changes needed to assure the firm's strategic competitiveness. By denying the need for change, difficult experiences can be avoided in the short run.[45] However, in the long run, the failure to change when needed leads to performance declines and, in the worst-case scenario, to failure. Recently IBM has been making significant changes to prepare for the future. For example, it sold its laptop computer manufacturing business to Lenova, a Chinese firm. It also streamlined its business operations in Europe. It is trying to reduce its bureaucracy and increase its capability to respond to rapid changes in its environment.[46] Similarly, Microsoft is continuously searching for new ways to provide value to consumers. Jeff Raikes, head of Microsoft's business applications, noted that a major focus to increase productivity in this decade will be the convergence of audio, video, and the computer network. In other words, Microsoft is developing products to allow workers to communicate and collaborate more efficiently. In particular, the company is

Microsoft is making an effort to integrate web conferencing, instant messaging, and connection to telephony infrastructure into Microsoft Office.

making an effort to integrate more technologies with Microsoft Office. It is trying to integrate web conferencing, instant messaging, and connection to telephony infrastructure.[47]

Resources, Capabilities, and Core Competencies

Resources, capabilities, and core competencies provide the foundation of competitive advantage. Resources are the source of a firm's capabilities. Resources are bundled to create organizational capabilities. Capabilities in turn are the source of a firm's core competencies, which are the basis of competitive advantages.[48] Later, we explain how some capabilities become core competencies. Figure 3.1 depicts these relationships. In this section, we define and provide examples of these building blocks of competitive advantage.

Resources

Broad in scope, resources cover a spectrum of individual, social, and organizational phenomena.[49] Typically, resources alone do not yield a competitive advantage.[50] In fact, a competitive advantage is generally based on the *unique bundling of several resources*.[51] For example, Amazon.com has combined service and distribution resources to develop its competitive advantages. The firm started as an online bookseller, directly shipping orders to customers. It quickly grew large and established a distribution network through which it could ship "millions of different items to millions of different customers." Lacking Amazon's combination of resources, traditional bricks-and-mortar companies, such as Borders, found it difficult to establish an effective online presence. These difficulties led them to develop partnerships with Amazon. Through these arrangements, Amazon now handles the online presence and the shipping of goods for several firms, including Borders—which now can focus on sales in its stores. Arrangements such as these are useful to the bricks-and-mortar companies because they are not accustomed to shipping so much diverse merchandise directly to individuals.[52]

Some of a firm's resources (defined in Chapter 1 as inputs to the firm's production process) are tangible while others are intangible. **Tangible resources** are assets that can be seen and quantified. Production equipment, manufacturing plants, and formal reporting structures are examples of tangible resources. **Intangible resources** include assets that typically are rooted deeply in the firm's history and have accumulated over time. Because they are embedded in unique patterns of routines, intangible resources are relatively difficult for competitors to analyze and imitate. Knowledge, trust between managers and employees, managerial capabilities, organizational routines (the unique ways people work together), scientific capabilities, the capacity for innovation, and the firm's reputation for its goods or services and how it interacts with people (such as employees, customers, and suppliers) are all examples of intangible resources.[53]

The four types of tangible resources are financial, organizational, physical, and technological (see Table 3.1). The three types of intangible resources are human, innovation, and reputational (see Table 3.2).

Tangible Resources

As tangible resources, a firm's borrowing capacity and the status of its plant and equipment are visible. The value of many tangible resources can be established through

Tangible Resources		TABLE 3.1
Financial Resources	• The firm's borrowing capacity	
	• The firm's ability to generate internal funds	
Organizational Resources	• The firm's formal reporting structure and its formal planning, controlling, and coordinating systems	
Physical Resources	• Sophistication and location of a firm's plant and equipment	
	• Access to raw materials	
Technological Resources	• Stock of technology, such as patents, trademarks, copyrights, and trade secrets	

Sources: Adapted from J. B. Barney, 1991, Firm resources and sustained competitive advantage, *Journal of Management,* 17: 101; R. M. Grant, 1991, *Contemporary Strategy Analysis,* Cambridge, U.K.: Blackwell Business, 100–102.

financial statements, but these statements do not account for the value of all of a firm's assets, because they disregard some intangible resources.[54] As such, each of the firm's sources of competitive advantage typically is not fully reflected on corporate financial statements. The value of tangible resources is also constrained because they are difficult to leverage—it is difficult to derive additional business or value from a tangible resource. For example, an airplane is a tangible resource or asset, but: "You can't use the same airplane on five different routes at the same time. You can't put the same crew on five different routes at the same time. And the same goes for the financial investment you've made in the airplane."[55]

Although production assets are tangible, many of the processes to use these assets are intangible. Thus, the learning and potential proprietary processes associated with a

Intangible Resources		TABLE 3.2
Human Resources	• Knowledge	
	• Trust	
	• Managerial capabilities	
	• Organizational routines	
Innovation Resources	• Ideas	
	• Scientific capabilities	
	• Capacity to innovate	
Reputational Resources	• Reputation with customers	
	• Brand name	
	• Perceptions of product quality, durability, and reliability	
	• Reputation with suppliers	
	• For efficient, effective, supportive, and mutually beneficial interactions and relationships	

Sources: Adapted from R. Hall, 1992, The strategic analysis of intangible resources, *Strategic Management Journal,* 13: 136–139; R. M. Grant, 1991, *Contemporary Strategy Analysis,* Cambridge, U.K.: Blackwell Business, 101–104.

tangible resource, such as manufacturing equipment, can have unique intangible attributes, such as quality control processes, unique manufacturing processes, and technology that develop over time and create competitive advantage.[56]

Intangible Resources

As suggested above, compared to tangible resources, intangible resources are a superior and more potent source of core competencies.[57] In fact, in the global economy, "the success of a corporation lies more in its intellectual and systems capabilities than in its physical assets. [Moreover], the capacity to manage human intellect—and to convert it into useful products and services—is fast becoming the critical executive skill of the age."[58]

Even though it is difficult to measure the value of intangible assets such as knowledge,[59] there is some evidence that the value of intangible assets is growing relative to that of tangible assets.[60] John Kendrick, a well-known economist studying the main drivers of economic growth, found a general increase in the contribution of intangible assets to U.S. economic growth since the early 1900s. In 1929, the ratio of intangible business capital to tangible business capital was 30 percent to 70 percent. However, that ratio is approaching 70 percent intangible business capital to about 30 percent of business capital today.[61]

Because intangible resources are less visible and more difficult for competitors to understand, purchase, imitate, or substitute for, firms prefer to rely on them rather than on tangible resources as the foundation for their capabilities and core competencies. In fact, the more unobservable (that is, intangible) a resource is, the more sustainable will be the competitive advantage that is based on it.[62] Another benefit of intangible resources is that, unlike most tangible resources, their use can be leveraged. With intangible resources, the larger the network of users, the greater the benefit to each party. For instance, sharing knowledge among employees does not diminish its value for any one person. To the contrary, two people sharing their individualized knowledge sets often can be leveraged to create additional knowledge that, although new to each of them, contributes to performance improvements for the firm.[63]

As shown in Table 3.2, the intangible resource of reputation is an important source of competitive advantage. Earned through the firm's actions as well as its words, a value-creating reputation is a product of years of superior marketplace competence as perceived by stakeholders.[64] A reputation indicates the level of awareness a firm has been able to develop among stakeholders[65] and the degree to which they hold the firm in high esteem.[66] A well-known and highly valued brand name is an application of reputation as a source of competitive advantage.[67]

A continuing commitment to innovation and aggressive advertising facilitates firms' efforts to take advantage of the reputation associated with their brands.[68] Because of the desirability of its reputation, the Harley-Davidson brand name, for example, has such status that it adorns a limited edition Barbie doll, a popular restaurant in New York City, and a line of L'Oréal cologne. Moreover, Harley-Davidson Motor-Clothes annually generates well in excess of $100 million in revenue for the firm and offers a broad range of clothing items, from black leather jackets to fashions for tots.[69] Other firms are trying to build their reputations. For example, Li-Ning, a manufacturer and marketer of athletic shoes, competes in the Chinese market against Nike and Adidas, firms with well-known

GETTY IMAGES

Harley-Davidson MotorClothes annually generates well in excess of $100 million in revenue for Harley-Davidson and offers a broad range of clothing items, including clothing for pets.

Human Capital: Underutilizing Valuable Intangible Assets

For many years firms have declared that their people are their most valuable resources. Yet they do not seem to practice what they proclaim to their stakeholders: When they experience performance difficulties, the first reductions made in costs often come through large layoffs of employees. Nevertheless, the data continue to grow suggesting that human capital is perhaps the most valuable resource held by most companies. Further indications of not fully valuing human capital is the fact that in the United States few women are in top management positions and their pay averages approximately 72 percent of the compensation paid to men in similar positions.

There are changes on the horizon in the use of women and minorities human capital. Women now hold approximately 47 percent of the executive and managerial jobs in U.S. companies. Carly Fiorina lost her CEO job with Hewlett-Packard, but there are other high-profile women top executives including Meg Whitman, CEO of eBay, and Anne Mulcahy, CEO of Xerox. Whitman argues that "good personnel decisions are about finding the right person for the right job at the right time." Late in 2004, she made changes in several key positions in her management team: Jeff Jordan, formerly head of eBay's U.S. operations, took over PayPal, an eBay subsidiary; Matt Bannick took over eBay's international operations; and Bill Cobb, former manager of the international arm, assumed responsibility for eBay's U.S. operations. By having them undertake new management tasks, Whitman is developing their human capital. All three are potential successors to Whitman when she decides to leave the CEO position.

Carol Bartz, CEO of Autodesk since 1992, is another successful female executive in a technology-based firm. Bartz attributes her success—she has turned the company around three times—to her "patient" and supportive board of directors. She has expressed concerns about having adequate human capital in the future given the seeming decline in math and engineering among U.S. students, especially because young girls are not encouraged to study in these areas. In fact, Bartz believes girls are often socialized to study liberal arts topics instead. Of course, this greatly underutilizes the available human capital.

PepsiCo has worked hard to better utilize its human capital with diversity programs. In 2005, PepsiCo was ranked fourth on DiversityInc's list of the best companies for diversity. PepsiCo's CEO, Steve Reinemund, argues that Pepsi's primary goals entail inclusion. To

reach these goals, he says, Pepsi must retain diverse and high-quality employees and integrate their perspectives to create and maintain the best marketing and innovation programs in the industry. The full potential of diversity cannot be realized without an inclusive culture. Managers are expected to well understand their employees' needs and to mentor them on a regular basis. At the end of 2004, women held 29 percent and people of color held 17 percent of PepsiCo's management jobs, both representing significant increases over 2000.

Executive pay levels have been controversial in recent years, but for many people they provide substantial incentive to work toward becoming a top-level manager. The median total compensation (salary and bonus) in 2004 was $2,470,600, a 14.5 percent gain over 2003. The controversy has focused on

GETTY IMAGES.

Carol Bartz of Autodesk.

executives who received significant pay when their firms performed poorly. In response, boards of directors have been trying to link more of executives' compensation to the firm's performance. It is an imperfect process because CEOs often receive too much credit for the good performance of their firms. The number of CEOs who are losing their jobs (see Chapter 12) also suggests that they may be receiving too much blame for bad performance as well. Regardless, all human capital is valuable and should receive commensurate rewards.

Sources: D. Kirkpatrick, 2005, The reigning queen of tech, *Fortune,* May 3, www.fortune.com; P. Gogoi, 2005, For women, a failure to negotiate, *Business Week,* April 22, www.businessweek.com; C. Terhune, 2005, Pepsi, vowing diversity isn't just image polish, seeks inclusive culture, *Wall Street Journal,* April 19, www.wsj.com; J. S. Lublin, 2005, Goodbye to pay for no performance, *Wall Street Journal,* April 11, www.wsj.com; C. Hymowitz, 2005, Chiefs with the skills of a COO gain favor as celebrity CEOs fade, *Wall Street Journal,* April 5, www.wsj.com; A. Lashinsky, 2004, Ebay's management merry-go-round, *Fortune,* December 13, www.fortune.com.

brands. Preparing for the Olympic Games to be held in Beijing in 2008, Li-Ning hired a veteran with experience at Procter & Gamble as vice president of marketing to build its image. His first initiative was to partner with the National Basketball Association to use its logo on Li-Ning shoes.[70]

As noted in the Strategic Focus, many companies espouse the importance of their employees and yet lay them off at the first sign of economic troubles. When they do so, they are more likely to experience longer-term declining performance.[71] Also, firms must make more effective use of their total human capital. Firms that do so, such as PepsiCo and eBay, are the most likely to develop competitive advantages and win competitive battles against their rivals. Reinforcing their efforts, recent research is finding that investments in firm-specific human capital increases learning and in turn, firm performance.[72] Clearly, some firms are recognizing the value of human capital for their strategic success, placing emphasis on trying to retain older workers because of their knowledge stocks developed over time. Such actions have created interfirm rivalry to acquire and retain high-quality human capital.[73] Emphasizing this rivalry, John Mack, the new CEO of Morgan Stanley, urged his managers to identify and recruit the most talented employees of rival banks because Morgan Stanley had lost significant numbers of top employees who accepted jobs from competitors. He said, "Nothing would underline the regime change more powerfully than pulling in a few big names."[74]

Capabilities

Capabilities exist when resources have been purposely integrated to achieve a specific task or set of tasks. These tasks range from human resource selection to product marketing and research and development activities.[75] Critical to the building of competitive advantages, capabilities are often based on developing, carrying, and exchanging information and knowledge through the firm's human capital.[76] Client-specific capabilities often develop from repeated interactions with clients and the learning about their needs that occurs.[77] As a result, capabilities often evolve and develop over time.[78] The foundation of many capabilities lies in the unique skills and knowledge of a firm's employees[79] and, often, their functional expertise. Hence, the value of human capital in developing and using capabilities and, ultimately, core competencies cannot be overstated.

Global business leaders increasingly support the view that the knowledge possessed by human capital is among the most significant of an organization's capabilities and may ultimately be at the root of all competitive advantages.[80] But firms must also be able to utilize the knowledge that they have and transfer it among their business units.[81] Given this reality, the firm's challenge is to create an environment that allows people to

Functional Areas	Capabilities	Examples of Firms
Distribution	Effective use of logistics management techniques	Wal-Mart, Dell
Human resources	Motivating, empowering, and retaining employees	Microsoft, Dell
Management information systems	Effective and efficient control of inventories through point-of-purchase data collection methods	Wal-Mart, Dell
Marketing	Effective promotion of brand-name products	Procter & Gamble
		Polo Ralph Lauren Corp.
		McKinsey & Co.
	Effective customer service	Nordstrom Inc.
		Norrell Corporation
	Innovative merchandising	Crate & Barrel
Management	Ability to envision the future of clothing	Gap Inc.
	Effective organizational structure	PepsiCo
Manufacturing	Design and production skills yielding reliable products	Komatsu
	Product and design quality	Gap Inc.
	Miniaturization of components and products	Sony
Research & development	Innovative technology	Caterpillar
	Development of sophisticated elevator control solutions	Otis Elevator Co.
	Rapid transformation of technology into new products and processes	Chaparral Steel
	Digital technology	Thomson Consumer Electronics

integrate their individual knowledge with that held by others in the firm so that, collectively, the firm has significant organizational knowledge.[82]

As illustrated in Table 3.3, capabilities are often developed in specific functional areas (such as manufacturing, R&D, and marketing) or in a part of a functional area (for example, advertising). Research indicates a relationship between capabilities developed in particular functional areas and the firm's financial performance at both the corporate and business-unit levels,[83] suggesting the need to develop capabilities at both levels. Table 3.3 shows a grouping of organizational functions and the capabilities that some companies are thought to possess in terms of all or parts of those functions.

Core Competencies

Defined in Chapter 1, *core competencies* are capabilities that serve as a source of competitive advantage for a firm over its rivals. Core competencies distinguish a company competitively and reflect its personality. Core competencies emerge over time through an organizational process of accumulating and learning how to deploy different resources and capabilities.[84] As the capacity to take action, core competencies are "crown jewels of a company," the activities the company performs especially well compared with competitors and through which the firm adds unique value to its goods or services over a long period of time.[85]

Not all of a firm's resources and capabilities are *strategic assets*—that is, assets that have competitive value and the potential to serve as a source of competitive advantage.[86] Some resources and capabilities may result in incompetence, because they represent competitive areas in which the firm is weaker than its competitors. Thus, some resources or capabilities may stifle or prevent the development of a core competence. Firms with the tangible resource of financial capital, such as Microsoft, which has a large amount of cash on hand, may be able to purchase facilities or hire the skilled workers required to manufacture products that yield customer value. However, firms without financial capital have a weakness in that they may be unable to buy or build new capabilities. To be successful, firms must locate external environmental opportunities that can be exploited through their capabilities, while avoiding competition in areas of weakness.[87]

An important question is, "How many core competencies are required for the firm to have a sustained competitive advantage?" Responses to this question vary. McKinsey & Co. recommends that its clients identify three or four competencies around which their strategic actions can be framed.[88] Supporting and nurturing more than four core competencies may prevent a firm from developing the focus it needs to fully exploit its competencies in the marketplace. Firms should take actions that are based on their core competencies.

Of course, not all capabilities are core competencies. And, some firms can have weaknesses in important capabilities that detract from their core competencies. For example, Unilever has a core competence in marketing, but its inability to execute caused it to suffer performance outcomes below expectations in 2004.[89] In contrast, Dell was named by *Fortune* magazine as America's Outstanding Company in 2005 largely on the basis of its several core competencies. It makes high-quality computers, holds costs low, has a highly efficient just-in-time inventory system, and has a direct marketing and distribution program second to none in its industry. Additionally, it implemented a new positive employee development, reward, and retention program in the early 2000s that substantially enhanced its growth and performance.[90]

Building Core Competencies

Two tools help the firm to identify and build its core competencies.[91] The first consists of four specific criteria of sustainable competitive advantage that firms can use to determine those capabilities that are core competencies. Because the capabilities shown in Table 3.3 have satisfied these four criteria, they are core competencies. The second tool is the value chain analysis. Firms use this tool to select the value-creating competencies that should be maintained, upgraded, or developed and those that should be outsourced.

Four Criteria of Sustainable Competitive Advantage

As shown in Table 3.4, capabilities that are valuable, rare, costly to imitate, and nonsubstitutable are core competencies. In turn, core competencies are sources of competitive advantage for the firm over its rivals. Capabilities failing to satisfy the four criteria of sustainable competitive advantage are not core competencies, meaning that although every core competence is a capability, not every capability is a core competence. In slightly different words, for a capability to be a core competence, it must be valuable and unique, from a customer's point of view. For the competitive advantage to be sustainable, the core competence must be inimitable and nonsubstitutable, from a competitor's point of view.

The Four Criteria of Sustainable Competitive Advantage		TABLE 3.4
Valuable Capabilities	• Help a firm neutralize threats or exploit opportunities	
Rare Capabilities	• Are not possessed by many others	
Costly-to-Imitate Capabilities	• Historical: A unique and a valuable organizational culture or brand name	
	• Ambiguous cause: The causes and uses of a competence are unclear	
	• Social complexity: Interpersonal relationships, trust, and friendship among managers, suppliers, and customers	
Nonsubstitutable Capabilities	• No strategic equivalent	

A sustained competitive advantage is achieved only when competitors cannot duplicate the benefits of a firm's strategy or when they lack the resources to attempt imitation. For some period of time, the firm may earn a competitive advantage by using capabilities that are, for example, valuable and rare, but imitable.[92] In this instance, the length of time a firm can expect to retain its competitive advantage is a function of how quickly competitors can successfully imitate a good, service, or process. Sustainable competitive advantage results only when all four criteria are satisfied.

Valuable

Valuable capabilities allow the firm to exploit opportunities or neutralize threats in its external environment. By effectively using capabilities to exploit opportunities, a firm creates value for customers. Under former CEO Jack Welch's leadership, GE built a valuable competence in financial services. It built this powerful competence largely through acquisitions and its core competence in integrating newly acquired businesses. In addition, to make such competencies as financial services highly successful required placing the right people in the right jobs. As Welch emphasizes, human capital is important in creating value for customers.[93]

Rare

Rare capabilities are capabilities that few, if any, competitors possess. A key question to be answered when evaluating this criterion is, "How many rival firms possess these valuable capabilities?" Capabilities possessed by many rivals are unlikely to be sources of competitive advantage for any one of them. Instead, valuable but common (i.e., not rare) resources and capabilities are sources of competitive parity.[94] Competitive advantage results only when firms develop and exploit valuable capabilities that differ from those shared with competitors.

Costly to Imitate

Costly-to-imitate capabilities are capabilities that other firms cannot easily develop. Capabilities that are costly to imitate are created because of one reason or a combination of three reasons (see Table 3.4). First, a firm sometimes is able to develop capabilities because of *unique historical conditions*. "As firms evolve, they pick up skills, abilities and resources that are unique to them, reflecting their particular path through history."[95]

A firm with a unique and valuable *organizational culture* that emerged in the early stages of the company's history "may have an imperfectly imitable advantage over firms founded in another historical period"[96]—one in which less valuable or less competitively useful values and beliefs strongly influenced the development of the firm's culture. This may be the case for the consulting firm McKinsey & Co. Briefly discussed in Chapter 1, organizational culture is a set of shared values by members in the organization, as we explain in Chapter 12. An organizational culture is a source of advantage when employees are held together tightly by their belief in it.[97]

UPS has been the prototype in many areas of the parcel delivery business because of its excellence in products, systems, marketing, and other operational business capabilities. "Its fundamental competitive strength, however, derives from the organization's unique culture, which has spanned almost a century, growing deeper all along. This culture provides solid, consistent roots for everything the company does, from skills training to technological innovation."[98]

A second condition of being costly to imitate occurs when the link between the firm's capabilities and its competitive advantage is *causally ambiguous*.[99] In these instances, competitors can't clearly understand how a firm uses its capabilities as the foundation for competitive advantage. As a result, firms are uncertain about the capabilities they should develop to duplicate the benefits of a competitor's value-creating strategy. For years, firms tried to imitate Southwest Airlines' low-cost strategy but most have been unable to duplicate Southwest's success. They did not realize that Southwest has a unique culture and attracts some of the top talent in the industry. The culture and excellent human capital worked together in implementing Southwest's strategy and are the basis for its competitive advantage.

Social complexity is the third reason that capabilities can be costly to imitate. Social complexity means that at least some, and frequently many, of the firm's capabilities are the product of complex social phenomena. Interpersonal relationships, trust, friendships among managers and between managers and employees, and a firm's reputation with suppliers and customers are examples of socially complex capabilities. Southwest Airlines is careful to hire people that fit with its culture. This complex interrelationship between the culture and human capital adds value in ways that other airlines cannot such as jokes by the stewardesses or the cooperation between gate personnel and pilots.

Nonsubstitutable

Nonsubstitutable capabilities are capabilities that do not have strategic equivalents. This final criterion for a capability to be a source of competitive advantage "is that there must be no strategically equivalent valuable resources that are themselves either not rare or imitable. Two valuable firm resources (or two bundles of firm resources) are strategically equivalent when they each can be separately exploited to implement the same strategies."[100] In general, the strategic value of capabilities increases as they become more difficult to substitute.[101] The more invisible capabilities are, the more difficult it is for firms to find substitutes and the greater the challenge is to competitors trying to imitate a firm's value-creating strategy. Firm-specific knowledge and trust-based working relationships between managers and non-managerial personnel, such as

Southwest Airlines' culture and excellent human capital worked together in implementing its strategy and are the basis for its competitive advantage.

ASSOCIATED PRESS, AP

Dell's direct sales model takes advantage of the firm's unique capabilities.

existed for years at Southwest Airlines, are examples of capabilities that are difficult to identify and for which finding a substitute is challenging. However, causal ambiguity may make it difficult for the firm to learn as well and may stifle progress, because the firm may not know how to improve processes that are not easily codified and thus are ambiguous.[102]

For example, competitors are deeply familiar with Dell Inc.'s successful direct sales model. However, to date, no competitor has been able to imitate Dell's capabilities, as suggested by the following comment: "There's no better way to make, sell, and deliver PCs than the way Dell does it, and nobody executes that model better than Dell."[103] Moreover, no competitor has been able to develop and use substitute capabilities that can duplicate the value Dell creates by using its capabilities. This experience suggests that Dell's direct sales model capabilities are nonsubstitutable.

In summary, only using valuable, rare, costly-to-imitate, and nonsubstitutable capabilities creates sustainable competitive advantage. Table 3.5 shows the competitive consequences and performance implications resulting from combinations of the four criteria of sustainability. The analysis suggested by the table helps managers determine the strategic value of a firm's capabilities. The firm should not emphasize capabilities that fit the criteria described in the first row in the table (that is, resources and capabilities that are neither valuable nor rare and that are imitable and for which strategic substitutes exist). Capabilities yield-

Outcomes from Combinations of the Criteria for Sustainable Competitive Advantage

TABLE **3.5**

Is the Resource or Capability Valuable?	Is the Resource or Capability Rare?	Is the Resource or Capability Costly to Imitate?	Is the Resource or Capability Nonsubstitutable?	Competitive Consequences	Performance Implications
No	No	No	No	Competitive disadvantage	Below-average returns
Yes	No	No	Yes/no	Competitive parity	Average returns
Yes	Yes	No	Yes/no	Temporary competitive advantage	Average returns to above-average returns
Yes	Yes	Yes	Yes	Sustainable competitive advantage	Above-average returns

ing competitive parity and either temporary or sustainable competitive advantage, however, will be supported. Some competitors such as Coca-Cola and PepsiCo may have capabilities that result in competitive parity. In such cases, the firms will nurture these capabilities while simultaneously trying to develop capabilities that can yield either a temporary or sustainable competitive advantage.

Value Chain Analysis

Value chain analysis allows the firm to understand the parts of its operations that create value and those that do not. Understanding these issues is important because the firm earns above-average returns only when the value it creates is greater than the costs incurred to create that value.[104]

The value chain is a template that firms use to understand their cost position and to identify the multiple means that might be used to facilitate implementation of a chosen business-level strategy.[105] As shown in Figure 3.3, a firm's value chain is segmented into primary and support activities. **Primary activities** are involved with a product's physical creation, its sale and distribution to buyers, and its service after the sale. **Support activities** provide the assistance necessary for the primary activities to take place.

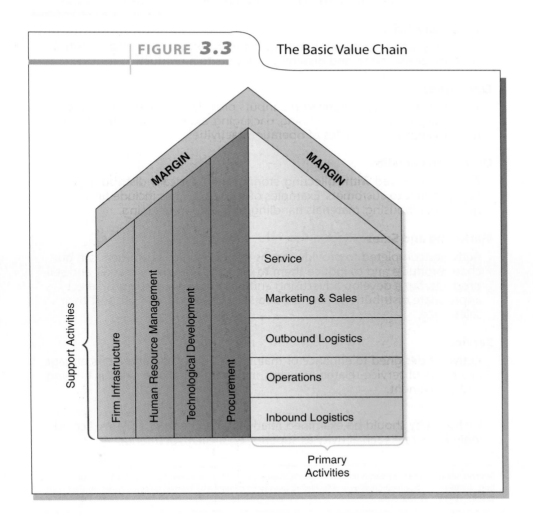

FIGURE 3.3 The Basic Value Chain

The value chain shows how a product moves from the raw-material stage to the final customer. For individual firms, the essential idea of the value chain is to create additional value without incurring significant costs while doing so and to capture the value that has been created. In a globally competitive economy, the most valuable links on the chain are people who have knowledge about customers. This locus of value-creating possibilities applies just as strongly to retail and service firms as to manufacturers. Moreover, for organizations in all sectors, the effects of e-commerce make it increasingly necessary for companies to develop value-adding knowledge processes to compensate for the value and margin that the Internet strips from physical processes.[106]

Table 3.6 lists the items that can be evaluated to determine the value-creating potential of primary activities. In Table 3.7, the items for evaluating support activities are shown. All items in both tables should be evaluated relative to competitors' capabilities. To be a source of competitive advantage, a resource or capability must allow the firm (1) to perform an activity in a manner that provides value superior to that provided by competitors, or (2) to perform a value-creating activity that competitors can-

Examining the Value-Creating Potential of Primary Activities	TABLE **3.6**

Inbound Logistics

Activities, such as materials handling, warehousing, and inventory control, used to receive, store, and disseminate inputs to a product.

Operations

Activities necessary to convert the inputs provided by inbound logistics into final product form. Machining, packaging, assembly, and equipment maintenance are examples of operations activities.

Outbound Logistics

Activities involved with collecting, storing, and physically distributing the final product to customers. Examples of these activities include finished-goods warehousing, materials handling, and order processing.

Marketing and Sales

Activities completed to provide means through which customers can purchase products and to induce them to do so. To effectively market and sell products, firms develop advertising and promotional campaigns, select appropriate distribution channels, and select, develop, and support their sales force.

Service

Activities designed to enhance or maintain a product's value. Firms engage in a range of service-related activities, including installation, repair, training, and adjustment.

Each activity should be examined relative to competitors' abilities. Accordingly, firms rate each activity as superior, equivalent, or inferior.

Source: Adapted with the permission of The Free Press, an imprint of Simon & Schuster Adult Publishing Group, from *Competitive Advantage: Creating and Sustaining Superior Performance,* by Michael E. Porter, pp. 39–40, Copyright © 1985, 1998 by Michael E. Porter.

TABLE **3.7**

Examining the Value-Creating Potential of Support Activities

Procurement

Activities completed to purchase the inputs needed to produce a firm's products. Purchased inputs include items fully consumed during the manufacture of products (e.g., raw materials and supplies, as well as fixed assets—machinery, laboratory equipment, office equipment, and buildings).

Technological Development

Activities completed to improve a firm's product and the processes used to manufacture it. Technological development takes many forms, such as process equipment, basic research and product design, and servicing procedures.

Human Resource Management

Activities involved with recruiting, hiring, training, developing, and compensating all personnel.

Firm Infrastructure

Firm infrastructure includes activities such as general management, planning, finance, accounting, legal support, and governmental relations that are required to support the work of the entire value chain. Through its infrastructure, the firm strives to effectively and consistently identify external opportunities and threats, identify resources and capabilities, and support core competencies.

Each activity should be examined relative to competitors' abilities. Accordingly, firms rate each activity as *superior, equivalent,* or *inferior.*

Source: Adapted with the permission of The Free Press, an imprint of Simon & Schuster Adult Publishing Group, from *Competitive Advantage: Creating and Sustaining Superior Performance,* by Michael E. Porter, pp. 40–43, Copyright © 1985, 1998 by Michael E. Porter.

not complete. Only under these conditions does a firm create value for customers and have opportunities to capture that value.

Sometimes start-up firms create value by uniquely reconfiguring or recombining parts of the value chain. FedEx changed the nature of the delivery business by reconfiguring outbound logistics (a primary activity) and human resource management (a support activity) to provide overnight deliveries, creating value in the process. As shown in Figure 3.4, the Internet has changed many aspects of the value chain for a broad range of firms. A key reason for this is that the Internet affects how people communicate, locate information, and buy goods and services.

Rating a firm's capability to execute its primary and support activities is challenging. Earlier in the chapter, we noted that identifying and assessing the value of a firm's resources and capabilities requires judgment. Judgment is equally necessary when using value chain analysis. The reason is that there is no obviously correct model or rule available to help in the process.

What should a firm do about primary and support activities in which its resources and capabilities are not a source of core competence and, hence, of competitive advantage? Outsourcing is one solution to consider.

FIGURE **3.4**   Prominent Applications of the Internet in the Value Chain

Firm Infrastructure
- Web-based, distributed financial and ERP systems
- Online investor relations (e.g., information dissemination, broadcast conference calls)

Human Resource Management
- Self-service personnel and benefits administration
- Web-based training
- Internet-based sharing and dissemination of company information
- Electronic time and expense reporting

Technology Development
- Collaborative product design across locations and among multiple value-system participants
- Knowledge directories accessible from all parts of the organization
- Real-time access by R&D to online sales and service information

Procurement
- Internet-enabled demand planning; real-time available-to-promise/capable-to-promise and fulfillment
- Other linkage of purchase, inventory, and forecasting systems with suppliers
- Automated "requisition to pay"
- Direct and indirect procurement via marketplaces, exchanges, auctions, and buyer-seller matching

Inbound Logistics	**Operations**	**Outbound Logistics**	**Marketing and Sales**	**After-Sales Service**
• Real-time integrated scheduling, shipping, warehouse management, demand management, and planning, and advanced planning and scheduling across the company and its suppliers • Dissemination throughout the company of real-time inbound and in-progress inventory data	• Integrated information exchange, scheduling and decision making in in-house plants, contract assemblers, and components suppliers • Real-time available-to-promise and capable-to-promise information available to the sales force and channels	• Real-time transaction of orders whether initiated by an end consumer, a salesperson, or a channel partner • Automated customer-specific agreements and contract terms • Customer and channel access to product development and delivery status • Collaborative integration with customer forecasting systems • Integrated channel management including information exchange, warranty claims, and contract management (process control)	• Online sales channels including websites and marketplaces • Real-time inside and outside access to customer information, product catalogs, dynamic pricing, inventory availability, online submission of quotes, and order entry • Online product configurators • Customer-tailored marketing via customer profiling • Push advertising • Tailored online access • Real-time customer feedback through Web surveys, opt-in/opt-out marketing, and promotion response tracking	• Online support of customer service representatives through e-mail response management, billing integration, co-browse, chat, "call me now," voice-over-IP, and other uses of video streaming • Customer self-service via websites and intelligent service request processing including updates to billing and shipping profiles • Real-time field service access to customer account review, schematic review, parts availability and ordering, work-order update, and service parts management

← · Web-distributed supply chain management ——————→

Outsourcing

Concerned with how components, finished goods, or services will be obtained, **outsourcing** is the purchase of a value-creating activity from an external supplier.[107] Not-for-profit agencies as well as for-profit organizations actively engage in outsourcing.[108]

Firms engaging in effective outsourcing increase their flexibility, mitigate risks, and reduce their capital investments.[109] In multiple global industries, the trend toward outsourcing continues at a rapid pace.[110] Moreover, in some industries virtually all firms seek the value that can be captured through effective outsourcing. The auto manufacturing industry and, more recently, the electronics industry are examples of this situation.[111] As with other strategic management process decisions, careful study is required before the firm decides to engage in outsourcing.[112]

Outsourcing can be effective because few, if any, organizations possess the resources and capabilities required to achieve competitive superiority in all primary and support activities. For example, research suggests that few companies can afford to develop internally all the technologies that might lead to competitive advantage.[113] By nurturing a smaller number of capabilities, a firm increases the probability of developing a competitive advantage because it does not become overextended. In addition, by outsourcing activities in which it lacks competence, the firm can fully concentrate on those areas in which it can create value.[114]

Other research suggests that outsourcing does not work effectively without extensive internal capabilities to coordinate external sourcing as well as core competencies.[115] Dell Inc., for example, outsources most of its customer service activities, allowing the firm to concentrate on creating value through its excellent efficiency in its just-in-time inventory system and its online distribution capabilities. In addition, the value generated by outsourcing must be sufficient to cover a firm's costs. For example, research indicates that for European banks outsourcing various information technology activities, "a provider must beat a bank's internal costs by about 40 percent."[116]

To verify that the appropriate primary and support activities are outsourced, four skills are essential for managers involved in outsourcing programs: strategic thinking, deal making, partnership governance, and change management.[117] Managers should understand whether and how outsourcing creates competitive advantage within their company—they need to be able to think strategically.[118] To complete effective outsourcing transactions, these managers must also be deal makers, able to secure rights from external providers that can be fully used by internal managers. They must be able to oversee and govern appropriately the relationship with the company to which the services were outsourced. Because outsourcing can significantly change how an organization operates, managers administering these programs must also be able to manage that change, including resolving employee resistance that accompanies any significant change effort.[119]

There are concerns about the consequences of outsourcing. For the most part, these concerns revolve around the potential loss in firms' innovative ability and the loss of jobs within companies that decide to outsource some of their work activities to others. Thus, innovation and technological uncertainty are two important issues to consider in making outsourcing decisions.[120] Companies should be aware of these issues and be prepared to fully consider the concerns about outsourcing when different stakeholders (e.g., employees) express them.

As explained in the Strategic Focus, outsourcing has several advantages for firms but also carries some important risks as well. Outsourcing can potentially reduce costs and increase the quality of the activities outsourced. In this way, it adds value to the product provided to consumers. Thus, outsourcing can contribute to a firm's competitive advantage and its ability to create value for its stakeholders. For these reasons many firms such as Dell, Hewlett-Packard, and Motorola are outsourcing the manufacturing and even the design of many of their products. Yet outsourcing does not always deliver the value expected, as shown by the study by Deloitte Consulting. Additionally, the risk of the outsourcing partner's learning the technology and becoming a competitor is highlighted by Motorola's experience with BenQ in China's lucrative mobile phone

Outsourcing—Boon or Bane to Competitiveness?

Outsourcing has become a popular strategic action but has also been highly controversial, even playing a role in major political debates in some countries. Its popularity is shown by the fact that major electronics companies in the United States outsource the manufacturing and often even the design of their products. In fact, 89 percent of the brand-name laptop computers sold by U.S. companies such as Dell and Hewlett-Packard are manufactured by firms located in other countries. The primary reasons for outsourcing are to lower costs of production and to have a partner with strong expertise in the outsourced area. If the company to which a firm outsources activities is chosen carefully, the product should be manufactured with higher quality and with more efficiency than the outsourcing company could have done. Yet some politicians are concerned about the loss of jobs, while others retort that such actions are necessary for companies to remain competitive in global markets. If firms are not allowed to outsource, they may lose their competitive advantage and be unable to compete on local or global markets. This outcome would most assuredly cost more jobs than outsourcing would.

Outsourcing has reached into all areas of the business. For example, medical doctors now often outsource MRI and CT scanning. Such outsourcing saves them from purchasing expensive equipment and from employing people to operate the machines and interpret the data from the scans. An outsourcing organization such as Imaging Solutions Inc., headquartered in Fargo, North Dakota, can potentially do the work more cheaply and more accurately. Companies such as Imaging Solutions, the India-based software outsourcer Infosys Technologies, and the Taiwanese computer manufacturing outsourcer Quanta have gained immensely from the outsourcing revolution in the United States and Western Europe. Wipro Technologies, an IT services outsourcer, has grown from 8,000 employees in 1999 to 42,000 employees in 2005. Some firms are now outsourcing functions that heretofore were considered to be core competencies or critical to their competitive position. Perhaps the most forbidden area of outsourcing in prior years has been research and development, but outsourcing has reached that as well. In some industries, even those where technology is critical, large amounts of R&D are outsourced. For example, large pharmaceutical firms now outsource 40 to 60 percent of their R&D activities. R&D operations can account for 5 to 18 percent of the total costs of major technology companies. To reduce these costs and remain competitive in global markets, many technology firms have been outsourcing parts of their R&D operations to specialized companies in India, China, and Eastern Europe. However, it is critical that they select the appropriate activities to outsource, maintain control, and ensure balance and smooth coordination along the R&D value chain. Essentially, firms must analyze their R&D value chains to identify and keep in house the strategic activities and outsource the nonstrategic activities. Care must be taken in the choice of activities to outsource and in selection of the partner to perform the outsourced activities.

One risk of outsourcing is that the partner will gain access to the technical knowledge needed to become a competitor at a future date. For example, Motorola contracted with BenQ Corporation to design and manufacture mobile phones. But, in 2004, BenQ began to manufacture and market mobile phones in China under its own brand name. Motorola cancelled its contract with BenQ but the damage was done. In addition to this type of risk, Deloitte Consulting found that approximately one third of the companies

India-based software outsourcer Infosys Technologies has gained immensely from the outsourcing revolution in the United States and Western Europe.

EPA/STR EPA/STR/LANDOV

that outsourced did not achieve the efficiencies and cost savings expected. Deloitte concluded that outsourcing introduces complexity and some potential coordination costs into the value chain, and recommended that firms take special care in choosing the functions or activities to outsource.

Sources: M. Kanellos, 2005, Outsourcing giant Wipro eyes consulting gigs, *New York Times*, www.nytimes.com, May 3; D. Armstrong, 2005, MRI and CT centers offer doctors way to profit on scans, *Wall Street Journal*, www.wsj.com, May 2; R. Christie, 2005, Outsourcing pitfalls await unwary firms seeking savings, *Wall Street Journal*, www.wsj.com, April 29; T. Hallett, 2005, Outsourcing your core competencies, silicon.com, www.silicon.com, April 28; E. Bellman, 2005, Outsourcing lifts India's Infosys, *Wall Street Journal*, www.wsj.com, April 15; P. Engardio, 2005, Online extra: R&D jobs: Who stays, who goes? *Business Week*, www.businessweek.com, March 21; C. Koch, 2005, Innovation ships out, *CIO*, www.cio.com, January 15; D. Kirkpatrick, 2004, Why outsourcing isn't really the issue, *Fortune*, www.fortune.com, October 29.

market. Therefore, outsourcing decisions are critical and must be made with strategic criteria in mind, including a thorough evaluation of potential partners and selection of effective and reliable partners.

Competencies, Strengths, Weaknesses, and Strategic Decisions

At the conclusion of the internal analysis, firms must identify their strengths and weaknesses in resources, capabilities, and core competencies. For example, if they have weak capabilities or do not have core competencies in areas required to achieve a competitive advantage, they must acquire those resources and build the capabilities and competencies needed. Alternatively, they could decide to outsource a function or activity where they are weak in order to improve the value that they provide to customers.[121]

Therefore, firms need to have the appropriate resources and capabilities to develop the desired strategy and create value for customers and shareholders as well.[122] Having many resources does not necessarily lead to success. Firms must have the right ones and the capabilities needed to produce superior value to customers. Undoubtedly, having the appropriate and strong capabilities required for achieving a competitive advantage is a primary responsibility of top-level managers.[123] These important leaders must focus on both the firm's strengths and weaknesses.

Tools such as outsourcing help the firm focus on its core competencies as the source of its competitive advantages. However, evidence shows that the value-creating ability of core competencies should never be taken for granted. Moreover, the ability of a core competence to be a permanent competitive advantage can't be assumed. The reason for these cautions is that all core competencies have the potential to become *core rigidities*. As Leslie Wexner, CEO of Limited Brands, says: "Success doesn't beget success. Success begets failure because the more that you know a thing works, the less likely you are to think that it won't work. When you've had a long string of victories, it's harder to foresee your own vulnerabilities."[124] Thus, a core competence is usually a strength because it is the source of competitive advantage. If emphasized when it is no longer competitively relevant, it can become a weakness, a seed of organizational inertia.

Events occurring in the firm's external environment create conditions through which core competencies can become core rigidities, generate inertia, and stifle innovation. "Often the flip side, the dark side, of core capabilities is revealed due to external events when new competitors figure out a better way to serve the firm's customers, when new technologies emerge, or when political or social events shift the ground underneath."[125] However, in the final analysis, changes in the external environment do not cause core competencies to become core rigidities; rather, strategic myopia and inflexibility on the part of managers are the cause.[126]

The Opening Case emphasized the importance of innovation for many firms. How important innovation is to firm success depends partly on the firm's industry and competitive environment as determined through the external environment analysis explained in Chapter 2. If it is important, a firm with a strength in technology development or technological knowledge held can base its strategy on this capability (or competence).[127] We conclude that determining what the firm *can do* through continuous and effective analyses of its internal environment increases the likelihood of long-term competitive success.

SUMMARY

- In the global landscape, traditional factors (e.g., labor costs and superior access to financial resources and raw materials) can still create a competitive advantage. However, this happens in a declining number of instances. In the new landscape, the resources, capabilities, and core competencies in the firm's internal environment may have a relatively stronger influence on its performance than do conditions in the external environment. The most effective organizations recognize that strategic competitiveness and above-average returns result only when core competencies (identified through the study of the firm's internal environment) are matched with opportunities (determined through the study of the firm's external environment).

- No competitive advantage lasts forever. Over time, rivals use their own unique resources, capabilities, and core competencies to form different value-creating propositions that duplicate the value-creating ability of the firm's competitive advantages. In general, the Internet's capabilities are reducing the sustainability of many competitive advantages. Because competitive advantages are not permanently sustainable, firms must exploit their current advantages while simultaneously using their resources and capabilities to form new advantages that can lead to competitive success in the future.

- Effective management of core competencies requires careful analysis of the firm's resources (inputs to the production process) and capabilities (resources that have been purposely integrated to achieve a specific task or set of tasks). The knowledge possessed by human capital is among the most significant of an organization's capabilities and may ultimately be at the root of all competitive advantages. The firm must create an environment that allows people to integrate their individual knowledge with that held by others so that, collectively, the firm has significant organizational knowledge.

- Individual resources are usually not a source of competitive advantage. Capabilities are a more likely source of competitive advantages, especially relatively sustainable ones. A key reason for this is that the firm's nurturing and support of core competencies that are based on capabilities is less visible to rivals and, as such, is harder to understand and imitate.

- Only when a capability is valuable, rare, costly to imitate, and nonsubstitutable is it a core competence and a source of competitive advantage. Over time, core competencies must be supported, but they cannot be allowed to become core rigidities. Core competencies are a source of competitive advantage only when they allow the firm to create value by exploiting opportunities in its external environment. When this is no longer the case, attention shifts to selecting or forming other capabilities that do satisfy the four criteria of sustainable competitive advantage.

- Value chain analysis is used to identify and evaluate the competitive potential of resources and capabilities. By studying their skills relative to those associated with primary and support activities, firms can understand their cost structure and identify the activities through which they can create value.

- When the firm cannot create value in either a primary or support activity, outsourcing is considered. Used commonly in the global economy, outsourcing is the purchase of a value-creating activity from an external supplier. The firm must outsource only to companies possessing a competitive advantage in terms of the particular primary or support activity under consideration. In addition, the firm must continuously verify that it is not outsourcing activities from which it could create value.

1. A. Andal-Ancion, P. A. Cartwright, & G. S. Yip, 2003, The digital transformation of traditional businesses, *MIT Sloan Management Review,* 44(4): 34–41.

2. R. R. Wiggins & T. W. Ruefli, 2002, Sustained competitive advantage: Temporal dynamics and the incidence of persistence of superior economic performance, *Organization Science,* 13: 82–105.

3. S. K. McEvily, K. M. Eisenhardt, & J. E. Prescott, 2004, The global acquisition, leverage, and protection of technological competencies, *Strategic Management Journal,* 25: 713–722.

4. Getting an edge on innovation, 2005, *BusinessWeek Online,* www .businessweek.com, March 21.

5. M. Iansiti, F. W. McFarlan, & G. Westerman, 2003, Leveraging the incumbent's advantage, *MIT Sloan Management Review,* 44(4): 58–64; P. W. Roberts & G. R. Dowling, 2002, Corporate reputation and sustained superior financial performance, *Strategic Management Journal,* 23: 1077–1093.

6. S. Dutta, M. J. Zbaracki, & M. Bergen, 2003, Pricing process as a capability: A resource-based perspective, *Strategic Management Journal,* 24: 615–630; A. M. Knott, 2003, Persistent heterogeneity and sustainable innovation, *Strategic Management Journal,* 24: 687–705.

7. C. G. Brush, P. G. Greene, & M. M. Hart, 2001, From initial idea to unique advantage: The entrepreneurial challenge of constructing a resource base, *Academy of Management Executive,* 15(1): 64–78.

8. T. J. Douglas & J. A. Ryman, 2003, Understanding competitive advantage in the general hospital industry: Evaluating strategic competencies, *Strategic Management Journal,* 24: 333–347; R. Makadok, 2001, Toward a synthesis of the resource-based and dynamic-capability views of rent creation, *Strategic Management Journal,* 22: 387–401.

9. D. G. Sirmon, M. A. Hitt, & R. D. Ireland, 2007, Managing firm resources in dynamic markets to create value: Looking inside the black box, *Academy of Management Review,* in press.

10. G. Hamel & L. Valikangas, 2003, The quest for resilience, Harvard Business Review, 81(9): 52–63; S. A. Way, 2002, High-performance work systems and intermediate indicators of firm performance within the U.S. small-business sector, Journal of Management, 28: 765–785; M. A. Hitt, L. Bierman, K. Shimizu, & R. Kochhar, 2001, Direct and moderating effects of human capital on strategy and performance in professional service firms: A resource-based perspective, Academy of Management Journal, 44: 13–28.

11. M. A. Hitt, C. C. Miller, & A. Colella, 2006. *Organizational Behavior: A Strategic Approach,* New York: John Wiley & Sons.

12. R. Florida, 2005, *The Flight of the Creative Class,* New York: HarperBusiness.

13. J. Shamsie, 2003, The context of dominance: An industry-driven framework for exploiting reputation, *Strategic Management Journal,* 24: 199–215; E. Autio, H. J. Sapienza, & J. G. Almeida, 2000, Effects of age at entry, knowledge intensity, and imitability on international growth, *Academy of Management Journal,* 43: 909–924.

14. M. Makhija, 2003, Comparing the resource-based and market-based view of the firm: Empirical evidence from Czech privatization, *Strategic Management Journal,* 24: 433–451; P. L. Yeoh & K. Roth, 1999, An empirical analysis of sustained advantage in the U.S. pharmaceutical industry: Impact of firm resources and capabilities, *Strategic Management Journal,* 20: 637–653.

15. D. F. Abell, 1999, Competing today while preparing for tomorrow, *Sloan Management Review,* 40(3): 73–81; D. Leonard-Barton, 1995, *Wellsprings of Knowledge: Building and Sustaining the Sources of Innovation,* Boston: Harvard Business School Press; R. A. McGrath, J. C. MacMillan, & S. Venkataraman, 1995, Defining and developing competence: A strategic process paradigm, *Strategic Management Journal,* 16: 251–275.

16. H. K. Steensma & K. G. Corley, 2000, On the performance of technology-sourcing partnerships: The interaction between partner interdependence and technology attributes, *Academy of Management Journal,* 43: 1045–1067.

17. J. B. Barney, 2001, Is the resource-based "view" a useful perspective for strategic management research? Yes, *Academy of Management Review,* 26: 41–56.

18. M. Subramani & N. Venkataraman, 2003, Safeguarding investments in asymmetric interorganizational relationships: Theory and evidence, *Academy of Management Journal,* 46: 46–62.

19. T. M. Begley & D. P. Boyd, 2003, The need for a corporate global mind-set, *MIT Sloan Management Review,* 44(2): 25–32.

20. Sirmon, Hitt, & Ireland, Managing resources in a dynamic environment.

21. Barney, Is the resource-based "view" a useful perspective for strategic management research? Yes; T. H. Brush & K. W. Artz, 1999, Toward a contingent resource-based theory: The impact of information asymmetry on the value of capabilities in veterinary medicine, *Strategic Management Journal,* 20: 223–250.

22. S. K. McEvily & B. Chakravarthy, 2002, The persistence of knowledge-based advantage: An empirical test for product performance and technological knowledge, *Strategic Management Journal,* 23: 285–305.

23. Sirmon, Hitt, & Ireland, Managing resources in a dynamic environment.

24. J. Benedict, E. M. Steenkamp, R. Batra, & D. L. Alden, 2003, How perceived brand globalness creates brand value, *Journal of International Business Studies,* 34: 53–65.

25. S. Nambisan, 2002, Designing virtual customer environments for new product development: Toward a theory, *Academy of Management Review,* 27: 392–413.

26. J. Wolf & W. G. Egelhoff, 2002, A reexamination and extension of international strategy-structure theory, *Strategic Management Journal,* 23: 181–189; R. Ramirez, 1999, Value co-production: Intellectual origins and implications for practice and research, *Strategic Management Journal,* 20: 49–65.

27. V. Shankar & B. L. Bayus, 2003, Network effects and competition: An empirical analysis of the home video game industry, *Strategic Management Journal,* 24: 375–384; S. W. Floyd & B. Wooldridge, 1999, Knowledge creation and social networks in corporate entrepreneurship: The renewal of organizational capability, *Entrepreneurship: Theory and Practice,* 23(3): 123–143.

28. G. Hawawini, V. Subramanian, & P. Verdin, 2003, Is performance driven by industry- or firm-specific factors? A new look at the evidence, *Strategic Management Journal,* 24: 1–16; M. A. Hitt, R. D. Nixon, P. G. Clifford, & K. P. Coyne, 1999, The development and use of strategic resources, in M. A. Hitt, P. G. Clifford, R. D. Nixon, & K. P. Coyne (eds.), *Dynamic Strategic Resources,* Chichester: John Wiley & Sons, 1–14.

29. M. R. Haas & M. T. Hansen, 2005, When using knowledge can hurt performance: The value of organizational capabilities in a management consulting company, *Strategic Management Journal,* 26: 1–24.

30. C. M. Christensen, 2001, The past and future of competitive advantage, *Sloan Management Review,* 42(2): 105–109.

31. J. R. Hough & M. A. White, 2003, Environmental dynamism and strategic decision-making rationality: An examination at the decision level, *Strategic Management Journal,* 24: 481–489.

32. C. J. Robertson & W. F. Crittenden, 2003, Mapping moral philosophies: Strategic implications for multinational firms, *Strategic Management Journal,* 24: 385–392.

33. C. M. Christensen & M. E. Raynor, 2003, Why hard-nosed executives should care about management theory, *Harvard Business Review,* 81(9): 66–74.

34. N. Checa, J. Maguire, & J. Barney, 2003, The new world disorder, *Harvard Business Review,* 81(8): 70–79; P. Westhead, M. Wright, & D. Ucbasaran, 2001, The internationalization of new and small firms: A resource-based view, *Journal of Business Venturing* 16(4): 333–358.

35. H. J. Smith, 2003, The shareholders vs. stakeholders debate, *MIT Sloan Management Review*, 44(4): 85–90; H. Collingwood, 2001, The earnings game: Everyone plays, nobody wins, *Harvard Business Review*, 79(6): 65–74.

36. P. C. Nutt, 2002, *Why decisions fail*, San Francisco: Berrett-Koehler Publishers.

37. J. M. Mezias & W. H. Starbuck, 2003, What do managers know, anyway? *Harvard Business Review*, 81(5): 16–17; M. Keil, 2000, Cutting your losses: Extricating your organization when a big project goes awry, *Sloan Management Review*, 41(3): 55–68.

38. P. G. Audia, E. Locke, & K. G. Smith, 2000, The paradox of success: An archival and a laboratory study of strategic persistence following radical environmental change, *Academy of Management Journal*, 43: 837–853; R. G. McGrath, 1999, Falling forward: Real options reasoning and entrepreneurial failure, *Academy of Management Review*, 24: 13–30.

39. G. P. West III & J. DeCastro, 2001, The Achilles heel of firm strategy: Resource weaknesses and distinctive inadequacies, *Journal of Management Studies*, 38: 417–442; G. Gavetti & D. Levinthal, 2000, Looking forward and looking backward: Cognitive and experimental search, *Administrative Science Quarterly*, 45: 113–137.

40. R. Amit & P. J. H. Schoemaker, 1993, Strategic assets and organizational rent, *Strategic Management Journal*, 14: 33–46.

41. R. E. Hoskisson & L. W. Busenitz, 2001, Market uncertainty and learning distance in corporate entrepreneurship entry mode choice, in M. A. Hitt, R. D. Ireland, S. M. Camp, & D. L. Sexton (eds.), *Strategic Entrepreneurship: Creating a New Integrated Mindset*, Oxford, UK: Blackwell Publishers, 151–172.

42. C. M. Fiol & E. J. O'Connor, 2003, Waking up! Mindfulness in the face of bandwagons, *Academy of Management Review*, 28: 54–70.

43. N. J. Hiller & D. C. Hambrick, 2005, Conceptualizing executive hubris: The role of (hyper-) core self-evaluations in strategic decision making, *Strategic Management Journal*, 26: 297–319.

44. P. Burrows & A. Park, 2002, What price victory at Hewlett-Packard? *Business Week*, April 1, 36–37.

45. J. M. Mezias, P. Grinyer, & W. D. Guth, 2001, Changing collective cognition: A process model for strategic change, *Long Range Planning*, 34(1): 71–95.

46. 2005, IBM plans restructuring, *Wall Street Journal Online*, www.wsj.com, May 4.

47. D. Kirkpatrick, 2005, Microsoft Office: Going beyond the cubicle, *Fortune Online*, www.fortune.com, April 27.

48. D. M. De Carolis, 2003, Competencies and imitability in the pharmaceutical industry: An analysis of their relationship with firm performance, *Journal of Management*, 29: 27–50.

49. G. Ahuja & R. Katila, 2004, Where do resources come from? The role of idiosyncratic situations, *Strategic Management Journal*, 25: 887–907.

50. D. L. Deeds, D. De Carolis, & J. Coombs, 2000, Dynamic capabilities and new product development in high-technology ventures: An empirical analysis of new biotechnology firms, *Journal of Business Venturing*, 15: 211–229; T. Chi, 1994, Trading in strategic resources: Necessary conditions, transaction cost problems, and choice of exchange structure, *Strategic Management Journal*, 15: 271–290.

51. Sirmon, Hitt, & Ireland, Managing resources in dynamic environments; S. Berman, J. Down, & C. Hill, 2002, Tacit knowledge as a source of competitive advantage in the National Basketball Association, *Academy of Management Journal*, 45: 13–31.

52. 2003, About Borders Group, www.borders.com, July 18; S. Shepard, 2001, Interview: "The company is not the stock," *Business Week*, April 30, 94–96.

53. K. G. Smith, C. J. Collins, & K. D. Clark, 2005, Existing knowledge, knowledge creation capability, and the rate of new product introduction in high-technology firms, *Academy of Management Journal*, 48: 346–357; S. G. Winter, 2005, Developing evolutionary theory for economics and management, in K. G. Smith and M. A. Hitt (eds.), *Great minds in management: The process of theory development*. Oxford, UK: Oxford University Press 509–546.

54. Subramani & Venkataraman, Safeguarding investments; R. Lubit, 2001, Tacit knowledge and knowledge management: The keys to sustainable competitive advantage, *Organizational Dynamics*, 29(3): 164–178.

55. A. M. Webber, 2000, New math for a new economy, *Fast Company*, January/February, 214–224.

56. M. Song, C. Droge, S. Hanvanich, & R. Calatone, 2005, Marketing and technology resource complementarity: An analysis of their interaction effect in two environmental contexts, *Strategic Management Journal*, 26: 259–276; R. G. Schroeder, K. A. Bates, & M. A. Junttila, 2002, A resource-based view of manufacturing strategy and the relationship to manufacturing performance, *Strategic Management Journal*, 23: 105–117.

57. M. A. Hitt & R. D. Ireland, 2002, The essence of strategic leadership: Managing human and social capital, *Journal of Leadership and Organization Studies*, 9(1): 3–14.

58. J. B. Quinn, P. Anderson, & S. Finkelstein, 1996, Making the most of the best, *Harvard Business Review*, 74(2): 71–80.

59. S. Tallman, M. Jenkins, N. Henry, & S. Pinch, 2004, Knowledge, clusters and competitive advantage, *Academy of Management Review*, 29: 258–271; A. W. King & C. P. Zeithaml, 2003, Measuring organizational knowledge: A conceptual and methodological framework, *Strategic Management Journal*, 24: 763–772.

60. 2003, Intellectual property, Special Advertising Section, *Business Week*, July 28.

61. Webber, New math, 217.

62. K. Funk, 2003, Sustainability and performance, *MIT Sloan Management Review*, 44(2): 65–70.

63. R. D. Ireland, M. A. Hitt, & D. Vaidyanath, 2002, Managing strategic alliances to achieve a competitive advantage, *Journal of Management*, 28: 416–446.

64. D. L. Deephouse, 2000, Media reputation as a strategic resource: An integration of mass communication and resource-based theories, *Journal of Management*, 26: 1091–1112.

65. Shamsie, The context of dominance.

66. Roberts & Dowling, Corporate reputation, 1078.

67. P. Berthon, M. B. Holbrook, & J. M. Hulbert, 2003, Understanding and managing the brand space, *MIT Sloan Management Review*, 44(2): 49–54; D. B. Holt, 2003, What becomes an icon most? *Harvard Business Review*, 81(3): 43–49.

68. J. Blasberg & V. Vishwanath, 2003, Making cool brands hot, *Harvard Business Review*, 81(6): 20–22.

69. 2003, Harley-Davidson MotorClothes Merchandise, www.harleydavidson.com, July 20.

70. D. Roberts & S. Holmes, 2005, China's real sports contest, *BusinessWeek Online*, www.businessweek.com, March 14.

71. R. D. Nixon, M. A. Hitt, H. Lee, & E. Jeong, 2004, Market reactions to announcements of corporate downsizing actions and implementation strategies, *Strategic Management Journal*, 25: 1121–1129.

72. N. W. Hatch & J. H. Dyer, 2004, Human capital and learning as a source of sustainable competitive advantage, *Strategic Management Journal*, 25: 1155–1178.

73. T. Gardner, 2005, Interfirm competition for human resources: Evidence from the software industry, *Academy of Management Journal*, 48: 237–256; S. J. Peterson & B. K. Spiker, 2005, Establishing the positive contributory value of older workers: A positive psychology perspective, *Organizational Dynamics*, 34(2): 153–167.

74. D. Wighton & D. Wells, 2005, Morgan Stanley to woo talent at rival banks, *Financial Times Online*, www.ft.com, July 4.

75. Sirmon, Hitt, & Ireland, Managing firm resources in dynamic environments; S. Dutta, O. Narasimhan, & S. Rajiv, 2005, Conceptualizing and measuring capabilities: Methodology and empirical application, *Strategic Management Journal*, 26: 277–285.

76. Hitt, Bierman, Shimizu, & Kochhar, Direct and moderating effects of human capital on strategy and performance in professional service firms: A resource-based perspective; M. A. Hitt, R. D. Ireland, & H. Lee, 2000, Technological learning, knowledge management, firm growth and performance: An introductory essay, *Journal of Engineering and Technology Management*, 17: 231–246.

77. S. K. Ethiraj, P. Kale, M. S. Krishnan, & J. V. Singh, 2005, Where do capabilities come from and do they matter? A study in the software services industry, *Strategic Management Journal*, 26: 25–45.

78. M. G. Jacobides & S. G. Winter, 2005, The co-evolution of capabilities and transaction costs: Explaining the institutional structure of production, *Strategic Management Journal*, 26: 395–413.

79. R. W. Coff & P. M. Lee, 2003, Insider trading as a vehicle to appropriate rent from R&D, *Strategic Management Journal*, 24: 183–190.

80. D. L. Deeds, 2003, Alternative strategies for acquiring knowledge, in S. E. Jackson, M. A. Hitt, & A. S. DeNisi (eds.), *Managing Knowledge for Sustained Competitive Advantage*, San Francisco: Jossey-Bass, 37–63.

81. R. A. Noe, J. A. Colquitt, M. J. Simmering, & S. A. Alvarez, 2003, Knowledge management: Developing intellectual and social capital, in S. E. Jackson, M. A. Hitt, & A. S. DeNisi (eds.), *Managing Knowledge for Sustained Competitive Advantage,* San Francisco: Jossey-Bass, 209–242; L. Argote & P. Ingram, 2000, Knowledge transfer: A basis for competitive advantage in firms, *Organizational Behavior and Human Decision Processes,* 82: 150–169.

82. M. J. Tippins & R. S. Sohi, 2003, IT competency and firm performance: Is organizational learning a missing link? *Strategic Management Journal,* 24: 745–761.

83. M. A. Hitt & R. D. Ireland, 1986, Relationships among corporate level distinctive competencies, diversification strategy, corporate structure, and performance, *Journal of Management Studies,* 23: 401–416; M. A. Hitt & R. D. Ireland, 1985, Corporate distinctive competence, strategy, industry, and performance, *Strategic Management Journal,* 6: 273–293; M. A. Hitt, R. D. Ireland, & K. A. Palia, 1982, Industrial firms' grand strategy and functional importance, *Academy of Management Journal,* 25: 265–298; M. A. Hitt, R. D. Ireland, & G. Stadter, 1982, Functional importance and company performance: Moderating effects of grand strategy and industry type, *Strategic Management Journal,* 3: 315–330; C. C. Snow & E. G. Hrebiniak, 1980, Strategy, distinctive competence, and organizational performance, *Administrative Science Quarterly,* 25: 317–336.

84. C. Zott, 2003, Dynamic capabilities and the emergence of intraindustry differential firm performance: Insights from a simulation study, *Strategic Management Journal,* 24: 97–125.

85. K. Hafeez, Y. B. Zhang, & N. Malak, 2002, Core competence for sustainable competitive advantage: A structured methodology for identifying core competence, *IEEE Transactions on Engineering Management,* 49(1): 28–35; C. K. Prahalad & G. Hamel, 1990, The core competence of the corporation, *Harvard Business Review,* 68(3): 79–93.

86. C. Bowman & V. Ambrosini, 2000, Value creation versus value capture: Towards a coherent definition of value in strategy, *British Journal of Management,* 11: 1–15.

87. C. Bowman, 2001, "Value" in the resource-based view of the firm: A contribution to the debate, *Academy of Management Review,* 26: 501–502.

88. C. Ames, 1995, Sales soft? Profits flat? It's time to rethink your business, *Fortune,* June 25, 142–146.

89. R. Thomlinson, 2005, Unilever: One company, two bosses, many problems, *Fortune Online,* www.fortune.com, January 13.

90. Hitt, Miller, & Colella, *Organizational Behavior.*

91. J. B. Barney, 1999, How a firm's capabilities affect boundary decisions, *Sloan Management Review,* 40(3): 137–145; J. B. Barney, 1995, Looking inside for competitive advantage, *Academy of Management Executive,* 9(4): 59–60; J. B. Barney, 1991, Firm resources and sustained competitive advantage, *Journal of Management,* 17: 99–120.

92. Barney, Looking inside for competitive advantage.

93. 2005, Jack Welch: It's all in the sauce, *Fortune Online,* www.fortune.com, April 4.

94. Barney, Looking inside for competitive advantage, 52.

95. Ibid., 53.

96. Barney, Firm resources, 108.

97. L. E. Tetrick & N. Da Silva, 2003, Assessing the culture and climate for organizational learning, in S. E. Jackson, M. A. Hitt, & A. S. DeNisi (eds.), *Managing Knowledge for Sustained Competitive Advantage,* San Francisco: Jossey-Bass, 333–359.

98. L. Soupata, 2001, Managing culture for competitive advantage at United Parcel Service, *Journal of Organizational Excellence,* 20(3): 19–26.

99. A. W. King & C. P. Zeithaml, 2001, Competencies and firm performance: Examining the causal ambiguity paradox, *Strategic Management Journal,* 22: 75–99.

100. Barney, Firm resources, 111.

101. Amit & Schoemaker, Strategic assets, 39.

102. M. J. Benner & M. L. Tushman, 2003, Exploitation, exploration, and process management: The productivity dilemma revisited, *Academy of Management Review,* 28: 238–256; S. K. McEvily, S. Das, & K. McCabe, 2000, Avoiding competence substitution through knowledge sharing, *Academy of Management Review,* 25: 294–311.

103. A. Serwer, 2005. America's most admired companies: The education of Michael Dell, *Fortune Online,* www.fortune.com, February 22.

104. Sirmon, Hitt, & Ireland, Managing firm resources in dynamic environments; M. E. Porter, 1985, *Competitive Advantage,* New York: Free Press, 33–61.

105. G. G. Dess, A. Gupta, J.-F. Hennart, & C. W. L. Hill, 1995, Conducting and integrating strategy research at the international corporate and business levels: Issues and directions, *Journal of Management,* 21: 376.

106. R. Amit & C. Zott, 2001, Value creation in e-business, *Strategic Management Journal,* 22(Special Issue): 493–520; M. E. Porter, 2001, Strategy and the Internet, *Harvard Business Review,* 79(3): 62–78.

107. T. W. Gainey & B. S. Klaas, 2003, The outsourcing of training and development: Factors impacting client satisfaction, *Journal of Management,* 29: 207–229.

108. M. Rola, 2002, Secrets to successful outsourcing management, *Computing Canada,* 28(23): 11.

109. P. Bendor-Samuel, 2003, Outsourcing: Transforming the corporation, *Forbes,* Special Advertising Section, May 26.

110. K. Madigan & M. J. Mandel, 2003, Commentary: Outsourcing jobs: Is it bad? *Business Week Online,* www.businessweek.com, August 25.

111. J. Palmer, 2003, Auto supplier stands out by focusing on the inside, *Wall Street Journal Online,* www.wsj.com, August 17; A. Takeishi, 2001, Bridging inter- and intra-firm boundaries: Management of supplier involvement in automobile product development, *Strategic Management Journal,* 22: 403–433; H. Y. Park, C. S. Reddy, & S. Sarkar, 2000, Make or buy strategy of firms in the U.S., *Multinational Business Review,* 8(2): 89–97.

112. M. J. Leiblein, J. J. Reuer, & F. Dalsace, 2002, Do make or buy decisions matter? The influence of organizational governance on technological performance, *Strategic Management Journal,* 23: 817–833.

113. J. C. Linder, S. Jarvenpaa, & T. H. Davenport, 2003, Toward an innovation sourcing strategy, *MIT Sloan Management Review,* 44(4): 43–49.

114. Hafeez, Zhang, & Malak, Core competence for sustainable competitive advantage; B. H. Jevnaker & M. Bruce, 1999, Design as a strategic alliance: Expanding the creative capability of the firm, in M. A. Hitt, P. G. Clifford, R. D. Nixon, & K. P. Coyne (eds.), *Dynamic Strategic Resources,* Chichester: John Wiley & Sons, 266–298.

115. Takeishi, Bridging inter- and intra-firm boundaries.

116. R. Lancellotti, O. Schein, & V. Stadler, 2003, When outsourcing pays off, *The McKinsey Quarterly,* Number 1, 10.

117. M. Useem & J. Harder, 2000, Leading laterally in company outsourcing, *Sloan Management Review,* 41(2): 25–36.

118. R. C. Insinga & M. J. Werle, 2000, Linking outsourcing to business strategy, *Academy of Management Executive,* 14(4): 58–70.

119. M. Katz, 2001, Planning ahead for manufacturing facility changes: A case study in outsourcing, *Pharmaceutical Technology,* March: 160–164.

120. M. J. Mol, P. Pauwels, P. Matthyssens, & L. Quintens, 2004, A technological contingency perspective on the depth and scope of international outsourcing, *Journal of International Management,* 10: 287–305.

121. M. A. Hitt, D. Ahlstrom, M. T. Dacin, E. Levitas, & L. Svobodina, 2004, The Institutional Effects on Strategic Alliance Partner Selection in Transition Economies: China versus Russia, *Organization Science,* 15: 173–185.

122. Y. Mishina, T. G. Pollock, & J. F. Porac, 2004, Are more resources always better for growth? Resource stickiness in market and product expansion, *Strategic Management Journal,* 25: 1179–1197.

123. D. S. Elenkov & I. M. Manev, 2005, Top management leadership and influence on innovation: The role of sociocultural context, *Journal of Management,* 31: 381–402.

124. M. Katz, 2001, Planning ahead for manufacturing facility changes: A case study in outsourcing, *Pharmaceutical Technology,* March: 160–164.

125. Leonard-Barton, *Wellsprings of Knowledge,* 30–31.

126. West & DeCastro, The Achilles heel of firm strategy; Keil, Cutting your losses.

127. D. J. Miller, 2004, Firms' technological resources and the performance effects of diversification: A longitudinal study, *Strategic Management Journal,* 25: 1097–1119.

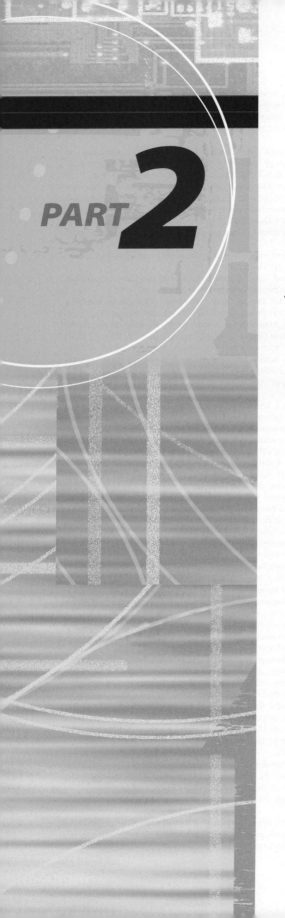

PART **2**

STRATEGIC ACTIONS: STRATEGY FORMULATION

Strategy at the Business Level

KNOWLEDGE OBJECTIVES

Studying this chapter should provide you with the strategic management knowledge needed to:

1. Define business-level strategy.

2. Discuss the relationship between customers and business-level strategies in terms of *who, what,* and *how.*

3. Explain the differences among business-level strategies.

4. Use the five forces of competition model to explain how above-average returns can be earned through each business-level strategy.

5. Describe the risks of using each of the business-level strategies.

Before its sale in August 2005, Frederick Cooper Lamp Company produced unique hand sewn lampshades like those being assembled here.

Lamps of Distinction: Where Did the Customers Go?

Frederick Cooper Lamp Company was founded in Chicago in 1923 by Frederick Cooper, an artist specializing in sculpture and watercolor art. The firm was launched in response to requests from clients that Cooper incorporate his works of art into lamps.

Relying on hand labor alone to make its lamps, chandeliers, and sconces, Cooper's company quickly became recognized as a manufacturer of high-quality, distinctive products. Throughout its history, one of Cooper Lamp's signature treatments was "the use of silk and other fine and exotic materials to produce unique hand sewn lampshades, many of which are adorned with distinctive bead and fringe treatments." The firm used the focused differentiation business-level strategy, which essentially means that Cooper Lamp made expensive products that provided unique value to a small group of customers who were willing to pay a premium to purchase uniqueness (we fully describe the focused differentiation strategy later in the chapter). The words of a company official reflect Cooper Lamp's strategy: "We offer a very high-quality product. Our shades are hand-sewn, using unique fabrics. We use unique materials. We put things together in a unique fashion and as a result we have a very good name among the designers and decorators, and the stores. We sell to very high-end stores, [including] Bloomingdale's, Neiman Marcus, [and] Horchow." Thus, Cooper made "really expensive lamps for a niche market." Cooper's cheapest lamps sold for $200, while its crystal chandeliers cost upwards of thousands of dollars.

The reason we use the past tense to describe Cooper's strategy is that the firm as it was known changed in August 2005. At that time, Cooper left its historic Chicago manufacturing facility, as required by the terms of its sale to developers who intend to convert its historic 240,000-square foot building into residential condos. The four-story building was sold and workers were laid off because the firm had to reduce the costs it incurred to manufacture its high-quality products. Some of the dismissed workers had been with the company for over 40 years. Other changes were in play as well, as indicated by the following comments from an employee: "We've sold the name but we can't say who bought it. That was part of the deal. But we can say Frederick Cooper will not be who it was before. But we're not going out of business. The new name will be Frederick Cooper Chicago."

What caused the demise of Frederick Cooper Lamp Company? The answer is perhaps familiar: declining demand for high-quality handmade products; inefficient, high-cost manufacturing facilities; and cheap imports from other nations that offer customers a reasonable degree of quality at a substantially lower price. From a strategic perspective, the firm's demise resulted from its below-average returns, which was a direct result of its not successfully implementing its business-level strategy.

Sources: R. Berg, 2005, Frederick Cooper workers to strike, *Chicago Indymedia*, www.chicago.indymedia.org, June 9; M. Brown, 2005, We can shape 'progress,' or let it punch our lights out, *Chicago Sun-Times*, www.suntimes.com, June 1; C. W. Ingram, 2005, Frederick Cooper sells building, plans to relocate, *Home Accents Today*, www.homeaccentstoday.com, March 1; P. Sherrod, 2005, Let there be light, *Chicago Tribune*, www.chicagotribune.com, June 19; N. Steinberg, 2005, Fancy lamps, *Granta*, 89: 136–150.

Increasingly important to firm success,[1] strategy is concerned with making choices among two or more alternatives.[2] As we noted in Chapter 1, when choosing a strategy, the firm decides to pursue one course of action instead of others. The choices made are influenced by opportunities and threats in the firm's external environment (see Chapter 2) as well as the nature and quality of its internal resources, capabilities, and core competencies[3] (see Chapter 3). Historically, Frederick Cooper Lamp Company used the unique skills of its artists to take advantage of an opportunity to satisfy the demand from a small group of customers who wanted to buy high-quality, unique lamps, chandeliers, and sconces.

The fundamental objective of using any type of strategy (see Figure 1.1) is to gain strategic competitiveness and earn above-average returns.[4] Strategies are purposeful, precede the taking of actions to which they apply, and demonstrate a shared understanding of the firm's vision and mission.[5] An effectively formulated strategy marshals, integrates, and allocates the firm's resources, capabilities, and competencies so that it will be properly aligned with its external environment.[6] A properly developed strategy also rationalizes the firm's vision and mission along with the actions taken to achieve them.[7] Information about a host of variables including markets, customers, technology, worldwide finance, and the changing world economy must be collected and analyzed to properly form and use strategies. Increasingly, Internet technology affects how organizations gather and study data and information that are related to decisions about the choice and use of strategy. In the final analysis, sound strategic choices, ones that reduce uncertainty regarding outcomes,[8] are the foundation on which successful strategies are built.[9]

Business-level strategy, this chapter's focus, is an integrated and coordinated set of commitments and actions the firm uses to gain a competitive advantage by exploiting core competencies in specific product markets.[10] This means that business-level strategy indicates the choices the firm has made about how it intends to compete in individual product markets. The choices are important, as there is an established link between a firm's strategies and its long-term performance.[11] Given the complexity of successfully competing in the global economy, these choices are difficult, often even gut-wrenching.[12] For example, to increase the effectiveness of its differentiation business-level strategy (we define and discuss this strategy later in the chapter), Kimberly-Clark executives recently decided to close some manufacturing facilities and to reduce its labor force. Describing his reaction to making these decisions, the firm's CEO said: "These are tough decisions, and these are ones that we don't take lightly. But I believe they are absolutely necessary to improve our competitive position."[13] Decisions made at Frederick Cooper such as the closing of the manufacturing facility were also difficult.

Every firm must form and use a business-level strategy.[14] However, every firm may not use all the strategies—corporate-level, acquisition and restructuring, international, and cooperative—that we examine in Chapters 6 through 9. For example, think of a local dry cleaner with only one location offering a single service (the cleaning and laundering of clothes) in a single storefront. A firm competing in a single-product market area in a single geographic location does not need a corporate-level strategy to deal with product diversity or an international strategy to deal with geographic

To keep customers coming back, even the local dry cleaner must successfully implement a business-level strategy.

diversity. In contrast, a diversified firm will use one of the corporate-level strategies as well as choose a separate business-level strategy for each product market area in which the company competes (the relationship between corporate-level and business-level strategies is further examined in Chapter 6). Every firm—from the local dry cleaner to the multinational corporation—chooses at least one business-level strategy. This means that business-level strategy is the *core* strategy—the strategy that the firm forms to describe how it intends to compete in a product market.[15]

We discuss several topics to examine business-level strategies. Because customers are the foundation of successful business-level strategies and should never be taken for granted,[16] we offer information about customers that is relevant to choosing a business-level strategy. In terms of customers, when selecting a business-level strategy the firm determines (1) *who* will be served, (2) *what* needs those target customers have that it will satisfy, and (3) *how* those needs will be satisfied. Selecting customers and deciding which of their needs the firm will try to satisfy, as well as how it will do so, are challenging tasks. Global competition, which has created many attractive options for customers, is one reason for this. In the current competitive environment, effective global competitors have become adept at identifying the needs of customers in different cultures and geographic regions as well as learning how to quickly and successfully adapt the functionality of the firms' good or service to meet those needs.

Descriptions of the purpose of business-level strategies and of the five business-level strategies follow the discussion of customers. The five strategies we examine are called *generic* because they can be used in any organization competing in any industry.[17] Our analysis describes how effective use of each strategy allows the firm to favorably position itself relative to the five competitive forces in the industry (see Chapter 2). In addition, we use the value chain (see Chapter 3) to show examples of the primary and support activities that are necessary to implement certain business-level strategies. Because no strategy is risk-free,[18] we also describe the different risks the firm may encounter when using one of these strategies.

In Chapter 11, we explain the organizational structures and controls that are linked with the successful use of each business-level strategy.

Customers: Their Relationship with Business-Level Strategies

Strategic competitiveness results only when the firm is able to satisfy a group of customers by using its competitive advantages as the basis for competing in individual product markets. A key reason firms must satisfy customers with their business-level strategy is that returns earned from relationships with customers are the lifeblood of all organizations.[19] In straightforward language, "Without customers, you don't have a business."[20]

The most successful companies try to find new ways to satisfy current customers and/or to meet the needs of new customers. Dell Inc. does this with an "unrelenting sense of urgency and speed,"[21] believing that solutions to customers' needs should be provided quickly and flawlessly. Recently, to meet the needs of home and small-office users and to increase its profitability while doing so, Dell started selling the first sub-$100 laser printer.[22] Dell, similar to other organizations interested in satisfying customers' needs, manages its relationships with customers in order to understand their current and future needs.[23]

Harrah's Entertainment prides itself on offering customers the best possible service.

Effectively Managing Relationships with Customers

The firm's relationships with its customers are strengthened when it delivers superior value to them. Strong interactive relationships with customers often provide the foundation for the firm's efforts to profitably serve customers' unique needs.

Harrah's Entertainment believes that it provides superior value to customers by "being the most service-oriented, geographically diversified company in gaming."[24] Importantly, delivering superior value often results in increased customer loyalty. In turn, customer loyalty has a positive relationship with profitability. In the financial services industry, for example, estimates are that companies "can boost profits by almost 100 percent by retaining just 5 percent more customers."[25] However, more choices and easily accessible information about the functionality of firms' products are creating increasingly sophisticated and knowledgeable customers, making it difficult to earn their loyalty.[26]

A number of companies have become skilled at the art of *managing* all aspects of their relationship with their customers.[27] For example, Amazon.com is an Internet-based venture widely recognized for the quality of information it maintains about its customers, the services it renders, and its ability to anticipate customers' needs.[28] Using the information it has, Amazon tries to serve what it believes are the unique needs of each customer. Based in Mexico, Cemex SA is a "leading global producer and marketer of quality cement and ready-mix concrete."[29] Cemex uses the Internet to link its customers, cement plants, and main control room, allowing the firm to automate orders and optimize truck deliveries in highly congested Mexico City. Analysts believe that Cemex's integration of Web technology with its cost leadership strategy is helping to differentiate it from competitors.[30] Lands' End is using the Internet to manage its relationships with women. The Swim Finder online feature, for example, "lets women choose swimsuits that 'enhance or de-emphasize' certain body areas, allowing a shopper to see a version of the suit on a three-dimensional likeness of her body."[31]

As we discuss next, there are three dimensions of firms' relationships with customers. Companies such as Amazon.com, Cemex, and Lands' End understand these dimensions and manage their relationships with customers in light of them.

Reach, Richness, and Affiliation

The *reach* dimension of relationships with customers is concerned with the firm's access and connection to customers. For instance, the largest physical retailer in bookstores, Barnes & Noble, carries 200,000-plus titles in over 820 stores.[32] By contrast, Amazon.com offers more than 4.5 million titles and is located on tens of millions of computer screens with additional customer connections being established across the globe. Indeed, Amazon "has virtually unlimited online shelf space and can offer customers a vast selection of products through an efficient search and retrieval interface."[33] Even though Barnes & Noble also has an Internet presence (barnesandnoble.com), Amazon.com's reach is significantly greater. In general, firms seek to extend their reach, adding customers in the process of doing so.

Richness, the second dimension, is concerned with the depth and detail of the two-way flow of information between the firm and the customer. The potential of the richness dimension to help the firm establish a competitive advantage in its relationship with customers led traditional financial services brokers, such as Merrill Lynch and Lehman Brothers, to offer online services in order to better manage information exchanges with their customers. Broader and deeper information-based exchanges allow firms to better understand their customers and their needs. Such exchanges also enable customers to become more knowledgeable about how the firm can satisfy them. Internet technology and e-commerce transactions have substantially reduced the costs of meaningful information exchanges with current and possible future customers.

Affiliation, the third dimension, is concerned with facilitating useful interactions with customers. Internet navigators such as Microsoft CarPoint help online clients find and sort information. CarPoint provides data and software to prospective car buyers that enable them to compare car models along multiple objective specifications. The program can supply this information at no charge to the consumer because Internet technology allows a great deal of information to be collected from a variety of sources at a low cost. A prospective buyer who has selected a specific car based on comparisons of different models can then be linked to dealers that meet the customer's needs and purchasing requirements. Because its revenues come not from the final customer or end user but from other sources (such as advertisements on its Web site, hyperlinks, and associated products and services), CarPoint represents the customer's interests, a service that fosters affiliation.[34] In contrast, an auto manufacturing company represents its own products, creating a situation in which its financial interests differ from those of consumers. Viewing the world through the customer's eyes and constantly seeking ways to create more value for the customer have positive effects in terms of affiliation.

As we discuss next, effective management of customer relationships (along the dimensions of reach, richness, and affiliation) helps the firm answer questions related to the issues of *who, what,* and *how.*

Who: Determining the Customers to Serve

Deciding *who* the target customer is that the firm intends to serve with its business-level strategy is an important decision.[35] Companies divide customers into groups based on differences in the customers' needs (needs are discussed further in the next section) to make this decision. Dividing customers into groups based on their needs is called **market segmentation,** which is a process that clusters people with similar needs into individual and identifiable groups.[36] In the animal health business, for example, the needs for food products of owners of companion pets (e.g., dogs and cats) differ from the needs for food products of those owning production animals (e.g., livestock).[37] As part of its business-level strategy, the firm develops a marketing program to effectively sell products to its particular target customer group.[38]

Almost any identifiable human or organizational characteristic can be used to subdivide a market into segments that differ from one another on a given characteristic. Common characteristics on which customers' needs vary are illustrated in Table 4.1. Based on their internal core competencies and opportunities in the external environment, companies choose a business-level strategy to deliver value to target customers and satisfy their specific needs.

Customer characteristics are often combined to segment markets into specific groups that have unique needs. In the consumer clothing market, for example, Gap learned that their female and male customers want different shopping experiences. In a company official's words, "Research showed that men want to come and go easily, while women want an exploration."[39] In light of these research results, newly developed

Consumer Markets

1. Demographic factors (age, income, sex, etc.)
2. Socioeconomic factors (social class, stage in the family life cycle)
3. Geographic factors (cultural, regional, and national differences)
4. Psychological factors (lifestyle, personality traits)
5. Consumption patterns (heavy, moderate, and light users)
6. Perceptual factors (benefit segmentation, perceptual mapping)

Industrial Markets

1. End-use segments (identified by SIC code)
2. Product segments (based on technological differences or production economics)
3. Geographic segments (defined by boundaries between countries or by regional differences within them)
4. Common buying factor segments (cut across product market and geographic segments)
5. Customer size segments

Source: Adapted from S. C. Jain, 2000, *Marketing Planning and Strategy,* Cincinnati: South-Western College Publishing, 120.

women's sections in Gap stores are organized by occasion (e.g., work, going out) with accessories for those occasions scattered throughout the section to facilitate browsing. The men's side of Gap stores is more straightforward, with signs used to direct male customers to clothing items that are commonly stacked by size. Thus, Gap is using its understanding of some of the psychological factors (see Table 4.1) influencing its customers' purchasing intentions to better serve unique groups' needs.

Demographic factors (see Table 4.1 and the discussion in Chapter 2) can also be used to segment markets into generations with unique interests and needs. Evidence suggests, for example, that direct mail is an effective communication medium for the World War II generation (those born before 1932). The Swing generation (those born between 1933 and 1945) values taking cruises and purchasing second homes. Once financially conservative but now willing to spend money, members of this generation seek product information from knowledgeable sources. The Baby Boom generation (born between 1946 and 1964) desires products that reduce the stress generated by juggling career demands and the needs of older parents with those of their own children. Ellen Tracy clothes, known for their consistency of fit and color, are targeted to Baby Boomer women. More conscious of hype, the 60-million-plus people

Gap caters to male and female customers by arranging the women's section of the store differently from the men's.

in Generation X (born between 1965 and 1976) want products that deliver as promised. The Xers use the Internet as a primary shopping tool and expect visually compelling marketing. Members of this group are the fastest-growing segment of mutual-fund shareholders, with their holdings overwhelmingly invested in stock funds. As employees, the top priorities of Xers are to work in a creative learning environment, to receive constant feedback from managers, and to be rewarded for using their technical skills.[40] Different marketing campaigns and distribution channels (e.g., the Internet for Generation X customers, direct mail for the World War II generation) affect the implementation of strategies for those companies interested in serving the needs of different generations.

What: Determining Which Customer Needs to Satisfy

After the firm decides *who* it will serve, it must identify the targeted customer group's needs that its goods or services can satisfy. This is important in that successful firms learn how to deliver to customers want they want and when they want it.[41]

In a general sense, *needs (what)* are related to a product's benefits and features.[42] Having close and frequent interactions with both current and potential customers helps the firm identify those individuals' and groups' current and future needs.[43] From a strategic perspective, a basic need of all customers is to buy products that create value for them. The generalized forms of value that goods or services provide are either low cost with acceptable features or highly differentiated features with acceptable cost. The most effective firms continuously strive to anticipate changes in customers' needs. Failure to do this results in the loss of customers to competitors who are offering greater value in terms of product features and functionalities. For example, some analysts believe that discounters, department stores, and other home furnishing chains are taking customers away from Pier 1 Imports Inc. Recent decisions to launch its first-ever catalog, to upgrade its Web site, and to improve its marketing programs are possible indicators that Pier 1 has not anticipated changes in its customers' needs in as timely a manner as should be the case.

In any given industry, there is great variety among consumers in terms of their needs.[44] The need some consumers have for high-quality, fresh sandwiches is what Pret A Manger seeks to satisfy with its menu items. In contrast, many large fast-food companies satisfy customer needs for lower-cost food items with acceptable quality that are delivered quickly.[45] Diversified food and soft-drink producer PepsiCo believes that "any one consumer has different needs at different times of the day." Through its soft drinks (Pepsi products), snacks (Frito-Lay), juices (Tropicana), and cereals (Quaker), PepsiCo is working on developing new products from breakfast bars to healthier potato chips "to make certain that it covers all those needs."[46] In general, and across multiple product groups (e.g., automobiles, clothing, food), evidence suggests that middle-market consumers in the United States want to trade up to higher levels of quality and taste. These customers "are willing to pay premiums of 20% to 200% for the kinds of well-designed, well-engineered, and well-crafted goods—often possessing the artisanal touches of traditional luxury goods—not before found in the mass middle market."[47] These needs represent opportunities for some firms to pursue through their business-level strategies.

To ensure success, a firm must be able to fully understand the needs of the customers in the target group it has selected to serve. In this sense, customer needs are neither right nor wrong, good nor bad. They are simply the desires, in terms of features and performance capabilities, of those customers the firm has targeted to serve. The most effective firms are filled with people committed to understanding the customers' current as well as future needs.

As explained in Chapters 1 and 3, *core competencies* are resources and capabilities that serve as a source of competitive advantage for the firm over its rivals. Firms use core competencies (*how*) to implement value-creating strategies and thereby satisfy customers' needs. Only those firms with the capacity to continuously improve, innovate, and upgrade their competencies can expect to meet and hopefully exceed customers' expectations across time.[48]

Companies draw from a wide range of core competencies to produce goods or services that can satisfy customers' needs. IBM, for example, emphasizes its core competence in technology to rapidly develop new service-related products. Beginning in 1993, then newly appointed CEO Lou Gerstner changed IBM by leveraging its "strength in network integration and consulting to transform [the firm] from a moribund maker of mainframe computers to a sexy services company that can basically design, build, and manage a corporation's entire data system."[49] SAS Institute is the world's largest privately owned software company and is the leader in business intelligence and analytics. Customers use SAS's programs for data warehousing, data mining, and decision support purposes. Allocating over 30 percent of revenues to research and development (R&D), SAS relies on its core competence in R&D to satisfy the data-related needs of such customers as the U.S. Census Bureau and a host of consumer goods firms (e.g., hotels, banks, and catalog companies).[50] Vans Inc. relies on its core competencies in innovation and marketing to design and sell skateboards and other products. The firm also pioneered thick-soled, slip-on sneakers that can absorb the shock of five-foot leaps on wheels. Vans uses what is recognized as an offbeat marketing mix to capitalize on its pioneering products. In lieu of mass media ads, the firm sponsors skateboarding events, supported the making of a documentary film that celebrates the "outlaw nature" of the skateboarding culture, and is building skateboard parks at malls around the country.[51]

All organizations, including IBM, SAS, and Vans Inc., must be able to use their core competencies (the *how*) to satisfy the needs (the *what*) of the target group of customers (the *who*) the firm has chosen to serve by using its business-level strategy.

Next, we describe the formal purpose of a business-level strategy and then the five business-level strategies available to all firms.

The Purpose of a Business-Level Strategy

The purpose of a business-level strategy is to create differences between the firm's position and those of its competitors.[52] To position itself differently from competitors, a firm must decide whether it intends to *perform activities differently* or to *perform different activities*.[53] In fact, "choosing to perform activities differently or to perform different activities than rivals" is the essence of business-level strategy.[54] Thus, the firm's business-level strategy is a deliberate choice about how it will perform the value chain's primary and support activities in ways that create unique value. Indeed, in the complex 21st-century competitive landscape, successful use of a business-level strategy results only when the firm learns how to integrate the activities it performs in ways that create competitive advantages that can be used to create value for customers.

Firms develop an activity map to show how they integrate the activities they perform. We show Southwest Airlines' activity map in Figure 4.1. The manner in which

FIGURE **4.1** | Southwest Airlines' Activity System

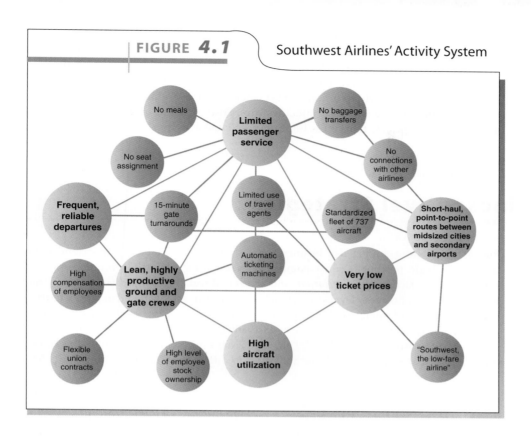

Southwest has integrated its activities is the foundation for the successful use of its integrated cost leadership/differentiation strategy (we discuss this strategy later in the chapter).[55] In Chapter 5's Opening Case, we describe how Southwest Airlines is *killing* (with killing defined as significantly outperforming) its competitors. The tight integration among Southwest's activities is a key source of the firm's ability to operate more profitably than its competitors.

As shown in Figure 4.1, Southwest Airlines has configured the activities it performs such that there are six strategic themes—limited passenger service; frequent, reliable departures; lean, highly productive ground and gate crews; high aircraft utilization; very low ticket prices; and short-haul, point-to-point routes between midsized cities and secondary airports. Individual clusters of tightly linked activities make it possible for the outcome of a strategic theme to be achieved. For example, no meals, no seat assignments, and no baggage transfers form a cluster of individual activities that support the strategic theme of limited passenger service (see Figure 4.1).

Southwest's tightly integrated activities make it difficult for competitors to imitate the firm's integrated cost leadership/differentiation strategy.[56] The firm's culture influences these activities and their integration and contributes to the firm's ability to continuously identify additional ways to differentiate Southwest's service from its competitors' as well as to lower its costs. In fact, the firm's unique culture and customer service, both of which are sources of differentiated customer features, are competitive advantages rivals have not been able to imitate, although some have tried. US Airways' Metro-Jet subsidiary, United Airlines' United Shuttle, and Continental Airlines' Continental Lite all failed in attempts to imitate Southwest's strategy. Hindsight shows that these competitors offered low prices to customers, but weren't able to operate at costs close to those of Southwest or to provide customers with any notable sources of differentiation, such as a unique experience while in the air.

Fit among activities is a key to the sustainability of competitive advantage for all firms, including Southwest Airlines. As Michael Porter comments, "Strategic fit among many activities is fundamental not only to competitive advantage but also to the sustainability of that advantage. It is harder for a rival to match an array of interlocked activities than it is merely to imitate a particular sales-force approach, match a process technology, or replicate a set of product features. Positions built on systems of activities are far more sustainable than those built on individual activities."[57]

Types of Business-Level Strategies

Firms choose from among five business-level strategies to establish and defend their desired strategic position against competitors: *cost leadership, differentiation, focused cost leadership, focused differentiation,* and *integrated cost leadership/differentiation* (see Figure 4.2). Each business-level strategy helps the firm to establish and exploit a particular *competitive advantage* within a particular *competitive scope*. How firms integrate the activities they perform within each different business-level strategy demonstrates how they differ from one another.[58] Thus, firms have different activity maps, meaning, for example, that Southwest Airlines' activity map differs from those of competitors Jet-

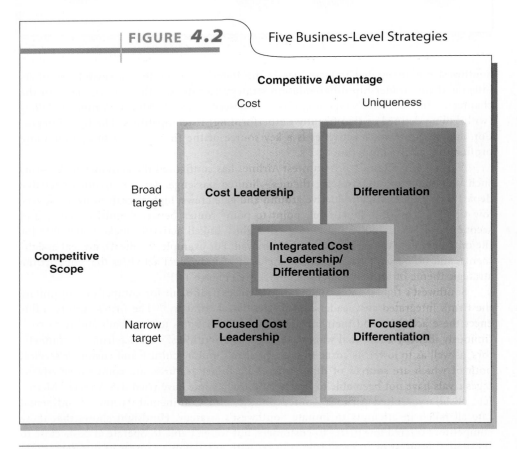

FIGURE 4.2 Five Business-Level Strategies

Competitive Advantage

Cost | Uniqueness

Competitive Scope

Broad target — Cost Leadership | Differentiation

Integrated Cost Leadership/ Differentiation

Narrow target — Focused Cost Leadership | Focused Differentiation

Source: Adapted with the permission of The Free Press, an imprint of Simon & Schuster Adult Publishing Group, from *Competitive Advantage: Creating and Sustaining Superior Performance,* by Michael E. Porter, 12. Copyright © 1985, 1998 by Michael E. Porter.

Blue, Continental, American Airlines, and so forth. Superior integration of activities increases the likelihood of being able to outperform competitors and to earn above-average returns as a result of doing so.

When selecting a business-level strategy, firms evaluate two types of potential competitive advantage: "lower cost than rivals, or the ability to differentiate and command a premium price that exceeds the extra cost of doing so."[59] Having lower cost derives from the firm's ability to perform activities differently than rivals; being able to differentiate indicates the firm's capacity to perform different (and valuable) activities.[60] Thus, based on the nature and quality of its internal resources, capabilities, and core competencies, a firm seeks to form either a cost competitive advantage or a uniqueness competitive advantage as the basis for implementing a particular business-level strategy.

There are two types of competitive scope—broad target and narrow target (see Figure 4.2). Firms serving a broad target market seek to use their competitive advantage on an industry-wide basis. A narrow competitive scope means that the firm intends to serve the needs of a narrow target customer group. With focus strategies, the firm "selects a segment or group of segments in the industry and tailors its strategy to serving them to the exclusion of others."[61] Buyers with particular needs and buyers located in specific geographic regions are examples of narrow target customer groups. As shown in Figure 4.2, a firm could also strive to develop a combined cost/uniqueness competitive advantage as the foundation for serving a target customer group that is larger than a narrow segment but not as comprehensive as a broad (or industry-wide) customer group. In this instance, the firm uses the integrated cost leadership/differentiation strategy.

None of the five business-level strategies shown in Figure 4.2 is inherently or universally superior to the others.[62] The effectiveness of each strategy is contingent both on the opportunities and threats in a firm's external environment and on the possibilities provided by the firm's unique resources, capabilities, and core competencies. It is critical, therefore, for the firm to select a business-level strategy that is based on a match between the opportunities and threats in its external environment and the strengths of its internal environment as shown by its core competencies.

Cost Leadership Strategy

The **cost leadership strategy** is an integrated set of actions taken to produce goods or services with features that are acceptable to customers at the lowest cost, relative to that of competitors.[63] Firms using the cost leadership strategy sell no-frills, standardized goods or services (but with competitive levels of differentiation) to the industry's most typical customers. Cost leaders' goods and services must have competitive levels of differentiation in terms of features that create value for customers. Indeed, emphasizing cost reductions while ignoring competitive levels of differentiation is ineffective. At the extreme, concentrating only on reducing costs could find the firm very efficiently producing products that no customer wants to purchase.

As shown in Figure 4.2, the firm using the cost leadership strategy targets a broad customer segment or group. Cost leaders concentrate on finding ways to lower their costs relative to those of their competitors by constantly rethinking how to complete their primary and support activities to reduce costs still further while maintaining competitive levels of differentiation.[64] Cost leader Greyhound Lines Inc., for example, continuously seeks ways to reduce the costs it incurs to provide bus service while offering customers an acceptable experience. Recently Greyhound sought to improve the quality of the experience customers have when paying the firm's low prices for its services by "refurbishing buses, updating terminals, adding greeters and improving customer service training."[65]

As primary activities, inbound logistics (e.g., materials handling, warehousing, and inventory control) and outbound logistics (e.g., collecting, storing, and distributing products to customers) often account for significant portions of the total cost to pro-

Greyhound's newly refurbished buses are part of its plan to improve its customers' experience.

duce some goods and services. Research suggests that having a competitive advantage in terms of logistics creates more value when using the cost leadership strategy than when using the differentiation strategy.[66] Thus, cost leaders seeking competitively valuable ways to reduce costs may want to concentrate on the primary activities of inbound logistics and outbound logistics.

Cost leaders also carefully examine all support activities to find additional sources of potential cost reductions. Developing new systems for finding the optimal combination of low cost and acceptable quality in the raw materials required to produce the firm's goods or services is an example of how the procurement support activity can facilitate successful use of the cost leadership strategy.

Big Lots Inc. uses the cost leadership strategy. With its vision of being "The World's Best Bargain Place," Big Lots is the largest broadline closeout discount chain in the United States. Operating under the format names of Big Lots, Big Lots Furniture, Wisconsin Toy, Consolidated International, Big Lots Capital, and Big Lots Wholesale, the firm strives constantly to drive its costs lower by relying on what some analysts see as a highly disciplined merchandise cost and inventory management system.[67] The firm's stores sell name-brand products at prices that are 15 to 35 percent below those of discount retailers and roughly 70 percent below those of traditional retailers.[68] Big Lots' buyers travel the country looking through manufacturer overruns and discontinued styles, finding goods priced well below wholesale prices. In addition, the firm buys from overseas suppliers. Big Lots thinks of itself as the undertaker of the retailing business, purchasing merchandise that others can't sell or don't want. The target customer is one seeking what Big Lots calls the "closeout moment," which is the feeling customers have after they recognize their significant savings from buying a brand name item at a steeply discounted price.[69] The customer need that Big Lots satisfies is to access the differentiated features and capabilities of brand-name products, but at a fraction of their initial cost. The tight integration of purchasing and inventory management activities across its full set of stores is the main core competence Big Lots uses to satisfy its customers' needs.

As described in Chapter 3, firms use value-chain analysis to determine the parts of the company's operations that create value and those that do not. Figure 4.3 demonstrates the primary and support activities that allow a firm to create value through the cost leadership strategy. Companies unable to link the activities shown in this figure through the activity map they form typically lack the core competencies needed to successfully use the cost leadership strategy.

Effective use of the cost leadership strategy allows a firm to earn above-average returns in spite of the presence of strong competitive forces (see Chapter 2). The next sections (one for each of the five forces) explain how firms are able to do this.

Rivalry with Existing Competitors

Having the low-cost position is a valuable defense against rivals. Because of the cost leader's advantageous position, rivals hesitate to compete on the basis of price, especially before evaluating the potential outcomes of such competition.[70] Wal-Mart is known for its ability to both control and reduce costs, making it difficult for firms to compete against it on the basis of costs. The discount retailer achieves strict cost control in several ways: "Wal-Mart's 660,000-square-foot main headquarters, with its drab gray interiors and frayed carpets, looks more like a government building than the home of one of the world's largest corporations. Business often is done in the no-frills cafeteria,

FIGURE 4.3 Examples of Value-Creating Activities Associated with the Cost Leadership Strategy

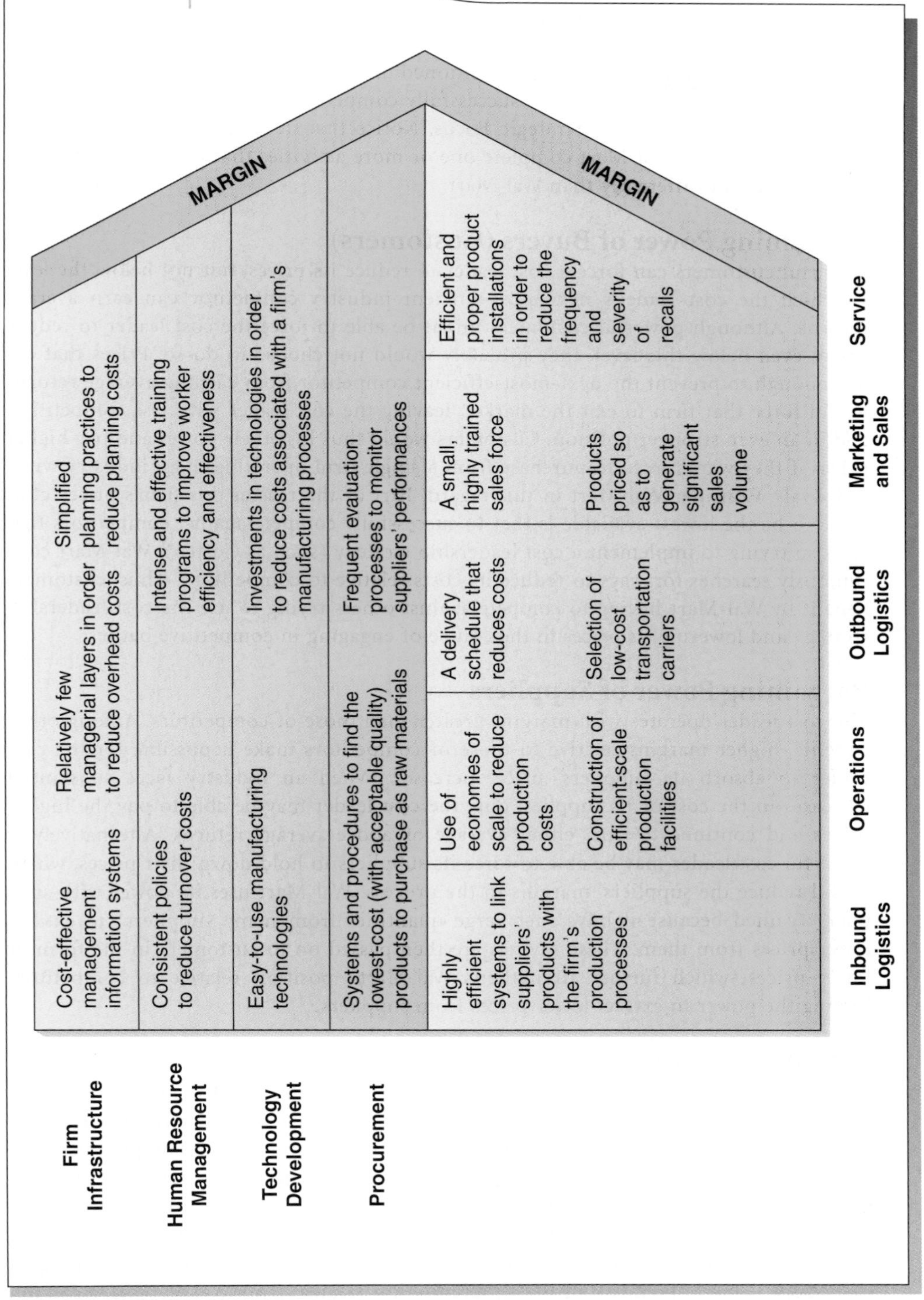

MARGIN
MARGIN
Firm Infrastructure
Cost-effective management information systems
Relatively few managerial layers in order to reduce overhead costs
Simplified planning practices to reduce planning costs
Human Resource Management
Consistent policies to reduce turnover costs
Intense and effective training programs to improve worker efficiency and effectiveness
Technology Development
Easy-to-use manufacturing technologies
Investments in technologies in order to reduce costs associated with a firm's manufacturing processes
Procurement
Systems and procedures to find the lowest-cost (with acceptable quality) products to purchase as raw materials
Frequent evaluation processes to monitor suppliers' performances
Highly efficient systems to link suppliers' products with the firm's production processes
Use of economies of scale to reduce production costs
Construction of efficient-scale production facilities
A delivery schedule that reduces costs
Selection of low-cost transportation carriers
A small, highly trained sales force
Products priced so as to generate significant sales volume
Efficient and proper product installations in order to reduce the frequency and severity of recalls
Inbound Logistics
Operations
Outbound Logistics
Marketing and Sales
Service

Source: Adapted with the permission of The Free Press, an imprint of Simon & Schuster Adult Publishing Group, from *Competitive Advantage: Creating and Sustaining Superior Performance,* by Michael E. Porter, 47. Copyright © 1985, 1998 by Michael E. Porter.

and suppliers meet with managers in stark, cramped rooms. Employees have to throw out their own garbage at the end of the day and double up in hotel rooms on business trips."[71] The former Kmart's decision to compete against Wal-Mart on the basis of cost contributed to the firm's failure and subsequent bankruptcy filing. Its competitively inferior distribution system—an inefficient and high-cost system compared with Wal-Mart's—is one of the factors that prevented Kmart from having a competitive cost structure.

Although Wal-Mart is favorably positioned in terms of rivalry with its competitors, there are actions firms can take to successfully compete against this retailing giant. We discuss these actions in the Strategic Focus. Notice that in each instance, competitors able to outperform Wal-Mart complete one or more activities that create value for customers better or differently than Wal-Mart.

Bargaining Power of Buyers (Customers)

Powerful customers can force a cost leader to reduce its prices, but not below the level at which the cost leader's next-most-efficient industry competitor can earn average returns. Although powerful customers might be able to force the cost leader to reduce prices even below this level, they probably would not choose to do so. Prices that are low enough to prevent the next-most-efficient competitor from earning average returns would force that firm to exit the market, leaving the cost leader with less competition and in an even stronger position. Customers would thus lose their power and pay higher prices if they were forced to purchase from a single firm operating in an industry without rivals. Consider Wal-Mart in this regard. Part of the reason this firm's prices continue to be the lowest available is that to successfully compete against competitors that are also trying to implement a cost leadership strategy (such as Costco), Wal-Mart continuously searches for ways to reduce its costs relative to competitors'. Thus, customers benefit by Wal-Mart having to compete against others trying to use the cost leadership strategy and lowering its prices in the course of engaging in competitive battles.

Bargaining Power of Suppliers

The cost leader operates with margins greater than those of competitors. Among other benefits, higher margins relative to those of competitors make it possible for the cost leader to absorb its suppliers' price increases. When an industry faces substantial increases in the cost of its supplies, only the cost leader may be able to pay the higher prices and continue to earn either average or above-average returns. Alternatively, a powerful cost leader may be able to force its suppliers to hold down their prices, which would reduce the suppliers' margins in the process. Wal-Mart uses its power with suppliers (gained because it buys such large quantities from many suppliers) to extract lower prices from them. These savings are then passed on to customers in the form of lower prices, which further strengthens Wal-Mart's position relative to competitors lacking the power to extract lower prices from suppliers.[72]

Potential Entrants

Through continuous efforts to reduce costs to levels that are lower than competitors', a cost leader becomes highly efficient. Because ever-improving levels of efficiency enhance profit margins, they serve as a significant entry barrier to potential competitors. New entrants must be willing and able to accept no-better-than-average returns until they gain the experience required to approach the cost leader's efficiency. To earn even average returns, new entrants must have the competencies required to match the cost levels of competitors other than the cost leader. The low profit margins (relative to margins earned by firms implementing the differentiation strategy) make it necessary for the cost leader to sell large volumes of its product to earn above-average returns. However, firms striving to be the cost leader must avoid pricing their products so low that their ability to operate profitably is reduced, even though volume increases.

Beating Wal-Mart: It's Tough, But It Can Be Done

Wal-Mart's size and success are almost staggering. Its 2004 annual revenue of over $285 billion exceeds the combined revenue totals of its five largest rivals. Analysts predict that within a decade Wal-Mart's annual revenues will be over half a trillion dollars. If it were a country today, Wal-Mart's revenue would be the third largest economy in the world.

A global powerhouse with locations in multiple countries, Wal-Mart was operating more than 663 million square feet of floor space at the close of its fiscal year 2005. However, some believe that Wal-Mart can be "had." The reason for this view is that, as discussed in Chapter 1, no competitive advantage is sustainable forever. In addition, all firms— including Wal-Mart—face savvy competitors who constantly strive to find ways to use their unique capabilities and core competencies to attack even a tough competitor's weaknesses. In one analyst's words: "As with all great powers, Wal-Mart has its imperfections, frailties that wily competitors have learned to exploit." Here are ways some firms have found to outperform Wal-Mart.

1. ***Target particular customers and fully understand their needs.*** The fifth largest retailer in the United States, Costco Warehouses "has vexed Wal-Mart for years." Costco continues to outperform Sam's Clubs, Wal-Mart's version of a warehouse store, both on sales per square foot and in profitability. Focusing on small business owners (who seem to "enjoy quality items on the cheap"), Costco sprinkles its regular lineup with brand-name goods (e.g., Godiva chocolates, Waterford crystal, and Cartier watches) at bargain-bin prices. Costco spends a great deal of time analyzing its customers to make certain the firm continues to provide them with unique products at very low prices.

2. ***Offer prices lower than Wal-Mart's.*** Dollar Tree is the largest single-price vendor operating in the United States. The firm does not sell any product for more than $1. "From picture frames and pet supplies to frozen food and fine china, Dollar Tree has sold every item on its shelves for a buck for the past 19 years." Wal-Mart sells many of the items carried in Dollar Tree stores, but often at higher prices. Relationships with buyers who scour the country for remainders, discards, and odd-lot, leftover merchandise are the key to the firm's success. Dollar Tree is always pleased to take excess inventory off a manufacturer's or retailer's shelves when it can do so at bargain-basement costs.

3. ***Re-create customer experiences.*** Save-A-Lot believes that there is a group of customers who values the role of a traditional, neighborhood grocer in a local community. To serve the needs of these people and to keep them from shopping at Wal-Mart, Save-A-Lot keeps its stores small (20–25 employees) and offers a limited selection of goods (1,250 items per location compared with upwards of 40,000 items at a Wal-Mart supercenter). Generating 75 percent of its sales from its own private-label brands, using its highly efficient distribution system, and concentrating on neighborhood customers with annual incomes of $35,000 or less, Save-A-Lot is able to sell its products for as much as 15 percent below Wal-Mart's prices.

Costco's success is due in part to its effort to provide its customers with the products they want.

4. ***Provide superior service.*** Wal-Mart's cost leadership strategy finds it offering "every day low prices" without much service. Firms able to fully understand their customers and "coddle" them with a highly trained sales force can do well competing against Wal-Mart. This is the case for Dick's Sporting Goods, where each store's sales force is given training so it can provide detailed information to customers about products and how they can satisfy a customer's needs. For example, the firm pays the costs for employees selling exercise equipment to become certified as personal fitness trainers. Dick's employs over 200 PGA pros in the in-store golf shops.

Sources: 2005, Outsmarting the B2B goliaths, *Re/Think Marketing,* www.rethinkmarketing.com, July 31; S. Hannaford, 2005, Both sides now, *Harvard Business Review,* 83(3): 17; M. Maier, 2005, How to beat Wal-Mart, *Business 2.0,* May, 108–114; J. Ewing, A. Zammert, W. Zellner, R. Tiplady, E. Groves, & M. Eidam, 2004, The next Wal-Mart? Like the U.S.-based giant, Germany's Aldi boasts awesome margins and huge clout, *Business Week,* April 26, 60–68; D. K. Rigby & D. Haas, 2004, Outsmarting Wal-Mart, *Harvard Business Review,* 82(12): 22; K. Naughton, 2003, Out of the box thinking, *Newsweek,* May 12, 40–44.

Product Substitutes

Compared with its industry rivals, the cost leader also holds an attractive position in terms of product substitutes. A product substitute becomes an issue for the cost leader when its features and characteristics, in terms of cost and differentiated features, are potentially attractive to the firm's customers. When faced with possible substitutes, the cost leader has more flexibility than its competitors. To retain customers, it can reduce the price of its good or service. With still lower prices and competitive levels of differentiation, the cost leader increases the probability that customers will prefer its product rather than a substitute.

Competitive Risks of the Cost Leadership Strategy

The cost leadership strategy is not risk free. One risk is that the processes used by the cost leader to produce and distribute its good or service could become obsolete because of competitors' innovations. These innovations may allow rivals to produce at costs lower than those of the original cost leader, or to provide additional differentiated features without increasing the product's price to customers.

A second risk is that too much focus by the cost leader on cost reductions may occur at the expense of trying to understand customers' perceptions of "competitive levels of differentiation." As noted earlier, Wal-Mart is well known for constantly and aggressively reducing its costs. At the same time, however, the firm must understand when a cost-reducing decision to eliminate differentiated features (e.g., extended shopping hours, a large number of checkout counters to reduce waits) would create a loss of value for customers.

A final risk of the cost leadership strategy concerns imitation. Using their own core competencies, competitors sometimes learn how to successfully imitate the cost leader's strategy. When this occurs, the cost leader must increase the value that its good or service provides to customers. Commonly, value is increased by selling the current product at an even lower price or by adding differentiated features that customers value while maintaining price.

Differentiation Strategy

The **differentiation strategy** is an integrated set of actions taken to produce goods or services (at an acceptable cost) that customers perceive as being different in ways that are important to them.[73] While cost leaders serve an industry's typical customer, differentiators target customers who perceive that value is created for them by the manner in which the firm's products differ from those produced and marketed by competitors.

Firms must be able to produce differentiated products at competitive costs to reduce upward pressure on the price customers pay for them. When a product's differentiated features are produced with noncompetitive costs, the price for the product can exceed what the firm's target customers are willing to pay. When the firm has a thorough understanding of what its target customers value, the relative importance they attach to the satisfaction of different needs, and for what they are willing to pay a premium, the differentiation strategy can be successfully used.[74]

Through the differentiation strategy, the firm produces nonstandardized products for customers who value differentiated features more than they value low cost. For example, superior product reliability and durability and high-performance sound systems are among the differentiated features of Toyota Motor Corporation's Lexus products. The Lexus promotional statement—"We pursue perfection, so you can pursue living"—suggests a strong commitment to overall product quality as a source of differentiation. However, Lexus offers its vehicles to customers at a competitive purchase price. As with Lexus products, a good's or service's unique attributes, rather than its purchase price, provide the value for which customers are willing to pay. Although it is currently experiencing difficulties, including ongoing investigations of the firm's finances, specialty retailer Krispy Kreme uses a differentiation strategy to produce premium-quality doughnuts.[75] A unique recipe to produce its products and The Doughnut Theatre (where customers watch doughnuts being made in the store and wait for the "Hot Now" sign to illuminate) are sources of differentiation for Krispy Kreme.

Continuous success with the differentiation strategy results when the firm consistently upgrades differentiated features that customers value, without significant cost increases. Because a differentiated product satisfies customers' unique needs, firms following the differentiation strategy are able to charge premium prices. For customers to be willing to pay a premium price, however, a "firm must truly be unique at something or be perceived as unique."[76] The ability to sell a good or service at a price that substantially exceeds the cost of creating its differentiated features allows the firm to outperform rivals and earn above-average returns. For example, shirt and neckwear manufacturer Robert Talbott follows stringent standards of craftsmanship and pays meticulous attention to every detail of production. The firm imports exclusive fabrics from the world's finest mills to make men's dress shirts and neckwear. Single-needle tailoring is used, and precise collar cuts are made to produce shirts. According to the company, customers purchasing one of its products can be assured that they are being provided with the finest fabrics available.[77] Thus, Robert Talbott's success rests on the firm's ability to produce and sell its differentiated products at a price significantly higher than the costs of imported fabrics and its unique manufacturing processes.

Rather than costs, a firm using the differentiation strategy always concentrates on investing in and developing features that differentiate a good or service in ways that customers value. Robert Talbott, for example, uses the finest silks from Europe and Asia to produce its "Best of Class" collection of ties. Overall, a firm using the differentiation strategy seeks to be different from its competitors on as many dimensions as possible. The less similarity between a firm's goods or services and those of competitors, the more buffered it is from rivals' actions. Commonly recognized differentiated goods include Toyota's Lexus, Ralph Lauren's wide array of product lines, and Caterpillar's heavy-duty earth-moving equipment. Thought by some to be the world's most expensive and prestigious consulting firm, McKinsey & Co. is a well-known example of a firm that offers differentiated services.

A good or service can be differentiated in many ways. Unusual features, responsive customer service, rapid product innovations and technological leadership, perceived prestige and status, different tastes, and engineering design and performance are examples of approaches to differentiation. There may be a limited number of ways to reduce costs (as demanded by successful use of the cost leadership strategy). In contrast, virtually anything a firm can do to create real or perceived value is a basis for differentiation.

Consider product design as a case in point. Because it can create a positive experience for customers,[78] design is becoming an increasingly important source of differentiation and hopefully for firms emphasizing it, of competitive advantage.[79] Product design is being counted on at General Motors (GM), for example, to help the firm deal with the types of performance problems we described in the Opening Case in Chapter 1 and in a Strategic Focus in Chapter 2. Indeed, product design may be a competitive dimension that will help GM get out of the 1970s mind-set in which the firm appears to remain grounded (GM's apparent mind-set is discussed in a Strategic Focus in Chapter 5). Some analysts believe that newly formed, interactive collaborations between GM designers and engineers are contributing to the development of car designs that are more stylish and visually appealing.[80] Firms using a differentiation strategy should remember that the work being completed in terms of all competitive dimensions (including design) should be oriented to satisfying customers' needs.[81]

A firm's value chain can be analyzed to determine whether the firm is able to link the activities required to create value by using the differentiation strategy. Examples of primary and support activities that are commonly used to differentiate a good or service are shown in Figure 4.4. Companies without the skills needed to link these activities cannot expect to successfully use the differentiation strategy. Next, we explain how firms using the differentiation strategy can successfully position themselves in terms of the five forces of competition (see Chapter 2) to earn above-average returns.

Rivalry with Existing Competitors

Customers tend to be loyal purchasers of products that are differentiated in ways that are meaningful to them. As their loyalty to a brand increases, customers' sensitivity to price increases is reduced. The relationship between brand loyalty and price sensitivity insulates a firm from competitive rivalry. Thus, Robert Talbott's "Best of Class" neckwear line is insulated from competition, even on the basis of price, as long as the company continues to satisfy the differentiated needs of its customer group. Likewise, Bose is insulated from intense rivalry as long as customers continue to perceive that its stereo equipment offers superior sound quality at a competitive purchase price.

Bargaining Power of Buyers (Customers)

The uniqueness of differentiated goods or services reduces customers' sensitivity to price increases. Customers are willing to accept a price increase when a product still satisfies their perceived unique needs better than a competitor's offering can. Thus, the golfer whose needs are uniquely satisfied by Callaway golf clubs will likely continue buying those products even if their cost increases. Similarly, the customer who has been highly satisfied with a 10-year-old Louis Vuitton wallet will probably replace that wallet with another one made by the same company even though the purchase price is higher than the original one. Purchasers of brand-name food items (e.g., Heinz ketchup and Kleenex tissues) will accept price increases in those products as long as they continue to perceive that the product satisfies their unique needs at an acceptable cost. Loyal customers of Abercrombie & Fitch Co.'s "preppy but edgy casual clothing at high prices" continue to buy the products even as they become more expensive.[82] In all of these instances, the customers are relatively insensitive to price increases because they do not think that an acceptable product alternative exists.

Bargaining Power of Suppliers

Because the firm using the differentiation strategy charges a premium price for its products, suppliers must provide high-quality components, driving up the firm's costs. However, the high margins the firm earns in these cases partially insulate it from the influence of suppliers in that higher supplier costs can be paid through these margins. Alternatively, because of buyers' relative insensitivity to price increases, the differentiated

FIGURE **4.4**

Examples of Value-Creating Activities Associated with the Differentiation Strategy

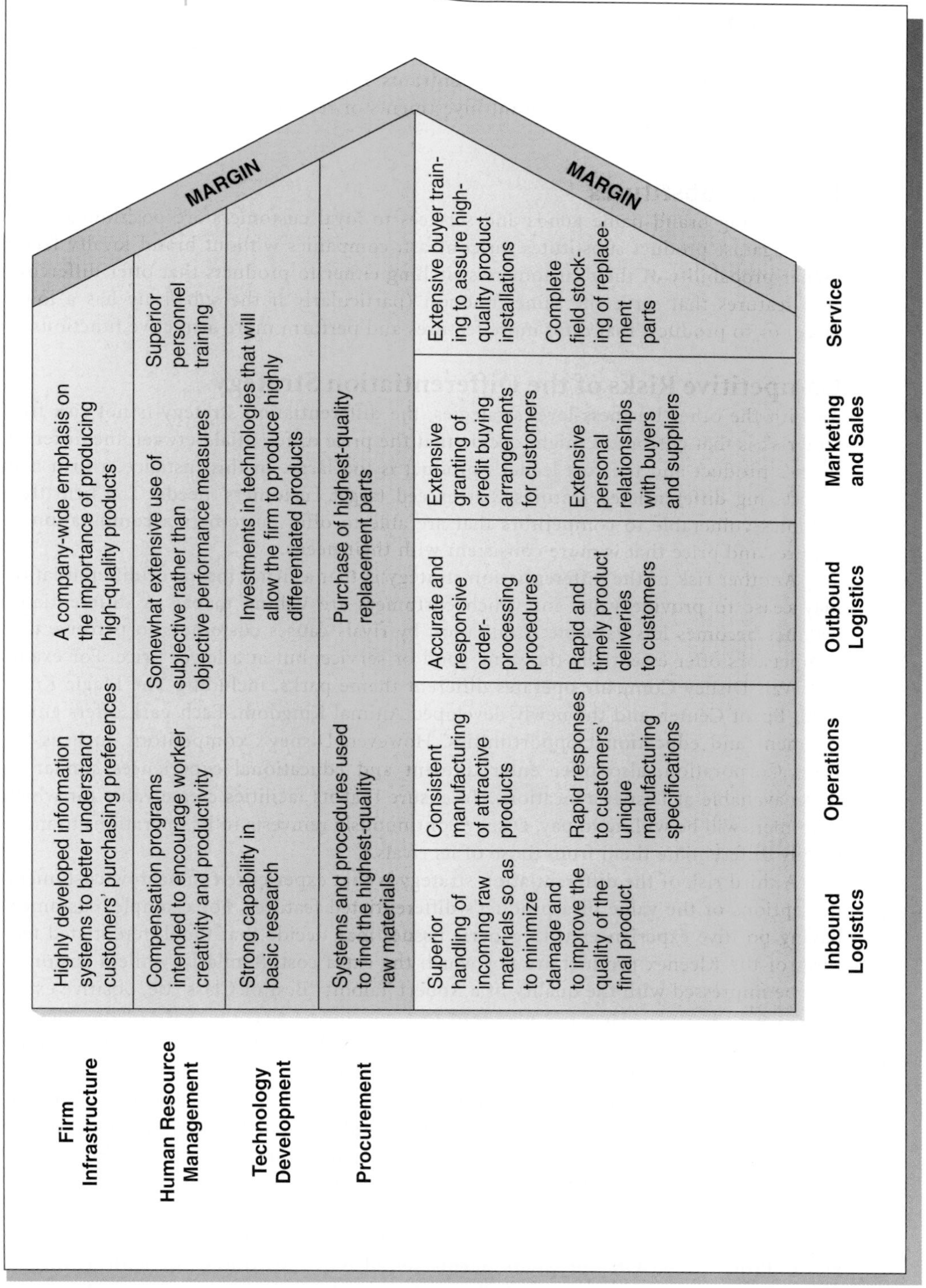

	Inbound Logistics	Operations	Outbound Logistics	Marketing and Sales	Service
Firm Infrastructure	Highly developed information systems to better understand customers' purchasing preferences				
Human Resource Management	Compensation programs intended to encourage worker creativity and productivity		Somewhat extensive use of subjective rather than objective performance measures		Superior personnel training
Technology Development	Strong capability in basic research		Investments in technologies that will allow the firm to produce highly differentiated products		
Procurement	Systems and procedures used to find the highest-quality raw materials		Purchase of highest-quality replacement parts		
	Superior handling of incoming raw materials so as to minimize damage and to improve the quality of the final product	Consistent manufacturing of attractive products	Accurate and responsive order-processing procedures	Extensive granting of credit buying arrangements for customers	Extensive buyer training to assure high-quality product installations
		Rapid responses to customers' unique manufacturing specifications	Rapid and timely product deliveries to customers	Extensive personal relationships with buyers and suppliers	Complete field stocking of replacement parts

Source: Adapted with the permission of The Free Press, an imprint of Simon & Schuster Adult Publishing Group, from *Competitive Advantage: Creating and Sustaining Superior Performance*, by Michael E. Porter, 47. Copyright © 1985, 1998 by Michael E. Porter.

firm might choose to pass the additional cost of supplies on to the customer by increasing the price of its unique product.

Potential Entrants

Customer loyalty and the need to overcome the uniqueness of a differentiated product present substantial barriers to potential entrants. Entering an industry under these conditions typically demands significant investments of resources and patience while seeking customers' loyalty.

Product Substitutes

Firms selling brand-name goods and services to loyal customers are positioned effectively against product substitutes. In contrast, companies without brand loyalty face a higher probability of their customers switching either to products that offer differentiated features that serve the same function (particularly if the substitute has a lower price) or to products that offer more features and perform more attractive functions.

Competitive Risks of the Differentiation Strategy

As with the other business-level strategies, the differentiation strategy is not risk free. One risk is that customers might decide that the price differential between the differentiator's product and the cost leader's product is too large. In this instance, a firm may be offering differentiated features that exceed target customers' needs. The firm then becomes vulnerable to competitors that are able to offer customers a combination of features and price that is more consistent with their needs.

Another risk of the differentiation strategy is that a firm's means of differentiation may cease to provide value for which customers are willing to pay. A differentiated product becomes less valuable if imitation by rivals causes customers to perceive that competitors offer essentially the same good or service, but at a lower price. For example, Walt Disney Company operates different theme parks, including The Magic Kingdom, Epcot Center, and the newly developed Animal Kingdom. Each park offers entertainment and educational opportunities. However, Disney's competitors, such as Six Flags Corporation, also offer entertainment and educational experiences similar to those available at Disney's locations. To ensure that its facilities create value for which customers will be willing to pay, Disney continuously reinvests in its operations to more crisply differentiate them from those of its rivals.[83]

A third risk of the differentiation strategy is that experience can narrow customers' perceptions of the value of a product's differentiated features. For example, customers having positive experiences with generic tissues may decide that the differentiated features of the Kleenex product are not worth the extra cost. Similarly, while a customer may be impressed with the quality of a Robert Talbott "Best of Class" tie, positive experiences with less expensive ties may lead to a conclusion that the price of the "Best of Class" tie exceeds the benefit. To counter this risk, firms must continue to meaningfully differentiate their product for customers at a price they are willing to pay.

Counterfeiting is the differentiation strategy's fourth risk. Makers of counterfeit goods—products that attempt to convey a firm's differentiated features to customers at significantly reduced prices—are a concern for many firms using the differentiation strategy. For example, Callaway Golf Company's success at producing differentiated products that create value, coupled with golf's increasing global popularity, has created great demand for counterfeited Callaway equipment. Through the U.S. Customs Service's "Project Teed Off" program, agents seized over 110 shipments with a total of more than 100,000 counterfeit Callaway golf club components over a three-year period.[84] Altria Group's domestic tobacco division, Philip Morris USA, files lawsuits against retailers selling counterfeit versions of its cigarettes, such as Marlboro. Judgments Philip Morris has won in these suits include immediate discontinuance of selling the counterfeit products as well as significant financial penalties for any future violations.[85] Pfizer is placing radio tags on bottles of Viagra. The small computer-like chips allow Pfizer to track each bottle of Viagra and confirm its legitimacy.[86]

Focus Strategies

Firms choose a focus strategy when they intend to use their core competencies to serve the needs of a particular industry segment or niche to the exclusion of others. Examples of specific market segments that can be targeted by a focus strategy include (1) a particular buyer group (e.g., youths or senior citizens), (2) a different segment of a product line (e.g., products for professional painters or those for "do-it-your-selfers"), or (3) a different geographic market (e.g., the East or the West in the United States).[87] Thus, the **focus strategy** is an integrated set of actions taken to produce goods or services that serve the needs of a particular competitive segment.

Goya Foods succeeds by offering a wide variety of products to consumers who form a particular segment of the market, in this case the Hispanic community.

To satisfy the needs of a certain size of company competing in a particular geographic market, Los Angeles–based investment banking firm Greif & Company positions itself as "The Entrepreneur's Investment Bank." Greif & Company is a leader in providing merger and acquisition advice to medium-sized businesses located in the western United States.[88] Partly because of costs and liability, governments are outsourcing health care to private companies. Nicknamed the "HMO behind bars," American Services Group Inc. (ASG) specializes in providing contract health care for prisons and jails such as New York's Rikers Island facility.[89] Goya Foods is the largest U.S.-based Hispanic-owned food company. Segmenting the Hispanic market into unique groups, Goya offers a total of over 1,000 products to consumers. The firm seeks "to be the be-all for the Latin community."[90] By successfully using a focus strategy, firms such as Greif & Company, ASG, and Goya Foods gain a competitive advantage in specific market niches or segments, even though they do not possess an industry-wide competitive advantage.[91]

Although the breadth of a target is clearly a matter of degree, the essence of the focus strategy "is the exploitation of a narrow target's differences from the balance of the industry."[92] Firms using the focus strategy intend to serve a particular segment of an industry more effectively than can industry-wide competitors. They succeed when they effectively serve a segment whose unique needs are so specialized that broad-based competitors choose not to serve that segment or when they satisfy the needs of a segment being served poorly by industry-wide competitors.[93]

Firms can create value for customers in specific and unique market segments by using the focused cost leadership strategy or the focused differentiation strategy.

Focused Cost Leadership Strategy

Based in Sweden, Ikea, a global furniture retailer with locations in 44 countries and sales revenue of $15.5 billion in 2004,[94] follows the focused cost leadership strategy.[95] The firm's vision is "Good design and function at low prices."[96] Young buyers desiring style at a low cost are Ikea's target customers.[97] For these customers, the firm offers home furnishings that combine good design, function, and acceptable quality with low prices. According to the firm, "low cost is always in focus. This applies to every phase of our activities."[98] The firm's intentions seem to be realized by customers, who see Ikea as a source of "stuff that's cool and cheap."[99] The firm continues its global expansion, recently opening stores in Russia and China.[100]

Ikea emphasizes several activities to keep its costs low.[101] For example, instead of relying primarily on third-party manufacturers, the firm's engineers design low-cost, modular furniture ready for assembly by customers. To eliminate the need for sales associates or decorators, Ikea positions the products in its stores so that customers can view different living combinations (complete with sofas, chairs, tables, and so forth) in a single roomlike setting, which helps the customer imagine how a grouping of furniture will look in the home. Typically, competitors' furniture stores display multiple varieties of a single item in separate rooms, so their customers examine living room sofas in one room, tables in another room, chairs in yet another location, and accessories in still another area. Ikea's approach requires fewer sales personnel, allowing the company to keep its costs low. A third practice that helps keep Ikea's costs low is requiring customers to transport their own purchases rather than providing delivery service.

Although it is a cost leader, Ikea also offers some differentiated features that appeal to its target customers, including in-store playrooms for children, wheelchairs for customer use, and extended hours. Stores outside those in the home country have "Sweden Shops" that sell Swedish specialties, such as herring, crisp bread, Swedish caviar, and gingerbread biscuits. Ikea believes that these services and products "are uniquely aligned with the needs of [its] customers, who are young, are not wealthy, are likely to have children (but no nanny), and, because they work for a living, have a need to shop at odd hours."[102] Thus, Ikea's focused cost leadership strategy finds the firm offering some differentiated features with its low-cost products.

Focused Differentiation Strategy

Other firms implement the focused differentiation strategy. As noted earlier, firms can differentiate their products in many ways. The Internet furniture venture Casketfurniture .com, for example, targets Generation X people who are interested in using the Internet as a shopping vehicle and who want to buy items with multiple purposes. The company considers itself to be "The Internet's Leading Provider of Top Quality Furniture Products." Casketfurniture.com offers a collection of products, including display cabinets, coffee tables, and entertainment centers, that can be easily converted into coffins if desired. The firm also makes custom casket products for customers.[103]

Founded in 1993, Anne Fontaine is a firm specializing in designing, producing, and selling white shirts for women. The firms sells its products in over 70 of its own stores that are located in major cities across the world. CEO and chief designer Anne Fontaine focuses on white because the color "represents light and purity, like a breath of fresh air." According to Fontaine, her design style is "eccentric, sensual, and above all feminine." The firm's shirt prices range from $165 to $550. Women desiring a "uniquely feminine" shirt that is made of the highest quality materials are Anne Fontaine's target customer.[104]

With its focus strategy, firms must be able to complete various primary and support activities in a competitively superior manner to develop and sustain a competitive advantage and earn above-average returns. The activities required to use the focused cost leadership strategy are virtually identical to those of the industry-wide cost leadership strategy (Figure 4.3), and activities required to use the focused differentiation strategy are largely identical to those of the industry-wide differentiation strategy (Figure 4.4). Similarly, the manner in which each of the two focus strategies allows a firm to deal successfully with the five competitive forces parallels those of the two broad strategies. The only difference is in the competitive scope, from an industry-wide market to a narrow industry segment. Thus, Figures 4.3 and 4.4 and the text regarding the five competitive forces also describe the relationship between each of the two focus strategies and competitive advantage.

Competitive Risks of Focus Strategies

With either focus strategy, the firm faces the same general risks as does the company using the cost leadership or the differentiation strategy, respectively, on an industry-wide basis. However, focus strategies have three additional risks.

First, a competitor may be able to focus on a more narrowly defined competitive segment and "outfocus" the focuser. For example, Confederate Motor Co. is producing a highly differentiated motorcycle that might appeal to some of Harley Davidson's customers. Obsessed with making a "fiercely American motorcycle" (one that is even more American than are Harley's products), Confederate's motorcycles are produced entirely by hand labor. In fact, a full week is required to make a single bike. Digital technology is used to design Confederate's products, which have a radical appearance. At a price of $62,000 or above, the firm's products will appeal only to customers wanting to buy a truly differentiated product such as the F113 Hellcat (which is receiving "rave reviews in the motorcycling press").[105]

Second, a company competing on an industry-wide basis may decide that the market segment served by the focus strategy firm is attractive and worthy of competitive pursuit. Consider the possibility that other manufacturers and marketers of women's clothing might determine that the profit potential in the narrow segment being served by Anne Fontaine is attractive. Gap Inc., for example, announced in spring 2005 that it was launching Forth & Towne, a new women's apparel retail concept, to "offer fashionable apparel and accessories targeting women over the age of 35."[106] If the Forth & Towne concept proves successful, Gap might begin to offer upscale, highly differentiated shirts that would compete against Anne Fontaine's.

The third risk involved with a focus strategy is that the needs of customers within a narrow competitive segment may become more similar to those of industry-wide customers as a whole. As a result, the advantages of a focus strategy are either reduced or eliminated. At some point, for example, the needs of Ikea's customers for stylish furniture may dissipate, although their desire to buy relatively inexpensive furnishings may not. If this change in needs were to happen, Ikea's customers might buy from large chain stores that sell somewhat standardized furniture at low costs. It is possible that the ability of competitors from other nations (especially from China) to inexpensively produce lamps with some levels of differentiation contributed to the decline in the size of Frederick Cooper Lamp's target market as illustrated in the Opening Case.

Integrated Cost Leadership/Differentiation Strategy

As stated earlier, many of today's customers have high expectations when purchasing a good or service. In a strategic context, this means that increasingly, customers want to purchase low-priced, differentiated products. Because of these expectations, a number of firms are trying to perform primary and support activities in ways that allow them to simultaneously pursue low cost and differentiation. Firms seeking to develop this type of activity map use the integrated cost leadership/differentiation strategy. The objective of using this strategy is to efficiently produce products with some differentiated attributes. Efficient production is the source of keeping costs low while some differentiation is the source of unique value. Firms that successfully use the integrated cost leadership/differentiation strategy have learned to quickly adapt to new technologies and rapid changes in their external environments. The reason for this is that simultaneously concentrating on developing two sources of competitive advantage (cost and differentiation) increases the number of primary and support activities in which the firm must become competent. In turn, having skills in a larger number of activities makes a firm more flexible.

Concentrating on the needs of its core customer group (higher-income, fashion-conscious discount shoppers), Target Stores uses an integrated cost leadership/differentiation strategy. The company's annual report describes this strategy: "Through careful nurturing and an intense focus on consistency and coordination throughout our organization, Target has built a strong, distinctive brand. At the core of our brand is our commitment to deliver the right balance of differentiation and value through our 'Expect More. Pay Less' brand promise."[107] Target relies on its relationships with, among others, Sonia Kashuk in cosmetics, Mossimo in apparel, Eddie Bauer in camping and outdoor gear, and Michael Graves in home, garden, and electronics products to offer differentiated products at discounted prices. Committed to presenting a consistent upscale image, the firm carefully studies trends to find new branded items that it believes can satisfy its customers' needs.[108]

Evidence suggests a relationship between successful use of the integrated strategy and above-average returns.[109] Thus, firms able to produce relatively differentiated products at relatively low costs can expect to perform well.[110] Indeed, a researcher found that the most successful firms competing in low-profit-potential industries were integrating the attributes of the cost leadership and differentiation strategies.[111] Other researchers have discovered that "businesses which combined multiple forms of competitive advantage outperformed businesses that only were identified with a single form."[112] The results of another study showed that the highest-performing companies in the Korean electronics industry combined the value-creating aspects of the cost leadership and differentiation strategies.[113] This finding suggests the usefulness of the integrated cost leadership/differentiation strategy in settings outside the United States.

Unlike Target, which uses the integrated cost leadership/differentiation strategy on an industry-wide basis, air-conditioning and heating-systems maker Aaon concentrates on a particular competitive scope. Thus, Aaon is implementing a focused integrated strategy. Aaon manufactures semicustomized rooftop air conditioning systems for large retailers, including Wal-Mart, Target, and Home Depot. Aaon positions its rooftop systems between low-priced commodity equipment and high-end customized systems. The firm's innovative manufacturing capabilities allow it to tailor a production line for units with special heat-recovery options unavailable on low-end systems. Combining custom features with assembly-line production methods results in significant cost savings. Aaon's prices are approximately 5 percent higher than low-end products but are only one-third the price of comparable customized systems.[114] Thus, the firm's narrowly defined target customers receive some differentiated features (e.g., special heat-recovery options) at a low, but not the lowest, cost.

Flexibility is required for firms to complete primary and support activities in ways that allow them to produce somewhat differentiated products at relatively low costs. Flexible manufacturing systems, information networks, and total quality management systems are three sources of flexibility that are particularly useful for firms trying to balance the objectives of continuous cost reductions and continuous enhancements to sources of differentiation as called for by the integrated strategy.

Flexible Manufacturing Systems

A flexible manufacturing system (FMS) increases the "flexibilities of human, physical, and information resources"[115] that the firm integrates to create relatively differentiated products at relatively low costs. A significant technological advance, FMS is a computer-controlled process used to produce a variety of products in moderate, flexible quantities with a minimum of manual intervention.[116]

The goal of an FMS is to eliminate the "low cost versus product variety" trade-off that is inherent in traditional manufacturing technologies. Firms use an FMS to change quickly and easily from making one product to making another.[117] Used properly, an FMS allows the firm to respond more effectively to changes in its customers' needs, while retaining low-cost advantages and consistent product quality.[118] Because an FMS also enables the firm to reduce the lot size needed to manufacture a product efficiently, the firm increases its capacity to serve the unique needs of a narrow competitive scope.

The effective use of an FMS is linked with a firm's ability to understand the constraints these systems may create (in terms of materials handling and the flow of supporting resources in scheduling, for example) and to design an effective mix of machines, computer systems, and people.[119] In industries of all types, effective mixes of the firm's tangible assets (e.g., machines) and intangible assets (e.g., people's skills) facilitate implementation of complex competitive strategies, especially the integrated cost leadership/differentiation strategy.[120]

Information Networks

By linking companies with their suppliers, distributors, and customers, information networks provide another source of flexibility. Among other outcomes, these networks, when used effectively,[121] facilitate the firm's efforts to satisfy customer expectations in terms of product quality and delivery speed.[122]

Earlier, we discussed the importance of managing the firm's relationships with its customers in order to understand their needs. Customer relationship management (CRM) is one form of an information-based network process that firms use to do this.[123] An effective CRM system provides a 360-degree view of the company's relationship with customers, encompassing all contact points, business processes, and communication media and sales channels.[124] The firm can then use this information to determine the trade-offs its customers are willing to make between differentiated features and low cost, which is vital for companies using the integrated cost leadership/differentiation strategy.

In addition to determining customers' product needs in terms of cost and differentiated features, effective information networks improve the flow of work and communications among employees producing a firm's good or service.[125] Better work flow and more effective communications allow workers to quickly identify problems and find flexible ways of dealing with them.[126]

Total Quality Management Systems

Total quality management (TQM) is a "managerial innovation that emphasizes an organization's total commitment to the customer and to continuous improvement of every process through the use of data-driven, problem-solving approaches based on empowerment of employee groups and teams."[127] Firms develop and use TQM systems in order to (1) increase customer satisfaction, (2) cut costs, and (3) reduce the amount of time required to introduce innovative products to the marketplace.[128] Ford Motor Company is relying on TQM to help "root out" its quality flaws,[129] while General Motors is "scrambling to narrow the quality gap that its executives say is the main reason consumers shy away from GM."[130] The focus by these firms on TQM to improve product and service quality is appropriate,[131] in that while U.S. auto manufacturers have made progress, "the Big Three still lag behind some foreign competitors, primarily the Japanese, by most quality measures."[132]

Firms able to simultaneously cut costs while enhancing their ability to develop innovative products increase their flexibility, an outcome that is particularly helpful to firms implementing the integrated cost leadership/differentiation strategy. Exceeding customers' expectations regarding quality is a differentiating feature, and eliminating process inefficiencies to cut costs allows the firm to offer that quality to customers at a relatively low price. Thus, an effective TQM system helps the firm develop the flexibility needed to spot opportunities to simultaneously increase differentiation and reduce costs.

Competitive Risks of the Integrated Cost Leadership/Differentiation Strategy

The potential to earn above-average returns by successfully using the integrated cost leadership/differentiation strategy is appealing. However, this is a risky strategy, as it is difficult for firms to perform primary and support activities in ways that allow them to produce relatively inexpensive products with levels of differentiation that create value for the target customer. Moreover, to properly use this strategy across time, firms must be able to simultaneously reduce costs incurred to produce products (as required by the cost leadership strategy) while increasing products' differentiation (as required by the differentiation strategy).

Firms that fail to perform the primary and support activities in an optimum manner become "stuck in the middle."[133] Being stuck in the middle means that the firm's cost structure is not low enough to allow it to attractively price its products and that its products are not sufficiently differentiated to create value for the target customer. When this happens, the firm will not earn above-average returns and will earn average returns only when the structure of the industry in which it competes is highly favorable.[134] Thus, companies implementing the integrated cost leadership/differentiation strategy must be able to perform the primary and support activities in ways that allow them to produce products that offer the target customer some differentiated features at a relatively low cost/price. As explained earlier, Southwest Airlines is able to do this and has avoided becoming stuck in the middle.

Firms can also become stuck in the middle when they fail to successfully implement *either* the cost leadership *or* the differentiation strategy. In other words, industry-wide competitors too can become stuck in the middle. Some speculate that this may be what happened at Hewlett-Packard under former CEO Carly Fiorina's leadership. Hewlett-Packard (HP) is competing against Dell with a strong low cost position and against IBM which has a strong differentiation strategy based on service. One analyst suggested that HP was "competing on price one week, service the next, while trying to sell through often conflicting, high-cost channels."[135] As explained in the Strategic Focus, Maytag Corporation is another firm that suffered from being stuck in the middle. As you will read, becoming stuck in the middle reduced the firm's ability to earn above-average returns and caused it to become a takeover target. You will learn more about Maytag's fate in a Strategic Focus in Chapter 6.

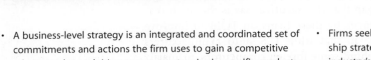

SUMMARY

- A business-level strategy is an integrated and coordinated set of commitments and actions the firm uses to gain a competitive advantage by exploiting core competencies in specific product markets. Five business-level strategies (cost leadership, differentiation, focused cost leadership, focused differentiation, and integrated cost leadership/differentiation) are examined in the chapter.

- Customers are the foundation of successful business-level strategies. When considering customers, a firm simultaneously examines three issues: *who*, *what*, and *how*. These issues, respectively, refer to the customer groups to be served, the needs those customers have that the firm seeks to satisfy, and the core competencies the firm will use to satisfy customers' needs. Increasing segmentation of markets throughout the global economy creates opportunities for firms to identify increasingly unique customer needs they can try to serve by using one of the business-level strategies.

- Firms seeking competitive advantage through the cost leadership strategy produce no-frills, standardized products for an industry's typical customer. However, these low-cost products must be offered with competitive levels of differentiation. Above-average returns are earned when firms continuously drive their costs lower than those of their competitors, while providing customers with products that have low prices and acceptable levels of differentiated features.

- Competitive risks associated with the cost leadership strategy include (1) a loss of competitive advantage to newer technologies, (2) a failure to detect changes in customers' needs, and (3) the ability of competitors to imitate the cost leader's competitive advantage through their own unique strategic actions.

- Through the differentiation strategy, firms provide customers with products that have different (and valued) features. Differentiated products must be sold at a cost that customers believe

Maytag Corporation: A Cost Leader? A Differentiator?

"For the better part of a century, Maytag brand appliances have been synonymous with dependability and quality." Appearing on the Maytag Corporation's Web site, this statement suggests that Maytag believes that dependability (or reliability) and product quality are competitive advantages for the firm. As competitive advantages, reliability and product quality are associated with use of a differentiation strategy rather than a cost leadership strategy for firms targeting a broad competitive scope.

It is arguably difficult in today's global appliance market to develop competitive advantages on the basis of reliability and quality. Lower-cost competitors have learned how to produce products that provide customers with years of solid, reliable service (because of this, repairmen for Maytag's competitors are also "lonely guys"). Global competitors from Korean, LG Electronics and Samsung, and China's Qingdao Haier Ltd. (more commonly referred to as the Haier Group), produce appliances with reliability levels close if not equal to Maytag's. Reliability is no longer a source of competitive advantage—it is the price of market entry. In the words of an analyst talking about Maytag's efforts to outperform competitors: "Reliable products or service is the table stakes. You've either got that or you aren't playing." The same can be said about product quality. For a host of products, including appliances, quality is increasingly becoming a necessary but not sufficient condition to attract customers' purchases. This means that without quality, customers won't consider buying a good or service. However, because virtually all firms are producing products with acceptable to high levels of quality, it is difficult for a firm to outperform competitors on the basis of the quality of its product.

If Maytag isn't able to differentiate its offerings in terms of reliability and quality as the basis for successfully using a differentiation strategy, might it have the ability to earn above-average returns through the cost leadership strategy? The evidence isn't encouraging here either. Maytag has high labor costs. Moreover, it is losing the battle to establish a firm position in low-cost distribution channels. Maytag recently exited Best Buy and is losing space to LG Electronics and Samsung at Home Depot. Relying on higher-cost distribution channels such as full-line department stores and independent retailers makes it difficult for Maytag to keep its costs low. In combination, then, Maytag has a host of operational issues: "High labor costs, lack of innovation, and Asia-based rivals." Stated very directly, Maytag's costs are too high to allow it to compete as the low-cost leader, and it lacks the innovation needed to consistently produce differentiated features that will create unique value for customers on an industry-wide basis.

But Maytag Corporation does own valuable brands such as Jenn-Air, Amana, and Hoover in addition to the core Maytag brand. Some competitors believe that there is hidden value in those brands and have launched bids to purchase the firm. In August 2005, Whirlpool Corp. offered the highest bid to purchase Maytag. If the transaction is completed, analysts expected that Whirlpool would be able to "drive significant efficiencies to help repair Maytag's overburdened cost structure [and] could better extend Maytag's pipeline of innovation." As part of another corporation such as Whirlpool, Maytag might be able to successfully implement the differentiation strategy and avoid being stuck in the middle.

Sources: 2005, About Maytag, Maytag Corporation Home Page, www.maytag.com, July 30; D. K. Berman & M. J. McCarthy, 2005, Whirlpool enters fight for Maytag with informal bid, *Wall Street Journal Online*, www.wsj.com, July 18; D. K. Berman, H. Sender, & M. J. McCarthy, 2005, China's Haier is said to drop offer for Maytag, *Wall Street Journal Online*, www.wsj.com, July 20; L. Grant & T. Howard, 2005, Maytag buyer would face repairs, *USA Today*, July 19, B3; M. J. McCarthy & J. T. Hallinan, 2005, Whirlpool to start due-diligence study on Maytag bid, *Wall Street Journal Online*, www.wsj.com, July 27.

is competitive given the product's features as compared with the cost/feature combination available through competitors' offerings. Because of their uniqueness, differentiated goods or services are sold at a premium price. Products can be differentiated along any dimension that some customer group values. Firms using this strategy seek to differentiate their products from competitors' goods or services along as many dimensions as possible. The less similarity with competitors' products, the more buffered a firm is from competition with its rivals.

- Risks associated with the differentiation strategy include (1) a customer group's decision that the differences between the differentiated product and the cost leader's good or service are no longer worth a premium price, (2) the inability of a differentiated product to create the type of value for which customers are willing to pay a premium price, (3) the ability of competitors to provide customers with products that have features similar to those associated with the differentiated product, but at a lower cost, and (4) the threat of counterfeiting, whereby firms produce a cheap "knockoff" of a differentiated good or service.

- Through the cost leadership and the differentiated focus strategies, firms serve the needs of a narrow competitive segment (e.g., a buyer group, product segment, or geographic area). This

strategy is successful when firms have the core competencies required to provide value to a narrow competitive segment that exceeds the value available from firms serving customers on an industry-wide basis.

- The competitive risks of focus strategies include (1) a competitor's ability to use its core competencies to "outfocus" the focuser by serving an even more narrowly defined competitive segment, (2) decisions by industry-wide competitors to focus on a customer group's specialized needs, and (3) a reduction in differences of the needs between customers in a narrow competitive segment and the industry-wide market.

- Firms using the integrated cost leadership/differentiation strategy strive to provide customers with relatively low-cost products that have some valued differentiated features. Flexibility is required for the firm to learn how to use primary and support activities in ways that allow them to produce somewhat differentiated products at relatively low costs. The primary risk of this strategy is that a firm might produce products that do not offer sufficient value in terms of either low cost or differentiation. When this occurs, the company is "stuck in the middle." Firms stuck in the middle compete at a disadvantage and are unable to earn more than average returns.

NOTES

1. G. Gavetti & J .W. Rivkin, 2005, How strategists really think, *Harvard Business Review*, 83(4): 54–63.
2. G. Gavetti, D. A. Levinthal, & J. W. Rivkin, 2005, Strategy making in novel and complex worlds: The power of analogy, *Strategic Management Journal*, 26: 691–712.
3. J. Tan & D. Tan, 2005, Environment-strategy co-evolution and co-alignment: A staged model of Chinese SOEs under transition, *Strategic Management Journal*, 26: 141–157.
4. G. George, J. Wiklund, & S. A. Zahra, 2005, Ownership and the internationalization of small firms, *Journal of Management*, 31: 210–233.
5. E. Kim, D. Nam, & J. L. Stimpert, 2004, The applicability of Porter's generic strategies in the digital age: Assumptions, conjectures, and suggestions, *Journal of Management*, 30: 569–589; R. D. Ireland, M. A. Hitt, S. M. Camp, & D. L. Sexton, 2001, Integrating entrepreneurship and strategic management actions to create firm wealth, *Academy of Management Executive*, 15(1): 49–63.
6. K. Shimizu & M. A. Hitt, 2004, Strategic flexibility: Organizational preparedness to reverse ineffective strategic decisions, *Academy of Management Executive*, 18(4): 44–59.
7. D. J. Ketchen Jr., C. C. Snow, & V. L. Street, 2004, Improving firm performance by matching strategic decision-making processes to competitive dynamics, *Academy of Management Executive*, 18(4): 29–43.
8. J. J. Janney & G. G. Dess, 2004, Can real-options analysis improve decision-making? Promises and pitfalls, *Academy of Management Executive*, 18(4): 60–75.
9. R. D. Ireland & C. C. Miller, 2005, Decision-making and firm success, *Academy of Management Executive*, 18(4): 8–12.
10. N. Park, J. M. Mezias, & J. Song, 2004, Increasing returns, strategic alliances, and the values of E-commerce firms, *Journal of Management*, 30: 7–27; G. G. Dess, A. Gupta, J. F. Hennart, & C. W. L. Hill, 1995, Conducting and integrating strategy research at the international, corporate, and business levels: Issues and directions, *Journal of Management*, 21: 357–393.
11. M. C. Mankins & R. Steele, 2005, Turning great strategy into great performance, *Harvard Business Review*, 83(7): 65–72; T. J. Douglas & J. A. Ryman, 2003, Understanding competitive advantage in the general hospital industry: Evaluating strategic competencies, *Strategic Management Journal*, 24: 333–347.
12. D. Lei & J. W. Slocum, 2005, Strategic and organizational requirements for competitive advantage, *Academy of Management Executive*, 19(1): 31–45.
13. B. M. Case, 2005, Irving firm to cut jobs, *Dallas Morning News*, July 23, D1, D9.
14. J. B. Barney & T. B. Mackey, 2005, Testing resource-based theory, In D. J. Ketchen Jr. & D. D. Bergh (eds.), *Research Methodology in Strategy and Management* (2nd ed.), London: Elsevier, 1–13.
15. C. B. Dobni & G. Luffman, 2003, Determining the scope and impact of market orientation profiles on strategy implementation and performance, *Strategic Management Journal*, 24: 577–585.
16. R. Gulati & J. B. Oldroyd, 2005, The quest for customer focus, *Harvard Business Review*, 83(4): 92–101.
17. M. E. Porter, 1980, *Competitive Strategy*, New York: Free Press.
18. A. J. Slywotzky & J. Drzik, 2005, Countering the biggest risk of all, *Harvard Business Review*, 83(4): 78–88.
19. F. E. Webster Jr., A. J. Malter, & S. Ganesan, 2005, The decline and dispersion of marketing competence, *MIT Sloan Management Review*, 6(4): 35–43.

20. D. Peppers & M. Rogers, 2005, Customers don't grow on trees, *Fast Company,* July, 25–26.

21. B. Breen & M. Aneiro, 2004, Living in Dell time, *Fast Company,* November, 86–95.

22. 2005, Dell selling first laser printer priced below $100, *Dallas Morning News,* www.dallasnews.com, June 21.

23. M. D. Johnson & F. Seines, 2005, Diversifying your customer portfolio, *MIT Sloan Management Review,* 46(3): 11.

24. 2005, About us, Harrah's Entertainment Home Page, www.harrahs.com, July 23.

25. 2005, The customer service center: CSR, www.knowlagent.com, July 23.

26. J. E. Blose, W. B. Tankersley, & L. R. Flynn, 2005, Managing service quality using data envelopment analysis, www.asq.org, June; B. Magura, 2003, What hooks M-commerce customers? *The McKinsey Quarterly,* 44(3): 9.

27. R. Dhar & R. Glazer, 2003, Hedging customers, *Harvard Business Review,* 81(5): 86–92.

28. 2005, Amazon.com, *Standard & Poor's Stock Report,* www.standardandpoors.com, June 25.

29. 2005, About Cemex, Cemex Home Page, www.cemex.com, July 23.

30. 2003, Fitch Mexico assigns AA qualifications to certificates of Cemex, *Emerging Markets Economy,* April 8, 3; L. Walker, 2001, Plugged in for maximum efficiency, *Washington Post,* June 20, G1, G4.

31. B. Tedeschi, 2005, Women are keen to shop online; merchants are eager to oblige, *New York Times,* www.nytimes.com, June 6.

32. 2005, Barnes & Noble, Inc., *Standard & Poor's Stock Reports,* www.standardandpoors.com, July 16.

33. 2005, Amazon.com, *Standard & Poor's Stock Reports,* www.standardandpoors.com, July 16.

34. 2005, www.carpoint.com, July 23.

35. A. Reed II & L. E. Bolton, 2005, The complexity of identity, *MIT Sloan Management Review,* 46(3): 18–22.

36. C. W. Lamb Jr., J. F. Hair Jr., & C. McDaniel, 2006, *Marketing* (8th Ed.), Mason, OH: Thomson South-Western, 224; A. Dutra, J. Frary, & R. Wise, 2004, Higher-order needs drive new growth in mature consumer markets, *Journal of Business Strategy,* 25(5): 26–34.

37. A. Baur, S. P. Hehner, & G. Nederegger, 2003, Pharma for Fido, *The McKinsey Quarterly,* Number 2, 7–10.

38. S. S. Hassan & S. H. Craft, 2005, Linking global market segmentation decisions with strategic positioning options, *Journal of Consumer Marketing,* 22(2/3): 81–88.

39. S. Hamner, 2005, Filling the Gap, *Business 2.0,* July, 30.

40. 2003, Unions and Gen-X: What does the future hold? *HR Focus,* March, 3; F. Marshall, 2003, Storehouse wakes up to Gen-X employees, *Furniture Today,* February 10, 2–3; J. Pereira, 2003, Best on the street, *Wall Street Journal,* May 12, R7; C. Burritt, 2001, Aging boomers reshape resort segment, *Lodging Hospitality,* 57(3): 31–32; J. D. Zbar, 2001, On a segmented dial, digital cuts wire finer, *Advertising Age,* 72(16): S12.

41. J. P. Womack, 2005, Lean consumption, *Harvard Business Review,* 83(3): 58–68.

42. A. Panjwani, 2005, Open source vs. proprietary software: The pluses and minuses, *The Financial Express online,* www.financialexpress.com, May 2.

43. M. E. Raynor & H. S. Weinberg, 2004, Beyond segmentation, *Marketing Management,* 13(6): 22–29.

44. W. Reinartz, J. S. Thomas, & V. Kumar, 2005, Balancing acquisition and retention resources to maximize customer profitability, *Journal of Marketing,* 69: 63–85.

45. L. Mazur, 2003, Forget risk-free rules to tap into customer needs, *Marketing,* April 10, 16.

46. D. Foust, F. F. Jespersen, F. Katzenberg, A. Barrett, & R. O. Crockett, 2003, The best performers, *BusinessWeek Online,* www.businessweek.com, March 24.

47. M. J. Silverstein & N. Fiske, 2003, Luxury for the masses, *Harvard Business Review,* 81(4): 48–57.

48. C. W. L. Hill & F. T. Rothaermel, 2003, The performance of incumbent firms in the face of radical technological innovation, *Academy of Management Review,* 28: 257–274; A. W. King, S. W. Fowler, & C. P. Zeithaml, 2001, Managing organizational competencies for competitive advantage: The middle-management edge, *Academy of Management Executive,* 15(2): 95–106.

49. S. N. Mehta, 2001, What Lucent can learn from IBM, *Fortune,* June 25, 40–44.

50. 2005, www.sas.com, July 25.

51. 2005, www.vans.com; A. Weintraub & G. Khermouch, 2001, Chairman of the board, *Business Week,* May 28, 94.

52. M. E. Porter, 1985, *Competitive Advantage,* New York: Free Press, 26.

53. M. E. Porter, 1996, What Is strategy? *Harvard Business Review,* 74(6): 61–78.

54. Porter, What Is strategy?

55. S. Warren & E. Perez, 2005, Southwest's net rises by 41%; Delta lifts cap on some fares, *Wall Street Journal Online,* www.wsj.com, July 15.

56. E. Souder, Update: Southwest aims to boost profit 15% in 2006, *Wall Street Journal Online,* www.wsj.com, July 14.

57. Porter, What is strategy?

58. C. Zott, 2003, Dynamic capabilities and the emergence of intraindustry differential firm performance: Insights from a simulation study, *Strategic Management Journal,* 24: 97–125.

59. M. E. Porter, 1994, Toward a dynamic theory of strategy, in R. P. Rumelt, D. E. Schendel, & D. J. Teece (eds.), *Fundamental Issues in Strategy,* Boston: Harvard Business School Press, 423–461.

60. Porter, What is strategy?, 62.

61. Porter, Competitive Advantage, 15.

62. G. G. Dess, G. T. Lumpkin, & J. E. McGee, 1999, Linking corporate entrepreneurship to strategy, structure, and process: Suggested research directions, *Entrepreneurship: Theory & Practice,* 23(3): 85–102; P. M. Wright, D. L. Smart, & G. C. McMahan, 1995, Matches between human resources and strategy among NCAA basketball teams, *Academy of Management Journal,* 38: 1052–1074.

63. Porter, Competitive Strategy, 35–40.

64. D. F. Spulber, 2004, *Management Strategy,* New York: McGrawHill/Irwin, 175.

65. K. Yung, 2005, Greyhound taking new direction, *Dallas Morning News,* www.dallasnews.com, June 26.

66. D. F. Lynch, S. B. Keller, & J. Ozment, 2000, The effects of logistics capabilities and strategy on firm performance, *Journal of Business Logistics,* 21(2): 47–68.

67. 2005, Big Lots, *Standard & Poor's Stock Reports,* www.standardandpoors.com, July 16.

68. 2005, Big Lots Inc. names Steve Fishman Chairman, Chief Executive Officer, and President, *Reuters,* www.reuters.com, June 10.

69. 2005, Big Lots, Inc. Home Page, www.biglots.com, July 23.

70. L. K. Johnson, 2003, Dueling pricing strategies, *The McKinsey Quarterly,* 44(3): 10–11.

71. A. D'Innocenzio, 2001, We are paranoid, *Richmond Times-Dispatch,* June 10, E1, E2.

72. M. Maier, 2005, How to beat Wal-Mart, *Business 2.0,* May, 108–114.

73. Porter, Competitive Strategy, 35–40.

74. Ibid., 65.

75. R. Brooks, 2005, Krispy Kreme ousts six executives, *Wall Street Journal Online,* www.wsj.com, June 22.

76. Porter, Competitive Advantage, 14.

77. 2005, History, Robert Talbott Home Page, www.roberttalbott.com, July 25.

78. J. H. Gilmore, 2005, Feedback, *Fast Company,* August, 17.

79. J. A. Byrne, 2005, The power of great design, *Fast Company,* June, 14.

80. D. Welch, 2005, GM's design push picks up speed, *Business Week,* July 18, 40–42.

81. S. Gluskoter, 2005, Let the customer drive design, *Fast Company,* June, 45.

82. R. Berner, 2005, Flip-flops, torn jeans—and control, *Business Week,* May 30, 68–70.

83. Barney, Gaining and Sustaining Competitive Advantage, 268.

84. 2003, Callaway Golf Company, *Standard & Poor's Stock Reports,* www.standardandpoors.com, May 3; H. R. Goldstein, A. E. Roth, T. Young, & J. D. Lawrence, 2001, US manufacturers take a swing at counterfeit golf clubs, *Intellectual Property & Technology Law Journal,* May, 23.

85. 2003, Philip Morris files to stop counterfeit cigarette sales, *Wall Street Journal,* www.wsj.com, March 3.

86. A. Cronin, 2004, Pfizer plans to put radio tags on Viagra to stop counterfeits, *Knight Ridder/Tribune Business News,* November 16, D1.

87. Porter, Competitive Strategy, 98.

88. 2005, Greif & Co. Home Page, www.greifco.com, July 26.

89. D. Raiford, 2002, Prison health ends contract with Philly, *Nashville Business Journal,* July 12; D. Foust & B. Grow, 2001, This company likes it in jail, *Business Week,* June 11, 112.

90. D. Kaplan, 2005, Lots of food for diverse culture, *Houston Chronicle,* July 19, D2.

91. Porter, Competitive Advantage, 15.

92. Ibid.

93. Ibid., 15–16.

94. B. Lodge, 2005, Tax incentives debated as Ikea primps, *Dallas Morning News,* July 25, A1, A2.

95. Porter, What is strategy?, 67.

96. 2005, About Ikea, Ikea Home Page, www.ikea.com, July 26.

97. K. Kling & I. Goteman, 2003, Ikea CEO Andres Dahlvig on international growth and Ikea's unique corporate culture and brand identity, *Academy of Management Executive,* 17(1): 31–37.

98. 2005, Our vision, Ikea Home Page, www.ikea.com, July 26.

99. T. Theis, 2005, Explore the store, *Dallas Morning News,* July 29, E1.

100. W. Stewart, 2003, Ikea's flat-pack revolution changing rooms in Russia, *Knight Ridder Tribune Business News,* www.knightridder.com, April 24; 2003, Ikea's RMB 500-million outlet opens in Shanghai, *SinoCast China Business Daily News,* April 18.

101. P. Szuchman, 2005, Can this kitchen be saved? *Wall Street Journal Online,* www.wsj.com, July 26.

102. G. Evans, 2003, Why some stores strike me as special, *Furniture Today,* 27(24): 91; Porter, What is strategy?, 65.

103. 2005, Welcome to CasketFurniture Store, CasketFurniture.com Home Page, www.casketfurniture.com, July 26.

104. 2005, Anne Fontaine Home Page, www.annefontaine.com, July 26.

105. B. Breen, 2005, Rebel yell, *Fast Company,* August, 60–61.

106. 2005, Gap Inc. introduces Forth & Towne, Gap Inc. Home Page, www.gap.com, July 26.

107. 2005, 2004 Annual Report, Target Corporation, www.target.com, July 26.

108. 2001, The engine that drives differentiation, *DSN Retailing Today,* April 2, 52.

109. Dess, Lumpkin, & McGee, Linking corporate entrepreneurship to strategy, 89.

110. P. Ghemawat, 2001, *Strategy and the Business Landscape,* Upper Saddle River, NJ: Prentice-Hall, 56.

111. W. K. Hall, 1980, Survival strategies in a hostile environment, *Harvard Business Review,* 58(5): 75–87.

112. Dess, Gupta, Hennart, & Hill, Conducting and integrating strategy research, 377.

113. L. Kim & Y. Lim, 1988, Environment, generic strategies, and performance in a rapidly developing country: A taxonomic approach, *Academy of Management Journal,* 31: 802–827.

114. S. A. Forest, 2001, When cool heads prevail, *Business Week,* June 11, 114.

115. R. Sanchez, 1995, Strategic flexibility in product competition, *Strategic Management Journal,* 16 (Special Issue): 140.

116. A. Faria, P. Fenn, & A. Bruce, 2005, Production technologies and technical efficiency: Evidence from Portuguese manufacturing industry, *Applied Economics,* 37: 1037–1046.

117. J. Baljko, 2003, Built for speed—When putting the reams of supply chain data they've amassed to use, companies are discovering that agility counts, *EBN,* 1352: 25–28.

118. E. K. Bish, A. Muriel, & S. Biller, 2005, Managing flexible capacity in a make-to-order environment, *Management Science,* 51: 167–180.

119. M. Savsar, 2005, Performance analysis of an FMS operating under different failure rates and maintenance policies, *International Journal of Flexible Manufacturing Systems,* 16: 229–249.

120. S. M. Iravani, M. P. van Oyen, & K. T. Sims, 2005, Structural flexibility: A new perspective on the design of manufacturing and service operations, *Management Science,* 51: 151–166.

121. A. McAfee, 2003, When too much IT knowledge is a dangerous thing, *The McKinsey Quarterly,* 44(2): 83–89.

122. F. Mattern, S. Schonwalder, & W. Stein, 2003, Fighting complexity in IT, *The McKinsey Quarterly,* Number 1, 57–65.

123. S. W. Brown, 2003, The employee experience, *Marketing Management,* 12(2): 12–13.

124. S. Isaac & R. N. Tooker, 2001, The many faces of CRM, *LIMRA's MarketFacts Quarterly,* 20(1): 84–89.

125. K. H. Doerr, T. R. Mitchell, C. A. Schriesheim, T. Freed, & X. Zhou, 2002, Heterogeneity and variability in the context of work flows, *Academy of Management Review,* 27: 594–607.

126. G. Edmondson, 2005, BMW keeps the home fires burning, *Business Week,* May 30, 52.

127. J. D. Westphal, R. Gulati, & S. M. Shortell, 1997, Customization or conformity: An institutional and network perspective on the content and consequences of TQM adoption, *Administrative Science Quarterly,* 42: 366–394.

128. V. W. S. Yeung & R. W. Armstrong, 2003, A key to TQM benefits: Manager involvement in customer processes, *International Journal of Services Technology and Management,* 4(1): 14–29.

129. J. Muller, 2001, Ford: Why it's worse than you think, *Business Week,* June 25, 80–89.

130. J. White, G. L. White, & N. Shirouzu, 2001, Soon, the big three won't be, as foreigners make inroads, *Wall Street Journal,* August 13, A1, A12.

131. D. Welch, K. Kerwin, & C. Tierney, 2003, Way to go, Detroit—Now go a lot farther, *Business Week,* May 26, 44.

132. N. Ganguli, T. V. Kumaresh, & A. Satpathy, 2003, Detroit's new quality gap, *The McKinsey Quarterly,* Number 1, 148–151.

133. Porter, Competitive Advantage, 16.

134. Ibid., 17.

135. 2005, Three reasons why good strategies fail: execution, execution, . . . *Knowledge@Wharton,* http://knowledge.wharton.upenn.edu, July 30.

The Competitive Nature of Strategy

KNOWLEDGE OBJECTIVES

Studying this chapter should provide you with the strategic management knowledge needed to:

1. Define competitors, competitive rivalry, competitive behavior, and competitive dynamics.

2. Describe market commonality and resource similarity as the building blocks of a competitor analysis.

3. Explain awareness, motivation, and ability as drivers of competitive behavior.

4. Discuss factors affecting the likelihood a competitor will take competitive actions.

5. Discuss factors affecting the likelihood a competitor will respond to actions taken against it.

6. Explain competitive dynamics in slow-cycle, fast-cycle, and standard-cycle markets.

ASSOCIATED PRESS, AP

Southwest Airlines owes its success in part to its excellent customer service.

Southwest Airlines: The King of the Hill That Is Changing an Industry

Much has been written about Southwest Airlines but more should be said. It is arguably the best airline in the United States and among the best in the world. Most competitors and analysts focus on Southwest's low-cost strategy. However, as we explained in Chapter 4, Southwest follows an integrated cost leadership/differentiation strategy. It differentiates its service with excellent human capital. The firm has fewer customer complaints than most competitors and has high "on-time" performance, among other distinctions.

Southwest's leadership in implementing the integrated strategy is changing the airline industry. Many of the "full service" airlines have tried to imitate Southwest's strategy but have been unable to manage costs effectively and/or offer comparable levels of service. Southwest continues to best most of its competitors such that they will have to change or die. In other words, Southwest is literally killing its competition. In the second quarter of 2005, Southwest announced a record increase in profits of 41 percent. Such an increase would be impressive enough under normal business conditions; coming at a time when the price of fuel is at record levels, causing most other airlines to announce major net losses, it is almost incredible. How was Southwest Airlines able to make such profits? It is effective in managing its costs, particularly through its hedging program. Gary Kelly, the CEO of Southwest Airlines, has suggested that no airline can make a profit when the price of oil is above $50 a barrel. As a result, Southwest has negotiated hedging agreements that extend through 2009 to pay no more than $35 a barrel for at least 25 percent of its fuel needs. It holds options for approximately 85 percent of its oil for $26 a barrel. It has been hedging the cost of its fuel since 2001, when the price of a barrel of oil was only $17. In recent times, the cost for a barrel of oil has been greater than $70. These types of decisions have helped Southwest to achieve 57 straight profitable quarters and allow the executives the flexibility to never lay off employees (even following September 11, 2001, when many large companies and most other airlines experienced major employee layoffs).

Southwest has also become increasingly aggressive in competitive actions. For example, it acquired an interest in AirTran Airways, thereby obtaining access to six additional gates at Midway Airport in Chicago. At a time when most of Southwest's competitors are reducing capacity, Southwest plans to add 29 planes to its fleet, bringing the total to 417, in order to increase its capacity for flights and passengers by 10 percent. "I feel very good about our competitive position as long as we continue to improve," Southwest's CEO Kelly said, adding that if Southwest's growth hurts a competitor, it is a byproduct of the growth. Most of his competitors, Kelly suggested, will have to manage their cost structure more effectively or they will be unlikely to survive.

Sources: S. Warren & E. Perez, 2005, Southwest's net rises by 41%; Delta lifts cap on some fares, *Wall Street Journal,* July 15, www.wsj.com; 2005, Southwest Airlines' profits skyrocket 41%, Rednova News, July 15, www.rednova.com; S. Warren, 2005, Hedge hog Southwest Air sharpens its teeth, *Wall Street Journal,* May 19, www.wsj.com; B. Gimbel, 2005, Southwest charts its course, *Fortune,* May 2, www.fortune.com; W. Zellner, 2005, Southwest: Dressed to kill . . . competitors, *Business Week,* February 21, www.businessweek.com; M. Maynard, 2004, From aw-shucks to cutthroat: Southwest's ascent, *New York Times,* December 26, www.nyt.com.

Firms operating in the same market, offering similar products, and targeting similar customers are **competitors**.[1] Southwest Airlines, Delta, United, Continental, and JetBlue are competitors, as are PepsiCo and Coca-Cola Company. Firms interact with their competitors as part of the broad context within which they operate while attempting to earn above-average returns.[2] The decisions firms make about their interactions with their competitors significantly affect their ability to earn above-average returns.[3] Because 80 to 90 percent of new firms fail, learning how to select the markets in which to compete and how to best compete within them is highly important.[4]

Competitive rivalry is the ongoing set of competitive actions and competitive responses that occur between competitors as they maneuver for an advantageous market position. Especially in highly competitive industries, firms constantly jockey for advantage as they launch strategic actions and respond or react to rivals' moves.[5] It is important for those leading organizations to understand competitive rivalry, in that "the central, brute empirical fact in strategy is that some firms outperform others,"[6] meaning that competitive rivalry influences an individual firm's ability to gain and sustain competitive advantages.[7]

A sequence of firm-level moves, rivalry results from firms initiating their own competitive actions and then responding to actions taken by competitors. **Competitive behavior** is the set of competitive actions and competitive responses the firm takes to build or defend its competitive advantages and to improve its market position.[8] Through competitive behavior, the firm tries to successfully position itself relative to the five forces of competition (see Chapter 2) and to defend current competitive advantages while building advantages for the future (see Chapter 3). Increasingly, competitors engage in competitive actions and responses in more than one market.[9] Firms competing against each other in several product or geographic markets are engaged in **multimarket competition**.[10] All competitive behavior—that is, the total set of actions and responses taken by all firms competing within a market—is called **competitive dynamics**. The relationships among these key concepts are shown in Figure 5.1.

This chapter focuses on competitive rivalry and competitive dynamics. The essence of these important topics is that a firm's strategies are dynamic in nature. Actions taken by one firm elicit responses from competitors that, in turn, typically result in responses from the firm that took the initial action.[11] To the extent possible, other airlines will need to react to Southwest's acquisition of additional gates in Chicago, as described in the Opening Case. In particular, America West and AirTran also wanted those gates. Southwest now controls 25 of the 43 gates at Chicago's Midway airport.[12]

Another way of highlighting competitive rivalry's effect on the firm's strategies is to say that a strategy's success is determined not only by the firm's initial competitive actions but also by how well it anticipates competitors' responses to them *and* by how well the firm anticipates and responds to its competitors' initial actions (also called attacks).[13] Although competitive rivalry affects all types of strategies (for example, corporate-level, acquisition, and international), its most dominant influence is on the firm's business-level strategy or strategies. Indeed, firms' actions and responses to those of their rivals are the basic building block of business-level strategies.[14] Recall from Chapter 4 that business-level strategy is concerned with what the firm does to successfully use its competitive advantages in specific product markets. In the global economy, competitive rivalry is intensifying,[15] meaning that the significance of its effect on firms' business-level strategies is increasing. However, firms that develop and use effective business-level strategies tend to outperform competitors in individual product markets, even when experiencing intense competitive rivalry.[16]

An expanding geographic scope contributes to the increasing intensity in the competitive rivalry between firms. Many firms from different parts of the world are beginning to emerge as formidable global competitors. Wipro, the Indian technology firm to which many activities have been outsourced in recent years, entered the global manage-

FIGURE **5.1**

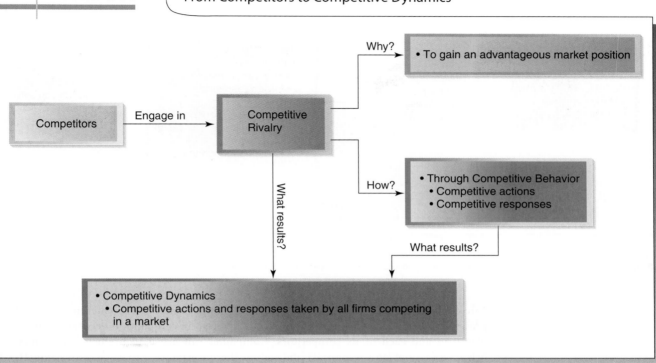

Source: Adapted from M.-J. Chen, 1996, Competitor analysis and interfirm rivalry: Toward a theoretical integration, *Academy of Management Review*, 21: 100–134.

ment consulting market in competition with many major firms in this industry. Major Chinese firms made acquisition bids for large U.S. firms in 2005. For example, the Haier Group bid to acquire Maytag, and China's state-owned oil company, CNOOC, made a bid to acquire Unocal.[17]

A Model of Competitive Rivalry

Over time, firms take many competitive actions and responses.[18] As noted earlier, competitive rivalry evolves from this pattern of actions and responses as one firm's competitive actions have noticeable effects on competitors, eliciting competitive responses from them.[19] This pattern shows that firms are mutually interdependent, that they feel each other's actions and responses, and that marketplace success is a function of both individual strategies and the consequences of their use.[20] Increasingly, too, executives recognize that competitive rivalry can have a major and direct effect on the firm's financial performance:[21] Research shows that intensified rivalry within an industry results in decreased average profitability for the competing firms.[22]

Figure 5.2 presents a straightforward model of competitive rivalry at the firm level but such rivalry is usually dynamic and complex.[23] The competitive actions and responses the firm takes are the foundation for successfully building and using its capabilities and

FIGURE **5.2**   A Model of Competitive Rivalry

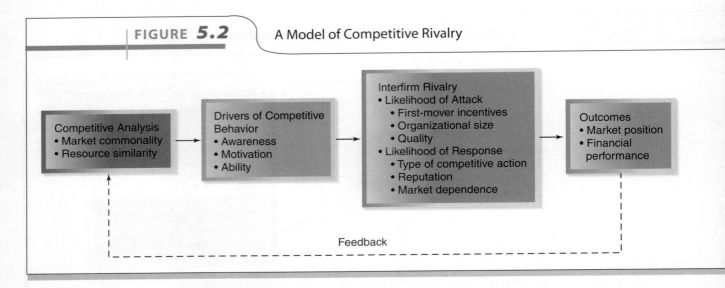

Source: Adapted from M.-J. Chen, 1996, Competitor analysis and interfirm rivalry: Toward a theoretical integration, *Academy of Management Review*, 21: 100–134.

core competencies to gain an advantageous market position.[24] The model in Figure 5.2 presents the sequence of activities commonly involved in competition between a particular firm and each of its competitors. Companies can use it to predict competitors' behavior (actions and responses) and reduce the uncertainty associated with competitors' actions.[25] Being able to predict competitors' actions and responses has a positive effect on the firm's market position and its subsequent financial performance.[26] The sum of all the individual rivalries modeled in Figure 5.2 that occur in a particular market reflects the competitive dynamics in that market.

The remainder of the chapter explains components of the model shown in Figure 5.2. We first describe market commonality and resource similarity as the building blocks of a competitor analysis. Next, we discuss the effects of three organizational characteristics—awareness, motivation, and ability—on the firm's competitive behavior. We then examine competitive rivalry between firms, or interfirm rivalry, in detail by describing the factors that affect the likelihood a firm will take a competitive action and the factors that affect the likelihood a firm will respond to a competitor's action. In the chapter's final section, we turn our attention to competitive dynamics to describe how market characteristics affect competitive rivalry in slow-cycle, fast-cycle, and standard-cycle markets.

Competitor Analysis

As previously noted, a competitor analysis is the first step the firm takes to be able to predict the extent and nature of its rivalry with each competitor. Recall that a competitor is a firm operating in the same market, offering similar products, and targeting similar customers. The number of markets in which firms compete against each other (called market commonality, defined below) and the similarity in their resources (called resource similarity, also defined below) determine the extent to which the firms are competitors. Firms with high market commonality and highly similar resources are "clearly direct and mutually acknowledged competitors."[27] However, being direct competitors does not necessarily mean that the rivalry between the firms will be intense. The drivers of competitive behavior—as well as factors influencing the likelihood that a competitor will initiate competitive actions and will respond to its competitor's competitive actions—influence the intensity of rivalry, even for direct competitors.[28]

In Chapter 2, we discussed competitor analysis as a technique firms use to understand their competitive environment. Together, the general, industry, and competitive environments comprise the firm's external environment. We also described how competitor analysis is used to help the firm *understand* its competitors. This understanding results from studying competitors' future objectives, current strategies, assumptions, and capabilities (see Figure 2.3). In this chapter, the discussion of competitor analysis is extended to describe what firms study to be able to *predict* competitors' behavior in the form of their competitive actions and responses. The discussions of competitor analysis in Chapter 2 and in this chapter are complementary in that firms must first *understand* competitors (Chapter 2) before their competitive actions and competitive responses can be *predicted* (this chapter).

Market Commonality

Each industry is composed of various markets. The financial services industry has markets for insurance, brokerage services, banks, and so forth. To concentrate on the needs of different, unique customer groups, markets can be further subdivided. The insurance market, for example, could be broken into market segments (such as commercial and consumer), product segments (such as health insurance and life insurance), and geographic markets (such as Western Europe and Southeast Asia). In general, the capabilities generated by the Internet's technology help to shape the nature of industries' markets along with the competition among firms operating in them.[29] For example, widely available electronic news sources affect how traditional print news distributors such as newspapers conduct their business.

In general, competitors agree about the different characteristics of individual markets that form an industry.[30] For example, in the transportation industry, there is an understanding that the commercial air travel market differs from the ground transportation market, which is served by such firms as Yellow Freight System and J.B. Hunt Transport Services Inc. Although differences exist, most industries' markets are somewhat related in terms of technologies used or core competencies needed to develop a competitive advantage.[31] For example, different types of transportation companies need to provide reliable and timely service. Commercial air carriers such as Southwest and JetBlue must therefore develop service competencies to satisfy their passengers, while Yellow Freight System and J.B. Hunt Transport Services Inc. must develop such competencies to serve the needs of those using their fleets to ship goods.

Firms competing in several markets, some of which may be in different industries, are likely to come into contact with a particular competitor several times,[32] a situation that involves the concept of market commonality. **Market commonality** is concerned with the number of markets with which the firm and a competitor are jointly involved and the degree of importance of the individual markets to each.[33] Firms competing against one another in several or many markets engage in multimarket competition.[34] McDonald's and Burger King compete against each other in multiple geographic markets across the world,[35] while Prudential and Cigna compete against each other in several market segments (such as institutional and retail) as well as product markets (such as life insurance and health insurance).[36] Airlines, chemicals, pharmaceuticals, and consumer foods are examples of other industries in which firms often simultaneously engage each other in competition in multiple markets.

Firms competing in several markets have the potential to respond to a competitor's actions not only within the market in which the actions are taken, but also in other markets where they compete with the rival. This potential creates a complicated competitive mosaic in which "the moves an organization makes in one market are designed to achieve goals in another market in ways that aren't immediately apparent to its rivals."[37] This potential complicates the rivalry between competitors. In fact, research suggests that "a firm with greater multimarket contact is less likely to initiate an attack, but more likely to move (respond) aggressively when attacked."[38] Thus, in general, multimarket competition reduces competitive rivalry.[39]

Resource Similarity

Resource similarity is the extent to which the firm's tangible and intangible resources are comparable to a competitor's in terms of both type and amount.[40] Firms with similar types and amounts of resources are likely to have similar strengths and weaknesses and use similar strategies.[41] The competition between Sony and Toshiba to establish the standard format for high-definition DVDs demonstrates these expectations. It is similar to the original battle they fought in the 1990s on DVDs, which ended in a draw with each firm sharing in the royalties from DVD sales. In the current battle, Sony has considerable support from major consumer electronics firms such as Matsushita, Samsung, Apple, Dell, and entertainment giant Walt Disney. Toshiba has powerful support from Intel, NEC, and many of the movie studios such as Paramount and Warner Bros. Pictures. They could compromise and pool their patents, but each firm would prefer to win the battle because of the significant returns a victory would provide.[42] Sony and Toshiba each serve only part of the market; yet establishing one standard requires that one firm wins and one firm loses. In other words, with one standard, one of the firms would serve the whole market. Additionally, they each have strong technological capabilities and the financial resources to develop the technology further as needed. In this case, intangible resources such as firm reputation could play a significant role in deciding the outcome of the competition between these companies.[43]

When performing a competitor analysis, a firm analyzes each of its competitors in terms of market commonality and resource similarity. The results of these analyses can be mapped for visual comparisons. In Figure 5.3, we show different hypothetical intersections between the firm and individual competitors in terms of market commonality and resource similarity. These intersections indicate the extent to which the firm and those with which it is compared are competitors.[44] For example, the firm and its competitor displayed in quadrant I of Figure 5.3 have similar types and amounts of resources (that is, the two firms have a similar portfolio of resources). The firm and its competitor in quadrant I would use their similar resource portfolios to compete against each other in many markets that are important to each. These conditions lead to the conclusion that the firms modeled in quadrant I are direct and mutually acknowledged competitors (e.g., Sony and Toshiba). In contrast, the firm and its competitor shown in quadrant III share few markets and have little similarity in their resources, indicating that they aren't direct and mutually acknowledged competitors. The firm's mapping of its competitive relationship with rivals is fluid as firms enter and exit markets and as companies' resources change in type and amount. Thus, the companies with which the firm is a direct competitor change across time.

Toyota Motor Corp. and General Motors (GM) have high market commonality, as they compete in many of the same global markets. In years past, the companies also had similar types and quantities of resources. This is changing, though, in that the companies' resources are becoming dissimilar, especially in terms of profitability and sales revenue. In fact, the companies are moving in opposite directions—Toyota's sales and

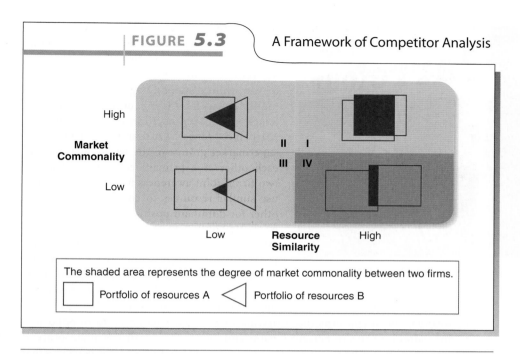

FIGURE 5.3 A Framework of Competitor Analysis

High

Market Commonality

II I

III IV

Low

Low   **Resource Similarity**   High

The shaded area represents the degree of market commonality between two firms.

☐ Portfolio of resources A   ◁ Portfolio of resources B

Source: Adapted from M.-J. Chen, 1996, Competitor analysis and interfirm rivalry: Toward a theoretical integration, *Academy of Management Review,* 21: 100–134.

profits are increasing while GM's sales and profits are decreasing. Thus, quadrant II in Figure 5.3 captures the degree to which Toyota and GM are direct competitors. In the Strategic Focus, we suggest the possibility that some of Toyota's recent competitive actions, such as moving into new international markets, are likely to increase the competition between Toyota and GM hastening GM's decline.

How will GM respond to the possibility of increased competition from Toyota in the global market? The challenge is daunting, in that it is difficult if not impossible to "out-Toyota Toyota."[45] Yet Toyota's chairman, Hiroshi Okuda, is worried about GM's weakness. While Toyota has targeted becoming the world's leading auto manufacturer, its managers are concerned that if GM is hurt too badly, there could be a public and political backlash in the United States, leading to restrictions on Toyota's actions in the U.S. market. Most analysts argue, however, that protectionism will only make firms weaker; market competition forces them to strengthen their capabilities. In so doing they will become more competitive over time.[46]

Drivers of Competitive Actions and Responses

As shown in Figure 5.2, market commonality and resource similarity influence the drivers (awareness, motivation, and ability) of competitive behavior. In turn, the drivers influence the firm's competitive behavior, as shown by the actions and responses it takes while engaged in competitive rivalry.[47]

Awareness, which is a prerequisite to any competitive action or response taken by a firm, refers to the extent to which competitors recognize the degree of their mutual

French supermarket chain Carrefour is aware of Wal-Mart as a primary competitor.

interdependence that results from market commonality and resource similarity.[48] Awareness tends to be greatest when firms have highly similar resources (in terms of types and amounts) to use while competing against each other in multiple markets. All U.S. airlines are aware of Southwest as a competitor, and certainly Wal-Mart and France's Carrefour, the two largest supermarket groups in the world, are aware of each other as a primary competitor. The last two firms' joint awareness has increased as they use similar resources to compete against each other for dominant positions in multiple European and South American markets.[49] Awareness affects the extent to which the firm understands the consequences of its competitive actions and responses. A lack of awareness can lead to excessive competition, resulting in a negative effect on all competitors' performance.[50]

Motivation, which concerns the firm's incentive to take action or to respond to a competitor's attack, relates to perceived gains and losses. Thus, a firm may be aware of competitors but may not be motivated to engage in rivalry with them if it perceives that its position will not improve or that its market position won't be damaged if it doesn't respond.[51]

Market commonality affects the firm's perceptions and resulting motivation. For example, all else being equal, the firm is more likely to attack the rival with whom it has low market commonality than the one with whom it competes in multiple markets. The primary reason is that there are high stakes involved in trying to gain a more advantageous position over a rival with whom the firm shares many markets. As we mentioned earlier, multimarket competition can find a competitor responding to the firm's action in a market different from the one in which the initial action was taken. Actions and responses of this type can cause both firms to lose focus on core markets and to battle each other with resources that had been allocated for other purposes. Because of the high stakes of competition under the condition of market commonality, there is a high probability that the attacked firm will respond to its competitor's action in an effort to protect its position in one or more markets.[52]

In some instances, the firm may be aware of the large number of markets it shares with a competitor and may be motivated to respond to an attack by that competitor, but it lacks the ability to do so. *Ability* relates to each firm's resources and the flexibility they provide. Without available resources (such as financial capital and people), the firm lacks the ability to attack a competitor or respond to its actions. However, similar resources suggest similar abilities to attack and respond. When a firm faces a competitor with similar resources, careful study of a possible attack before initiating it is essential because the similarly resourced competitor is likely to respond to that action.[53]

Resource *dissimilarity* also influences competitive actions and responses between firms, in that "the greater is the resource imbalance between the acting firm and competitors or potential responders, the greater will be the delay in response"[54] by the firm with a resource disadvantage. For example, Wal-Mart initially used a focused cost leadership strategy to compete only in small communities (those with a population of 25,000 or less). Using sophisticated logistics systems and extremely efficient purchasing practices as advantages, among others, Wal-Mart created what was at that time a new type of value (primarily in the form of wide selections of products at the lowest competitive prices) for customers in small retail markets. Local competitors lacked the ability

PART 2 / Strategic Actions: Strategy Formulation

Is General Motors Stuck in the 1970s?

At times it seems that General Motors (GM) operates as if it is still in the 1970s, when its market share was over 50 percent. In 2005 GM remained the largest auto manufacturer in the world, but second-place Toyota is gaining fast. Its competitive actions in recent years to produce exceptionally high quality and differentiated automobiles, sell them in multiple product segments (e.g., luxury, small fuel efficient, and moderate cost) and expand sales all over the world (e.g., Europe, China) have increased its growth and enhanced its market share. GM's annual sales are the fifth largest in the world across all industries, but the company is faltering. In 2005, its market share was only slightly above 25 percent and it was on track to have a net loss of billions of dollars.

GM's problems are many. Importantly, managerial hubris led the firm to use tunnel vision in formulating its strategies, and the firm did not respond effectively (or at all) to major changes in the auto industry. One analyst commented that "GM has found itself stuck in second gear for a quarter of a century." It did not respond quickly or effectively to the earlier popularity of compact cars or to the more recent trend toward hybrid vehicles. It has negotiated poorly with unions, incurring massive costs and future liabilities. Because of these contractual cost requirements, it has accepted compromises in car design and engineering. The result has been automobiles with outdated designs for the marketplace, unable to compete with more attractive designs from competitors. According to one analyst, "The bedrock principle upon which GM was built—offering a car to feed every market segment—has degraded into a series of contrived brands, most with little identity, and bland, overlapping product lines."

GM has two major assets at present, a well-known brand name and cash. Unfortunately, the brand name has begun to suffer because of poor designs and weak quality relative to competitors and cash must be invested wisely if it is to be of value other than keeping a firm out of bankruptcy court. While the decline in sales and profits show the need to shut down plants and reduce production, GM cannot do so. Its union contracts require that all plants be operated at no less than 80 percent capacity.

GM's executives have also shown a penchant for poor strategic decisions and an inability to capitalize on opportunities. For example, GM was an early mover into China. It has invested more than $1 billion in China since 1998, but due to intense competition in 2005, it experienced a 35 percent decline in sales in Shanghai, the largest auto market in the country. In contrast, Hyundai and a local company, Chery, had substantial sales increases in this market. Simply put, these competitors have done a better job of designing and manufacturing cars that Chinese consumers desire.

Addressing the continuing reductions in performance, GM's CEO, Rick Wagoner, implied that the company was not making the progress needed, partly because of the "intense competitive conditions and pricing pressures." Further, he suggests that GM must increase its efficiency and productivity.

Although GM entered China early, it saw sales drop by 35 percent in 2005.

Sources: J. B. White, 2005, General Motors swings to loss on weakness in North America, *Wall Street Journal*, July 20, www.wsj.com; M. Ihlwan & J. B. Bush, 2005, Hyundai: Crowding into the fast lane, *Business Week*, June 20, www.businessweek .com; D. Welch & D. Beucke, 2005, Why GM's plan won't work, *Business Week*, May 9, www.businessweek.com; D. Roberts, 2005, First-mover disadvantage, *Business Week*, May 9, www.businessweek.com; J.W. Peters, 2005, Ford and G.M. suffer as buyers shun S.U.V.'s, *New York Times*, May 4, www.nytimes.com; P. Hjelt, 2005, World's most admired companies, *Fortune*, March 1, www.fortune.com.

to marshal needed resources at the pace required to respond quickly and effectively. However, even when facing competitors with greater resources (greater ability) or more attractive market positions, firms should eventually respond, no matter how daunting the task seems.[55] Choosing not to respond can ultimately result in failure, as happened with at least some local retailers who didn't respond to Wal-Mart's competitive actions.

As explained in the Strategic Focus, GM was once the market leader but now is having trouble competing in the global auto market. In the near future, Toyota is likely to exceed GM as the largest auto maker in the world. Some speculate whether GM can survive and compete effectively over time. In a disadvantageous competitive position, firms might best try to serve a special niche in the market to avoid direct competition.[56] Those serving market niches effectively often enjoy positive performance outcomes. Unfortunately, GM attempts to serve the broader market. and so is unlikely to have a positive future unless major changes are made.

Competitive Rivalry

The ongoing competitive action/response sequence between a firm and a competitor affects the performance of both firms;[57] thus it is important for companies to carefully study competitive rivalry to select and implement successful strategies. Understanding a competitor's awareness, motivation, and ability helps the firm to predict the likelihood of an attack by that competitor and the probability that a competitor will respond to actions taken against it.

As we described earlier, the predictions drawn from studying competitors in terms of awareness, motivation, and ability are grounded in market commonality and resource similarity. These predictions are fairly general. The value of the final set of predictions the firm develops about each of its competitors' competitive actions and responses is enhanced by studying the "Likelihood of Attack" factors (such as first-mover incentives and organizational size) and the "Likelihood of Response" factors (such as the actor's reputation) that are shown in Figure 5.2. Evaluating and understanding these factors allows the firm to refine the predictions it makes about its competitors' actions and responses.

Strategic and Tactical Actions

Firms use both strategic and tactical actions when forming their competitive actions and competitive responses in the course of engaging in competitive rivalry.[58] A **competitive action** is a strategic or tactical action the firm takes to build or defend its competitive advantages or improve its market position. A **competitive response** is a strategic or tactical action the firm takes to counter the effects of a competitor's competitive action. A **strategic action or a strategic response** is a market-based move that involves a significant commitment of organizational resources and is difficult to implement and reverse. A **tactical action or a tactical response** is a market-based move that is taken to fine-tune a strategy; it involves fewer resources and is relatively easy to implement and reverse. Hyundai Motor Co.'s expenditures on research and development and plant expansion to support the firm's desire to be one of the world's largest carmakers by 2010, selling at least one million units annually in the United States,[59] are strategic actions. Likewise, Boeing Corp.'s decision to commit the resources required to build the super-efficient 787 midsized jetliner for delivery in 2008[60] demonstrates a strategic action. Changes in airfares are somewhat frequently announced by airlines. As tactical actions that are easily reversed, pricing decisions are often taken by these firms to increase demand in certain markets during certain periods.

Coca-Cola Company, PepsiCo Inc., and Nestlé SA are aware of one another as they compete in the bottled water market. Moreover, this awareness influences the competitive actions and responses these firms initiate as they engage in competitive rivalry. Of course, bottled water isn't the only product category (outside of soft drinks) in which multimarket competitors Coca-Cola and PepsiCo compete against each other. Because of the degree of their market commonality and resource similarity and the fact that they engage in multimarket competition, Coca-Cola and PepsiCo will continue to carefully monitor each other's competitive actions and responses in multiple product areas as part of their competitive rivalry.

Likelihood of Attack

In addition to market commonality, resource similarity, and the drivers of awareness, motivation, and ability, other factors affect the likelihood a competitor will use strategic actions and tactical actions to attack its competitors. Three of these factors—first-mover incentives, organizational size, and quality—are discussed next.

First-Mover Incentives

A **first mover** is a firm that takes an initial competitive action in order to build or defend its competitive advantages or to improve its market position. The first-mover concept has been influenced by the work of the famous economist Joseph Schumpeter, who argued that firms achieve competitive advantage by taking innovative actions[61] (innovation is defined and described in detail in Chapter 13). In general, first movers "allocate funds for product innovation and development, aggressive advertising, and advanced research and development."[62]

The benefits of being a successful first mover can be substantial. Especially in fast-cycle markets (discussed later in the chapter), where changes occur rapidly and where it is virtually impossible to sustain a competitive advantage for any length of time, "a first mover may experience five to ten times the valuation and revenue of a second mover."[63] This evidence suggests that although first-mover benefits are never absolute, they are often critical to firm success in industries experiencing rapid technological developments and relatively short product life cycles.[64] In addition to earning above-average returns until its competitors respond to its successful competitive action, the first mover can gain (1) the loyalty of customers who may become committed to the goods or services of the firm that first made them available and (2) market share that can be difficult for competitors to take during future competitive rivalry.[65] The general evidence that first movers have greater survival rates than later market entrants[66] is perhaps the culmination of first-mover benefits.

The firm trying to predict its competitors' competitive actions might conclude that they will take aggressive strategic actions to gain first movers' benefits. However, while a firm's competitors might be motivated to be first movers, they may lack the ability to do so. First movers tend to be aggressive and willing to experiment with innovation and take higher, yet reasonable, levels of risk.[67] To be a first mover, the firm must have readily available the resources to significantly invest in R&D as well as to rapidly and successfully produce and market a stream of innovative products.[68]

Organizational slack makes it possible for firms to have the ability (as measured by available resources) to be first movers. *Slack* is the buffer or cushion provided by actual or obtainable resources that aren't currently in use and are in excess of the minimum resources needed to produce a given level of organizational output.[69] In 2005, many of the large oil companies, such as ExxonMobil, had considerable slack resources: With oil prices in excess of $70 per barrel, they had significant amounts of cash on hand.

As a liquid resource, slack can quickly be allocated to support the competitive actions, such as R&D investments and aggressive marketing campaigns that lead to first-mover benefits. This relationship between slack and the ability to be a first mover allows the firm to predict that a competitor who is a first mover likely has available slack and will probably take aggressive competitive actions to continuously introduce innovative products. Furthermore, the firm can predict that as a first mover, a competitor will try to rapidly gain market share and customer loyalty in order to earn above-average returns until its competitors are able to effectively respond to its first move.

Firms evaluating their competitors should realize that being a first mover carries risk. For example, it is difficult to accurately estimate the returns that will be earned from introducing product innovations to the marketplace.[70] Additionally, the first mover's cost to develop a product innovation can be substantial, reducing the slack available to it to support further innovation. Thus, the firm should carefully study the results a competitor achieves as a first mover. Continuous success by the competitor suggests additional product innovations, while lack of product acceptance over the course of the competitor's innovations may indicate less willingness in the future to accept the risks of being a first mover.

A **second mover** is a firm that responds to the first mover's competitive action, typically through imitation. More cautious than the first mover, the second mover studies customers' reactions to product innovations. In the course of doing so, the second mover also tries to find any mistakes the first mover made so that it can avoid them and the problems they created. Often, successful imitation of the first mover's innovations allows the second mover "to avoid both the mistakes and the huge spending of the pioneers [first movers]."[71]

Second movers also have the time to develop processes and technologies that are more efficient than those used by the first mover.[72] Greater efficiencies could result in lower costs for the second mover. American Home Mortgage Holdings Inc. (AHMH) is a second mover with its Internet-based offering, MortgageSelect.com. In the words of the firm's CEO, being the second mover allowed it "to see where other firms had failed." Based on its observations of earlier Internet mortgage market entrants, AHMH decided not to brand its own services (instead providing mortgages for other companies) and has fine-tuned the offering of a "high-touch" call center to support its Web site.[73] Overall, the outcomes of the first mover's competitive actions may provide an effective blueprint for second and even late movers as they determine the nature and timing of their competitive responses.[74]

Determining that a competitor is an effective second mover (based on its past actions) allows a first-mover firm to predict that the competitor will respond quickly to successful, innovation-based market entries. The first mover can expect a successful second-mover competitor to study its market entries and to respond with its own new entry into the market within a short time period. As a second mover, the competitor will try to respond with a product that provides greater customer value than does the first mover's product. The most successful second movers are able to rapidly and meaningfully interpret market feedback to respond quickly, yet successfully, to the first mover's successful innovations.

A **late mover** is a firm that responds to a competitive action a significant amount of time after the first mover's action and the second mover's response. Typically, a late response is better than no response at all, although any success achieved from the late competitive response tends to be considerably less than that achieved by first and second movers. Thus, the firm competing against a late mover can predict that the competitor will likely enter a particular market only after both the first and second movers have achieved success in that market. Moreover, on a relative basis, the firm can predict that the late mover's competitive action will allow it to earn average returns only after the considerable time required for it to understand how to create at least as much customer value as that offered by the first and second movers' products. Although exceptions exist, most of the late mover's competitive actions will be ineffective relative to those initiated by first and second movers.

Organizational Size

An organization's size affects the likelihood that it will take competitive actions as well as the types of actions it will take and their timing.[75] In general, small firms are more likely than large companies to launch competitive actions and tend to do it more quickly. Smaller firms are thus perceived as nimble and flexible competitors who rely on speed and surprise to defend their competitive advantages or develop new ones while engaged in competitive rivalry, especially with large companies, to gain an advantageous market position.[76] Small firms' flexibility and nimbleness allow them to develop variety in their competitive actions; large firms tend to limit the types of competitive actions used.[77]

Large firms, however, are likely to initiate more competitive actions along with more strategic actions during a given period.[78] Thus, when studying its competitors in terms of organizational size, the firm should use a measurement such as total sales revenue or total number of employees. The competitive actions the firm likely will encounter from competitors larger than it is will be different than the competitive actions it will encounter from competitors that are smaller.

The organizational-size factor adds another layer of complexity. When engaging in competitive rivalry, the firm often prefers a large number of unique competitive actions. Ideally, the organization has the amount of slack resources held by a large firm to launch a greater *number* of competitive actions and a small firm's flexibility to launch a greater *variety* of competitive actions. Herb Kelleher, cofounder and former CEO of Southwest Airlines, addressed this matter: "Think and act big and we'll get smaller. Think and act small and we'll get bigger."[79]

In the context of competitive rivalry, Kelleher's statement can be interpreted to mean that relying on a limited number or types of competitive actions (which is the large firm's tendency) can lead to reduced competitive success across time, partly because competitors learn how to effectively respond to the predictable. In contrast, remaining flexible and nimble (which is the small firm's tendency) in order to develop and use a wide variety of competitive actions contributes to success against rivals.

Wal-Mart is a large firm that has the flexibility required to take many types of competitive actions. With almost \$288 billion in sales revenue in 2004, Wal-Mart is the world's largest company.

Herb Kelleher, cofounder and former CEO of Southwest Airlines.

In less than a decade, Wal-Mart has become one of the largest grocery retailers in the United States. This accomplishment demonstrates Wal-Mart's ability to successfully compete against its various rivals, even long-established grocers. Not far behind Wal-Mart in 2004 sales revenue were British Petroleum ($285 billion in sales), ExxonMobil ($271 billion in sales), and Royal Dutch Shell ($269 billion in sales), all large oil companies.[80]

Analysts believe that Wal-Mart's tactical actions are as critical to its success as its strategic actions and that its tactical actions demonstrate a great deal of flexibility. For example, "every humble store worker has the power to lower the price on any Wal-Mart product if he spots it cheaper elsewhere."[81] Decision-making responsibility and authority have been delegated to the level of the individual worker to make certain that the firm's cost leadership business-level strategy always results in the lowest prices for customers. Managers and employees both spend a good deal of time thinking about additional strategic and tactical actions, respectively, that might enhance the firm's performance. Wal-Mart has met the expectation suggested by Kelleher's statement, in that it is a large firm that "remains stuck to its small-town roots" in order to think and act like the small firm capable of using a wide variety of competitive actions. Wal-Mart is continuing to apply this type of thinking to its major expansion in China. In 2005, China is building 15 new stores, including supercenters in Beijing and Shanghai.[82] Wal-Mart's competitors might feel confident in predicting that the firm's competitive actions will be a combination of the tendencies shown by small and large companies.

Quality

Quality has many definitions, including well-established ones relating it to the production of goods or services with zero defects[83] and seeing it as a never-ending cycle of continuous improvement.[84] From a strategic perspective, we consider quality to be an outcome of how the firm completes primary and support activities (see Chapter 3). Thus, **quality** exists when the firm's goods or services meet or exceed customers' expectations. Some evidence suggests that quality may be the most critical component in satisfying the firm's customers.[85]

In the eyes of customers, quality is about doing the right things relative to performance measures that are important to them.[86] Customers may be interested in measuring the quality of a firm's goods and services against a broad range of dimensions. Sample quality dimensions in which customers commonly express an interest are shown in Table 5.1. Quality is possible only when top-level managers support it and when its importance is institutionalized throughout the entire organization.[87] When quality is institutionalized and valued by all, employees and managers alike become vigilant about continuously finding ways to improve quality.[88]

Quality is a universal theme in the global economy and is a necessary but not sufficient condition for competitive success.[89] Without quality, a firm's products lack credibility, meaning that customers don't think of them as viable options. Indeed, customers won't consider buying a product until they believe that it can satisfy at least their base-level expectations in terms of quality dimensions that are important to them. Quality is important for firm performance. For example, innovative new products lead to higher firm performance only when they are of high quality.[90]

Quality affects competitive rivalry. The firm evaluating a competitor whose products suffer from poor quality can predict that the competitor's sales revenue will likely decline until the quality issues are resolved. In addition, the firm can predict that the competitor likely won't be aggressive in its competitive actions until the quality problems are corrected in order to gain credibility with customers. However, after the problems are corrected, that competitor is likely to take more aggressive competitive actions. Hyundai Motor Co.'s experiences illustrate these expectations.

Quality Dimensions of Goods and Services

TABLE 5.1

Product Quality Dimensions

1. *Performance*—Operating characteristics
2. *Features*—Important special characteristics
3. *Flexibility*—Meeting operating specifications over some period of time
4. *Durability*—Amount of use before performance deteriorates
5. *Conformance*—Match with preestablished standards
6. *Serviceability*—Ease and speed of repair
7. *Aesthetics*—How a product looks and feels
8. *Perceived quality*—Subjective assessment of characteristics (product image)

Service Quality Dimensions

1. *Timeliness*—Performed in the promised period of time
2. *Courtesy*—Performed cheerfully
3. *Consistency*—Giving all customers similar experiences each time
4. *Convenience*—Accessibility to customers
5. *Completeness*—Fully serviced, as required
6. *Accuracy*—Performed correctly each time

Sources: Adapted from J. W. Dean, Jr., & J. R. Evans, 1994, *Total Quality: Management, Organization and Society,* St. Paul, MN: West Publishing Company; H. V. Roberts & B. F. Sergesketter, 1993, *Quality Is Personal,* New York: The Free Press; D. Garvin, 1988, *Managed Quality: The Strategic and Competitive Edge,* New York: The Free Press.

Immediately upon becoming CEO of Hyundai Motor Co. in March 1999, Mong Koo Chung started touring the firm's manufacturing facilities. Appalled at what he saw, he told workers and managers alike, "The only way we can survive is to raise our quality to Toyota's level."[91] To dramatically improve quality, a quality-control unit was established, and significant resources (over $1 billion annually) were allocated to research and development (R&D) in order to build cars that could compete on price and deliver on quality. Today, quality is still viewed as the firm's number one priority.[92] In 2003, the director of automotive quality research at J.D. Power observed, "Since 1998, Hyundai is the most improved car in the initial quality survey. They have dropped their number of quality problems by 50 percent."[93] Signaling a strong belief in its products' quality, Hyundai offers a 10-year drive-train warranty in the United States, which the firm has selected as a key market. As noted in the earlier Strategic Focus, Hyundai is taking market share from GM in the Chinese market.[94] Improvements to the quality of Hyundai's products helped the firm to become a more aggressive competitor.

Thanks to its focus on quality, Hyundai is considered the most improved car since 1998.

REUTERS/HENNY RAY ABRAMS/LANDOV

Likelihood of Response

The success of a firm's competitive action is affected by the likelihood that a competitor will respond to it as well as by the type (strategic or tactical) and effectiveness of that response. As noted earlier, a competitive response is a strategic or tactical action the firm takes to counter the effects of a competitor's competitive action. In general, a firm is likely to respond to a competitor's action when (1) the action leads to better use of the competitor's capabilities to gain or produce stronger competitive advantages or an improvement in its market position, (2) the action damages the firm's ability to use its capabilities to create or maintain an advantage, or (3) the firm's market position becomes less defensible.[95]

In addition to market commonality and resource similarity and awareness, motivation, and ability, firms evaluate three other factors—type of competitive action, reputation, and market dependence—to predict how a competitor is likely to respond to competitive actions (see Figure 5.2).

Type of Competitive Action

Competitive responses to strategic actions differ from responses to tactical actions. These differences allow the firm to predict a competitor's likely response to a competitive action that has been launched against it. In general, strategic actions receive strategic responses and tactical actions receive tactical responses.

In general, strategic actions elicit fewer total competitive responses because strategic responses, such as market-based moves, involve a significant commitment of resources and are difficult to implement and reverse.[96] Moreover, the time needed for a strategic action to be implemented and its effectiveness assessed delays the competitor's response to that action.[97] In contrast, a competitor likely will respond quickly to a tactical action, such as when an airline company almost immediately matches a competitor's tactical action of reducing prices in certain markets. Either strategic actions or tactical actions that target a large number of a rival's customers are likely to elicit strong responses.[98] In fact, if the effects of a competitor's strategic action on the focal firm are significant (e.g., loss of market share, loss of major resources such as critical employees), a response is likely to be swift and strong.[99]

Actor's Reputation

In the context of competitive rivalry, an *actor* is the firm taking an action or a response while *reputation* is "the positive or negative attribute ascribed by one rival to another based on past competitive behavior."[100] A positive reputation may be a source of above-average returns, especially for consumer goods producers.[101] Thus, a positive corporate reputation is of strategic value[102] and affects competitive rivalry. To predict the likelihood of a competitor's response to a current or planned action, firms evaluate the responses that the competitor has taken previously when attacked—past behavior is assumed to a predictor of future behavior.

Competitors are more likely to respond to strategic or tactical actions when they are taken by a market leader.[103] In particular, evidence suggests that commonly successful actions, especially strategic actions, will be quickly imitated. For example, although a second mover, IBM committed significant resources to enter the PC market. When IBM was immediately successful in this endeavor, competitors such as Dell, Compaq, and Gateway responded with strategic actions to enter the market. IBM's reputation as well as its successful strategic action strongly influenced entry by these competitors. Today, though, Dell is the PC market leader and a strong performer (IBM is a much smaller force in the market); in 2005, Dell was chosen as *Fortune*'s "Most Admired Corporation" in the United States.[104] Competitors now target Dell as the market leader.

In contrast to a firm with a strong reputation, such as IBM, competitors are less likely to take responses against a company with a reputation for competitive behavior that is risky, complex, and unpredictable. The firm with a reputation as a price predator (an actor that frequently reduces prices to gain or maintain market share) generates few responses to its pricing tactical actions because price predators, which typically increase prices once their market share objective is reached, lack credibility with their competitors.[105]

Dependence on the Market

Market dependence denotes the extent to which a firm's revenues or profits are derived from a particular market.[106] In general, firms can predict that competitors with high market dependence are likely to respond strongly to attacks threatening their market position.[107] Interestingly, the threatened firm in these instances may not always respond quickly, although an effective response to an attack on the firm's position in a critical market is very important.

Boeing and Airbus each have significant shares of the global passenger airplane market. They also compete in another market, airplane defense contracts. When an opportunity is presented to one, the other is likely to be a competitor in the same market and for specific contracts. For example, in 2005 the U.S. Air Force was considering replacing its aging fleet of aerial tankers used for refueling aircraft in the air. Given that the Air Force has 540 of these aircraft, the contract is likely to be lucrative. Boeing and Airbus are aggressively competing for the opportunity to receive the contract for the new fleet because they depend greatly on the aircraft industry. These two firms are the primary competitors so that when one receives a contract, it normally means that the other one lost out.[108] Similarly, there is significant competition in the luxury automobile market. A few years ago, Mercedes introduced a series of new "classes" of its luxury automobile. BMW, whose performance is similar to Mercedes' and who is substantially dependent on its success in the luxury auto market, followed by introducing its own new series. Mercedes recently announced a new generation of its M-Class autos. Given that the new series of vehicles represents an upgrade, it will be interesting to see if BMW and other competitors (e.g., Lexus) respond.[109]

Coca-Cola has been losing its competitive capabilities over the last few years. It seems unable to defend its market position against attacks made by PepsiCo, even though it is highly dependent on the beverage market. Since the death of its highly regarded CEO, Roberto Goizueta, in 1997, Coca-Cola has struggled through a series of CEOs and other top executives. As a result of this turmoil, and because PepsiCo made the right competitive moves by introducing valued new products, PepsiCo has gained in the market and is earning profits while Coke's profits are falling along with its fortunes. Coke's current CEO, Neville Isdell, is trying to meet the challenge by advertising heavily to support existing brands and by introducing new products. We must now observe how the competition between Coke and Pepsi plays out over time to see the results of the competitive actions and reponses between these major competitors.

The Continuing Saga of Coke and Pepsi Competition: Has Coke Fizzled While Pepsi Popped the Top?

In 2004, the Coca-Cola Company named a new CEO, but some referred to it as another public spectacle by Coke. Procter & Gamble's CEO, A.G. Lafley, called it one of the strangest processes he had observed. After the unsuccessful tenure of a couple of short-term CEOs and a controversial tenure, Neville Isdell was brought out of retirement to become Coke's CEO in 2004. The once vaunted company had fallen on hard times.

In 1998 Coca-Cola was considered a crown jewel, one of the best-known brands in the world. Since that time, however, the company has experienced a number of unsettling dysfunctional actions (some would call them management blunders). The musical chairs in the top executive jobs and the "good old boys" on the board of directors, which one analyst refers to as the "Coca-Cola Keiretsu," have added to the company's problems. In the period 2000–2005, the 13 highest-level executives in the company all left their jobs, suggesting chaos at the top of the company.

Coca-Cola has gone flat and needs a new formula. In the first quarter of 2005, Coke reported an 11 percent decline in profits because of continuing weak sales in North America and Europe. In contrast, PepsiCo reported a 13 percent increase in profits for the second quarter of 2005. These results for PepsiCo exceeded predictions by Wall Street analysts. PepsiCo attributed the profits increase to continued aggressive investments in North American beverages and in its international business operations, and its plan to increase these investments still further in future quarters. This may spell further trouble for Coca-Cola. Both companies are heavily dependent on their beverage businesses, although PepsiCo has significant snack food operations as well. The increases in PepsiCo's business in North American and international markets likely has come at least partly at the benefit of Coca-Cola losses. PepsiCo has reported strong increases in drinks and snack food sales in India, China, Russia, Turkey, Argentina, and the Middle East. It reported significant jumps in the sales of noncarbonated beverages. Neville Isdell, Coke's CEO, recognizes the challenges ahead of him. He says the "system isn't broken," with which some analysts might quarrel. However, he is investing heavily in advertising to shore up Coke's stronger brands and also investing in new drinks as well.

One analyst pointed out that Coca-Cola has not produced a successful new soda brand since 1982. Consultant Tom Pirko recommends that the company invest heavily in developing new brands and new icons. He believes the firm needs to take some risks again so that consumers will once more become excited about Coke products. Perhaps Isdell has been listening, because in 2005 Coke invested in the no-calorie market with Coca-Cola Zero; it acquired a majority stake in a milk drinks firm; it bought a stake in a Danone bottled-water venture; and it began distributing a new citrus-flavored drink and the Rockstar energy drink. Only time will tell if this is enough to overcome PepsiCo's big push in new products such as Pepsi Lime, Pepsi One, and Propel fitness water.

Coke is branching out in an effort to stop declining sales and catch up to Pepsi.

DANIEL ACKER/BLOOMBERG NEWS/LANDOV

Sources: A. K. Walker, 2005, Coca-Cola zeros in on growing no-calorie soda market, *Nashua Telegraph,* July 17, www.nashuatelegraph.com; 2005, Coca-Cola to acquire majority stake in milk drinks firm, *Rednova News,* July 15, www.rednova.com; 2005, Pepsi profit up 13% in quarter, *Los Angeles Times,* July 13, www.latimes.com; B. Morris, 2004, Coca-Cola: The Real Story, *Fortune,* May 17, www.fortune.com; C. Terhune, 2005, Coca-Cola plans to test new citrus-flavored soda, *Wall Street Journal,* April 28, www.wsj.com; C. Terhune, 2005, Coke, bottler to distribute Rockstar energy drink, *Wall Street Journal,* April 28, www.wsj.com; C. Terhune, 2005, Coke to buy stake from Danone in bottle-water joint venture, *Wall Street Journal,* April 25, www.wsj.com; C. Terhune, 2005, Coke's profit falls 11% as sales remain weak in North America, *Wall Street Journal,* April 20, www.wsj.com; Coca-Cola, 2005, The Coca-Cola Company announces changes to senior management and operating structure, March 23, www.2.coca-cola.com; D. Foust, 2004, Gone flat, *Business Week,* December 20, www.businessweek.com; M. Clayton, How to fix Coca-Cola, *Fast Company,* November, www.fastcompany.com.

Competitive Dynamics

Whereas competitive rivalry concerns the ongoing actions and responses between a firm and its competitors for an advantageous market position, competitive dynamics concerns the ongoing actions and responses taking place among *all* firms competing within a market for advantageous positions.

To explain competitive rivalry, we described (1) factors that determine the degree to which firms are competitors (market commonality and resource similarity), (2) the drivers of competitive behavior for individual firms (awareness, motivation, and ability) and (3) factors affecting the likelihood that a competitor will act or attack (first-mover incentives, organizational size, and quality) and respond (type of competitive action, reputation, and market dependence). Building and sustaining competitive advantages are at the core of competitive rivalry, in that advantages are the key to creating value for shareholders.[110]

To explain competitive dynamics, we discuss the effects of varying rates of competitive speed in different markets (called slow-cycle, fast-cycle, and standard-cycle markets, defined below) on the behavior (actions and responses) of all competitors within a given market. Competitive behaviors as well as the reasons or logic for taking them are similar within each market type, but differ across market type.[111] Thus, competitive dynamics differ in slow-cycle, fast-cycle, and standard-cycle markets. The sustainability of the firm's competitive advantages differs across the three market types.

As noted in Chapter 1, firms want to sustain their competitive advantages for as long as possible, although no advantage is permanently sustainable. The degree of sustainability is affected by how quickly competitive advantages can be imitated and how costly it is to do so.

Slow-Cycle Markets

Slow-cycle markets are those in which the firm's competitive advantages are shielded from imitation commonly for long periods of time and where imitation is costly.[112] Thus, competitive advantages are sustainable in slow-cycle markets.

Building a unique and proprietary capability produces a competitive advantage and success in a slow-cycle market. This type of advantage is difficult for competitors to understand. As discussed in Chapter 3, a difficult-to-understand and costly-to-imitate resource or capability usually results from unique historical conditions, causal ambiguity, and/or social complexity. Copyrights, geography, patents, and ownership of an information resource are examples of resources.[113] After a proprietary advantage is developed, the firm's competitive behavior in a slow-cycle market is oriented to protecting, maintaining, and extending that advantage. Thus, the competitive dynamics in slow-cycle markets usually concentrate on competitive actions and responses that enable firms to protect, maintain, and extend their competitive advantage. Major strategic actions in these markets, such acquisitions, usually carry less risk than in faster cycle markets.[114]

Walt Disney Co. continues to extend its proprietary characters, such as Mickey Mouse, Minnie Mouse, and Goofy. These characters have a unique historical development as a result of Walt and Roy Disney's creativity and vision for entertaining people. Products based on the characters seen in Disney's animated films are sold through Disney's theme park shops as well as freestanding retail outlets called Disney Stores. Because patents shield it, the proprietary nature of Disney's advantage in terms of animated characters protects the firm from imitation by competitors.

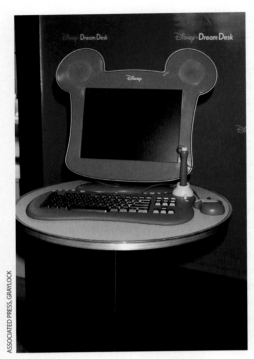

Disney has an advantage over its competitors because it can prevent imitation of products based on its characters, such as the computer pictured here.

Consistent with another attribute of competition in a slow-cycle market, Disney protects its exclusive rights to its characters and their use as shown by the fact that "the company once sued a day-care center, forcing it to remove the likeness of Mickey Mouse from a wall of the facility."[115] As with all firms competing in slow-cycle markets, Disney's competitive actions (such as building theme parks in France, Japan, and China) and responses (such as lawsuits to protect its right to fully control use of its animated characters) maintain and extend its proprietary competitive advantage while protecting it.

Patent laws and regulatory requirements such as those in the United States requiring FDA (Food and Drug Administration) approval to launch new products shield pharmaceutical companies' positions. Competitors in this market try to extend patents on their drugs to maintain advantageous positions that the patents provide. However, after a patent expires, the firm is no longer shielded from competition, allowing generic imitations and usually leading to a loss of sales.

As is true with Walt Disney Co., pharmaceutical companies aggressively pursue legal actions to protect their patents. This is demonstrated by recent actions taken by Pfizer Inc., the maker and seller of Lipitor, the world's most prescribed cholesterol-lowering drug. Pfizer filed a suit asking a judge to prohibit Ranbaxy from making and marketing Lipitor before Pfizer's 1987 U.S. patent expires in 2010. The stakes are high in these suits because Pfizer generates over $10 billion annually on Lipitor sales.[116] But it is a continuous battle; Pfizer lost a case in 2005 when the Australian patent office eliminated Pfizer's patent protection on Lipitor in a challenge filed by Ranbaxy. Also, in 2005, the U.S. Patent and Trademark Office ruled that one of Pfizer's several patents on Lipitor was based on invalid arguments.[117]

The competitive dynamics generated by firms competing in slow-cycle markets are shown in Figure 5.4. In slow-cycle markets, firms launch a product (e.g., a new drug) that has been developed through a proprietary advantage (e.g., R&D) and then exploit it for as long as possible while the product is shielded from competition. Eventually, competitors respond to the action with a counterattack. In markets for drugs, this counterattack commonly occurs as patents expire or are broken through legal means, creating the need for another product launch by the firm seeking a protected market position.

Fast-Cycle Markets

Fast-cycle markets are markets in which the firm's capabilities that contribute to competitive advantages aren't shielded from imitation and where imitation is often rapid and inexpensive. Thus, competitive advantages aren't sustainable in fast-cycle markets. Firms competing in fast-cycle markets recognize the importance of speed; these companies appreciate that "time is as precious a business resource as money or head count—and that the costs of hesitation and delay are just as steep as going over budget or missing a financial forecast."[118] Such high-velocity environments place considerable pressures on top managers to make strategic decisions quickly but they must also be effective.[119] The often substantial competition and technology-based strategic focus make the strategic decision complex, increasing the need for a comprehensive approach integrated with decision speed, two often-conflicting characteristics of the strategic decision process.[120]

Reverse engineering and the rate of technology diffusion in fast-cycle markets facilitate rapid imitation. A competitor uses reverse engineering to quickly gain the knowl-

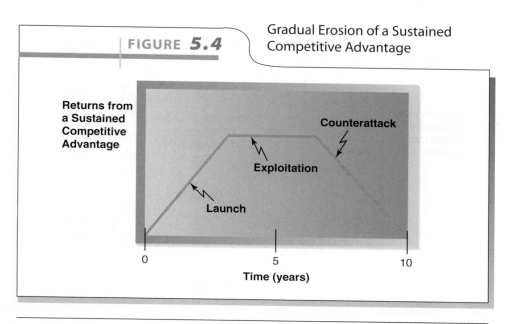

FIGURE 5.4 Gradual Erosion of a Sustained Competitive Advantage

Source: Adapted from I. C. MacMillan, 1988, Controlling competitive dynamics by taking strategic initiative, *Academy of Management Executive,* II(2): 111–118.

edge required to imitate or improve the firm's products. Technology is diffused rapidly in fast-cycle markets, making it available to competitors in a short period. The technology often used by fast-cycle competitors isn't proprietary, nor is it protected by patents as is the technology used by firms competing in slow-cycle markets. For example, only a few hundred parts, which are readily available on the open market, are required to build a PC. Patents protect only a few of these parts, such as microprocessor chips.[121]

Fast-cycle markets are more volatile than slow-cycle and standard-cycle markets. Indeed, the pace of competition in fast-cycle markets is almost frenzied, as companies rely on innovations as the engines of their growth. Because prices fall quickly in these markets, companies need to profit quickly from their product innovations. Imitation of many fast-cycle products is relatively easy, as demonstrated by Dell Inc. and Hewlett-Packard, along with a host of local PC vendors, that have partly or largely imitated IBM's PC design to create their products. Continuous declines in the costs of parts, as well as the fact that the information required to assemble a PC isn't especially complicated and is readily available, make it possible for additional competitors to enter this market without significant difficulty.[122]

The fast-cycle market characteristics described above make it virtually impossible for companies in this type of market to develop sustainable competitive advantages. Recognizing this, firms avoid "loyalty" to any of their products, preferring to cannibalize their own before competitors learn how to do so through successful imitation. This emphasis creates competitive dynamics that differ substantially from those found in slow-cycle markets. Instead of concentrating on protecting, maintaining, and extending competitive advantages, as in slow-cycle markets, companies competing in fast-cycle markets focus on learning how to rapidly and continuously develop new competitive advantages that are superior to those they replace. Commonly, they search for fast and effective means of developing new products. For example, it is common in some industries for firms to use strategic alliances to gain access to new technologies and thereby develop and introduce more new products into the market.[123]

The competitive behavior of firms competing in fast-cycle markets is shown in Figure 5.5. As suggested by the figure, competitive dynamics in this market type entail taking

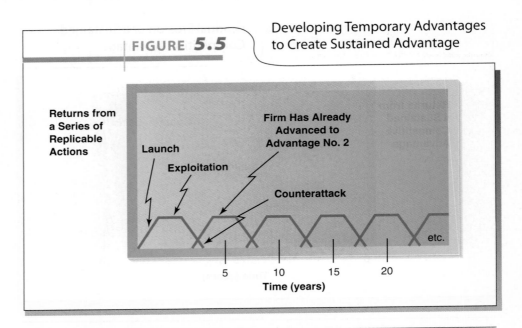

Source: Adapted from I. C. MacMillan, 1988, Controlling competitive dynamics by taking strategic initiative, *Academy of Management Executive*, II(2): 111–118.

actions and responses that are oriented to rapid and continuous product introductions and the development of a stream of ever-changing competitive advantages. The firm launches a product to achieve a competitive action and then exploits the advantage for as long as possible. However, the firm also tries to develop another temporary competitive advantage before competitors can respond to the first one (see Figure 5.5). Thus, competitive dynamics in fast-cycle markets often result in rapid product upgrades as well as quick product innovations.[124]

As our discussion suggests, innovation plays a dominant role in the competitive dynamics in fast-cycle markets. For individual firms, this means that innovation is a key source of competitive advantage. Through innovation, the firm can cannibalize its own products before competitors successfully imitate them.

As noted earlier, it is difficult for firms competing in fast-cycle markets to maintain a competitive advantage in terms of their products. Partly because of this, both IBM and Hewlett-Packard (HP) experienced problems in competing effectively over time. In fact, IBM sold its PC business to Lenovo, China's largest PC manufacturer. Changes may be in store for HP's PC business as well. Neither firm has been able to compete effectively with Dell, the current PC market leader.[125]

Standard-Cycle Markets

Standard-cycle markets are markets in which the firm's competitive advantages are moderately shielded from imitation and where imitation is moderately costly. Competitive advantages are partially sustainable in standard-cycle markets, but only when the firm is able to continuously upgrade the quality of its capabilities, making the competitive advantages dynamic. The competitive actions and responses that form a standard-cycle market's competitive dynamics are designed to seek large market shares, to gain customer loyalty through brand names, and to carefully control their operations in order to consistently provide the same positive experience for customers.[126]

Standard-cycle companies serve many customers in competitive markets. Because the capabilities and core competencies on which their competitive advantages are based are less specialized, imitation is faster and less costly for standard-cycle firms than for those competing in slow-cycle markets. However, imitation is slower and more expensive in these markets than in fast-cycle markets. Thus, competitive dynamics in standard-cycle markets rest midway between the characteristics of dynamics in slow-cycle and fast-cycle markets. Imitation comes less quickly and is more expensive for standard-cycle competitors when a firm is able to develop economies of scale by combining coordinated and integrated design and manufacturing processes with a large sales volume for its products.

Because of large volumes, the size of mass markets, and the need to develop scale economies, the competition for market share is intense in standard-cycle markets. This form of competition is readily evident in the battles between Coca-Cola and PepsiCo, as discussed in the Strategic Focus. As noted, they compete in markets all over the world. In recent years, PepsiCo has been winning the battles in domestic and international markets. This outcome is partly due to effective strategic actions by PepsiCo and ineffective actions by Coca-Cola's top management, which evidenced chaos in the period of 1998–2004.

Innovation can also drive competitive actions and responses in standard-cycle markets, especially when rivalry is intense. Some innovations in standard-cycle markets are incremental rather than radical in nature (incremental and radical innovations are discussed in Chapter 13). One of the reasons for PepsiCo's success in competition against Coca-Cola has been the innovative new products it has introduced. As described in the Strategic Focus, Coke's current CEO, Neville Isdell, is emphasizing heavy advertising to support its existing strong brand and to support the introduction of a variety of new beverage products in the market. Thus, both Coca-Cola and PepsiCo are emphasizing innovation in their competition.

In the final analysis, innovation has a substantial influence on competitive dynamics as it affects the actions and responses of all companies competing within a slow-cycle, fast-cycle, or standard-cycle market. We have emphasized the importance of innovation to the firm's strategic competitiveness in earlier chapters and will do so again in Chapter 13. Our discussion of innovation in terms of competitive dynamics extends the earlier discussions by showing its importance in all types of markets in which firms compete.

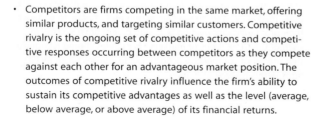

SUMMARY

- Competitors are firms competing in the same market, offering similar products, and targeting similar customers. Competitive rivalry is the ongoing set of competitive actions and competitive responses occurring between competitors as they compete against each other for an advantageous market position. The outcomes of competitive rivalry influence the firm's ability to sustain its competitive advantages as well as the level (average, below average, or above average) of its financial returns.

- For the individual firm, the set of competitive actions and responses it takes while engaged in competitive rivalry is called competitive behavior. Competitive dynamics is the set of actions and responses taken by all firms that are competitors within a particular market.

- Firms study competitive rivalry in order to be able to predict the competitive actions and responses that each of their competitors likely will take. Competitive actions are either strategic or tactical in nature. The firm takes competitive actions to defend or build its competitive advantages or to improve its market position. Competitive responses are taken to counter the effects of a competitor's competitive action. A strategic action or a strategic response requires a significant commitment of organizational resources, is difficult to successfully implement, and is difficult to reverse. In contrast, a tactical action or a tactical response requires fewer organizational resources and is easier to implement and reverse. For an airline company, for example, entering major new markets is an example of a strategic action or a strategic response; changing its prices in a particular market is an example of a tactical action or a tactical response.

- A competitor analysis is the first step the firm takes to be able to predict its competitors' actions and responses. In Chapter 2, we discussed what firms do to *understand* competitors. This discussion is extended in this chapter as we described what the firm does to *predict* competitors' market-based actions. Thus, understanding precedes prediction. Market commonality (the number of markets with which competitors are jointly involved and their importance to each) and resource similarity (how comparable competitors' resources are in terms of type and amount) are studied to complete a competitor analysis. In general, the greater the market commonality and resource similarity, the more that firms acknowledge that they are direct competitors.

- Market commonality and resource similarity shape the firm's awareness (the degree to which it and its competitor understand their mutual interdependence), motivation (the firm's incentive to attack or respond), and ability (the quality of the resources available to the firm to attack and respond). Having knowledge of a competitor in terms of these characteristics increases the quality of the firm's predictions about that competitor's actions and responses.

- In addition to market commonality and resource similarity and awareness, motivation, and ability, three more specific factors affect the likelihood a competitor will take competitive actions. The first of these concerns first-mover incentives. First movers, those taking an initial competitive action, often earn above-average returns until competitors can successfully respond to their action and gain loyal customers. Not all firms can be first movers in that they may lack the awareness, motivation, or ability required to engage in this type of competitive behavior. Moreover, some firms prefer to be a second mover (the firm responding to the first mover's action). One reason for this is that second movers, especially those acting quickly, can successfully compete against the first mover. By evaluating the first mover's product, customers' reactions to it, and the responses of other competitors to the first mover, the second mover can avoid the early entrant's mistakes and find ways to improve upon the value created for customers by the first mover's good or service. Late movers (those that respond a long time after the

original action was taken) commonly are lower performers and are much less competitive.

- Organizational size, the second factor, tends to reduce the variety of competitive actions that large firms launch while it increases the variety of actions undertaken by smaller competitors. Ideally, the firm would like to initiate a large number of diverse actions when engaged in competitive rivalry. The third factor, quality, is a base denominator to successful competition in the global economy. It is a necessary prerequisite to achieve competitive parity. It is a necessary but insufficient condition for gaining an advantage.

- The type of action (strategic or tactical) the firm took, the competitor's reputation for the nature of its competitor behavior, and that competitor's dependence on the market in which the action was taken are studied to predict a competitor's response to the firm's action. In general, the number of tactical responses taken exceeds the number of strategic responses. Competitors respond more frequently to the actions taken by the firm with a reputation for predictable and understandable competitive behavior, especially if that firm is a market leader. In general, the firm can predict that when its competitor is highly dependent for its revenue and profitability in the market in which the firm took a competitive action, that competitor is likely to launch a strong response. However, firms that are more diversified across markets are less likely to respond to a particular action that affects only one of the markets in which they compete.

- Competitive dynamics concerns the ongoing competitive behavior occurring among all firms competing in a market for advantageous positions. Market characteristics affect the set of actions and responses firms take while competing in a given market as well as the sustainability of firms' competitive advantages. In slow-cycle markets, where competitive advantages can be maintained, competitive dynamics finds firms taking actions and responses that are intended to protect, maintain, and extend their proprietary advantages. In fast-cycle markets, competition is almost frenzied as firms concentrate on developing a series of temporary competitive advantages. This emphasis is necessary because firms' advantages in fast-cycle markets aren't proprietary and, as such, are subject to rapid and relatively inexpensive imitation. Standard-cycle markets experience competition between slow-cycle and fast-cycle markets; firms are moderately shielded from competition in these markets as they use capabilities that produce competitive advantages that are moderately sustainable. Competitors in standard-cycle markets serve mass markets and try to develop economies of scale to enhance their profitability. Innovation is vital to competitive success in each of the three types of markets. Companies should recognize that the set of competitive actions and responses taken by all firms differs by type of market.

1. D. F. Spulber, 2004, *Management Strategy,* Boston: McGraw-Hill/Irwin, 87–88; M.-J. Chen, 1996, Competitor analysis and interfirm rivalry: Toward a theoretical integration, *Academy of Management Review,* 21: 100–134.

2. T. Galvin, 2002, Examining institutional change: Evidence from the founding dynamics of U.S. health care interest associations, *Academy of Management Journal,* 45: 673–696.

3. B. Pittman, 2003, Leading for value, *Harvard Business Review,* 81(4): 41–46.

4. A. M. Knott & H. E. Posen, 2005, Is failure good? *Strategic Management Journal,* 26: 617–641.

5. A. Nair & L. Filer, 2003, Cointegration of firm strategies within groups: A long-run analysis of firm behavior in the Japanese steel industry, *Strategic Management Journal,* 24: 145–159.

6. T. C. Powell, 2003, Varieties of competitive parity, *Strategic Management Journal,* 24: 61–86.

7. S. Jayachandran, J. Gimeno, & P. R. Varadarajan, 1999, Theory of multimarket competition: A synthesis and implications for marketing strategy, *Journal of Marketing,* 63: 49–66.

8. C. M. Grimm, H. Lee, & K. G. Smith, 2005, *Strategy as Action: Competitive dynamics and competitive advantage,* New York: Oxford University Press; G. Young, K. G. Smith, C. M. Grimm, & D. Simon, 2000, Multimarket contact and resource dissimilarity: A competitive dynamics perspective, *Journal of Management,* 26: 1217–1236.

9. H. A. Haveman & L. Nonnemaker, 2000, Competition in multiple geographic markets: The impact on growth and market entry, *Administrative Science Quarterly,* 45: 232–267.

10. K. G. Smith, W. J. Ferrier, & H. Ndofor, 2001, Competitive dynamics research: Critique and future directions, in M. A. Hitt, R. E. Freeman, & J. S. Harrison (eds.), *Handbook of Strategic Management,* Oxford, UK: Blackwell Publishers, 326.

11. G. Young, K. G. Smith, & C. M. Grimm, 1996, "Austrian" and industrial organization perspectives on firm-level competitive activity and performance, *Organization Science,* 73: 243–254.

12. W. Zellner, 2005, Southwest: Dressed to kill . . . Competitors, *BusinessWeek Online,* www.businessweek.com, February 21.

13. H. D. Hopkins, 2003, The response strategies of dominant U.S. firms to Japanese challengers, *Journal of Management,* 29: 5–25; G. S. Day & D. J. Reibstein, 1997, The dynamic challenges for theory and practice, in G. S. Day & D. J. Reibstein (eds.), *Wharton on Competitive Strategy,* New York: John Wiley & Sons, 2.

14. M.-J. Chen & D. C. Hambrick, 1995, Speed, stealth, and selective attack: How small firms differ from large firms in competitive behavior, *Academy of Management Journal,* 38: 453–482.

15. D. L. Deeds, D. De Carolis, & J. Coombs, 2000, Dynamic capabilities and new product development in high technology ventures: An empirical analysis of new biotechnology firms, *Journal of Business Venturing,* 15: 211–299.

16. T. J. Douglas & J. A. Ryman, 2003, Understanding competitive advantage in the general hospital industry: Evaluating strategic competencies, *Strategic Management Journal,* 24: 333–347.

17. H. Sender, 2005, Meet China inc.: Topping Japan inc. of 1980s, *Wall Street Journal,* www.wsj.com, June 24.

18. S. J. Marsh, 1998, Creating barriers for foreign competitors: A study of the impact of anti-dumping actions on the performance of U.S. firms, *Strategic Management Journal,* 19: 25–37; K. G. Smith, C. M. Grimm, G. Young, & S. Wally, 1997, Strategic groups and rivalrous firm behavior: Toward a reconciliation, *Strategic Management Journal,* 18: 149–157.

19. W. J. Ferrier, 2001, Navigating the competitive landscape: The drivers and consequences of competitive aggressiveness, *Academy of Management Journal,* 44: 858–877.

20. Smith, Ferrier, & Ndofor, Competitive dynamics research, 319.

21. J. Shamsie, 2003, The context of dominance: An industry-driven framework for exploiting reputation, *Strategic Management Journal,* 24: 199–215; K. Ramaswamy, 2001, Organizational ownership, competitive intensity, and firm performance: An empirical study of the Indian manufacturing sector, *Strategic Management Journal,* 22: 989–998.

22. K. Cool, L. H. Roller, & B. Leleux, 1999, The relative impact of actual and potential rivalry on firm profitability in the pharmaceutical industry, *Strategic Management Journal,* 20: 1–14.

23. D. R. Gnyawali & R. Madhavan, 2001, Cooperative networks and competitive dynamics: A structural embeddedness perspective, *Academy of Management Review,* 26: 431–445.

24. Y. Y. Kor & J. T. Mahoney, 2005, How dynamics, management, and governance of resource deployments influence firm-level performance, *Strategic Management Journal,* 26: 489–496; Young, Smith, Grimm, & Simon, Multimarket contact and resource dissimilarity, 1217.

25. R. L. Priem, L. G. Love, & M. A. Shaffer, 2002, Executives' perceptions of uncertainty scores: A numerical taxonomy and underlying dimensions, *Journal of Management,* 28: 725–746.

26. I. C. MacMillan, A. B. van Putten, & R. S. McGrath, 2003, Global gamesmanship, *Harvard Business Review,* 81(5): 62–71; S. Godin, 2002, Survival is not enough, *Fast Company,* January, 90–94.

27. Chen, Competitor analysis, 108.

28. Ibid., 109.

29. K. Uhlenbruck, M. A. Hitt, & M. Semadeni, 2005, Market value effects of acquisitions of Internet firms: A resource-based analysis, working paper, University of Montana; A. Afuah, 2003, Redefining firm boundaries in the face of the Internet: Are firms really shrinking? *Academy of Management Review,* 28: 34–53.

30. G. K. Deans, F. Kroeger, & S. Zeisel, 2002, The consolidation curve, *Harvard Business Review,* 80(12): 20–21; E. Abrahamson & C. J. Fombrun, 1994, Macrocultures: Determinants and consequences, *Academy of Management Review,* 19: 728–755.

31. C. Salter, 2002, On the road again, *Fast Company,* January, 50–58.

32. Young, Smith, Grimm, & Simon, Multimarket contact, 1219.

33. Chen, Competitor analysis, 106.

34. J. Gimeno & C. Y. Woo, 1999, Multimarket contact, economies of scope, and firm performance, *Academy of Management Journal,* 42: 239–259.

35. K. MacArthur, 2001, McDonald's flips business strategy, *Advertising Age,* April 2, 1, 36.

36. 2003, Prudential Financial Inc., *Standard & Poor's Stock Reports,* www.standardandpoors.com, May 17.

37. MacMillan, van Putten, & McGrath, Global gamesmanship, 63.

38. Young, Smith, Grimm, & Simon, Multimarket contact, 1230.

39. J. Gimeno, 1999, Reciprocal threats in multimarket rivalry: Staking out "spheres of influence" in the U.S. airline industry, *Strategic Management Journal,* 20: 101–128; N. Fernandez & P. L. Marin, 1998, Market power and multimarket contact: Some evidence from the Spanish hotel industry, *Journal of Industrial Economics,* 46: 301–315.

40. Jayachandran, Gimeno, & Varadarajan, Theory of multimarket competition, 59; Chen, Competitor analysis, 107.

41. J. Gimeno & C. Y. Woo, 1996, Hypercompetition in a multimarket environment: The role of strategic similarity and multimarket contact on competitive de-escalation, *Organization Science,* 7: 322–341.

42. A. Lashinsky, 2005, Sony vs. Toshiba: A DVD shootout, *Fortune,* www.fortune.com, May 3.

43. K. Lamertz, P. M. Pursey, A. R. Heugens, & L. Calmet, 2005, The configuration of organizational images among firms in the Canadian beer brewing industry, *Journal of Management Studies,* 42: 817–843.

44. Chen, Competitor analysis, 107–108.
45. L. Ulrich, 2003, Outside the box, *Money*, 32(6): 137–138.
46. Toyota's bad memories, 2005, *Wall Street Journal Online*, www.wsj.com, April 28.
47. Chen, Competitor analysis, 110.
48. Ibid.; W. Ocasio, 1997, Towards an attention-based view of the firm, *Strategic Management Journal*, 18 (Special Issue): 187–206; Smith, Ferrier, & Ndofor, Competitive dynamics research, 320.
49. M. Selva, 2003, Wal-Mart, France's Carrefour set sights on Ahold businesses, *Sunday Business*, April 6, B3; 2001, Wal around the world, *The Economist*, December 8, 55–56.
50. S. Tallman, M. Jenkins, N. Henry, & S. Pinch, 2004, Knowledge, clusters and competitive advantage, *Academy of Management Review*, 29: 258–271; J. F. Porac & H. Thomas, 1994, Cognitive categorization and subjective rivalry among retailers in a small city, *Journal of Applied Psychology*, 79: 54–66.
51. S. H. Park & D. Zhou, 2005, Firm heterogeneity and competitive dynamics in alliance formation, *Academy of Management Review*, 30: 531–554; Smith, Ferrier, & Ndofor, Competitive dynamics research, 320
52. Chen, Competitor analysis, 113.
53. R. Belderbos & L. Sleuwaegen, 2005, Competitive drivers and international plant configuration strategies: A product-level test, *Strategic Management Journal*, 26: 577–593.
54. C. M. Grimm & K. G. Smith, 1997, *Strategy as Action: Industry rivalry and coordination*, Cincinnati: South-Western Publishing Co., 125.
55. 2002, Blue light blues, *The Economist*, January 29, 54; D. B. Yoffie & M. Kwak, 2001, Mastering strategic movement at Palm, *MIT Sloan Management Review*, 43(1): 55–63.
56. A. Echols & W. Tsai, 2004, Niche and performance: The moderating role of network embeddedness, *Strategic Management Journal*, 26: 219–238.
57. K. G. Smith, W. J. Ferrier, & C. M. Grimm, 2001, King of the hill: Dethroning the industry leader, *Academy of Management Executive*, 15(2): 59–70.
58. W. J. Ferrier & H. Lee, 2003, Strategic aggressiveness, variation, and surprise: How the sequential pattern of competitive rivalry influences stock market returns, *Journal of Managerial Issues*, 14: 162–180; G. S. Day, 1997, Assessing competitive arenas: Who are your competitors? in G. S. Day & D. J. Reibstein (eds.), *Wharton on Competitive Strategy*, New York: John Wiley & Sons, 25–26.
59. R. Truett, 2003, A chance to shape design destiny, *Automotive News*, April 7, D2; M. Ihlwan, L. Armstrong, & K. Kerwin, 2001, Hyundai gets hot, *Business Week*, December 17, 84–86.
60. 2003, Boeing says to build new 7E7 in United States, *Reuters*, www.reuters.com, May 16.
61. J. Schumpeter, 1934, *The Theory of Economic Development*, Cambridge, MA: Harvard University Press.
62. J. L. C. Cheng & I. F. Kesner, 1997, Organizational slack and response to environmental shifts: The impact of resource allocation patterns, *Journal of Management*, 23: 1–18.
63. F. Wang, 2000, Too appealing to overlook, *America's Network*, December, 10–12.
64. D. P. Forbes, 2005, Managerial determinants of decision speed in new ventures, *Strategic Management Journal*, 26: 355–366; G. Hamel, 2000, *Leading the Revolution*, Boston: Harvard Business School Press, 103.
65. W. T. Robinson & S. Min, 2002, Is the first to market the first to fail? Empirical evidence for industrial goods businesses, *Journal of Marketing Research*, 39: 120–128.
66. T. Cottrell & B. R. Nault, 2004, *Strategic Management Journal*, 25: 1005–1025; R. Agarwal, M. B. Sarkar, & R. Echambadi, 2002, The conditioning effect of time on firm survival: An industry life cycle approach, *Academy of Management Journal*, 45: 971–994.
67. A. Nerer & P. W. Roberts, 2004, Technological and product-market experience and the success of new product introductions in the pharmaceutical industry, *Strategic Management Journal*, 25: 779–799; A. Srivastava & H. Lee, 2005, Predicting order and timing of new product moves: The role of top management in corporate entrepreneurship, *Journal of Business Venturing*, 20: 459–481.
68. J. W. Spencer & T. P. Murtha, 2005, How do governments matter to new industry creation? *Academy of Management Review*, 30: 321–337.
69. S. W. Geiger & L. H. Cashen, 2002, A multidimensional examination of slack and its impact on innovation, *Journal of Managerial Issues*, 14: 68–84.
70. M. B. Lieberman & D. B. Montgomery, 1988, First-mover advantages, *Strategic Management Journal*, 9: 41–58.
71. 2001, Older, wiser, webbier, *The Economist*, June 30, 10.
72. M. Shank, 2002, Executive strategy report, IBM business strategy consulting, www.ibm.com, March 14; W. Boulding & M. Christen, 2001, First-mover disadvantage, *Harvard Business Review*, 79(9): 20–21.
73. B. Finkelstein, 2003, AHMH took two-pronged approach to building volume, *Origination News*, 11(4): 19.
74. J. Gimeno, R. E. Hoskisson, B. B. Beal, & W. P. Wan, 2005, Explaining the clustering of international expansion moves: A critical test in the U.S. telecommunications industry, *Academy of Management Journal*, 48: 297–319; K. G. Smith, C. M. Grimm, & M. J. Gannon, 1992, *Dynamics of Competitive Strategy*, Newberry Park, CA.: Sage Publications.
75. S. D. Dobrev & G. R. Carroll, 2003, Size (and competition) among organizations: Modeling scale-based selection among automobile producers in four major countries, 1885–1981, *Strategic Management Journal*, 24: 541–558; Smith, Ferrier, & Ndofor, Competitive dynamics research, 327.
76. F. K. Pil & M. Hoiweg, 2003, Exploring scale: The advantage of thinking small, *The McKinsey Quarterly*, 44(2): 33–39; Chen & Hambrick, Speed, stealth, and selective attack.
77. D. Miller & M.-J. Chen, 1996, The simplicity of competitive repertoires: An empirical analysis, *Strategic Management Journal*, 17: 419–440.
78. Young, Smith, & Grimm, "Austrian" and industrial organization perspectives.
79. B. A. Melcher, 1993, How Goliaths can act like Davids, *Business Week*, Special Issue, 193.
80. J. Guyon, 2005, Fortune Global 500, *Fortune*, July 25, 97–142.
81. 2001, Wal around the world, 55.
82. C. Chandler, 2005, The great Wal-Mart of China, *Fortune*, July 25, 104–116.
83. P. B. Crosby, 1980, *Quality Is Free*, New York: Penguin.
84. W. E. Deming, 1986, *Out of the Crisis*, Cambridge, MA: MIT Press.
85. L. B. Crosby, R. DeVito, & J. M. Pearson, 2003, Manage your customers' perception of quality, *Review of Business*, 21(1): 18–24.
86. R. S. Kaplan & D. P. Norton, 2001, *The Strategy-Focused Organization*, Boston: Harvard Business School Press.
87. R. Cullen, S. Nicholls, & A. Halligan, 2001, Measurement to demonstrate success, *British Journal of Clinical Governance*, 6(4): 273–278.
88. K. E. Weick & K. M. Sutcliffe, 2001, *Managing the Unexpected*, San Francisco: Jossey-Bass, 81–82.
89. G. Yeung & V. Mok, 2005, What are the impacts of implementing ISOs on the competitiveness of manufacturing industry in China, *Journal of World Business*, 40: 139–157.
90. H.-J. Cho & V. Pucik, 2005, Relationship between innovativeness, quality, growth, profitability, and market value, *Strategic Management Journal*, 26: 555–575.
91. Ihlwan, Armstrong, & Kerwin, Hyundai gets hot, 84.
92. J. C. Armstrong, 2003, Hyundai Motor begins sourcing 2006 Santa Fe, *Automotive News*, April 28, 21.
93. T. Box, 2003, Accelerating quality, *Dallas Morning News*, May 17, D1, D3.
94. M. Ihlwan & J. B. Bush, 2005, Hyundai: Crowding into the fast lane, *Business Week*, June 20, www.businessweek.com.
95. J. Schumpeter, 1950, *Capitalism, Socialism and Democracy*, New York: Harper; Smith, Ferrier, & Ndofor, Competitive dynamics research, 323.
96. M.-J. Chen & I. C. MacMillan, 1992, Nonresponse and delayed response to competitive moves, *Academy of Management Journal*, 35: 539–570; Smith, Ferrier, & Ndofor, Competitive dynamics research, 335.
97. M.-J. Chen, K. G. Smith, & C. M. Grimm, 1992, Action characteristics as predictors of competitive responses, *Management Science*, 38: 439–455.
98. M.-J. Chen & D. Miller, 1994, Competitive attack, retaliation and performance: An expectancy-valence framework, *Strategic Management Journal*, 15: 85–102.

99. T. Gardner, 2005, Interfirm competition for human resources: Evidence from the software industry, *Academy of Management Journal,* 48: 237–258; N. Huyghebaert & L. M. van de Gucht, 2004, Incumbent strategic behavior in financial markets and the exit of entrepreneurial start-ups, *Strategic Management Journal,* 25: 669–688.

100. Smith, Ferrier, & Ndofor, Competitive dynamics research, 333.

101. J. Shamsie, 2003, The context of dominance: An industry-driven framework for exploiting reputation, *Strategic Management Journal,* 24: 199–215.

102. P. W. Roberts & G. R. Dowling, 2003, Corporate reputation and sustained superior financial performance, *Strategic Management Journal,* 24: 1077–1093.

103. W. J. Ferrier, K. G. Smith, & C. M. Grimm, 1999, The role of competitive actions in market share erosion and industry dethronement: A study of industry leaders and challengers, *Academy of Management Journal,* 42: 372–388.

104. M. A. Hitt, C. C. Miller, A. Colella, 2006, *Organizational behavior: A strategic approach,* New York: John Wiley & Sons.

105. Smith, Grimm, & Gannon, Dynamics of Competitive Strategy.

106. A. Karnani & B. Wernerfelt, 1985, Multiple point competition, *Strategic Management Journal,* 6: 87–97.

107. Smith, Ferrier, & Ndofor, Competitive dynamics research, 330.

108. L. Wayne, 2005, New Boeing-Airbus rivalry: Tanker contracts, *New York Times,* www.nytimes.com, June 16.

109. D. Neil, 2005, It's a step up in class: Mercedes ditches the old M-Class design for sturdy power and southern comfort, *Los Angeles Times,* www.latimes.com, June 15.

110. G. McNamara, P. M. Vaaler, & C. Devers, 2003, Same as it ever was: The search for evidence of increasing hypercompetition, *Strategic Management Journal,* 24: 261–278.

111. A. Kalnins & W. Chung, 2004, Resource-seeking agglomeration: A study of market entry in the lodging industry, *Strategic Management Journal,* 25: 689–699.

112. J. R. Williams, 1992, How sustainable is your competitive advantage? *California Management Review,* 34(3): 29–51.

113. Ibid., 6.

114. N. Pangarkar & J. R. Lie, 2004, The impact of market cycle on the performance of Singapore acquirers, *Strategic Management Journal,* 25: 1209–1216.

115. Ibid., 57.

116. 2005, Pfizer loses Lipitor patent suit, Red Herring, www.redherring.com, March 29; 2003, Pfizer suit is for a blockbuster drug, *Businessline,* February 26, 13.

117. 2005, Pfizer's Lipitor patent rejected on re-examination, Patent Baristas, www.patentbaristas.com, June 23; R. Steyer, 2005, Pfizer contests Lipitor rule, TheStreet.com, www.thestreet.com, March 29.

118. 2003, How fast is your company? *Fast Company,* June, 18.

119. T. Talaulicar, J. Grundei, & A. V. Werder, 2005, Strategic decision making in start-ups: The effect of top management team organization and processes on speed and comprehensiveness, *Journal of Business Venturing,* 20: 519–541.

120. M. Song, C. Droge, S. Hanvanich, & R. Calatone, 2005, Marketing and technology resource complementarity: An analysis of their interaction effect in two environmental contexts, *Strategic Management Journal,* 26: 259–276.

121. R. Williams, 1999, Renewable advantage: Crafting strategy through economic time, New York: Free Press, 8.

122. Ibid.

123. D. Gerwin, 2004, Coordinating new product development in strategic alliances, *Academy of Management Review,* 29: 241–257.

124. R. Sanchez, 1995, Strategic flexibility in production competition, *Strategic Management Journal,* 16 (Special Issue): 9–26.

125. Hitt, Miller, & Colella, *Organizational behavior;* J. Radigan, 2004, The rival visions of IBM and HP, *BusinessWeek Online,* www.businessweek.com, December 16.

126. Williams, Renewable Advantage, 7.

Strategy at the Corporate Level

KNOWLEDGE OBJECTIVES

Studying this chapter should provide you with the strategic management knowledge needed to:

1. Define corporate-level strategy and discuss its purpose.

2. Describe different levels of diversification with different corporate-level strategies.

3. Explain three primary reasons firms diversify.

4. Describe how firms can create value by using a related diversification strategy.

5. Explain the two ways value can be created with an unrelated diversification strategy.

6. Discuss the incentives and resources that encourage diversification.

7. Describe motives that can encourage managers to overdiversify a firm.

© KRISTINA MILLAR

Of Brinker's five concepts, Chili's is the one responsible for most of the firm's revenue—over 70 percent.

Brinker International is a diversified company using a portfolio of food-related concepts to compete in the casual dining segment of the restaurant industry. Casual dining is a segment in which firms offer moderately priced food in casual atmospheres. Analysts believe that demographic trends in the United States favor continuing growth in the casual dining segment.

Using its "diversified portfolio of casual dining concepts," Brinker believes that it is able to offer customers dining options that will "suit almost any appetite and lifestyle." As you will learn in Chapter 11, Outback Steakhouse Inc. is another food company using a corporate-level strategy of diversification as the foundation for its growth and profitability. Commenting about Brinker, an analyst recently observed that this firm's "portfolio strategy is difficult to manage." Discussions in this chapter will show that although they can help a firm earn above-average returns, diversification (portfolio) strategies are difficult to successfully use in all industries—not just in the restaurant industry or in the casual dining segment of that industry.

Although the number of concepts in Brinker's portfolio changes in response to each unit's success or lack of success, Brinker currently competes with five concepts—concepts that the firm believes are distinctive and that satisfy a wide range of dining tastes: Chili's Grill & Bar, Romano's Macaroni Grill, On the Border, Maggiano's Little Italy, and Rockfish (Brinker owns a 43 percent interest in this company). These concepts compete in different parts of the casual dining segment: bar & grill (Chili's); upscale Italian (Romano's Macaroni Grill); Tex-Mex (On the Border); historical Italian settings (Maggiano's Little Italy, whose atmosphere is intended to recall New York's Little Italy in 1945); and seafood (Rockfish). Chili's generates the largest percentage of Brinker's revenue (over 70 percent). With just five concepts, Brinker is using a strategy of relatively low diversification—the dominant business corporate-level diversification strategy (this strategy is defined and discussed later in this chapter).

To successfully use the firm's corporate-level strategy, personnel at Brinker's headquarters office constantly evaluate the performance of each dining concept. A key corporate objective is to offer customers a set of dining options that are complementary rather than competitive. In this way, Brinker customers have a chance to "eat at a different Brinker restaurant every day of the week without overloading on any one cuisine."

Concepts failing to satisfy various performance criteria, including financial expectations and the need to be complementary rather than competitive, are divested. In fiscal year 2004, for example, Brinker sold its Cozymel's Coastal Mexican Grill chain. In fiscal year 2005, it divested its Big Bowl Asian Kitchen chain and expected to complete the sale of its Corner Bakery chain in 2006. Corner Bakery's experiences demonstrate how Brinker uses its corporate-level strategy to find the best combination of dining concepts. Corner Bakery failed to successfully compete against fast-growing, highly profitable Panera Bread in the bakery café niche of the casual dining segment. Rather than invest further in a concept that was losing ground to its major competitor, Brinker decided to sell the chain so the company could concentrate on its other concepts with growth potential. To successfully use its corporate-level strategy, Brinker's upper-level decision makers make decisions about the dining segments in which the firm will compete and how to manage its concepts in those segments.

Sources: 2005, Brinker International Home Page, About us, www.brinker.com, August 24; 2005, Brinker International, *Standard & Poor's Stock Report,* www.standardandpoors.com, August 20; 2005, Brinker International named to *Fortune* magazine's 'Top 50 employers for minorities', *Yahoo! Finance,* www.yahoo.com, August 25; R. Gibson, 2005, Outback tries to diversify in new strategy, *Wall Street Journal* (Eastern edition), April 27, B8; S. D. Simpson, 2005, Brinker's not on the brink, *Yahoo! Finance,* www.yahoo.com, August 12.

Our discussions of business-level strategies (Chapter 4) and the competitive rivalry and competitive dynamics associated with them (Chapter 5) concentrate on firms competing in a single industry or product market.[1] In this chapter, we introduce you to corporate-level strategies, which are strategies firms use to *diversify* their operations from a single business competing in a single market into several product markets and most commonly, into several businesses. Thus, a **corporate-level strategy** specifies actions a firm takes to gain a competitive advantage by selecting and managing a group of different businesses competing in different product markets. Corporate-level strategies help companies select new strategic positions—positions that are expected to increase the firm's value.[2] As explained in the Opening Case, Brinker International competes in five different markets of the casual dining segment of the restaurant industry. Each of Brinker's dining concepts (e.g., Chili's, On the Border) represents a different business holding a different strategic position in the casual dining segment.

As is the case with Brinker International, firms use corporate-level strategies as a means to grow revenues and profits. But the decision to take actions to pursue growth is never a risk-free choice for firms to make.[3] Indeed, effective firms carefully evaluate their growth options (including the different corporate-level strategies) before committing firm resources to any of them.[4]

Because the diversified firm operates in several different and unique product markets and likely in several businesses, it forms two types of strategies: corporate level (or company-wide) and business level (or competitive).[5] Corporate-level strategy is concerned with two key issues: in what product markets and businesses the firm should compete and how corporate headquarters should manage those businesses.[6] For the diversified corporation, a business-level strategy (see Chapter 4) must be chosen for each of the businesses in which the firm has decided to compete. In this regard, each of Brinker's dining concepts or businesses uses a differentiation business-level strategy.

As is the case with a business-level strategy, a corporate-level strategy is expected to help the firm earn above-average returns by creating value.[7] Some suggest that few corporate-level strategies actually create value.[8] This may have been the case at Morgan Stanley under former CEO Philip Purcell's leadership, as some analysts contend that the corporate-level strategy he put into place lacked coherence and was poorly implemented.[9] In fact, the degree to which corporate-level strategies create value beyond the sums of the value created by all of a firm's business units remains an important research question.[10]

Evidence suggests that a corporate-level strategy's value is ultimately determined by the degree to which "the businesses in the portfolio are worth more under the management of the company than they would be under any other ownership."[11] Thus, an effective corporate-level strategy creates, across all of a firm's businesses, aggregate returns that exceed what those returns would be without the strategy[12] and contributes to the firm's strategic competitiveness and its ability to earn above-average returns.[13]

Product diversification, a primary form of corporate-level strategies, concerns the scope of the markets and industries in which the firm competes as well as "how managers buy, create and sell different businesses to match skills and strengths with opportunities presented to the firm."[14] Successful diversification is expected to reduce variability in the firm's profitability as earnings are generated from different businesses. Brinker International executives have this expectation, in that they believe that "even when market factors or internal challenges impact one or more concepts, the other restaurants in our portfolio are there to balance our overall performance."[15] In another example, recent weakness in Boeing Co.'s defense business is being offset by increasing strength in its commercial plane business.[16] Because firms incur development and monitoring costs when diversifying, the ideal portfolio of businesses balances diversification's costs and benefits.[17] CEOs and their top-management teams are responsible for determining the ideal portfolio for their company.

We begin this chapter by examining different levels of diversification (from low to high). After describing the different reasons firms diversify their operations, we focus on two types of related diversification (related diversification signifies a moderate to a high level of diversification for the firm). When properly used, these strategies help create value in the diversified firm, either through the sharing of resources (the related constrained strategy) or the transferring of core competencies across the firm's different businesses (the related linked strategy). We then discuss unrelated diversification, which is another corporate-level strategy that can create value. The chapter then shifts to the topic of incentives and resources that may stimulate diversification, although the effects of this type of diversification tend to be value neutral. However, managerial motives to diversify, the final topic in the chapter, can actually destroy some of the firm's value.

Boeing is focusing on its commercial plane business to support its weakening defense business.

Levels of Diversification

Diversified firms vary according to their level of diversification and the connections between and among their businesses. Figure 6.1 lists and defines five categories of businesses according to increasing levels of diversification. The single- and dominant-business categories denote relatively low levels of diversification; more fully diversified firms are classified into related and unrelated categories. A firm is related through its diversification when there are several links between its businesses; for example, businesses may share products (goods or services), technologies, or distribution channels. The more links among businesses, the more "constrained" is the relatedness of diversification. Unrelatedness refers to the absence of direct links between businesses.

Low Levels of Diversification

A firm pursing a low level of diversification uses either a single- or a dominant-business corporate-level diversification strategy. A *single-business diversification strategy* is a

FIGURE **6.1** | Levels and Types of Diversification

Low Levels of Diversification

    Single business: 95% or more of revenue comes from a single business.

    Dominant business: Between 70% and 95% of revenue comes from a single business.

Moderate to High Levels of Diversification

    Related constrained: Less than 70% of revenue comes from the dominant business, and all businesses share product, technological, and distribution linkages.

    Related linked   Less than 70% of revenue comes from
    (mixed related and   the dominant business, and there are
     unrelated):   only limited links between businesses.

Very High Levels of Diversification

    Unrelated: Less than 70% of revenue comes from the dominant business, and there are no common links between businesses.

Source: Adapted from R. P. Rumelt, 1974, *Strategy, Structure and Economic Performance*, Boston: Harvard Business School.

Life Savers and Altoids are two of the brands Wrigley has acquired from Kraft Foods in order to diversify its product portfolio.

corporate-level strategy wherein the firm generates 95 percent or more of its sales revenue from its core business area.[18] For example, Wm. Wrigley Jr. Company, the world's largest producer of chewing and bubble gums, historically used a single-business strategy while operating in relatively few product markets. Wrigley's trademark chewing gum brands include Spearmint, Doublemint, and Juicy Fruit, although the firm produces other products as well. Sugar-free Extra, which holds the largest share of the U.S. chewing gum market, was introduced in 1984. Alpine is a "throat relief" gum and in 2005 remained the only gum of this type in the market.

Wrigley is beginning to diversify its product portfolio to become an important player in the confectionery market. In 2005, Wrigley acquired certain confectionary assets from Kraft Foods Inc., including the well-known brands Life Savers and Altoids. The purpose of this diversification is to weave the firm's "brands even deeper into the fabric of everyday life around the world."[19] With increasing diversification of its product lines, Wrigley may soon begin using the dominant-business corporate-level strategy.

With the *dominant-business diversification strategy,* the firm generates between 70 and 95 percent of its total revenue within a single business area. United Parcel Service (UPS) uses this strategy. Recently UPS generated 74 percent of its revenue from its U.S. package delivery business and 17 percent from its international package business, with the remaining 9 percent coming from the firm's non-package business.[20] Though the U.S. package delivery business currently generates the largest percentage of UPS's sales revenue, the firm anticipates that in the years to come its other two businesses will account for the majority of growth in revenues. This expectation suggests that UPS may become more diversified, both in terms of the goods and services it offers and the number of countries in which those goods and services are offered. If this were to happen, UPS would likely become a moderately diversified firm.

Moderate and High Levels of Diversification

A firm generating more than 30 percent of its revenue outside a dominant business and whose businesses are related to each other in some manner uses a related diversification corporate-level strategy. When the links between the diversified firm's businesses are rather direct, a *related constrained diversification strategy* is being used. Campbell Soup, Procter & Gamble, Kodak, and Merck & Company all use a related constrained strategy, as do some large cable companies. With a related constrained strategy, a firm shares resources and activities between its businesses. Cable firms such as Comcast and Time Warner Inc., for example, share technology-based resources and activities across their television programming, high-speed Internet connection, and phone service businesses. Currently, Comcast and Time Warner are seeking to add another related product offering, wireless services, to their portfolios of businesses. For each firm, adding wireless would provide another opportunity to share resources and activities to create more value for stakeholders.[21]

The diversified company with a portfolio of businesses with only a few links between them is called a mixed related and unrelated firm and is using the *related linked diversification strategy* (see Figure 6.1). Johnson & Johnson, General Electric (GE), and Cendant use this corporate-level diversification strategy. Compared with related constrained firms, related linked firms share fewer resources and assets between their businesses, concentrating instead on transferring knowledge and core competencies between the businesses. As with firms using each type of diversification strategy, companies implementing the related linked strategy constantly adjust the mix in their portfolio of businesses as well as make decisions about how to manage their businesses. As explained in the Strategic Focus, GE recently reorganized its businesses in an effort to better manage them and to facilitate the firm's transition from an industrial firm to a more technology-driven company. GE is seeking to create value through its corporate-level strategy both in terms of the choices made about the businesses in which the firm will compete and how to manage those businesses.

A highly diversified firm that has no relationships between its businesses follows an *unrelated diversification strategy*. United Technologies, Textron, Samsung, and Hutchison Whampoa Limited (HWL) are examples of firms using this type of corporate-level strategy. Commonly, firms using this strategy are called *conglomerates.*

HWL is a leading international corporation committed to innovation and technology with businesses spanning the globe.[22] Ports and related services, telecommunications, property and hotels, retail and manufacturing, and energy and infrastructure are HWL's five core businesses. These businesses are not related to each other, and the firm makes no efforts to share activities or to transfer core competencies between or among them. Each of these five businesses is quite large; for example,

The HWL building in Hong Kong. HWL is a good example of unrelated diversification, having five core businesses that are not related to each other.

What Is the Best Way to Manage Product Diversification at GE?

General Electric (GE) is a diversified technology, media, manufacturing, and financial services company. The firm feels that by providing "Imagination at Work," it is able to produce goods and provide services that help its customers solve some of the world's most difficult problems. In 2004, GE's revenue reached $154 billion while its earnings exceeded $16.5 billion. An indicator of the firm's stature is that it topped *Fortune* magazine's "Global Most Admired Corporation" list in 2005. Jeffrey Immelt, the firm's CEO, believes that becoming more of a high-technology company and strengthening GE's positions in emerging markets such as China, India, and some Middle East countries are key to his firm's efforts to increase revenue and profitability.

Using the related linked corporate-level strategy, GE was organized into 11 core businesses in 2004. As called for by the related linked strategy, very few resources and activities were shared between or among these 11 businesses. While there was little sharing between what were rather independent businesses, activities were shared between divisions housed within each business while corporate headquarters personnel worked to transfer corporate-level core competencies between or among the businesses.

In 2005, things changed in terms of the businesses in GE's portfolio as well as how those businesses were managed. In mid-2005, Immelt announced that he was reorganizing GE into six, rather than 11, core businesses: Infrastructure, Industrial, Commercial Financial Services, NBC Universal, Healthcare, and Consumer Finance. According to Immelt, "[T]hese changes will accelerate GE's growth in key industries." In addition, the reorganization is expected to help GE become a more "customer-focused" organization—one capable of delivering increasingly effective solutions to problems that customers want to solve.

Changes in how GE would manage its portfolio of businesses followed decisions about what businesses would be in the portfolio. The changes in GE's portfolio that have taken place under Immelt's leadership demonstrate his intention of making GE even more of a high-technology company rather than an industrial firm. In only four years under Immelt's leadership, GE spent over $60 billion to acquire technology-based assets and divested approximately $15 billion of non-technology assets. The newly acquired assets were coupled with GE's remaining assets to batch the firm's operations into six major, technology-oriented businesses. Immelt and his top management team will help to manage these six businesses from the corporate headquarters office. The focus of these managerial efforts will be on transferring core competencies in different types of technologies from one business to one or more of the remaining five businesses. As in all firms, at GE the skills of top-level managers influence the degree to which the transfers of corporate-level core competencies create value.[23]

In general, analysts responded positively to GE's new mix of businesses and its reorganization, agreeing that it was occurring at a time when the firm was strong and had opportunities to strengthen its standing in international markets. In addition, analysts responded positively to the announcement that GE would report key financial data for significant units in each of the six businesses, increasing the overall transparency of the firm's operations.

ZACK SECKLER/BLOOMBERG NEWS/LANDOV

GE's recent reorganization split it into six businesses instead of 11 in the hope of becoming more customer-focused.

Sources: 2005, Imagination at work, GE Home Page, www.ge.com, August 23; 2005, GE assigns insurance division to financial services, *Kansas City Star*, www.kansascity.com, June 24; 2005, GE to reorganize into 6 business units, *Wall Street Journal Online*, www.wsj.com, June 23; K. Kranhold & J. S. Lublin, 2005, GE is expected to tap two of its executives as vice chairman, *Wall Street Journal Online*, www.wsj.com, June 17; D. Wakabayashi, 2005, GE streamlines businesses, *Reuter's*, www.reuters.com, June 23.

the retailing arm of the retail and manufacturing business has more than 6,200 stores in 31 countries. Groceries, cosmetics, electronics, wine, and airline tickets are some of the product categories featured in these stores.[24] This firm's size and diversity suggest the challenge of successfully managing the unrelated diversification strategy.

Reasons for Diversification

There are many reasons firms use a corporate-level diversification strategy (see Table 6.1). Typically, a diversification strategy is used to increase the firm's value by improving its overall performance. Value is created either through related diversification or through unrelated diversification when the strategy allows a company's businesses to increase revenues or reduce costs while implementing their business-level strategies.

Other reasons for using a diversification strategy may have nothing to do with increasing the firm's value; in fact, diversification can have neutral effects or even reduce a firm's value. Value-neutral reasons for diversification include those of a desire to match and thereby neutralize a competitor's market power (such as to neutralize another firm's advantage by acquiring a similar distribution outlet). Decisions to expand a firm's portfolio of businesses to reduce managerial risk can have a negative

Reasons for Diversification	TABLE 6.1

Value-Creating Diversification
- Economies of scope (related diversification)
  - Sharing activities
  - Transferring core competencies
- Market power (related diversification)
  - Blocking competitors through multipoint competition
  - Vertical integration
- Financial economies (unrelated diversification)
  - Efficient internal capital allocation
  - Business restructuring

Value-Neutral Diversification
- Antitrust regulation
- Tax laws
- Low performance
- Uncertain future cash flows
- Risk reduction for firm
- Tangible resources
- Intangible resources

Value-Reducing Diversification
- Diversifying managerial employment risk
- Increasing managerial compensation

FIGURE **6.2**

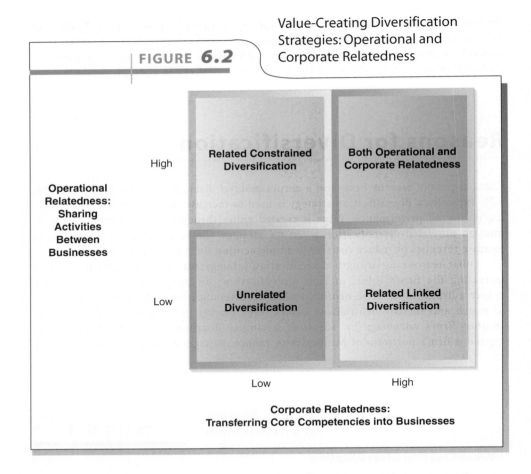

Operational
Relatedness:
Sharing
Activities
Between
Businesses

High — Related Constrained Diversification | Both Operational and Corporate Relatedness

Low — Unrelated Diversification | Related Linked Diversification

Low   High

Corporate Relatedness:
Transferring Core Competencies into Businesses

effect on the firm's value. Greater amounts of diversification reduce managerial risk in that if one of the businesses in a diversified firm fails, the top executive of that business remains employed by the corporation. In addition, because diversification can increase a firm's size and thus managerial compensation, managers have motives to diversify a firm to a level that reduces its value.[25] Diversification rationales that may have a neutral or negative effect on the firm's value are discussed later in the chapter.

Operational relatedness and corporate relatedness are two ways diversification strategies can create value (see Figure 6.2). Study of these independent relatedness dimensions shows the importance of resources and key competencies.[26] The figure's vertical dimension depicts opportunities to share operational activities between businesses (operational relatedness) while the horizontal dimension suggests opportunities for transferring corporate-level core competencies (corporate relatedness). The firm with a strong capability in managing operational synergy, especially in sharing assets between its businesses, falls in the upper left quadrant, which also represents vertical sharing of assets through vertical integration. The lower right quadrant represents a highly developed corporate capability for transferring one or more core competencies across businesses. This capability is located primarily in the corporate headquarters office. Unrelated diversification is also illustrated in Figure 6.2 in the lower left quadrant. Financial economies (discussed later), rather than either operational or corporate relatedness, are the source of value creation for firms using the unrelated diversification strategy.

Value-Creating Diversification: Related Constrained and Related Linked Diversification

With the related diversification corporate-level strategy, the firm builds upon or extends its resources and capabilities to create value.[27] The company using the related diversification strategy wants to develop and exploit economies of scope between its businesses.[28] Available to companies operating in multiple product markets or industries,[29] **economies of scope** are cost savings that the firm creates by successfully sharing some of its resources and capabilities or transferring one or more corporate-level core competencies that were developed in one of its businesses to another of its businesses.

As illustrated in Figure 6.2, firms seek to create value from economies of scope through two basic kinds of operational economies: sharing activities (operational relatedness) and transferring corporate-level core competencies (corporate relatedness). The difference between sharing activities and transferring competencies is based on how separate resources are jointly used to create economies of scope. To create economies of scope, tangible resources, such as plant and equipment or other business-unit physical assets, often must be shared. Less tangible resources, such as manufacturing know-how, also can be shared.[30] However, know-how transferred between separate activities with no physical or tangible resource involved is a transfer of a corporate-level core competence, not an operational sharing of activities.

Operational Relatedness: Sharing Activities

Firms can create operational relatedness by sharing either a primary activity (such as inventory delivery systems) or a support activity (such as purchasing practices)—see Chapter 3's discussion of the value chain. Firms using the related constrained diversification strategy share activities in order to create value. Procter & Gamble (P&G) uses this corporate-level strategy. P&G's paper towel business and baby diaper business both use paper products as a primary input to the manufacturing process. The firm's paper production plant produces inputs for both businesses and is an example of a shared activity. In addition, because they both produce consumer products, these two businesses are likely to share distribution channels and sales networks.

P&G recently acquired Gillette Co. Although the exact nature of the sharing of activities that will be possible after these firms combine their operations is to be determined, there is little doubt that the innovation capabilities of the two firms will be integrated to facilitate activity sharing.[31] In one analyst's words, here is an example of what might happen: "P&G prides itself on what it calls its 'technology transfer' ability, mainly its drive to take technology from one brand and use it in another. For example, it potentially could apply some of its Olay skin-care ability to Gillette's women's razors, since razors are increasingly trying to include skin-care features."[32] Early reactions to the value-creating possibilities of the transaction between P&G and Gillette were quite favorable, with one analyst saying that that the combination of the two firms was "likely to be a match made in heaven."[33] The ability to share technology from one part of the firm to another may be a cause of the analyst's optimism. If the newly formed P&G becomes more innovative, this is a positive outcome, in that increasingly, "innovation is the driving force behind value creation and competitive advantage."[34]

Firms expect activity sharing among units to result in increased strategic competitiveness and improved financial returns.[35] For example, Fidelity Investments has established a money-management unit, called Pyramis Global Advisors. This unit of the giant financial services powerhouse is responsible for overseeing all of Fidelity's equity accounts for institutional investors. At the time of Pyramis's launching, Fidelity was a minor player in the market to manage money for large institutions. Although Pyramis is to operate separately from Fidelity's other businesses, some activities such as the work of financial analysts will be shared to reduce costs and to generate economies of scope.[36]

Other issues affect the degree to which activity sharing creates positive outcomes. For example, managers of other businesses in the firm may feel that a newly created business is unfairly receiving assets. This could be the case at Fidelity where in the short run at least, Robert J. Haber will serve as the chief investment officer for the new business. The issue here is that Haber will also continue managing Fidelity's Focused Stock Fund, which was up 13 percent toward the end of the third quarter in 2005 (a performance that was superior to most of its peer funds). Thus, analysts working in the successful Focused Stock Fund group may feel that Haber's simultaneously serving as the chief investment office for a newly formed business within Fidelity could reduce his effectiveness with their group.[37]

Activity sharing is also risky because ties among a firm's businesses create links between outcomes. For instance, if demand for one business's product is reduced, there may not be sufficient revenues to cover the fixed costs required to operate the facilities being shared. Organizational difficulties such as these can reduce activity sharing success.[38]

Although activity sharing across business businesses isn't risk free, research shows that it can create value. For example, studies that examined acquisitions of firms in the same industry (horizontal acquisitions), such as the banking industry, have found that sharing resources and activities and thereby creating economies of scope contributed to postacquisition increases in performance and higher returns to shareholders.[39] Additionally, firms that sold off related units in which resource sharing was a possible source of economies of scope have been found to produce lower returns than those that sold off businesses unrelated to the firm's core business.[40] Still other research discovered that firms with very closely related businesses had lower risk.[41] These results suggest that gaining economies of scope by sharing activities across a firm's businesses may be important in reducing risk and in creating value. Further, more attractive results are obtained through activity sharing when a strong corporate headquarters office facilitates it.[42]

Corporate Relatedness: Transferring of Core Competencies

Over time, the firm's intangible resources, such as its know-how, become the foundation of core competencies. **Corporate-level core competencies** are complex sets of resources and capabilities that link different businesses, primarily through managerial and technological knowledge, experience, and expertise.[43] The ability to successfully price new products in all of the firm's businesses is an example of what research has shown to be a value-creating, corporate-level competence.[44] Firms seeking to create value through corporate relatedness use the related linked diversification strategy.

There are at least two ways the related linked diversification strategy helps firms to create value.[45] First, because the expense of developing a core competence has been incurred in one of the firm's businesses, transferring it to a second business eliminates the need for that second business to allocate resources to develop it. This is the case at Henkel KGaA, where the firm intends to transfer its competence in nanotechnology from its commercial adhesives business to its industrial adhesives business.[46] Resource intangibility is a second source of value creation through corporate relatedness. Intangible resources are difficult for competitors to understand and imitate. Because of this difficulty, the unit receiving a transferred corporate-level competence often gains an immediate competitive advantage over its rivals.[47]

A number of firms have successfully transferred one or more corporate-level core competencies across their businesses. Virgin Group Ltd. transfers its marketing core competence across travel, cosmetics, music, drinks, mobile phones, health clubs, and a number of other businesses.[48] Thermo Electron uses its entrepreneurial core competence to start new ventures and maintain a new-venture network.[49] Honda has developed and transferred its competence in engine design and manufacturing to its businesses making products such as motorcycles, lawnmowers, and cars and trucks. With respect to smaller engines, for example, these transfers of the corporate-level competence in terms of engine design and manufacturing have been very successful, in that company officials believe that "Honda has become known as the leader in creating four-stroke engines that are reliable, technologically advanced and easy to start."[50]

One way managers facilitate the transfer of corporate-level core competencies is by moving key people into new management positions.[51] However, the manager of an older business may be reluctant to transfer key people who have accumulated knowledge and experience critical to the business's success. Thus, managers with the ability to facilitate the transfer of a core competence may come at a premium, or the key people involved may not want to transfer. Additionally, the top-level managers from the transferring business may not want the competencies transferred to a new business to fulfill the firm's diversification objectives. This could be the case at Fidelity Investments, where managers of the firm's other businesses (e.g., its 401(k) business) may not want one or more of their competencies transferred to the newly established Pyramis Global Advisors business. Research partly supports some hesitancy on managers' parts when it comes to transfers, in that those studying this activity have found that transferring expertise in manufacturing-based businesses often does not result in improved performance.[52] Moreover, it seems that businesses in which performance does improve often demonstrate a corporate-wide passion for pursuing skill transfer and appropriate coordination mechanisms for realizing economies of scope.

Market Power

Firms using a related diversification strategy may gain market power when successfully using their related constrained or related linked strategy. **Market power** exists when a firm is able to sell its products above the existing competitive level or to reduce the costs of its primary and support activities below the competitive level, or both.[53] Federated Department Stores Inc. (parent of Macy's) acquired May Department Stores Co. (parent of Foley's) in part to give the combined company the clout it needs to reduce various costs such as purchasing and distribution below those of competitors.[54] Having market power helps firms successfully use their related diversification strategy.

As explained in the Strategic Focus, market power is one of the forces driving Whirlpool Corp.'s proposed acquisition of Maytag Corp. The transaction between these two firms may face regulatory challenges, primarily because the combined company would have a large part of certain U.S. markets (e.g., washing machines). If approved, though, Whirlpool and Maytag may have complementary resources and capabilities that, when integrated, could result in increased market power. The combined firm might have the clout to reduce costs (through global purchasing and strategic restructurings, for example)[55] and to increase product sales by using compatible design and innovation skills to crisply differentiate products from competitors' offerings.[56] Achieving one or both outcomes would increase Whirlpool's market power relative to its competitors. However, increasing its market power is challenging, because competitors are not standing still. China's Haier Group (a large conglomerate), for example, is seeking to establish a global brand name for its array of products.[57]

In addition to efforts to gain scale as a means of increasing market power, as Whirlpool is attempting to do by acquiring Maytag, firms can create market power through multipoint competition[58] and vertical integration. **Multipoint competition**

Adding Maytag's Products to Whirlpool's: An Effort to Develop Market Power

With sales exceeding $13 billion, over 68,000 employees, and approximately 50 manufacturing and technology centers located across the globe at the end of 2004, Whirlpool Corp. was a leading maker and seller of major home appliances. Offering products for the kitchen (refrigerators, cooktops, freezers, icemakers, microwaves), laundry room (washers and dryers), and whole home (air treatment, water treatment, central heating and cooling) businesses, Whirlpool makes products for virtually every aspect of home life.

Product innovation is critical to Whirlpool's efforts to successfully use its related constrained corporate-level strategy. Making items almost exclusively for homes, Whirlpool's products are grouped into businesses called Kitchen (refrigerators, ranges, etc.), Laundry Room (washers and dryers), and Whole Home (air purifiers and water treatment units, etc.). The sharing of innovation-based technologies and distribution channels among these businesses is critical to the firm's efforts to develop market power.

The new Duet washer is a recent product innovation. Compared with standard units, this washer uses 70 percent less water and 61 percent less electricity. Another Duet advantage is that certain wool fabrics can be washed in the Duet, eliminating the cost of dry cleaning. According to the company, the "Duet became the first appliance in North America to be certified by The Woolmark Company, the world's leading wool textile organization, to safely clean washable wool."

But not everything is well for Whirlpool. As is the case for many manufacturers, the firm's growth and profitability are being threatened by global competitors such as South Korea's LG Electronics and Samsung and China's Haier Group. In addition to reducing its internal costs, Whirlpool decided that increasing the size of its operations would give it the scale it needs to lower costs still further, perhaps even below those of its low-cost competitors. In slightly different words, Whirlpool wanted to reduce costs as a means of increasing its market power.

After watching others bid for Maytag Corporation (the third-largest American maker of home appliances, following Whirlpool and GE), Whirlpool entered the competition and received word in August 2005 that Maytag's board of directors had approved its $1.68 billion acquisition offer. At the end of the third quarter of 2005, the deal was waiting for regulatory approval. If approved, the transaction would result in the newly created company having about 72 percent of the U.S. washing machine market in unit sales, 81 percent of gas dryers, 74 percent of electric dryers, and 31 percent of refrigerators. It is the sheer size of these market shares that caused some to conclude that the proposed transaction may face regulatory challenges.

Assuming the acquisition moves forward, Whirlpool intends to use its global purchasing power and its manufacturing operations located in China and other low-cost facilities to develop "significant efficiencies" as the foundation for reducing Maytag's overburdened cost structure. Whirlpool also intends to share its innovation-based skills with Maytag's operations as the source for developing new products for the still well-recognized and valuable Maytag brand name. If these innovation efforts are successful, the newly formed firm might also be able to gain market power by selling truly innovative products at prices above those of competitors.

DANA MIXER/BLOOMBERG NEWS/LANDOV

Maytag has accepted Whirlpool's acquisition offer, but the transaction is still waiting on regulatory approval.

Sources: 2005, Whirlpool bid accepted, *Dallas Morning News,* August 23, D11; 2005, Whirlpool Corporation, Whirlpool Corporation Home Page, www.whirlpool.com, August 23; 2005, Whirlpool Corporation Worldwide, Whirlpool Corporation Home Page, www.whirlpool.com, August 23; W. Ryberg, 2005, Maytag board OKs $1.68 billion deal with Whirlpool, *Des Moines Register,* www.desmoinesregister.com, August 18; W. Ryberg, 2005, Purchase may face antitrust trouble, *Des Moines Register,* www.desmoinesregister.com, August 20; A. R. Sorkin, 2005, Group led by Chinese appliance maker bids for Maytag, *New York Times,* www.nytimes.com, June 21.

exists when two or more diversified firms simultaneously compete in the same product areas or geographic markets.[59] The actions taken by United Parcel Service (UPS) and FedEx in two markets, overnight delivery and ground shipping, illustrate multipoint competition. UPS has moved into overnight delivery, FedEx's stronghold; FedEx has been buying trucking and ground shipping assets to move into ground shipping, UPS's stronghold. Moreover, there is geographic competition for markets as DHL, the strongest shipping company in Europe, tries to move into the U.S. market.[60] All three competitors (UPS, FedEx and DHL) are trying to move into large foreign markets to either gain a stake in a market or to expand their existing share of a market. For instance, because China was allowed into the World Trade Organization (WTO) and government officials have declared the market more open to foreign competition, the battle for global market share among these three top shippers is raging in China and other countries throughout the world.[61] If one of these firms successfully gains strong positions in several markets while competing against its rivals, its market power may increase.

Some firms using a related diversification strategy engage in vertical integration to gain market power. **Vertical integration** exists when a company produces its own inputs (backward integration) or owns its own source of output distribution (forward integration). In some instances, firms partially integrate their operations, producing and selling their products by using company businesses as well as outside sources.[62]

Vertical integration is commonly used in the firm's core business to gain market power over rivals. Market power is gained as the firm develops the ability to save on its operations, avoid market costs, improve product quality, and, possibly, protect its technology from imitation by rivals.[63] Market power also is created when firms have strong ties between their assets for which no market prices exist. Establishing a market price would result in high search and transaction costs, so firms seek to vertically integrate rather than remain separate businesses.[64]

There are limits to vertical integration. For example, an outside supplier may produce the product at a lower cost. As a result, internal transactions from vertical integration may be expensive and reduce profitability relative to competitors. Also, bureaucratic costs may occur with vertical integration. And, because vertical integration can require substantial investments in specific technologies, it may reduce the firm's flexibility, especially when technology changes quickly. Finally, changes in demand create capacity balance and coordination problems. If one business is building a part for another internal business, but achieving economies of scale requires the first division to manufacture quantities that are beyond the capacity of the internal buyer to absorb, it would be necessary to sell the parts outside the firm as well as to the internal business. Thus, although vertical integration can create value, especially through market power over competitors, it is not without risks and costs.[65]

For example, Merck, the pharmaceutical company, previously owned a pharmacy-benefits management company called Medco Health. Medco acts as a middleman between patients, insurers, and drugmakers, which led to conflicts of interest with its parent company. By revenue, Medco was 50 percent larger than Merck, but had a much smaller profit margin. Because of the legal headaches caused by the conflicts of interest, as well as the small profit margin and a desire to focus more attention on its own underlying profitability, Merck spun off Medco in mid-2003. This decision indicates that the benefits Merck expected from vertical integration did not fully materialize.[66]

Many manufacturing firms no longer pursue vertical integration as a means of gaining market power.[67] In fact, deintegration is the focus of most manufacturing firms, such as Intel and Dell, and even some large auto companies, such as Ford and General Motors, as they develop independent supplier networks.[68] Solectron Corp., a contract manufacturer, represents a new breed of large contract manufacturers that is helping to foster this revolution in supply-chain management.[69] Such firms often manage their customers' entire product lines and offer services ranging from inventory management to delivery and after-sales service. Conducting business through e-commerce also allows vertical integration to be changed into "virtual integration."[70] Thus, closer relationships are possible with suppliers and customers through virtual integration or electronic means of integration, allowing firms to reduce the costs of processing transactions while improving their supply-chain management skills and tightening the control of their inventories. This evidence suggests that *virtual integration* rather than *vertical integration* may be a more common source of market power gains for today's firms.

Simultaneous Operational Relatedness and Corporate Relatedness

As Figure 6.2 suggests, some firms simultaneously seek operational and corporate relatedness to create economies of scope.[71] Although difficult, the ability to simultaneously create economies of scope by sharing activities (operational relatedness) and transferring core competencies (corporate relatedness) is very hard for competitors to understand and learn how to imitate. However, firms that fail in their efforts to simultaneously obtain operational and corporate relatedness may create the opposite of what they seek—namely, diseconomies of scope instead of economies of scope.[72]

Disney's related diversification strategy relies on knowledge of its customers to sell products based on movie characters through its Consumer Products business, for example.

Walt Disney Co. uses a related diversification strategy to simultaneously create economies of scope through operational and corporate relatedness. Within the firm's Studio Entertainment business, for example, Disney can gain economies of scope by sharing activities among its different movie distribution companies such as Touchstone Pictures, Hollywood Pictures, and Dimension Films, among others. Broad and deep knowledge about its customers is a capability on which Disney relies to develop corporate-level core competencies in terms of advertising and marketing. With these competencies, Disney is able to create economies of scope through corporate relatedness as it cross-sells products that are highlighted in its movies through the distribution channels that are part of its Parks and Resorts and Consumer Products businesses. Thus, characters created in movies (think of those in *The Lion King*) become figures that are marketed through Disney's retail stores (which are part of the Consumer Products business). In addition, themes established in movies become the source of new rides in the firm's theme parks, which are part of the Parks and Resorts business.[73]

As we have described, Walt Disney Co. successfully uses related diversification as a corporate-level strategy through which it creates economies of scope by sharing some activities and by transferring core competencies. However, it is difficult for investors to actually observe the value created by a firm (such as Walt Disney Co.) as it shares activities and transfers core competencies. Because of this, the value of the assets of a firm using a diversification strategy to create economies of scope in these manners tend to be discounted by investors. In general, the reason for this discount is that investors face a "lingering question [about] whether multiple revenue streams will outpace multiple-platform overhead."[74]

Unrelated Diversification

Firms do not seek either operational relatedness or corporate relatedness when using the unrelated diversification corporate-level strategy. An unrelated diversification strategy (see Figure 6.2) can create value through two types of financial economies. **Financial economies** are cost savings realized through improved allocations of financial resources based on investments inside or outside the firm.[75]

Efficient internal capital allocations can lead to financial economies. Efficient internal capital allocations reduce risk among the firm's businesses—for example, by leading to the development of a portfolio of businesses with different risk profiles. The second type of financial economy concerns the purchasing of other corporations and then the restructuring of their assets. Here, the diversified firm buys another company, restructures that company's assets in ways that allow it to operate more profitably, and then sells the company for a profit in the external market.[76] Next, we discuss the two types of financial economies in greater detail.

Efficient Internal Capital Market Allocation

In a market economy, capital markets are thought to efficiently allocate capital. Efficiency results as investors take equity positions (ownership) with high expected future cash-flow values. Capital is also allocated through debt as shareholders and debtholders try to improve the value of their investments by taking stakes in businesses with high growth and profitability prospects.

In large diversified firms, the corporate headquarters office distributes capital to its businesses to create value for the overall corporation. The nature of these distributions may generate gains from internal capital market allocations that exceed the gains that would accrue to shareholders as a result of capital being allocated by the external capital market.[77] This happens because while managing the firm's portfolio of businesses, those in a firm's corporate headquarters may gain access to detailed and accurate information regarding those businesses' actual and prospective performance.

Compared with corporate office personnel, investors have relatively limited access to internal information and can only estimate the performances of individual businesses as well as their future prospects. Moreover, although businesses seeking capital must provide information to potential suppliers (such as banks or insurance companies), firms with internal capital markets may have at least two informational advantages. First, information provided to capital markets through annual reports and other sources may not include negative information, instead emphasizing positive prospects and outcomes. External sources of capital have limited ability to understand the operational dynamics of large organizations. Even external shareholders who have access to information have no guarantee of full and complete disclosure.[78] Second, although a firm must disseminate information, that information also becomes simultaneously available to the firm's current and potential competitors. With insights gained by studying such information, competitors might attempt to duplicate a firm's value-creating strategy. Thus, an ability to efficiently allocate capital through an internal market may help the firm protect the competitive advantages it develops while using its corporate-level strategy as well as its various business-unit level strategies.

If intervention from outside the firm is required to make corrections to capital allocations, only significant changes are possible, such as forcing the firm into bankruptcy or changing the top management team. Alternatively, in an internal capital market, the corporate headquarters office can fine-tune its corrections, such as choosing to adjust managerial incentives or suggesting strategic changes in one of the firm's businesses.

Thus, capital can be allocated according to more specific criteria than is possible with external market allocations. Because it has less accurate information, the external capital market may fail to allocate resources adequately to high-potential investments. The corporate headquarters office of a diversified company can more effectively perform such tasks as disciplining underperforming management teams through resource allocations.[79]

Research suggests, however, that in efficient capital markets, the unrelated diversification strategy may be discounted.[80] "For years, stock markets have applied a 'conglomerate discount': they value diversified manufacturing conglomerates at 20 percent less, on average, than the value of the sum of their parts. The discount still applies, in good economic times and bad. Extraordinary manufacturers (like GE) can defy it for a while, but more ordinary ones (like Philips and Siemens) cannot."[81] One reason for this discount could be that firms sometimes substitute acquisitions for innovation. In these instances, too many resources are allocated to analyzing and completing acquisitions to further diversify a firm instead of allocating an appropriate amount of resources to nurture internal innovations. This happened for some Japanese drug firms between 1975 and 1995, a time period during which "corporate diversification was a strategic substitute for significant innovation."[82]

In spite of the challenges associated with it, a number of corporations continue to use the unrelated diversification strategy.[83] This is certainly the case in Europe, where the use of unrelated diversification is increasing,[84] and in emerging markets as well. The Achilles' heel for firms using the unrelated diversification strategy in a developed economy is that competitors can imitate financial economies more easily than they can replicate the value gained from the economies of scope developed through operational relatedness and corporate relatedness. This is less of a problem in emerging economies, where the absence of a "soft infrastructure" (including effective financial intermediaries, sound regulations, and contract laws) supports and encourages use of the unrelated diversification strategy.[85] In fact, in emerging economies such as those in India and Chile, diversification increases the performance of firms affiliated with large diversified business groups.[86] The increasing skill levels of people working in corporations located in emerging markets may support the successful use of the unrelated diversification strategy.[87]

Restructuring of Assets

Financial economies can also be created when firms learn how to create value by buying, restructuring, and then selling other companies' assets in the external market.[88] As in the real estate business, buying assets at low prices, restructuring them, and selling them at a price exceeding their cost generates a positive return on the firm's invested capital.[89] In recent years, Blackstone Group, a private equity firm, has bought and restructured hotel assets. Blackstone acquired Wyndham International Inc. in 2005 with the intention of building the brand name as the foundation for positively restructuring the chain's assets. Previously, Blackstone bought and then restructured the assets of the 143-hotel AmeriSuites chain before profitably selling the chain to Hyatt Corp.[90]

Creating financial economies by acquiring and restructuring other companies' assets requires an understanding of significant trade-offs. Success usually calls for a focus on mature, low-technology businesses because of the uncertainty of demand for high-technology products. In high-technology businesses, resource allocation decisions become too complex, creating information-processing overload on the small corporate headquarters offices that are common in unrelated diversified firms. High-technology businesses are often human-resource dependent; these people can leave or demand higher pay and thus appropriate or deplete the value of an acquired firm.[91]

Buying and then restructuring service-based assets so they can be profitably sold in the external market is also difficult. Here, sales often are a product of close personal relationships between a client and the representative of the firm being restructured. Thus, for both high-technology firms and service-based companies, relatively few tangible assets can be restructured to create value that can be profitably sold. It is difficult to restructure intangible assets such as human capital and effective relationships that have evolved over time between buyers (customers) and sellers (firm personnel).

Value-Neutral Diversification: Incentives and Resources

The objectives firms seek when using related diversification and unrelated diversification strategies all have the potential to help the firm create value by using a corporate-level strategy. However, these strategies, as well as single- and dominant-business diversification strategies, are sometimes used with value-neutral rather than value-creating objectives in mind. As we discuss next, different incentives to diversify sometimes surface, and the quality of the firm's resources may permit only diversification that is value neutral rather than value creating.

Incentives to Diversify

Incentives to diversify come from both the external environment and a firm's internal environment. External incentives include antitrust regulations and tax laws. Internal incentives include low performance, uncertain future cash flows, and the pursuit of synergy and reduction of risk for the firm.

Antitrust Regulation and Tax Laws

Government antitrust policies and tax laws provided incentives for U.S. firms to diversify in the 1960s and 1970s.[92] Antitrust laws prohibiting mergers that created increased market power (via either vertical or horizontal integration) were stringently enforced during that period.[93] Merger activity that produced conglomerate diversification was encouraged primarily by the Celler-Kefauver Antimerger Act (1950), which discouraged horizontal and vertical mergers. As a result, many of the mergers during the 1960s and 1970s were "conglomerate" in character, involving companies pursuing different lines of business. Between 1973 and 1977, 79.1 percent of all mergers were conglomerate.[94]

During the 1980s, antitrust enforcement lessened, resulting in more and larger horizontal mergers (acquisitions of target firms in the same line of business, such as a merger between two oil companies).[95] In addition, investment bankers became more open to the kinds of mergers facilitated by regulation changes; as a consequence, takeovers increased to unprecedented numbers.[96] The conglomerates, or highly diversified firms, of the 1960s and 1970s became more "focused" in the 1980s and early 1990s as merger constraints were relaxed and restructuring was implemented.[97]

In the late 1990s and early 2000s, antitrust concerns emerged again with the large volume of mergers and acquisitions (see Chapter 7).[98] Mergers are now receiving more scrutiny than they did in the 1980s and through the early 1990s.[99] As we noted in a Strategic Focus, the proposed transaction between Whirlpool and Maytag is expected to be carefully examined by regulators.

The tax effects of diversification stem not only from corporate tax changes but also from individual tax rates. Some companies (especially mature ones) generate more cash from their operations than they can reinvest profitably. Some argue that *free cash flows* (liquid financial assets for which investments in current businesses are no longer economically viable) should be redistributed to shareholders as dividends.[100] However, in the 1960s and 1970s, dividends were taxed more heavily than were capital gains. As a result, before 1980, shareholders preferred that firms use free cash flows to buy and build companies in high-performance industries. If the firm's stock value appreciated over the long term, shareholders might receive a better return on those funds than if the funds had been redistributed as dividends, because returns from stock sales would be taxed more lightly than dividends would.

Under the 1986 Tax Reform Act, however, the top individual ordinary income tax rate was reduced from 50 to 28 percent, and the special capital gains tax was changed to treat capital gains as ordinary income. These changes created an incentive for shareholders to stop encouraging firms to retain funds for purposes of diversification. These tax law changes also influenced an increase in divestitures of unrelated business units after 1984. Thus, while individual tax rates for capital gains and dividends created a shareholder incentive to increase diversification before 1986, they encouraged less diversification after 1986, unless it was funded by tax-deductible debt. The elimination of personal interest deductions, as well as the lower attractiveness of retained earnings to shareholders, might prompt the use of more leverage by firms, for which interest expense is tax deductible.

Corporate tax laws also affect diversification. Acquisitions typically increase a firm's depreciable asset allowances. Increased depreciation (a non-cash-flow expense) produces lower taxable income, thereby providing an additional incentive for acquisitions. Before 1986, acquisitions may have been the most attractive means for securing tax benefits,[101] but the 1986 Tax Reform Act diminished some of the corporate tax advantages of diversification.[102] The recent changes recommended by the Financial Accounting Standards Board—eliminating the "pooling of interests" method for accounting for the acquired firm's assets and eliminating the write-off for research and development in process—reduce some of the incentives to make acquisitions, especially acquisitions in related high-technology industries (these changes are discussed further in Chapter 7).[103]

Although there was a loosening of federal regulations in the 1980s and a retightening in the late 1990s, a number of industries have experienced increased merger activity due to industry-specific deregulation activity, including banking, telecommunications, oil and gas, and electric utilities. Regulations changes have also affected convergence between media and telecommunications industries, which has allowed a number of mergers, such as the successive Time Warner and AOL Time Warner mergers. The Federal Communications Commission (FCC) has made a highly contested ruling "allowing broadcasters to own TV stations that reach 45 percent of U.S. households, up from 35 percent, own three stations in the largest markets (up from two) and own a TV station and newspaper in the same town."[104] Critics argued that the change in regulations would allow "an orgy of mergers and acquisitions" and that "it is a victory for free enterprise, but it is not a victory for free speech."[105] Although the FCC has put forth new rules, those rule revisions were found to be substantially unjustified by Congress, which remanded them to the FCC for further deliberation. Also, Congress is considering legislation that may affect regulation of broadcasting, including ownership restrictions.[106] Because of the impending regulatory change, a number of firms have considered potential acquisitions. For example, the FCC has allowed cable companies to get into local phone service. In Orange County, California, cable TV companies now provide 25 percent of local phone service. Phone companies have also been moving into selling TV service, although technology has been hindered until recently because high frequencies, which TV signals use, fade out on thin copper wires. At one point, to overcome this problem, SBC, a large local telephone operator, considered acquiring DirecTV, a satellite TV market leader.[107] Thus, regulatory changes such as the ones we have described create incentives for diversification.

Low Performance

Some research shows that low returns are related to greater levels of diversification.[108] If "high performance eliminates the need for greater diversification,"[109] then low performance may provide an incentive for diversification. Poor performance may lead to increased diversification, as it did with the formerly independent Sears, Roebuck and Co., especially if resources exist to do so.[110]

During the 1990s and early into the 21st century, Sears struggled and teetered on the edge of bankruptcy. During these times, Sears endured competitive threats from a number of fronts, including Home Depot and Lowe's strong movements into appliances (which were high-margin items for Sears).

One of Sears' responses to the threats it faced was to diversify its operations. The purchase of Lands' End in 2002, for example, moved Sears into a different type of clothing. However, in total, the efforts Sears undertook to improve its performance, including diversification-related decisions, weren't successful. In November 2004, Sears and Kmart merged to form what the firms called "a major new retail company." The newly created firm, Sears Holdings Company, is widely diversified and is the third largest retailer in the United States.[111] Time will tell if creating a widely diversified corporation will be the pathway to the strategic success that eluded both Sears and Kmart when they were independent companies.

Research evidence and the experience of a number of firms suggest that an overall curvilinear relationship, as illustrated in Figure 6.3, may exist between diversification

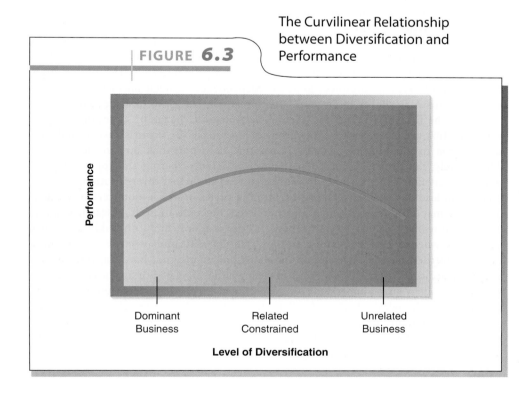

FIGURE 6.3

The Curvilinear Relationship between Diversification and Performance

Performance

Dominant Business   Related Constrained   Unrelated Business

Level of Diversification

and performance.[112] The German media company Bertelsmann was led by then CEO Thomas Middelhoff into a variety of new ventures, especially Internet ones, that have proved to be a drag on the company's resources and have provided very little return on investment. The current CEO, Gunter Thielen, is emphasizing a return to basics by getting rid of non-core businesses, such as the Internet ventures. "The course has been pretty clear since Middelhoff left," says a German consultant: "Focus on the businesses that they understand and dominate." These businesses include producing books, magazines, music, and TV shows. Under Thielen's leadership, Bertelsmann has regrouped and refocused on what it does best.[113]

Uncertain Future Cash Flows

As a firm's product line matures or is threatened, diversification may be taken as an important defensive strategy.[114] Small firms and companies in mature or maturing industries sometimes find it necessary to diversify for long-term survival.[115] For example, uncertainty was one of the dominant reasons for diversification among railroad firms during the 1960s and 1970s. Railroads diversified primarily because the trucking industry was thought to have the capability to have substantially negative effects on the rail business. The trucking industry created uncertainty for railroad operators regarding the future levels of demand for their services.

Diversifying into other product markets or into other businesses can reduce the uncertainty about a firm's future cash flows. Competing in five parts of the casual dining segment helps to reduce demand uncertainty for Brinker International, for example. In this instance, while the demand for one of Brinker's dining concepts might decline at a point in time, demand for one or more of its other concepts might increase at the same moment. The uncertainty of cash flows is one of the reasons Brinker has diversified into different parts of the casual dining segment of the restaurant industry.

Synergy and Firm Risk Reduction

Diversified firms pursuing economies of scope often have investments that are too inflexible to realize synergy between business units. As a result, a number of problems may arise. **Synergy** exists when the value created by business units working together exceeds the value that those same units create working independently. But as a firm increases its relatedness between business units, it also increases its risk of corporate failure, because synergy produces joint interdependence between businesses that constrains the firm's flexibility to respond. This threat may force two basic decisions.

First, the firm may reduce its level of technological change by operating in environments that are more certain. This behavior may make the firm risk averse and thus uninterested in pursuing new product lines that have potential, but are not proven. Alternatively, the firm may constrain its level of activity sharing and forgo synergy's potential benefits. Either or both decisions may lead to further diversification. The former would lead to related diversification into industries in which more certainty exists. The latter may produce additional, but unrelated, diversification.[116] Research suggests that a firm using a related diversification strategy is more careful in bidding for new businesses, whereas a firm pursuing an unrelated diversification strategy may be more likely to overprice its bid, because an unrelated bidder may not have full information about the acquired firm.[117] However, firms using either a related or an unrelated diversification strategy must understand the consequences of paying large premiums. For example, even though the P&G and Gillette transaction is being viewed positively, as we previously noted, the annual growth rate of Gillette's product lines in the newly created company will need to average 12.1 percent or more for P&G's shareholders to benefit financially from the additional diversification resulting from this merger.[118]

Resources and Diversification

As we have discussed, there are several value-neutral incentives for firms to diversify as well as value-creating incentives (such as the ability to create economies of scope). However, even when incentives to diversify exist, a firm must have the types and levels of resources and capabilities needed to successfully use a corporate-level diversification strategy.[119] Although both tangible and intangible resources facilitate diversification, they vary in their ability to create value. Indeed, the degree to which resources are valuable, rare, difficult to imitate, and nonsubstitutable (see Chapter 3) influence their ability to create value through diversification. For instance, free cash flows are a tangible, financial resource that may be used to diversify the firm. However, compared with diversification that is grounded in intangible resources, diversification based on financial resources only is more visible to competitors and thus more imitable and less likely to create value on a long-term basis.[120]

Tangible resources usually include the plant and equipment necessary to produce a product and tend to be less-flexible assets. Any excess capacity often can be used only for closely related products, especially those requiring highly similar manufacturing technologies. Excess capacity of other tangible resources, such as a sales force, can be used to diversify more easily. Again, excess capacity in a sales force is more effective with related diversification, because it may be utilized to sell similar products. The sales force would be more knowledgeable about related-product characteristics, customers, and distribution channels.[121] Tangible resources may create resource interrelationships in production, marketing, procurement, and technology, defined earlier as activity sharing. Intangible resources are more flexible than tangible physical assets in facilitating diversification. Although the sharing of tangible resources may induce diversification, intangible resources such as tacit knowledge could encourage even more diversification.[122]

Sometimes, however, the benefits expected from using resources to diversify the firm for either value-creating or value-neutral reasons are not gained.[123] For example, Wendy's International decided to sell up to 18 percent of its Tim Horton's doughnut chain through an initial public offering (IPO) that was to be completed by the end of the first quarter of 2006. Influencing this decision was the fact that the doughnut chain had "posted break-even results over the past three years."[124] Thus, Wendy's resources were being used for value-neutral purposes through its diversification into the doughnut business. Wendy's expected to use the resources generated through the IPO to focus on product development improvements in its core restaurants and perhaps to pursue other diversification possibilities that would create value rather than being only value neutral.[125] Similarly, Sara Lee Corporation is "embarking on an aggressive strategic plan that will transform the entire enterprise into a tightly focused food, beverage and household products company."[126] Through these efforts, Sara Lee intends to eliminate both the value-creating and value-neutral diversification choices that were not helping the firm substantially improve its financial performance. Under the direction of the firm's new CEO, resources generated by selling off assets were to be redeployed toward strategic acquisitions and product innovation.[127]

Sara Lee Corporation will sell off diversification choices that were not profitable enough and focus instead on food, beverage and household products.

Value-Reducing Diversification: Managerial Motives to Diversify

Managerial motives to diversify can exist independently of value-neutral reasons (i.e., incentives and resources) and value-creating reasons (e.g., economies of scope). The desire for increased compensation and reduced managerial risk are two motives for top-level executives to diversify their firm beyond value-creating and value-neutral levels.[128] In slightly different words, top-level executives may diversify a firm in order to diversify their own employment risk, as long as profitability does not suffer excessively.[129]

Diversification provides additional benefits to top-level managers that shareholders do not enjoy. Research evidence shows that diversification and firm size are highly correlated, and as firm size increases, so does executive compensation.[130] Because large firms are complex, difficult-to-manage organizations, top-level managers commonly receive substantial levels of compensation to lead them.[131] Greater levels of diversification can increase a firm's complexity, resulting in still more compensation for executives to lead an increasingly diversified organization. Governance mechanisms, such as the board of directors, monitoring by owners, executive compensation practices, and the market for corporate control, may limit managerial tendencies to overdiversify. These mechanisms are discussed in more detail in Chapter 10.

In some instances, though, a firm's governance mechanisms may not be strong, resulting in a situation in which executives may diversify the firm to the point that it fails to earn even average returns.[132] The loss of adequate internal governance may result in poor relative performance, thereby triggering a threat of takeover. Although takeovers may improve efficiency by replacing ineffective managerial teams, managers may avoid takeovers through defensive tactics, such as "poison pills," or may reduce their own exposure with "golden parachute" agreements.[133] Therefore, an external governance threat, although restraining managers, does not flawlessly control managerial motives for diversification.[134]

Most large publicly held firms are profitable because the managers leading them are positive stewards of firm resources, and many of their strategic actions, including those related to selecting a corporate-level diversification strategy, contribute to the firm's success.[135] As mentioned, governance mechanisms should be designed to deal with exceptions to the managerial norms of making decisions and taking actions that will increase the firm's ability to earn above-average returns. Thus, it is overly pessimistic to assume that managers usually act in their own self-interest as opposed to their firm's interest.[136]

Top-level executives' diversification decisions may also be held in check by concerns for their reputation. If a positive reputation facilitates development and use of managerial power, a poor reputation may reduce it. Likewise, a strong external market for managerial talent may deter managers from pursuing inappropriate diversification.[137] In addition, a diversified firm may police other firms by acquiring those that are poorly managed in order to restructure its own asset base. Knowing that their firms could be acquired if they are not managed successfully encourages executives to use value-creating, diversification strategies.

As shown in Figure 6.4, the level of diversification that can be expected to have the greatest positive effect on performance is based partly on how the interaction of resources, managerial motives, and incentives affects the adoption of particular diversification strategies. As indicated earlier, the greater the incentives and the more flexible the resources, the higher the level of expected diversification. Financial resources (the most flexible) should have a stronger relationship to the extent of diversification than either tangible or intangible resources. Tangible resources (the most inflexible) are useful primarily for related diversification.

As discussed in this chapter, firms can create more value by effectively using diversification strategies. However, diversification must be kept in check by corporate gover-

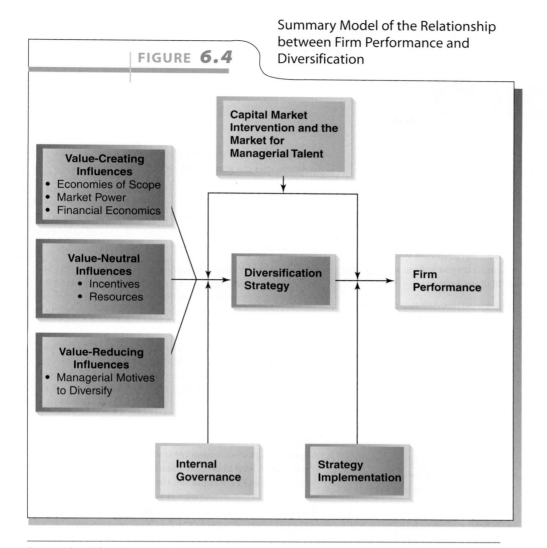

FIGURE **6.4**

Summary Model of the Relationship between Firm Performance and Diversification

Capital Market Intervention and the Market for Managerial Talent

Value-Creating Influences
- Economies of Scope
- Market Power
- Financial Economics

Value-Neutral Influences
- Incentives
- Resources

Value-Reducing Influences
- Managerial Motives to Diversify

Diversification Strategy

Firm Performance

Internal Governance

Strategy Implementation

Source: Adapted from R. E. Hoskisson & M. A. Hitt, 1990, Antecedents and performance outcomes of diversification: A review and critique of theoretical perspectives, *Journal of Management,* 16: 498.

nance (see Chapter 10). Appropriate strategy implementation tools, such as organizational structures, are also important (see Chapter 11).

We have described corporate-level strategies in this chapter. In the next one, we discuss mergers and acquisitions as prominent means for firms to diversify and to grow profitably while doing so.[138] These trends toward more diversification through acquisitions, which have been partially reversed due to restructuring (see Chapter 7), indicate that learning has taken place regarding corporate-level diversification strategies.[139] Accordingly, firms that diversify should do so cautiously, choosing to focus on relatively few, rather than many, businesses.[140] In fact, research suggests that although unrelated diversification has decreased, related diversification has increased, possibly due to the restructuring that continued into the 1990s and early 21st century.[141] This sequence of diversification followed by restructuring is now taking place in Europe and other places such as Korea, mirroring actions of firms in the United States and the United Kingdom.[142] Firms can improve their strategic competitiveness when they pursue a level of diversification that is appropriate for their resources (especially financial resources) and core competencies and the opportunities and threats in their country's institutional and competitive environments.[143]

- The primary reason a firm uses a corporate-level strategy to become more diversified is to create additional value. Using a single- or dominant-business corporate-level strategy may be preferable to seeking a more diversified strategy, unless a corporation can develop economies of scope or financial economies between businesses, or unless it can obtain market power through additional levels of diversification. Economies of scope and market power are the main sources of value creation when the firm diversifies by using a corporate-level strategy with moderate to high levels of diversification.

- The corporate-level strategy of related diversification helps the firm to create value by sharing activities or transferring competencies between different businesses in the company's portfolio of businesses.

- Sharing activities usually involves sharing tangible resources between businesses. Transferring core competencies involves transferring core competencies developed in one business to another one. It also may involve transferring competencies between the corporate headquarters office and a business unit.

- Sharing activities is usually associated with the related constrained diversification corporate-level strategy. Activity sharing is costly to implement and coordinate, may create unequal benefits for the divisions involved in the sharing, and may lead to fewer managerial risk-taking behaviors.

- Transferring core competencies is often associated with related linked (or mixed related and unrelated) diversification, although firms pursuing both sharing activities and transferring core competencies can also use the related linked strategy.

- Efficiently allocating resources or restructuring a target firm's assets and placing them under rigorous financial controls are two ways to accomplish successful unrelated diversification. Firms using the unrelated diversification strategy focus on creating financial economies to generate value.

- Diversification is sometimes pursued for value-neutral reasons. Incentives from tax and antitrust government policies, performance disappointments, or uncertainties about future cash flow are examples of value-neutral reasons that firms may choose to become more diversified.

- Managerial motives to diversify (including to increase compensation) can lead to overdiversification and a subsequent reduction in a firm's ability to create value. Evidence suggests, however, that certainly the majority of top-level executives seek to be good stewards of the firm's assets and to avoid diversifying the firm in ways and amounts that destroy value.

- Managers need to pay attention to their firm's internal environment and its external environment when making decisions about the optimum level of diversification for their company. Of course, internal resources are important determinants of the direction that diversification should take. However, conditions in the firm's external environment may facilitate additional levels of diversification, as might unexpected threats from competitors.

1. M. E. Porter, 1980, *Competitive Strategy,* New York: The Free Press, xvi.

2. G. Gavetti, D. A. Levinthal, & J. W. Rivkin, 2005, Strategy making in novel and complex worlds: The power of analogy, *Strategic Management Journal,* 26: 691–712.

3. G. Probst & S. Raisch, 2005, Organizational crisis: The logic of failure, *Academy of Management Executive,* 19(1): 90–105; S. P. Viguerie & C. Thompson, 2005, The faster they fall, *Harvard Business Review,* 83(3): 22.

4. N. J. Moss, 2005, The relative value of growth, *Harvard Business Review,* 83(4): 102–112.

5. M. E. Porter, 1987, From competitive advantage to corporate strategy, *Harvard Business Review,* 65(3): 43–59.

6. Ibid.; C. A. Montgomery, 1994, Corporate diversification, *Journal of Economic Perspectives,* 8: 163–178.

7. P.-Y. Chu, M.-J. Teng, C.-H. Huang, & H.-S. Lin, 2005, Virtual integration and profitability: Some evidence from Taiwan's IC industry, *International Journal of Technology Management,* 29: 152–172; M. Kwak, 2002, Maximizing value through diversification, *MIT Sloan Management Review,* 43(2): 10.

8. S. A. Mansi & D. M. Reeb, 2002, Corporate diversification: What gets discounted? *Journal of Finance,* 57: 2167–2183; P. Wright, M. Kroll, A. Lado, & B. Van Ness, 2002, The structure of ownership and corporate acquisition strategies, *Strategic Management Journal,* 23: 41–53; C. C. Markides & P. J. Williamson, 1996, Corporate diversification and organizational structure: A resource-based view, *Academy of Management Journal,* 39: 340–367.

9. E. Thorton, 2005, How Purcell lost his way, *Business Week,* July 11, 68–70.

10. C. E. Helfat & K. M. Eisenhardt, 2004, Inter-temporal economies of scope organizational modularity, and the dynamics of diversification, *Strategic Management Journal,* 25: 1217–1232.

11. A. Campbell, M. Goold, & M. Alexander, 1995, Corporate strategy: The question for parenting advantage, *Harvard Business Review,* 73(2): 120–132.

12. M. Goold & A. Campbell, 2002, Parenting in complex structures, *Long Range Planning,* 35(3): 219–243; T. H. Brush, P. Bromiley, & M. Hendrickx, 1999, The relative influence of industry and corporation on business segment performance: An alternative estimate, *Strategic Management Journal,* 20: 519–547; T. H. Brush & P. Bromiley, 1997, What does a small corporate effect mean? A variance components simulation of corporate and business effects, *Strategic Management Journal,* 18: 825–835.

13. D. J. Miller, 2004, Firms' technological resources and the performance effects of diversification: A longitudinal study, *Strategic Management Journal,* 25: 1097–1119.

14. D. D. Bergh, 2001, Diversification strategy research at a crossroads: Established, emerging and anticipated paths, in M. A. Hitt, R. E. Freeman, & J. S. Harrison (eds.), *Handbook of Strategic Management,* Oxford, UK: Blackwell Publishers, 363–383.

15. 2004, Brinker International Annual Report, 4.

16. S. Holmes, 2005, 'I like a challenge—And I've got one,' *Business Week,* July 18, 44.

17. D. E. M. Sappington, 2003, Regulating horizontal diversification, *International Journal of Industrial Organization,* 21: 291–315.

18. R. P. Rumelt, *Strategy, Structure, and Economic Performance,* Boston: Harvard Business School, 1974; L. Wrigley, 1970, *Divisional Autonomy and Diversification* (Ph.D. dissertation), Harvard Business School.

19. 2005, Wrigley to add Life Savers and Altoids to its confectionery portfolio, Wrigley Home Page, www.wrigley.com, February 17.

20. R. D. Ireland, R. E. Hoskisson, & M. A. Hitt, 2006, *Understanding Business Strategy,* Mason, OH: Thomson South-Western, 139.

21. P. Grant, J. Drucker, & D. K. Berman, 2005, Cable's eyes on wireless prize, *Wall Street Journal Online,* www.wsj.com, May 18.

22. 2005, About Us, Hutchison Whampoa Limited Home Page, www.hutchison-whampoa.com, August 29.

23. M. Goold & D. Young, 2005, When lean isn't mean, *Harvard Business Review,* 83(4): 16–18.

24. B. Einhorn & R. Tiplady, 2005, What does Li see in this wallflower? *Business Week,* May 23, 58.

25. R. K. Aggarwal & A. A. Samwick, 2003, Why do managers diversify their firms? Agency reconsidered, *Journal of Finance,* 58: 71–118; P. Wright, M. Kroll, & D. Elenkov, 2002, Acquisition returns, increase in firm size, and chief executive officer compensation: The moderating role of monitoring, *Academy of Management Journal,* 45: 599–608.

26. W. S. DeSarbo, C. A. Di Benedetto, M. Song, & I. Sinha, 2005, Revisiting the Miles and Snow strategic framework: Uncovering interrelationships between strategic types, capabilities, environmental uncertainty, and firm performance, *Strategic Management Journal,* 26: 47–74; J. Song, 2002, Firm capabilities and technology ladders, *Strategic Management Journal,* 23: 191–210; J. Lampel & J. Shamsie, 2000, Probing the unobtrusive link: Dominant logic and the design of joint ventures at General Electric, *Strategic Management Journal,* 21: 593–602.

27. M. S. Gary, 2005, Implementation strategy and performance outcomes in related diversification, *Strategic Management Journal,* 26: 643–664; H. Tanriverdi & N. Venkatraman, 2005, Knowledge relatedness and the performance of multibusiness firms, *Strategic Management Journal,* 26: 97–119.

28. M. W. Peng, S.-H. Lee, & D. Y. L. Wang, 2005, What determines the scope of the firm over time? A focus on institutional relatedness, *Academy of Management Review,* 30: 622–633.

29. M. E. Porter, 1985, *Competitive Advantage,* New York: The Free Press, 328.

30. J. W. Lu & P. W. Beamish, 2004, International diversification and firm performance: The S-curve hypothesis, *Academy of Management Journal,* 47: 598–609; R. G. Schroeder, K. A. Bates, & M. A. Junttila, 2002, A resource-based view of manufacturing strategy and the relationship to manufacturing performance, *Strategic Management Journal,* 23: 105–117.

31. N. Byrnes, R. Berner, W. Zellner, & W. C. Symonds, 2005, Branding: Five new lessons, *Business Week,* February 14, 26–28.

32. N. Deogun, C. Forelle, D. K. Berman, & E. Nelson, 2005, P&G to buy Gillette for $54 billion, *Wall Street Journal Online,* www.wsj.com, January 28.

33. R. G. Blumenthal, 2005, P&G looks underrated in eve of buying Gillette, *Bryan-College Station Eagle,* August 29, E4.

34. D. Wince-Smith, 2005, Innovate at your own risk, *Harvard Business Review,* 83(5): 25.

35. D. Gupta & Y. Gerchak, 2002, Quantifying operational synergies in a merger/acquisition, *Management Science,* 48: 517–533.

36. A. Pressman, 2005, Fidelity trolls for bigger fish, *Business Week,* August 15, 70–71.

37. Ibid.

38. M. L. Marks & P. H. Mirvis, 2000, Managing mergers, acquisitions, and alliances: Creating an effective transition structure, *Organizational Dynamics,* 28(3): 35–47.

39. C. Park, 2003, Prior performance characteristics of related and unrelated acquirers, *Strategic Management Journal,* 24: 471–480; G. Delong, 2001, Stockholder gains from focusing versus diversifying bank mergers, *Journal of Financial Economics,* 2: 221–252; T. H. Brush, 1996, Predicted change in operational synergy and post-acquisition performance of acquired businesses, *Strategic Management Journal,* 17: 1–24; H. Zhang, 1995, Wealth effects of U.S. bank takeovers, *Applied Financial Economics,* 5: 329–336.

40. D. D. Bergh, 1995, Size and relatedness of units sold: An agency theory and resource-based perspective, *Strategic Management Journal,* 16: 221–239.

41. M. Lubatkin & S. Chatterjee, 1994, Extending modern portfolio theory into the domain of corporate diversification: Does it apply? *Academy of Management Journal,* 37: 109–136.

42. A. Van Oijen, 2001, Product diversification, corporate management instruments, resource sharing, and performance, *Academy of Management Best Paper Proceedings* (on CD-ROM, Business Policy and Strategy Division); T. Kono, 1999, A strong head office makes a strong company, *Long Range Planning,* 32(2): 225.

43. M. Kotabe, X. Martin, & H. Domoto, 2003, Gaining from vertical partnerships: Knowledge transfer, relationship duration, and supplier performance improvement in the U.S. and Japanese automotive industries, *Strategic Management Journal,* 24: 293–316; L. Capron, P. Dussauge, & W. Mitchell, 1998, Resource redeployment following horizontal acquisitions in Europe and the United States, 1988–1992, *Strategic Management Journal,* 19: 631–661; A. Mehra, 1996, Resource and market based determinants of performance in the U.S. banking industry, *Strategic Management Journal,* 17: 307–322; S. Chatterjee & B. Wernerfelt, 1991, The link between resources and type of diversification: Theory and evidence, *Strategic Management Journal,* 12: 33–48.

44. S. Dutta, M. J. Zbaracki, & M. Bergen, 2003, Pricing process as a capability: A resource-based perspective, *Strategic Management Journal,* 24: 615–630.

45. L. Capron & N. Pistre, 2002, When do acquirers earn abnormal returns? *Strategic Management Journal,* 23: 781–794.

46. 2005, Henkel's Lehner to expand adhesives unit through acquisitions, *Bloomberg.com,* www.bloomberg.com, August 17.

47. J. W. Spencer, 2003, Firms' knowledge-sharing strategies in the global innovation system: Empirical evidence from the flat panel display industry, *Strategic Management Journal,* 24: 217–233.

48. 2005, Virgin Group Ltd., *Hoovers,* www.hoovers.com, August 17.

49. 2005, About Thermo, Thermo Electron Home Page, www.thermoelectron.com, August 12.

50. 2005, Honda engines, Honda Motor Company Home Page, www.honda.com, August 29.

51. G. Stalk Jr., 2005, Rotate the core, *Harvard Business Review,* 83(3): 18–19; C. Zellner & D. Fornahl, 2002, Scientific knowledge and implications for its diffusion, *Journal of Knowledge Management,* 6(2): 190–198.

52. C. St. John & J. S. Harrison, 1999, Manufacturing-based relatedness, synergy, and coordination, *Strategic Management Journal,* 20: 129–145.

53. S. Chatterjee & J. Singh, 1999, Are tradeoffs inherent in diversification moves? A simultaneous model for type of diversification and mode of expansion decisions, *Management Science,* 45: 25–41.

54. M. Halkias, 2005, Federated, May agree to merge, *Dallas Morning News,* www.dallasnews.com, February 27.

55. T. Muck, 2005, Arkansas Business reports Whirlpool to lay off 400 in Ft. Smith, *Today's THV KTHV Little Rock,* www.kthv.com, August 26.

56. C. Salter, 2005, Whirlpool finds its cool, *Fast Company*, June, 73–75.

57. M. Dickie, 2005, Haier gets to top but must work to stay there, *Financial Times Online*, www.ft.com, August 29.

58. Bergh, Diversification strategy research at a crossroads, 369.

59. G. Symeonidis, 2002, Cartel stability with multiproduct firms, *International Journal of Industrial Organization*, 20: 339–352; J. Gimeno & C. Y. Woo, 1999, Multimarket contact, economies of scope, and firm performance, *Academy of Management Journal*, 42: 239–259.

60. 2005, DHL import express, DHL Home Page, yourdhl.com, August 29.

61. 2005, UPS expanding logistics options for Intra-Asia customers, *Supply & Demand Chain Executive*, www.sdcexec.com, April 11.

62. R. Gulati, P. R. Lawrence, & P. Puranam, 2005, Adaptation in vertical relationships: Beyond incentive conflict, *Strategic Management Journal*, 26: 415–440.

63. D. A. Griffin, A. Chandra, & T. Fealey, 2005, Strategically employing natural channels in an emerging market, *Thunderbird International Business Review*, 47(3): 287–311; A. Darr & I. Talmud, 2003, The structure of knowledge and seller-buyer networks in markets for emergent technologies, *Organization Studies*, 24: 443–461.

64. O. E. Williamson, 1996, Economics and organization: A primer, *California Management Review*, 38(2): 131–146.

65. M. G. Jacobides, 2005, Industry change through vertical disintegration: How and why markets emerged in mortgage banking, *Academy of Management Journal*, 48: 465–498.

66. R. Barker, 2003, How high will Medco fly on its own? *Business Week*, May 26, 118.

67. L. R. Kopczak & M. E. Johnson, 2003, The supply-chain management effect, *MIT Sloan Management Review*, 3: 27–34; K. R. Harrigan, 2001, Strategic flexibility in the old and new economies, in M. A. Hitt, R. E. Freeman, & J. S. Harrison (eds.), *Handbook of Strategic Management*, Oxford, UK: Blackwell Publishers, 97–123.

68. M. R. Subramani & N. Venkatraman, 2003, Safeguarding investments in asymmetric interorganizational relationships: Theory and evidence, *Academy of Management Journal*, 46: 46–62; R. E. Kranton & D. F. Minehart, 2001, Networks versus vertical integration, *Rand Journal of Economics*, 3: 570–601.

69. C. Serant, 2003, Mexico spins a new orbit—The country's venerable contract manufacturing complex is assuming a dramatic new form as China asserts its position as the EMS industry's cost leader, *EBN*, January 20, 27.

70. P. Kothandaraman & D. T. Wilson, 2001, The future of competition: Value-creating networks, *Industrial Marketing Management*, 30: 379–389.

71. K. M. Eisenhardt & D. C. Galunic, 2000, Coevolving: At last, a way to make synergies work, *Harvard Business Review*, 78(1): 91–111.

72. R. Schoenberg, 2001, Knowledge transfer and resource sharing as value creation mechanisms in inbound continental European acquisitions, *Journal of Euro-Marketing*, 10: 99–114.

73. 2005, The Walt Disney Company—Company overview, Walt Disney Home Page, http://corporate.disney.go.com, August 30.

74. M. Freeman, 2002, Forging a model for profitability, *Electronic Media*, January 28, 1, 13.

75. D. D. Bergh, 1997, Predicting divestiture of unrelated acquisitions: An integrative model of ex ante conditions, *Strategic Management Journal*, 18: 715–731; C. W. L. Hill, 1994, Diversification and economic performance: Bringing structure and corporate management back into the picture, in R. P. Rumelt, D. E. Schendel, & D. J. Teece (eds.), *Fundamental Issues in Strategy*, Boston: Harvard Business School Press, 297–321.

76. Porter, *Competitive Advantage*.

77. O. E. Williamson, 1975, *Markets and Hierarchies: Analysis and Antitrust Implications*, New York: Macmillan Free Press.

78. J. McTague, 2002, Security in numbers, *Barron's*, December 30, 26; C. Botosan & M. Harris, 2000, Motivations for changes in disclosure frequency and its consequences: An examination of voluntary quarterly segment disclosure, *Journal of Accounting Research*, 38: 329–353; R. Kochhar & M. A. Hitt, 1998, Linking corporate strategy to capital structure: Diversification strategy, type, and source of financing, *Strategic Management Journal*, 19: 601–610.

79. D. Miller, R. Eisenstat, & N. Foote, 2002, Strategy from the inside out: Building capability-creating organizations, *California Management Review*, 44(3): 37–54; M. E. Raynor & J. L. Bower, 2001, Lead from the center: How to manage divisions dynamically, *Harvard Business Review*, 79(5): 92–100; P. Taylor & J. Lowe, 1995, A note on corporate strategy and capital structure, *Strategic Management Journal*, 16: 411–414.

80. J. M. Campa & S. Kedia, 2002, Explaining the diversification discount, *Journal of Finance*, 57: 1731–1762; M. Kwak, 2001, Spinoffs lead to better financing decisions, *MIT Sloan Management Review*, 42(4): 10; O. A. Lamont & C. Polk, 2001, The diversification discount: Cash flows versus returns, *Journal of Finance*, 56: 1693–1721; R. Rajan, H. Servaes, & L. Zingales, 2001, The cost of diversity: The diversification discount and inefficient investment, *Journal of Finance*, 55: 35–79.

81. 2001, Spoilt for choice, *The Economist*, www.economist.com, July 5.

82. L. G. Thomas III, 2004, Are we all global now? Local vs. foreign sources of corporate competence: The case of the Japanese pharmaceutical industry, *Strategic Management Journal*, 25 (Special Issue): 865–886.

83. D. J. Denis, D. K. Denis, & A. Sarin, 1999, Agency theory and the reference of equity ownership structure on corporate diversification strategies, *Strategic Management Journal*, 20: 1071–1076; R. Amit & J. Livnat, 1988, A concept of conglomerate diversification, *Journal of Management*, 14: 593–604.

84. Whittington, In praise of the evergreen conglomerate, 4.

85. T. Khanna, K. G. Palepu, & J. Sinha, 2005, Strategies that fit emerging markets, *Harvard Business Review*, 83(6): 63–76.

86. T. Khanna & K. Palepu, 2000, Is group affiliation profitable in emerging markets? An analysis of diversified Indian business groups, *Journal of Finance*, 55: 867–892; T. Khanna & K. Palepu, 2000, The future of business groups in emerging markets: Long-run evidence from Chile, *Academy of Management Journal*, 43: 268–285.

87. S. Sams, 2005, Emerging expertise, *Harvard Business Review*, 83(5): 24–26.

88. R. E. Hoskisson, R. A. Johnson, D. Yiu, & W. P. Wan, 2001. Restructuring strategies and diversified business groups: Differences associated with country institutional environments, in M. A. Hitt, R. E. Freeman, & J. S. Harrison (eds.), Handbook of Strategic Management, Oxford, UK: Blackwell Publishers, 433–463; S. J. Chang & H. Singh, 1999, The impact of entry and resource fit on modes of exit by multibusiness firms, Strategic Management Journal, 20: 1019–1035.

89. W. Ng & C. de Cock, 2002, Battle in the boardroom: A discursive perspective, Journal of Management Studies, 39: 23–49.

90. J. Robertson, 2005, Hotel chain to be sold, Dallas Morning News, www.dallasnews.com, June 14.

91. R. Coff, 2003, Bidding wars over R&D-intensive firms: Knowledge, opportunism, and the market for corporate control, Academy of Management Journal, 46: 74–85.

92. M. Lubatkin, H. Merchant, & M. Srinivasan, 1997, Merger strategies and shareholder value during times of relaxed antitrust enforcement: The case of large mergers during the 1980s, Journal of Management, 23: 61–81.

93. D. P. Champlin & J. T. Knoedler, 1999, Restructuring by design? Government's complicity in corporate restructuring, Journal of Economic Issues, 33(1): 41–57.

94. R. M. Scherer & D. Ross, 1990, Industrial Market Structure and Economic Performance, Boston: Houghton Mifflin.

95. A. Shleifer & R. W. Vishny, 1994, Takeovers in the 1960s and 1980s: Evidence and implications, in R. P. Rumelt, D. E. Schendel, & D. J. Teece (eds.), Fundamental Issues in Strategy, Boston: Harvard Business School Press, 403–422.

96. S. Chatterjee, J. S. Harrison, & D. D. Bergh, 2003, Failed takeover attempts, corporate governance and refocusing, Strategic Management Journal, 24: 87–96; Lubatkin, Merchant, & Srinivasan, Merger strategies and shareholder value; D. J. Ravenscraft & R. M. Scherer, 1987, Mergers, Sell-Offs and Economic Efficiency, Washington, DC: Brookings Institution, 22.

97. D. A. Zalewski, 2001, Corporate takeovers, fairness, and public policy, Journal of Economic Issues, 35: 431–437; P. L. Zweig, J. P. Kline, S. A. Forest, & K. Gudridge, 1995, The case against mergers, Business Week, October 30, 122–130; J. R. Williams, B. L. Paez, & L. Sanders, 1988, Conglomerates revisited, Strategic Management Journal, 9: 403–414.

98. E. J. Lopez, 2001, New anti-merger theories: A critique, Cato Journal, 20: 359–378; 1998, The trustbusters' new tools, The Economist, May 2, 62–64.

99. R. Croyle & P. Kager, 2002, Giving mergers a head start, Harvard Business Review, 80(10): 20–21.

100. M. C. Jensen, 1986, Agency costs of free cash flow, corporate finance, and takeovers, American Economic Review, 76: 323–329.

101. R. Gilson, M. Scholes, & M. Wolfson, 1988, Taxation and the dynamics of corporate control: The uncertain case for tax motivated acquisitions, in J. C. Coffee, L. Lowenstein, & S. Rose-Ackerman (eds.), Knights, Raiders, and Targets: The Impact of the Hostile Takeover, New York: Oxford University Press, 271–299.

102. C. Steindel, 1986, Tax reform and the merger and acquisition market: The repeal of the general utilities, Federal Reserve Bank of New York Quarterly Review, 11(3): 31–35.

103. M. A. Hitt, J. S. Harrison, & R. D. Ireland, 2001, Mergers and Acquisitions: A Guide to Creating Value for Stakeholders, New York: Oxford University Press.

104. D. B. Wilkerson & Russ Britt, 2003, It's showtime for media deals: Radio lessons fuel debate over control of TV, newspapers, MarketWatch, www.marketwatch.com, May 30.

105. S. Labaton, 2003, Senators move to restore F.C.C. limits on the media, New York Times, www.nytimes.com, June 5.

106. A. M. Squeo, 2004, FCC's Powell sits on horns of dilemma: Chairman must assuage industry without compromising his deregulation agenda, Wall Street Journal, July 19, A4.

107. S. Wooley, 2003, Telco TV (take 2), Forbes, May 12, 68.

108. C. Park, 2002, The effects of prior performance on the choice between related and unrelated acquisitions: Implications for the performance consequences of diversification strategy, Journal of Management Studies, 39: 1003–1019.

109. Rumelt, Strategy, Structure and Economic Performance, 125.

110. J. G. Matsusaka, 2001, Corporate diversification, value maximization, and organizational capabilities, Journal of Business, 74: 409–432.

111. 2005, About Sears, Sears Holding Company Home Page, www.sears.com, August 30.

112. L. E. Palich, L. B. Cardinal, & C. C. Miller, 2000, Curvilinearity in the diversification-performance linkage: An examination of over three decades of research, Strategic Management Journal, 21: 155–174.

113. J. Ewing, 2003, Back to basics, Business Week, March 10, 46–47.

114. A. E. Bernardo & B. Chowdhry, 2002, Resources, real options, and corporate strategy, Journal of Financial Economics, 63: 211–234.

115. N. W. C. Harper & S. P. Viguerie, 2002, Are you too focused? McKinsey Quarterly, Mid-Summer, 29–38; J. C. Sandvig & L. Coakley, 1998, Best practices in small firm diversification, Business Horizons, 41(3): 33–40; C. G. Smith & A. C. Cooper, 1988, Established companies diversifying into young industries: A comparison of firms with different levels of performance, Strategic Management Journal, 9: 111–121.

116. N. M. Kay & A. Diamantopoulos, 1987, Uncertainty and synergy: Towards a formal model of corporate strategy, Managerial and Decision Economics, 8: 121–130.

117. R. W. Coff, 1999, How buyers cope with uncertainty when acquiring firms in knowledge-intensive industries: Caveat emptor, Organization Science, 10: 144–161.

118. S. Tully, 2005, The urge to merge, Fortune, February 21, 21–22.

119. S. J. Chatterjee & B. Wernerfelt, 1991, The link between resources and type of diversification: Theory and evidence, Strategic Management Journal, 12: 33–48.

120. W. Keuslein, 2003, The Ebitda folly, Forbes, March 17, 165–167; Kochhar & Hitt, Linking corporate strategy to capital structure.

121. L. Capron & J. Hulland, 1999, Redeployment of brands, sales forces, and general marketing management expertise following horizontal acquisitions: A resource-based view, Journal of Marketing, 63(2): 41–54.

122. A. M. Knott, D. J. Bryce, & H. E. Pose, 2003, On the strategic accumulation of intangible assets, Organization Science, 14: 192–207; J. Castillo, 2002, A note on the concept of tacit knowledge, Journal of Management Inquiry, 11(1): 46–57; R. D. Smith, 2000, Intangible strategic assets and firm performance: A multi-industry study of the resource-based view, Journal of Business Strategies, 17(2): 91–117.

123. K. Shimizu & M. A. Hitt, 2005, What constrains or facilitates divestitures of formerly acquired firms? The effects of organizational inertia, Journal of Management, 31: 50–72.

124. 2005, Wendy's announces strategic plan, Forbes, www.forbes.com, July 29.

125. 2005, Wendy's to sell part of Tim Horton's chain, Chicago Tribune, www.chicagotribune.com, July 29.

126. 2005, Sara Lee Corporation announces bold transformation plan to drive long-term growth and performance, Sara Lee Corporation Home Page, www.saralee.com, February 21.

127. 2005, Sara Lee cleans out its cupboards, Fortune, March 7, 38.

128. J. G. Combs & M. S. Skill, 2003, Managerialist and human capital explanation for key executive pay premiums: A contingency perspective, Academy of Management Journal, 46: 63–73; M. A. Geletkanycz, B. K. Boyd, & S. Finkelstein, 2001, The strategic value of CEO external directorate networks: Implications for CEO compensation, Strategic Management Journal, 9: 889–898; W. Grossman & R. E. Hoskisson, 1998, CEO pay at the crossroads of Wall Street and Main: Toward the strategic design of executive compensation, Academy of Management Executive, 12(1): 43–57; S. Finkelstein & D. C. Hambrick, 1996, Strategic Leadership: Top Executives and Their Effects on Organizations, St. Paul, MN: West Publishing Company.

129. W. Shen & A. A. Cannella Jr., 2002, Power dynamics within top management and their impacts on CEO dismissal followed by inside succession, Academy of Management Journal, 45: 1195–1206; W. Shen & A. A. Cannella Jr., 2002, Revisiting the performance consequences of CEO succession: The impacts of successor type, postsuccession senior executive turnover, and departing CEO tenure, Academy of Management Journal, 45: 717–733; P. J. Lane, A. A. Cannella Jr., & M. H. Lubatkin, 1998, Agency problems as antecedents to unrelated mergers and diversification: Amihud and Lev reconsidered, Strategic Management Journal, 19: 555–578; D. L. May, 1995, Do managerial motives influence firm risk reduction strategies? Journal of Finance, 50: 1291–1308; Y. Amihud and B. Lev, 1981, Risk reduction as a managerial motive for conglomerate mergers, Bell Journal of Economics, 12: 605–617.

130. J. J. Cordeiro & R. Veliyath, 2003, Beyond pay for performance: A panel study of the determinants of CEO compensation, American Business Review, 21(1): 56–66; Wright, Kroll, & Elenkov, Acquisition returns, increase in firm size, and chief executive officer compensation; S. R. Gray & A. A. Cannella Jr., 1997, The role of risk in executive compensation, Journal of Management, 23: 517–540.

131. R. Bliss & R. Rosen, 2001, CEO compensation and bank mergers, Journal of Financial Economics, 1: 107–138; W. G. Sanders & M. A. Carpenter, 1998, Internationalization and firm governance: The roles of CEO compensation, top team composition, and board structure, Academy of Management Journal, 41: 158–178.

132. J. J. Janney, 2002, Eat or get eaten? How equity ownership and diversification shape CEO risk-taking, Academy of Management Executive, 14(4): 157–158; J. W. Lorsch, A. S. Zelleke, & K. Pick, 2001, Unbalanced boards, Harvard Business Review, 79(2): 28–30; R. E. Hoskisson & T. Turk, 1990, Corporate restructuring: Governance and control limits of the internal market, Academy of Management Review, 15: 459–477.

133. M. Kahan & E. B. Rock, 2002, How I learned to stop worrying and love the pill: Adaptive responses to takeover law, University of Chicago Law Review, 69(3): 871–915.

134. R. C. Anderson, T. W. Bates, J. M. Bizjak, & M. L. Lemmon, 2000, Corporate governance and firm diversification, *Financial Management,* 29(1): 5–22; J. D. Westphal, 1998, Board games: How CEOs adapt to increases in structural board independence from management, *Administrative Science Quarterly,* 43: 511–537; J. K. Seward & J. P. Walsh, 1996, The governance and control of voluntary corporate spin offs, *Strategic Management Journal,* 17: 25–39; J. P. Walsh & J. K. Seward, 1990, On the efficiency of internal and external corporate control mechanisms, *Academy of Management Review,* 15: 421–458.

135. M. Wiersema, 2002, Holes at the top: Why CEO firings backfire, *Harvard Business Review,* 80(12): 70–77

136. V. Kisfalvi & P. Pitcher, 2003, Doing what feels right: The influence of CEO character and emotions on top management team dynamics, *Journal of Management Inquiry,* 12(10): 42–66; R. Larsson, K. R. Brousseau, M. J. Driver, & M. Homqvist, 2003, International growth through cooperation: Brand-driven strategies, leadership, and career development in Sweden, *Academy of Management Executive,* 17(1): 7–21; W. G. Rowe, 2001, Creating wealth in organizations: The role of strategic leadership, *Academy of Management Executive,* 15(1): 81–94.

137. E. F. Fama, 1980, Agency problems and the theory of the firm, *Journal of Political Economy,* 88: 288–307.

138. F. Vermeulen, 2005, How acquisitions can revitalize companies, *MIT Sloan Management Review,* 46(4): 45–51.

139. M. L. A. Hayward, 2002, When do firms learn from their acquisition experience? Evidence from 1990–1995, *Strategic Management Journal,* 23: 21–39; L. Capron, W. Mitchell, & A. Swaminathan, 2001, Asset divestiture following horizontal acquisitions: A dynamic view, *Strategic Management Journal,* 22: 817–844.

140. W. M. Bulkeley, 1994, Conglomerates make a surprising come-back—with a '90s twist, *Wall Street Journal,* March 1, A1, A6.

141. J. P. H. Fan & L. H. P. Lang, 2000, The measurement of relatedness: An application to corporate diversification, *Journal of Business,* 73: 629–660.

142. Khanna & Palepu, The future of business groups in emerging markets; P. Ghemawat & T. Khanna, 1998, The nature of diversified business groups: A research design and two case studies, Journal of Industrial Economics, 46: 35–61.

143. Wan & Hoskisson, Home country environments, corporate diversification strategies, and firm performance.

Acquisitions and Mergers

Studying this chapter should provide you with the strategic management knowledge needed to:

1. Explain the popularity of acquisition strategies in firms competing in the global economy.

2. Discuss reasons why firms use an acquisition strategy to achieve strategic competitiveness.

3. Describe seven problems that work against developing a competitive advantage using an acquisition strategy.

4. Name and describe attributes of effective acquisitions.

5. Define the restructuring strategy and distinguish among its common forms.

6. Explain the short- and long-term outcomes of the different types of restructuring strategies.

ASSOCIATED PRESS, AP

Edward E. Whitacre, Jr. of SBC and David W. Dorman of AT&T on February 1, 2005; SBC acquired AT&T's long distance business.

Domestic and Cross-Border Acquisitions: Meeting Competitive Challenges and Acquiring Critical Resources

As a firm analyzes its external environment and assesses its internal resources and capabilities to meet environmental challenges, acquisitions as well as adjustments to the firm's set of businesses are often considered. Domestically, a number of U.S. firms have found that horizontal acquisitions (acquisitions of potential competitors) meet their needs to handle these environmental challenges and resource considerations. For example, Sears and Kmart merged in order to meet the competitive challenge by Wal-Mart and other large discount retailers. Likewise, consumer product firms Gillette and Procter & Gamble merged. Phone companies have partially met aggressive challenges from cable companies offering local phone service by making acquisitions in the long distance area. For instance, SBC Communications acquired AT&T's long distance business. In response to this move, Verizon and Quest have been battling over the opportunity to acquire MCI, a long distance service company. Most of these horizontal acquisitions have been directed at obtaining more efficiency and market power. Others have been directed at diversifying into new areas of business where the competitive challenge is not as significant as it is in the telecommunications acquisitions.

Still other horizontal acquisitions have been undertaken in order to respond to industry overcapacity. For instance, the proposed acquisition of America West Airlines by U.S. Airways will create more critical mass for the merged airline to compete with larger legacy carriers as well as with discounters such as Southwest Airlines and AirTran Airways. Once the merger is complete, this combination will allow these airlines to reduce some of the overcapacity in the industry.

There have also been a number of cross-border acquisitions announced, especially from Chinese firms seeking to obtain opportunities and especially critical resources allowing them to compete in the important U.S. market. Many of these acquisitions appear to be horizontal. In 2005, Lenovo Group, the largest personal computer manufacturer in China, acquired the PC assets of IBM and is allowed to use the IBM brand label for five years following the acquisition. Lenovo plans to introduce its own brand in association with IBM during this five-year period to build up brand equity in the U.S. market, a critical resource necessary to compete globally. Similarly, the Haier Group, the largest manufacturer of appliances in China, proposed (but later withdrew its offer) to purchase Maytag Corp. in order to build its presence in the United States through the Maytag brand. Chinese National Offshore Oil Corporation (CNOOC), a major oil and natural gas producer in the Chinese domestic market, sought to break up a deal between Chevron and Unocal Corp. by offering a higher takeover bid for Unocal.

Although many of these acquisition attempts appear to be horizontal, much of the impetus for these proposed deals is to obtain brand equity to allow opportunities for distribution. In addition to intangible brand opportunities, the acquiring companies also gain tangible outlets and relationships with distributors, which are necessary to market products in consolidating distribution channels. The CNOOC bid for Unocal would have allowed more sourcing opportunities to produce oil and gas. Thus, these acquisitions also have a vertical acquisition objective.

Cross-border acquisition activity is also taking place in services. For instance, Bank of America,

Chinese National Offshore Oil Corporation is one of the Chinese companies acquiring assets to help them compete in the U.S. market.

which purchased Fleet Boston Financial Corporation in 2004 in the United States, is now building its share of China Construction Bank, headquartered in Beijing. (Foreign investors can buy up to 20 percent of a Chinese bank.) This deal will give Bank of America a seat on Construction Bank's board of directors. Europe has lagged the United States as far as acquiring other banks across borders. However, in 2005 Italy's UniCredito Italiano SpA established an agreement with Germany's HVB Group AG to create Europe's biggest cross-border banking deal. This will give UniCredito branches across a large portion of Western Europe and the former Soviet bloc nations. Both banks have been making acquisitions in Eastern Europe.

To preserve the brand names, each bank will maintain its own brand identity in the short term.

As shown above and as will be explained further in this chapter, acquisition strategies are undertaken for a variety of objectives, including creating efficiencies, gaining market power, improving resources necessary to be more competitive, and overcoming entry barriers. A major question, however, is what the net benefits are after the costs of integration are considered. Many acquisitions have led to increased costs and thus have failed, ending in restructuring divestures. It will be interesting to see which of the acquisitions illustrated above are successful and which create problems for the acquiring firm.

Sources: D. Barboza & A. R. Sorkin, 2005, Chinese oil giant in takeover bid for U.S. corporation, *New York Times*, www.nytimes.com, June 23; J. Biediger, T. Decicco, T. Green, G. Hoffman, D. Lei, K. Mahadaven, J. Ojeda, J. Slocum, & K. Ward, 2005, Strategic action at Lenovo, *Organization Dynamics*, 34(1): 89–102; C. Buckley & J. Creswell, 2005, U.S. bank buys stake in China, *New York Times*, www.nytimes.com, June 17; D. W. Conklin, 2005, Cross-border mergers and acquisitions: A response to environmental transformation, *Journal of World Business*, 40(1): 29–40; G. A. Fowler, 2005, Buying spree by China firms is a bet on value of U.S. brands, *Wall Street Journal*, June 23, B1, B6; M. Krantz, 2005, Warren Buffett raves about Gillette-P&G deal, buys stock, *USA Today*, www.usatoday.com, February 2; A. Merrick, 2005, Shoppers believe retail mergers are a poor bargain, survey finds, *Wall Street Journal*, May 11, A1; S. Rosenbush, 2005, Ready for Chinese merger mania? *Business Week Online*, www.businessweek.com, June 27; J. Singer, C. Mollenkamp & E. Taylor, 2005, UniCredito agrees to acquire HVB; Deal totaling $18.81 billion would create huge lender spanning European borders, *Wall Street Journal*, June 13, A3; J. Singer, E. Taylor & G. Kahn, 2005, Two EU banks discuss merger worth $20 billion, *Wall Street Journal*, May 27, A1, A6; E. B. Smith, 2005, Chinese snap up brand-name U.S. firms, *USA Today*, www.usatoday.com, June 21.

EPA/DING JIANZHOU/LANDOV

In Chapter 6 we studied corporate-level strategies, focusing on types and levels of product diversification strategies that can build core competencies and create competitive advantage. As noted in that chapter, diversification allows a firm to create value by productively using excess resources.[1] In this chapter, we explore mergers and acquisitions, often combined with a diversification strategy, as a prominent strategy employed by firms throughout the world. The acquisition of AT&T's long distance service by SBC Communications is a diversifying acquisition that allows SBC to offer its business customers more phone service options while AT&T can develop its local phone service options. As described in the Opening Case, combining the two firms creates an opportunity for complementarity but also allows SBC to meet the competitive challenge of cable companies offering local phone service. This objective is achieved much faster by using this approach than by developing a new business internally.

In the latter half of the 20th century, acquisition became a prominent strategy used by major corporations to achieve growth and meet competitive challenges. Even smaller and more focused firms began employing acquisition strategies to grow and to enter new markets.[2] However, acquisition strategies are not without problems; a number of acquisitions fail. Thus, we focus on how acquisitions can be used to produce value for the firm's stakeholders.[3] Before describing attributes associated with effective acquisitions, we examine the most prominent problems companies experience when using an acquisition strategy. For example, when acquisitions contribute to poor performance, a firm may deem it necessary to restructure its operations. Closing the chapter are descriptions of three restructuring strategies, as well as the short- and long-term outcomes resulting from their use. Setting the stage for these topics is an examination of the popularity of mergers and acquisition and a discussion of the differences among mergers, acquisitions, and takeovers.

The Popularity of Merger and Acquisition Strategies

The acquisition strategy has been a popular strategy among U.S. firms for many years. Some believe that this strategy played a central role in an effective restructuring of U.S. businesses during the 1980s and 1990s and into the 21st century.[4] Increasingly, acquisition strategies are becoming more popular with firms in other nations and economic regions, including Europe. In fact, about 40 to 45 percent of the acquisitions in recent years have been made across country borders (i.e., a firm headquartered in one country acquiring a firm headquartered in another country).[5] For example, 40 percent of Wal-Mart's international growth has come through acquisitions, "and management remains open to further acquisitions."[6]

Five waves of mergers and acquisitions took place in the 20th century, with the last two occurring in the 1980s and 1990s.[7] There were 55,000 acquisitions valued at $1.3 trillion in the 1980s, and acquisitions in the 1990s exceeded $11 trillion in value.[8] World economies, particularly the U.S. economy, slowed in the new millennium, reducing the number of mergers and acquisitions completed.[9] The annual value of mergers and acquisitions peaked in 2000 at about $3.4 trillion and fell to about $1.75 trillion in 2001.[10] However, as the worldwide economy improved, the global volume of announced acquisition agreements was up 41 percent from 2003 to $1.95 trillion for 2004, the highest level since 2000, and the pace in 2005 was significantly above the level of 2004.[11]

Although the frequency of acquisitions has slowed, their number remains high. In fact, an acquisition strategy is sometimes used because of the uncertainty in the competitive landscape. A firm may make an acquisition to increase its market power because of a competitive threat, to enter a new market because of the opportunity available in that market, or to spread the risk due to the uncertain environment.[12] In addition, as volatility brings undesirable changes to its primary markets, a firm may acquire other companies to shift its core business into different markets.[13] Such options may arise because of industry or regulatory changes. For instance, Clear Channel Communications built its business by buying radio stations in many geographic markets when the Telecommunications Act of 1996 changed the regulations regarding such acquisitions.[14] However, more recently Clear Channel has been suggested to have too much market power and is now likely to split into three different businesses (see the Strategic Focus later in the chapter).

The strategic management process (see Figure 1.1) calls for an acquisition strategy to increase a firm's strategic competitiveness as well as its returns to shareholders. Thus, an acquisition strategy should be used only when the acquiring firm will be able to increase its value through ownership of an acquired firm and the use of its assets.[15]

However, evidence suggests that, at least for the acquiring firms, acquisition strategies may not always result in these desirable outcomes.[16] Researchers have found that shareholders of acquired firms often earn above-average returns from an acquisition, while shareholders of acquiring firms are less likely to do so, typically earning returns from the transaction that are close to zero. In the latest acquisition boom between 1998 and 2000, acquiring firm shareholders experienced significant losses relative to the losses in all of the 1980s. Acquiring firm shareholders lost $0.12 on average for the acquisitions between 1998 and 2000 whereas in the 1980s shareholders lost $.016 per dollar spent. This may suggest that for large firms, it is now more difficult to create sustainable value by using an acquisition strategy to buy publicly traded companies.[17] In approximately two-thirds of all acquisitions, the acquiring firm's stock price falls immediately after the intended transaction is announced. This negative response is an indication of investors' skepticism about the likelihood that the acquirer will be able to achieve the synergies required to justify the premium.[18]

Mergers, Acquisitions, and Takeovers: What Are the Differences?

A **merger** is a strategy through which two firms agree to integrate their operations on a relatively coequal basis. There are few true mergers, because one party is usually dominant in regards to market share or firm size. DaimlerChrysler AG was termed a "merger of equals" and, although Daimler-Benz was the dominant party in the automakers' transaction, Chrysler managers would not allow the business deal to be completed unless it was termed a merger.[19]

An **acquisition** is a strategy through which one firm buys a controlling, or 100 percent, interest in another firm with the intent of making the acquired firm a subsidiary business within its portfolio. In this case, the management of the acquired firm reports to the management of the acquiring firm. While most mergers are friendly transactions, acquisitions can be friendly or unfriendly.

A **takeover** is a special type of an acquisition strategy wherein the target firm does not solicit the acquiring firm's bid. The number of unsolicited takeover bids increased in the economic downturn of 2001–2002, a common occurrence in economic recessions, because the poorly managed firms that are undervalued relative to their assets are more easily identified.[20] Many takeover attempts are not desired by the target firm's managers and are referred to as hostile. In a few cases, unsolicited offers may come from parties familiar and possibly friendly to the target firm.

On a comparative basis, acquisitions are more common than mergers and takeovers. Accordingly, this chapter focuses on acquisitions.

Reasons for Acquisitions

In this section, we discuss reasons that support the use of an acquisition strategy. Although each reason can provide a legitimate rationale for an acquisition, the acquisition may not necessarily lead to a competitive advantage.

Increased Market Power

A primary reason for acquisitions is to achieve greater market power.[21] Defined in Chapter 6, *market power* exists when a firm is able to sell its goods or services above competitive levels or when the costs of its primary or support activities are below those of its competitors. Market power usually is derived from the size of the firm and its resources and capabilities to compete in the marketplace.[22] It is also affected by the firm's share of the market. Therefore, most acquisitions that are designed to achieve greater market power entail buying a competitor, a supplier, a distributor, or a business in a highly related industry to allow the exercise of a core competence and to gain competitive advantage in the acquiring firm's primary market. One goal in achieving market power is to become a market leader.[23] In 2005, Federated Department Stores, Inc. completed an acquisition of May Department Stores Co. This represents a horizontal acquisition in the large department store retail segment of the "big box" retail store industry. Both Federated and May have been squeezed at the discount end by Wal-Mart and at the high luxury end by firms such as Neiman Marcus. This acquisition represents Federated's hope that by increasing the size of the firm it can maintain enough efficiency to be competitive. Federated is the parent of Macy's and Bloomingdale's, while May's chains include Lord & Taylor, Marshall Field's, and Filene's. These two firms are a good match geographically and across concept (e.g., high quality versus cost conscious), but some malls will probably lose stores because of the overlap in store concepts. This will, however, improve local market power and reduce costs for these businesses.[24] Research in marketing suggests that performance of the merged firm increases if marketing-related issues are involved. The performance improvement of the merged firm subsequent to a horizontal acquisition is even more significant than the average potential cost savings if marketing of the combined firms improves economies of scope.[25] To increase their market power, firms often use horizontal, vertical, and related acquisitions.

Horizontal Acquisitions

The acquisition of a company competing in the same industry as the acquiring firm is referred to as a *horizontal acquisition*. Horizontal acquisitions increase a firm's market power by exploiting cost-based and revenue-based synergies.[26] Research suggests that horizontal acquisitions result in higher performance when the firms have similar characteristics.[27] Examples of important similar characteristics include strategy, managerial styles, and resource allocation patterns. Similarities in these characteristics make the integration of the two firms proceed more smoothly.[28] Horizontal acquisitions are often most effective when the acquiring firm integrates the acquired firm's assets with its assets, but only after evaluating and divesting excess capacity and assets that do not complement the newly combined

Federated Chief Executive Officer Terry Lundgren speaks during a news conference; Federated Department Stores' acquisition of May Dept. Stores is an attempt to remain competitive with firms like Neiman Marcus.

RICK MAIMAN/BLOOMBERG NEWS/LANDOV

firm's core competencies.[29] As the acquisition of May by Federated illustrates, the merged firm will likely have to divest itself of some stores in order to reduce costs associated with the acquisition.

Vertical Acquisitions

A *vertical acquisition* refers to a firm acquiring a supplier or distributor of one or more of its goods or services.[30] A firm becomes vertically integrated through this type of acquisition in that it controls additional parts of the value chain (see Chapters 3 and 6). Kodak's acquisition of Creo, a Canadian producer of devices that "convert computer-generated print files directly to plates used for printing," represents a vertical acquisition. Because Kodak's sales of traditional film and developing have been declining as more people turn to digital photography, Kodak has been acquiring firms that move it into the "filmless imaging" area. These acquisitions have included digital printing (as in the Creo acquisition), health-care imaging, and consumer photography markets. Although the Creo acquisition is primarily focused on a corporate market, other acquisitions will allow Kodak to sell imaging products across a range of specialty (e.g., health care) and consumer markets.[31]

Vertical acquisitions also occur in service and entertainment businesses. Sony's acquisition of Columbia Pictures in the late 1980s was a vertical acquisition in which Columbia's movie content could be used by Sony's hardware devices. Sony's additional acquisition of CBS Records, a music producer, and development of the PlayStation hardware have formed the bases for more vertical integration. The spread of broadband and the technological shift from analog to digital hardware require media firms to find new ways to sell their content to consumers. Sony's former CEO, Nobuyuki Idei, believed that this shift created a new opportunity to sell hardware that integrates this change by selling "televisions, personal computers, game consoles and handheld devices through which all of that wonderful content will one day be streaming."[32]

However, this vision has not functioned well, and Idei was replaced by Howard Stringer as CEO, the first American CEO in Sony's history. Sony's businesses were quite autonomous and the coordination proved difficult to establish between them to realize Idei's vision. Furthermore, the lack of coordination caused a slowdown in innovation such that "Sony's reputation as an innovator" has suffered as "the snazziest gadgets from competitors, like the iPod and the TiVo digital video recorder, increasingly depend on the specific juggling act that Sony can't do well: integrating hardware, software and services."[33]

Related Acquisitions

The acquisition of a firm in a highly related industry is referred to as a *related acquisition*. Sun Microsystems Inc.'s main business has been selling computer workstations and servers. However, Sun's performance has suffered because its server business is highly competitive. Because of increased storage needs that are readily accessible by servers, servers and disk storage devices (versus tapes, which are not as accessible) are more often now sold together. In order to take advantage of this growing opportunity, Sun agreed to acquire Storage Technology Corp. for $4.1 billion. "The purchase also will add about 1,000 Storage Technology's sales representatives to sell Sun's disk-based storage systems against tough rivals such as EMC Corp., Hewlett-Packard Co. and International Business Machines Corp."[34] However, because of the difficulty in achieving synergy, related acquisitions are often difficult to value.[35]

Acquisitions intended to increase market power are subject to regulatory review as well as to analysis by financial markets.[36] For example, as noted in the Opening Case, the takeover attempt of Gillette by Procter & Gamble received a significant amount of government scrutiny as well as close examination by financial analysts. Although European regulators did not approve GE's acquisition of Honeywell, Procter & Gamble's acquisition of Gillette was approved.[37] Thus, firms seeking growth and market power through acquisitions must understand the political/legal segment of the general environment (see Chapter 2) in order to successfully use an acquisition strategy.

Overcoming Entry Barriers

Barriers to entry (introduced in Chapter 2) are factors associated with the market or with the firms currently operating in it that increase the expense and difficulty faced by new ventures trying to enter that particular market. For example, well-established competitors may have substantial economies of scale in the manufacture or service of their products. In addition, enduring relationships with customers often create product loyalties that are difficult for new entrants to overcome. When facing differentiated products, new entrants typically must spend considerable resources to advertise their goods or services and may find it necessary to sell at prices below competitors' to entice customers.

Facing the entry barriers created by economies of scale and differentiated products, a new entrant may find acquiring an established company to be more effective than entering the market as a competitor offering a good or service that is unfamiliar to current buyers. In fact, the higher the barriers to market entry, the greater the probability that a firm will acquire an existing firm to overcome them. Although an acquisition can be expensive, it does provide the new entrant with immediate market access.

For example, Nortel Networks Corp., a Canadian telecom producer, recently purchased PEC Solutions for $448 million. Through this acquisition, the new subsidiary, called Nortel PEC Solutions, inherited government contracts in the growing market pertaining to homeland security, intelligence, and defense. This gives Nortel a stronger stake in the federal computer networks market. Although other federal programs have been cut, the budget for information technology has increased from the proposed $60 billion in 2005 to $65 billion in 2006. Before the purchase, only 40 of Nortel's 30,000 employees worldwide had security clearances from the U.S. government. Nortel's purchase of PEC significantly increased this number, allowing Nortel to overcome considerable barriers to entry in this growing market. Furthermore, the combined company allows Nortel PEC to compete with the nation's largest contractors such as Lockheed Martin and Northrup Grumman. The acquisition has allowed Nortel to transition into this government service market much more rapidly than it would have been able to without buying a current player in the market. It also has given Nortel improved access to a market for its "large-scale telecommunications equipment."[38]

As in the Nortel example, firms trying to enter international markets often face steep entry barriers. However, acquisitions are commonly used to overcome those barriers.[39] At least for large multinational corporations, another indicator of the importance of entering and then competing successfully in international markets is the fact that five emerging markets (China, India, Brazil, Mexico, and Indonesia) are among the 12 largest economies in the world, with a combined purchasing power that is already one-half that of the Group of Seven industrial nations (United States, Japan, Britain, France, Germany, Canada, and Italy). Furthermore, the emerging markets are among the fastest growing economies in the world.[40]

Cross-Border Acquisitions

Acquisitions made between companies with headquarters in different countries are called *cross-border acquisitions*. These acquisitions are often made to overcome entry barriers. In Chapter 9, we examine cross-border alliances and the reason for their use. Compared with a cross-border alliance, a cross-border acquisition gives a firm more control over its international operations.[41]

Mittal Steel Becomes the Largest Worldwide Steel Producer through a Strategy of Cross-Border Acquisitions

Mittal Steel Company was formed in 2004 through the combination of Ispat/LNM Holdings and International Steel Group (ISG). At the close of these deals, Lakshmi N. Mittal became CEO of the largest steel company in the world. The company has the capacity to ship 60 million metric tons annually and predicts annual revenues of over $32 billion. With this combination it will outpace its closest rival, Arcelor SA, which was formed in 2002 by a merger among Arbed SA of Luxembourg, Usinor SA of France, and Aceraliasa SA of Spain. Early in 2004 Arcelor SA invested $1.2 billion to obtain a 60 percent interest in Companhia Siderurgica de Tubarao, Brazil's second largest crude-steel producer. Thus, significant consolidation in the industry is taking place through cross-border horizontal acquisitions.

Mittal Steel has the current lead as the largest firm, at least for now. LNM Holdings, privately held by the Mittal family, was acquired by Ipsat, a publicly traded firm. Ipsat was then combined with ISG to form the Mittal Steel Company. Upon the announcement of the deal, Ipsat stock jumped 27 percent. Through ISG, Mittal Steel now has about 40 percent of the U.S. market in the flat-rolled-steel used in automobiles.

ISG, a combination of LTV Steel, Acme Steel, Bethlehem Steel, Weirton Steel, and Georgetown Steel, was created through deals put together by Wilbur Ross, a private equity investor. Most of these ventures had been bankrupt and Ross picked them up rather cheaply during the steel industry downturn of 1999–2000. The bankrupt firms did not have large pension fund liabilities, which would be a drag on earnings. Even though Mittal Steel and Arcelor produce, respectively, 60 million and 44 million metric tons of steel annually, together they account for less than 10 percent of the total capacity in this global industry. There is still significant room for additional cross-border and domestic horizontal acquisitions to build more concentration in the globalized steel industry.

Mittal Steel's predecessor company, LNM Holdings, had bought many steel businesses in emerging market countries, especially in Eastern Europe, and sought to consolidate and invest significant amounts to improve productivity in the steel firms. Mittal is similarly looking for deals in Turkey, India and China.

Arcelor has been using a cross-border strategy to reduce costs by moving much of its higher-cost European capacity to lower-cost countries such as Brazil, hence the 2004 deal with Siderurgica de Tubarao. Brazil is a great place to manufacture steel because it has plentiful raw materials for steel making and also a surging demand for products that use steel, such as autos. Because the raw product is cheaper to manufacture there, Brazil has become the world's ninth-largest producer of crude steel. Arcelor is seeking to build more value-added products in Brazil but now can also ship steel at a lower price where Arcelor's European rolling mills can convert them into higher quality steel. Thus, the Brazilian operations provide a significant center of cost advantage for Arcelor through its cross-border acquisition in Brazil.

All of this activity has been supported by high steel prices, a result of the high demand for steel created by the hyper growth in China and other emerging market countries. However, China was

Wilbur Ross (left), chairman and CEO of WL Ross & Co., and Lakshmi N. Mittal (Mittal Steel Company); cross-border acquisitions have made Mittal Steel Company the largest steel company in the world.

recently identified as a net exporter, suggesting that the country's domestic demand is slowing. This implies that steel-making capacity around the world may soon grow into oversupply and signal decreasing prices and difficult times in the years ahead. This would be even more problematic because many nations have supported subsidies and loan guarantees to increase production around the world. Thus, besides the consolidation through acquisitions, a significant increase in productive capacity is also being projected. Although the stock gain by Mittal Steel is well earned in the present time, it may be that in the future, as overcapacity is realized in the industry, larger firms may have a difficult time unless they are much more productive than their competitors and can reduce costs as the price comes down. However, such competition may also lead to further consolidation and additional cross-border acquisitions of companies that are not competitive.

Sources: 2005, Mittal completes buy of ISG, *Platt's Metal Week*, April 18, 20; 2005, Business: The wrong worry; steel, *The Economist*, March 12, 80; S. Reed & A. Ashton, 2005, Steel: The mergers aren't over yet, *Business Week*, February 21, 6; P. Barta & P. Glader, 2004, China's steel threat may be excess not shortage, *Wall Street Journal*, December 30, A1, A2; P. Glader, 2004, Mittals see Turkey, Asia as next stops, *Wall Street Journal*, October 28, A3; P. Glader & V. Knight, 2004, Arcelor to invest as much as $1.2 billion in Brazil, *Wall Street Journal*, June 29, A2; M. Pinkham & C. C. Petry, 2004, Merger of Ipsat, ISG forms steel giant, *Metal Standard News*, November, 48–49; S. Reed & M. Arndt, 2004, The raja of steel, *Business Week*, December 20, 50–52; A. Sloan, 2004, The tough deal that saved steel, *Newsweek*, November 8, 46.

Historically, U.S. firms have been the most active acquirers of companies outside their domestic market.[42] However, in the global economy, companies throughout the world are choosing this strategic option with increasing frequency. In recent years, cross-border acquisitions have represented as much as 45 percent of the total number of annual acquisitions.[43] Because of relaxed regulations, the amount of cross-border activity among nations within the European community also continues to increase. The fact that many large European corporations have approached the limits of growth within their domestic markets and thus seek growth in other markets is what some analysts believe accounts for the growth in the range of cross-border acquisitions. Research has indicated that many European and U.S. firms participated in cross-border acquisitions across Asian countries that experienced a financial crisis due to significant currency devaluations in 1997. These acquisitions, it is argued, facilitated the survival and restructuring of many large Asian companies such that these economies recovered more quickly than they would have without the cross-border acquisitions.[44]

As illustrated in the Strategic Focus, firms in the steel industry are completing a number of large cross-border acquisitions. Although cross-border acquisitions are taking place across a wide variety of industries to overcome entry barriers (see the Opening Case), such acquisitions can be difficult to negotiate and operate because of the differences in foreign cultures.[45]

Cost of New Product Development and Increased Speed to Market

Developing new products internally and successfully introducing them into the marketplace often require significant investments of a firm's resources, including time, making it difficult to quickly earn a profitable return.[46] Also of concern to firms' managers is achieving adequate returns from the capital invested to develop and commercialize new products—an estimated 88 percent of innovations fail to achieve adequate returns. Perhaps contributing to these less-than-desirable rates of return is the successful imitation of approximately 60 percent of innovations within four years after the patents are obtained. Because of outcomes such as these, managers often perceive internal product development as a high-risk activity.[47]

Acquisitions are another means a firm can use to gain access to new products and to current products that are new to the firm. Compared with internal product development processes, acquisitions provide more predictable returns as well as faster market entry. Returns are more predictable because the performance of the acquired firm's products can be assessed prior to completing the acquisition.[48] For these reasons, extensive bidding wars and acquisitions are more frequent in high-technology industries.[49]

Acquisition activity is also extensive throughout the pharmaceutical industry, where firms frequently use acquisitions to enter markets quickly, to overcome the high costs of developing products internally, and to increase the predictability of returns on their investments. The cost of bringing a new drug to market in 2005 was "pushing $900 million and the average time to launch stretched to 12 years." Interestingly, there was one large deal between pharmaceutical firms in 2004, the merger between French firms Sanofi Synthelabo and Avenus that created Sanofi-Avenus. This $67 billion deal accounted for most of the $77.5 billion total value of deals between pharmaceutical firms. Although merger activity continued in 2005, most deals were smaller, as many companies targeted small acquisitions to supplement market power and reinvigorate or create innovative drug pipelines. Usually it is larger biotech or pharmaceutical firms acquiring smaller biotech firms that have drug opportunities close to market entry.[50]

As indicated previously, compared with internal product development, acquisitions result in more rapid market entries.[51] Acquisitions often represent the fastest means to enter international markets and help firms overcome the liabilities associated with such strategic moves.[52] Acquisitions provide rapid access both to new markets and to new capabilities. Using new capabilities to pioneer new products and to enter markets quickly can create advantageous market positions.[53] Pharmaceutical firms, for example, access new products through acquisitions of other drug manufacturers. They also acquire biotechnology firms both for new products and for new technological capabilities. Pharmaceutical firms often provide the manufacturing and marketing capabilities to take the new products developed by biotechnology firms to the market.[54] In early 2005, Pfizer, for example, agreed to acquire Angiosyn, Inc., a smaller biotech company, which has developed a promising drug to avoid blindness. The deal, valued near $527 million, could extend Pfizer's lead in drugs for eye diseases. This deal "spotlights the interest among the largest pharmaceutical makers to purchasing fledgling biotech concerns."[55]

Lower Risk Compared to Developing New Products

Because the outcomes of an acquisition can be estimated more easily and accurately than the outcomes of an internal product development process, managers may view acquisitions as lowering risk.[56] The difference in risk between an internal product development process and an acquisition can be seen in the results of Pfizer's strategy and that of its competitors described above.[57]

As with other strategic actions discussed in this book, the firm must exercise caution when using a strategy of acquiring new products rather than developing them internally. While research suggests that acquisitions have become a common means of avoiding risky internal ventures (and therefore risky R&D investments), they may also become a substitute for innovation.[58] Thus, acquisitions are not a risk-free alternative to entering new markets through internally developed products.

Increased Diversification

Acquisitions are also used to diversify firms. Based on experience and the insights resulting from it, firms typically find it easier to develop and introduce new products in markets currently served by the firm. In contrast, it is difficult for companies to develop products that differ from their current lines for markets in which they lack experience.[59] Thus, it is uncommon for a firm to develop new products internally to diversify its product lines.[60] Using acquisitions to diversify a firm is the quickest and, typically, the easiest way to change its portfolio of businesses.[61] For example, since 2002 Advanced Medical Optics Inc. (AMO) has used an acquisition strategy to develop a set of products and services that focus on the "vision care lifecycle." AMO provides contact lenses to customers in their teens, laser surgery to patients in their 30s and 40s, and post-cataract-surgery implantable lenses to seniors. In 2004 AMO acquired Pfizer's surgical ophthalmology business. In early 2005, the firm acquired Quest Vision Technologies, Inc., which focuses on developing lenses for presbyopia, or nearsightedness, a common condition among people in their 40s that causes them to wear bifocals or reading glasses. Finally, in 2005 they closed a deal to acquire Visx, Inc., the leader in laser surgery treatment machines based on sales volume. For the present, it appears that AMO's related diversification strategy is creating value as the market has valued its acquisitions positively.[62]

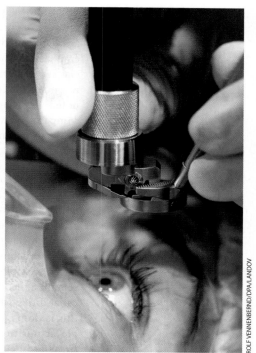

AMO's diversification strategy led it to expand into the area of laser surgery.

Both related diversification and unrelated diversification strategies can be implemented through acquisitions.[63] For example, United Technologies Corp. (UTC) has used acquisitions to build a conglomerate. Since the mid-1970s it has been building a portfolio of stable and noncyclical businesses, including Otis Elevator Co. and Carrier Corporation (air conditioners), in order to reduce its dependence on the volatile aerospace industry. Its main businesses have been Pratt & Whitney (jet engines), Sikorsky (helicopters), and Hamilton Sundstrand (aerospace parts). UTC has also acquired a hydrogen-fuel-cell business. Perceiving an opportunity in security caused by problems at airports and because security has become a top concern both for governments and for corporations, United Technologies in 2003 acquired Chubb PLC, a British electronic-security company, for $1 billion. With its acquisition of Kidde PLC, in the same general business, in 2004 for $2.84 billion, UTC will have obtained 10 percent of the world's market share in electronic security. All businesses UTC purchases are involved in manufacturing industrial and commercial products. However, many are relatively low technology (e.g., elevators and air conditioners).[64]

Research has shown that the more related the acquired firm is to the acquiring firm, the greater the probability is that the acquisition will be successful.[65] Thus, horizontal acquisitions (through which a firm acquires a competitor) and related acquisitions tend to contribute more to the firm's strategic competitiveness than would the acquisition of a company that operates in product markets quite different from those in which the acquiring firm competes.[66]

Reshaping the Firm's Competitive Scope

As discussed in Chapter 2, the intensity of competitive rivalry is an industry characteristic that affects the firm's profitability.[67] To reduce the negative effect of an intense rivalry on their financial performance, firms may use acquisitions to lessen their dependence on one or more products or markets. Reducing a company's dependence on specific markets alters the firm's competitive scope.

ROLF VENNENBERND/DPA/LANDOV

As the Opening Case illustrates, SBC is acquiring AT&T to help it shift its scope toward corporate long distance customers to help it compete against cable firms, which are increasingly entering SBC's local phone service business. Similarly, GE reduced its emphasis in the electronics market many years ago by making acquisitions in the financial services industry. Today, GE is considered a service firm because a majority of its revenue now comes from services instead of from industrial products.[68] However, as we noted in Chapter 6, GE is now attempting to become more of a high-technology company, allowing it to take advantage of opportunities in a number of domestic and international markets.

Learning and Developing New Capabilities

Some acquisitions are made to gain capabilities that the firm does not possess. For example, acquisitions may be used to acquire a special technological capability. Research has shown that firms can broaden their knowledge base and reduce inertia through acquisitions.[69] Therefore, acquiring a firm with skills and capabilities that differ from its own helps the acquiring firm to gain access to new knowledge and remain agile.[70] For example, research suggests that firms increase the potential of their capabilities when they acquire diverse talent through cross-border acquisitions. When this is done, greater value is created through the international expansion versus a simple acquisition without such diversity and resource creation potential.[71] Of course, firms are better able to learn these capabilities if they share some similar properties with the firm's current capabilities. Thus, firms should seek to acquire companies with different but related and complementary capabilities in order to build their own knowledge base.[72]

One of Cisco Systems' primary goals in its early acquisitions was to gain access to capabilities that it needed to compete in the fast-changing networking equipment industry that connects the Internet. Cisco developed an intricate process to quickly integrate the acquired firms and their capabilities (knowledge). Cisco's processes accounted for its phenomenal success in the latter half of the 1990s. However, the goal is now more internal cooperation to "avoid the diving catch."[73] Although Cisco continues to pursue acquisitions that build new capabilities, it completed only 10 acquisitions from January 2001 through July 2003, including four companies that Cisco cultivated through prior alliance relationships, versus 23 acquisitions in 2000 alone. It picked up the pace in 2004 with 12 acquisitions, but none were more than $200 million, although Cisco acquired Airespace in 2005 for $450 million.[74] With this recent acquisition Cisco is trying to build up its capability for wireless transmission of data inside a corporation.

Problems in Achieving Acquisition Success

Acquisition strategies based on reasons described in this chapter can increase strategic competitiveness and help firms earn above-average returns. However, acquisition strategies are not risk-free. Reasons for the use of acquisition strategies and potential problems with such strategies are shown in Figure 7.1.

Research suggests that perhaps 20 percent of all mergers and acquisitions are successful, approximately 60 percent produce disappointing results, and the remaining 20 percent are clear failures.[75] Successful acquisitions generally involve having a well-conceived strategy for selecting the target, not paying too high a premium, and

FIGURE **7.1**

Reasons for Acquisitions and Problems in Achieving Success

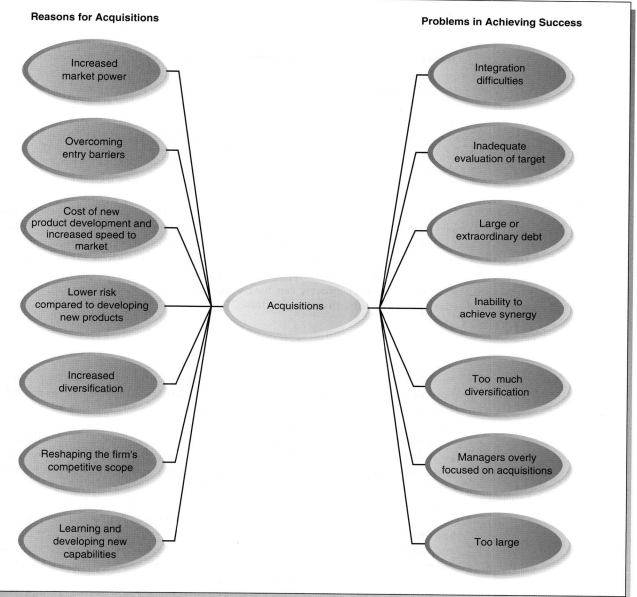

employing an effective integration process.[76] As shown in Figure 7.1, several problems may prevent successful acquisitions.

Integration Difficulties

Integrating two companies following an acquisition can be quite difficult. Integration challenges include melding two disparate corporate cultures, linking different financial and control systems, building effective working relationships (particularly when management styles differ), and resolving problems regarding the status of the newly acquired firm's executives.[77]

The importance of a successful integration should not be underestimated.[78] Without it, an acquisition is unlikely to produce positive returns. Thus, as suggested by a researcher studying the process, "managerial practice and academic writings show that the post-acquisition integration phase is probably the single most important determinant of shareholder value creation (and equally of value destruction) in mergers and acquisitions."[79]

Integration is complex and involves a large number of activities, which if overlooked can lead to significant difficulties. For instance, HealthSouth Corporation developed into a major power in the hospital and health-care industries through an aggressive acquisition strategy. However, the strategy's success was based primarily on generous government Medicare reimbursements. When Congress slashed the budget for such reimbursements, HealthSouth was not in a position to take advantage of its scale because the managers had not sought possible improved cost savings through integration. In fact, the CEO was accused of fraudulent reporting to make up for the significant losses, which went unreported. "Acquisition covered up a lot of sins," said one health-care analyst. "It allowed the company to layer on a lot of growth without necessarily digesting any of its purchases."[80]

It is important to maintain the human capital of the target firm after the acquisition. Much of an organization's knowledge is contained in its human capital.[81] Turnover of key personnel from the acquired firm can have a negative effect on the performance of the merged firm.[82] The loss of key personnel, such as critical managers, weakens the acquired firm's capabilities and reduces its value. If implemented effectively, the integration process can have a positive effect on target firm managers and reduce the probability that they will leave.[83]

Inadequate Evaluation of Target

Due diligence is a process through which a potential acquirer evaluates a target firm for acquisition. In an effective due-diligence process, hundreds of items are examined in areas as diverse as the financing for the intended transaction, differences in cultures between the acquiring and target firm, tax consequences of the transaction, and actions that would be necessary to successfully meld the two workforces. Due diligence is commonly performed by investment bankers, accountants, lawyers, and management consultants specializing in that activity, although firms actively pursuing acquisitions may form their own internal due-diligence team.[84]

The failure to complete an effective due-diligence process may easily result in the acquiring firm paying an excessive premium for the target company. In fact, research shows that without due diligence, "the purchase price is driven by the pricing of other 'comparable' acquisitions rather than by a rigorous assessment of where, when, and how management can drive real performance gains. [In these cases], the price paid may have little to do with achievable value."[85] Analysts have questioned whether Nortel, for instance, paid too much for PEC Solutions mentioned earlier; PEC's stock price increased by $4.01 to close at $15.32 on the day the acquisition was announced,[86] suggesting the size of the premium Nortel paid.

Many firms once used investment banks to perform their due diligence, but in the post-Enron era the process is increasingly performed in-house. While investment bankers such as Credit Suisse First Boston and Citibank still play a large role in due diligence for large mergers and acquisitions, their role in smaller mergers and acquisitions seems to be decreasing. A growing number of companies are building their own internal operations to offer advice about and to finance mergers. However, although investment banks are playing a lesser role, there will always be the need for an outside opinion for a company's board of directors—to reassure them about a planned merger and reduce their liability.[87]

Large or Extraordinary Debt

To finance a number of acquisitions completed during the 1980s and 1990s, some companies significantly increased their levels of debt. A financial innovation called junk bonds helped make this increase possible. *Junk bonds* are a financing option through which risky acquisitions are financed with money (debt) that provides a large potential return to lenders (bondholders). Because junk bonds are unsecured obligations that are not tied to specific assets for collateral, interest rates for these high-risk debt instruments sometimes reached between 18 and 20 percent during the 1980s.[88] Some prominent financial economists viewed debt as a means to discipline managers, causing them to act in the shareholders' best interests.[89]

Junk bonds are now used less frequently to finance acquisitions, and the conviction that debt disciplines managers is less strong. Nonetheless, some firms still take on significant debt to acquire companies. For example, when Time Warner acquired AOL, it increased its total debt to $26 billion. Although current CEO Dick Parsons has spent three years cutting Time Warner's debt in half, the market has still not lifted its stock price. The firm may ultimately need to break up and sell off some of its businesses (especially its Internet asset, AOL) to remain appealing to investors given its diverse businesses in cable TV, filmed entertainment, network TV, music, and publishing.[90]

High debt can have several negative effects on the firm. For example, because high debt increases the likelihood of bankruptcy, it can lead to a downgrade in the firm's credit rating by agencies such as Moody's and Standard and Poor's.[91] In addition, high debt may preclude needed investment in activities that contribute to the firm's long-term success, such as R&D, human resource training, and marketing.[92] Still, leverage can be a positive force in a firm's development, allowing it to take advantage of attractive expansion opportunities. However, too much leverage (such as extraordinary debt) can lead to negative outcomes, including postponing or eliminating investments, such as R&D expenditures, that are necessary to maintain strategic competitiveness over the long term.

Inability to Achieve Synergy

Derived from *synergos,* a Greek word that means "working together," *synergy* exists when the value created by units working together exceeds the value those units could create working independently (see Chapter 6). That is, synergy exists when assets are worth more when used in conjunction with each other than when they are used separately.[93] For shareholders, synergy generates gains in their wealth that they could not duplicate or exceed through their own portfolio diversification decisions.[94] Synergy is created by the efficiencies derived from economies of scale and economies of scope and by sharing resources (e.g., human capital and knowledge) across the businesses in the merged firm.[95]

A firm develops a competitive advantage through an acquisition strategy only when a transaction generates private synergy. *Private synergy* is created when the combination and integration of the acquiring and acquired firms' assets yields capabilities and core competencies that could not be developed by combining and integrating either firm's assets with another company. Private synergy is possible when firms' assets are complementary in unique ways; that is, the unique type of asset complementarity is not possible by combining either company's assets with another firm's assets.[96] Because of its uniqueness, private synergy is difficult for competitors to understand and imitate. However, private synergy is difficult to create.

A firm's ability to account for costs that are necessary to create anticipated revenue- and cost-based synergies affects the acquisition's success. Firms experience several expenses when trying to create private synergy through acquisitions. Called transaction costs, these expenses are incurred when firms use acquisition strategies to create synergy.[97] Transaction costs may be direct or indirect. Direct costs include legal fees and charges from investment bankers who complete due diligence for the acquiring firm. Indirect costs include managerial time to evaluate target firms and then to complete negotiations, as well as the loss of key managers and employees following an acquisition.[98] Firms tend to underestimate the sum of indirect costs when the value of the synergy that may be created by combining and integrating the acquired firm's assets with the acquiring firm's assets is calculated.

Monsanto is one of the leading firms in developing strains of seed for basic food sources such as corn and soy beans. To pursue additional opportunities it purchased Seminis for $1.4 billion.[99] This deal "marks Monsanto's entry into the market for non-genetically modified fruits and vegetable seeds." Seminis has significant market share in these basic seed areas. For example, it has 36 percent of cucumber, 34 percent of hot pepper, and 23 percent of the tomato seed market shares. However, Monsanto's stock fell 10 percent in the few days after announcement of the deal. Analysts indicated "the acquisition could pose integration problems and results in few immediate synergies."[100] The concern is that more direct biotechnology shaping of fruits and vegetables sold in grocery stores will not be accepted by the public, although consumers have accepted indirect shaping of corn and soy bean seeds.

Too Much Diversification

As explained in Chapter 6, diversification strategies can lead to strategic competitiveness and above-average returns. In general, firms using related diversification strategies outperform those employing unrelated diversification strategies. However, conglomerates, formed by using an unrelated diversification strategy, also can be successful, as demonstrated by United Technologies Corp.

At some point, however, firms can become overdiversified. The level at which overdiversification occurs varies across companies because each firm has different capabilities to manage diversification. Recall from Chapter 6 that related diversification requires more information processing than does unrelated diversification. Because of this additional information processing, related diversified firms become overdiversified with a smaller number of business units than do firms using an unrelated diversification strategy.[101] Regardless of the type of diversification strategy implemented, however, overdiversification results in declines in performance, after which business units are often divested.[102] The pattern of excessive diversification followed by divestments of underperforming business units acquired earlier is currently taking place in the media industry. We discuss this later in a Strategic Focus. Many firms in the media industry have been seeking to divest businesses bought in the boom era of the late 1990s through 2001, when the Internet economy collapsed.[103] These cycles were also frequent among U.S. firms during the 1960s through the 1980s.[104]

Even when a firm is not overdiversified, a high level of diversification can have a negative effect on the firm's long-term performance. For example, the scope created by additional amounts of diversification often causes managers to rely on financial rather than strategic controls to evaluate business units' performances (financial and strategic controls are defined and explained in Chapters 11 and 12). Top-level executives often rely on financial controls to assess the performance of business units when they do not have a rich understanding of business units' objectives and strategies. Use of financial controls, such as return on investment (ROI), causes individual business-unit managers to focus on short-term outcomes at the expense of long-term investments. When long-term investments are reduced to increase short-term profits, a firm's overall strategic competitiveness may be harmed.[105]

Another problem resulting from too much diversification is the tendency for acquisitions to become substitutes for innovation. Typically, managers do not intend acquisitions to be used in that way. However, a reinforcing cycle evolves. Costs associated with acquisitions may result in fewer allocations to activities, such as R&D, that are linked to innovation. Without adequate support, a firm's innovation skills begin to atrophy. Without internal innovation skills, the only option available to a firm to gain access to innovation is to complete still more acquisitions. Evidence suggests that a firm using acquisitions as a substitute for internal innovations eventually encounters performance problems.[106]

Managers Overly Focused on Acquisitions

Typically, a considerable amount of managerial time and energy is required for acquisition strategies to contribute to the firm's strategic competitiveness. Activities with which managers become involved include (1) searching for viable acquisition candidates, (2) completing effective due-diligence processes, (3) preparing for negotiations, and (4) managing the integration process after the acquisition is completed.

Top-level managers do not personally gather all of the data and information required to make acquisitions. However, these executives do make critical decisions on the firms to be targeted, the nature of the negotiations, and so forth. Company experiences show that participating in and overseeing the activities required for making acquisitions can divert managerial attention from other matters that are necessary for long-term competitive success, such as identifying and taking advantage of other opportunities and interacting with important external stakeholders.[107]

Both theory and research suggest that managers can become overly involved in the process of making acquisitions.[108] One observer suggested: "The urge to merge is still like an addiction in many companies: doing deals is much more fun and interesting than fixing fundamental problems. So, as in dealing with any other addiction or temptation, maybe it is best to just say no."[109] The overinvolvement can be surmounted by learning from mistakes and by not having too much agreement in the board room. Dissent is helpful to make sure that all sides of a question are considered (see Chapter 10).[110] When failure does occur, leaders may be tempted to blame the failure on others and on unforeseen circumstances rather than on their excessive involvement in the acquisition process.[111]

A strong example of being overly focused on making a deal is the acquisition of Compaq Computer Corporation by Hewlett Packard Company (HP). Carly Fiorina, CEO at the time of the acquisition, waged a highly controversial battle with other significant shareholders over whether these two firms should merge (see the Opening Case in Chapter 12). Fiorina won the battle and the deal was carried out in 2002. In the process, both HP and Compaq employees and managers became overly consumed with the deal and in the course of time lost significant focus on ongoing operations. In the end, "HP's shareholders

Carly Fiorina was the CEO of Hewlett Packard at the time of its unsuccessful acquisition of Compaq.

GETTY IMAGES

paid $24 billion in stock to buy Compaq and in exchange got relatively little value."[112] Fiorina lost her job and Mark Hurd, the new CEO, has a major job retrenching and reorganizing HP's businesses.[113]

Too Large

Most acquisitions create a larger firm, which should help increase its economies of scale. These economies can then lead to more efficient operations—for example, the two sales organizations can be integrated using fewer sales reps because a sales rep can sell the products of both firms (particularly if the products of the acquiring and target firms are highly related).

Many firms seek increases in size because of the potential economies of scale and enhanced market power (discussed earlier). At some level, the additional costs required to manage the larger firm will exceed the benefits of the economies of scale and additional market power. Additionally, there is an incentive to grow larger because size serves as a takeover defense.[114] Research in the United Kingdom indicates that firms that acquire other firms and grow larger are less likely to be taken over.[115]

The complexities generated by the larger size often lead managers to implement more bureaucratic controls to manage the combined firm's operations. *Bureaucratic controls* are formalized supervisory and behavioral rules and policies designed to ensure consistency of decisions and actions across different units of a firm. However, through time, formalized controls often lead to relatively rigid and standardized managerial behavior. Certainly, in the long run, the diminished flexibility that accompanies rigid and standardized managerial behavior may produce less innovation. Because of innovation's importance to competitive success, the bureaucratic controls resulting from a large organization (that is, built by acquisitions) can have a detrimental effect on performance.[116]

Sara Lee Corporation, for example, has decided to spin off its apparel business in a "massive restructuring that will shed operations with annual revenue of $8.2 billion." It will try "to focus on its strongest brands in bakery, meat and household products." Sara Lee had struggled to increase sales and innovate across is "vast portfolio that includes diverse products such as Jimmy Dean sausage, Playtex bras and Kiwis shoe polish." The restructuring will trim revenues that used to account for 40 percent of sales. The company plans to use some of the savings to research and develop new products in its top selling brands.[117]

Effective Acquisitions

Earlier in the chapter, we noted that acquisition strategies do not consistently produce above-average returns for the acquiring firm's shareholders.[118] Nonetheless, some companies are able to create value when using an acquisition strategy.[119] For example, few companies have grown so successfully by acquisition as Cisco has. A number of other network companies tried to pursue acquisitions to build up their ability to sell into the network equipment binge, but only Cisco retained much of its value in the post-bubble era. Many firms, such as Lucent, Nortel, and Ericsson, teetered on the edge of bankruptcy after the Internet bubble burst. When it makes an acquisition, "Cisco has gone much further in its thinking about integration. Not only is retention important, but Cisco also works to minimize the distractions caused by an acquisition. This is important, because the speed of change is so great, that even if the target firm's product development teams are distracted, they will be slowed contributing to acquisition failure. So, integration must be rapid and reassuring."[120]

Results from a research study shed light on the differences between unsuccessful and successful acquisition strategies and suggest that there is a pattern of actions that can improve the probability of acquisition success.[121] The study shows that when the target firm's assets are complementary to the acquired firm's assets, an acquisition is more successful. With complementary assets, integrating two firms' operations has a higher probability of creating synergy. In fact, integrating two firms with complementary assets frequently produces unique capabilities and core competencies.[122] With complementary assets, the acquiring firm can maintain its focus on core businesses and leverage the complementary assets and capabilities from the acquired firm. Often, targets were selected and "groomed" by establishing a working relationship prior to the acquisition.[123] As discussed in Chapter 9, strategic alliances are sometimes used to test the feasibility of a future merger or acquisition between the involved firms.[124]

The study's results also show that friendly acquisitions facilitate integration of the firms involved in an acquisition. Through friendly acquisitions, firms work together to find ways to integrate their operations to create synergy.[125] In hostile takeovers, animosity often results between the two top-management teams, a condition that in turn affects working relationships in the newly created firm. As a result, more key personnel in the acquired firm may be lost, and those who remain may resist the changes necessary to integrate the two firms.[126] With effort, cultural clashes can be overcome, and fewer key managers and employees will become discouraged and leave.[127]

Additionally, effective due-diligence processes involving the deliberate and careful selection of target firms and an evaluation of the relative health of those firms (financial health, cultural fit, and the value of human resources) contribute to successful acquisitions.[128] Financial slack in the form of debt equity or cash, in both the acquiring and acquired firms, also has frequently contributed to success in acquisitions. While financial slack provides access to financing for the acquisition, it is still important to maintain a low or moderate level of debt after the acquisition to keep debt costs low. When substantial debt was used to finance the acquisition, companies with successful acquisitions reduced the debt quickly, partly by selling off assets from the acquired firm, especially noncomplementary or poorly performing assets. For these firms, debt costs do not prevent long-term investments such as R&D, and managerial discretion in the use of cash flow is relatively flexible.

Another attribute of successful acquisition strategies is an emphasis on innovation, as demonstrated by continuing investments in R&D activities. Significant R&D investments show a strong managerial commitment to innovation, a characteristic that is increasingly important to overall competitiveness, as well as acquisition success.

Flexibility and adaptability are the final two attributes of successful acquisitions. When executives of both the acquiring and the target firms have experience in managing change and learning from acquisitions, they will be more skilled at adapting their capabilities to new environments.[129] As a result, they will be more adept at integrating the two organizations, which is particularly important when firms have different organizational cultures.

Efficient and effective integration may quickly produce the desired synergy in the newly created firm. Effective integration allows the acquiring firm to keep valuable human resources in the acquired firm from leaving.[130]

The attributes and results of successful acquisitions are summarized in Table 7.1. Managers seeking acquisition success should emphasize the seven attributes that are listed. Berkshire Hathaway is a conglomerate holding company for Warren Buffett, one of the world's richest men. The company operates widely in the insurance industry and also has stakes in gems, candy, apparel, pilot training, and shoes. The company owns an

Attributes of Successful Acquisitions

TABLE 7.1

Attributes	Results
1. Acquired firm has assets or resources that are complementary to the acquiring firm's core business	1. High probability of synergy and competitive advantage by maintaining strengths
2. Acquisition is friendly	2. Faster and more effective integration and possibly lower premiums
3. Acquiring firm conducts effective due diligence to select target firms and evaluate the target firm's health (financial, cultural, and human resources)	3. Firms with strongest complementarities are acquired and overpayment is avoided
4. Acquiring firm has financial slack (cash or a favorable debt position)	4. Financing (debt or equity) is easier and less costly to obtain
5. Merged firm maintains low to moderate debt position	5. Lower financing cost, lower risk (e.g., of bankruptcy), and avoidance of trade-offs that are associated with high debt
6. Acquiring firm has sustained and consistent emphasis on R&D and innovation	6. Maintain long-term competitive advantage in markets
7. Acquiring firm manages change well and is flexible and adaptable	7. Faster and more effective integration facilitates achievement of synergy

interest in such well-known firms as Wal-Mart, American Express, Coca-Cola, The Washington Post Company, and Wells Fargo. Recently, Buffett has sought to buy an interest in a U.S. utility firm, PacifiCorp.[131] His acquisition strategy in insurance and other business has been particularly successful because he has followed many of the suggestions in Table 7.1.

As we have learned, some acquisitions enhance strategic competitiveness. However, the majority of acquisitions that took place from the 1970s through the 1990s did not enhance firms' strategic competitiveness. In fact, "history shows that anywhere between one-third [and] more than half of all acquisitions are ultimately divested or spun-off."[132] Thus, firms often use restructuring strategies to correct for the failure of a merger or an acquisition.

Restructuring

Defined formally, **restructuring** is a strategy through which a firm changes its set of businesses or its financial structure.[133] From the 1970s into the 2000s, divesting businesses from company portfolios and downsizing accounted for a large percentage of firms' restructuring strategies. Restructuring is a global phenomenon.[134]

The failure of an acquisition strategy is often followed by a restructuring strategy. Morgan Stanley, a large U.S. investment bank, merged with Dean Witter, a retail investment company, in 1997. The merger was touted to become a financial supermarket. However, the two company's cultures did not fit together well; "beneath the surface the two sides didn't try very hard to conceal their mutual scorn."[135] Although Philip Purcell, from Dean Witter, won the political battle to retrain his CEO position after a number of key personal left calling for his resignation, ultimately Purcell was forced to resign. John Mack, a former CEO, is back in the CEO position. However, Morgan Stanley will likely restructure in order to improve its position by selling off its Discover Card division and possibly even the retail brokerage business.

In other instances, however, firms use a restructuring strategy because of changes in their external and internal environments. For example, opportunities sometimes surface in the external environment that are particularly attractive to the diversified firm in light of its core competencies. In such cases, restructuring may be appropriate to position the firm to create more value for stakeholders, given the environmental changes.[136]

As discussed next, there are three restructuring strategies that firms use: downsizing, downscoping, and leveraged buyouts.

Downsizing

Once thought to be an indicator of organizational decline, downsizing is now recognized as a legitimate restructuring strategy.[137] *Downsizing* is a reduction in the number of a firm's employees and, sometimes, in the number of its operating units, but it may or may not change the composition of businesses in the company's portfolio. Thus, downsizing is an intentional proactive management strategy, whereas "decline is an environmental or organizational phenomenon that occurs involuntarily and results in erosion of an organization's resource base."[138]

In the late 1980s, early 1990s, and early 2000s, thousands of jobs were lost in private and public organizations in the United States. One study estimates that 85 percent of *Fortune* 1000 firms have used downsizing as a restructuring strategy.[139] Moreover, *Fortune* 500 firms laid off more than one million employees, or 4 percent of their collective workforce, in 2001 and into the first few weeks of 2002.[140] This trend continues in many industries. For instance, in 2005 GM signaled that it will lay off 25,000 people through 2008 due to poor competitive performance, especially as a result of the improved performance of foreign competitors.[141]

Downscoping

Downscoping has a more positive effect on firm performance than downsizing does.[142] *Downscoping* refers to divestiture, spin-off, or some other means of eliminating businesses that are unrelated to a firm's core businesses. Commonly, downscoping is described as a set of actions that causes a firm to strategically refocus on its core businesses.[143] Sara Lee, as mentioned, is spinning off its apparel business. Restructuring spin-offs in the media industry are also described in the Strategic Focus; both Viacom and Clear Channel Communications have participated in such restructurings and are considering further moves.

A firm that downscopes often also downsizes simultaneously. However, it does not eliminate key employees from its primary businesses in the process, because such action could lead to a loss of one or more core competencies. Instead, a firm that is simultaneously downscoping and downsizing becomes smaller by reducing the diversity of businesses in its portfolio.[144]

Restructuring through Firm Spin-offs Allows for Value Creation

Restructuring divestitures (often in the form of spin-offs) are done for many reasons. *Spin-offs* result when a single firm creates at least two firms in a nontaxable break-off, creating at least one new equity share offering. Usually the parent maintains the original stock price symbol and the break-off firm uses a new symbol. Such restructuring spin-offs are sparked by both internal and external events. Often such restructuring is preceded internally by a downturn in performance. Externally, such downscoping may be necessitated by environmental changes in demand that cause some businesses to become more peripheral, and the core set of businesses evolves. Core businesses may have evolved towards maturity where they are throwing off cash, but new businesses are required to drive future growth. Although there may be pressure for a change in strategy, often such restructurings are triggered by some internal event such as a change in leadership or an external event in the environment such as a devaluation in a country's currency, as in the Asian currency crisis in 1997.

A number of media acquisitions took place in the late 1990s and early part of the 21st century. However, the media business has evolved significantly and problems arose with the media mergers. For instance, the Time Warner acquisition of AOL has led Time Warner to consider splitting off the AOL business as it has reconfigured the business to more effectively compete with Yahoo and Microsoft Corporation's MSN. Viacom made a number of acquisitions including the CBS network, which, in the beginning, added significant value to Viacom's MTV and other cable networks and Paramount Film Studios. However, Viacom's stock price has lagged and Sumner Redstone, Viacom CEO, has considered ways to increase value. One strategy under consideration is to divide the large media business into two operational units, one focused on smaller growing businesses such as MTV, Nickelodeon, The Movie Channel, and Paramount Pictures, among others, and another that would include CBS Television and Infinity Broadcasting as well as other entertainment businesses such as Viacom Outdoor, which schedules outdoor advertising and concerts. Although the latter set of businesses are slow-growing, they generate a lot of cash and allow the separate company to offer a more generous dividend policy—a policy that attracts more conservative investors. The growth operation focused on MTV and other channels would allow a different type of investor focus. Other media companies, including Vivendi Universal, Time Warner, and Liberty Media Corporation, have also sold off assets in restructuring moves that are similar to the one being considered by Viacom.

Clear Channel Communications has also signaled that it will consider breaking up into three separate businesses: Clear Channel Communications (radio and broadcasting), Clear Channel Outdoor (advertising), and Clear Channel Entertainment (scheduling of live entertainment venues). Clear Channel's performance dropped and regulatory agencies complained of "monopolistic behavior between the entertainment and radio divisions." This concern, as well as performance concerns similar to those of the potential Viacom split-up, have created a situation where Clear Channel executives are signaling this strategic restructuring and spin-off strategy.

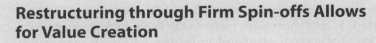

DANIEL ACKER/BLOOMBERG NEWS/LANDOV

To address its performance concerns, Clear Channel Communications will consider separating into three businesses.

Many of the media mergers were vertical acquisitions, such as Viacom's acquisition of CBS, in which the television network and other venues were considered opportunities for the content side to be fed directly into the broadcasting channel distribution business. However, as events changed with increased competition, other opportunities for media such as video game substitution for entertainment, and other outlets for content such as DVD sales, many of the firms unwound their vertical acquisitions into slower-growth distribution outlets. Furthermore, many of the distribution outlets such as the Internet and broadband have not generated significant revenue, and the cable firms have turned to alternative businesses such as offering phone service. Thus the split-ups of former acquisitions have been warranted and many times firms signaling such restructurings have seen an increase in their stock price. This certainly was the case for Viacom when it announced its possible split-up into three businesses.

Viacom had already spun off a previous vertical acquisition, Blockbuster, due to increased competition from the online video rental company NetFlix and the growth of DVD sales through regular retail channels. Viacom found that although the Blockbuster chain was continuing to make a profit, its revenues were decreasing. Accordingly, Blockbuster was spun off as a separate company from Viacom. Apparently, Viacom learned from this experience and is considering its next move in regard to further split-ups as described above.

Sources: K. Bachman, 2005, Clear Channel breaking up, *Media Week*, May 2, 5; S. McBride, 2005, Clear Channel posts earnings drop, plans spin-off, *Wall Street Journal*, May 2, B6, B8; J. Flint, 2005, Split and polish: As Viacom ponders a breakup, industry rethinks old notions, *Wall Street Journal*, March 17, A1, A9; T. Lowry, 2005, Antenna adjustment, *Business Week*, June 20, 64; M. Peers, 2005, Liberty Media unveils plans to spin off its Discovery stake, *Wall Street Journal*, March 16, A3; M. Sikora, 2005, Working overtime to ensure tax shields for big spin-offs, *Mergers and Acquisitions*, May, 34–36; J. Angwin, 2004, Time Warner may sell AOL shares, *Wall Street Journal*, May 23, A3; D. Desjardins, 2004, Blockbuster looks ahead after Viacom spin-off, *DSN Retailing Today*, July 19; J. Harrison, 2004, Retreating from troubled businesses, *Mergers and Acquisitions*, October, 10–13.

By refocusing on its core businesses, the firm can be managed more effectively by the top management team. Managerial effectiveness increases because the firm has become less diversified, allowing the top management team to better understand and manage the remaining businesses.[145]

In general, U.S. firms use downscoping as a restructuring strategy more frequently than European companies do, while the trend in Europe, Latin America, and Asia has been to build conglomerates. In Latin America, these conglomerates are called *grupos*. Many Asian and Latin American conglomerates have begun to adopt Western corporate strategies in recent years and have been refocusing on their core businesses. This downscoping has occurred simultaneously with increasing globalization and with more open markets that have greatly enhanced the competition. By downscoping, these firms have been able to focus on their core businesses and improve their competitiveness.[146]

Downscoping has been practiced recently by many emerging market firms. For example, the Tata Group, founded by Jamsetji Nusserwanji Tata in 1868 as a private trading firm and now India's largest business group, includes 91 firms in a wide range of industries. The group covers chemicals, communications, consumer products, energy, engineering, information systems, materials, and services industries. The group's revenue in 2003–2004 was $14.25 billion, about 2.6 percent of India's GDP. Tata's member companies employ about 220,000 people and export their products to 140 countries. However, as India has changed, Tata executives have sought to restructure its member businesses to "build a more focused company without abandoning the best of Tata's manufacturing tradition."[147] Over a 10-year period Tata has restructured from 250 businesses to its current set.

Leveraged Buyouts

Leveraged buyouts are commonly used as a restructuring strategy to correct for managerial mistakes or because the firm's managers are making decisions that primarily serve their own interests rather than those of shareholders.[148] A *leveraged buyout* (LBO) is a restructuring strategy whereby a party buys all of a firm's assets in order to take the firm private. Once the transaction is completed, the company's stock is no longer traded publicly. Firms that facilitate or engage in taking public firms or a business unit of a firm private are called *private equity firms.*

Usually, significant amounts of debt are incurred to finance a buyout; hence the term "leveraged" buyout. To support debt payments and to downscope the company to concentrate on the firm's core businesses, the new owners may immediately sell a number of assets.[149] It is not uncommon for those buying a firm through an LBO to restructure the firm to the point that it can be sold at a profit within a five- to eight-year period.

Management buyouts (MBOs), employee buyouts (EBOs), and whole-firm buyouts, in which one company or partnership purchases an entire company instead of a part of it, are the three types of LBOs. In part because of managerial incentives, MBOs, more so than EBOs and whole-firm buyouts, have been found to lead to downscoping, increased strategic focus, and improved performance.[150] Research has shown that management buyouts can also lead to greater entrepreneurial activity and growth.[151]

While there may be different reasons for a buyout, one is to protect against a capricious financial market, allowing the owners to focus on developing innovations and bringing them to the market.[152] As such, buyouts can represent a form of firm rebirth to facilitate entrepreneurial efforts and stimulate strategic growth.[153]

Restructuring Outcomes

The short-term and long-term outcomes resulting from the three restructuring strategies are shown in Figure 7.2. As indicated, downsizing does not commonly lead to a higher firm performance.[154] Still, in free-market-based societies at large, downsizing has generated an incentive for individuals who have been laid off to start their own businesses.

Research has shown that downsizing contributed to lower returns for both U.S. and Japanese firms. The stock markets in the firms' respective nations evaluated downsizing negatively. Investors concluded that downsizing would have a negative effect on companies' ability to achieve strategic competitiveness in the long term. Investors also seem to assume that downsizing occurs as a consequence of other problems in a company.[155] This assumption may be caused by a firm's diminished corporate reputation when a major downsizing is announced.[156] This is clear in the GM layoffs mentioned above.

An unintentional outcome of downsizing, however, is that laid-off employees often start new businesses in order to live through the disruption in their lives. Accordingly, downsizing has generated a host of entrepreneurial new ventures.

As shown in Figure 7.2, downsizing tends to result in a loss of human capital in the long term. Losing employees with many years of experience with the firm represents a major loss of knowledge. As noted in Chapter 3, knowledge is vital to competitive success in the global economy. Thus, in general, research evidence and corporate experience

FIGURE **7.2** | Restructuring and Outcomes

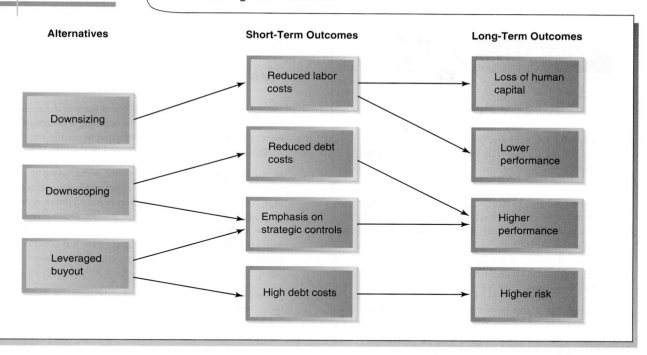

suggest that downsizing may be of more tactical (or short-term) value than strategic (or long-term) value.[157]

Downscoping generally leads to more positive outcomes in both the short and the long term than does downsizing or engaging in a leveraged buyout (see Figure 7.2). Downscoping's desirable long-term outcome of higher performance is a product of reduced debt costs and the emphasis on strategic controls derived from concentrating on the firm's core businesses. In so doing, the refocused firm should be able to increase its ability to compete.[158]

While whole-firm LBOs have been hailed as a significant innovation in the financial restructuring of firms, there can be negative trade-offs.[159] First, the resulting large debt increases the financial risk of the firm, as is evidenced by the number of companies that filed for bankruptcy in the 1990s after executing a whole-firm LBO. Sometimes, the intent of the owners to increase the efficiency of the bought-out firm and then sell it within five to eight years creates a short-term and risk-averse managerial focus.[160] As a result, these firms may fail to invest adequately in R&D or take other major actions designed to maintain or improve the company's core competence.[161] Research also suggests that in firms with an entrepreneurial mind-set, buyouts can lead to greater innovation, especially if the debt load is not too great.[162] However, because buyouts more often result in significant debt, most LBOs have taken place in mature industries where stable cash flows are possible. This enables the buyout firm to meet the recurring debt payments as exemplified by Wilbur Ross's buyouts in the steel industry described in the Strategic Focus dealing with Mittal Steel.

- Acquisition strategies are increasingly popular. Because of globalization, deregulation of multiple industries in many different economies, and favorable legislation, the number and size of domestic and cross-border acquisitions continues to increase.

- Firms use acquisition strategies to (1) increase market power, (2) overcome entry barriers to new markets or regions, (3) avoid the costs of developing new products and increase the speed of new market entries, (4) reduce the risk of entering a new business, (5) become more diversified, (6) reshape their competitive scope by developing a different portfolio of businesses, and (7) enhance their learning, thereby adding to their knowledge base.

- Among the problems associated with the use of an acquisition strategy are (1) the difficulty of effectively integrating the firms involved, (2) incorrectly evaluating the target firm's value, (3) creating debt loads that preclude adequate long-term investments (e.g., R&D), (4) overestimating the potential for synergy, (5) creating a firm that is too diversified, (6) creating an internal environment in which managers devote increasing amounts of their time and energy to analyzing and completing the acquisition, and (7) developing a combined firm that is too large, necessitating extensive use of bureaucratic, rather than strategic, controls.

- Effective acquisitions have the following characteristics: (1) the acquiring and target firms have complementary resources that can be the basis of core competencies in the newly created firm, (2) the acquisition is friendly thereby facilitating integration of the two firms' resources, (3) the target firm is selected and purchased based on thorough due diligence, (4) the acquiring and target firms have considerable slack in the form of cash or debt capacity, (5) the merged firm maintains a low or moderate level of debt by

selling off portions of the acquired firm or some of the acquiring firm's poorly performing units, (6) the acquiring and acquired firms have experience in terms of adapting to change, and (7) R&D and innovation are emphasized in the new firm.

- Restructuring is used to improve a firm's performance by correcting for problems created by ineffective management. Restructuring by downsizing involves reducing the number of employees and hierarchical levels in the firm. Although it can lead to short-term cost reductions, they may be realized at the expense of long-term success, because of the loss of valuable human resources (and knowledge) and overall corporate reputation.

- The goal of restructuring through downscoping is to reduce the firm's level of diversification. Often, the firm divests unrelated businesses to achieve this goal. Eliminating unrelated businesses makes it easier for the firm and its top-level managers to refocus on the core businesses.

- Leveraged buyouts (LBOs) represent an additional restructuring strategy. Through an LBO, a firm is purchased so that it can become a private entity. LBOs usually are financed largely through debt. There are three types of LBOs: management buyouts (MBOs), employee buyouts (EBOs), and whole-firm LBOs. Because they provide clear managerial incentives, MBOs have been the most successful of the three. Often, the intent of a buyout is to improve efficiency and performance to the point where the firm can be sold successfully within five to eight years.

- Commonly, restructuring's primary goal is gaining or reestablishing effective strategic control of the firm. Of the three restructuring strategies, downscoping is aligned the most closely with establishing and using strategic controls.

NOTES

1. J. Anand, 2004, Redeployment of corporate resources: A study of acquisition strategies in the US defense industries, 1978–1996, *Managerial and Decision Economics,* 25: 383–400; L. Capron & N. Pistre, 2002, When do acquirers earn abnormal returns? *Strategic Management Journal,* 23: 781–794.
2. R. A. Krishnan, S. Joshi, & H. Krishnan, 2004, The influence of mergers on firms' product-mix strategies, *Strategic Management Journal,* 25: 587–611.
3. H. Shahrur, 2005, Industry structure and horizontal takeovers: Analysis of wealth effects on rivals, suppliers, and corporate customers, *Journal of Financial Economics,* 76: 61–98; K. Fuller, J. Netter, & M. Stegemoller, 2002,

What do returns to acquiring firms tell us? Evidence from firms that make many acquisitions, *Journal of Finance,* 57: 1763–1793; M. A. Hitt, J. S. Harrison, & R. D. Ireland, 2001, *Mergers and Acquisitions: A Guide to Creating Value for Stakeholders,* New York: Oxford University Press.
4. B. E. Chappuis, K. A. Frick, & P. J. Roche, 2004, High-tech mergers take shape, *McKinsey Quarterly,* (1): 60–69; G. K. Deans, F. Kroeger, & S. Zeisel, 2002, The consolidation curve, *Harvard Business Review,* 80(12): 20–21; 2000, How M&As will navigate the turn into a new century, *Mergers and Acquisitions,* January, 29–35.

5. J. A. Schmidt, 2002, Business perspective on mergers and acquisitions, in J. A. Schmidt (ed.), *Making Mergers Work,* Alexandria, VA: Society for Human Resource Management, 23–46.

6. 2005, Wal-Mart open to more international acquisitions, *Forbes,* www.forbes.com, June 14.

7. E. R. Auster & M. L. Sirower, 2002, The dynamics of merger and acquisition waves: A three-stage conceptual framework with implications for practice, *Journal of Applied Behavioral Science,* 38: 216–244.

8. M. A. Hitt, R. D. Ireland, & J. S. Harrison, 2001, Mergers and acquisitions: A value creating or a value destroying strategy? in M. A. Hitt, R. E. Freeman, & J. S. Harrison, *Handbook of Strategic Management,* Oxford, UK: Blackwell Publishers, 385–408.

9. L. Saigol, 2002, Thin pickings in dismal year for dealmaking, *Financial Times,* www.ft.com, January 2; 2001, Waiting for growth, *The Economist,* www.economist.com, April 27.

10. 2002, Mergers snapshot: 2001 deal volume, *Wall Street Journal,* January 4, C12; 2001, The great merger wave breaks, *The Economist,* January 27, 59–60.

11. D. K. Berman, 2005, Lots of merger activity—a few big deals, *Wall Street Journal,* July 1, C12; D. K. Berman, 2005, Year-end review of markets & finance 2004; simmering M&A sector reaches a boil; crush of December activity signals M&A is heating up; will 'deals beget deals'? *Wall Street Journal,* January 5, R10.

12. R. Coff, 2003, Bidding wars over R&D-intensive firms: Knowledge, opportunism, and the market for corporate control, *Academy of Management Journal,* 46: 74–85; P. Chattopadhyay, W. H. Glick, & G. P. Huber, 2001, Organizational actions in response to threats and opportunities, *Academy of Management Journal,* 44: 937–955.

13. J. J. Reuer & T. W. Tong, 2005, Real options in international joint ventures, *Journal of Management,* 31: 403–423; A. E. M. A. Schilling & H. K. Steensma, 2002, Disentangling the theories of firm boundaries: A path model and empirical test, *Organization Science,* 13: 387–401; H. T. J. Smit, 2001, Acquisition strategies as option games, *Journal of Applied Corporate Finance,* 14(2): 79–89.

14. A. Bednarski, 2003, From diversity to duplication: Mega-mergers and the failure of the marketplace model under the Telecommunications Act of 1996, *Federal Communications Law Journal,* 55(2): 273–295.

15. G. Cullinan, J.-M. Le Roux, & R.-M. Weddigen, 2004, When to walk away from a deal, *Harvard Business Review,* 82(4): 96–104; L. Selden & G. Colvin, 2003, M&A needn't be a loser's game, *Harvard Business Review,* 81(6): 70–73;.

16. J. J. Reuer, 2005, Avoiding lemons in M&A deals, *MIT Sloan Management Review,* 46(3): 15–17; M. C. Jensen, 1988, Takeovers: Their causes and consequences, *Journal of Economic Perspectives,* 1(2): 21–48.

17. Moeller, Schlingemann, & Stulz, Wealth destruction on a massive scale.

18. D. K. Berman, 2005, Mergers horror II: The rhetoric, *Wall Street Journal,* May 24, C1; T. Wright, M. Kroll, A. Lado, & B. Van Ness, 2002, The structure of ownership and corporate acquisition strategies, *Strategic Management Journal,* 23: 41–53; A. Rappaport & M. L. Sirower, 1999, Stock or cash? *Harvard Business Review,* 77(6): 147–158.

19. A. Keeton, 2003, Class-action is approved against DaimlerChrysler, *Wall Street Journal,* June 13, B2.

20. E. Thornton, F. Keesnan, C. Palmeri, & L. Himelstein, 2002, It sure is getting hostile, *Business Week,* January 14, 28–30.

21. P. Haspeslagh, 1999, Managing the mating dance in equal mergers, "Mastering Strategy" (Part Five), *Financial Times,* October 25, 14–15.

22. P. Wright, M. Kroll, & D. Elenkov, 2002, Acquisition returns, increase in firm size and chief executive officer compensation: The moderating role of monitoring, *Academy of Management Journal,* 45: 599–608.

23. G. Anders, 2002, Lessons from WaMu's M&A playbook, *Fast Company,* January, 100–107.

24. B. K. Berman & E. Bryon, 2005, Federated clinches deal to buy May, *Wall Street Journal,* February 28, A3, A6.

25. C. Hamburg, M. Bucerius, & M. Bucerius, 2005, A marketing perspective on mergers and acquisitions: How marketing integration affects post-merger performance, *Journal of Marketing,* 69: 95–113.

26. Capron & Pistre, When do acquirers earn abnormal returns?; L. Capron, 1999, Horizontal acquisitions: The benefits and risks to long-term performance, *Strategic Management Journal,* 20: 987–1018.

27. C. E. Fee & S. Thomas, 2004, Sources of gains in horizontal mergers: Evidence from customer, supplier, and rival firms, *Journal of Financial Economics,* 74: 423–460.

28. M. Lubatkin, W. S. Schulze, A. Mainkar, & R. W. Cotterill, 2001, Ecological investigation of firm effects in horizontal mergers, *Strategic Management Journal,* 22: 335–357; K. Ramaswamy, 1997, The performance impact of strategic similarity in horizontal mergers: Evidence from the U.S. banking industry, *Academy of Management Journal,* 40: 697–715.

29. L. Capron, W. Mitchell, & A. Swaminathan, 2001, Asset divestiture following horizontal acquisitions: A dynamic view, *Strategic Management Journal,* 22: 817–844.

30. M. R. Subramani & N. Venkatraman, 2003, Safeguarding investments in asymmetric interorganizational relationships: Theory and evidence, *Academy of Management Journal,* 46: 46–62; T. S. Gabrielsen, 2003, Conglomerate mergers: Vertical mergers in disguise? *International Journal of the Economics of Business,* 10(1): 1–16.

31. W. M. Bulkeley & S. Weinberg, 2005, Kodak to buy printing supplier for $980 million, *Wall Street Journal,* February 1, B5.

32. 2003, Special Report: The complete home entertainer? Sony, *The Economist,* March 1, 62–64.

33. P. Dvorak, 2005, Out of tune: at Sony, rivalries were encouraged; then came iPod, *Wall Street Journal,* June 29, A1, A6.

34. D. Clark & C. Forelle, 2005, Sun Microsystems to buy Storagetek for $4.1 billion, *Wall Street Journal,* June 3, A3.

35. D. Gupta & Y. Gerchak, 2002, Quantifying operational synergies in a merger/acquisition, *Management Science,* 48: 517–533.

36. D. E. M. Sappington, 2003, Regulating horizontal diversification, *International Journal of Industrial Organization,* 21: 291–315.

37. A. Cohen & M. Jacoby, 2005, EU's Kroes puts antitrust stance in line with U.S.; Shift on deal reviews gives less weight to competitors, more to consumer benefits, *Wall Street Journal,* October 1, A17; M. Jacoby, 2005, P&G's planned Gillette takeover nears approval by EU regulators, *Wall Street Journal,* June 30, B7; A. Barrett, 2003, "In the credibility penalty box": Can Honeywell CEO Cote restore investors' confidence? *Business Week,* April 28, 80–81.

38. G. Witte, 2005, Nortel to buy PEC Solutions for $448 million, *Washington Post,* April 27, E01.

39. S.-F. S. Chen & M. Zeng, 2004, Japanese investors' choice of acquisitions vs. startups in the US: The role of reputation barriers and advertising outlays, *International Journal of Research in Marketing,* 21(2): 123–136; S. J. Chang & P. M. Rosenzweig, 2001, The choice of entry mode in sequential foreign direct investment, *Strategic Management Journal,* 22: 747–776.

40. 2004, Leaders: Grow up; emerging economies, *The Economist,* October 16, 12; N. Dawar & A. Chattopadhyay, 2002, Rethinking marketing programs for emerging markets, *Long Range Planning,* 35(5): 457–474; J. A. Gingrich, 1999, Five rules for winning emerging market consumers, *Strategy & Business,* 15: 19–33.

41. K. Shimizu, M. A. Hitt, D. Vaidyanath, & V. Pisano, 2004, Theoretical foundations of cross-border mergers and acquisitions: A review of current research and recommendations for the future, *Journal of International Management,* 10: 307–353; J. A. Doukas & L. H. P. Lang, 2003, Foreign direct investment, diversification and firm performance, *Journal of International Business Studies,* 34: 153–172; Hitt, Harrison, & Ireland, *Mergers and Acquisitions,* Chapter 10.

42. A. Seth, K. P. Song, & R. R. Pettit, 2002, Value creation and destruction in cross-border acquisitions: An empirical analysis of foreign acquisitions of U.S. firms, *Strategic Management Journal,* 23: 921–940.

43. Schmidt, Business perspective on mergers and acquisitions.

44. A. M. Agami, 2002, The role that foreign acquisitions of Asian companies played in the recovery of the Asian financial crisis, *Multinational Business Review,* 10(1): 11–20.

45. P. Quah & S. Young, 2005, Post-acquisition management: A phases approach for cross-border M&As, *European Management Journal,* 17(1),

65–75; J. K. Sebenius, 2002, The hidden challenge of cross-border negotiations, *Harvard Business Review*, 80(3): 76–85.

46. V. Bannert & H. Tschirky, 2004, Integration planning for technology intensive acquisitions, *R&D Management*, 34(5): 481–494; W. Vanhaverbeke, G. Duysters, & N. Noorderhaven, 2002, External technology sourcing through alliances or acquisitions: An analysis of the application-specific integrated circuits industry, *Organization Science*, 6: 714–733.

47. H. Gatignon, M. L. Tushman, W. Smith, & P. Anderson, 2002, A structural approach to assessing innovation: Construct development of innovation locus, type, and characteristics, *Management Science*, 48: 1103–1122; Hitt, Harrison, & Ireland, *Mergers and Acquisitions*.

48. M. A. Hitt, R. E. Hoskisson, R. A. Johnson, & D. D. Moesel, 1996, The market for corporate control and firm innovation, *Academy of Management Journal*, 39: 1084–1119.

49. Coff, Bidding wars over R&D-intensive firms: Knowledge, opportunism, and the market for corporate control.

50. L. Jarvis, 2005, Pharma M&A cooling slightly in 2005, *Chemical Market Reporter*, Jun 6–Jun 12, 20–21.

51. P. Kale & P. Puranam, 2004, Choosing equity stakes in technology-sourcing relationships: An integrative framework, *California Management Review*, 46(3): 77–99; T. Yoshikawa, 2003, Technology development and acquisition strategy, *International Journal of Technology Management*, 25(6,7): 666–674.

52. Y. Luo, O. Shenkar, & M.-K. Nyaw, 2002, Mitigating liabilities of foreignness: Defensive versus offensive approaches, *Journal of International Management*, 8: 283–300; J. W. Lu & P. W. Beamish, 2001, The internationalization and performance of SMEs, *Strategic Management Journal*, 22 (Special Issue): 565–586.

53. C. W. L. Hill & F. T. Rothaermel, 2003, The performance of incumbent firms in the face of radical technological innovation, *Academy of Management Review*, 28: 257–274; G. Ahuja & C. Lampert, 2001, Entrepreneurship in the large corporation: A longitudinal study of how established firms create breakthrough inventions, *Strategic Management Journal*, 22 (Special Issue): 521–543.

54. F. Rothaermel, 2001, Incumbent's advantage through exploiting complementary assets via interfirm cooperation, *Strategic Management Journal*, 22 (Special Issue): 687–699.

55. A. Grimes & S. Hensley, 2005, Pfizer nears a deal to acquire Angiosyn, pad eye-drug roster, *Wall Street Journal*, January 20, C1, C5.

56. L.-F. Hsieh; Y.-T. Tsai, 2005, Technology investment mode of innovative technological corporations: M & A strategy intended to facilitate innovation, *Journal of American Academy of Business*, 6(1): 185–194; G. Ahuja & R. Katila, 2001, Technological acquisitions and the innovation performance of acquiring firms: A longitudinal study, *Strategic Management Journal*, 22: 197–220; M. A. Hitt, R. E. Hoskisson, & R. D. Ireland, 1990, Mergers and acquisitions and managerial commitment to innovation in M-form firms, *Strategic Management Journal*, 11 (Special Issue): 29–47.

57. J. Whalen & A. L. Abboud, 2005, Big pharma, flush with cash, is looking acquisitive, *Wall Street Journal*, February 16, C1, C4.

58. Hitt, Hoskisson, Johnson, & Moesel, The market for corporate control.

59. Hill & Rothaermel, The performance of incumbent firms in the face of radical technological innovation.

60. M. A. Hitt, R. E. Hoskisson, R. D. Ireland, & J. S. Harrison, 1991, Effects of acquisitions on R&D inputs and outputs, *Academy of Management Journal*, 34: 693–706.

61. Capron, Mitchell, & Swaminathan, Asset divestiture following horizontal acquisitions; D. D. Bergh, 1997, Predicting divestiture of unrelated acquisitions: An integrative model of ex ante conditions, *Strategic Management Journal*, 18: 715–731.

62. R. L. Rundle, 2005, Eye-care firm gets focused, *Wall Street Journal*, May 27, B3.

63. C. E. Helfat & K. M. Eisenhardt, 2004, Inter-temporal economies of scope, organizational modularity, and the dynamics of diversification, *Strategic Management Journal*, 25: 1217–1232; C. Park, 2003, Prior performance characteristics of related and unrelated acquirers, *Strategic Management Journal*, 24: 471–480.

64. 2005, How to streamline $14 billion of annual supply chain purchasing, *World Trade*, June, 48; 2004, Kidde accepts $2.84 billion bid from United Technologies, *Wall Street Journal*, December 17, A6; D. Brady, 2004, The unsung CEO, *Business Week*, October 25, 76–84.

65. Hitt, Harrison, & Ireland, *Mergers and Acquisitions*.

66. J. Anand & H. Singh, 1997, Asset redeployment, acquisitions and corporate strategy in declining industries, *Strategic Management Journal*, 18 (Special Issue): 99–118.

67. Helfat & Eisenhardt, Inter-temporal economies of scope, organizational modularity, and the dynamics of diversification; W. J. Ferrier, 2001, Navigating the competitive landscape: The drivers and consequences of competitive aggressiveness, *Academy of Management Journal*, 44: 858–877.

68. 2004, Cultural shift at GE, *Strategic Direction*, 28(4): 10–13; M. Warner, 2002, Can GE light up the market again? *Fortune*, November 11, 108–117; R. E. Hoskisson & M. A. Hitt, 1994, *Downscoping: How to Tame the Diversified Firm*, New York: Oxford University Press.

69. J. Anand & A. Delios, 2002, Absolute and relative resources as determinants of international acquisitions, *Strategic Management Journal*, 23(2): 119–134; F. Vermeulen & H. Barkema, 2001, Learning through acquisitions, *Academy of Management Journal*, 44: 457–476.

70. F. Vermeulen, 2005, How acquisitions can revitalize firms, *MIT Sloan Management Review*, 46(4): 45–51; J. Gammelgaard, 2004, Access to competence: An emerging acquisition motive, *European Business Forum*, Spring, 44–48; M. L. A. Hayward, 2002, When do firms learn from their acquisition experience? Evidence from 1990–1995, *Strategic Management Journal*, 23: 21–39.

71. J. Anand, L. Capron, & W. Mitchell, 2005, Using acquisitions to access multinational diversity: Thinking beyond the domestic versus cross-border M&A comparison, *Industrial and Corporate Change*, 14(2): 191–224.

72. J. S. Harrison, M. A. Hitt, R. E. Hoskisson, & R. D. Ireland, 2001, Resource complementarity in business combinations: Extending the logic to organizational alliances, *Journal of Management*, 27: 679–690.

73. J. Chatman, C. O'Reilly, & V. Chang, 2005, Cisco Systems: Developing a human capital strategy, *California Management Review*, 47(2): 137–167; S. Thurm, 2003, After the boom: A go-go giant of Internet age, Cisco is learning to go slow, *Wall Street Journal*, May 7, A1.

74. S. Thurm, 2005, Cisco to acquire wi-fi company for $450 million technology from Airespace may help company remain leader in corporate market, *Wall Street Journal*, January 13, B4.

75. Schmidt, Business perspective on mergers and acquisitions.

76. M. Zollo & H. Singh, 2004, Deliberate learning in corporate acquisitions: Post-acquisition strategies and integration capability in U.S. bank-mergers, *Strategic Management Journal*, 25: 1233–1256; P. Mallette, C. L. Fowler, & C. Hayes, 2003, The acquisition process map: Blueprint for a successful deal, *Southern Business Review*, 28(2): 1–13; Hitt, Harrison, & Ireland, *Mergers and Acquisitions*.

77. R. A. Weber & C. F. Camerer, 2003, Cultural conflict and merger failure: An experimental approach, *Management Science*, 49: 400–415; J. Vester, 2002, Lessons learned about integrating acquisitions, *Research Technology Management*, 45(3): 33–41; D. K. Datta, 1991, Organizational fit and acquisition performance: Effects of post-acquisition integration, *Strategic Management Journal*, 12: 281–297.

78. J. R. Carleton & C. S. Lineberry, 2004, *Achieving Post-Merger Success*, New York: John Wiley & Sons; Y. Weber & E. Menipaz, 2003, Measuring cultural fit in mergers and acquisitions, *International Journal of Business Performance Management*, 5(1): 54–72.

79. M. Zollo, 1999, M&A—The challenge of learning to integrate, "Mastering Strategy" (Part Eleven), *Financial Times*, December 6, 14–15.

80. C. Haddad, A. Weintraub, & B. Grow, 2003, Too good to be true, *Business Week*, April 14, 70–72.

81. M. A. Hitt, L. Bierman, K. Shimizu, & R. Kochhar, 2001, Direct and moderating effects of human capital on strategy and performance in professional service firms, *Academy of Management Journal*, 44: 13–28.

82. J. A. Krug, 2003, Why do they keep leaving? *Harvard Business Review*, 81(2): 14–15; H. A. Krishnan & D. Park, 2002, The impact of workforce reduction on subsequent performance in major mergers and acquisi-

tions: An exploratory study, *Journal of Business Research,* 55(4): 285–292; G. G. Dess & J. D. Shaw, 2001, Voluntary turnover, social capital and organizational performance, *Academy of Management Review,* 26: 446–456.

83. T. McIntyre, 2004, A model of levels of involvement and strategic roles of human resource development (HRD) professionals as facilitators of due diligence and the integration process, *Human Resource Development Review,* 3(2): 173–182; J. A. Krug & H. Hegarty, 2001, Predicting who stays and leaves after an acquisition: A study of top managers in multinational firms, *Strategic Management Journal,* 22: 185–196.

84. G. Cullinan, J.-M. Le Roux, & R.-M. Weddigen, 2004, When to walk away from a deal, *Harvard Business Review,* 82(4): 96–104.

85. Rappaport & Sirower, Stock or cash? 149.

86. Witte, Nortel to buy PEC Solutions for $448 million.

87. E. Thornton, 2003, Bypassing the street, *Business Week,* June 2, 79.

88. G. Yago, 1991, Junk Bonds: How High Yield Securities Restructured Corporate America, New York: Oxford University Press, 146–148.

89. M. C. Jensen, 1986, Agency costs of free cash flow, corporate finance, and takeovers, *American Economic Review,* 76: 323–329.

90. S. N. Mehta, 2005, Will Wall Street ever trust Time Warner?, *Fortune,* May 30, 76–81.

91. M. A. Hitt & D. L. Smart, 1994, Debt: A disciplining force for managers or a debilitating force for organizations? *Journal of Management Inquiry,* 3: 144–152.

92. Hitt, Harrison, & Ireland, *Mergers and Acquisitions.*

93. T. N. Hubbard, 1999, Integration strategies and the scope of the company, "Mastering Strategy" (Part Eleven), *Financial Times,* December 6, 8–10.

94. Hitt, Harrison, & Ireland, *Mergers and Acquisitions.*

95. T. Saxton & M. Dollinger, 2004, Target reputation and appropriability: Picking and deploying resources in acquisitions, *Journal of Management,* 30: 123–147.

96. Harrison, Hitt, Hoskisson, & Ireland, Resource complementarity in business combinations; J. B. Barney, 1988, Returns to bidding firms in mergers and acquisitions: Reconsidering the relatedness hypothesis, *Strategic Management Journal,* 9 (Special Issue): 71–78.

97. O. E. Williamson, 1999, Strategy research: Governance and competence perspectives, *Strategic Management Journal,* 20: 1087–1108.

98. Hitt, Hoskisson, Johnson, & Moesel, The market for corporate control.

99. S. Killman, 2005, Monsanto Co. to pay $1 billion for produce-seed firm Seminis, *Wall Street Journal,* January 25, A3.

100. K. Sissell, 2005, Monsanto acquires seeds firm for $1.4 billion, *Chemical Week,* February 2, 9.

101. C. W. L. Hill & R. E. Hoskisson, 1987, Strategy and structure in the multiproduct firm, *Academy of Management Review,* 12: 331–341.

102. R. A. Johnson, R. E. Hoskisson, & M. A. Hitt, 1993, Board of director involvement in restructuring: The effects of board versus managerial controls and characteristics, *Strategic Management Journal,* 14 (Special Issue): 33–50; C. C. Markides, 1992, Consequences of corporate refocusing: Ex ante evidence, *Academy of Management Journal,* 35: 398–412.

103. G. Garai, 2002, Take our outfit—Please! How do you start a small business? Maybe by relieving a corporation of a rashly acquired division, as our expert explains, *BusinessWeek Online,* www.businessweek.com, December 18.

104. D. Palmer & B. N. Barber, 2001, Challengers, elites and families: A social class theory of corporate acquisitions, *Administrative Science Quarterly,* 46: 87–120.

105. Hitt, Harrison, & Ireland, *Mergers and Acquisitions;* R. E. Hoskisson & R. A. Johnson, 1992, Corporate restructuring and strategic change: The effect on diversification strategy and R&D intensity, *Strategic Management Journal,* 13: 625–634.

106. Hitt, Harrison, & Ireland, *Mergers and Acquisitions.*

107. Hughes, Lang, Mester, Moon, & Pagano, Do bankers sacrifice value to build empires? Managerial incentives, industry consolidation, and financial performance; Hitt, Hoskisson, Johnson, & Moesel, The market for corporate control; Hitt, Hoskisson, & Ireland, Mergers and acquisitions and managerial commitment to innovation in M-form firms.

108. M. L. A. Hayward & D. C. Hambrick, 1997. Explaining the premiums paid for large acquisitions: Evidence of CEO hubris, *Administrative Science Quarterly* 42: 103–127; R. Roll, 1986, The hubris hypothesis of corporate takeovers, *Journal of Business,* 59: 197–216.

109. J. Pfeffer, 2003, The human factor: Curbing the urge to merge, *Business 2.0,* July, 58.

110. Hayward, When do firms learn from their acquisition experience?

111. Weber & Camerer, Cultural conflict and merger failure: An experimental approach.

112. C. J. Loomis, 2005, Why Carly's big bet is failing, *Fortune,* February 7, 50–59.

113. P. Burrows & P. Elgin, 2005, The un-Carly unveils his plan, *Business Week,* www.businessweek.com, June 16.

114. R. M. Cyert, S.-H. Kang, & P. Kumar, 2002, Corporate governance, takeovers, and top-management compensation: Theory and evidence, *Management Science,* 48: 453–469.

115. A. P. Dickerson, H. D. Gibson, & E. Tsakalotos, 2003, Is attack the best form of defence? A competing risks analysis of acquisition activity in the UK, *Cambridge Journal of Economics,* 27: 337–357.

116. Hitt, Harrison, & Ireland, *Mergers and Acquisitions.*

117. J. Adamy, 2005, Sara Lee to spin off apparel arm, *Wall Street Journal,* February 11, A5.

118. A. P. Dickerson, H. D. Gibson, & E. Tsakalotos, 2002. Takeover risk and the market for corporate control: The experience of British firms in the 1970s and 1980s, *International Journal of Industrial Organization,* 20: 1167–1195.

119. Reuer, Avoiding lemons in M&A deals; R. M. Di Gregorio, 2003, Making mergers and acquisitions work: What we know and don't know—Part II, *Journal of Change Management,* 3(3): 259–274; R. M. Di Gregorio, 2002, Making mergers and acquisitions work: What we know and don't know—Part I, *Journal of Change Management,* 3(2): 134–148.

120. D. Mayer & M. Kenney, 2004, Economic action does not take place in a vacuum: Understanding Cisco's acquisition and development strategy, *Industry and Innovation,* 11(4): 299–325.

121. M. A. Hitt, R. D. Ireland, J. S. Harrison, & A. Best, 1998, Attributes of successful and unsuccessful acquisitions of U.S. firms, *British Journal of Management,* 9: 91–114.

122. Harrison, Hitt, Hoskisson, & Ireland, Resource complementarity in business combinations.

123. J. Hagedoorn & G. Dysters, 2002, External sources of innovative capabilities: The preference for strategic alliances or mergers and acquisitions, *Journal of Management Studies,* 39: 167–188.

124. P. Porrini, 2004, Can a previous alliance between an acquirer and a target affect acquisition performance? *Journal of Management,* 30: 545–562; J. Reuer, 2001, From hybrids to hierarchies: Shareholder wealth effects of joint venture partner buyouts, *Strategic Management Journal,* 22: 27–44.

125. R. J. Aiello & M. D. Watkins, 2000, The fine art of friendly acquisition, *Harvard Business Review,* 78(6): 100–107.

126. P. Gwynne, 2002, Keeping the right people, *MIT Sloan Management Review,* 43(2): 19; D. D. Bergh, 2001, Executive retention and acquisition outcomes: A test of opposing views on the influence of organizational tenure, *Journal of Management,* 27: 603–622; J. P. Walsh, 1989, Doing a deal: Merger and acquisition negotiations and their impact upon target company top management turnover, *Strategic Management Journal,* 10: 307–322.

127. M. L. Marks & P. H. Mirvis, 2001, Making mergers and acquisitions work: Strategic and psychological preparation, *Academy of Management Executive,* 15(2): 80–92.

128. Cullinan, Le Roux, & Weddigen, When to walk away from a deal; S. Rovit & C. Lemire, 2003, Your best M&A strategy, *Harvard Business Review,* 81(3): 16–17.

129. Hitt, Harrison, & Ireland, *Mergers and Acquisitions;* Q. N. Huy, 2001, Time, temporal capability and planned change, *Academy of Management Review,* 26: 601–623; L. Markoczy, 2001, Consensus formation during strategic change, *Strategic Management Journal,* 22: 1013–1031.

130. R. W. Coff, 2002, Human capital, shared expertise, and the likelihood of impasse in corporate acquisitions, *Journal of Management,* 28: 107–128.

131. R. Smith, 2005, Buffett to invest more in energy sector, *Wall Street Journal,* June 22, A3.

132. J. Anand, 1999, How many matches are made in heaven, Mastering Strategy (Part Five), *Financial Times,* October 25, 6–7.

133. R. A. Johnson, 1996, Antecedents and outcomes of corporate refocusing, *Journal of Management,* 22: 437–481; J. E. Bethel & J. Liebeskind, 1993, The effects of ownership structure on corporate restructuring, *Strategic Management Journal,* 14 (Special Issue): 15–31.

134. R. E. Hoskisson, A. A. Cannella, L. Tihanyi, & R. Faraci, 2004. Asset restructuring and business group affiliation in French civil law countries, *Strategic Management Journal,* 25: 525–539; R. E. Hoskisson, R. A. Johnson, D. Yiu, & W. P. Wan, 2001, Restructuring strategies of diversified groups: Differences associated with country institutional environments, in M. A. Hitt, R. E. Freeman, & J. S. Harrison (eds.), *Handbook of Strategic Management,* Oxford, UK: Blackwell Publishers, 433–463.

135. B. McLean, A. Serwer, & N. Varchaver, 2005, Brahmins at the gate, *Fortune,* May 2, 59–65.

136. J. L. Morrow Jr., R. A. Johnson, & L. W. Busenitz, 2004, The effects of cost and asset retrenchment on firm performance: The overlooked role of a firm's competitive environment, *Journal of Management,* 30: 189–208; T. A. Kruse, 2002, Asset liquidity and the determinants of asset sales by poorly performing firms, *Financial Management,* 31(4): 107–129.

137. R. D. Nixon, M. A. Hitt, H.-U. Lee, & E. Jeong, 2004, Market reactions to announcements of corporate downsizing actions and implementation strategies, *Strategic Management Journal,* 25: 1121–1129.

138. G. J. Castrogiovanni & G. D. Bruton, 2000, Business turnaround processes following acquisitions: Reconsidering the role of retrenchment, *Journal of Business Research,* 48: 25–34; W. McKinley, J. Zhao, & K. G. Rust, 2000, A sociocognitive interpretation of organizational downsizing, *Academy of Management Review,* 25: 227–243.

139. W. McKinley, C. M. Sanchez, & A. G. Schick, 1995, Organizational downsizing: Constraining, cloning, learning, *Academy of Management Executive,* 9(3): 32–44.

140. P. Patsuris, 2002, Forbes.com layoff tracker surpasses 1M mark, *Forbes,* www.forbes.com, January 16.

141. J. B. White & L. Hawkins Jr., 2005, GM plans to cut 25,000 jobs by '08 in restructuring; Analysts, unions question whether moves will work; A steady work-force decline, *Wall Street Journal,* June 8, A1.

142. Hoskisson & Hitt, *Downscoping.*

143. L. Dranikoff, T. Koller, & A. Schneider, 2002, Divestiture: Strategy's missing link, *Harvard Business Review,* 80(5): 74–83.

144. M. Rajand & M. Forsyth, 2002, Hostile bidders, long-term performance, and restructuring methods: Evidence from the UK, *American Business Review,* 20(1): 71–81.

145. Johnson, Hoskisson, & Hitt, Board of director involvement; R. E. Hoskisson & M. A. Hitt, 1990, Antecedents and performance outcomes of diversification: A review and critique of theoretical perspectives, *Journal of Management,* 16: 461–509.

146. R. E. Hoskisson, R. A. Johnson, L. Tihanyi, & R. E. White, 2005, Diversified business groups and corporate refocusing in emerging economies, *Journal of Management,* forthcoming.

147. M. Kripalani, 2004, Ratan Tata: No one's doubting now, *Business Week,* July 26, 50–51.

148. D. D. Bergh & G. F. Holbein, 1997, Assessment and redirection of longitudinal analysis: Demonstration with a study of the diversification and divestiture relationship, *Strategic Management Journal,* 18: 557–571; C. C. Markides & H. Singh, 1997, Corporate restructuring: A symptom of poor governance or a solution to past managerial mistakes? *European Management Journal,* 15: 213–219.

149. M. F. Wiersema & J. P. Liebeskind, 1995, The effects of leveraged buyouts on corporate growth and diversification in large firms, *Strategic Management Journal,* 16: 447–460.

150. R. Harris, D. S. Siegel, & M. Wright, 2005, Assessing the impact of management buyouts on economic efficiency: Plant-level evidence from the United Kingdom, *Review of Economics and Statistics,* 87: 148–153; A. Seth & J. Easterwood, 1995, Strategic redirection in large management buyouts: The evidence from post-buyout restructuring activity, *Strategic Management Journal,* 14: 251–274; P. H. Phan & C. W. L. Hill, 1995, Organizational restructuring and economic performance in leveraged buyouts: An ex-post study, *Academy of Management Journal,* 38: 704–739.

151. C. M. Daily, P. P. McDougall, J. G. Covin, & D. R. Dalton, 2002, Governance and strategic leadership in entrepreneurial firms, *Journal of Management,* 3: 387–412.

152. M. Wright, R. E. Hoskisson, L. W. Busenitz, & J. Dial, 2000, Entrepreneurial growth through privatization: The upside of management buyouts, *Academy of Management Review,* 25: 591–601.

153. M. Wright, R. E. Hoskisson, & L. W. Busenitz, 2001, Firm rebirth: Buyouts as facilitators of strategic growth and entrepreneurship, *Academy of Management Executive,* 15(1): 111–125.

154. Bergh, Executive retention and acquisition outcomes: A test of opposing views on the influence of organizational tenure.

155. H. A. Krishnan & D. Park, 2002, The impact of work force reduction on subsequent performance in major mergers and acquisitions: An exploratory study, *Journal of Business Research,* 55(4): 285–292; P. M. Lee, 1997, A comparative analysis of layoff announcements and stock price reactions in the United States and Japan, *Strategic Management Journal,* 18: 879–894.

156. D. J. Flanagan & K. C. O'Shaughnessy, 2005, The effect of layoffs on firm reputation, *Journal of Management,* 31: 445–463.

157. N. Mirabal & R. DeYoung, 2005, Downsizing as a Strategic Intervention, *Journal of American Academy of Business,* 6(1): 39–45.

158. K. Shimizu & M. A. Hitt, 2005, What constrains or facilitates divestitures of formerly acquired firms? The effects of organizational inertia, *Journal of Management,* 31: 50–72.

159. S. Toms & M. Wright, 2005, Divergence and convergence within Anglo-American corporate governance systems: Evidence from the US and UK, 1950–2000, *Business History,* 47(2): 267–295.

160. P. Desbrieres & A. Schatt, 2002, The impacts of LBOs on the performance of acquired firms: The French case, *Journal of Business Finance & Accounting,* 29 (5,6): 695–729.

161. G. D. Bruton, J. K. Keels, & E. L. Scifres, 2002, Corporate restructuring and performance: An agency perspective on the complete buyout cycle, *Journal of Business Research,* 55: 709–724; W. F. Long & D. J. Ravenscraft, 1993, LBOs, debt, and R&D intensity, *Strategic Management Journal,* 14 (Special Issue): 119–135.

162. Wright, Hoskisson, Busenitz, & Dial, Entrepreneurial growth through privatization; S. A. Zahra, 1995, Corporate entrepreneurship and financial performance: The case of management leveraged buyouts, *Journal of Business Venturing,* 10: 225–248.

Strategy Abroad

Studying this chapter should provide you with the strategic management knowledge needed to:

1. Explain traditional and emerging motives for firms to pursue international diversification.

2. Explore the four factors that lead to a basis for international business-level strategies.

3. Define the three international corporate-level strategies: multidomestic, global, and transnational.

4. Discuss the environmental trends affecting international strategy, especially liability of foreignness and regionalization.

5. Name and describe the five alternative modes for entering international markets.

6. Explain the effects of international diversification on firm returns and innovation.

7. Name and describe two major risks of international diversification.

8. Explain why the positive outcomes from international expansion are limited.

REUTERS/CHINA NEWSPHOTO/LANDOV

Fu Chengyu, chairman of China National Offshore Oil Corp. (CNOOC), which attempted to take over Unocal Corp. but lost out to Chevron.

In 2004, China's foreign-exchange reserves—assets of the Chinese government that are held in different hard currencies such as the dollar, euro, and yen—increased $200 billion to reach $609.9 billion by year end. These reserves result from China's trade surplus with businesses in foreign countries, including the United States. Because of this trade imbalance, other governments have pressured China to increase the value of its currency, the yuan, which would reduce the competitive position of export-related businesses in China. One way the Chinese government can reduce this pressure is by encouraging Chinese companies to reduce the trade imbalance by buying assets overseas. Goods produced by Chinese firms in other nations have the potential to reduce the trade surplus.

With this encouragement many Chinese businesses have been searching the world for acquisitions. South America topped Hong Kong and the rest of Asia as the top destination for Chinese foreign investment in 2004. Through the first 11 months of 2004, South America garnered $899 million of the $1.8 billion invested abroad by Chinese firms. This is primarily due to South America's abundant supply of commodity assets. However, the adjustment of Chinese companies to South American countries has been difficult at times.

A pioneer in such investments, Shougang International Trade and Engineering Company purchased a state-run ironworks, Hierro de Peru, in 1993. However, Shougang did not fulfill its promises to invest to grow the operation, creating significant disappointment. Furthermore, the firm's practices such as not hiring locals for key positions alienated Peruvian workers and the community, in part because mine safety declined and the number of fatal accidents increased. Other Chinese companies have learned from Shougang's mistakes and are adapting to the local environment. Huwei Technologies Company, China's largest maker of telecommunications and network equipment, has been making acquisitions and doing business in Latin America for over six years. Although it had difficulty adjusting to the local economy and cultures, the firm has adapted more fully to the culture in learning to follow government policies and make better local hires.

In 2004 and into 2005, Chinese companies dramatically increased bidding for foreign assets. In early 2004, TCL Corp., a large television manufacturer, purchased the television operations of France's Thomson SA (RCA brand) and the mobile handset operations of France's Alcatel SA. In December 2004, Lenovo Group, the largest personal computer manufacturer in China, proposed to acquire the PC assets of IBM. With this bid, the Chinese foreign direct investment increased to $3 billion in 2004. When the deal closed in 2005, Lenovo was allowed to use the IBM label for five years as it builds its brand in the United States.

Also in 2005, the Haier Group, the largest appliance manufacturer in China, proposed to purchase Maytag Corporation for $1.3 billion in order to build its presence in the United States through the Maytag brand. The China National Offshore Oil Corporation (CNOOC), a large producer of oil and natural gas in China, made a bid to take over Unocal Corp. for $18.5 billion after Chevron and Unocal had agreed for the firms to merge at $16.5 billion. Chevron offered a counter bid that was ultimately successful, even though it was lower than the CNOOC bid. Although the Haier and the CNOOC transactions were not successfully completed, they demonstrate the incentive of Chinese firms to engage in foreign entry, in part due to the excessive foreign reserves incentive.

These foreign reserves are also being invested domestically and abroad in the steel industry. Although China does not have the largest steel firm in the world—that honor belongs to Netherlands-based Mittal Steel, which, as described in Chapter 7, has the capacity to produce approximately 60 million metric tons of steel per year—Chinese mills turned out 273 million tons of crude steel in 2004. This is about the same amount of steel produced in the United States, Japan, and Russia combined, approximately 25 percent of the world's total production.

In 2005 the output is expected to exceed 300 million tons as Chinese firms build up their capacity. China consumed about 258 million tons last year, approximately one third of all steel used worldwide. Demand in China is expected to reach 310 million tons in 2005. Six major producers—Shanghai Baosteel Group, Anshan Iron and Steel Group, Wuhan Iron and Steel Group, Magang Group, Shougang Group, and Handan Iron and Steel Group—annually produce 21.6, 10, 8, 7, 6, and 4 tons of steel, respectively. Industry observers worry about both China and Brazil building capacity to the extent that it will outpace global demand and thus drive down prices. This is another example of the industrial and financial power evolving in China and the influence Chinese firms and industries are having through the implementation of global strategies and worldwide competition.

Sources: A. Browne, O. Brown, S. Yang, & V. Ruan, 2005, China's reserves of foreign money surged last year, *Wall Street Journal,* January 12, A2; J. Kahn, 2005, China's costly quest for energy control, *New York Times,* www.nytimes.com, June 27; E. Kurtenbach, 2005, Steel heating up in China; Industry, demand booming, *Arizona Republic,* July 3, D3; S. Lohr, 2005, The big tug of war over Unocal, *New York Times,* www.nytimes.com, July 6; J. Millman, N. P. Wonacott, & Q. Haixu, 2005, For China, a cautionary tale; Insularity, unfamiliar ways strain investments in South America, *Wall Street Journal,* January 11, A18; S. Moffett & C. Hulzler, 2005, Protests in China against Japan reflect regional power struggle, *Wall Street Journal,* April 20, A1, A13; D. Normile, 2005, Branded in China, *Electronic Business,* March, 61–65; E. B. Smith, 2005, Chinese snap up brand-name U.S. firms, *USA Today,* www.usatoday.com, June 21; C. Chandler, 2004, TV's Mr. Big, *Fortune,* February 9, 84–87.

As the Opening Case indicates, China's firms are exercising their financial muscle due to high levels of foreign reserves from a $600 billion trade surplus by entering other markets through foreign direct investment by acquisitions and other modes of entry. China's entrance into the World Trade Organization (WTO) has brought change not only to China and its trading partners but also to industries and firms throughout the world. Despite its underdeveloped market and institutional environment, China is taking advantage of the size of its market with its foreign direct investment. Many firms choose direct investment over indirect investment because it provides better protection for the assets invested.[1] Domestic firms are becoming more competitive and building up capacity. As indicated by the overall capacity of Chinese firms in the steel industry and overall demand for steel as China builds up its infrastructure and manufacturing capacity (for instance, in the auto industry), the potential global market power of China is astounding.[2]

As foreign firms enter China and as Chinese firms enter into other foreign markets, both opportunities and threats for firms competing in global markets are exemplified. This chapter examines opportunities facing firms as they seek to develop and exploit core competencies by diversifying into global markets. In addition, we discuss

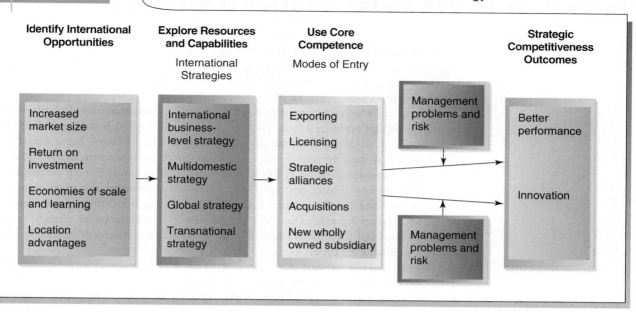

different problems, complexities, and threats that might accompany a firm's international strategy.[3] Although national boundaries, cultural differences, and geographical distances all pose barriers to entry into many markets, significant opportunities draw businesses into the international arena. A business that plans to operate globally must formulate a successful strategy to take advantage of these global opportunities.[4] Furthermore, to mold their firms into truly global companies, managers must develop global mind-sets.[5] Especially in regard to managing human resources, traditional means of operating with little cultural diversity and without global sourcing are no longer effective.[6]

As firms move into international markets, they develop relationships with suppliers, customers, and partners, and then learn from these relationships. Such activity is evident in the pharmaceuticals industry as firms compete against each other in global markets and invest in all areas of the world in order to learn about new markets and new potential drugs.[7]

In this chapter, as illustrated in Figure 1.1, we discuss the importance of international strategy as a source of strategic competitiveness and above-average returns. The chapter focuses on the incentives to internationalize. Once a firm decides to compete internationally, it must select its strategy and choose a mode of entry into international markets. It may enter international markets by exporting from domestic-based operations, licensing some of its products or services, forming joint ventures with international partners, acquiring a foreign-based firm, or establishing a new subsidiary. Such international diversification can extend product life cycles, provide incentives for more innovation, and produce above-average returns. These benefits are tempered by political and economic risks and the problems of managing a complex international firm with operations in multiple countries.

Figure 8.1 provides an overview of the various choices and outcomes of strategic competitiveness. The relationships among international opportunities, the resources and capabilities that result in strategies, and the modes of entry that are based on core competencies are explored in this chapter.

Identifying International Opportunities:
Incentives to Use an International Strategy

An **international strategy** is a strategy through which the firm sells its goods or services outside its domestic market.[8] One of the primary reasons for implementing an international strategy (as opposed to a strategy focused on the domestic market) is that international markets yield potential new opportunities.[9]

Raymond Vernon captured the classic rationale for international diversification.[10] He suggested that typically a firm discovers an innovation in its home-country market, especially in an advanced economy such as that of the United States. Some demand for the product may then develop in other countries, and exports are provided by domestic operations. Increased demand in foreign countries justifies direct foreign investment in production capacity abroad, especially because foreign competitors also organize to meet increasing demand. As the product becomes standardized, the firm may rationalize its operations by moving production to a region with low manufacturing costs.[11] Vernon, therefore, observed that one reason why firms pursue international diversification is to extend a product's life cycle.

Another traditional motive for firms to become multinational is to secure needed resources. Key supplies of raw material—especially minerals and energy—are important in some industries, as illustrated in the Opening Case by the proposed acquisition of Unocal by CNOOC. For instance, aluminum producers need a supply of bauxite, tire firms need rubber, and oil companies scour the world to find new petroleum reserves. Other industries, such as clothing, electronics, watchmaking, and many others, have moved portions of their operations to foreign locations in pursuit of lower production costs.

Although these traditional motives persist, other emerging motivations also drive international expansion (see Chapter 1). For instance, pressure has increased for a global integration of operations, mostly driven by more universal product demand. As nations industrialize, the demand for some products and commodities appears to become more similar. This "nationless," or borderless, demand for globally branded products may be due to similarities in lifestyle in developed nations. Increases in global communication media also facilitate the ability of people in different countries to visualize and model lifestyles in different cultures.[12] IKEA, for example, has become a global brand by selling furniture in 44 countries through 224 stores that it owns and operates through franchisees. It generated $15.5 billion in sales in 2004. All of its furniture is sold in components that can be packaged in flat packs and assembled by the consumer after purchase. This arrangement has allowed for easier shipping and handling than fully assembled units and has facilitated the development of the global brand.[13]

In some industries, technology drives globalization because the economies of scale necessary to reduce costs to the lowest level often require an investment greater than that needed to meet domestic market demand. Hyundai, a Korean car maker, certainly found this to be true; accordingly, they have sought to enhance their operations in the United States and elsewhere.[14] There is also pressure for cost reductions, achieved by purchasing from the lowest-cost global suppliers. For instance, research and development expertise for an emerging business start-up may not exist in the domestic market.[15]

New large-scale, emerging markets, such as China and India, provide a strong internationalization incentive because of their high potential demand for consumer products and services.[16] Because of currency fluctuations, firms may also choose to distribute their operations across many countries, including emerging ones, in order to reduce the risk of devaluation in one country.[17] However, the uniqueness of emerging markets presents both opportunities and challenges.[18] While India, for example, differs from Western countries in many respects, including culture, politics, and the precepts of its economic system, it also offers a huge potential market and its government is becoming more supportive of foreign direct investment.[19] However, the differences between China and India and Western countries pose serious challenges to Western competitive paradigms that emphasize the skills needed to manage financial, economic, and political risks.[20]

A large majority of U.S.-based companies' international business is in European markets, where 60 percent of U.S. firms' assets that are located outside the domestic market are invested.[21] Companies seeking to internationalize their operations in Europe, as elsewhere, need to understand the pressure on them to respond to local, national, or regional customs, especially where goods or services require customization because of cultural differences or effective marketing to entice customers to try a different product.[22]

The need for local repair and service capabilities, for example, influence a firm to be responsive to local country conditions through its internationalization strategy.[23] This localization may affect even industries that are seen as needing more global economies of scale, as in the white goods (e.g., home appliances, such as refrigerators) industry.

Employment contracts and labor forces differ significantly in international markets. For example, it is more difficult to lay off employees in Europe than in the United States because of employment contract differences. In many cases, host governments demand joint ownership with a local company in order to invest in local operations, which allows the foreign firm to avoid tariffs. Also, host governments frequently require a high percentage of procurements, manufacturing, and R&D to use local sources.[24] These issues increase the need for local investment and responsiveness as opposed to seeking global economies of scale.

We've discussed incentives that influence firms to use international strategies. When these strategies are successful, firms can derive four basic benefits: (1) increased market size; (2) greater returns on major capital investments or on investments in new products and processes; (3) greater economies of scale, scope, or learning; and (4) a competitive advantage through location (for example, access to low-cost labor, critical resources, or customers). We examine these benefits in terms of both their costs (such as higher coordination expenses and limited access to knowledge about host country political influences[25]) and their managerial challenges.

Increased Market Size

Firms can expand the size of their potential market—sometimes dramatically—by moving into international markets. Pharmaceutical firms have been doing significant foreign direct investment into China due to the size of the market. One researcher who sampled 117 pharmaceutical firms found that "ninety-nine firms (84.6 percent) chose a joint venture entry operation with a local Chinese partner as their entry mode for the Chinese market and the remaining firms (15.4 percent) established a 100 percent foreign-owned venture operation in China."[26]

Although changing consumer tastes and practices linked to cultural values or traditions is not simple, following an international strategy is a particularly attractive option to firms competing in domestic markets that have limited growth opportunities. For example, firms in the beer industry lack significant growth opportunities in their domestic markets. Accordingly, most large global brewers have pursued a strategy of acquiring other brewers, both in developed markets and in emerging economies. For instance, Heineken NV has purchased a Russian brewer, Patra, increasing Heineken's

SANDY HUFFAKER/BLOOMBERG NEWS/LANDOV

Heineken expanded into international markets by purchasing Patra, a Russian brewer.

market share in Russia from 7.5 percent to 8.3 percent. The Dutch brewer is now the third largest shareholder of the Russian beer market, behind Baltic Beverages Holdings (a joint venture between Copenhagen-based Carlsberg AS and Edinburgh-based Scottish and Newcastle PLC) and Belgian brewer InBevsa (formerly Interbrew SA), which have 34.2 percent and 14.2 percent, respectively.[27]

The size of an international market also affects a firm's willingness to invest in R&D to build competitive advantages in that market.[28] Larger markets usually offer higher potential returns and thus pose less risk for a firm's investments. The strength of the science base in the country in question also can affect a firm's foreign R&D investments. Most firms prefer to invest more heavily in those countries with the scientific knowledge and talent to produce value-creating products and processes from their R&D activities.[29] Research suggests that German multinationals are increasingly investing in international R&D opportunities for resource development and learning purposes as opposed to market-seeking motives.[30]

Return on Investment

Large markets may be crucial for earning a return on significant investments, such as plant and capital equipment or R&D. Therefore, most R&D-intensive industries such as electronics are international. In addition to the need for a large market to recoup heavy investment in R&D, the development pace for new technology is increasing. New products become obsolete more rapidly, and therefore investments need to be recouped more quickly. Moreover, firms' abilities to develop new technologies are expanding, and because of different patent laws across country borders, imitation by competitors is more likely. Through reverse engineering, competitors are able to take apart a product, learn the new technology, and develop a similar product. Because their competitors can imitate the new technology relatively quickly, firms need to recoup new product development costs even more rapidly. Consequently, the larger markets provided by international expansion are particularly attractive in many industries such as pharmaceutical firms, because they expand the opportunity for the firm to recoup significant capital investments and large-scale R&D expenditures.[31]

Regardless of other issues, however, the primary reason for investing in international markets is to generate above-average returns on investments. Still, firms from different countries have different expectations and use different criteria to decide whether to invest in international markets.[32] Turkey, for example, has experienced significant growth since 2001 due to foreign direct investment and better management. Companies are noticing its fairly large market and entry point for other markets in the Mideast. Turkey was expected to draw $6 billion of foreign direct investment in 2005, up from $0.8 billion in the 2002–2004 period.[33]

Economies of Scale and Learning

By expanding their markets, firms may be able to enjoy economies of scale, particularly in their manufacturing operations. To the extent that a firm can standardize its products across country borders and use the same or similar production facilities, thereby coordinating critical resource functions, it is more likely to achieve optimal economies of scale.[34]

Economies of scale are critical in the global auto industry. China's decision to join the World Trade Organization will allow carmakers from other countries to enter the country and lower tariffs to be charged (in the past, Chinese carmakers have had an advantage over foreign carmakers due to tariffs). Ford, Honda, General Motors, and Volkswagen are each producing an economy car to compete with the existing cars in China. Because of global economies of scale (allowing them to price their products competitively) and local investments in China, all of these companies are likely to obtain significant market share in China. Shanghai Automotive Industry Corp. (SAIC) is one of the local Chinese firms that has helped these foreign car companies achieve their significant success in manufacturing cars in China. SAIC has joint ventures, for instance, with both GM and Volkswagen and produced 612,216 cars with these two companies in 2004. Furthermore, SAIC is seeking to develop opportunities for exporting vehicles overseas as well. It aspires to be one of the six largest automakers in the world by 2020.[35]

Firms may also be able to exploit core competencies in international markets through resource and knowledge sharing between units across country borders.[36] This sharing generates synergy, which helps the firm produce higher-quality goods or services at lower cost. In addition, working across international markets provides the firm with new learning opportunities.[37] Multinational firms have substantial occasions to learn from the different practices they encounter in separate international markets. However, research finds that to take advantage of the international R&D investments, firms need to already have a strong R&D system in place to absorb the knowledge.[38]

Location Advantages

Firms may locate facilities in other countries to lower the basic costs of the goods or services they provide. These facilities may provide easier access to lower-cost labor, energy, and other natural resources. Other location advantages include access to critical supplies and to customers.[39] Once positioned favorably with an attractive location, firms must manage their facilities effectively to gain the full benefit of a location advantage.

Such location advantages can be influenced by costs of production and transportation requirements as well as by the needs of the intended customers.[40] Cultural influences may also affect location advantages and disadvantages. If there is a strong match between the cultures in which international transactions are carried out, the liability of foreignness is lower than if there is high cultural distance.[41] Research also suggests that regulation distances influence the ownership positions of multinational firms as well as their strategies for managing expatriate human resources.[42]

China's Internet market has increased dramatically such that 94 million Chinese are now online, a market size second only to the United States. Thus China is a great location for Internet-oriented companies. In May 2005 Microsoft announced it had formed a joint venture with a Shanghai company to offer its MSN Internet portal. Earlier, Google opened an office in Shanghai, having formed a deal with Tencent to provide search services for the Chinese company. Yahoo formed a joint venture with Alibaba.com to focus on business-to-business and consumer-auction sites; Yahoo provides search engine capacity to the venture.[43] Amazon.com, eBay, and Expedia have been examining China for opportunities as well. However, it is difficult for firms to enter the market without having a local operating partner, as the ventures by Microsoft, Google, and Yahoo indicate.[44]

International Strategies

Firms choose to use one or both of two basic types of international strategies: business-level international strategy and corporate-level international strategy. At the business level, firms follow generic strategies: cost leadership, differentiation, focused cost leadership, focused differentiation, or integrated cost leadership/differentiation. There are three corporate-level international strategies: multidomestic, global, or transnational (a combination of multidomestic and global). To create competitive advantage, each strategy must realize a core competence based on difficult-to-duplicate resources and capabilities.[45] As discussed in Chapters 4 and 6, firms expect to create value through the implementation of a business-level strategy and a corporate-level strategy.[46]

International Business-Level Strategy

Each business must develop a competitive strategy focused on its own domestic market. We discussed business-level strategies in Chapter 4 and competitive rivalry and competitive dynamics in Chapter 5. International business-level strategies have some unique features. In an international business-level strategy, the home country of operation is often the most important source of competitive advantage.[47] The resources and capabilities established in the home country frequently allow the firm to pursue the strategy into markets located in other countries. However, research indicates that as a firm continues its growth into multiple international locations, the country of origin is less important for competitive advantage.[48]

Michael Porter's model, illustrated in Figure 8.2, describes the factors contributing to the advantage of firms in a dominant global industry and associated with a specific home country or regional environment.[49] The first dimension in Porter's model is *factors of production*. This dimension refers to the inputs necessary to compete in any industry—labor, land, natural resources, capital, and infrastructure (such as transportation, postal, and communication systems). There are basic factors (for example, natural and labor resources) and advanced factors (such as digital communication systems and a highly educated workforce). Other production factors are generalized (highway systems and the supply of debt capital) and specialized (skilled personnel in a specific industry, such as the workers in a port that specialize in handling bulk chemicals). If a country has both advanced and specialized production factors, it is likely to serve an industry well by spawning strong home-country competitors that also can be successful global competitors.

Ironically, countries often develop advanced and specialized factors because they lack critical basic resources. For example, some Asian countries, such as South Korea, lack abundant natural resources but offer a strong work ethic, a large number of engineers, and systems of large firms to create an expertise in manufacturing. Similarly, Germany developed a strong chemical industry, partially because Hoechst and BASF spent years creating a synthetic indigo dye to reduce their dependence on imports, unlike Britain, whose colonies provided large supplies of natural indigo.[50]

The second dimension in Porter's model, *demand conditions,* is characterized by the nature and size of buyers' needs in the home market for the industry's goods or services. The sheer size of a market segment can produce the demand necessary to create scale-efficient facilities.

Chinese manufacturing companies have spent years focused on building their businesses in China, and only recently are beginning to look at markets beyond their borders. As the opening case suggests, companies such as Lenovo (personal computers)

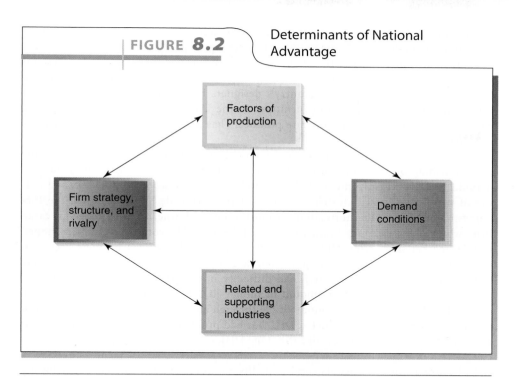

FIGURE 8.2 Determinants of National Advantage

Factors of production

Firm strategy, structure, and rivalry

Demand conditions

Related and supporting industries

Source: Adapted with the permission of The Free Press, an imprint of Simon & Schuster Adult Publishing Group, from *Competitive Advantage of Nations*, by Michael E. Porter, p. 72. Copyright ©1990, 1998 by Michael E. Porter.

and Haier (small appliances) have begun the difficult process of building their brand equity in other countries, beginning in the Far East and seeking to make subsequent moves into the West. These companies have been helped by China's entry to the World Trade Organization and are looking to overseas markets to increase market share and profits. The efficiency built in a large-scale market could help lead to ultimate domination of the industry in other countries, although this could be difficult for firms coming from an emerging economy.

Specialized demand may also create opportunities beyond national boundaries. For example, Swiss firms have long led the world in tunneling equipment because of the need to tunnel through mountains for rail and highway passage in Switzerland. Japanese firms have created a niche market for compact, quiet air conditioners, which are important in Japan because homes are often small and close together.[51]

Related and supporting industries are the third dimension in Porter's model. Italy has become the leader in the shoe industry because of related and supporting industries; a well-established leather-processing industry provides the leather needed to construct shoes and related products. Also, many people travel to Italy to purchase leather goods, providing support in distribution. Supporting industries in leather-working machinery and design services also contribute to the success of the shoe industry. In fact, the design services industry supports its own related industries, such as ski boots, fashion apparel, and furniture. In Japan, cameras and copiers are related industries. Similarly, it is argued that the "creative resources nurtured by [the] popular cartoons and animation sector, combined with technological knowledge accumulated in the consumer electronics industry, facilitated the emergence of a successful video game industry in Japan."[52]

Firm strategy, structure, and rivalry make up the final country dimension and also foster the growth of certain industries. The dimension of strategy, structure, and rivalry among firms varies greatly from nation to nation. Because of the excellent technical training system in Germany, there is a strong emphasis on methodical product and process improvements. In Japan, unusual cooperative and competitive systems have facilitated the cross-functional management of complex assembly operations. In Italy, the national pride of the country's designers has spawned strong industries in sports cars, fashion apparel, and furniture. In the United States, competition among computer manufacturers and software producers has favored the development of these industries.

The four basic dimensions of the "diamond" model in Figure 8.2 emphasize the environmental or structural attributes of a national economy that contribute to national advantage. Government policy also clearly contributes to the success and failure of many firms and industries. In 2003, DHL Worldwide Express entered the U.S. domestic shipping market through the acquisition of Airborne, a Seattle-based air cargo firm, which put it in competition with UPS and FedEx. The combined company hoped to take market share from UPS's and FedEx's small and midsized business accounts, which tended to have higher margins than large corporate accounts that are typically heavily discounted. However, DHL had difficulty in competing with FedEx and UPS; the company lost a significant amount of money in 2004 and did not expect to break even until 2006. It has become more visible through an ad campaign and a great deal of yellow paint on its delivery vehicles. DHL has had problems with its service quality, but it takes time to build a business like this. One DHL executive stated, "Awareness leads to consideration, which leads to trial, which leads to loyalty. That's what it's all about."[53] DHL has sought to improve its service quality to ultimately gain the customer loyalty desired.

Although each firm must create its own success, not all firms will survive to become global competitors—not even those operating with the same country factors that spawned the successful firms. The actual strategic choices managers make may be the most compelling reason for success or failure. Accordingly, the factors illustrated in Figure 8.2 are likely to produce competitive advantages only when the firm develops and implements an appropriate strategy that takes advantage of distinct country factors. Thus, these distinct country factors are necessary to consider when analyzing the business-level strategies (i.e., cost leadership, differentiation, focused cost leadership, focused differentiation, and integrated cost leadership/differentiation, discussed in Chapter 4) in an international context. However, pursuing an international strategy leads to more adjustment and learning as the firm adjusts to competition in the host country, as illustrated in the DHL example.

International Corporate-Level Strategy

The international business-level strategies are based at least partially on the type of international corporate-level strategy the firm has chosen. Some corporate strategies give individual country units the authority to develop their own business-level strategies; other corporate strategies dictate the business-level strategies in order to standardize the firm's products and sharing of resources across countries.[54]

International corporate-level strategy focuses on the scope of a firm's operations through both product and geographic diversification.[55] International corporate-level strategy is required when the firm operates in multiple industries and multiple countries or regions.[56] The headquarters unit guides the strategy, although business- or country-level managers can have substantial strategic input, depending on the type of international corporate level strategy followed. The three international corporate-level strategies are multidomestic, global, and transnational, as shown in Figure 8.3.

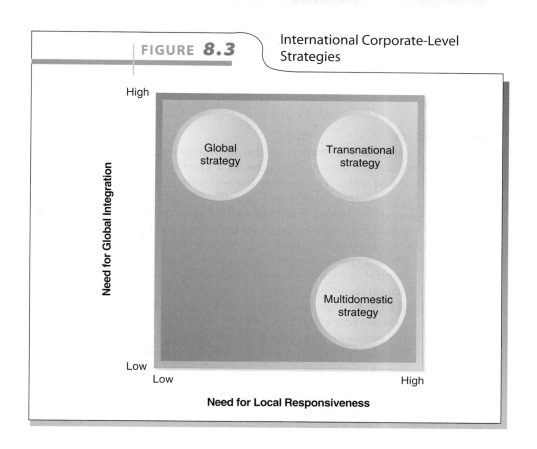

FIGURE **8.3** International Corporate-Level Strategies

Need for Global Integration (vertical axis, Low to High)

Need for Local Responsiveness (horizontal axis, Low to High)

Global strategy

Transnational strategy

Multidomestic strategy

Multidomestic Strategy

A **multidomestic strategy** is an international strategy in which strategic and operating decisions are decentralized to the strategic business unit in each country so as to allow that unit to tailor products to the local market.[57] A multidomestic strategy focuses on competition within each country. It assumes that the markets differ and therefore are segmented by country boundaries. The multidomestic strategy uses a highly decentralized approach, allowing each division to focus on a geographic area, region, or country.[58] In other words, consumer needs and desires, industry conditions (e.g., the number and type of competitors), political and legal structures, and social norms vary by country. With multidomestic strategies, the firm can customize its products to meet the specific needs and preferences of local customers. Therefore, these strategies should maximize a firm's competitive response to the idiosyncratic requirements of each market.[59]

The use of multidomestic strategies usually expands the firm's local market share because the firm can pay attention to the needs of the local clientele.[60] However, the use of these strategies results in more uncertainty for the corporation as a whole, because of the differences across markets and thus the different strategies employed by local country units.[61] Moreover, multidomestic strategies do not allow for the achievement of economies of scale and can be more costly. As a result, firms employing a multidomestic strategy decentralize their strategic and operating decisions to the business units operating in each country. Historically, Unilever, a large European consumer products firm, has had a very decentralized approach to managing its international operations.[62] The French defense contractor French Thomson-CSF has transformed into a new global defense and aerospace electronics group called Thales SA. Thales has won contracts worldwide by using a multidomestic strategy. It has become a local player in six countries outside

France: Britain, the Netherlands, Australia, South Africa, South Korea, and Singapore.[63] It implemented its strategy with a series of joint ventures with and acquisitions of local players in each of these markets. The multidomestic strategy has been commonly used by European multinational firms because of the variety of cultures and markets found in Europe.[64]

Global Strategy

In contrast to a multidomestic strategy, a global strategy assumes more standardization of products across country markets.[65] As a result, a global strategy is centralized and controlled by the home office. The strategic business units operating in each country are assumed to be interdependent, and the home office attempts to achieve integration across these businesses.[66] A **global strategy** is an international strategy through which the firm offers standardized products across country markets, with competitive strategy being dictated by the home office. Thus, a global strategy emphasizes economies of scale and offers greater opportunities to take innovations developed at the corporate level or in one country and utilize them in other markets. Improvements in global accounting and financial reporting standards are facilitating this strategy.[67]

While a global strategy produces lower risk, it may cause the firm to forgo growth opportunities in local markets, either because those markets are less likely to be identified as opportunities or because the opportunities require that products be adapted to the local market.[68] The global strategy is not as responsive to local markets and is difficult to manage because of the need to coordinate strategies and operating decisions across country borders. Vodafone, in implementing a global strategy, has had difficulty in Japan: "By focusing too much on building a globally oriented brand, Vodafone failed to give Japanese customers what they wanted, chiefly a wide lineup of phones with fancy features."[69]

Achieving efficient operations with a global strategy requires sharing resources and facilitating coordination and cooperation across country boundaries, which in turn require centralization and headquarters control. Furthermore, research suggests that the performance of the global strategy is enhanced if it deploys in areas where regional integration among countries is occurring, such as the European Union.[70] Many Japanese firms have successfully used the global strategy.[71]

Cemex is the third largest cement company in the world, behind France's Lafarge and Switzerland's Holcim, and is the largest producer of ready mix, a prepackaged product that contains all the ingredients needed to make localized cement products. In 2005, Cemex acquired RMC for $4.1 billion. RMC is a large U.K. cement producer with two-thirds of its business in Europe. Cemex was already the number one producer in Spain through its acquisition of a Spanish company in 1992. In 2000 Cemex acquired Southdown, a large manufacturer in the United States. Accordingly,

Cemex's global strategy works because it can integrate its subsidiaries through the use of the Internet.

Cemex has strong market power in the Americas as well as in Europe. Because Cemex pursues a global strategy effectively, its integration of its centralization process has resulted in a quick payoff for its merger integration process. To integrate its businesses globally, Cemex uses the Internet as one way of increasing revenue and lowering its cost structure. By using the Internet to improve logistics and manage an extensive supply network, Cemex can significantly reduce costs. Connectivity between the operations in different countries and universal standards dominates its approach.[72] As explained in the Strategic Focus, Whirlpool originally used the global strategy but has begun to pursue the transnational strategy, which is described next.

Transnational Strategy

A **transnational strategy** is an international strategy through which the firm seeks to achieve both global efficiency and local responsiveness. Realizing these goals is difficult: one requires close global coordination while the other requires local flexibility. "Flexible coordination"—building a shared vision and individual commitment through an integrated network—is required to implement the transnational strategy. Such integrated networks allow a firm to manage its connections with customers, suppliers, partners, and other parties more efficiently rather than using arms-length transactions.[73] The transnational strategy is difficult to use because of its conflicting goals (see Chapter 11 for more on the implementation of this and other corporate-level international strategies). On the positive side, the effective implementation of a transnational strategy often produces higher performance than does the implementation of either the multidomestic or global international corporate-level strategies.[74]

The Strategic Focus on Whirlpool's strategy in the global appliance industry suggests how one large global player has evolved towards the transnational strategy in order to deal with the competitive trends in this industry. Renault has used this strategy to reinvigorate Nissan, in which Renault bought a controlling interest in 1999. Since then, Carlos Ghosn, CEO of Nissan, has brought Nissan back from being a very poor performer to being one of the top performers in the industry. The business units of Renault cooperate to achieve global and regional efficiencies and adapt to local market conditions successfully.[75]

Environmental Trends

Although the transnational strategy is difficult to implement, emphasis on global efficiency is increasing as more industries begin to experience global competition. To add to the problem, there is also an increased emphasis on local requirements: global goods and services often require some customization to meet government regulations within particular countries or to fit customer tastes and preferences. In addition, most multinational firms desire coordination and sharing of resources across country markets to hold down costs, as illustrated by the Cemex example above.[76] Furthermore, some products and industries may be more suited than others for standardization across country borders.

As a result, most large multinational firms with diverse products employ a multidomestic strategy with certain product lines and a global strategy with others. Many multinational firms may require this type of flexibility if they are to be strategically competitive, in part due to trends that change over time. Two important trends are the liability of foreignness, which has increased after the terrorist attacks and the war in Iraq, and regionalization.

Whirlpool's Progress toward the Transnational Strategy

In the late 1980s, Whirlpool analyzed the international appliance industry and concluded that over time the industry would be dominated by a handful of global players. With that vision, Whirlpool planned a global strategy that would allow it to pursue worldwide leadership as the industry evolved. In 1989 Whirlpool acquired Philips NV's European appliance business for $2 billion. This acquisition gave Whirlpool not only a strong position in Europe but also an entrance into Asian distribution. In 1994 then CEO David Whitwam described Whirlpool's progress toward its vision: "[O]ur vision at Whirlpool is to integrate our geographical businesses wherever possible, so that our most advanced expertise in any given area, whether it's refrigeration technology, financial reporting systems, or distribution strategy, isn't confined to one location or division." In the process of achieving this vision, Whirlpool purchased a majority stake in an Indian firm, established four joint ventures in China, and made new investments in Latin America.

However, by the mid-1990s serious setbacks had emerged in Whirlpool's international operations. In 1995, Whirlpool's European profit fell by 50 percent and in 1996 the company reported a $13 million loss in Europe. The Asian situation was even worse: Whirlpool lost $70 million and $62 million in Asia in 1996 and 1997, respectively. Its centralized global strategy of producing worldwide products with some adaptation to local markets was not functioning as anticipated.

Although Whirlpool made a number of mistakes in its global strategy, the strategy began to evolve once the company became established in these foreign countries and many suppliers began to form networks around Whirlpool's local host country facilities. At first, Whirlpool pursued a strategy of reducing costs and focusing on standardized products. Over time, however, as its foreign operations evolved, each center of production began to develop various skills and designs that were fitting for a particular region. Ultimately these centers became centers of excellence for technology and production. For instance, Whirlpool's Duet front-loading washers and dryers were developed and continue to be manufactured in Germany. Even though German-made washers have extremely high labor costs—$32 per hour including benefits, versus $23 per hour in the United States—the front-loading technology, long popular in Europe because it uses less water and electricity, was available in Germany at a very small incremental investment. The Germans had worked out the technology exceptionally well for a front door and a basket that runs at high speeds. Designing and manufacturing the Duet in Germany was the fastest route for getting the appliances to the American market. Once the Duet gained favor among American consumers it was still much cheaper for washers to be made in Germany and shipped to the United States. Maytag's Neptune model stumbled in the United States because of its high repair rate, which gave Whirlpool's Duet, with its "kink-free German technology," the advantage. Since 2001, almost 2 million Duets have been sold in the United States at $1,200 apiece.

Besides the washer technology centered in Germany, Whirlpool has a global network of appliance-manufacturing centers, including "microwave ovens engineered in Sweden and made in China for American consumers; stoves designed in

The Whirlpool Duet, manufactured in Germany, has been successful in the U.S. because of its excellent technology.

DANIEL ACKER/BLOOMBERG NEWS/LANDOV

America and made in Tulsa, Oklahoma, for American consumers; refrigerators assembled in Brazil and exported to Europe; and top-loading washers made at a sprawling factory in Clyde, Ohio, for American consumers, although some are sold in Mexico."

Whirlpool and other multinationals are evolving toward more sophistication in their global approach by using a transnational strategy. Interestingly, in the United States more than 40 percent of imports are from U.S. overseas subsidiaries. These overseas subsidiaries thus contribute to the lopsided trade deficit in the United States. Furthermore, Whirlpool's employment in the United States has not risen in years while it has tripled abroad. However, Whirlpool has not had to downsize in the United States, where its centers of excellence co-exist with the high skills necessary to allow its global network to function competitively. In implementing its transnational strategy, Whirlpool has maintained a strong cost focus and has improved its designs in order to more fully adapt to specific regional and country environments and enhance its global competitive position.

Sources: C. K. Prahalad, 2005, The art of outsourcing, *Wall Street Journal,* June 8, A14; C. Salter, 2005, Whirlpool finds its cool, *Fast Company,* June, 73–75; L. Uchitelle, 2005, Globalization: It's not just wages, *New York Times,* www.nytimes.com, June 17; R. E. Sloane, 2004, Leading a supply chain turnaround, *Harvard Business Review,* 82(10): 114–120; K. K. Spors, 2004, *World Business* (a special report); Against the grain: A Chinese appliance maker has placed its bet on a counterintuitive strategy: It brings jobs to the U.S., *Wall Street Journal,* September 27, R6; A. C. Inkpen, 2000, Whirlpool Corporation's global strategy, Thunderbird's Case Collection, The Garvin School of International Management; C. Quintanilla, 1997, Despite setbacks, Whirlpool pursues overseas markets—foreign restructuring in a European recovery may hold promise, *Wall Street Journal,* December 9, 1; R. J. Babyak, 1995, Strategic imperative, *Appliance Manufacturer,* February, W-21-W-24; R. F. Maruca, 1994, The right way to go global: An interview with Whirlpool CEO David Whitwam, *Harvard Business Review,* 72(2): 137–148.

Liability of Foreignness

The dramatic success of Japanese firms such as Toyota and Sony in the United States and other international markets in the 1980s was a powerful jolt to U.S. managers and awakened them to the importance of international competition in what were rapidly becoming global markets. In the 21st century, China, India, Brazil, and Eastern Europe represent potential major international market opportunities for firms from many countries, including the United States, Japan, Korea, and the European Union.[77] However, there are legitimate concerns about the relative attractiveness of global strategies. This is illustrated by the experience of Walt Disney Company in opening theme parks in foreign countries. For example, Disney suffered "law suits in France, at Disneyland Paris, because of the lack of fit between its transferred personnel policies and the French employees charged to enact them."[78] Research shows that global strategies are not as prevalent as once thought and are very difficult to implement, even when using Internet-based strategies.[79] The September 11, 2001, attacks and the 2003 war in Iraq are two explanations for these concerns.[80]

As such, firms may focus less on truly global markets and more on regional adaptation. Although parallel developments in the Internet and mobile telecommunication facilitate communications across the globe, as noted earlier, the implementation of Web-based strategies also requires local adaptation.

The globalization of businesses with local strategies is demonstrated by the online operation of Lands' End, Inc., which uses local Internet portals to offer its products for sale. Lands' End, formerly a direct-mail catalog business and now a part of Sears, Roebuck and Co., launched the Web-based portion of its business in 1995. The firm established Web sites in the United Kingdom and Germany in 1999 and in France, Italy, and Ireland in 2000 prior to initiating a catalog business in those countries. With word of mouth and limited online advertising, a Web site business can be built in a foreign country without a lot of initial marketing expenses. Once the online business is large enough, a catalog business can be launched with mailings targeted to customers who have used the business online. Thus, even smaller companies can sell their goods and services globally when facilitated by electronic infrastructure without having significant (brick-and-mortar) facilities outside of their home location. Lands' End and other retailers are going further by creating personal customization for fitting apparel sizes over the Internet. Service can be enhanced by being able to order online and pick up at a store. Even with custom ordering systems, significant local adaptation is still needed in each country or region.[81]

Regionalization

Regionalization is a second trend that has become more common in global markets. Because a firm's location can affect its strategic competitiveness,[82] it must decide whether to compete in all or many global markets, or to focus on a particular region or regions. Competing in all markets provides economies that can be achieved because of the combined market size. Research suggests that firms that compete in risky emerging markets can also have higher performance.[83]

However, a firm that competes in industries where the international markets differ greatly (in which it must employ a multidomestic strategy) may wish to narrow its focus to a particular region of the world. In so doing, it can better understand the cultures, legal and social norms, and other factors that are important for effective competition in those markets. For example, a firm may focus on Far East markets only rather than competing simultaneously in the Middle East, Europe, and the Far East. Or, the firm may choose a region of the world where the markets are more similar and some coordination and sharing of resources would be possible. In this way, the firm may be able not only to better understand the markets in which it competes, but also to achieve some economies, even though it may have to employ a multidomestic strategy. For instance, research suggests that most large retailers are better at focusing on a particular region rather than being truly global.[84]

Countries that develop trade agreements to increase the economic power of their regions may promote regional strategies. The European Union (EU) and South America's Organization of American States (OAS) are country associations that developed trade agreements to promote the flow of trade across country boundaries within their respective regions.[85] Many European firms acquire and integrate their businesses in Europe to better coordinate pan-European brands as the EU creates more unity in European markets. With this process likely to continue as new countries are added to the agreement, some international firms may prefer to pursue regional strategies versus global strategies because the size of the market is increasing.[86]

The North American Free Trade Agreement (NAFTA), signed by the United States, Canada, and Mexico, facilitates free trade across country borders in North America. NAFTA loosens restrictions on international strategies within this region and provides greater opportunity for regional international strategies. NAFTA does not exist for the sole purpose of U.S. businesses moving across its borders. In fact, Mexico is the number two trading partner of the United States, and NAFTA greatly increased Mexico's exports to this country. Research suggests

President Bush meets with Central American presidents about CAFTA, a trade agreement intended to reduce tariffs.

that managers of small and medium-sized firms are influenced by the strategy they implement (those with a differentiation strategy are more positively disposed to the agreement than are those pursuing a cost leadership strategy) and by their experience and rivalry with exporting firms.[87] The Central American Free Trade Agreement (CAFTA), signed into U.S. law in 2005 but not yet implemented, would reduce tariffs with five countries in Central America plus the Dominican Republic in the Caribbean Sea.[88]

Most firms enter regional markets sequentially, beginning in markets with which they are more familiar. They also introduce their largest and strongest lines of business into these markets first, followed by their other lines of business once the first lines are successful. They also usually invest in the same area as their original investment location.[89]

After the firm selects its international strategies and decides whether to employ them in regional or world markets, it must choose a market entry mode.[90]

Choice of International Entry Mode

International expansion is accomplished by exporting products, participating in licensing arrangements, forming strategic alliances, making acquisitions, and establishing new wholly owned subsidiaries. These means of entering international markets and their characteristics are shown in Table 8.1. Each means of market entry has its advantages and disadvantages. Thus, choosing the appropriate mode or path to enter international markets affects the firm's performance in those markets.[91]

Exporting

Many industrial firms begin their international expansion by exporting goods or services to other countries.[92] Exporting does not require the expense of establishing operations in the host countries, but exporters must establish some means of marketing and distributing their products. Usually, exporting firms develop contractual arrangements with host-country firms.

Global Market Entry: Choice of Entry	TABLE 8.1

Type of Entry	Characteristics
Exporting	High cost, low control
Licensing	Low cost, low risk, little control, low returns
Strategic alliances	Shared costs, shared resources, shared risks, problems of integration (e.g., two corporate cultures)
Acquisition	Quick access to new market, high cost, complex negotiations, problems of merging with domestic operations
New wholly owned subsidiary	Complex, often costly, time consuming, high risk, maximum control, potential above-average returns

The disadvantages of exporting include the often high costs of transportation and possible tariffs placed on incoming goods. Furthermore, the exporter has less control over the marketing and distribution of its products in the host country and must either pay the distributor or allow the distributor to add to the price to recoup its costs and earn a profit.[93] As a result, it may be difficult to market a competitive product through exporting or to provide a product that is customized to each international market.[94] However, evidence suggests that cost leadership strategies enhance the performance of exports in developed countries, whereas differentiation strategies are more successful in emerging economies.[95]

Firms export mostly to countries that are closest to their facilities because of the lower transportation costs and the usually greater similarity between geographic neighbors. For example, U.S. NAFTA partners Mexico and Canada account for more than half of the goods exported from Texas. The Internet has also made exporting easier, as illustrated by the Lands' End system described earlier.[96] Even small firms can access critical information about foreign markets, examine a target market, research the competition, and find lists of potential customers.[97] Governments also use the Internet to facilitate applications for export and import licenses. Although the terrorist threat is likely to slow its progress, high-speed technology is still the wave of the future.[98]

Small businesses are most likely to use the exporting mode of international entry.[99] Currency exchange rates are one of the most significant problems small businesses face. The Bush administration has supported a weak dollar against the euro, which makes imports to the United States more expensive to U.S. consumers and U.S. goods less costly to foreign buyers, thus providing some economic relief for U.S. exporters.[100]

Licensing

Licensing is an increasingly common form of organizational network, particularly among smaller firms.[101] A licensing arrangement allows a foreign company to purchase the right to manufacture and sell the firm's products within a host country or set of countries.[102] The licenser is normally paid a royalty on each unit produced and sold. The licensee takes the risks and makes the monetary investments in facilities for manufacturing, marketing, and distributing the goods or services. As a result, licensing is possibly the least costly form of international expansion.

China is a large and growing market for cigarettes, while the U.S. market is shrinking due to health concerns. But U.S. cigarette firms have had trouble entering the Chinese market because state-owned tobacco firms have lobbied against such entry. As such, cigarette firms such as Altria Group, parent company of Philip Morris International, have an incentive to form a deal with such state-owned firms. The state-owned firms would get access to the most famous brand in the world, Marlboro. Accordingly, both the Chinese firms and Philip Morris have formed a licensing agreement to take advantage of the opportunity as China opens its markets more fully.[103] Because it is a licensing agreement rather than foreign direct investment by Philip Morris, China maintains control of the distribution.

Licensing is also a way to expand returns based on previous innovations.[104] Even if product life cycles are short, licensing may be a useful tool. For instance, because the toy industry faces relentless change and an unpredictable buying public, licensing is used and contracts are often completed in foreign markets where labor may be less expensive.[105] The Sesame Street Workshop, creator of the Muppet figures, has created a large business by licensing figures such as Elmo, Snuffleupagus, and the Count to Target and other specialty stores focused on apparel for "a previously untapped teen/adult market."[106]

Licensing also has disadvantages. For example, it gives the firm very little control over the manufacture and marketing of its products in other countries. Thus, license deals must be structured properly.[107] In addition, licensing provides the least potential returns, because returns must be shared between the licenser and the licensee. Worse, the international firm may learn the technology and produce and sell a similar competitive product after the license expires. Komatsu, for example, first licensed much of its technology from International Harvester, Bucyrus-Erie, and Cummins Engine to compete against Caterpillar in the earthmoving equipment business. Komatsu then dropped these licenses and developed its own products using the technology it had gained from the U.S. companies.[108]

Marriott International Inc. has achieved distinction as a franchise licenser of hotel chains. One analyst noted that Marriott has "become the industry leader by obsessively whipping its troops into line—not just employees, but franchised hotel owners—while pampering loyal customers and winning bookings away from rivals."[109] However, Marriott owns less than 3 percent of the properties, unlike Hilton and Starwood (St. Regis, Sheraton, and Westin hotel chains), which own over 30 percent. Although Marriott has used franchise licensing successfully, if a firm wants to move to a different ownership arrangement, licensing may create some inflexibility. Thus, it is important that a firm think ahead and consider sequential forms of entry in international markets.[110]

Sesame Street Workshop has licensed many of its characters, including Elmo, to specialty stores such as Target.

TIME LIFE PICTURES/GETTY IMAGES

Strategic Alliances

In recent years, strategic alliances have become a popular means of international expansion.[111] Strategic alliances allow firms to share the risks and the resources required to enter international markets.[112] Moreover, strategic alliances can facilitate the development of new core competencies that contribute to the firm's future strategic competitiveness.[113]

GE Finance recently agreed to take a 49.9 percent stake in BAC International Bank, one of Central America's largest banks. BAC International has 178 branches in Costa Rica, El Salvador, Guatemala, Honduras, Nicaragua, and Panama. GE Finance is also one of the largest issuers of credit cards in the region. GE is using a joint venture strategy in order to reduce risk in an emerging market economy where a free market agreement, CAFTA, is in the works. GE Finance expects to get 60 percent of its revenue growth from developing or emerging market countries over the next decade compared with 20 percent in the previous decade.[114]

As in the GE example, most strategic alliances are formed with a host-country firm that knows and understands the competitive conditions, legal and social norms, and cultural idiosyncrasies of the country, which should help the expanding firm manufacture and market a competitive product. Often, firms in emerging economies want to form international alliances and ventures to gain access to sophisticated technologies that are new to them. This type of arrangement can benefit the non-emerging economy firm as well, in that it gains access to a new market and doesn't have to pay tariffs to do so (because it is partnering with a local company).[115] In return, the host-country firm may find its new access to the expanding firm's technology and innovative products attractive.

Each partner in an alliance brings knowledge or resources to the partnership.[116] Indeed, partners often enter an alliance with the purpose of learning new capabilities. Common among those desired capabilities are technological skills.[117] Managing these expectations can facilitate improved performance.

The alliance mentioned above between Renault, a French automaker, and its Japanese partner, Nissan, has been successful over the years because of the way it was managed. Research suggests that company executives need to know their own firm well, understand factors that determine the norms in different countries, know how the firm is seen by other partners in the venture, and learn to adapt while remaining consistent with their own company cultural values. Such a multi-faceted and versatile approach has helped the Renault and Nissan alliance succeed over the years.[118]

Not all alliances are successful; in fact, many fail.[119] The primary reasons for failure include incompatible partners and conflict between the partners.[120] International strategic alliances are especially difficult to manage.[121] Several factors may cause a relationship to sour. Trust between the partners is critical and is affected by at least four fundamental issues: the initial condition of the relationship, the negotiation process to arrive at an agreement, partner interactions, and external events.[122] Trust is also influenced by the country cultures involved in the alliance or joint venture.[123]

Research has shown that equity-based alliances, over which a firm has more control, tend to produce more positive returns[124] (strategic alliances are discussed in greater depth in Chapter 9). However, if trust is required to develop new capabilities in a research collaboration, equity can serve as a barrier to the necessary relationship building.[125] If conflict in a strategic alliance or joint venture will not be manageable, an acquisition may be a better option.[126] Research suggests that alliances are more favorable in the face of high uncertainty and where cooperation is needed to share knowledge between partners and where strategic flexibility is important, such as with small and medium-sized firms.[127] Acquisitions are better in situations with less need for strategic flexibility and when the transaction is used to maintain economies of scale or scope.[128] Alliances can also lead to an acquisition, which is discussed next.

Acquisitions

As free trade has continued to expand in global markets, cross-border acquisitions have also been increasing significantly. In recent years, cross-border acquisitions have comprised more than 45 percent of all acquisitions completed worldwide.[129] As explained in Chapter 7, acquisitions can provide quick access to a new market. In fact, acquisitions may provide the fastest, and often the largest, initial international expansion of any of the alternatives.[130] Thus, entry is much quicker than by other modes. For example, Wal-Mart has entered Germany and the United Kingdom by acquiring local firms.[131] Also, acquisitions are the mode used by many firms to enter Eastern European markets.

Unicredito Italiano SPA has agreed to buy Germany's HVB Group AG. The rationale behind this acquisition is that the market for banking will ultimately be unified for financial services across European Union country boundaries. Both of these firms have also been buying banks in other parts of Europe, especially in Eastern Europe. Therefore the combination would allow better market power within Western Europe and emerging economies in Eastern Europe.[132]

Although acquisitions have become a popular mode of entering international markets, they are not without costs. International acquisitions carry some of the disadvantages of domestic acquisitions, as indicated in the Opening Case (also see Chapter 7). In addition, they can be expensive and also often require debt financing, which carries an extra cost. International negotiations for acquisitions can be exceedingly complex and are generally more complicated than domestic acquisitions. For example, it is estimated that only 20 percent of cross-border bids lead to a completed acquisition, compared with 40 percent of bids for domestic acquisitions.[133] Dealing with the legal and regulatory requirements in the target firm's country and obtaining appropriate information to negotiate an agreement frequently present significant problems. Finally, the problems of merging the new firm into the acquiring firm often are more complex than in domestic acquisitions. The acquiring firm must deal not only with different corporate cultures, but also with potentially different social cultures and practices. Therefore, while international acquisitions have been popular because of the rapid access to new markets they provide, they also carry with them important costs and multiple risks.

China is home to several large energy companies that are finally forming a global strategy. China's increasing petroleum needs and dependence on the Middle East are spurring the companies to seek foreign oil sources. This is illustrated by the attempted takeover bid of Unocal by CNOOC described in the Opening Case. This bid was unsuccessful largely due to U.S. government opposition. SAIC, a China-based automobile producer, has made an acquisition bid for the assets of MG Rover Group, a historic British auto producer, which is now in insolvency. This acquisition would give the Chinese firm an entry point into Europe and an opportunity to establish its own brand through the MG Rover label. SAIC had previously considered a joint venture but has now fully funded the bid, worth $104 million.[134] However, the SAIC bid has formidable government opposition in the UK and must clear extra regulatory hurdles to receive approval.

New Wholly Owned Subsidiary

The establishment of a new wholly owned subsidiary is referred to as a **greenfield venture.** This process is often complex and potentially costly, but it affords maximum control to the firm and has the most potential to provide above-average returns. This potential is especially true of firms with strong intangible capabilities that might be leveraged through a greenfield venture.[135] A firm maintains full control of its operations with a greenfield venture. More control is especially advantageous if the firm has proprietary technology. Research also suggests that "wholly-owned subsidiaries and expatriate staff are preferred" in service industries where "close contacts with end customers" and "high levels of professional skills, specialized know-how, and customization" are required.[136] Other research suggests that greenfield investments are more prominent where physical capital-intensive plants are planned and that acquisitions are more likely preferred when a firm is human capital intensive—that is, where a strong local degree of unionization and high cultural distance would cause difficulty in transferring knowledge to a host nation through a greenfield approach.[137]

The risks are also high, however, because of the costs of establishing a new business operation in a new country. The firm may have to acquire the knowledge and expertise of the existing market by hiring either host-country nationals, possibly from competitors, or consultants, which can be costly. Still, the firm maintains control over the technology, marketing, and distribution of its products.[138] Furthermore, the company must build new manufacturing facilities, establish distribution networks, and learn and implement appropriate marketing strategies to compete in the new market.[139] Research also suggests that if a policy change emerges, firms prefer to move toward a wholly owned approach. For instance, after the Asian financial crisis many countries had to change their institutional policy to allow more foreign ownership. As the institutional policy changed, many firms chose to go with a wholly owned approach rather than a joint venture.[140]

The globalization of the air cargo industry has implications for companies such as UPS and FedEx. The impact of this globalization is especially pertinent to the China and Asia Pacific region. China's air cargo market is expected to grow 11 percent per year through 2023. Accordingly, both UPS and FedEx have announced that they will build hubs in Shanghai and Guangzhou, respectively. DHL already has a hub in the Hong Kong airport. These investments will be wholly owned because these firms need to maintain the integrity of their IT and logistics systems in order to maximize efficiency. Greenfield ventures also help the firms to maintain the proprietary nature of their systems.[141]

Dynamics of Mode of Entry

A firm's choice of mode of entry into international markets is affected by a number of factors.[142] Initially, market entry will often be achieved through export, which requires no foreign manufacturing expertise and investment only in distribution. Licensing can facilitate the product improvements necessary to enter foreign markets, as in the Komatsu example. Strategic alliances have been popular because they allow a firm to connect with an experienced partner already in the targeted market. Strategic alliances also reduce risk through the sharing of costs. Therefore, all three modes—export, licensing, and strategic alliance—are good tactics for early market development. Also, the strategic alliance is often used in more uncertain situations, such as an emerging economy.[143] However, if intellectual property rights in the emerging economy are not well protected, the number of firms in the industry is growing fast, and the need for global integration is high, the wholly owned entry mode is preferred.[144]

To secure a stronger presence in international markets, acquisitions or greenfield ventures may be required. Large aerospace firms Airbus and Boeing have used joint ventures, while military equipment firms such as Thales SA, as noted above, have used acquisitions to build a global presence.[145] Many Japanese auto manufacturers, such as Honda, Nissan, and Toyota, have gained a presence in the United States through both greenfield ventures and joint ventures.[146] Toyota, for example, has two advantages that must be maintained internally: efficient manufacturing techniques using a team approach and a reputation for producing high-quality automobiles.[147] These advantages for Toyota are based on effective management; if Toyota outsourced manufacturing, it would likely lose these advantages. Therefore, Toyota uses some form of foreign direct investment (e.g., greenfield ventures, joint ventures) rather than another mode of entry. Both acquisitions and greenfield ventures are likely to come at later stages in the development of an international strategy. In addition, both strategies tend to be more successful when the firm making the investment possesses valuable core competencies.[148] Large diversified business groups, often found in emerging economies, not only gain resources through diversification but also have specialized abilities in managing differences in inward and outward flows of foreign direct investment. In particular, Korean *chaebols* have been adept at making acquisitions in emerging economies.[149]

Thus, to enter a global market, a firm selects the entry mode that is best suited to the situation at hand. In some instances, the various options will be followed sequentially, beginning with exporting and ending with greenfield ventures.[150] In other cases, the firm may use several, but not all, of the different entry modes, each in different markets. The decision regarding which entry mode to use is primarily a result of the industry's competitive conditions, the country's situation and government policies, and the firm's unique set of resources, capabilities, and core competencies.

Strategic Competitiveness Outcomes

Once its international strategy and mode of entry have been selected, the firm turns its attention to implementation issues (see Chapter 11). It is important to do this, because as explained next, international expansion is risky and may not result in a competitive advantage (see Figure 8.1). The probability the firm will achieve success by using an international strategy increases when that strategy is effectively implemented.

International Diversification and Returns

As noted earlier, firms have numerous reasons to diversify internationally. **International diversification** is a strategy through which a firm expands the sales of its goods or services across the borders of global regions and countries into different geographic locations or markets. Because of its potential advantages, international diversification should be related positively to firms' returns. Research has shown that, as international diversification increases, firms' returns decrease and then increase as firms learn to manage international expansion.[151] In fact, the stock market is particularly sensitive to investments in international markets. Firms that are broadly diversified into multiple international markets usually achieve the most positive stock returns, especially when they diversify geographically into core business areas.[152] There are also many reasons for the positive effects of international diversification, such as potential economies of scale and experience, location advantages, increased market size, and the opportunity to stabilize returns. The stabilization of returns helps reduce a firm's overall risk.[153] All of these outcomes can be achieved by smaller and newer ventures, as well as by larger and established firms. New ventures can also enjoy higher returns when they learn new technologies from their international diversification.[154]

Firms in the Japanese auto industry, particularly Toyota, have found that international diversification may allow them to better exploit their core competencies, because sharing knowledge resources between operations can produce synergy. Also, a firm's returns may affect its decision to diversify internationally. For example, poor returns in a domestic market may encourage a firm to expand internationally in order to enhance its profit potential. In addition, internationally diversified firms may have access to more flexible labor markets, as the Japanese do in the United States, and may thereby benefit from global scanning for competition and market opportunities. Also, through global networks with assets in many countries, firms can develop more flexible structures to adjust to changes that might occur. "Offshore outsourcing" has created significant value-creation opportunities for firms engaged in it, especially as firms move into markets with more flexible labor markets. Furthermore, offshoring increases exports to firms that receive the offshoring contract.[155]

The Malaysian oil company Petronas, like China's CNOOC, is state-owned. However, Petronas' operations are profitable, which is usually counter to most state-owned monopolies. Because Malaysia's oil reserves have dwindled and because few domestic opportunities exist to drill for new reserves, Petronas expanded its operations abroad to fill the potentially growing reserve challenge. It has done so successfully and has operations in 32 countries.[156] It has gone to Iraq and the Sudan, among other places, where more technologically developed Western rivals have been apprehensive to venture. Although multinational firms such as Petronas can produce above-average returns, international diversification can be carried too far, as explained later.

International Diversification and Innovation

In Chapter 1, we indicated that the development of new technology is at the heart of strategic competitiveness. As noted in Porter's model (see Figure 8.2), a nation's competitiveness depends, in part, on the capacity of its industry to innovate. Eventually and inevitably, competitors outperform firms that fail to innovate and improve their operations and products. Therefore, the only way to sustain a competitive advantage is to upgrade it continually.[157]

International diversification provides the potential for firms to achieve greater returns on their innovations (through larger or more numerous markets) and lowers the often substantial risks of R&D investments. Therefore, international diversification provides incentives for firms to innovate.[158]

In addition, international diversification may be necessary to generate the resources required to sustain a large-scale R&D operation. An environment of rapid technological obsolescence makes it difficult to invest in new technology and the capital-intensive operations required to take advantage of such investment. Firms operating solely in domestic markets may find such investments problematic because of the length of time required to recoup the original investment. If the time is extended, it may not even be possible to recover the investment before the technology becomes obsolete.[159] As a result, international diversification improves a firm's ability to appropriate additional and necessary returns from innovation before competitors can overcome the initial competitive advantage created by the innovation. For instance, research suggests that Japanese foreign direct investment in developing countries is focused more on market-seeking and labor cost-saving purposes, whereas investment in developed economies is more focused on strategy development as well as market-seeking purposes. In these firms, a relatively strong ownership advantage is evident versus in developing economies.[160] In addition, firms moving into international markets are exposed to new products and processes. If they learn about those products and processes and integrate this knowledge into their operations, further innovation can be developed.[161] Research, however, finds that to take advantage of R&D investment, knowledge absorptive capacity needs to be in place as well.[162]

The relationship among international diversification, innovation, and returns is complex. Some level of performance is necessary to provide the resources to generate international diversification, which in turn provides incentives and resources to invest in research and development. The latter, if done appropriately, should enhance the returns of the firm, which then provides more resources for continued international diversification and investment in R&D.[163]

Because of the potential positive effects of international diversification on performance and innovation, such diversification may even enhance returns in product-diversified firms. International diversification would increase market potential in each of these firms' product lines, but the complexity of managing a firm that is both product-diversified and internationally diversified is significant. Research indicates that media firms gain from both product and geographic diversification. However, international diversification often contributes more than product diversification in developed countries.[164] Research also suggests that firms in less developed countries gain more from being product-diversified than firms in developed countries. This is especially true when partnering with multinational firms from a more developed country that are looking to enter a less developed country in pursuit of increased international diversification.[165]

Evidence suggests that more culturally diverse top-management teams often have a greater knowledge of international markets and their idiosyncrasies[166] (top-management teams are discussed further in Chapter 12). Moreover, an in-depth understanding of diverse markets among top-level managers facilitates intrafirm coordination and the use of long-term, strategically relevant criteria to evaluate the performance of managers and their units.[167] In turn, this approach facilitates improved innovation and performance.[168]

Complexity of Managing Multinational Firms

Although firms can realize many benefits by implementing an international strategy, doing so is complex and can produce greater uncertainty.[169] For example, multiple risks are involved when a firm operates in several different countries. Firms can grow only so large and diverse before becoming unmanageable, or before the costs of managing them exceed their benefits.[170] For example, the Body Shop has retail outlets in over 50 countries. One of the difficulties it has is coordinating the different IT platforms and managing the different accounting and reporting standards used in each country.[171] Other complexities include the highly competitive nature of global markets, multiple cultural environments, potentially rapid shifts in the value of different currencies, and the instability of some national governments.

Risks in an International Environment

International diversification carries multiple risks.[172] Because of these risks, international expansion is difficult to implement and manage. The chief risks are political and economic. Taking these risks into account, highly internationally diversified firms are accustomed to market conditions yielding competitive situations that differ from what was predicted. Sometimes, these situations contribute to the firm's strategic competitiveness; on other occasions, they have a negative effect on the firm's efforts. Specific examples of political and economic risks are shown in Figure 8.4.

Political Risks

Political risks are risks related to instability in national governments and to war, both civil and international. Instability in a national government creates numerous problems, including economic risks and uncertainty created by government regulation; the existence of many, possibly conflicting, legal authorities or corruption; and the potential nationalization of private assets.[173] Foreign firms that invest in another country may have concerns about the stability of the national government and what might happen to their investments or assets because of unrest and government instability.[174]

Russia has reduced foreign direct investment by prosecuting powerful private firm executives as well as seeking to gain state control of firm assets. For example, Yukos, a thriving oil and gas firm, was penalized for alleged tax fraud and broken up. The CEO was jailed because of the accusations. As a result, the assets of Yukos were partly assimilated into Gazprom, a government-owned oil and gas enterprise. Furthermore, other acquisitions of Russian businesses such as by Seimens AG were not approved by the Russian government. This trend has given pause to some firms considering significant foreign direct investment in Russia. Although Vladimir Putin, Russia's president, has tried to create more reassurance with regard to property rights, firms are still leery of investing in Russia given the current trend toward more government control over the private sector.[175]

| FIGURE **8.4** | Risk in the International Environment

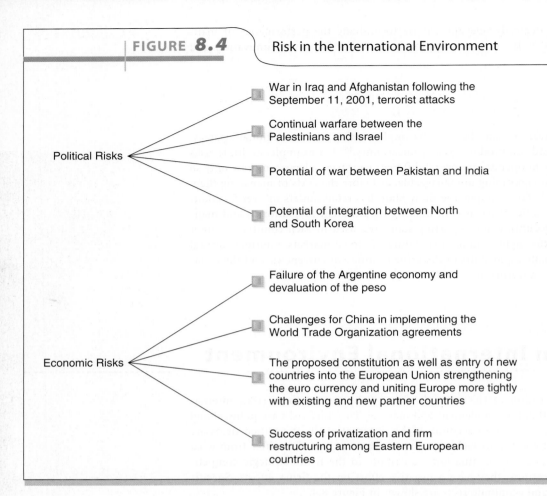

Political Risks
- War in Iraq and Afghanistan following the September 11, 2001, terrorist attacks
- Continual warfare between the Palestinians and Israel
- Potential of war between Pakistan and India
- Potential of integration between North and South Korea

Economic Risks
- Failure of the Argentine economy and devaluation of the peso
- Challenges for China in implementing the World Trade Organization agreements
- The proposed constitution as well as entry of new countries into the European Union strengthening the euro currency and uniting Europe more tightly with existing and new partner countries
- Success of privatization and firm restructuring among Eastern European countries

Sources: 2003, Finance and economics: The perils of convergence; Economics focus, *The Economist,* April 5, 71; K. D. Brouthers, 2003, Institutional, cultural and transaction cost influences on entry mode choice and performance, *Journal of International Business Studies,* 33: 203–221; F. Bruni, 2003, With a constitution to ponder, Europeans gather in Greece, *New York Times,* www.nytimes.com, June 20; B. Davis, R. Buckman, & C. Rhoads, 2003, A global journal report: For global economy, much rides on how the U.S. war plays out, *Wall Street Journal,* March 20, A1; J. Flint, 2003, China: How big, how fast, how dangerous? *Forbes,* www.forbes.com, July 1; G. A. Fowler, 2003, Copies `R' Us—Pirates in China move fast to pilfer toy makers' ideas, *Wall Street Journal,* January 31, B1;W. Rugg, 2003, A down dollar's lure—and peril, *BusinessWeek Online,* www.businessweek.com, May 22; J. H. Zhao, S. H. Kim, & J. Du, 2003, The impact of corruption and transparency on foreign direct investment: An empirical analysis, *Management International Review,* 43(1): 41–62.

Economic Risks

As illustrated in the example of Russia and property rights, economic risks are interdependent with political risks. As discussed in the Strategic Focus, if firms cannot protect their intellectual property, they will not make foreign direct investments. Countries therefore need to create and sustain strong intellectual property rights and their enforcement, or they risk losing their reputation in the eyes of potential investing firms and might also risk sanctions from international political bodies such as the WTO.

Another economic risk is the security risk posed by terrorists. For instance, concerns about terrorism in Indonesia have kept firms from investing in the Indonesian

Are China and India Changing Their Approach to Intellectual Property Enforcement?

The lack of intellectual property protection in large nations such as China and India has made it difficult for Western innovation-oriented firms to be successful there. This problem exists for a large variety of industries from movies and music to software and pharmaceuticals. However, as China and India open their markets, government officials in these countries are reconsidering their current laws and enforcement arrangements for intellectual property rights.

Interestingly, many of India's most innovative companies are welcoming the possibility of stronger patent protections for scientific intellectual property. In the early stages of a country's economic development, lax intellectual property laws allow the imitation of more highly developed countries' intellectual property. India's previous patent system, for example, allowed Indian pharmaceutical companies to copy drug patents created abroad by merely changing the manufacturing process. This allowed a local pharmaceutical industry focused on generic drug manufacturing to keep medicines quite inexpensive for local consumers—as little as one-tenth the original prices. However, as Indian companies consider foreign direct investment and developing multinational enterprises in the pharmaceutical industry outside of India, stronger international patent protection becomes more reasonable. For instance, Indian pharmaceutical companies applied for nearly 800 patents at the World Intellectual Property Organization (WIPO) in 2004, twice as many as were applied for in the previous four years combined. Accordingly, stronger intellectual property laws and enforcement create a better environment for Indian pharmaceutical, software, and other knowledge-industry participants to retain profits for their product innovations.

Similar experiences are being encountered in the Chinese market. There are few recent cases in which the Chinese courts have protected a foreign firm's intellectual property. Other Asian and European business groups besides U.S. firms have been cajoling Beijing to do a better job of marshalling intellectual property protection. Fostering better intellectual property protection is important for any firms considering locating a new R&D and manufacturing facility in China. Microsoft claimed that 90 percent of the Microsoft-labeled software used in China is actually counterfeit. Philips Electronics NV has continually faced counterfeiting in their compact sales with little recourse in the Chinese courts, especially in remote parts of the country. Honda confronted a company producing a scooter that it called a "Hongda."

Of course, China has taken on more intellectual property rights obligations with its entrance into the World Trade Organization. However, the culture in China is a difficult one to overcome. Because during the Communist era in China property belonged "collectively" to the state and to the people and not to individuals or to enterprises, intellectual property ownership is a difficult concept to adjust to for the Chinese. William Lash, U.S. Assistant Secretary of Commerce, has suggested that China, instead of imposing fines for people caught violating patents, trademarks, and

The sale of counterfeit products is a problem in China; here, a shopper looks over some of the counterfeit handbags on display at a shop in the Lowu Commercial Center in Shenzhen, China.

ANDREW LOITERTON/BLOOMBERG NEWS/LANDOV

copyrights, should launch criminal actions against counterfeiters. Such an enforcement approach, he argues, would send a stronger signal to counterfeiters.

However, others argue that the government ownership and control of intellectual property rights in the economy undermines private property rights, especially intangible knowledge such as those associated with patents and copyrights. New invention and innovation that would take place in private laboratories and startup companies throughout the country, if successful, may undermine the power and employment opportunities associated with state-owned firms. Thus, China's state-owned firms' political interests are potentially in conflict with its private enterprises' commercial and entrepreneurial interests.

However, as Chinese firms enter world markets, there needs to be a shift in managerial mind-set in moving from an orientation of imitation toward innovation. It will be a significant strategic leap when state-owned firms move from a focus on products "made in China" to "created in China." If other nations begin to pirate their hard-earned innovations and wisdom, it is likely to follow that the government will implement stronger structural safeguards protecting intellectual property rights. One analyst concluded, "Such enlightened self-interest can be the only driver for the true cultural change needed." Furthermore, to create an incentive for increased foreign direct investment of high value-added investment of technology companies such as research and development centers, China will need to change its anti-intellectual property right culture.

Sources: 2005, Official questions China piracy claims, *Managing Intellectual Property,* May, 1; F. M. R. Armbrecht, 2005, "Created in China" should speed its respect for IP rights, *Research Technology Management,* 48(2): 2–5; E. Bellman, 2005, India senses patent appeal; Local companies envision benefits in stronger protections, *Wall Street Journal,* April 21, A20; P. Choate, 2005, *Hot Property: The Stealing of Ideas in an Age of Globalization,* New York: Alfred A. Knopf; I. P. Mahmood & C. Rufin, 2005, Government's dilemma: The role of government in imitation and innovation, *Academy of Management Review,* 30: 338–360; A. Stevenson-Yang & K. DeWoskin, 2005, China destroys the IP paradigm, *Far Eastern Economic Review,* March, 9–18.

economy. Although many foreign investors in the energy and mining sectors have stuck with Indonesia through political and economic instability, the nation needs to attract new investors to sustain economic growth. Indonesia, with the world's biggest Muslim population, has a hard time competing for investment against the comparatively faster growth in China and India, which have fewer security risks.[176]

As noted earlier, foremost among the economic risks of international diversification are the differences and fluctuations in the value of different currencies.[177] The value of the dollar relative to other currencies determines the value of the international assets and earnings of U.S. firms; for example, an increase in the value of the U.S. dollar can reduce the value of U.S. multinational firms' international assets and earnings in other countries. Furthermore, the value of different currencies can also, at times, dramatically affect a firm's competitiveness in global markets because of its effect on the prices of goods manufactured in different countries.[178]

An increase in the value of the dollar can harm U.S. firms' exports to international markets because of the price differential of the products. Although the dollar was weak historically, it was gaining more strength in 2005. As such, overseas profits for American companies do not look as good as they might otherwise. However, it makes the assets of firms where the currency is higher look stronger but weakens the pricing power of their exports.

Limits to International Expansion: Management Problems

Firms tend to earn positive returns on early international diversification, but the returns often level off and become negative as the diversification increases past some point.[179] There are several reasons for the limits to the positive effects of international diversification. First, greater geographic dispersion across country borders increases the costs of coordination between units and the distribution of products. Second, trade barriers, logistical costs, cultural diversity, and other differences by country (e.g., access to raw materials and different employee skill levels) greatly complicate the implementation of an international diversification strategy.[180]

Institutional and cultural factors can present strong barriers to the transfer of a firm's competitive advantages from one country to another.[181] Marketing programs often have to be redesigned and new distribution networks established when firms expand into new countries. In addition, firms may encounter different labor costs and capital charges. In general, it is difficult to effectively implement, manage, and control a firm's international operations.

Wal-Mart made significant mistakes in markets around the world as it internationalized. For example, its first Mexican stores carried ice skates, riding lawn mowers, fishing tackle—even clay pigeons for skeet shooting. To get rid of the clay pigeons, the stores would radically discount them, "only to have automated inventory systems linked to Wal-Mart's corporate headquarters in Bentonville, Arkansas, order a fresh batch."[182] As Wal-Mart began to get the right mix of products, it became very successful in Latin America, especially in Mexico, and elsewhere in the world. The company has accelerated that growth through international acquisitions; 40 percent of the international sales growth from 2001 to 2005 has come from foreign-acquired retailers. One analyst reported that "More than 2,000 of Wal-Mart's 5,700 stores are now located outside the United States. Of the 500 stores Wal-Mart will open across all divisions this year [2005], about a third will be international."[183]

The amount of international diversification that can be managed varies from firm to firm and according to the abilities of each firm's managers. The problems of central coordination and integration are mitigated if the firm diversifies into more friendly countries that are geographically close and have cultures similar to its own country's culture. In that case, there are likely to be fewer trade barriers, the laws and customs are better understood, and the product is easier to adapt to local markets.[184] For example, U.S. firms may find it less difficult to expand their operations into Mexico, Canada, and Western European countries than into Asian countries.

Management must also be concerned with the relationship between the host government and the multinational corporation.[185] Although government policy and regulations are often barriers, many firms, such as Toyota and General Motors, have turned to strategic alliances to overcome those barriers.[186] By forming interorganizational networks, such as strategic alliances (see Chapter 9), firms can share resources and risks but also build flexibility.[187] However, large networks can be difficult to manage.[188]

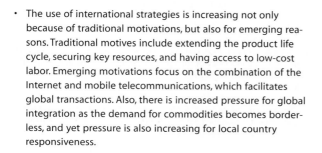

SUMMARY

- The use of international strategies is increasing not only because of traditional motivations, but also for emerging reasons. Traditional motives include extending the product life cycle, securing key resources, and having access to low-cost labor. Emerging motivations focus on the combination of the Internet and mobile telecommunications, which facilitates global transactions. Also, there is increased pressure for global integration as the demand for commodities becomes borderless, and yet pressure is also increasing for local country responsiveness.

- An international strategy usually attempts to capitalize on four benefits: increased market size; the opportunity to earn a return on large investments; economies of scale and learning; and advantages of location.

- International business-level strategies are usually grounded in one or more home-country advantages, as Porter's diamond model suggests. The diamond model emphasizes four determinants: factors of production; demand conditions; related and supporting industries; and patterns of firm strategy, structure, and rivalry.

- There are three types of international corporate-level strategies. A multidomestic strategy focuses on competition within each country in which the firm competes. Firms using a multidomestic strategy decentralize strategic and operating decisions to the business units operating in each country, so that each unit can tailor its goods and services to the local market. A global strategy assumes more standardization of products across country boundaries; therefore, competitive strategy is centralized and controlled by the home office. A transnational strategy seeks to combine aspects of both multidomestic and global strategies in order to emphasize both local responsiveness and global integration and coordination. This strategy is difficult to implement, requiring an integrated network and a culture of individual commitment.

- Although the transnational strategy's implementation is a challenge, environmental trends are causing many multinational firms to consider the need for both global efficiency and local responsiveness. Many large multinational firms—particularly those with many diverse products—use a multidomestic strategy with some product lines and a global strategy with others.

- The threat of wars and terrorist attacks increases the risks and costs of international strategies. Furthermore, research suggests that the liability of foreignness is more difficult to overcome than once thought.

- Some firms decide to compete only in certain regions of the world, as opposed to viewing all markets in the world as potential opportunities. Competing in regional markets allows firms and managers to focus their learning on specific markets, cultures, locations, resources, etc.

- Firms may enter international markets in one of several ways, including exporting, licensing, forming strategic alliances, making acquisitions, and establishing new wholly owned subsidiaries, often referred to as greenfield ventures. Most firms begin with exporting or licensing, because of their lower costs and risks, but later may expand to strategic alliances and acquisitions. The most expensive and risky means of entering a new international market is through the establishment of a new wholly owned subsidiary. On the other hand, such subsidiaries provide the advantages of maximum control by the firm and, if they are successful, the greatest returns.

- International diversification facilitates innovation in a firm, because it provides a larger market to gain more and faster returns from investments in innovation. In addition, international diversification may generate the resources necessary to sustain a large-scale R&D program.

- In general, international diversification is related to above-average returns, but this assumes that the diversification is effectively implemented and that the firm's international operations are well managed. International diversification provides greater economies of scope and learning, which, along with greater innovation, help produce above-average returns.

- Several risks are involved with managing multinational operations. Among these are political risks (e.g., instability of national governments) and economic risks (e.g., fluctuations in the value of a country's currency).

- There are also limits to the ability to manage international expansion effectively. International diversification increases coordination and distribution costs, and management problems are exacerbated by trade barriers, logistical costs, and cultural diversity, among other factors.

NOTES

1. S. Li, 2005, Why a poor governance environment does not deter foreign direct investment: The case of China and its implications for investment protection, *Business Horizons*, 48(4): 297–302.
2. E. Kurtenbach, 2005, Steel heating up in China; industry, demand booming, *The Arizona Republic*, July 3, D3.
3. W. P. Wan, 2005, Country resource environments, firm capabilities, and corporate diversification strategies. *Journal of Management Studies*, 42: 161–182; S. Werner, 2002, Recent developments in international management research: A review of 20 top management journals, *Journal of Management*, 28: 277–305.
4. R. E. Hoskisson, H. Kim, R. E. White, & L. Tihanyi, 2004, A framework for understanding international diversification by business groups from emerging economies. In M. A. Hitt & J. L. C. Cheng (eds.), Theories of the multinational enterprise: Diversity, complexity, and relevance. *Advances in International Management*, Oxford, UK: Elsevier/JAI Press, 137–163;

A. K. Gupta & V. Govindarajan, 2001, Converting global presence into global competitive advantage, *Academy of Management Executive*, 15(2): 45–57.
5. T. M. Begley & D. P. Boyd, 2003, The need for a corporate global mind-set, *MIT Sloan Management Review*, 44(2): 25–32; A. K. Gupta & V. Govindarajan, 2002, Cultivating a global mindset, *Academy of Management Executive*, 16(1): 116–126.
6. V. Mok & G. Yeung, 2005, Employee motivation, external orientation and the technical efficiency of foreign-financed firms in China: A stochastic frontier analysis, *Managerial and Decision Economics*, 26(3): 175–190; R. L. Mecham III, 2003, Success for the new global manager: What you need to know to work across distances, countries, and cultures, *Leadership Quarterly*, 14: 347–352; A. McWilliams, D. D. Van Fleet, & P. M. Wright, 2001, Strategic management of human resources for global competitive advantage, *Journal of Business Strategies*, 18(1): 1–24;.

7. D. M. De Carolis, 2003, Competencies and imitability in the pharmaceutical industry: An analysis of their relationship with firm performance, *Journal of Management,* 29: 27–50; J. S. Childers Jr., R. L. Somerly, & K. E. Bass, 2002, Competitive environments and sustained economic rents: A theoretical examination of country-specific differences within the pharmaceutical industry, *International Journal of Management,* 19(1): 89–98; G. Bottazzi, G. Dosi, M. Lippi, F. Pammolli, & M. Riccaboni, 2001, Innovation and corporate growth in the evolution of the drug industry, *International Journal of Industrial Organization,* 19: 1161–1187.

8. L. Tongli, E. J. Ping, & W. K. C. Chiu, 2005, International diversification and performance: Evidence from Singapore, *Asia Pacific Journal of Management,* 22: 65–88; S. Tallman & K. Fladmoe-Lindquist, 2002, Internationalization, globalization, and capability-based strategy, *California Management Review,* 45(1): 116–135; S. Tallman, 2001, Global strategic management, in M. A. Hitt, R. E. Freeman, & J. S. Harrison (eds.), *Handbook of Strategic Management,* Oxford, UK: Blackwell Publishers, 462–490.

9. J.E. Ricart, M.J. Enright, P. Ghemawat, S.L. Hart, & T. Khanna, 2004, New frontiers in international strategy, *Journal of International Business Studies,* 35: 175–200; W. Hejazi & P. Pauly, 2003, Motivations for FDI and domestic capital formation, *Journal of International Business Studies,* 34: 282–289.

10. R. Vernon, 1996, International investment and international trade in the product cycle, *Quarterly Journal of Economics,* 80: 190–207.

11. J. M.-S. Cheng, C. Blankson, P. C. S. Wu, & S. S. M. Chen, 2005, A stage model of an international brand development: The perspectives of manufacturers from two newly industrialized economies—South Korea and Taiwan, *Industrial Marketing Management,* 34: 504–514; S. Andersson, 2004, Internationalization in different industrial contexts, *Journal of Business Venturing,* 19: 851–875; H. F. Lau, C. C. Y. Kwok, & C. F. Chan, 2000, Filling the gap: Extending international product life cycle to emerging economies, *Journal of Global Marketing,* 13(4): 29–51.

12. L. Yu, 2003, The global-brand advantage, *MIT Sloan Management Review,* 44(3): 13.

13. 2005, IKEA, a household name, *Journal of Commerce,* May 30, 1.

14. 2005, Business: A better drive; Hyundai Motor, *The Economist,* May 21, 75; Y. S. Pak, J. Lee, & J. M. An, 2002, Lessons learned from Daewoo Motors' experience in emerging markets, *Multinational Business Review,* 10(2): 122–128; B. Kim & Y. Lee, 2001, Global capacity expansion strategies: Lessons learned from two Korean carmakers, *Long Range Planning,* 34(3): 309–333.

15. D. Rigby & C. Zook, 2003, Open-market innovation, *Harvard Business Review,* 89(10): 80–89; J.-R. Lee & J.-S. Chen, 2003, Internationalization, local adaptation and subsidiary's entrepreneurship: An exploratory study on Taiwanese manufacturing firms in Indonesia and Malaysia, *Asia Pacific Journal of Management,* 20: 51–72; K. Macharzina, 2001, The end of pure global strategies? *Management International Review,* 41(2): 105.

16. Y. Luo, 2003, Market-seeking MNEs in an emerging market: How parent-subsidiary links shape overseas success, *Journal of International Business Studies,* 34: 290–309; 2003, Special Report: Two systems, one grand rivalry—India and China, *The Economist,* June 21, 66–68; Y. Luo, 2000, Entering China today: What choices do we have? *Journal of Global Marketing,* 14(2): 57–82.

17. C. C. Y. Kwok & D. M. Reeb, 2000, Internationalization and firm risk: An upstream-downstream hypothesis, *Journal of International Business Studies,* 31: 611–629; J. J. Choi & M. Rajan, 1997, A joint test of market segmentation and exchange risk factor in international capital markets, *Journal of International Business Studies,* 28: 29–49.

18. M. Wright, I. Filatotchev, R. E. Hoskisson, & M. W. Peng, 2005, Strategy research in emerging economies: Challenging the conventional wisdom, *Journal of Management Studies,* 42: 1–30; T. London & S. Hart, 2004, Reinventing strategies for emerging markets: Beyond the transnational model, *Journal of International Business Studies,* 35: 350–370; R. E. Hoskisson, L. Eden, C. M. Lau, & M. Wright, 2000, Strategy in emerging economies, *Academy of Management Journal,* 43: 249–267.

19. H. Sender, 2005, The economy; the outlook: India comes of age, as focus on returns lures foreign capital, *Wall Street Journal,* June 6, A2.

20. M. W. Peng, S.-H. Lee, & D. Y. L. Wang, 2005, What determines the scope of the firm over time? A focus on institutional relatedness, *Academy of Man-agement Review,* 30: 622–633; M. Peng, 2003, Institutional transitions and strategic choices, *Academy of Management Review,* 28: 275–296.

21. 2005, EU economy: Building transatlantic bridges, *EIU ViewsWire,* May 27; T. Aeppel, 2003, Manufacturers spent much less abroad last year—U.S. firms cut investing overseas by estimated 37 percent; the "high-wage paradox," *Wall Street Journal,* May 9, A8.

22. T. Stein, 2005, Globe Trotters: Venture firms are increasingly looking beyond U.S. shores, encouraged by the explosive growth, low development costs and surging entrepreneurship in emerging markets. But can U.S.-style venture capital be exported successfully? *Venture Capital Journal,* May 2, 1; W. Kuemmerle, 2001, Go global—or not? *Harvard Business Review,* 79(6): 37–49; Y. Luo & M. W. Peng, 1999, Learning to compete in a transition economy: Experience, environment and performance, *Journal of International Business Studies,* 30: 269–295.

23. O. Gadiesh, 2004, Risk-proofing your brand, *European Business Forum,* Summer, 82; Lee & Chen, Internationalization, local adaptation and subsidiary's entrepreneurship.

24. J. W. Spencer, T. P. Murtha, & S. A. Lenway, 2005, How governments matter to new industry creation, *Academy of Management Review,* 30: 321–337; I. P. Mahmood & C. Rufin, 2005, Government's dilemma: The role of government in imitation and innovation, *Academy of Management Review,* 30: 338–360.

25. L. Eden & S. Miller, 2004, Distance matters: Liability of foreignness, institutional distance and ownership strategy, In M. Hitt & J. L. Cheng (eds.), *Advances in International Management,* Oxford, UK: Elsevier/JAI Press, 187–221; T. Kostova & S. Zaheer, 1999, Organizational legitimacy under conditions of complexity: The case of the multinational enterprise, *Academy of Management Review,* 24: 64–81; S. Zaheer & E. Mosakowski, 1997, The dynamics of the liability of foreignness: A global study of survival in financial services, *Strategic Management Journal,* 18: 439–464.

26. F. Jiang, 2005, Driving forces of international pharmaceutical firms' FDI into China, *Journal of Business Research,* 22(1): 21–39.

27. W. Echikson, 2005, Beer makers want to tap Russia, an increasingly frothy market, *Wall Street Journal,* September 14; B3; 2005, Heineken NV: Russian brewer is acquired, lifting marketshare to 8.3 percent, *Wall Street Journal,* May 9, A1.

28. K. Asakawa & M. Lehrer, 2003, Managing local knowledge assets globally: The role of regional innovation relays, *Journal of World Business,* 38: 31–42.

29. Cantwell, Dunning, & Janne, Towards a technology-seeking explanation of U.S. direct investment in the United Kingdom; W. Chung & J. Alcacer, 2002, Knowledge seeking and location choice of foreign direct investment in the United States, *Management Science,* 48(12): 1534–1554.

30. B. Ambos, 2005, Foreign direct investment in industrial research and development: A study of German MNCs, *Research Policy,* 34: 395–410.

31. Jiang, Driving forces of international pharmaceutical firms' FDI into China.

32. W. Chung, 2001, Identifying technology transfer in foreign direct investment: Influence of industry conditions and investing firm motives, *Journal of International Business Studies,* 32: 211–229.

33. J. C. Cooper & K. Madigan, 2005, Turkey: Leaving the bloom-bust cycle behind, *Business Week,* May 23, 34.

34. K. J. Petersen, R. B. Handfield, & G. L. Ragatz, 2005, Supplier integration into new product development: Coordinating product, process and supply chain design, *Journal of Operations Management,* 23: 371–388; S. Prasad, J. Tata, & M. Madan, 2005, Build to order supply chains in developed and developing countries, *Journal of Operations Management,* 23: 551–568; A. J. Mauri & A. V. Phatak, 2001, Global integration as inter-area product flows: The internalization of ownership and location factors influencing product flows across MNC units, *Management International Review,* 41(3): 233–249.

35. A. Taylor, 2004, Shanghai Auto wants to be the world's next great car company, *Fortune,* October 4, 103–109.

36. W. Kuemmerle, 2002, Home base and knowledge management in international ventures, *Journal of Business Venturing,* 2: 99–122; H. Bresman, J. Birkinshaw, & R. Nobel, 1999, Knowledge transfer in international acquisitions, *Journal of International Business Studies,* 30: 439–462;

J. Birkinshaw, 1997, Entrepreneurship in multinational corporations: The characteristics of subsidiary initiatives, *Strategic Management Journal*, 18: 207–229.

37. J. Cantwell, J. Dunning, & O. Janne, 2004, Towards a technology-seeking explanation of U.S. direct investment in the United Kingdom, *Journal of International Management*, 10, 5–20; S. Makino, C. M. Lau, & R. S. Yeh, 2002, Asset-exploitation versus asset-seeking: Implications for location choice of foreign direct investment from newly industrialized economies, *Journal of International Business Studies*, 33(3): 403–421.

38. J. Penner-Hahn & J. M. Shaver, 2005, Does international research increase patent output? An analysis of Japanese pharmaceutical firms, *Strategic Management Journal*, 26: 121–140.

39. K. Ito & E. L. Rose, 2002, Foreign direct investment location strategies in the tire industry, *Journal of International Business Studies*, 33(3): 593–602.

40. R. Tahir & J. Larimo, 2004, Understanding the location strategies of the European firms in Asian countries, *Journal of American Academy of Business*, 5: 102–110.

41. D. Xu & O. Shenkar, 2004, Insitutional distance and the multinational enterprise, *Academy of Management Review*, 27: 608–618.

42. D. Xu, Y. Pan, & P. W. Beamish, 2004, The effect of regulative and normative distances on MNE ownership and expatriate strategies, *Management International Review*, 44(3): 285–307.

43. J. Dean & J. Cheng, 2005, Meet Jack Ma, who will guide Yahoo in China, *Wall Street Journal*, August 12, B1.

44. B. Einhorn, B. Elgin, & R. D. Hof, 2005, The great Web race, *Business Week*, June 13, 54.

45. Tallman & Fladmoe-Lindquist, Internationalization, globalization, and capability-based strategy; D. A. Griffith & M. G. Harvey, 2001, A resource perspective of global dynamic capabilities, *Journal of International Business Studies*, 32: 597–606; Y. Luo, 2000, Dynamic capabilities in international expansion, *Journal of World Business*, 35(4): 355–378.

46. D. Tan & J. T. Mahoney, 2005, Examining the Penrose effect in an international business context: The dynamics of Japanese firm growth in U.S. industries, *Managerial and Decision Economics*, 26(2): 113–127; K. Uhlenbruck, 2004, Developing acquired foreign subsidiaries: The experience of MNEs for multinationals in transition economies, *Journal of International Business Studies*, 35: 109–123.

47. J. Gimeno, R. E. Hoskisson, B.D. Beal, & W. P. Wan, 2005, Explaining the clustering of international expansion moves: A critical test in the U.S. telecommunications industry, *Academy of Management Journal*, 48: 297–319.

48. L. Nachum, 2001, The impact of home countries on the competitiveness of advertising TNCs, *Management International Review*, 41(1): 77–98.

49. M. E. Porter, 1990, *The Competitive Advantage of Nations*, New York: The Free Press.

50. Ibid., 84.

51. Porter, *The Competitive Advantage of Nations*, 89.

52. Y. Aoyama & H. Izushi, 2003, Hardware gimmick or cultural innovation? Technological, cultural, and social foundations of the Japanese video game industry, *Research Policy*, 32: 423–443.

53. T. Mucha, 2005, Pouring it on to compete with UPS and FedEx, DHL underwent a corporate makeover, with new colors, new commercials, and 17,000 new painted trucks, *Business 2.0*, March, 60.

54. P. Ghemawat, 2004, Global standardization vs. localization: A case study and model, in J.A. Quelch & R. Deshpande (eds.), *The Global Market: Developing a Strategy to Manage Across Borders*, New York: Jossey-Bass; J. Birkinshaw, 2001, Strategies for managing internal competition, *California Management Review*, 44(1): 21–38.

55. W. P. Wan & R. E. Hoskisson, 2003, Home country environments, corporate diversification strategies and firm performance, *Academy of Management Journal*, 46: 27–45; J. M. Geringer, S. Tallman, & D. M. Olsen, 2000, Product and international diversification among Japanese multinational firms, *Strategic Management Journal*, 21: 51–80.

56. Wan & Hoskisson, Home country environments, corporate diversification strategies and firm performance; M. A. Hitt, R. E. Hoskisson, & R. D. Ireland,

1994, A mid-range theory of the interactive effects of international and product diversification on innovation and performance, *Journal of Management*, 20: 297–326.

57. L. Li, 2005, Is regional strategy more effective than global strategy in the U.S. service industries?, *Management International Review*, 45: 37–57; B. B. Alred & K. S. Swan, 2004, Global versus multidomestic: Culture's consequences on innovation, *Management International Review*, 44: 81–105; A.-W. Harzing, 2000, An empirical analysis and extension of the Bartlett and Ghoshal typology of multinational companies, *Journal of International Business Studies*, 32: 101–120.

58. A. Ferner, P. Almond, I. Clark, T. Colling, & T. Edwards, 2004, The dynamics of central control and subsidiary anatomy in the management of human resources: Case study evidence from US MNCs in the UK, *Organization Studies*, 25: 363–392.

59. L. Nachum, 2003, Does nationality of ownership make any difference and if so, under what circumstances? Professional service MNEs in global competition, *Journal of International Management*, 9: 1–32; Sheth, From international to integrated marketing; J. Taggart & N. Hood, 1999, Determinants of autonomy in multinational corporation subsidiaries, *European Management Journal*, 17: 226–236.

60. Y. Luo, 2001, Determinants of local responsiveness: Perspectives from foreign subsidiaries in an emerging market, *Journal of Management*, 27: 451–477.

61. M. Geppert, K. Williams, & D. Matten, 2003, The social construction of contextual rationalities in MNCs: An Anglo-German comparison of subsidiary choice, *Journal of Management Studies*, 40: 617–641; M. Carpenter & J. Fredrickson, 2001, Top management teams, global strategic posture, and the moderating role of uncertainty, *Academy of Management Journal*, 44: 533–545; T. T. Herbert, 1999, Multinational strategic planning: Matching central expectations to local realities, *Long Range Planning*, 32: 81–87.

62. G. Jones, 2002, Control, performance, and knowledge transfers in large multinationals: Unilever in the United States, 1945–1980, *Business History Review*, 76(3): 435–478.

63. D. Michaels, 2003, World business (a special report); victory at sea: How did a French company capture several British naval contracts? Think 'multidomestic', *Wall Street Journal Europe*, September 26, R5.

64. A.-W. Harzing & A. Sorge, 2003, The relative impact of country of origin and universal contingencies in internationalization strategies and corporate control in multinational enterprises: Worldwide and European perspectives, *Organization Studies*, 24: 187–214.

65. Li, Is regional strategy more effective than global strategy in the U.S. service industries?; Alred & Swan, Global versus multidomestic: Culture's consequences on innovation; Harzing, An empirical analysis and extension of the Bartlett and Ghoshal typology.

66. I. C. MacMillan, A. B. van Putten, & R. G. McGrath, 2003, Global gamesmanship, *Harvard Business Review*, 81(5): 62–71.

67. R. G. Barker, 2003, Trend: Global accounting is coming, *Harvard Business Review*, 81(4): 24–25.

68. A. Yaprak, 2002, Globalization: Strategies to build a great global firm in the new economy, *Thunderbird International Business Review*, 44(2): 297–302; D. G. McKendrick, 2001, Global strategy and population level learning: The case of hard disk drives, *Strategic Management Journal*, 22: 307–334.

69. G. Parker, 2005, Going global can hit snags, Vodafone finds, *Wall Street Journal*, June 16, B1.

70. A. Delios & P. W. Beamish, 2005, Regional and global strategies of Japanese firms, *Management International Review*, 45: 19–36.

71. H. D. Hopkins, 2003, The response strategies of dominant US firms to Japanese challengers, *Journal of Management*, 29: 5–25; S. Massini, A. Y. Lewin, T. Numagami, & A. Pettigrew, 2002, The evolution of organizational routines among large Western and Japanese firms, *Research Policy*, 31(8,9): 1333–1348; J. K. Johansson & G. S. Yip, 1994, Exploiting globalization potential: U.S. and Japanese strategies, *Strategic Management Journal*, 15: 579–601.

72. K. A. Garrett, 2005, Cemex, *Business Mexico,* April, 23.

73. T. B. Lawrence, E. A. Morse, & S. W. Fowler, 2005, Managing your portfolio of connections, *MIT Sloan Management Review,* 46(2): 59–65; Y. Doz, J. Santos, & P. Williamson, 2001, *From Global to Metanational: How Companies Win in the Knowledge Economy,* Boston: Harvard Business School Press; C. A. Bartlett & S. Ghoshal, 1989, *Managing across Borders: The Transnational Solution,* Boston: Harvard Business School Press.

74. A. Abbott & K. Banerji, 2003, Strategic flexibility and firm performance: The case of US based transnational corporations, *Global Journal of Flexible Systems Management,* 4(1/2): 1–7; J. Child & Y. Yan, 2001, National and transnational effects in international business: Indications from Sino-foreign joint ventures, *Management International Review,* 41(1): 53–75.

75. J. P. Millikin & D. Fu, 2005, The global leadership of Carlos Ghosn at Nissan, *Thunderbird International Business Review,* 47(1): 121–137; B. James, 2003, Ghosn's local vision plays on a world stage, *International Herald Tribune,* May 3, 9.

76. A. M. Rugman & A. Verbeke, 2003, Extending the theory of the multinational enterprise: Internalization and strategic management perspectives, *Journal of International Business Studies,* 34: 125–137.

77. Wright, Filatotchev, Hoskisson, & Peng, Strategy research in emerging economies: Challenging the conventional wisdom.

78. N. Y. Brannen, 2004, When Mickey loses face: Recontextualization, semantic fit and Semiotics of foreignness, *Academy of Management Review,* 29: 593–616.

79. S. Zaheer & A. Zaheer, 2001, Market microstructure in a global B2B network, *Strategic Management Journal,* 22: 859–873.

80. J. A. Trachtenberg & B. Steinberg, 2003, Plan B for Marketers–in a time of global conflict, companies consider changing how they push products, *Wall Street Journal,* March 20, B7.

81. J. Schlosser, 2004, Cashing in on the new world of me, *Fortune,* December 13, 244–248.

82. A. Rugman & A. Verbeke, 2004, A perspective on regional and global strategies of multinational enterprises, *Journal of International Business Studies,* 35: 3–18; B. Elango, 2004, Geographic scope of operations by multinational companies: An exploratory study of regional and global strategies, *European Management Journal,* 22(4): 431–441.

83. C. Pantzalis, 2001, Does location matter? An empirical analysis of geographic scope and MNC market valuation, *Journal of International Business Studies,* 32: 133–155.

84. A. Rugman & S. Girod, 2003, Retail multinationals and globalization: The evidence is regional, *European Management Journal,* 21(1): 24–37.

85. R. D. Ludema, 2002, Increasing returns, multinationals and geography of preferential trade agreements, *Journal of International Economics,* 56: 329–358; L. Allen & C. Pantzalis, 1996, Valuation of the operating flexibility of multinational corporations, *Journal of International Business Studies,* 27: 633–653.

86. Delios & Beamish, Regional and global strategies of Japanese firms.

87. T. L. Pett & J. A. Wolff, 2003, Firm characteristic and managerial perceptions of NAFTA: An assessment of export implications for U.S. SMEs, *Journal of Small Business Management,* 41(2): 117–132.

88. G. Hitt, 2005, Senate pushes toward passage of CAFTA accord, *Wall Street Journal,* July 1, A7.

89. W. Chung & J. Song, 2004, Sequential investment, firm motives, and agglomeration of Japanese electronics firms in the United States, *Journal of Economics and Management Strategy,* 13: 539–560; D. Xu & O. Shenkar, 2002, Institutional distance and the multinational enterprise, *Academy of Management Review,* 27(4): 608–618; J. Chang & P. M. Rosenzweig, 1998, Industry and regional patterns in sequential foreign market entry, *Journal of Management Studies,* 35: 797–822.

90. K. D. Brouthers, L. E. Brouthers, & S. Werner, 2003, Industrial sector, perceived environmental uncertainty and entry mode strategy, *Journal of Business Research,* 55: 495–507; S. Zahra, J. Hayton, J. Marcel, & H. O'Neill, 2001, Fostering entrepreneurship during international expansion: Managing key challenges, *European Management Journal,* 19: 359–369.

91. H. Zhao, Y. Luo, & T. Suh, 2004, Transaction costs determinants and ownership-based entry mode choice: A meta-analytical review, *Journal of International Business Studies,* 35: 524–544; K. D. Brouthers, 2003, Institutional, cultural and transaction cost influences on entry mode choice and performance, *Journal of International Business Studies,* 33: 203–221; R. Konopaske, S. Werner, & K. E. Neupert, 2002, Entry mode strategy and performance: The role of FDI staffing, *Journal of Business Research,* 55: 759–770.

92. C. Lages, C. R. Lages, & L. F. Lages, 2005, The RELQUAL scale: A measure of relationship quality in export market ventures, Journal of Business Research, 58: 1040–1048; R. Isaak, 2002, Using trading firms to export: What can the French experience teach us? Academy of Management Executive, 16(4): 155–156; M. W. Peng, C. W. L. Hill, & D. Y. L. Wang, 2000, Schumpeterian dynamics versus Williamsonian considerations: A test of export intermediary performance, Journal of Management Studies, 37: 167–184.

93. Y. Chui, 2002, The structure of the multinational firm: The role of ownership characteristics and technology transfer, *International Journal of Management,* 19(3): 472–477.

94. Luo, Determinants of local responsiveness.

95. L. E. Brouthers & K. Xu, 2002, Product stereotypes, strategy and performance satisfaction: The case of Chinese exporters, Journal of International Business Studies, 33: 657–677; M. A. Raymond, J. Kim, & A. T. Shao, 2001, Export strategy and performance: A comparison of exporters in a developed market and an emerging market, Journal of Global Marketing, 15(2): 5–29; P. S. Aulakh, M. Kotabe, & H. Teegen, 2000, Export strategies and performance of firms from emerging economies: Evidence from Brazil, Chile and Mexico, Academy of Management Journal, 43: 342–361.

96. W. Dou, U. Nielsen, & C. M. Tan, 2003, Using corporate Websites for export marketing, *Journal of Advertising Research,* 42(5): 105–115.

97. A. Haahti, V. Madupu, U. Yavas, & E. Babakus, 2005, Cooperative strategy, knowledge intensity and export performance of small and medium sized enterprises, *Journal of World Business,* 40(2): 124–138.

98. K. A. Houghton & H. Winklhofer, 2004, The effect of Web site and ecommerce adoption on the relationship between SMEs and their export intermediaries, *International Small Business Journal,* Volume 22: 369–385.

99. P. Westhead, M. Wright, & D. Ucbasaran, 2001, The internationalization of new and small firms: A resource-based view, *Journal of Business Venturing,* 16: 333–358.

100. M. N. Baily & R. Z. Lawrence, 2005, Don't blame trade for U.S. job losses, *The McKinsey Quarterly,* 1, 86.

101. D. Kline, 2003, Sharing the corporate crown jewels, *MIT Sloan Management Review,* 44(3): 83–88; M. A. Hitt & R. D. Ireland, 2000, The intersection of entrepreneurship and strategic management research, in D. L. Sexton & H. Landstrom (eds.), *Handbook of Entrepreneurship,* Oxford, UK: Blackwell Publishers, 45–63.

102. A. Arora & A. Fosfuri, 2000, Wholly-owned subsidiary versus technology licensing in the worldwide chemical industry, *Journal of International Business Studies,* 31: 555–572.

103. N. Zamiska & V. O'Connell, 2005, Philip Morris is in talks to make Marlboros in China, *Wall Street Journal,* April 21, B1, B2.

104. Y. J. Kim, 2005, The impact of firm and industry characteristics on technology licensing, *S. A. M. Advanced Management Journal,* 70(1): 42–49.

105. M. Johnson, 2001, Learning from toys: Lessons in managing supply chain risk from the toy industry, *California Management Review,* 43(3): 106–124.

106. B. Ebenkamp, 2005, Tamra Seldin, *Brandweek,* April 11, 40, 50.

107. Rigby & Zook, Open-market innovation.

108. C. A. Bartlett & S. Rangan, 1992, Komatsu limited, in C. A. Bartlett & S. Ghoshal (eds.), *Transnational Management: Text, Cases and Readings in Cross-Border Management,* Homewood, IL: Irwin, 311–326.

109. S. Fitch, 2004, Soft pillows and sharp elbows, *Forbes,* May 10, 66.

110. J. J. Reuer & T. W. Tong, 2005, Real options in international joint ventures, *Journal of Management,* 31: 403–423; B. Petersen, D. E. Welch, & L. S. Welch,

2000, Creating meaningful switching options in international operations, *Long Range Planning,* 33(5): 688–705.

111. R. Larsson, K. R. Brousseau, M. J. Driver, & M. Homqvist, 2003, International growth through cooperation: Brand-driven strategies, leadership, and career development in Sweden, *Academy of Management Executive,* 17(1): 7–21; J. W. Lu & P. W. Beamish, 2001, The internationalization and performance of SMEs, *Strategic Management Journal,* 22 (Special Issue): 565–586; M. Koza & A. Lewin, 2000, Managing partnerships and strategic alliances: Raising the odds of success, *European Management Journal,* 18(2): 146–151.

112. J. S. Harrison, M. A. Hitt, R. E. Hoskisson, & R. D. Ireland, 2001, Resource complementarity in business combinations: Extending the logic to organization alliances, *Journal of Management,* 27: 679–690; T. Das & B. Teng, 2000, A resource-based theory of strategic alliances, *Journal of Management,* 26: 31–61.

113. M. A. Hitt, D. Ahlstrom, M. T. Dacin, E. Levitas, & L. Svobodina, 2004, The institutional effects on strategic alliance partner selection in transition economies: China versus Russia, *Organization Science,* 15: 173–185; M. Peng, 2001, The resource-based view and international business, *Journal of Management,* 27: 803–829.

114. K. Kranhold, 2005, GE Finance to expand into Central America, *Wall Street Journal,* May 12, C6.

115. J. Bamford, D. Ernst, & D. G. Fubini, 2004, Launching a world-class joint venture, *Harvard Business Review,* 82(2): 91–100.

116. E. W. K. Tsang, 2002, Acquiring knowledge by foreign partners for international joint ventures in a transition economy: Learning-by-doing and learning myopia, *Strategic Management Journal,* 23(9): 835–854; P. J. Lane, J. E. Salk, & M. A. Lyles, 2002, Absorptive capacity, learning, and performance in international joint ventures, *Strategic Management Journal,* 22: 1139–1161; B. L. Simonin, 1999, Transfer of marketing know-how in international strategic alliances: An empirical investigation of the role and antecedents of knowledge ambiguity, *Journal of International Business Studies,* 30: 463–490.

117. A. T. Mohr & J. F. Puck, 2005, Managing functional diversity to improve the performance of international joint ventures, *Long Range Planning,* 38(2): 163–182; P. Almeida, J. Song, & R. M. Grant, 2002, Are firms superior to alliances and markets? An empirical test of cross-border knowledge building, *Organization Science,* 13(2): 147–161; M. A. Hitt, M. T. Dacin, E. Levitas, J. L. Arregle, & A. Borza, 2000, Partner selection in emerging and developed market contexts: Resource based and organizational learning perspectives, *Academy of Management Journal,* 43: 449–467.

118. R. Pooley, 2005, The model alliance of Renault and Nissan, *Human Resource Management International Digest,* 13(2): 29–32.

119. M. W. Peng & O. Shenkar, 2002, Joint venture dissolution as corporate divorce, *Academy of Management Executive,* 16(2): 92–105; O. Shenkar & A. Yan, 2002, Failure as a consequence of partner politics: Learning from the life and death of an international cooperative venture, *Human Relations,* 55: 565–601.

120. J. A. Robins, S. Tallman, & K. Fladmoe-Lindquist, 2002, Autonomy and dependence of international cooperative ventures: An exploration of the strategic performance of U.S. ventures in Mexico, *Strategic Management Journal,* 23(10): 881–901; Y. Gong, O. Shenkar, Y. Luo, & M.-K. Nyaw, 2001, Role conflict and ambiguity of CEOs in international joint ventures: A transaction cost perspective, *Journal of Applied Psychology,* 86: 764–773.

121. P. K. Jagersma, 2005, Cross-border alliances: Advice from the executive suite, *Journal of Business Strategy,* 26(1): 41–50; D. C. Hambrick, J. Li, K. Xin, & A. S. Tsui, 2001, Compositional gaps and downward spirals in international joint venture management groups, *Strategic Management Journal,* 22: 1033–1053; M. T. Dacin, M. A. Hitt, & E. Levitas, 1997, Selecting partners for successful international alliances: Examination of U.S. and Korean Firms, *Journal of World Business,* 32: 3–16.

122. J. Child & Y. Yan, 2003, Predicting the performance of international joint ventures: An investigation in China, *Journal of Management Studies,* 40(2):

283–320; J. P. Johnson, M. A. Korsgaard, & H. J. Sapienza, 2002, Perceived fairness, decision control, and commitment in international joint venture management teams, *Strategic Management Journal,* 23(12): 1141–1160; A. Arino, J. de la Torre, & P. S. Ring, 2001, Relational quality: Managing trust in corporate alliances, *California Management Review,* 44(1): 109–131.

123. L. Huff & L. Kelley, 2003, Levels of organizational trust in individualist versus collectivist societies: A seven-nation study, *Organization Science,* 14(1): 81–90.

124. Y. Pan & D. K. Tse, 2000, The hierarchical model of market entry modes, *Journal of International Business Studies,* 31: 535–554; Y. Pan, S. Li, & D. K. Tse, 1999, The impact of order and mode of market entry on profitability and market share, *Journal of International Business Studies,* 30: 81–104.

125. J. J. Reuer & M. Zollo, 2005, Termination outcomes of research alliances, *Research Policy,* 34(1): 101–115.

126. P. Porrini, 2004, Can a previous alliance between an acquirer and a target affect acquisition performance? *Journal of Management,* 30: 545–562; J. J. Reuer, 2002, Incremental corporate reconfiguration through international joint venture buyouts and selloffs, *Management International Review,* 42: 237–260.

127. J. J. Reuer, 2005, Avoiding lemons in M&A deals, *MIT Sloan Management Review,* 46(3): 15–17; G. A. Knight & P. W. Liesch, 2002, Information internalisation in internationalising the firm, *Journal of Business Research,* 55(12): 981–995.

128. J. H. Dyer, P. Kale, & H. Singh, 2004, When to ally and when to acquire. *Harvard Business Review,* 82(7): 108–117; W. H. Hoffmann & W. Schaper-Rinkel, 2001, Acquire or ally? A strategy framework for deciding between acquisition and cooperation, *Management International Review,* 41(2): 131–159.

129. K. Shimizu, M.A. Hitt, D. Vaidyanath, & V. Pisano, 2004, Theoretical foundations of cross-border mergers and acquisitions: A review of current research and recommendations for the future. *Journal of International Management,* 10: 307–353; M. A. Hitt, J. S. Harrison, & R. D. Ireland, 2001, *Mergers and Acquisitions: A Guide to Creating Value for Stakeholders,* New York: Oxford University Press.

130. M. A. Hitt & V. Pisano, 2003, The cross-border merger and acquisition strategy, *Management Research,* 1: 133–144.

131. J. Levine, 2004, Europe: Gold mines and quicksand, *Forbes,* April 12, 76.

132. J. Singer, C. Mollenkamp, & E. Taylor, 2005, Unicredito agrees to acquire HVB: Deal totaling $18.8 billion would create huge leader spanning European borders, *Wall Street Journal,* June 13, A3; G. Edmondson & M. Kline, 2005, An Italian bank pulls the trigger, *Business Week,* June 27, 34.

133. 1999, French dressing, *The Economist,* July 10, 53–54.

134. C. Buckley, 2005, SAIC to fund MG Rover bid, *The Times of London,* www.timesonline.co.uk, July 18.

135. A.-W. Harzing, 2002, Acquisitions versus greenfield investments: International strategy and management of entry modes, *Strategic Management Journal,* 23: 211–227; K. D. Brouthers & L. E. Brouthers, 2000, Acquisition or greenfield start-up? Institutional, cultural and transaction cost influences, *Strategic Management Journal,* 21: 89–97.

136. C. Bouquet, L. Hebert, & A. Delios, 2004, Foreign expansion in service industries: Separability and human capital intensity, *Journal of Business Research,* 57: 35–46.

137. D. Elango, 2005, The influence of plant characteristics on the entry mode choice of overseas firms, *Journal of Operations Management,* 23(1): 65–79.

138. P. Deng, 2003, Determinants of full-control mode in China: An integrative approach, *American Business Review,* 21(1): 113–123.

139. R. Belderbos, 2003, Entry mode, organizational learning, and R&D in foreign affiliates: Evidence from Japanese firms, *Strategic Management Journal,* 34: 235–259.

140. K. E. Meyer & H. V. Nguyen, 2005, Foreign investment strategies in subnational institutions in emerging markets: Evidence from Vietnam, *Journal of Management Studies,* 42: 63–93; J. Reuer, O. Shenkar, & R. Ragozzino, 2004, Mitigating risks in international mergers and acquisitions: The role

of contingent payouts, *Journal of International Business Studies,* 35: 19–32.

141. B. Stanley, 2005, United Parcel Service to open a hub in Shanghai, *Wall Street Journal,* July 8, B2; B. Stanley, 2005, FedEx plans hub in Guangzhou: Facility to begin operation in 2008 as cargo industry tries to claim turf in Asia, *Asian Wall Street Journal,* July 14, A3.

142. V. Gaba, Y. Pan, & G. R. Ungson, 2002, Timing of entry in international market: An empirical study of U.S. Fortune 500 firms in China, *Journal of International Business Studies,* 33(1): 39–55; S.-J. Chang & P. Rosenzweig, 2001, The choice of entry mode in sequential foreign direct investment, *Strategic Management Journal,* 22: 747–776.

143. K. E. Myer, 2001, Institutions, transaction costs, and entry mode choice in Eastern Europe, *Journal of International Business Studies,* 32: 357–367.

144. S. Li, 2004, Why are property rights protections lacking in China? An institutional explanation, *California Management Review,* 46(3): 100–115; Y. Luo, 2001, Determinants of entry in an emerging economy: A multilevel approach, *Journal of Management Studies,* 38: 443–472.

145. A. Antoine, C. B. Frank, H. Murata, & E. Roberts, 2003, Acquisitions and alliances in the aerospace industry: An unusual triad, *International Journal of Technology Management,* 25(8): 779–790.

146. L. J. Howell & J. C. Hsu, 2002, Globalization within the auto industry, *Research Technology Management,* 45(4): 43–49; A. Takeishi, 2001, Bridging inter- and intra-firm boundaries: Management of supplier involvement in automobile product development, *Strategic Management Journal,* 22: 403–433.

147. S.J. Spear, 2004, Learning to lead at Toyota, *Harvard Business Review,* 82(5): 78–86.

148. J. Hagedoorn & G. Dysters, 2002, External sources of innovative capabilities: The preference for strategic alliances or mergers and acquisitions, *Journal of Management Studies,* 39: 167–188; H. Chen, 1999, International performance of multinationals: A hybrid model, *Journal of World Business,* 34: 157–170.

149. J. E. Garten, 2005, A new threat to America, Inc., *Business Week,* July 25, 114; Hoskisson, Kim, Tihanyi, & White, A framework for understanding international diversification by business groups from emerging economies.

150. J. Song, 2002, Firm capabilities and technology ladders: Sequential foreign direct investments of Japanese electronics firms in East Asia, *Strategic Management Journal,* 23: 191–210.

151. J. W. Lu & P. W. Beamish, 2004, International diversification and firm performance: The S-curve hypothesis, *Academy of Management Journal,* 47: 598–609.

152. S. E. Christophe & H. Lee, 2005, What matters about internationalization: A market-based assessment, *Journal of Business Research,* 58: 536–643; J. A. Doukas & L. H. P. Lang, 2003, Foreign direct investment, diversification and firm performance, *Journal of International Business Studies,* 34: 153–172.

153. Kwok & Reeb, 2000, Internationalization and firm risk; J. M. Geringer, P. W. Beamish, & R. C. daCosta, 1989, Diversification strategy and internationalization: Implications for MNE performance, *Strategic Management Journal,* 10: 109–119; R. E. Caves, 1982, *Multinational Enterprise and Economic Analysis,* Cambridge, MA: Cambridge University Press.

154. Zahra, Ireland, & Hitt, International expansion by new venture firms.

155. D. Farrell, 2005, Offshoring: Value creation through economic change, *Journal of Management Studies,* 42: 675–683; J. P. Doh, 2005, Offshore outsourcing: Implications for international business and strategic management theory and practice, *Journal of Management Studies,* 42: 695–704.

156. L. Lopez, 2005, Petronas's net soared in year; high oil, petroleum prices fueled 41 percent rise in revenue; widening global stature, *Asian Wall Street Journal,* July 1, A3; L. Lopez, 2003, A well-oiled money machine, *Far Eastern Economic Review,* March 13, 40–43.

157. J. Penner-Hahn & J. M. Shaver, 2005, Does international research and development increase patent output? An analysis of Japanese pharmaceutical firms, *Strategic Management Journal,* 26: 121–140; Hagedoorn & Dysters,

External sources of innovative capabilities; G. Hamel, 2000, *Leading the Revolution,* Boston: Harvard Business School Press.

158. L. Tihanyi, R. A. Johnson, R. E. Hoskisson, & M. A. Hitt, 2003, Institutional ownership differences and international diversification: The effects of board of directors and technological opportunity, *Academy of Management Journal,* 46: 195–211.

159. Ambos, Foreign direct investment in industrial research and development; F. Bradley & M. Gannon, 2000, Does the firm's technology and marketing profile affect foreign market entry? *Journal of International Marketing,* 8(4): 12–36; M. Kotabe, 1990, The relationship between offshore sourcing and innovativeness of U.S. multinational firms: An empirical investigation, *Journal of International Business Studies,* 21: 623–638.

160. S. Makino, P. W. Beamish, & N. B. Zhao, 2004, The characteristics and performance of Japanese FDI in less developed and developed countries, *Journal of World Business,* 39(4): 377–392.

161. Asakawa & Lehrer, Managing local knowledge assets globally: The role of regional innovation relays; I. Zander & O. Solvell, 2000, Cross border innovation in the multinational corporation: A research agenda, *International Studies of Management and Organization,* 30(2): 44–67.

162. Penner-Hahn & Shaver, Does international research increase patent output?

163. O. E. M. Janne, 2002, The emergence of corporate integrated innovation systems across regions: The case of the chemical and pharmaceutical industry in Germany, the UK and Belgium, *Journal of International Management,* 8: 97–119; N. J. Foss & T. Pedersen, 2002, Transferring knowledge in MNCs: The role of sources of subsidiary knowledge and organizational context, *Journal of International Management,* 8: 49–67.

164. J. Jung & S. M. Chan-Olmsted, 2005, Impacts of media conglomerates' dual diversification on financial performance, *Journal of Media Economics,* 18(3): 183–202.

165. Wan & Hoskisson, Home country environments, corporate diversification strategies and firm performance.

166. D. S. Elenkov, W. Judge, & P. Wright, 2005, Strategic leadership and executive innovation influence: an international multi-cluster comparative study, *Strategic Management Journal,* 26: 665–682; P. Herrmann, 2002, The influence of CEO characteristics on the international diversification of manufacturing firms: An empirical study in the United States, *International Journal of Management,* 19(2): 279–289.

167. H. A. Krishnan & D. Park, 2003, Power in acquired top management teams and post-acquisition performance: A conceptual framework, *International Journal of Management,* 20: 75–80; A. McWilliams, D. D. Van Fleet, & P. M. Wright, 2001, Strategic management of human resources for global competitive advantage, *Journal of Business Strategies,* 18(1): 1–24.

168. M. A. Hitt, R. E. Hoskisson, & H. Kim, 1997, International diversification: Effects on innovation and firm performance in product-diversified firms, *Academy of Management Journal,* 40: 767–798.

169. Y. Li, L. Li, Y. Liu, & L. Wang, 2005, Linking management control system with product development and process decisions to cope with environment complexity. *International Journal of Production Research,* 43: 2577–2591; J. Child, L. Chung, & H. Davies, 2003, The performance of cross-border units in China: A test of natural selection, strategic choice and contingency theories, *Journal of International Business Studies,* 34: 242–254.

170. Y.-H. Chiu, 2003, The impact of conglomerate firm diversification on corporate performance: An empirical study in Taiwan, *International Journal of Management,* 19: 231–237; Luo, Market-seeking MNEs in an emerging market: How parent-subsidiary links shape overseas success.

171. 2005, Keeping IT together, *Chain Store Age,* June, 48.

172. Y. Paik, 2005, Risk management of strategic alliances and acquisitions between western MNCs and companies in central Europe, *Thunderbird International Business Review,* 47(4): 489–511; A. Delios & W. J. Henisz, 2003, Policy uncertainty and the sequence of entry by Japanese firms,

1980–1998, Journal of International Business Studies, 34: 227–241; D. M. Reeb, C. C. Y. Kwok, & H. Y. Baek, 1998, Systematic risk of the multinational corporation, Journal of International Business Studies, 29: 263–279.

173. P. Rodriguez, K. Uhlenbruck, & L. Eden, 2005, Government corruption and the entry strategies of multinationals, Academy of Management Review, 30: 383–396; J. H. Zhao, S. H. Kim, & J. Du, 2003, The impact of corruption and transparency on foreign direct investment: An empirical analysis, Management International Review, 43(1): 41–62.

174. P. S. Ring, G. A. Bigley, T. D'aunno, & T. Khanna, 2005, Perspectives on how governments matter, Academy of Management Review, 30: 308–320; S. Globerman & D. Shapiro, 2003, Governance infrastructure and US foreign direct investment, Journal of International Business Studies, 34(1): 19–39.

175. G. Chazan, 2005, Putin pledges to help foreign investors, Wall Street Journal, June 27, A13.

176. T. Mapes, 2005, Terror still keeps foreign investors out of Indonesia, Wall Street Journal, May 31, A14.

177. T. Vestring, T. Rouse, & U. Reinert, 2005, Hedging your offshoring bets, MIT Sloan Management Review, 46(3): 26–29; L. L. Jacque & P. M. Vaaler, 2001, The international control conundrum with exchange risk: An EVA framework, Journal of International Business Studies, 32: 813–832.

178. T. G. Andrews & N. Chompusri, 2005, Temporal dynamics of crossvergence: Institutionalizing MNC integration strategies in post-crisis ASEAN, Asia Pacific Journal of Management, 22(1): 5–22; S. Mudd, R. Grosse, & J. Mathis, 2002, Dealing with financial crises in emerging markets, Thunderbird International Business Review, 44(3): 399–430.

179. Lu & Beamish, International diversification and firm performance: The s-curve hypothesis; Wan & Hoskisson, Home country environments, corporate diversification strategies and firm performance; Hitt, Hoskisson, & Kim, International diversification; S. Tallman & J. Li, 1996, Effects of international diversity and product diversity on the performance of multinational firms, Academy of Management Journal, 39: 179–196.

180. F. J. Contractor, S. K. Kundu, & C. C. Hsu, 2003, A three-stage theory of international expansion: The link between multinationality and performance in the service sector, Journal of International Business Studies, 34(1), 5–19; A. K. Rose & E. van Wincoop, 2001, National money as a barrier to international trade: The real case for currency union, American Economic Review, 91: 386–390.

181. I. Bjorkman, W. Barner-Rasmussen, & L. Li, 2004, Managing knowledge transfer in MNCs: The impact of headquarters control mechanisms, Journal of International Business Studies, 35: 443–455.

182. D. Luhnow, 2001, How NAFTA helped Wal-Mart transform the Mexican market. Wall Street Journal, August 31, A1, A2.

183. B. Felgner, 2005, Wal-Mart offers growth sequence, Home Textiles Today, June 20, 4.

184. P. S. Barr & M. A. Glynn, 2004, Cultural variations in strategic issue interpretation: Relating cultural uncertainty avoidance to controllability in discriminating threat and opportunity, Strategic Management Journal, 25: 59–67; V. Miroshnik, 2002, Culture and international management: A review, Journal of Management Development, 21(7,8): 521–544.

185. W. P. J. Henisz & B. A. Zelner, 2005, Legitimacy, interest group pressures and change in emergent institutions, the case of foreign investors and host country governments, Academy of Management Review, 30: 361–382; T. P. Blumentritt & D. Nigh, 2002, The integration of subsidiary political activities in multinational corporations, Journal of International Business Studies, 33: 57–77.

186. N. Shirouzu, 2005, Mean but lean, Toyota seeks outside help, Wall Street Journal, July 14, B4.

187. J. W. Lu & P. W. Beamish, 2004, Network development and firm performance: A field study of internationalizing Japanese firms, Multinational Business Review, 12(3): 41–61; U. Andersson, M. Forsgren, & U. Holm, 2002, The strategic impact of external networks: Subsidiary performance and competence development in the multinational corporation, Strategic Management Journal, 23: 979–996.

188. S.-J. Chang & S. Park, 2005, Types of firms generating network externalities and MNCs' co-location decisions, Strategic Management Journal, 26: 595–616.

Cooperative Strategic Management

Studying this chapter should provide you with the strategic management knowledge needed to:

1. Define cooperative strategies and explain why firms use them.

2. Define and discuss three types of strategic alliances.

3. Name the business-level cooperative strategies and describe their use.

4. Discuss the use of corporate-level cooperative strategies in diversified firms.

5. Understand the importance of cross-border strategic alliances as an international cooperative strategy.

6. Explain cooperative strategies' risks.

7. Describe two approaches used to manage cooperative strategies.

The strategic alliance between Northwest and KLM is being disputed because of Air France's acquisition of KLM.

Strategic alliances have become an essential ingredient in companies' strategies. There are many reasons for this, but the bottom line is that when firms form appropriate alliances and manage them effectively, they help create value. For example, Fujitsu has developed a number of successful strategic alliances that have played a major role in the firm's success in recent years. Fujitsu has had a successful partnership with Siemens AG for over 20 years. One outcome of the partnership was the merger of the two companies' European computer operations into a joint venture (JV) named Fujitsu Siemens Computers. This JV manufactures and sells a variety of information systems products. In 1993, Fujitsu and Advanced Micro Devices (AMD) formed a JV, Fujitsu AMD Semiconductor Ltd., to design, develop, and sell flash memory chips. These chips are sold to each of the parent firms, which then use them in products sold in international markets. In 1997 Fujitsu formed a strategic alliance with Computer Associates to develop and market Jasmine, a software product offered as a standard for global solutions. In 1998, Fujitsu formed a strategic alliance with Cisco Systems to provide sales and support for Cisco products in Europe. Fujitsu has developed alliances with other firms such as Dell, EDS, Intel, Microsoft, Novell, Oracle, Sun Microsystems, and Veritas. Thus, strategic alliances have served as a critical means of populating international markets for Fujitsu.

Strategic alliances have been critically important to other firms as well. For example, Northwest Airlines' alliance with KLM, formed in 1989, provides each firm approximately $1 billion in additional revenue annually. To develop this alliance originally required Northwest to obtain immunity from U.S. antitrust laws so that the two airlines could share sensitive price information, necessary to implement the code-share arrangement. However, Air France acquired KLM and now Northwest must obtain a new agreement from the U.S. government to share the pricing information with the new owner. American Airlines has filed a statement opposing the arrangement, and the decision is currently in doubt. Losing $1 billion annually could severely harm Northwest.

While Fujitsu and Northwest apparently developed strategic alliances to take advantage of opportunities, others may form alliances out of necessity. For example, many computer manufacturers have formed alliances with foreign manufacturers in order to hold down costs, allowing them to compete more effectively in the global markets for PCs. In 2004 Dell, Apple, Gateway, and Acer outsourced 100 percent of the manufacturing of their laptop computers. IBM outsourced only 40 percent, lost money on its laptops, and sold the business to Lenovo, the leading Chinese PC company. Thus, computer firms must find ways to keep their costs down in order to compete in the industry and do so by developing strategic alliances with foreign manufacturers. Now 80 percent of laptop computers are manufactured by Taiwanese companies, mostly in mainland China, where costs are even lower.

Strategic alliances are critical in Europe's information technology (IT) services industry as well. The industry has become highly competitive in recent years with the entry of global IT service providers such as IBM and the growth of others such as Siemens. An example of the competitive challenge is IBM's acquisition of the IT group from the Danish firm Maersk and another smaller Danish firm for $575 million. As a part of the deal, IBM will provide IT services to these companies. Siemens did the same with BBC Technology in a 10-year deal worth $3.7 billion. In this way the services firms entered the market and shut out competition from these potentially lucrative deals. The stakes are high, as analysts estimate that the market for IT services in Europe is $212 billion annually with the global market at $636 billion annually. Thus, strategic alliances can be highly important to individual firms, and they are critical to certain industries (e.g., IT services).

Sources: 2005, Strategic alliances, Fujitsu, www.fujitsu.com, July 23; S. Carey & D. Michaels, 2005, Northwest could lose its lucrative pact with KLM, 2005, *Wall Street Journal Online*, www.wsj.com, July 18; J. Dean & P. Tam, 2005, The laptop trail, *Wall Street Journal Online*, www.wsj.com, June 9,; A. Reinhardt, 2005, Europe's tech outfits hurry to the alter, *BusinessWeek Online*, wwwbusinessweek.com, May 9.

In previous chapters, we examined important strategies for achieving growth, innovation, and strategic execution (internal growth) and acquisitions (external growth). In this chapter, we examine cooperative strategies, which are another means by which firms grow, and differentiate themselves from competitors to develop value-creating competitive advantages.[1]

A **cooperative strategy** is a strategy in which firms work together to achieve a shared objective.[2] Thus, cooperating with other firms is another strategy that is used to create value for a customer that exceeds the cost of providing that value and to establish a favorable position relative to competition (see Chapters 2, 4, 5, and 8).[3] The Opening Case examines several types of strategic alliances that we explore in this chapter. Fujitsu forms equity-based alliances designed to take advantage of market opportunities. Northwest Airlines has had a valuable nonequity strategic alliance through a code-share arrangement with KLM since 1989 that appears to offer both firms a competitive advantage. They both derive substantial revenue from the alliance each year. Losing the alliance would greatly harm Northwest Airlines' probability of survival. The increasing importance of cooperative strategies as a growth engine shouldn't be underestimated. Increasingly, cooperative strategies are formed by competitors, as shown by the Northwest-KLM alliance. Because they each reach many destinations that the other does not, the alliance provided greater value to each airline's customers; the companies' cooperation created more value than their competition.[4] The alliances formed by Dell and Hewlett Packard with foreign computer manufacturers were a competitive necessity. They also drove IBM out of the laptop computer business. We refer to this form of alliance as outsourcing.[5] The competition for IT alliances in Europe is fierce as evidenced by the acquisition of IT groups by Siemens and IBM as a means of obtaining IT services contracts with major European firms. This means that effective competition in the 21st-century landscape results when the firm learns how to cooperate with firms and use this cooperation as a means of competing against competitors.[6]

Because they are the primary type of cooperative strategy used by firms, strategic alliances are this chapter's focus. Although not frequently used, collusive strategies are another type of cooperative strategy discussed in this chapter. In a *collusive strategy*, two or more firms cooperate to increase prices above the fully competitive level.[7]

We examine several topics in this chapter. First, we define and offer examples of different strategic alliances as primary types of cooperative strategies. Next, we discuss the extensive use of cooperative strategies in the global economy and reasons for this use. In succession, we then describe business-level (including collusive strategies), corporate-level, international, and network cooperative strategies—most in the form of strategic alliances. The chapter closes with discussion of the risks of using cooperative strategies as well as how effective management of them can reduce those risks.

Strategic Alliances as a Primary Type of Cooperative Strategy

A **strategic alliance** is a cooperative strategy in which firms combine some of their resources and capabilities to create a competitive advantage.[8] Thus, as linkages between them, strategic alliances involve firms with some degree of exchange and sharing of resources and capabilities to co-develop or distribute goods or services.[9] Strategic alliances allow firms to leverage their existing resources and capabilities while working with partners to develop additional resources and capabilities as the foundation for new competitive advantages.[10]

Many firms, especially large global competitors, establish multiple strategic alliances. This is evident in the Opening Case with Fujitsu forming alliances with AMD, Cisco, Dell, and Microsoft, among others. Focusing on developing advanced technologies, Lockheed Martin has formed over 250 alliances with firms in more than 30 countries as it concentrates on its primary business of defense modernization.[11] In general, strategic alliance success requires cooperative behavior from all partners. Actively solving problems, being trustworthy, and consistently pursuing ways to combine partners' resources and capabilities to create value are examples of cooperative behavior known to contribute to alliance success.[12]

A competitive advantage developed through a cooperative strategy often is called a collaborative or relational advantage.[13] As previously discussed, particularly in Chapter 4, competitive advantages enhance the firm's marketplace success.[14] Rapid technological changes and the global economy are examples of factors challenging firms to constantly upgrade current competitive advantages while they develop new ones to maintain strategic competitiveness.[15]

Three Types of Strategic Alliances

There are three major types of strategic alliances—joint venture, equity strategic alliance, and nonequity strategic alliance.

A **joint venture** is a strategic alliance in which two or more firms create a legally independent company to share some of their resources and capabilities to develop a competitive advantage. Joint ventures are effective in establishing long-term relationships and in transferring tacit knowledge. Because it can't be codified, tacit knowledge is learned through experiences[16] such as those taking place when people from partner firms work together in a joint venture. As discussed in Chapter 3, tacit knowledge is an important source of competitive advantage for many firms.[17]

Typically, partners in a joint venture own equal percentages and contribute equally to its operations. In China, Shui On Construction and entrepreneur Paul S. P. Tung created a 50–50 joint venture called TH Group to invest in cement factories. Cement is big business in China as the government seeks to develop the infrastructure (ports, highways, etc.) of the western provinces. Mr. Tung contributed the money and Shui On the expertise necessary to develop a large, well-run cement company.[18] Overall, evidence suggests that a joint venture may be the optimal alliance when firms need to combine their resources and capabilities to create a competitive advantage that is substantially different from any they possess individually and when the partners intend to enter highly uncertain markets.[19]

An **equity strategic alliance** is an alliance in which two or more firms own different percentages of the company they have formed by combining some of their resources and capabilities to create a competitive advantage. Many foreign direct investments, such as those made by Japanese and U.S. companies in China, are completed through equity strategic alliances.[20]

For example, Citigroup Inc. formed a strategic alliance with Shanghai Pudong Development Bank (SPDB), China's ninth largest bank, through an initial equity investment totaling 5 percent. Citibank was allowed to raise that stake to almost 25 percent, making it a significant shareholder, and was the first foreign bank to own more than 20 percent of a bank in the PRC (People's Republic of China). This equity strategic alliance served "as a launchpad for Citigroup to enter the Chinese credit-card business." In 2004 SPDB and Citibank jointly launched their first credit card in China.[21]

A **nonequity strategic alliance** is an alliance in which two or more firms develop a contractual relationship to share some of their unique resources and capabilities to create a competitive advantage. In this type of strategic alliance, firms do not establish a separate independent company and therefore don't take equity positions. Because of this, nonequity strategic alliances are less formal and demand fewer partner commitments than do joint ventures and equity strategic alliances.[22] The relative informality and lower commitment levels characterizing nonequity strategic alliances make them unsuitable for complex projects where success requires effective transfers of tacit knowledge between partners.[23]

However, firms today increasingly use this type of alliance in many different forms, such as licensing agreements, distribution agreements, and supply contracts.[24] For example, the former Sears, Roebuck and Co. agreed to outsource its credit card business to Citigroup Inc. for $3 billion. Sears was one of the few companies that still held total control over its private-label credit cards, as most department stores favored co-branding nonequity alliances with financial institutions. Under a 10-year marketing-and-servicing agreement, Citigroup will absorb costs associated with Sears' 0 percent financing program, which Sears said will save it more than $200 million a year. Sears also said that it expects to receive approximately $200 million in annual performance payments from Citigroup under the agreement. This strategic alliance will give Sears a chance to refocus on its struggling retail business and gives Citibank control over Sears' credit card operation.[25] A key reason for the growth in types of cooperative strategies is the complexity and uncertainty that characterize most global industries, making it difficult for firms to be successful without partnerships.[26] For example, Citibank is a global company competing in markets all over the world. While Sears is a domestic company, it must compete with global firms, such as Wal-Mart, which have significant economies of scale.

Cirque du Soleil's alliance with Clear Channel Communications has helped them organize a North American tour.

Typically, outsourcing commitments take the form of a nonequity strategic alliance.[27] Discussed in Chapter 3, *outsourcing* is the purchase of a value-creating primary or support activity from another firm. Dell and most other computer firms outsource most or all of their production of laptop computers as discussed in the Opening Case. Other forms of nonequity alliance are exemplified by the joint agreement between Aetna and CVS to develop outreach programs to inform Medicare beneficiaries about the Medicare Modernization Act. Likewise, Cirque du Soleil formed a partnership with Clear Channel Communications to implement a 100-date tour of North American cities.[28]

Reasons Firms Develop Strategic Alliances

Cooperative strategies have become an integral part of the competitive landscape and are quite important to many companies. For example, surveyed executives of technology companies stated that strategic alliances are central to their firms' success.[29] Speaking directly to the issue of technology acquisition and development for these firms, a manager noted that "you have to partner today or you will miss the next wave. You cannot possibly acquire the technology fast enough, so partnering is essential."[30]

Among other benefits, strategic alliances allow partners to create value that they couldn't develop by acting independently[31] and to enter markets more quickly.[32] Moreover, most (if not all) firms lack the full set of resources and capabilities needed to reach their objectives, which indicates that partnering with others will increase the probability of reaching them.[33]

The effects of the greater use of cooperative strategies—particularly in the form of strategic alliances—are noticeable. In large firms, for example, alliances account for more than 20 percent of revenue.[34] Supporting this expectation is the belief of many senior-level executives that alliances are a prime vehicle for firm growth.[35] In some industries, alliance versus alliance is becoming more prominent than firm versus firm as a point of competition. In the global airline industry, for example, competition is increasingly between large alliances rather than between airlines.[36]

Essentially, firms form strategic alliances to reduce competition, enhance their competitive capabilities, gain access to resources, take advantage of opportunities, and build strategic flexibility. To do so means that they must select the right partners and develop trust.[37] Thus, firms attempt to develop a network portfolio of alliances in which they create social capital that affords them flexibility.[38] Because of the social capital, they can call on their partners for help when needed. Of course, social capital means reciprocity exists: Partners can ask them for help as well (and they are expected to provide it).[39]

The individually unique competitive conditions of slow-cycle, fast-cycle, and standard-cycle markets[40] cause firms using cooperative strategies to achieve slightly different objectives (see Table 9.1). We discussed these three market types in Chapter 5, on competitive rivalry and competitive dynamics. *Slow-cycle markets* are markets where the firm's competitive advantages are shielded from imitation for relatively long periods of time and where imitation is costly. These markets are close to monopolistic conditions. Railroads and, historically, telecommunications, utilities, and financial services are examples of industries characterized as slow-cycle markets. In *fast-cycle markets*, the firm's competitive advantages aren't shielded from imitation, preventing their long-term sustainability. Competitive advantages are moderately shielded from imitation in *standard-cycle markets*, typically allowing them to be sustained for a longer period of time than in fast-cycle market situations, but for a shorter period of time than in slow-cycle markets.

Market	Reason
Slow-Cycle	• Gain access to a restricted market
	• Establish a franchise in a new market
	• Maintain market stability (e.g., establishing standards)
Fast-Cycle	• Speed up development of new goods or services
	• Speed up new market entry
	• Maintain market leadership
	• Form an industry technology standard
	• Share risky R&D expenses
	• Overcome uncertainty
Standard-Cycle	• Gain market power (reduce industry overcapacity)
	• Gain access to complementary resources
	• Establish better economies of scale
	• Overcome trade barriers
	• Meet competitive challenges from other competitors
	• Pool resources for very large capital projects
	• Learn new business techniques

Reasons for Strategic Alliances by Market Type

TABLE 9.1

Slow-Cycle Markets

Firms in slow-cycle markets often use strategic alliances to enter restricted markets or to establish franchises in new markets. For example, due to consolidating acquisitions, the American steel industry has three major players: U.S. Steel, ISG, and Nucor. In an effort to compete in a global steel market, these companies are focused on obtaining international partners and foreign markets. They have made strategic alliances in Europe and Asia and are invested in ventures in South America and Australia. For example, Nucor is investing in joint ventures in Brazil and Australia. While the global consolidation continues, these companies are increasing their competitiveness through their strategic alliances overseas.[41]

Slow-cycle markets are becoming rare in the 21st-century competitive landscape for several reasons, including the privatization of industries and economies, the rapid expansion of the Internet's capabilities for the quick dissemination of information, and the speed with which advancing technologies make quickly imitating even complex products possible.[42] Firms competing in slow-cycle markets should recognize the future likelihood that they'll encounter situations in which their competitive advantages become partially sustainable (in the instance of a standard-cycle market) or unsustainable (in the case of a fast-cycle market). Cooperative strategies can be helpful to firms making the transition from relatively sheltered markets to more competitive ones.[43]

Fast-Cycle Markets

Fast-cycle markets tend to be unstable, unpredictable, and complex.[44] Combined, these conditions virtually preclude establishing long-lasting competitive advantages, forcing firms to constantly seek sources of new competitive advantages while creating value by using current ones. Alliances between firms with current excess resources and capabilities and those with promising capabilities help companies competing in fast-cycle markets to make an effective transition from the present to the future and also to gain rapid entry to new markets.

The information technology (IT) industry is a fast-cycle market. The IT landscape continues to change rapidly as businesses are becoming more focused on selecting a handful of strategic partners to help drive down costs, integrate technologies that provide significant business advantages or productivity gains, and aggressively look for applications that can be shifted to more flexible and cost-effective platforms. We learned about the highly competitive European IT market in the Opening Case. In fact, IBM and Siemens' actions exemplify the aggressiveness with which firms try to obtain and solidify a market position. Dell, also mentioned in the Opening Case, strives to maintain its market leadership through responsiveness to customers. As a result of customers' requests, it has made servers and storage more modular and more customizable. Dell's connection to customers also helped it to identify wireless technology as critical for corporations, and thus made it a standard feature on all corporate laptops in 2004. Dell's strategic partners incorporate much of this technology into the machines manufactured for and sold by Dell.[45]

Standard-Cycle Markets

In standard-cycle markets, which are often large and oriented toward economies of scale (e.g., commercial aerospace), alliances are more likely to be made by partners with complementary resources and capabilities. While airline alliances were originally set up to increase revenue, airlines have realized that they could also be used to reduce costs. SkyTeam (chaired by Delta and Air France) developed an internal Web site to speed joint buying and let member carriers swap tips on pricing. Managers at Oneworld (American Airlines and British Airways) say the alliance's members have already saved up to $200 million through joint purchasing, and Star Alliance (United and Lufthansa) estimates that its member airlines save up to 25 percent on joint orders. Some airlines have taken this new buying power up to their biggest-ticket item: airplanes. Four airlines (Air Canada, Lufthansa, Austrian Airlines, and Scandinavian Airlines System) are seeking to buy together as many as 100 planes. Alitalia and Air France are attempting to purchase regional jets together. As these examples illustrate, alliances of companies in this standard-cycle market are often geared toward obtaining potential economies of scale.[46]

Companies also may cooperate in standard-cycle markets to gain market power. As discussed in Chapter 6, market power allows the firm to sell its product above the existing competitive level or to reduce its costs below the competitive level, or both. Verizon Communications developed a joint venture with Vodafone Group named Verizon Wireless to offer wireless services in multiple U.S. markets in 2003. The partners were able to share the risk and enter more markets, thereby giving the venture greater market power early in its life. By 2005, Verizon Wireless provided services in 43 markets. As a first mover and operating in a significant number of markets, the firm has substantial market power.[47]

Business-Level Cooperative Strategy

A **business-level cooperative strategy** is used to help the firm improve its performance in individual product markets. As discussed in Chapter 4, business-level strategy details what the firm intends to do to gain a competitive advantage in specific

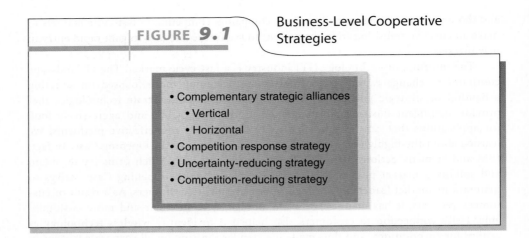

FIGURE **9.1** | Business-Level Cooperative Strategies

- Complementary strategic alliances
  - Vertical
  - Horizontal
- Competition response strategy
- Uncertainty-reducing strategy
- Competition-reducing strategy

product markets. Thus, the firm forms a business-level cooperative strategy when it believes that combining its resources and capabilities with those of one or more partners will create competitive advantages that it can't create by itself and that will lead to success in a specific product market. There are four business-level cooperative strategies (see Figure 9.1).

Complementary Strategic Alliances

Complementary strategic alliances are business-level alliances in which firms share some of their resources and capabilities in complementary ways to develop competitive advantages.[48] There are two types of complementary strategic alliances—vertical and horizontal (see Figure 9.1).

Vertical Complementary Strategic Alliance

In a *vertical complementary strategic alliance,* firms share their resources and capabilities from different stages of the value chain to create a competitive advantage (see Figure 9.2).[49] Oftentimes, vertical complementary alliances are formed in reaction to environmental changes. In other words, they serve as a means of adaptation to the environmental changes.[50] The alliances formed by Dell, Hewlett-Packard, and other computer firms with Taiwanese manufacturers represent this type of cooperative arrangement. Personal computers had became more of a commodity product with little differentiation among them. As a result, price became a major competitive factor, requiring firms to control their costs. To substantially reduce the cost of their manufacturing each unit, many of the computer firms turned to outsourcing. IBM outsourced only about 40 percent of its manufacturing and could not control its costs as well as its competitors. Subsequently, IBM essentially left the market, selling its laptop business to Lenovo. As exemplified in the computer industry, these types of changes in industries and in the global competitive environments have led to *vertical disintegration.*[51] As explained in the Opening Case, Dell and several other computer firms outsource 100 percent of their laptop computer manufacturing rather than performing it in-house. The Taiwanese manufacturers have the technological capabilities and access to low cost labor, thereby providing complementary capabilities. A critical issue for firms is how much technological knowledge they should share with their partner. They need the partners to have adequate knowledge to perform the task effectively and to be complementary to their capabilities. Part of this decision depends on the trust and social capital developed between the partners.[52]

FIGURE **9.2**   Vertical and Horizontal Complementary Strategic Alliances

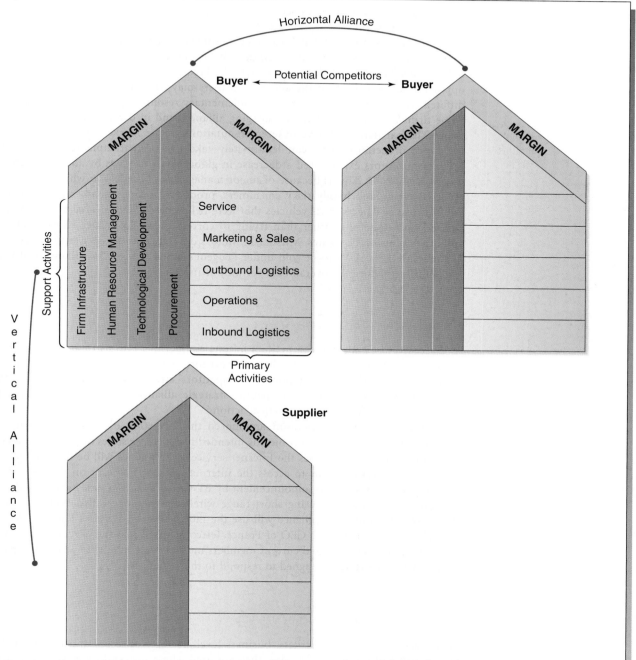

Horizontal Complementary Strategic Alliance

A *horizontal complementary strategic alliance* is an alliance in which firms share some of their resources and capabilities from the same stage of the value chain to create a competitive advantage (see Figure 9.2). Commonly, firms use this type of alliance to focus on long-term product development and distribution opportunities.[53] Bell Canada and

Microsoft Canada entered into an alliance to provide Internet services in Canada through a new portal. Although they share the day-to-day operations of the portal, Bell Canada is responsible for content development and for customer support, billing, and marketing. Microsoft provides access to its portal infrastructure and to online services such as Hotmail and MSN Messenger.[54]

Importantly, horizontal alliances may require equal investments of resources by the partners but they rarely provide equal benefits to the partners. There are several potential reasons for the imbalance in benefits.[55] Frequently, the partners have different opportunities as a result of the alliance. Partners may learn at different rates and have different capabilities to leverage the complementary resources provided in the alliance. Some firms are more effective in managing alliances and in deriving the benefits from them. The partners may have different reputations in the market thus differentiating the types of actions firms can legitimately take in the marketplace. For example, Mitsubishi Motors experienced a decrease in global sales revenues by about 50 percent during 2004–2005. This is because of major management blunders in which loans were made to young and highly risky consumers, producing a large number of bad loans, and because of defects in its vehicles that were believed to result in fatalities. Managers covered up the defects rather than trying to correct them. To bolster its productivity and capacity utilization rates, Mitsubishi Motors developed an alliance with Peugeot to manufacture new SUVs to be sold under Peugeot's brand name. This alliance will help Mitsubishi to reduce the overall cost per unit of its own vehicles.[56]

Competition Response Strategy

As discussed in Chapter 5, competitors initiate competitive actions to attack rivals and launch competitive responses to their competitors' actions. Strategic alliances can be used at the business level to respond to competitors' attacks. Because they can be difficult to reverse and expensive to operate, strategic alliances are primarily formed to respond to strategic rather than tactical actions.

France Telecom and Microsoft announced the formation of an alliance with two initial major projects. The first project is intended to develop a series of phones based on Microsoft technology that uses the Internet services. The phones will be designed to use as traditional cell phones or to access the Internet while at home or on the road. This project is in response to the announcement by BT Group PLC of a new hybrid fixed-line and mobile phone service using short-range wireless technology called Bluetooth. The France Telecom–Microsoft alliance will use the more powerful Wireless Fidelity (Wi-Fi) technology. Didier Lombard, CEO of France Telecom, stated that the telecom industry is undergoing rapid changes and current members must also act rapidly to adapt. The partnership with Microsoft is designed to respond to these changes.[57]

Uncertainty-Reducing Strategy

Particularly in fast-cycle markets, business-level strategic alliances are used to hedge against risk and uncertainty.[58] Also, they are used where uncertainty exists, such as in entering new product markets or emerging economies. For example, Dutch bank ABN AMRO developed a venture called ShoreCap International involving a multisector partnership of organizations, including private businesses, financial institutions, development funds, and foundations. ShoreCap invests capital in and advises local financial institutions that do small and microbusiness lending in developing economies, targeting Asia, Africa, and Central and Eastern Europe. The venture's leading sponsor,

ShoreBank Corporation, is a for-profit community development and environmental bank. It has a history of collaboration with financial institutions and other partners, including the World Bank. Through this cooperative strategy with other financial institutions, ShoreBank's goal is to reduce the risk of providing credit to smaller borrowers in disadvantaged regions. It also hopes to reduce poverty in the regions where it invests.[59]

In other instances, firms form business-level strategic alliances to reduce the uncertainty associated with developing new products or establishing a technology standard.[60] Interestingly, the alliance between France Telecom and Microsoft is a competition response alliance for France Telecom but it is an uncertainty-reducing alliance for Microsoft. Microsoft is using the alliance to learn more about the telecom industry and business. It wants to learn how it can develop software to satisfy needs in this industry. By partnering with a firm in this industry, it is reducing its uncertainty about the market and software needs. And, the alliance is clearly designed to develop new products so the alliance reduces the uncertainty for both firms by combining their knowledge and capabilities.

Competition-Reducing Strategy

Used to reduce competition, collusive strategies differ from strategic alliances in that collusive strategies are often an illegal type of cooperative strategy. There are two types of collusive strategies—explicit collusion and tacit collusion.

Explicit collusion "exists when firms directly negotiate production output and pricing agreements in order to reduce competition."[61] Explicit collusion strategies are illegal in the United States and most developed economies (except in regulated industries).

Firms that use explicit collusion strategies may face litigation and may be found guilty of noncompetitive actions. For instance, in 2004, the Attorney General for New York, Eliot Spitzer, charged Marsh & McLennan with price fixing and collusion. The charges accused the company of recommending clients go to favored insurance providers and in colluding with insurers to rig the bid process for property and casualty insurance. Insurance companies (e.g., American International Group—AIG) and other insurers were also accused in Spitzer's charges. The CEO of AIG is the father of the CEO of Marsh McLennan, making the charges more intriguing. These are serious charges affecting the future of the companies charged and thus their current market values.[62]

Tacit collusion exists when several firms in an industry indirectly coordinate their production and pricing decisions by observing each other's competitive actions and responses.[63] Tacit collusion results in below fully competitive production output and above fully competitive prices. Unlike explicit collusion, firms engaging in tacit collusion do not directly negotiate output and pricing decisions.

Discussed in Chapter 6, *mutual forbearance* is a form of tacit collusion "in which firms avoid competitive attacks against those rivals they meet in multiple markets." Rivals learn a great deal about each other when engaging in multimarket competition, including how to deter the effects of their rival's competitive attacks and responses. Given what they know about each other as a competitor, firms choose not to engage in what could be destructive competitions in multiple product markets.[64]

AOL dominates the instant-messaging (IM) business, with almost 60 million users. Yahoo! and MSN also operate IM services, but unlike e-mail, instant messages cannot cross over programs, which irritates many users. AOL and Microsoft quietly announced in 2003 that they would integrate their IM services for consumers. MSN has the next largest group of IM users (23.6 million) and through this strategic agreement with AOL was able to reduce the level of competition.[65]

Tacit collusion has ensured that the cereals in this aisle are overwhelmingly from four companies: Kellogg, General Mills, Post, and Quaker.

Tacit collusion tends to be used as a business-level competition-reducing strategy in highly concentrated industries, such as breakfast cereals. Firms in these industries recognize that they are interdependent and that their competitive actions and responses significantly affect competitors' behavior toward them. Understanding this interdependence and carefully observing competitors because of it tend to lead to tacit collusion.

Four firms (Kellogg, General Mills, Post, and Quaker) have accounted for as much as 80 percent of sales volume in the ready-to-eat segment of the U.S. cereal market.[66] Some believe that this high degree of concentration results in "prices for branded cereals that are well above [the] costs of production."[67] Prices above the competitive level in this industry suggest the possibility that the dominant firms use a tacit collusion cooperative strategy.

In general, governments in free-market economies need to determine how rivals can collaborate to increase their competitiveness without violating established regulations.[68] However, this is challenging when evaluating collusive strategies, particularly tacit ones. For example, regulation of pharmaceutical and biotech firms who must collaborate to meet global competition might lead to too much price fixing and, therefore, regulation is required to make sure that the balance is right, although sometimes the regulation gets in the way of efficient markets.[69] Individual companies must analyze the effect of a competition-reducing strategy on their performance and competitiveness.

Assessment of Business-Level Cooperative Strategies

Firms use business-level strategies to develop competitive advantages that can contribute to successful positions and performance in individual product markets. To develop a competitive advantage using an alliance, the particular set of resources and capabilities that is integrated through the alliance must be valuable, rare, imperfectly imitable, and nonsubstitutable (see Chapter 3).

Evidence suggests that complementary business-level strategic alliances, especially vertical ones, have the greatest probability of creating a sustainable competitive advantage.[70] Horizontal complementary alliances are sometimes difficult to maintain because they are often between rivalrous competitors. As noted earlier, the international airline industry, in an effort to avoid laws blocking international mergers, has been forming global partnerships for a number of years. The largest is Star Alliance, built around United Airlines, Lufthansa, and All Nippon Airways. The fact that United entered Chapter 11 bankruptcy proceedings in 2003 and continues to threaten Chapter 7 bankruptcy (liquidation) has destabilized this partnership. KLM, based in The Netherlands, originally was only a partner to a minor partnership, the strategic alliance noted earlier with Northwest Airlines on transatlantic routes. Delta and Continental then joined the alliance to participate on joint domestic flights, and are cooperating with KLM on international flights. It seems natural that all should join the SkyTeam alliance, the partnership anchored by Delta and Air France. However, regulatory approval is now required from the European Union for the Northwest strategic alliance with KLM because of KLM's acquisition by Air France. Approval is required because the consolidation in the industry is reducing competition and prior approval was based on KLM not Air France. Because of the weak position of several of the airlines—United, for one, is on the brink of further bankruptcy—and the high rivalry among partners in the airline industry, the horizontal alliances formed are often unstable.[71]

Although strategic alliances designed to respond to competition and to reduce uncertainty can also create competitive advantages, these advantages often are more temporary than those developed through complementary (both vertical and horizontal) strategic alliances. The primary reason is that complementary alliances have a stronger focus on creating value than do competition-reducing and uncertainty-reducing alliances, which are formed to respond to competitors' actions or reduce uncertainty rather than to attack competitors.

Of the four business-level cooperative strategies, the competition-reducing strategy has the lowest probability of creating a sustainable competitive advantage. For example, research suggests that firms following a foreign direct investment strategy using alliances as a follow-the-leader imitation approach may not have strong strategic or learning goals. Thus, such investment could be attributable to tacit collusion among the participating firms rather than intended to obtain a competitive advantage.[72] Companies using such competition-reducing business-level strategic alliances should carefully monitor the degree to which they are facilitating the creation of competitive advantages.

Corporate-Level Cooperative Strategy

A firm uses a **corporate-level cooperative strategy** to help it diversify in terms of products offered or markets served, or both. Diversifying alliances, synergistic alliances, and franchising are the most commonly used corporate-level cooperative strategies (see Figure 9.3).

Firms use diversifying alliances and synergistic alliances to grow and diversify their operations through a means other than a merger or an acquisition.[73] When a firm seeks to diversify into markets in which the host nation's government prevents mergers and acquisitions, alliances become an especially appropriate option. Corporate-level strategic alliances are also attractive compared with mergers and particularly acquisitions, because they require fewer resource commitments[74] and permit greater flexibility in terms of efforts to diversify partners' operations.[75] An alliance can be used as a way to determine if the partners might benefit from a future merger or acquisition between them. This "testing" process often characterizes alliances formed to combine firms' unique technological resources and capabilities.[76]

FIGURE 9.3 Corporate-Level Cooperative Strategies

- Diversifying alliances
- Synergistic alliances
- Franchising

Diversifying Strategic Alliance

A **diversifying strategic alliance** is a corporate-level cooperative strategy in which firms share some of their resources and capabilities to diversify into new product or market areas. Shell Petrochemicals and China National Offshore Oil Corporation (CNOOC) formed a joint venture to construct a $4.3 billion petrochemicals complex in southern China. The goal of the venture is to produce products for "Guangdong and high-consumption areas along the country's coastal economic zones."[77] CNOOC's business has been mainly upstream, especially in offshore oil production. The joint venture represents CNOOC's continuing diversification from its core upstream business. After the venture began operating, the partners experienced some tense times. CNOOC's bid to acquire Unocal was discouraged by Shell, because Unocal was a competitor. Fortunately for Shell, CNOOC's bid was rejected by Unocal in favor of a bid by Chevron.[78]

It should be noted that highly diverse networks of alliances can lead to poorer performance by partner firms.[79] However, cooperative ventures are also used to reduce diversification in firms that have overdiversified.[80] Japanese chipmakers Fujitsu, Mitsubishi Electric, Hitachi, NEC, and Toshiba have been using joint ventures to consolidate and then spin off diversified businesses that were performing poorly. For example, Fujitsu, realizing that memory chips were becoming a financial burden, dumped its flash memory business into a joint venture company controlled by Advanced Micro Devices. This alliance helped Fujitsu to refocus on its core businesses.[81]

Synergistic Strategic Alliance

A **synergistic strategic alliance** is a corporate-level cooperative strategy in which firms share some of their resources and capabilities to create economies of scope. Similar to the business-level horizontal complementary strategic alliance, synergistic strategic alliances create synergy across multiple functions or multiple businesses between partner firms.

PanAmSat developed a joint venture with Jsat Corporation to develop and send into orbit a small satellite ($140 million in expenses) to provide high-definition video programming and Internet services to the Eastern part of the United States. PanAmSat will move its current customers off of its old satellite onto the new one and will also provide technical and marketing expertise to the venture. By doing this as a joint venture rather than solo, PanAmSat expects to save more than $200 million. It is synergistic because it will allow PanAmSat to send up more satellites and thus compete effectively in more markets and against smaller regional providers that have only a few satellites. It also benefits Jsat with a lucrative opportunity. In this case, the alliance diversifies PanAmSat geographically and Jsat in product markets.[82] Thus, a synergistic strategic alliance is different from a complementary business-level alliance in that it diversifies both firms into a new business, but in a synergistic way.

The Strategic Focus suggests that franchises are a major means of growth for some firms such as Wendy's and Dunkin' Donuts. By contrast, Outback has used franchises to a much lesser extent. Because franchising helps firms grow faster, it simultaneously helps the firms build their brand, if they closely control the quality of franchise operations.

Franchising

Franchising is a corporate-level cooperative strategy in which a firm (the franchisor) uses a franchise as a contractual relationship to describe and control the sharing of its resources and capabilities with partners (the franchisees).[83] A *franchise* is a "contractual agreement between two legally independent companies whereby the franchisor grants

Franchising Finger Foods the American Way

Franchising has been used as a primary growth mode for many retail food operations such as McDonald's, Subway, and Outback Steakhouse. Franchises have been especially valuable in international markets. While the firms have to maintain strong controls to ensure quality and no harm to their brand, they can also use franchisors to help them adapt to the cultural environment. For example, when Subway first entered China, it experienced problems because the Chinese do not like to eat with their hands. However, each Subway has at least one item that is tailored to Chinese tastes. According to Subway, China could handle well over 20,000 Subway outlets. Thus, if Subway is able to help the Chinese accept its sandwiches, it has substantial opportunities in China.

Franchises had a rough beginning in China. There was no word for the concept, but one was eventually developed: *jia meng,* meaning "person joins a group of other people." Subway has become the third largest fast-food chain in China, behind McDonald's and KFC. While these three franchisors have experienced success, the environment remains challenging. A&W, Chili's, and Dunkin' Donuts tried and failed; they closed all their Chinese stores and departed Chinese markets. Still, the Chinese market can be lucrative. The Chinese division of KFC's parent firm, Yum! Brands, is earning over $1 billion sales revenue annually. Because of the huge potential market and KFC's success, the Guatemala-based fried-chicken chain Pollo Campero SA is opening outlets in Shanghai. This same company has enjoyed recent success in the U.S. market.

Other restaurants have grown and succeeded using franchises to complement their wholly-owned stores. For example, Outback Steakhouse International is the third-largest restaurant company in the United States. With almost 1,200 locations in 20 countries, it has annual sales of about $3.2 billion. While Outback has used franchising as a means of growth, it has maintained tight controls and owns a large majority of its stores—less than 15 percent are franchises. Other food chains such as Wendy's and Dunkin' Donuts have used franchising much more extensively. Just over 40 percent of Wendy's 6,600 restaurants are franchised. Even more significant, 78 percent of Dunkin' Donuts outlets are franchised. Thus, Dunkin' Donuts has used franchising as its primary growth strategy.

GETTY IMAGES

Subway's success in China is dependent on the ability of Chinese consumers to accept Subway's sandwiches.

Sources: R. Gibson, 2005, Hedge fund urges Wendy's to spin off coffee chain, *Wall Street Journal Online,* www. wsj.com, July 12; J. T. Areddy, 2005, Guatemala-based chicken chain plans to open stores in China, *Wall Street Journal Online,* www.wsj.com, July 10; M. Overfelt, 2005, How we got started, *Fortune,* www.fortune.com, June 1; C. Adler, 2005, How China eats a sandwich, *Fortune,* www. fortune.com, March 10; L. Tischler, 2004, It's not about the doughnuts, *Fast Company,* www.fastcompany.com, December.

the right to the franchisee to sell the franchisor's product or do business under its trademarks in a given location for a specified period of time."[84]

Franchising is a popular strategy; companies using it account for $1 trillion in annual U.S. retail sales and compete in more than 75 industries. Already frequently used in developed nations, franchising is expected to account for significant portions of growth in emerging economies in the 21st century's first two decades. This is shown by the number of food chains selling franchises in China in recent years as described in the Strategic Focus.[85] As with diversifying and synergistic strategic alliances, franchising is an alternative to pursuing growth through mergers and acquisitions.

McDonald's, Hilton International, and Krispy Kreme are well-known examples of firms that use the franchising corporate-level cooperative strategy. The convenience store company 7-Eleven, Inc. has successfully used franchising in its expansion, both domestically and internationally. The chain now has over 25,000 franchised outlets worldwide. 7-Eleven is especially popular in Asia, where convenience stores are more like pantries for city dwellers short on space. There are 77 stores per million people in Japan and 148 per million in Taiwan, far more than the 20 per million in the United States.[86]

In the most successful franchising strategy, the partners (the franchisor and the franchisees) closely work together.[87] A primary responsibility of the franchisor is to develop programs to transfer to the franchisees the knowledge and skills that are needed to successfully compete at the local level.[88] In return, franchisees should provide feedback to the franchisor regarding how their units could become more effective and efficient.[89] Working cooperatively, the franchisor and its franchisees find ways to strengthen the core company's brand name, which is often the most important competitive advantage for franchisees operating in their local markets.[90]

Franchising is a particularly attractive strategy to use in fragmented industries, such as retailing and commercial printing. In fragmented industries, a large number of small and medium-sized firms compete as rivals; however, no firm or small set of firms has a dominant share, making it possible for a company to gain a large market share by consolidating independent companies through contractual relationships.[91] That is why franchising is a common strategy used by food chains as described in the Strategic Focus.

Assessment of Corporate-Level Cooperative Strategies

Costs are incurred with each type of cooperative strategy.[92] Compared with those at the business-level, corporate-level cooperative strategies commonly are broader in scope and more complex, making them relatively more costly. Those forming and using cooperative strategies, especially corporate-level ones, should be aware of alliance costs and carefully monitor them.

In spite of these costs, firms can create competitive advantages and value when they effectively form and use corporate-level cooperative strategies.[93] The likelihood of this being the case increases when successful alliance experiences are internalized. In other words, those involved with forming and using corporate-level cooperative strategies can also use them to develop useful knowledge about how to succeed in the future. To gain maximum value from this knowledge, firms should organize it and verify that it is always properly distributed to those involved with the formation and use of alliances.[94]

We explain in Chapter 6 that firms answer two questions to form a corporate-level strategy—in which businesses will the diversified firm compete, and how will those businesses be managed? These questions are also answered as firms form corporate-level cooperative strategies. Thus, firms able to develop corporate-level cooperative strategies and manage them in ways that are valuable, rare, imperfectly imitable, and nonsubstitutable (see Chapter 3) develop a competitive advantage that is in addition to advantages gained through the activities of individual cooperative strategies. Later in the chapter, we further describe alliance management as a source of competitive advantage.

International Cooperative Strategy

A **cross-border strategic alliance** is an international cooperative strategy in which firms with headquarters in different nations combine some of their resources and capabilities to create a competitive advantage. For example, British Petroleum (BP) invested over $6 billion in a joint venture with Russian oil company Tyumen Oil. The venture combined BP's Russian assets, a stake in Russian oil company Sidanco, with Tyumen. The new company is the 10th largest oil producer in the world, increasing its competitive advantage against other, smaller oil companies.[95] Taking place in virtually all industries, the number of cross-border alliances being completed continues to increase,[96] in some cases at the expense of mergers and acquisitions.[97] However, as the Strategic Focus on franchising suggests, there is a significant amount of international cooperative activity. While cross-border alliances can be complex, they may be necessary to improve technology as indicated by the international alliance among IBM, Sony, and Toshiba to develop a new microprocessor (described in the next Strategic Focus).

There are several reasons for the increasing use of cross-border strategic alliances. In general, multinational corporations outperform domestic-only firms.[98] Thus, a firm may form cross-border strategic alliances to leverage core competencies that are the foundation of its domestic success to expand into international markets.[99] Nike has used its core competence with celebrity marketing as it expands overseas, especially because its U.S. business growth has slowed. It has sought to duplicate its marketing strategy in international markets, signing big-name athletes to sell shoes and apparel. Nike has alliance agreements with Brazilian soccer star Ronaldo and the world's most popular soccer team, Manchester United. The firm also has alliance agreements with two world-famous athletes, golfer Tiger Woods and cyclist Lance Armstrong, who won his seventh straight Tour de France in 2005. These alliances have helped Nike achieve considerable financial success over time.[100]

Limited domestic growth opportunities and foreign government economic policies are additional reasons firms use cross-border alliances. As discussed in Chapter 8, local ownership is an important national policy objective in some nations. In India and China, for example, governmental policies reflect a strong preference to license local companies. Thus, in some countries, the full range of entry mode choices that we described in Chapter 8 may not be available to firms wishing to internationally diversify. Indeed, investment by foreign firms in these instances may be allowed only through a partnership with a local firm, such as in a cross-border alliance. Especially important, strategic alliances with local partners can help firms overcome certain liabilities of moving into a foreign country, such as lack of knowledge of the local culture or institutional norms.[101] A cross-border strategic alliance can also be helpful to foreign partners from an operational perspective, because the local partner has significantly more information about factors contributing to competitive success such as local markets, sources of capital, legal procedures, and politics.[102]

Firms also use cross-border alliances to help transform themselves or to better use their advantages to benefit from opportunities surfacing in the rapidly changing global economy. In these cases, the firm leverages its distinctive capabilities through the alliance. This is the case in the alliance among IBM, Sony, and Toshiba. As explained in the Strategic Focus, Sony and Toshiba plan to use the new "Cell" microprocessor in high-definition televisions that they are developing, using their knowledge of the consumer electronics market. The microprocessor takes advantage of IBM's strong technological capabilities.

In general, cross-border alliances are more complex and risky than domestic strategic alliances.[103] However, the fact that firms competing internationally tend to outperform domestic-only competitors suggests the importance of learning how to diversify into international markets. Compared with mergers and acquisitions, cross-border alliances may be a better way to learn this process, especially in the early stages of the firms' geographic diversification efforts. When Starbucks was looking to expand overseas, it wanted to do so quickly in order to keep its first-mover advantage. Thus, it agreed to a complex series of joint ventures in many countries in the interest of speed. While the company receives a percentage of the revenues and profits as well as licensing fees for supplying its coffee, controlling costs abroad is more difficult than in the United States.[104] However, as noted above, the firm hopes to learn a great deal from serving multiple markets. Careful and thorough study of a proposed cross-border alliance contributes to success,[105] as do precise specifications of each partner's alliance role.[106] These points are explored later in our discussion of how to best manage alliances.

Network Cooperative Strategy

Increasingly, firms use several cooperative strategies. In addition to forming their own alliances with individual companies, a growing number of firms are joining forces in multiple networks.[107] A **network cooperative strategy** is a cooperative strategy wherein several firms agree to form multiple partnerships to achieve shared objectives.

A network cooperative strategy is particularly effective when it is formed by geographically clustered firms,[108] as in California's Silicon Valley and Singapore's Silicon Island.[109] Effective social relationships and interactions among partners while sharing their resources and capabilities make it more likely that a network cooperative strategy will be successful,[110] as does having a productive *strategic center firm* (discussed further in Chapter 11). Firms involved in networks gain information and knowledge from multiple sources. They can use these heterogeneous knowledge sets to produce more and better innovation. As a result, firms involved in networks of alliances tend to be more innovative.[111] The research evidence suggests that the positive financial effects of network cooperative strategies will make these strategies important contributors to the 21st-century success of both supplier and buyer partners involved.[112] However, there are disadvantages to participating in networks as a firm can be locked in to its partners, precluding the development of alliances with others. In certain types of networks, such as Japanese *keiretsus,* firms in the network are expected to help other firms in the network whenever they need aid. Such expectations can become a burden and reduce the focal firm's performance over time.[113]

Alliance Network Types

An important advantage of a network cooperative strategy is that firms gain access "to their partners' partners."[114] Having access to multiple collaborations increases the

Forming an International Alliance Network for Innovation and Its Use

In 2005, IBM, Sony (and Sony Computer Entertainment Inc.), and Toshiba announced the development of a microprocessor called the Cell and the introduction to the market of new products using the Cell from their alliance. The Cell represents a major break-through in architectural design, resulting in a small but powerful microprocessor. Engineers from the three companies have been collaborating at a joint design center in Austin, Texas, since 2001. The Cell's ultra-high-speed communication capabilities are especially suited for entertainment and media applications. The alliance partners describe it as a "supercomputer on a chip." The Cell incorporates many of the positive attributes of IBM's sophisticated servers, Sony's computer entertainment systems, and Toshiba's advanced semiconductor technology. Sony and Toshiba expect to use the Cell in a broad range of new products including digital televisions, home servers, and supercomputers.

William Zeitler, senior vice president for IBM, stated that "we see tangible results of our collaboration . . . that portends a new era in graphics and multi-media performance." Ken Kutaragi, executive deputy president and COO for Sony, stated that "With Cell opening a doorway, a new chapter in computer science is about to begin." Masashi Muromachi, corporate vice president of Toshiba Corporation, stated that "we are very proud . . . [of] the first development of the Cell project, initiated with the aspirations by the joint team of IBM, Sony Group, and Toshiba . . . sustaining a whole spectrum of advanced information-rich broadband applications from consumer electronics [to] home entertainment through various industrial systems."

Sony plans to launch home servers and high-definition television systems in 2006. Sony Computer Entertainment Inc. announced plans to introduce a new generation computer entertainment system powered by the Cell. Toshiba expects to have diverse applications for the Cell. Its first product using the Cell will be a high-definition television in 2006 (which will compete with its collaborator, Sony).

This new microprocessor has a different technical base from Intel's chips, which were developed for data processing. The Cell was designed for communicating over broadband networks, requiring new software as well. Intel chips can carry out two

ASSOCIATED PRESS, AP

Jim Kahle, IBM Director of Technology for Cell Technology, shows a new Cell Technology chip during a news conference in San Francisco.

277

sequences of instructions simultaneously, while the Cell can carry out ten simultaneously. A workstation with multiple Cell chips can perform 16 trillion mathematical operations in a second, matching the world's fastest supercomputers.

IBM is involved in multiple alliances, as explained earlier in this chapter. Thus, it is involved in a network, providing it with exposure to many sets of technological knowledge. For example, IBM is involved in an alliance with Microsoft and ATI Technologies that developed the game machine Xenon in 2005. The chip it uses does not match the Cell's power but is easier to program. In fact, the two chips are likely to be semi-competitors. IBM has benefited by participating in the network of alliances in the development of the new technologies. These technological developments are the result of a new strategy launched by IBM in the first years of this century to stay on the cutting edge of technology. The new chips developed will allow IBM to compete in almost all markets requiring semiconductors, which includes a growing array of products today. Thus, alliance networks have helped IBM be at the forefront in the development of new technologies and new products.

Sources: S. Hamm, 2005, IBM discovers the power of one, *Business Week,* February 14, 80; D. Clark & R. A. Guth, 2005, Sony, IBM, Toshiba to offer first peek of "Cell" chip design, *Wall Street Journal,* February 7, B1; 2005, IBM, Sony, Sony Computer Entertainment Inc., and Toshiba disclose key details of the Cell chip, Press Release, Sony Corporation, February 7; D. Hug, 2004, IBM, Sony, SCEI, and Toshiba to unveil next-generation cell processor, JCNN News Summaries, December 1.

likelihood that additional competitive advantages will be formed as the set of shared resources and capabilities expands.[115] In turn, development of new capabilities further stimulates the development of product innovations that are so critical to strategic competitiveness in the global economy.[116]

The set of strategic alliance partnerships resulting from the use of a network cooperative strategy is commonly called an *alliance network.* The alliance networks that companies develop vary by industry conditions. A *stable alliance network* is formed in mature industries where demand is relatively constant and predictable. Through a stable alliance network, firms try to extend their competitive advantages to other settings while continuing to profit from operations in their core, relatively mature industry. Thus, stable networks are built for *exploitation* of the economies (scale and/or scope) available between firms.[117] *Dynamic alliance networks* are used in industries characterized by frequent product innovations and short product life cycles.[118] For instance, the pace of innovation in the information technology (IT) industry is too fast for any one company to maintain success over time. Therefore, the ability to develop and nurture strategic partnerships can make the difference between success and failure. As such, independent software vendors earn more than 40 percent of their revenue through successful partnering. After IBM's "near-death experience" in the early 1990s, the power of its alliances with more than 90,000 business partners helped shape its turnaround. By partnering, companies play on "teams," fielding the best players at every position and thus providing stamina and flexibility for customers. Through partnerships, a company can offer a broader range of IT solutions and improve the probability of market success.[119]

Thus, dynamic alliance networks are primarily used to stimulate rapid, value-creating product innovations and subsequent successful market entries, demonstrating that their purpose is often *exploration* of new ideas.[120] Often, large firms in such industries as software and pharmaceuticals create networks of smaller entrepreneurial start-up firms to accomplish this goal.[121] Small firms also build credibility faster by being engaged in such joint network relationships.[122]

Firms are regularly using strategic alliances to enter international markets; they help these firms survive in those markets early and to be competitive later. In fact, as noted in the Strategic Focus, firms are increasingly participating in international network alliances. IBM has alliances with Sony and Toshiba to develop the Cell microprocessor and another alliance with Microsoft and ATI Technologies to develop a different chip. However, Microsoft and ATI gain value indirectly from IBM's other alliance because it adds to IBM's technological capabilities. While these alliances appear to be successful, there are risks with alliances as well.

Competitive Risks with Cooperative Strategies

Stated simply, many cooperative strategies fail.[123] In fact, evidence shows that two-thirds of cooperative strategies have serious problems in their first two years and that as many as 70 percent of them fail. This failure rate suggests that even when the partnership has potential complementarities and synergies, alliance success is elusive.[124]

Although failure is undesirable, it can be a valuable learning experience. Companies need to carefully study a cooperative strategy's failure to gain insights that can be used to successfully develop future cooperative strategies.[125] Companies should work hard to avoid cooperative strategy failure and to learn from failure if it occurs. In the construction industry, cooperation on a project between the main contractor and subcontractors is very important. Without managing areas of mistrust, including suspected incompetence and potential dishonesty, success can be elusive, and failure of the alliance can be very costly.[126] Prominent cooperative strategy risks are shown in Figure 9.4.

One cooperative strategy risk is that a partner may act opportunistically. Opportunistic behaviors surface either when formal contracts fail to prevent them or when an alliance is based on a false perception of partner trustworthiness. Not infrequently, the opportunistic firm wants to acquire as much of its partner's tacit knowledge as it can.[127] Full awareness of what a partner wants in a cooperative strategy reduces the likelihood that a firm will suffer from another's opportunistic actions.[128]

FIGURE 9.4 Managing Competitive Risks in Cooperative Strategies

Competitive Risks
- Inadequate contracts
- Misrepresentation of competencies
- Partners fail to use their complementary resources
- Holding alliance partner's specific investments hostage

Risk and Asset Management Approaches
- Detailed contracts and monitoring
- Developing trusting relationships

Desired Outcome
- Creating value

HP dissolved its alliance with Apple to distribute iPods because HP was not profiting enough from the arrangement.

In January 2004, Hewlett Packard and Apple made a surprise announcement of an alliance for HP to distribute Apple's iPod machines to retail outlets. HP explained that the iPod would become the center of its digital entertainment strategy. It was a surprise because the two firms are strong competitors in the personal computer market. However, in July 2005, HP announced that selling the iPod no longer fits its digital media strategy. HP accounted for about 5 percent of iPod's sales, slightly over 6 million units valued at over $4 billion in revenue to Apple annually. HP did not profit greatly from these sales and it had to use the Apple name, though the firms originally stated that iPods sold by HP would carry the HP logo. Furthermore, it was reported that Apple had control of the financial characteristics of the deal. It appears that the partnership favored Apple and that HP decided that it was not gaining adequate value from the alliance for it to continue. Therefore, the alliance was dissolved. However, the non-compete clause remained in place until its expiration in August of 2006.[129]

Some cooperative strategies fail when it is discovered that a firm has misrepresented the competencies it can bring to the partnership. The risk of competence misrepresentation is more common when the partner's contribution is grounded in some of its intangible assets. Superior knowledge of local conditions is an example of an intangible asset that partners often fail to deliver. Asking the partner to provide evidence that it does possess the resources and capabilities (even when they are largely intangible) it is to share in the cooperative strategy may be an effective way to deal with this risk.

Another risk is that a firm won't actually make available to its partners the resources and capabilities (such as its most sophisticated technologies) that it committed to the cooperative strategy. This risk surfaces most commonly when firms form an international cooperative strategy.[130] In these instances, different cultures and languages can cause misinterpretations of contractual terms or trust-based expectations.

A final risk is that one firm may make investments that are specific to the alliance while its partner does not. For example, the firm might commit resources and capabilities to develop manufacturing equipment that can be used only to produce items coming from the alliance. If the partner isn't also making alliance-specific investments, the firm is at a relative disadvantage in terms of returns earned from the alliance compared with investments made to earn the returns.

Pixar and Disney partnered to develop and market several computer-animated features, including *Toy Story, Monsters Inc.,* and *A Bug's Life,* all of which have been box-office hits. However, Disney perceived risks in its partnership with Pixar. Pixar had significant bargaining power to strike another deal—with Disney or with another company. All of Pixar's films have done better at the box office than have Disney's recent animated features, and Pixar contributed 35 percent of Disney's studio operating profits in 2002. Pixar's chairman, Steve Jobs, met with executives from other studios during the negotiations for a new agreement, thereby putting pressure on Disney to sweeten its offer for a continued partnership, perhaps by allowing Pixar to keep more of its profits.[131] Disney and Pixar were unable to reach a new agreement and thus parted ways.

Managing Cooperative Strategies

As our discussion has shown, cooperative strategies represent important strategic alternatives for firms competing in the global economy.[132] However, our study of cooperative strategies also shows that they are complex and challenging to manage successfully.[133]

Firms gain the most benefit from cooperative strategies when they are effectively managed. The firm that learns how to manage cooperative strategies better than its competitors may develop a competitive advantage in terms of this activity.[134] Because the ability to effectively manage cooperative strategies is unevenly distributed across organizations in general, assigning managerial responsibility for a firm's cooperative strategies to a high-level executive or to a team improves the likelihood that the strategies will be well managed.

Those responsible for managing the firm's set of cooperative strategies coordinate activities, categorize knowledge learned from previous experiences, and make certain that what the firm knows about how to effectively form and use cooperative strategies is in the hands of the right people at the right time. Firms use one of two primary approaches to manage cooperative strategies—cost minimization and opportunity maximization[135] (see Figure 9.4). This is the case whether or not the firm has formed a separate cooperative strategy management function.

In the *cost minimization* management approach, the firm develops formal contracts with its partners. These contracts specify how the cooperative strategy is to be monitored and how partner behavior is to be controlled. The goal of this approach is to minimize the cooperative strategy's cost and to prevent opportunistic behavior by a partner. The focus of the second managerial approach—*opportunity maximization*—is on maximizing a partnership's value-creation opportunities. In this case, partners are prepared to take advantage of unexpected opportunities to learn from each other and to explore additional marketplace possibilities. Less formal contracts, with fewer constraints on partners' behaviors, make it possible for partners to explore how their resources and capabilities can be shared in multiple value-creating ways.

Firms can successfully use both approaches to manage cooperative strategies. However, the costs to monitor the cooperative strategy are greater with cost minimization, in that writing detailed contracts and using extensive monitoring mechanisms is expensive, even though the approach is intended to reduce alliance costs. Although monitoring systems may prevent partners from acting in their own best interests, they also often preclude positive responses to new opportunities that surface to use the alliance's competitive advantages. Thus, formal contracts and extensive monitoring systems tend to stifle partners' efforts to gain maximum value from their participation in a cooperative strategy and require significant resources to put into place and use.[136]

For example, Sony Ericsson Mobile Communications was a joint venture formed by Sony and Ericsson to become the top seller of multimedia mobile-phone handsets. Although it was growing at three times the overall market rate in its core areas, the

© CLARO CORTES IV/REUTERS/CORBIS

Wal-Mart's partnership with Szitic will help it expand its market into China.

venture posted a loss. Notably, the loss was attributed to costs from job cuts and closing units, such as research parks in Munich, Germany, and North Carolina. Such cost-cutting activities may create difficulties for strategic alliances built to explore opportunities.[137]

The relative lack of detail and formality that is a part of the contract developed by firms using the second management approach of opportunity maximization means that firms need to trust each other to act in the partnership's best interests. A psychological state, *trust* is a willingness to be vulnerable because of the expectations of positive behavior from the firm's alliance partner.[138] When partners trust each other, there is less need to write detailed formal contracts to specify each firm's alliance behaviors,[139] and the cooperative relationship tends to be more stable.[140] On a relative basis, trust tends to be more difficult to establish in international cooperative strategies compared with domestic ones. Differences in trade policies, cultures, laws, and politics that are part of cross-border alliances account for the increased difficulty. When trust exists, partners' monitoring costs are reduced and opportunities to create value are maximized. Essentially, in these cases, the firms have built social capital as described earlier in the chapter.[141]

Research showing that trust between partners increases the likelihood of alliance success seems to highlight the benefits of the opportunity maximization approach to managing cooperative strategies. Trust may also be the most efficient way to influence and control alliance partners' behaviors.[142] Research indicates that trust can be a capability that is valuable, rare, imperfectly imitable, and often nonsubstitutable.[143] Thus, firms known to be trustworthy can have a competitive advantage in terms of how they develop and use cooperative strategies both internally and externally.[144] One reason is that it is impossible to specify all operational details of a cooperative strategy in a formal contract. Confidence that its partner can be trusted reduces the firm's concern about the inability to contractually control all alliance details.

In 2005, CapitaLand Ltd. of Singapore signed a contract to acquire a 65 percent ownership in 15 malls in which Wal-Mart is the anchor. The deal represented an extension of Wal-Mart's partnership with Shenzhen International Trust & Investment Co. (Szitic). The malls are managed by a joint venture between CapitaLand and Szitic. The agreement among the parties allows CapitaLand an option to invest in 17 other malls to be anchored by Wal-Mart. This deal suggests that the partners have built a level of trust and social capital in prior relationships. Otherwise they would not have extended the relationship with further partnerships nor would they have agreed to grant options for future joint activities. With China's substantial growth potential and Wal-Mart's significant expansion plans, the social capital among these partners may have valuable benefits for all parties over time.[145]

- A cooperative strategy is one in which firms work together to achieve a shared objective. Strategic alliances, in which firms combine some of their resources and capabilities to create a competitive advantage, are the primary form of cooperative strategies. Joint ventures (where firms create and own equal shares of a new venture that is intended to develop competitive advantages), equity strategic alliances (where firms own different shares of a newly created venture), and nonequity strategic alliances (where firms cooperate through a contractual relationship) are the three basic types of strategic alliances. Outsourcing, discussed in Chapter 3, commonly occurs as firms form nonequity strategic alliances.

- Collusive strategies are the second type of cooperative strategies (with strategic alliances being the other). In many economies and certainly in developed ones, explicit collusive strategies are illegal unless sanctioned by government policies. With increasing globalization, fewer government-sanctioned situations of explicit collusion exist. Tacit collusion, also called mutual forbearance, is a cooperative strategy through which firms tacitly cooperate to reduce industry output below the potential competitive output level, thereby raising prices above the competitive level.

- The reasons firms use cooperative strategies vary by slow-cycle, fast-cycle, and standard-cycle market conditions. To enter restricted markets (slow-cycle), to move quickly from one competitive advantage to another (fast-cycle), and to gain market power (standard-cycle) are among the reasons by market type for use of cooperative strategies.

- There are four business-level cooperative strategies (a business-level cooperative strategy is used to help the firm improve its performance in individual product markets). Through vertical and horizontal complementary alliances, companies combine their resources and capabilities to create value in different parts (vertical) or the same parts (horizontal) of the value chain. Competition-responding strategies are formed to respond to competitors' actions, especially strategic ones. Competition-reducing strategies are used to avoid excessive competition while the firm marshals its resources and capabilities to improve its competitiveness. Uncertainty-reducing strategies are used to hedge against the risks created by the conditions of uncertain competitive environments (such as new product markets). Complementary alliances have the highest probability of yielding a sustainable competitive advantage; competition-reducing alliances have the lowest probability of doing so.

- Corporate-level cooperative strategies are used when the firm wants to pursue product and/or geographic diversification. Through diversifying strategic alliances, firms agree to share some of their resources and capabilities to enter new markets or produce new products. Synergistic alliances are ones where firms share resources and capabilities to develop economies of scope. This alliance is similar to the business-level horizontal complementary alliance in which firms try to develop operational synergy, except that synergistic alliances are used to develop synergy at the corporate level. Franchising is a corporate-level cooperative strategy where the franchisor uses a franchise as a contractual relationship to specify how resources and capabilities will be shared with franchisees.

- As an international cooperative strategy, a cross-border alliance is used for several reasons, including the performance superiority of firms competing in markets outside their domestic market and governmental restrictions on growth through mergers and acquisitions. Cross-border alliances tend to be riskier than their domestic counterparts, particularly when partners aren't fully aware of each other's purpose for participating in the partnership.

- A network cooperative strategy is one wherein several firms agree to form multiple partnerships to achieve shared objectives. One of the primary benefits of a network cooperative strategy is the firm's opportunity to gain access "to its partner's other partnerships." When this happens, the probability greatly increases that partners will find unique ways to share their resources and capabilities to form competitive advantages. Network cooperative strategies are used to form either a stable alliance network or a dynamic alliance network. Used in mature industries, partners use stable networks to extend competitive advantages into new areas. In rapidly changing environments where frequent product innovations occur, dynamic networks are primarily used as a tool of innovation.

- Cooperative strategies aren't risk free. If a contract is not developed appropriately, or if a partner misrepresents its competencies or fails to make them available, failure is likely. Furthermore, a firm may be held hostage through asset-specific investments made in conjunction with a partner, which may be exploited.

- Trust is an increasingly important aspect of successful cooperative strategies. Firms recognize the value of partnering with companies known for their trustworthiness. When trust exists, a cooperative strategy is managed to maximize the pursuit of opportunities between partners. Without trust, formal contracts and extensive monitoring systems are used to manage cooperative strategies. In this case, the interest is to minimize costs rather than to maximize opportunities by participating in a cooperative strategy. The key is to build trust and social capital.

1. S. J. Chang, 2004, Venture capital financing, strategic alliances, and the initial public offerings of Internet startups, *Journal of Business Venturing,* 19: 721–741; J. Hagedoorn & G. Dysters, 2002, External sources of innovative capabilities: The preference for strategic alliances or mergers and acquisitions, *Journal of Management Studies,* 39: 167–188.

2. T. A. Hemphill, 2003, Cooperative strategy, technology innovation and competition policy in the United States and the European Union, *Technology Analysis & Strategic Management,* 15(1): 93–101; J. B. Barney, 2002, *Gaining and Sustaining Competitive Advantage,* 2nd ed., Upper Saddle River, NJ: Prentice-Hall, 339.

3. K. Singh & W. Mitchell, 2005, Growth dynamics: The bidirectional relationship between interfirm collaboration and business sales in entrant and incumbent alliances, *Strategic Management Journal,* 26: 497–521; C. Young-Ybarra & M. Wiersema, 1999, Strategic flexibility in information technology alliances: The influence of transaction cost economics and social exchange theory, *Organization Science,* 10: 439–459.

4. J. Bowser, 2001, Strategic co-opetition: The value of relationships in the networked economy, *IBM Business Strategy Consulting,* www.ibm.com, March 12.

5. M. J. Mol, P. Pauwels, P. Matthyssens, & L. Quintens, 2004, A technological contingency perspective on the depth and scope of international outsourcing, *Journal of International Management,* 10: 287–305.

6. C. Hardy, T. B. Lawrence, & D. Grant, 2005, Discourse and collaboration: The role of conversations and collective identity, *Academy of Management Review,* 30: 58–77; A. Haahti, V. Madupu, U. Yavas, & E. Babakus, 2005, Cooperative strategy, knowledge intensity and export performance of small and medium sized enterprises, *Journal of World Business,* 40: 124–138; R. Vassolo, J. Anand, & T. B. Folta, 2004, Non-additivity in portfolios of exploration activities: A real options-based analysis of equity alliances in biotechnology, *Strategic Management Journal,* 25: 1045–1061.

7. Barney, *Gaining and Sustaining Competitive Advantage,* 339.

8. R. D. Ireland, M. A. Hitt, & D. Vaidyanath, 2002, Alliance management as a source of competitive advantage, *Journal of Management,* 28: 413–446; J. G. Coombs & D. J. Ketchen, 1999, Exploring interfirm cooperation and performance: Toward a reconciliation of predictions from the resource-based view and organizational economics, *Strategic Management Journal,* 20: 867–888.

9. M. R. Subramani & N. Venkatraman, 2003, Safeguarding investments in asymmetric interorganizational relationships: Theory and evidence, *Academy of Management Journal,* 46(1): 46–62.

10. P. Kale, J. H. Dyer, & H. Singh, 2002, Alliance capability, stock market response, and long-term alliance success: The role of the alliance function, *Strategic Management Journal,* 23: 747–767; D. F. Kuratko, R. D. Ireland, & J. S. Hornsby, 2001, Improving firm performance through entrepreneurial actions: Acordia's corporate entrepreneurship strategy, *Academy of Management Executive,* 15(4): 60–71.

11. A. Antoine, C. B. Frank, H. Murata, & E. Roberts, 2003, Acquisitions and alliances in the aerospace industry: An unusual triad, *International Journal of Technology Management,* 25(8): 779–790; 2002, Lockheed Martin, Responsive global partnerships, www.lockheedmartin.com, March 17.

12. D. Gerwin, 2004, Coordinating new product development in strategic alliances, *Academy of Management Review,* 29: 241–257; Ireland, Hitt, & Vaidyanath, Alliance management as a source of competitive advantage.

13. M. Harvey, M. B. Myers, & M. M. Novicevic, 2003, The managerial issues associated with global account management: A relational contract perspective, *Journal of Management Development,* 22(1,2): 103–129; T. K. Das & B.-S. Teng, 2001, A risk perception model of alliance structuring, *Journal of International Management,* 7: 1–29.

14. A. Afuah, 2002, Mapping technological capabilities into product markets and competitive advantage: The case of cholesterol drugs, *Strategic Management Journal,* 23: 171–179; A. Arino, 2001, To do or not to do? Non-cooperative behavior by commission and omission in interfirm ventures, *Group & Organization Management,* 26(1): 4–23; C. Holliday, 2001, Sustainable growth, the DuPont way, *Harvard Business Review,* 79(8): 129–134.

15. Y. Kim & K. Lee, 2003, Technological collaboration in the Korean electronic parts industry: Patterns and key success factors, *R&D Management,* 33(1): 59–77; M. A. Geletkanycz & S. S. Black, 2001, Bound by the past? Experience-based effects on commitment to the strategic status quo, *Journal of Management,* 27: 3–21.

16. S. L. Berman, J. Down, & C. W. L. Hill, 2002, Tacit knowledge as a source of competitive advantage in the National Basketball Association, *Academy of Management Journal,* 45: 13–31.

17. H. Hoang & F. T. Rothaermel, 2005, The effect of general and partner-specific alliance experience on joint R&D project performance, *Academy of Management Journal,* 48: 332–345.

18. M. Clifford, 2003, Concrete lessons in reform, *BusinessWeek Online,* www.businessweek.com, June 16.

19. R. E. Hoskisson & L. W. Busenitz, 2002, Market uncertainty and learning distance in corporate entrepreneurship entry mode choice, in M. A. Hitt, R. D. Ireland, S. M. Camp, & D. L. Sexton (eds.), *Strategic Entrepreneurship: Creating a New Mindset,* Oxford, UK: Blackwell Publishers, 151–172.

20. A.-W. Harzing, 2002, Acquisitions versus greenfield investments: International strategy and management of entry modes, *Strategic Management Journal,* 23: 211–227; S.-J. Chang & P. M. Rosenzweig, 2001, The choice of entry mode in sequential foreign direct investment, *Strategic Management Journal,* 22: 747–776.

21. 2004, Shanghai Pudong Development Bank and Citibank Launch, www.spdb.com, February 4; J. T. Areddy, 2003, Citigroup may bolster 5% stake in Pudong Development Bank, *Wall Street Journal,* January 6, C7; 2003, Citibank can boost China stake, *Wall Street Journal,* April 28, C11.

22. S. Das, P. K. Sen, & S. Sengupta, 1998, Impact of strategic alliances on firm valuation, *Academy of Management Journal,* 41: 27–41.

23. P. Bierly & E. Kessler, 1999. The timing of strategic alliances. In M. A. Hitt, P. G. Clifford, R. D. Nixon, & K. P. Coyne (eds.), *Dynamic Strategic Resources.* West Sussex, England: John Wiley & Sons, 299–321.

24. T. B. Folta & K. D. Miller, 2002, Real options in equity partnerships, *Strategic Management Journal,* 23: 77–88; Barney, *Gaining and Sustaining Competitive Advantage,* 339; S. D. Hunt, C. J. Lambe, & C. M. Wittmann, 2002, A theory and model of business alliance success, *Journal of Relationship Marketing,* 1(1): 17–35.

25. M. Pacelle, R. Sidel, & A. Merrick, 2003, Citigroup agrees to buy Sears's credit-card unit, *Wall Street Journal Online,* www.wsj.com, July 15.

26. A. Hinterhuber, 2002, Value chain orchestration in action and the case of the global agrochemical industry, *Long Range Planning,* 35(6): 615–635; A. C. Inkpen, 2001, Strategic alliances, in M. A. Hitt, R. E. Freeman, & J. S. Harrison (eds.), *Handbook of Strategic Management,* Oxford, UK: Blackwell Publishers, 409–432.

27. M. Delio, 1999, Strategic outsourcing, *Knowledge Management,* 2(7): 62–68.

28. L. Tischler, 2005, Join the circus, *Fast Company,* www.fastcompany.com, July 18; Aetna and CVS intend to form strategic alliance to help Medicare beneficiaries make decisions on new prescription drug plans, Aetna, www.aetna. com, July 7.

29. M. J. Kelly, J.-L. Schaan, & H. Jonacas, 2002, Managing alliance relationships: Key challenges in the early stages of collaboration, *R&D Management,* 32(1): 11–22.

30. A. C. Inkpen & J. Ross, 2001, Why do some strategic alliances persist beyond their useful life? *California Management Review,* 44(1): 132–148.

31. C. Hardy, N. Phillips, & T. B. Lawrence, 2003, Resources, knowledge and influence: The organizational effects of interorganizational collaboration, *Journal of Management Studies,* 40(2): 321–347; Inkpen, Strategic alliances, 411.

32. L. Fuentelsaz, J. Gomez, & Y. Polo, 2002, Followers' entry timing: Evidence from the Spanish banking sector after deregulation, *Strategic Management Journal,* 23: 245–264.

33. K. R. Harrigan, 2001, Strategic flexibility in the old and new economies, in M. A. Hitt, R. E. Freeman, & J. S. Harrison (eds.), *Handbook of Strategic Management,* Oxford, UK: Blackwell Publishers, 97–123.

34. G. W. Dent, Jr., 2001, Gap fillers and fiduciary duties in strategic alliances, *Business Lawyer,* 57(1): 55–104.

35. M. Gonzalez, 2001, Strategic alliances, *Ivey Business Journal,* 66(1): 47–51.

36. M.-J. Oesterle & K. Macharzina, 2002, Editorial: De-regulation, liberalization, and concentration in the airline industry, *Management International Review,* 42(2): 115–119; M. Johnson, 2001, Airlines rush for comfort alliances, *Global Finance,* 15(11): 119–120.

37. M. A. Hitt, D. Ahlstrom, M. T. Dacin, E. Levitas, & L. Svobodina, 2004, The institutional effects of strategic alliance partner selection in transition economies: China versus Russia, *Organization Science,* 15: 173–185; P. A. Saparito, C. C. Chen, & H. J. Sapienza, 2004, The role of relational trust in bank-small firm relationships, *Academy of Management Journal,* 47: 400–410.

38. A. C. Inkpen & E. W. K. Tsang, 2005, Social capital, networks and knowledge transfer, *Academy of Management Review,* 30: 146–165.

39. A. Bollingtoft & J. P. Ulhoi, 2005, The networked business incubator—leveraging entrepreneurial agency, 2005, *Journal of Business Venturing,* 20: 265–290; T. G. Pollock, J. F. Porac, & J. B. Wade, 2004, Constructing deal networks: Brokers as network "architects" in the U.S. IPO market and other examples, *Academy of Management Review,* 29: 50–72.

40. J. R. Williams, 1998, *Renewable Advantage: Crafting Strategy through Economic Time,* New York: The Free Press.

41. M. Arndt, 2003, Up from the scrap heap, *BusinessWeek Online,* www.businessweek.com, July 21.

42. S. A. Zahra, R. D. Ireland, I. Gutierrez, & M. A. Hitt, 2000, Privatization and entrepreneurial transformation: Emerging issues and a future research agenda, *Academy of Management Review,* 25: 509–524.

43. I. Filatotchev, M. Wright, K. Uhlenbruck, L. Tihanyi, & R. E. Hoskisson, 2003, Governance, organizational capabilities, and restructuring in transition economies, *Journal of World Business,* 38(4): 331–347.

44. K. M. Eisenhardt, 2002, Has strategy changed? *MIT Sloan Management Review,* 43(2): 88–91.

45. M. Dell, 2003, Collaboration equals innovation, *InformationWeek,* January 27, 24–26; H. D'Antoni, 2003, Behind the numbers: Business alliances merit closer examination, *InformationWeek,* January 27, 88.

46. D. Michaels & J. L. Lunsford, 2003, Airlines move about buying planes jointly, *Wall Street Journal,* May 20, A3.

47. 2005, Sprint joins rival Verizon in wireless broadband sector, *Los Angeles Times,* www.latimes.com, July 18.

48. D. R. King, J. G. Covin, & H. Hegarty, 2003, Complementary resources and the exploitation of technological innovations, *Journal of Management,* 29: 589–606; J. S. Harrison, M. A. Hitt, R. E. Hoskisson, & R. D. Ireland, 2001, Resource complementarity in business combinations: Extending the logic to organizational alliances, *Journal of Management,* 27: 679–699.

49. Subramani & Venkatraman, Safeguarding investments in asymmetric interorganizational relationships.

50. R. Gulati, P. R. Lawrence, & P. Puranam, 2005, Adaptation in vertical relationships beyond incentive conflict, *Strategic Management Journal,* 26: 415–440.

51. M. G. Jacobides, 2005, Industry change through vertical disintegration: How and why markets emerged in mortgage banking, *Academy of Management Journal,* 48: 465–498.

52. G. Hoetker, 2005, How much you know versus how well I know you: Selecting a supplier for a technically innovative component, *Strategic Management Journal,* 26: 75–96.

53. M. Kotabe & K. S. Swan, 1995, The role of strategic alliances in high technology new product development, *Strategic Management Journal,* 16: 621–636.

54. J. Li, 2003, Bell Canada, Microsoft in Internet service alliance, *Wall Street Journal Online,* www.wsj.com, June 16.

55. P. Dussauge, B. Garrette, & W. Mitchel, 2004, Asymmetric performance: The market share impact of scale and link alliances in global auto industry, *Strategic Management Journal,* 25: 701–711.

56. 2005, Peugeot in pact with Mitsubishi for new SUVs, *Wall Street Journal Online,* www.wsj.com, July 12.

57. C. Bryan-Low & B. Lagrotteria, 2005, France Telecom and Microsoft forge product alliance, *Wall Street Journal Online,* www.wsj.com, July 7.

58. J. J. Reuer & T. W. Tong, 2005, Real options in international joint ventures, *Journal of Management,* 31: 403–423; S. Chatterjee, R. M. Wiseman, A. Fiegenbaum, & C. E. Devers, 2003, Integrating behavioural and economic concepts of risk into strategic management: The twain shall meet, *Long Range Planning,* 36(1), 61–80; Hitt, Ireland, Camp, & Sexton, *Strategic Entrepreneurship,* 9.

59. Dow Jones, 2003, ABN, ShoreBank set up co to invest in developing economies, *Wall Street Journal Online,* www.wsj.com, July 10.

60. Hoetker, How much you know versus how well I know you, 75.

61. Barney, *Gaining and Sustaining Competitive Advantage,* 339.

62. T. Valdmanis, A. Shell, & E. B. Smith, 2004, Marsh & McLennan accused of price fixing, collusion, *USA Today,* www.usatoday.com, October 15.

63. D. Leahy & S. Pavelin, 2003, Follow-my-leader and tacit collusion, *International Journal of Industrial Organization,* 21(3): 439–454.

64. B. R. Golden & H. Ma, 2003, Mutual forbearance: The role of intrafirm integration and rewards, *Academy of Management Review,* 28: 479–493.

65. 2003, AOL, Microsoft vow messaging cooperation, *New York Times,* www.nytimes.com, June 4.

66. G. K. Price & J. M. Connor, 2003, Modeling coupon values for ready-to-eat breakfast cereals, *Agribusiness,* 19(2): 223–244.

67. G. K. Price, 2000, Cereal sales soggy despite price cuts and reduced couponing, *Food Review,* 23(2): 21–28.

68. S. B. Garland & A. Reinhardt, 1999, Making antitrust fit high tech, *Business Week,* March 22, 34–36.

69. E. G. Rogoff & H. S. Guirguis, 2002, Legalized price-fixing, *Forbes,* December 9, 48.

70. Jacobides, Industry change through vertical disintegrations; Dussauge, Garrette, & Mitchell, Asymmetric performance.

71. 2005, Northwest could lose its lucrative pact with KLM, *Wall Street Journal Online,* www.wsj.com, July 18; 2003, Who gains if United should die? *The Economist,* May 10, 56.

72. Leahy & Pavelin, Follow-my-leader and tacit collusion.

73. Harrison, Hitt, Hoskisson, & Ireland, Resource complementarity, 684–685; S. Chaudhuri & B. Tabrizi, 1999, Capturing the real value in high-tech acquisitions, *Harvard Business Review,* 77(5): 123–130.

74. A. E. Bernardo & B. Chowdhry, 2002, Resources, real options, and corporate strategy, *Journal of Financial Economics,* 63: 211–234; Inkpen, Strategic alliances, 413.

75. J. L. Johnson, R. P.-W. Lee, A. Saini, & B. Grohmann, 2003, Market-focused strategic flexibility: Conceptual advances and an integrative model, *Academy of Marketing Science Journal,* 31: 74–90; Young-Ybarra & Wiersema, Strategic flexibility, 439.

76. Folta & Miller, Real options in equity partnerships, 77.

77. A. R. Sorkin, 2005, Bid by Chevron in big oil deal thwarts China, *New York Times,* www.nytimes.com, July 20; 2005, Shell may discourage CNOOC from purchasing American Unocal, *China Chemical Reporter,* www.highbeam.com, March 6; 2002, CNOOC adds petrochemicals to downstream strategy, *Petroleum Economist,* December, 39.

78. Ibid.

79. A. Goerzen & P. W. Beamish, 2005, The effect of alliance network diversity on multinational enterprise performance, *Strategic Management Journal,* 333–354.

80. M. V. Shyam Kumar, 2005, The value from acquiring and divesting a joint venture: A real options approach, *Strategic Management Journal,* 26: 321–331.

81. J. Yang, 2003, One step forward for Japan's chipmakers, *Business Week Online,* www.businessweek.com, July 7.

82. A. Pasztor, 2005, PanAmSat adopts lower-cost strategy, *Wall Street Journal Online,* www.wsj.com, July 5.

83. J. G. Combs & D. J. Ketchen Jr., 2003, Why do firms use franchising as an entrepreneurial strategy? A meta-analysis, *Journal of Management,* 29: 427–443.

84. F. Lafontaine, 1999, Myths and strengths of franchising, "Mastering Strategy" (Part Nine), *Financial Times,* November 22, 8–10.

85. C. Adler, 2005, How China eats a sandwich, *Fortune,* www.fortune.com, March 10; L. Fenwick, 2001, Emerging markets: Defining global opportunities, *Franchising World,* 33(4): 54–55.

86. 2005, 7-Eleven, Inc., www.entrepreneur.com, July 28; J. Wilgoren, 2003, In the urban 7-Eleven, the Slurpee looks sleeker, *New York Times,* www .nytimes.com, July 13.

87. S. C. Michael, 2002, Can a franchise chain coordinate? *Journal of Business Venturing,* 17: 325–342.

88. M. Gerstenhaber, 2000, Franchises can teach us about customer care, *Marketing,* March 16, 18.

89. P. J. Kaufmann & S. Eroglu, 1999, Standardization and adaptation in business format franchising, *Journal of Business Venturing,* 14: 69–85.

90. S. C. Michael, 2002, First mover advantage through franchising, *Journal of Business Venturing,* 18: 61–81.

91. Barney, *Gaining and Sustaining Competitive Advantage,* 110–111.

92. M. Zollo, J. J. Reuer, & H. Singh, 2002, Interorganizational routines and performance in strategic alliances, *Organization Science,* 13: 701–714.

93. Ireland, Hitt, & Vaidyanath, Alliance management.

94. P. Almeida, G. Dokko, & L. Rosenkopf, 2003, Startup size and the mechanisms of external learning: Increasing opportunity and decreasing ability? *Research Policy,* 32(2): 301–316; B. L. Simonin, 1997, The importance of collaborative know-how: An empirical test of the learning organization, *Academy of Management Journal,* 40: 1150–1174.

95. H. Timmons, 2003, BP signs deal with Russian firm for venture in oil and gas, *New York Times,* June 27, W1.

96. R. Narula & G. Duysters, 2004, Globalization and trends in international R&D alliances, *Journal of International Management,* 10: 199–218; M. A. Hitt, M. T. Dacin, E. Levitas, J.-L. Arregle, & A. Borza, 2000, Partner selection in emerging and developed market contexts: Resource-based and organizational learning perspectives, *Academy of Management Journal,* 43: 449–467.

97. D. Kovaleski, 2003, More firms shaking hands on strategic partnership agreements, *Pensions & Investments,* February 3, 20; A. L. Velocci Jr., 2001, U.S.-Euro strategic alliances will outpace company mergers, *Aviation Week & Space Technology,* 155(23): 56.

98. I. M. Manev, 2003, The managerial network in a multinational enterprise and the resource profiles of subsidiaries, *Journal of International Management,* 9: 133–152; M. A. Hitt, R. E. Hoskisson, & H. Kim, 1997, International diversification: Effects on innovation and firm performance in product diversified firms, *Academy of Management Journal,* 40: 767–798.

99. H. K. Steensma, L. Tihanyi, M. A. Lyles, & C. Dhanaraj, 2005, The evolving value of foreign partnerships in transitioning economies, *Academy of Management Journal,* 48: 213–235; L. Nachum & D. Keeble, 2003, MNE linkages and localized clusters: Foreign and indigenous firms in the media cluster of Central London, *Journal of International Management,* 9: 171–192.

100. 2005, Tiger Woods leads the charge for Nike Golf as an outstanding year unfolds, Yahoo! Finance, biz.yahoo.com, July 18; C. Noon, 2005, Armstrong, sets the pace in the Alps, *Forbes,* Forbes.com, July 15; S. Holmes, 2003, The real Nike news is happening abroad, *BusinessWeek Online,* www.businessweek.com, July 21.

101. Y. Luo, O. Shenkar, & M.-K. Nyaw, 2002, Mitigating the liabilities of foreignness: Defensive versus offensive approaches, *Journal of International Management,* 8: 283–300.

102. S. R. Miller & A. Parkhe, 2002, Is there a liability of foreignness in global banking? An empirical test of banks' x-efficiency, *Strategic Management Journal,* 23: 55–75; Y. Luo, 2001, Determinants of local responsiveness: Perspectives from foreign subsidiaries in an emerging market, *Journal of Management,* 27: 451–477.

103. J. E. Oxley & R. C. Sampson, 2004, The scope and governance of international R&D alliances, *Strategic Management Journal,* 25: 723–749.

104. S. Holmes, 2003, For Starbucks, there's no place like home, *BusinessWeek Online,* www.businessweek.com, June 9.

105. H. J. Teegen & J. P. Doh, 2002, US-Mexican alliance negotiations: Impact of culture on authority, trust, performance, *Thunderbird International Business Review,* 44(6): 749–775; P. Ghemawat, 2001, Distance matters: The hard reality of global expansion, *Harvard Business Review,* 79(8): 137–147.

106. J. K. Sebenius, 2002, The hidden challenge of cross-border negotiations, *Harvard Business Review,* 80(3): 76–85.

107. Z. Zhao, J. Anand, & W. Mitchell, 2005, A dual networks perspective on inter-organizational transfer of R&D capabilities: International joint ventures in the Chinese automotive industry, *Journal of Management Studies,* 42: 127–160.

108. C. B. Copp & R. L. Ivy, 2001, Networking trends of small tourism businesses in post-socialist Slovakia, *Journal of Small Business Management,* 39: 345–353.

109. M. Ferrary, 2003, Managing the disruptive technologies life cycle by externalising the research: Social network and corporate venturing in the Silicon Valley, *International Journal of Technology Management,* 25(1,2): 165–180; S. S. Cohen & G. Fields, 1999, Social capital and capital gains in Silicon Valley, *California Management Review,* 41(2): 108–130; J. A. Matthews, 1999, A silicon island of the east: Creating a semiconductor industry in Singapore, *California Management Review,* 41(2): 55–78.

110. A. C. Cooper, 2002, Networks, alliances, and entrepreneurship, in M. A. Hitt, R. D. Ireland, S. M. Camp, & D. L. Sexton (eds.), *Strategic Entrepreneurship: Creating a New Mindset,* Oxford, UK: Blackwell Publishers, 203–222.

111. G. G. Bell, 2005, Custers, networks, and firm innovativeness, *Strategic Management Journal,* 26: 287–295.

112. A. Echols & W. Tsai, 2005, Niche and performance: The moderating role of network embeddedness, *Strategic Management Journal,* 26: 219–238; S. Chung & G. M. Kim, 2003, Performance effects of partnership between manufacturers and suppliers for new product development: The supplier's standpoint, *Research Policy,* 32: 587–604.

113. H. Kim, R. E. Hoskisson, & W. P. Wan, 2004, Power, dependence, diversification strategy and performance in keiretsu member firms, *Strategic Management Journal,* 25: 613–636.

114. R. S. Cline, 2001, Partnering for strategic alliances, *Lodging Hospitality,* 57(9): 42.

115. M. Rudberg & J. Olhager, 2003, Manufacturing networks and supply chains: An operations strategy perspective, *Omega,* 31(1): 29–39.

116. G. J. Young, M. P. Charns, & S. M. Shortell, 2001, Top manager and network effects on the adoption of innovative management practices: A study of TQM in a public hospital system, *Strategic Management Journal,* 22: 935–951.

117. E. Garcia-Canal, C. L. Duarte, J. R. Criado, & A. V. Llaneza, 2002, Accelerating international expansion through global alliances: A typology of cooperative strategies, *Journal of World Business,* 37(2): 91–107; F. T. Rothaermel, 2001, Complementary assets, strategic alliances, and the incumbent's advantage: An empirical study of industry and firm effects in the bio-pharmaceutical industry, *Research Policy,* 30: 1235–1251.

118. V. Shankar & B. L. Bayus, 2003, Network effects and competition: An empirical analysis of the home video game industry, *Strategic Management Journal,* 24: 375–384.

119. B. Duncan, 2003, Five steps to successful strategic partnering, *Information Week,* www.informationweek.com, July 21.

120. Z. Simsek, M. H. Lubatkin, & D. Kandemir, 2003, Inter-firm networks and entrepreneurial behavior: A structural embeddedness perspective, *Journal of Management,* 29: 401–426; H. W. Volberda, C. Baden-Fuller, & F. A. J. van den Bosch, 2001, Mastering strategic renewal: Mobilising renewal journeys in multi-unit firms, *Long Range Planning,* 34(2): 159–178.

121. King, Covin, & Hegarty, Complementary resources and the exploitation of technological innovations.

122. A. I. Goldberg, G. Cohen, & A. Fiegenbaum, 2003, Reputation building: Small business strategies for successful venture development, *Journal of Small Business Management,* 41(2): 168–186; S. Das, P. K. Sen, & S. Sengupta, 2003, Strategic alliances: A valuable way to manage intellectual capital? *Journal of Intellectual Capital,* 4(1): 10–19.

123. D. C. Hambrick, J. Li, K. Xin, & A. S. Tsui, 2001, Compositional gaps and downward spirals in international joint venture management groups, *Strategic Management Journal,* 22: 1033–1053; T. K. Das & B.-S. Teng, 2000, Instabilities of strategic alliances: An internal tensions perspective, *Organization Science,* 11: 77–101.

124. Ireland, Hitt, & Vaidyanath, Alliance management; A. Madhok & S. B. Tallman, 1998, Resources, transactions and rents: Managing value through interfirm collaborative relationships, *Organization Science,* 9: 326–339.

125. D. De Cremer & D. van Knippenberg, 2002, How do leaders promote cooperation? The effects of charisma and procedural fairness, *Journal of Applied Psychology,* 87: 858–867.

126. S.-O. Cheung, T. S. T. Ng, S.-P. Wong, & H. C. H. Suen, 2003, Behavioral aspects in construction partnering, *International Journal of Project Management,* 21: 333–344.

127. P. M. Norman, 2002, Protecting knowledge in strategic alliances—Resource and relational characteristics, *Journal of High Technology Management Research,* 13(2): 177–202; P. M. Norman, 2001, Are your secrets safe? Knowledge protection in strategic alliances, *Business Horizons,* November/December, 51–60.

128. M. A. Hitt, M. T. Dacin, B. B. Tyler, & D. Park, 1997, Understanding the differences in Korean and U.S. executives strategic orientations, *Strategic Management Journal,* 18: 159–168.

129. N. Wingfield & P.-W. Tam, 2005, H-P to stop reselling iPods, unwinding a high-profile deal, *Wall Street Journal Online,* www.wsj.com, July 29.

130. R. Abratt & P. Motlana, 2002, Managing co-branding strategies: Global brands into local markets, Business Horizons, 45(5): 43–50; P. Lane, J. E. Salk, & M. A. Lyles, 2001, Absorptive capacity, learning, and performance in international joint ventures, Strategic Management Journal, 22: 1139–1161.

131. R. Grover, 2003, Is Steve about to move his cheese? *Business Week,* February 10, 72.

132. R. Larsson, K. R. Brousseau, M. J. Driver, & M. Homqvist, 2003, International growth through cooperation: Brand-driven strategies, leadership, and career development in Sweden, *Academy of Management Executive,* 17(1): 7–21; R. Larsson, L. Bengtsson, K. Henriksson, & J. Sparks, 1998, The interorganizational learning dilemma: Collective knowledge development in strategic alliances, *Organization Science,* 9: 285–305.

133. Ireland, Hitt, & Vaidyanath, Alliance management.

134. J. H. Dyer, P. Kale, & H. Singh, 2001, How to make strategic alliances work, *MIT Sloan Management Review,* 42(4): 37–43.

135. J. H. Dyer, 1997, Effective interfirm collaboration: How firms minimize transaction costs and maximize transaction value, *Strategic Management Journal,* 18: 535–556.

136. J. H. Dyer & C. Wujin, 2003, The role of trustworthiness in reducing transaction costs and improving performance: Empirical evidence from the United States, Japan, and Korea, *Organization Science,* 14: 57–69.

137. 2003, Sony Ericsson venture to close sites and cut 500 jobs, *New York Times,* www.nytimes.com, June 25; J. L. Schenker, 2003, Sony Ericsson posts loss despite sales gain, *New York Times,* www.nytimes.com, July 16.

138. Hutt, Stafford, Walker, & Reingen, Case study: Defining the social network, 53.

139. D. L. Ferrin & K. T. Dirks, 2003, The use of rewards to increase and decrease trust: Mediating processes and differential effects, *Organization Science,* 14(1): 18–31; D. F. Jennings, K. Artz, L. M. Gillin, & C. Christodouloy, 2000, Determinants of trust in global strategic alliances: Amrad and the Australian biomedical industry, *Competitiveness Review,* 10(1): 25–44.

140. V. Perrone, A. Zaheer, & B. McEvily, 2003, Free to be trusted? Boundary constraints on trust in boundary spanners, *Organization Science,* 14: 422–439; H. K. Steensma, L. Marino, & K. M. Weaver, 2000, Attitudes toward cooperative strategies: A cross-cultural analysis of entrepreneurs, *Journal of International Business Studies,* 31: 591–609.

141. Inkpen and Tsang, Social capital; L. Huff & L. Kelley, 2003, Levels of organizational trust in individualist versus collectivist societies: A seven-nation study, *Organization Science,* 14(1): 81–90.

142. Dyer & Wujin, The role of trustworthiness in reducing transaction costs and improving performance.

143. J. H. Davis, F. D. Schoorman, R. C. Mayer, & H. H. Tan, 2000, The trusted general manager and business unit performance: Empirical evidence of a competitive advantage, *Strategic Management Journal,* 21: 563–576.

144. B. Hillebrand & W. G. Biemans, 2003, The relationship between internal and external cooperation: literature review and propositions, *Journal of Business Research,* 56: 735–744.

145. K. Lim, 2005, CapitaLand will boost its presence in China, *Wall Street Journal Online,* www.wsj.com, July 11.

PART **3**

Strategic Actions: Strategy Implementation

Corporate Governance

KNOWLEDGE OBJECTIVES

Studying this chapter should provide you with the strategic management knowledge needed to:

1. Define corporate governance and explain why it is used to monitor and control managers' strategic decisions.

2. Explain why ownership has been largely separated from managerial control in the modern corporation.

3. Define an agency relationship and managerial opportunism and describe their strategic implications.

4. Explain how three internal governance mechanisms— ownership concentration, the board of directors, and executive compensation—are used to monitor and control managerial decisions.

5. Discuss the types of compensation executives receive and their effects on strategic decisions.

6. Describe how the external corporate governance mechanism—the market for corporate control—acts as a restraint on top-level managers' strategic decisions.

7. Discuss the use of corporate governance in international settings, in particular in Germany and Japan.

8. Describe how corporate governance fosters ethical strategic decisions and the importance of such behaviors on the part of top-level executives.

ASSOCIATED PRESS, AP

Carlos Gutierrez, former Kellogg CEO; during his tenure, Kellogg's stock price doubled.

Is Managerial Incentive Compensation Too High?

As incentive compensation for managers, many firms grant stock options to their top executives. In 1992, S&P 500 firms granted stock options worth approximately $11 billion. By the year 2000, such options granted by the S&P 500 firms increased to $119 billion. However, by 2002, the S&P 500 option grants had fallen to $71 billion—a significant decline from the previous year, caused by the burst of the technology-firm bubble, but still a sixfold increase over the previous decade. In contrast, an executive pay scoreboard produced by *Business Week* disclosed that salary increases were moderate in 2004 relative to 2003. S&P 500 firms' CEO pay increased 11.3 percent in 2004, which is close to the gain in the S&P 500 stock index of 10.9 percent. Comparatively though, CEO raises and total pay were significantly higher than those of the average worker, who saw a pay increase of 2.9 percent. Thus, although CEO pay raises have moderated relative to the past, they are still significantly higher than the average worker in the firms managed by these CEOs.

Stock option grants have been moderated partly because of legislation such as the Sarbanes-Oxley Act (discussed later in the chapter), as well as by criticisms from corporate-governance activists such as the California Public Employees' Retirement System (CalPERS) and TIAA-CREF regarding excessive stock option incentive grants. Additionally, a new rule by the Financial Accounting Standards Board (FASB Statement No. 123) required firms to record stock options as an expense beginning in July 2005.

Many firms argued against the ruling, suggesting that expensing options would hurt earnings in high-technology companies, because much of the excessive compensation has come from technological companies. They argued that many firms would dispense with options and the incentive for employees to share in and foster company growth. Research suggests, however, that although expensing options will reduce the number of options granted, it will not significantly dampen technology companies' dependence on this incentive. About 20 percent of the technology companies are reducing the grants offered, and many are reducing the number of employees involved, especially lower-level employees. Thus, it is likely that stock option plans will be more oriented toward management than toward lower-level employees. This will likely increase the already significant disparity between CEO and worker pay.

Many companies have been able to avoid expensing options, at least in the short term, by vesting executive options before the original expiration date and thus accelerating executives' potential payoff several years earlier than would otherwise have been the case. Other firms have been seeking to complete a leveraged buyout or an acquisition because expensing options would significantly reduce income. For instance, expensing its options at fair market value would have caused Ask Jeeves, the fourth-ranked Internet search engine, to reduce its 2004 earnings from $53.16 million to $21.78 million. However, before this happened, IAC, an Internet conglomerate headed by Barry Diller, announced it would acquire Ask Jeeves as a hub for its other Internet businesses.

The concern about expensing options has been driving down the number of stock options being granted. The average number of stock options granted per employee in 2004 was 123, down 56 percent from 277 in 2001 for S&P 500 companies. It is likely that overall pay will begin to moderate as shareholder pressure and expected changes in accounting procedures will reduce stock option awards in the future. Although lower stock price gains may be partly to blame for the devaluation of stock option packages, media attention was also moderating the total compensation for executives. Other firms have been researching the accounting formulas used to value options, seeking to use a formula that lowers option valuation to the least admissible value and thus expense options at the lowest possible cost. Additionally, to facilitate stock options as a viable incentive, a number of company executives' stock options have been repriced when a firm's stock price drops significantly. The ethics of such repricing will continue to be debated in corporate-governance circles.

Source: B. Barnes & P. Grant, 2005, Barry Diller's IAC sells NBC Universal stake, *Wall Street Journal,* June 9, A3; L. Lavelle, 2005, A payday for performance, *Business Week,* April 28, 78; E. MacDonald, 2005, Optional end run, *Forbes,* June 20, 62; E. MacDonald, 2005, A volatile brew: Companies have found how to ease the impact of strict new stock options rules, *Forbes,* August 15, 70–71; J. S. McClenahen, 2005, The new rules, *Industry Week,* July, 40–48; C. M. O'Connor, 2005, Are tech LBOs driven by option expensing? In June, FASB will make companies deduct option cost from earnings, *The Investment Dealer's Digest,* April 4, 10–12; M. K. Ozanian & E. MacDonald, 2005, Paychecks on steroids, *Forbes,* May 9, 134–138; K. Richardson, 2005, Stock options remain alive and well, *Wall Street Journal,* July 25, C3; A. E. Sheng, 2005, Stock-option cuts to hit employees in lower ranks, *Wall Street Journal,* July 13, D3; A. Arya & H.-L. Sun, 2004, Stock option repricing: Heads I win, tails you lose, *Journal of Business Ethics,* 50(4): 297–312; R. Simon, 2004, Stock-option awards sharply cut; Value fell 41 percent for CEOs, 53 percent for lower-level, *Wall Street Journal,* December 14, D3.

As the Opening Case illustrates, executive compensation as a governance device is an increasingly important part of the strategic management process.[1] If the board makes the wrong decision in compensating the firm's strategic leader (e.g., CEO), the shareholders and the firm suffer. Compensation is used to motivate CEOs to act in the best interests of the firm—in particular, the shareholders. When they do, the firm's value should increase.

What are a CEO's actions worth? The Opening Case suggests that they are increasingly worth a significant amount in the United States. While some critics argue that U.S. CEOs are paid too much, the hefty increases in their incentive compensation in recent years ostensibly have come from linking their pay to their firms' performance, and U.S. firms have performed better than many companies in other countries. However, research suggests that firms with a smaller pay gap between the CEO and other top executives perform better, especially when collaboration among top management team members is more important.[2] The performance improvement is attributed to better cooperation among the top management team members. Other research suggests that CEOs receive excessive compensation when corporate governance is the weakest.[3] Also, as noted in the Opening Case, there has been a shift in compensation practices used for top executives over the last several years, given new policies regarding governance and increasingly critical media attention.

Corporate governance is the set of mechanisms used to manage the relationship among stakeholders that is used to determine and control the strategic direction and performance of organizations.[4] At its core, corporate governance is concerned with identifying ways to ensure that strategic decisions are made effectively.[5] Governance can also be thought of as a means corporations use to establish order between parties (the firm's owners and its top-level managers) whose interests may conflict. Thus, corporate governance reflects and enforces the company's values.[6] In modern corporations—especially those in the United States and the United Kingdom—a primary objective of corporate governance is to ensure that the interests of top-level managers are aligned with the interests of the shareholders. Corporate governance involves oversight in areas where owners, managers, and members of boards of directors may have conflicts of interest. These areas include the election of directors, the general supervision of CEO pay and more focused supervision of director pay, and the corporation's overall structure and strategic direction.[7]

Corporate governance has been emphasized in recent years because, as the Opening Case illustrates, corporate governance mechanisms occasionally fail to adequately monitor and control top-level managers' decisions. This situation has resulted in changes in governance mechanisms in corporations throughout the world, especially with respect to efforts intended to improve the performance of boards of directors. These changes often cause confusion about the proper role of the board. According to one observer, "Depending on the company, you get very different perspectives: Some boards are settling for checking the boxes on compliance regulations, while others are thinking about changing the fundamental way they govern, and some worry that they've gotten themselves into micromanaging the CEO and company. There's a fair amount of turmoil and collective searching going on."[8] A second and more positive reason for this interest is that evidence suggests that a well-functioning corporate governance and control system can create a competitive advantage for an individual firm.[9] For example, one governance mechanism—the board of directors—has been suggested to be rapidly evolving into a major strategic force in U.S. business firms.[10] Thus, in this chapter, we describe actions designed to implement strategies that focus on monitoring and controlling mechanisms, which can help to ensure that top-level managerial actions contribute to the firm's strategic competitiveness and its ability to earn above-average returns.

Effective corporate governance is also of interest to nations.[11] As stated by one scholar, "Every country wants the firms that operate within its borders to flourish and grow in such ways as to provide employment, wealth, and satisfaction, not only to improve standards of living materially but also to enhance social cohesion. These aspirations cannot be met unless those firms are competitive internationally in a sustained way, and it is this medium- and long-term perspective that makes good corporate governance so vital."[12]

Corporate governance, then, reflects company standards, which in turn collectively reflect societal standards.[13] In many corporations, shareholders hold top-level managers accountable for their decisions and the results they generate. As with these firms and their boards, nations that effectively govern their corporations may gain a competitive advantage over rival countries. In a range of countries, but especially in the United States and the United Kingdom, the fundamental goal of business organizations is to maximize shareholder value.[14] Traditionally, shareholders are treated as the firm's key stakeholders, because they are the company's legal owners. The firm's owners expect top-level managers and others influencing the corporation's actions (for example, the board of directors) to make decisions that will result in the maximization of the company's value and, hence, of the owners' wealth.[15]

In the first section of this chapter, we describe the relationship that is the foundation on which the modern corporation is built: the relationship between owners and managers. The majority of this chapter is used to explain various mechanisms owners use to govern managers and to ensure that they comply with their responsibility to maximize shareholder value.

Three internal governance mechanisms and a single external one are used in the modern corporation. The three internal governance mechanisms we describe in this chapter are (1) ownership concentration, as represented by types of shareholders and their different incentives to monitor managers; (2) the board of directors; and (3) executive compensation. We then consider the market for corporate control, an external corporate governance mechanism. Essentially, this market is a set of potential owners seeking to acquire undervalued firms and earn above-average returns on their investments by replacing ineffective top-level management teams.[16] The chapter's focus then shifts to the issue of international corporate governance. We briefly describe governance approaches used in German and Japanese firms whose traditional governance structures are being affected by the realities of global competition. In part, this discussion suggests that the structures used to govern global companies in many different countries, including Germany, Japan, the United Kingdom, and the United States, are becoming more, rather than less, similar. Closing our analysis of corporate governance is a consideration of the need for these control mechanisms to encourage and support ethical behavior in organizations.

Importantly, the mechanisms discussed in this chapter can positively influence the governance of the modern corporation, which has placed significant responsibility and authority in the hands of top-level managers. The most effective managers understand their accountability for the firm's performance and respond positively to corporate governance mechanisms.[17] In addition, the firm's owners should not expect any single mechanism to remain effective over time. Rather, the use of several mechanisms allows owners to govern the corporation in ways that maximize strategic competitiveness and increase the financial value of their firm. With multiple governance mechanisms operating simultaneously, however, it is also possible for some of the governance mechanisms to be in conflict.[18] Later, we review how these conflicts can occur.

Separation of Ownership and Managerial Control

Historically, U.S. firms were managed by the founder-owners and their descendants. In these cases, corporate ownership and control resided in the same persons. As firms grew larger, "the managerial revolution led to a separation of ownership and control in most large corporations, where control of the firm shifted from entrepreneurs to professional managers while ownership became dispersed among thousands of unorganized stockholders who were removed from the day-to-day management of the firm."[19] These changes created the modern public corporation, which is based on the efficient separation of ownership and managerial control. Supporting the separation is a basic legal premise suggesting that the primary objective of a firm's activities is to increase the corporation's profit and, thereby, the financial gains of the owners (the shareholders).[20]

The separation of ownership and managerial control allows shareholders to purchase stock, which entitles them to income (residual returns) from the firm's operations after paying expenses. This right, however, requires that they also take a risk that the firm's expenses may exceed its revenues. To manage this investment risk, shareholders maintain a diversified portfolio by investing in several companies to reduce their overall risk.[21] As shareholders diversify their investments over a number of corporations, their risk declines. The poor performance or failure of any one firm in which they invest has less overall effect. Thus, shareholders specialize in managing their investment risk.

In small firms, managers often are high percentage owners, so there is less separation between ownership and managerial control. In fact, there are a large number of family-owned firms in which ownership and managerial control are not separated. In the United States, at least one-third of the S&P top 500 firms have substantial family ownership, holding on average about 18 percent of the outstanding equity. And family-owned firms perform better when a member of the family is the CEO than when the CEO is an outsider.[22] In many countries outside the United States, such as in Latin America, Asia, and some European countries, family-owned firms represent the dominant form.[23] The primary purpose of most of these firms is to increase the family's wealth, which explains why a family CEO often is better than an outside CEO.[24] There are at least two critical issues for family-controlled firms. First, as they grow, they may not have access to all of the skills needed to effectively manage the firm and maximize its returns for the family. Thus, they may need outsiders. Also, as they grow, they may need to seek outside capital and thus give up some of the ownership. In these cases, protection of the minority owners' rights becomes important.[25] To avoid these potential problems, when these firms grow and become more complex, their owner-managers may contract with managerial specialists. These managers make major decisions in the owner's firm and are compensated on the basis of their decision-making skills. As decision-making specialists, managers are agents of the firm's owners and are expected to use their decision-making skills to operate the owners' firm in ways that will maximize the return on their investment.[26]

Without owner (shareholder) specialization in risk bearing and management specialization in decision making, a firm may be limited by the abilities of its owners to manage and make effective strategic decisions. Thus, the separation and specialization of ownership (risk bearing) and managerial control (decision making) should produce the highest returns for the firm's owners.

Shareholder value is reflected by the price of the firm's stock. As stated earlier, corporate governance mechanisms, such as the board of directors or compensation based on the performance of a firm, is the reason that CEOs show general concern about the firm's stock price. As the Opening Case describes, CEO incentive compensation generally reflected the gain in the S&P 500 firms in 2004.

Agency Relationships

The separation between owners and managers creates an agency relationship. An **agency relationship** exists when one or more persons (the principal or principals) hire another person or persons (the agent or agents) as decision-making specialists to perform a service.[27] Thus, an agency relationship exists when one party delegates decision-making responsibility to a second party for compensation (see Figure 10.1).[28] In addition to shareholders and top executives, other examples of agency relationships are consultants and clients and insured and insurer. Moreover, within organizations, an agency relationship exists between managers and their employees, as well as between top executives and the firm's owners.[29] In the modern corporation, managers must understand the links between these relationships and the firm's effectiveness.[30] Although the agency relationship between managers and their employees is important, in this chapter we focus on the agency relationship between the firm's owners (the principals) and top-level managers (the principals' agents), because this relationship is related directly to how the firm's strategies are implemented.

The separation between ownership and managerial control can be problematic. Research evidence documents a variety of agency problems in the modern corporation.[31] Problems can surface because the principal and the agent have different interests and goals, or because shareholders lack direct control of large publicly traded corporations. Problems also arise when an agent makes decisions that result in the pursuit of goals that conflict with those of the principals. Thus, the separation of ownership and control potentially allows divergent interests (between principals and agents) to surface, which can lead to managerial opportunism.

Managerial opportunism is the seeking of self-interest with guile (i.e., cunning or deceit).[32] Opportunism is both an attitude (e.g., an inclination) and a set of behaviors (i.e., specific acts of self-interest).[33] It is not possible for principals to know beforehand which agents will or will not act opportunistically. The reputations of top executives are an imperfect predictor, and opportunistic behavior cannot be observed until it has

FIGURE **10.1** | An Agency Relationship

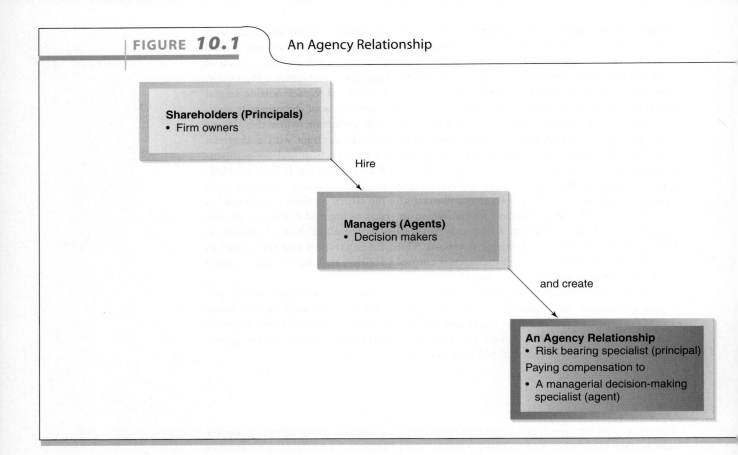

occurred. Thus, principals establish governance and control mechanisms to prevent agents from acting opportunistically, even though only a few are likely to do so.[34] Any time that principals delegate decision-making responsibilities to agents, the opportunity for conflicts of interest exists. Top executives, for example, may make strategic decisions that maximize their personal welfare and minimize their personal risk.[35] Decisions such as these prevent the maximization of shareholder wealth. Decisions regarding product diversification demonstrate these possibilities.

Product Diversification as an Example of an Agency Problem

As explained in Chapter 6, a corporate-level strategy to diversify the firm's product lines can enhance a firm's strategic competitiveness and increase its returns, both of which serve the interests of shareholders and the top executives. However, product diversification can result in two benefits to managers that shareholders do not enjoy, so top executives may prefer product diversification more than shareholders do.[36]

First, diversification usually increases the size of a firm, and size is positively related to executive compensation. Also, diversification increases the complexity of managing a firm and its network of businesses and may thus require more pay because of this complexity.[37] Thus, increased product diversification provides an opportunity for top executives to increase their compensation.[38]

Second, product diversification and the resulting diversification of the firm's portfolio of businesses can reduce top executives' employment risk. Managerial employment risk is the risk of job loss, loss of compensation, and loss of managerial reputation.[39]

These risks are reduced with increased diversification, because a firm and its upper-level managers are less vulnerable to the reduction in demand associated with a single or limited number of product lines or businesses. For example, Kellogg Co. was almost entirely focused on breakfast cereal in 2001 when it suffered its first ever market share leadership loss to perennial number two, General Mills, Inc. Upon appointing Carlos Gutierrez, a longtime manager at Kellogg, to the CEO position, the company embarked on a new strategy to overcome its poor performance. The competitive environment was difficult because of the emergence of premium-product private labels and frequent price wars. Furthermore, retail consolidation squeezed overall industry sales and caused an extensive focus on cost reduction. In order to reduce the risk of a takeover attempt because of low stock price, Kellogg purchased Keebler Foods Co. in 2001. As a result, its overall revenue increased from $6 billion to $8.3 billion in 2002. While its diversified scope increased, it also focused on a change from "volume to value" and implemented a second strategy called "managing for cash," in which it significantly increased its incentive compensation for division managers, encouraging them to focus on improved innovation at more decentralized divisions.[40] Through this approach, Kellogg's earnings were substantial enough so that it could raise its dividend by 10 percent in 2005, which was the first dividend increase in five years. Kellogg's stock price doubled during Gutierrez's tenure as CEO, and through this diversification move, his risk of job loss was substantially reduced.[41]

Another concern that may represent an agency problem is a firm's free cash flows over which top executives have control. Free cash flows are resources remaining after the firm has invested in all projects that have positive net present values within its current businesses.[42] In anticipation of positive returns, managers may decide to invest these funds in products that are not associated with the firm's current lines of business to increase the firm's level of diversification. The managerial decision to use free cash flows to overdiversify the firm is an example of self-serving and opportunistic managerial behavior. In contrast to managers, shareholders may prefer that free cash flows be distributed to them as dividends, so they can control how the cash is invested.[43]

Curve *S* in Figure 10.2 depicts the shareholders' optimal level of diversification. Owners seek the level of diversification that reduces the risk of the firm's total failure while simultaneously increasing the company's value through the development of economies of scale and scope (see Chapter 6). Of the four corporate-level diversification strategies shown in Figure 10.2, shareholders likely prefer the diversified position noted by point *A* on curve *S*—a position that is located between the dominant business and related-constrained diversification strategies. Of course, the optimum level of diversification owners seek varies from firm to firm.[44] Factors that affect shareholders' preferences include the firm's primary industry, the intensity of rivalry among competitors in that industry, and the top management team's experience with implementing diversification strategies.

As do principals, upper-level executives—as agents—also seek an optimal level of diversification. Declining performance resulting from too much product diversification increases the probability that corporate control of the firm will be acquired in the market. After a firm is acquired, the employment risk for the firm's top executives increases substantially. Furthermore, a manager's employment opportunities in the external managerial labor market (discussed in Chapter 12) are affected negatively by a firm's poor performance. Therefore, top executives prefer diversification, but not to a point that it increases their employment risk and reduces their employment opportunities.[45] Curve *M* in Figure 10.2 shows that executives prefer higher levels of product diversification than do shareholders. Top executives might prefer the level of diversification shown by point *B* on curve *M*.

In general, shareholders prefer riskier strategies and more focused diversification. They reduce their risk through holding a diversified portfolio of equity investments.

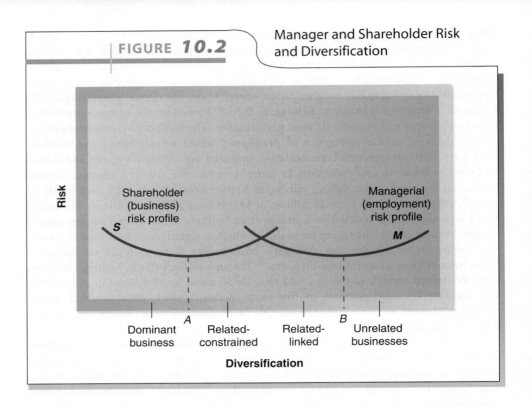

FIGURE 10.2 Manager and Shareholder Risk and Diversification

Risk

Shareholder (business) risk profile

S

Managerial (employment) risk profile

M

A

B

Dominant business

Related-constrained

Related-linked

Unrelated businesses

Diversification

Alternatively, managers obviously cannot balance their employment risk by working for a diverse portfolio of firms. Therefore, top executives may prefer a level of diversification that maximizes firm size and their compensation and that reduces their employment risk. Product diversification, therefore, is a potential agency problem that could result in principals incurring costs to control their agents' behaviors.

Agency Costs and Governance Mechanisms

The potential conflict illustrated by Figure 10.2, coupled with the fact that principals do not know which managers might act opportunistically, demonstrates why principals establish governance mechanisms. However, the firm incurs costs when it uses one or more governance mechanisms. **Agency costs** are the sum of incentive costs, monitoring costs, enforcement costs, and individual financial losses incurred by principals because governance mechanisms cannot guarantee total compliance by the agent. If a firm is diversified, governance costs increase because it is more difficult to monitor what is going on inside the firm.[46]

In general, managerial interests may prevail when governance mechanisms are weak, as is exemplified by allowing managers a significant amount of autonomy to make strategic decisions. If, however, the board of directors controls managerial autonomy, or if other strong governance mechanisms are used, the firm's strategies should better reflect the interests of the shareholders. More recently, governance observers have been concerned about more egregious behavior beyond inefficient corporate strategy.

Due to fraudulent behavior such as that found in Enron and WorldCom, concerns regarding corporate governance has been increasing. In 2002, the U.S. Congress enacted the Sarbanes-Oxley (SOX) Act, which increased the intensity of corporate governance mechanisms as it was implemented in 2003 and 2004.[47] These governance changes and associated reactions are described in the Strategic Focus detailing the changes enacted by the SOX Act.

Sarbanes-Oxley Act Increases Governance Intensity

Firms in the United States are experiencing a significant trend to reform corporate governance practices. This reform movement has been driven by a series of corporate governance failures beginning in 2002 when stockholders from a large number of firms experienced fraud due to internal control failures or poor internal controls allowing unethical executives in firms such as Enron, WorldCom, Adelphia, and Tyco too much discretion. In response to this perceived crisis in governance, the U.S. Congress enacted the 2002 Sarbanes-Oxley Act.

This act extended the regulatory powers of the U.S. Securities and Exchange Commission (SEC) regarding corporate governance procedures. The SEC was born after another failure, the 1929 collapse of the U.S. stock market. In particular, the nascent SEC fostered the introduction of independent outside auditors to verify that firms' financial statements were accurate. Furthermore, public companies had to submit their quarterly and annual financial statements to the SEC. This system worked well until the likes of Enron and WorldCom surmounted the principal SEC safeguard, the independent assessment of financial statements by external auditors.

As forensic accountants examined Enron's and WorldCom's processes, they found that Arthur Andersen, Enron's external auditor, was co-opted into these fraudulent schemes primarily because Andersen had a significant consulting services business that had nothing to do with external auditing of Enron. The amount of consulting services did not allow its auditing service to act independently from the consulting business. If they had been independent, Arthur Andersen would probably have survived. However, when similarities to the Enron case were found at WorldCom, another external auditing client, and it became known that Arthur Andersen had similar consulting service business with WorldCom, Arthur Andersen lost too much credibility and ultimately was liquidated due to its significant lapses in ethics.

The bankruptcy of Enron took place in 2001. And the SOX Act was implemented in 2002 with the effects coming into play in 2003 and especially 2004. The Sarbanes-Oxley Act has "introduced a new era of corporate governance, including requirements for auditor independence, the restriction of firms engaging in accounting from both auditing and consulting services, independence of firms' board committees, management assessment of internal controls and personal certification of financial reports by firms' CEOs and CFOs." This act passed the Senate with a vote of 99 to zero. Since its enactment, however, there have been a number of arguments over some controversial guidelines.

Foremost among the controversies has been the expense large firms have incurred to come into compliance with the law. According to the American Institute of Certified Public Accountants, internal auditing costs have increased by 32 percent because of SOX. The Financial Executive Institute has calculated the average firm's costs for compliance to be $3.14 million. Some private firms have decided to remain

The Securities and Exchange Commission (SEC) audits companies to ensure the accuracy of their financial statements.

J. CARRIER/BLOOMBERG NEWS/LANDOV

private in order to avoid compliance, and a number of public companies have announced their intention to privatize; one report suggests a 30 percent increase in privatization since the enactment of Sarbanes-Oxley. Furthermore, some foreign firms have decided to delist on U.S. exchanges in order to avoid the costs of Sarbanes-Oxley.

A number of states—including California, Colorado, Illinois, Kentucky, Maryland, Montana, New Jersey, New Mexico, New York, Ohio, Pennsylvania, Massachusetts, and Texas—have adopted or are considering adopting Sarbanes-Oxley-like provisions that would also apply to private companies within their state boundaries. The laws often reflect the principles found in the SOX Act, including "transparency, independence and accountability." As such, the implementation of the SOX Act indicates an increased monitoring intensity for firm stakeholders involved in corporate governance.

Sources: D. R. Dalton & C. M. Dalton, 2005, Sarbanes-Oxley legislation and the private company: If not a marriage, then certainly an engagement, *Journal of Business Strategy,* 26(2): 7–8; W. J. Hass & S. G. Pryor, IV, 2005, The board's role in corporate renewal, *Journal of Private Equity,* 8(2): 12; D. Henry, A. Borrus, L. Lavelle, D. Brady, M. Arndt, & J. Weber, 2005, Death, taxes and Sarbanes-Oxley? Executives may be frustrated with the law's burdens, but corporate performance is here to stay, *Business Week,* January 17, 28–31; R. Marden & R. Edwards, 2005, The Sarbanes-Oxley 'axe,' *The CPA Journal,* April, 6–10; J. McTague, 2005, Corporate tangle, *Barron's,* April 4, 19; B. McLean & P. Elkind, 2003, *The Smartest Guy in the Room: The Amazing Rise and Scandalous Fall of Enron,* New York: Penguin Group.

Research suggests that more intensive application of governance mechanisms may produce significant changes in strategies. William Donaldson, then chairman of the SEC, argued that the collapse of investor confidence after the Enron and other scandals suggests that corporate America needs more intense governance in order for continued investment in the stock market to facilitate growth. Donaldson has said, "The short-term costs of compliance, particularly efforts to improve internal control and corporate governance over financial reporting, should be viewed as an investment. In the long term, the reforms realized from SOX will result in more sound corporate practices and more reliable financial reporting."[48]

However, others argue that the indirect costs of SOX—the impact on strategy formulation and implementation—are even more influential.[49] That is, because of more intense governance, firms may make a lot fewer risky decisions and thus decrease potential shareholder wealth significantly. Stephen Odland, the new CEO of Office Depot, is a supporter of the law but has said, "If we frighten managers to the point that they're not willing to risk anything we could damage our economy and our ability to compete in the world."[50] Jack Lambeth, vice president of information technology and leading the SOX-compliant effort at Blackboard, an education-technology company, will spend about $1.5 million implementing SOX by the end of 2005. Blackboard went public in 2004 and earned $5.6 million in its initial year. Accordingly, the money spent on implementing SOX is costing the company a significant portion of its earnings power. Lambeth said, "A dollar spent making sure we are SOX-compliant could have been spent increasing our sales territory or investing in our Web-hosting infrastructure." As a result, he suggests, SOX will force many start-up companies to consider selling out to a large company rather than going public, as for example Ask Jeeves was acquired by IAC (see the Opening Case).

This could reduce the number of venture capital investments and ultimately reduce the number of IPOs. One observer noted: "Many boards have been vigilant in their oversight role in regard to corporate value. However, CEOs and directors have been distracted from more important strategic issues in order to meet detailed compliance deadlines provided by the Sarbanes-Oxley Act. Boards need to refocus on three critical strategic processes: strategic planning, risk assessment and renewal which includes succession planning."[51]

Next, we explain the effects of different governance mechanisms on the decisions managers make about the choice and the use of the firm's strategies.

Ownership Concentration

Both the number of large-block shareholders and the total percentage of shares they own define **ownership concentration. Large-block shareholders** typically own at least 5 percent of a corporation's issued shares. Ownership concentration as a governance mechanism has received considerable interest because large-block shareholders are increasingly active in their demands that corporations adopt effective governance mechanisms to control managerial decisions.[52]

In general, diffuse ownership (a large number of shareholders with small holdings and few, if any, large-block shareholders) produces weak monitoring of managers' decisions. Among other problems, diffuse ownership makes it difficult for owners to effectively coordinate their actions. Diversification of the firm's product lines beyond the shareholders' optimum level can result from ineffective monitoring of managers' decisions. Higher levels of monitoring could encourage managers to avoid strategic decisions that harm shareholder value. In fact, research evidence shows that ownership concentration is associated with lower levels of firm product diversification.[53] Thus, with high degrees of ownership concentration, the probability is greater that managers' strategic decisions will be intended to maximize shareholder value.

As noted, such concentration of ownership has an influence on strategies and firm value. Interestingly, research in Spain showed a curvilinear relationship between shareholder concentration and firm value. At moderate levels of shareholder concentration, firm value increased; at high levels of concentration, firm value decreased for shareholders, especially minority shareholders.[54] When large shareholders have a high degree of wealth, they have power relative to minority shareholders in extracting wealth from the firm, especially when they are in managerial positions. The importance of boards of directors in mitigating expropriation of minority shareholder value has been found in the United States relative to strong family ownership who have incentives to appropriate shareholder wealth.[55] Such expropriation is often found in countries such as Korea where minority shareholder rights are not as protected as they are in the United States.[56] However, in the United States much of this concentration has come from increasing equity ownership by institutional investors.

The Growing Influence of Institutional Owners

A classic work published in the 1930s argued that the "modern" corporation had become characterized by a separation of ownership and control.[57] This change occurred primarily because growth prevented founders-owners from maintaining their dual positions in their increasingly complex companies. More recently, another shift has occurred: Ownership of many modern corporations is now concentrated in the hands of institutional investors rather than individual shareholders.[58]

Rob Feckner (right) of the California Employees Retirement System (CALpers), which provides public employees with retirement and health coverage.

Institutional owners are financial institutions such as stock mutual funds and pension funds that control large-block shareholder positions. Because of their prominent ownership positions, institutional owners, as large-block shareholders, are a powerful governance mechanism. Institutions of these types now own more than 50 percent of the stock in large U.S. corporations, and of the top 1,000 corporations, they own, on average, 56 percent of the stock. Pension funds alone control at least one-half of corporate equity.[59]

These ownership percentages suggest that as investors, institutional owners have both the size and the incentive to discipline ineffective top-level managers and can significantly influence a firm's choice of strategies and overall strategic decisions.[60] Research evidence indicates that institutional and other large-block shareholders are becoming more active in their efforts to influence a corporation's strategic decisions. Initially, these shareholder activists and institutional investors concentrated on the performance and accountability of CEOs and contributed to the ouster of a number of them. They are now targeting what they believe are ineffective boards of directors.[61]

For example, CalPERS provides retirement and health coverage to over 1.3 million current and retired public employees. As the largest public employee pension fund in the United States, CalPERS is generally thought to act aggressively to promote governance decisions and actions that it believes will enhance shareholder value in companies in which it invests.[62] The largest institutional investor, TIAA-CREF, has taken actions similar to those of CalPERS, but with a less publicly aggressive stance. To date, research suggests that these institutions' activism may not have a direct effect on firm performance, but that its influence may be indirect through its effects on important strategic decisions, such as those concerned with international diversification and innovation.[63] With the increased intensity of governance associated with the passage of the SOX Act, institutional investors as well as other groups have been emboldened in their activism.

Board of Directors

Typically, shareholders monitor the managerial decisions and actions of a firm through the board of directors. Shareholders elect members to their firm's board. Those who are elected are expected to oversee managers and to ensure that the corporation is operated in ways that will maximize its shareholders' wealth. Even with large institutional investors having major equity ownership in U.S. firms, diffuse ownership continues to exist in most firms, which means that in large corporations, monitoring and control of managers by individual shareholders is limited. Furthermore, large financial institutions, such as banks, are prevented from directly owning stock in firms and from having representatives on companies' boards of directors, although this is not the case in Europe and elsewhere.[64] These conditions highlight the importance of the board of directors for corporate governance. Unfortunately, over time, boards of directors have not been highly effective in monitoring and controlling top management's actions.[65] As noted in the Strategic Focus, boards are experiencing increasing pressure from shareholders, lawmakers, and regulators to become more forceful in their oversight role and thereby forestall inappropriate actions by top executives. If changes are instituted as explained in the Strategic Focus, boards will have even more power to influence the actions of managers and the directions of their companies. Furthermore, boards not only serve a monitoring role, but they also provide resources to firms. These resources include their personal knowledge and expertise as well as their access to resources of other firms through their external contacts and relationships.[66]

The **board of directors** is a group of elected individuals whose primary responsibility is to act in the owners' interests by formally monitoring and controlling the corporation's top-level executives.[67] Boards have the power to direct the affairs of the organization, punish and reward managers, and protect shareholders' rights and interests.[68] Thus, an appropriately structured and effective board of directors protects owners from managerial opportunism such as that found in Enron and WorldCom. Board members are seen as stewards of their company's resources, and the way they carry out these responsibilities affects the society in which their firm operates.[69]

Generally, board members (often called directors) are classified into one of three groups (see Table 10.1). *Insiders* are active top-level managers in the corporation who are elected to the board because they are a source of information about the firm's day-to-day operations.[70] *Related outsiders* have some relationship with the firm, contractual or otherwise, that may create questions about their independence, but these individuals are not involved with the corporation's day-to-day activities. *Outsiders* provide independent counsel to the firm and may hold top-level managerial positions in other companies or may have been elected to the board prior to the beginning of the current CEO's tenure.[71]

Historically boards of directors were primarily dominated by inside managers. A widely accepted view is that a board with a significant percentage of its membership drawn from the firm's top executives tends to provide relatively weak monitoring and control of managerial decisions.[72] Managers have been suspected of using their power to

Classifications of Boards of Directors' Members
TABLE 10.1

Insiders
- The firm's CEO and other top-level managers

Related outsiders
- Individuals not involved with the firm's day-to-day operations, but who have a relationship with the company

Outsiders
- Individuals who are independent of the firm in terms of day-to-day operations and other relationships

select and compensate directors and exploiting their personal ties with them. In response to the Securities and Exchange Commission's proposal to require audit committees to be made up of outside directors, in 1984 the New York Stock Exchange, possibly to preempt formal legislation, implemented an audit committee rule requiring outside directors to head the audit committee. Subsequently, other rules required important committees such as the compensation committee and the nomination committees to be headed by independent outside directors.[73] These requirements were instituted after the Sarbanes-Oxley Act was passed, and policies of the New York Stock Exchange as well as the American Exchange now require companies to maintain boards of directors that are composed of a majority of outside independent directors and to maintain full independent audit committees. Thus one can clearly see that corporate governance is becoming more intense through the board of directors mechanism.

Critics advocate reforms to ensure that independent outside directors represent a significant majority of the total membership of a board.[74] Alternatively, others argue that having outside directors is not enough to resolve the problems; it depends on the power of the CEO. In some cases, the CEO is powerful enough to reduce the effectiveness of outside board members.[75] The Strategic Focus proposes that boards need to reduce the power of the CEO by separating the chairperson of the board's role and the CEO's role on the board so that the same person does not hold both positions.[76]

From the Strategic Focus, it is clear that the increased emphasis on separating the roles of the CEO and the chairperson provides more power and independence to the independent outside directors relative to the CEOs. This should lead to more CEO dismissals when things go wrong such as when Carly Fiorina was fired from Hewlett-Packard (see the Opening Case in Chapter 12). Because of recent problems associated with egregious use of CEO power, CEOs who have recently been appointed by boards must meet tougher standards. As a result, often the selection process takes longer. At Computer Associates, John Swainson, replacing a CEO who was accused of unethical behavior, was scrutinized for three months before being appointed to the position: "[E]very aspect of my personal life was investigated before I took the job."[77] Most companies no longer prohibit consensual romances between employees, but because of high ethical standards at Boeing, especially due to ethical concerns associated with government contracting, Harry Stonecipher lost his CEO position at Boeing because of an affair with a female employee. Although the Sarbanes-Oxley implementation has created stronger scrutiny in regard to finances, the legislation and concern in the media has heightened scrutiny on a range of candidate traits beyond the leader's actual ability to run the company's businesses.[78]

Alternatively, having a large number of outside board members can also create some problems. Outsiders do not have contact with the firm's day-to-day operations and typically do not have easy access to the level of information about managers and their skills that is required to effectively evaluate managerial decisions and initiatives.[79] Outsiders can, however, obtain valuable information through frequent interactions with inside board members, during board meetings and otherwise. Insiders possess such information by virtue of their organizational positions. Thus, boards with a critical mass of insiders typically are better informed about intended strategic initiatives, the reasons for the initiatives, and the outcomes expected from them.[80] Without this type of information, outsider-dominated boards may emphasize the use of financial, as opposed to strategic, controls to gather performance information to evaluate managers' and business units' performances. A virtually exclusive reliance on financial evaluations shifts risk to top-level managers, who, in turn, may make decisions to maximize their interests and reduce their employment risk. Reductions in R&D investments, additional diversification of the firm, and the pursuit of greater levels of compensation are some of the results of managers' actions to achieve financial goals set by outsider-dominated boards.[81]

Governing the CEO

Many believe that despite the increased governance and power of independent outside directors populating boards of directors, boardrooms are still dominated by CEOs. A case in point is insurance company AIG, whose CEO, Maurice Greenberg, was dramatically ousted even though he had dominated this corporation and, in fact, the global insurance industry for decades. Similarly, CEO Philip Purcell fought and lost an internal campaign against a mutiny of former managers who were ousted at investment bank Morgan Stanley. These CEOs were accustomed to getting their way. Enron, WorldCom, Tyco, and Adelphia provide further examples of the power of the top executives overcoming internal controls and taking fraudulent actions. Internal auditors exist within a power structure that creates the opportunity for fraud, especially when one person has all the power through being both chairperson of the board and CEO of the corporation. Thus, there is a significant push currently to create a way to overcome this power by separating the roles of chairperson of the board and CEO.

In the pharmaceutical industry, for example, a diverse mixture of religious-based organizations, corporate governance groups, and disgruntled shareholders have joined together to pressure large firms to split the chairperson and CEO positions. Wyeth, Eli Lilly, Abbott Laboratories, Merck, Pfizer, and Bristol-Myers Squibb companies have been urged to name an independent outside director as chairperson of the board and have received proposals that require a shareholder vote. Some of these proposals have come very close to passing. Almost universally these companies have responded that the proposals were not in the best interest of the company because, as Bristol-Myers Squibb put it, having the same person serve as chairperson and CEO is important "to provide unified leadership and direction." The Interfaith Center on Corporate Responsibility (ICCR) met with two other firms, Johnson & Johnson and Schering-Plough. These firms did not receive a proxy vote solicitation, but instead were lobbied to implement split roles as well as ethics policies. Instead of splitting the roles, the firms agreed to strong ethical policy statements and to strongly consider providing lifesaving medicines for applications in developing countries where the populace cannot afford to pay for newly discovered treatments. Institutional Shareholder Services, a powerful association of institutional investors, suggested that its members vote on the proxies in favor of splitting the two jobs to improve corporate governance. Although unsuccessful on this point, the firms have been much more sensitive to governance activist concerns.

The SEC has gone further in the mutual fund industry by requiring mutual fund firms to have split roles because independent directors on boards colluded in ways that reduced shareholder returns at mutual funds. Thus, this was being forced on mutual funds in order to do away with cliquish behavior that has been evidenced in the past.

The unification of power where the CEO concurrently serves as board chairperson might be useful especially when a firm is in crisis and needs to have a consistent message. In regard to governance oversight and evaluation of strategic proposals, however, it's rather like the fox guarding the hen house. In other words, the chairperson of the board has effective control of the oversight of corporate management, which likely will lead to continued governance problems.

An alternative proposal is to have a lead independent outside director (LID) chosen from the ranks of the outside independent board members. The LID serves as a liaison between corporate management and the outside board members. Thus, the outside directors no longer have direct contact with the CEO if an evaluation of the CEO's performance is required. This allows for more arm's-length evaluation of the CEO and also protects the CEO from being unnecessarily distracted, especially when only routine matters are brought up. Of course, the effectiveness of any position rests upon the ability and character of the person in the position. No amount of structural independence can overcome a desire or intent to be fraudulent and escape accountability.

Either of these approaches, splitting the roles or creating the role of the LID, increases the scrutiny of the CEO and the strategic decisions that he or she makes. Thus, either approach intensifies the governance associated with board of director monitoring.

Sources: 2005, Leaders: Bossing the bosses; corporate governance in America, *The Economist,* April 9, 15; J. Burnes, 2005, Board chairman rule is challenged, *Wall Street Journal,* April 18, C15; A. Dale, 2005, Declaration of independence issued, *Wall Street Journal,* January 20, C15; C. M. Dalton & D. R. Dalton, 2005, Corporate governance: Follow the leader, *Journal of Business Strategy,* 26(1): 8–9; P. Davies, 2005, Drug firms urged to split top jobs, *Wall Street Journal,* April 22, C3; M. Karnitschnig, 2005, Too many chiefs at Siemens? German consensus culture may hamper forward-looking CEO, *Wall Street Journal,* January 20, A12; J. W. Lorsch & A. Zelleke, 2005, Should the CEO be the Chairman, *MIT Sloan Management Review,* 46(2): 71–74; A. T. Palmer, 2005, Should the top roles be split? *Chief Executive,* May, 16–18; S. T. Petra, 2005, Do outside independent directors strengthen corporate boards? *Corporate Governance,* 5(1): 55–64.

Enhancing the Effectiveness of the Board of Directors

Because of the importance of boards of directors in corporate governance and as a result of increased scrutiny from shareholders—in particular, large institutional investors—the performances of individual board members and of entire boards are being evaluated more formally and with greater intensity.[82] Given the demand for greater accountability and improved performance, many boards have initiated voluntary changes. Among these changes are (1) increases in the diversity of the backgrounds of board members (for example, a greater number of directors from public service, academic, and scientific settings; a greater percentage of ethnic minorities and women; and members from different countries on boards of U.S. firms), (2) the strengthening of internal management and accounting control systems, and (3) the establishment and consistent use of formal processes to evaluate the board's performance.[83] Additional changes include (4) the creation of a "lead director" role that has strong powers with regard to the board agenda and oversight of nonmanagement board member activities, as suggested in the Strategic Focus, and (5) modification of the compensation of directors, especially reducing or eliminating stock options as a part of the package.

Boards have become more involved in the strategic decision-making process, so they must work collaboratively. Some argue that improving the processes used by boards to make decisions and monitor managers and firm outcomes is the key to increasing board effectiveness.[84] Moreover, because of the increased pressure from owners and the potential conflict among board members, procedures are necessary to help boards function effectively in facilitating the strategic decision-making process.[85]

Increasingly, outside directors are being required to own significant equity stakes as a prerequisite to holding a board seat. In fact, some research suggests that firms perform better if outside directors have such a stake.[86] Other research suggests that diverse boards help firms make more effective strategic decisions and perform better over time.[87] One activist concludes that boards need three foundational characteristics to be effective: director stock ownership, executive meetings to discuss important strategic issues, and a serious nominating committee that truly controls the nomination process to strongly influence the selection of new board members.[88] Once on the job, the outside director needs to seek effectiveness through three linked sets of behaviors that suggest the non-executive director should be "engaged but non-executive" (not seek to micro manage), "challenging but supportive" (help improve decisions and then support the decision made), and "independent but involved" (make independent evaluation of important decisions and be involved in the strategic decision processes of the board).[89]

Executive Compensation

As the Opening Case illustrates, the compensation of top-level managers, and especially of CEOs, generates a great deal of interest and strongly held opinions. One reason for this widespread interest can be traced to a natural curiosity about extremes and excesses. Another stems from a more substantive view, that CEO pay is tied in an indirect but tangible way to the fundamental governance processes in large corporations: Who has power? What are the bases of power? How and when do owners and managers exert their relative preferences? How vigilant are boards? Who is taking advantage of whom?[90]

Executive compensation is a governance mechanism that seeks to align the interests of managers and owners through salaries, bonuses, and long-term incentive compensation, such as stock awards and options.[91] As noted in the Opening Case, long-term incentive plans have become a critical part of compensation packages in U.S. firms. The use of longer-term pay helps firms cope with or avoid potential agency problems by linking managerial wealth to the wealth of common shareholders.[92] Because of this, the stock market generally reacts positively to the introduction of a long-range incentive plan for top executives.[93]

Sometimes the use of a long-term incentive plan prevents major stockholders (e.g., institutional investors) from pressing for changes in the composition of the board of directors, because they assume that the long-term incentives will ensure that top executives will act in shareholders' best interests. Alternatively, stockholders largely assume that top-executive pay and the performance of a firm are more closely aligned when firms have boards that are dominated by outside members.[94]

However, sometimes the persistence of institutional investors pays off in regard to questioning actions by boards regarding pay packages. This is certainly the case at Hollinger International, Inc. where the persistent questions of Christopher H. Browne, a managing director of Tweedy, Browne Company, who is Hollinger's largest shareholder, lead to the CEO's dismissal. Conrad Black, Hollinger's then CEO, and other managers were overpaid for a number of years. Brown simply asked the important question as to the background of the pay being provided to Black and others. A report sponsored by the board found that over $400 million between 1997 and 2003 had been transferred to Hollinger's key managers, including Black. This amounted to approximately 95 percent of the company's entire net income during this period. Ultimately, key managers lost their positions and the firm was broken up into pieces; the collective share price went from $7.70 in March 2003 to around $17.00 in late 2004.[95]

Effectively using executive compensation as a governance mechanism is particularly challenging to firms implementing international strategies. For example, the interests of owners of multinational corporations may be best served when there is less uniformity among the firm's foreign subsidiaries' compensation plans.[96] Developing an array of unique compensation plans requires additional monitoring and increases the firm's potential agency costs. Importantly, levels of pay vary by regions of the world. For example, managerial pay is highest in the United States and much lower in Asia. Compensation is lower in India partly because many of the largest firms have strong family ownership and control.[97] As corporations acquire firms in other countries, the managerial compensation puzzle becomes more complex and may cause additional executive turnover.[98]

A Complicated Governance Mechanism

Executive compensation—especially long-term incentive compensation—is complicated for several reasons. First, the strategic decisions made by top-level managers are typically complex and nonroutine, so direct supervision of executives is inappropriate for judging the quality of their decisions. The result is a tendency to link the compensation of top-level managers to measurable outcomes, such as the firm's financial performance. Second, an executive's decision often affects a firm's financial outcomes over an extended period, making it difficult to assess the effect of current decisions on the corporation's performance. In fact, strategic decisions are more likely to have long-term, rather than short-term, effects on a company's strategic outcomes. Third, a number of other factors affect a firm's performance besides top-level managerial decisions and behavior. Unpredictable economic, social, or legal changes (see Chapter 2) make it difficult to discern the effects of strategic decisions. Thus, although performance-based compensation may provide incentives to top management teams to make decisions that best serve shareholders' interests,[99] such compensation plans alone are imperfect in their ability to monitor and control managers.[100] Still, incentive compensation represent a significant portion of many executives' total pay.

Although incentive compensation plans may increase the value of a firm in line with shareholder expectations, such plans are subject to managerial manipulation. For instance, as firms are being forced to expense stock options, *Forbes* magazine has reported that many firms are using "creative accounting" to reduce the expense associated with these options by changing the "expectations of volatility." The idea is that the value of options increases as the stock price varies. If the stock price does not vary as much, then stock options are valued lower. This creates a lower expense for firms using options simply by changing the accounting formula.[101]

Additionally, annual bonuses may provide incentives to pursue short-run objectives at the expense of the firm's long-term interests. Supporting this conclusion, some research has found that bonuses based on annual performance were negatively related to investments in R&D when the firm was highly diversified, which may affect the firm's long-term strategic competitiveness.[102] However, research has found a positive relationship between investments in R&D and long-term compensation in non-family firms.[103]

Although long-term, performance-based incentives may reduce the temptation to underinvest in the short run, they increase executive exposure to risks associated with uncontrollable events, such as market fluctuations and industry decline. The longer term the focus of incentive compensation, the greater are the long-term risks borne by top-level managers. Also, because long-term incentives tie a manager's overall wealth to the firm in a way that is inflexible, such incentives and ownership may not be valued as highly by a manager as by outside investors who have the opportunity to diversify their wealth in a number of other financial investments.[104] Thus, firms may have to overcompensate managers using long-term incentives, as the next section suggests.

The Effectiveness of Executive Compensation

The primary reason for compensating executives in stock is that the practice affords them an incentive to keep the stock price high and hence aligns managers' interests with shareholders' interests. However, there may be some unintended consequences. Managers who own more than 1 percent of their firm's stock may be less likely to be forced out of their jobs, even when the firm is performing poorly.[105] Furthermore, a review of the research suggests that over time, firm size has accounted for more than 50 percent of the variance in total CEO pay, while firm performance has accounted for less than 5 percent of the variance.[106] Thus, the effectiveness of pay plans as a governance mechanism is suspect.

While some stock option–based compensation plans are well designed with option strike prices substantially higher than current stock prices, too many have been designed simply to give executives more wealth that will not immediately show up on the balance sheet. Research of stock option repricing where the strike price value of the option has been lowered from its original position suggests that action is taken more frequently in high-risk situations.[107] However, repricing also happens when firm performance was poor, to restore the incentive effect for the option. Evidence also suggests that politics are often involved.[108] Additionally, research has found that repricing stock options does not appear to be a function of management entrenchment or ineffective governance. These firms often have had sudden and negative changes to their growth and profitability. They also frequently lose their top managers.[109] Interestingly, institutional investors prefer compensation schemes that link pay with performance, including the use of stock options.[110] Again, this evidence shows that no internal governance mechanism is perfect.

While stock options became highly popular as a means of compensating top executives and linking pay with performance, they also have become controversial of late.[111] It seems that option awards became a means of providing large compensation packages, and the options awarded did not relate to the firm's performance, particularly when boards showed a propensity to reprice options at a lower strike price when stock prices fell precipitously.[112] Because of the large number of options granted in recent years and the increasingly common practice of repricing them, this was one of the reasons for the pressure to expense options. As noted in the Opening Case, this action is quite costly to many firms' stated profits and appears to have dampened the excessive use of options.

Market for Corporate Control

The **market for corporate control** is an external governance mechanism that becomes active when a firm's internal controls fail.[113] The market for corporate control is composed of individuals and firms that buy ownership positions in or take over potentially undervalued corporations so they can form new divisions in established diversified companies or merge two previously separate firms. Because the undervalued firm's executives are assumed to be responsible for formulating and implementing the strategy that led to poor performance, they are usually replaced. Thus, when the market for corporate control operates effectively, it ensures that managers who are ineffective or act opportunistically are disciplined.[114]

The market for corporate control is often viewed as a "court of last resort."[115] This suggests that the takeover market as a source of external discipline is used only when internal governance mechanisms are relatively weak and have proven to be ineffective. Alternatively, other research suggests that the rationale for takeovers as a corporate governance strategy is not as strong as the rationale for takeovers as an ownership investment in target candidates where the firm is performing well and does not need discipline.[116] Additionally, a study of active corporate raiders in the 1980s showed that takeover attempts often were focused on above-average performance firms in an industry.[117] Taken together, this research suggests that takeover targets are not always low performers with weak governance. As such, this research suggests that the market for corporate control may not be as efficient as a governance device as theory suggests. At

ASSOCIATED PRESS, AP

Despite attracting the attention of regulatory authorities, Oracle eventually took over PeopleSoft, whose CEO had to step down.

the very least, internal governance controls would be much more precise relative to this external control mechanism.

Although the market for corporate control may be a blunt instrument as far as corporate governance is concerned, the takeover market has continued to be very active. In fact, research suggests that more intense governance environment may have fostered an increasingly active takeover market. Because institutional investors have more concentrated ownership, they may be interested in firms that are targeted for acquisition. Target firms earn a substantial premium over the acquiring firm. At the same time, managers who have ownership positions or stock options are likely to gain in making a transaction with an acquiring firm. There is even more evidence that this may be the case given the increasing number of firms that have golden parachutes which allow up to three years of additional compensation plus other incentives if a firm is taken over. These compensation contracts reduce the risk for managers if a firm is taken over. In fact, research suggests that there was a friendlier environment in the 1990s for takeovers due to these ownership and governance arrangements.[118] Although the 1980s had more defenses put up against hostile takeovers, the current environment has been much more friendly, most likely due to the increased intensity of the governance devices on both the buyer (institutional investor) side as well as the corporate management side. The idea that CEOs who have substantial ownership or stock options in the target firm do well in the friendly transactions in the 1990s and into the 21st century is also supported by research.[119]

The market for corporate control governance mechanism should be triggered by a firm's poor performance relative to industry competitors. A firm's poor performance, often demonstrated by the firm's earning below-average returns, is an indicator that internal governance mechanisms have failed; that is, their use did not result in managerial decisions that maximized shareholder value. This market has been active for some time. As noted in Chapter 7, the decade of the 1990s produced the largest number and value of mergers and acquisitions. The major reduction in the stock market resulted in a significant drop in acquisition activity in the first part of the 21st century. However, the number of mergers and acquisitions began to increase and the market for corporate control has become increasingly international, with over 40 percent of the merger and acquisition activity involving two firms from different countries.[120]

While some acquisition attempts are intended to obtain resources important to the acquiring firm, most of the *hostile* takeover attempts are due to the target firm's poor performance.[121] Therefore, target firm managers and members of the boards of directors are highly sensitive about hostile takeover bids. It frequently means that they have not done an effective job in managing the company. If they accept the offer, they are likely to lose their jobs; the acquiring firm will insert its own management. If they reject the offer and fend off the takeover attempt, they must improve the performance of the firm or risk losing their jobs as well.[122]

For example, Oracle made a hostile bid for PeopleSoft; PeopleSoft rejected the offer, but Oracle remained in the takeover battle. The takeover attempt invited considerable attention from regulatory authorities in both the United States and Europe. Ultimately, the takeover was consummated and the CEO of PeopleSoft was dismissed before the two firms were integrated.[123]

Managerial Defense Tactics

Hostile takeovers are the major activity in the market for corporate control governance mechanism. Not all hostile takeovers are prompted by poorly performing targets, and firms targeted for hostile takeovers may use multiple defense tactics to fend off the takeover attempt. Historically, the increased use of the market for corporate control has enhanced the sophistication and variety of managerial defense tactics that are used to reduce the influence of this governance mechanism. The market for corporate control tends to increase risk for managers. As a result, managerial pay is often augmented indirectly through golden parachutes (wherein, as mentioned, a CEO can receive up to three years' salary if his or her firm is taken over). Golden parachutes, similar to most other defense tactics, are controversial.

Among other outcomes, takeover defenses increase the costs of mounting a takeover, causing the incumbent management to become entrenched, while reducing the chances of introducing a new management team.[124] For example, though People-Soft's management ultimately succumbed to a takeover by Oracle, the company's takeover defense strategy allowed it to hold Oracle at bay for roughly a year and a half. As one observer noted, "PeopleSoft had a number of defense mechanisms, including a board with staggered terms. In addition, its board was authorized to increase or decrease its own size without shareholder approval, and its directors could only be removed for cause and only by a vote of 66.67 percent of entitled voters."[125] In addition, PeopleSoft had a poison pill in place "entitling holders of its common stock to buy any acquirer's shares at a very cheap price in the event of a hostile takeover. That provision forced Oracle to take it to court in an effort to avoid the hefty dilution that might be triggered by the poison pill."[126]

Table 10.2 lists a number of takeover defense strategies. Some defense tactics necessitate only changes in the financial structure of the firm, such as repurchasing shares of the firm's outstanding stock.[127] Some tactics (e.g., reincorporation of the firm in another state) require shareholder approval, but the greenmail tactic, wherein money is used to repurchase stock from a corporate raider to avoid the takeover of the firm, does not. These defense tactics are controversial, and the research on their effects is inconclusive. Alternatively, most institutional investors oppose the use of defense tactics. TIAA-CREF and CalPERS have taken actions to have several firms' poison pills eliminated. Many institutional investors have also been opposed to severance packages (golden parachutes), and the opposition is growing significantly in Europe as well.[128] But there can be advantages to severance packages because they may encourage executives to accept takeover bids that are attractive to shareholders.[129] Also, as in the case of Carly Fiorina at HP, a severance package may encourage a CEO doing a poor job to depart.[130]

A potential problem with the market for corporate control is that it may not be totally efficient. A study of several of the most active corporate raiders in the 1980s showed that approximately 50 percent of their takeover attempts targeted firms with above-average performance in their industry—corporations that were neither undervalued nor poorly managed.[131] The targeting of high-performance businesses may lead to acquisitions at premium prices and to decisions by managers of the targeted firm to establish what may prove to be costly takeover defense tactics to protect their corporate positions.[132]

Although the market for corporate control lacks the precision of internal governance mechanisms, the fear of acquisition and influence by corporate raiders is an effective constraint on the managerial-growth motive. The market for corporate control has been responsible for significant changes in many firms' strategies and, when used appropriately, has served shareholders' interests. But this market and other means of corporate governance vary by region of the world and by country. Accordingly, we next address the topic of international corporate governance.

TABLE 10.2

Defense strategy	Category	Popularity among firms	Effectiveness as a defense	Stockholder wealth effects
Poison pill Preferred stock in the merged firm offered to shareholders at a highly attractive rate of exchange.	Preventive	High	High	Positive
Corporate charter amendment An amendment to stagger the elections of members to the board of directors of the attacked firm so that all are not elected during the same year, which prevents a bidder from installing a completely new board in the same year.	Preventive	Medium	Very low	Negative
Golden parachute Lump-sum payments of cash that are distributed to a select group of senior executives when the firm is acquired in a takeover bid.	Preventive	Medium	Low	Negligible
Litigation Lawsuits that help a target company stall hostile attacks; areas may include antitrust, fraud, inadequate disclosure.	Reactive	Medium	Low	Positive
Greenmail The repurchase of shares of stock that have been acquired by the aggressor at a premium in exchange for an agreement that the aggressor will no longer target the company for takeover.	Reactive	Very low	Medium	Negative
Standstill agreement Contract between the parties in which the pursuer agrees not to acquire any more stock of the target firm for a specified period of time in exchange for the firm paying the pursuer a fee.	Reactive	Low	Low	Negative
Capital structure change Dilution of stock, making it more costly for a bidder to acquire; may include employee stock option plans (ESOPs), recapitalization, new debt, stock selling, share buybacks.	Reactive	Medium	Medium	Inconclusive

Source: J. A. Pearce II & R. B. Robinson, Jr., 2004, Hostile takeover defenses that maximize shareholder wealth, *Business Horizons*, 47(5): 15–24.

International Corporate Governance

Understanding the corporate governance structure of the United Kingdom and the United States is inadequate for a multinational firm in today's global economy.[133] While the stability associated with German and Japanese governance structures has historically been viewed as an asset, the governance systems in these is changing, just as it is in other parts of the world.[134] These changes are partly the result of multinational firms operating in many different countries and attempting to develop a more global governance system.[135] While the similarity is increasing, differences remain evident, and firms employing an international strategy must understand these differences in order to operate effectively in different international markets.[136]

Corporate Governance in Germany

In many private German firms, the owner and manager may still be the same individual. In these instances, there is no agency problem.[137] Even in publicly traded German corporations, there is often a dominant shareholder. Thus, the concentration of ownership is an important means of corporate governance in Germany, as it is in the United States.[138]

Historically, banks have been at the center of the German corporate governance structure, as is also the case in many other European countries, such as Italy and France. As lenders, banks become major shareholders when companies they financed earlier seek funding on the stock market or default on loans. Although the stakes are usually under 10 percent, the only legal limit on how much of a firm's stock banks can hold is that a single ownership position cannot exceed 15 percent of the bank's capital. Through their shareholdings, and by casting proxy votes for individual shareholders who retain their shares with the banks, three banks in particular—Deutsche, Dresdner, and Commerzbank—exercise significant power. Although shareholders can tell the banks how to vote their ownership position, they generally do not do so. A combination of their own holdings and their proxies results in majority positions for these three banks in many German companies. Those banks, along with others, monitor and control managers, both as lenders and as shareholders, by electing representatives to supervisory boards.

German firms with more than 2,000 employees are required to have a two-tiered board structure that places the responsibility for monitoring and controlling managerial (or supervisory) decisions and actions in the hands of a separate group.[139] While all the functions of direction and management are the responsibility of the management board (the Vorstand), appointment to the Vorstand is the responsibility of the supervisory tier (the Aufsichtsrat). Employees, union members, and shareholders appoint members to the Aufsichtsrat. Proponents of the German structure suggest that it helps prevent corporate wrongdoing and rash decisions by "dictatorial CEOs." However, critics maintain that it slows decision-making and often ties a CEO's hands. In Germany the power sharing may have gone too far because it includes representation from the local community as well as unions. Accordingly, the corporate governance framework in Germany has made it difficult to restructure companies as quickly as can be done in the United States when performance suffers.[140]

Because of the role of local government (through the board structure) and the power of banks in Germany's corporate governance structure, private shareholders rarely have major ownership positions in German firms. Large institutional investors, such as pension funds and insurance companies, are also relatively insignificant owners of corporate stock. Thus, at least historically, German executives generally have not been dedicated to the maximization of shareholder value that occurs in many countries.[141]

However, corporate governance in Germany is changing, at least partially, because of the increasing globalization of business. Many German firms are beginning to gravitate toward the U.S. system. Recent

The structure of German firms arguably helps prevent bad decisions by a CEO, but it can also slow the process of decision-making.

research suggests that the traditional system produced some agency costs because of a lack of external ownership power. Alternatively, firms with stronger external ownership power were less likely to undertake governance reforms. Firms that adopted governance reforms often divested poorly performing units and achieved higher levels of market performance.[142]

Corporate Governance in Japan

Attitudes toward corporate governance in Japan are affected by the concepts of obligation, family, and consensus.[143] In Japan, an obligation "may be to return a service for one rendered or it may derive from a more general relationship, for example, to one's family or old alumni, or one's company (or Ministry), or the country. This sense of particular obligation is common elsewhere but it feels stronger in Japan."[144] As part of a company family, individuals are members of a unit that envelops their lives; families command the attention and allegiance of parties throughout corporations. Moreover, a *keiretsu* (a group of firms tied together by cross-shareholdings) is more than an economic concept; it, too, is a family. Consensus, an important influence in Japanese corporate governance, calls for the expenditure of significant amounts of energy to win the hearts and minds of people whenever possible, as opposed to top executives issuing edicts.[145] Consensus is highly valued, even when it results in a slow and cumbersome decision-making process.

As in Germany, banks in Japan play an important role in financing and monitoring large public firms. The bank owning the largest share of stocks and the largest amount of debt—the main bank—has the closest relationship with the company's top executives. The main bank provides financial advice to the firm and also closely monitors managers. Thus, Japan has a bank-based financial and corporate governance structure, whereas the United States has a market-based financial and governance structure.[146]

Aside from lending money, a Japanese bank can hold up to 5 percent of a firm's total stock; a group of related financial institutions can hold up to 40 percent. In many cases, main-bank relationships are part of a horizontal keiretsu. A keiretsu firm usually owns less than 2 percent of any other member firm; however, each company typically has a stake of that size in every firm in the keiretsu. As a result, somewhere between 30 and 90 percent of a firm is owned by other members of the keiretsu. Thus, a keiretsu is a system of relationship investments.

As is the case in Germany, Japan's structure of corporate governance is changing. For example, because of Japanese banks' continuing development as economic organizations, their role in the monitoring and control of managerial behavior and firm outcomes is less significant than in the past.[147] The Asian economic crisis in the latter part of the 1990s made the governance problems in Japanese corporations apparent. The problems were readily evidenced in the large and once-powerful Mitsubishi keiretsu. Many of its core members lost substantial amounts of money in the late 1990s.[148]

Still another change in Japan's governance system has occurred in the market for corporate control, which was nonexistent in past years.[149] Japan experienced three recessions in the 1990s and is dealing with another early in the 21st century. As a whole, managers are unwilling to make the changes necessary to turn their companies around. As a result, many firms in Japan are performing poorly, but could, under the right guidance, improve their performance. For example, Sony Corporation was shaken by the appointment of Howard Stringer, originally from Wales in the United Kingdom, as the new CEO. It is likely that the appointment of a non-Japanese CEO would not have been possible without a set of strong independent outsiders on the board such as Carlos Ghosn, a Brazilian CEO who facilitated Nissan's return to profitability. Outside directors are increasing their influence. Cross-shareholding, which has largely prevented the market for corporate control from developing, has been reduced from 50 to 20 percent over the last decade.[150] As Japan's commercial legal code softens in regard to foreign ownership, foreign investment banks have been looking to buy Japanese domestic firms in order to enter the market, filling the vacuum left by lower cross-shareholding.[151]

Interestingly, research suggests that the Japanese stewardship-management approach, historically dominated by inside managers, produces greater investments in long-term R&D projects than does the more financially oriented system in the United States.[152] As the potential for a stronger takeover market increases, some Japanese firms are considering delisting and taking their firms private in order to maintain long-term "strategic flexibility."[153]

The increasing influence of outside directors resulted in the appointment of Howard Stringer as CEO of Sony Corporation.

Global Corporate Governance

The 21st-century competitive landscape is fostering the creation of a relatively uniform governance structure that will be used by firms throughout the world.[154] For example, as markets become more global and customer demands more similar, shareholders are becoming the focus of managers' efforts in an increasing number of companies in Korea and Taiwan.[155] Investors are becoming more and more active throughout the world, as evidenced by the growing shareholder outrage at severance packages given to executives in Europe.

Changes in governance are evident in many countries and are moving the governance models closer to that of the United States.[156] Firms in Europe, especially in France and the United Kingdom, are developing boards of directors with more independent members. Similar actions are occurring in Japan, where the boards are being reduced in size and foreign members added.

Even in transitional economies, such as those of China and Russia, changes in corporate governance are occurring.[157] However, changes are implemented more slowly in these economies. Chinese firms have found it helpful to use stock-based compensation plans, thereby providing an incentive for foreign companies to invest in China.[158] Because Russia has reduced controls on the economy and on business activity much faster than China has, the country needs more effective governance systems to control its managerial activities. In fact, research suggests that ownership concentration leads to lower performance in Russia, primarily because minority shareholder rights are not well protected through adequate governance controls.[159]

Governance Mechanisms and Ethical Behavior

The governance mechanisms described in this chapter are designed to ensure that the agents of the firm's owners—the corporation's top executives—make strategic decisions that best serve the interests of the entire group of stakeholders, as described in Chapter 1. In the United States, shareholders are recognized as a company's most significant stakeholder. Thus, governance mechanisms focus on the control of managerial decisions to ensure that shareholders' interests will be served, but product market stakeholders (e.g., customers, suppliers, and host communities) and organizational stakeholders

WorldCom is just one of the companies that has recently experienced a scandal due to the unethical behavior of employees.

(e.g., managerial and nonmanagerial employees) are important as well.[160] Therefore, at least the minimal interests or needs of all stakeholders must be satisfied through the firm's actions. Otherwise, dissatisfied stakeholders will withdraw their support from one firm and provide it to another (for example, customers will purchase products from a supplier offering an acceptable substitute).

The firm's strategic competitiveness is enhanced when its governance mechanisms take into consideration the interests of all stakeholders. Although the idea is subject to debate, some believe that ethically responsible companies design and use governance mechanisms that serve all stakeholders' interests. There is, however, a more critical relationship between ethical behavior and corporate governance mechanisms. The Enron disaster illustrates the devastating effect of poor ethical behavior not only on a firm's stakeholders, but also on other firms. This issue is being taken seriously in other countries such as Japan as well.[161]

In addition to Enron, scandals at WorldCom, HealthSouth, and Tyco show that all corporate owners are vulnerable to unethical behaviors by their employees, including top-level managers—the agents who have been hired to make decisions that are in shareholders' best interests. The decisions and actions of a corporation's board of directors can be an effective deterrent to these behaviors. In fact, some believe that the most effective boards participate actively to set boundaries for their firms' business ethics and values.[162] Once formulated, the board's expectations related to ethical decisions and actions of all of the firm's stakeholders must be clearly communicated to its top-level managers. Moreover, as shareholders' agents, these managers must understand that the board will hold them fully accountable for the development and support of an organizational culture that increases unethical decisions and behaviors. As explained in Chapter 12, CEOs can be positive role models for improved ethical behavior.

Only when the proper corporate governance is exercised can strategies be formulated and implemented that will help the firm achieve strategic competitiveness and earn above-average returns. As the discussion in this chapter suggests, corporate governance mechanisms are a vital, yet imperfect, part of firms' efforts to select and successfully use strategies.

SUMMARY

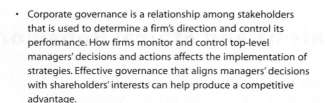

- Corporate governance is a relationship among stakeholders that is used to determine a firm's direction and control its performance. How firms monitor and control top-level managers' decisions and actions affects the implementation of strategies. Effective governance that aligns managers' decisions with shareholders' interests can help produce a competitive advantage.

- There are three internal governance mechanisms in the modern corporation—ownership concentration, the board of directors, and executive compensation. The market for corporate control is the single external governance mechanism influencing managers' decisions and the outcomes resulting from them.

- Ownership is separated from control in the modern corpora[te]. Owners (principals) hire managers (agents) to make decisio[ns] that maximize the firm's value. As risk-bearing specialists, owners diversify their risk by investing in multiple corporati[ons] with different risk profiles. As decision-making specialists, ow[n]ers expect their agents (the firm's top-level managers) to m[ake] decisions that will lead to maximization of the value of thei[r] firm. Thus, modern corporations are characterized by an age[ncy] relationship that is created when one party (the firm's owne[rs]) hires and pays another party (top-level managers) to use its decision-making skills.

- Separation of ownership and control creates an agency problem when an agent pursues goals that conflict with principals' goals. Principals establish and use governance mechanisms to control this problem.

- Ownership concentration is based on the number of large-block shareholders and the percentage of shares they own. With significant ownership percentages, such as those held by large mutual funds and pension funds, institutional investors often are able to influence top executives' strategic decisions and actions. Thus, unlike diffuse ownership, which tends to result in relatively weak monitoring and control of managerial decisions, concentrated ownership produces more active and effective monitoring. Institutional investors are an increasingly powerful force in corporate America and actively use their positions of concentrated ownership to force managers and boards of directors to make decisions that maximize a firm's value.

- In the United States and the United Kingdom, a firm's board of directors, composed of insiders, related outsiders, and outsiders, is a governance mechanism expected to represent shareholders' collective interests. The percentage of outside directors on many boards now exceeds the percentage of inside directors. Through the implementation of the SOX Act, outsiders are expected to be more independent of a firm's top-level managers compared with directors selected from inside the firm.

- Executive compensation is a highly visible and often criticized governance mechanism. Salary, bonuses, and long-term incentives are used to strengthen the alignment between managers' and shareholders' interests. A firm's board of directors is responsible for determining the effectiveness of the firm's executive compensation system. An effective system elicits managerial decisions that are in shareholders' best interests.

- In general, evidence suggests that shareholders and boards of directors have become more vigilant in their control of managerial decisions. Nonetheless, these mechanisms are insufficient to govern managerial behavior in many large companies. Therefore, the market for corporate control is an important governance mechanism. Although it, too, is imperfect, the market for corporate control has been effective in causing corporations to combat inefficient diversification and to implement more effective strategic decisions.

- Corporate governance structures used in Germany and Japan differ from each other and from that used in the United States. Historically, the U.S. governance structure has focused on maximizing shareholder value. In Germany, employees, as a stakeholder group, have a more prominent role in governance. By contrast, until recently, Japanese shareholders played virtually no role in the monitoring and control of top-level managers. However, all of these systems are becoming increasingly similar, as are many governance systems both in developed countries, such as France and Spain, and in transitional economies, such as Russia and China.

- Effective governance mechanisms ensure that the interests of all stakeholders are served. Thus, long-term strategic success results when firms are governed in ways that permit at least minimal satisfaction of capital market stakeholders (e.g., shareholders), product market stakeholders (e.g., customers and suppliers), and organizational stakeholders (managerial and non-managerial employees; see Chapter 2). Moreover, effective governance produces ethical behavior in the formulation and implementation of strategies.

NOTES

1. K. Hendry & G. C. Kiel, 2004, The role of the board in firm strategy: Integrating agency and organisational control perspectives, *Corporate Governance*, 12(4), 500–520; M. Carpenter & J. Westphal, 2001, Strategic context of external network ties: Examining the impact of director appointments on board involvement in strategic decision making, *Academy of Management Journal*, 44: 639–660.

2. A. Henderson & J. Fredrickson, 2001, Top management team coordination needs and the CEO pay gap: A competitive test of economic and behavioral views, *Academy of Management Journal*, 44: 96–117.

3. S. Werner, H. L. Tosi, & L. Gomez-Mejia, 2005, Organizational governance and employee pay: How ownership structure affects the firm's compensation strategy, *Strategic Management Journal*, 26: 377–384; J. E. Core, R. W. Holthausen, & D. F. Larcker, 1999, Corporate governance, chief executive officer compensation, and firm performance, *Journal of Financial Economics*, 51: 371–406.

4. M. D. Lynall, B. R. Golden, & A. J. Hillman, 2003, Board composition from adolescence to maturity: A multitheoretic view, *Academy of Management Review*, 28: 416–431; A. J. Hillman, G. D. Keim, & R. A. Luce, 2001, Board composition and stakeholder performance: Do stakeholder directors make a difference? *Business and Society*, 40: 295–314.

5. A. Desai, M. Kroll, & P. Wright, 2005, Outside board monitoring and the economic outcomes of acquisitions: A test of the substitution hypothesis, *Journal of Business Research*, 58, 926–934; C. M. Daily, D. R. Dalton, & A. A. Cannella, 2003, Corporate governance: Decades of dialogue and data, *Academy of Management Review*, 28: 371–382; P. Stiles, 2001, The impact of the board on strategy: An empirical examination, *Journal of Management Studies*, 38: 627–650.

6. M. S. Schwartz, T. W. Dunfee, & M. J. Kline, 2005, Tone at the top: An ethics code for directors? *Journal of Business Ethics*, 58: 79–100; D. Finegold, E. E. Lawler III, & J. Conger, 2001, Building a better board, *Journal of Business Strategy*, 22(6): 33–37.

7. E. F. Fama & M. C. Jensen, 1983, Separation of ownership and control, *Journal of Law and Economics,* 26: 301–325.

8. C. Hymowitz, 2004, Corporate Governance (a special report); Experiments in corporate governance: Finding the right way to improve board oversight isn't easy; but plenty of companies are trying, *Wall Street Journal,* June 21, R1.

9. M. Carney, 2005, Corporate governance and competitive advantage in family-controlled firms, *Entrepreneurship Theory and Practice,* 29: 249–265; R. Charan, 1998, *How Corporate Boards Create Competitive Advantage,* San Francisco: Jossey-Bass.

10. G. J. Nicholson & G. C. Kiel, 2004, Breakthrough board performance: How to harness your board's intellectual capital, *Corporate Governance,* 4(1): 5–23; A. Cannella Jr., A. Pettigrew, & D. Hambrick, 2001, Upper echelons: Donald Hambrick on executives and strategy, *Academy of Management Executive,* 15(3): 36–52; J. D. Westphal & E. J. Zajac, 1997, Defections from the inner circle: Social exchange, reciprocity and diffusion of board independence in U.S. corporations, *Administrative Science Quarterly,* 42: 161–212.

11. X. Wu, 2005, Corporate governance and corruption: A cross-country analysis, *Governance,* 18(2): 151–170; J. McGuire & S. Dow, 2002, The Japanese keiretsu system: An empirical analysis, *Journal of Business Research,* 55: 33–40.

12. J. Charkham, 1994, *Keeping Good Company: A Study of Corporate Governance in Five Countries,* New York: Oxford University Press, 1.

13. R. E. Hoskisson, D. Yiu, & H. Kim, 2004, Corporate governance systems: Effects of capital and labor market congruency on corporate Innovation and global competitiveness, *Journal of High Technology Management,* 15: 293–315.

14. R. Aguilera & G. Jackson, 2003, The cross-national diversity of corporate governance: Dimensions and determinants, *Academy of Management Review,* 28: 447–465; Cadbury Committee, 1992, *Report of the Cadbury Committee on the Financial Aspects of Corporate Governance,* London: Gee.

15. R. P. Wright, 2004, Top managers' strategic cognitions of the strategy making process: Differences between high and low performing firms, *Journal of General Management,* 30(1): 61–78.

16. T. Moeller, 2005, Let's make a deal! How shareholder control impacts merger payoffs, *Journal of Financial Economics,* 76(1): 167–190; M. A. Hitt, R. E. Hoskisson, R. A. Johnson, & D. D. Moesel, 1996, The market for corporate control and firm innovation, *Academy of Management Journal,* 39: 1084–1119.

17. K. Berryman & T. Stephenson, 2004, A new era in corporate governance, www.mckinseyquarterly.com, April 15; K. Ramaswamy, M. Li, & R. Veliyath, 2002, Variations in ownership behavior and propensity to diversify: A study of the Indian context, *Strategic Management Journal,* 23: 345–358.

18. R. E. Hoskisson, M. A. Hitt, R. A. Johnson, & W. Grossman, 2002, Conflicting voices: The effects of ownership heterogeneity and internal governance on corporate strategy, *Academy of Management Journal,* 45: 697–716.

19. G. E. Davis & T. A. Thompson, 1994, A social movement perspective on corporate control, *Administrative Science Quarterly,* 39: 141–173.

20. R. Bricker & N. Chandar, 2000, Where Berle and Means went wrong: A reassessment of capital market agency and financial reporting, *Accounting, Organizations and Society,* 25: 529–554; M. A. Eisenberg, 1989, The structure of corporation law, *Columbia Law Review,* 89(7): 1461 as cited in R. A. G. Monks & N. Minow, 1995, *Corporate Governance,* Cambridge, MA: Blackwell Business, 7.

21. R. M. Wiseman & L. R. Gomez-Mejia, 1999, A behavioral agency model of managerial risk taking, *Academy of Management Review,* 23: 133–153.

22. R. C. Anderson & D. M. Reeb, 2004, Board composition: Balancing family influence in S&P 500 firms, *Administrative Science Quarterly,* 49: 209–237.

23. Carney, Corporate governance and competitive advantage in family-controlled firms; N. Anthanassiou, W. F. Crittenden, L. M. Kelly, & P. Marquez, 2002, Founder centrality effects on the Mexican family firm's top management group: Firm culture, strategic vision and goals and firm performance, *Journal of World Business,* 37: 139–150.

24. G. Redding, 2002, The capitalist business system of China and its rationale, *Asia Pacific Journal of Management,* 19: 221–249.

25. T.-S. Lee & Y.-H. Yeh, 2004, Corporate governance and financial distress: Evidence from Taiwan, *Corporate Governance,* 12(3): 378–388; M. Carney & E. Gedajlovic, 2003, Strategic innovation and the administrative heritage of East Asian family business groups, *Asia Pacific Journal of Management,* 20: 5–26; D. Miller & I. Le Breton-Miller, 2003, Challenge versus advantage in family business, *Strategic Organization,* 1: 127–134.

26. E. E. Fama, 1980, Agency problems and the theory of the firm, *Journal of Political Economy,* 88: 288–307.

27. D. Dalton, C. Daily, T. Certo, & R. Roengpitya, 2003, Meta-analyses of financial performance and equity: Fusion or confusion? *Academy of Management Journal,* 46: 13–26; M. Jensen & W. Meckling, 1976, Theory of the firm: Managerial behavior, agency costs, and ownership structure, *Journal of Financial Economics,* 11: 305–360.

28. D. C. Hambrick, S. Finkelstein, & A. C. Mooney, 2005, Executive job demands: New insights for explaining strategic decisions and leader behaviors, *Academy of Management Review,* 30: 472–491; L. R. Gomez-Mejia, M. Nunez-Nickel, & I. Gutierrez, 2001, The role of family ties in agency contracts, *Academy of Management Journal,* 44: 81–95.

29. M. G. Jacobides & D. C. Croson, 2001, Information policy: Shaping the value of agency relationships, *Academy of Management Review,* 26: 202–223.

30. H. E. Ryan Jr. & R. A. Wiggins III, 2004, Who is in whose pocket? Director compensation, board independence, and barriers to effective monitoring, *Journal of Financial Economics,* 73: 497–524.

31. M. W. Peng, 2004, Outside directors and firm performance during institutional transitions, *Strategic Management Journal,* 25: 453–471; A. J. Hillman & T. Dalziel, 2003, Boards of directors and firm performance: Integrating agency and resource dependence perspectives, *Academy of Management Review,* 28: 383–396.

32. Hoskisson, Hitt, Johnson, & Grossman, Conflicting voices; O. E. Williamson, 1996, *The Mechanisms of Governance,* New York: Oxford University Press, 6.

33. R. W. Coff & P. M. Lee, 2003, Insider trading as a vehicle to appropriate rent from R&D. *Strategic Management Journal,* 24: 183–190; C. C. Chen, M. W. Peng, & P. A. Saparito, 2002, Individualism, collectivism, and opportunism: A cultural perspective on transaction cost economics, *Journal of Management,* 28: 567–583; S. Ghoshal & P. Moran, 1996, Bad for practice: A critique of the transaction cost theory, *Academy of Management Review,* 21: 13–47.

34. K. H. Wathne & J. B. Heide, 2000, Opportunism in interfirm relationships: Forms, outcomes, and solutions, *Journal of Marketing,* 64(4): 36–51.

35. T. Yoshikawa, P. H. Phan, & J. Linton, 2004, The relationship between governance structure and risk management approaches in Japanese venture capital firms, *Journal of Business Venturing,* 19: 831–849; L. Tihanyi, R. A. Johnson, R. E. Hoskisson, & M. A. Hitt, 2003, Institutional ownership differences and international diversification: The effects of boards of directors and technological opportunity, *Academy of Management Journal,* 46: 195–211; Y. Amihud & B. Lev, 1981, Risk reduction as a managerial motive for conglomerate mergers, *Bell Journal of Economics,* 12: 605–617.

36. R. C. Anderson, T. W. Bates, J. M. Bizjak, & M. L. Lemmon, Corporate governance and firm diversification, *Financial Management,* 29(1): 5–22; R. E. Hoskisson & T. A. Turk, 1990, Corporate restructuring: Governance and control limits of the internal market, *Academy of Management Review,* 15: 459–477.

37. R. Bushman, Q. Chen, E. Engel, & A. Smith, 2004, Financial accounting information, organizational complexity and corporate governance systems, *Journal of Accounting & Economics,* 7: 167–201; M. A. Geletkanycz, B. K. Boyd, & S. Finkelstein, 2001, The strategic value of CEO external directorate networks: Implications for CEO compensation, *Strategic Management Journal,* 9: 889–898.

38. Y. Grinstein & P. Hribar, 2004, CEO compensation and incentives: Evidence from M&A bonuses, *Journal of Financial Economics,* 73: 119–143; P. Wright, M. Kroll, & D. Elenkov, 2002, Acquisition returns, increase in firm size and chief executive officer compensation: The moderating role of monitoring, *Academy of Management Journal,* 45: 599–608; S. Finkelstein & D. C. Hambrick, 1989, Chief executive compensation: A study of the inter-

section of markets and political processes, *Strategic Management Journal,* 16: 221–239.

39. Gomez-Mejia, Nunez-Nickel, & Gutierrez, The role of family ties in agency contracts.

40. J. A. Fraser, 2004, A return to basics at Kellogg, *MIT Sloan Management Review,* 45(4): 27–30.

41. J. Adamy, 2005, Kellogg profit and revenue rise, as high prices seem to stick, *Wall Street Journal,* April 29, B3; 2005, A return to health for Kellogg, *Strategic Direction,* February, 11–14; R. Barker, 2004, Kellogg: A little payoff in the box? *Business Week,* December 27, 189.

42. M. S. Jensen, 1986, Agency costs of free cash flow, corporate finance, and takeovers, *American Economic Review,* 76: 323–329.

43. M. Jensen & E. Zajac, 2004, Corporate elites and corporate strategy: How demographic preferences and structural position shape the scope of the firm, *Strategic Management Journal,* 25: 507–524; T. H. Brush, P. Bromiley, & M. Hendrickx, 2000, The free cash flow hypothesis for sales growth and firm performance, *Strategic Management Journal,* 21: 455–472.

44. K. Ramaswamy, M. Li, & B. S. P. Petitt, 2004, Who drives unrelated diversification? A study of Indian manufacturing firms, *Asia Pacific Journal of Management,* 21: 403–423; Ramaswamy, Li, & Veliyath, Variations in ownership behavior and propensity to diversify.

45. A. Desai, M. Kroll, & P. Wright, 2005, Outside board monitoring and the economic outcomes of acquisitions: A test of the substitution hypothesis, *Journal of Business Research,* 58: 926–934; P. Wright, M. Kroll, A. Lado, & B. Van Ness, 2002, The structure of ownership and corporate acquisition strategies, *Strategic Management Journal,* 23: 41–53.

46. T. K. Mukherjee, H. Kiymaz, & H. K. Baker, 2004, Merger motives and target valuation: A survey of evidence from CFOs, *Journal of Applied Finance,* 14(2): 7–24; R. Rajan, H. Servaes, & L. Zingales, 2001, The cost of diversity: The diversification discount and inefficient investment, *Journal of Finance,* 55: 35–79; A. Sharma, 1997, Professional as agent: Knowledge asymmetry in agency exchange, *Academy of Management Review,* 22: 758–798.

47. A. Borrus, L. Lavelle, D. Brady, M. Arndt, & J. Weber, 2005, Death, taxes and Sarbanes-Oxley? Executives may be frustrated with the law's burdens, but corporate performance is here to stay, *Business Week,* January 17, 28–31.

48. R. Marden & R. Edwards, 2005, The Sarbanes-Oxley 'axe,' *CPA Journal,* April, 6–10.

49. J. Fox, 2005, Calling off the dogs, *Fortune,* June 27, 27–29.

50. J. McTague, 2005, Corporate tangle, *Barron's,* April 4, 19.

51. W. J. Hass & S. G. Pryor IV, 2005, The board's role in corporate renewal, *Journal of Private Equity,* 8(2): 12.

52. A. de Miguel, J. Pindado, & C. de la Torre, 2004, Ownership structure and firm value: New evidence from Spain, *Strategic Management Journal,* 25: 1199–1207; J. Coles, N. Sen, & V. McWilliams, 2001, An examination of the relationship of governance mechanisms to performance, *Journal of Management,* 27: 23–50.

53. M. Singh, I. Mathur, & K. C. Gleason, 2004, Governance and performance implications of diversification strategies: Evidence from large U.S. firms, *Financial Review,* 39: 489–526; S.-S. Chen & K. W. Ho, 2000, Corporate diversification, ownership structure, and firm value: The Singapore evidence, *International Review of Financial Analysis,* 9: 315–326; R. E. Hoskisson, R. A. Johnson, & D. D. Moesel, 1994, Corporate divestiture intensity in restructuring firms: Effects of governance, strategy, and performance, *Academy of Management Journal,* 37: 1207–1251.

54. De Miguel, Pindado, & de la Torre, Ownership structure and firm value: New evidence from Spain.

55. R. C. Anderson & D. M. Reeb, 2004, Board composition: Balancing family influence in S&P 500 firms, *Administrative Science Quarterly,* 49: 209–237.

56. S. J. Chang, 2003, Ownership structure, expropriation and performance of group-affiliated companies in Korea, *Academy of Management Journal,* 46: 238–253.

57. A. Berle & G. Means, 1932, *The Modern Corporation and Private Property,* New York: Macmillan.

58. B. Ajinkya, S. Bhojraj, & P. Sengupta, 2005, The association between outside directors, institutional investors and the properties of management earn-ings forecasts, *Journal of Accounting Research,* 43: 343–376; P. A. Gompers & A. Metrick, 2001, Institutional investors and equity prices, *Quarterly Journal of Economics,* 116: 229–259; M. P. Smith, 1996, Shareholder activism by institutional investors: Evidence from CalPERS, *Journal of Finance,* 51: 227–252.

59. Hoskisson, Hitt, Johnson, & Grossman, Conflicting voices; C. M. Dailey, 1996, Governance patterns in bankruptcy reorganizations, *Strategic Management Journal,* 17: 355–375.

60. Hoskisson, Hitt, Johnson, & Grossman, Conflicting voices; R. E. Hoskisson & M. A. Hitt, 1994, *Downscoping: How to Tame the Diversified Firm,* New York: Oxford University Press.

61. K. Rebeiz, 2001, Corporate governance effectiveness in American corporations: A survey, *International Management Journal,* 18(1): 74–80.

62. R. Parloff, 2004, Pension politics, *Fortune,* December 27, 27–32.

63. Tihanyi, Johnson, Hoskisson, & Hitt, Institutional ownership differences and international diversification; Hoskisson, Hitt, Johnson, & Grossman, Conflicting voices; P. David, M. A. Hitt, & J. Gimeno, 2001, The role of institutional investors in influencing R&D, *Academy of Management Journal,* 44: 144–157.

64. S. Thomsen & T. Pedersen, 2000, Ownership structure and economic performance in the largest European companies, *Strategic Management Journal,* 21: 689–705.

65. R. V. Aguilera, 2005, Corporate governance and director accountability: An institutional comparative perspective, *British Journal of Management,* 16(S1), S39–S53; E. H. Fram, 2004, Governance reform: It's only just begun, *Business Horizons,* 47(6): 10–14.

66. Hillman & Dalziel, Boards of directors and firm performance.

67. Rebeiz, Corporate governance effectiveness in American corporations; J. K. Seward & J. P Walsh, 1996, The governance and control of voluntary corporate spinoffs, *Strategic Management Journal,* 17: 25–39.

68. S. Young, 2000, The increasing use of non-executive directors: Its impact on UK board structure and governance arrangements, *Journal of Business Finance & Accounting,* 27(9/10): 1311–1342; P. Mallete & R. L. Hogler, 1995, Board composition, stock ownership, and the exemption of directors from liability, *Journal of Management,* 21: 861–878.

69. C. Caldwell & R. Karri, 2005, Organizational governance and ethical systems: A covenantal approach to building trust, *Journal of Business Ethics,* 58: 249–259; J. Chidley, 2001, Why boards matter, *Canadian Business,* October 29, 6; D. P. Forbes & F. J. Milliken, 1999, Cognition and corporate governance: Understanding boards of directors as strategic decision-making groups, *Academy of Management Review,* 24: 489–505.

70. Hoskisson, Hitt, Johnson, & Grossman, Conflicting voices; B. D. Baysinger & R. E. Hoskisson, 1990, The composition of boards of directors and strategic control: Effects on corporate strategy, *Academy of Management Review,* 15: 72–87.

71. Carpenter & Westphal, Strategic context of external network ties: Examining the impact of director appointments on board involvement in strategic decision making; E. J. Zajac & J. D. Westphal, 1996, Director reputation, CEO-board power, and the dynamics of board interlocks, *Administrative Science Quarterly,* 41: 507–529.

72. J. Westphal & L. Milton, 2000, How experience and network ties affect the influence of demographic minorities on corporate boards, *Administrative Science Quarterly,* June, 45(2): 366–398.

73. S. T. Petra, 2005, Do outside independent directors strengthen corporate boards? *Corporate Governance,* 5(1): 55–65.

74. 2003, The hot seat, *Wall Street Journal Online,* www.wsj.com, February 24; 2001, The fading appeal of the boardroom series, *The Economist,* February 10 (Business Special): 67–69.

75. H. L. Tosi, W. Shen, & R. J. Gentry, 2003, Why outsiders on boards can't solve the corporate governance problem, *Organizational Dynamics,* 32: 180–192.

76. J. W. Lorsch & A. Zelleke, 2005, Should the CEO be the Chairman, *MIT Sloan Management Review,* 46(2): 71–74.

77. C. Hymowitz, 2005, The perils of picking CEOs: Add character's character to board's lists of concerns as openings at the top grow, *Wall Street Journal,* March 15, B2.

78. Ibid.

79. J. Roberts, T. McNulty, P. Stiles, 2005, Beyond agency conceptions of the work of the non-executive director: Creating accountability in the boardroom, *British Journal of Management,* 16(S1): S5–S26.

80. J. Coles & W. Hesterly, 2000, Independence of the chairman and board composition: Firm choices and shareholder value, *Journal of Management,* 26: 195–214; S. Zahra, 1996, Governance, ownership and corporate entrepreneurship among the Fortune 500: The moderating impact of industry technological opportunity, *Academy of Management Journal,* 39: 1713–1735.

81. Yoshikawa, Phan, & Linton, The relationship between governance structure and risk management approaches in Japanese venture capital firms; Hoskisson, Hitt, Johnson, & Grossman, Conflicting voices.

82. E. E. Lawler III & D. L. Finegold, 2005, The changing face of corporate boards, *MIT Sloan Management Review,* 46(2): 67–70; A. Conger, E. E. Lawler, & D. L. Finegold, 2001, *Corporate Boards: New Strategies for Adding Value at the Top,* San Francisco: Jossey-Bass; J. A. Conger, D. Finegold, & E. E. Lawler III, 1998, Appraising boardroom performance, *Harvard Business Review,* 76(1): 136–148.

83. J. Marshall, 2001, As boards shrink, responsibilities grow, *Financial Executive,* 17(4): 36–39.

84. S. Finkelstein & A. C. Mooney, 2003, Not the usual suspects: How to use board process to make boards better, *Academy of Management Executive,* 17: 101–113.

85. Hoskisson, Hitt, Johnson, & Grossman, Conflicting voices.

86. W. Shen, 2005, Improve board effectiveness: The need for incentives, *British Journal of Management,* 16(S1): S81–S89; M. Gerety, C. Hoi, & A. Robin, 2001, Do shareholders benefit from the adoption of incentive pay for directors? *Financial Management,* 30: 45–61; D. C. Hambrick & E. M. Jackson, 2000, Outside directors with a stake: The linchpin in improving governance, *California Management Review,* 42(4): 108–127.

87. I. Filatotchev & S. Toms, 2003, Corporate governance, strategy and survival in a declining industry: A study of UK cotton textile companies, *Journal of Management Studies,* 40: 895–920.

88. J. Kristie, 2001, The shareholder activist: Nell Minow, *Directors and Boards,* 26(1): 16–17.

89. Roberts, McNulty, & Stiles, Beyond agency conceptions of the work of the non-executive director: Creating accountability in the boardroom.

90. L. A. Bebchuk & J. M Fried, 2004, *Pay Without Performance: The Unfulfilled Promise of Executive Compensation,* Cambridge, MA: Harvard University Press; M. A. Carpenter & W. G. Sanders, 2002, Top management team compensation: The missing link between CEO pay and firm performance, *Strategic Management Journal,* 23: 367–375; D. C. Hambrick & S. Finkelstein, 1995, The effects of ownership structure on conditions at the top: The case of CEO pay raises, *Strategic Management Journal,* 16: 175.

91. J. S. Miller, R. M. Wiseman, & L. R. Gomez-Mejia, 2002, The fit between CEO compensation design and firm risk, *Academy of Management Journal,* 45: 745–756; L. Gomez-Mejia & R. M. Wiseman, 1997, Reframing executive compensation: An assessment and outlook, *Journal of Management,* 23: 291–374.

92. J. McGuire & E. Matta, 2003, CEO stock options: The silent dimension of ownership, *Academy of Management Journal,* 46: 255–265; W. G. Sanders & M. A. Carpenter, 1998, Internationalization and firm governance: The roles of CEO compensation, top team composition and board structure, *Academy of Management Journal,* 41: 158–178.

93. N. T. Hill & K. T. Stevens, 2001, Structuring compensation to achieve better financial results, *Strategic Finance,* 9: 48–51; J. D. Westphal & E. J. Zajac, 1999, The symbolic management of stockholders: Corporate governance reform and shareholder reactions, *Administrative Science Quarterly,* 43: 127–153.

94. L. Gomez-Mejia, M. Larraza-Kintana, & M. Makri, 2003, The determinants of executive compensation in family-controlled public corporations, *Academy of Management Journal,* 46: 226–237; F. Elloumi & J. P. Gueyie, 2001, CEO compensation, IOS and the role of corporate governance, *Corporate Governance,* 1(2): 23–33; M. J. Conyon & S. I. Peck, 1998, Board control, remuneration committees, and top management compensation, *Academy of Management Journal,* 41: 146–157.

95. N. Byrnes, 2004, Not so fast, Lord Black, *Business Week,* September 27, 104.

96. S. O'Donnell, 2000, Managing foreign subsidiaries: Agents of headquarters, or an interdependent network? *Strategic Management Journal,* 21: 521–548; K. Roth & S. O'Donnell, 1996, Foreign subsidiary compensation: An agency theory perspective, *Academy of Management Journal,* 39: 678–703.

97. K. Ramaswamy, R. Veliyath, & L. Gomes, 2000, A study of the determinants of CEO compensation in India, *Management International Review,* 40(2): 167–191.

98. J. Krug & W. Hegarty, 2001, Predicting who stays and leaves after an acquisition: A study of top managers in multinational firms, *Strategic Management Journal,* 22: 185–196.

99. Carpenter & Sanders, Top management team compensation.

100. Werner, Tosi, & Gomez-Mejia, Organizational governance and employee pay: How ownership structure affects the firm's compensation strategy; S. Bryan, L. Hwang, & S. Lilien, 2000, CEO stock-based compensation: An empirical analysis of incentive-intensity, relative mix, and economic determinants, *Journal of Business,* 73: 661–693.

101. E. MacDonald, 2005, A volatile brew: Companies have found how to ease the impact of strict new stock option rules, *Forbes,* August 15, 70–71.

102. R. E. Hoskisson, M. A. Hitt, & C. W. L. Hill, 1993, Managerial incentives and investment in R&D in large multiproduct firms, *Organization Science,* 4: 325–341.

103. Gomez-Mejia, Larraza-Kintana, & Makri, 2003, The determinants of executive compensation in family-controlled public corporations.

104. L. K. Meulbroek, 2001, The efficiency of equity-linked compensation: Understanding the full cost of awarding executive stock options, *Financial Management,* 30(2): 5–44.

105. J. Dahya, A. A. Lonie, & D. A. Power, 1998, Ownership structure, firm performance and top executive change: An analysis of UK firms, *Journal of Business Finance & Accounting,* 25: 1089–1118.

106. L. Gomez-Mejia, 2003, What should be done about CEO pay? *Academy of Management Issues Forum,* July; H. Tosi, S. Werner, J. Katz, & L. Gomez-Mejia, 2000, How much does performance matter? A meta-analysis of CEO pay studies, *Journal of Management,* 26: 301–339.

107. J. C. Bettis, J. M. Biziak, & M. L. Lemmon, 2005, Exercise behavior, valuation and the incentive effects of employee stock options, *Journal of Financial Economics,* 76: 445–470.

108. T. G. Pollock, H. M. Fischer, & J. B. Wade, 2002, The role of politics in repricing executive options, *Academy of Management Journal,* 45: 1172–1182; M. E. Carter & L. J. Lynch, 2001, An examination of executive stock option repricing, *Journal of Financial Economics,* 59: 207–225; D. Chance, R. Kumar, & R. Todd, 2001, The "repricing" of executive stock options, *Journal of Financial Economics,* 59: 129–154.

109. N. K. Chidambaran & N. R. Prabhala, 2003, Executive stock option repricing, internal governance mechanisms and management turnover, *Journal of Financial Economics,* 69: 153–189.

110. J. C. Hartzell & L. T. Starks, 2003, Institutional investors and executive compensation, *Journal of Finance,* 58: 2351–2374.

111. P. T. Chingos, 2004, *Responsible Executive Compensation for a New Era of Accountability,* Hoboken, NJ: Wiley.

112. M. A. Chen, 2004, Executive option repricing, incentives, and retention, *Journal of Finance,* 59: 1167–1199; P. Brandes, R. Dharwadkar, & G. V. Lemesis, 2003, Effective stock option design: Reconciling stake-

holder, strategic and motivational factors, *Academy of Management Executive,* 17(1): 77–93.

113. Moeller, Let's make a deal! How shareholder control impacts merger payoffs; R. Coff, 2002, Bidding wars over R&D intensive firms: Knowledge, opportunism and the market for corporate control, *Academy of Management Journal,* 46: 74–85; Hitt, Hoskisson, Johnson, & Moesel, The market for corporate control and firm innovation.

114. R. Sinha, 2004, The role of hostile takeovers in corporate governance, *Applied Financial Economics,* 14: 1291–1305; D. Goldstein, 2000, Hostile takeovers as corporate governance? Evidence from 1980s, *Review of Political Economy,* 12: 381–402.

115. O. Kini, W. Kracaw, & S. Mian, 2004, The nature of discipline by corporate takeovers, *Journal of Finance,* 59: 1511–1551.

116. R. Sinha, 2004, The role of hostile takeovers in corporate governance, *Applied Financial Economics,* 14: 1291–1305.

117. J. P. Walsh & R. Kosnik, 1993, Corporate raiders and their disciplinary role in the market for corporate control, *Academy of Management Journal,* 36: 671–700.

118. Moeller, Let's make a deal! How shareholder control impacts merger payoffs.

119. J. Hartzell, E. Ofek, & D. Yermack, 2004, What's in it for me? CEOs whose firms are acquired, *Review of Financial Studies,* 17: 37–61.

120. K. Shimizu, M. A. Hitt, D. Vaidyanath, & P. Vincenzo, 2004, Theoretical foundations of cross-border mergers and acquisitions: A review of current research and recommendations for the future, *Journal of International Management,* 10: 307–353; M. A. Hitt & V. Pisano, 2003, The cross-border merger and acquisition strategy, *Management Research,* 1: 133–144.

121. Sinha, The role of hostile takeovers in corporate governance; J. Anand & A. Delios, 2002, Absolute and relative resources as determinants of international acquisitions, *Strategic Management Journal,* 23: 119–134.

122. J. Harford, 2003, Takeover bids and target directors' incentives: The impact of a bid on directors' wealth and board seats, *Journal of Financial Economics,* 69: 51–83; S. Chatterjee, J. S. Harrison, & D. D. Bergh, 2003, Failed takeover attempts, corporate governance and refocusing, *Strategic Management Journal,* 24: 87–96.

123. P. Brickley & D. Bank, 2004, PeopleSoft saga described at trial: Director testifies behavior of CEO led board to weigh dismissal several times, *Wall Street Journal,* October 5, A3.

124. C. Sundaramurthy, J. M. Mahoney, & J. T. Mahoney, 1997, Board structure, antitakeover provisions, and stockholder wealth, *Strategic Management Journal,* 18: 231–246.

125. B. E. Tunick, 2005, The Oracle from Oracle: Will other tech giants follow the M&A call? *Investment Dealers' Digest,* February 7, 1.

126. Ibid.

127. W. G. Sanders & M. A. Carpenter, 2003, Strategic satisficing? A behavioral-agency theory perspective on stock repurchase program announcements, *Academy of Management Journal,* 46: 160–178; J. Westphal & E. Zajac, 2001, Decoupling policy from practice: The case of stock repurchase programs, *Administrative Science Quarterly,* 46: 202–228.

128. A. Cala, 2005, Carrying golden parachutes; France joins EU trend to reign in executive severance deals, *Wall Street Journal,* June 8, A13.

129. J. A. Pearce II & R. B. Robinson Jr., 2004, Hostile takeover defenses that maximize shareholder wealth, *Business Horizons,* 47(5): 15–24.

130. P. Burrows & P. Elgin, 2005, The un-Carly unveils his plan, *Business Week,* www.businessweek.com, June 16.

131. Walsh & Kosnik, Corporate raiders.

132. A. Chakraborty & R. Arnott, 2001, Takeover defenses and dilution: A welfare analysis, *Journal of Financial and Quantitative Analysis,* 36: 311–334.

133. C. C. J. M. Millar, T. I. Eldomiaty, C. J. Choi, & B. Hilton, 2005, Corporate governance and institutional transparency in emerging markets, *Journal of Business Ethics,* 59: 163–174; D. Norburn, B. K. Boyd, M. Fox, & M. Muth,

2000, International corporate governance reform, *European Business Journal,* 12(3): 116–133; M. Useem, 1998, Corporate leadership in a globalizing equity market, *Academy of Management Executive,* 12(3): 43–59.

134. S. M. Jacoby, 2004, *The Embedded Corporation: Corporate Governance and Employment Relations in Japan and the United States,* Princeton, NJ: Princeton University Press.

135. P. Witt, 2004, The competition of international corporate governance systems—A German perspective, *Management International Review,* 44: 309–333; L. Nanchum, 2003, Does nationality of ownership make any difference and if so, under what circumstances? Professional service MNEs in global competition, *Journal of International Management,* 9: 1–32.

136. Aguilera & Jackson, The cross-national diversity of corporate governance: Dimensions and determinants.

137. Carney, Corporate governance and competitive advantage in family-controlled firms; S. Klein, 2000, Family businesses in Germany: Significance and structure, *Family Business Review,* 13: 157–181.

138. A. Tuschke & W. G. Sanders, 2003, Antecedents and consequences of corporate governance reform: The case of Germany, *Strategic Management Journal,* 24: 631–649; J. Edwards & M. Nibler, 2000, Corporate governance in Germany: The role of banks and ownership concentration, *Economic Policy,* 31: 237–268; E. R. Gedajlovic & D. M. Shapiro, 1998, Management and ownership effects: Evidence from five countries, *Strategic Management Journal,* 19: 533–553.

139. S. Douma, 1997, The two-tier system of corporate governance, *Long Range Planning,* 30(4): 612–615.

140. M. Karnitschnig, 2005, Too many chiefs at Siemens? German consensus culture may hamper forward-looking CEO, *Wall Street Journal,* January 20, A12.

141. P. C. Fiss & E. J. Zajac, 2004, The diffusion of ideas over contested terrain: The (non) adoption of a shareholder value orientation among German firms, *Administrative Science Quarterly,* 49: 501–534.

142. Tuschke & Sanders, Antecedents and consequences of corporate governance reform: The case of Germany.

143. T. Hoshi, A. K. Kashyap, & S. Fischer, 2001, *Corporate Financing and Governance in Japan,* Boston: MIT Press.

144. Charkham, *Keeping Good Company,* 70.

145. M. A. Hitt, H. Lee, & E. Yucel, 2002, The importance of social capital to the management of multinational enterprises: Relational networks among Asian and Western Firms, *Asia Pacific Journal of Management,* 19: 353–372.

146. Jacoby, *The embedded corporation;* P. M. Lee & H. M. O'Neill, 2003, Ownership structures and R&D investments of U.S. and Japanese firms: Agency and stewardship perspectives, *Academy of Management Journal,* 46: 212–225.

147. A. Kawaura, 2004, Deregulation and governance: Plight of Japanese banks in the 1990s, *Applied Economics,* 36: 479–484; B. Bremner, 2001, Cleaning up the banks—finally, *Business Week,* December 17, 86; 2000, Business: Japan's corporate-governance u-turn, *The Economist,* November 18, 73.

148. B. Bremner, E. Thornton, & I. M. Kunii, 1999, Fall of a keiretsu, *Business Week,* March 15, 87–92.

149. C. L. Ahmadjian & G. E. Robbins, 2005, A clash of capitalisms: Foreign shareholders and corporate restructuring in 1990s Japan, *American Sociological Review,* 70: 451–471.

150. J. Sapsford & M. Fackler, 2005, Directors' role shift in Japan, *Wall Street Journal,* March 10, A15.

151. M. Takebe, 2005, Ex-finance aid of Japan resigns post at Lehman, *Wall Street Journal,* March 10, B7.

152. P. M. Lee, 2004, A comparison of ownership structures and innovations of U.S. and Japanese firms, *Managerial and Decision Economics,* 26(1):

39–50; Lee & O'Neill, Ownership structures and R&D investments of U.S. and Japanese firms.

153. Y. Hayashi, 2005, Japan firms ponder private life, *Wall Street Journal,* August 1, C14.

154. J. B. White, 2000, The company we'll keep, *Wall Street Journal Online,* www.wsj.com, January 17.

155. J.-S. Baek, J.-K. Kang, & K. S. Park, 2004, Corporate governance and firm value: Evidence from the Korean financial crisis, *Journal of Financial Economics,* 71: 265–313; T.-S. Lee & Y.-H. Yeh, 2004, Corporate governance and financial distress: Evidence from Taiwan, *Corporate Governance,* 12: 378–388.

156. T. Edwards, 2004, Corporate governance, industrial relations and trends in company-level restructuring in Europe: Convergence towards the Anglo-American model? *Industrial Relations Journal,* 35: 518–535.

157. N. Boubarkri, J.-C. Cosset, & O. Guedhami, 2004, Postprivatization corporate governance: The role of ownership structure and investor protection, *Journal of Financial Economics,* 76: 369–399; K. Uhlenbruck, K. E. Meyer, & M. A. Hitt, 2003, Organizational transformation in transition economies: Resource-based and organizational learning perspectives, *Journal of Management Studies,* 40: 257–282; P. Mar & M. Young, 2001, Corporate governance in transition economies: A case study of 2 Chinese airlines, *Journal of World Business,* 36(3): 280–302.

158. J. Li, K. Lam, & J. W. Moy, 2005, Ownership reform among state firms in China and its implications, *Management Decision,* 43: 568–588; L. Chang,

1999, Chinese firms find incentive to use stock-compensation plans, *Wall Street Journal,* November 1, A2; T. Clarke & Y. Du, 1998, Corporate governance in China: Explosive growth and new patterns of ownership, *Long Range Planning,* 31(2): 239–251.

159. M. A. Hitt, D. Ahlstrom, M. T. Dacin, E. Levitas, & L. Svobodina, 2004, The institutional effects on strategic alliance partner selection in transition economies: China versus Russia, *Organization Science,* 15: 173–185; I. Filatotchev, R. Kapelyushnikov, N. Dyomina, & S. Aukutsionek, 2001, The effects of ownership concentration on investment and performance in privatized firms in Russia, *Managerial and Decision Economics,* 22(6): 299–313; E. Perotti & S. Gelfer, 2001, Red barons or robber barons? Governance and investment in Russian financial-industrial groups, *European Economic Review,* 45(9): 1601–1617.

160. S. Sharma & I. Henriques, 2005, Stakeholder influences on sustainability practices in the Canadian Forest products industry, *Strategic Management Journal,* 26: 159–180; Hillman, Keim, & Luce, Board composition and stakeholder performance; R. Oliver, 2000, The board's role: Driver's seat or rubber stamp? *Journal of Business Strategy,* 21: 7–9.

161. N. Demise, 2005, Business ethics and corporate governance in Japan, *Business and Society,* 44: 211–217.

162. Caldwell & Karri, Organizational governance and ethical systems: A covenantal approach to building trust; A. Felo, 2001, Ethics programs, board involvement, and potential conflicts of interest in corporate governance, *Journal of Business Ethics,* 32: 205–218.

Organizational Structure

KNOWLEDGE OBJECTIVES

Studying this chapter should provide you with the strategic management knowledge needed to:

1. Define organizational structure and controls and discuss the difference between strategic and financial controls.

2. Describe the relationship between strategy and structure.

3. Discuss the functional structures used to implement business-level strategies.

4. Explain the use of three versions of the multidivisional (M-form) structure to implement different diversification strategies.

5. Discuss the organizational structures used to implement three international strategies.

6. Define strategic networks and discuss how strategic center firms implement such networks at the business, corporate and international levels.

FRANCK ROBICHON/EPA/LANDOV

The competition between divisions that once helped Sony develop highly successful new products is now hurting its reputation for innovation.

Sony's Struggles with Its Online Music Business: Organization and Cooperation Difficulties among Its Businesses

Sony has had great historical success in implementing its strategy worldwide in consumer electronics. Its Sony Walkman and Sony PlayStation products have been exemplary in this regard. Recently, however, Sony has experienced difficulty in pursuing its competitive strategy in the online music business. In part, its problems have been due to the same organizational structure that helped to create its past successes.

Sony's decentralized product divisions have fostered innovation through an entrepreneurial spirit within its separate divisions. The organizational structure encourages competition, so that, for example, engineers in separate divisions are encouraged to outdo each other. This approach created "monster hits" that turned Sony into one of the most successful global brands in consumer products over the past few decades.

However, Sony's reputation as an innovator has suffered recently because it has been beaten by the competition with products such as iPod and TiVo digital video recorders. These products require the integration of hardware, software, and online services—but Sony's structure has worked against it, causing the divisions to be competitive at product efforts that require more coordination.

Sony has used an SBU multidivisional structure (defined later in the chapter), which allows strong decentralization to each product group or division. These groups compete for resources with each other but are highly autonomous business units focused on a particular set of related businesses. Using this structure has made it difficult to "communicate with everybody when you have that many silos." This is exemplified by the Connect service, Sony's attempt to revamp the Walkman line of products in competition with the iPod digital music players and iTunes online music distribution service by Apple Computer Company.

To develop a competing product, the Connect service was created, which coordinates all the various Sony businesses. Sony's U.S. music group, which was purchased from CBS Records in 1988, however, was concerned that it would lose power to control its copyrighted music through free music downloads that might be initiated through Connnect service. To make matters worse, the PC and Walkman groups had each developed competing digital music players that they wished to promote. Theoretically, given Sony's market presence and prowess in these separate areas, it could outcompete Apple iPod and iTunes. However, the Connect service required coordination with the PC and Walkman groups as well as with the music-business group, which was reluctant to participate.

This significant coordination problem took center stage in 2005, ultimately causing significant product delays. As a result of this organizational debacle the then CEO, Nobuyuki Idei, was forced to retire and was replaced by Howard Stringer. This example illustrates how important structure and execution can be when seeking to implement a firm's newly chosen strategy.

Sources: 2005, With Sony trailing, can anything stop Samsung?, *Marketing Week,* July 28, 9; B. Carter, 2005, Sony seeks new beginning, *Marketing,* March 16, 16; P. Dvorak, 2005, Out of tune: At Sony, rivalries were encouraged; then came iPod, *Wall Street Journal,* A1, A6; P. Dvorak, 2005, Stringer takes control at Sony with plans to streamline firm, *Wall Street Journal,* June 23, B4; K. Kelly & E. Smith, 2005, Past as prologue: New CEO to seek synergies, *Wall Street Journal,* March 8, B1; A. Lashinsky, 2005, Saving face at Sony, *Fortune,* February 21, 79–83.

As described in Chapter 4, all firms use one or more business-level strategies. In Chapters 6–9, we discuss the other strategies that might be used (corporate-level, international, and cooperative). Once selected, strategies can't be implemented in a vacuum. Organizational structure and controls, this chapter's topic, provide the framework within which strategies are used in both for-profit organizations and not-for-profit agencies.[1] However, as we explain, separate structures and controls are required to successfully implement different strategies. For example, Sony uses a form of the multidivisional structure to support use of its related linked corporate-level strategy, while each of its business units employs a version of the functional structure to effectively implement the differentiation business-level strategy. Top-level managers have the final responsibility for ensuring that the firm has matched each of its strategies with the appropriate organizational structure and that changes to both take place when needed. The match or degree of fit between strategy and structure influences the firm's attempts to earn above-average returns.[2] Thus, the ability to select an appropriate strategy and match it with the appropriate structure is an important characteristic of effective strategic leadership.[3]

This chapter opens with an introduction to organizational structure and controls. We then provide more details about the need for the firm's strategy and structure to be properly matched. As suggested in the Opening Case, the new CEO at Sony, Howard Stringer, is aware of this need and is committed to improving a proper match between Sony's corporate-level strategy and the structure used to implement it. Currently, more cooperation between rivalrous business units is needed to effectively implement Sony's online music business strategy. Affecting firms' efforts to match strategy and structure is the fact that they influence each other.[4] As we discuss, strategy has a more important influence on structure, although once in place, structure influences strategy,[5] as illustrated in the Opening Case.

The chapter describes the relationship between growth and structural change that successful firms experience. This is followed with discussions of the different organizational structures that firms use to implement the separate business-level, corporate-level, international, and cooperative strategies. A series of figures highlights the different structures firms match with strategies. Across time and based on their experiences, organizations, especially large and complex ones, customize these general structures to meet their unique needs.[6] Typically, the firm tries to form a structure that is complex enough to facilitate use of its strategies but simple enough for all parties to understand and implement.[7]

Organizational Structure and Controls

Research shows that organizational structure and the controls that are a part of the structure affect firm performance.[8] In particular, evidence suggests that performance declines when the firm's strategy is not matched with the most appropriate structure and controls.[9] As the Opening Case illustrated, an ineffective match between strategy and structure is thought to account for Sony's difficulty in creating a successful online music business. Recognizing this mismatch, the firm has selected a new CEO to facilitate better cooperation among its separate business units. Even though mismatches between strategy and structure do occur, such as the one at Sony, research evidence suggests that managers try to act rationally when forming or changing their firm's structure.[10]

Organizational Structure

Organizational structure specifies the firm's formal reporting relationships, procedures, controls, and authority and decision-making processes.[11] Developing an organizational structure that effectively supports the firm's strategy is difficult,[12] especially because of the uncertainty (or unpredictable variation[13]) about cause-effect relationships in the global economy's rapidly changing and dynamic competitive environments.[14] When a structure's elements (e.g., reporting relationships, procedures, and so forth) are properly aligned with one another, this structure facilitates effective implementation of the firm's strategies.[15] Thus, organizational structure is a critical component of effective strategy implementation processes.[16]

A firm's structure specifies the work to be done and how to do it, given the firm's strategy or strategies.[17] Thus, organizational structure influences how managers work and the decisions resulting from that work.[18] Supporting the implementation of strategies, structure is concerned with processes used to complete organizational tasks.[19] Effective structures provide the stability a firm needs to successfully implement its strategies and maintain its current competitive advantages, while simultaneously providing the flexibility to develop competitive advantages that will be needed for its future strategies.[20] Thus, *structural stability* provides the capacity the firm requires to consistently and predictably manage its daily work routines,[21] while *structural flexibility* provides the opportunity to explore competitive possibilities and then allocate resources to activities that will shape the competitive advantages the firm will need to be successful in the future.[22] An effective organizational structure allows the firm to *exploit* current competitive advantages while *developing* new ones.[23]

Modifications to the firm's current strategy or selection of a new strategy call for changes to its organizational structure. However, research shows that once in place, organizational inertia often inhibits efforts to change structure, even when the firm's performance suggests that it is time to do so.[24] In his pioneering work, Alfred Chandler found that organizations change their structures only when inefficiencies force them to do so.[25] Firms seem to prefer the structural status quo and its familiar working relationships until the firm's performance declines to the point where change is absolutely necessary.[26] In addition, top-level managers hesitate to conclude that there are problems with the firm's structure (or its strategy, for that matter), in that doing so suggests that their previous choices weren't the best ones.[27] Because of these inertial tendencies, structural change is often induced instead by the actions of stakeholders who are no longer willing to tolerate the firm's performance. For example, continuing losses of customers who have become dissatisfied with the value created by the firm's products could force change, as could reactions from capital market stakeholders (see Chapter 2 and Chapter 10).

Appropriate timing of structural change happens when top-level managers recognize that a current organizational structure no longer provides the coordination and direction needed for the firm to successfully implement its strategies.[28] As indicated in the Strategic Focus on the structural change at Kellogg Co., effectively implementing a firm's strategy can have significant positive effects on its performance. The structural change at Kellogg allowed the company both to regain its market share leadership over General Mills and to increase profitability and associated value creation for shareholders. As we discuss next, effective organizational controls help managers recognize when it is time to adjust the firm's structure.

Organizational Controls

As illustrated in the Strategic Focus on Kellogg, organizational controls are an important aspect of structure.[29] **Organizational controls** guide the use of strategy, indicate

A Change in Structure Leads to Improved Strategy Implementation at Kellogg Co.

In the late 1990s Kellogg Co. of Battle Creek, Michigan, had $6 billion in annual sales, but its brands as well as its profit margins were quite weak. Two important events in 1999 led to significant structural change. First, Carlos Gutierrez, a longtime inside manager, was appointed as CEO. Second, a corporate crisis stimulated significant motivation for change: Though Kellogg had been the leader in the industry for a number of decades, it was suddenly surpassed in market share by the industry's perennial number two firm, General Mills Inc. Kellogg managers recognized that change was needed.

Kellogg had long been committed to sales volume, which meant pushing its highest-selling brands of cereal regardless of their profitability. This approach made it susceptible to competition, especially to generic-brand competitors, and to a significant loss in brand equity. In 2001, Kellogg substantially changed its structure. The company had been organized in a way that the managers and employees associated with major products were unable to understand and unable to track their own impact on profitability. Although separate divisions had been organized, they focused on disciplines such as brand, supply chain, and innovation. Gutierrez reorganized the system in way that "fully integrated the business units" and resulted in allowing "a brand's sales staff, innovation team, marketers, managers and other relevant personnel" to focus "on achieving the same realistic targets for net sales, cash flow and operating profits."

Under the new structure, the sales force could more easily see the connection between how and what they sold and specific profits and losses. The change enabled the divisions to "operate like small businesses." In essence, this allowed the units to operate like they would in a multidivisional structure (see the discussion later in this chapter) having the operating profits associated with each division or brand.

Additionally, Gutierrez facilitated the acquisition of Keebler Foods Company. At the time of the acquisition (in 2001), Keebler was the second-leading cookie and cracker manufacturer in the United States. New cereal and snack food products and mixed products were introduced after the acquisition of Keebler. Accordingly, innovation was spurred through the acquisition of Keebler. Some of the most effective products were those that mixed cereal and snack food concepts to create increased profit margins. The Keebler acquisition as well as the new product units could be organized as separate business units under the new structure.

Performance incentives were also aligned with business units, and "compensation became consequential." "It used to be, if you had a good year, you got 120 percent of your salary; in a bad year you got 80 percent. Now it can be anywhere from zero to 200 percent."

The company established more realistic goals for the divisions as well. Although stock-market analysts were worried about the lower projected growth of earnings and sales, Kellogg was able to meet and exceed Wall Street's expectations. One analyst commented, "When it comes to cost reductions, management of the balance sheet, the development of new products and growing categories profitably, Kellogg has surpassed everyone's expectations."

ASSOCIATED PRESS, AP

Kellogg's reorganization, instituted by Carlos Gutierrez and continued by James Jenness (pictured), helped the company regain its spot as the number one cereal maker.

In 2005, Carlos Gutierrez was selected as President Bush's Secretary of the U.S. Department of Commerce. James Jenness, Kellogg's new CEO, is seeking to continue Gutierrez's strategies. Kellogg is again the number one cereal maker ahead of General Mills. This significant resurgence is due, primarily, to the structural change instituted by Carlos Gutierrez and continued by James Jenness.

Sources: J. Adamy, 2005, Kellogg Co.: Departing CEO Gutierrez to get annual pension of $1.3 million, *Wall Street Journal*, January 5, A1; J. Adamy, 2005, Kellogg's profit increases by 9.1 percent on cereal sales, *Wall Street Journal*, July 28, B3; J. Adamy, 2005, Kellogg profit and revenue rise, as high prices seem to stick, *Wall Street Journal*, April 29, B3; 2005, A return to health for Kellogg, *Strategic Direction*, February, 11–14; R. Barker, 2004, Kellogg: A little payoff in the box?, *Business Week*, December 27, 189; J. A. Fraser, 2004, A return to basics at Kellogg, *MIT Sloan Management Review*, 45(4): 27–30.

how to compare actual results with expected results, and suggest corrective actions to take when the difference is unacceptable. When there are fewer differences between actual and expected outcomes, the organization's controls are more effective.[30] It is difficult for the company to successfully exploit its competitive advantages without effective organizational controls.[31] Properly designed organizational controls provide clear insights regarding behaviors that enhance firm performance.[32] Firms rely on strategic controls and financial controls as part of their structures to support use of their strategies.

Strategic controls are largely subjective criteria intended to verify that the firm is using appropriate strategies for the conditions in the external environment and the company's competitive advantages. Thus, strategic controls are concerned with examining the fit between what the firm *might do* (as suggested by opportunities in its external environment) and what it *can do* (as indicated by its competitive advantages). Effective strategic controls help the firm understand what it takes to be successful.[33] Strategic controls demand rich communications between managers responsible for using them to judge the firm's performance and those with primary responsibility for implementing the firm's strategies (such as middle- and first-level managers). These frequent exchanges are both formal and informal in nature.[34]

Strategic controls are also used to evaluate the degree to which the firm focuses on the requirements to implement its strategies. For a business-level strategy, for example, the strategic controls are used to study primary and support activities (see Tables 3.6 and 3.7) to verify that those critical to successful implementation of the business-level strategy are being properly emphasized and executed. With related corporate-level strategies, strategic controls are used to verify the sharing of appropriate strategic factors such as knowledge, markets, and technologies across businesses. To effectively use strategic controls when evaluating related diversification strategies, executives must have a deep understanding of each unit's business-level strategy.[35]

Intel is focused on improving strategic control of its operations. To accomplish this, Paul S. Otellini, Intel's CEO, has shifted the chip maker's organization and control systems to focus the employees on different product platforms. As such, he has reorganized Intel into five market-focused units: corporate computing, the digital home, mobile computing, health care, and channel products (PCs produced by smaller manufacturers). Each platform brings together engineers, software writers, and marketers to focus on creating and selling platform products for particular market-oriented customer groups. In doing this he has used "two men in a box," meaning there are two executives in charge of each of the largest groups, mobile computing and corporate computing.[36] This approach has facilitated improved strategic control; the overall structure has more key executives and affiliated functional teams overseeing the development of each market platform.

Partly because strategic controls are difficult to use with extensive diversification,[37] financial controls are emphasized to evaluate the performance of the firm using the unrelated diversification strategy. The unrelated diversification strategy's focus on financial outcomes (see Chapter 6) requires the use of standardized financial controls to compare performances between units and managers.[38] **Financial controls** are largely objective criteria used to measure the firm's performance against previously established quantitative standards. Accounting-based measures, such as return on investment and return on assets, and market-based measures, such as economic value added, are examples of financial controls.

When using financial controls, firms evaluate their current performance against previous outcomes as well as against competitors and industry averages. In the global economy, technological advances are being used to develop highly sophisticated financial controls, making it possible for firms to more thoroughly analyze their performance results and to assure compliance with regulations. For example, companies such as Oracle Corp. and SAP developed software tools that automate processes firms can use to meet the financial reporting requirements specified by the Sarbanes-Oxley Act.[39] (As noted in Chapter 10, this act requires a firm's principal executive and financial officers to certify corporate financial and related information in quarterly and annual reports submitted to the Securities and Exchange Commission.)

For example, John Swainson took over as CEO of Computer Associates (CA) in late 2004, a time during which CA was struggling to deal with legal and financial difficulties. In particular, CA lacked strong internal controls and with the implementation of the Sarbanes-Oxley Act, needed to create better financial and ethical accountability. Due to these difficulties, CA had been forced to restate its financial results for fiscal years 2000 and 2001, a scandal that resulted in the firing and resignation of dozens of executives in 2004. In order to manage the business and create a corporate structure with better financial accountability, Swainson organized CA into five business units: enterprise-systems management, security management, storage management, business service optimization, and a products group. CA has also implemented an SAP system through which it will manage these business units' profit and loss responsibility. Following the reorganization, each business unit will be required to report financial metrics and earnings quarterly. It is hoped that this approach will build trust with regulators, customers, and shareholders. As illustrated by the CA example, proper financial controls are important to maintain trust with key stakeholders as they are used to create more financial transparency and accountability.[40]

Both strategic and financial controls are important aspects of each organizational structure, and any structure's effectiveness is determined by using a combination of strategic and financial controls. However, the relative use of controls varies by type of strategy. For example, companies and business units of large diversified firms using the cost leadership strategy emphasize financial controls (such as quantitative cost goals), while companies and business units using the differentiation strategy emphasize strategic controls (such as subjective measures of the effectiveness of product development teams).[41] As explained above, a corporate-wide emphasis on sharing among business units (as called for by related diversification strategies) results in an emphasis on strategic controls, while financial controls are emphasized for strategies in which activities or capabilities are not shared (e.g., in an unrelated diversification).

John Swainson, CEO of Computer Associates, has reorganized the company in hopes of regaining the trust of customers and investors.

Relationships between Strategy and Structure

Strategy and structure have a reciprocal relationship.[42] This relationship highlights the interconnectedness between strategy formulation (Chapter 4 and Chapters 6–9) and strategy implementation (Chapters 10–13). In general, this reciprocal relationship finds structure flowing from or following the selection of the firm's strategy. Once in place, structure can influence current strategic actions as well as choices about future strategies. The general nature of the strategy/structure relationship means that changes to the firm's strategy create the need to change how the organization completes its work. In the "structure influences strategy" direction, firms must be vigilant in their efforts to verify that how their structure calls for work to be completed remains consistent with the implementation requirements of chosen strategies. Research shows, however, that "strategy has a much more important influence on structure than the reverse."[43]

Regardless of the strength of the reciprocal relationships between strategy and structure, those choosing the firm's strategy and structure should be committed to matching each strategy with a structure that provides the stability needed to use current competitive advantages as well as the flexibility required to develop future advantages. This means, for example, that when changing strategies, the firm should simultaneously consider the structure that will be needed to support use of the new strategy. As illustrated in the Strategic Focus on Kellogg, a proper strategy/structure match can be a competitive advantage and contribute to a firm's earning above-average returns.[44]

Evolutionary Patterns of Strategy and Organizational Structure

Research suggests that most firms experience a certain pattern of relationships between strategy and structure. Chandler[45] found that firms tended to grow in somewhat predictable patterns: "first by volume, then by geography, then integration (vertical, horizontal) and finally through product/business diversification"[46] (see Figure 11.1). Chandler interpreted his findings to indicate that the firm's growth patterns determine its structural form.

As shown in Figure 11.1, sales growth creates coordination and control problems that the existing organizational structure cannot efficiently handle. Organizational growth creates the opportunity for the firm to change its strategy to try to become even more successful. However, the existing structure's formal reporting relationships, procedures, controls, and authority and decision-making processes lack the sophistication required to support use of the new strategy.[47] A new structure is needed to help decision makers gain access to the knowledge and understanding required to effectively integrate and coordinate actions to implement the new strategy.[48]

Three major types of organizational structures are used to implement strategies: simple structure, functional structure, and multidivisional structure.

Simple Structure

The **simple structure** is a structure in which the owner-manager makes all major decisions and monitors all activities while the staff serves as an extension of the manager's

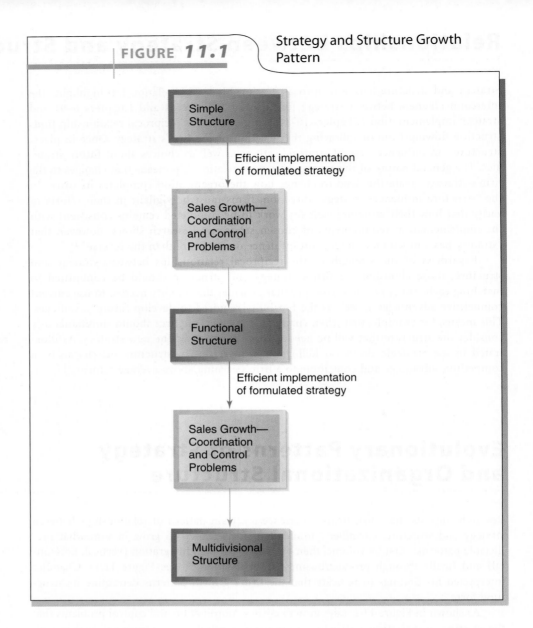

FIGURE **11.1** | Strategy and Structure Growth Pattern

Simple Structure

Efficient implementation of formulated strategy

Sales Growth— Coordination and Control Problems

Functional Structure

Efficient implementation of formulated strategy

Sales Growth— Coordination and Control Problems

Multidivisional Structure

supervisory authority.[49] Typically, the owner-manager actively works in the business on a daily basis. Informal relationships, few rules, limited task specialization, and unsophisticated information systems characterize the simple structure. Frequent and informal communications between the owner-manager and employees make it relatively easy to coordinate the work that is to be done. The simple structure is matched with focus strategies and business-level strategies, as these firms commonly compete by offering a single product line in a single geographic market. Local restaurants, repair businesses, and other specialized enterprises are examples of firms relying on the simple structure to implement their strategy.

As the small firm grows larger and becomes more complex, managerial and structural challenges emerge. For example, the amount of competitively relevant information requiring analysis substantially increases, placing significant pressure on the owner-manager. Additional growth and success may cause the firm to change its strategy. Even if the strategy remains the same, the firm's larger size dictates the need for more sophisticated workflows and integrating mechanisms. At this evolutionary point, firms tend to move from the simple structure to a functional organizational structure.[50]

Casketfurniture.com, mentioned in Chapter 4 as an example of a company using the focus differentiation strategy, may soon move from the simple structure to a functional structure. Family-owned and managed, this venture is a part of MHP Enterprises Ltd.'s operations. As a small family firm, MHP has long been managed through the simple structure. In 1997, MHP decided to expand its distribution to mortuaries by selling products related to death and funerals by establishing Casketfurniture.com. Using the Internet, this venture sells what it believes are creative products throughout the world. The continuing success of Casketfurniture.com could create coordination and control problems for MHP that may be solved only by the firm changing from the simple to the functional structure.[51]

Functional Structure

The **functional structure** consists of a chief executive officer and a limited corporate staff, with functional line managers in dominant organizational areas, such as production, accounting, marketing, R&D, engineering, and human resources.[52] This structure allows for functional specialization,[53] thereby facilitating active sharing of knowledge within each functional area. Knowledge sharing facilitates career paths as well as the professional development of functional specialists. However, a functional orientation can have a negative effect on communication and coordination among those representing different organizational functions. Because of this, the CEO must work hard to verify that the decisions and actions of individual business functions promote the entire firm rather than a single function.[54] The functional structure supports implementation of business-level strategies and some corporate-level strategies (e.g., single or dominant business) with low levels of diversification.

Multidivisional Structure

With continuing growth and success, firms often consider greater levels of diversification. However, successful diversification requires analysis of substantially greater amounts of data and information when the firm offers the same products in different markets (market or geographic diversification) or offers different products in several markets (product diversification). In addition, trying to manage high levels of diversification through functional structures creates serious coordination and control problems.[55] Thus, greater diversification leads to a new structural form.[56]

The **multidivisional (M-form) structure** consists of operating divisions, each representing a separate business or profit center in which the top corporate officer delegates responsibilities for day-to-day operations and business-unit strategy to division managers. Each division represents a distinct, self-contained business with its own functional hierarchy.[57] As initially designed, the M-form was thought to have three major benefits: "(1) it enabled corporate officers to more accurately monitor the performance of each business, which simplified the problem of control; (2) it facilitated comparisons between divisions, which improved the resource allocation process; and (3) it stimulated managers of poorly performing divisions to look for ways of improving performance."[58] Active monitoring of performance through the M-form increases the likelihood that decisions made by managers heading individual units will be in shareholders' best interests. Because diversification is a dominant corporate-level strategy used in the global economy, the M-form is a widely adopted organizational structure.[59]

Used to support implementation of related and unrelated diversification strategies, the M-form helps firms successfully manage the many demands (including those related to processing vast amounts of information) of diversification.[60] Chandler viewed the M-form as an innovative response to coordination and control problems that surfaced during the 1920s in the functional structures then used by large firms such as DuPont and General Motors.[61] Research shows that the M-form is appropriate when the firm grows through diversification.[62] Partly because of its value to diversified corporations, some consider the multidivisional structure to be one of the 20th century's most significant organizational innovations.[63]

No one organizational structure (simple, functional, or multidivisional) is inherently superior to the others.[64] In Peter Drucker's words: "There is no one right organization. . . . Rather, the task . . . is to select the organization for the particular task and mission at hand."[65] In our context, Drucker is saying that the firm must select a structure that is "right" for the particular strategy that has been selected to pursue the firm's vision and mission. Because no single structure is optimal in all instances, managers concentrate on developing proper matches between strategies and organizational structures rather than searching for an "optimal" structure.

We now describe the strategy/structure matches that evidence shows positively contribute to firm performance.

Matches between Business-Level Strategies and the Functional Structure

Different forms of the functional organizational structure are used to support implementation of the cost leadership, differentiation, and integrated cost leadership/differentiation strategies. The differences in these forms are accounted for primarily by different uses of three important structural characteristics or dimensions: *specialization* (concerned with the type and number of jobs required to complete work[66]), *centralization* (the degree to which decision-making authority is retained at higher managerial levels[67]), and *formalization* (the degree to which formal rules and procedures govern work[68]).

Using the Functional Structure to Implement the Cost Leadership Strategy

Firms using the cost leadership strategy want to sell large quantities of standardized products to an industry's or a segment's typical customer. Simple reporting relationships, few layers in the decision-making and authority structure, a centralized corporate staff, and a strong focus on process improvements through the manufacturing function rather than the development of new products by emphasizing product R&D characterize the cost leadership form of the functional structure[69] (see Figure 11.2). This structure contributes to the emergence of a low-cost culture—a culture in which all employees constantly try to find ways to reduce the costs incurred to complete their work.

In terms of centralization, decision-making authority is centralized in a staff function to maintain a cost-reducing emphasis within each organizational function (engineering, marketing, etc.). While encouraging continuous cost reductions, the centralized staff also verifies that further cuts in costs in one function won't adversely affect the productivity levels in other functions.[70]

Jobs are highly specialized in the cost leadership functional structure. Job specialization is accomplished by dividing work into homogeneous subgroups. Organizational functions are the most common subgroup, although work is sometimes batched on the basis of products produced or clients served. Specializing in their work allows employees to increase their efficiency, reducing the firm's costs as a result. Highly formalized rules and procedures, often emanating from the centralized staff, guide the work completed in the cost leadership form of the functional structure. Predictably following formal rules and procedures creates cost-reducing efficiencies. Known for its commitment to EDLP

FIGURE **11.2**

Functional Structure for Implementing a Cost Leadership Strategy

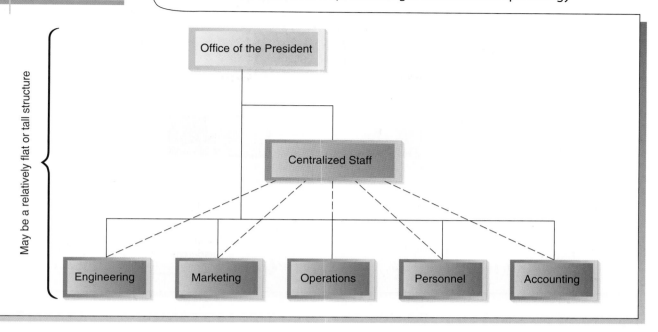

Notes:
- Operations is the main function
- Process engineering is emphasized rather than new product R&D
- Relatively large centralized staff coordinates functions
- Formalized procedures allow for emergence of a low-cost culture
- Overall structure is mechanistic; job roles are highly structured

("everyday low price"), Wal-Mart's functional organizational structures in its retail divisions (e.g., Wal-Mart Stores, Supercenters, Sam's Club) are formed to continuously drive costs lower.[71] As discussed in Chapter 4, competitors' efforts to duplicate the success of Wal-Mart's cost leadership strategies have failed, partly because of the effective strategy/structure matches in Wal-Mart's business units.

Using the Functional Structure to Implement the Differentiation Strategy

Firms using the differentiation strategy produce products that customers perceive as being different in ways that create value for them. With this strategy, the firm wants to sell nonstandardized products to customers with unique needs. Relatively complex and flexible reporting relationships, frequent use of cross-functional product development teams, and a strong focus on marketing and product R&D rather than manufacturing and process R&D (as with the cost leadership form of the functional structure) characterize the differentiation form of the functional structure (see Figure 11.3). This structure contributes to the emergence of a development-oriented culture—a culture in which employees try to find ways to further differentiate current products and to develop new, highly differentiated products.[72]

Continuous product innovation demands that people throughout the firm be able to interpret and take action based on information that is often ambiguous, incomplete, and uncertain. With a strong focus on the external environment to identify new opportunities, employees often gather this information from people outside the firm, such as

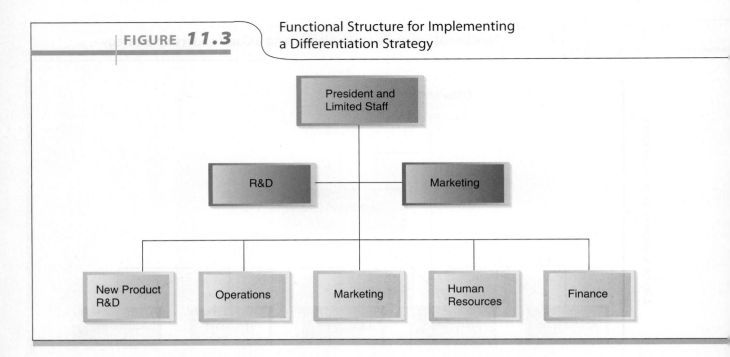

FIGURE 11.3 Functional Structure for Implementing a Differentiation Strategy

President and Limited Staff

R&D | Marketing

New Product R&D | Operations | Marketing | Human Resources | Finance

Notes:
- Marketing is the main function for keeping track of new product ideas
- New product R&D is emphasized
- Most functions are decentralized, but R&D and marketing may have centralized staffs that work closely with each other
- Formalization is limited so that new product ideas can emerge easily and change is more readily accomplished
- Overall structure is organic; job roles are less structured

customers and suppliers. Commonly, rapid responses to the possibilities indicated by the collected information are necessary, suggesting the need for decision-making responsibility and authority to be decentralized. To support creativity and the continuous pursuit of new sources of differentiation and new products, jobs in this structure are not highly specialized. This lack of specialization means that workers have a relatively large number of tasks in their job descriptions. Few formal rules and procedures are also characteristics of this structure. Low formalization, decentralization of decision-making authority and responsibility, and low specialization of work tasks combine to create a structure in which people interact frequently to exchange ideas about how to further differentiate current products while developing ideas for new products that can be differentiated to create value for customers.

Using the Functional Structure to Implement the Integrated Cost Leadership/Differentiation Strategy

Firms using the integrated cost leadership/differentiation strategy want to sell products that create value because of their relatively low cost and reasonable sources of differentiation. The cost of these products is low "relative" to the cost leader's prices while their differentiation is "reasonable" compared with the clearly unique features of the differentiator's products.

The integrated cost leadership/differentiation strategy is used frequently in the global economy, although it is difficult to successfully implement. This difficulty is due largely to the fact that different primary and support activities (see Chapter 3) must be emphasized when using the cost leadership and differentiation strategies. To achieve the cost leadership position, production and process engineering are emphasized, with infrequent product changes. To achieve a differentiated position, marketing and new product R&D are emphasized while production and process engineering are not. Thus, effective use of the integrated strategy results when the firm successfully combines activities intended to reduce costs with activities intended to create additional differentiation features. As a result, the integrated form of the functional structure must have decision-making patterns that are partially centralized and partially decentralized. Additionally, jobs are semi-specialized, and rules and procedures call for some formal and some informal job behavior.

Matches between Corporate-Level Strategies and the Multidivisional Structure

As explained earlier, Chandler's research showed that the firm's continuing success leads to product or market diversification or both.[73] The firm's level of diversification is a function of decisions about the number and type of businesses in which it will compete as well as how it will manage the businesses (see Chapter 6). Geared to managing individual organizational functions, increasing diversification eventually creates information processing, coordination, and control problems that the functional structure cannot handle. Thus, use of a diversification strategy requires the firm to change from the functional structure to the multidivisional structure to develop an appropriate strategy/structure match.

As defined in Figure 6.1 in Chapter 6, corporate-level strategies have different degrees of product and market diversification. The demands created by different levels of diversification highlight the need for a unique organizational structure to effectively implement each strategy (see Figure 11.4).

Using the Cooperative Form of the Multidivisional Structure to Implement the Related Constrained Strategy

The **cooperative form** is a structure in which horizontal integration is used to bring about interdivisional cooperation.[74] The divisions in the firm using the related constrained

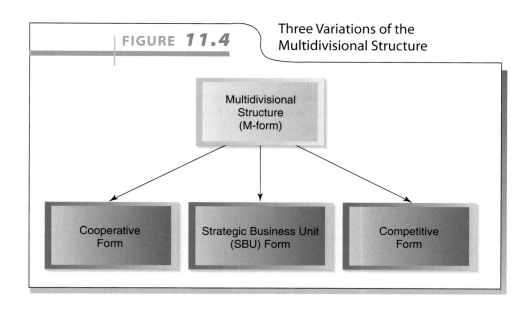

FIGURE 11.4 Three Variations of the Multidivisional Structure

FIGURE **11.5**

Cooperative Form of the Multidivisional Structure
for Implementing a Related Constrained Strategy

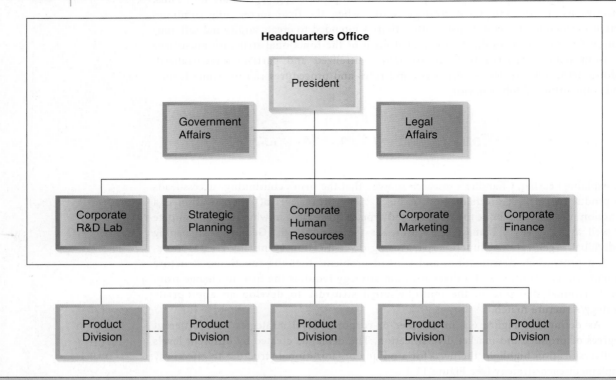

Notes:
- Structural integration devices create tight links among all divisions
- Corporate office emphasizes centralized strategic planning, human resources, and marketing to foster cooperation between divisions
- R&D is likely to be centralized
- Rewards are subjective and tend to emphasize overall corporate performance in addition to divisional performance
- Culture emphasizes cooperative sharing

diversification strategy commonly are formed around products, markets, or both. As the Opening Case illustrates, Sony would likely experience better coordination among its divisions if it were to implement the cooperative form of the multidivisional structure, given the lack of divisional coordination in its poorly executed online music strategy. In Figure 11.5, we use product divisions as part of the representation of the cooperative form of the multidivisional structure, although market divisions could be used instead of or in addition to product divisions to develop the figure.

All of the related constrained firm's divisions share one or more corporate strengths. Production competencies, marketing competencies, and channel dominance are examples of strengths that the firm's divisions might share.[75] Production expertise is one of the strengths of Sony's divisions. However, as the Opening Case illustrates, Sony has had difficulties in coordinating across divisions to create joint products in online music. Outback Steakhouse, Inc. has sought to diversify across the eight chains it owns or operates: its namesake flagship brand, Carrabba's Italian Grill (178 units), Fleming's Prime Steakhouse & Wine Bar (32 units), Bonefish Grill (75 units), Roy's (19 units), Lee Roy Selmon's (two units), Paul Lee's Chinese Kitchens (three units), and Cheeseburger in Paradise restaurants (15 units). In implementing its cooperative M-form structure,

Outback Steakhouse centralized a number of critical functions across the businesses, causing the firm to share the results of real estate development and purchasing and leasing actions. It also shares its expertise with its restaurants in running franchise operations in such areas as contracting, advertising, and training.[76]

The sharing of divisional competencies facilitates the corporation's efforts to develop economies of scope. As explained in Chapter 6, economies of scope (cost savings resulting from the sharing of competencies developed in one division with another division) are linked with successful use of the related constrained strategy. Interdivisional sharing of competencies depends on cooperation, suggesting the use of the cooperative form of the multidivisional structure.[77] Increasingly, it is important that the links resulting from effective use of integration mechanisms support the cooperative sharing of both intangible resources (such as knowledge) and tangible resources (such as facilities and equipment).[78]

The cooperative structure uses different characteristics of structure as integrating mechanisms to facilitate interdivisional cooperation. Defined earlier in the discussion of functional organizational structures, centralization is one of these mechanisms. As illustrated in the example of Outback Steakhouse, centralizing some organizational functions (such as human resource management, R&D, marketing, and finance) at the corporate level allows the linking of activities among divisions. Work completed in these centralized functions is managed by the firm's central office with the purpose of exploiting common strengths among divisions by sharing competencies.[79] The intent is to develop competitive advantages in the divisions as they imple-

Outback Steakhouse shares strengths across its eight different chains.

© LON C. DIEHL/PHOTOEDIT

ment their cost leadership, differentiation, or integrated cost leadership/differentiation business-unit strategies that allows the firm to create more value compared to the value that is created by nondiversified rivals' use of business-level strategies.[80]

Frequent, direct contact between division managers, another integrating mechanism, encourages and supports cooperation and the sharing of competencies or resources that could be used to create new advantages. Sometimes, liaison roles are established in each division to reduce the time division managers spend integrating and coordinating their unit's work with the work occurring in other divisions. Temporary teams or task forces may be formed around projects whose success depends on sharing competencies that are embedded within several divisions. Formal integration departments might be established in firms frequently using temporary teams or task forces. Ultimately, a matrix organization may evolve in firms implementing the related constrained strategy. A *matrix organization* is an organizational structure in which there is a dual structure combining both functional specialization and business product or project specialization.[81] Although complicated, an effective matrix structure can lead to improved coordination among a firm's divisions.[82]

The success of the cooperative multidivisional structure is significantly affected by how well information is processed among divisions. But because cooperation among divisions implies a loss of managerial autonomy, division managers may not readily commit themselves to the type of integrative information-processing activities that this structure demands. Moreover, coordination among divisions sometimes results in an unequal flow of positive outcomes to divisional managers. In other words, when managerial rewards are based at least in part on the performance of individual divisions, the manager of the division that is able to benefit the most by the sharing of corporate competencies might be viewed as receiving relative gains at others' expense. Strategic controls are important in these instances, as divisional managers' performance can be evaluated at least partly on the basis of how well they have facilitated interdivisional cooperative efforts. Furthermore, using reward systems that emphasize overall company performance, besides outcomes achieved by individual divisions, helps overcome problems associated with the cooperative form.

Using the Strategic Business Unit Form of the Multidivisional Structure to Implement the Related Linked Strategy

When the firm has fewer links or less constrained links among its divisions, the related linked diversification strategy is used. The strategic business unit form of the multidivisional structure supports implementation of this strategy. The **strategic business unit (SBU) form** consists of three levels: corporate headquarters, strategic business units (SBUs), and SBU divisions (see Figure 11.6).

FIGURE 11.6

SBU Form of the Multidivisional Structure for Implementing a Related Linked Strategy

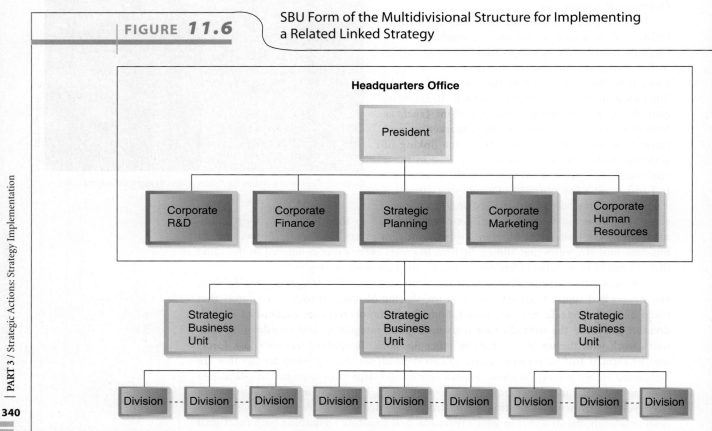

Notes:
• Structural integration among divisions within SBUs, but independence across SBUs
• Strategic planning may be the most prominent function in headquarters for managing the strategic planning approval process of SBUs for the president
• Each SBU may have its own budget for staff to foster integration
• Corporate headquarters staff serve as consultants to SBUs and divisions, rather than having direct input to product strategy, as in the cooperative form

The divisions within each SBU are related in terms of shared products or markets or both, but the divisions of one SBU have little in common with the divisions of the other SBUs. Divisions within each SBU share product or market competencies to develop economies of scope and possibly economies of scale. The integration mechanisms used by the divisions in a cooperative structure can be equally well used by the divisions within the individual strategic business units that are part of the SBU form of the multidivisional structure. In this structure, each SBU is a profit center that is controlled and evaluated by the headquarters office. Although both financial and strategic controls are important, on a relative basis financial controls are vital to headquarters' evaluation of each SBU; strategic controls are critical when the heads of SBUs evaluate their divisions' performance. Strategic controls are also critical to the headquarters' efforts to determine if the company has chosen an effective portfolio of businesses and if those businesses are being successfully managed.

The SBU structure is used by large firms and can be complex, with the complexity reflected by the organization's size and product and market diversity. Sony used the related linked strategy but it needed to pursue the related constrained strategy accompanied by the cooperative M-form structure, as exemplified in the Opening Case about its difficulty in getting separate SBUs to cooperate in creating an online music business.

Cendant Corporation employs the SBU structure to implement the related linked strategy. Cendant was created in December 1997 by a merger between CUC International, a marketing company, and HFS, a diversified firm with franchising operations in several industries, including real estate, hospitality, and vehicle services. Cendant owns a diversified set of services businesses, including its fee-for-services businesses: hotels (Ramada, Howard Johnson, Days Inn), real estate (Coldwell Banker, Century 21), tax preparation services, rental cars (Budget Rent A Car, Avis), travel (Web sites Orbitz and CheapTickets; Galileo, a computerized-reservation network used by travel agents and airlines around the globe), among others. Cendant grows through acquisitions as well as through internal means, such as development of new product lines, to implement its corporate-level diversification strategy. Cendant also uses joint ventures and franchising to complement each of its separate SBUs.[83]

Each SBU has a number of related businesses that are coordinated by the SBU managers. For example, Cendant's real estate franchises include some of the best-known names in the commercial and residential real estate brokerage market. It also has a relocation service, Cendant Mobility. Real estate services generate approximately 40 percent of revenues for this diversified company; Cendant collects fees on close to 30 percent of U.S. home sales. The sharing of competencies among units within an SBU is an important characteristic of the SBU form of the multidivisional structure (see the notes to Figure 11.6). Additionally, each SBU receives strategic help from corporate headquarters on contracting and training new franchised businesses and generally running

Ramada Inn is only one of Cendant's diversified services businesses; it also owns rental car businesses, including Avis.

fee-for-service businesses using more centralized functions. One drawback to the SBU structure is that multifaceted businesses often have difficulties in communicating this complex business model to stockholders.[84] Furthermore, if coordination between SBUs is needed, as noted in the Opening Case about Sony, problems can arise because the SBU structure, similar to the competitive form discussed next, does not readily foster cooperation across SBUs.

Using the Competitive Form of the Multidivisional Structure to Implement the Unrelated Diversification Strategy

Firms using the unrelated diversification strategy want to create value through efficient internal capital allocations or by restructuring, buying, and selling businesses.[85] The competitive form of the multidivisional structure supports implementation of this strategy.

The **competitive form** is a structure in which there is complete independence among the firm's divisions (see Figure 11.7). Unlike the divisions included in the cooperative structure, the divisions that are part of the competitive structure do not share common corporate strengths (e.g., marketing competencies or channel dominance). Because strengths aren't shared, integrating devices aren't developed for use by the divisions included in the competitive structure.

FIGURE 11.7 Competitive Form of the Multidivisional Structure for Implementing an Unrelated Strategy

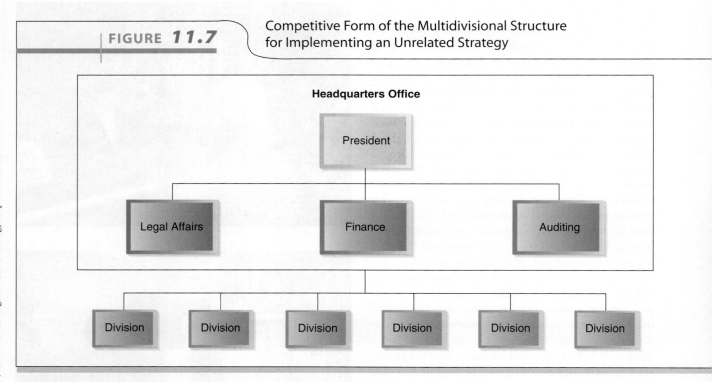

Notes:
- Corporate headquarters has a small staff
- Finance and auditing are the most prominent functions in the headquarters office to manage cash flow and assure the accuracy of performance data coming from divisions
- The legal affairs function becomes important when the firm acquires or divests assets
- Divisions are independent and separate for financial evaluation purposes
- Divisions retain strategic control, but cash is managed by the corporate office
- Divisions compete for corporate resources

The efficient internal capital market that is the foundation for use of the unrelated diversification strategy requires organizational arrangements that emphasize divisional competition rather than cooperation.[86] Three benefits are expected from the internal competition that the competitive form of the multidivisional structure facilitates. First, internal competition creates flexibility—corporate headquarters can have divisions working on different technologies to identify those with the greatest potential, for example. Resources can then be allocated to the division that is working with the most promising technology to fuel the entire firm's success. Second, internal competition challenges the status quo and inertia, because division heads know that future resource allocations are a product of excellent current performance as well as superior positioning of their division in terms of future performance. Last, internal competition motivates effort. The challenge of competing against internal peers can be as great as the challenge of competing against external marketplace competitors.[87]

Independence among divisions, as shown by a lack of sharing of corporate strengths and the absence of integrating devices, allows the firm using the unrelated diversification strategy to form specific profit performance expectations for each division to stimulate internal competition for future resources. The benefits of internal capital allocations or restructuring cannot be fully realized unless divisions are held accountable for their own independent performance. In the competitive structure, organizational controls (primarily financial controls) are used to emphasize and support internal competition among separate divisions and as the basis for allocating corporate capital based on divisions' performances. Textron Inc., a large "multi-industry" company, for example, seeks "to identify, research, select, acquire and integrate companies, and has developed a set of rigorous criteria to guide decision-making." As such, it continuously looks "to enhance and reshape its portfolio by divesting non-core assets and acquiring branded businesses in attractive industries with substantial long-term growth potential." It runs a number of independent businesses including units that manufacture fasteners, golf carts, and Bell helicopters. Textron uses return on invested capital (ROIC) as the "compass for guiding" the evaluation of its diversified set of businesses as they compete internally for resources.[88]

To emphasize competitiveness among divisions, the headquarters office maintains an arms-length relationship with them, intervening in divisional affairs only to audit operations and discipline managers whose divisions perform poorly. In emphasizing competition between divisions, the headquarters office relies on strategic controls to set rate-of-return targets and financial controls to monitor divisional performance relative to those targets. The headquarters office then allocates cash flow on a competitive basis, rather than automatically returning cash to the division that produced it. Thus, the focus of the headquarters' work is on performance appraisal, resource allocation, and long-range planning to verify that the firm's portfolio of businesses will lead to financial success.[89]

The three major forms of the multidivisional structure should each be paired with a particular corporate-level strategy. Table 11.1 shows these structures' characteristics. Differences are seen in the degree of centralization, the focus of the performance appraisal, the horizontal structures (integrating mechanisms), and the incentive compensation schemes. The most centralized and most costly structural form is the cooperative structure. The least centralized, with the lowest bureaucratic costs, is the competitive structure. The SBU structure requires partial centralization and involves some of the mechanisms necessary to implement the relatedness between divisions. Also, the divisional incentive compensation awards are allocated according to both SBUs and corporate performance.

Characteristics of the Structures Necessary to Implement the Related
Constrained, Related Linked, and Unrelated Diversification Strategies

TABLE *11.1*

Structural Characteristics	Overall Structural Form		
	Cooperative M-Form (Related Constrained Strategy)[a]	SBU M-Form (Related Linked Strategy)[a]	Competitive M-Form (Unrelated Diversification Strategy)[a]
Centralization of operations	Centralized at corporate office	Partially centralized (in SBUs)	Decentralized to divisions
Use of integration mechanisms	Extensive	Moderate	Nonexistent
Divisional performance appraisals	Emphasize subjective (strategic) criteria	Use a mixture of subjective (strategic) and objective (financial) criteria	Emphasize objective (financial) criteria
Divisional incentive compensation	Linked to overall corporate performance	Mixed linkage to corporate, SBU, and divisional performance	Linked to divisional performance

[a]Strategy implemented with structural form.

Matches between International Strategies and Worldwide Structures

As explained in Chapter 8, international strategies are becoming increasingly important for long-term competitive success.[90] Among other benefits, international strategies allow the firm to search for new markets, resources, core competencies, and technologies as part of its efforts to outperform competitors.[91]

As with business-level and corporate-level strategies, unique organizational structures are necessary to successfully implement the different international strategies.[92] Forming proper matches between international strategies and organizational structures facilitates the firm's efforts to effectively coordinate and control its global operations.[93] More importantly, research findings confirm the validity of the international strategy/ structure matches we discuss here.[94]

Using the Worldwide Geographic Area Structure to Implement the Multidomestic Strategy

The *multidomestic strategy* decentralizes the firm's strategic and operating decisions to business units in each country so that product characteristics can be tailored to local preferences. Firms using this strategy try to isolate themselves from global competitive forces by establishing protected market positions or by competing in industry segments that are most affected by differences among local countries. The worldwide geographic area structure is used to implement this strategy. The **worldwide geographic area structure** emphasizes national interests and facilitates the firm's efforts to satisfy local or cultural differences (see Figure 11.8).

Because using the multidomestic strategy requires little coordination between different country markets, integrating mechanisms among divisions in the worldwide geographic area structure are not needed. Hence, formalization is low, and coordination among units in a firm's worldwide geographic area structure is often informal.

FIGURE **11.8**

Worldwide Geographic Area Structure for Implementing a Multidomestic Strategy

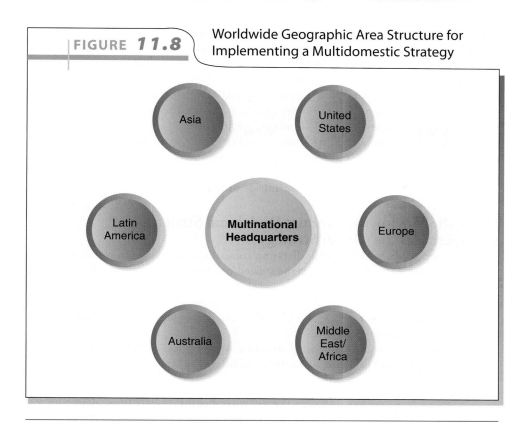

Notes:
- The perimeter circles indicate decentralization of operations
- Emphasis is on differentiation by local demand to fit an area or country culture
- Corporate headquarters coordinates financial resources among independent subsidiaries
- The organization is like a decentralized federation

The multidomestic strategy/worldwide geographic area structure match evolved as a natural outgrowth of the multicultural European marketplace. Friends and family members of the main business who were sent as expatriates into foreign countries to develop the independent country subsidiary often implemented this type of structure for the main business. The relationship to corporate headquarters by divisions took place through informal communication among "family members."[95]

SABMiller was created through a merger of South African Breweries and Miller Brewing in 2002. Over a three-year period, SABMiller's stock price has nearly doubled under the direction of CEO Graham Mackay. When Philip Morris sold Miller Brewing to SAB, Anheuser-Busch was the largest brewer in the United States and also the most profitable. However, SABMiller has been very successful as a strong number two in market share, especially in the United States with its Miller Light brand. More importantly, SAB-Miller has been pursuing the multidomestic strategy using acquisitions to buy strong local and regional brands throughout the world. Using an acquisition strategy, SAB-Miller has purchased Peroni in Italy, Pilsner Urquell in the Czech Republic, Tyskie in Poland, and, most recently, Bavaria, the second-largest brewer in Latin America. Global brewers Inbev (the largest global brewer by volume) and Heineken have also acquired firms as a means of implementing their multidomestic strategies.[96]

To implement its multidomestic strategy, SABMiller uses the worldwide geographic area structure with regional and country division headquarters throughout the world. Decentralization to these regional and country headquarters allows for strong marketing to adapt the acquired brands to the local cultures and for some improved cost structures, especially in avoiding significant transportation costs across geographic regions. SABMiller expects to make further acquisitions in developing markets such as China and India to contribute to future growth. But the strategy and structure combination has worked well even in the United States, where Miller's profits have exceeded their expectations. Thus, the strategy/structure fit in SABMiller has contributed significantly to the success of the firm not only in the United States but also throughout the world.[97]

A key disadvantage of the multidomestic strategy/worldwide geographic area structure match is the inability to create strong global efficiency. With an increasing emphasis on lower-cost products in international markets, the need to pursue worldwide economies of scale has also increased. These changes have fostered the use of the global strategy and its structural match, the worldwide product divisional structure.

Using the Worldwide Product Divisional Structure to Implement the Global Strategy

With the corporation's home office dictating competitive strategy, the *global strategy* is one through which the firm offers standardized products across country markets. The firm's success depends on its ability to develop and take advantage of economies of scope and economies of scale on a global level. Decisions to outsource some primary or support activities to the world's best providers are particularly helpful when the firm tries to develop economies of scale.[98]

The worldwide product divisional structure supports use of the global strategy. In the **worldwide product divisional structure,** decision-making authority is centralized in

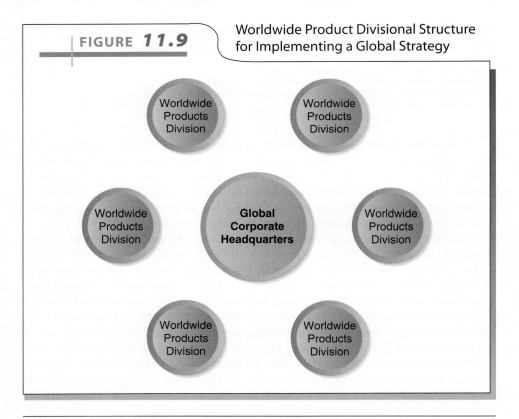

FIGURE **11.9**

Worldwide Product Divisional Structure for Implementing a Global Strategy

Notes:
- The headquarters' circle indicates centralization to coordinate information flow among worldwide products
- Corporate headquarters uses many intercoordination devices to facilitate global economies of scale and scope
- Corporate headquarters also allocates financial resources in a cooperative way
- The organization is like a centralized federation

the worldwide division headquarters to coordinate and integrate decisions and actions among divisional business units (see Figure 11.9). This structure is often used in rapidly growing firms seeking to manage their diversified product lines effectively, as in Japan's Canon, Inc.

Canon Inc. is a large Japanese firm focused on business machines, cameras, and optical products. Canon uses the global strategy by focusing continuously on integrating its production operations and driving costs lower through processes as well as new product R&D. It implements its strategy through the worldwide product divisional structure. There are four main product groups in this structure: consumer products including digital single lens reflex cameras, inkjet printers, binoculars, and image scanners; office products including copiers and large printing systems as well as associated toner cartridges; industrial products including semi-conductor production equipment and broadcasting equipment; and Canon product groups including document scanners, color card and label printers, and personal information products. Although there are regional marketing headquarters, they are subject to the product groups, and sales are organized globally through these product groups.[99]

Canon's sales are organized globally through its four main product groups: consumer products, office products, industrial products, and Canon products.

Integrating mechanisms are important in the effective use of the worldwide product divisional structure. Direct contact between managers, liaison roles between departments, and temporary task forces as well as permanent teams are examples of these mechanisms. One researcher describes the use of these mechanisms in the worldwide structure: "There is extensive and formal use of task forces and operating committees to supplement communication and coordination of worldwide operations."[100] The evolution of a shared vision of the firm's strategy and how structure supports its implementation is one of the important outcomes resulting from these mechanisms' effective use. The disadvantages of the global strategy/worldwide structure combination are the difficulty involved with coordinating decisions and actions across country borders and the inability to quickly respond to local needs and preferences.

Using the Combination Structure to Implement the Transnational Strategy

The *transnational strategy* calls for the firm to combine the multidomestic strategy's local responsiveness with the global strategy's efficiency. Thus, firms using this strategy are trying to gain the advantages of both local responsiveness and global efficiency. The combination structure is used to implement the transnational strategy. The **combination structure** is a structure drawing characteristics and mechanisms from both the worldwide geographic area structure and the worldwide product divisional structure. The transnational strategy is often implemented through two possible combination structures: a global matrix structure or a hybrid global design.[101]

The global matrix design brings together both local market and product expertise into teams that develop and respond to the global marketplace. The global matrix design (the basic matrix structure was defined earlier) promotes flexibility in designing products and responding to customer needs. However, it has severe limitations in that it places employees in a position of being accountable to more than one manager. At any given time, an employee may be a member of several functional or product group teams. Relationships that evolve from multiple memberships can make it difficult for employees to be simultaneously loyal to all of them. Although the matrix places authority in the hands of managers who are most able to use it, it creates problems in regard

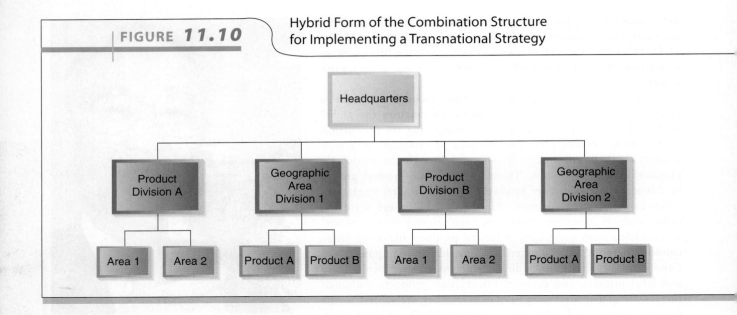

to corporate reporting relationships that are so complex and vague that it is difficult and time-consuming to receive approval for major decisions.

The hybrid structure is illustrated in Figure 11.10. In this design, some divisions are oriented toward products while others are oriented toward market areas. Thus, in some products where the geographic area is more important, the division managers are area-oriented. In other divisions where worldwide product coordination and efficiencies are more important, the division manager is more product oriented. For instance, at Philips Electronic NV, a number of products are consumer oriented (for example, coffeemakers) while others are industrial products (for example, semiconductor chips for mobile phones or medical equipment such as X-ray or ultrasound scanners).[102] In consumer-oriented products, divisions might be more geographic-area oriented and decentralized, while in semiconductors, divisions might be more product oriented and centralized.

The fits between the multidomestic strategy and the worldwide geographic area structure and between the global strategy and the worldwide product divisional structure are apparent. However, when a firm wants to implement the multidomestic and the global strategies simultaneously through a combination structure, the appropriate integrating mechanisms for the two structures are less obvious. The structure used to implement the transnational strategy must be simultaneously centralized and decentralized; integrated and nonintegrated; formalized and nonformalized. These seemingly opposite characteristics must be managed by an overall structure that is capable of encouraging all employees to understand the effects of cultural diversity on a firm's operations. This is illustrated in the Strategic Focus on Unilever's teams approach.

The teams approach exemplified in the Strategic Focus on Unilever highlights the need for a strong educational component to change an organization's entire culture. If the cultural change is effective, the combination structure should allow the firm to learn how to gain competitive benefits in local economies by adapting its core competencies, which often have been developed and nurtured in less culturally diverse competitive environments. As firms globalize and move toward the transnational strategy, the idea of a corporate headquarters has become increasingly important in fostering leadership and a shared vision to create a stronger company identity.[103]

Unilever is Reorganizing to Implement the Transnational Strategy by Using the Combination Structure

Unilever is a large consumer products firm headquartered historically in two locations, the Netherlands and the United Kingdom. Unilever is adopting a structure similar to the reorganization adopted by Procter & Gamble (P&G), with global managers overseeing consumer marketing and product development and regional bosses controlling areas such as sales, media buying, and trade marketing. The new organizational structure, which has been shaped over the last six years and more dramatically by CEO Patrick Cescau in 2005, is moving Unilever away from the location-specific dominance that is associated with a multidomestic strategy and worldwide area structure. In the restructuring, "Unilever sought to reduce the influence of country heads by forming global teams for some products." As such, it is clear that Unilever is using the combination structure to implement a transnational strategy.

Unilever's organization system differs from P&G's in a significant respect: "profit-and-loss responsibilities lie with regional presidents rather than with global category organizations that control marketing, product mixes and strategy." Although brand managers and directors in global brand categories sign off on overall strategic plans for each business unit, regional organizations have the power to set marketing budgets and to buy actual media applications (e.g., TV, radio, Internet, or newspaper advertisements). This power was previously in the hands of local country managers. One veteran P&G executive commented on that restructuring by noting: "You are essentially moving decision rights around, and that is very difficult since new kings are crowned and others dethroned." In the new system, "country managers can't tinker with [the product's] packaging, formulation or advertising."

For example, under the new structure regional marketers in the personal care brands such as Dove, Lux, and Axe/Lynx report directly to Simon Clift, marketing director for personal care branded products. This greatly expands the number of people he oversees, from 60 people to thousands, and thus he will now focus only on personal care products. In turn Mr. Clift reports to board-level personal care president Ralph Kugler.

One example of how the restructuring works in the regions is the home and personal care business in Asia. Country heads for Asian countries have been relocating to Singapore to form a team to manage investments in innovation and marketing across the region. Instead of reporting to marketing directors in each country, they will build a regional team to manage brands across the region, and thus only sales will remain an exclusively local function. Although this realignment may speed up decision-making processes, improve cost management, and provide stronger brand consistency in the region, there is the risk that it could weaken insights from local-consumer-oriented marketers. "It's not exactly clear how a strategy devised in Singapore for the Thai market will work in the Indian context." The bottom line is that there is more global and regional brand-management centralization than under the previous strategy. Thus Unilever is moving from a multidomestic strategy developed in continental Europe to a transnational strategy as it moves globally. It mirrors to a degree the strategy that competitors such P&G and L'Oreal have previously implemented but with more regional area control versus product control.

Unilever is restructuring by forming global teams for some products, rather than location-specific teams. Ben & Jerry's is one of the brands owned by Unilever.

© LON C. DIEHL/PHOTOEDIT

If the restructuring does not function as proposed, many stockholders hope that the company can be split into two different companies, one focusing on food and the other on soaps and personal care products. This way the separate businesses might pursue mergers that would strengthen each business. This pressure is felt even more since P&G's recent takeover of Gillette, which could spark further consolidation in the consumer and household products industries in which Unilever competes.

Sources: 2005, Can Unilever create a masterpiece? *Strategic Direction,* May, 11–14; 2005, Unilever's restructure "makes us more like P&G," *Marketing Week,* February 24, 8; D. Ball, 2005, Too many cooks: Despite revamp, unwieldy Unilever falls behind rivals, *Wall Street Journal,* January 3, A1; D. Ball, 2005, Unilever weighs adding CEO post to alter structure, *Wall Street Journal,* February 7, B5; D. Baishya, 2005, Will realignment aid Unilever marketing strategies?, *Media,* January 4, A20; G. Jones & P. Miskell, 2005, European integration and corporate restructuring: The strategy of Unilever c.1957–c.1990, *Economic History Review,* 58(1): 113–139; J. Neff, 2005, Unilever gets snarled in its own untangling, *Advertising Age,* May 2, 63–64; J. Neff, 2005, Unilever reorganization shifts P&L responsibility, *Advertising Age,* February 28, 13.

Matches between Cooperative Strategies and Network Structures

As discussed in Chapter 9, a network strategy exists when partners form several alliances in order to improve the performance of the alliance network itself through cooperative endeavors.[104] The greater levels of environmental complexity and uncertainty companies face in today's competitive environment are causing increasing numbers of firms to use cooperative strategies such as strategic alliances and joint ventures.[105]

The breadth and scope of firms' operations in the global economy create many opportunities for firms to cooperate.[106] In fact, a firm can develop cooperative relationships with many of its stakeholders, including customers, suppliers, and competitors.[107] When a firm becomes involved with combinations of cooperative relationships, it is part of a strategic network, or what others call an alliance constellation.[108]

A *strategic network* is a group of firms that has been formed to create value by participating in multiple cooperative arrangements, such as alliances and joint ventures. An effective strategic network facilitates the discovery of opportunities beyond those identified by individual network participants.[109] A strategic network can be a source of competitive advantage for its members when its operations create value that is difficult for competitors to duplicate and that network members can't create by themselves.[110] Strategic networks are used to implement business-level, corporate-level, and international cooperative strategies.

Commonly, a strategic network is a loose federation of partners who participate in the network's operations on a flexible basis. At the core or center of the strategic network, the *strategic center firm* is the one around which the network's cooperative relationships revolve (see Figure 11.11).

Because of its central position, the strategic center firm is the foundation for the strategic network's structure. Concerned with various aspects of organizational structure, such as formal reporting relationships and procedures, the strategic center firm manages what are often complex, cooperative interactions among network partners. In order to perform the primary tasks discussed next, the strategic center must make sure that incentives for participation in the network are aligned so that network firms continue to have a reason to remain connected.[111] The strategic center firm is engaged in four primary tasks as it manages the strategic network and controls its operations:[112]

Strategic outsourcing. The strategic center firm outsources and partners with more firms than do other network members. At the same time, the strategic center firm

FIGURE **11.11** | A Strategic Network

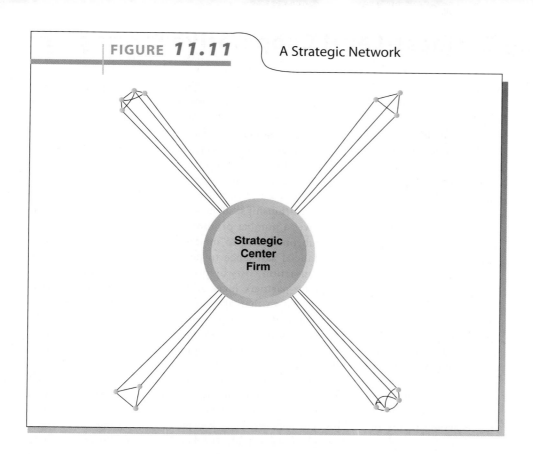

requires network partners to be more than contractors. Members are expected to find opportunities for the network to create value through its cooperative work.

Competencies. To increase network effectiveness, the strategic center firm seeks ways to support each member's efforts to develop core competencies that can benefit the network.

Technology. The strategic center firm is responsible for managing the development and sharing of technology-based ideas among network members. The structural requirement that members submit formal reports detailing the technology-oriented outcomes of their efforts to the strategic center firm facilitates this activity.[113]

Race to learn. The strategic center firm emphasizes that the principal dimensions of competition are between value chains and between networks of value chains. Because of this, the strategic network is only as strong as its weakest value-chain link. With its centralized decision-making authority and responsibility, the strategic center firm guides participants in efforts to form network-specific competitive advantages. The need for each participant to have capabilities that can be the foundation for the network's competitive advantages encourages friendly rivalry among participants seeking to develop the skills needed to quickly form new capabilities that create value for the network.[114]

Interestingly, strategic networks are being used more frequently, partly because of the ability of a strategic center firm to execute a strategy that links other firms more cheaply. Improved information systems and communication capabilities (e.g., the Internet) make this possible.[115]

Implementing Business-Level Cooperative Strategies

As noted in Chapter 9, there are two types of business-level complementary alliances: vertical and horizontal. Firms with competencies in different stages of the value chain form a vertical alliance to cooperatively integrate their different, but complementary, skills. Firms that agree to combine their competencies to create value in the same stage of the value chain form a horizontal alliance. Vertical complementary strategic alliances, such as those developed by Toyota Motor Company, are formed more frequently than horizontal alliances. Acting as the strategic center firm, Toyota fashioned its lean production system around a network of supplier firms.[116]

A strategic network of vertical relationships, such as the network in Japan between Toyota and its suppliers, often involves a number of implementation issues.[117] First, the strategic center firm encourages subcontractors to modernize their facilities and provides them with technical and financial assistance to do so, if necessary. Second, the strategic center firm reduces its transaction costs by promoting longer-term contracts with subcontractors, so that supplier-partners increase their long-term productivity. This approach is diametrically opposed to that of continually negotiating short-term contracts based on unit pricing. Third, the strategic center firm enables engineers in upstream companies (suppliers) to have better communication with those companies with whom it has contracts for services. As a result, suppliers and the strategic center firm become more interdependent and less independent.[118]

The lean production system pioneered by Toyota and others has been diffused throughout the global auto industry.[119] However, no auto company has learned how to duplicate the manufacturing effectiveness and efficiency Toyota derives from the cooperative arrangements in its strategic network.[120] A key factor accounting for Toyota's manufacturing-based competitive advantage is the cost other firms would incur to imitate the structural form used to support Toyota's application. In part, then, the structure of Toyota's strategic network that it created as the strategic center firm facilitates cooperative actions among network participants that competitors can't fully understand or duplicate.

In vertical complementary strategic alliances, such as the one between Toyota and its suppliers, the strategic center firm is obvious, as is the structure that firm establishes. However, this is not always the case with horizontal complementary strategic alliances where firms try to create value in the same part of the value chain, as with airline alliances that are commonly formed to create value in the marketing and sales primary activity segment of the value chain (see Table 3.6).[121] Because air carriers commonly participate in multiple horizontal complementary alliances, such as the Star Alliance between Lufthansa, United, Thai, Air Canada, SAS, and others, it is difficult to determine the strategic center firm. Moreover, participation in several alliances can cause firms to question partners' true loyalties and intentions. Also, if rivals band together in too many collaborative activities, one or more governments may suspect the possibility of illegal collusive activities. For these reasons, horizontal complementary alliances are used less frequently than their vertical counterpart.

Implementing Corporate-Level Cooperative Strategies

Corporate-level cooperative strategies (such as franchising) are used to facilitate product and market diversification. As a cooperative strategy, franchising allows the firm to use its competencies to extend or diversify its product or market reach, but without completing a merger or an acquisition.[122] Research suggests that knowledge embedded in corporate-level cooperative strategies facilitates synergy.[123] For example, "McDonald's is the leading global foodservice retailer with more than 30,000 local restaurants serving nearly 50 million people in more than 119 countries each day."[124] The McDonald's franchising system is a strategic network. McDonald's headquarters office serves as the strategic center firm for the network's franchisees. The headquarters office uses strategic controls and financial controls to verify that the franchisees' operations create the greatest value for the entire network. One strategic control issue is the location of franchisee units. McDonald's believes that its greatest expansion opportunities are outside the United States. For instance, McDonald's "expects to open at least 100 units a year in China through 2008."[125] As a result, as the strategic center firm, McDonald's is devoting its capital expenditures (over 70 percent in the last three years) primarily to develop units in non–U.S. markets. Financial controls are framed around requirements an interested party must satisfy to become a McDonald's franchisee as well as performance standards that are to be met when operating a unit. [126]

Implementing International Cooperative Strategies

Strategic networks formed to implement international cooperative strategies result in firms competing in several countries.[127] Differences among countries' regulatory environments increase the challenge of managing international networks and verifying that at a minimum, the network's operations comply with all legal requirements.[128]

Distributed strategic networks are the organizational structure used to manage international cooperative strategies. As shown in Figure 11.12, several regional strategic center firms are included in the distributed network to manage partner firms' multiple cooperative arrangements.[129]

Regional strategic centers for Dell Inc. are located in countries throughout the world, instead of only in the United States where the firm is headquartered. For example, Dell has a large European center in Limerick, Ireland. In Limerick, as at its other regional locations, Dell has developed a strong strategic network for its "built to order" business model that functions throughout its supply chain. When an order comes into Dell, the first stage involves a parts system that includes a just-in-time (JIT) hub of suppliers, most of which are very near to the Dell location of focus. Usually the components necessary to build

Dell has developed strategic networks at each of its regional centers, and as a result the firm's profitability has increased by five to seven percent.

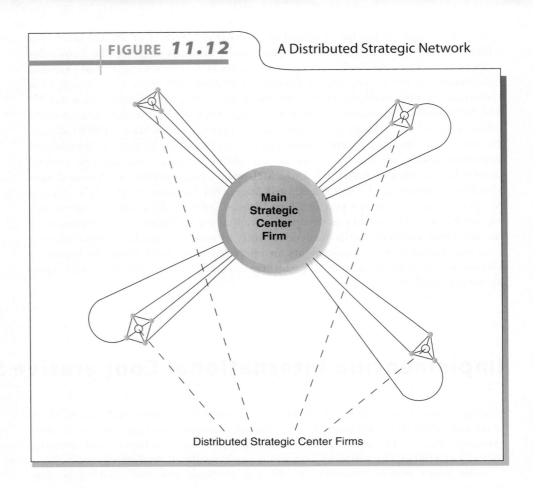

FIGURE 11.12 A Distributed Strategic Network

Main
Strategic
Center
Firm

Distributed Strategic Center Firms

the order are delivered within four hours after an order is received. This demand-driven supply network creates on average 15 percent less inventory and 17 percent better order performance. AMR Research suggests that Dell's network realizes a 5 to 7 percent improvement in profitability.[130]

SUMMARY

- Organizational structure specifies the firm's formal reporting relationships, procedures, controls, and authority and decision-making processes. Influencing managerial work, structure essentially details the work to be done and how that work is to be accomplished. Organizational controls guide the use of strategy, indicate how to compare actual and expected results, and suggest actions to take to improve performance when it falls below expectations. When properly matched with the strategy for which they were intended, structure and controls can be a competitive advantage.

- Strategic controls (largely subjective criteria) and financial controls (largely objective criteria) are the two types of organizational controls used to implement the firm's chosen strategy. Both types of controls are critical, although their degree of emphasis varies based on individual matches between strategy and structure.

- Strategy and structure influence each other, although overall, strategy has a stronger influence on structure. Research indicates that firms tend to change structure when declining performance forces them to do so. Effective managers anticipate the need for structural change, quickly modifying structure to better accommodate the firm's strategy implementation needs when evidence calls for that action.

- The functional structure is used to implement business-level strategies. The cost leadership strategy requires a centralized functional structure—one in which manufacturing efficiency and process engineering are emphasized. The differentiation strategy's functional structure decentralizes implementation-related decisions, especially those concerned with marketing, to those involved with individual organizational functions. Focus strategies, often used in small firms, require a simple structure until such time that the firm diversifies in terms of products and/or markets.

- Unique combinations of different forms of the multidivisional structure are matched with different corporate-level diversification strategies to properly implement these strategies. The cooperative M-form, used to implement the related constrained corporate-level strategy, has a centralized corporate office and extensive integrating mechanisms. Divisional incentives are linked to overall corporate performance. The related linked SBU M-form structure establishes separate profit centers within the diversified firm. Each profit center may have divisions offering similar products, but the

centers are unrelated to each other. The competitive M-form structure, used to implement the unrelated diversification strategy, is highly decentralized, lacks integrating mechanisms, and utilizes objective financial criteria to evaluate each unit's performance.

- The multidomestic strategy, implemented through the worldwide geographic area structure, emphasizes decentralization and locates all functional activities in the host country or geographic area. The worldwide product divisional structure is used to implement the global strategy. This structure is centralized in order to coordinate and integrate different functions' activities so as to gain global economies of scope and economies of scale. Decision-making authority is centralized in the firm's worldwide division headquarters.

- The transnational strategy—a strategy through which the firm seeks the local responsiveness of the multidomestic strategy and the global efficiency of the global strategy—is implemented through the combination structure. Because it must be simultaneously centralized and decentralized, integrated and non-integrated, and formalized and nonformalized, the combination structure is difficult to organize and manage successfully. However, two structural designs are suggested: the matrix and the hybrid structure with both geographic and product-oriented divisions.

- Increasingly important to competitive success, cooperative strategies are implemented through organizational structures framed around strategic networks. Strategic center firms play a critical role in managing strategic networks.

NOTES

1. M. S. Gary, 2005, Implementation strategy and performance outcomes in related diversification, *Strategic Management Journal*, 26: 643–664; J. Hauser, 2003, Organizational lessons for nonprofits, *The McKinsey Quarterly*, Special Edition: 60–69.
2. H. Barth, 2003, Fit among competitive strategy, administrative mechanisms, and performance: A comparative study of small firms in mature and new industries, *Journal of Small Business Management*, 41(2), 133–147; R. E. Miles & C. C. Snow, 1978, *Organizational Strategy, Structure and Process*, New York: McGraw-Hill.
3. N. Nohria, W. Joyce, & B. Roberson, 2003, What really works, *Harvard Business Review*, 81(7): 42—52.
4. T. Amburgey & T. Dacin, 1994, As the left foot follows the right? The dynamics of strategic and structural change, *Academy of Management Journal*, 37: 1427–1452.
5. B. Keats & H. O'Neill, 2001, Organizational structure: Looking through a strategy lens, in M. A. Hitt, R. E. Freeman, & J. S. Harrison (eds.), *Hand-

book of Strategic Management*, Oxford, UK: Blackwell Publishers, 520–542.
6. R. E. Hoskisson, C. W. L. Hill, & H. Kim, 1993, The multidivisional structure: Organizational fossil or source of value? *Journal of Management*, 19: 269–298.
7. E. M. Olson, S. F. Slater, G. Tomas, & M. Hult., 2005, The performance implications of fit among business strategy, marketing organization structure, and strategic behavior, *Journal of Marketing*, 69(3): 49–65.
8. T. Burns & G. M. Stalker, 1961, *The Management of Innovation*, London: Tavistok; P. R. Lawrence & J. W. Lorsch, 1967, *Organization and Environment*, Homewood, IL: Richard D. Irwin; J. Woodward, 1965, *Industrial Organization: Theory and Practice*, London: Oxford University Press.
9. H. Kim, R. E. Hoskisson, L. Tihanyi, & J. Hong, 2004, Evolution and restructuring of diversified business groups in emerging markets: The lessons from chaebols in Korea, *Asia Pacific Journal of Management*, 21: 25–48; M. Bower, 2003, Organization: Helping people pull together, *The McKinsey Quarterly*, Number 2, www.premium.mckinseyquarterly.com.

10. Keats & O'Neill, Organizational structure, 520–542; J. R. Galbraith, 1995, *Designing Organizations,* San Francisco: Jossey-Bass, 6.

11. Keats & O'Neill, Organizational structure, 533; Galbraith, *Designing Organizations,* 6.

12. H. J. Leavitt, 2003, Why hierarchies thrive, *Harvard Business Review,* 81(3): 96–102.

13. R. L. Priem, L. G. Love, & M. A. Shaffer, 2002, Executives' perceptions of uncertainty sources: A numerical taxonomy and underlying dimensions, *Journal of Management,* 28: 725–746.

14. S. K. Ethiraj & D. Levinthal, 2004, Bounded rationality and the search for organizational architecture: An evolutionary perspective on the design of organizations and their evolvability, *Administrative Science Quarterly,* 49: 404–437; J. D. Day, 2003, The value in organization, *The McKinsey Quarterly,* Number 2: 4–5; V. P. Rindova & S. Kotha, 2001, Continuous "morphing": Competing through dynamic capabilities, form, and function, *Academy of Management Journal,* 44: 1263–1280.

15. Barth, Fit among competitive strategy, administrative mechanisms, and performance; J. G. Covin, D. P. Slevin, & M. B. Heeley, 2001, Strategic decision making in an intuitive vs. technocratic mode: Structural and environmental consideration, *Journal of Business Research,* 52: 51–67.

16. E. M. Olson, S. F. Slater, & G. T. M. Hult, 2005, The importance of structure and process to strategy implementation, *Business Horizons,* 48(1): 47–54; H. Barkema, J. A. C. Baum, & E. A. Mannix, 2002, Management challenges in a new time, *Academy of Management Journal,* 45: 916–930.

17. L. Donaldson, 2001, *The contingency theory of organizations,* Thousand Oaks, CA: Sage; Jenster & Hussey, *Company Analysis,* 169; L. Donaldson, 1997, A positivist alternative to the structure-action approach, *Organization Studies,* 18: 77–92.

18. M. A. Schilling & H. K. Steensma, 2001, The use of modular organizational forms: An industry-level analysis, *Academy of Management Journal,* 44: 1149–1168.

19. C. B. Dobni & G. Luffman, 2003, Determining the scope and impact of market orientation profiles on strategy implementation and performance, *Strategic Management Journal,* 24: 577–585; D. C. Hambrick & J. W. Fredrickson, 2001, Are you sure you have a strategy? *Academy of Management Executive,* 15(4): 48–59.

20. T. J. Andersen, 2004, Integrating decentralized strategy making and strategic planning processes in dynamic environments, *Journal of Management Studies,* 41: 1271–1299.

21. J. Rivkin & N. Siggelkow, 2003, Balancing search and stability: Interdependencies among elements of organizational design, *Management Science,* 49: 290–321; G. A. Bigley & K. H. Roberts, 2001, The incident command system: High-reliability organizing for complex and volatile task environments, *Academy of Management Journal,* 44: 1281–1299.

22. K. D. Miller & A. T. Arikan, 2004, Technology search investments: Evolutionary, option reasoning, and option pricing approaches, *Strategic Management Journal,* 25: 473–485; J. Child & R. M. McGrath, 2001, Organizations unfettered: Organizational form in an information-intensive economy, *Academy of Management Journal,* 44: 1135–1148.

23. S. K. Ethiraj & Daniel Levinthal, 2004, Modularity and innovation in complex systems, *Management Science,* 50: 159–173; T. W. Malnight, 2001, Emerging structural patterns within multinational corporations: Toward process-based structures, *Academy of Management Journal,* 44: 1187–1210; A. Sharma, 1999, Central dilemmas of managing innovation in firms, *California Management Review,* 41(3): 146–164; H. A. Simon, 1991, Bounded rationality and organizational learning, *Organization Science,* 2: 125–134.

24. S. K. Maheshwari & D. Ahlstrom, 2004, Turning around a state owned enterprise: The case of Scooters India Limited, *Asia Pacific Journal of Management,* 21(1–2): 75–101; B. W. Keats & M. A. Hitt, 1988, A causal model of linkages among environmental dimensions, macroorganizational characteristics, and performance, *Academy of Management Journal,* 31: 570–598.

25. A. Chandler, 1962, *Strategy and Structure,* Cambridge, MA: MIT Press.

26. R. E. Hoskisson, R. A. Johnson, L. Tihanyi, & R. E. White, 2005, Diversified business groups and corporate refocusing in emerging economies, *Journal of Management,* 31: 941–965; J. D. Day, E. Lawson, & K. Leslie, 2003, When reorganization works, *The McKinsey Quarterly,* Number 2, 20–29.

27. M. Robb, P. Todd, & D. Turnbull, 2003, Untangling underperformance, *The McKinsey Quarterly,* Number 2, 52–59; Keats & O'Neill, Organizational structure, 535.

28. C. H. Noble, 1999, The eclectic roots of strategy implementation research, *Journal of Business Research,* 45: 119–134.

29. P. K. Mills & G. R. Ungson, 2003, Reassessing the limits of structural empowerment: Organizational constitution and trust as controls, *Academy of Management Review,* 28: 143–153.

30. R. Reed, W. J. Donoher, & S. F. Barnes, 2004, Predicting misleading disclosures: The effects of control, pressure, and compensation, *Journal of Managerial Issues,* 16: 322–336.

31. C. Sundaramurthy & M. Lewis, 2003, Control and collaboration: Paradoxes of governance, *Academy of Management Review,* 28: 397–415.

32. Y. Li, L. Li, Y. Liu, & L. Wang, 2005, Linking management control system with product development and process decisions to cope with environment complexity, *International Journal of Production Research,* 43: 2577–2591; D. F. Kuratko, R. D. Ireland, & J. S. Hornsby, 2001, Improving firm performance through entrepreneurial actions: Acordia's corporate entrepreneurship strategy, *Academy of Management Executive,* 15(4): 60–71.

33. S. D. Julian & E. Scifres, 2002, An interpretive perspective on the role of strategic control in triggering strategic change, *Journal of Business Strategies,* 19: 141–159.

34. R. E. Hoskisson, M. A. Hitt, & R. D. Ireland, 1994, The effects of acquisitions and restructuring strategies (strategic refocusing) on innovation, in G. von Krogh, A. Sinatra, & H. Singh (eds.), *Managing Corporate Acquisition,* London: MacMillan, 144–169.

35. M. A. Hitt, R. E. Hoskisson, R. A. Johnson, & D. D. Moesel, 1996, The market for corporate control and firm innovation, *Academy of Management Journal,* 39: 1084–1119.

36. C. Edwards, 2005, Shaking up Intel's insides, *Business Week,* January 31, 35; W. Lazonick & A. Prencipe, 2005, Dynamic capabilities and sustained innovation: Strategic control and financial commitment at Rolls-Royce PLC, *Industrial and Corporate Change,* 14: 501–542.

37. R. E. Hoskisson & M. A. Hitt, 1988, Strategic control and relative R&D investment in multiproduct firms, *Strategic Management Journal,* 9: 605–621.

38. D. J. Collis, 1996, Corporate strategy in multibusiness firms, *Long Range Planning,* 29: 416–418.

39. M. L. Songini, 2003, Oracle tools designed to help monitor financial controls, *Computerworld,* 37(22): 49.

40. S. Cowley, 2005, New CEO shuffles CA deck, *Info World,* April 11, 19; B. Dunn, 2005, CA starts buying again amid reorganization, *Information Week,* April 11, 24; M. Hamblen, 2005, CA's top exec aims for more-focused operations, *Computer World,* April 11, 10.

41. J. B. Barney, 2002, *Gaining and Sustaining Competitive Advantage,* 2nd ed., Upper Saddle River, NJ: Prentice Hall.

42. X. Yin & E. J. Zajac, 2004, The strategy/governance structure fit relationship: Theory and evidence in franchising arrangements, *Strategic Management Journal,* 25: 365–383.

43. Keats & O'Neill, Organizational structure, 531.

44. D. Miller & J. O. Whitney, 1999, Beyond strategy: Configuration as a pillar of competitive advantage, *Business Horizons,* 42(3): 5–17.

45. Chandler, Strategy and Structure.

46. Keats & O'Neill, Organizational structure, 524.

47. M. E. Sosa, S. D. Eppinger, & C. M. Rowles, 2004, The misalignment of product architecture and organizational structure in complex product development, *Management Science,* 50: 1674–1689.

48. S. Karim & W. Mitchell, 2004, Innovating through acquisition and internal development: A quarter-century of boundary evolution at Johnson &

Johnson, *Long Range Planning,* 37: 525–547; C. Williams & W. Mitchell, 2004, Focusing firm evolution: The impact of information infrastructure on market entry by U.S. telecommunications companies, 1984–1998, *Management Science,* 50: 1561–1575.

49. C. Levicki, 1999, *The Interactive Strategy Workout,* 2nd ed., London: Prentice Hall.

50. J. J. Chrisman, A. Bauerschmidt, & C. W. Hofer, 1998, The determinants of new venture performance: An extended model, Entrepreneurship Theory & Practice, 23(3): 5–29; H. M. O'Neill, R. W. Pouder, & A. K. Buchholtz, 1998, Patterns in the diffusion of strategies across organizations: Insights from the innovation diffusion literature, Academy of Management Review, 23: 98–114.

51. 2005, Welcome to CasketFurniture Store, CasketFurniture.com Home Page, www.casketfurniture.com, August 25.

52. Galbraith, Designing Organizations, 25.

53. Keats & O'Neill, Organizational structure, 539.

54. Lawrence & Lorsch, Organization and Environment.

55. O. E. Williamson, 1975, Markets and Hierarchies: Analysis and Anti-trust Implications, New York: The Free Press.

56. Chandler, Strategy and Structure.

57. J. Greco, 1999, Alfred P. Sloan Jr. (1875–1966): The original organizational man, *Journal of Business Strategy,* 20(5): 30–31.

58. Hoskisson, Hill, & Kim, The multidivisional structure, 269–298.

59. H. Zhou, 2005, Market structure and organizational form, *Southern Economic Journal,* 71: 705–719; H. Itoh, 2003, Corporate restructuring in Japan Part I: Can M-form organization manage diverse businesses? *Japanese Economic Review,* 54: 49–73; W. G. Rowe & P. M. Wright, 1997, Related and unrelated diversification and their effect on human resource management controls, *Strategic Management Journal,* 18: 329–338.

60. C. E. Helfat & K. M. Eisenhardt, 2004, Inter-temporal economies of scope, organizational modularity, and the dynamics of diversification, *Strategic Management Journal,* 25: 1217–1232; A. D. Chandler, 1994, The functions of the HQ unit in the multibusiness firm, in R. P. Rumelt, D. E. Schendel, & D. J. Teece (eds.), *Fundamental Issues in Strategy,* Cambridge, MA: Harvard Business School Press, 327.

61. O. E. Williamson, 1994, Strategizing, economizing, and economic organization, in R. P. Rumelt, D. E. Schendel, & D. J. Teece (eds.), *Fundamental Issues in Strategy,* Cambridge, MA: Harvard Business School Press, 361–401.

62. R. M. Burton & B. Obel, 1980, A computer simulation test of the M-form hypothesis, *Administrative Science Quarterly,* 25: 457–476.

63. O. E. Williamson, 1985, The Economic Institutions of Capitalism: Firms, Markets, and Relational Contracting, New York: Macmillan.

64. Keats & O'Neill, Organizational structure, 532.

65. M. F. Wolff, 1999, In the organization of the future, competitive advantage will be inspired, *Research Technology Management,* 42(4): 2–4.

66. R. H. Hall, 1996, *Organizations: Structures, Processes, and Outcomes,* 6th ed., Englewood Cliffs, NJ: Prentice Hall, 13; S. Baiman, D. F. Larcker, & M. V. Rajan, 1995, Organizational design for business units, *Journal of Accounting Research,* 33: 205–229.

67. L. G. Love, R. L. Priem, & G. T. Lumpkin, 2002, Explicitly articulated strategy and firm performance under alternative levels of centralization, *Journal of Management,* 28: 611–627.

68. Hall, Organizations, 64–75.

69. Barney, Gaining and Sustaining Competitive Advantage, 257.

70. Olson, Slater, Tomas, & Hult, The performance implications of fit among business strategy, marketing organization structure, and strategic behavior.

71. 2005, Wal-Mart stores "pricing philosophy," www.walmart.com, August 26.

72. Olson, Slater, Tomas, & Hult, The performance implications of fit among business strategy, marketing organization structure, and strategic behavior.

73. Chandler, Strategy and Structure.

74. Gary, Implementation strategy and performance outcomes in related diversification.

75. R. Rumelt, 1974, *Strategy, Structure and Economic Performance,* Boston: Harvard University Press.

76. R. Gibson, 2005, Outback tries to diversify in new strategy, *Wall Street Journal,* April 27, B8.

77. C. C. Markides & P. J. Williamson, 1996, Corporate diversification and organizational structure: A resource-based view, *Academy of Management Journal,* 39: 340–367; C. W. L. Hill, M. A. Hitt, & R. E. Hoskisson, 1992, Cooperative versus competitive structures in related and unrelated diversified firms, *Organization Science,* 3: 501–521.

78. P. F. Drucker, 2002, They're not employees, they're people, *Harvard Business Review,* 80(2): 70–77; J. Robins & M. E. Wiersema, 1995, A resource-based approach to the multibusiness firm: Empirical analysis of portfolio interrelationships and corporate financial performance, *Strategic Management Journal,* 16: 277–299.

79. J. R. Baum & S. Wally, 2003, Strategic decision speed and firm performance, *Strategic Management Journal,* 24: 1107–1129.

80. C. C. Markides, 1997, To diversify or not to diversify, *Harvard Business Review,* 75(6): 93–99.

81. J. G. March, 1994, *A Primer on Decision Making: How Decisions Happen,* New York: The Free Press, 117–118.

82. M. Goold & A. Campbell, 2003, Structured networks: Towards the well designed matrix, *Long Range Planning,* 36(5): 427–439.

83. D. DeFotis, 2005, Reversal of Fortune?, *Barron's,* May 2, T7.

84. P. A. Argenti, R. A. Howell, & K. A. Beck, 2005, The strategic communication imperative, *MIT Sloan Management Review,* 46(3): 84–89.

85. Hoskisson, Hill, & Kim, The multidivisional structure; R. E. Hoskisson & M. A. Hitt, 1990, Antecedents and performance outcomes of diversification: A review and critique of theoretical perspectives, *Journal of Management,* 16: 461–509.

86. Hill, Hitt, & Hoskisson, Cooperative versus competitive structures, 512.

87. J. Birkinshaw, 2001, Strategies for managing internal competition, *California Management Review,* 44(1): 21–38.

88. 2005, Textron profile, www.textron.com, August 27.

89. M. Maremont, 2004, Leadership (a special report); more can be more: Is the conglomerate a dinosaur from a bygone era? The answer is no—with a caveat, *Wall Street Journal,* October 24, R4; T. R. Eisenmann & J. L. Bower, 2000, The entrepreneurial M-form: Strategic integration in global media firms, *Organization Science,* 11: 348–355.

90. S. E. Christophe & H. Lee, 2005, What matters about internationalization: A market-based assessment, *Journal of Business Research,* 58: 636–643; Y. Luo, 2002, Product diversification in international joint ventures: Performance implications in an emerging market, *Strategic Management Journal,* 23: 1–20.

91. T. M. Begley & D. P. Boyd, 2003, The need for a corporate global mind-set, *MIT Sloan Management Review,* 44(2): 25–32; Tallman, Global strategic management, 467.

92. T. Kostova & K. Roth, 2003, Social capital in multinational corporations and a micro-macro model of its formation, *Academy of Management Review,* 28: 297–317.

93. Malnight, Emerging structural patterns, 1188.

94. J. Wolf & W. G. Egelhoff, 2002, A reexamination and extension of international strategy-structure theory, *Strategic Management Journal,* 23: 181–189.

95. C. A. Bartlett & S. Ghoshal, 1989, *Managing across Borders: The Transnational Solution,* Boston: Harvard Business School Press.

96. P. Sellers, 2005, SAB brews up big trouble for Bud, *Fortune,* August 22, 26; D. Bilefsky & J. Singer, 2005, SABMiller pursues Columbian brewer, *Wall Street Journal,* July 19, A3.

97. G. Makay, 2005, Challenging conventional wisdom in the global beer business, www.sabmiller.com, August 29.

98. S. T. Cavusgil, S. Yeniyurt, & J. D. Townsend, 2004, The framework of a global company: A conceptualization and preliminary validation, *Industrial Marketing Management,* 33: 711–716.

99. I. Rowley, H. Tashiro, & L. Lee, 2005, Canon: Combat-ready, *Business Week,* September 5, 48–49; 2005, About Canon, www.canon.com, August 29.

100. Malnight, Emerging structural patterns, 1197.

101. Goold & Campbell, Structured networks: Towards the well designed matrix.

102. C. Bryan-Low & S. Simons, 2005, Philips to buy health-care tech firm, *Wall Street Journal,* July 7, B5.

103. R. J. Kramer, 1999, Organizing for global competitiveness: The corporate headquarters design, *Chief Executive Digest,* 3(2): 23–28.

104. Y. L. Doz & G. Hamel, 1998, *Alliance Advantage: The Art of Creating Value through Partnering,* Boston: Harvard Business School Press, 222.

105. K. Moller, A. Rajala, & S. Svahn, 2005, Strategic business nets—their type and management, *Journal of Business Research,* 58: 1274–1284; S. X. Li & T. J. Rowley, 2002, Inertia and evaluation mechanisms in interorganizational partner selection: Syndicate formation among U.S. investment banks, *Academy of Management Journal,* 45: 1104–1119; A. C. Inkpen, 2001, Strategic alliances, in M. A. Hitt, R. E. Freeman, & J. S. Harrison (eds.), *Handbook of Strategic Management,* Oxford, UK: Blackwell Publishers, 409–432.

106. T. H. Reus & W. J. Ritchie III, 2004, Interpartner, parent, and environmental factors influencing the operation of international joint ventures: 15 years of research, *Management International Review,* 44: 369–395; Luo, Product diversification in international joint ventures, 2.

107. Goold & Campbell, Structured networks: Towards the well designed matrix; M. Sawhney, E. Prandelli, & G. Verona, 2003, The power of innomediation, *MIT Sloan Management Review,* 44(2): 77–82; R. Gulati, N. Nohria, & A. Zaheer, 2000, Strategic networks, *Strategic Management Journal,* 21 (Special Issue): 203–215; B. Gomes-Casseres, 1994, Group versus group: How alliance networks compete, *Harvard Business Review,* 72(4): 62–74.

108. B. Comes-Casseres, 2003, Competitive advantage in alliance constellations, *Strategic Organization,* 1: 327–335; T. K. Das & B.-S. Teng, 2002, Alliance constellations: A social exchange perspective, *Academy of Management Review,* 27: 445–456.

109. S. Tallman, M. Jenkins, N. Henry, & S. Pinch, 2004, Knowledge, clusters, and competitive advantage, *Academy of Management Review,* 29: 258–271; C. Lee, K. Lee, & J. M. Pennings, 2001, Internal capabilities, external networks, and performance: A study on technology-based ventures, *Strategic Management Journal,* 22 (Special Issue): 615–640.

110. A. Zaheer & G. G. Bell, 2005, Benefiting from network position: Firm capabilities, structural holes, and performance, *Strategic Management Journal,* 26: 809–825; M. B. Sarkar, R. Echambadi, & J. S. Harrison, 2001, Alliance entrepreneurship and firm market performance, *Strategic Management Journal,* 22 (Special Issue): 701–711.

111. V. G. Narayanan & A. Raman, 2004, Aligning incentives in supply chains, *Harvard Business Review,* 82(11): 94–102.

112. S. Harrison, 1998, *Japanese Technology and Innovation Management,* Northampton, MA: Edward Elgar.

113. T. Keil, 2004, Building external corporate venturing capability, *Journal of Management Studies,* 41: 799–825.

114. P. Dussauge, B. Garrette, & W. Mitchell, 2004, Learning from competing partners: Outcomes and duration of scale and link alliances in Europe, North America and Asia, *Strategic Management Journal,* 21: 99–126; G. Lorenzoni & C. Baden-Fuller, 1995, Creating a strategic center to manage a web of partners, *California Management Review,* 37(3): 146–163.

115. N. C. Carr, 2005, In praise of walls, *MIT Sloan Management Review,* 45(3): 10–13.

116. J. H. Dyer & K. Nobeoka, 2000, Creating and managing a high-performance knowledge-sharing network: The Toyota case, *Strategic Management Journal,* 21 (Special Issue): 345–367; J. H. Dyer, 1997, Effective interfirm collaboration: How firms minimize transaction costs and maximize transaction value, *Strategic Management Journal,* 18: 535–556.

117. M. Kotabe, X. Martin, & H. Domoto, 2003, Gaining from vertical partnerships: Knowledge transfer, relationship duration and supplier performance improvement in the U.S. and Japanese automotive industries, *Strategic Management Journal,* 24: 293–316.

118. T. Nishiguchi, 1994, *Strategic Industrial Sourcing: The Japanese Advantage,* New York: Oxford University Press.

119. P. Dussauge, B. Garrette, & W. Mitchell, 2004, Asymmetric performance: The market share impact of scale and link alliances in the global auto industry, *Strategic Management Journal,* 25: 701–711.

120. C. Dawson & K. N. Anhalt, 2005, A 'China price' for Toyota, *Business Week,* February 21, 50–51; W. M. Fruin, 1992, *The Japanese Enterprise System,* New York: Oxford University Press.

121. A. Andal-Ancion & G. Yip, 2005, Smarter ways to do business with the competition, *European Business Forum,* April 1, 32–36.

122. P. J. Brews & C. L. Tucci, 2004, Exploring the structural effects of internetworking, *Strategic Management Journal,* 25: 429–451.

123. B. B. Nielsen, 2005, The role of knowledge embeddedness in the creation of synergies in strategic alliances, *Journal of Business Research,* 58: 1194–1204.

124. 2005, About McDonald's, www.mcdonalds.com, August 31.

125. 2005, McDonald's plans for the future, *Restaurant and Institutions,* June 1, 19.

126. 2005, McDonald's USA franchising, www.mcdonalds.com, August 31.

127. P. H. Andersen & P. R. Christensen, 2005, Bridges over troubled water: Suppliers as connective nodes in global supply networks, *Journal of Business Research,* 58: 1261–1273; C. Jones, W. S. Hesterly, & S. P. Borgatti, 1997, A general theory of network governance: Exchange conditions and social mechanisms, *Academy of Management Review,* 22: 911–945.

128. A. Goerzen, 2005, Managing alliance networks: Emerging practices of multinational corporations, *Academy of Management Executive,* 19(2): 94–107; J. M. Mezias, 2002, Identifying liabilities of foreignness and strategies to minimize their effects: The case of labor lawsuit judgments in the United States, *Strategic Management Journal,* 23: 229–244.

129. R. E. Miles, C. C. Snow, J. A. Mathews, G. Miles, & J. J. Coleman Jr., 1997, Organizing in the knowledge age: Anticipating the cellular form, *Academy of Management Executive,* 11(4): 7–20.

130. M. Wheatley, 2005, Yours, mine, and ours, *Manufacturing Business Technology,* 23(8): 40–42.

Leadership

Studying this chapter should provide you with the strategic management knowledge needed to:

1. Define strategic leadership and describe the importance of top-level managers.

2. Define top management teams and explain their effects on firm performance.

3. Describe the managerial succession process using internal and external managerial labor markets.

4. Discuss the value of strategic leadership in determining the firm's strategic direction.

5. Describe the importance of strategic leaders in managing the firm's resources, with emphasis on exploiting and maintaining core competencies, human capital, and social capital.

6. Define organizational culture and explain what must be done to sustain an effective culture.

7. Explain what strategic leaders can do to establish and emphasize ethical practices.

8. Discuss the importance and use of organizational controls.

REUTERS/LOU DEMATTEIS/LANDOV

Mark Hurd, Carly Fiorina's successor as CEO of Hewlett-Packard.

Long-Term Vision or Operational Performance? The "Un-Carly" Takes Hewlett-Packard's Reins

After almost six years as CEO of Hewlett-Packard, Carly Fiorina was fired by the firm's board of directors. They were unhappy with the stock price, which closely paralleled the operating performance of the firm. At the time she lost her job, Fiorina was well known and perhaps the most powerful woman executive in the world. Why did this smart, powerful woman lose her job? One reason relates to a season of discontent with top executives in many U.S. firms: A large number of top executives lost their jobs in 2004–2005 because investors and boards of directors wanted stronger firm performance. Other reasons Fiorina lost her job were because of her presence and some of the decisions that she made.

Perhaps the biggest decision Fiorina made during her tenure was to acquire Compaq. She encountered significant resistance to this decision from within and outside the company. Her decision to acquire Compaq was based on the charge given her by the board of directors when she was hired. They asked her to change the company and enhance its competitiveness. She felt that integrating Compaq would give HP market power in the personal computer market and would also enrich HP's ability to compete with IBM in information services. Because it was a high-profile acquisition and because many such mergers are not successful, her decision was risky. She had to fight members of the board, major investors, and some managers in her own company. She won the battle but staked her future on the performance of the combined company.

Three years after the merger of HP and Compaq, the new company could not compete with Dell or IBM. Some analysts believe that Fiorina overlooked critical operating concerns that were necessary especially to compete with the super-efficient Dell. HP's cost structure is much weaker than Dell's and its efficiency in production and inventory control is not in the same competitive space as Dell. In late 2004, HP badly missed its sales and profit targets, and Fiorina fired three top sales executives. But she also did not heed the warnings of analysts and her own board to shore up HP's operations. Some believe that she did not have the right talent in this area. Because of HP's poor operating performance, the firm's stock price lagged badly and investors were quite concerned.

Some believe that Fiorina was unlikely to succeed because she was an outsider. She had a significantly different approach than her predecessors. She was the spokesperson for the company. She appeared in commercials for the company and held high-profile pep rallies for employees. Because of these actions, many current and former HP executives and managers never accepted her leadership. They viewed her more in a promotional role than as a strategic leader. In short, Fiorina had a vision but was unable to muster the support needed to achieve the vision.

After firing Fiorina, the HP board then hired Mark Hurd as CEO and president. Many have referred to the quiet, unassuming Hurd as the "un-Carly." Hurd is a "nuts-and-bolts" operations person with seemingly no grand vision of his own. It is reported that Hurd is in the process of revamping much of Fiorina's strategy. He is likely to remake the sales force and to effect large layoffs to reduce costs. This approach is traditional for large companies and thus more comfortable to investors and Wall Street analysts. However, operating on short-term goals to reduce costs without a long-range vision is not a good plan for recapturing HP's lost glory. Mark Hurd is "executing" but without a long-term sense of direction. Perhaps HP would have done better to team Fiorina and Hurd. Then they might have a big thinker with vision and a doer who can execute and increase efficiency. Both are needed to provide the strategic leadership necessary to compete effectively in the current competitive landscape.

Sources: D. K. Berman & A. Latour, 2005, Too big: learning from mistakes, *Wall Street Journal,* www.wsj.com, February 10; B. Elgin, 2005, The inside story of Carly's ouster, *Business Week,* www.businessweek.com; February 10; J. Markoff, 2005, Fiorina's confrontational tenure at Hewlett comes to a close, *New York Times,* www.nytimes.com, February 10; C. de Aenlle, 2005, See you, Carly, goodbye, Harry, hello, investors, *New York Times,* www.nytimes.com. March 13; J. Markoff, 2005, A break with style not with strategy, *New York Times,* www.nytimes.com. March 30; P. Burrows & P. Elgin, The un-Carly unveils his plan, 2005, *Business Week,* www.businessweek.com, June 16.

As the Opening Case illustrates, all CEOs encounter significant risk, but they also can make a major difference in how a firm performs. If a strategic leader can create a strategic vision for the firm using forward thinking, she may be able to energize the firm's human capital and achieve positive outcomes. However, the challenge of strategic leadership is significant. Carly Fiorina was hired with much publicity and she had the media spotlight on her during much of her tenure with HP. The controversial acquisition of Compaq and the attempts to change the company appeared to be unsuccessful as the firm suffered weakening performance. And Fiorina paid the ultimate price: losing her job. Her replacement is unlike Fiorina in many ways and is focusing on improving HP's operational performance, which should increase the firm's financial performance. However, it is difficult to build and maintain success over a sustained period of time. Emphasis on the operational performance should be helpful in the short term but a focus on the long term is likely necessary if HP is to regain its competitive position over time relative to Dell and IBM.

As this chapter makes clear, it is through effective strategic leadership that firms are able to successfully use the strategic management process. As strategic leaders, top-level managers must guide the firm in ways that result in the formation of a vision and mission (as explained in Chapter 1). This guidance may lead to goals that stretch everyone in the organization to improve performance.[1] Moreover, strategic leaders must facilitate the development of appropriate strategic actions and determine how to implement them. These actions on the part of strategic leaders culminate in strategic competitiveness and above-average returns,[2] as shown in Figure 12.1.

As noted in the Opening Case, it is difficult to be a successful strategic leader. The Opening Case also suggests that the job of CEO is challenging and stressful, even more so now than it was in previous years. Research suggests that CEO tenure on the job is likely to be three to 10 years. The average tenure of a CEO in 1995 was 9.5 years. In the early 21st century, the average had decreased to 7.3 years. And it continues to decrease, with the largest number of CEOs ever losing their jobs in early 2005.[3] Additionally, company boards of directors are showing an increased tendency to go outside the firm for new CEOs or to select "dark horses" from within the firm. They seem to be searching for an executive who is unafraid to make changes in the firm's traditional practices. Still, many new CEOs fail (as we learn later in this chapter).[4]

This chapter begins with a definition of strategic leadership, its importance as a potential source of competitive advantage, and the styles that are the most effective. Next, we examine top management teams and their effects on innovation, strategic change, and firm performance. Following this discussion is an analysis of the internal and external managerial labor markets from which strategic leaders are selected. Closing the chapter are descriptions of the five key components of effective strategic leadership: determining

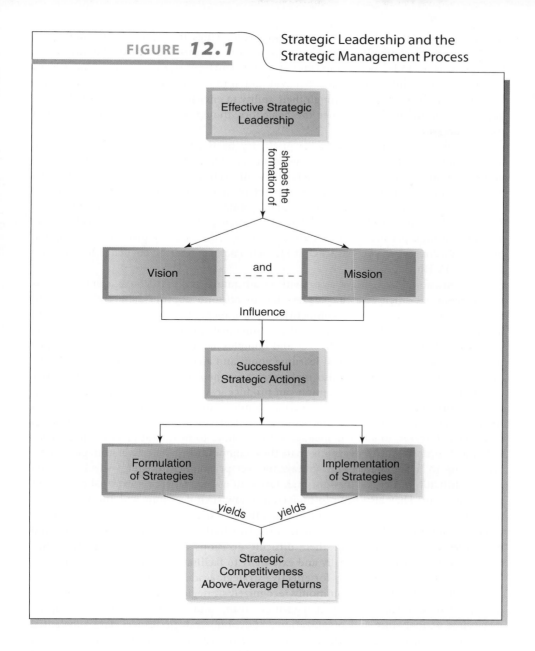

FIGURE **12.1** Strategic Leadership and the Strategic Management Process

Effective Strategic
Leadership

*shapes the
formation of*

Vision — *and* — Mission

Influence

Successful
Strategic Actions

Formulation
of Strategies

Implementation
of Strategies

yields   *yields*

Strategic
Competitiveness
Above-Average Returns

a strategic direction, effectively managing the firm's resource portfolio (which includes exploiting and maintaining core competencies along with developing human capital and social capital), sustaining an effective organizational culture, emphasizing ethical practices, and establishing balanced organizational control systems.

Strategic Leadership and Style

Strategic leadership is the ability to anticipate, envision, maintain flexibility, and empower others to create strategic change as necessary. Multifunctional in nature, strategic leadership involves managing through others, managing an entire enterprise rather than a functional subunit, and coping with change that continues to increase in the 21st-century competitive landscape, as is clearly illustrated in the Opening Case. Because of this landscape's complexity and global nature, strategic leaders must learn how to effectively influence human behavior, often in uncertain environments. By word or by personal example, and through their ability to envision the future, effective strategic leaders meaningfully influence the behaviors, thoughts, and feelings of those with whom they work.[5]

The ability to manage human capital may be the most critical of the strategic leader's skills.[6] In the 21st century, intellectual capital, including the ability to manage knowledge and create and commercialize innovation, affects a strategic leader's success.[7] Competent strategic leaders also establish the context through which stakeholders (such as employees, customers, and suppliers) can perform at peak efficiency.[8] The crux of strategic leadership is the ability to manage the firm's operations effectively and sustain high performance over time.[9] This was the primary problem encountered by Carly Fiorina when she was CEO at Hewlett-Packard, and the challenge for her successor, Mark Hurd.

A firm's ability to achieve a competitive advantage and earn above-average returns is compromised when strategic leaders fail to respond appropriately and quickly to changes in the complex global competitive environment. The inability to respond or to identify the need for change is one of the reasons that some CEOs fail. Strategic leaders must learn how to deal with diverse and complex competitive situations. Individual judgment is an important part of learning about and analyzing the firm's external conditions.[10] However, managers also make errors in their evaluation of the competitive conditions. These errors in perception can produce less-effective decisions. But, usually, it means that managers must make decisions under more uncertainty. Some can do this well, but some cannot. Those who cannot are likely to be ineffective and short-term managers. However, to survive, managers do not have to make optimal decisions. They only need to make better decisions than their competitors.[11] Effective strategic leaders are willing to make candid and courageous, yet pragmatic, decisions—decisions that may be difficult, but necessary—through foresight as they reflect on external conditions facing the firm. They also need to understand how such decisions will affect the internal systems currently in use in the firm. Effective strategic leaders use visioning to motivate employees. They often solicit corrective feedback from peers, superiors, and employees about the value of their difficult decisions and vision. Ultimately, they develop strong partners internally and externally to facilitate execution of their vision.[12]

The primary responsibility for effective strategic leadership rests at the top, in particular with the CEO. Other commonly recognized strategic leaders include members of the board of directors, the top management team, and divisional general managers. Regardless of their title and organizational function, strategic leaders have substantial decision-making responsibilities that cannot be delegated.[13] Strategic leadership is an extremely complex, but critical, form of leadership. Strategies cannot be formulated and implemented to achieve above-average returns without effective strategic leaders.

The styles used to provide leadership often affect the productivity of those being led. The most effective leadership style used by strategic leaders is transformational leadership. Transformational leadership entails motivating followers to do more than expected, to continuously enrich their capabilities, and to place the interests of the organization above their own.[14] Transformational leaders develop and communicate a vision for the organization and formulate a strategy to achieve the vision. They make the followers aware of the need to achieve valued organizational outcomes. And, they encourage followers to continuously strive for higher levels of achievement. Such leaders often have high emotional intelligence. Emotionally intelligent leaders understand themselves well, have strong motivation, are empathetic with others, and have effective interpersonal skills.[15]

The Role of Top-Level Managers

Top-level managers play a critical role in firms as they are charged with formulating and implementing strategies effectively.[16] The strategic decisions made by top-level managers influence how the firm is designed and whether or not goals will be achieved. Thus, a critical element of organizational success is having a top management team with superior managerial skills.[17]

Managers often use their discretion (or latitude for action) when making strategic decisions, including those concerned with the effective implementation of strategies.[18] Managerial discretion differs significantly across industries. The primary factors that determine the amount of decision-making discretion held by a manager (especially a top-level manager) are (1) external environmental sources such as the industry structure, the rate of market growth in the firm's primary industry, and the degree to which products can be differentiated; (2) characteristics of the organization, including its size, age, resources, and culture; and (3) characteristics of the manager, including commitment to the firm and its strategic outcomes, tolerance for ambiguity, skills in working with different people, and aspiration levels (see Figure 12.2). Because strategic leaders' decisions are intended to help the firm gain a competitive advantage, how managers exercise discretion when determining appropriate strategic actions is critical to the firm's success.[19] Top executives must be action oriented; thus, their decisions should spur the company to action.

In addition to determining new strategic initiatives, top-level managers develop the appropriate organizational structure and reward systems of a firm. In Chapter 11, we described how the organizational structure and reward systems affect strategic actions taken to implement different strategies. Top executives also have a major effect on a firm's culture. Evidence suggests that managers' values are critical in shaping a firm's cultural values.[20] Accordingly, top-level managers have an important effect on organizational activities and performance.[21] Because of the challenges top executives face, they often are more effective when they operate as top management teams.

Top Management Teams

In most firms, the complexity of challenges and the need for substantial amounts of information and knowledge require strategic leadership by a team of executives. Use of a team to make strategic decisions also helps to avoid another potential problem when these decisions are made by the CEO alone: managerial hubris. Research has shown that when CEOs begin to believe glowing press accounts and to feel that they are unlikely to make errors, they are more likely to make poor strategic decisions.[22] Some felt that part of Carly Fiorina's problem was that she seemed to be the primary spokesperson for HP, and her refusal to focus more on the operational details of the business may have been partly the result of her celebrity status. Top executives need to have self-confidence but must guard against allowing it to become arrogance and a false belief in their own invincibility.[23] To guard against CEO overconfidence and poor strategic decisions, firms often use the top management team to consider strategic opportunities and problems and to make strategic decisions. The **top management team** is composed of the key managers who are responsible for selecting and implementing the firm's strategies. Typically, the top management team includes the officers of the corporation, defined by the title of vice-president and above or by service as a member of the board of directors.[24] The quality of the strategic decisions made by a top management team affects the firm's ability to innovate and engage in effective strategic change.[25]

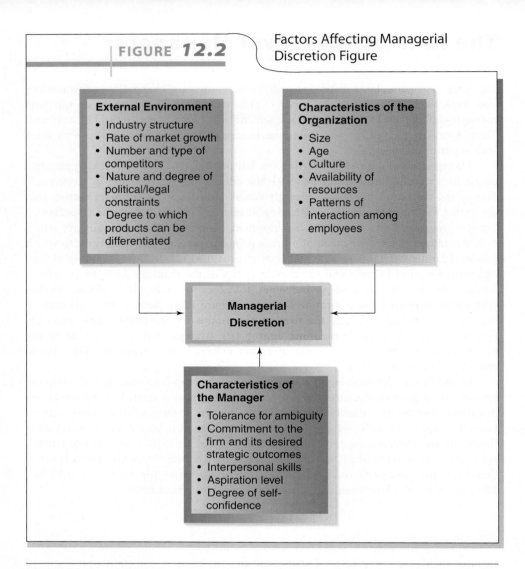

FIGURE **12.2**

Factors Affecting Managerial
Discretion Figure

External Environment

- Industry structure
- Rate of market growth
- Number and type of
  competitors
- Nature and degree of
  political/legal
  constraints
- Degree to which
  products can be
  differentiated

**Characteristics of the
Organization**

- Size
- Age
- Culture
- Availability of
  resources
- Patterns of
  interaction among
  employees

**Managerial
Discretion**

**Characteristics of
the Manager**

- Tolerance for ambiguity
- Commitment to the
  firm and its desired
  strategic outcomes
- Interpersonal skills
- Aspiration level
- Degree of self-
  confidence

Source: Adapted from S. Finkelstein & D. C. Hambrick, 1996, *Strategic Leadership: Top Executives and Their Effects on Organizations,* St. Paul, MN: West Publishing Company.

Top Management Team, Firm Performance, and Strategic Change

The job of top-level executives is complex and requires a broad knowledge of the firm's operations, as well as the three key parts of the firm's external environment—the general, industry, and competitor environments, as discussed in Chapter 2. Therefore, firms try to form a top management team that has the appropriate knowledge and expertise to operate the internal organization, yet that also can deal with all the firm's stakeholders as well as its competitors.[26] This normally requires a heterogeneous top management team. A **heterogeneous top management team** is composed of individuals with different functional backgrounds, experience, and education. The more heterogeneous a top management team is, with varied expertise and knowledge, the more capacity it has to *formulate* an effective strategy.

Members of a heterogeneous top management team benefit from discussing the different perspectives advanced by team members. In many cases, these discussions increase the quality of the top management team's decisions, especially when a synthesis emerges from the diverse perspectives that is generally superior to any one individual perspective.[27] The net benefit of such actions by heterogeneous teams has been positive in terms of market share and above-average returns. Research shows that more heterogeneity among top management team members promotes debate, which often leads to better strategic decisions. In turn, better strategic decisions produce higher firm performance.[28]

It is also important that the top management team members function cohesively. In general, the more heterogeneous and larger the top management team is, the more difficult it is for the team to effectively implement strategies.[29] Comprehensive and long-term strategic plans can be inhibited by communication difficulties among top executives who have different backgrounds and different cognitive skills.[30] Alternatively, communication among diverse top management team members can be facilitated through electronic communications, sometimes reducing the barriers before face-to-face meetings.[31] However, a group of top executives with diverse backgrounds may inhibit the process of decision making if it is not effectively managed. In these cases, top management teams may fail to comprehensively examine threats and opportunities, leading to a sub-optimal strategic decision. Thus, the CEO must attempt to achieve behavioral integration among the team members.[32]

Having members with substantive expertise in the firm's core functions and businesses is also important to the effectiveness of a top management team. In a high-technology industry, it may be critical for a firm's top management team members to have R&D expertise, particularly when growth strategies are being implemented.[33] Yet their eventual effect on strategic decisions depends not only on their expertise and the way the team is managed but also on the context in which they make the decisions (the governance structure, incentive compensation, etc.).[34]

The characteristics of top management teams are related to innovation and strategic change.[35] For example, more heterogeneous top management teams are associated positively with innovation and strategic change. The heterogeneity may force the team or some of the members to "think outside of the box" and thus be more creative in making decisions. Therefore, firms that need to change their strategies are more likely to do so if they have top management teams with diverse backgrounds and expertise. When a new CEO is hired from outside the industry, the probability of strategic change is greater than if the new CEO is from inside the firm or inside the industry.[36] While hiring a new CEO from outside the industry adds diversity to the team, the top management team must be managed effectively to use the diversity in a positive way. Thus, to create strategic change, the CEO should exercise transformational leadership.[37] A top management team with various areas of expertise is more likely to identify environmental changes (opportunities and threats) or changes within the firm that require a different strategic direction.

The CEO and Top Management Team Power

As noted in Chapter 10, the board of directors is an important governance mechanism for monitoring a firm's strategic direction and for representing stakeholders' interests, especially those of shareholders. In fact, higher performance normally is achieved when the board of directors is more directly involved in shaping a firm's strategic direction.[38]

Boards of directors, however, may find it difficult to direct the strategic actions of powerful CEOs and top management teams.[39] It is not uncommon for a powerful CEO to appoint to the board a number of sympathetic outside members or to have inside board members who are also on the top management team and report to the CEO.[40] In either case, the CEO may have significant control over the board's actions. Thus the amount of discretion a CEO has in making strategic decisions is related to the board of directors and how it chooses to oversee the CEO's actions and the top management team. In the poor performance of Hewlett-Packard explained in the Opening Case, the

The board of directors of the San Francisco Ballet.

board of directors shares part of the blame. While some members on the board opposed Fiorina's decision to acquire Compaq, the majority supported her. Interestingly, recent research shows that social ties between the CEO and board members may actually increase board members' involvement in strategic decisions. Thus, strong relationships between the CEO and the board of directors may have positive or negative outcomes.[41]

CEOs and top management team members can achieve power in other ways. A CEO who also holds the position of chairman of the board usually has more power than the CEO who does not.[42] Although this practice of CEO duality (when the CEO and the chairperson of the board are the same) has become more common in U.S. businesses, it has come under heavy criticism. Duality has been blamed for poor performance and slow response to change in a number of firms.[43]

The problems with poor top management decisions and lack of board oversight are evident in the recent problems at General Motors and Ford. Some have suggested that both firms seem stuck in neutral while customers buy automobiles from other manufacturers. In fact, following continuing losses of market share, in 2005 GM announced that it planned to close more U.S. manufacturing plants and lay off approximately 25,000 workers. Rather than focus on a long-term vision to make the firm's products competitive again, top management emphasized the need to cut costs, particularly benefits costs of line employees.[44] Toyota is taking advantage of GM's and Ford's lack of vision; Toyota's vision is to become the largest and most important auto manufacturer in the world.[45]

GM's continued loss of market share is forcing it to close plants and lay off workers.

Although it varies across industries, CEO duality (where one person serves as both the CEO and the chair of the board of directors) occurs most commonly in the largest firms. Increased shareholder activism, however, has brought CEO duality under scrutiny and attack in both U.S. and European firms. Historically, an independent board leadership structure in which the same person did not hold the positions of CEO and chair was believed to enhance a board's ability to monitor top-level managers' decisions and actions, particularly in terms of the firm's financial performance.[46] And, as reported in Chapter 10, many believe these two positions should be separate in most companies today to make the board more independent from the CEO. Stewardship theory, on the other hand, suggests that CEO duality facilitates effective decisions and actions. In these instances, the increased effectiveness gained through CEO duality accrues from the individual who wants to perform effectively and desires to be the best possible steward of the firm's assets. Because of this person's positive orientation and actions, extra governance and the coordination costs resulting from an independent board leadership structure would be unnecessary.[47]

Top management team members and CEOs who have long tenure—on the team and in the organization—have a greater influence on board decisions. And CEOs with greater influence may take actions in their own best interests, the outcomes of which increase their compensation from the company.[48] Long tenure is known to restrict the breadth of an executive's knowledge base. With the limited perspectives associated with a restricted knowledge base, long-tenured top executives typically develop fewer alternatives to evaluate in making strategic decisions.[49] However, long-tenured managers also may be able to exercise more effective strategic control, thereby obviating the need for board members' involvement because effective strategic control generally produces higher performance.[50]

To strengthen the firm, boards of directors should develop an effective relationship with the firm's top management team. The relative degrees of power held by the board and top management team members should be examined in light of an individual firm's situation. For example, the abundance of resources in a firm's external environment and the volatility of that environment may affect the ideal balance of power between boards and top management teams. Moreover, a volatile and uncertain environment may create a situation where a powerful CEO is needed to move quickly, but a diverse top management team may create less cohesion among team members and prevent or stall necessary strategic actions. Through the development of effective working relationships, boards, CEOs, and other top management team members are able to serve the best interests of the firm's stakeholders.[51]

Managerial Succession

The choice of top executives—especially CEOs—is a critical decision with important implications for the firm's performance.[52] Many companies use leadership screening systems to identify individuals with managerial and strategic leadership potential. The most effective of these systems assess people within the firm and gain valuable information about the capabilities of other companies' managers, particularly their strategic leaders.[53] Based on the results of these assessments, training and development programs are provided for current managers in an attempt to pre-select and shape the skills of people who may become tomorrow's leaders. The "ten-step talent" management development program at General Electric, for example, is considered one of the most effective in the world.[54]

Organizations select managers and strategic leaders from two types of managerial labor markets—internal and external.[55] An **internal managerial labor market** consists of a firm's opportunities for managerial positions and the qualified employees within that firm. An **external managerial labor market** is the collection of managerial career opportunities and the qualified people who are external to the organization in which the opportunities exist. Several benefits are thought to accrue to a firm when the internal labor market is used to select an insider as the new CEO. Because of their experience with the firm and the industry environment in which it competes, insiders are familiar with company products, markets, technologies, and operating procedures. Also, internal

Robert Iger, formerly Disney's chief strategy officer, is Michael Eisner's replacement as CEO.

hiring produces lower turnover among existing personnel, many of whom possess valuable firm-specific knowledge. When the firm is performing well, internal succession is favored to sustain high performance. It is assumed that hiring from inside keeps the important knowledge necessary to sustain the performance. The management consultant Jim Collins found that high-performing firms almost always appoint an insider to be the new CEO. He argues that bringing in a well-known outsider, to whom he refers as a "white knight," is a recipe for mediocrity.[56] Perhaps this is what happened with Carly Fiorina at HP. Of course, her successor is also from the outside but is less of a "white knight."

Given the phenomenal success of GE and its highly effective management development program, an insider, Jeffrey Immelt, was chosen to succeed Jack Welch.[57] Firms generally have succession management programs to develop managers so that one will eventually be prepared to ascend to the top.[58] Immelt was well prepared to take over the CEO job at GE.

Even in the case where performance is below par, some boards still select an insider. This is exemplified by the choice of Robert Iger to replace longtime Disney CEO Michael Eisner. There was some initial criticism of the choice, with a few analysts expressing doubts about Iger's capabilities or ability to be independent from Eisner. Yet, he began to establish his own course for the firm shortly after his appointment. His independence received a boost when Eisner's chief strategy officer was demoted.[59]

It is not unusual for employees to strongly prefer that the internal managerial labor market be used to select top management team members and the CEO. In the past, companies have also had a preference for insiders to fill top-level management positions because of a desire for continuity and a continuing commitment to the firm's current vision, mission, and chosen strategies.[60] However, because of a changing competitive landscape and varying levels of performance, an increasing number of boards of directors have been turning to outsiders to succeed CEOs.[61] A firm often has valid reasons to select an outsider as its new CEO: Long tenure with a firm seems to reduce the number of innovative ideas top executives are able to develop to cope with conditions facing their firm. Given the importance of innovation for a firm's success in today's competitive landscape (see Chapter 13), an inability to innovate or to create conditions that stimulate innovation throughout a firm is a liability for a strategic leader. Figure 12.3 shows how the composition of the top management team and the CEO succession (managerial labor market) interact to affect strategy. For example, when the top management team is homogeneous (its members have similar functional experiences and educational backgrounds) and a new CEO is selected from inside the firm, the firm's current strategy is unlikely to change.

Alternatively, when a new CEO is selected from outside the firm and the top management team is heterogeneous, there is a high probability that strategy will change. When the new CEO is from inside the firm and a heterogeneous top management team is in place, the strategy may not change, but innovation is likely to continue. An external CEO succession with a homogeneous team creates a more ambiguous situation. The recent selection of Sir Howard Stringer as CEO of Sony suggests changes in that firm's future. He is not only an outsider but also a foreigner. His selection as Sony's new CEO may be a result of increasing globalization and may be a harbinger of future appointments like this one.[62]

To have an adequate number of top managers, firms must take advantage of a highly qualified labor pool, including one source of managers as strategic leaders that has been

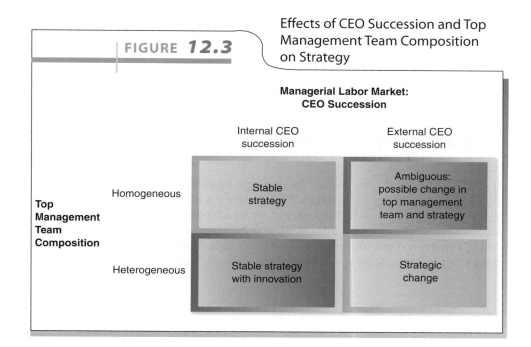

FIGURE 12.3

Effects of CEO Succession and Top Management Team Composition on Strategy

Managerial Labor Market: CEO Succession

	Internal CEO succession	External CEO succession
Homogeneous	Stable strategy	Ambiguous: possible change in top management team and strategy
Heterogeneous	Stable strategy with innovation	Strategic change

Top Management Team Composition

overlooked in prior years: women. Firms have begun to utilize women's potential managerial talents with substantial success. Trailblazers such as Catherine Elizabeth Hughes (the first African American woman to head a firm that was publicly traded on a U.S. stock exchange), Muriel Siebert (the first woman to purchase a seat on the New York Stock Exchange), and publisher Judith Regan have made important contributions as strategic leaders. A few firms have gained value by using the significant talents of women leaders. But many more have not done so, which represents an opportunity cost to them. Alternatively, women are being recognized for their leadership skill and are being selected for prominent strategic leadership positions, such as those held by Anne Mulcahy, CEO of Xerox, and Meg Whitman, CEO of eBay.

The New York Thruway Authority is one of the firms to utilize women's leadership skills on its board of directors.

More women are also being appointed to the boards of directors for organizations in both the private and public sectors. These additional appointments suggest that women's ability to represent stakeholders' and especially shareholders' best interests in for-profit companies at the level of the board of directors is being more broadly recognized. However, in addition to appointments to the board of directors, firms competing in the complex and demanding global economy may be well served by adding more female executives to their top management teams. It is important for firms to create diversity in leadership positions. Organizations such as Johnson & Johnson, the World Bank, and Royal Dutch Shell are creating more diverse leadership teams in order to deal with complex, heterogeneous, and ambiguous environments.[63] To build diverse teams, firms must break down their glass ceilings to allow all people regardless of gender or ethnicity to move into key leadership positions.[64] In so doing, firms more effectively use the human capital in their workforce. They also provide more opportunities for all people in the firm to satisfy their needs, such as their need for self-actualization; therefore, employees should be more highly motivated, leading to higher productivity for the firm.[65]

Key Strategic Leadership Actions

Several identifiable actions characterize strategic leadership that positively contributes to effective use of the firm's strategies.[66] We present the most important of these actions in Figure 12.4. Many of the actions interact with each other. For example, managing the firm's resources effectively includes developing human capital and contributes to establishing a strategic direction, fostering an effective culture, exploiting core competencies, using effective organizational control systems, and establishing ethical practices.

Determining Strategic Direction

Determining the strategic direction involves specifying the image and character the firm seeks to develop over time.[67] The strategic direction is framed within the context of the conditions (such as opportunities and threats) strategic leaders expect their firm to face in five, ten or more years.

The ideal long-term strategic direction has two parts: a core ideology and an envisioned future. While the core ideology motivates employees through the company's heritage, the envisioned future encourages employees to stretch beyond their expectations of accomplishment and requires significant change and progress in order to be realized.[68] The envisioned future serves as a guide to many aspects of a firm's strategy

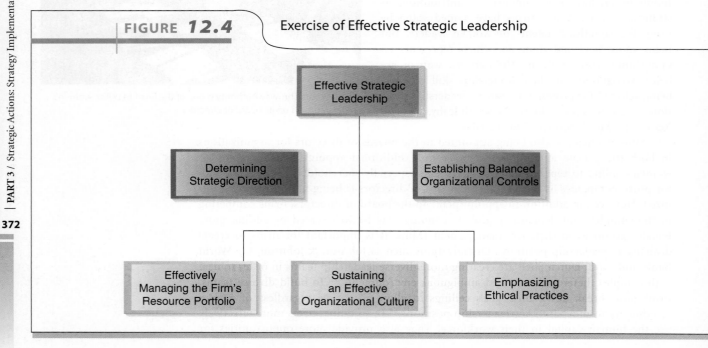

FIGURE **12.4**   Exercise of Effective Strategic Leadership

implementation process, including motivation, leadership, employee empowerment, and organizational design.

Most changes in strategic direction are difficult to design and implement, but Jeffrey Immelt has an even greater challenge at GE. GE performed exceptionally well under Jack Welch's leadership. While there is need for a change because the competitive landscape is shifting, stakeholders accustomed to Jack Welch and high performance may not readily accept Immelt's changes, especially in strategy. Immelt is trying to effect critical changes in the firm's culture, strategy, and governance and simultaneously gain stakeholders' commitment to them. He is shifting GE managers' mind-set to innovation that he believes is critical to GE's future competitiveness. He is linking managerial bonuses to the development and introduction of new ideas, customer satisfaction, and sales growth as opposed to bottom-line results as used in the past. He is investing significant resources (billions of dollars) into a fund called "Imagination Breakthrough" for projects that extend the boundary of GE. Finally, he expects to rotate key people less frequently and bring in more outsiders as industry experts than was done in Welch's era.[69] A charismatic CEO may foster stakeholders' commitment to a new vision and strategic direction. Nonetheless, it is important not to lose sight of the organization's strengths when making changes required by a new strategic direction. Immelt must use the strengths of GE to ensure continued positive performance. The goal is to pursue the firm's short-term need to adjust to a new vision and strategic direction while maintaining its long-term survivability by managing its portfolio of resources effectively.

Effectively Managing the Firm's Resource Portfolio

Probably the most important task for strategic leaders is effectively managing the firm's portfolio of resources. Firms have multiple resources that can be categorized into one of the following: financial capital, human capital, social capital, and organizational capital (including organizational culture).[70] The importance of these resources is shown in the Strategic Focus. The importance of managing financial capital is well accepted although managers use different approaches.[71] Many small business owners, as discussed in the Strategic Focus, use personal forms of credit to obtain access to needed financing. More to the point, the Strategic Focus argues the need for firms to use their full complement of human capital, especially making full use of the capabilities of women employees. Finally, the Strategic Focus shows the value of intangible resources such as brand and information/knowledge of customers. Wal-Mart has a large amount of valuable data on its customers that allows it and its suppliers to better serve them. Abro, on the other hand, has a valuable brand but is experiencing problems in protecting it against counterfeiters. In all cases, effective management of a firm's resources is essential in order to extract the value from them.

Strategic leaders manage the firm's portfolio of resources by organizing them into capabilities, structuring the firm to use the capabilities, and developing and implementing a strategy to leverage those resources to achieve a competitive advantage.[72] In particular, strategic leaders must exploit and maintain the firm's core competencies and develop and retain the firm's human and social capital.

Exploiting and Maintaining Core Competencies

Examined in Chapters 1 and 3, *core competencies* are capabilities that serve as a source of competitive advantage for a firm over its rivals. Typically, core competencies relate to an organization's functional skills, such as manufacturing, finance, marketing, and research and development. As shown by the descriptions that follow, firms develop and exploit core competencies in many different functional areas. Strategic leaders must verify that the firm's competencies are emphasized when implementing strategies. Intel,

How Do Managers Acquire, Protect, and Use Resources Wisely?

Resources are the lifeblood of companies. Firms must have them to operate and they must protect them because of their value to competitors. Finally, resources must be used effectively in order to create value for customers and gain an advantage over competitors. A critical resource for all organizations is financial capital, but it is especially important for smaller companies. Entrepreneurs often experience problems in maintaining an adequate cash flow to continue operations. However, large firms can also experience such problems. For example, when United Airlines filed for bankruptcy protection, it was because it did not have adequate cash flow to pay all of its expenses. Entrepreneurs need access to cash quickly. The U.S. Small Business Administration reports that 46 percent of small businesses use a personal credit card (of the entrepreneur/owner) and only 28 percent of the businesses have access to a line of credit, usually from a local bank. They receive financing in other ways as well, such as a business credit card (34 percent) and vehicle loans (21 percent).

While financial capital is highly important to businesses, other resources are equally or perhaps even more important. One highly important resource for most firms is human capital. Because of its importance, firms must make certain that it accesses and uses human capabilities to the greatest extent possible. Some firms have not made full use of all of their human capital, especially women. In the early 1970s, women received less than 10 percent of all graduate degrees in law, medicine, dentistry, and veterinary medicine. Today, women receive about two-thirds of the degrees in veterinary medicine, almost 50 percent in law, greater than 40 percent in medicine, and about one third of the degrees in dentistry. Additionally, women received over 41 percent of the MBA degrees in 2002, up from 3.6 percent in 1970. Finally, in 1970, women received 13.3 percent of all Ph.D. degrees; that figure increased to over 46 percent of all Ph.D. degrees awarded in 2002. Women are increasingly entering the professional labor markets with 60 percent participation rate, up from less than 40 percent three decades ago. Therefore, women are capable, educated, and available. Firms must fully utilize their human capital and break glass ceilings that stall women's opportunities for higher-level positions.

Not all resources are as easy to identify as financial capital and human capital. For example, a valuable resource held by Wal-Mart is information about its customers and their purchases. Wal-Mart amasses data on the types of products consumers buy, their buying habits, when they are most likely to buy, and so forth. In fact, Wal-Mart stores 460 terabytes of data, more than twice as much as the entire Internet. Wal-Mart shares part of these data with suppliers. For example, Kraft can access a private extranet provided by Wal-Mart to obtain real-time information on how its products are selling. However, Wal-Mart is careful about sharing its information with others. The information can be highly valuable to the

Wal-Mart's information about customers' purchases helped it estimate the expected sales due to Hurricane Frances.

JOE SKIPPER/REUTERS/LANDOV

company. For example, when Hurricane Frances was predicted to hit Florida, Wal-Mart was able to analyze its data on sales prior to previous hurricanes to identify the expected sales of flashlights and many other products in order to have adequate amounts on hand for the customers. Such predictive knowledge translates into profits for the firm.

Intellectual property rights and brand names also represent valuable resources to some companies. For example, one relatively small company, Abro Industries, has found both to be important. Abro develops and sells several different types of glues, tapes, and epoxy. It sells its products in more than 130 countries and has annual revenues of approximately $100 million. It is profitable and has strong shares of the markets in several countries. In fact, the generic name for masking tape in India is "Abro." The president of Abro, Peter Baranay, said, "We live and die by our brand." Yet the company started experiencing trouble with companies in other countries selling counterfeit products using the Abro brand. It started in India, Turkey, and parts of the former Soviet Union and has spread to China. Abro finds it difficult to protect its brand and sale of its products. These counterfeit products take sales and profits from Abro. Thus, Baranay has a major challenge in protecting his firm's products and profits from illegal uses of its brand.

Sources: W. M. Cox & R. Alm, 2005, Scientists are made, not born, *New York Times,* www.nytimes.com, February 28; G. Bounds, 2004, The great money hunt, *Wall Street Journal,* www.wsj.com, November 29; N. King, 2004, Stuck on you: A tiny glue seller claims identity theft, *Wall Street Journal,* www.wsj.com, November 22; C. L. Hays, 2004, Wal-Mart's hoard of data staggering, *Houston Chronicle,* November 14, D-4.

for example, has core competencies of *competitive agility* (an ability to act in a variety of competitively relevant ways) and *competitive speed* (an ability to act quickly when facing environmental and competitive pressures).[73] Capabilities are developed over time as firms learn from their actions and enhance their knowledge about specific actions needed. For example, some firms have excellent capabilities to deal with customers developed over time with increasing knowledge of their customers and their needs.[74] Firms with capabilities in R&D that develop into core competencies are rewarded by the market because of the critical nature of innovation in many industries.[75]

In many large firms, and certainly in related diversified ones, core competencies are effectively exploited when they are developed and applied across different organizational units (see Chapter 6). For example, PepsiCo purchased Quaker Oats, which makes the sports drink Gatorade. PepsiCo uses its competence in distribution systems to exploit the Quaker assets. For example, Pepsi soft drinks (e.g., Pepsi Cola and Mountain Dew) and Gatorade share the logistics activity. Similarly, PepsiCo uses this competence to distribute Quaker Oats' healthy snacks and Frito Lay's salty snacks through the same channels. PepsiCo launched the Heart and Soul-Mates Support Network offering nutritional tips, motivational messages, and coaching advice to jointly promote its Tropicana Pure Premium and Quaker Oatmeal products.[76]

Firms must continuously develop and when appropriate, change their core competencies to stay ahead of competitors. If they have a competence that provides an advantage but do not change it, competitors will eventually imitate that competence and reduce or eliminate the firm's competitive advantage. Additionally, firms must guard against the competence becoming a liability thereby preventing change. Some firms are reluctant to change competencies because they helped them gain competitive advantages. However, competencies can become outdated and result in the loss of competitive advantages if not changed. If this occurs, competitors will eventually develop a more valuable competence, eliminating the firm's competitive advantage and taking its market share away.[77] Most core competencies require high-quality human capital.

Developing Human Capital and Social Capital

Human capital refers to the knowledge and skills of a firm's entire workforce. From the perspective of human capital, employees are viewed as a capital resource that requires investment.[78] These investments are productive, in that much of the development of U.S. industry can be attributed to the effectiveness of its human capital. This fact suggests that "as the dynamics of competition accelerate, people are perhaps the only truly sustainable source of competitive advantage."[79] Human capital's increasing importance suggests a significant role for the firm's human resource management activities.[80] As a support activity (see Chapter 3), human resource management practices facilitate people's efforts to successfully select and especially to use the firm's strategies.[81]

Human capital is important in all types of organizations, large and small, new and established. For example, a major factor in the decision by venture capitalists to invest in an entrepreneurial venture is the quality of the human capital involved. In fact, it may be of equal or more importance to the quality of the entrepreneurial opportunity.[82] J. W. Marriott, Jr., CEO of Marriott International, argued strongly that the primary reason for the long-term success of the company has been the belief that its human capital is the most important asset of the firm. Thus, the company built and maintained a homelike and friendly environment that supports the growth and development of its employees, called "associates in Marriott." He also suggested that the firm invests significant effort in hiring caring and dependable people who are ethical and trustworthy. The firm then trains and rewards them for high-quality performance.[83]

Effective training and development programs increase the probability that a manager will be a successful strategic leader. These programs have grown progressively important to the success of firms as knowledge has become more integral to gaining and sustaining a competitive advantage.[84] Additionally, such programs build knowledge and skills, inculcate a common set of core values, and offer a systematic view of the organization, thus promoting the firm's vision and organizational cohesion. The programs also contribute to the development of core competencies.[85] Furthermore, they help strategic leaders improve skills that are critical to completing other tasks associated with effective strategic leadership, such as determining the firm's strategic direction, exploiting and maintaining the firm's core competencies, and developing an organizational culture that supports ethical practices. Thus, building human capital is vital to the effective execution of strategic leadership.[86]

Strategic leaders must acquire the skills necessary to help develop human capital in their areas of responsibility. When human capital investments are successful, the result is a workforce capable of learning continuously. Continuous learning and leveraging the firm's expanding knowledge base are linked with strategic success.[87] Dell's success in recent years has been attributed to the quality of its leadership. In fact, it evaluates leaders' performance on how well they maintain high levels of employee satisfaction among their associates and help maintain the "soul of Dell"—its values and culture—as well as on business outcomes. As a result, leaders in Dell are highly responsive to employees' needs.[88]

Learning also can preclude making errors. Strategic leaders tend to learn more from their failures than their successes because they sometimes make the wrong attributions for the successes.[89] For example, the effectiveness of certain approaches and knowledge can be context specific.[90] Some "best practices," for example, may not work well in all situations. We know that using teams to make decisions can be effective, but there are times when it is better for leaders to make decisions alone, especially when the decisions must be made and implemented quickly (e.g., in crisis situations).[91] It is important to learn from both successes and failures.

Learning and building knowledge are important for creating innovation in firms.[92] Innovation leads to competitive advantage.[93] Overall, firms that create and maintain greater knowledge usually achieve and maintain competitive advantages. However, as noted with core competencies, strategic leaders must guard against allowing high levels of knowledge in one area to lead to myopia and overlooking knowledge development opportunities in other important areas of the business.[94]

Because of the economic downturn in 2001–2002 and the continuing economic malaise for some time thereafter, many firms laid off key people. Layoffs can result in a significant loss of the knowledge possessed by a firm's human capital. Research has shown that moderate-sized layoffs may improve firm performance, but large layoffs produce stronger performance downturns in firms because of the loss of human capital.[95] Although it is also not uncommon for restructuring firms to reduce their expenditures on, or investments in, training and development programs, restructuring may actually be an important time to increase investments in these programs. Restructuring firms have less slack and cannot absorb as many errors; moreover, the employees who remain after layoffs may find themselves in positions without all of the skills or knowledge they need to perform the required tasks effectively.[96] Improvements in information technology can facilitate better use of human resources when a downsizing event occurs.[97]

Viewing employees as a resource to be maximized rather than a cost to be minimized facilitates the successful implementation of a firm's strategies as does the strategic leader's ability to approach layoffs in a manner that employees believe is fair and equitable.[98] A critical issue for employees is the fairness in the layoffs and in treatment in their jobs.[99]

Social capital involves relationships inside and outside the firm that help the firm accomplish tasks and create value for customers and shareholders.[100] Social capital is a critical asset for a firm. Inside the firm, employees and units must cooperate to get the work done. In multinational organizations, units often must cooperate across country boundaries on activities such as R&D to produce outcomes needed by the firm (e.g., new products).[101]

External social capital has become critical to firm success in the last several years. Few, if any, firms have all of the resources that they need to compete in global (or domestic) markets. Thus, they establish alliances with other firms that have complementary resources in order to gain access to them. These relationships must be effectively managed to ensure that the partner trusts the firm and is willing to share the desired resources.[102] In fact, the success of many types of firms may partially depend on social capital. Large multinational firms often must establish alliances in order to enter new foreign markets. Likewise, entrepreneurial firms often must establish alliances to gain access to resources, venture capital, or other types of resources (e.g., special expertise that the entrepreneurial firm cannot afford to maintain in-house.)[103] Retaining quality human capital and maintaining strong internal social capital can be affected strongly by the firm's culture.

Sustaining an Effective Organizational Culture

We defined **organizational culture** as a complex set of ideologies, symbols, and core values that is shared throughout the firm and influences the way business is conducted in Chapter 1. Evidence suggests that a firm can develop core competencies in terms of both the capabilities it possesses and the way the capabilities are leveraged by strategies to produce desired outcomes. In other words, because the organizational culture influences how the firm conducts its business and helps regulate and control employees' behavior, it can be a source of competitive advantage.[104] Thus, shaping the context within which the firm formulates and implements its strategies—that is, shaping the organizational culture—is a central task of strategic leaders.[105]

Entrepreneurial Mind-Set

An organizational culture often encourages (or discourages) the pursuit of entrepreneurial opportunities, especially in large firms.[106] Entrepreneurial opportunities are an important source of growth and innovation.[107] Therefore, a key role of strategic leaders is to encourage and promote innovation by pursuing entrepreneurial opportunities.[108] One way in which this activity might be promoted is to invest in opportunities as real options—that is, invest in an opportunity to provide the potential of exercising the option of taking advantage of the opportunity at some point in the future.[109] For example, a firm might buy a piece of land to have the option to build on it at some time in the future should the company need more space and should that location increase in value to the firm. Firms might enter strategic alliances for similar reasons. For example, they might do so to have the option of acquiring the partner later or of building a stronger relationship with it (e.g., developing a joint new venture).[110] In Chapter 13, we describe how large firms use strategic entrepreneurship to pursue entrepreneurial opportunities and to gain first-mover advantages. Medium- and small-sized firms also rely on strategic entrepreneurship when trying to develop innovations as the foundation for profitable growth. In firms of all sizes, strategic entrepreneurship is more likely to be successful when employees have an entrepreneurial mind-set.[111] Five dimensions characterize a firm's entrepreneurial mind-set: autonomy, innovativeness, risk taking, proactiveness, and competitive aggressiveness.[112] In combination, these dimensions influence the actions a firm takes to be innovative and launch new ventures.

The first of an entrepreneurial orientation's five dimensions, *autonomy,* allows employees to take actions that are free of organizational constraints and permits individuals and groups to be self-directed. The second dimension, *innovativeness,* "reflects a firm's tendency to engage in and support new ideas, novelty, experimentation, and creative processes that may result in new products, services, or technological processes."[113] Cultures with a tendency toward innovativeness encourage employees to think beyond existing knowledge, technologies, and parameters in efforts to find creative ways to add value. *Risk taking* reflects a willingness by employees and their firm to accept risks when pursuing entrepreneurial opportunities. These risks can include assuming significant levels of debt and allocating large amounts of other resources (e.g., people) to projects that may not be completed. The fourth dimension of an entrepreneurial orientation, *proactiveness,* describes a firm's ability to be a market leader rather than a follower. Proactive organizational cultures constantly use processes to anticipate future market needs and to satisfy them before competitors learn how to do so. Finally, *competitive aggressiveness* is a firm's propensity to take actions that allow it to consistently and substantially outperform its rivals.[114]

Changing the Organizational Culture and Restructuring

Changing a firm's organizational culture is more difficult than maintaining it, but effective strategic leaders recognize when change is needed. Incremental changes to the firm's culture typically are used to implement strategies.[115] More significant and, sometimes, even radical changes to organizational culture are used to support the selection of strategies that differ from those the firm has implemented historically. Regardless of the reasons for change, shaping and reinforcing a new culture require effective communication and problem solving, along with the selection of the right people (those who have the values desired for the organization), effective performance appraisals (establishing goals and measuring individual performance toward goals that fit in with the new core values), and appropriate reward systems (rewarding the desired behaviors that reflect the new core values).[116]

Evidence suggests that cultural changes succeed only when the firm's CEO, other key top management team members, and middle-level managers actively support

Change Lost in a 'Sea' of Organizational Politics

In 1997 Morgan Stanley's investment banking unit and Dean Witter, a financial retailer, merged and an internal struggle ensued for the top position at the company. Philip Purcell, the CEO of Dean Witter, eventually won the battle for the CEO position over insiders at Morgan Stanley. However, because of a lagging stock price, investors were unhappy with Purcell's leadership. More to the point, a number of Morgan Stanley executives also expressed concern about his leadership. In fact, a group of eight former Morgan executives, who collectively owned a large amount of stock in the company, called for Purcell to be replaced. They did not think that he understood the Morgan Stanley culture and its businesses.

The internal political turmoil boiled over in March 2005 when Purcell ousted a popular top executive, Vikram Pandit, and named co-presidents, one of whom was Zoe Cruz, with whom Pandit often clashed. These changes brought more expressions of concern from external parties, especially the former executives and other prominent shareholders. Yet the changes were intended to address the performance problems the firm had been experiencing.

The internal conflict not only caused executives to "take their eye off the ball" but also presented opportunities for competitors to steal some of the company's top talent. For example, there were reports that rivals Goldman Sachs, Merrill Lynch, UBS, and Lehman Brothers were developing lists of Morgan Stanley managers they wished to pursue. When there is turmoil inside a firm, professionals are more likely to consider opportunities at other companies because of the uncertainty created by the internal conflict. During the several-month-long conflict, a number of top managers resigned from their positions at Morgan Stanley, some in protest of Purcell's leadership. Purcell changed the style, values, and culture of Morgan Stanley, according to the former executives who were encouraging his dismissal.

Eventually, Purcell lost the battle to keep his job, chiefly due to a lagging stock price. He tendered his resignation on June 13, 2005. The board of directors, largely composed of Purcell loyalists, began to search for a new CEO. However, they also announced that former Morgan Stanley executives would not be considered. This caused objections and the board eventually gave in to pressures and began intense talks with John Mack, a former Morgan Stanley executive, who lost a

The internal conflict between Morgan Stanley and Dean Witter caused stock prices to drop and top managers to leave the company.

ADAM ROUNTREE/BLOOMBERG NEWS/LANDOV

Chapter 12 / Leadership

379

political battle with Purcell in 2001 and left the firm. As a condition of his acceptance, he demanded to rehire some key executives who had departed the firm, including Pandit. When it was announced that Mack was a candidate for the CEO position, Morgan Stanley's stock increased 2.7 percent, indicating a positive shareholder and investor reaction. John Mack was rehired as CEO of Morgan Stanley in 2005.

However, it will take considerable time to reduce the chaos created by the intense organizational politics and conflict in the first half of 2005. It may take years to restore the firm's culture and human capital to its former effectiveness levels.

Sources: A. Davis, 2005, Morgan Stanley discusses CEO post with John Mack, *Wall Street Journal,* www.wsj.com, June 24; R. Smith & A. Davis, 2005, At Morgan Stanley, chance increases for exiles' return, *Wall Street journal,* www.wsj.com. June 18; L. Thomas, 2005, The ties that bind at Morgan Stanley, *New York Times,* www.nytimes.com, April 24; L. Thomas & A. R. Sorkin, 2005, Hoping to steal some talent, rivals circle Morgan Stanley, *New York Times,* www.nytimes.com, April 18; L. Thomas, 2005, 2 executives are out as intrigue engulfs Morgan Stanley, *New York Times,* www.nytimes.com, March 30; D. Wells, 2005, Morgan Stanley in management shake-up, *Financial Times,* www.ft.com, March 29.

them.[117] To effect change, middle-level managers in particular need to be highly disciplined to energize the culture and foster alignment with the strategic vision.[118]

Attempts to change a culture and approaches to a business are often resisted by current employees and managers. This is evident in the Strategic Focus discussion of Morgan Stanley. In fact, the current and former employees were successful in stopping the changes by ousting the CEO. However, the several months of turmoil and conflict likely left serious injuries to Morgan Stanley's culture and human capital. One might even question the motives of the people on both sides of the conflict. Were they acting in the best interests of the firm and its shareholders, or were they trying to protect more for their personal interests? If the latter, their actions suggest important ethical concerns and the need for strategic leaders to emphasize ethical practices when using the strategic management process.

Emphasizing Ethical Practices

The effectiveness of processes used to implement the firm's strategies increases when they are based on ethical practices. Ethical companies encourage and enable people at all organizational levels to act ethically when doing what is necessary to implement the firm's strategies. In turn, ethical practices and the judgment on which they are based create "social capital" in the organization in that "goodwill available to individuals and groups" in the organization increases.[119] Alternately, when unethical practices evolve in an organization, they may become acceptable to many managers and employees throughout the organization. One study found that in these circumstances, managers were particularly likely to engage in unethical practices if they had not been able to meet their goals. In other words, they engaged in such practices to help them meet their goals.[120]

To properly influence employees' judgment and behavior, ethical practices must shape the firm's decision-making process and be an integral part of its culture. In fact, research has found that a value-based culture is the most effective means of ensuring that employees comply with the firm's ethical requirements.[121] As discussed in

Chapter 10, in the absence of ethical requirements, managers may act opportunistically, making decisions that are in their own best interests but not in the firm's best interests. In other words, managers acting opportunistically take advantage of their positions, making decisions that benefit themselves to the detriment of the firm's owners (shareholders).[122] But managers are most likely to integrate ethical values into their decisions when the company has explicit ethics codes, the code is integrated into the business through extensive ethics training, and shareholders expect ethical behavior.[123]

Recently, reported financial results for Royal Ahold, a Dutch-based firm with operations in many parts of the world such as North America and South America, were alleged to contain irregularities. The concern was that the irregularities led to inflated earnings reports. The CEO and the CFO of Ahold lost their jobs when the irregularities came to light. Thus, in addition to the firms' shareholders, they paid a high price for the indiscretions. While there have been numerous and well-publicized incidences of unethical (and unlawful) behavior by top executives in recent years, examples of ethical practices exist. Dell stands out as an ethical company. Dell has an explicit statement of its values in what the firm refers to as the "Soul of Dell." The statement of values on Dell's website includes such points as "We are committed to behaving ethically. . . . We believe in participating responsibly in the global marketplace . . . understanding and respecting the laws, values and cultures where we do business . . . contributing positively in every community we call home." These values are incorporated into evaluations of managers' performance.[124]

Firms should employ ethical strategic leaders—leaders who include ethical practices as part of their strategic direction for the firm, who desire to do the right thing, and for whom honesty, trust, and integrity are important.[125] Strategic leaders who consistently display these qualities inspire employees as they work with others to develop and support an organizational culture in which ethical practices are the expected behavioral norms.[126]

The effects of white-collar fraud are substantial.[127] Estimates in the United States suggest that white-collar fraud ranges from $200 billion to as much as $600 billion annually. Furthermore, this fraud usually equals from 1 to 6 percent of the firm's sales, and white-collar crime causes as much as 30 percent of new venture firms to fail. These amounts are incredibly high when compared with the total cost of approximately $20 billion for street crime in the United States.[128] Certainly, executives in multinational firms must understand that there are differences in ethical values across cultures globally.[129] Beyond this, however, research has shown that a positive relationship exists between ethical values (character) and an executive's health. So, ethical practices have many possible benefits to the firm and the executive.[130] Strategic leaders are challenged to take actions that increase the probability that an ethical culture will prevail in their organizations. One action that has gained favor is to institute a formal program to manage ethics. Operating much like control systems, these programs help inculcate values throughout the organization.[131] When these efforts are successful, the practices associated with an ethical culture become institutionalized in the firm; that is, they become the set of behavioral commitments and actions accepted by most of the firm's employees and other stakeholders with whom employees interact.

Additional actions strategic leaders can take to develop an ethical organizational culture include (1) establishing and communicating specific goals to describe the firm's ethical standards (e.g., developing and disseminating a code of conduct); (2) continuously revising and updating the code of conduct, based on inputs from people throughout the firm and from other stakeholders (e.g., customers and suppliers); (3) disseminating the code of conduct to all stakeholders to inform them of the firm's ethical standards and practices; (4) developing and implementing methods and procedures to use in achieving the firm's ethical standards (e.g., using internal auditing practices that are consistent with the standards); (5) creating and using explicit reward systems that recognize acts of courage (e.g., rewarding those who use proper channels and procedures to report observed wrongdoings); and (6) creating a work environment in which all people are treated with dignity.[132] The effectiveness of these actions increases when they are taken simultaneously and thereby are mutually supportive. When managers and employees do not engage in such actions—perhaps because an ethical culture has not been created—problems are likely to occur. As we discuss next, formal organizational controls can help prevent further problems and reinforce better ethical practices.

Establishing Balanced Organizational Controls

Organizational controls are basic to a capitalistic system and have long been viewed as an important part of strategy implementation processes.[133] Controls are necessary to help ensure that firms achieve their desired outcomes.[134] Defined as the "formal, information-based . . . procedures used by managers to maintain or alter patterns in organizational activities," controls help strategic leaders build credibility, demonstrate the value of strategies to the firm's stakeholders, and promote and support strategic change.[135] Most critically, controls provide the parameters within which strategies are to be implemented, as well as corrective actions to be taken when implementation-related adjustments are required. In this chapter, we focus on two organizational controls—strategic and financial—that were introduced in Chapter 11. Our discussion of organizational controls here emphasizes strategic and financial controls because strategic leaders, especially those at the top of the organization, are responsible for their development and effective use.

Evidence suggests that, although critical to the firm's success, organizational controls are imperfect. *Control failures* have a negative effect on the firm's reputation and divert managerial attention from actions that are necessary to effectively use the strategic management process.

As explained in Chapter 11, financial control focuses on short-term financial outcomes. In contrast, strategic control focuses on the *content* of strategic actions, rather than their *outcomes*. Some strategic actions can be correct but still result in poor financial outcomes because of external conditions, such as a recession in the economy, unexpected domestic or foreign government actions, or natural disasters.[136] Therefore, an emphasis on financial control often produces more short-term and risk-averse managerial decisions, because financial outcomes may be caused by events beyond managers' direct control. Alternatively, strategic control encourages lower-level managers to make decisions that incorporate moderate and acceptable levels of risk because outcomes are shared between the business-level executives making strategic proposals and the corporate-level executives evaluating them.

The Balanced Scorecard

The **balanced scorecard** is a framework that firms can use to verify that they have established both strategic and financial controls to assess their performance.[137] This technique is most appropriate for use when dealing with business-level strategies, but can also apply to corporate-level strategies.

The underlying premise of the balanced scorecard is that firms jeopardize their future performance possibilities when financial controls are emphasized at the expense of strategic controls,[138] in that financial controls provide feedback about outcomes achieved from past actions, but do not communicate the drivers of the firm's future performance.[139] Thus, an overemphasis on financial controls could promote managerial behavior that has a net effect of sacrificing the firm's long-term value-creating potential for short-term performance gains.[140] An appropriate balance of strategic controls and financial controls, rather than an overemphasis on either, allows firms to effectively monitor their performance.

Four perspectives are integrated to form the balanced scorecard framework: *financial* (concerned with growth, profitability, and risk from the shareholders' perspective), *customer* (concerned with the amount of value customers perceive was created by the firm's products), *internal business processes* (with a focus on the priorities for various business processes that create customer and shareholder satisfaction), and *learning and growth* (concerned with the firm's effort to create a climate that supports change, innovation, and growth). Thus, using the balanced scorecard framework allows the firm to understand how it looks to shareholders (financial perspective), how customers view it (customer perspective), the processes it must emphasize to successfully use its competitive advantage (internal perspective), and what it can do to improve its performance in order to grow (learning and growth perspective).[141] Generally speaking, strategic controls tend to be emphasized when the firm assesses its performance relative to the learning and growth perspective, while financial controls are emphasized when assessing performance in terms of the financial perspective.

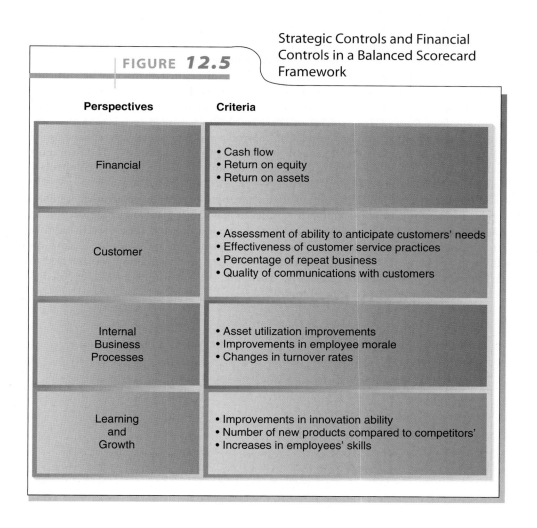

| FIGURE **12.5** | Strategic Controls and Financial Controls in a Balanced Scorecard Framework |

Perspectives	Criteria
Financial	• Cash flow • Return on equity • Return on assets
Customer	• Assessment of ability to anticipate customers' needs • Effectiveness of customer service practices • Percentage of repeat business • Quality of communications with customers
Internal Business Processes	• Asset utilization improvements • Improvements in employee morale • Changes in turnover rates
Learning and Growth	• Improvements in innovation ability • Number of new products compared to competitors' • Increases in employees' skills

Firms use different criteria to measure their standing relative to the scorecard's four perspectives. Sample criteria are shown in Figure 12.5. The firm should select the number of criteria that will allow it to have both a strategic understanding and a financial understanding of its performance without becoming immersed in too many details.[142] For example, we know from research that a firm's innovation, quality of its goods and services, growth of its sales, and its profitability are all interrelated.[143]

Strategic leaders play an important role in determining a proper balance between strategic controls and financial controls for their firm. This is true in single-business firms as well as in diversified firms. A proper balance between controls is important, in that "wealth creation for organizations where strategic leadership is exercised is possible because these leaders make appropriate investments for future viability [through strategic control], while maintaining an appropriate level of financial stability in the present [through financial control]."[144] In fact, most corporate restructuring is designed to refocus the firm on its core businesses, thereby allowing top executives to reestablish strategic control of their separate business units.[145] Thus, as emphasized in Chapter 11, both strategic controls and financial controls support effective use of the firm's corporate-level strategy.

Successful use of strategic control by top executives frequently is integrated with appropriate autonomy for the various subunits so that they can gain a competitive advantage in their respective markets.[146] Strategic control can be used to promote the sharing of both tangible and intangible resources among interdependent businesses within a firm's portfolio. In addition, the autonomy provided allows the flexibility necessary to take advantage of specific marketplace opportunities. As a result, strategic leadership promotes the simultaneous use of strategic control and autonomy.[147]

Balancing strategic and financial controls in diversified firms can be difficult. Failure to maintain an effective balance between strategic controls and financial controls in these firms often contributes to a decision to restructure the company. For example, Jean-Pierre Garnier, CEO of GlaxoSmithKline, worked to reinvent the company by streamlining its costs (financial controls) and simultaneously enhancing its development of innovative and valuable new drugs (strategic controls). The firm must achieve a balance in these controls in order to survive in the strongly competitive pharmaceuticals industry.[148]

After Porsche regained its position among the top sports car manufacturers, it implemented a balanced scorecard approach in order to maintain a market-leading position. In particular, it used the balanced scorecard to promote learning and continuously improve the business. For example, knowledge was collected from all Porsche dealerships throughout the world. The instrument used to collect the information was referred to as "Porsche Key Performance Indicators." Therefore, the balanced scorecard was used as a learning tool more than a control tool.[149]

- Effective strategic leadership is a prerequisite to successfully using the strategic management process. Strategic leadership entails the ability to anticipate events, envision possibilities, maintain flexibility, and empower others to create strategic change.

- Top-level managers are an important resource for firms to develop and exploit competitive advantages. In addition, when they and their work are valuable, rare, imperfectly imitable, and nonsubstitutable, strategic leaders can themselves be a source of competitive advantage.

- The top management team is composed of key managers who play a critical role in selecting and implementing the firm's strategies. Generally, they are officers of the corporation or members of the board of directors.

- There is a relationship among the top management team's characteristics, a firm's strategies, and its performance. For example, a top management team that has significant marketing and R&D knowledge positively contributes to the firm's use of growth strategies. Overall, most top management teams are more effective when they have diverse skills.

- When the board of directors is involved in shaping a firm's strategic direction, that firm generally improves its performance. However, the board may be less involved in decisions about strategy formulation and implementation when CEOs have more power. CEOs increase their power when they appoint people to the board and when they simultaneously serve as the CEO and board chair.

- In managerial succession, strategic leaders are selected from either the internal or the external managerial labor market. Because of their effect on performance, the selection of strategic leaders has implications for a firm's effectiveness. There are valid reasons to use either the internal or the external market when choosing the firm's strategic leaders. In most instances, the internal market is used to select the firm's CEO, but the number of outsiders chosen is increasing. Outsiders often are selected to initiate changes.

- Effective strategic leadership has five major components: determining the firm's strategic direction, effectively managing the firm's resource portfolio (including exploiting and maintaining core competencies and managing human capital and social capital), sustaining an effective organizational culture, emphasizing ethical practices, and establishing balanced organizational controls.

- Strategic leaders must develop the firm's strategic direction. The strategic direction specifies the image and character the firm wants to develop over time. To form the strategic direction, strategic leaders evaluate the conditions (e.g., opportunities and threats in the external environment) they expect their firm to face over the next five to ten or more years.

- Strategic leaders must ensure that their firm exploits its core competencies, which are used to produce and deliver products that create value for customers, through the implementation of strategies. In related diversified and large firms in particular, core competencies are exploited by sharing them across units and products.

- A critical element of strategic leadership and the effective implementation of strategy is the ability to manage the firm's resource portfolio. This includes integrating resources to create capabilities and leveraging those capabilities through strategies to build competitive advantages. Human capital and social capital are perhaps the most important resources.

- As a part of managing the firm's resources, strategic leaders must develop a firm's human capital. Effective strategic leaders and firms view human capital as a resource to be maximized, rather than as a cost to be minimized. Resulting from this perspective is the development and use of programs intended to train current and future strategic leaders to build the skills needed to nurture the rest of the firm's human capital.

- Effective strategic leaders also build and maintain internal and external social capital. Internal social capital promotes cooperation and coordination within and across units in the firm. External social capital provides access to resources that the firm needs to compete effectively.

- Shaping the firm's culture is a central task of effective strategic leadership. An appropriate organizational culture encourages the development of an entrepreneurial orientation among employees and an ability to change the culture as necessary.

- In ethical organizations, employees are encouraged to exercise ethical judgment and to behave ethically at all times. Improved ethical practices foster social capital. Setting specific goals to describe the firm's ethical standards, using a code of conduct, rewarding ethical behaviors, and creating a work environment in which all people are treated with dignity are examples of actions that facilitate and support ethical behavior within the firm.

- Developing and using balanced organizational controls is the final component of effective strategic leadership. The balanced scorecard is a tool used by the firm and its strategic leaders to develop an appropriate balance between its strategic and financial controls. An effective balance between strategic and financial controls allows for the flexible use of core competencies, but within the parameters indicated by the firm's financial position.

1. R. D. Ireland, M. A. Hitt, S. M. Camp, & D. L. Sexton, 2001, Integrating entrepreneurship and strategic management actions to create firm wealth, *Academy of Management Executive,* 15(1): 49–63; K. R. Thompson, W. A. Hochwarter, & N. J. Mathys, 1997, Stretch targets: What makes them effective? *Academy of Management Executive,* 11(3): 48–59.

2. A. Cannella Jr., A. Pettigrew, & D. Hambrick, 2001, Upper echelons: Donald Hambrick on executives and strategy, *Academy of Management Executive,* 15(3): 36–52; R. D. Ireland & M. A. Hitt, 1999, Achieving and maintaining strategic competitiveness in the 21st century: The role of strategic leadership, *Academy of Management Executive,* 12(1): 43–57.

3. C. de Aenlle, 2005, See you, Carly. Goodbye, Harry. Hello investors, *New York Times Online,* www.nytimes.com, March 13.

4. A. Barrionuevo, 2005, As directors feel their oats, chiefs are put out to pasture, *New York Times Online,* www.nytimes.com, March 15; L. Greiner, T. Cummings, & A. Bhambri, 2002, When new CEOs succeed and fail: 4-D theory of strategic transformation, *Organizational Dynamics,* 32: 1–16.

5. S. Green, F. Hassan, J. Immelt, M. Marks, & D. Meiland, 2003, In search of global leaders, *Harvard Business Review,* 81(8): 38–45; T. J. Peters, 2001, Leadership: Sad facts and silver linings, *Harvard Business Review,* 79(11): 121–128.

6. M. A. Hitt, C. Miller, & A. Collella, 2005, *Organizational Behavior: A Strategic Approach,* New York: John Wiley & Sons; M. A. Hitt & R. D. Ireland, 2002, The essence of strategic leadership: Managing human and social capital, *Journal of Leadership and Organizational Studies,* 9: 3–14.

7. A. S. DeNisi, M. A. Hitt, & S. E. Jackson, 2003, The knowledge-based approach to sustainable competitive advantage, in S. E. Jackson, M. A. Hitt, & A. S. DeNisi (eds.), *Managing Knowledge for Sustained Competitive Advantage,* San Francisco: Jossey-Bass, 3–33; D. J. Teece, 2000, *Managing Intellectual Capital: Organizational, Strategic and Policy Dimensions,* Oxford: Oxford University Press.

8. J. E. Post, L. E. Preston, & S. Sachs, 2002, Managing the extended enterprise: The new stakeholder view, *California Management Review,* 45(1): 6–28.

9. M. Maccoby, 2001, Making sense of the leadership literature, *Research Technology Management,* 44(5): 58–60; T. Kono, 1999, A strong head office makes a strong company, *Long Range Planning,* 32: 225–246.

10. C. L. Shook, R. L. Priem, & J. E. McGee, 2003, Venture creation and the enterprising individual: A review and synthesis, *Journal of Management,* 29: 379–399.

11. J. M. Mezias & W. H. Starbuck, 2003, Studying the accuracy of managers' perceptions: A research odyssey, *British Journal of Management,* 14: 3–17.

12. M. Maccoby, 2001, Successful leaders employ strategic intelligence, *Research Technology Management,* 44(3): 58–60.

13. S. Finkelstein & D. C. Hambrick, 1996, *Strategic Leadership: Top Executives and Their Effects on Organizations,* St. Paul, MN: West Publishing Company, 2.

14. Hitt, Miller, & Colella, *Organizational Behavior;* D. Vera & M. Crossan, 2004, Strategic leadership and organizational learning, *Academy of Management Review,* 29: 222–240.

15. D. Goleman, 2004, What makes a leader? *Harvard Business Review,* 82(1): 82–91.

16. R. Castanias & C. Helfat, 2001, The managerial rents model: Theory and empirical analysis, *Journal of Management,* 27: 661–678; H. P. Gunz & R. M. Jalland, 1996, Managerial careers and business strategy, *Academy of Management Review,* 21: 718–756.

17. M. Beer & R. Eisenstat, 2000, The silent killers of strategy implementation and learning, *Sloan Management Review,* 41(4): 29–40; C. M. Christensen, 1997, Making strategy: Learning by doing, *Harvard Business Review,* 75(6): 141–156.

18. R. Whittington, 2003, The work of strategizing and organizing: For a practice perspective, *Strategic Organization,* 1: 117–125; M. Wright, R. E. Hoskisson, L. W. Busenitz, & J. Dial, 2000, Entrepreneurial growth through privatization: The upside of management buyouts, *Academy of Management Review,* 25: 591–601; M. J. Waller, G. P. Huber, & W. H. Glick, 1995, Functional background as a determinant of executives' selective perception, *Academy of Management Journal,* 38: 943–974; N. Rajagopalan, A. M. Rasheed, & D. K. Datta, 1993, Strategic decision processes: Critical review and future directions, *Journal of Management,* 19: 349–384.

19. W. Rowe, 2001, Creating wealth in organizations: The role of strategic leadership, *Academy of Management Executive,* 15(1): 81–94; Finkelstein & Hambrick, *Strategic Leadership,* 26–34.

20. J. A. Petrick & J. F. Quinn, 2001, The challenge of leadership accountability for integrity capacity as a strategic asset, *Journal of Business Ethics,* 34: 331–343; R. C. Mayer, J. H. Davis, & F. D. Schoorman, 1995, An integrative model of organizational trust, *Academy of Management Review,* 20: 709–734.

21. S. Gove, D. Sirmon, & M. A. Hitt, 2003, Relative resource advantages: The effect of resources and resource management on organizational performance, Paper presented at the Strategic Management Society Conference, Baltimore; J. J. Sosik, 2001, Self-other agreement on charismatic leadership: Relationships with work attitudes and managerial performance, *Group & Organization Management,* 26: 484–511.

22. M. L. A. Hayward, V. P. Rindova, & T. G. Pollock, 2004, Believing one's own press: The causes and consequences of CEO celebrity, *Strategic Management Journal,* 25: 637–653.

23. N. J. Hiller & D. C. Hambrick, 2005, Conceptualizing executive hubris: The role of (hyper-) core self-evaluations in strategic decision making, *Strategic Management Journal,* 26: 297–319.

24. I. Goll, R. Sambharya, & L. Tucci, 2001, Top management team composition, corporate ideology, and firm performance, *Management International Review,* 41(2): 109–129.

25. J. Bunderson, 2003, Team member functional background and involvement in management teams: Direct effects and the moderating role of power and centralization, *Academy of Management Journal,* 46: 458–474; L. Markoczy, 2001, Consensus formation during strategic change, *Strategic Management Journal,* 22: 1013–1031.

26. Post, Preston, & Sachs, Managing the extended enterprise; C. Pegels, Y. Song, & B. Yang, 2000, Management heterogeneity, competitive interaction groups, and firm performance, *Strategic Management Journal,* 21: 911–923.

27. Markoczy, Consensus formation during strategic change; D. Knight, C. L. Pearce, K. G. Smith, J. D. Olian, H. P. Sims, K. A. Smith, & P. Flood, 1999, Top management team diversity, group process, and strategic consensus, *Strategic Management Journal,* 20: 446–465.

28. J. J. Distefano & M. L. Maznevski, 2000, Creating value with diverse teams in global management, *Organizational Dynamics,* 29(1): 45–63; T. Simons, L. H. Pelled, & K. A. Smith, 1999, Making use of difference, diversity, debate, and decision comprehensiveness in top management teams, *Academy of Management Journal,* 42: 662–673.

29. Finkelstein & Hambrick, *Strategic Leadership,* 148.

30. S. Barsade, A. Ward, J. Turner, & J. Sonnenfeld, 2000, To your heart's content: A model of affective diversity in top management teams, *Administrative Science Quarterly,* 45: 802–836; C. C. Miller, L. M. Burke, & W. H. Glick, 1998, Cognitive diversity among upper-echelon executives: Implications for strategic decision processes, *Strategic Management Journal,* 19: 39–58.

31. B. J. Avolio & S. S. Kahai, 2002, Adding the "e" to e-leadership: How it may impact your leadership, *Organizational Dynamics,* 31: 325–338.

32. Z. Simsek, J. F. Veiga, M. L. Lubatkin, & R. H. Dino, 2005, Modeling the multi-level determinants of top management team behavioral integration, *Academy of Management Journal*, 48: 69–84.

33. U. Daellenbach, A. McCarthy, & T. Schoenecker, 1999, Commitment to innovation: The impact of top management team characteristics, *R&D Management*, 29(3): 199–208; D. K. Datta & J. P. Guthrie, 1994, Executive succession: Organizational antecedents of CEO characteristics, *Strategic Management Journal*, 15: 569–577.

34. M. Jensen & E. J. Zajac, 2004, Corporate elites and corporate strategy: How demographic preferences and structural position shape the scope of the firm, *Strategic Management Journal*, 25: 507–524.

35. W. B. Werther, 2003, Strategic change and leader-follower alignment, *Organizational Dynamics*, 32: 32–45; S. Wally & M. Becerra, 2001, Top management team characteristics and strategic changes in international diversification: The case of U.S. multinationals in the European community, *Group & Organization Management*, 26: 165–188.

36. Y. Zhang & N. Rajagopalan, 2003, Explaining the new CEO origin: Firm versus industry antecedents, *Academy of Management Journal*, 46: 327–338.

37. T. Dvir, D. Eden, B. J. Avolio, & B. Shamir, 2002, Impact of transformational leadership on follower development and performance: A field experiment, *Academy of Management Journal*, 45: 735–744.

38. L. Tihanyi, R. A. Johnson, R. E. Hoskisson, & M. A. Hitt, 2003, Institutional ownership and international diversification: The effects of boards of directors and technological opportunity, *Academy of Management Journal*, 46: 195–211.

39. B. R. Golden & E. J. Zajac, 2001, When will boards influence strategy? Inclination times power equals strategic change, *Strategic Management Journal*, 22: 1087–1111.

40. M. Carpenter & J. Westphal, 2001, Strategic context of external network ties: Examining the impact of director appointments on board involvement in strategic decision making, *Academy of Management Journal*, 44: 639–660.

41. J. D. Westphal, 1999, Collaboration in the boardroom: Behavioral and performance consequences of CEO-board social ties, *Academy of Management Journal*, 42: 7–24.

42. J. Roberts & P. Stiles, 1999, The relationship between chairmen and chief executives: Competitive or complementary roles? *Long Range Planning*, 32(1): 36–48.

43. J. Coles, N. Sen, & V. McWilliams, 2001, An examination of the relationship of governance mechanisms to performance, *Journal of Management*, 27: 23–50; J. Coles & W. Hesterly, 2000, Independence of the chairman and board composition: Firm choices and shareholder value, *Journal of Management*, 26: 195–214.

44. B. Simon, 2005, GM shuts plants and cuts 25,000 jobs, *Financial Times Online*, www.ft.com, June 7; D. Hakim, 2005, G.M. and Ford stuck in neutral as buyers look beyond Detroit, *New York Times Online*, www.nytimes.com, April 15.

45. Y. Kageyama, 2005, Toyota sets it sights on being no. 1 in the world, *Houston Chronicle*, March 18, D4.

46. C. M. Daily & D. R. Dalton, 1995, CEO and director turnover in failing firms: An illusion of change? *Strategic Management Journal*, 16: 393–400.

47. R. Albanese, M. T. Dacin, & I. C. Harris, 1997, Agents as stewards, *Academy of Management Review*, 22: 609–611; J. H. Davis, F. D. Schoorman, & L. Donaldson, 1997, Toward a stewardship theory of management, *Academy of Management Review*, 22: 20–47.

48. J. G. Combs & M. S. Skill, 2003, Managerialist and human capital explanations for key executive pay premiums: A contingency perspective, *Academy of Management Journal*, 46: 63–73.

49. N. Rajagopalan & D. Datta, 1996, CEO characteristics: Does industry matter? *Academy of Management Journal*, 39: 197–215.

50. R. A. Johnson, R. E. Hoskisson, & M. A. Hitt, 1993, Board involvement in restructuring: The effect of board versus managerial controls and characteristics, *Strategic Management Journal*, 14 (Special Issue): 33–50.

51. M. Schneider, 2002, A stakeholder model of organizational leadership, *Organization Science*, 13: 209–220.

52. M. Sorcher & J. Brant, 2002, Are you picking the right leaders? *Harvard Business Review*, 80(2): 78–85; D. A. Waldman, G. G. Ramirez, R. J. House, & P. Puranam, 2001, Does leadership matter? CEO leadership attributes and profitability under conditions of perceived environmental uncertainty, *Academy of Management Journal*, 44: 134–143.

53. W. Shen & A. A. Cannella, 2002, Revisiting the performance consequences of CEO succession: The impacts of successor type, postsuccession senior executive turnover, and departing CEO tenure, *Academy of Management Journal*, 45: 717–734.

54. R. Charan, 2000, GE's ten-step talent plan, *Fortune*, April 17, 232.

55. R. E. Hoskisson, D. Yiu, & H. Kim, 2000, Capital and labor market congruence and corporate governance: Effects on corporate innovation and global competitiveness, in S. S. Cohen & G. Boyd (eds.), *Corporate Governance and Globalization*, Northampton, MA: Edward Elgar, 129–154.

56. M. Hurlbert, 2005, Lo! A white knight! So why isn't the market cheering? *New York Times Online*, www.nytimes.com, March 27.

57. S. B. Shepard, 2002, A talk with Jeff Immelt: Jack Welch's successor charts a course for GE in the 21st century, *Business Week*, January 28, 102–104.

58. D. C. Carey & D. Ogden, 2000, *CEO Succession: A Window on How Boards Can Get It Right When Choosing a New Chief Executive*, New York: Oxford University Press.

59. I. Anabtawi & L. A. Stout, 2005, An inside job, *New York Times Online*, www.nytimes.com, March 27; T. Burt, 2005, Disney demotes chief strategy officer, *Financial Times Online*, www.ft.com, March 27; M. Marr & M. Mangalinden, 2005, Walt Disney board is expected to name Iger as new CEO, *Wall Street Journal Online*, www.wsj.com, March 13.

60. W. Shen & A. A. Cannella, 2003, Will succession planning increase shareholder wealth? Evidence from investor reactions to relay CEO successions, *Strategic Management Journal*, 24: 191–198.

61. Greiner, Cummings, & Bhambri, When new CEOs succeed and fail.

62. K. Belson & T. Zaun, 2005, Land of the rising gaijin chief executive, *New York Times Online*, www.nytimes.com, March 27.

63. R. M. Fulmer & M. Goldsmith, 2000, *The Leadership Investment: Promoting Diversity in Leadership*, New York: American Management Association.

64. S. Foley, D. L. Kidder, & G. N. Powell, 2002, The perceived glass ceiling and justice perceptions: An investigation of Hispanic law associates, *Journal of Management*, 28: 471–496.

65. Hitt, Miller, & Colella, *Organizational Behavior*; N. M. Carter, W. B. Gartner, K. G. Shaver, & E. J. Gatewood, 2003, The career reasons of nascent entrepreneurs, *Journal of Business Venturing*, 18: 13–39.

66. B. Dyck, M. Mauws, F. Starke, & G. Mischke, 2002, Passing the baton: The importance of sequence, timing, technique and communication in executive succession, *Journal of Business Venturing*, 17: 143–162.

67. M. A. Hitt, B. W. Keats, & E. Yucel, 2003, Strategic leadership in global business organizations, in W. H. Mobley & P. W. Dorfman (eds.), *Advances in Global Leadership*, Oxford, UK: Elsevier Science, Ltd., 9–35.

68. I. M. Levin, 2000, Vision revisited, *Journal of Applied Behavioral Science*, 36: 91–107; J. C. Collins & J. I. Porras, 1996, Building your company's vision, *Harvard Business Review*, 74(5): 65–77.

69. D. Brady, 2005, The Immelt revolution, *Business Week*, March 28, 64–73.

70. J. Barney & A. M. Arikan, 2001, The resource-based view: Origins and implications, in M. A. Hitt, R. E. Freeman, & J. S. Harrison (eds.), *Handbook of Strategic Management*, Oxford, UK: Blackwell Publishers, 124–188.

71. E. T. Prince, 2005, The fiscal behavior of CEOs, *Managerial Economics*, 46(3): 23–26.

72. D. G. Sirmon, M. A. Hitt, & R. D. Ireland, 2006, Managing firm resources in dynamic markets to create value: Looking inside the black box, *Academy of Management Review*, in press.

73. R. A. Burgelman, 2001, *Strategy Is Destiny: How Strategy-Making Shapes a Company's Future*, New York: The Free Press.

74. S. K. Ethiraj, P. Kale, M. S. Krishnan, & J. V. Singh, 2005, Where do capabilities come from and how do they matter? A study in the software services industry, *Strategic Management Journal*, 26: 25–45.

75. S. Dutta, O. Narasimhan, & S. Rajiv, 2005, Conceptualizing and measuring capabilities: Methodology and empirical application, *Strategic Management Journal*, 26: 277–285.

76. 2003, History, www.pepsico.com, July; 2003, PepsiCo, Inc., www.hoovers.com, July; S. Jaffe, 2001, Do Pepsi and Gatorade mix? *BusinessWeek Online*, www.businessweek.com, August 14.

77. Barney & Arikan, The resource-based view.

78. N. W. Hatch & J. H. Dyer, 2004, Human capital and learning as a source of sustainable competitive advantage, *Strategic Management Journal*, 25: 1155–1178; C. A. Lengnick-Hall & J. A. Wolff, 1999, Similarities and contradictions in the core logic of three strategy research streams, *Strategic Management Journal*, 20: 1109–1132.

79. M. A. Hitt, L. Bierman, K. Shimizu, & R. Kochhar, 2001, Direct and moderating effects of human capital on strategy and performance in professional service firms: A resource-based perspective, *Academy of Management Journal*, 44: 13–28.

80. S. E. Jackson, M. A. Hitt, & A. S. DeNisi (eds.), 2003, *Managing Knowledge for Sustained Competitive Advantage: Designing Strategies for Effective Human Resource Management*, Oxford, UK: Elsevier Science, Ltd.

81. A. McWilliams, D. D. Van Fleet, & P. M. Wright, 2001, Strategic management of human resources for global competitive advantage, *Journal of Business Strategies*, 18(1): 1–24; J. Pfeffer, 1994, *Competitive Advantage through People*, Cambridge, MA: Harvard Business School Press, 4.

82. W. Watson, W. H. Stewart, & A. Barnir, 2003, The effects of human capital, organizational demography, and interpersonal processes on venture partner perceptions of firm profit and growth, *Journal of Business Venturing*, 18: 145–164.

83. H. B. Gregersen & J. S. Black, 2002, J. W. Marriott Jr. on growing the legacy, *Academy of Management Executive*, 16(2): 33–39.

84. R. A. Noe, J. A. Colquitt, M. J. Simmering, & S. A. Alvarez, 2003, Knowledge management: Developing intellectual and social capital, in S. E. Jackson, M. A. Hitt, & A. S. DeNisi (eds.), 2003, *Managing Knowledge for Sustained Competitive Advantage: Designing Strategies for Effective Human Resource Management*, Oxford, UK: Elsevier Science, Ltd., 209–242.

85. G. P. Hollenbeck & M. W. McCall Jr. 2003, Competence, not competencies: Making a global executive development work, in W. H. Mobley & P. W. Dorfman (eds.), *Advances in Global Leadership*, Oxford, UK: Elsevier Science, Ltd., 101–119; J. Sandberg, 2000, Understanding human competence at work: An interpretative approach, *Academy of Management Journal*, 43: 9–25.

86. Hitt, Keats, & Yucel, Strategic leadership in global business organizations; J. J. Distefano & M. L. Maznevski, 2003, Developing global managers integrating theory, behavior, data and performance, in W. H. Mobley & P. W. Dorfman (eds.), *Advances in Global Leadership*, Oxford, UK: Elsevier Science, Ltd., 341–371.

87. J. S. Bunderson & K. M. Sutcliffe, 2003, Management team learning orientation and business unit performance, *Journal of Applied Psychology*, 88: 552–560; C. R. James, 2003, Designing learning organizations, *Organizational Dynamics*, 32(1): 46–61.

88. Hitt, Miller, & Colella, *Organizational Behavior*.

89. J. D. Bragger, D. A. Hantula, D. Bragger, J. Kirnan, & E. Kutcher, 2003, When success breeds failure: History, Hysteresis, and delayed exit decisions, *Journal of Applied Psychology*, 88: 6–14.

90. M. R. Haas & M. T. Hansen, 2005, When using knowledge can hurt performance: The value of organizational capabilities in a management consulting company, *Strategic Management Journal*, 26: 1–24; G. Ahuja & R. Katila, 2004, Where do resources come from? The role of idiosyncratic situations, *Strategic Management Journal*, 25: 887–907.

91. Hitt, Miller, & Colella, *Organizational Behavior*.

92. J. W. Spencer, 2003, Firms' knowledge-sharing strategies in the global innovation system: Empirical evidence from the flat-panel display industry, *Strategic Management Journal*, 24: 217–233; M. Harvey & M. M. Novice

vic, 2002, The hypercompetitive global marketplace: The importance of intuition and creativity in expatriate managers, *Journal of World Business*, 37: 127–138.

93. S. Rodan & C. Galunic, 2004, More than network structure: How knowledge heterogeneity influences managerial performance and innovativeness, *Strategic Management Journal*, 25: 541–562; S. K. McEvily & B. Chakravarthy, 2002, The persistence of knowledge-based advantage: An empirical test for product performance and technological knowledge, *Strategic Management Journal*, 23: 285–305.

94. K. D. Miller, 2002, Knowledge inventories and managerial myopia, *Strategic Management Journal*, 23: 689–706.

95. R. D. Nixon, M. A. Hitt, H. Lee, & E. Jeong, 2004, Market reactions to corporate announcements of downsizing actions and implementation strategies, *Strategic Management Journal*, 25: 1121–1129.

96. J. Di Frances, 2002, 10 reasons why you shouldn't downsize, *Journal of Property Management*, 67(1): 72–73

97. A. Pinsonneault & K. Kraemer, 2002, The role of information technology in organizational downsizing: A tale of two American cities, *Organization Science*, 13: 191–208.

98. Nixon, Hitt, Lee, & Jeong, Market reactions to corporate announcements of downsizing actions.

99. T. Simons & Q. Roberson, 2003, Why managers should care about fairness: The effects of aggregate justice perceptions on organizational outcomes, *Journal of Applied Psychology*, 88: 432–443; M. L. Ambrose & R. Cropanzano, 2003, A longitudinal analysis of organizational fairness: An examination of reactions to tenure and promotion decisions, *Journal of Applied Psychology*, 88: 266–275.

100. P. S. Adler & S.-W. Kwon, 2002, Social capital: Prospects for a new concept, *Academy of Management Review*, 27: 17–40.

101. A. Mendez, 2003, The coordination of globalized R&D activities through project teams organization: An exploratory empirical study, *Journal of World Business*, 38: 96–109.

102. R. D. Ireland, M. A. Hitt, & D. Vaidyanath, 2002, Managing strategic alliances to achieve a competitive advantage, *Journal of Management*, 28: 413–446.

103. J. Florin, M. Lubatkin, & W. Schulze, 2003, *Academy of Management Journal*, 46: 374–384; P. Davidsson & B. Honig, 2003, The role of social and human capital among nascent entrepreneurs, *Journal of Business Venturing*, 18: 301–331.

104. A. K. Gupta & V. Govindarajan, 2000, Knowledge management's social dimension: Lessons from Nucor Steel, *Sloan Management Review*, 42(1): 71–80; C. M. Fiol, 1991, Managing culture as a competitive resource: An identity-based view of sustainable competitive advantage, *Journal of Management*, 17: 191–211; J. B. Barney, 1986, Organizational culture: Can it be a source of sustained competitive advantage? *Academy of Management Review*, 11: 656–665.

105. V. Govindarajan & A. K. Gupta, 2001, Building an effective global business team, *Sloan Management Review*, 42(4): 63–71; S. Ghoshal & C. A. Bartlett, 1994, Linking organizational context and managerial action: The dimensions of quality of management, *Strategic Management Journal*, 15: 91–112.

106. D. F. Kuratko, R. D. Ireland, & J. S. Hornsby, 2001, Improving firm performance through entrepreneurial actions: Acordia's corporate entrepreneurship strategy, *Academy of Management Executive*, 15(4): 60–71.

107. A. Ardichvili, R. Cardoza, & S. Ray, 2003, A theory of entrepreneurial opportunity identification and development, *Journal of Business Venturing*, 18: 105–123; T. E. Brown, P. Davidsson, & J. Wiklund, 2001, An operationalization of Stevenson's conceptualization of entrepreneurship as opportunity-based firm behavior, *Strategic Management Journal*, 22: 953–968.

108. D. S. Elenkov, W. Judge, & P. Wright, 2005, Strategic leadership and executive innovation influence: An international multi-cluster comparative study, *Strategic Management Journal*, 26: 665–682.

109. R. G. McGrath, W. J. Ferrier, & A. L. Mendelow, 2004, Real options as engines of choice and heterogeneity, *Academy of Management Review*, 29: 86–101.

110. R. S. Vassolo, J. Anand, & T. B. Folta, 2004, Non-additivity in portfolios of exploration activities: A real options analysis of equity alliances in biotechnology, *Strategic Management Journal*, 25: 1045–1061.

111. R. D. Ireland, M. A. Hitt, & D. Sirmon, 2003, A model of strategic entrepreneurship: The construct and its dimensions, *Journal of Management*, 29: 963–989.

112. G. T. Lumpkin & G. G. Dess, 1996, Clarifying the entrepreneurial orientation construct and linking it to performance, *Academy of Management Review*, 21: 135–172; R. G. McGrath & I. MacMillan, 2000, *Entrepreneurial mindset*, Boston: Harvard Business School Press.

113. Lumpkin & Dess, Clarifying the entrepreneurial orientation construct, 142.

114. Ibid., 137.

115. R. R. Sims, 2000, Changing an organization's culture under new leadership, *Journal of Business Ethics*, 25: 65–78.

116. R. A. Burgelman & Y. L. Doz, 2001, The power of strategic integration, *Sloan Management Review*, 42(3): 28–38.

117. J. S. Hornsby, D. F. Kuratko, & S. A. Zahra, 2002, Middle managers' perception of the internal environment for corporate entrepreneurship: Assessing a measurement scale, *Journal of Business Venturing*, 17: 253–273.

118. B. Axelrod, H. Handfield-Jones, & E. Michaels, 2002, A new game plan for C players, *Harvard Business Review*, 80(1): 80–88.

119. Adler & Kwon, Social capital.

120. M. E. Scheitzer, L. Ordonez, & M. Hoegl, 2004, Goal Setting as a motivator of unethical behavior, *Academy of Management Journal*, 47: 422–432.

121. L. K. Trevino, G. R. Weaver, D. G. Toffler, & B. Ley, 1999, Managing ethics and legal compliance: What works and what hurts, *California Management Review*, 41(2): 131–151.

122. C. W. L. Hill, 1990, Cooperation, opportunism, and the invisible hand: Implications for transaction cost theory, *Academy of Management Review*, 15: 500–513.

123. J. M. Stevens, H. K. Steensma, D. A. Harrison, & P. L. Cochran, 2005, Symbolic or substantive document? Influence of ethics codes on financial executives decisions, *Strategic Management Journal*, 26: 181–195.

124. 2005, www.us.dell.com, June 24.

125. C. J. Robertson & W. F. Crittenden, 2003, Mapping moral philosophies: Strategic implications for multinational firms, *Strategic Management Journal*, 24: 385–392; E. Soule, 2002, Managerial moral strategies—In search of a few good principles, *Academy of Management Review*, 27: 114–124.

126. L. M. Leinicke, J. A. Ostrosky, & W. M. Rexroad, 2000, Quality financial reporting: Back to the basics, *CPA Journal*, August, 69–71.

127. J. Ivancevich, T. N. Duening, J. A. Gilbert, & R. Konopaske, 2003, Deterring white-collar crime, *Academy of Management Executive*, 17(2): 114–127.

128. K. Schnatterly, 2003, Increasing firm value through detection and prevention of white-collar crime, *Strategic Management Journal*, 24: 587–614.

129. P. Rodriguez, K. Uhlenbruck, & L. Eden, 2005, Government corruption and the entry strategies of multinationals, *Academy of Management Review*, 30: 383–396; J. B. Cullen, K. P. Parboteeah, & M. Hoegl, 2004, Cross-national differences in managers' willingness to justify ethically suspect behaviors: A test of institutional anomie theory, *Academy of Management Journal*, 47: 411–421.

130. J. H. Gavin, J. C. Quick, C. L. Cooper, & J. D. Quick, 2003, A spirit of personal integrity: The role of character in executive health, *Organizational Dynamics*, 32: 165–179.

131. J. R. Cohen, L. W. Pant, & D. J. Sharp, 2001, An examination of differences in ethical decision-making between Canadian business students and accounting professionals, *Journal of Business Ethics*, 30: 319–336.

132. P. E. Murphy, 1995, Corporate ethics statements: Current status and future prospects, *Journal of Business Ethics*, 14: 727–740.

133. G. Redding, 2002, The capitalistic business system of China and its rationale, *Asia Pacific Journal of Management*, 19: 221–249.

134. J. H. Gittell, 2000, Paradox of coordination and control, *California Management Review*, 42(3): 101–117.

135. M. D. Shields, F. J. Deng, & Y. Kato, 2000, The design and effects of control systems: Tests of direct- and indirect-effects models, *Accounting, Organizations and Society*, 25: 185–202.

136. K. J. Laverty, 1996, Economic "short-termism": The debate, the unresolved issues, and the implications for management practice and research, *Academy of Management Review*, 21: 825–860.

137. R. S. Kaplan & D. P. Norton, 2001, The strategy-focused organization, *Strategy & Leadership*, 29(3): 41–42; R. S. Kaplan & D. P. Norton, 2000, *The Strategy-Focused Organization: How Balanced Scorecard Companies Thrive in the New Business Environment*, Boston: Harvard Business School Press.

138. B. E. Becker, M. A. Huselid, & D. Ulrich, 2001, *The HR Scorecard: Linking People, Strategy, and Performance*, Boston: Harvard Business School Press, 21.

139. Kaplan & Norton, The strategy-focused organization.

140. R. S. Kaplan & D. P. Norton, 2001, Transforming the balanced scorecard from performance measurement to strategic management: Part I, *Accounting Horizons*, 15(1): 87–104.

141. R. S. Kaplan & D. P. Norton, 1992, The balanced scorecard—measures that drive performance, *Harvard Business Review*, 70(1): 71–79.

142. M. A. Mische, 2001, *Strategic Renewal: Becoming a High-Performance Organization*, Upper Saddle River, NJ: Prentice-Hall, 181.

143. H.-J. Cho & V. Pucik, 2005, Relationship between innovativeness, quality, growth, profitability and market value, *Strategic Management Journal*, 26: 555–575.

144. Rowe, Creating wealth in organizations: The role of strategic leadership.

145. R. E. Hoskisson, R. A. Johnson, D. Yiu, & W. P. Wan, 2001, Restructuring strategies of diversified business groups: Differences associated with country institutional environments, in M. A. Hitt, R. E. Freeman, & J. S. Harrison (eds.), *Handbook of Strategic Management*, Oxford, UK: Blackwell Publishers, 433–463; R. A. Johnson, 1996, Antecedents and outcomes of corporate refocusing, *Journal of Management*, 22: 437–481; R. E. Hoskisson & M. A. Hitt, 1994, *Downscoping: How to Tame the Diversified Firm*, New York: Oxford University Press.

146. J. Birkinshaw & N. Hood, 2001, Unleash innovation in foreign subsidiaries, *Harvard Business Review*, 79(3): 131–137.

147. Ireland & Hitt, Achieving and maintaining strategic competitiveness.

148. R. C. Morais, 2003, Mind the gap, *Forbes*, www.forbes.com, July 21.

149. J. D. Gunkel & G. Probst, 2003, Implementation of the balanced scorecard as a means of corporate learning: The Porsche case, European Case Clearing House, Cranfield, UK.

Entrepreneurship

Studying this chapter should provide you with the strategic management knowledge needed to:

1. Define strategic entrepreneurship and corporate entrepreneurship.

2. Define entrepreneurship and entrepreneurial opportunities and explain their importance.

3. Define invention, innovation, and imitation and describe the relationship among them.

4. Describe entrepreneurs and the entrepreneurial mind-set.

5. Explain international entrepreneurship and its importance.

6. Describe how firms internally develop innovations.

7. Explain how firms use cooperative strategies to innovate.

8. Describe how firms use acquisitions as a means of innovation.

9. Explain how strategic entrepreneurship helps firms create value.

W. L. Gore, maker of Gore-Tex products, is as inventive in its company structure as it is in its product development.

© RACHEL EPSTEIN/PHOTOEDIT

W. L. Gore & Associates: The Most Innovative Company in America?

For many athletes, especially those living in cold or wet climates, Gore-Tex is a familiar name. The breathable and water-resistant fabric has been developed into a range of outerwear products that provide comfort and protection from cold, wet, and windy weather.

The maker of these products, W. L. Gore & Associates, is actually quite diversified and remains a privately held company. Using its world-class expertise with fluorocarbon polymers, the firm's products "provide innovative solutions throughout the industry, in next-generation electronics, for medical products, and with high-performance fabrics." As an example of the breadth of the firm's product lines, consider the fact that during their path-breaking flight to the moon, Neil Armstrong and Buzz Aldrin installed seismographic equipment with lightweight, high-temperature cable made by Gore (as part of this flight, Armstrong was the first astronaut to walk on the moon's surface). Operating with four divisions (fabrics, medical, industrial, and electronics), Gore has annual sales in excess of $1.35 billion. The firm employs over 6,000 people in more than 45 manufacturing plants and sales locations around the globe.

What contributes to this firm's initial and continuing success? According to Gore employees, at the core of the firm's success is a belief in product *and* organizational innovations and a commitment to technical excellence.

From its inception as an entrepreneurial venture, Gore has always been about product innovation. Indeed, the firm was founded in 1958 by Bill and Vieve Gore to explore opportunities for fluorocarbon polymers, especially polytetrafluorethylene (PTFE). Bill had the idea of seeking applications with PTFE while working as a scientist for DuPont Corporation. Because of a lack of interest at DuPont, Bill purchased the patent on which PTFE was based and launched his own business venture.

Since its founding, W. L. Gore has produced a constant stream of product innovations. "They've defined new standards for comfort and protection for workwear and activewear (Gore-Tex); advanced the science of regenerating tissues destroyed by disease or traumatic injuries; developed next-generation materials for printed circuit boards and fiber optics; and pioneered new methods to detect and control environmental pollution." Filing hundreds of patents annually as the basis of its products, Gore has been recognized many times for the innovativeness of what it manufactures. In 1997, the European Patent Office included a number of the firm's products in an exhibit of product innovations shown at The Hague.

As noted above, organizational innovations are also part of the lifeline to Gore's success. In the words of a business analyst: "Gore's uniqueness comes from being as innovative in its operation principles as it is in its diverse product lines." The firm's organizational structure is flat, allowing frequent and direct communications among all associates. Essentially, the firm operates by developing a "bunch of small task forces." Teams, which are organized around what are perceived to be opportunities to create innovative products, are small, as are manufacturing plants (no plant has more than 200 associates). When new hires join Gore, they choose a mentor who helps them develop and find a team to which they believe they can contribute. Instead of bosses, associates have leaders, a prestigious position in that team members elect their own leader. And any associate can become a leader by launching a product idea that attracts other associates who are willing to form a team to pursue it. Members of teams evaluate each other, creating a situation in which the team is really the party to whom each associate feels responsible. Associates are encouraged to spend about 10 percent of their time on speculative ideas. Four principles are central to Gore's culture: (1) "fairness to each other and everyone with whom we come in contact, (2) freedom to encourage, help, and allow other associates to grow in knowledge, skill, and scope of responsibility, (3) the ability to make one's own commitments and keep them, and (4) consultation with other associates before undertaking actions that could impact the reputation of the company."

Gore's organizational innovations have helped the company to garner many awards recognizing its attractiveness as a place to work. Gore has been included multiple times on the "100 Best Companies to Work for in America" list, ranked number one among the "100 Best Places to Work in the U.K." (2004 and 2005), and was selected by *Fast Company* in 2004 as "The Most Innovative Company in America."

Sources: D. Miller & I. L. Breton-Miller, 2005, Leveraging the mission in family business, *Harvard Business School Working Knowledge*, www.hbswk.hbs.edu, February 14; 2005, W. L. Gore, *Times Online*, www.business.timesonline.co.uk, March 6; 2005, Gore cited as American's most innovative company, W. L. Gore & Associates Home page, www.gore.com, July 11; 2005, About Gore, W. L. Gore & Associates Home page, www.gore.com, July 11; A. Deutschman, 2004, The fabric of creativity, *Fast Company*, 54–61.

In Chapter 1, we indicated that *organizational culture* refers to the complex set of ideologies, symbols, and core values that are shared throughout the firm and that influence how the firm conducts business. Thus, culture is the social energy that drives—or fails to drive—the organization. Having read this chapter's Opening Case, you can easily see that W. L. Gore's culture is oriented toward and supportive of continuous product and organizational innovations. Increasingly, a firm's ability to engage in both types of innovation is linked to performance improvements.[1]

Is W. L. Gore the most innovative company in the United States and one of the most innovative in the world? Obviously, answering this question in either direction could stir debate. What can not be legitimately debated is that Gore consistently produces product innovations as well as organizational innovations. You will see from reading this chapter that Gore's ability to innovate in both ways shows that the firm successfully practices strategic entrepreneurship. While product innovation's importance has long been recognized, the equally critical importance of organizational innovations is a more recent recognition.[2]

Strategic entrepreneurship is taking entrepreneurial actions using a strategic perspective. When engaging in strategic entrepreneurship, the firm simultaneously focuses on finding opportunities in its external environment that it can try to exploit through innovations. Identifying opportunities to exploit through innovations is the *entrepreneurship* part of strategic entrepreneurship, while determining the best way to manage the firm's innovation efforts is the *strategic* part. Thus, strategic entrepreneurship finds firms integrating their actions to find opportunities and to successfully innovate as a primary means of pursuing them.[3] In the 21st-century competitive landscape, firm survival and success increasingly is a function of a firm's ability to continuously find new opportunities and quickly produce innovations to pursue them.[4]

To examine strategic entrepreneurship, we consider several topics in this chapter. First, we examine entrepreneurship and innovation in a strategic context. Definitions of entrepreneurship, entrepreneurial opportunities, and entrepreneurs as those who engage in entrepreneurship to pursue entrepreneurial opportunities are included as parts of this analysis. We then describe international entrepreneurship, a phenomenon reflecting the increased use of entrepreneurship in economies throughout the world. After this discussion, the chapter shifts to descriptions of the three ways firms innovate. Internally, firms innovate through either autonomous or induced strategic behavior. We then describe actions firms take to implement the innovations resulting from those two types of strategic behavior.

In addition to innovating through internal activities, firms can develop innovations by using cooperative strategies, such as strategic alliances, and by acquiring other companies to gain access to their innovations and innovative capabilities. Most large, complex firms use all three methods to innovate. The method the firm chooses to innovate can be affected by the firm's governance mechanisms. Research evidence suggests, for example, that inside board directors with equity positions favor internal innovation while outside directors with equity positions prefer acquiring innovation.[5] The chapter closes with summary comments about how firms use strategic entrepreneurship to create value and earn above-average returns.

As you will see from studying this chapter, innovation and entrepreneurship are vital for young and old and for large and small firms, for service companies as well as manufacturing firms and for high-technology ventures.[6] In the global competitive landscape, the long-term success of new ventures and established firms is a function of the ability to meld entrepreneurship with strategic management.[7]

Before moving to the next section, we should mention that our focus in this chapter is on innovation and entrepreneurship within established organizations. This phenomenon is called **corporate entrepreneurship**, which is the use or application of entrepreneurship within an established firm.[8] An important part of the entrepreneurship discipline, corporate entrepreneurship increasingly is thought to be linked to survival and success of established corporations.[9] Indeed, established firms use entrepreneurship to strengthen their performance and to enhance growth opportunities.[10] Of course, innovation and entrepreneurship play a critical role in the degree of success achieved by start-up entrepreneurial ventures as well.

Our focus in this chapter is on corporate entrepreneurship. However, the materials we will describe are equally important in entrepreneurial ventures (sometimes called "start-ups"). Moreover, we will make specific reference to entrepreneurial ventures in a few parts of the chapter as we discuss the importance of strategic entrepreneurship for firms competing in the 21st-century competitive landscape.

Entrepreneurship and Entrepreneurial Opportunities

Entrepreneurship is the process by which individuals or groups identify and pursue entrepreneurial opportunities without being immediately constrained by the resources they currently control.[11] **Entrepreneurial opportunities** are conditions in which new goods or services can satisfy a need in the market. These opportunities exist because of competitive imperfections in markets and among the factors of production used to produce them[12] and when information about these imperfections is distributed asymmetrically (that is, not equally) among individuals.[13] Entrepreneurial opportunities come in a host of forms (e.g., the chance to develop and sell a new product and the chance to sell an existing product in a new market).[14] Firms should be receptive to pursuing entrepreneurial opportunities whenever and wherever they may surface.

As these two definitions suggest, the essence of entrepreneurship is to identify and exploit entrepreneurial opportunities—that is, opportunities others do not see or for which they do not recognize the commercial potential.[15] As a process, entrepreneurship results in the "creative destruction" of existing products (goods or services) or methods of producing them and replaces them with new products and production methods.[16] Thus, firms engaging in entrepreneurship place high value on individual innovations as well as the ability to continuously innovate across time.[17]

We study entrepreneurship at the level of the individual firm. However, evidence suggests that entrepreneurship is the economic engine driving many nations' economies in the global competitive landscape.[18] Thus, entrepreneurship, and the innovation it spawns, is important for companies competing in the global economy and for countries seeking to stimulate economic climates with the potential to enhance the living standard of their citizens.[19]

Innovation

Peter Drucker argued that "innovation is the specific function of entrepreneurship, whether in an existing business, a public service institution, or a new venture started by a lone individual."[20] Moreover, Drucker suggested that innovation is "the means by which the entrepreneur either creates new wealth-producing resources or endows existing resources with enhanced potential for creating wealth."[21] Thus, entrepreneurship and the innovation resulting from it are important for large and small firms, as well as for start-up ventures, as they compete in the 21st-century competitive landscape.[22] In fact, some argue that firms failing to innovate will stagnate.[23] The realities of competition in the 21st-century competitive landscape suggest that "No company can maintain a long-term leadership position in a category unless it is in a continuous process of developing innovative new products desired by customers."[24] This means that innovation should be an intrinsic part of virtually all of a firm's activities.[25]

Innovation is a key outcome firms seek through entrepreneurship and is often the source of competitive success, especially in turbulent, highly competitive environments.[26] For example, research results show that firms competing in global industries that invest more in innovation also achieve the highest returns.[27] In fact, investors often react positively to the introduction of a new product, thereby increasing the price of a firm's stock. Innovation, then, is an essential feature of high-performance firms.[28] Furthermore, "innovation may be required to maintain or achieve competitive parity, much less a competitive advantage in many global markets."[29] The most innovative firms understand that financial slack should be available at all times to support the pursuit of entrepreneurial opportunities.[30]

In his classic work, Schumpeter argued that firms engage in three types of innovative activity.[31] **Invention** is the act of creating or developing a new product or process. **Innovation** is the process of creating a commercial product from an invention. Innovation begins after an invention is chosen for development.[32] Thus, an invention brings something new into being, while an innovation brings something new into use. Accordingly, technical criteria are used to determine the success of an invention, whereas commercial criteria are used to determine the success of an innovation.[33] Finally, **imitation** is the adoption of an innovation by similar firms. Imitation usually leads to product or process standardization, and products based on imitation often are offered at lower prices, but without as many features. Entrepreneurship is critical to innovative activity in that it acts as the linchpin between invention and innovation.[34]

In the United States in particular, innovation is the most critical of the three types of innovative activity. Many companies are able to create ideas that lead to inventions, but commercializing those inventions through innovation has, at times, proved difficult. This difficulty is suggested by the fact that approximately 80 percent of R&D occurs in large firms, but these same firms produce fewer than 50 percent of the patents.[35] Patents are a strategic asset and the ability to regularly produce them can be an important source of competitive advantage, especially for firms competing in knowledge-intensive industries[36] (e.g., pharmaceuticals).

Entrepreneurs

Entrepreneurs are individuals, acting independently or as part of an organization, who see an entrepreneurial opportunity and then take risks to develop an innovation to pursue it. Often, entrepreneurs are the individuals who receive credit for making things happen![37] Entrepreneurs are found throughout an organization—from top-level managers to those working to produce a firm's goods or services. Entrepreneurs are found throughout W. L. Gore & Associates, for example. Recall from the Opening Case's analysis of this firm that part of the job of all Gore associates is to use roughly 10 percent of their time to develop innovations. Entrepreneurs tend to demonstrate several characteristics, including those of being optimistic,[38] highly motivated, willing to take responsibility for their projects, and courageous.[39] In addition, entrepreneurs tend to be passionate and emotional about the value and importance of their innovation-based ideas.[40]

Evidence suggests that successful entrepreneurs have an entrepreneurial mind-set. The person with an **entrepreneurial mind-set** values uncertainty in the marketplace and seeks to continuously identify opportunities with the potential to lead to important innovations.[41] Because it has the potential to lead to continuous innovations, individuals' entrepreneurial mind-sets can be a source of competitive advantage for a firm.[42] Howard Schultz, founder of Starbucks, believes that his firm has a number of individuals with an entrepreneurial mind-set. Making music a meaningful part of Starbucks' customers' experiences is an example of an evolving product offering resulting from an entrepreneurial mind-set. In Schultz's words: "The music world is changing, and Starbucks and Starbucks Hear Music will continue to be an innovator in the industry. It takes passion, commitment, and even a bit of experimentation to maintain that position."[43] Of course, changes in the music industry create the uncertainties that lead to entrepreneurial opportunities that can be pursued by relying on an entrepreneurial mind-set.

As our discussions have suggested, "innovation is an application of knowledge to produce new knowledge."[44] As such, entrepreneurial mind-sets are fostered and supported when knowledge

Starbucks' decision to offer music in its stores is the result of an entrepreneurial mind-set.

GETTY IMAGES

The entrepreneurial mind-set of HP employees led them to develop new printing technology that cuts printing time in half.

is readily available throughout a firm. Indeed, research has shown that units within firms are more innovative when they have access to new knowledge.[45] Transferring knowledge, however, can be difficult, often because the receiving party must have adequate absorptive capacity (or the ability) to learn the knowledge.[46] This requires that the new knowledge be linked to the existing knowledge. Thus, managers need to develop the capabilities of their human capital to build on their current knowledge base while incrementally expanding that knowledge[47] to facilitate the development of entrepreneurial mind-sets.

Recent actions at Hewlett-Packard Co. (HP) demonstrate the use of knowledge as part of the entrepreneurial mind-set many employees have developed. In response to inroads into the firm's lucrative computer printers being made by competitors such as Dell Inc. and Lexmark International, HP introduced a new technology for inkjet printers that reduces photo-printing time by half. An analyst commented, "This seems to be a pattern we've seen before—competitors gain on HP by slashing prices, then HP introduces new technology that lets them move ahead."[48] Thus, HP employees use their entrepreneurial mind-set to identify opportunities (e.g., to reduce the time needed to print photos) and then integrate knowledge available throughout the firm to develop an innovation to exploit the identified opportunity.

International Entrepreneurship

International entrepreneurship is a process in which firms creatively discover and exploit opportunities that are outside their domestic markets in order to develop a competitive advantage.[49] As the practices suggested by this definition shown, entrepreneurship is a global phenomenon.[50]

A key reason that entrepreneurship has become a global phenomenon is that in general, internationalization leads to improved firm performance.[51] Nonetheless, decision makers should recognize that the decision to internationalize exposes their firms to various risks, including those of unstable foreign currencies, problems with market efficiencies, insufficient infrastructures to support businesses, and limitations on market size.[52] Thus, the decision to engage in international entrepreneurship should be a product of careful analysis.[53]

Because of its positive benefits, entrepreneurship is at the top of public policy agendas in many of the world's countries, including Finland, Germany, Ireland, and Israel. Some argue that placing entrepreneurship on these agendas may be appropriate in that regulation hindering innovation and entrepreneurship is the root cause of Europe's productivity problems.[54] In Ireland, for example, the government is

PART 3 / Strategic Actions: Strategy Implementation

396

"particularly focused on encouraging new innovative enterprises that have growth potential and are export oriented."[55] Some believe that entrepreneurship is flourishing in New Zealand, a trend having a positive effect on the productivity of the nation's economy.[56]

While entrepreneurship is a global phenomenon, the rate of entrepreneurship differs across countries. A study of 29 countries found that the percentage of adults involved in entrepreneurial activity ranged from a high of more than 20 percent in Mexico to a low of approximately 5 percent in Belgium. The United States had a rate of about 13 percent. Importantly, this study also found a strong positive relationship between the rate of entrepreneurial activity and economic development in a country.[57]

Culture is one of the reasons for the differences in rates of entrepreneurship among different countries. For example, the tension between individualism and collectivism is important in that entrepreneurship declines as collectivism is emphasized. Simultaneously, however, research results suggest that exceptionally high levels of individualism might be dysfunctional for entrepreneurship. Viewed collectively, these results appear to call for a balance between individual initiative and a spirit of cooperation and group ownership of innovation. For firms to be entrepreneurial, they must provide appropriate autonomy and incentives for individual initiative to surface, but also promote cooperation and group ownership of an innovation if it is to be implemented successfully. Thus, international entrepreneurship often requires teams of people with unique skills and resources, especially in cultures where collectivism is a valued historical norm.[58]

The level of investment outside of the home country made by young ventures is also an important dimension of international entrepreneurship. In fact, with increasing globalization, a greater number of new ventures have been "born global."[59] Research has shown that new ventures that enter international markets increase their learning of new technological knowledge and thereby enhance their performance.[60] Because of the positive outcomes associated with its use, the amount of international entrepreneurship has been increasing in recent years.[61]

The probability of entering international markets increases when the firm has top executives with international experience.[62] Furthermore, the firm has a higher likelihood of successfully competing in international markets when its top executives have international experience.[63] Because of the learning and economies of scale and scope afforded by operating in international markets, both young and established internationally diversified firms often are stronger competitors in their domestic market as well. Additionally, as research has shown, internationally diversified firms are generally more innovative.[64]

Next, we discuss the three ways firms innovate.

Internal Innovation

In established organizations, most innovation comes from efforts in research and development (R&D). This is the case with the innovations through which Toyota Motor Company produced the Prius, a gas-electric hybrid.[65] As explained in the Strategic Focus, this is also the case at Panera Bread Company. While reading about Panera, observe how the firm relies on its R&D activities to continuously improve the quality of the breads it makes as well as to continuously provide customers with innovative food items.

Panera Bread Company: Thriving through Internal Innovation

St. Louis–based Panera Bread Company is a chain of specialty bakery-cafés. The firm was founded in 1981 as the Au Bon Pain Co. with three bakery-cafés and one cookie store. The firm grew slowly until the mid-1990s. At that time, company leaders observed what they believed were two important trends: (1) customers wanted more than the run-of-the-mill offerings available from well-established franchised concepts such as McDonald's, Wendy's, Pizza Hut, and so forth, and (2) while they desired "better" food, customers still wanted to receive that food quickly. Combining these competitive dimensions resulted in what today is known as the "fast casual" dining experience, an experience in which customers quickly receive good food they can eat in an enjoyable restaurant environment. Given its new, innovative focus, the firm changed its name to Panera Bread Company (in Latin, "panera" roughly translates as "time for bread").

Operating with the vision of "a loaf of bread in every arm" and the mission of "providing high-quality products and exceptional service to our customers," Panera is a leader in the fast-casual segment restaurant business. The firm has close to 800 locations in 35 states. Roughly 70 percent of the locations are operated by franchisees. The firm's products include made-to-order sandwiches that are built around "a variety of artisan breads, including Asiago cheese bread, focaccia, and its classic sourdough bread." Soups, salads, and gourmet coffee are other staples on Panera's menu. Atlanta Bread, Bruegger's, and Cosi are Panera's main competitors.

Internally developed product innovations are critical to Panera's original and continuing success. For example, the firm's "fresh dough concept" is the innovative basis for how it makes its breads. The company sees the facilities it uses to manufacture its fresh-baked dough on a daily basis as a competitive advantage. Viewed as a "proprietary innovation," how Panera manufacturers its dough is based on intangible assets. Consider comments from a company official as proof: "When it comes to the exacts of our method, we take a proprietary attitude. [But] our manufacturing facilities don't use any technologies you haven't seen in a bakery before. Our sourdough is based on a perpetual starter, refreshed regularly, and the usual bakery manufacturing steps follow: mixing, makeup, retarding and/or cooling." Panera uses its resources to find ways to innovatively improve the quality of the distribution system it uses to provide fresh dough to its stores and to improve the quality of the dough itself.

Panera also concentrates on internal innovation to continuously "improve the menu." John Taylor, who is in charge of research and development for the customer experience, and Scott Davis, senior vice president and chief concept officer, are the Panera managers responsible for many of the new breads, sandwiches, soups, and salads that are continuously introduced to keep Panera's menu new and exciting. Consider the approach to the firm's soups as an example of internal innovations. Five times per year, the firm "rotates in two specialty flavors for a typical run of a couple of months before they are replaced by the next

Internal innovation at Panera keeps the menu fresh and the customers happy.

© ROBIN NELSON/PHOTOEDIT

limited-time offerings." These offerings are in addition to the soups available to customers on a year-round basis. To develop new soups, Panera works closely with manufacturing partners to complete a process that usually requires four to six months to finish and involves obtaining customer feedback.

Sources: B. R. Barringer & R. D. Ireland, 2006, *Entrepreneurship: Successfully Launching New Ventures,* Upper Saddle River, NJ: Pearson Prentice Hall, 95–96; S. Kirsner, 2005, 4 leaders you need to know, *Fast Company,* February, 68–76; 2005, Panera Bread Company Fact Sheet, *Hoover's Online,* www.hoovers.com, July 8; 2005, Panera Bread, *Nation's Restaurant News,* 39(19): 94; N. Kruse, 2004, Custom fitting: One kind definitely does not fit all, *Nation's Restaurant News,* 38(44): 34.

Effective R&D often leads to firms' filing for patents to protect their innovative work. Increasingly, successful R&D results from integrating the skills available in the global workforce. Firms seeking internal innovations through their R&D must understand that "Talent and ideas are flourishing everywhere—from Bangalore to Shanghai to Kiev—and no company, regardless of geography, can hesitate to go wherever those ideas are."[66] Thus, in the years to come, the ability to have a competitive advantage based on innovation may accrue to firms able to meld the talent of human capital from countries around the world. W. L. Gore & Associates and Panera Bread Company appear to be two companies with an ability to do this.

Research and development could be the major source of innovation in the 21st century.

Increasingly, it seems possible that in the 21st-century competitive landscape, R&D may be the most critical factor in gaining and sustaining a competitive advantage in some industries, such as pharmaceuticals. Larger, established firms, certainly those competing globally, often try to use their R&D labs to create competence-destroying new technologies and products.[67] Being able to innovate in this manner can create a competitive advantage for a firm in many industries.[68] Although critical to long-term corporate success, the outcomes of R&D investments are uncertain and often not achieved in the short term,[69] meaning that patience is required as firms evaluate the outcomes of their R&D efforts.

Incremental and Radical Innovation

Firms produce two types of internal innovations—incremental and radical innovations—when using their R&D activities. Most innovations are *incremental*—that is, they build on existing knowledge bases and provide small improvements in the current product lines. Incremental innovations are evolutionary and linear in nature.[70] "The markets for incremental innovations are well-defined, product characteristics are well understood, profit margins tend to be lower, production technologies are efficient, and competition is primarily on the basis of price."[71] Adding a different kind of whitening agent to a soap detergent is an example of an incremental innovation, as are improvements in televisions over the last few decades (moving from black-and-white to color, improving existing audio capabilities, etc.). Panera Bread Company's introduction of new soups is another example of incremental innovations. Companies launch far more incremental innovations than radical innovations.[72]

In contrast to incremental innovations, *radical innovations* usually provide significant technological breakthroughs and create new knowledge.[73] Recall from the Opening Case that W. L. Gore & Associates seeks to develop primarily radical rather than incremental innovations through its R&D activities. Radical innovations, which are revolutionary and non-linear in nature, typically use new technologies to serve newly created markets. The development of the personal computer (PC) is an example of a radical innovation. Reinventing the computer by developing a "radically new computer-brain chip" is an example of what could be a radical innovation. If researchers are successful in their efforts, superchips (with the capability to process a trillion calculations per second) will be developed.[74] Obviously, such a radical innovation would seem to have the capacity to revolutionize the tasks computers could perform.

Because they establish new functionalities for users, radical innovations have strong potential to lead to significant growth in revenue and profits.[75] Developing new processes is a critical part of producing radical innovations. Both types of innovation can create value, meaning that firms should determine when it is appropriate to emphasize either incremental or radical innovation.[76] However, radical innovations have the potential to contribute more significantly to a firm's efforts to earn above-average returns.

Radical innovations are rare because of the difficulty and risk involved in developing them.[77] The value of the technology and the market opportunities are highly uncertain.[78] Because radical innovation creates new knowledge and uses only some or little of a firm's current product or technological knowledge, creativity is required. However, creativity does not create something from nothing. Rather, creativity discovers, combines, or synthesizes current knowledge, often from diverse areas.[79] This knowledge is then used to develop new products that can be used in an entrepreneurial manner to move into new markets, capture new customers, and gain access to new resources.[80] Such innovations are often developed in separate business units that start internal ventures.[81]

Internally developed incremental and radical internal innovations result from deliberate efforts. These deliberate efforts are called *internal corporate venturing,* which is the set of activities firms use to develop internal inventions and especially innovations.[82] As shown in Figure 13.1, autonomous and induced strategic behavior are the two types of internal corporate venturing. Each venturing type facilitates incremental and radical innovations. However, a larger number of radical innovations spring from autonomous strategic behavior while the greatest percentage of incremental innovations come from induced strategic behavior.

Autonomous Strategic Behavior

Autonomous strategic behavior is a bottom-up process in which product champions pursue new ideas, often through a political process, by means of which they develop and coordinate the commercialization of a new good or service until it achieves success in the marketplace. A *product champion* is an organizational member with an entrepreneurial vision of a new good or service who seeks to create support for its commercialization. Product champions play critical roles in moving innovations forward.[83] Indeed, in many corporations, "Champions are widely acknowledged as pivotal to innovation speed and success."[84] The primary reason for this is that "no business idea takes root purely on its own merits; it has to be sold."[85] Commonly, product champions use their social capital to develop informal networks within the firm. As

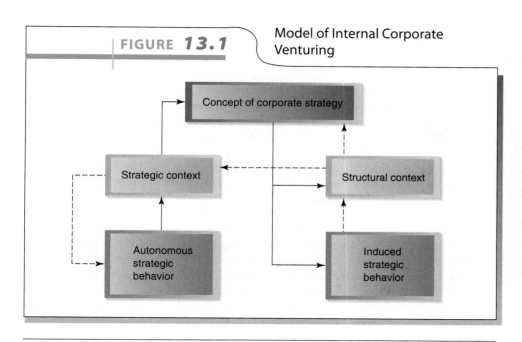

FIGURE **13.1** Model of Internal Corporate Venturing

Source: Adapted from R. A. Burgelman, 1983, A model of the interactions of strategic behavior, corporate context, and the concept of strategy, *Academy of Management Review,* 8: 65.

progress is made, these networks become more formal as a means of pushing an innovation to the point of successful commercialization.[86] Internal innovations springing from autonomous strategic behavior tend to diverge from the firm's current strategy, taking it into new markets and perhaps new ways of creating value for customers and other stakeholders.

Autonomous strategic behavior is based on a firm's wellsprings of knowledge and resources that are the sources of the firm's innovation. Thus, a firm's technological capabilities and competencies are the basis for new products and processes.[87] GE depends on autonomous strategic behavior on a regular basis to produce innovations.[88] Essentially, "the search for marketable services can start in any of GE's myriad businesses. [For example], an operating unit seeks out appropriate technology to better do what it already does. Having mastered the technology, it then incorporates it into a service it can sell to others."[89]

Changing the concept of corporate-level strategy through autonomous strategic behavior results when a product is championed within strategic and structural contexts (see Figure 13.1). The strategic context is the process used to arrive at strategic decisions (often requiring political processes to gain acceptance). The best firms keep changing their strategic context and strategies because of the continuous changes in the current competitive landscape. Thus, some believe that the most competitively successful firms reinvent their industry or develop a completely new one across time as they compete with current and future rivals.[90]

To be effective, an autonomous process for developing new products requires that new knowledge be continuously diffused throughout the firm. In particular, the diffusion of tacit knowledge is important for development of more effective new products.[91] Interestingly, some of the processes important for the promotion of autonomous new product development behavior vary by the environment and country in which a firm operates. For example, the Japanese culture is high on uncertainty avoidance. As such, research has found that Japanese firms are more likely to engage in autonomous behaviors under conditions of low uncertainty.[92]

Stokke used the design of its existing high chair to develop a successful baby stroller.

Induced Strategic Behavior

The second of the two forms of internal corporate venturing, *induced strategic behavior,* is a top-down process whereby the firm's current strategy and structure foster innovations that are closely associated with that strategy and structure. In this form of venturing, the strategy in place is filtered through a matching structural hierarchy. In essence, induced strategic behavior results in internal innovations that are highly consistent with the firm's current strategy.

Norwegian furniture manufacturer Stokke recently introduced a high-end baby stroller (at the time of its introduction, the base price was $749). This stroller is based on the company's design of its most famous product, a high chair called the KinderZeat. Using the KinderZeat's design concept (which was to develop a seat that can "grow" with babies), the firm relied on its existing strategy and structure to develop its high-end stroller. When contemplating the product, the firm's managers knew that they wanted a different "design approach to create a vehicle that would both bring baby closer to mom and dad and be flexible enough to navigate the modern landscape (everything from Starbucks tables to escalators)."[93] Thus, by using the differentiation strategy and a particular form of the functional structure (see Chapter 11), Stokke's strategy and structure have created a very successful product through an internal innovation.

Implementing Internal Innovations

An entrepreneurial mind-set is required to be innovative and to develop successful internal corporate ventures. When valuing environmental and market uncertainty, which are key parts of an entrepreneurial mind-set, individuals and firms demonstrate their willingness to take risks to commercialize innovations. While they must continuously attempt to identify opportunities, they must also select and pursue the best opportunities and do so with discipline. Thus, employing an entrepreneurial mind-set entails not only developing new products and markets but also placing an emphasis on execution. Those with an entrepreneurial mind-set "engage the energies of everyone in their domain," both inside and outside the organization.[94]

Having processes and structures in place through which a firm can successfully implement the outcomes of internal corporate ventures and commercialize the innovations is critical. Indeed, the successful introduction of innovations into the marketplace reflects implementation effectiveness.[95] In the context of internal corporate ventures, processes are the "patterns of interaction, coordination, communication, and decision making employees use" to convert the innovations resulting from either autonomous or induced strategic behaviors into successful market entries.[96] As we describe in Chapter 11, organizational structures are the sets of formal relationships supporting organizational processes.

Effective integration of the various functions involved in innovation processes—from engineering to manufacturing and, ultimately, market distribution—is required to implement the incremental and radical innovations resulting from internal corporate ventures.[97] Increasingly, product development teams are being used to integrate the activities associated with different organizational functions. Such integration involves coordinating and applying the knowledge and skills of different functional areas in order to maximize innovation.[98] Effective product development teams also create value when they "pull the plug" on a project.[99] Although ending a project is difficult, sometimes because of emotional commitments to innovation-based projects, effective teams recognize when conditions change in ways that preclude the innovation's ability to create value as originally anticipated.

Cross-Functional Product Development Teams

Cross-functional teams facilitate efforts to integrate activities associated with different organizational functions, such as design, manufacturing, and marketing.[100] In addition, new product development processes can be completed more quickly and the products more easily commercialized when cross-functional teams work effectively.[101] Using cross-functional teams, product development stages are grouped into parallel or overlapping processes to allow the firm to tailor its product development efforts to its unique core competencies and to the needs of the market.

Horizontal organizational structures support the use of cross-functional teams in their efforts to integrate innovation-based activities across organizational functions.[102] Therefore, instead of being built around vertical hierarchical functions or departments, the organization is built around core horizontal processes that are used to produce and manage innovations. Some of the core horizontal processes that are critical to innovation efforts are formal; they may be defined and documented as procedures and practices. More commonly, however, these processes are informal: "They are routines or ways of working that evolve over time."[103] Often invisible, informal processes are critical to successful innovations and are supported properly through horizontal organizational structures more so than through vertical organizational structures.

Two primary barriers that may prevent the successful use of cross-functional teams as a means of integrating organizational functions are independent frames of reference of team members and organizational politics.[104]

Team members working within a distinct specialization (e.g., a particular organizational function) may have an independent frame of reference typically based on common backgrounds and experiences. They are likely to use the same decision criteria to evaluate issues such as product development efforts as they do within their functional units. Research suggests that functional departments vary along four dimensions: time orientation, interpersonal orientation, goal orientation, and formality of structure.[105] Thus, individuals from different functional departments having different orientations on these dimensions can be expected to perceive product development activities in different ways. For example, a design engineer may consider the characteristics that make a product functional and workable to be the most important of the product's characteristics. Alternatively, a person from the marketing function may hold characteristics that satisfy customer needs most important. These different orientations can create barriers to effective communication across functions.[106]

Organizational politics is the second potential barrier to effective integration in cross-functional teams. In some organizations, considerable political activity may center on allocating resources to different functions. Interunit conflict may result from aggressive competition for resources among those representing different organizational functions. This dysfunctional conflict between functions creates a barrier to their integration.[107] Methods must be found to achieve cross-functional integration without excessive political conflict and without changing the basic structural characteristics necessary for task specialization and efficiency.

Facilitating Integration and Innovation

Shared values and effective leadership are important for achieving cross-functional integration and implementing innovation.[108] Highly effective shared values are framed around the firm's vision and mission, and become the glue that promotes integration between functional units. Thus, the firm's culture promotes unity and internal innovation.[109]

Strategic leadership is also highly important for achieving cross-functional integration and promoting innovation. Leaders set the goals and allocate resources. The goals include integrated development and commercialization of new goods and services. Effective strategic leaders also ensure a high-quality communication system to facilitate cross-functional integration. A critical benefit of effective communication is the sharing of knowledge among team members.[110] Effective communication thus helps create synergy and gains team members' commitment to an innovation throughout the organization. Shared values and leadership practices shape the communication systems that are formed to support the development and commercialization of new products.[111]

Creating Value from Internal Innovation

The model in Figure 13.2 shows how firms can create value from the internal corporate venturing processes they use to develop and commercialize new goods and services. An entrepreneurial mind-set is necessary so that managers and employees will consistently try to identify entrepreneurial opportunities the firm can pursue by developing new goods and services and new markets. Cross-functional teams are important for promoting integrated new product design ideas and commitment to their subsequent implementation. Effective leadership and shared values promote integration and vision for innovation and commitment to it. The end result for the firm is the creation of value for the customers and shareholders by developing and commercializing new products.[112]

In the next two sections, we discuss the other ways firms innovate—by using cooperative strategies and by acquiring companies.

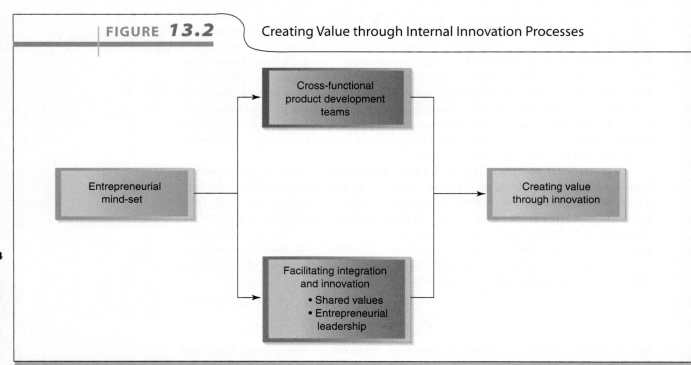

FIGURE 13.2   Creating Value through Internal Innovation Processes

Innovation through Cooperative Strategies

Virtually all firms lack the breadth and depth of resources (e.g., human capital and social capital) in their R&D activities needed to internally develop a sufficient number of innovations. Even in light of its success and widely respected ability to consistently produce incremental and primarily radical innovations, W. L. Gore & Associates, for example, frequently uses cooperative strategies to develop new innovations and to quicken the pace at which some of their own innovations are distributed.[113] In other instances, firms use cooperative strategies to align what they believe are complementary assets with the potential to lead to future innovations. This is the reason for the recent cooperative arrangement formed between Netflix and Wal-Mart. As explained in the Strategic Focus, the exact innovations that may result from these firms' cooperation are unknown, although both companies are interested in such possibilities.

The rapidly changing technologies of the 21st-century competitive landscape, globalization, and the need to innovate at world-class levels are primary influences on firms' decisions to innovate by cooperating with other companies. Evidence shows that the skills and knowledge contributed by firms forming a cooperative strategy to innovate tend to be technology-based, a fact suggesting how technologies and their applications continue to influence the choices firms make while competing in the 21st-century competitive landscape.[114] Indeed, some believe that because of these conditions, firms are becoming increasingly dependent on cooperative strategies as a path to successful competition in the global economy.[115] This may be the case with Netflix and Wal-Mart, as these firms seek ways to integrate their skills to develop an innovative way to deliver VoD (Video on Demand) to a significant number of customers.

Both entrepreneurial ventures and established firms use cooperative strategies (e.g., strategic alliances and joint ventures) to innovate. An entrepreneurial venture, for example, may seek investment capital as well as established firms' distribution capabilities to successfully introduce one of its innovative products to the market.[116] Alternatively, more established companies may need new technological knowledge and can gain access to it by forming a cooperative strategy with entrepreneurial ventures.[117] To increase its financial returns, Sony Corp. is forming alliances with smaller firms to develop innovative technologies.[118] Alliances between large pharmaceutical firms and biotechnology companies increasingly have been formed to integrate the knowledge and resources of both to develop new products and bring them to market.[119]

Because of the importance of strategic alliances, particularly in the development of new technology and in commercializing innovations, firms are beginning to build networks of alliances that represent a form of social capital to them.[120] This social capital in the form of relationships with other firms helps them to obtain the knowledge and other resources necessary to develop innovations.[121] Knowledge from these alliances helps firms develop new capabilities.[122] Some firms now even allow other companies to participate in their internal new product development processes. It is not uncommon, for example, for firms to have supplier representatives on their cross-functional innovation teams because of the importance of the suppliers' input to ensure quality materials for any new product developed.[123]

However, alliances formed for the purpose of innovation are not without risks. In addition to conflict that is natural when firms try to work together to reach a mutual goal,[124] cooperative strategy participants also take a risk that a partner will appropriate a firm's technology or knowledge and use it to enhance its own competitive abilities.[125] To prevent or at least minimize this risk, firms, particularly new ventures, need to select their partners carefully. The ideal partnership is one in which the firms have complementary skills as well as compatible strategic goals.[126] However, because companies are

Cooperating to Innovate in the DVD Rental and Sales Markets

Prior to 1999, here was the drill. As customers wishing to rent movies to watch in our homes, we went to a store, sorted through racks and racks of items to find a product that interested us, perhaps stood in line to pay for the rental, sometimes waiting to pay while the clerk answered questions for a person who had called on the telephone wanting to know what movies were actually in stock, paid for the rental, then took our rented item home for a defined period of time. Occasionally, we forgot to return the rental product on time, an error in judgment that led to paying the dreaded "late fee." Late fees generated significant amounts of revues for some companies; at its peak, Blockbuster Inc. collected an estimated $300 million annually in late fees. Then entrepreneur Reed Hastings revolutionized our rental experience.

Founded largely because of his frustration with not being able to find older movies to rent and because of his hatred for paying late fees, Hastings launched Netflix in 1999 as a Web-based catalog service. Grounded in a distribution system innovation (namely, using the postal service to deliver products to customers at any location), Netflix initially offered options to consumers to rent lesser-known and typically older movies in DVD format. Hastings and those working with him in their entrepreneurial venture quickly realized, though, that what their customers truly valued was the ability to avoid the hassle of choosing, renting, and returning videos to conventional retailers—not the ability to rent hard-to-find movies. "Thus was born Netflix's innovative subscription service, which allowed customers to keep videos for as long as they wished." This innovation is the foundation for Netflix's rapid growth. Now the world's largest DVD movie rental service, Netflix recently was offering over 45,000 titles to over 3 million subscribers, who were choosing from eight different subscription plans to find the one suiting their needs.

Not unexpectedly, Netflix's success attracted competitors, one of whom was mega-retailer Wal-Mart, which entered the on-line rental business in October 2002. Using its Wal-Mart.com platform, Wal-Mart's service plans were quite similar to Netflix's. But Wal-Mart never achieved the levels of success it desired. A reason for this could be that Wal-Mart's distribution expertise is in delivering huge numbers and quantities of products to central locations for subsequent deliveries to stores. As it turned out, Wal-Mart does not have the level of expertise Netflix possesses when it comes to distributing a small number of items to a huge number of different locations.

The competition between Netflix and Wal-Mart formally ended on May 19, 2005, with an announcement that the firms had formed a joint agreement to cooperate in the on-line movie businesses. The agreement is intended to meld Wal-Mart's movie sales expertise with Netflix's rental expertise. Under this agreement, Wal-Mart will sell but will not rent DVDs. "In return, Netflix will promote Wal-Mart's on-line movie sales business, including the pre-order price guarantee option at Walmart.com, both at its Web site and in mailers sent to Netflix subscribers." Thus, these firms combined their respective skills to offer innovative delivery capabilities to two sets of customers. The market reacted favorably to this cooperative arrangement, sending Netflix's share price some 30 percent higher on the day the joint agreement was announced.

Video on demand (VoD) may be the next frontier for these firms to tackle

Netflix, the world's largest DVD rental service, recently made an agreement with Wal-Mart to cooperate in the on-line movie business.

through their cooperative agreement. Currently, the number of Netflix and Wal-Mart customers interested in downloading is quite small. But Hastings expects this to change: "We are actively investing in VoD and will continue to try and find niches where downloading is actually a better solution for the customer." Being able to deliver VoD to mainstream rather than niche customer segments is a huge technological challenge. Some analysts believe that melding Netflix's understanding of rental customers and their needs with Wal-Mart's technological capabilities could result in a successful VoD offering that would give them a first-mover advantage in this emerging market.

Sources: J. Heilemann, 2005, Showtime for Netflix, *Business 2.0,* March, 36–39; W. Civils, 2005, Bulls, bears debate Netflix, *Wall Street Journal Online,* www.wsj.com, May 25; J. Seid, 2005, Can Netflix stay on top? *CNNMoney,* www.cnnmoney.com, May 24; 2005, About Netflix, Netflix Home Page, www.netflix.com, July 16; 2005, Wal-Mart.com and Netflix announce new promotional agreement, Netflix Home Page, www.netflix.com, May 19.

operating in a network of firms and thus may be participating in multiple alliances simultaneously, they encounter challenges in managing the alliances.[127] Research has shown that firms can become involved in too many alliances, which can harm rather than facilitate their innovation capabilities.[128] Thus, effectively managing a cooperative strategy to produce innovation is critical.

Innovation through Acquisitions

Firms sometimes acquire companies to gain access to their innovations and to their innovative capabilities. One reason companies do this is that the capital market values growth; acquisitions provide a means to rapidly extend one or more product lines and increase the firm's revenues. Acquisitions pursued for this reason should, nonetheless, have a strategic rationale. Pharmaceutical company Novartis AG, for example, is acquiring other companies to make progress toward its growth goal of becoming one of the world's pharmaceutical giants. However, the transactions being completed are part of what Novartis envisions as a set of "strategic acquisitions to create the world leader in the generic drug industry."[129] Pfizer Inc. also uses acquisitions to innovate. In fact, Pfizer recently announced that it intends to intensify its ". . . efforts to acquire new products and technologies to further strengthen (its) new product pipeline."[130]

Similar to internal corporate venturing and strategic alliances, acquisitions are not a risk-free approach to innovating. A key risk of acquisitions is that a firm may substitute an ability to buy innovations for an ability to produce innovations internally. In support of this contention, research shows that firms engaging in acquisitions introduce fewer new products into the market.[131] This substitution may take place because firms lose strategic control and focus instead on financial control of their original and especially of their acquired business units.

We note in Chapter 7 that companies can also learn new capabilities from firms they acquire. In the case of this chapter's topic, this would mean that firms may gain capabilities to produce innovation from an acquired company. Additionally, firms that emphasize innovation and carefully select companies for acquisition that also emphasize innovation are likely to remain innovative.[132]

This chapter closes with an assessment of how strategic entrepreneurship, as we have discussed it, helps firms create value for stakeholders through its operations.

Newer entrepreneurial firms often are more effective than larger established firms when it comes to identifying entrepreneurial opportunities.[133] As a consequence, it seems that entrepreneurial ventures produce more radical innovations than do their larger, more established counterparts. Entrepreneurial ventures' strategic flexibility and willingness to take risks may account for their ability to spot opportunities and then develop radical innovations to pursue them.

On the other side of the coin, larger and well-established firms often have more resources and capabilities to exploit identified opportunities.[134] Younger, entrepreneurial firms generally excel with the opportunity-seeking part of strategic entrepreneurship while more established firms generally excel with the advantage-seeking part. However, to compete effectively in the 21st-century competitive landscape, firms must not only identify and exploit opportunities but do so while achieving and sustaining a competitive advantage.[135] Thus, on a relative basis, newer entrepreneurial firms must learn how to gain a competitive advantage, and older, more established firms must relearn how to identify entrepreneurial opportunities. Another way of saying this is that in general, entrepreneurial ventures need to improve their advantage-seeking behaviors while larger firms need to improve their opportunity-seeking skills.

In some large organizations, action is being taken to deal with these matters. For example, an increasing number of widely known, large firms, including Blockbuster Inc., Williams-Sonoma, Inc., Wendy's International, AstraZeneca, and Choice Hotels, have created a new, top-level managerial position commonly called President or Executive Vice President of Emerging Brands. The essential responsibility for people holding these positions is to find entrepreneurial opportunities for their firms. If innovations are to be developed to pursue one or more identified opportunities, this person also leads the analysis to determine if the innovations should be internally developed, pursued through a cooperative venture, or acquired. The objective is for these activities to help firms successfully develop both incremental and radical innovations.

To be entrepreneurial, firms must develop an entrepreneurial mind-set among their managers and employees. Managers must emphasize the management of their resources, particularly human capital and social capital.[136] The importance of knowledge to identify and exploit opportunities as well as to gain and sustain a competitive advantage suggests that firms must have strong human capital.[137] Social capital is critical for access to complementary resources from partners in order to compete effectively in domestic and international markets.[138]

Many entrepreneurial opportunities continue to surface in international markets, a reality that is contributing to firms' willingness to engage in international entrepreneurship. By entering global markets that are new to them, firms can learn new technologies and management practices and diffuse this knowledge throughout the entire enterprise. Furthermore, the knowledge firms gain can contribute to their innovations. Research has shown that firms operating in international markets tend to be more innovative.[139] Entrepreneurial ventures and large firms now regularly enter international markets. Both types of firms must also be innovative to compete effectively. Thus, by developing resources (human and social capital), taking advantage of opportunities in domestic and international markets, and using the resources and knowledge gained in these markets to be innovative, firms achieve competitive advantages.[140] In so doing, they create value for their customers and shareholders.

Firms practicing strategic entrepreneurship contribute to a country's economic development. In fact, some countries such as Ireland have made dramatic economic progress by changing the institutional rules for businesses operating in the country. This could be construed as a form of institutional entrepreneurship. Likewise, firms that seek to establish their technology as a standard, also representing institutional entrepreneurship, are engaging in strategic entrepreneurship because creating a standard produces a competitive advantage for the firm.[141]

Research shows that because of its economic importance and individual motives, entrepreneurial activity is increasing around the globe. Furthermore, more women are becoming entrepreneurs because of the economic opportunity entrepreneurship provides and the individual independence it affords.[142] In the United States, for example, women are the nation's fastest-growing group of entrepreneurs.[143] In future years, entrepreneurial activity may increase the wealth of less-affluent countries and continue to contribute to the economic development of the more-affluent countries. Regardless, the entrepreneurial ventures and large, established firms that choose to practice strategic entrepreneurship are likely to be the winners in the 21st century.[144]

After identifying opportunities, entrepreneurs must act to develop capabilities that will become the basis of their firm's core competencies and competitive advantages. The process of identifying opportunities is entrepreneurial, but this activity alone is not sufficient to create maximum wealth or even to survive over time.[145] As we learned in Chapter 3, to successfully exploit opportunities, a firm must develop capabilities that are valuable, rare, difficult to imitate, and nonsubstitutable. When capabilities satisfy these four criteria, the firm has one or more competitive advantages to exploit the identified opportunities (as described in Chapter 3). Without a competitive advantage, the firm's success will be only temporary (as explained in Chapter 1). An innovation may be valuable and rare early in its life, if a market perspective is used in its development. However, competitive actions must be taken to introduce the new product to the market and protect its position in the market against competitors to gain a competitive advantage. These actions combined represent strategic entrepreneurship.

SUMMARY

- Strategic entrepreneurship is taking entrepreneurial actions using a strategic perspective. Firms engaging in strategic entrepreneurship find themselves simultaneously engaging in opportunity-seeking and advantage-seeking behaviors. The purpose of doing this is to continuously find new opportunities and quickly develop innovations to take advantage of them.

- Entrepreneurship is a process used by individuals and groups to identify entrepreneurial opportunities without being immediately constrained by the resources they control. Corporate entrepreneurship, the focus of this chapter, is the application of entrepreneurship (including the identification of entrepreneurial opportunities) within ongoing, established organizations. Entrepreneurial opportunities are conditions in which new goods or services can satisfy a need in the market. Increasingly, entrepreneurship is positively contributing to individual firms' performances and is stimulating growth in entire economies.

- Firms engage in three types of innovative activity: (1) invention, which is the act of creating a new good or process, (2) innovation, or the process of creating a commercial product from an invention, and (3) imitation, which is the adoption of an innova-

tion by similar firms. Invention brings something new into being while innovation brings something new into use.

- Entrepreneurs see or envision entrepreneurial opportunities and then take actions to develop innovations to pursue them. The most successful entrepreneurs (whether they are establishing their own venture or are working in an ongoing organization) have an entrepreneurial mind-set, which is an orientation that values the possibilities suggested by market-place uncertainties.

- International entrepreneurship, or the process of identifying and exploiting entrepreneurial opportunities outside the firm's domestic markets, is becoming important to firms around the globe. Some evidence suggests that firms capable of effectively engaging in international entrepreneurship outperform those competing only in their domestic markets.

- Three basic approaches are used to produce innovation: (1) internal innovation, which takes place by forming internal corporate ventures, (2) cooperative strategies such as strategic alliances, and (3) acquisitions. Autonomous strategic behavior and induced strategic behavior are the two forms of internal corporate venturing. Autonomous strategic behavior is a bottom-up process through which a product champion facilitates the commercialization of an innovative good or service. Induced strategic behavior is a top-down process in which a firm's current strategy and structure facilitate product or process innovations that are associated with them. Thus, induced strategic behavior is driven by the organization's current corporate strategy and structure while autonomous strategic behavior can result in a change to the firm's current strategy and structure arrangements.

- Firms create two types of innovation—incremental and radical—through internal innovation that takes place in the form of autonomous strategic behavior or induced strategic behavior. Overall, firms produce more incremental innovations although radical innovations have a higher probability of significantly increasing sales revenue and profits. Increasingly, cross-functional integration is vital to a firm's efforts to develop and implement internal corporate venturing activities and to commercialize the resulting innovation. Additionally, integration and innovation can be facilitated

by developing shared values and effectively using strategic leadership.

- To gain access to the kind of specialized knowledge that often is required to innovate in the complex global economy, firms may form a cooperative relationship such as a strategic alliance with other companies, some of whom may be competitors.

- Acquisitions are another means firms use to innovate. Innovation can be acquired through direct acquisition, or firms can learn new capabilities from an acquisition, thereby enriching their internal innovation abilities.

- The practice of strategic entrepreneurship by all types of firms, large and small, new and more established, creates value for all stakeholders, especially for shareholders and customers. Strategic entrepreneurship also contributes to the economic development of entire nations.

NOTES

1. D. S. Elenkov & I. M. Manev, 2005, Top management leadership and influence on innovation: The role of sociocultural context, *Journal of Management,* 31: 381–402.

2. S. D. Dobrev & W. P. Barnett, 2005, Organizational roles and transition to entrepreneurship, *Academy of Management Journal,* 48: 433–449; V. Govindarajan & C. Trimble, 2005, Building breakthrough businesses within established organizations, *Harvard Business Review,* 83(5): 58–68.

3. M. A. Hitt, R. D. Ireland, S. M. Camp, & D. L. Sexton, 2002, Strategic entrepreneurship: Integrating entrepreneurial and strategic management perspectives, in M. A. Hitt, R. D. Ireland, S. M. Camp, & D. L. Sexton (eds.), *Strategic Entrepreneurship: Creating a New Mindset,* Oxford, UK: Blackwell Publishers, 1–16; M. A. Hitt, R. D. Ireland, S. M. Camp, & D. L. Sexton, 2001, Strategic entrepreneurship: Entrepreneurial strategies for wealth creation, *Strategic Management Journal,* 22 (Special Issue): 479–491; R. D. Ireland, M. A. Hitt, S. M. Camp, & D. L. Sexton, 2001, Integrating entrepreneurship and strategic management actions to create firm wealth, *Academy of Management Executive,* 15(1): 49–63.

4. D. A. Shepherd & D. R. DeTienne, 2005, Prior knowledge, potential financial reward, and opportunity identification, *Entrepreneurship Theory and Practice,* 29(1): 91–112; W. J. Baumol, 2004, Entrepreneurial cultures and countercultures, *Academy of Learning & Education,* 3(3): 316–326.

5. R. E. Hoskisson, M. A. Hitt, R. A. Johnson, & W. Grossman, 2002, Conflicting voices: The effects of institutional ownership heterogeneity and internal governance on corporate innovation strategies, *Academy of Management Journal,* 45: 697–716.

6. K. G. Smith, C. J. Collins, & K. D. Clark, 2005, Existing knowledge, knowledge creation capability, and the rate of new product introduction in high-technology firms, *Academy of Management Journal,* 48: 346–357.

7. R. D. Ireland, M. A. Hitt, & D. G. Sirmon, 2003, A model of strategic entrepreneurship: The construct and its dimensions, *Journal of Management,* 29: 963–989.

8. B. R. Barringer & R. D. Ireland, 2006, *Entrepreneurship: Successfully Launching New Ventures,* Upper Saddle River, NJ: Pearson Prentice Hall, 5; G. G. Dess, R. D. Ireland, S. A. Zahra, S. W. Floyd, J. J. Janney, & P. J. Lane, 2003, Emerging issues in corporate entrepreneurship, *Journal of Management,* 29: 351–378.

9. H. A. Schildt, M. V. J. Maula, & T. Keil, 2005, Explorative and Exploitative learning from external corporate ventures, *Entrepreneurship Theory and Practice,* 29: 493–515.

10. G. T. Lumpkin & B. B. Lichtenstein, 2005, The role of organizational learning in the opportunity-recognition process, *Entrepreneurship Theory and Practice,* 29: 451–472.

11. Barringer & Ireland, *Entrepreneurship;* H. H. Stevenson & J. C. Jarillo, 1990, A paradigm for entrepreneurship: Entrepreneurial management, *Strategic Management Journal,* 16 (Special Issue): 17–27.

12. S. A. Alvarez & J. B. Barney, 2005, Organizing rent generation and appropriation: Toward a theory of the entrepreneurial firm, *Journal of Business Venturing,* 19: 621–635.

13. M. Minniti, 2005, Entrepreneurial alertness and asymmetric information in a spin-glass model, *Journal of Business Venturing,* 19: 637–658.

14. W. Kuemmerle, 2005, The entrepreneur's path to global expansion, *MIT Sloan Management Review,* 46(2): 42–49.

15. S. Shane & S. Venkataraman, 2000, The promise of entrepreneurship as a field of research, *Academy of Management Review,* 25: 217–226.

16. J. Schumpeter, 1934, *The Theory of Economic Development,* Cambridge, MA: Harvard University Press.

17. R. Katila, 2002, New product search over time: Past ideas in their prime? *Academy of Management Journal,* 45: 995–1010; B. R. Barringer & A. C. Bluedorn, 1999, The relationship between corporate entrepreneurship and strategic management, *Strategic Management Journal,* 20: 421–444.

18. R. G. Holcombe, 2003, The origins of entrepreneurial opportunities, *Review of Austrian Economics,* 16: 25–54; C. M. Daily, P. P. McDougall,

J. G. Covin, & D. R. Dalton, 2002, Governance and strategic leadership in entrepreneurial firms, *Journal of Management,* 28: 387–412.

19. R. D. Ireland, J. W. Webb, & J. E. Coombs, 2005, Theory and methodology in entrepreneurship research, in D. J. Ketchen Jr. & D. D. Bergh (eds.), *Research Methodology in Strategy and Management* (Volume 2), San Diego: Elsevier Publishers, 111–141; S. D. Sarasvathy, 2005, The questions we ask and the questions we care about: Reformulating some problems in entrepreneurship research, *Journal of Business Venturing,* 19: 707–717.

20. P. F. Drucker, 1998, The discipline of innovation, *Harvard Business Review,* 76(6): 149–157.

21. Ibid.

22. J. D. Wolpert, 2002, Breaking out of the innovation box, *Harvard Business Review,* 80(8): 77–83.

23. K. Karnik, 2005, Innovation's importance: Powering economic growth, *National Association of Software and Service Companies,* www.nasscom.org, January 24.

24. 2005, Innovation challenge, *Extraordinary Dairy,* www.extraordinarydairy .com, January 24.

25. M. Subramaniam & M. A. Youndt, 2005, The influence of intellectual capital on the types of innovative capabilities, *Academy of Management Journal,* 48: 450–463.

26. J. E. Perry-Smith & C. E. Shalley, 2003, The social side of creativity: A static and dynamic social network perspective, *Academy of Management Review,* 28: 89–106.

27. R. Price, 1996, Technology and strategic advantage, *California Management Review,* 38(3): 38–56; L. G. Franko, 1989, Global corporate competition: Who's winning, who's losing and the R&D factor as one reason why, *Strategic Management Journal,* 10: 449–474.

28. J. W. Spencer, 2003, Firms' knowledge-sharing strategies in the global innovation system: Empirical evidence from the flat panel display industry, *Strategic Management Journal,* 24: 217–233; K. M. Kelm, V. K. Narayanan, & G. E. Pinches, 1995, Shareholder value creation during R&D innovation and commercialization stages, *Academy of Management Journal,* 38: 770–786.

29. M. A. Hitt, R. D. Nixon, R. E. Hoskisson, & R. Kochhar, 1999, Corporate entrepreneurship and cross-functional fertilization: Activation, process and disintegration of a new product design team, *Entrepreneurship: Theory and Practice,* 23(3): 145–167.

30. J. P. O'Brien, 2003, The capital structure implications of pursuing a strategy of innovation, *Strategic Management Journal,* 24: 415–431.

31. Schumpeter, *The Theory of Economic Development.*

32. R. Katila & S. Shane, 2005, When does lack of resources make new firms innovative? *Academy of Management Journal,* 48: 814–829.

33. P. Sharma & J. L. Chrisman, 1999, Toward a reconciliation of the definitional issues in the field of corporate entrepreneurship, *Entrepreneurship: Theory and Practice,* 23(3): 11–27; R. A. Burgelman & L. R. Sayles, 1986, *Inside Corporate Innovation: Strategy, Structure, and Managerial Skills,* New York: Free Press.

34. D. K. Dutta & M. M. Crossan, 2005, The nature of entrepreneurial opportunities: Understanding the process using the 4I organizational learning framework, *Entrepreneurship Theory and Practice* 29: 425–449.

35. R. E. Hoskisson & L. W. Busenitz, 2002, Market uncertainty and learning distance in corporate entrepreneurship entry mode choice, in M. A. Hitt, R. D. Ireland, S. M. Camp, & D. L. Sexton (eds.), *Strategic Entrepreneurship: Creating a New Mindset,* Oxford, UK: Blackwell Publishers, 151–172.

36. D. Somaya, 2003, Strategic determinants of decisions not to settle patent litigation, *Strategic Management Journal,* 24: 17–38.

37. S. D. Sarasvathy, 2004, Making it happen: Beyond theories of the firm to theories of firm design, *Entrepreneurship Theory and Practice,* 28: 519–531.

38. 2004, Rules to live by, and break, *Knowledge@Wharton,* http://knowledge .wharton.upenn.edu, June 17.

39. D. Duffy, 2004, Corporate entrepreneurship: Entrepreneurial skills for personal and corporate success, *Center for Excellence,* www.centerforexcellence .net, June 14.

40. M. S. Cardon, C. Zietsma, P. Saparito, B. P. Matheren, & C. Davis, 2005, A tale of passion: New insights into entrepreneurship from a parenthood metaphor, *Journal of Business Venturing,* 19: 23–45.

41. R. G. McGrath & I. MacMillan, 2000, *The Entrepreneurial Mindset,* Boston, MA: Harvard Business School Press.

42. R. D. Ireland, M. A. Hitt, & J. W. Webb, 2005, Entrepreneurial alliances and networks, in O. Shenkar and J. J. Reuer (eds.), *Handbook of Strategic Alliances,* Thousand Oaks, CA: Sage Publications, 333–352; T. M. Begley & D. P. Boyd, 2003, The need for a corporate global mind-set, *MIT Sloan Management Review,* 44(2): 25–32.

43. H. D. Schultz, 2005, Starbucks' founder on innovation in the music biz, *Business Week,* July 4, 16–17.

44. H.-J. Cho & V. Pucik, 2005, Relationship between innovativeness, quality, growth, profitability, and market value, *Strategic Management Journal,* 26: 555–575.

45. W. Tsai, 2001, Knowledge transfer in intraorganizational networks: Effects of network position and absorptive capacity on business unit innovation and performance, *Academy of Management Journal,* 44: 996–1004.

46. S. A. Zahra & G. George, 2002, Absorptive capacity: A review, reconceptualization, and extension, *Academy of Management Review,* 27: 185–203.

47. M. A. Hitt, L. Bierman, K. Shimizu, & R. Kochhar, 2001, Direct and moderating effects of human capital on strategy and performance in professional service firms, *Academy of Management Journal,* 44: 13–28.

48. 2005, H-P printer zips through photos, *Dallas Morning News,* July 12, D10.

49. Zahra & George, Absorptive capacity: 261.

50. T. M. Begley, W.-L. Tan, & H. Schoch, 2005, Politico-Economic factors associated with interest in starting a business: A multi-country study, *Entrepreneurship Theory and Practice,* 29: 35–52; J. W. Lu & P. W. Beamish, 2001, The internationalization and performance of SMEs, *Strategic Management Journal,* 22 (Special Issue): 565–585.

51. L. Tihanyi, R. A. Johnson, R. E. Hoskisson, & M. A. Hitt, 2003, Institutional ownership differences and international diversification: The effects of boards of directors and technological opportunity, *Academy of Management Journal,* 46: 195–211.

52. R. D. Ireland & J. W. Webb, 2006, International entrepreneurship in emerging economies: A resource-based perspective, in S. Alvarez, A. Carrera, L. Mesquita, & R. Vassolo (eds.), *Entrepreneurship and Innovation in Emerging Economies,* Oxford, UK: Blackwell Publishers: in press; A. E. Ellstrand, L. Tihanyi, & J. L. Johnson, 2002, Board structure and international political risk, *Academy of Management Journal,* 45: 769–777.

53. S. Andersson, 2004, Internationalization in different industrial contexts, *Journal of Business Venturing,* 19: 851–875.

54. D. Farrell, H. Fassbender, T. Kneip, S. Kriesel, & E. Labaye, 2003, Reviving French and German productivity, *The McKinsey Quarterly,* Number One, 40–53.

55. 2004, *GEM 2004 Irish Report,* www.gemconsortium.org/download, July 13.

56. J. McMillan, 2005, Creative destruction thrives, *New Zealand Herald,* January 13, C2.

57. P. D. Reynolds, S. M. Camp, W. D. Bygrave, E. Autio, & M. Hay, 2002, *Global Entrepreneurship Monitor,* Kauffman Center for Entrepreneurial Leadership, Ewing Marion Kauffman Foundation.

58. M. H. Morris, 1998, *Entrepreneurial Intensity: Sustainable Advantages for Individuals, Organizations, and Societies,* Westport, CT: Quorum Books, 85–86.

59. N. Nummeia, S. Saarenketo, & K. Puumalainen, 2005, Rapidly with a rifle or more slowly with a shotgun? Stretching the company boundaries of internationalizing ICT firms, *Journal of International Entrepreneurship,* 2: 275–288; S. A. Zahra & G. George, 2002, International entrepreneurship: The state of the field and future research agenda, in M. A. Hitt, R. D. Ireland, S. M. Camp, & D. L. Sexton (eds.), *Strategic Entrepreneurship: Creating a New Mindset,* Oxford, UK: Blackwell Publishers, 255–288.

60. S. A. Zahra, R. D. Ireland, & M. A. Hitt, 2000, International expansion by new venture firms: International diversity, mode of market entry, technological learning and performance, *Academy of Management Journal,* 43: 925–950.

61. P. P. McDougall & B. M. Oviatt, 2000, International entrepreneurship: The intersection of two paths, *Academy of Management Journal,* 43: 902–908.

62. A. Yan, G. Zhu, & D. T. Hall, 2002, International assignments for career building: A model of agency relationships and psychological contracts, *Academy of Management Review,* 27: 373–391.

63. H. Barkema & O. Chvyrkov, 2002, What sort of top management team is needed at the helm of internationally diversified firms? in M. A. Hitt, R. D. Ireland, S. M. Camp, & D. L. Sexton (eds.), *Strategic Entrepreneurship: Creating a New Mindset,* Oxford, UK: Blackwell Publishers, 290–305.

64. T. S. Frost, 2001, The geographic sources of foreign subsidiaries' innovations, *Strategic Management Journal,* 22: 101–122.

65. C. Dawson, 2005, Proud papa of the Prius, *Business Week,* July 20, 20.

66. R. Underwood, 2005, Walking the talk? *Fast Company,* March, 25–26.

67. J. Battelle, 2005, Turning the page, *Business 2.0,* July, 98–100.

68. J. Santos, Y. Doz, & P. Williamson, 2004, Is your innovation process global? *MIT Sloan Management Review,* 45(4): 31–37; C. D. Charitou & C. C. Markides, 2003, Responses to disruptive strategic innovation, *MIT Sloan Management Review,* 44(2): 55–63.

69. J. A. Fraser, 2004, A return to basics at Kellogg, *MIT Sloan Management Review,* 45(4): 27–30; P. M. Lee & H. M. O'Neill, 2003, Ownership structures and R&D investments of U.S. and Japanese firms: Agency and stewardship perspectives, *Academy of Management Journal,* 46: 212–225.

70. S. Kola-Nystrom, 2003, Theory of conceuptualizing the challenge of corporate renewal, Lappeenranta University of Technology, Working Paper.

71. 2005, Radical and incremental innovation styles, *Strategies 2 innovate,* www.strategies2innovate.com, July 12.

72. W. C. Kim & R. Mauborgne, 2005, Navigating toward blue oceans, *Optimize,* February: 44–52.

73. G. Ahuja & M. Lampert, 2001, Entrepreneurship in the large corporation: A longitudinal study of how established firms create breakthrough inventions, *Strategic Management Journal,* 22 (Special Issue): 521–543.

74. O. Port, 2005, Mighty morphing power processors, *Business Week,* June 6, 60–61.

75. 2005, Getting an edge on innovation, *Business Week,* March 21, 124.

76. J. E. Ashton, F. X. Cook Jr., & P. Schmitz, 2003, Uncovering hidden value in a midsize manufacturing company, *Harvard Business Review,* 81(6): 111–119; L. Fleming & O. Sorenson, 2003, Navigating the technology landscape of innovation, *MIT Sloan Management Review,* 44(2): 15–23.

77. J. Goldenberg, R. Horowitz, A. Levav, & D. Mazursky, 2003, Finding your innovation sweet spot, *Harvard Business Review,* 81(3): 120–129.

78. G. C. O'Connor, R. Hendricks, & M. P. Rice, 2002, Assessing transition readiness for radical innovation, *Research Technology Management,* 45(6): 50–56.

79. R. I. Sutton, 2002, Weird ideas that spark innovation, *MIT Sloan Management Review,* 43(2): 83–87.

80. K. G. Smith & D. Di Gregorio, 2002, Bisociation, discovery, and the role of entrepreneurial action, in M. A. Hitt, R. D. Ireland, S. M. Camp, & D. L. Sexton (eds.), *Strategic Entrepreneurship: Creating a New Mindset,* Oxford, UK: Blackwell Publishers, 129–150.

81. J. G. Covin, R. D. Ireland, & D. F. Kuratko, 2005, Exploration through internal corporate ventures, Indiana University, Working Paper; Hoskisson & Busenitz, Market uncertainty and learning distance.

82. R. A. Burgelman, 1995, *Strategic Management of Technology and Innovation,* Boston: Irwin.

83. S. K. Markham, 2002, Moving technologies from lab to market, *Research Technology Management,* 45(6): 31–42.

84. J. M. Howell, 2005, The right stuff: Identifying and developing effective champions of innovation, *Academy of Management Executive,* 19(2): 108–119.

85. T. H. Davenport, L. Prusak, & H. J. Wilson, 2003, Who's bringing you hot ideas and how are you responding? *Harvard Business Review,* 81(2): 58–64.

86. M. D. Hutt & T. W. Seph, 2004, *Business Marketing Management* (8th ed.), Cincinnati, OH: Thomson South-Western.

87. M. A. Hitt, R. D. Ireland, & H. Lee, 2000, Technological learning, knowledge management, firm growth and performance, *Journal of Engineering and Technology Management,* 17: 231–246; D. Leonard-Barton, 1995, *Well springs of Knowledge: Building and Sustaining the Sources of Innovation,* Cambridge, MA: Harvard Business School Press.

88. A. Taylor III, 2005, Billion-dollar bets, *Fortune,* June 27, 139–154.

89. S. S. Rao, 2000, General Electric, software vendor, *Forbes,* January 24, 144–146.

90. H. W. Chesbrough, 2002, Making sense of corporate venture capital, *Harvard Business Review,* 80(3): 90–99.

91. M. Subramaniam & N. Venkatraman, 2001, Determinants of transnational new product development capability: Testing the influence of transferring and deploying tacit overseas knowledge, *Strategic Management Journal,* 22: 359–378.

92. M. Song & M. M. Montoya-Weiss, 2001, The effect of perceived technological uncertainty on Japanese new product development, *Academy of Management Journal,* 44: 61–80.

93. R. Underwood, 2005, Hot wheels, *Fast Company,* May, 64–65.

94. McGrath & MacMillan, *Entrepreneurial Mindset.*

95. 2002, Building scientific networks for effective innovation, *MIT Sloan Management Review,* 43(3): 14.

96. C. M. Christensen & M. Overdorf, 2000, Meeting the challenge of disruptive change, *Harvard Business Review,* 78(2): 66–77.

97. L. Yu, 2002, Marketers and engineers: Why can't we just get along? *MIT Sloan Management Review,* 43(1):13.

98. P. S. Adler, 1995, Interdepartmental interdependence and coordination: The case of the design/manufacturing interface, *Organization Science,* 6: 147–167.

99. I. Royer, 2003, Why bad projects are so hard to kill, *Harvard Business Review,* 81(2): 48–56.

100. P. Evans & B. Wolf, 2005, Collaboration rules, *Harvard Business Review,* 83(7): 96–104.

101. B. Fischer & A. Boynton, 2005, Virtuoso teams, *Harvard Business Review,* 83(7): 116–123.

102. Hitt, Nixon, Hoskisson, & Kochhar, Corporate entrepreneurship.

103. Christensen & Overdorf, Meeting the challenge of disruptive change.

104. Hitt, Nixon, Hoskisson, & Kochhar, Corporate entrepreneurship.

105. A. C. Amason, 1996, Distinguishing the effects of functional and dysfunctional conflict on strategic decision making: Resolving a paradox for top management teams, *Academy of Management Journal,* 39: 123–148; P. R. Lawrence & J. W. Lorsch, 1969, *Organization and Environment,* Homewood, IL: Richard D. Irwin.

106. D. Dougherty, L. Borrelli, K. Muncir, & A. O'Sullivan, 2000, Systems of organizational sensemaking for sustained product innovation, *Journal of Engineering and Technology Management,* 17: 321–355; D. Dougherty, 1992, Interpretive barriers to successful product innovation in large firms, *Organization Science,* 3: 179–202.

107. Hitt, Nixon, Hoskisson, & Kochhar, Corporate entrepreneurship.

108. E. C. Wenger & W. M. Snyder, 2000, Communities of practice: The organizational frontier, *Harvard Business Review,* 78(1): 139–144.

109. Gary Hamel, 2000, *Leading the Revolution,* Boston: Harvard Business School Press.

110. McGrath & MacMillan, *Entrepreneurial Mindset.*

111. Q. M. Roberson & J. A. Colquitt, 2005, Shared and configural justice: A social network model of justice in teams, *Academy of Management Review,* 30: 595–607.

112. S. W. Fowler, A. W. King, S. J. Marsh, & B. Victor, 2000, Beyond products: New strategic imperatives for developing competencies in dynamic environments, *Journal of Engineering and Technology Management,* 17: 357–377.

113. 2005, W. L. Gore & Associates joins Global Healthcare exchange, W. L. Gore & Associates Home Page, www.gore.com, April 20.

114. F. T. Rothaermel & D. L. Deeds, 2004, Exploration and exploitation alliances in biotechnology: A system of new product development, *Strategic Management Journal,* 25: 201–221; R. Gulati & M. C. Higgins, 2003, Which ties matter when? The contingent effects of interorganizational partnerships on IPO success, *Strategic Management Journal,* 24: 127–144.

115. J. Hagel III & J. S. Brown, 2005, Productive friction, *Harvard Business Review,* 83(2): 82–91.

116. A. C. Cooper, 2002, Networks, alliances and entrepreneurship, in M. A. Hitt, R. D. Ireland, S. M. Camp, & D. L. Sexton (eds.), *Strategic Entrepreneurship: Creating a New Mindset,* Oxford, UK: Blackwell Publishers, 204–222.

117. S. A. Alvarez & J. B. Barney, 2001, How entrepreneurial firms can benefit from alliances with large partners, *Academy of Management Executive,* 15(1): 139–148; F. T. Rothaermel, 2001, Incumbent's advantage through exploiting complementary assets via interfirm cooperation, *Strategic Management Journal,* 22 (Special Issue): 687–699.

118. B. Brenner, C. Edwards, R. Grover, T. Lowry, & E. Thornton, 2005, Sony's sudden samurai, *Business Week,* March 21, 28–32.

119. Alvarez & Barney, How entrepreneurial firms can benefit from alliances with large partners; F. T. Rothaermel, 2001, Incumbent's advantage through exploiting complementary assets via interfirm cooperation, *Strategic Management Journal,* 22 (Special Issue): 687–699.

120. D. Kline, 2003, Sharing the corporate crown jewels, *MIT Sloan Management Review,* 44(3): 89–93.

121. H. Yli-Renko, E. Autio, & H. J. Sapienza, 2001, Social capital, knowledge acquisition and knowledgeexploitation in young technology-based firms, *Strategic Management Journal,* 22 (Special Issue): 587–613.

122. C. Lee, K. Lee, & J. M. Pennings, 2001, Internal capabilities, external networks and performance: A study of technology-based ventures, *Strategic Management Journal,* 22 (Special Issue): 615–640.

123. A. Takeishi, 2001, Bridging inter- and intra-firm boundaries: Management of supplier involvement in automobile product development, *Strategic Management Journal,* 22: 403–433.

124. J. Weiss & J. Hughes, 2005, Want collaboration? Accept—and actively manage—conflict, *Harvard Business Review,* 83(3): 92–101.

125. R. D. Ireland, M. A. Hitt, & D. Vaidyanath, 2002, Strategic alliances as a pathway to competitive success, *Journal of Management,* 28: 413–446.

126. M. A. Hitt, M. T. Dacin, E. Levitas, J.-L. Arregle, & A. Borza, 2000, Partner selection in emerging and developed market contexts: Resource-based and organizational learning perspectives, *Academy of Management Journal,* 43: 449–467.

127. J. J. Reuer, M. Zollo, & H. Singh, 2002, Post-formation dynamics in strategic alliances, *Strategic Management Journal,* 23: 135–151.

128. F. Rothaermel & D. Deeds, 2002, More good things are not always necessarily better: An empirical study of strategic alliances, experience effects, and new product development in high-technology start-ups, in M. A. Hitt, R. Amit, C. Lucier, & R. Nixon (eds.), *Creating Value: Winners in the New Business Environment,* Oxford, UK: Blackwell Publishers, 85–103.

129. 2005, Novartis announces completion of Hexal AG acquisition, Novartis Home Page, www.novartis.com, June 6.

130. 2005, Pfizer sees sustained long-term growth, Pfizer Home Page, www.pfizer.com, April 5.

131. M. A. Hitt, R. E. Hoskisson, R. A. Johnson, & D. D. Moesel, 1996, The market for corporate control and firm innovation, *Academy of Management Journal,* 39: 1084–1119.

132. M. A. Hitt, J. S. Harrison, & R. D. Ireland, 2001, *Mergers and Acquisitions: A Guide to Creating Value for Stakeholders,* New York: Oxford University Press.

133. Ireland, Hitt, & Sirmon, A model of strategic entrepreneurship.

134. Ibid.

135. Hitt, Ireland, Camp, & Sexton, Strategic entrepreneurship.

136. D. G. Sirmon, M. A. Hitt, & R. D. Ireland, 2007, Managing firm resources in dynamic environment to create value: Looking inside the black box, *Academy of Management Review,* in press.

137. Hitt, Bierman, Shimizu, & Kochhar, Direct and moderating effects of human capital.

138. M. A. Hitt, H. Lee, & E. Yucel, 2002, The importance of social capital to the management of multinational enterprises: Relational networks among Asian and Western firms, *Asia Pacific Journal of Management,* 19: 353–372.

139. M. A. Hitt, R. E. Hoskisson, & H. Kim, 1997, International diversification: Effects on innovation and firm performance in product diversified firms, *Academy of Management Journal,* 40: 767–798.

140. M. A. Hitt & R. D. Ireland, 2002, The essence of strategic leadership: Managing human and social capital, *Journal of Leadership and Organization Studies,* 9(1): 3–14.

141. R. Garud, S. Jain, & A. Kumaraswamy, 2002, Institutional entrepreneurship in the sponsorship of common technological standards: The case of Sun Microsystems and JAVA, *Academy of Management Journal,* 45: 196–214.

142. Reynolds, Camp, Bygrave, Autio, & Hay, *Global Entrepreneurship Monitor.*

143. J. D. Jardins, 2005, I am woman (I think), *Fast Company,* May, 25–26.

144. Hitt, Ireland, Camp, & Sexton, Strategic entrepreneurship.

145. C. W. L. Hill & F. T. Rothaermel, 2003, The performance of incumbent firms in the face of radical technological innovation, *Academy of Management Review,* 28: 257–274.

Case Studies

Preparing an Effective Case Analysis

WHAT TO EXPECT FROM IN-CLASS CASE DISCUSSIONS

As you will learn, classroom discussions of cases differ significantly from lectures. The case method calls for your instructor to guide the discussion and to solicit alternative views as a way of encouraging your active participation when analyzing a case. When alternative views are not forthcoming, your instructor might take a position just to challenge you and your peers to respond thoughtfully as a way of generating additional alternatives. Instructors will often evaluate your work in terms of both the quantity and the quality of your contributions to in-class case discussions. The in-class discussions are important in that you can derive significant benefit from having your ideas and recommendations examined against those of your peers and from responding to challenges by other class members and/or the instructor.

During case discussions, your instructor will likely listen, question, and probe to extend the analysis of case issues. In the course of these actions, your peers and/or your instructor may challenge an individual's views and the validity of alternative perspectives that have been expressed. These challenges are offered in a constructive manner; their intent is to help all who are analyzing a case develop their analytical and communication skills. Commonly, instructors will encourage you and your peers to be innovative and original when developing and presenting ideas. Over the course of an individual discussion, you are likely to develop a more complex view of the case as a result of listening to and thinking about the diverse inputs offered by your peers and instructor. Among other benefits, experience with multiple case discussions will increase your knowledge of the advantages and disadvantages of group decision-making processes.

Both your peers and your instructor will value comments that help identify problems and solutions. To offer relevant contributions, you are encouraged to use independent thought and, through discussions with your peers outside class, to refine your thinking. We also encourage you to avoid using phrases such as "I think," "I believe," and "I feel" when analyzing a case. Instead, consider using a less emotion-laden phrase, such as "My analysis shows. . . ." This highlights the logical nature of the approach you have taken to analyze the case. When preparing for an in-class case discussion, plan to use the case data to explain your assessment of the situation. Assume that your peers and instructor are familiar with the basic facts of the case. In addition, it is good practice to prepare notes regarding your analysis of case facts before class discussions and use them when explaining your perspectives. Effective notes signal to classmates and the instructor that you are prepared to discuss the case thoroughly. Moreover, thorough notes eliminate the need for you to memorize the facts and figures needed to successfully discuss a case.

The case analysis process described here will help prepare you to effectively discuss a case during class meetings. Using this process helps you consider the issues required to identify a focal firm's problems and to propose strategic actions through which the firm can improve its competitiveness. In some instances, your instructor may ask you to prepare an oral or written analysis of a particular case. Typically, such an assignment demands even more thorough study and analysis of the case contents. At your instructor's discretion, oral and written analyses may be completed by

C

| TABLE 1 | An Effective Case Analysis Process |

Step 1: Gaining Familiarity	a. In general—determine who, what, how, where, and when (the critical facts of the case).
	b. In detail—identify the places, persons, activities, and contexts of the situation.
	c. Recognize the degree of certainty/uncertainty of acquired information.
Step 2: Recognizing Symptoms	a. List all indicators (including stated "problems") that something is not as expected or as desired.
	b. Ensure that symptoms are not assumed to be the problem (symptoms should lead to identification of the problem).
Step 3: Identifying Goals	a. Identify critical statements by major parties (for example, people, groups, the work unit, and so on).
	b. List all goals of the major parties that exist or can be reasonably inferred.
Step 4: Conducting the Analysis	a. Decide which ideas, models, and theories seem useful.
	b. Apply these conceptual tools to the situation.
	c. As new information is revealed, cycle back to substeps a and b.
Step 5: Making the Diagnosis	a. Identify predicaments (goal inconsistencies).
	b. Identify problems (discrepancies between goals and performance).
	c. Prioritize predicaments/problems regarding timing, importance, and so on.
Step 6: Doing the Action Planning	a. Specify and prioritize the criteria used to choose action alternatives.
	b. Discover or invent feasible action alternatives.
	c. Examine the probable consequences of action alternatives.
	d. Select a course of action.
	e. Design an implementation plan/schedule.
	f. Create a plan for assessing the action to be implemented.

Source: C. C. Lundberg and C. Enz, 1993, A framework for student case preparation, *Case Research Journal,* 13 (Summer): 144. Reprinted by permission of NACRA, North American Case Research Association.

individuals or by groups of three or more people. The information and insights gained through completing the six steps shown in Table 1 are often valuable when developing an oral or written analysis. However, when preparing an oral or written presentation, you must consider the overall framework in which your information and inputs will be presented. Such a framework is the focus of the next section.

PREPARING AN ORAL OR WRITTEN CASE PRESENTATION

Experience shows that two types of thinking (analysis and synthesis) are necessary to develop an effective oral or written presentation (see Exhibit 1). In the analysis stage, you should first analyze the general external environmental issues affecting the firm. Next,

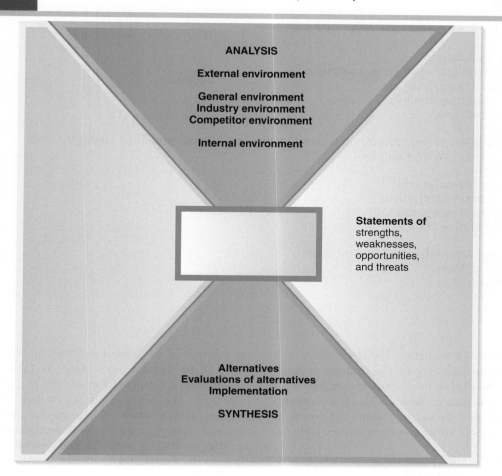

ANALYSIS

External environment

General environment
Industry environment
Competitor environment

Internal environment

Statements of strengths, weaknesses, opportunities, and threats

Alternatives
Evaluations of alternatives
Implementation

SYNTHESIS

your environmental analysis should focus on the particular industry or industries in which a firm operates. Finally, you should examine companies against which the focal firm competes. By studying the three levels of the external environment (general, industry, and competitor), you will be able to identify a firm's opportunities and threats. Following the external environmental analysis is the analysis of the firm's internal environment, which identifies the firm's strengths and weaknesses.

As noted in Exhibit 1, you must then change the focus from analysis to synthesis. Specifically, you must synthesize information gained from your analysis of the firm's internal and external environments. Synthesizing information enables you to generate alternatives that can resolve the problems or challenges facing the focal firm. Once you identify a best alternative from an evaluation based on predetermined criteria and goals, you must explore implementation actions.

Types of Thinking in Case Preparation: Analysis and Synthesis

Table 2 outlines the sections that should be included in either an oral or a written presentation: introduction (strategic profile and purpose), situation analysis, statements of strengths/weaknesses and opportunities/threats, strategy formulation, and implementation. These sections are described in the following discussion. Familiarity with the contents of your book's 13 chapters is helpful because the general outline for an

TABLE 2	General Outline for an Oral or Written Presentation

I. Strategic Profile and Case Analysis Purpose

II. Situation Analysis
 A. General environmental analysis
 B. Industry analysis
 C. Competitor analysis
 D. Internal analysis

III. Identification of Environmental Opportunities and Threats and Firm Strengths and Weaknesses (SWOT Analysis)

IV. Strategy Formulation
 A. Strategic alternatives
 B. Alternative evaluation
 C. Alternative choice

V. Strategic Alternative Implementation
 A. Action items
 B. Action plan

oral or a written presentation shown in Table 2 is based on an understanding of the strategic management process detailed in those chapters. We follow the discussions of the parts of Table 2 with a few comments about the "process" to use to present the results of your case analysis in either an oral or written format.

Strategic Profile and Case Analysis Purpose

The strategic profile should briefly present the critical facts from the case that have affected the focal firm's historical strategic direction and performance. The case facts should not be restated in the profile; rather, these comments should show how the critical facts lead to a particular focus for your analysis. This primary focus should be emphasized in this section's conclusion. In addition, this section should state important assumptions about case facts on which your analyses may be based.

Situation Analysis

As shown in Table 2, a general starting place for completing a situation analysis is the general environment.

General Environmental Analysis Your analysis of the general environment should focus on trends in the

six segments of the general environment (see Table 3). Many of the segment issues shown in Table 3 for the six segments are explained more fully in Chapter 2 of your book. The objective you should have in evaluating these trends is to be able to predict the segments that you expect to have the most significant influence on your focal firm over the next several years (say three to five years) and to explain your reasoning for your predictions.

Industry Analysis Porter's five-forces model is a useful tool for analyzing the industry or industries in which your firm competes. We explain how to use this tool in Chapter 2. In this part of your analysis, you want to determine the attractiveness of the industry or industries in which the focal firm is competing. As attractiveness increases, so does the possibility that your focal firm will be able to earn above-average returns by using its chosen strategies. After evaluating the power of the five forces relative to your focal firm, you should evaluate how attractive the industry is in which your focal firm is competing.

Competitor Analysis Firms also need to analyze each of their primary competitors. This analysis should identify competitors' current strategies, vision, mission, capabilities, core competencies, and a competitive response profile. We explain these items in

| TABLE 3 | Sample General Environmental Categories |

Technological Trends

- Information technology continues to become cheaper with more practical applications
- Database technology enables organization of complex data and distribution of information
- Telecommunications technology and networks increasingly provide fast transmission of all sources of data, including voice, written communications, and video information
- Computerized design and manufacturing technologies continue to facilitate quality and flexibility

Demographic Trends

- Regional changes in population due to migration
- Changing ethnic composition of the population
- Aging of the population
- Aging of the "baby boom" generation

Economic Trends

- Interest rates
- Inflation rates
- Savings rates
- Exchange rates
- Trade deficits
- Budget deficits

Political/Legal Trends

- Antitrust enforcement
- Tax policy changes
- Environmental protection laws
- Extent of regulation/deregulation
- Privatizing state monopolies
- State-owned industries

Sociocultural Trends

- Women in the workforce
- Awareness of health and fitness issues
- Concern for the environment
- Concern for customers

Global Trends

- Currency exchange rates
- Free-trade agreements
- Trade deficits

Chapter 2. This information is useful to the focal firm in formulating an appropriate strategy and in predicting competitors' probable responses. Sources that can be used to gather information about an industry and companies with whom the focal firm competes are listed in Appendix I. Included in this list is a wide range of publications, such as periodicals, newspapers, bibliographies, directories of companies, industry ratios, forecasts, rankings/ratings, and other valuable statistics.

Internal Analysis Assessing a firm's strengths and weaknesses through a value-chain analysis facilitates moving from the external environment to the internal environment. Analyzing the primary and support activities of the value chain will help you understand how external environmental trends affect the specific activities of a firm. Such analysis helps highlight strengths and weaknesses (see Chapter 3 for an explanation and use of the value chain).

For purposes of preparing an oral or a written presentation, it is important to note that strengths are internal resources and capabilities that have the potential to be core competencies. Weaknesses, on the other hand, are internal resources and capabilities that have the potential to place a firm at a competitive disadvantage relative to its rivals. Therefore, some of a firm's resources and capabilities are strengths; others are weaknesses.

When you evaluate the internal characteristics of the firm, your analysis of the functional activities emphasized is critical. For instance, if the strategy of the firm is primarily technology-driven, it is important to evaluate the firm's R&D activities. If the strategy is market-driven, marketing activities are of paramount importance. If a firm has financial difficulties, critical financial ratios would require careful evaluation. In fact, because of the importance of financial health, most cases require financial analyses. Appendix II lists and operationally defines several common financial ratios. Included are tables describing profitability, liquidity, leverage, activity, and shareholders' return ratios. Leadership, organizational culture, structure, and control systems are other characteristics of firms you should examine to fully understand the "internal" part of your firm.

IDENTIFICATION OF ENVIRONMENTAL OPPORTUNITIES AND THREATS AND FIRM STRENGTHS AND WEAKNESSES (SWOT ANALYSIS)

The outcome of the situation analysis is the identification of a firm's strengths and weaknesses and its environmental threats and opportunities. The next step requires that you analyze the strengths and weaknesses and the opportunities and threats for configurations that benefit or do not benefit your firm's efforts to perform well. Case analysts, and organizational strategists as well, seek to match a firm's strengths with its external environmental opportunities. In addition, strengths are chosen to prevent any serious environmental threat from negatively affecting the firm's performance. The key objective of conducting a SWOT

analysis is to determine how to position the firm so it can take advantage of opportunities, while simultaneously avoiding or minimizing environmental threats. Results from a SWOT analysis yield valuable insights into the selection of a firm's strategies. The analysis of a case should not be overemphasized relative to the synthesis of results gained from your analytical efforts. You may be tempted to emphasize the results from the analysis in your oral or written case analysis. It is important, however, that you make an equal effort to develop and evaluate alternatives and to design implementation of the chosen strategy.

STRATEGY FORMULATION—STRATEGIC ALTERNATIVES, ALTERNATIVE EVALUATION, AND ALTERNATIVE CHOICE

Developing alternatives is often one of the most difficult steps in preparing an oral or written presentation. Development of three to four alternative strategies is common (see Chapter 4 for business-level strategy alternatives and Chapter 6 for corporate-level strategy alternatives). Each alternative should be feasible (it should match the firm's strengths, capabilities, and especially core competencies), and feasibility should be demonstrated. In addition, you should show how each alternative takes advantage of environmental opportunities or protects against environmental threats. Developing carefully thought-out alternatives requires synthesis of your analyses' results and creates greater credibility in oral and written case presentations.

Once you develop strong alternatives, you must evaluate the set to choose the best one. Your choice should be defensible and provide benefits over the other alternatives. Therefore, it is important that both alternative development and evaluation of alternatives are thorough. You should explain and defend your choice of the best alternative.

STRATEGIC ALTERNATIVE IMPLEMENTATION—ACTION ITEMS AND ACTION PLAN

After selecting the most appropriate strategy (the one most likely to help your firm earn above-average returns), you must turn your attention to implementation-related issues. Effective synthesis is important to ensure that you have considered and evaluated all critical

C

implementation issues. Issues you might consider include the structural changes necessary to implement the new strategy. In addition, leadership changes and new controls or incentives may be necessary to implement strategic actions. The implementation actions you recommend should be explicit and thoroughly explained. Occasionally, careful evaluation of implementation actions may show the strategy to be less favorable than you thought originally. A strategy is only as good as the firm's ability to implement it.

PROCESS ISSUES

You should ensure that your presentation (either oral or written) is logical and consistent throughout. For example, if your presentation identifies one purpose, but your analysis focuses on issues that differ from the stated purpose, the logical inconsistency will be apparent. Likewise, your alternatives should flow from the configuration of strengths, weaknesses, opportunities, and threats you identified by analyzing your firm's external and internal environments.

Thoroughness and clarity also are critical to an effective presentation. Thoroughness is represented by the comprehensiveness of the analysis and alternative generation. Furthermore, clarity in the results of the analyses, selection of the best alternative strategy, and design of implementation actions are important. For example, your statement of the strengths and weaknesses should flow clearly and logically from your analysis of your firm's internal environment.

Presentations (oral or written) that show logical consistency, thoroughness, clarity of purpose, effective analyses, and feasible recommendations (strategy and implementation) are more effective and are likely to be more positively received by your instructor and peers. Furthermore, developing the skills necessary to make such presentations will enhance your future job performance and career success.

NOTES

1. C. Christensen, 1989, *Teaching and the Case Method,* Boston: Harvard Business School Publishing Division; C. C. Lundberg, 1993, Introduction to the case method, in C. M. Vance (ed.), *Mastering Management Education,* Newbury Park, Calif.: Sage.
2. C. C. Lundberg and C. Enz, 1993, A framework for student case preparation, *Case Research Journal* 13 (Summer): 133.
3. J. Soltis, 1971, John Dewey, in L. E. Deighton (ed.), *Encyclopedia of Education,* New York: Macmillan and Free Press.

APPENDIX I: SOURCES FOR INDUSTRY AND COMPETITOR ANALYSES

Abstracts and Indexes

Periodicals

ABI/Inform
Business Periodicals Index
EBSCO Business Source Premier
InfoTrac Custom Journals
InfoTrac Custom Newspapers
InfoTrac OneFile
Lexis/Nexis Academic
Public Affairs Information Service Bulletin (PAIS)
Readers' Guide to Periodical Literature

Newspapers

NewsBank—Foreign Broadcast Information
NewsBank—Global NewsBank
New York Times Index
Wall Street Journal/Barron's Index
Wall Street Journal Index
Washington Post Index

Bibliographies

Encyclopedia of Business Information Sources

Directories

Companies—General

America's Corporate Families and International Affiliates
D&B Million Dollar Database (http://www.dnbmdd.com)
Hoover's Online: The Business Network (http://www
   .hoovers.com/free)
Standard & Poor's Corporation Records
Standard & Poor's Register of Corporations, Directors
   & Executives (http://www.netadvantage
   .standardandpoors.com)
Ward's Business Directory of Largest U.S. Companies

Companies—International

America's Corporate Families and International
   Affiliates
Business Asia
Business China
Business Eastern Europe
Business Europe
Business International
Business International Money Report
Business Latin America
Directory of American Firms Operating in Foreign
   Countries
Directory of Foreign Firms Operating in the
   United States

Preparing an Effective Case Analysis

C

Hoover's Handbook of World Business
International Directory of Company Histories
Mergent International Manual
Mergent Online (http://www.fisonline.com)
Who Owns Whom

Companies—Manufacturers

Thomas Register of American Manufacturers
U.S. Manufacturer's Directory, Manufacturing &
    Distribution, USA
U.S. Office of Management and Budget, Executive
    Office of the President, Standard Industrial
    Classification Manual

Companies—Private

D&B Million Dollar Database (http://www.dnbmdd.com)
Ward's Business Directory of Largest U.S. Companies

Companies—Public

Annual reports and 10-K reports
Disclosure (corporate reports)
Mergent's Manuals:
    Mergent's Bank and Finance Manual
    Mergent's Industrial Manual
    Mergent's International Manual
    Mergent's Municipal and Government Manual
    Mergent's OTC Industrial Manual
    Mergent's OTC Unlisted Manual
    Mergent's Public Utility Manual
    Mergent's Transportation Manual
Standard & Poor's Corporation, Standard Corporation
    Descriptions (http://www.netadvantage
    .standardandpoors.com)
    Standard & Poor's Analyst's Handbook
    Standard & Poor's Industry Surveys
    Standard & Poor's Statistical Service
Q-File

Companies—Subsidiaries and Affiliates

America's Corporate Families and International Affiliates
Mergent's Industry Review
Standard & Poor's Analyst's Handbook
Standard & Poor's Industry Surveys (2 volumes)
U.S. Department of Commerce, U.S. Industrial Outlook
Who Owns Whom

Industry Ratios

Dun & Bradstreet, Industry Norms and Key Business
    Ratios
RMA's Annual Statement Studies
Troy Almanac of Business and Industrial Financial Ratios

Industry Forecasts

International Trade Administration, U.S. Industry & Trade Outlook

Rankings and Ratings

Annual Report on American Industry in Forbes
Business Rankings Annual
Mergent's Industry Review
   (http://www.worldcatlibraries.org)
Standard & Poor's Industry Report Service
   (http://www.netadvantage.standardandpoors.com)
Value Line Investment Survey
Ward's Business Directory of Largest U.S. Companies

Statistics

Bureau of the Census, U.S. Department of Commerce, American Statistics Index (ASI)
Bureau of the Census, U.S. Department of Commerce, Economic Census publications
Bureau of the Census, U.S. Department of Commerce, Statistical Abstract of the United States
Bureau of Economic Analysis, U.S. Department of Commerce, Survey of Current Business
Internal Revenue Service, U.S. Department of the Treasury, Statistics of Income: Corporation Income Tax Returns
Statistical Reference Index (SRI)

APPENDIX II: FINANCIAL ANALYSIS IN CASE STUDIES

TABLE A-1	Profitability Ratios	
Ratio	**Formula**	**What It Shows**
1. Return on total assets	$\dfrac{\text{Profits after taxes}}{\text{Total assets}}$	The net return on total investments of the firm
	or	or
	$\dfrac{\text{Profits after taxes} + \text{Interest}}{\text{Total assets}}$	The return on both creditors' and shareholders' investments
2. Return on stockholder's equity (or return on net worth)	$\dfrac{\text{Profits after taxes}}{\text{Total stockholder's equity}}$	How profitably the company is utilizing shareholders' funds
3. Return on common equity	$\dfrac{\text{Profits after taxes} - \text{Preferred stock dividends}}{\text{Total stockholder's equity} - \text{Par value of preferred stock}}$	The net return to common stockholders
4. Operating profit margin (or return on sales)	$\dfrac{\text{Profits before taxes and before interest}}{\text{Sales}}$	The firm's profitability from regular operations
5. Net profit margin (or net return on sales)	$\dfrac{\text{Profits after taxes}}{\text{Sales}}$	The firm's net profit as a percentage of total sales

TABLE A-2	Liquidity Ratios	
Ratio	**Formula**	**What It Shows**
1. Current ratio	$\dfrac{\text{Current assets}}{\text{Current liabilities}}$	The firm's ability to meet its current financial liabilities
2. Quick ratio (or acid-test ratio)	$\dfrac{\text{Current assets} - \text{Inventory}}{\text{Current liabilities}}$	The firm's ability to pay off short-term obligations without relying on sales of inventory
3. Inventory to net working capital	$\dfrac{\text{Inventory}}{\text{Current assets} - \text{Current liabilities}}$	The extent to which the firm's working capital is tied up in inventory

TABLE A-3   Leverage Ratios

Ratio	Formula	What It Shows
1. Debt-to-assets	$\dfrac{\text{Total debt}}{\text{Total assets}}$	Total borrowed funds as a percentage of total assets
2. Debt-to-equity	$\dfrac{\text{Total debt}}{\text{Total shareholders' equity}}$	Borrowed funds versus the funds provided by shareholders
3. Long-term debt-to-equity	$\dfrac{\text{Long-term debt}}{\text{Total shareholders' equity}}$	Leverage used by the firm
4. Times-interest-earned (or coverage ratio)	$\dfrac{\text{Profits before interest and taxes}}{\text{Total interest charges}}$	The firm's ability to meet all interest payments
5. Fixed charge coverage	$\dfrac{\text{Profits before taxes and interest} + \text{Lease obligations}}{\text{Total interest charges} + \text{Lease obligations}}$	The firm's ability to meet all fixed-charge obligations including lease payments

TABLE A-4   Activity Ratios

Ratio	Formula	What It Shows
1. Inventory turnover	$\dfrac{\text{Sales}}{\text{Inventory of finished goods}}$	The effectiveness of the firm in employing inventory
2. Fixed-assets turnover	$\dfrac{\text{Sales}}{\text{Fixed assets}}$	The effectiveness of the firm in utilizing plant and equipment
3. Total assets turnover	$\dfrac{\text{Sales}}{\text{Total assets}}$	The effectiveness of the firm in utilizing total assets
4. Accounts receivable turnover	$\dfrac{\text{Annual credit sales}}{\text{Accounts receivable}}$	How many times the total receivables has been collected during the accounting period
5. Average collecting period	$\dfrac{\text{Accounts receivable}}{\text{Average daily sales}}$	The average length of time the firm waits to collect payment after sales

C

Ratio	Formula	What It Shows
1. Dividend yield on common stock	$\dfrac{\text{Annual dividend per share}}{\text{Current market price per share}}$	A measure of return to common stockholders in the form of dividends
2. Price-earnings ratio	$\dfrac{\text{Current market price per share}}{\text{After-tax earnings per share}}$	An indication of market perception of the firm; usually, the faster-growing or less risky firms tend to have higher PE ratios than the slower-growing or more risky firms
3. Dividend payout ratio	$\dfrac{\text{Annual dividends per share}}{\text{After-tax earnings per share}}$	An indication of dividends paid out as a percentage of profits
4. Cash flow per share	$\dfrac{\text{After-tax profits + Depression}}{\text{Number of common shares outstanding}}$	A measure of total cash per share available for use by the firm

Tata Steel: A Century of Corporate Social Responsibilities

Kathryn Hughes
Jean-Francois Manzoni
Vikas Tibrewala

INSEAD

It is the story of a company that is doing well because of, not in spite of, its relations with its community. . . In the past, we were good in business ethics, but poor in business processes, acumen, and marketing. We are trying to make the transition from an imbalance to a more proper balance.

— Managing Director B. Muthuraman

Jamshedpur, India: January 2003. The Tata Steel plant was plastered with "EVA+" stickers. The battle cry was also shouted from workers' helmets, windshields of managers' cars, and entrances to production facilities. A departure from the slogan of the 1980s, "We Also Make Steel," which emphasized the company's focus on community and society, the EVA[1] emphasis reflected a new outlook at Tata Steel. The walls of the steel mills were painted with enormous Balanced Scorecards. The pristine property was virtually free of the coal dust and grime prevalent in steel plants; potted plants and flowers adorned the plant instead. Such a scene would be difficult to envision at any steel plant in the world, let alone at Tata Steel, located in the underdeveloped state of Jharkhand in eastern India.[2]

Tata Steel, the largest private steel maker in the country and part of the renowned Indian conglomerate the Tata Group, had undergone a dramatic transformation over the previous decade. Following Independence in 1947, India had implemented restrictive trade regulations. Administered through innumerable permits from Delhi, the extensive directives led some to quip that the country had traded the "British Raj" for the "Licence Raj." Despite production, pricing and plant expansion limitations, Tata Steel thrived against its only major competitor, the inefficient state-owned Steel Authority of India Ltd. (SAIL). In the face of a foreign currency crisis in 1991, Prime Minister P. V. Narasimha Rao introduced liberalisation, gradually dismantling the regulations and dissolving the protected economic environment. Under the leadership of then Managing Director, Dr. J. J. Irani, Tata Steel confronted these wrenching changes. Irani drove a transformation effort (dubbed "modernisation of the mind") involving dramatic cost cutting, workforce reduction, and plant renovations (Exhibit 1). Despite a significant slash in workforce numbers ("family size" in Tata parlance), Irani maintained the company's generous community practices. By maintaining healthcare, education, and infrastructure support to residents of Jamshedpur, Tata Steel reaffirmed its nationally renowned reputation for benevolent relations with society.

In 2001, Dr. Irani completed his tenure as Managing Director. A selection process nominated B. Muthuraman as his successor. Formerly Vice President of Sales and Marketing and more recently responsible for overseeing construction of the plant's Cold Rolling Mill at a world record setting pace, Muthuraman's background diverged from the engineering focus that had characterized Irani's management. Under Irani, Tata Steel had survived liberalisation. Muthuraman's remit as leader would be to confront the challenge of intensified global competition.

This case, funded by the INSEAD-PricewaterhouseCoopers Research Initiative on High Performance Organizations, was written by Kathryn Hughes, Research Program Manager, Jean-Francois Manzoni, Associate Professor of Management, and Vikas Tibrewala, Senior Affiliate Professor of Marketing, all at INSEAD. It is intended to be used as a basis for class discussion rather than to illustrate either effective or ineffective handling of an administrative situation. Copyright © 2004 INSEAD, Fontainebleau, France. Reprinted by permission.

EXHIBIT 1

Tata Steel Key Data (Rs Crore)

	1980–81	1985–86	1990–91	1995–96	1997–98	2000–01	2002–03
Turnover	521	1,286	2,331	5,880	6,517	7,812	9,844
Net Sales	492	1,222	2,142	5,854	6,433	7,759	9,793
Volume Production (m tons)	1.537	1.772	1.90	2.66	2.971	3.413	3.975
Operating Profit	59	197	304	1,154	995	1,707	2,302
Profit After Tax	26	108	160	566	322	553	1,012
Employee Figures	62,695	79,505	75,153	72,621	64,753	48,821	46,234

Source: Tata Steel.

To adapt to the new buyer's market and the increased influence of international capital, Tata Steel sought greater focus on its shareholders. As Tata Group Chairman Ratan Tata described in a July 2001 interview, "We [have] recognized that, regrettably, the steel industry does not cover the cost of capital . . . If you have to invest thousands of crores,[3] as we did in the modernization of the plant, and if it doesn't give us a return that is equal to the cost of capital, then we have destroyed shareholder value . . .[We have awakened] to the fact that we have to do much more in steel to make it an investor-attractive area of business."[i]

Muthuraman sought a means to structure and communicate the challenges that faced Tata Steel. At a two-day retreat in December 2001, forty-five senior executives, led by Boston Consulting Group's Arun Maira, worked on an outline for a new vision statement. The results of the brainstorming were posted on the company intranet; executives solicited feedback from workers and managers, and consulted the President of the Tata Workers Union. Through various communications forums, 4000 employees contributed ideas. After a small team digested the 7,000 suggestions, Tata Steel unveiled its new vision statement. Launched on May 2, 2002, "Vision 2007" laid out two main pillars:

- To seize the opportunities of tomorrow and create a future that will make us an EVA© positive company, and
- To continue to improve the quality of life of our employees and the communities we serve.

Despite the heavy groundwork entailed in creating the vision statement, the more difficult test of implementation still lay ahead (Exhibit 2). The vision raised the spectre of contradictory challenges for Muthuraman and his team. In practical terms, how would Tata Steel manage its resource commitment to the "community" while pursuing its EVA+ vision? It seemed inevitable that the new emphasis on shareholder return would dilute Tata Steel's historic focus on its community.

A TRADITION OF COMPASSION

While a shareholder focus and EVA emphasis were relatively recent mantras at Tata Steel, its social orientation predated the company's foundation in the late 19th century. Convinced of the national benefits of a strong industrial base, Jamsetji N. Tata sought to develop textiles, hydroelectric power, steel operations, and scientific education facilities to fuel "the increased prosperity of India" and prepare for independence from British colonial rule.[4] J. N. Tata's endeavours were visionary both for their boldness and for their progressive employment practices, including the first fire-sprinklers in India (1886) and a Pension Fund (1895).

Initially, the Raj scorned Tata's ambitions in heavy industry. The (British) Chief Commissioner of Indian Railways scoffed, "Why, I will undertake to eat every pound of steel rail they succeed in making." He was not the only sceptic. An initial share offering in 1906 received a lukewarm response in London, and it was only a year later that the Tata Iron and Steel Company was able to raise the necessary capital, through an overwhelmingly popular share issue in Bombay, subscribed to by 8000 shareholders. J. N. Tata also devoted half his personal wealth to establish the Indian Institute of Science in Bangalore, even after warnings that the school would receive insufficient applicants. No less a figure than Jawaharlal Nehru later commented, "When you have to give the lead in action, in ideas, a lead which does not fit in with the very climate of opinion, that is true courage . . . it is this type of courage and vision that Jamsetji Tata showed."

EXHIBIT
2

Vision 2007

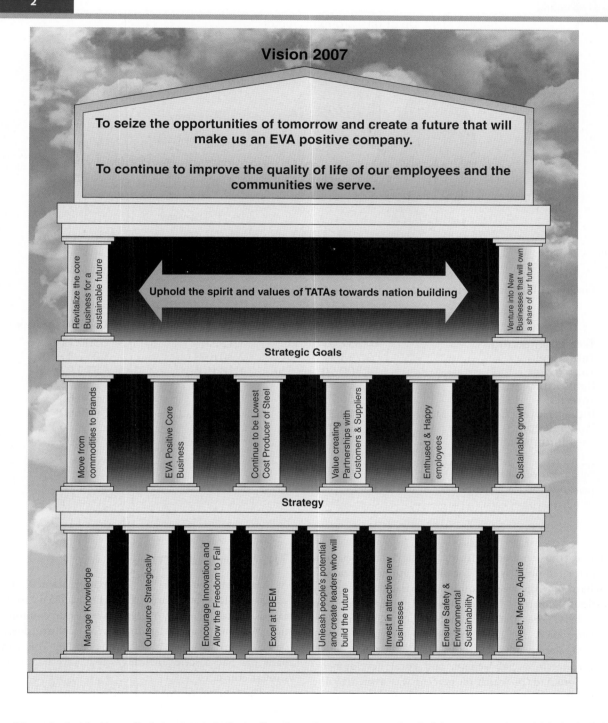

Though J. N. Tata died in 1904 before all of his bold ventures had come to fruition, subsequent generations of Tata leadership cultivated his vision of India's development through industrial development. A century later, this commitment resulted in the Tata Group, a network of eighty companies which included an automotive producer, a power company, a telecom, a hotel chain, a tea producer, and an IT consultancy, the first global billion-dollar Indian software organization (Exhibit 3). These businesses were linked by their

EXHIBIT
3

The Tata Group

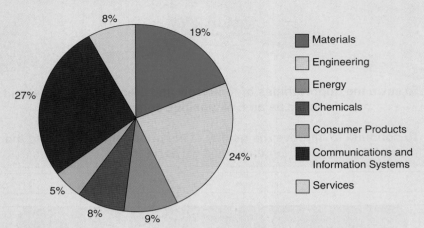

Percent Make-Up of Tata Group by Sector

- 19% Materials
- 24% Engineering
- 9% Energy
- 8% Chemicals
- 5% Consumer Products
- 27% Communications and Information Systems
- 8% Services

Financial Results for Fiscal Year Ending March 31, 2003 (Rs Crore)

	Net Sales (Income from Operations)	Operating Profit	Profit/Loss After Tax
Tata Engineering	10,837.01	1,139.41	300.11
Tata Steel	9,793.27	2,301.98	1,012.31
Tata Power	4,300.50	1,184.16	519.92
Rallis International	1,037.68	79.65	58.75
Tata Tea	760.75	97.78	70.60
Indian Hotels Company Ltd.	569.27	54.74	70.60*
Tata Telecom	319.02	29.97	18.56
Tata Infomedia Ltd.	118.12	19.03	13.08

*Includes income from investments.

Source: www.tata.com.

shared ethos, embodied in the Articles of Association, which cited objectives of social obligations beyond the welfare of employees. Common partial ownership by various Tata trusts further bolstered ties among group members. The first, created by J. N. Tata in 1892, mushroomed, by 2003, into eleven trusts that supported, among other issues, women's education, medical research, social welfare, and rural development. Tata Sons Ltd, of which 66 percent was owned by the philanthropic trusts in 2003, acted as the sole proprietor of the TATA brand name and functioned as the group management company. It maintained a shareholding in each of the major operating companies, some of whose Chief Executives served on its board. In 2003, Tata Sons owned nearly 20 percent of Tata Steel (Exhibit 4).

THE LEGACY IN ACTION

As Managing Director Muthuraman explained, "Our values at Tata Steel are well acknowledged, to the extent we take care of our employees, our communities. We have a special culture here. Culture doesn't come overnight or because of one leader. This company has had a series of leaders that have had a very similar ethos."

The foundations of the group's progressive policies originated with J. N. Tata's philosophy on industrial development, and the catalogue of forward-thinking worker practices introduced throughout the 20th century at Tata Steel testified to his legacy. In many cases, Tata Steel pioneered employment policies well before its contemporaries in the industrialized West, let alone

EXHIBIT 4   Pattern of Shareholding at Tata Steel in 2003

Category	Holdings (Number of shares)	% of Holdings
Promoters' holdings		
Indian promoters		
Tata Sons Ltd.	73,048,744	19.86
Tata Engineering & Locomotive Co. Ltd.	17,204,486	4.68
Others	6,880,566	1.87
Foreign promoters	–	–
Subtotal	*97,133,796*	*26.41*
Nonpromoters holdings		
Institutional investors, banks,		
and public bodies	108,767,236	29.57
Foreign institutional investors	15,474,798	4.21
Subtotal	*124,242,034*	*33.78*
Private corporate bodies	24,930,200	6.78
Indian public	118,017,325	32.09
Other	3,448,546	0.94
Subtotal	*146,396,071*	*39.81*
Grand total	*367,771,901*	*100.00*

Note: Total foreign holding = 5.13% (includes 0.94% for other foreign investors).

Source: www.tatasteel.com

those in India. For example, while steel workers in England continued to work minimum twelve-hour shifts, Tata Steel instituted eight-hour working systems in 1912. Similarly, the company introduced a Free Medical Scheme in 1915 and a Workers' Provident Fund in 1920, both thirty years before they were mandated by government (Exhibit 5). The group's efforts were even supported by the intervention of the renowned Fabian socialists Sydney and Beatrix Potter Webb. As leading lights of the British Labour Party and founders of the London School of Economics, they were invited in 1924 by the Managing Director, Dorabji Tata, to make recommendations for social, medical and cooperative services in Jamshedpur.[ii] Receiving tailored advice in rural India from socialist-theory titans such as the Webbs was an impressive coup for the Tatas.

In an industry notorious for frequent strikes and walkouts, Tata Steel maintained harmony through leadership in labour relations. It developed a collaborative partnership with its union, signing in 1956 a Joint Consultation agreement with the Tata Workers' Union that formed Joint Department Councils (JDCs). That labour pact, upheld over the following five decades, enabled the 47 JDCs, comprised equally of management and employees, to decide by consensus upon issues of working conditions, environment, safety, and productivity.

While India experienced heavy political unrest during the 1970s, with as much as 47 percent of the entire "organised sector" workforce simultaneously on strike, not a single strike against management had arisen at Tata Steel since 1928.[5,6] During 1975 when a state of emergency was called across India, the national union announced a strike throughout the steel industry.[7] When the Tata Workers' Union refused to join the strike, national union representatives came to Jamshedpur to block incoming shipments on the railway tracks. Together, Tata Steel management and workers charged the protesting outsiders, jointly dispersing the threat to operations.

Earlier, in 1971, the Indian government decided to nationalise the coal sector to "bring about improvement in the health and safety scenario."[8] The only private mines it explicitly spared from this nationalisation were those belonging to Tata Steel, which were preserved as a benchmark for sector peers. In 1977, when George Fernandes, the Minister of Industry, proposed nationalisation of Tata Steel, the Tata Workers' Union immediately cabled a protest to the Prime Minister. While previous nationalisations had been politically popular, the government quickly realised that there was no support for the nationalisation of Tata Steel. The Chairman at the time, J. R. D. Tata, said, "[I run Tata Steel] partly because of Jamsetji's tradition. Profit was not the sole aim. Partly, to save it from being taken over and ruined.

| EXHIBIT 5 | Labor Welfare at Tata Steel |

	Introduced at Tata Steel	Enforced by Law	Legal Measure
Eight-hour working day	1912	1948	Factories Act
Free medical aid	1915	1948	Employees State Insurance Act
Establishment of Welfare Department	1917	1948	Factories Act
Schooling facilities for children	1917		
Formation of Works Committee for handling complaints concerning service conditions and grievances	1919	1947	Industrial Disputes Act
Leave with pay	1920	1948	Factories Act
Workers' Provident Fund scheme	1920	1924	Workmen's Compensation Act
Technical institute for training apprentices, craftsmen, & engineering graduates	1921	1961	Apprentices Act
Maternity benefit	1928	1946	Bihar Maternity Benefit Act
Profit sharing bonus	1934	1965	Bonus Act
Retiring gratuity	1937	1972	Payment of Gratuity Act
Ex-gratia payment: road accident while coming to or returning from duty	1979		

Source: R. M. Lala, *The Creation of Wealth* (Bombay: IBH Publishers, 1992).

That is why I fought for Tata Steel against nationalisation. The spirit of goodwill and cooperation we have built up between management and labour will be no more if Tata Steel is nationalised."[9,10]

Tata's policies spawned worker loyalty exemplary for the steel industry. "The employees have a sense of ownership, they feel involved. Tata Steel schemes imply good forward thinking and a general concern for the employees," observed Rajeev Dubey, Managing Director of Rallis India.[11] "The company vision has become sacrosanct, even to workers. The attrition rates in this company are the lowest in the country," noted U. K. Chaturvedi, Executive in Charge of Long Products.

The company's compassionate approach proved equally inspiring to senior managers. Attuned to employees' needs, they endorsed and extended the company-wide policies instituted early in Tata Steel's development. Targeting to ease the burden of difficult working conditions for labourers had become ingrained as a management responsibility over the decades. For example, Santosh Gupta, Managing Director of TRF Limited, recalled that, when Tata Steel acquired a bearings business in 1983, the only pharmacy was located in a neighbouring village, a difficult two kilometre walk away.[12] After he

asked the village pharmacy to open a facility at the plant, women and children mobbed his home. "They told me they were coming to thank me for reducing the stress and hassle of obtaining medicines. A healthy person will give us much more on the job. A healthy body leads to a healthy mind, and that is influenced by a worker's surroundings, neighbours, and family. Motivations come best when workers are hassle-free. India is a high-hassle country. If we can be a low-hassle company within it, I think that is impressive."

The company's code of ethics and commitment also helped attract senior executives. As Bharat Wakhlu, Chief of Supply Chain, explained, "We have used the 'talent issue' to explain to investors why we have given so much on the social side at Tata Steel. It is not necessarily a given that you can attract top talent to Jamshedpur! The quality of life is as good as anywhere else; I have been educated in the United States, I have worked outside of India, I speak several languages, and yet I choose to work in Jamshedpur."

Tata Steel's practices generated similar reactions beyond Jamshedpur. P. Roy, Executive in Charge of the Ferro-Alloy Mineral Division, explained that domestically they could ask for a 30–50 percent higher premium from customers due to brand reputation and reliability. "Values work in India. Customers may tell themselves, 'I can rely on this pipe because Tata is a trusted company.' That premium is comprised of brand value, ethics and product quality. It does open doors." H. M. Nerurkar, Executive in Charge, Flat Products, concurred, noting a similar response from suppliers. "In India we get a lot of mileage right away due to our reputation. Everyone knows that thanks to our performance and values they can count on this player. Some values in a social context, add value in a business context. When negotiating contracts, we have been able to bring the price down by about half." Even those who attempted to bribe Tata Steel developed a "healthy respect for its adamancy to operate with a certain code of ethics."[13]

"CITY OF JAMSHED"

Jamshedpur, named in tribute to Jamsetji N. Tata in 1919, was a vivid illustration of the pioneering steel town the founder had exhorted his son to build. "Be sure to lay wide streets planted with shady trees, every other one of a quick growing variety. Be sure that there is plenty of space for lawns and gardens. Reserve large areas for football, hockey and parks. Earmark areas for Hindu temples, Mohammedan mosques and Christian churches."[iii] Jamshedpur was considered an "oasis" across India, and the Town Division was the only civic services provider in the country to be ISO 14001 certified for its Environmental Management Systems.

Initial prospecting by the American and English geological experts brought by Tata Steel to Central India had proved futile. The eastern site for the plant was finally determined by its relative proximity to raw materials, but primarily due to the presence of water, essential for steel production. As Dubey explained, "It is important to understand the geographical context of Tata Steel's business. In Bihar, there was no infrastructure; Tata Steel selected it purely based on the raw materials that had been available." Two hundred and fifty kilometres from Calcutta, the nearest large city, Jamshedpur developed into a self-sustained community, ensconced between the Subarnarekha and Kharkai rivers (Exhibit 6).[14] The chosen site was so remote that

EXHIBIT 6	Location of Jamshedpur

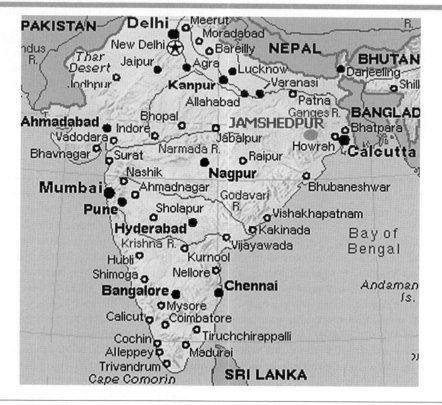

Source: www.jamshedpurlive.com

EXHIBIT 7   Comparative Statistics, Jamshedpur vs. India

Tata Steel Actions	Results for Tata Steel	Rest of India
Labour: Tata Steel coordinates with union representatives via the Joint Departmental Council, including unions in internal planning.	No employee strike against Tata Steel since 1928. (Labour Strike of 1920 ended in a day thanks to Dorabji Tata's intervention).	The national average for number of man days lost per year due to strikes in India between 1988 and 1997 was 9.35 million.
Education: Tata Steel provides schools for employee families and contracts with private-sector education providers to provide for non-employee children.	In 2001, Jamshedpur boasts an overall literacy rate of 76%; 71% for women.	The 2001 literacy rate in India was 55%; 46% for women. In the state of Jharkhand, the literacy rate was 44%; 32% for women.
Infrastructure: Tata Steel has built 1,000 km of roads, provided 202 MW of power, and cleans and distributes running water to Jamshedpur; pumped 7.5 MGD sewerage daily in 2000–2001, and removed 120,000 tons of garbage.	Electricity constantly available.	• In 2001, 55.8% of households had electricity for lighting; 24.3% in the state of Jharkhand • In 2001, 9.1% of households in India had a telephone; 3.3% in the state of Jharkhand • In 2001, 36.7% of Indian households had a tap as a source for drinking water; 12.6% in Jharkhand.
Medical: Tata Steel provides 16 medical centres including the 740-bed Tata Main hospital.	TRSD treated a total of 2,857 tuberculosis cases between 1996 and 2000.	• From 1996 to 2001, India had an infant mortality rate of 64 per 1000; the state of Jharkhand (2000), 70. • From 1996 to 2001, life expectancy from birth was 65.4 years in India overall and 62.1 years in Bihar.

Source: 2001 Indian National Census, Statistical Outline of India, 2001–2002, Tata Services Limited, Department of Economics and Statistics, Tata Steel Corporate Sustainability Report, 2000–2001.

Tata Steel had to employ guards to ward off tigers and wild elephants, whose continuing presence was reaffirmed by a dangerous rampage through Jamshedpur in 2001.

Over the subsequent decades, Tata Steel provided a growing range of services and infrastructure for Jamshedpur citizens (Exhibit 7). Formalized as the "Town Division" of Tata Steel, it was responsible for constructing and maintaining water works, highway systems, bridges and public transportation, and emergency services such as the fire brigade. As of 2001, the Town Division oversaw water purification and supply, maintenance of more than 500 kilometres of public roads, and the distribution of power to the Jamshedpur area's 750,000 inhabitants.

Additionally, the Town Division ran educational and medical services for the community. In 2001, Tata Steel schools educated 11,000 pupils. The 740-bed Tata Main Hospital, further supplemented by sixteen medical centres, treated 40,000 patients in 2000–2001. The Town Division operated numerous recreational programs for youth and constructed extensive athletic grounds including a 22,000-seat cricket stadium and an eight-lane athletics track.

Tata Steel's care for its employees encompassed their lives both on and off the plant grounds. Santosh Gupta explained, "In another group, management may pay a very poor salary, but they provide exotic free meals. That worker may be loyal because of the meal, but with this meal and meagre salary, can he support his family? We at Tata Steel don't believe in that philosophy."

The seniority of Tata Steel managers deployed to the Town Division further signified its importance to the company. Rather than being seen as relegation to a non-core division of the business, a posting in town services was a sign of recognition. Town Division General Managers often went on to assume prominent positions at Tata Steel and within the Tata group. As Dubey, former General Manager of Town Services reflected, "The humanity I learned from working at that position was tremendous. Was I in production? Was I in operations? No, but I learned so much. It was a tremendous experience, where I learned to connect with myself on a spiritual level." In addition to assigning top managers to run town administration, numerous executives served on committees, interacting with Jamshedpur community groups to gauge services that should be provided or improved.

The Indian public equated socially responsible business with Tata Steel, leading the company to produce a television commercial and a print advertisement in the 1980s, featuring happy customers and employees, with the "We Also Make Steel" slogan. The community unambiguously appreciated the Town Division. When the Bihar government tried to wrest control of public services from Tata Steel in 1991, Irani asked Jamshedpur citizens to voice their administration preference. The subsequent referendum overwhelmingly supported Tata Steel; the government received less than a 5 percent vote and "stayed away."

EXTENDED "FAMILY"

With its broad definition, "community" did not stop at the borders of Jamshedpur. Tata Steel assisted in the development of areas near Jamshedpur and its mines. In 1979, it established the Tata Steel Rural Development Society (TSRDS), which operated in 600 villages both in Jamshedpur's state of Jharkhand and in the neighbouring state of Orissa. TSRDS embraced three chief goals: accessible health care, enhanced income generation for communities, and empowerment of the rural population (Exhibit 8). Indigenous tribes, many living in proximity to Tata Steel's captive mines, benefited from the efforts. In 2001–2002, water from the irrigation projects brought an additional 1,624 acres of rural land under cultivation. Self-help groups of women developed entrepreneurial initiatives, supplementing agricultural income. Health services reached numerous recipients through immunisations and AIDS awareness programmes.

Tata Steel's care further encompassed the natural environment that surrounded its plants and mines. It emphasized the "greening" of its own plant facilities as well as the reforestation of lands around its mines. As one executive noted, "Sometimes we leave places cleaner than we find them." The Millennium Project, launched in 1997, pledged to plant one million trees by the turn of the century. Jamshedpur alone welcomed 75,000 new trees. Mining areas, such as those surrounding its Noamundi site, productive since 1925, reclaimed 165 hectares of forest, as a result of both the Project and a four-phase environmental regulation effort begun in 1980. While efforts were touted as a success, Tata Steel admitted naïveté in some of its efforts. On one occasion, reforestation efforts had been stymied after tribes, desperate for cooking fuel, cut down young saplings.

FINANCING COMPASSION

Tata Steel created the town of Jamshedpur during its economically challenged early years, when the British government favoured its own imports over domestically produced goods. Post World War I, plummeting prices, transportation difficulties, and an earthquake in Japan, its chief pig iron customer, brought Tata Steel to the verge of closure in 1924. While the company stabilised and rebounded, Tata Steel did not lay off a single worker, though its shareholders went without dividends for thirteen years. Managing Director Dorabji Tata said, in 1923, "We are constantly accused by people of wasting money in the town of Jamshedpur. We are asked why it should be necessary to spend so much on housing, sanitation, roads, hospitals and on welfare . . . Gentlemen, people who ask these questions are sadly lacking in imagination. We are not putting up a row of workman's huts in Jamshedpur, we are building a city." Though post-Independence government policies initially swung domestic economics in favour of Tata Steel, the push by the central government for rapid industrialisation spawned the emergence of a number of steel plants, later consolidated under SAIL in 1973. Despite this rising competitive presence within India in the 1950s and 1960s, social provisions at Tata Steel continued unabated.

After independence, customs tariffs rose 200–300 percent on some imports, while other products carried a total physical ban. The central government controlled the right to open new plants, expand production at existing facilities, alter prices and decide import/export quotas via issuance of licences. Demand for steel products consistently outpaced supply due to production restraints set by the government. Eccentricities in

C

EXHIBIT
8
Tata Steel Rural Development Society 2001–2002 Highlights

Activity	Count	No. of Beneficiaries	No. of Villages
Income Generation			
Land brought under cultivation (acre)	1,623.95	2,100	116
Income from cash crop (Rs in lakhs)	77.40	2,259	114
Animal Husbandry			
United established (piggery, poultry) (number)	93	212	33
Kruiler poultry	372	372	30
Sale (Rs in lakhs)	13.28	229	54
Forestry			
Sale of saplings (Rs in lakhs)	68,970	125	24
Other Income Generation Activities			
Units established (number)	15	391	20
Sale (Rs in lakhs)	4.7052	23	12
Self-Help Groups			
SHG formation (women/men)	108/39	1,256/100	29/10
Family Welfare			
Temp. methods of contraception		8,907	
Tubectomy/Vasectomy		1,334/1	
Low-cost toilet	372	2,774	94
AIDS awareness	270	3,545	87
Anaemia/iron folic acid tablet		53,108	
Blood donation		496	
Community based primary health station	30	60	30
Drinking Water Project			
Tubewell installed/repair	69/140	11,426/8,898	56/31
Tubewell training	10	100	10
Well constructed/repaired	11/18	855/625	8/6
Empowerment			
Equipment (kg)	567	740	91
Seeds (kg)	35,172.52	771	68
Land brought under irrigation (acre)	662	660	37
Wastelands/fallow land for agriculture (acre)	9	15	3
Agriculture training	253	2,408	100
Forestry			
Tree plantation	38,360	486	20
Gobar-gas plants	52	180	8
Save forest meeting	11	895	11
Veterinary Services			
Animals treated	24,295	5,544	83
Training in veterinary services/poultry	63/22	133/60	32/37
Assistance for construction/young ones	3/2,441	26/1	3/40
Education & Awareness			
Education programs	52	525	44
Adult literacy/preschool literacy	24/38	799/1,135	52/37
Sports & Culture			
Coaching	11	185	39
Outside participation	38	459	68
Inter-village tournaments	86	2,338	348
Cultural programs	16	7,052	46

legislation determined that defective products were exempt from pricing regulations. Unlike many other companies, Tata Steel refused to exploit this loophole, even though it would have returned higher margins, instead quoting products at government determined rates, well below market price. With excessive customer demand, quality of output was not a competitive point among manufacturers. State-supported steel plants limped along with inefficient production methods in the 1970s. Meanwhile, Tata Steel incorporated front-running production techniques adopted from foreign competitors in Japan and England. It developed technologies with a German oven maker to effectively utilize the unique variety of coal in Bihar.[15] Its proactive management combined with the unusual market dynamics created by the "Licence Raj" significantly bolstered Tata Steel's bottom line.

Prevented from reinvestment or facility expansion by government mandate, and unable to acquire additional businesses due to the draconian Monopolies and Restrictive Trade Practices Act (MRTP), Tata Steel funnelled its surplus earnings into community works. By directing revenue to "community expenditure" rather than profits that would be hit with corporate taxes, Tata Steel provided Jamshedpur with superior services. Tata Steel could additionally afford to recognize all its employees equally in its labour agreements. As a result its wage expenses exploded, since gardeners and teachers received compensation and employment contracts commensurate with those of steelworkers. Management rewarded worker loyalty by guaranteeing a job to the son of any employee with a twenty-five year tenure at Tata Steel.

The onset of liberalisation, however, turned the tide for stricter cost control in company operations. Taking over as Managing Director in 1993, Dr. Irani recognized oncoming competitive pressures. He drove a "modernising of the mind" and a renovation of the plant's production, which continued over the subsequent eight years. Irani introduced improved employee performance measurement systems. He approved construction of the Cold Rolling Mill, overseen by Muthuraman, which produced refined, higher margin steel products. He implemented rigorous cost reduction efforts. His endeavours earned a lengthy list of accolades for Tata Steel, including the Prime Minister's Trophy for Best Integrated Steel Mill for three successive years (1998–2000) and being named "the lowest cost steel producer in the world" by New York consultancy World Steel Dynamics in 2001. There were a number of individual leadership awards for Irani himself, including an Honorary Knighthood by the Queen of the United Kingdom.

However, Irani's renovation efforts were not without controversy, most notably concerning the significant downsizing of the bloated workforce. In 1992, when Irani and Chairman Ratan Tata embarked on a road show to generate international interest in a $100 million convertible bond issue, investors in Zurich lambasted the company's enormous employee figures. Recognizing the disproportionate growth of worker numbers relative to the increase in production levels over the previous decades, Irani embarked on a massive reduction in "family size." He reduced employee numbers from 78,000 in 1992 to 48,800 in 2001 via a generous Voluntary Redundancy Scheme.

Significantly, even in these turbulent times of workforce reductions, the company respected the labour pact signed several decades earlier. As Dr. J. J. Irani observed, "We always maintained a partnership with the unions. We formed Joint Plant Committees, included unions in cost decisions. It is necessary that they understand our cost structures extremely well. You must communicate with them in terms of money. When we told them that the family size had to go down, they accepted the change with codified rules. Once those rules have been outlined and agreed upon, you *cannot* change them or you will be opening a Pandora's box."

Mr. R. B. B. Singh, the union president, echoed this view, "We didn't contest their approach to the downsizing. It was necessary, given the political changes, and management stuck to the tenets of the 1956 agreement." On exploratory trips to Japan and Southeast Asia to assess the competitive steel environment in the 1990s, Irani invited union leaders to join him. Their first-hand encounter with the productivity discrepancy at home and abroad fortified a unified effort between Tata Steel and its union to adjust to the changing economic context by boosting efficiency and the quality of production.

Irani also decided to cap expenditure on town services in 1996, emphasizing increased efficiency on service provision. Reflecting back on that decision, Irani noted that, before liberalisation, "We had never asked ourselves the question, how much are we actually spending on social services that don't benefit our employees or communities?" When inflation soared in the 1980s, spending on social services ballooned from Rs 20 crore in 1980 to Rs 100 crore by the mid 1990s.[16]

Upon taking the helm in 2001, Muthuraman maintained the budgetary limit for the Town Division at Rs 100 crore. Of that sum, Rs 25 crore went towards running the Tata Main Hospital and other health services, with the remainder dedicated to municipal services. Managers estimated in 2003 that

C

34 percent of hospital services went to those not employed by Tata Steel, while an overall 20 percent of the company's social spending benefited those not directly employed by the company. In addition to immediate Jamshedpur expenses, Tata Steel dedicated Rs 38 crore to its community beyond town borders and employees, through the Tata Steel Rural Development Society.

ENLIGHTENED SELF-INTEREST

While few questioned Tata Steel's devotion to its community or the sincerity of its ethos, its social services were incontestably, if indirectly, self-serving. The Chief Information Officer, Varun Jha, conceded, "Of course, we realize that this compassion has beneficial implications." Ishaat Hussain, Finance Director of Tata Sons, also recognised, "Tata's social spending is not altruistic, it is enlightened self-interest. If Tata Steel didn't do it, would the company have survived until today? Tata Steel is still a shining example, an oasis. To operate in that region, you really have to be."

Santosh Gupta concurred, "In India the employee looks to his employer as if it is the government. Don't forget, there is no social security in India. Parents come back to live with their children because there is no wage coming in for them after retirement." Continuing, he explained, "For the last 25 years we have befriended the neighbouring villages. If they want a school, we give them a school. To say that we are 'buying peace' would be uncharitable, but we have maintained a pre-eminent position in their favour. I have thought of the benefits of that spending in qualitative terms, not quantitative terms. By being accommodating and understanding, we have created innumerable benefits for ourselves."

Jha reflected that if another service provider emerged, the altruistic and the required services provided by Tata Steel would be more readily distinguishable. "It is important not to confuse what we need to do out of commitment to our employees and what we do out of social good will. We would like to maintain a presence in both areas." "The challenge," added Manzer Hussain, General Manager of Town Services, "lies in finding a sustainable way of doing things."

"Now with the EVA and shareholder emphasis, Tata Steel is trying to prove that you can be both profitable and socially responsible. When there is no social safety net, where corporate entities play the role of the former maharajas . . . Until the government begins to start providing these services, we need to do so," summed up Irani.

TRADITION QUESTIONED

While Tata Steel survived liberalisation due to Irani's renovations, the oncoming years were forecast to be challenging. Global levels of manufactured steel were chronically above demand, often depressing world steel prices. The imposition of U.S. anti-dumping duties upset the international trade balance, indirectly affecting Indian steel export volumes and increasing overall competition levels. In 2000, the European Union had asked the Steel Exporters Forum of India to cut exports by 60 percent, down to 1995 levels.[iv] In the coming years, the Indian government intended to divest itself of SAIL. With margins already squeezed, steel producers had minimal latitude for further belt tightening.

The head of the Ferro-Alloy Mineral Division could feel the pressure from customers, particularly international ones: "My customers are highly conscious of quality. They are aware of our ethics, but they do want the lowest cost. International business is quite selfish. Domestically, people recognize our values, but not internationally. They care about price, price, price."

As company ownership grew among institutional investors and within the international capital markets, they also started to question the community ethos at Tata Steel. *Fortune* magazine asked whether there was a "sell-by date for Tata Steel's corporate generosity."[v] Ratan Tata, Chairman of Tata Steel, noted, "In particular, foreign shareholders think that this is baggage we are carrying and, in a manner of speaking, it is. But you have to look at the industrial harmony and so on, so I don't think you can ascribe a value to it."[vi] Manzer Hussain of Town Services made an allusion to the same dilemma: "There has been increasing financial pressure to reduce this spending, but at the same time people within the Indian context support our efforts. But where we are not competing in an Indian context, when capital is coming from the international scene, this argument for spending is less compelling."

The level of foreign share ownership was in fact relatively small, at just over 5 percent in 2003. India's long-standing investment tradition had rebounded with liberalisation. The capital markets in India boomed, with market value capitalisation multiplying over 20-fold between 1984 and 2001; and going from 14 stock exchanges to 23. By 2003, the Indian public held 32 percent of Tata Steel's shares. "The customer woke up around the time of liberalisation. Only in the last two years have our shareholders sat up. How does our total welfare orientation trickle down to the customer? To the shareholder?" asked the Vice President of Human Resources, Niroop Mahanty.

The ownership structure within the Tata Group had shifted as well. In 1991, Tata Sons was 79 percent owned by the Tata Charitable Trusts, but by 2001 that percentage had been reduced to 66 percent. At the same time, Tata Sons stake in Tata Steel had surged from under 9 percent at the outset of Irani's tenure as leader to over 26 percent in 2001. Tata Sons' growing influence emerged via subtle pressure on Tata Steel, for example, by encouraging it to invest in non-core sectors such as telecom in 2001.

The changing ownership structure, disbursing shares among a growing number of investors, prompted management to reflect on the company's community-minded philosophy. "When there is a single owner of a company, that owner has a set of values so that the culture of that person emanates through the company. J. N. Tata wanted temples, so we built temples. But in a publicly owned company, whose values are you trying to propagate?" queried Jha.

Internal debates arose concerning who should receive services and the level of expenditure. Manzer Hussain, General Manager Town Services, asked, "Where do we stop providing services? Jamshedpur is two-thirds enclosed by rivers, so those are our natural boundaries, but we continue to receive requests and demands from communities just beyond town reach for services we provide here." Yet A. D. Baijal, Executive in Charge of Raw Materials and Iron Making, countered, "At some point you have to stop giving. We teach to grow crops, provide education. We give them basic tools. They are growing wheat and making a good profit. Soon the tribes around us will want tractors. But there has to be a limit to the extent we can give."

"We don't measure the benefits to the company of our social spending. Hypothetically, if we have a new owner, how are we going to justify that expenditure? The accolades we receive for our efforts and community involvement is only the paint. We need to scratch deeper to understand what the benchmarks really are," claimed Niroop Mahanty.

WHAT NOW?

To increase the efficiency and cost effectiveness of social expenditure, Tata Steel decided to alter the delivery system of its services. Management wished to "continue the objective of the model, changing the model but not the objective." When it announced impending outsourcing of electricity services, water distribution, and schools, consternated responses poured in from towns-people and employees. There were anxious inquiries as to whether Tata Steel was abandoning its commitment

to Jamshedpur. "When we first thought of doing more outsourcing, we thought it was only between the unions and us. So we talked to the unions and then proceeded. But then letters and calls started coming in. Is Tata Steel stepping away? Now the mindset has been reconditioned. The community is far more willing to accept changes. There is a large credibility issue, and I think we do well in that category," said Hussain. In 1996, Tata Steel cared for 33,000 children in its schools. By 2003, that figure was reduced to 11,000; the other children were enrolled in schools spun off to alternative education providers. Some managers maintained that Tata Steel's core competency was not in social services, but in steel manufacturing. Determining services that required Tata Steel's monetary and human resources was essential yet not clear-cut. As Niroop Mahanty contested,

> We need to think about what is making steel and what is not making steel. We are now outsourcing water management to Vivendi, but that is an essential part of our steel business. You cannot say that it isn't core. What is core and what is not core? Education? That is definitely not core, and if I can find a company who can maintain it at the same level, it is better for students to have those specialists running it. But while we want to hand off running some services, we don't plan to sell anything. We are creating joint ventures.

Managing Director Muthuraman emphasized that outsourcing would revise the cost structure but not the benefits to the community. Attention that management previously lavished on the community was now absorbed in its new EVA campaign. "We are concentrating on EVA now because of the fact that we had not focused on it historically. Shareholders are one entity of Tata Steel which we have not treated so well in the past."

"The current vision is to be EVA positive. Past consultants, such as McKinsey, Arthur D. Little, BCG, have all said that steel does not create shareholder value . Current management is trying to do everything possible to prove that incorrect," said Sudhir Deoras, Managing Director of Tata International Limited. Widespread internal publicity, such as the EVA+ sticker campaign, had increased focus on the challenge ahead for Tata Steel. As Muthuraman confirmed, "Every worker knows what EVA is, how it translates into their daily responsibilities."

Still, dissenting opinions within Tata Steel were unconvinced that a disproportionate focus on EVA would hold long-term value for the company. "Our vision needs to inspire more than just EVA positive. We need to continue to attract people who will perpetuate

C

Country	Competitor	1999 EVA	1999 Profits	1999 Production
Brazil	Gerdau	(BRL172 m)	BRL360.1 m	5 mt
France	Usinor	(Frf5,306 m)	(€178 m)	21 mt
United States	U.S. Steel	($230 m)	$44 m	12 mt
United States	Nucor	($60 m)	$244.59 m	10.4 mt
Netherlands	Ispat International	(€140 m)	$85 m	~15.5 mt

Source: Stern Stewart and Company Web sites.

the Tata Steel culture," noted D. R. Mody of the Tata Management Development Centre.

A former executive commented, "The vision is stated in two parts. EVA they will know their success in achieving. What attempt has Tata Steel made to measure the second-half, the community benefits side of their vision? They should have the form, and they do, but they need to go beyond the form of their vision to the content. Will they neglect, or be forced to neglect, the second part? The EVA+ sticker is everywhere. But where is the sticker for community?"

NOTES

i. Kanavi, S. (2001) "Given the right incentives, India can be a steel supplier to the world," *Business India*, July 23.

ii. United Nations website: www.un.org/partners.

iii. Lala, R. M. (1981) *The Creation of Wealth: The Tata Story*, IBH Publishers Limited, Bombay: 17.

iv. Author unknown (2000) "EU to review import duties against Indian steelmakers" *American Metal Market*, August 2: 4.

v. Ellis, E. (2002) "Tata Steels itself for change," *Fortune*, April 29: 60.

vi. Kanavi, S. (2001) "Given right incentives, India can be a steel supplier to the world," *Business India*, July 23.

1. EVA (Economic Value Added) is a registered trademark of Stern Stewart & Co.

2. In November 2001, the state of Jharkhand was created from territory previously part of the state of Bihar.

3. This case uses Indian monetary and numerical conventions throughout. The rupee is the primary unit of Indian currency and, in 2004, traded at approximately 45 INR (Indian Rupees) to the U.S. dollar. One lakh = 100,000 (typically written as 1,00,000) and one crore = 100 lakhs.

4. A detailed historical account of the community works provided by Tata Steel can be found in: Pandey, S. N. (1991) *Social Side of Tata Steel*, Tata McGraw-Hill Publishing Company Limited, New Delhi.

5. For a comparative measure, in the U.S., the cost of steel strikes to the economy averaged $116 million annually between 1950 and 1972. At a total expense of $2.55 billion over the twenty-two year period, the present day conversion of the 1960 value according to the consumer price index, would be $15.92 billion.

6. A communist-led union tried to take over the plant in 1958, and the ensuing inter-union conflict resulted in a work stoppage for several days.

7. In June 1975, Prime Minister Indira Gandhi declared a 21-month state of national emergency, thus creating what amounted to a constitutional dictatorship.

8. Report of the National Commission on Labour of India, Ministry of Labour.

9. Lala, R. M. (1981) *The Creation of Wealth*, IBH Publishers, Bombay: 219.

10. J. R. D. Tata had already witnessed the nationalisation and subsequent economic downfall of his Air-India International. Though he continued as Chairman after nationalisation in 1953, his services were later terminated by the Prime Minister in 1978. At the time of Fernandes' nationalisation attempt, Tata ownership was less than 4 percent of Tata Steel.

11. Rallis India is a Tata group company in the agro-chemical industry; Rajeev Dubey was previously with Tata Steel.

12. TRF Limited, an engineering equipment provider, is a Tata Group company located in Jamshedpur.

13. In the 2002 Corruption Perceptions Index from Transparency International, India was ranked 71st of 102 most corrupt countries in terms of the degree to which corruption is perceived to exist among public officials and politicians.

14. Even in 2003, train travel between Calcutta and Jamshedpur took five hours.

15. This coal was generally considered to be of inferior quality and thus had little market value.

16. According to the Time Series of Wholesale Price Index in India from *Statistical Outline of India, 2001–2002*, published by Tata Services Limited, if 1993–1994 is taken as the base at 100, 1970–1971=14.4, 1980–1981=37.1, 1990–1991=73.7, 2000–2001=155.7.

Doing the Right Thing: Bank One's Response to the Mutual Fund Scandal

Christine Uber Grosse

Thunderbird, The Garvin School of International Management

INTRODUCTION

Jamie Dimon, CEO of Bank One Corporation, sipped his coffee in the boardroom of J.P. Morgan Chase & Co. while he waited for William B. Harrison, Jr. to arrive. Although the merger between their two banks wouldn't be finalized for a few more days, he felt at home in the World Headquarters building at 270 Park Avenue in midtown Manhattan. It was good to be back in New York. He'd left the city and number two position at Citibank after a falling out with its CEO, Sandy Weil, in 1999. A year later, Dimon became CEO of Bank One and moved to Chicago.

The merger of Bank One and J.P. Morgan Chase would be finalized on July 1, 2004, creating the second largest financial institution in the world. Mr. Harrison, CEO of J.P. Morgan Chase, had called the meeting today with Mr. Dimon to discuss the final settlement of the charges brought by the Securities and Exchange Commission (SEC) and New York State Attorney General Eliot Spitzer against Banc One Investment Advisors Corporation.

As he waited for Harrison, Dimon went over the events of the last ten months that had rocked the pristine mutual fund industry. The widespread probe into trading practices could have tarnished Bank One's reputation in the financial community. Dimon was relieved that the situation would be resolved shortly. He was ready to brief Harrison on the final details of the settlement before it became public.

BACKGROUND OF THE INVESTIGATION

In September 2003, the mutual fund scandal started when Bank One, Bank of America, Janus, and Strong Capital came under investigation for improper and/or illegal trading practices. They were named in a complaint brought by the SEC and Eliot Spitzer's office against Canary Capital Partners. Bank One was the last of the four companies to reach a settlement with the SEC. Under pressure to reach an agreement before the merger with J.P. Morgan Chase took place, Bank One agreed to a $90 million settlement. Although the company neither admitted nor denied wrongdoing, it agreed to pay $50 million in fines and restitution, and reduce fees charged to investors in its mutual funds by $40 million over the next five years. In addition, Mark Beeson, former head of Bank One's mutual fund division, agreed to pay a $100,000 fine. He was also banned from the industry for two years.

Bank One's $90 million settlement was considerably less than the $675 million in fines and restitution that Bank of America/Fleet Boston paid for its role in the scandal. Like Bank One, Bank of America reached an agreement with the SEC just before its merger with Fleet Boston. Bank of America paid a higher price because of a broader case in which one of its brokers faced criminal charges. The scandal spread far beyond the four companies named in the complaint against Canary Capital. Less than a year after the original charges were brought, dozens of

THUNDERBIRD
THE GARVIN SCHOOL OF
INTERNATIONAL MANAGEMENT

Case 2 / Doing the Right Thing: Bank One's Response to the Mutual Fund Scandal |

mutual fund companies had paid over $2.5 billion in fines, restitution, and fee cuts (Brewster, 2004).

Nothing is more important to us than maintaining the highest ethical standards.

— Jamie Dimon, September 9, 2003

Long known in the financial community for his integrity, Dimon addressed the allegations of improper trading as soon as they became public in September 2003. Quickly, he developed a strategy that involved cooperation, transparency, and communication to lead the bank out of the crisis. He focused on "doing the right thing," a value he consistently emphasized at the bank. In a message to employees, Dimon (September 9, 2003) wrote, "At Bank One we talk a lot about doing the right thing, and I promise we will do the right thing in this situation."

In the same message, Dimon outlined the steps that Bank One would take to respond to the mutual fund scandal. Echoing the theme of doing the right thing, Dimon wrote, "Nothing is more important to us than maintaining the highest ethical standards." He also emphasized that the bank took its responsibility to shareholders very seriously. He mentioned that the bank shared the interests of the New York Attorney General and regulators to safeguard the integrity of the mutual fund industry.

Dimon's message to employees established the major components of his strategy that were followed throughout the crisis:

- Do the right thing
- Maintain the highest ethical standards
- Take the bank's responsibility to mutual fund shareholders seriously
- Cooperate fully with the New York Attorney General and regulators
- Review and evaluate policies and procedures quickly and thoroughly
- Take disciplinary action as needed against employees
- Make restitution to shareholders
- Communicate and promote transparency

Dimon promised a swift and thorough gathering of the facts. In the interest of transparency and communication, Dimon pledged to communicate with bank employees and mutual fund shareholders as appropriate, and encouraged bank employees to share his letter with any Bank One customers who were interested. However, Dimon requested employees to withhold comment or speculation until the investigation uncovered the facts. He also asked for their patience, since it

would clearly take some time before the investigation was completed.

Throughout the crisis, the bank adhered to the basic strategy outlined in that letter to employees. How well did his strategy pay off? Did his leadership, commitment to doing the right thing, transparent action, and communication help Bank One regain customer trust and move beyond the mutual fund scandal?

ABOUT BANK ONE AND J.P. MORGAN CHASE & CO.

Bank One Corporation's wholly owned indirect subsidiary, Banc One Investment Advisors (BOIA), came under investigation in the mutual fund probe. BOIA offered investment management services, including One Group Mutual Funds, to individuals and companies. One Group Mutual Funds managed over $100 billion in assets. BOIA, whose headquarters were in Columbus, OH, registered with the SEC as an investment adviser on November 22, 1991. BOIA was a wholly owned subsidiary of Bank One, National Association (Ohio), which in turn was a wholly owned subsidiary of Bank One Corporation.

Before its merger with J.P. Morgan Chase & Co. on July 1, 2004, Bank One was the sixth largest bank in the United States, with assets of around $320 billion. Bank One served about 20,000 middle market clients and approximately seven million retail households. The bank issued over 51 million credit cards and managed investment assets of about $188 billion.

On July 1, 2004, Bank One merged with J.P. Morgan Chase & Co. The combined financial services firm had assets of about $1.12 trillion. Operating in over 50 countries, the company provided financial services for consumers and businesses, investment banking, asset and wealth management, financial transaction processing, and private equity. With corporate headquarters in New York, J.P. Morgan Chase would maintain headquarters for U.S. retail financial services and commercial banking in Chicago (*Wall Street Journal Online*, 2004).

SITUATION LEADING UP TO THE SCANDAL

On September 3, 2003, New York State Attorney General Eliot L. Spitzer and the SEC brought charges against Canary Capital Partners, a hedge fund, for illegal after-hours trading and improper market timing. In this complaint, Bank One and three other mutual fund firms were named for making special deals with Canary to conduct the improper mutual fund trades.

C

Probes into mutual fund trading focused on late trading and market timing. Late trading, an illegal practice, occurs when mutual fund orders that are placed after 4 p.m. are processed at the same-day price rather than the price set on the following day. Law requires that late trades be placed at the following day's price.

Although market timing, also known as timing, is not illegal, many mutual fund prospectuses discourage investors from doing it. Timing involves the rapid buying and selling of mutual fund shares by short-term investors who try to take advantage of inefficiencies in the pricing of mutual funds. Timers hope to profit from fund share prices that lag behind the value of the underlying securities.

Share prices of mutual funds are set at 4 p.m. Eastern Standard Time (EST) based on the values of their portfolio holdings. Any trades placed after 4 p.m. EST are supposed to be charged at the next day's prices to keep investors from taking advantage of news that happens after the close of trading (Carey, 2003).

Like many other funds, One Group Mutual Funds had policies that discouraged market timing, because it skimmed profits from the accounts of other shareholders. By giving special permission to certain large investors to market time, BOIA earned higher management fees from those investors' accounts (Lauricella, 2004).

Market timing could hurt long-term investors by driving up costs and reducing their profits (Johnson, 2003). The rapid in-and-out trading can cause an increase in transaction costs since the portfolio manager may have to buy and sell securities in response to the hedge fund's trades. These costs are normally borne by the mutual fund.

In addition, the *dilution effect* occurs when the fund has to pay for the timers' profits out of its own finite pool of assets (Carey, 2003). The profits usually are paid from the fund's cash holdings or a sale of securities to cover the payment. In either case, shareholders are hurt because the total amount of assets available in the mutual fund is diminished.

Some blame the practice of market timing on stale pricing. Because mutual fund prices are adjusted only once a day, they frequently go out of date, hence stale. The fund's underlying securities change value throughout the day, and may be spread across different time zones. Large investors can use sophisticated technology to take advantage of the differences between the prices of the fund's shares and the fund's assets (*Arizona Republic*, 2003).

The effects of Canary's market timing apparently took a toll on Bank One mutual fund managers. According to the Canary settlement document, the managers complained to One Group President Mark Beeson about the impact of Canary's timing activity on their funds (Atlas, 2003). In April 2003, Canary stopped trading in Bank One's mutual funds when Beeson no longer felt comfortable waiving penalties for their frequent trading.

ONE GROUP RESTRICTIONS AGAINST TIMING

Mark A. Beeson held the positions of President and CEO of One Group Mutual Funds from January 2000 until his resignation in October 2003. In 1994 Beeson began working at BOIA as the chief financial officer. After two years, he was promoted to chief administrative officer.

From June 2002 until May 2003, Mark A. Beeson and One Group allowed Canary Capital to make 300 buy-and-sell transactions in several domestic and international stock funds. Canary earned a profit of around $5.2 million from this market timing. In addition, Canary was not charged around $4 million in penalties that it should have paid for market timing (SEC Order, 2004).

Prospectuses in the One Group put restrictions on excessive exchange activity in all the One Group mutual funds. Exchange of any investment in the funds was limited to "two substantive exchange redemptions within 30 days of each other." In November 2001, One Group set a 2% early redemption fee for any international fund redemption made within 90 days of purchase. It also reserved the right to refuse any exchange request that would negatively affect shareholders. In fact, over 300 exchange privilege violations were identified by Beeson and BOIA between January 2002 and September 2003 (SEC Order, 2004).

Late in 2001, Edward Stern, head of Canary Capital, made a proposal through Security Trust Corporation to BOIA. He offered to borrow $25 million from Bank One and match it with $25 million of his own funds if he were allowed to trade in certain mutual funds. Beeson refused the proposal several times. But after talking it over with Security Trust Corporation and Bank One employees, Beeson decided to consider letting Stern trade in certain Bank One funds in March 2002.

Although Bank One's chief operating officer advised against it, Beeson allowed Edward Stern to trade in several domestic and two international funds for up to half of one percent of the fund's value. For trading purposes, Bank One loaned $15 million to Stern, who matched it with his own $15 million. Stern agreed that the entire amount would stay within Bank One as security for the loan. BOIA did not charge Stern the 2% redemption fee normally required for any trade made less than 90 days after an initial purchase. This would have amounted to around $4.2 million in redemption fees.

In January 2003, Stern received a second Bank One loan of $15 million, which he again matched with $15 million of his own funds. He also used this money to trade in One Group funds. Between June 2002 and April 2003, Stern earned a net profit of about $5.2 million from approximately 300 in-and-out trades. From this arrangement, Bank One gained the interest on the loans and BOIA increased mutual fund sales and associated fees. According to the SEC settlement document (2004), the agreements with Canary Capital were never discussed with the One Group Board of Trustees.

Another possible reason why Beeson agreed to the arrangement was the hope of doing future business with Stern. On several occasions, he discussed Stern's possible investment in a Bank One hedge fund, but that investment never took place (SEC Order, 2004).

Other customers besides Canary Capital received special treatment from BOIA. Apparently without Beeson's knowledge, a Texas hedge fund was excused from paying the 2% redemption fee in March 2003. Although the Texas company invested $43 million in two international funds and redeemed the investment three days later, it did not have to pay about $840,000 in redemption fees. BOIA did not reimburse the two international funds for the fees that it didn't collect.

As standard procedure, the portfolio holdings of One Group mutual funds were considered confidential information that was published only as required by law. Nonetheless, Stern asked for and received monthly updates on the eight funds in which he had investments from July 2002 until April 2003 when the relationship ended. Beeson provided him with this information without any confidentiality agreement. The investigation also found that BOIA provided One Group's portfolio holdings to other special clients over a period of ten years. This information was given out as often as once a week to seven clients, eight prospective clients, and several dozen consultants from pension funds or fund advisers.

The special trading arrangements for Stern and others began to unravel in July 2003. Noreen Harrington, a former Hartz investments officer, blew the whistle on improper trading practices at Canary Capital. She quoted Eddie Stern as saying, "If I ever get in trouble, they're not going to want me, they're going to want the mutual funds" (Vickers, 2004). New York Attorney General Eliot Spitzer subpoenaed Stern and named him in a complaint for having engaged in "fraudulent" schemes of late trading and market tim-

ing of mutual funds. Two months later, Canary Capital settled with the SEC and Attorney General's office for $40 million. Canary agreed to pay $30 million in restitution for profits gained by improper trading, as well as a $10 million penalty. Canary neither admitted nor denied wrongdoing.

THE MUTUAL FUND INDUSTRY

Shock waves hit Wall Street when Spitzer's investigations began into trading abuses in the mutual fund industry. Few outside the financial community expected to see a scandal occur there. As the probe continued, it uncovered improper trading practices at dozens of mutual fund companies. New York Attorney General Eliot Spitzer called the industry "a cesspool" (Waggoner, Dugas & Fogarty, 2003). Half of the 88 largest mutual fund groups had permitted favored investors to buy mutual fund shares at stale prices, skimming profits from long-term shareholders (Quinn, 2003).

Pricing had been an issue in the mutual fund industry for a long time. In the 1930s, mutual funds often had two prices: a public price, as well as a more up-to-date price that a few big investors could access just before the price became public. The privileged investors who knew where mutual fund prices were going could make fast profits. In response, Congress passed the Investment Company Act of 1940 in an attempt to make mutual fund pricing policies fairer. Among other rules, it required funds to have just one public price.

According to Mr. Spitzer, mutual fund companies made over $50 billion in management fees in 2002. He was the first to suggest that the widespread practice of preferential trading for big investors could be channeling billions of dollars away from everyday long-term investors in mutual funds. Mr. Spitzer commented on ways that companies could make amends. "If they're expecting to get settlements (with regulators), they're going to have to give much more back than just (investors') losses. They're going to be paying stiff fines and giving back their management fees. They violated their trust with the American investor" (Gordon, 2003).

Spitzer also expressed dissatisfaction with the SEC's oversight of the industry. Paul Roye headed the mutual fund division of the SEC. "Heads should roll at the SEC. There is a whole division at the SEC that is supposed to be looking at mutual funds. Where have they been?" According to SEC Chairman William Donaldson, the SEC was considering new curbs on fund trading (Gordon, 2003).

The question remained how the scandal would affect the mutual fund industry. Arthur Levitt, former

SEC chair, said, "This seems to be the most egregious violation of the public trust of any of the events of recent years. Investors may realize they can't trust the bond market or they can't trust a stock broker or analysts, but mutual funds have been havens of security and integrity" (Lauricella, 10/20/03). How many of the 95 million customers would cash in their shares?

Investors apparently didn't lose faith in all mutual funds. John C. Bogle, founder of the Vanguard Group, believed that money was flowing out of companies that had lost investor confidence and into companies that had kept their good reputations for being well managed or holding down costs and fees (Lauricella, 10/20/03).

Indeed, stock funds gained $23.2 billion in December 2003, up from $14 billion in November 2003, according to AMG Data Services in Arcata, California. More than half of the new money went into three funds which were not implicated in the investigations: Fidelity, Vanguard, and American Funds (McGeehan, 2004). As of November 2003, Putnam lost a net $11.1 billion from its stock funds, while investors withdrew about $2.2 billion from Janus Capital's stock funds. Much of that may have been reinvested in other mutual funds.

DEVELOPMENTS AT BANK ONE

Bank One took a number of actions as the investigation progressed. Several weeks after the probe began, Mark Beeson, the head of One Group, resigned. To replace him, Dimon appointed Dave Kundert, head of the bank's investment management group.

Peter C. Marshall, Chairman of the Board of Trustees of One Group Mutual Funds, sent a letter and prospectus supplement on October 10, 2003, to all mutual fund customers informing them of the complaint filed by the New York State Attorney General against Canary Capital Partners, LLC. The prospectus supplement included detailed information about legal proceedings related to the complaint which found that Canary engaged in improper trading practices with certain Bank One mutual funds.

In the letter Marshall wrote, "Nothing is more important to your Board than to get all the facts and to resolve this matter as soon as possible" (Marshall, 2003). He echoed Jamie Dimon's commitment to find out the facts quickly and do the right thing. He informed shareholders that a special review committee had been created to help gather and review information concerning the alleged trading activities. He assured the shareholders that they would receive restitution if they had been harmed by the wrongful conduct of any Bank

One employee. Furthermore, he made it clear that every member of the One Group Board of Trustees was independent. As Jamie Dimon had done in September, Marshall affirmed that the Board was committed to meeting the highest standards in the industry and putting shareholders' interests first.

Shortly after Marshall's letter came out, Jamie Dimon sent an e-mail update to employees concerning the mutual fund investigation (October 15, 2003). He summarized the key findings. Canary Capital Partners, hedge fund was allowed to trade eleven One Group funds more often than other customers over an 11-month period ending in May, 2003. The investment by Canary averaged 0.5% of the fund's assets and never went over 1%. Dimon regretted the special arrangement with Canary and stated that it never should have happened.

The investigation into whether shareholders were financially harmed was continuing. The bank would make full restitution if it found this to be true. The bank would continue to see if other clients had similar arrangements, but so far they had not found the problem to be widespread or systemic.

Bank One terminated its contract with Security Trust Company, a back-office firm that processed Canary's transactions in One Group mutual funds. Although it was not accused of any wrongdoing in Spitzer's suit, the firm could not assure Bank One that they had abided by their contract, which stated that the only trades that could be sent to One Group for same-day pricing were those "received prior to market close." No evidence was found that Bank One or Bank One employees made after-market trading arrangements.

Next, Dimon announced five changes that would strengthen oversight and transparency of mutual fund policies and procedures at Bank One. First, Dave Kundert took over as President of One Group. Second, the bank implemented improved computer monitoring and compliance measures. Third, employees would receive internal training on how to identify inappropriate timing practices. Fourth, the bank enhanced agreements with service providers to receive assurance that they had internal policies and controls to prevent going around One Group's policies concerning market timing and excessive trading. Fifth, the bank continued to review mutual fund policies in order to meet the highest standards.

As he had done in a previous message, Dimon promoted transparency and communication by encouraging employees to share his letter with any Bank One customers who had questions. He also promised to give additional updates as appropriate.

TAKING THE MATTER SERIOUSLY

It was important for Bank One to convince the SEC, shareholders, and customers that it was taking the charges seriously. As a result, this theme appears in each public communication from the Bank. In Marshall's letter to One Group Shareholders (2003), he emphasizes how seriously the Board of Trustees is taking the matter. "On behalf of the One Group Board of Trustees, I want to convey to you the seriousness with which your board takes its responsibility to One Group mutual fund shareholders."

Dan McNeela, an analyst for Morningstar, Inc., responded to Dimon's personnel changes and plans for change. "This confirms our opinion that Jamie Dimon is taking the matter seriously, but it may not be enough simply to ask a couple of executives to leave and say everything is okay" (Manor, 2003).

Dave Kundert, President of One Group Funds, addressed the mutual fund scandal at Bank One in a message sent to employees on November 26, 2004. He explained that it was likely that the bank would face enforcement action against Banc One Investment Advisors. However, he expressed optimism that "we can avoid regulatory litigation and reach an amicable resolution with the regulators over the next several months."

Kundert outlined to employees the broad changes in policies and procedures that Bank One had recently implemented in the One Group mutual funds. They had established a 100% independent Board of Trustees. They would continue to cooperate with the Attorney General's and SEC's investigations.

After holding a public dialog on best practices in the industry, they selected and implemented a number of best practices which included the following:

- Hiring a new compliance officer
- Increase training for employees
- Disclosure of more information about fund managers' salaries
- Change how research fees are negotiated, paid, and disclosed to investors (Johnson, 2003)
- Addition of redemption fees to certain funds
- Allow employees of the fund company to only buy One Group fund shares through Banc One Securities Corp. accounts or One Group, and require holding the One Group funds for at least 90 days (Shipman, 2003)
- Disclosure of portfolio holdings quarterly on the fund company's Web site
- Cap individual purchases of Class B shares. These shares had a back-end sales charge and higher expenses than Class A shares, which had a front-end

charge that declined as people invested more (Stempel, 2003)

Richard Bove, analyst at Hoefer and Arnett, confirmed that "Jamie Dimon has indicated that if Bank One had done anything inappropriate, he would take any action necessary to correct what was wrong." He commented that "it's pretty clear that Bank One will pay sizable fines, not because it did anything malicious but because of a lack of control" (Stempel, 2003).

On a conference call discussing third quarter earnings with executives at Bank One Corporation, Jamie Dimon reaffirmed his commitment to doing the right thing. "I look at this as a chance for Bank One, even though we made some errors here, to earn your and our customers' respect by standing tall and doing the right thing, and not only look at these problems, (but try) to improve other things that should be fixed in the mutual fund business" (Siegel, 2003).

SETTLEMENT AGREEMENTS

On June 29, 2004, Banc One Investment Advisors agreed on a settlement with the Securities and Exchange Commission and the New York Attorney General's office concerning issues related to One Group mutual fund trading. The mutual fund unit of Bank One had "allowed improper short-term trading of its fund shares at the expense of other shareholders." According to Stephen Cutler, director of the SEC's division of enforcement, "Bank One and Mark Beeson blatantly disregarded the well-being of One Group funds' long-term shareholders" (Lauricella, 2004).

Bank One agreed to the settlement without admitting or denying any wrongdoing. Philip Khinda, counsel to the One Group of funds and their board of trustees, commented on the settlement agreement. "It's a very fair result and a product of the commitment of everyone involved to doing right by the shareholders of the funds" (Lauricella, 2004).

The Securities and Exchange Commission found that Banc One Investment Advisors (BOIA) and Mark Beeson, President and Chief Executive Officer of One Group Mutual Funds and a senior managing director of BOIA, violated and/or aided and abetted or caused violations of the antifraud provisions of the Advisers Act and the Investment Company Act by the following:

1. Allowing excessive short-term trading in One Group funds by a hedge-fund manager that was inconsistent with the terms of the funds' prospectuses and that was potentially harmful to the funds;
2. Failing to disclose to the One Group Board of Trustees or to shareholders the conflict of interest

C

created when Respondents entered into a market-timing arrangement with a hedge-fund manager that was potentially harmful to One Group, but that would increase BOIA's advisory fees and potentially attract additional business;

3. Failing to charge the hedge-fund manager redemption fees as required by the international funds' prospectuses when other investors were charged the redemption fees;

4. Having no written procedures in place to prevent the nonpublic disclosure of One Group portfolio holdings and improperly providing confidential portfolio holdings to the hedge-fund manager when shareholders were not provided with or otherwise privy to the same information;

5. Causing One Group funds, without the knowledge of the funds' trustees, to participate in joint transactions, raising a conflict of interest in violation of the Investment Company Act (from the SEC Order, June 29, 2004, p. 2).

In the settlement agreement, Bank One agreed that Banc One Investment Advisors would pay $10 million in restitution, as well as pay $40 million as a penalty. The entire amount of $50 million would be paid to shareholders. It would be placed in an escrow account to be distributed to eligible shareholders through a plan created by an independent consultant and approved by the SEC and One Group Board of Trustees.

In addition, Banc One Investment Advisors agreed to reduce advisory fees by $8 million per year for five years. In addition, BOIA would not raise advisory fees for five years.

Mark Beeson, former President and Chief Executive Officer of the One Group Mutual Funds unit of Bank One, was banned for two years from the mutual fund industry and fined $100,000 for his role in improper short-term trading. Beeson neither admitted nor denied any wrongdoing.

THE AFTERMATH

After the settlement, David J. Kundert, Chairman and CEO of Banc One Investment Advisors, remarked, "Soon after we first learned of these investigations, we committed to cooperate with regulators, make restitution to shareholders, and review and change our policies as appropriate. The monetary and governance

actions outlined in these agreements build upon the controls and policies we initiated last fall to fulfill that commitment. Strong procedures are now in place to further protect the interests of our mutual fund shareholders and prevent a recurrence of similar issues in the future" (CT News Archive, June 29, 2004).

Peter C. Marshall, Chairman of the One Group Board of Trustees, explained the settlement in an August 2004 letter to One Group Mutual Fund shareholders. The prospectus that was enclosed with Marshall's letter outlined the steps that the bank would take to implement the settlement. The One Group Mutual Funds Supplement that accompanied the letter informed investors that they would receive a proportionate share of the money lost from market-timing, as well as advisory fees paid by the affected funds during the market-timing. Payment was expected to be made in 2005.

The final lines of the enclosed prospectus cautions shareholders that "It is possible, although not likely, that these matters and/or related developments may result in increased Fund redemptions and reduced sales of Fund shares, which could result in increased costs and expenses or otherwise adversely affect the Funds." The outcomes of the settlements and reforms implemented by Bank One, now J.P. Morgan Chase and Co., remained to be seen.

Would Dimon's strategy of ethical behavior, transparency, and communication restore confidence in the funds? Or would fund redemptions increase and sales of shares decrease? What would be the effect of the investigations and resulting settlements on the industry? What reforms would be adopted by, or imposed on, the mutual fund industry?

ACKNOWLEDGMENTS

The author gratefully acknowledges the support and assistance of Beth Dowie, Vice President of Support Services, J.P. Morgan Chase & Co. She also thanks Andrew Inkpen, Director of the Thunderbird Case Clearinghouse, for financial support of the project; Helen Grassbaugh, Administrative Assistant for the Thunderbird Case Clearinghouse; and Georgia Lessard, Documentation Specialist. She also appreciates the patience and insights of Robert E. Grosse, professor of international business at Thunderbird.

REFERENCES

Arizona Republic. "Mutual Fund Woes Blamed on 'Stale Pricing'," November 11, 2003, D7.

Atlas, Riva D. "Justice Obstruction Charges Called Possible in Fund Case," *New York Times,* October 16, 2003.

CT News Archive. "Banc One Investment Advisors Confirms Mutual Funds Settlement Agreements," June 29, 2004.

Brewster, Deborah. "Banc One Pays $50m on Market Timing," *Financial Times,* June 30, 2004, p. 18.

Carey, Susan. "Fund Probe Spurs Bank One Exits," *Wall Street Journal,* October 16, 2003.

Dimon, Jamie. Internal Message, September 9, 2003.

Dimon, Jamie. Internal Message, October 15, 2003.

Gordon, Marcy. "Congress Joins Probe of Mutual Fund Scam," AOL News November 3, 2003. http://aolsvc.news.aol.com/news/.

Johnson, Carrie. "Bank One Expecting Regulatory Actions: Firm was Named Early in Mutual Funds Probe," *Washington Post,* November 27, 2003.

Kundert, Dave. Bank One Internal Message to Employees, November 26, 2003.

Lauricella, Tom. "Probe Signals Shake-Up for Mutual Fund Industry," *Wall Street Journal,* October 20, 2003.

Lauricella, Tom. "Bank One Unit Agrees to Pay $90 Million Over Fund Trades." *Wall Street Journal,* June 30, 2004, pp. A1, A5.

Manor, Robert. "Bank One Exec Quits over Fund Trading," *Chicago Tribune,* October 16, 2003.

Marshall, Peter C. Letter to Bank One Mutual Fund Customers, October 10, 2003.

Marshall, Peter C. Letter to Bank One Mutual Fund Customers, July 8, 2004.

McGeehan, Patrick. "Mutual Fund Industry Booms Despite Scandal," *The New York Times,* January 11, 2004.

One Group Mutual Funds Supplement, dated July 8, 2004, to all One Group Mutual Fund prospectuses dated on or after February 28, 2004.

Quinn, Jane Bryant. "Mutual Funds' Greed Machine," *Newsweek,* November 24, 2003, p. 45.

Shipman, John. "Bank One's Fund Unit Told to Expect Enforcement Action," Dow Jones Newswire, November 26, 2003.

Siegel, Tara. "Bank One CEO Reiterates Restitution for Hurt Fund Holders," Dow Jones Newswire, October 22, 2003.

Stempel, Jonathan. "Bank One Expects Enforcement Action," Reuters News Service, November 26, 2003.

Vickers, Marcia. "Dynasty in Distress," *Business Week,* February 9, 2004, pp. 63–70.

Waggoner, John, Christine Dugas, and Thomas A. Fogarty. "SEC Wades through a Mutual-Fund 'Cesspool'," *The Arizona Republic,* November 4, 2003, pp. D1, D3.

Wall Street Journal Online. "JPMorgan Chase, Bank One Complete Merger," Press Release July 1, 2004, http://online.wsj.com/article/0,,PR_CO_20040701_000009,00.html.

Wall Street Journal Online. "Securities and Exchange Commission Order to Banc One Investment Advisors Corporation and Mark A. Beeson," June 29, 2004.

Louis V. Gerstner Jr.—The Man Who Turned IBM Around

Konakanchi Prashanth
Vivek Gupta

ICFAI University Press, Business School Case Development Centre

Louis is an incredibly focused executive, he makes it very clear to everyone what his expectations are.

—John W. Thompson, former general manager of IBM's North American Sales Group[1]

He's thinking like a businessman and IBM hasn't had someone at the top thinking like a businessman for many years. IBM's chairmen have for years treated the company like an institution that couldn't be changed. But Gerstner is going through a methodical, unsentimental resuscitation of IBM.

—Edwin Black, publisher of *OS/2 Professionals*, an IT magazine in the United States[2]

INTRODUCTION

In 1993, IBM, a global leader in the information technology (IT) industry, was in deep financial trouble. The company had reported a record net loss of $8.1 billion. Many analysts wrote off IBM as dead. However, eight years down the line in 2001, the company reported a net income of $7.7 billion (see Exhibit 1). During the period 1993–2001, the share price of IBM shot up by nearly 800 percent. This was the period in which Louis V. Gerstner Jr. headed IBM.

Under the leadership of Gerstner, IBM made a remarkable comeback and proved its critics wrong. In doing so, IBM seemed to have made significant changes which had an impact on the entire IT industry. It strategically positioned its server family to suit the needs of the emerging Enterprise Resource Planning (ERP) and e-commerce applications. IBM also changed its emphasis from being product-centric to being customer-centric in order to provide complete solutions to its clients.

Gerstner played a major role in reviving the fortunes of IBM. Under Gerstner, the image of IBM was transformed from a company that primarily manufactured mainframes to a company that offered complete solutions in hardware, software, and other technologies. Gerstner brought about a radical change in the work culture of IBM. The turnaround was achieved by a series of well calculated and unconventional moves, which appeared unreasonable to many employees of IBM as well as industry analysts.

According to analysts, Gerstner's style of functioning was quite different from that of his predecessors. He was a man of conviction and always followed his own instincts. He was seldom disturbed by what his critics said. He believed that his deeds spoke for himself. He wanted results and expected his employees to give the results at any cost. He did not mince words when it came to expressing his views on their performance.

Gerstner never believed in setting long-term plans. Instead, he focused on immediate problems, and evolved strategies to solve them. He identified the needs of customers, and developed solutions to satisfy their needs. Gerstner watched the IT industry closely and carefully and was quick to foresee the trends that were likely to emerge in the future. He was among the few people who visualized that networking could transform the way people worked. While visualizing these changes was not exceptional, converting these visions into the potential opportunities was indeed exceptional.

This case was written by Konakanchi Prashanth, under the direction of Vivek Gupta. Reprinted by permission of ICFAI Center for Management Research.

EXHIBIT 1	Financial Performance of IBM for the Period 1992–2001									
	1992	**1993**	**1994**	**1995**	**1996**	**1997**	**1998**	**1999**	**2000**	**2001**
Sales revenues ($ bn)	64.5	62.7	64.1	71.9	75.9	78.5	81.7	87.5	88.4	85.9
Net income ($ bn)	(4.97)	(8.1)	3.0	4.2	5.4	6.1	6.3	7.7	8.1	7.7
Earnings per share (in $)	(2.17)	(3.55)	1.24	1.76	2.5	3.00	3.29	4.12	4.44	4.35
Employees (000s)	301.5	256.2	219.8	225.3	240.6	269.5	291.1	307.4	316.3	319.9

Source: Louis Gerstner, *Who Says Elephants Can't Dance*, pp. 356–358, 361.

BACKGROUND NOTE

Gerstner was born on March 1, 1942 in Minolta, New York. His father was a traffic manager at F&M Schaefer Corporation Brewery. Right from his childhood, his parents stressed the importance of education and discipline. Thus, they helped to a great extent in shaping his attitude towards life. Gerstner graduated in engineering at Dartmouth[3] in 1963. Two years later, he earned a business management degree from Harvard Business School.

Fresh out of college, Gerstner joined the reputed management consultancy firm McKinsey & Company in 1965, earning the distinction of being the youngest manager to be hired by the firm at that time. He soon became noted as a hard taskmaster. Within four years of joining, he was promoted to partner. He was among the selected few who were offered partnership before six years, which was the general practice. In 1973, he was promoted to senior partner in the firm and was responsible for handling major clients. Two years later, in 1975, he was appointed as a director of the firm. He was the youngest director of the firm. During his 13 years' tenure at McKinsey, Gerstner had many accomplishments to his credit, prominent among them being devising the financial strategy practice for McKinsey, helping the transportation firm Penn Central Railway[4] turn around from the verge of bankruptcy, and helping American Express[5] to expand its business. He was also a member of the leadership committee at the firm. An important leadership lesson that Gerstner learned at McKinsey was to thoroughly focus on the problem at hand and create an environment that encouraged people to come out with their ideas, irrespective of their designation in the firm.

In 1978, Gerstner joined American Express as an Executive Vice President in the credit card division. A year later, he was promoted to Executive Vice President of American Express cards and the President of the Travel Related Services (TRS) division.[6] Gerstner went on to become the president of American Express in 1985. During his stint with the firm (which lasted for 11 years), the TRS division grew at a compounded annual rate of 18 percent, becoming one of the best performing divisions of American Express. Under his leadership, customers' needs and preferences were accorded top priority and many new products[7] were developed and new services were offered, keeping in mind their viability in the domestic and international markets. He constantly set high targets and motivated his colleagues towards achieving them. Instead of simply reacting to the strategies of his competitors, Gerstner believed in devising strategies depending upon the situation. He laid stress on adopting new technologies to constantly improve upon the quality of service provided to customers.

Gerstner's penchant for challenge was more profoundly noticed in 1989, when he left his job at American Express and joined RJR Nabisco, which manufactured food and tobacco products. During his four-year stint, Gerstner helped transform the company from being a loss-making one (net loss of $1.1 billion) in 1989 to a profitable one (earning a net income of $299 million) in 1992.

He undertook several cost-cutting initiatives and reduced the company's debt significantly. He formed a new executive team, devised a new compensation system, and developed new rules for capital spending. All these moves were undertaken within 100 days of becoming CEO. By doing so, Gerstner demonstrated his ability to make quick decisions. He also pruned some non-performing products such as Chung King, Baby Ruth, and Butterfinger candies from Nabisco's product line and invested more money in high-performing products such as Winston and Camel cigarettes. Gerstner pushed executives to set targets for the future and devise their strategies accordingly, to meet those targets. He further learned that communicating directly with employees and maintaining a rapport with them was one of the most effective ways to win their confidence and motivate them to give their best.

From 1965 to 1992, Gerstner had changed three jobs, and learned from all his experiences. He implemented the knowledge and experience he acquired in each successive assignment he undertook. By 1992, he had become well known in industry circles for his turnaround strategies. In April 1993, Gerstner quit Nabisco to join IBM as its CEO.

THE TENURE AT IBM

When Gerstner joined IBM, he was sarcastically referred to as "the guy from a cookie company." During that time, IBM was passing through the worst phase ever in its nearly eight-decade-long history. IBM recorded an operating loss of $325 million in the first half of 1993, and the stock price dipped by about 15 percent within a few months of Gerstner becoming CEO. The financial situation of the company was deteriorating. The company posted a net loss of $2.86 billion in 1991, followed by a net loss of $4.97 billion in the financial year 1992.

During the period 1986–1992, IBM's overall market share in the IT industry in the United States had declined 37 percent, while its global market share had fallen by 30 percent. The company had 24 product units that functioned independently, even though they were a part of IBM. In fact, the former CEO, John Akers, had already announced a restructuring plan to split the company into independent units. To make matters worse, the mainframes and storage systems division, which contributed nearly half of IBM's revenues, was losing ground both in terms of revenues as well as market share. Moreover, the company's personal computers division was not generating any profits. The morale of the employees was also low as 105,000 employees had been asked to quit in the previous six years.

Owing to his lack of experience in the computer industry and having observed the state of affairs at IBM, Gerstner was initially reluctant to take up the post, but he later conceded. He was excited at the challenge of leading one of the top hardware companies in the United States. Responding to the Herculean task ahead at IBM, Gerstner said,[8] "The challenge they have laid down is immense. I don't underestimate its magnitude, but I take up that challenge with a great determination to succeed. We will build on IBM's traditions, but we will not hesitate to make every change necessary to meet the challenge of a very rapidly adjusting market place."

THE EARLY INITIATIVES

After joining IBM, Gerstner's immediate task was to make the company profitable. He spent the initial period at the firm learning about the prevalent situation. Gerstner visited different IBM facilities all over the world and met customers, competitors, senior executives, financial analysts, and consultants to get a first hand account of the actual state of affairs. During these interactions, he learned that customers still appreciated IBM since it offered solutions for a host of their computer-related needs under one roof. But having seen the facilities himself, Gerstner realized that the quality of the IBM products needed to be significantly improved. He felt that the different business units of IBM needed to be integrated in order to produce products of better quality within a specified time period. This led him to make a crucial decision to reverse Akers' plans to split IBM into 11 entities. He argued that customers wanted IBM to remain a single entity.

In his first e-mail message to the employees of IBM, he assured them that he would put in his best efforts to help the company recover from its existing state. At the same time, he mentally prepared them to face certain tough decisions, primarily further reductions in the workforce. Gerstner summoned the top 12 managers of IBM and asked them to clearly define their respective businesses, in terms of parameters such as nature of business, customers, competitors, markets, and their strengths and weaknesses. He tried to boost confidence in the IBM ranks by insisting that the company's strengths were formidable and that it would definitely emerge from the crisis. Soon after, Gerstner announced a set of objectives that he intended to pursue in his first year at IBM (see Exhibit 2).

In an effort to right size, in July 1993, Gerstner reduced the workforce by a further 35,000. Though during the period 1986–1992, the workforce at IBM had been reduced by 20 percent, it was through attractive voluntary retirement schemes, which in turn had led to an increase in the expenses of the company. A series of other cost-cutting initiatives were undertaken by Gerstner in the same year. These included the sale of the Federal Systems[9] unit for $1.575 billion, the sale of IBM's

EXHIBIT 2	Gerstner's Objectives for 1993

- Paring IBM to a more efficient size
- Taking more care of IBM's customers
- Decentralizing decision making
- Developing a strategy that would make clear which business the company would focus on

Source: 1999, Robert Slater, *Saving Big Blue*, p. 63.

art collection,[10] worth $25 million, and the sale of IBM property worth $248 million. For the financial year 1993, IBM registered a record net loss of $8.1 billion.

Within six months of becoming CEO, Gerstner announced several human resource initiatives. He abolished the lifetime employment policy followed by the company. Though this policy was aimed at improving the loyalty of employees towards the organization, Gerstner felt that it was no longer relevant in the highly competitive scenario. He tried to foster a performance-driven culture at IBM and insisted on results.

Before Gerstner became the CEO, the employees of IBM had to strictly adhere to a formal dress code prescribed by the management. They were expected to follow certain ethical standards in their professional as well as personal life. Smoking and consuming alcohol were prohibited during office hours. Gerstner tried to minimize these restrictions and create an informal culture at IBM. Employees were no longer required to adhere to a formal dress code. Gerstner believed that employees should present themselves in a simple manner before the customers, and try to solve their problems, instead of just focusing on selling IBM's products. He restricted his interference in the affairs of employees to official matters only. Employees were given more freedom in their work-related affairs.

In the pre-Gerstner days, meetings at IBM lasted for hours. A large number of people attended these meetings. The meetings were more like discussions and nothing concrete emerged out of them. However, under Gerstner, the meetings were made shorter. He was focused on the central issues, and wanted decisions to evolve out of each meeting. Only those persons who were required for the meeting were permitted to attend, and they were expected to present the relevant facts as concisely as possible.

Gerstner also brought about major changes in the compensation structure of employees. Before, compensation was generally in the form of salary. Stock options were not common, and were awarded as incentives only to employees belonging to the executive cadre, on the basis of their performance. Employees were awarded bonuses depending upon the performance of the unit to which they belonged. They also received other benefits such as membership in clubs, medical benefits, and a post-retirement pension. The annual compensation hike was conferred to all IBM employees, barring those whose performance was not found satisfactory. The rates at which the compensation increased did not differ much across the hierarchy. Further, the compensation structure was uniform for all employees who belonged to a certain salary grade, irrespective of the difference in the nature of work they handled.

However, Gerstner believed that stock options must be an inherent part of the compensation structure. He believed that this would make the employees more responsible, as their performance would affect the stock prices, and hence, their personal financial gains. Further, by providing stock options the company could retain its skilled manpower. Thus, during his tenure, stock options were awarded to more employees. For the executives, the stock options formed a major part of their compensation. The number of options varied according to the employee's grade, their annual base salary, and the annual incentive target. The number of employees who received stock options increased from 1,300 in 1992 to 72,500 in 2001.

Employees were also awarded bonuses, which varied according to the overall performance of IBM. As they moved up the hierarchy, the performance-linked bonus component of their total remuneration also grew. This move was aimed at enhancing the commitment of employees. However, Gerstner scrapped other benefits such as club memberships, medical benefits, and pension schemes.

Gerstner also felt that at IBM, marketing was not given the importance it deserved. In 1993, he appointed Abby Kohnstamm as the head of corporate marketing. Initial research revealed that the goodwill enjoyed by IBM helped push its products into the market, but there was no marketing strategy in place. Gerstner therefore decided to evolve a uniform marketing strategy for IBM. A major decision in this direction was to centralize the advertising and media strategy. The advertising contract for IBM's operations across the world was awarded to Ogilvy & Mather.[11] Before Gerstner, IBM managers across the world had around 70 different advertising agencies, and there wasn't much coordination between them. As a result, monitoring the agencies was quite difficult. Gerstner's decision played an important role in strengthening the image of IBM.

Due to the huge size of IBM's operations spread all across the world, it was very difficult for Gerstner to closely monitor their functioning. He decided to delegate the authority to make decisions regarding the regular operations of these units to the heads of the respective units while the crucial strategic decisions were taken by him. Gerstner created a corporate executive committee comprising ten executives to monitor and integrate the operations of different units and keep him updated about the same. To make them more accountable, Gerstner declared that the bonuses earned by the executives would depend on the overall performance of the company and not on their individual performance. He also created a Worldwide

Management Council comprising 35 executives to discuss new initiatives undertaken by IBM and the probable impact of these on operations across the world. These measures were a major step towards Gerstner's efforts to decentralize decision making at IBM.

THE TURNAROUND STRATEGY

In 1994, Gerstner made efforts to improve the reporting procedures across different units of the firm. This helped him to closely monitor the production schedules, cost schedules, and sale of different products. He also started focusing on specific problems related to individual units. He realized that the personal computers division, which had good potential, was performing very poorly. The division was facing tough competition from companies such as Dell, Hewlett-Packard, and Compaq. With the objective of improving the situation, Gerstner appointed Richard Thomson, who was his colleague at American Express and RJR Nabisco, as the head of the unit.

Gerstner took various measures to improve IBM's customer orientation. When customers complained about the high prices of mainframe software, Gerstner quickly ordered price cuts of up to 30 percent. Since IBM hardware and software were not compatible with other systems, customers were often not willing to invest in IBM's proprietary products. IBM started developing hardware and software using Java[12] in order to make its products compatible with other systems.

Gerstner always tried to solve the problems faced by IBM's customers. He understood that the massive scale of IBM's operations made it very difficult for it to provide its customers the personalized attention they desired. In what was perceived to be the largest restructuring exercise of IBM's work force, he split IBM's entire sales force into 14 vertical marketing groups, each catering to a specific industry. Gerstner divided his existing and potential customers around the world on the basis of the industry to which they belonged such as banking, insurance, and so on. Further, each industry was allotted to a team of research people, software engineers, and industry consultants so that they could develop solutions according to the industry-specific needs of customers.

It was generally believed that the popularity of PCs would lead to a decline in the demand for mainframes. An important decision that Gerstner made in 1994 was to continue with mainframes, thus removing all speculation about IBM's commitment to the mainframes business. He strongly felt that IBM must build on its core business, rather than deviate from it. Gerstner instructed his executives to replace IBM's aging line of mainframes with smaller, faster, cheaper, but still highly profitable machines. In order to make mainframes more affordable, he shifted from "bi-polar" to CMOS (Complementary Metal Oxide Semiconductor) technology, which helped reduce production costs considerably. During the period 1994–2001, Gerstner slashed the unit price of mainframes by 96 percent from $63,000 to $2,500. By the end of 1994, Gerstner had reduced IBM's manpower strength by 80,000, lowering the annual operating costs significantly. The total amount saved as a result of the cost-cutting initiatives undertaken by Gerstner in 1994 amounted to $2.86 billion. IBM earned a net income of $3 billion in 1994, indicating that IBM was well on its way to recovery.

In 1995, IBM witnessed some significant developments under Gerstner's leadership. Gerstner always stressed that IT had become more than just a productivity tool. It had become fundamental to how a company operated and the prime source of a company's competitive advantage. Clients wanted to integrate different computing platforms and applications together in networks, and they turned to specialist computer service companies like EDS and the consulting arms of big accounting firms. Gerstner expressed his confidence that IBM's size and scope could provide "complete solutions" to its customers. If IBM did not have the product being demanded, it offered third party alternatives to its customers.

Gerstner also felt that IBM was moving in the direction of using the same computer architecture for different product lines. This required tight integration of different businesses. He argued that the PC era would come to an end and PCs would be replaced by network computing. While PCs would still exist on every desk, the programs, data, and other information would reside on powerful servers linked by networks. In such a scenario, systems integration capabilities would be crucial. To strengthen its technological capabilities, IBM acquired the software company Lotus (famous for developing the 1-2-3 spreadsheet) for $3.52 billion in 1995.

Later in the year, Gerstner introduced a concept known as network-centered computing.[13] He believed that networking technologies could enable the computers around the world to get connected at a faster rate and have wider applications for such technologies. Gerstner decided that 25 percent of the expenses incurred in R&D would be shifted to the projects that were related to network-centered computing. He felt that the existing client/server technology[14] was quite expensive and that a more powerful networking technology could be offered at a competitive price to the customers. As a first step towards offering networking solutions to the customers, IBM offered Lotus Notes and IBM network software and services to customers in late 1995.

In 1996, Gerstner continued to aggressively pursue the network-centered computing strategy. In April 1996, he appointed Sam Palmisino[15] as the head of the PC division. Palmisino's strategy was to design and launch innovative products at competitive prices and reduce the cycle time for launching new products. He pushed his sales force to market products even before they were launched. These efforts led to the IBM's PC unit, for the first time, generating profits for the financial year 1996–1997. Another development in the same year was the acquisition of the software firm Tivoli Systems, the developer of software that managed client-server computer networks. It was bought for around $1.2 billion. In the same year, IBM sold one of its non-performing units, Prodigy,[16] for $250 million. The year ended on a positive note for IBM, with its profits amounting to $5.4 billion on revenues of $75.9 billion.

EMPHASIS ON E-BUSINESS

In 1997, Gerstner's network-centered computing strategy evolved into a full-fledged "e-business" strategy for IBM. This strategy sought to leverage IBM's strengths in big servers, huge storage capability, bullet-proof databases, massive processing power, and expert systems integration. IBM provided the complete package for e-business (e.g. hardware, software, training, security, networking, and services). Lotus Notes Groupware added another powerful feature to IBM's e-business solutions. Notes ensured that various forms of communication including e-mail were made available to all persons in an organization for whom they were relevant. Each Notes server periodically checked the status of other servers in the network and copied the updated contents of its database to others. Hence, users were able to access the latest information in real time. During the period 1995–1998, the number of Notes users increased from 3 million to 22 million. IBM also launched a web-server program called Go that made the company's hardware products suitable for e-commerce transactions.

Later in the year, Gerstner launched a huge marketing campaign in both the print and electronic media across the world to promote IBM as a company that offered world class e-business solutions to its customers. Existing and prospective customers were directly contacted through mail. Senior executives spoke of e-business in all their presentations and speeches. Executives were encouraged to interact with each other on a regular basis to exchange their views on the topic, thereby enabling them to widen their knowledge on the subject. The campaign on which Gerstner spent millions of dollars depicted real-world managers struggling with Web-related problems and was a huge success. *Fortune* reported that the campaign made a tremendous impact on the audience. During the period 1997–2002, IBM had spent over $5 billion on advertising of its e-business initiative. Acknowledging the success of the e-business campaign, Gerstner said, "I consider the e-business campaign to be one of the finest jobs of brand positioning I've seen in my entire career."[17]

One of the press reports described how Gerstner revamped IBM's marketing approach by setting an example. "When Gerstner ran into the P&G chairman and CEO, John E. Pepper, at a business function, he came to know that the top management at P&G was wrestling with how to better exploit new technology such as the Internet to streamline operations. He later called Pepper to suggest that he bring his management team out to P&G for a day long briefing on their vision of a new era of e-commerce. This proactive call surprised Pepper, and the initiative paid off handsomely."[18]

Gerstner also advised his executives to concentrate on providing "complete solutions" to their clients. He stressed that in a competitive era where it was difficult to distinguish products, good customer service was the key to higher sales and stronger customer loyalty. In just a few years, IBM developed the world's largest computer service business, IBM Global Service (IBMGS), overtaking its nearest competitor, Electronic Data Systems (EDS). In 1997, IBM reported a net income of $6.09 billion, while revenues amounted to $78.5 billion. Revenues from IBMGS formed a quarter of the total sales. Gerstner had given a new thrust to customer service, and his efforts seemed to pay rich dividends. Pat Zilvitis, chief information officer of Gillette, said, "I don't view IBM as a hardware vendor anymore. I think of them as an IT vendor that can help me in a number of different ways. If I have got a problem, I go to my IBM rep and expect to get the right expert."[19]

Gerstner continued to aggressively pursue the e-business strategy in 1998 as well. IBM extended the benefits of e-business to its customers. Rather than investing a large amount of money on call centers and other related activities, it solved the problems of customers through online support systems. In mid-1998, Gerstner signed seven computer services deals, of which five were outside the United States. He also announced plans to make IBM the premier supplier of e-commerce software and services. He indicated that IBM would soon have the technology to build a variety of net-ready information appliances ranging from Internet phones to handheld computers to TV set-top boxes.[20] In 1998, IBM reported a net profit of $6.33 billion on revenues of $81.6 billion.

In 1999, the world was waking up to the Year 2000 problem,[21] popularly known as the Y2K. To address this problem, Gerstner quickly established customer support teams. This gesture of IBM reiterated its standing as a customer-driven company. Gerstner was named Man of the Year[22] by a leading U.S. magazine, *Industry Week*. IBM ended the year with revenues of $87.55 billion and a net income of $7.7 billion.

Under the guidance of Gerstner, IBM continued its good financial performance. The company generated revenues of $88.4 billion and a net profit of $8.1 billion in 2000. However, in the financial year ending December 2001, IBM's net income fell to $7.7 billion while revenues dipped to $85.9 billion, as a result of the global recession in the IT industry.

After working for almost nine years with IBM, Gerstner retired on March 1, 2002. According to analysts, Gerstner had engineered IBM's remarkable transformation from a hardware seller to service provider. Appreciating his leadership skills, Palmisino, the new CEO of IBM, said, "I feel very fortunate to succeed Lou Gerstner as CEO. Against all odds, he led IBM back from its darkest days. He transformed the company's culture and reignited growth. IBM's unflagging focus on both the customer and technology innovation is a direct result of Lou's leadership over the last nine years. He will leave a significant legacy."[23]

Addressing the annual shareholders meeting in April 2001, Gerstner summed up his vision for IBM, "Today, the agenda for IBM is dominated by this once-in-a-lifetime opportunity to separate from the pack, to stand apart, and to lead. That's about more than our marketplace performance. We think leaders are expected to lead on multiple dimensions. That means leadership in technology, leadership in imagining how business and society can be changed, and certainly leadership in crafting the public policy frameworks required for a networked world."[24]

THE CRITICISM

Though Gerstner has been credited for his remarkable efforts to turn around IBM, the manner in which he went about this task drew much criticism. His early moves to keep IBM intact and change the corporate culture of IBM were severely criticized by the employees. An executive who had served the company for approximately three decades, criticizing Gerstner's approach in 1998, said, "When I joined IBM, I was so proud. . . . It was the best company in the world. Today, it's just another company. . . . Gerstner's made it a pedestrian company. The pride, the culture he's effectively destroyed. You could argue that if he hadn't kept IBM intact, the company would have been destroyed. My sense is that Gerstner inherited something that was about to hit a wall. The way he went about doing it from a Wall Street perspective was very successful. But from the perspective of someone who knew how special this company was, it was a tragedy. I would have liked to see the company broken up. There is no entrepreneurial spirit any more. A lot of people are going through the motions. This is no longer a lifestyle company. Gerstner is running it as just another financial institution. So, what bothers me is that they had something so precious. My sense is that as smaller entities, they could have maintained some of the culture they created, some of the entrepreneurial spirit. That's lost now. I remember the way it was."[25]

It was also felt that Gerstner achieved better financial results for IBM at the cost of employee welfare. For example, in 1999, IBM decided to reduce medical coverage and pension of employees, as a cost-cutting measure. The employees alleged that Gerstner was increasing his personal gains at the cost of their interests (as he would earn more money through incentives by showing more profits for IBM). Jimmy Leas, an IBM engineer and a patent lawyer, remarked, "Gerstner slashed retirement pay for employees to make profits look higher because part of his salary depends on earnings going up. Gerstner put his interests ahead of company interests."[26] His allegation was justified by the fact that Gerstner received a higher compensation of $73.6 million in 2000, while employees suffered as a result of cuts in benefits in 1999.

Analysts also alleged that Gerstner had not been successful in capitalizing on IBM's capabilities in high-level, high-margin consulting. This sector remained largely dominated by McKinsey and Andersen Consulting. They also felt that though Gerstner was a good manager, he was a poor entrepreneur. Bob Djurdjevic, president of an Arizona-based firm, Annex Research,[27] said, "Gerstner did an excellent job of cutting costs and returning IBM to profitability. That job was done by about 1995. Ever since, his main challenge was to generate growth. He did poorly at that. He will be remembered as a good manager, but a poor entrepreneur."[28]

NOTES

1. "Top 25 Managers of the Year," *BusinessWeek*, January 14, 2002.
2. Quoted in *Saving Big Blue* by Robert Slater, p. 115.
3. Established in 1769, Dartmouth offers several undergraduate and graduate programs. The institution offers 16 graduate programs in arts and sciences, apart from conducting programs in specialized fields such as engineering (Thayer School of Engineering), medicine (Dartmouth Medical College) and business administration (Tuck School of Business).
4. The oldest railway company in the United States, later renamed Conrail.
5. American Express provides international banking, financial advisory and travel-related services in more than 200 countries all over the world. The company offers charge and credit cards, travelers' checks, travel services, financial planning, and investment and insurance products.
6. The arm of American Express that deals with credit cards, travelers' checks, travel agencies, and more.
7. New products such as Platinum and Optima cards were developed.
8. As quoted in the book *Saving Big Blue* by Robert Slater, p. 54.
9. A division of IBM that sold computers and electronic components to defense and public agencies of the U.S. government.
10. A collection of paintings that was started by IBM's founder, Thomas Watson Sr.
11. An advertising agency with operations spread all over the world.
12. A platform-independent language developed by Sun Microsystems. An application written in Java can run on any platform.
13. A model of computing based on networks, most notably the Internet. Gerstner believed that in the future, networking technologies would play an important role in business.
14. A network architecture in which each computer or process on the network is either a client or a server. Servers are powerful computers or processes dedicated to managing disk drives (file servers), printers (print servers), or network traffic (network servers). Clients are PCs or workstations on which users run applications. Clients rely on servers for resources, such as files, devices, and processing power.
15. Palmisino worked for IBM for over three decades, during which he held several key positions. He was later promoted as the CEO in 2002.
16. Prodigy was an Internet service provider that was jointly owned by IBM and Sears, Roebuck & Company.
17. Quoted in *Who Says Elephants Can't Dance*, by Louis Gerstner, p. 173.
18. "How IBM became a Growth Company Again," *BusinessWeek*, December 9, 1996.
19. "IBM: From Big Blue Dinosaur to E-Business Animal," *Fortune*, April 7, 1999.
20. A set-top box is used to select television channels offered by satellite/cable television providers as well as to play video games.
21. Many software applications were designed to handle dates that begin with "19___." In the new millennium, the dates begin with "20___," which required necessary upgrades in the software applications, particularly accounting and database-related ones.
22. It is the award given by *Industry Week* to recognize people who have attained tremendous success in their respective fields.
23. Press release, January 29, 2002, "Samuel J. Palmisino elected IBM CEO; Louis V. Gerstner, Jr. to remain chairman through 2002," www.ibm.com.
24. Press release, April 24, 2001, "L.V. Gerstner, Jr. 2001 Annual Meeting," www.ibm.com.
25. Quoted in *Saving Big Blue*, by Robert Slater, p. 86.
26. "IBM Workers Continue to Fight Pension Changes," *Washington Post*, April 17, 2001.
27. A U.S.-based market intelligence and computer industry consulting firm with operations spread all over the world.
28. "Gerstner: The Untold Story," December 27, 2002, www.djurdjevic.com.

ADDITIONAL READINGS AND REFERENCES

"The Top 25 Managers," www.businessweek.com, February, 1997.

www.brown.edu, May 22, 1997.

Cortese, Amy, and Ira Sager, "Lou Gerstner, Web Plumber," www.businessweek.com, June 15, 1997.

Santosus, Megan, "Leaders of the Information Age," www.cio.com, September 15, 1997.

"AT&T to Acquire IBM's Global Network Business for $5 Billion," www.att.com, December 8, 1998.

Sager, Ira, "E.Biz—The E.Biz 25," www.businessweek.com, 1999.

Teresko, John, "Driving Success At New Blue," www.industryweek.com, June 12, 1999.

Teresko, John, "Gerstner, e-Business, And Management," www.industryweek.com, June 12, 1999.

"1999 Top 50," www.time.com.

"Louis V. Gerstner, Jr. Retired Chairman and CEO," www.ibm.com.

Wolf, Craig, "IBM Lauds Science that Sells," www.poughkeepsiejournal.com, June 17, 2001.

Olin, Dirk, *The New York Times*, "In a memoir, Louis V. Gerstner Jr. recalls how he rescued a floundering I.B.M." www.deccanherald.com, December 1, 2001.

www.businessweek.com, January 14, 2002.

Di Carlo, Lisa, "A Successor for IBM's Silent Man," www.forbes.com, January 29, 2002.

Dodge, John, "IBM Decided Not to Die," www.bio-itworld.com, July 5, 2002.

Poletti, Therese, "How to teach an elephant to dance," www.siliconvalley.com, Nov. 17, 2002.

Pruitt, Scarlet, "Gerstner says Internet saved IBM," www.free.idg.net, November 21, 2002.

"Lou Gerstner Discusses Changing the Culture at IBM," www.hbs.edu, December 9, 2002.

"Reformer of Big Blue's Corporate Culture," www.nni.nikkei.co.jp.

"Louis V. Gerstner Jr., Chairman & CEO, International Business Machines Corporation (IBM), Armonk, New York," www.proudofmymom.com.

www.harvard.edu.

www.globalcompetition.net.

www.americanexpress.com.

yosemite.epa.gov.

www.djurdjevic.com.

www.netlingo.com.

www.webopedia.com.

Lufthansa 2003: Energizing a Decade of Change

Heike Bruch

University of St. Gallen/Lufthansa School of Business

Lufthansa was almost bankrupt in 1992. Ten years later, Lufthansa had become one of the most robust airlines and top aviation groups in the world.

By 2002, Lufthansa had undergone a decade of fundamental change. After the turnaround was initiated, the Executive and Supervisory Boards systematically maintained the change momentum. Lufthansa was transformed from a state-owned, monolithic, unprofitable national airline into one of the most profitable, privately owned aviation groups in the industry. From the brink of bankruptcy, Lufthansa turned a record loss of €350 million in 1992 into a pre-tax profit of €952 million in 2002.

This financial result reflected Lufthansa's major competitive advantage—its ability to respond rapidly, act flexibly, and withstand crises. Lufthansa proved its unique change management competence, especially after September 11, 2001, when it coped with the most serious crisis in the airline industry since World War II. In contrast to the general trend in the industry and the prevailing overall economic situation, Deutsche Lufthansa pulled ahead of its competitors and reversed a loss of €744 million in 2001 into an operating profit of €718 million in 2002 (equivalent to an increase of 78 percent over 2001).

In 2003, the war in Iraq and the SARS disease demanded that, more than ever before, Lufthansa draw on its ability to cope with crises. In fact, overcoming change-tiredness and continuous re-energizing were seen as the key management challenges in 2003.

At the beginning of the 1990s, Lufthansa was almost bankrupt. When Jürgen Weber's tenure as CEO began, Lufthansa was *the* national airline carrier of the Federal Republic of Germany—state-owned, monolithic and unprofitable.

In 2003, when the Weber era ended, Lufthansa was a privately owned, profitable aviation group aspiring to become the leading provider of air transportation services in the world: Lufthansa went from a record loss of €350 million to a profit of €718 between 1992 and 2002. The number of passengers increased from 33.7 million in 1992 to 43.9 million in 2002 (see Exhibit 1).

THE TURNAROUND (1992–1993)

The 1991–1992 Crisis

In 1991, Lufthansa was an embodiment of the strengths or desirable characteristics thought to be associated with firms competing within German industries: high reliability, order and technical excellence. Majority-owned by the German government, Lufthansa's strategy, organization, and culture stemmed from its role as an organ of the state. Under the leadership of Heinz Ruhnau in the 1980s, Lufthansa pursued a policy of rapid fleet expansion based on the belief that only the largest airlines would survive in an era of global competition. By 1991, when Weber was appointed CEO, Lufthansa had enlarged its fleet by some 120 aircraft to 275.

The sharp decline in air traffic during the Gulf War and the recession thereafter led to serious overcapacity in the airline industry worldwide. In 1991, seat load factor (SLF—proportion of available seats filled) sank to about 57 percent in Europe.

Lufthansa became fully aware of the crisis and its potential effects later than other airlines. In 1991, while overall traffic dropped by 9 percent in Europe, Lufthansa had an 11 percent increase in passengers because of the German reunification. Despite this growth, however, Lufthansa reported an after-tax loss

This case was written in cooperation between the University of St. Gallen and the Lufthansa School of Business by Prof. Heike Bruch (University of St. Gallen, Switzerland). It is intended to be used as a basis of discussion rather than to illustrate either effective or ineffective handling of a business solution. Reprinted by permission of Prof. Heike Bruch and Lufthansa.

EXHIBIT 1   Ten-Year Statistics 1993–2002

	2002	2001	2000	1999	1998	1997	1996	1995	1994	1993
Consolidated Income Statement[1]										
Revenue[2] (€m)	16,971.4	16,690.0	15,200.4	12,794.7	11,736.6	11,048.9	10,666.9	10,174.9	9,630.5	9,065.6
Result										
Operating result[3] (€m)	717.6	28.3	1,041.6	723.4	1,059.5	840.7	—	—	—	—
Profit from operating activities (€m)	1,592.1	−315.6	1,482.0	1,012.3	1,454.6	1,089.6	344.8	428.1	305.0	166.7
Profit from ordinary activities[4] (€m)	952.4	−744.7	1,215.3	1,002.9	1,269.1	894.1	350.7	386.7	375.3	38.1
Profit before taxes (€m)[10]	952.4	−744.7	1,215.3	1,002.9	1,269.1	894.1	350.7	836.1	175.7	−4.2
Taxes (€m)	230.5	−140.2	529.3	363.3	537.1	341.7	65.3	81.3	21.3	42.6
Net profit/loss for the period[5] (€m)[10]	716.8	−633.2	689.0	630.4	731.5	550.5	285.4	754.8	154.4	−46.8
Main Cost Items										
Staff costs (€m)	4,660.1	4,480.6	3,624.9	3,232.2	2,867.2	2,823.1	2,943.1	2,761.0	2,687.0	2,770.5
Fees and charges (€m)	2,239.3	2,310.8	2,250.3	2,095.3	1,930.1	1,843.9	1,995.1	1,868.2	1,684.8	1,568.3
Fuel for aircraft (€m)	1,347.2	1,621.0	1,498.6	908.0	864.0	948.0	911.9	747.0	755.0	839.7
Depreciation and amortization (€m)	1,243.3	1,714.1	1,022.4	933.4	865.9	861.5	710.3	696.4	673.9	647.1
Net interest (€m)	−415.1	−397.9	−256.2	−219.3	−195.7	−280.0	−44.6	−63.0	−156.4	−207.0
Consolidated Balance Sheet[1]										
Asset Structure										
Non-current assets (€m)	12,102.8	13,244.8	11,082.0	9,691.6	8,712.6	7,947.7	6,396.0	6,368.0	6,573.9	6,152.2
Current and other assets (€m)	7,034.1	4,961.9	3,728.4	3,215.5	3,579.0	3,712.0	3,161.1	3,049.6	2,699.7	2,749.4
of which liquid assets (€m)	3,637.8	1,182.2	969.8	777.7	1,666.7	1,858.5	958.1	1,097.9	720.9	485.1

Capital Structure

Capital and reserves[6] (€m)[10]	4,125.2	3,498.1	4,113.5	3,691.5	3,303.8	2,690.5	2,737.0	2,527.3	2,090.8	1,490.1
of which issued capital (€m)	976.9	976.9	976.9	976.9	975.5	975.5	975.5	975.5	975.5	780.2
of which reserves (€m)[10]	2,431.5	3,154.4	2,447.6	2,084.2	1,596.8	1,164.5	1,656.8	1,444.5	797.7	360.8
of which profit/loss for the period (€m)	716.8	−633.2	689.0	630.4	731.5	550.5	97.6	97.6	88.2	−56.7
Minority interest (€m)	46.8	30.1	51.3	41.5	9.9	2.9	7.1	9.7	4.7	8.0
Debt[7] (€m)	14,964.9	14,677.7	10,645.6	9,154.1	8,977.9	8,966.4	6,820.0	6,890.3	7,182.8	7,411.5
of which retirement benefit obligations €m	4,019.5	3,700.5	3,354.3	2,993.0	2,760.4	2,577.7	1,875.1	1,688.8	1,585.8	719.9
of which liabilities[8] (€m)	4,713.4	4,445.7	2,408.4	2,229.8	2,374.9	2,988.2				
Total assets (€m)	19,136.9	18,205.9	14,810.4	12,887.1	12,291.6	11,659.7	9,557.1	9,417.6	9,273.6	8,901.6

Other Financial Data, Lufthansa Group[1]

Capital expenditure (€m)	879.7	2,978.6	2,446.5	1,937.5	1,897.9	1,208.6	1,016.0	698.1	1,066.6	890.2
of which on tangible and intangible assets (€m)	645.9	2,549.1	1,769.2	1,337.6	1,669.4	1,036.2	830.5	594.4	903.1	754.4
of which on financial assets (€m)	233.8	429.5	677.3	599.9	228.5	172.4	185.4	103.7	163.4	135.8
Cash flow[9] (€m)	2,311.6	1,735.7	2,140.2	808.9	1,860.0	1,996.9	1,247.7	1,268.9	1,293.8	987.0

Indebtedness

Gross (€m)	4,771.2	4,994.6	2,444.3	2,319.8	2,403.8	3,043.0	1,690.0	2,108.2	2,515.9	3,477.3
Net (€m)	1,133.4	3,812.4	1,474.5	1,542.1	737.1	1,184.5	731.9	1,010.3	1,835.7	2,992.2

Deutsche Lufthansa AG

Net profit/loss for the year (€m)	1,111.0	−797.2	445.1	402.4	401.1	441.2	97.6	97.6	144.9	−56.7
Accumulated losses (€m)	−797.2	—	—	—	—	—	—	—	−56.7	−190.6

EXHIBIT 1 *(Cont'd)*

Consolidated Income Statement[1] Deutsche Lufthansa AG	2002	2001	2000	1999	1998	1997	1996	1995	1994	1993
Transfers to/withdrawals from reserves (€m)	−84.8	—	−216.1	−187.7	−186.5	−265.6	0.0	0.0	0.0	190.6
Dividends proposed/paid (€m)	229.0	—	229.0	214.7	214.6	175.6	97.6	97.6	88.2	—
Dividends per share proposed/paid[11] (€)	0.60	—	0.60	0.56	0.56	0.46	0.26	0.26	0.20[12]	—
Operational ratios[1]										
Profit/loss revenue ratio (loss/profit from ordinary activities[4]/revenue,[2] %)	5.6	−4.5	8.0	7.8	11.0	8.1	3.3	3.8	3.9	0.4
Return on total capital (profit from ordinary activities[4] plus interest on debt/total assets, %)	7.9	−1.4	10.7	10.3	13.0	10.9	4.9	5.7	6.3	3.4
Return on equity (net profit/loss for the period[5]/shareholders' equity,[6] %)[10]	17.4	−18.1	16.7	17.1	22.1	20.5	10.4	21.1[12]	7.4	−3.1
Return on equity (profit from ordinary activities[4]/shareholders' equity,[6] %)[10]	23.1	−21.3	29.5	27.2	38.4	33.2	12.8	15.3	17.9	2.6
Equity ratio (shareholders' equity[6]/total assets, %)[10]	21.6	23.1	27.8	28.7	26.9	23.1	28.6	26.8	22.5	16.7
Gearing (net indebtedness/shareholders' equity,[6] %)[10]	27.5	109.0	35.8	41.8	22.3	44.0	26.7	40.0	87.8	200.8

Operational ratios[1]										
Net indebtedness—total assets ratio (%)	33.6	19.8	10.8	7.7	10.2	6.0	12.0	10.0	20.9	5.9
Internal financing ratio (cash flow[9]/capital expenditure, %)	110.9	121.3	181.8	122.8	165.2	98.0	41.8	87.5	58.3	262.8
Net indebtedness—cash flow[9] ratio (%)	303.1	141.9	79.6	58.7	59.3	39.6	190.6	68.9	219.6	49.0
Revenue efficiency (cash flow[9])/revenue,[2] %	0.9	13.4	2.5	11.7	18.1	15.8	6.3	14.1	10.4	13.6
Net working capital (current assets less short-term debt, €bn)	1.3	1.3	1.2	1.7	0.2	−0.02	−1.1	−1.0	−1.5	−0.40
Personnel Ratios										
Annualized average employee total	60,514	58,044	57,586	57,999	55,520	54,867	66,207	69,523	87,957	94,135
Revenue[2]/employee (€)	149,809	165,918	176,691	183,916	199,008	213,910	193,253	218,638	189,713	180,288
Staff costs/revenue,[2] %	30.6	27.9	27.1	27.6	25.6	24.8	25.3	23.8	26.8	27.5
Output Data Lufthansa Group[14]										
Total available metric ton-kilometers (millions)	17,123.4	18,209.8	19,983.2	20,697.5	19,324.6	20,133.6	21,838.8	23,562.8	23,941.3	22,755.6
Total revenue metric ton-kilometers (millions)	11,768.4	12,890.0	14,063.1	14,532.8	13,620.9	14,170.4	15,529.1	16,918.0	16,186.9	16,080.8
Overall load factor (%)	68.7	70.8	70.4	70.2	70.5	70.4	71.1	71.8	67.6	70.7
Available seat-kilometers (millions)	98,295.3	103,876.9	112,147.2	116,183.1	98,750.0	102,354.4	116,383.1	123,800.8	126,400.4	119,876.4
Revenue passenger-kilometers (millions)	67,017.5	72,750.9	79,085.3	81,716.3	70,581.4	74,668.4	84,443.1	92,160.4	90,388.5	88,570.0
Passenger load carried (%)	68.2	70.0	70.5	70.3	71.5	73.0	72.6	74.4	71.5	73.9

EXHIBIT 1 *(Cont'd)*

Consolidated Income Statement[1] Output Data Lufthansa Group[14]	2002	2001	2000	1999	1998	1997	1996	1995	1994	1993
Passengers carried (millions)	43.9	45.7	47.0	43.8	40.5	37.2	41.4	40.7	37.7	35.6
Revenue passenger metric ton-kilometers (millions)	8,922.8	9,105.4	9,251.9	8,458.3	7,474.1	7,071.1	8,084.8	7,828.4	7,202.4	6,636.6
Cargo/mail (metric tons)	1,624,983	1,655,870	1,801,817	1,745,306	1,702,733	1,703,657	1,684,729	1,576,210	1,435,636	1,263,698
Cargo/mail metric ton-kilometers (millions)	7,158.0	7,081.5	7,666.1	7,070.7	6,696.3	6,548.0	6,448.0	6,234.7	5,687.6	5,131.8
Number of flights[16]	517,922	540,674	550,998	655,589	618,615	596,456	595,120	580,108	536,687	501,139
Flight kilometers (millions)	668.1	687.9	678.0	668.7	636.4	614.6	720.5	659.0	620.9	561.1
Aircraft utilization (block hours)	1,112,062	1,157,982	1,154,442	1,092,893	1,010,987	963,675	1,000,723	1,070,238	992,452[15]	973,504
Aircraft in service	344	345	331	306	302	286	314	314	308	301

*Figures are converted from DM into €.

1. As from the 1997 financial year, the financial statements are prepared according to the International Accounting Standards. Previous years' figures are not comparable.
2. The figures for 1998 have been adjusted for the changed allocation of commission payments.
3. Before 1997 operating results were not revealed.
4. Up to 1995 before net changes in special items with an equity portion.
5. Up to 1996 before withdrawal from/transfer to retained earnings and before minority interest.
6. Up to 1995 including the equity portion of special items and up to 1996 including minority interest.
7. Up to 1995 including the debt portion of special items.
8. Prior to 1997 liabilities were not shown separately as a sub-item of overall debt.
9. Calculated as net cash from operating activities as per cash flow statement, up to 1996 financial cash flow.
10. As from the 1995 financial year, the special items with an equity portion set up in individual company financial statements for tax purposes are not included in the consolidated financial statements according to the HGB. The special items brought forward from the 1994 financial year were released in 1995 as extraordinary income amounting to €449 million. This additional income was allocated to retained earnings. As a result of this reclassification, earnings before taxes, the net profit for the year, retained earnings and equity (including the equity portion of special items) were all shown with correspondingly higher totals.
11. In 1996 the face value of the shares was diluted to €2.56; previous years' figures were adjusted.
12. €0.58 on preference shares.
13. Net profit less extraordinary result.
14. As from the 1997 financial year, Condor is no longer included.
15. Method of calculation changed.
16. From 2000 number of flights includes only "real flights." "The discontinuation of ground transports particularly by Lufthansa Cargo has led to marked divergences compared to previous years.

of DM 444 million in 1991. Although an awareness of a serious crisis began to spread in early 1992, employment continued to rise during the first six months:

> *There was a general conviction that we were immortal. And even when the crisis became obvious, people still thought, "We are the German airline company, state-owned and a prestige organization. They will never let us die."*
>
> — Jürgen Weber, Lufthansa CEO until June 2003

In 1992, with only 14 days of operating cash requirements in hand, Weber went to all the major German banks and asked them for money to pay employee salaries. No private bank believed in Lufthansa's survival. Only one state-owned institution, the Kreditanstalt für Wiederaufbau, agreed to fund the company.

Redevelopment Workshops

The starting point of the turnaround was a four-week program on change management in which a group of young managers convinced Weber of the need for a fundamental redevelopment process.

As a result, Weber invited about 20 senior managers to the training centre at Seeheim for a "mental change" meeting, which would later be christened the "crisis management meeting" to express the urgency of the situation.

Before the meeting, people's awareness of the need for change was low. After three days in Seeheim, everyone agreed on the need for radical change. The facts were too obvious and dramatic.

> *No one had an idea of the gravity and brutality of the crisis. After a long phase of denial . . . , people began to look for scapegoats, after which they accepted that urgent need to act. After that, everything went very fast. The goals we committed ourselves to . . . were very ambitious and nobody believed that we could ever meet them. . . . The critical question was how to get other managers and employees involved.*
>
> — Wolfgang Mayrhuber, since June 2003 CEO of Lufthansa and former member of the Operations Team

One way of spreading the sense of urgency was to repeat the Seeheim workshop three times with different groups, each having 50 managers. This was done to let other managers live through the same process and feel the threat and urgency, rather than just tell them the facts and the appropriate strategy to implement. The Seeheim experience convinced most senior managers, who then committed to extremely ambitious goals.

The Seeheim meetings yielded 131 projects or key actions concerning drastic staff cuts (8,000 positions), lower non-personnel costs—including downsizing the fleet (savings of DM 400 million)—and increasing revenues (DM 700 million) in order to compensate for DM 1.3 billion in losses.

Managing the Turnaround

The executive board appointed the "OPS Team" (Operations Team), a small, powerful group that became an important motor in the implementation of the 131 "Programm 93" projects. The OPS Team put in enormous effort and succeeded in activating Programm 93 initiatives by defining concrete activities and by constantly monitoring, advising and supporting the line managers, who were ultimately responsible for implementation.

To demonstrate his unconditional commitment to the OPS Team, Weber initiated a number of both symbolic and substantive measures. These included, for example, locating the OPS Team office next to his own and investing in a great deal of personal communication, for example, holding town meetings.

> *Our openness to employees about the situation was key for the turnaround. That allowed us to develop common goals between employees, management, work councils and unions. We were even able to discuss issues such as reducing staff and increasing productivity openly and personally.*
>
> — Jürgen Weber

Weber led as many such meetings himself as possible. Other senior managers also held town meetings in their departments and in 2003, this practice was still very prevalent throughout Lufthansa. Weber's involvement was accompanied by various visible actions such as the executive board's 10 percent waiver on their annual salaries in 1992 or reducing the size of their company cars.

About 70 percent of the Programm or roughly 93 projects were successfully implemented during the turnaround. The remaining 30 percent were put into action later and implementation was still going on in 2003. So as not to lose the unions' consensus, Weber intentionally did not insist on the immediate implementation of the remaining 30 percent. The absence of strikes and a high level of consensus between management and other stakeholders, in particular the labor unions, was a remarkable feature of the Lufthansa crisis management. This philosophy was upheld as the change process continued into the 1990s.

SUSTAINABLE RENEWAL (1993–2001)

In November 1993, 18 months after the crisis management meeting, the first effects of the effort became visible, and Lufthansa announced its first success to the public.

C

However, Lufthansa was quite aware that such superficial recovery could not sustain success and that more fundamental change had to follow. To secure its future, the company had to deal with broader issues, e.g. privatization, organizational structure, and strategic cost savings. As Jürgen Weber said:

> We have learned our lesson: Don't invest in growth counting on "automatic" economies of scale. We need a second phase in this transformation. People cannot practice new thinking and acting in the old structures. In order to achieve a real mental change, we have to restructure Lufthansa, create transparency, and sustain cost consciousness. And this process is much harder than acute crisis management.

From State-Owned Airline to Private Aviation Group

At the outset of the turnaround, Lufthansa began negotiating privatization with the German government. A critical stumbling block was replacing the "VBL" pension fund (VBL—Versorgungsanstalt des Bundes und der Länder), binding Lufthansa to the German state. It was extremely difficult to break these "golden chains."

In May 1994, the problem of the pension fund was resolved. The German government diluted its holdings to 36 percent and agreed to a payment of DM 1 billion into the VBL to cover disbursements to present retirees as well as to offer an allowance and guarantee for constituting a separate Lufthansa pension fund. Lufthansa became fully privatized in 1997.

At the beginning of the 1990s, Lufthansa had six departments (finance, personnel, sales, marketing, maintenance, and flight operations), each led by a member of the executive board (see Exhibit 2). This structure was inefficient, showing symptoms such as high involvement of top management in operational problems, slow decision processes, low transparency, lack of accountability, insufficient market proximity, and high sensitivity for the considerable fluctuations on the airline market.

Lufthansa realized that it could not effectively respond to emerging competitive challenges with its existing structure. The purpose of the restructuring process was therefore to increase cost and revenue transparency as well as market proximity and to reduce the fragmentation in decision processes.

In the process of considering different organizational alternatives, the basic idea emerged that Lufthansa would be more successful as a federative group of small, independent units than as a functional, monolithic block. As a result, Lufthansa's goal was to evolve from an airline company into an aviation group and more specifically to become the leading provider of air transport services in the world.

> The second half of the '90s was a phase in which everything just worked out for Lufthansa. Everything we touched turned to gold. We no longer had an external enemy. This period of time gave us breathing room to move ahead in other fields of business.

— Holger Hätty, Head of Corporate Strategy

Ultimately, six business areas were formally separated as legally autonomous, strategically independent subsidiaries: Lufthansa Passage Airline (Passenger Service; Lufthansa German Airline and Cityline), Lufthansa Cargo AG (logistics), Lufthansa Technik AG (maintenance, repair, and overhaul service), Lufthansa Systems GmbH (IT services), Thomas Cook (leisure travel), and LSG Sky Chefs (catering). (See Exhibit 3.) With more than 30,000 employees in the cockpit and cabin, at ground stations, and worldwide sales, only Passenger Service—the original core of what was formerly Lufthansa—remained under the everyday influence of the top management.

In 2003, the Lufthansa Group Management Board directed the activities of the entire group through four central functions: the Chairman's Office, Passenger Service, Finance, and Human Resources Management.

Each of the six main business units was to aim for profitable, sustainable growth and a top position in its world market segment (see Exhibit 4). Most of these business areas were already leaders. However, their strategies for growth and globalization varied significantly.

With time, each of the various subsidiaries also developed a unique strategic relationship to the Lufthansa brand. For example, Passenger Service increasingly associated itself with Star Alliance brand in addition to the Lufthansa name. Technical Services as well as Cargo also relied on the Lufthansa name extensively for business. However, LSG Sky Chefs intentionally distanced itself from the Lufthansa brand in order to better establish itself as an international name in the local markets it served.

In 2002, the Lufthansa Group generated a total revenue of €17.0 billion, which was 1.7 percent more than in 2001. The Group's airlines earned traffic revenue amounting to €12.0 billion, a decrease of 1.8 percent on the previous year. Thanks to its forward-looking capabilities and pricing policy, however, Lufthansa was able to increase its capacity utilization and to keep average yields steady. Other operating revenues rose by 11.3 percent to €4.9 billion owing to the expansion of the consolidated Group. Other operating income climbed by 42.7 percent to €2.1 billion.

> Our strategy has been confirmed over and over since 2000. Growth through partnerships and the idea of the aviation group makes us less vulnerable to fluctuation in the more narrow context of the airline market.

— Holger Hätty

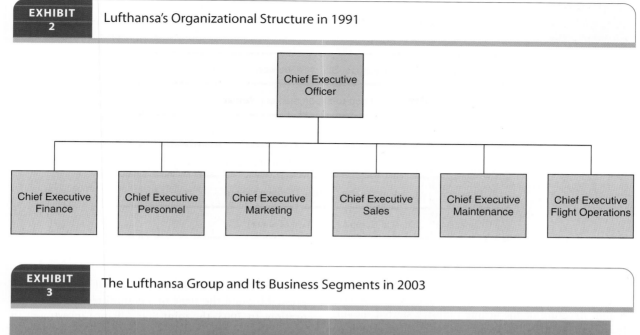

EXHIBIT 2 — Lufthansa's Organizational Structure in 1991

- Chief Executive Officer
  - Chief Executive Finance
  - Chief Executive Personnel
  - Chief Executive Marketing
  - Chief Executive Sales
  - Chief Executive Maintenance
  - Chief Executive Flight Operations

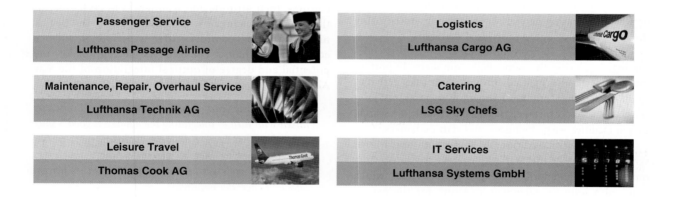

EXHIBIT 3 — The Lufthansa Group and Its Business Segments in 2003

Deutsche Lufthansa AG, Cologne

Passenger Service	Logistics
Lufthansa Passage Airline	Lufthansa Cargo AG
Maintenance, Repair, Overhaul Service	Catering
Lufthansa Technik AG	LSG Sky Chefs
Leisure Travel	IT Services
Thomas Cook AG	Lufthansa Systems GmbH

Building a Strategic Network—The Star Alliance

Apart from the focus on structural redevelopment within the company, Lufthansa worked constantly on its external relationships. Having experienced extreme overcapacity as a result of following the philosophy of "growth through internal strength," the company decided to choose an alternative strategy: "growth through partnerships."

Lufthansa was one of the founding members of the Star Alliance—the most comprehensive, and probably the most competitive, airline network in the world (see Exhibit 5). By 2003, the number of members of the Star Alliance had grown to 14 members operating from 894 destinations in 129 countries.

Another three airlines, Asiana Airlines, LOT Polish Airlines, and Spanair, were to join that same year.

The Star Alliance started functioning on 14 May 1997. Entering the Star Alliance had an immediately visible effect on Lufthansa's profit. Lufthansa reported that in 1997, an extra €492 million in profit from business operations came as a result of the alliance.

By 2003, three other global alliances had emerged: Oneworld, World-Wide Reliability, and Skyteam (see Exhibit 6). With the launch of Oneworld in February 1999, competition in the airline industry had taken on a new dimension. This new alliance had five founding members, a common logo, and shared the Star Alliance vision of seamlessly linking the partner airlines' route networks.

EXHIBIT 4

Competitive Position of the Lufthansa Companies in 2003

Passage	No. 1 in Europe, Star Alliance world leader (23% market share)
Logistik	No. 1 in airport-to-airport market (7% market share)
Technik	No. 1 in civil MRO branch (10% market share)
Catering	No. 1 in airline catering (35% market share)
IT Services	Leading specialist airline IT market share
Touristik	No. 2 in Europe (20% market share)

Strategically, these developments were of vital importance. At the end of the 20th century, the economic structure of the airline industry started moving from competition between airlines to competition between networks. Consequently, airline networks began to work toward intensifying integration and common alliance strategies. However, the biggest challenge for the Star Alliance in 2003 lay in finding a balance between integrating network management and ensuring the independence of the individual members.

Traditionally, the core of airline alliances was code-sharing, i.e., using the same flight numbers. Important synergies were also realized through joint sales activities (joint advertising, common frequent flyer programs, joint travel agency contracts, etc.), collective market research, shared facilities—e.g., lounges—and staff exchanges.

Beyond these traditionally important operational synergies, in 1999 the Star Alliance started integrating much more demanding management activities, which required a joint management structure for the overall alliance.

In December 1998, the airlines in the Star Alliance formed a focused management team to lead the alliance on a day-to-day basis. Jürgen Weber personally championed the need for a permanent management structure in order to give further force and dynamism to the Alliance. The newly appointed Alliance Management Board consisted of six executives who were made responsible for dealing with all the strategic issues of the network (see Exhibit 7).

There were four key issues of major strategic importance:

- The global network
- Marketing and sales
- Device and product development
- Information technology

With the new structure in place, the Alliance progressed beyond the stage of a committee-based collaboration. In 2003, the joint Star Alliance investment in global advertisement for more than five years resulted in a strong market position and effective branding. Despite the awareness that a true strategic integration demanded a fusion of the partners' different corporate cultures, their attitude and willingness to go further in this direction changed within Lufthansa at the beginning of the 21st century. After a period of alliance euphoria, Lufthansa changed its perception of the potential and degree of optimal integration of the Star Alliance.

In the early years, Lufthansa's motto was, "Everything linked with further integrating the alliance is good." Since 2000, there has been a different approach, more in line with the thinking that 80 percent solutions that every partner can really get behind are better than 99 percent ones that engender negativity.

— Carsten Spohr, Head of Passage, Alliance Management

One central reason for the change in Lufthansa's perceptions was that further integration within the alliance would affect the other Lufthansa companies. A common network strategy and cultural integration were inevitably connected to critical issues concerning branding and identity within the Lufthansa Group. The specialization within the Star Alliance, and particularly the planned extension of joint procurement, could cause serious economic problems for certain Lufthansa subsidiaries.

For example, the search for synergies within the Star Alliance included the joint development of IT solutions. In April 1999, the management board of the Star Alliance assigned the United Airlines IT department to

| EXHIBIT 5 | Evolution of the Star Alliance |

May 14, 1997
Air Canada, Lufthansa, SAS, Thai Airways International and United Airlines launch the Star Alliance network.

March 1999
Ansett Australia and Air New Zealand join the Star Alliance network.

March 2000
The Austrian Airlines Group, Comprising Australian Airlines, Lauda Air and Tyrolean Airways becomes the 10th member of Star Alliance.

March 2003
Asiana Airlines joins the Star Alliance network.

April 2003
Spanair joins the Star Alliance network.

October 1997
VARIG Brazilian Airlines joins the Star Alliance network.

October 1999
With an official Launch Eent in Tokyo, ANA joins the Star Alliance network and Singapore Airlines officially gains Observer Status to join the Alliance.

April 2000
Singapore Airlines joins Star Alliance.

July 2000
British Midland and Mexicana Airlines join Star Alliance.

October 2003
LOT joins Star Alliance

| EXHIBIT 6 | Alliances in Comparison (July 2001) |

		Passengers (in thousands)	Fleet	Employees	Destinations
	Star Alliance	292,000	2,058	277,600	729
	Oneworld	209,000	1,852	270,044	565
	Sky Team	176,700	1,013	155,000	472
	Worldwide	168,542	1,263	160,797	~ 500

develop a central Star Alliance IT Organization, which at that time represented a major threat to LH IT Services' main market.

Another critical issue lay in the serious economic problems that various members of the Star Alliance were experiencing. For example, while Star Alliance saved Air Canada from bankruptcy in 1999 with a financial booster of €490 million, it did not lend the same assistance to Australian airline Ansett, which would ultimately file for bankruptcy in September 2001 and fly for the last time on April 2, 2002.

At the end of 2002, United Airlines, a founding partner of the Alliance and its largest member, reported record losses of €3.2 billion and was declared as being in Chapter 11 of the U.S. Bankruptcy Code as of December 9, 2002. Jan Albrecht, CEO of the Star Alliance, said:

Things will be business as usual at United and the entire Alliance. Customers won't notice the difference.

In addition to conventional cost reduction measures of €1.1 billion and material cost reductions

C

EXHIBIT 7 Alliance GmbH structure in 2003

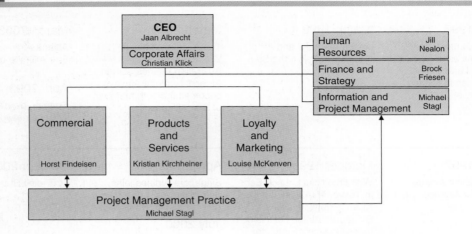

of €1.4 billion annually, United planned to further expand its code and revenue sharing in order to deal with the crisis. Toward that end, United renegotiated with Lufthansa on sales in North America, which would bring United an additional €90 million annually.

> *In addition to our finance rationalization, we will be utilizing more fully our core competencies—the unparalleled route network, our strong alliance, and our best-in-market frequent-flyer program—so as to put United back among the leading global air carriers.*

> — Glenn Tilton, CEO, United Airlines

The significance of United Airlines as the key Alliance partner was unquestioned at Lufthansa. It was clear that Lufthansa's financial situation would change fundamentally without its strong U.S. partner and that finding another U.S. equivalent in 2003 was not an option.

> *The Alliance is not a solution when members begin having serious financial problems. We are not in a position to save United financially. Although they are our most important partner, we can't help them beyond know-how transfer; otherwise, we would be risking our own well-being. That is the only realistic strategy in view of current events.*

> — Carsten Spohr

Lufthansa ruled out financial assistance and began to discuss initial scenarios. At the same time, efforts were made to support United with experience exchange and know-how transfer in crisis management.

Programm 15

In addition to long-term organization and strategic restructuring, the Lufthansa management constantly gave strategic cost saving priority after the turnaround.

> *Looking at our current financial situation, if we don't take action now, we will face a serious crisis once again in a couple of years.*

> — Jürgen Weber in 1996

In the mid-1990s, after a large portion of the Programm 93 projects had been implemented and the crisis from 1991 withstood, Weber decided to pursue the transformation process further and to give Programm 15 renewed vigor.

Programm 15 was a broad-range, strategic cost management program designed to make Lufthansa more competitive through cost management and cultural change, resulting in more cost consciousness among staff at every organizational level.

The number "15" stood for 15 German pfennig per SKO ("seat kilometers offered," the cost target for transporting one aircraft seat one kilometer). Lufthansa intended to reduce costs from 17.7 pfennig in 1996 to 15 pfennig in 2001. This implied an overall cost reduction of 20 percent within five years (4 percent annual reduction throughout the Lufthansa Group).

Programm 15 purposely set goals that were challenging but achievable. Line managers were responsible for cost reductions, so the realization of Programm 15 was integrated into their "normal" management goals and constituted part of their performance expectations.

As with the turnaround, a project team was put in place to monitor and maintain in Programm 15. No compromises were made on goals, but the Programm 15 team consulted with line management on how to cut costs and tried to solve problems through open discussion with those who were responsible for implementation. Close monitoring and sharing results openly (actual performance data for each individual manager were published regularly) ensured accountability and continuous feedback.

To draw attention to and preserve the focus on strategic cost goals, Programm 15 relied on top management support and a number of both symbolic and substantive measures. Just as the OPS Team, Programm 15 was located next to Weber's office. Cost reduction measures were set in the center of town meetings, weekly reports in the *Lufthanseat* (the staff journal), and widespread publications on a few, impressive success stories.

As Programm 15 came to a conclusion in 2002, Lufthansa posted a profit of €689 million, the second best results in the firm's history.

THE PILOTS' STRIKE (2001)

Although the annual results for 2000 were extraordinarily good, by the end of the year, the first weak signals of an economic slump, particularly in sales growth, had already appeared on Weber's radar screen.

While Weber was planning the first measures for renewed cost-savings initiatives for spring 2001, the pilots, with 2000's strong annual figures in sight, began to call for an exceptionally high raise in compensation.

As early as autumn 2000, the pilots' labor union, "Vereinigung Cockpit" (VC), informed Lufthansa's top management that negotiations regarding wages and compensation would be extremely harsh.

> In October of 2000, VC terminated all cooperation with us and announced that they were not going to talk about anything else until a solution for the compensation had been found. And they were as good as their word. They refused all communication for some four months until negotiations on wage and compensation agreements began February 2001.

— Oliver Kaden, Head of Industrial Relations Flight Crews 1999–2003 and Head of the CEO's Office as of June 2003

And so the toughest round of wage negotiations in Lufthansa's history began with the pilots in the spring of 2001. Cockpit (VC) demanded an increase in salary of approximately 30 percent and underscored its demands during a warning strike by threatening to take confrontational measures.

In line with the consensus-oriented corporate culture at Lufthansa, executive board member Stefan Lauer tried to negotiate with the pilots in an informal, personal talk. But VC, allegedly "under pressure" from its members, would not be satisfied with quiet talks. Consequently, Lufthansa's management decided to step up the negotiations in their own way by refusing to make any voluntary concessions whatsoever. It seemed more like an exchange of positions rather than an actual negotiation process intended for changing things. The barriers grew to such heights on both fronts that they failed to come to an agreement on their own over the course of 13 days in May. On May 23, after seven unsuccessful negotiation rounds, Hans-Dietrich Genscher, formerly the German Secretary of State, was asked to arbitrate. With his help, a new wage agreement was finally concluded on June 8, 2001.

What made it possible for a group of professionals to articulate its demands and to escalate negotiations to such huge proportions? First of all, as a professional group, the pilots were less fully integrated into the company. They spent most of their working hours in the air and were at the company only a minimum amount of time. As a result, they developed their own subculture, which was detached from the rest of the company.

This development was augmented by the fact that pilots were in general increasingly networking across companies, as could for example be seen since 1991 in the European Cockpit Association (ECA) and in the progressive growth of the Star Alliance, and since 1998 in the cross-alliance Association of Star Alliance Pilots (ASAP). In this context, in 2000 an international benchmarking study on pilots' wages and working conditions was conducted jointly by Lufthansa and VC. It was found that among European pilots (KLM, SR, SK, AF, and BA), Lufthansa pilots were in the middle wage-earning bracket, but that all European carriers were paid considerably less than U.S. airlines. Based on this assessment, Lufthansa pilots began to feel disadvantaged, even though they were among the Group's top wage-earners.

> The pilots are identifying more and more with the network-based international sphere, while the other professional groups identify with Lufthansa.

— Christoph Fay, Head of Lufthansa Group Human Resources Marketing

A large portion of the disgruntlement and severity associated with the argument had emotional roots. During the crisis years at the beginning of the 1990s, the pilots, just as everyone at Lufthansa, made considerable concessions voluntarily.

> The causes of the pilots' strike go back ten years. During the turnaround at the beginning of the '90s, the company convinced the pilots that Lufthansa could only

survive if all the employee groups made a considerable sacrifice. Subsequently, the pilots agreed to irreversible concessions. Some of the strongest opponents of the solution back then led the strike in 2001. The situation was exacerbated by the fact that the pilots felt they had been unjustly treated and were not appreciated enough. This provided immense potential for industrial action. Cockpit deliberately brought this "dynamite" into the company with little regard for the impact of their actions. They just wanted to send out a signal.

— Stefan Lauer, Executive Board, Human Resources

The situation around the pilots' strike escalated primarily because of emotional reasons, specifically the feeling of not being appreciated or acknowledged. After the '92 crisis had been dealt with successfully, the company turned into something of a mass production operation, so now the pilots are treated with more distance—or more technocratically, if you will.

— Oliver Kaden

The pilots' strike had a far-reaching effect on Lufthansa. Aside from the one-time costs of €75 million that the two-and-a-half-day strike caused and the additional permanent annual staff costs totaling about €125 million, the company's culture, especially its community spirit, suffered great damage. The pilots' unwillingness to compromise ultimately ended up further widening the gap that had existed historically between the pilots and ground crew.

The fact that an occupational group could pursue its own interests so unswervingly and so obviously neglect the interests of the company as a whole triggered disgust, restlessness, and counteractions throughout the company. Countless indignant comments were submitted to the management by employees, expressing their anger toward and incomprehension of the pilots' actions.

The discord came to a head on May 17 in the form of a counter-demonstration by ground crew. The pilots had convened for a demonstration in the waiting lounge at the airport, their intention being to explain their perspective to the stranded passengers. Ground crew employees wanted to publicly demonstrate that the pilots' strike was causing unrest within Lufthansa. The meeting of the two groups in the airport set off an aggressive argument in which it was only barely possible to avoid physical fighting.

In addition, this turn of events was a source of personal disappointment for Weber. For the first time, Lufthansa had not been able to generate a constructive atmosphere for negotiations with a professional group. A professional group had promoted its own interests

without considering the impact on the company as a whole. To Weber, this was a personal slap in the face after so many years of working to develop Lufthansa's strategy, organization, and culture.

The pilots' strike really hurt Jürgen Weber. In a nutshell, everything he had fought for for ten years was put in jeopardy by the pilots. That left scars in the organization which are visible even today.

— Ursel Reininger, Head of Management Development

The Lufthansa signature community-oriented culture, which had made it possible to deal with the crisis in the 1990s and which was seen as being critical for coping with current events, had failed.

In hindsight, a certain understanding for the pilots' demands arose from various corners of the management. Debate about whether the internal negotiating strategy had been the right one continued to persist. The events of September 11 temporarily strengthened the community spirit within Lufthansa.

Although 9/11 put the rift in the organization on the back burner, it can still be sensed—suspicion, aversion and great disappointment have not disappeared completely.

— Ursel Reininger

RE-ENERGIZING THE ONGOING CHANGE (2001–2004)

D-Check

By the end of 2000, Lufthansa's management had already begun developing a sequel initiative to Programm 15.

By the end of 2000, we had already started picking up the first signals telling us that we could not afford to rest on the laurels of the past but would instead always have to be proactive and ensure our success.

— Peter Gerber, Senior Vice President and Head of D-Check

By the end of 2000, we had the feeling that the end of a golden era was nigh. 2000 was the second-best fiscal year in the history of Lufthansa—it was all sunny days and blue skies for us. But we saw dark clouds on the horizon. It's just that no one believed us.

— Holger Hätty

Even in good times, Jürgen Weber is a prudent businessman. His motto has always been "keep from becoming too tranquil." He tries to prevent such calm.

— Ursel Reininger

The decision with regard to D-Check—the third cost-oriented program in Lufthansa's change process—was made in April 2001. The positive experiences with predecessor programs Programm 93 and Programm 15 moved Weber to utilize a similar program structure for the next phase of the strategic cost-saving process.

Lufthansa's experience with programs is double-sided. On the one hand, past programs have proven to impact the organization in a positive way; but on the other, some people have also learned how to just "make it through" the program without really doing anything.

— Peter Gerber

In order to counter potential weariness for change and new measures in the company, which had in any event been subject to great trial, the management decided to make a clear distinction between D-Check and its predecessors both with respect to its content and the way in which it was to be communicated.

In contrast to Programm 15, which was nothing more than a cost-cutting program, D-Check was to have a long-term effect and to focus on cash flow. The business units were consulted in order to determine the volume of the program. Specifically, the business units were asked to estimate the scope of the risks (e.g., price fluctuations, sudden drops in load capacity, or infrastructural bottlenecks) they might encounter over the next three years. By considering all these potential risks in sum, they then determined a worst-case scenario in which Lufthansa would have to generate €1 billion over the long term in order to prepare the Group for future risks. So this was to be the purpose of D-Check: to raise €1 billion over the medium term from June 2001 to May 2004.

The name "D-Check" recalled the most comprehensive routine check performed to ensure the functionality of an airplane, thereby calling for a systematic "organizational check-up" to ensure the company's ability to compete. The basic idea of the program was take apart, test, and—wherever they proved risky or defective—exchange every "part" in the company.

A total of 26 full-time employees were responsible for these projects at headquarters. Ten employees worked in the corporate project team, which reported directly to Weber. The individuals involved had to apply for the job and underwent a stringent selection process.

Responsibility for generating cash flow lay in the hands of line and business unit managers. In line with the risks of its business, Passenger Service bore by far the greatest burden in D-Check (see Exhibit 8).

In 2003, a total of 600 individual projects were initiated in association with D-Check. Of those, 70 percent focused on cost reduction, the remaining 30 percent on making a profit. All activities were subject to constant, strict monitoring.

During the initial months, an organization tries to resist new initiatives, and if you communicate a program ineffectively during that time, you're dead.

— Peter Gerber

D-Check was accompanied by a comprehensive communication strategy based on three pillars. First, printed media were used, including the monthly barometer reporting on the current cash-flow status in *Lufthanseat*, the employee magazine; a thank-you letter to project leaders in the implementation of a D-Check project; venues discussing specific topics and background information for the business and corporate units; and internal media such as *InTouch* at LH Systems. The next pillar entailed electronic media, such as comments by Weber on achieving D-Check goals on the intranet or current information from individual D-Check projects. Finally, the third pillar, which was given particular emphasis, consisted of personal communication. Specifically, in light of Lufthansa's good financial situation, the significance of D-Check had to be demonstrated during the beginning phase.

Jürgen Weber and the remainder of the top management showed their commitment to the program by communicating it comprehensively—e.g., at town meetings; at other events with up to 250 Group managers; and through measures such as "Board on Tour," in which executive board members visited selected project leaders, among other things.

In addition to the senior management's considerable personal investment in the program, a large number of other measures were deployed for initiating it, including business unit workshops, a series of ten large events which reached 1,250 managers within the space of a week, or the graphic communication of worst-case scenarios and benchmarks. Nevertheless, at first, the program had serious problems that were primarily associated with a lack of commitment. This outlook changed radically with September 11.

Initially, not all employees understood that another change project was necessary. We were living in a lush phase and had slipped a bit into a state of inertia. Nine-eleven caused a complete about-face. The attacks transformed our world completely in a matter of seconds. We found ourselves in a crisis situation from one second to the next. After that, there was no longer any debate about the necessity for change.

— Peter Gerber

The Basic Tenets of the D-Check Program Philosophy

1. Prophylactic measures for ensuring and reinforcing Lufthansa's competitive position over the long term ("Ensuring the future")
2. Company-wide program, including central units and business units (Passage, logistics, technology, catering, IT services and the service and finance companies)
3. The detailed review of structure and processes customized especially for Lufthansa in terms of time, cost, and quality in analogy to the D-Check process performed for airplanes
4. Goal definition on a cash-flow basis (cost-benefit); subsequent derival of company objectives
5. Uniform and transparent external and internal communication

Project Team Tasks

- Controlling and monitoring of D-Check throughout the entire Group
- Doing D-Check in central units
- Heading up of projects in Group units
- Coordination of interface projects between business units
- Support of projects in the business units
- Coordination of measures to improve e-capabilities
- Digitizing of processes
- Communication of D-Check (along with Lufthansa communication)

EXHIBIT 8   D-Check Projects and Generated Cash Flow

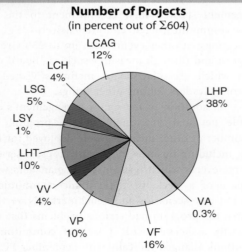

Number of Projects
(in percent out of Σ604)

LCAG 12%
LCH 4%
LSG 5%
LSY 1%
LHT 10%
VV 4%
VP 10%
VF 16%
VA 0.3%
LHP 38%

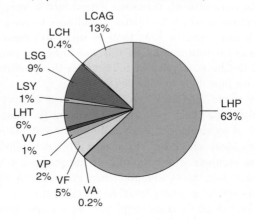

Planned Cashflow from 2004
(in percent out of Σ1326 Mio. Euro)

LCAG 13%
LCH 0.4%
LSG 9%
LSY 1%
LHT 6%
VV 1%
VP 2%
VF 5%
VA 0.2%
LHP 63%

After 9/11, D-Check was complemented by "D-Check acute"—an additional program package with a special focus on cash spending for 2002. Energized by external events, the program surpassed even its own goals: by July 2002, it had already met its objectives for all of fiscal 2002 (see Exhibit 9).

September 11

At Lufthansa, the news of the attacks on the World Trade Center traveled like wildfire throughout the Group. Countless Lufthansa people spent the entire afternoon on September 11 in front of the television in shock and filled with great sorrow and fear for their colleagues in the air and for the consequences to themselves and Lufthansa.

The emotional impact, which at first catalyzed stunned trauma, turned into highly active involvement for dealing with the crisis only a short while later.

Paralysis, sorrow, and shock—a sort of apocalyptic time—predominated some days after 9/11. After about ten days, the Group Management got the employees into the cafeteria and talked with them about next steps. Once people knew about the action plan, the atmosphere changed right away, thereby setting free an immense force for taking action.

— Christoph Fay

Thirteen of the 28 Lufthansa airplanes en route to the United States were able to turn back. The remainder had to find alternate airports in Gander and Halifax (Canada). The Special Assistance Team (SAT), whose job was actually to provide assistance in the event of a plane crash, was activated.

The SAT provided immediate assistance on site, for example by supporting the people waiting in the planes. The Gander airport was not equipped for large planes, so it had no portable staircase. Moreover, some passengers did not have a visa for Canada and were not authorized to disembark. Lufthansa was the only airline worldwide to take care of its stranded passengers and to offer support by providing essentials such as clothing, food, diapers, medicine, counseling, and assistance with administrative formalities associated with their continuing journey. Furthermore, the SAT developed emergency measures to preempt further danger, such as retracting Lufthansa employees and their families from the Near East, cancellation of flights to insecure regions, and the like.

The reports from the aid teams were extremely emotional and communicated far and wide. Mr. Lauer told us of first-class passengers in Gander cowering on cots in a church and cooking food and of people's gratitude that we took care of them. These anecdotes helped us to digest these experiences together and to develop pride in the helpful, service-oriented mentality at Lufthansa.

— Silke Lehnhardt, Head of the Lufthansa School of Business

| EXHIBIT 9 | D-Check Barometer |

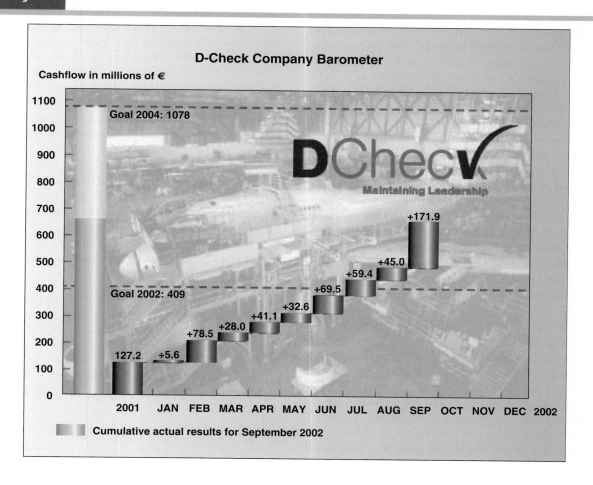

New York City, Tuesday, September 11, 2001

8:45 a.m.:	American Airlines Flight 11 with 92 passengers on board flies into the North Tower of the World Trade Center.
9:03 a.m.:	United Airlines Flight 175, a Boeing 767 on its way with 65 passengers from Newark to Los Angeles, flies into the South Tower of the World Trade Center.
9:43 a.m.:	American Airlines Flight 77 hits the Pentagon in Arlington, Virginia.
10:05 a.m.:	The South Tower collapses.
10:28 a.m.:	The North Tower collapses.
10:29 a.m.:	United Airlines Flight 93 with 45 passengers on board crashes about 80 kilometers outside Pittsburgh, Pennsylvania.

9/11 triggered the greatest crisis in the airline industry since World War II. In addition to dramatic declines in passenger numbers and freight, the industry was also suddenly confronted with additional costs associated with reinforced security measures and increased insurance rates. The direct results alone added up to €15 billion in losses for the airlines, which is equivalent to over 20 years' profit from flights for the entire industry. As early as October 2001, airlines that had already been experiencing serious difficulty, such as Swissair and Sabena, filed for bankruptcy. Approximately 400,000 people in the airline industry lost their jobs all over the world.

The consequences of 9/11 far exceeded the risks calculated in worst-case scenarios. During the four-day national airspace shutdown over the United States, Lufthansa cancelled 233 flights, the result being that 56,000 passengers were not able to travel as scheduled. The number of no-show passengers also rose considerably, sometimes even 50 percent more than on a normal business day. The loss in profit combined with the cost of supporting passengers and employees approximated €46 million.

In addition, costs were also incurred for security measures at airports (security checks on passengers, baggage, and freight) and in the planes themselves (installment of reinforced cockpit doors, removal of tips and sharp objects from on-board silverware, and hiring of Sky Marshals) as well as for the considerable increase in insurance for the fleet. Within seven days after 9/11, the insurance companies cancelled the airlines' coverage for war and war-like events. The rates for full war coverage increased by more than tenfold. Basic coverage for the fleet alone represented another financial burden of about €50 million for the Group. With increases in cost in 2002 by 224.2 percent over 2001, insurance expenses amounted to €107 million.

Lufthansa's exploding costs were a stark contrast to the sharp drop in demand for flights to North America by 30 percent and for flights to the Far East by 17 percent. During the first months after the attacks, Lufthansa was transporting about 30,000 passengers per day, about 25 percent less than usual. Demand particularly fell for first and business class seats, which meant €50 million in losses per week. Not only was the airline's business hit hard, but the other Lufthansa Group companies were, too. In particular, Lufthansa Cargo also suffered dramatic losses.

The incomparability and unique difficulty that went hand in hand with 9/11 made it impossible to make forecasts about business. The insecurity, previously unwitnessed in such magnitude, complicated planning strategic measures for managing the crisis.

Only weeks after the attacks, three different scenarios were defined in terms of how demand would develop: V, U and L. "V" anticipated a sharp drop in demand with a rapid recovery. "U" anticipated that after the initial sharp drop, demand would table out at average levels over the medium term and then increase again. "L" anticipated that demand would remain low over the long term. More than ever before, Lufthansa was called upon to draw on its ability to cope with crises.

To manage the crisis, Lufthansa once again deployed several of the measures used during the turnaround in the early 1990s.

Dealing with 9/11 went very smoothly. People knew what they had to do. It was as if we just went to a drawer and opened it, pulled out the crisis plan, and implemented it.

— Holger Hätty

What we needed nine months for at the beginning of the 90s now only took us nine weeks; even with the same set of tools.

— Jürgen Weber

To immediately reduce capacity, all routes were reviewed for profitability and the route network reduced. Even before 9/11, Lufthansa had already decided to downsize its original flight offering and to withdraw 12 short-range aircraft from its fleet. Now, however, Lufthansa chose to ground another four. The new policy put 20 of Lufthansa's 236 aircraft out of commission, and people expected more to follow.

With the additional project "D-Check acute" with special focus on cash spending for 2002, D-Check was turned into Lufthansa's program for systematic cost and multi-project management. It was key for overcoming the crisis after September 11.

We altered our message immediately and said, "Only three things matter now: costs, costs, and costs." All the cost-effective parts of a program were given priority as of that moment.

— Peter Gerber

Within 17 days, an action plan had been developed, presented to the labor unions and approved by the executive board. In addition to capacity reduction, this comprehensive, radical action plan included other drastic measures, such as the immediate stop on investment and hiring, the postponement of the Airbus A380 and cancellation of the planned purchase of four Boeing 747-400 planes. All other plans for making investments and all other current and planned projects were reviewed and shelved wherever necessary.

The greatest challenge consisted of reducing human resources' costs in accordance with the law while remaining flexible and being able to quickly return the crew to full capacity when the crisis started to wear off.

We developed ad hoc measures which we classified into three levels. Level 1 included measures that were easily and quickly implemented. Level 2 included tougher measures that had to be coordinated first, such as temporary employment or employee dismissals during the trial period. Level 3 included measures for a catastrophe scenario that we wanted to avoid taking but could have taken in the most extreme emergency in order to survive. Luckily, we never had to use Level 2 or 3 measures.

— Dr. Martin Schmitt, Senior Vice President, Executive Personnel and Services

In order to reduce capacity, other measures were also used along with the hiring stop, such as unpaid vacation time, time off in lieu of overtime and vacation, and offering more part-time work. The extension of the wage agreement for ground and cabin crew and the postponement of the wage increase for cockpit personnel was agreed with the labor unions.

The entire executive board waived 10 percent of its salary. Other members of the management and the non-tariff employees were asked to contribute to the crisis management effort by voluntarily waiving 5 to 10 percent of their salaries. Three-fourths did so. All personnel were encouraged to voluntarily lend the company their Christmas bonuses at zero interest until August of the following year.

Except for Air France, Lufthansa was the only airline not to dismiss employees as a result of September 11. Thanks to the "D-Check acute" action plan and security surcharges on tickets and cargo goods, a cash flow of €530 million was generated within three and a half months (see Exhibit 10). Despite the considerable efforts made to manage the crisis, the operating results of €700–750 million projected for 2001 were now no longer realistic. In 2001, Lufthansa concluded fiscal 2001 by posting a loss of €633 million. Despite the poor results, Weber decided to pay out a bonus at the end of the year 2001. Personal investment was weighted unusually high in order to acknowledge the immense effort made to manage the crisis. The company's community spirit and confidence were reinforced through the successful handling of the 9/11 crisis.

It still was not clear how the crisis would develop even into April 2002. Fear, pulling together, and the belief that we were going to make it dominated. Although the situation seemed hopeless, the experiences from the '91–'92 turnaround were still very fresh in everyone's mind and that gave us incredible strength as a community. Jürgen Weber was very important for this optimism during the crisis—he was an embodiment of our successes with handling crises and of our belief in ourselves.

— Peter Gerber

One of the most difficult tasks is to motivate people when times are good. After 9/11, people once again became aware of the fact that we would have to constantly exert ourselves, even when there was no acute threat looming. Sad though it is, this is one of the positive effects of those terrible events. People are once again full of energy and all on their own, thus ensuring that costs don't explode again.

— Jürgen Weber

CHALLENGES IN 2003

Ongoing Crisis Management

After the airline stabilized with its reduced capacities in 2002, the first half of 2003 presented Lufthansa with an even worse crisis than 9/11. The industry experienced the worst crisis yet in terms of air traffic.

EXHIBIT
10

Cashflow Generated from D-Check Acute

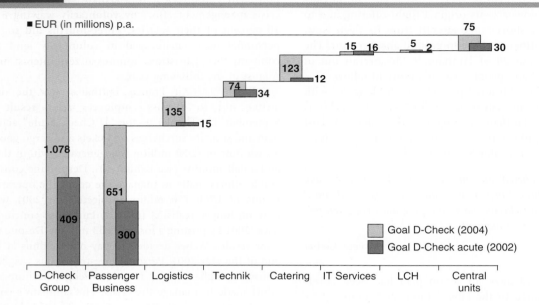

■ EUR (in millions) p.a.

Goal D-Check (2004)
Goal D-Check acute (2002)

| D-Check Group | Passenger Business | Logistics | Technik | Catering | IT Services | LCH | Central units |

Lufthansa had to post unexpectedly high losses of €415 million in the first quarter of 2003. The persisting economic downturn, the impact of the Iraq war, and the consequences of the SARS lung disease weakened demand in air traffic in the first half of 2003.

In January of 2003, the executive board decided to further reduce capacities. The new plan included a capacity reduction of another 31 from Lufthansa AG and 15 more from Lufthansa CityLine, investment reductions worth €200 million, as well as an immediate hiring freeze throughout the Group and a supplementary D-Check initiative called "Cash 100." With this initiative, the executive board requested all business units to immediately present tangible measures for meeting these objectives. The purpose of Cash 100 was to create an additional cash flow of €100 million before the end of 2003.

In March of 2003, the executive board approved further comprehensive measures intended for securing the projected year-end results.

The executive board decided to declare a state of crisis in April of 2003, as a result of which, temporary work had been introduced by April 15 of that year.

In June of 2003, when the crisis started to bottom out, Lufthansa promptly raised capacity on routes to North America and Asia in a rapid response to emerging market opportunities. In face of an increase in demand, flexible capacity management was considered the special strength of the Lufthansa Group.

There is an urgent need for action and yet at the same time there seems to be no end in sight for this trend. War in Iraq and SARS are causing our passenger volume and thus also our revenue to decline even more and that necessitates tough measures which can be rapidly implemented. Our competitive advantage is that we are faster and better prepared than our competitors.

— Jürgen Weber

We are currently experiencing a different type of crisis, and it is as yet unclear as to whether our tried-and-trusted methods for managing crises will be effective. A certain mentality has developed around here that if anyone can pull away from the brink of crisis, we can. There is the danger of people failing to recognize that this time, we have a totally different crisis on our hands, namely long-term decreases in yield due to a new competitor with a more efficient business model. We are at the end of a phase of mere cost reduction. At some point, you just can't squeeze any more juice from a lemon, no matter how hard you try. So now we have to start thinking about where to get juice.

— Karl-Heinz Steinke, Senior Vice President, Corporate Controlling and Cost Management

Organizational Burnout

By 2003, Lufthansa had a decade of constant energetic exertion behind it. One challenge was to counter the threat of overexertion in the company. A challenge at Lufthansa was how to handle or prevent exhaustion, change-tiredness, or even organizational burnout.

We are in a business in which the only thing we are ever able to say to our employees is, "Economize, economize, economize!" And our people respond by asking, "When is the economizing going to come to an end?" They are exhausted and every time they slow down to catch their breath, there we are at their heels telling them, "Economize!" They want something playful and light-hearted now and then. The sex appeal of working constantly is clearly coming to an end. The pilots' strike and excessive demands were no coincidence. This problem will return to haunt us. Maintaining the change momentum is becoming increasingly difficult.

— Holger Hätty

There is a sort of weariness for change in the company. Up to now, we have tended more to talk of a crisis in order to cut costs. We had to manage to integrate a positive, innovative spirit in the cost-saving effort so that it would be exciting and trendy. Otherwise, we will always be battling exhaustion and inertia and never able to achieve sustainable change through our programs.

— Peter Gerber

Burnout is a challenge. Everywhere, people are feeling the need for peace and quiet and hoping that once we've stood this through, everything will return to normal and we'll be able to rest. People still have not sufficiently grasped that that moment will probably never come.

— Silke Lehnhardt

Business Model

The growth of low-cost airlines' structure and business model called into question the traditional model for an airline company. One possible answer was strong, internal segmentation, which would enable Lufthansa to offer services to the low-cost market so as to be able to defend its market share against airlines such as Ryan Air, easyJet, and others. On the other hand, it would be necessary to pinpoint one focus in order to fully exploit Lufthansa's economies of scale and cost efficiencies over the other cheap airline carriers.

In Europe, there is 25 percent overcapacity and enormous competition. There are no barriers for getting into the market, but the ones for leaving it are massive, especially because of the high gearing and emotional attachment to the idea of a national carrier. We are an airline for business people and must therefore service routes several times a day. That is only profitable for certain routes and is easy prey for cheap airline carriers.

— Holger Hätty

Our business model is associated with extremely high risk that is gaining in significance now and in future probably will continue to do so. On the one hand, we have huge fixed costs and a very volatile market on the other.

— Silke Lehnhardt

One challenge will be to develop a well-thought-out strategy on short-haul European routes. At the moment, the conventional system is under massive attack on the continent. We will have to undergo a massive "fitness program" to cope with these new challenges.

— Stefan Lauer

Changing Seats at the Top

The Lufthansa Supervisory Board nominated Wolfgang Mayrhuber, then deputy chairman of the executive board of Deutsche Lufthansa AG, as Jürgen Weber's successor.

This early decision will ensure continuity within Lufthansa's executive management.

— Supervisory Board Chairman Dr. Klaus Schlede

With Wolfgang Mayrhuber at the helm, the company will be well equipped for the future at this difficult time, and that is an important sign for our customers, shareholders, and employees.

— Jürgen Weber

At his last annual press conference, Jürgen Weber presented outstanding annual results for 2002 that exceeded those of all other airlines worldwide.

The year 2002, as well as the first months of 2003, had been marked by geopolitical uncertainty; a persistent, cyclical slowdown in the economy; insolvency; threats of further terrorist attacks and war; and the SARS disease, which when taken en masse made both markets and consumers extremely nervous. Yet it was precisely in this turbulent phase that Lufthansa had managed to buck this sector-wide trend. Weber summarized this fact while expressing his optimism for the future:

Wolfgang Mayrhuber will captain a well-run ship. We are in a leading position in our industry, and we shall continue to work hard to maintain and extend this position. The Lufthansa Group has proved that it can respond rapidly, act flexibly and withstand crises.

On June 18, 2003, Mayrhuber began his tenure as Weber's successor. Weber left behind him a crisis-resistant, healthy organization, but one that had been strongly influenced by him as a person and that had oriented itself toward him and sought strength from him in times of crisis. Weber worked for Lufthansa for 35 years and led it for 12.

When Wolfgang Mayrhuber became CEO, he had been in service with Lufthansa for 30 years. He had been a key figure in Lufthansa's turnaround, privatization, and strategic renewal. In his new function, Mayrhuber wasted no time in calling for a high level of company innovation, creativity, and flexibility.

From autumn 2003 Lufthansa therefore planned to offer its passengers a new business class with greater comfort and a radically revamped seat that converted into a bed. These redesigned seats were to be installed in the modern fleet of long-haul Airbus 340-600 first. Lufthansa intended to invest around €30 million in a comprehensive customer program that would be implemented by summer 2004.

Especially our premium customers deserve outstanding service. They will be given their own dedicated terminals in Frankfurt and Munich as well as exclusive transfer lounges. State-of-the-art technology currently under development in cooperation with the German Federal Ministry of the Interior, including for security, will help to make air travel a pleasure once again.

— Wolfgang Mayrhuber

However, Mayrhuber also said that Lufthansa would be able to retain its top ranking in the industry and creative force if only costs were also reduced at the same time:

We shall remain the generator of innovation within our industry. This will require leaner structures and thus even more efficient lines of decision. These are Lufthansa's answers to the changing conditions on the global market.

— Wolfgang Mayrhuber

As had been the case under Weber, the firm's primary objectives continued to be the systematic, continued development of Lufthansa well as ensuring the continuity of its strategic development.

The group is ideally equipped for the future in times of crisis. Under Wolfgang Mayrhuber's leadership, Lufthansa will remain ready for change and continue to develop its strengths, such as vigilance, speed, and flexibility.

— Jürgen Weber

General Motors Defense

Changwha Chung
Paul W. Beamish

Richard Ivey School of Business, The University of Western Ontario

If you don't like change, you're going to like irrelevance a lot less.

—General Eric K. Shinseki, Chief of Staff, U.S. Army

In October 1999 the recently appointed Chief of Staff of the U.S. Army, Eric Shinseki, held a meeting with eight leading defense industry manufacturers. During this meeting he went into detail regarding his vision for the type of equipment he felt the U.S. Army currently lacked. Of particular importance, he felt, was the need for a new medium-weight armored vehicle. Contrary to past practice, Shinseki planned to award a multibillion-dollar contract within only 11 months. Any manufacturers wishing to be considered were asked to have a prototype ready by May 2000 for testing at Fort Knox.

Bill Pettipas, executive director of General Motors Defense in London, Ontario, was among the industry leaders present during the meeting. Pettipas was convinced that an existing GM-developed platform was ideal for the Army's needs. At issue, however, was how to pursue the contract. Should they go it alone, or form a joint venture? A possible JV partner was General Dynamics. General Dynamics was interested in exploring the possibility of a joint venture with GM for the contract, but made it clear that the firm would also submit its own bid. For Pettipas, the question was which arrangement would result in the greatest likelihood of success.

GENERAL MOTORS

General Motors (GM), the world's largest vehicle manufacturer, designed, built, and marketed cars and trucks worldwide. GM had been the global automotive sales leader since 1931. GM employed about 355,000 people. GM cars and trucks were sold under the following brands: Buick, Cadillac, Chevrolet, GMC, Pontiac, Saab, Saturn, and Oldsmobile. GM also produced cars through its Holden, Opel, and Vauxhall units. Non-automotive operations included Hughes Electronics (DirecTV), Allison Transmission (heavy-duty automatic transmissions), GM Locomotive (locomotives, diesel engines), and GM Defense (light armored vehicles). GM had a 49 percent stake in Isuzu Motors and 20 percent stakes in Fuji Heavy Industries (Subaru), Suzuki Motor, and Fiat Auto (Alfa Romeo, Lancia). The GMAC subsidiary provided financing.

GENERAL MOTORS DEFENSE

In 1999, less than 1 percent of GM's total annual revenues of $167 billion came from defense. GM had a rich history of military vehicle production. GM supplied its

Richard Ivey School of Business
The University of Western Ontario **IVEY**

Changwha Chung prepared this case under the supervision of Paul W. Beamish solely to provide material for class discussion. The authors do not intend to illustrate either effective or ineffective handling of a managerial situation. The authors may have disguised certain names and other identifying information to protect confidentiality.

first vehicle for the U.S. military during World War I and had continued to supply vehicles ever since. After World War II, GM continued producing armored vehicles including the M551 Sheridan light tank.

General Motors Defense (GMD), London, Ontario, was a group of GM-owned business units engaged in the design, production, and support of light armored vehicles, their supporting turret systems, and a wide range of commercially based military trucks. GMD consisted of research, design, and manufacturing facilities in London, Ontario; Goleta, California; Troy, Michigan; Adelaide, Australia; and Kreuzlingen, Switzerland. GMD also had offices in Washington, D.C.; Ottawa, Canada; and Canberra, Australia, for government relations.

GMD was a proven manufacturer of quality armored vehicles and turrets. Its two main platforms were light armored vehicle (LAV) and Piranha. GMD supplied these platforms to numerous military forces in over 15 countries, including Australia, Canada, Saudi Arabia, Switzerland, and the United States. These vehicles had been used in operations in Bosnia, Somalia, Cyprus, Panama, Haiti, and as part of Operation Desert Storm. GMD was also well equipped to provide services in project/program management, subcontract management, and product support. GMD's North American chassis operation had a large plant, which was comprised of a manufacturing and test facility covering 34,000 square meters, a 1.2-kilometer banked test track, and a 310,000-liter swim tank. GMD's advanced production technologies included computer-driven laser cutters, rectilinear robotic welders, CAD-CAM systems, and flexible machining centers.

GMD's weapons and electronics operation also had proven experience in designing, manufacturing, and integrating turrets and fire control systems. GMD was recognized globally as the leading manufacturer in multi-purpose lightweight turrets. GMD had recently acquired MOWAG of Switzerland. MOWAG was in charge of designing and developing the Piranha family of vehicles as well as the HMMWV-based Eagle 4×4. GMD greatly benefited from MOWAG's innovative design and world-class manufacturing techniques. GMD had also recently acquired Military Trucks in Detroit, Michigan. Military Trucks sold commercially based GM vehicles adapted for use by military customers. Lastly, General Motors Defense Australia (GMDA) was a center of production for LAV-25 turret systems, and responsible for Asia-Pacific markets.

Main Platform of GM Defense

GMD's light armored vehicles (LAVs) were produced in a number of different variants. These included mortar, anti-tank, ambulance, logistic, personnel carrier, recovery, air defense, command and control, electronic warfare, mobile repair, reconnaissance, and assault guns with 90mm and 105mm main guns.

In the LAV family, the LAV III had been recently developed and was being placed into production. The LAV III was a four-wheel drive (selective eight-wheel drive), armored vehicle weighing approximately 18 tons. It was designed and manufactured with a common hull configuration and was well suited for multiple capability, joint, and combined arms formations. The LAV III could attain speeds of 62 mph (100 kph) on the highway and had a maximum range of 312 miles. The basic infantry carrier vehicle (ICV) had armor that protected the two-man crew and seven on-board soldiers from machine gun bullets, mortar, and artillery fragments. The LAV III ICV variant included configurations such as the reconnaissance, anti-tank guided missile, and medical evacuation vehicles, as well as carriers for mortars, engineer squads, command groups, reconnaissance, and fire support teams. The Mobile Gun System variant comprised a General Dynamics Land Systems 105mm cannon mounted in a low-profile turret integrated on the General Motors LAV III chassis.

Bill Pettipas

In 1982, Bill Pettipas worked at Canadian Forces headquarters in Ottawa. During his 28 years in the Canadian military, he had once served as commanding officer of the Royal Canadian Regiment in London, Ontario. When he was sent to Norway to look at a missile system in 1982, he was approached by a General Motors executive who offered him a sales position at GMD. Pettipas rejected the offer but a year later changed his mind, retired from the Canadian Forces, and joined GMD.

Pettipas started his new job as a domestic sales manager. His responsibility was to sell to the Canadian military. However, Pettipas struggled as he made the transition from the armed forces to business. He did not initially know much about the business, but soon determined that people did not buy a product as much as they did the personality that sold it. He believed that sales success was based on building relationships, even in an industry in which sales were about a $700,000 to $2 million armored vehicle. Not only did he focus on the final customer, the soldier, he also really believed in his products.

In the 1980s, GM Diesel (the former name of GM Defense) grew at a slow, steady pace as small contracts gave way to larger ones, including deals with Australia, New Zealand, Saudi Arabia, and the U.S. Marines. There were, however, hard times in the late 1980s when GM attempted to sell its Diesel division, but it turned out that there were no takers that were acceptable to General

Motors. The division itself then made a bid for greater freedom and won and convinced GM Corporation to allow the GM Locomotive Group, of which GM Defense was a part, to have its own Strategy Board, giving it more autonomy to conduct its business.

Early in 1999, Bill Kienapple, former executive director of GMD, handpicked Pettipas as his successor. Kienapple recognized the value of Pettipas' military background and charismatic leadership style. Kienapple believed that employees were very loyal to Pettipas, and that he had a well-rounded understanding of the business as well as of the customer. Pettipas could walk the GMD shop floor and call to just about everyone by name. Pettipas was both visionary and possessed a keen ability to focus on the core of an issue. With common sense, he could get an idea of how to achieve his goals, and do it through the power of personality.

THE U.S. ARMY

The U.S. Army was made up of ten active duty divisions—six heavy divisions and four light divisions. The brigades, battalions, and companies within a heavy division were organized around the conveyances—tanks or Bradley fighting vehicles—that take that unit to the fight. The brigades in a light division such as the 82nd Airborne were organized around infantry who parachute, march, or helicopter to the fight.

The U.S. Army was well suited for the war it was designed to fight: a huge counterstrike against an invading Soviet Army on the plains of Central Europe. The U.S. Army's institutional identity was reflected by its heavy pieces, especially the near-invincible Abrams tanks. None of these tanks was destroyed by the enemy in the 1991 Gulf War. The Abrams had first been completed in 1980, and it had been a peerless war machine. It could kill enemy tanks at standoff range, beyond the reach of enemy fire. Because of its armor, the Abrams could survive almost any strike. It had a layer of metal protection so thick that the tank weighed 70 tons.

The Abrams was too big to be transported efficiently to the battlefield by air. The only means to transport the Abrams was by ship, a process that took weeks. Even after the Abrams was transported to the battlefield by ship, it guzzled a gallon of fuel per half mile traveled. Because a huge fuel supply followed the Abrams and other armored vehicles to war, it created a division's cumbersome logistic tail. Support units, such as those handling fuel, spare parts, and maintenance, comprised more than 80 percent of the heavy Army's lift requirement, the effort of getting itself to war. The material that had to be loaded, transported, unloaded, and set up just to support the fighting was often discussed in terms of the tooth-to-tail ratio.

Among the U.S. military services, the Army had 480,000 active members, as against 375,000 in the Navy, 359,000 in the Air Force, and 175,000 in the Marines. The personnel budget allocated to the active Army was 40 percent more than the Navy and the Air Force and more than three times of that for the Marines.

The U.S. Army was fragmented in terms of culture. Any plan to blend the light and heavy elements of the Army would create a more common culture. The Army valued its specialization. For example, a cadet at West Point chose his branch during his senior year at the Academy. Each branch had a set of rituals and traditions. Thus, only a minority of those in the army saw transformation as something that they needed to contemplate.

The U.S. Army's Equipment Need

During the 1990s, the U.S. Army faced missions that it did not welcome and found itself ill-equipped to perform. During the Cold War era, the U.S. Army knew exactly who the enemy was, how it would fight, and where. Even though the U.S. Army's two main combat vehicles—the Abrams tank and the Bradley fighting vehicle—did not share a common chassis and each thus required its own logistics tail, the Army managed to find ways to circumvent the problems. For the enormous logistic tail problem, the U.S. Army positioned fuel, spare parts, and support material in the battlefield in advance. For the tanks' weight problem, the U.S. Army reinforced the various European bridges the tanks would likely cross to engage the Soviet armor.

However, the need for the transformation became apparent during and after the 1991 Gulf War. The desert war revealed two potentially disastrous flaws. The first problem was that the armored units could not reach the battlefield quickly. After the Iraqi Army took Kuwait in August 1990, the U.S. Army immediately began to amass its forces in the desert. On the eve of the war, in January 1991, the U.S. Army eventually had a full set-up of its heavy and light divisions: nearly 600 Bradley fighting vehicles and Abrams tanks with 200,000 soldiers in the theatre. The five-month build-up was a tremendous accomplishment by U.S. Army standards. However, this very fact sounded alarm in the U.S. military. The second problem was that the U.S. Army's quick-response light forces needed to have different equipment to stop Iraqi forces by themselves. Even though three battalions of the 82nd Airborne, about 4,000 soldiers, arrived in Saudi Arabia within a week, they were too vulnerable to fight against the Iraqi Army in the desert.

In 1994, Bradley fighting vehicles were transported to Cap Haitien, Haiti, but the heavy vehicles could not move even two blocks beyond the port because of their 30-ton bulk. In 1995, when a mechanized infantry brigade attempted to make its way in Bosnia, it got bogged down on the inferior roads and bridges of the Balkans. In the Kosovo War, the Serb Army maneuvered at will in Kosovo, but the U.S. Army had to watch helplessly from the other side of bridges they could not cross. The operational problems of the U.S. Army in the Gulf, Haiti, Bosnia, and Kosovo made it clear that there was an apparent gap between the U.S. Army's light units, which were too vulnerable, and its heavy units, which were too slow. Politically, the Army was losing ground to the more glamorous sister services operating from the sea and especially, from the air and space.

General Shinseki

In November 1942, Shinseki was born on the Hawaiian island of Kauai. His grandfather had immigrated to Hawaii from Hiroshima, and his parents were Nisei, American-born children of Japanese immigrants. During World War II after Pearl Harbor, Nisei were categorized as enemy aliens in spite of their status as American citizens.

Shinseki nonetheless had a typical American childhood. By the end of high school, he had many colleges to choose from, and he opted to go to West Point.

After graduation, Shinseki shipped out to Vietnam. However, his first duty only lasted three months. Shinseki's infantry company was hit by mortar. While being evacuated to medical facilities, he was even more seriously wounded in a helicopter crash. Shinseki was in the hospital for the next seven months recovering from his injuries. In February 1970, Shinseki went back to Vietnam again. This time, he took charge of an armored cavalry unit. Seven weeks later, he stepped on a mine and lost his right foot and part of his lower leg. Shinseki again had to be evacuated to hospital where he remained for a year.

During those painful months of recovery, Shinseki initially decided to leave the U.S. Army and return to civilian life, but changed his mind again. He had observed many officers leaving the Army and thought that some of them ought to stay and pass along what they had learned from the experiences in the Vietnam war. Even though he had an artificial foot, he worked hard to make himself responsible for reaching and maintaining the necessary physical requirements in the U.S. Army.

In the 1980s, as a colonel, Shinseki commanded American forces in Germany. While in charge of a heavy brigade of the U.S. Army, he witnessed the Soviet Union collapse. In the absence of a major confrontation with the Soviet Union, he was later responsible for peacekeeping in Bosnia. In 1998, Shinseki became Vice-Chief of Staff, serving under General Dennis Reimer. Reimer wanted to drastically reorganize the Army's echelon structure, which was outlined in *Breaking the Phalanx: A New Design for Land Power in the 21st Century*, a book by Colonel D. A. Macgregor. Reimer believed that the drastic reorganization would make the U.S. Army leaner and more efficient. Even though Reimer distributed copies of the book to every general in the U.S. Army, he faced strong resistance from senior officers.

In June of 1999, General Shinseki was appointed the U.S. Army's 34th Chief of Staff. Shinseki promised to reform the bulky U.S. Army. He proposed to make the U.S. Army nimble as well as lethal. He wanted to create a U.S. Army that would be flexible enough to perform peacekeeping missions or to fight an all-out war against Iraq and North Korea. Moving away from traditional, ponderous tanks and armored vehicles, Shinseki proposed to bring whole new advanced systems and technologies into the Army.

COMPETITORS TO GMD

General Dynamics

General Dynamics (GD) was a leading defense company. GD operated in four areas: combat systems (tanks, amphibious assault vehicles, and munitions), marine (warships and nuclear submarines), aerospace (business jets), and information systems and technology (command and control systems). It employed 43,000 people worldwide and had annual sales of $10 billion.

In 1952, GD was established after its predecessor and current operating division, Electric Boat, acquired the aircraft company Canadair Ltd. As a subsidiary, Electric Boat built nuclear-powered submarines (Seawolf, Ohio, and Los Angeles classes). In 1982, GD added its Combat Systems business unit, General Dynamics Land Systems (GDLS). GDLS built the M1 tank and Abrams combat vehicle. In 1997, GD added an information systems and technology business unit, Advanced Technology Systems, and returned to the aerospace business with Gulfstream in 1999.

GD's corporate headquarters was in Falls Church, Virginia, near Washington D.C. Government relations, international affairs, legal affairs, public relations, human resources, and finance were among the functions managed by the headquarters staff. In particular,

Government Relations served as the company's liaison with Congress and all branches and agencies of the U.S. federal government that bought or oversaw the procurement of GD's products and services. GD's International department represented the company's interest before the elements of the U.S. Government responsible for defense trade policy and international arms and technology transfers. For most of the U.S. Department of Defense programs, General Dynamics had shared the market with United Defense. Representing the ground combat system of the United States, the signature product line of GD was the Abrams main battle tank; that of United Defense was the Bradley fighting vehicle.

General Dynamics Land System (GDLS)

General Dynamics Land System (GDLS) was a wholly owned subsidiary of General Dynamics based in Sterling Heights, Michigan. GDLS manufactured tracked and wheeled armored vehicles, as well as amphibious combat vehicles, for the U.S. Army, the U.S. Marine Corps, and international allies. In 1982, GDLS was formed after its parent company acquired and integrated Chrysler Corporation's defense operations. GDLS's principal products were the U.S. Army's M1A2 Abrams SEP main battle tank, internationally recognized as the world's finest main battle tank, and the U.S. Marine Corps Advanced Amphibious Assault Vehicle (AAAV).

GDLS had delivered more than 8,500 Abrams main battle tanks to the U.S. Army and international allies. GDLS had been a great contributor in the U.S. Army's core programs: Abrams Tank, Future Combat System, Crusader, Future Scout & Cavalry System, Wolverine, and Fox programs. GDLS had worked in partnership with the U.S. Army on all of these programs to ensure its mission success.

GDLS employed 3,500 people in eight states and had annual sales that exceeded $1.1 billion. GDLS operated the United States' only main battle tank production facility, in Lima, Ohio. In the other satellite plants, GDLS machined Abrams components. Recently, GDLS was trying to develop more medium- and light-weight armored vehicle systems. GDLS had a proven record in engineering research, development, and technological innovation in the defense industry. GDLS had a strong array of capabilities: precision machining, experience with steel and aluminum and special armor, product fabrication, assembly, technical training, total package fielding, manufacturing technical assistance, contract logistics support services, systems integration, combat systems development, electronic

production and assembly, software development, and prototype development. To enhance its capabilities, GDLS acquired AV Technology in 1998 and Robotics Systems Technology in 1999.

United Defense

United Defense (UD) was a leader in designing, developing and producing combat vehicles (the Bradley armored infantry vehicle), fire support equipment (self-propelled howitzers), combat support vehicles, weapons delivery systems (missile launchers, artillery systems), and amphibious assault vehicles. For several defense programs comprising critical elements of the U.S. military forces, UD had been a sole-source prime contractor. The U.S. government thus accounted for almost 80 percent of sales. The board of United Defense included former Secretary of Defense Frank Carlucci and former Chairman of the Joint Chiefs of Staff John M. Shalikashvili. For the past 60 years, United Defense had produced more than 100,000 combat vehicles and 100,000 weapon systems that the U.S. Department of Defense and its international allies were using.

Its Ground Systems Division (GSD) produced the U.S. Army's primary armored infantry vehicle, the Bradley fighting vehicle family. Since United Defense had introduced its first Bradley fighting vehicle in 1981, the company had consistently improved the Bradley vehicles to meet and exceed the requirements of the changing battlefield. GD's Abrams, as a battle tank, was suited for fighting a war against an invading Soviet Army on the plains of Central Europe. On the other hand, United Defense's Bradley provided more nimble mobility, lethal firepower, and superior protection that gave it a fighting edge in the changing battlefield of the post-Cold War era.

THE CONTRACT PROPOSAL

Pettipas knew that GMD's existing platform would be a perfect match with the transformation requirement of the U.S. Army. Nevertheless, he had to decide how to pursue the multibillion-dollar contract, and do so within an incredibly short amount of time. He was contemplating whether GMD should go it alone or form a joint venture bid with another industry leader.

In anticipation of a possible program start, GMD explored cooperating with GDLS in 1997 to pursue the Canadian Armored Combat Vehicle (ACV) program. Thus, GD seemed a possible joint venture partner for the new U.S. Army contract. Pettipas had been informed that GDLS was also interested in exploring the possibility of a joint venture with GM for the contract.

The anticipated $600 million Canadian ACV program was to develop and field a replacement for the Canadian Army's nearly 200 Cougar vehicles. GMD in London, Ontario, was intended to be the prime contractor and provide the light armored vehicle chassis. GDLS would provide the 105mm, two-man automated turret. Computing Devices Canada would provide the turret electronics and fire control software. GMD and GDLS implicitly agreed that GDLS would become the prime contractor if there would be U.S. military programs, integrating the turret on GMD's chassis. The ACV program was considerably delayed by the Canadian Department of National Defense, and no contract was made available prior to the 1999 joint bid possibility. Pettipas realized that the previous joint effort with GDLS had created a close bond between GMD and GDLS.

Pettipas recalled that GDLS and Vickers Defense Systems (VDS) had formed another joint venture company ten months ago. The joint venture company, Vehicle Armor and Armament Ltd. (VAA Ltd.), was established to work on the Future Scout and Cavalry System program (FSCS). Vickers Defense Systems was a subsidiary of Vickers PLC. Vickers PLC was a UK-based international engineering company, focusing on land defense systems and equipment, marine propulsion systems and motion control equipment, superalloys, and components for the gas turbine and automotive industries.

Both GDLS and VDS were members of the SIKA International consortium. The consortium had been established to compete for the multibillion-dollar FSCS program, and it was later awarded a three-and-a-half-year development contract. The consortium consisted of Lockheed Martin, British Aerospace, GDLS, Vickers Defense Systems, Computing Devices Company, Northrop Grumman, Pilkington Optronics, Shorts Missile Systems, and Smiths Industries. The joint venture company was to provide the SIKA consortium with the most cost-effective chassis and weapon system solutions for the FSCS requirement. By creating synergy between its engineering staffs to facilitate the best technical solution for the SIKA consortium, the joint venture, located in Newcastle, England, was responsible for the design and production of a demonstrator as well as providing other significant design and management support activities. GDLS joined with VDS to ensure that GDLS could maintain its leading positions in the design, development, and manufacture of armored vehicles for the future. Recalling all these movements of GDLS, Pettipas began to wonder about the real (or hidden) intention of GDLS.

Perplexed, Pettipas had yet to decide which approach—solo or joint venture—would result in the greatest likelihood of success. It wasn't helping to know that GD was planning to submit a bid of its own.

Reasons to Go Solo

In 1982, GMD made a sole bid for a vehicle program for the U.S. Marines offering to provide nine different variants. It won the program, and was asked to provide six variants. Subsequently, GMD went into production and supplied 750 light armored vehicles. GMD won this program because it was technically capable of designing and manufacturing advanced 8×8 prototypes (with a license from MOWAG), whereas its competitors made a bid with less advanced 6×6 prototypes. GMD's leading technologies on 8×8 light armored vehicles led to winning other programs as well. Through the U.S. Department of Defense, GMD supplied 1,117 light armored vehicles (with 10 different variants) to Saudi Arabia.

When GMD developed a teaming arrangement with GDLS for the proposed Canadian Army program in 1997, the plan was for GM to share design and manufacturing responsibilities with GD. GMD would provide the light armored vehicle chassis, and GD the turret. In 1999, GMD acquired its long-time licensor, MOWAG of Switzerland. This greatly enhanced GMD's design and manufacturing capabilities for both light armored vehicle chassis and automated turrets.

With superior design and manufacturing capabilities, GMD focused on commonality across its product lines of light armored vehicles. GMD also emphasized its commonality with the U.S. Army support units. The U.S. Army had long suffered from logistics tail problems. The operational problems of the U.S. Army in the Gulf, Haiti, Bosnia, Somalia, and Kosovo made it clear that the U.S. Army would need some commonality across its armored units. Somewhat surprisingly, the U.S. Army had not had major programs to improve commonality in the last 20 years.

Even though Pettipas believed that GMD's 8×8 light armored vehicles were technically competitive and would provide significant benefits to the U.S. Army, he was concerned about their relatively high prices. Notwithstanding this, he did not want to compete with competitors on price. For him, soldiers' lives were at stake. He did not want to trade inferior low-priced products for soldiers' lives on the battlefield.

If GMD made a sole bid for the BCT program, it would not have to worry about coordination problems with partners. More importantly, GMD might face even more serious problems if it formed a JV with GD. Because proprietary data and knowledge would have to be disseminated to lower levels for manufacturing processes, GMD would have no other choice but to share some proprietary information with a JV partner.

Pettipas knew that GD would make its own bid for 6×6 prototypes. He was not too concerned about GD's bid because he saw little chance for GD to win the program with what he believed to be inferior vehicles. However, a serious problem might occur if the JV proposal won the BCT program. Even though GD, at the time, was behind GMD in terms of technologies for 8×8 light armored vehicles, it could certainly enhance its 8×8 capabilities through learning processes in the proposed JV. In the worst case, GMD might breed a future competitor by forming a GMD–GD joint venture. Longer term, it could thus create a potentially disastrous outcome that could never be reversed. Pettipas's concern was, "What if GD caught up on our design and manufacturing capabilities right after the end of the proposed JV, and offered its own bid for 8×8 light armored vehicles in future programs?"

Reasons to Form a Joint Venture

If GMD and GD formed a JV, GD might add value by contributing its Mobile Gun Systems (MGS) that would be installed on turrets of light armored vehicles. In 1997, GMD joined with GD and Computing Devices Canada (CDC) for the proposed Canadian ACV Program. At that time, CDC provided the turret electronics and fire control software. Recently, GD had acquired CDC (renamed GD Canada) and enhanced its technologies on MGS. To save in-house development costs, the MGS for GMD's light armored vehicles was being outsourced from GD Canada.

Pettipas also considered the merits of partnering with United Defense (UD). He felt however that GD was a better fit than UD, in every aspect. GMD focused on commonality across its product lines. He thus believed that GD would be a better candidate for a JV because GMD not only shared the manufacturing processes of Canadian combat vehicles with GD in 1997 but also it outsourced MGS from GD Canada. Besides, UD was not a public firm. Even though UD had strong connections with the U.S. government (George H. W. Bush was on the board), there were some rumors that UD might be sold to another competitor (possibly to GD) or it might be broken up. Considering that there was consolidation underway between the major European players, Pettipas would not hesitate in choosing GD as a partner, if he decided to form a JV for the BCT program.

Even though Pettipas was confident that GMD (with a sole bid) would have no problem in winning the BCT program on technical grounds, he was not quite sure about the political front. If GMD would make a sole bid, it would have to compete against two major players in the U.S. armored tanks/vehicles industry. GD and UD were in fact the only players in the industry, and they thus had significant political power regarding U.S. Army programs, relative to all foreign competitors. Both GD and UD engaged in heavy lobbying activities through their strong Government Relations departments. Pettipas reflected on a common practice in the U.S. defense industry—"kill the program."

"Kill the Program"

It was a common practice in the U.S. defense industry for firms to try to kill any program they could not compete in, or any program they did compete in but had lost. The logic was that by seeing to the cancellation of programs, the funds from the canceled programs would be available for new programs in which they would have opportunities. Numerous existing programs could be canceled to fund a major new program. Thus, even if a contractor won a multibillion-dollar program for delivering orders for multiple years, it could not be sure that it would be able to continue its contract with the U.S. military because of this industry-specific practice.

Although the U.S. military sometimes canceled programs, they did not necessarily face hefty penalties at the time of cancellation. Because of uncertain environments in the U.S. defense industry, contractors usually hedged against any possibilities of canceled programs by amortizing non-recurring expenses (or contingent penalties) into their development costs. In other words, they factored the chance of cancellation into the price of the early-delivered vehicles. This was a common industry practice agreed upon both by the U.S. military and contractors. There was also a straightforward way to pay penalties for canceled programs. However, the former was more commonly used in the industry.

Pettipas wondered whether GM might need a U.S. partner for political reasons when bidding for the BCT program, or for political assistance from the U.S. partner after winning the program, so as to keep the program rolling. He thought about winning the program with a sole bid. He envisioned GM would be against two major U.S. competitors, if it won with a sole bid, and both would presumably be lobbying heavily for the program cancellation.

GD's Solo Bid

GD clarified that it would make a sole bid for the BCT program with its 6×6 prototypes. GDLS aimed for the

BCT program with a low-cost approach. Because GD licensed 6×6 technologies from an Austrian engineering company, it intended to fully exploit its resources/capabilities by bidding its prototype. Even though 6×6 light armored vehicles were technically inferior to 8×8 ones, GD felt they had a great chance of winning the program because of its price attractiveness. With a license from the Austrian company, GDLS had supplied its 6×6 light armored vehicles to Kuwait, and made a bid for the Polish Army program.

A few years earlier, GD and UD had competed head-to-head for the U.S. Marine program Advanced Amphibious Assault Vehicle (AAAV). Historically, UD had supplied medium-sized amphibious vehicles to the U.S. military because of its superior technologies for the medium-sized armored vehicles (thanks to the Bradley family). However, for the U.S. Marine AAAV program, GD won the contract.

Mass Retailing in Asia (B) Competition

Neil Jones
Philippe Lasserre
Claudia Gehlen

INSEAD

WAL-MART

Founded in 1962 in Bentonville, Arkansas by Sam Walton, Wal-Mart became the top-ranked retail company in the United States in 1990. By 2004, Wal-Mart was the world's largest company with 1.5 million employees and annual sales totaling US$256 billion. Wal-Mart operated discount stores, neighborhood stores, hypermarkets (Wal-Mart supercenters) and membership warehouses (Sam's Club).

Wal-Mart's astonishing success in the United States came from several competitive dimensions in which it differed from its many competitors: its everyday low price (EDLP) approach to merchandising and marketing and its management of internal operations and supply chain operations. Wal-Mart invested over half a billion dollars in IT and satellite facilities to connect its worldwide stores to headquarters. Headquarters could complete stock-taking of each item for more than 4,000 stores worldwide within an hour. Moreover, Wal-Mart's top executives spent up to four days per week physically visiting stores to observe local conditions and speak with store managers. At headquarters, the massive amounts of data that had been collected by store and by item were analyzed by advanced data mining systems to identify patterns and trends that could help increase sales. Some observers emphasized Wal-Mart's reputation for hard bargaining. It famously made suppliers pay for their own phone calls and forced negotiations to take place in small rooms fitted with uncomfortable chairs. Trips to visit suppliers were to cost less than 1% of the purchase. Even top executives were expected to be frugal and share hotel rooms.

However, Wal-Mart did not simply rely on its ability to negotiate low prices and source from low wage countries. It also tried to create competitive advantages by managing its suppliers: it devoted considerable attention to choosing the best suppliers and it concentrated volumes in the latter to help them achieve economies of scale. It also set specific targets for response time and quality. Moreover, it tended to force suppliers to invest in new systems and technology that could lower overall system costs and increase delivery speed and order accuracy, thus reducing costly stock-outs. To do this, Wal-Mart developed a surprising openness with its suppliers: it shared its daily sales data as well as forecasts and strategic plans. Wal-Mart was an early adopter of technologies to allow such an exchange (such as EDI).

Above all, Wal-Mart is famed for its distinctive culture inherited from Sam Walton (Exhibit 1).

In the 1990s, Wal-Mart started to expand abroad. In 1991 it opened its first store in Mexico, and in 1994 it began operations in Canada. Further overseas expansion included Argentina and Brazil in 1995, China in 1996, Germany in 1997, South Korea in 1998, the UK in 1999, and Japan in 2002. By 2003, Wal-Mart operated more than 2,740 discount stores and supercenters and 500 membership warehouses in the United States, as well as more than 1,170 stores of different formats in international markets.

Mass Retailing in Asia (B) Competition. This case was written by Neil Jones, Affiliate Professor of Strategy and Technology, Philippe Lasserre, Emeritus Professor of Strategy and Asian Business, with the assistance of Claudia Gehlen, Research Associate, all at INSEAD. It is intended to be used as a basis for class discussion rather than to illustrate either effective or ineffective handling of an administrative situation. Copyright © 2005 INSEAD, Singapore. Reprinted by permission.

EXHIBIT 2	Wal-Mart International Expansion

Year	Country entered	Mode of entry	Store number Initially	Store number in 2002/03	Employees	Sales in 2002 in million $
1991	Mexico	Joint Venture	1	595	92,708	10,980
1992	Puerto Rico	International Expansion	1	55	7,500	2,000
1994	Canada	Acquisition	122	213	52,000	5,643
1995	Brazil	International Expansion	5	22	6,000	421
	Argentina	International Expansion	3	11	4,000	100
1996	China	Joint Venture	2	26	15,000	517
	Indonesia	Joint Venture	exited in 1997	0	0	–
1997	Germany	Acquisition	95	94	15,500	2,408
1998	South Korea	Acquisition	4	15	3,000	741
1999	Britain	Acquisition	229	259	125,000	17,430
2002	Japan	Acquisition	400	400	30,000	–

Source: Company documents.

Although the company derived the bulk of its revenue from the United States, international expansion would continue, particularly in Asia (Exhibit 2). Wal-Mart experienced some disappointments in Asia. In Indonesia it was forced to dissolve its joint venture in 1997 and it pulled out of Hong Kong in the 1990s, having failed to crack the local market. Consumers seemed to prefer neighborhood chain stores that were familiar to them. However, Wal-Mart continued to expand into larger and more stable markets.

Wal-Mart had a significant presence in only a few countries in Asia. One of its key challenges was to persuade Asian customers to embrace the hypermarket and warehouse concept. Most Asian customers were used to shopping daily at wet markets or neighborhood stores. They tended to take public transport or walk to shops near their homes, and they preferred fresh produce rather than refrigerated foods. The result was that Asian customers tended to make smaller, more frequent purchases than Wal-Mart's typical customers.

In Indonesia, Wal-Mart was forced to dissolve its joint venture in 1997. The Indonesian partner sued, seeking nearly US$200 million in damages for mismanagement from the retailer. Wal-Mart entered South Korea through acquisitions. In 1997 the retailer had 11 stores, but sales were below expectations (US$160 million). Like its rival Carrefour, Wal-Mart pulled out of Hong Kong in the 1990s, having failed to crack the

Hong Kong market. Consumers seemed to prefer familiar neighborhood chain stores. In 2003 Wal-Mart closed down its Taiwan branch and moved the branch's purchasing business to the parent company's Asia-Pacific purchasing headquarters in Shenzhen. Since Taiwan's manufacturing sector had been losing competitiveness in recent years, Wal-Mart relocated its employees from the Taiwan branch to Mainland China. The branch's staff shrank from 150 at the peak to 30.

Wal-Mart made major efforts in both China and Japan. Wal-Mart entered China, Asia's second-largest retail market behind Japan, in 1996, one year after Carrefour. The first attempts were unsuccessful as the joint venture in China fell through due to management differences. Between 1996 and 2003, Wal-Mart operated and aggressively expanded its retail business in partnership with joint venture partners and suppliers in China.

By mid-2004 Wal-Mart was operating 39 stores in 19 cities, mainly supercenters and Sam's Clubs, from Shenzhen in the south to Kunming in the west, Harbin in the north, and Guiyang in the Guizhou province, but was still witnessing losses in some outlets (Exhibit 3). Despite its desire to penetrate the buoyant Shanghai market, by mid-2004 it had not yet succeeded in opening the three stores that it had planned to establish in this city. The same year, the retailer's sales rose 23% to 5.85 billion yuan (US$707 million), ranking seventh among 22 foreign-funded store chains in the country.

According to Beijing Chenbao, Wal-Mart also had plans to open two more stores in Beijing.

Wal-Mart opened a global procurement center in Shanghai to buy merchandise in northern and eastern China for export. Ninety-five percent of Wal-Mart's merchandise in its China stores was sourced domestically. In its drive to provide customers with the widest choice and selection possible at an "everyday lowest price," Wal-Mart centralized its supply chain through two distribution centers, Shenzhen in the south and, more recently, Tianjin in the north. China was home to more than 80% of Wal-Mart's suppliers, and in 2003 Wal-Mart alone spent US$15 billion, the equivalent of 1% of China's GDP. If Wal-Mart were a country, it would be China's eighth biggest trading partner, ahead of the United Kingdom. It was quick to capitalize on the production glut from which China suffered: Wal-Mart demanded rock-bottom prices and forced managers to cut costs. As an example, the average wholesale price for fans, juicers and toasters has tumbled to US$4 from US$7 a decade ago.

In Japan, Wal-Mart spent four years studying the market before concluding that it needed a local partner. In March 2002 Wal-Mart invested in Seiyu, a prominent Japanese retailing chain, purchasing an initial 6.1% of the company. Within 18 months it had acquired over 38% of the company with an option to increase this to 67% by 2007. It had significantly restructured its

EXHIBIT 3	Wal-Mart in China				
		Number of stores per format in 2004			**Total**
Province	**City**	**Supercenters**	**SAM'S Clubs**	**Neighborhood Stores**	
Guangdong	Shenzhen	6	1	2	9
	Dongguan	1	0	0	1
	Shantou	1	0	0	1
Yunnan	Kunming	3	0	0	3
Fujian	Fuzhou	2	1	0	3
	Xiamen	2	0	0	2
Hunan	Changsha	1	0	0	1
Jiangxi	Nanchang	1	0	0	1
Liaoning	Dalian	2	0	0	2
	Shenyang	2	0	0	2
Jilin	Changchun	2	1	0	3
Heilongjiang	Harbin	1	0	0	1
Shandong	Jinan	1	0	0	1
	Qingdao	1	0	0	1
Jiangsu	Nanjing	1	0	0	1
	Tianjin	1	0	0	1
	Beijing	0	1	0	1
Total		28	4	2	34

relationships with suppliers as well as its in-store look and feel, and had imparted some of the Wal-Mart culture as well. Seiyu's chairman of the board, Noriyuki Watanabe, stated in September 2003 that, "Seiyu has already adopted Wal-Mart's three basic beliefs." But Wal-Mart's results in Japan were disappointing. It faced stiff competition from local retailers revamping their systems, and still needed to win over demanding shoppers who were suspicious of low prices. Its best effort so far has been the four-story Seiyu store in Futamatagawa, where sales are up 15% since remodeling (Exhibit 4).

In 2004 Wal-Mart opened its first warehouse-sized supercenter located in the fishing town of Numazu, 100km west of Tokyo. Despite plans to open new stores, Wal-Mart's main focus was still on making existing stores more efficient.

In October 2004 the Japanese restructuring agency announced that it would not rescue Daiei, a general merchandise store. This opened the way for Wal-Mart, in association with Marubeni, to make a bid to take over the troubled retailer, thereby allowing Wal-Mart to expand significantly into Japan.

CARREFOUR

In 2003 Carrefour was the second-largest mass retailer in the world, operating 10,378 stores of different formats in 29 countries with almost 400,000 employees and sales totaling nearly €69 billion in 2002. The company has always been significantly more international than Wal-Mart, deriving 49% of its revenues from markets outside France. During the past 30 years Carrefour has built strong store networks across three continents. It was therefore able to initiate the virtuous circle early in its expansion efforts.

Carrefour started in 1959 when the Defforey and Fournier families created their first hypermarket in the suburbs of Paris. It operated exclusively in France before expanding into Spain in the late 1960s. However, Carrefour initially experienced failure in a number of markets including Germany, Belgium, the United Kingdom, Switzerland and the United States.

During the 1980s and 1990s, Carrefour continued its international expansion through a combination of organic growth and mergers, extending its reach into Latin America and Asia (Exhibit 5).

In 1999, Carrefour acquired Promodes, France's second-largest mass retailer. During the following two years the company wrestled with integrating Promodes' businesses into its existing operations.

Although known as a hypermarket pioneer, Carrefour operates various other types of outlets including

EXHIBIT 4	Wal-Mart in Japan: The Seiyu, Ltd (2003)	
Sales in million $		9,694.40
Number of employees		14,138
Sales by area as of February 2003, in %		
Tokyo		38.8
Kansai		14.0
Kanagawa		10.2
Chubu, Hokuriku		10.1
Saitama		10.0
Chiba		6.9
Tohoku		6.7
Kanto		2.1
Chugoku		1.2
% of total sales by product segment		
Clothing		17.1
Household-related goods		14.5
Fresh food		18.1
Processed food		37.1
Others		13.2
Sales per Unit in 2003		
Sales floor space (average m²)		1,114
Sales per m² (thousands of yen*)		716
Sales per employee (thousands of yen)		46,095

EXHIBIT 5	Carrefour in the World: Sales by Regions 2003				
	Hypermarkets	**Supermarkets**	**Hard discounts**	**Others**	**Total**
France	23,948	13,151	2,037	5,576	44,712
Europe	17,900	8,302	4,405	2,453	33,060
Latin America	4,059	1,139	245	–	5,443
Asia	5,152	–	4	–	5,156
Total	**51,059**	**22,592**	**6,691**	**8,029**	**88,371**

supermarkets (Champion and Stoc), discount stores (Ed and Dia), as well as several convenience stores in different formats (Shopi, Marché Plus, 8 à Huit, Proxi). Ooshop, online shopping, was introduced in 2000 in the Paris region, offering 6,000 products at the same price as in the hypermarkets via a Web site designed to enable customers to complete their purchases in less than 20 minutes.

Outside France, Carrefour has concentrated on two or three formats. The company's strategy consists of selecting a format best suited to a particular market and adapting that format to local needs. This ability to creatively adapt to customer needs in international markets has been Carrefour's primary strength. Shared processes and systems, as well as the international introduction of product ranges, have helped to complement its locally sensitive strategy and increase operational efficiency.

Carrefour's move into Asia started with its entry into Taiwan in 1987 (Exhibit 6). As René Brillet, Director of the Asia Region, put it: "*This explains why we have roots on this continent, which offers us the potential for tremendous growth, because of its size, its cultural diversity and its enormous population.*" The company benefited from the collaboration of its local joint-venture partner, the President Group. Another advantage of the Taiwanese experience was that it served as a human resource hub for other Asian markets, especially China. Carrefour did not have an easy start in Taiwan; it had to learn how to adapt its business model to the local conditions and it took almost two years to set up the first hypermarket. But by 2003 Carrefour had established its leadership over the island's modern mass retail market with sales of €1,381 million in 2002.

EXHIBIT 6	Carrefour in Asia

a) Number and Location of Stores

	1993	1994	1995	1996	1997	1998	1999	2000	2001	2002	2003	Surface (1000 m²)
China			2	3	7	14	20	24	24	36	95	337
Hypermarkets											40	322
Hard Discounts											55	15
South Korea				3	3	6	12	20	22	25	27	253
Hong Kong				1	2	4	4					
Indonesia						1	5	7	8	10	11	73
Japan								1	3	4	7	65
Malaysia		1	1	2	3	5	6	6	6	6	7	69
Singapore					1	1	1	1	1	1	2	15
Taiwan	7	8	10	13	17	21	23	24	26	28	31	243
Thailand				2	6	7	9	11	15	17	19	172
Total	7	9	13	24	39	59	80	94	105	127	199	1227
Hypermarkets											144	1212
Hard Discounts											55	15

Note: Except in China all other countries are under the Hypermarket format.
Source: ACNielsen Retailer Services: Carrefour Annual Report 2003

b) Sales per Country (2002)

Country	Year of entry	Sales in 2002 in million euros
Taiwan	1989	1,381.00
Malaysia	1994	225.9
China	1995	1,396.50
South Korea	1996	1,242.90
Thailand	1996	416.4
Singapore	1997	86
Indonesia	1998	313.2
Japan	2000	156.9
Total		**5,191.80**

| EXHIBIT 7 | Carrefour Locations in China (2003) |

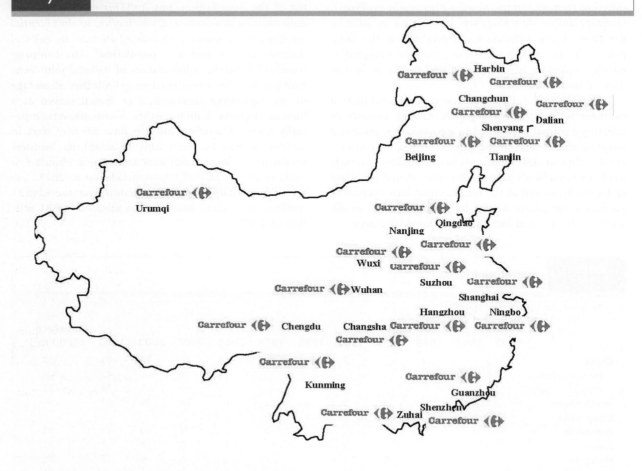

Carrefour ⟨C⟩ Harbin
Carrefour ⟨C⟩
Changchun
Carrefour ⟨C⟩
Shenyang
Carrefour ⟨C⟩
Dalian
Carrefour ⟨C⟩ Carrefour ⟨C⟩
Beijing   Tianjin
Carrefour ⟨C⟩
Urumqi
Carrefour ⟨C⟩
Qingdao
Nanjing
Carrefour ⟨C⟩
Carrefour ⟨C⟩
Wuxi
Carrefour ⟨C⟩
Suzhou   Carrefour ⟨C⟩
Shanghai
Carrefour ⟨C⟩ Wuhan
Hangzhou   Ningbo
Carrefour ⟨C⟩ Chengdu   Changsha Carrefour ⟨C⟩ Carrefour ⟨C⟩
Carrefour ⟨C⟩
Carrefour ⟨C⟩
Kunming
Carrefour ⟨C⟩
Guanzhou
Shenzhen
Carrefour ⟨C⟩ Zuhai
Carrefour ⟨C⟩

After its success in Taiwan, Carrefour moved into China where it is the most prolific foreign retailer with gross sales of €1,369.5 million, 42 hypermarkets and 55 hard discount stores in 2003, employing around 23,000 local people. Ninety-five percent of all managers are Chinese. In 2003, Dia discount stores opened in Shanghai and Beijing. And in March 2004 Carrefour opened its 42nd hypermarket in Urumqi, capital of Xinjiang Uygur Autonomous Region (Exhibit 7).

Having overcome its legal tribulations, Carrefour has resumed expansion and has just started making profits in all its stores in 19 cities.

Carrefour moved into South Korea and Thailand just prior to the Asian crisis. Both countries recovered rather quickly, allowing Carrefour to pursue its expansion. In South Korea, Carrefour became the No. 4 food retailer, operating 25 stores and posting gross sales of €1,242.9 million in 2002.

In Thailand, Carrefour operated 19 stores with gross sales of €416.4 million in 2002.

Despite the financial crisis that hit Indonesia in 1997, Carrefour opened its first hypermarket in 1998, and by 2002 was the leading foreign retailer with 12 stores and gross sales of €313.2 million. It has plans to develop its presence outside Jakarta.

In Malaysia, Carrefour initially met little competition when it entered the market in 1994. But after the financial crisis it encountered increasing competition from strong local or foreign retailers like Tesco. In 2002, Carrefour's gross sales were €225.9 million for six hypermarkets.

As Japan was known to be one of the most complex markets, Carrefour postponed entering the Japanese market until 2000. The first three stores were showing major losses and it was obliged to revise its ambitious plans to expand to 13 stores by 2003. A change in policy was necessary to adjust to local expectations. Carrefour decided to bring a "French Touch" to its stores, which was very successful and a clear departure from its existing policy of sourcing its merchandise locally.

In October 2004, the *Asian Wall Street Journal* printed a rumor that, according to a consultant, Carrefour was planning to sell its eight stores in Japan, due to "difficulties in acquiring real estate for new stores and the lack of touch with Japanese consumers' tastes."

TESCO

In 2003, Tesco was the world's sixth-largest grocery store operator with sales of US$52.7 billion. In the United Kingdom, Tesco was the No. 1 food retailer with 1,100 stores (Exhibit 8).

Founded in 1919 as a full-service downtown operator, the company has since expanded into non-food items and larger discount retailing formats, and has become a pioneer of US-style supermarkets in the United Kingdom. During the 1980s, Tesco underwent a reorganization of its strategy, moving its operations from smaller city locations to larger superstores in the suburbs. In 2001 Tesco achieved an impressive 18% growth rate. It has further become the world leader in Internet grocery sales, cementing an agreement with Safeway to use its profitable online system in the United States.

Like other major retail chains, Tesco has focused on international expansion and on increasing its market share. In 1993 Tesco began to look outside the United Kingdom for new markets. The company made its first acquisitions in other parts of Europe and by 1997 had opened stores in Poland, Hungary, Slovakia, and the Czech Republic. By 2000 it had penetrated Asia, notably Thailand, Taiwan, and South Korea. Tesco has continued to grow organically as well as by acquisition to expand its foothold in the region.

During 2003, Tesco continued to grow at 10%, a rate several percentage points faster than Carrefour. Seventy-five percent of the new businesses opened was in international markets, with the result that by the end of 2003 the company had 189 hypermarkets overseas.

Tesco chose to expand abroad using the hypermarket format, although non-food products had not traditionally been part of its offering, and at a time when Tesco did not have any hypermarkets in the United Kingdom. The advantage was that Tesco started with a clean sheet: it has not taken UK-style stores to emerging markets but has been more flexible and up-to-date. In these growth markets Tesco is capable of selling 45% to 55% non-food products.

According to David Reid, Tesco has aimed to establish an operating platform that provides the systems and key processes to run the business, because expanding internationally is a big financial challenge. Furthermore, it has invested heavily in recruiting and training the right local staff to complement its localized product offerings and store formats. Even though the company has been moving quickly, it has remained very focused and careful not to stake too many flags in too many countries.

Tesco's entry into Asia was in Thailand in 1998, in association with Charoen Pokphand Group (CP). Thai local competitors tried to impede the United Kingdom retailer's progress with a wall of lawsuits. But such legal actions were a minor nuisance compared with the bombing in 2001 of two Tesco/Lotus outlets. Another outlet was hit by a rocket-propelled grenade and yet another came under fire from automatic weapons. But Tesco/Lotus, Thailand's No. 1 retailer with 26 stores, did not consider relocating to more hospitable territory. It planned to open more stores, in line with rival retailers Carrefour and Wal-Mart. In 2001, anticipating new regulations aiming to curb its expansion, Tesco launched an advertising campaign to convince Thais of its support for Thai suppliers, consumers (more choice and lower prices) and exporters (Thai goods sold in its stores elsewhere). In Thailand, Tesco employs 19,000 people in 47 hypermarkets and 17 Express stores.

In Ulsan, South Korea, Tesco opened its 100th international store in 2002. It has also launched its online grocery sales system in South Korea, which has one of the highest Internet penetration rates in the world.

It has established Hong Kong as its global sourcing superhub.

China would mark the next landmark in Tesco's rapid expansion through selective acquisition. Being present in Taiwan, Tesco has had a team in China since 2002 studying potential acquisitions. In its bid to catch up with two of its larger global rivals, Wal-Mart and Carrefour, Tesco may acquire a 50% stake in Hymall, a Chinese mainland subsidiary of the Taiwan-based Ting Hsin International Group. Hymall had 25 hypermarket outlets in Shanghai and other major cities on the Chinese Mainland and Tesco planned to open another 15 hypermarkets in China in 2004, bringing its total to 40. The projected store number would be 150 by 2008. Compared to Carrefour and Wal-Mart, companies that had been building up their own 'empires' from the 1990s onwards, Tesco was late entering the market. Moreover, Tesco lacked experience in global operations, especially in developing countries.

However, the experience in Japan proved that the chain could move very fast. Breaking with its previous tried and tested formula, in which it focused on hypermarket operations in Asia, in 2003 Tesco bought C Two-Network, a small but profitable convenience store operator that operated 78 stores and some wholesaling activities, mainly in the Tokyo metropolitan area. In

EXHIBIT 8 Tesco in Asia

Region	Number of stores	Sales area	New stores opened in 2003/04	Planned openings in 2004/05
Japan (2003)	78	0.3 m sq ft	78	2
Malaysia (2003)	5	0.5 m sq ft	2	2
South Korea (1999)	28	2.9 m sq ft	7	4
Taiwan (2000)	4	0.4 m sq ft	1	–
Thailand (1998)	64	5.4 m sq ft	12	57
Total for Asia	179	9.5 m sq ft	100	65
Total Worldwide	2,318	45.4 m sq ft	199	184

April 2004 it announced plans to acquire Fre'c, a highly indebted Japanese chain with 27 stores in the dense residential outskirts of Tokyo. Tesco is expected to use C Two-Network's links to processed-food wholesalers and Fre'c's knowledge of fresh produce to open between five and 10 small stores a year.

In 2003, Tesco moved into Malaysia. In view of its success, the Malaysian authorities felt the need to protect the interests of small traders and warned Tesco in March 2004 not to continue to open its stores round the clock.

MAKRO

Makro, a Dutch cash-&-carry chain, is more a wholesaler than a retailer. Its format has proved attractive in China and other Asian countries, especially Thailand.

As hypermarkets have expanded, Makro's margins on non-food goods have eroded. Cost control rather than sales growth appeared to be the key to success. Makro's annual sales growth has been in single figures since 2000, but its return on investment capital has been 20% or more. This may be attributed largely to the company's logistics system.

Unlike Ahold, Makro has been pursuing its expansion in Asia. Experience has shown that the wholesale format suited even little-developed markets. It has been successful in China and other Asian countries.

Makro first entered Taiwan and captured more than 30% market share in 1989, but was quickly followed by Carrefour, who provided free parking and a full range of products at low prices.

In Thailand, Makro has become one of the largest retailers. Siam Makro operated 20 stores and sold to "mom & pop" stores rather than competing with them. Thanks to its clientele and because it is the only big player in the sector, the company's expansion has been different. It has moved patiently, buying most of its sites instead of renting them.

Makro has large stores in all the major provincial cities. Its rule of thumb is that customers will drive up to 80km to purchase goods. Makro has adopted a new format hoping to accelerate expansion. Its smaller stores, with only 10,000 items instead of 25,000, have been generating an operating profit since virtually the first day of their operations. The stores were built on land big enough to expand if business grew. In order to reduce the visibility of foreign management, Siam Makro has had a Thai president since 2001.

In 1991, Makro arrived in Indonesia, and operated 14 stores by 2003. During the riots in 1998, Makro lost one store in Jakarta, which later reopened. In 2004 it added four new outlets and refurbished its current stores to accommodate a wider variety of fresh foods. The new Makro store design for Indonesia was a single-storey warehouse building with 10,000 m^2 of floor space including a 1,300 m^2 fresh produce section for hotel, restaurant and catering customers.

According to the president director, Simon Collins, Makro's aim has been—from the very beginning—to join forces and grow together with Indonesia's small-to-medium-scale businesses. Makro believed that its existence did not threaten smaller local players, and the ease with which it obtained approval and licenses showed that there was no opposition from traditional business.

Makro, which in 2003 operated 60 stores totaling more than 500,000 m^2 in five Asian countries, also planned to open two new retail warehouses in the Philippines and another two in Thailand in 2004.

METRO

With 3,200 stores, German retailer Metro Holding AG was Europe's largest retailer in 1997 and No. 2 worldwide, behind Wal-Mart. In Germany, it also owned department stores under the well-known Kaufhof name. But by 2003, Metro had been overtaken by its competitors to become the world's fifth-largest retailer.

In China, the company chose Shanghai as its commercial hub, as did many other retailers, and, together with Carrefour, it was one of the big retail players there.

In India, Metro AG received approval in 2004 for 100% foreign direct investment in wholesale cash-and-carry operations (whereas Carrefour did not manage to obtain the green light for its hypermarkets). However, Metro has come under attack from the old guard of the Indian trading sector, accusing the wholesaler of using cash-and-carry as a cover to indulge in direct retailing to the consumer.

In 2002, Metro carefully entered Japan by opening a 5,000 m^2 store on the outskirts of Tokyo. The store was a cash-and-carry wholesale outlet targeted at restaurants, retail and hotel professionals. Metro planned to open another store in the greater Tokyo area but has preferred to adopt a slow, patient approach for future expansion in Japan.

Ito-Yokado

The Ito-Yokado Group was the largest Japanese retailing group and the world's 15th largest in 2003, with sales of US$28.4 billion. The group was closely linked with the 7-Eleven chain of convenience stores, of which it owned 73% and which accounted for a substantial proportion of its revenues. Superstores and other types of retail operations accounted for 48%, however, making Ito-Yokado a highly diversified retail conglomerate not limited by the success of its convenience store operations.

Although founded in 1913, Ito-Yokado did not begin growing until 21-year-old Masayoshi Ito took control of the single store operation in 1956. By the 1960s, Ito had implemented US-style self-service in his new hypermarkets (six of which were opened in 1965), and was ready to expand into other businesses.

During the 1970s and 1980s, Ito-Yokado acquired the Japanese franchise rights to 7-Eleven convenience stores, Denny's restaurants, Robinson's department stores, and Oshman's sporting goods, among others. Through this growth process the group became one of the largest retail employers in Japan, with 51,000 employees across its diverse outlets.

Japanese labor is among the world's most costly, and land and rents were still expensive even after 11 years of price declines. Floor space costs were, on average, eight times higher for Ito-Yokado than for Wal-Mart, and Ito-Yokado spent, on average, three times as much as Wal-Mart on labor. The strong service culture in the retail sector also meant that Japanese retailers typ-ically needed more staff per square meter than did their Western counterparts, pushing up costs still further.

The 1990s saw the company diversify into the online shopping and financial services markets. At the same time it continued to invest in international expansion, entering the large and fast-growing China market.

Aeon

Japan's second and the world's 17th largest retailer, Aeon has established a reputation as one of the most aggressive players. Aeon, the parent company of Jusco, operated 368 stores with US$24.3 billion sales in 2003. The company has chosen an unusual growth strategy for a Japanese retailer: acquiring stores from failed competitors. For example, it absorbed some 50 stores belonging to Kotobukiya and supported Mycal's rehabilitation, partly to thwart Wal-Mart, which had expressed an interest in Mycal's stores.

In raising its store count, Aeon hopes to bolster its nationwide distribution network, to reduce inventory risk and boost its buying power. It also intends to shift wholly to performance-related pay.

The chain is also planning to expand into China and aims to establish around 60 stores by 2006.

Dairy Farm

Dairy Farm is a pan-Asian retailer. It was incorporated in 1886 by a Scottish surgeon, Sir Patrick Manson, with five prominent Hong Kong businessmen. The company's objectives were threefold: to import a herd of dairy cattle in order to lower the price of milk by more than half; to improve the health of Hong Kong's people by supplying them with cows' milk kept free from contamination by means of stringent hygiene; and to realize a profit for the company's shareholders.

1n 1957, Dairy Farm had three retail stores and began to expand its product range, marking the start of its transformation to a major food retailer and distributor.

In 1964, the company acquired the Wellcome grocery chain, which expanded its food retailing business and gave it significant access to the Chinese market in Hong Kong. In 1979, it acquired the 75-store Franklins "No Frills" chain in Australia. Since then it has acquired 228 Seven-Eleven convenience stores in Hong Kong, entered Taiwan in 1987, acquired chain stores in New Zealand and Spain, developed a joint venture with Cold Storage, acquired Guardian Pharmacy retailer, and taken a 32% participation in Hero, the Indonesian retail chain, and a 90% participation in Giant hypermarkets from Malaysia.

EXHIBIT 9

Dairy Farm: Format and Location of Stores in Asia 2002

Banner	Format	Honk Kong	Guangzhou	Taiwan	Singapore	Malaysia	Indonesia	India
					Countries/Regions			
Wellcome	Supermarkets	243		154				
FoodWorld	Supermarkets							92
Cold Storage	Supermarkets				75			
Shop N Save	Supermarkets				35			
Hero	Supermarkets						105	
Tops	Supermarkets	34						
Giant	Supermarkets/Hypermarkets				4	56	6	
7-Eleven	Convenience Stores	484	150			206		
Starmart	Convenience Stores						39	
Guardian	Pharmacy				107	123	72	

In December 2002, it commenced operations in South Korea through a 50/50 joint venture with CJ Corporation to operate health and beauty stores, and in 2003 it acquired 22 Kayo supermarket chain stores, increasing Wellcome's network to 144 stores in Taiwan.

Following the strategic restructuring of Ahold, Dairy Farm's 37% affiliate, PT Hero Supermarkets acquired 22 Tops supermarkets from PT Ahold Indonesia, increasing Hero's network total to 111 supermarkets in the country.

In May 2003 Dairy Farm acquired 34 Tops supermarkets in Malaysia from Royal Ahold. The Tops supermarkets were re-branded as Giant and Cold Storage, taking the number of supermarkets owned by Dairy Farm to 47 in Malaysia.

At 31 December 2003, Diary Farm and its associates operated 2,570 outlets including supermarkets, hypermarkets, health and beauty stores, convenience stores, home furnishing stores and restaurants, employed 56,800 people in the region, and reported 2003 total sales of US$4.5 billion. The group operates under different banners (Exhibit 9):

- *Supermarkets* — Wellcome in Hong Kong and Taiwan, Cold Storage in Singapore and Malaysia, Giant in Malaysia, Shop N Save in Singapore, Hero in Indonesia and Foodworld in India.

- *Hypermarkets* — Giant in Malaysia, Singapore and Indonesia.

- *Health and beauty stores* — Mannings in Hong Kong, Guardian in Singapore, Malaysia and Indonesia, Health and Glow in India, and Olive Young in South Korea.

- *Convenience stores* — 7-Eleven in Hong Kong, Singapore and Southern China and Starmart in Indonesia.

- *Home furnishing stores* — IKEA in Hong Kong and Taiwan.

The group also has a 50% interest in Maxim's, Hong Kong's leading restaurant chain.

Dairy Farm International Holdings Limited, managed from Hong Kong, is incorporated in Bermuda and listed on the London stock exchange and the Singapore and Bermuda stock exchanges. Dairy Farm is part of the Jardine Matheson Group.

AHOLD

At the end of 2002, Ahold operated 156 stores in several Asian countries, accounting for 1% of its total sales. As part of its strategy to optimize its portfolio and to strengthen its financial position by reducing debt, Ahold decided to divest its Asian operations. In 2003, Ahold completed the sale of its Indonesian and Malaysian operations after pulling out of China and Singapore. In 2004, Ahold sold its stake in CRC Ahold, which operated 48 stores in Thailand, to its partner, the Central Group. The divestment was the final step in the overall sale of Ahold's Asian operations.

ONGC's Growth Strategy

K Yamini Aparna
Vivek Gupta

ICFAI University Press, Business School Case Development Centre

ONGC, the most valuable company in India by market capitalization, is on a high growth trajectory. It is on its way to be a truly integrated oil and gas player.[1]

— Jigar Shah, Head, Research Wing, KR Choksey Shares & Securities Pvt Ltd.

In the coming six to seven years' time, one would see ONGC on an assured growth path. It should have increased production and recovery factor, reserve accretion, best-in-class technology, competent, motivated human resource and strong financials. I would like ONGC to meet India's hydrocarbon needs to the maximum possible extent. I would also like to see ONGC recognized within and outside the country, for its competencies and achievements. We should be accepted globally as one of the best E&P companies.[2]

— Subir Raha, Chairman & Managing Director, ONGC

INTRODUCTION

The Oil and Natural Gas Corporation Limited (ONGC) was the largest oil exploration and production (E&P) company in India. The company enjoyed a dominant position in the country's hydrocarbon sector with 84 percent market share of crude oil & gas production. Around 57 percent petroleum exploration licenses in India for over 588,000 square kilometers belonged to ONGC. The company was the first to achieve Rs 100 billion net profits in the Indian corporate history.

ONGC's major products included petroleum, crude natural gas, liquefied petroleum gas (LPG), kerosene, and petrochemical feedstock. For the fiscal year ended 2002–2003, the company reported gross revenues of Rs 353.872 billion and net profit of Rs 105.293 billion. With market capitalization of US$15 billion, ONGC was ranked 260 in *BusinessWeek*'s Global 1000 list of the world's top companies by market value for 2003–2004.

Since the mid-1990s, ONGC had faced the problem of declining crude oil and gas production. The company made efforts to consolidate its position in the business by acquiring foreign oil equity through its wholly owned subsidiary ONGC Videsh Limited (OVL). OVL was formed to help ONGC secure a strong foothold in the international oil market. With the acquisition of Mangalore Refinery and Petrochemicals Limited (MRPL), ONGC became the first integrated oil company in India.

With ONGC's core business showing signs of stagnation, the company chalked out a massive diversification plan to go into downstream activities such as LNG marketing, diesel, naphtha, and kerosene. ONGC was also contemplating forward integration opportunities in gas, petrochemicals, and the power sector. The company also announced its intentions of entering the insurance and shipping business in the next couple of years. However, ONGC's diversification plans received a major setback when the Government of India (GoI) announced that the company should stick to its core business rather than venturing into "unrelated" areas.

71

C

ONGCs Growth Strategy by K Yamini Aparna, under the direction of Vivek Gupta. Reprinted by permission of ICFAI Center for Management Research.

BACKGROUND NOTE

Prior to independence, there were two companies in India involved in the exploration of oil—the Assam Oil Company in the northeastern region and the Attock Oil Company in the northwestern region. Both companies had meager oil exploration outputs as major parts of India were deemed unfit for exploration of oil and gas resources. After independence, the GoI realized the importance of developing the oil and gas sector to achieve rapid industrialization. In the 1950s, private oil companies carried out exploration of hydrocarbon resources in the country. However, a large portion of offshore regions remained largely unexplored.

In the mid-1950s, the GoI decided to explore oil and natural gas resources in various regions of the country. This resulted in the formation of the Oil and Natural Gas Directorate at the end of 1955, as a subordinate office under the then Ministry of Natural Resources and Scientific Research. The department was constituted with a team of geoscientists from the Geological Survey of India. However, soon after the Directorate's formation, it became evident that it would not be possible for the new body to function efficiently due to limited financial and administrative powers.

In August 1956, the Directorate was raised to the status of a Commission with enhanced powers, but it continued to be under GoI control. In October 1959, the body received further elevation, both in status and powers, with the Commission being converted into a statutory body by an act of Parliament. This act came to be known as the ONGC Act in 1959. According to the act, the Oil and Natural Gas Commission's main functions were "to plan, promote, organize and implement programmes for the development of Petroleum Resources and the production and sale of petroleum and petroleum products produced by it, and to perform such other functions as the Central Government may, from time to time, assign to it."

ONGC began its work. In inland areas, ONGC discovered new oil resources in Assam and established a new oil province in the Cambay basin of Gujarat. The company started offshore operations in the early 1970s and discovered a rich oil field in Bombay High. With other subsequent discoveries of huge oil and gas fields, over five billion metric tons of hydrocarbons were discovered.

In the early 1990s, when the GoI adopted a policy of economic liberalization, core sectors including petroleum were deregulated and delicensed, coupled with partial disinvestment of government equity in public sector undertakings (PSUs). As a result, ONGC

EXHIBIT 1	ONGC'S Equity Distribution (April 2004)

Major Stakeholder	Share %
Government	74.1
Public	13.9
IOC	9.6
GAIL	2.4

Source: www.ongcindia.com.

was reorganized as a company with limited liability under the Indian Company's Act, 1956, in February 1994, and all the business of the Oil and Natural Gas Commission was transferred to the Oil and Natural Gas Corporation Limited. After the transfer in 1993, the GoI disinvested 2 percent equity stake through competitive bidding. Subsequently, ONGC expanded its equity by another 2 percent by offering shares to employees. In 1997, the company was granted "Navaratna status."[3] In March 1999, the GoI further sold its 10 percent equity stake in ONGC to the Indian Oil Corporation (IOC) and 2.5 percent stake to the Gas Authority of India Limited (GAIL). This further reduced the GoI holding in ONGC (see Exhibit 1 for Equity Distribution of ONGC).

In the late 1990s, ONGC faced several problems. Apart from global economic recession, the company witnessed declining crude oil production and depleting reserves (see Exhibit 2 for production of crude oil and natural gas by ONGC during the 1992–1999 period). Lack of sophisticated technology made it difficult to cut down on reserves depletion or improve extraction of crude oil from existing reserves. Analysts claimed that ONGC was over-exploiting oil from Bombay High wells. ONGC consultants recommended that the company should cut down production at Bombay High by 25 percent to rehabilitate these oil wells.

In the fiscal year 2000–2001, ONGC's oil production had come down to 25.05 million metric tons. In the midst of a crisis, ONGC realized that it was relying heavily on its core business, i.e., exploration and production of crude oil. With these core businesses facing problems, the company was compelled to diversify into new businesses.

In a significant development in 2002, ONGC was granted rights for marketing transportation fuels on the condition of assured sourcing of products. To fulfill this, ONGC acquired a 37.39 percent equity stake[4] in Mangalore Refineries and Petrochemicals Limited (MRPL) from the AV Birla (AVB) Group,

EXHIBIT 2	ONGC: Production of Crude Oil and Natural Gas (1992–1999)	
Year	**Crude Oil (millions of metric tons)**	**Natural Gas (billions of cubic meters)**
1992–1993	24.43	16.50
1993–1994	24.12	16.81
1994–1995	29.36	17.95
1995–1996	31.64	20.88
1996–1997	29.21	21.29
1997–1998	27.73	18.62
1998–1999	26.39	22.75

Source: www.flonnet.com.

VERTICAL INTEGRATION

Industry experts felt that ONGC's new strategy was essential. They felt that there was a pricing cycle for crude (see Exhibit 3 for world oil prices for three decades), gas, refinery margin, marketing margin, and petrochemical margin and that international prices operated on different cycles in each case. This meant that confinement to one sector, whether upstream or downstream or petrochemicals, would make any organization vulnerable to the ups and downs of a particular cycle. The integration of these activities would ensure profitable operation across a number of cycles and financial stability.

ONGC acquired 297 million shares of MRPL from the AVB group for Rs 2 per share in March 2003. The company pumped in Rs 6 billion by issuing fresh equity of MRPL, increasing its equity stake to 51 percent. Later on, ONGC purchased 356 million shares from institutional investors and increased its stake in MRPL to 71.5 percent. This deal was worth about Rs 3.9 billion. The total amount invested by

a leading business conglomerate in India. It thus diversified into the downstream (refining and retailing) business. Grant of marketing rights and acquisition of MRPL were the major steps in transforming ONGC into an integrated oil and gas corporation.

EXHIBIT 3	World Oil Prices Chronology (1970–2003)

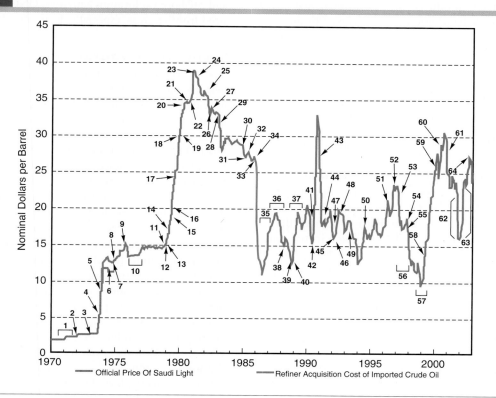

Source: www.eia.doe.gov.

ONGC in MRPL was about Rs 10.494 billion. In addition to equity, ONGC lent Rs 24 billion to MRPL at a rate of 6 percent, saving MRPL an estimated interest cost of Rs 820 million per annum.

MRPL had a refining capacity of 9.69 million metric tons per year. This company had been established when the Administered Pricing Mechanism (APM)[5] was in practice in the Indian oil industry. The GoI's regulatory framework provided assured returns. However, after the refining sector was deregulated in 1998, MRPL lost the regulatory protection and became vulnerable to price fluctuations in the international market. This affected the company's operating profitability significantly and it posted continuous losses for four years in a row.

Despite this poor financial performance, ONGC acquired MRPL to venture into the retail business because it possessed advanced technology, including the capability to meet Euro II norms for transportation fuel quality. The acquisition was considered good for ONGC in the long term, as setting up a similar state-of-the-art nine million metric ton refinery would cost four times the acquisition amount. Moreover, by taking over a loss-making company, ONGC was entitled to huge tax concessions.

The retail business also promised growing demand for petroleum products and consequent stability to ONGC's financial position, even if its core business was in trouble. Because of MRPL, ONGC could divert oil from Bombay High to the refinery for captive consumption. The GoI permitted ONGC to set up 600 retail outlets for marketing products from the MRPL refinery. MRPL was also a partner in the Mangalore-Hassan-Bangalore product pipeline, which helped mobilize products into remote areas.

Due to the injection of funds and operational and managerial support of ONGC, the operational performance and credit profile of MRPL improved considerably. During 2002–2003, it registered an operating profit of Rs 3.48 billion, in spite of a net loss of Rs 4.12 billion. Due to the access to Bombay High Crude, for the year 2002–2003, MRPL processed 7.25 million metric tons of crude against 5.5 million metric tons in 2001–2002.

In April 2004, ONGC announced plans to buy out HPCL's equity stake[6] in MRPL for about Rs 5.5 billion. The proposal had been sent to the GoI and if it materialized, ONGC's equity stake in MRPL would increase to 87.95 percent.

THE GROWTH PLAN

ONGC tried to overcome the declining production of oil and natural gas by focusing on new domestic production enhancement programs, offshore exploration, and technology upgrades. To improve productivity and financial performance, ONGC concentrated on human resources development and financial restructuring.

For the fiscal year 2004–2005, ONGC planned to spend approximately Rs 100 billion on capital expenditure relating to exploration and development of domestic oil and gas properties. As part of production enhancement, redevelopment of Bombay High oil wells was given top priority. This involved two projects called Bombay High North Redevelopment and Bombay High South Redevelopment, which were expected to cost around Rs 82 billion. The program aimed to achieve an additional 76 million metric tons of producible reserves of oil and gas.

ONGC expanded its global operations through its subsidiary OVL, by making sizeable capital investments in Vietnam, Sakhalin (Russia), and Sudan. OVL acquired a 25 percent stake in the Greater Nile Project in Sudan and a 20 percent stake in the Sakhalin Oil Fields in Russia and obtained major projects in Myanmar, Libya, Angola, Syria, and Iran. For the fiscal year 2004–2005, ONGC earmarked Rs 35 billion on capital expenditure relating to existing overseas exploration and development. Apart from regular onshore and offshore exploration activities, ONGC also emphasized frontier areas, especially deepwater drilling.

Technology Upgrades

ONGC found that a main reason for disappointing performance during the late 1990s was its reliance on outdated and obsolete technology, leading to high operation and maintenance costs. Therefore, greater stress was given to technology in the early 2000s. Most ONGC exploration basins were near their maturity phase. To enhance the recovery quantities from these basins, the company decided to employ advanced technology-enabled measures such as Increased Oil Recovery (IOR) and Enhanced Oil Recovery (EOR).[7] Another modern technology adopted was SCADA (Supervisory Control and Data Acquisition), which facilitated around-the-clock monitoring and an automated sensory system for each oil well.

ONGC also adopted modern technology called Virtual Reality Interpretation Centers,[8] which were one of the ten best such systems in the world for applications in exploration, drilling, and engineering. ONGC engaged its team of experts for redesigning the wells to reduce well spaces and draw out the undrained oil embedded between existing wells. Other measures included greater use of horizontal drilling, side-tracks, in-fill drilling, and water injection, as well as technologies using chemical and thermal methods to enhance oil recovery.

Substantial investments were made in IT, covering three major areas—enterprise resource planning (ERP), control systems, and communication networks. ONGC's ERP system covered all aspects of a corporate management information system (MIS) and inventory control. To avoid problems faced in the past due to technological obsolescence, the entire communication system was revamped under a project named Promise launched in 2001. ONGC introduced state-of-the-art fiber optic cables and land and satellite communication systems. The company also acquired the best possible system for data exploration, compilation, monitoring, and processing. ONGC's totally digitalized magnetic media seismic library, entirely handled by robots, was considered the most extensive in the world.

Human Resources Development

ONGC's HR policy aimed at creating a highly motivated, enthusiastic, and self-driven work force (see Exhibit 4 for HR Objectives of ONGC). To heighten motivation levels, the company developed many built-in appraisal systems to identify employee potential and reward exceptional performance. Like other PSUs in India, ONGC also faced the problem of overstaffing and procedural delays. A leaner structure was considered essential to be cost effective and, therefore, ONGC planned to reduce the strength of its workforce of 40,000 by 10 percent in 2003. To get rid of bureaucratic delay, all internal systems and processes were reorganized to facilitate faster file processing. Earlier, each proposal had to pass through various departments, requiring the approval of innumerable functional heads, which made quick decisions impossible and hampered performance. This system was done away with and fast track file clearance was introduced.

ONGC also made efforts to comprehensively redesign its HR appraisal system. New result-oriented incentive and reward schemes were introduced, including the Productivity Honorarium Scheme, Quarterly Incentive Scheme, Group Incentives for Cohesive Team Working, and Reward and Recognition Scheme. Emphasis was placed on greater empowerment of staff to facilitate faster decision making. The positive impact of this was soon obvious. In an international bidding project, a decision was made in just 26 days. Earlier, the time frame for such decisions was roughly one year.

To further develop employees' skill sets, ONGC established the Institute of Management Development, later renamed ONGC Academy. It had an ISO 9001 certification for designing parameters to measure the performance of human resources, succession planning, work climate and work culture analysis, managing change, and other areas of research related to management development. The academy was responsible for executive training and development programs and for conducting seminars and conventions for executives in India and abroad to help the workforce achieve global standards. Exclusive workshops and interactive brainstorming sessions were organized at regular intervals in various work centers to facilitate employee participation in all these projects. All such programs were intended to enhance the productivity and performance of employees by identifying and developing their potential and competency.

In 2001, ONGC launched the Shramik Project (Integrated System of Human Resource Automated Management Information). It was an integrated, online human resource system where all transactions were done through computers. The new system was expected to help streamline systems and procedures, minimizing processing time and administrative costs, improving level of employee satisfaction, and enhancing the quality of decision making.

EXHIBIT 4	HR Objectives of ONGC

- To develop and sustain core values.
- To develop business leaders for tomorrow.
- To provide job contentment through empowerment, accountability, and responsibility.
- To build and upgrade competencies through virtual learning, opportunities for growth, and providing challenges in the job.
- To foster a climate of creativity, innovation, and enthusiasm.
- To enhance the quality of life of employees and their families.
- To inculcate high understanding of "Service" to a greater cause.

Source: Adapted from www.ongcindia.com.

Financial Restructuring

Financial restructuring involved employing better financial management techniques aimed at cost reduction and improving operational efficiency. Special care was taken to streamline related functions such as treasury management, budget control, expenditure monitoring, and reporting. The internal audit system was revamped so that the finance department could provide value-added services to operating divisions.

ONGC was also weighed down by a heavy corporate tax and interest burden during the late 1990s. The company possessed huge cash reserves that were lying idle in the bank. At the same time, a substantial amount of money was being paid out as interest on foreign loans. The company decided to utilize its huge cash reserves and reduce its tax and interest burden. All outstanding foreign exchange loans were prepaid, curtailing the interest outgo and making ONGC a zero-debt company. The excess cash was invested to acquire better technology and assets in India and abroad. Financial restructuring resulted in significant tax savings in the fiscal years 2002 and 2003.

The above measures resulted in more efficient operations, increasing production output from 24.7 million metric tons in 2001 to 26 million metric tons in 2003. The company expected to achieve an output of 29 million metric tons by 2006 (see Exhibits 5 and 6 for ONGC's oil and gas production for 2001–2003).

DEREGULATION

The GoI deregulated the Indian oil industry from April 1, 2002, by doing away with APM. This meant that domestic oil companies could make independent decisions based on import parity and market forces in pricing petroleum products. It also meant that oil PSUs would lose state protection and would have to face the global competitive business environment.

Industry experts felt that deregulation would give an edge to domestic PSUs in marketing their products

EXHIBIT 5	ONGC Natural Gas Production 2001–2003 (billions of cubic meters)		
Year	2001	2002	2003
Onshore	20	20	20
Offshore	6	6	6
Overseas	–	–	0.1
Total	**26**	**26**	**26.1**

Source: www.ongcindia.com.

due to their strong investment base, superior infrastructure, and extended distribution network. They felt that dismantling APM would also result in increased profitability for oil companies.

As expected, the dismantling of APM benefited ONGC significantly. For the fiscal year 2002–2003, ONGC reported a 70 percent jump in net profits to Rs 105.293 billion as opposed to Rs 61.979 billion in the previous year. ONGC's revenues increased from Rs 225.142 billion in 2001–2002 to Rs 342.773 billion in 2002–2003, an increase of 53.4 percent. According to industry experts, deregulation coinciding with steady rise in global oil prices was responsible for increase in revenues and net profits.

However, analysts expressed concern that ONGC oil fields were aging and production of crude oil in 2003–2004 was flat at 26 million metric tons compared to the previous year. The company's expenditure on redevelopment of oil fields increased but its efforts to boost production through improved techniques in Bombay High had not paid off yet.

ONGC's financial performance recorded a fall in the fiscal year 2003–2004. Revenues declined by 7 percent from Rs 342.773 billion in the fiscal year 2002–2003 to Rs 320.639 billion in the fiscal year 2003–2004 and net profit went down by 18 percent, from Rs 105.293 billion to Rs 86.64 billion, for the same period. The company attributed this decline in financial performance to external factors like the government policies and depreciation of the dollar vis-à-vis the rupee (see Exhibit 7 for the latest financial performance of ONGC). The appreciation of the rupee against the U.S. dollar made a dent in the company's profits to the tune of around Rs 11 billion.

Moreover, irrespective of increasing crude oil prices in the international market, ONGC had to sell crude oil to distribution and marketing PSUs at subsidized prices, which led to lower realizations. Apart from this, subsidies for natural gas created a further dent to the tune of Rs 10.5 billion. Despite the dismantling of

EXHIBIT 6	ONGC Crude Oil Production 2001–2003 (millions of barrels)		
Year	2001	2002	2003
Onshore	137	132	63
Offshore	63	65	144
Overseas	–	–	1
Total	**200**	**197**	**208**

Source: www.ongcindia.com.

EXHIBIT 7   ONGC Financial Performance (Rs millions)

Particulars	2003	2004	Change %
Net Sales	342,773	320,639	−6.5
Other Income	19,593	15,471	−21.0
Expenditure	158,718	143,834	−9.4
Operating Profit	184,055	176,806	−3.9
Operating Profit Margin %	53.7%	55.1%	
Interest	1,132	468	−58.7
Depreciation	41,277	55,719	35.0
Profit Before Tax	161,238	136,090	−15.6
Tax	55,945	49,446	−11.6
Profit After Tax	105,293	86,644	−17.7
Net Profit Margin %	30.7%	27.0%	
No. of Shares (m)	1,425.9	1,425.9	
Diluted Earnings per share (Rs)	73.8	60.8	
P/E Ratio		10.1	

Source: www.equitymaster.com.

APM, subsidies were retained on LPG, kerosene, and largely on petrol and diesel as well. As a result, ONGC reported under-recoveries of Rs 27 billion.

FUTURE PLANS

In mid-2004, ONGC was contemplating forward integration opportunities in gas, petrochemicals, and the power sector. It announced plans to set up major power plants using natural gas at Dahej in Gujarat and another plant at Mangalore in Karnataka. An agreement was entered into with the Gujarat government for setting up a Special Economic Zone (SEZ) for this purpose, including a 2,000 megawatt power plant based on regasified natural gas. In addition, another SEZ was planned in Kakinada, Andhra Pradesh, to establish a power plant and an LNG import terminal.

Another 2,000 megawatt plant was planned adjacent to the company's subsidiary, MRPL, in Karnataka. However, ONGC did not plan to venture into transmission and distribution of electricity or power trading. As gas transportation was uneconomical, power plants were planned at gas fields and the power generated was proposed to be sold to grids or captive users.

ONGC also planned to foray into areas such as LNG marketing, diesel, naphtha, and kerosene, which promised higher realizations. ONGC also announced its plans to enter into the insurance and shipping business in the next couple of years. Speaking on the company's future plans, Raha said his vision was to transform ONGC into a fully integrated global oil and gas power-house within the next five years. However, industry experts had some doubts about ONGC's diversification plans, including its venture into unrelated areas such as insurance and shipping. For instance, analysts were unsure about the chances for success in the insurance business. The Indian insurance industry was already fiercely competitive, with several major national and international players dominating the scene.

In August 2004, in a significant development that could radically change the face of the Indian oil industry, the GoI announced plans to merge major oil companies. The petroleum ministry proposed that HPCL and BPCL should be merged with ONGC, while Oil India would be merged with IOC. HPCL and BPCL together had about 11,000 petrol stations and a refining capacity of 32 million metric tons per annum. Their merger with ONGC would create India's largest oil producer and a vertically integrated firm. Along with Oil India, ONGC's Assam and Gujarat oil fields were also proposed to be given to IOC to create India's largest retailing firm, controlling nearly 12 million metric tons of crude oil. There was also a proposal to merge GAIL with ONGC. This way there would be only two mega, state-owned enterprises, having combined expertise in the field of oil and gas exploration and oil retail and marketing.

However, the merger proposal was vehemently opposed by the managements of HPCL and BPCL on the grounds that they wanted the freedom to enter the oil and gas E&P business on their own to become vertically integrated firms. In the light of this negative response, the ministry had to put on hold the proposed merger plans and decided to continue discussions with the management of the two companies. The ministry also said that in the event of the merger not taking place, it had no alternative but to restrict oil and energy companies to their core business. The ministry also announced that in that case, oil producers would not be allowed to venture into fuel marketing, while retailing companies would not be able to enter upstream business. Analysts felt this would hamper ONGC's forward integration and diversification plans.

In September 2004, the petroleum ministry was reportedly drafting a formal order asking ONGC to stay focused exclusively on its E&P business. The order is believed to specify that ONGC's refinery assets must be limited to capital investment/holding and not operatorship. Refining should be left to downstream oil companies, as it was their core business. It mentioned that ONGC was not expected to get into downstream marketing and retailing. The reports said ONGC may even be asked to invest at least half its net profit plus depreciation every year in oil and gas E&P business both in India and abroad. Analysts felt that if the order came into force, it would be major setback for ONGC, which had ambitious diversification plans.

NOTES

1. "Analysts upbeat about the future of ONGC," www.ongcindia.com, June 28, 2003.
2. *Drilling & Exploration World*, Vol. 11, No. 10, August 2002.
3. Navaratna status is conferred by the GoI on selected public enterprises to turn them into global giants by granting autonomy and other privileges. The apex committee headed by the Cabinet Secretary regularly reviews the performance of such companies. A comprehensive review of operations is conducted every three years to determine whether the privileged status should be continued or not.
4. HPCL and AVB Group companies, including Grasim Industries (18.92), Hindalco Industries (12.04), Indian Rayon & Industries (5.16), and Indo Gulf Corporation (1.27), had 37.39 percent equity stake each in MRPL. The remaining stake was with financial institutions and the public.
5. Prior to deregulation, the Indian government tried to offset the effects of price changes in crude oil by maintaining an Oil Pool Account, which built financial reserves when crude oil prices were down and released them back as subsidies when crude

oil prices rose. However, in practice, the April 2002 reforms did not completely remove the government's influence on petroleum product prices. Subsidies had been maintained on some products, such as kerosene, which is commonly used as a cooking fuel by low-income households in India.
6. HPCL originally had a 37.39 percent stake. However, as part of the acquisition deal, financial institutions were to convert their Rs. 5.5 billion debt into equity, which meant bringing down the stake of HPCL to 15–16 percent.
7. Enhanced oil recovery is the third stage in hydrocarbon production during which sophisticated techniques that alter the original properties of the oil are used. The purpose of this program is not only to restore formation pressure but also to improve oil displacement or fluid flow in the reservoir.
8. Virtual reality refers to an electronic artificial/manmade immersive environment. The experiences in such an artificial environment are interpreted to analyze the experiences in the actual environment. This exercise is expected to reduce the risks involved in initial experiments in the actual environment.

ADDITIONAL READINGS AND REFERENCES

Sridhar, V., "ONGC: Coping with Competition," *Frontline*, April 11–24, 1998.

Srinivasan, Raghuvir, "What MRPL Means to ONGC," *Business Line*, August 4, 2002.

"ONGC: India's First National Integrated Oil & Gas Corporate," *Drilling & Exploration World*, August 2002.

Srinivasan, Raghuvir, "ONGC: Hold," *Business Line*, November 10, 2002.

Subramaniam, T. S., "Vertical Integration Is Essential," Interview with Subir Raha, *Frontline*, January 15–31, 2003.

India: ONGC Emerges as Global Energy Leader, *Oxford Analytica*, April 14, 2003.

"Analysts upbeat about the future of ONGC," www.ongcindia.com, June 28, 2003.

Shankara, Jai, "ONGC: India's trillion rupee powerhouse," *Business Barons*, April 1, 2004.

Chaudhary, Archana And Narayanan, Dinesh, "We Would Be a $50 Billion Company in Five Years," Interview with Subir Raha, *Business Line*, June 17, 2004.

"ONGC: Being Wasted," www.equitymaster.com, June 22, 2004.

Thomas, E. C., "New Era in Oil Sector," http://pib.nic.in.

"Competitive Environment Would Force ONGC to Redefine Its Business Strategy," Interview with I. N. Chatterjee, Director (Finance), ONGC, www.shilpabichitra.com.

www.ongcindia.com.
www.indiainfoline.com.
www.sify.com.
www.tribuneindia.com.
www.economictimes.indiatimes.com.
www.ndtv.com.
www.dpe.nic.in.
www.rigzone.com.
www.eia.doe.gov.
www.capitalmarket.com.
www.indiatodayconclave.com.
www.ipan.com.
www.ciionline.com.
www.teriin.org.
www.oilfieldprofessionals.com.
www.petrosilicon.com.
www.msnbc.msn.com.

9Live: Birth of a TV Channel

Dominik Boskamp
Holger Materlik
Franziska May
Dominik Steinküler
Prof. Lutz Kaufmann
Daniel Schmidt

WHU, Otto Beisheim Graduate School of Management

It was a cold and very clear night in April 2001. Christiane zu Salm, roughly one month on her job as CEO of the television station tm3, looked out of her office in Munich, the epicenter of the German media industry. For her, a new direction was the only possible route to take the heavily troubled firm to a safe haven. The TV channel would have to make a complete turn-around. Now big discussions were looming back and forth about what to do, and where to start. At the moment, Ms. zu Salm looked again at her favorite concept, the project 9Live. Today her team had finished a detailed concept draft of the project: Interactive television. Ms. zu Salm reviewed again the concept she and her staff had worked out in the last weeks. The main question remaining now was if the new program would find its place in the German television market. Would enough people watch them? Would enough people call in to their shows? How could they finance the channel, and what were their profit drivers?

Christiane zu Salm felt the excitement of the big challenges she was facing. In any case, she was brought in to make the turnaround, and find a viable concept that was independent of advertising revenue. Not moving in any direction while watching one's ship sink certainly was no option anymore. Now it was on her to decide which path to take, and to take the risks the best way she could.

COMPANY INFORMATION: TM3

Before the idea of 9Live and "interactive TV" was established, the TV station tm3 went through a history of frequent strategic changes. The TV channel was founded in 1995 by Vienna-born Herbert Kloiber and his company Tele München in cooperation with the Heinrich Bauer publishing house. The initial strategy of the program was to be a women's station offering content not available in the German television environment. As further progress was difficult in light of the predominance of the two media conglomerates Kirch Group and Bertelsmann, Kloiber sought options away from these two giants: by offering a 45 percent stake to the newly formed EM.TV (the producer and merchandiser of children's television programs), he formed a strategic alliance with the children's content provider.

However, after EM.TV's overambitious plans (after its initial public offering it acquired a stake in Formula 1 racing) to ascend into the world class failed

Dominik Boskamp, Holger Materlik, Franziska May, and Dominik Steinkühler prepared this case under the supervision of Professor Lutz Kaufmann and Ph.D. student Daniel Schmidt to provide material for class discussion. The authors do not intend to illustrate either effective or ineffective handling of a managerial situation. The authors may have disguised certain names and other identifying information described to protect confidentiality. The case study is based on facts; the surrounding story describing the concrete situation of Christiane zu Salm on the night in April 2001 is illustrative and is not based on information from Christiane zu Salm herself.

to materialize as the Kirch Group and Bertelsmann held against it, a rivalry among the German media conglomerate escalated. The Munich-based film distributor Kinowelt, which many considered to be the third force in the industry, tried in 1998 to take over Kloiber's stake in tm3. But in late 1998, Rupert Murdoch, the biggest international media mogul, bought a majority stake (66 percent) in the women's channel tm3 in order to gain a foothold into the German market.

This led to a major strategic change: It was widely speculated that Murdoch was about to transform tm3 into a fitness channel similar to one he already held in the US. In 1999/2000, after acquiring the remaining 34 percent stake from Herbert Kloiber, who had difficulties keeping the money-losing venture alive by himself, Murdoch also successfully bid for the rights for the champions league in order to transform the channel into "The Champions League Station." This strategy was not successful either because tm3 just did not have the reputation with the viewer community to push market share significantly above 1 percent.

In May 2000, after years of negotiating with both rivals, Kirch and Bertelsmann, Rupert Murdoch announced plans to buy into Kirch's digital pay-TV venture, Premiere. Right after the agreement with Kirch was closed, Murdoch withdrew tm3's rights to air the Champions League soccer games, and relocated his sports program onto the new pay-TV platform.

Since Murdoch's strategic interest in the channel vanished, H.O.T. Networks GmbH and ProSiebenSat.1 Media AG (Kirch Group) took over tm3 in early 2001. In the initial shareholding structure, H.O.T. held 48.6 percent of shares, pooled with Christiane zu Salm's share of 3 percent. The ProSiebenSat.1 group held 48.4 percent of the channel.

H.O.T. Networks was owned by Barry Diller, who was a very well-known luminary in the international media landscape heading USA Interactive, a diversified group of companies that had in common a transformation into interactive businesses such as Expedia, the online travel agency and the TV travel shop. With his experience as chief executive officer of Paramount Pictures (1974–1984), Fox Inc. (1984–1992), and Sega Enterprises Inc., he was appointed CEO of the home shopping channel QVC in 1992, which was introduced in Germany in 1996.

Barry Diller together with the whole team of shareholders introduced a completely new focus, away from women's TV and fitness. They wanted to introduce something new and innovative into the German television market. At the beginning of April Christiane zu Salm was brought in to turn the newly acquired sinking ship around.

Christiane zu Salm looked back on a successful past. After an apprenticeship with the major German publishing house Fischer, she had studied business in Munich and at Harvard. After her graduation she had held different positions for the UFA Film- und Fernseh-GmbH, a major German movie and cinema corporation. Before her new job at tm3, Ms. zu Salm had been head of MTV Central Europe (responsible for Germany, Austria, and Switzerland) for three years, being the youngest head of a TV channel in Germany up to that time, winning her various awards for her successful management, e.g. the Echo as "media personality of the year 2001."

MARKET OVERVIEW

The German television market had a history of its own. Before the 1980s merely three public TV channels, namely ARD, ZDF, and a regional program known as "the Third," were available to the average German household. Only when close to foreign military bases or borders could some foreign channels be received. The electromagnetic broadcasting technique via terrestrial frequencies as it was originally employed in Germany had limited geographical reach and transmission frequencies.

The public broadcasting networks were legally committed to offer a basic supply of information, education, and entertainment. For this purpose, in 1950 the federal states of West Germany founded broadcasting corporations governed under public law which were affiliated in the ARD, and which started to jointly broadcast the "Erstes Deutsches Fernsehen," the first German TV channel, two years later. Thirteen years later, with increasing demand for program variety, the ZDF ("Zweites Deutsches Fernsehen") was going on air with the same legal framework. The sixties also saw the establishment of the Channel Three TV programs, which were broadcast on a regional basis by the ARD units. The conduct of business and the general direction of the program were monitored by broadcasting councils consisting of social groups that should represent the interests of the general public, and thus maintain a neutral political stance and a balanced view of facts in the program composition. Monthly viewer license fees determined by the state parliaments were the main source of financing for the public television channels.

In 1978 the state prime ministers decided to establish cable pilot projects in several German cities in order to assess public demand for program variety as well as the viability of the broadband cable network as a means to overcome the bottleneck in transmission capacity of terrestrial frequencies. On June 16, 1981, the so-called FRAG sentence of the German Federal Constitutional Court paved the way for the establishment of private television. Subsequently, on January 1, 1984, the "Programmgesellschaft für Kabel und Satellitenrundfunk" (PKS) as the first private television channel started broadcasting. One day later, Radio Tele Luxemburg Plus (RTL plus) started broadcasting terrestrially out of Luxemburg and could be received with the help of an extra antenna. The initial success led the government to push the expansion of the cable network. In 1985 PKS was renamed to SAT.1, and launched a nationwide program in all cable and satellite networks. Only one year later, RTL plus changed its name to RTL, and turned nationwide as well. Additionally, the launch of the first ASTRA satellite in December 1988, which presented a substantial improvement over former satellite systems, supported the development of direct satellite reception, especially in the more rural regions which were not yet connected to the cable network. The private TV stations generated more than 90 percent of their revenues from advertising. To support this, many of them also started to show erotic night programs, primarily to generate cash flows early on in their life cycles. These programs, which were only allowed to be screened late at night, made the most money with erotic hotline commercials in blocks between the programs. The companies of such telephone services paid solid advertisement fees, which were otherwise very hard to obtain, especially at the late night time slots. Until 2001, however, most of the bigger private channels reduced broadcasting such content, usually due to image reasons. Moreover, a channel's program content was to some degree constrained by the necessary adherence to the agreements in the licenses of the channels, which were allotted by the federal regulatory authority (the "Landesmedienanstalt").

As a result of this rapid expansion and improvement in technology, the number of programs that an average of the 30 million German households could receive increased to 33 by the end of 1997. This development was accompanied by the emergence of TV stations with different, more focused concepts, and programs like the 24-hour news channel n-tv (established in 1992) or the sport channel DSF (established in 1993). In 1995, the first teleshopping channel, H.O.T. (Home Order Television), started broadcasting, followed by QVC only one year later. Exhibits 1 and 2 provide an overview of private and pay TV channels with a nationwide reach in Germany at the end of 1999.

EXHIBIT 1	Overview of the German Television Market

Program	Category		Reach (million households)		
	Full Service	**Limited Content**	**Terrestrial**[1]	**Cable**[1]	**Satellite**[1]
RTL	X		3.17	18.57	10.4
RTL II	X		1.07	18.9	11.2
Super RTL		X		15.88	10.4
VOX	X		1.42	18.4	10.38
SAT. 1	X		5.08	17.46	9.71
ProSieben	X		5.2	17.7	11.4
Kabel 1	X		0.4	17.5	11.4
N24		X	X	X	X
DSF		X	0.4	18	10.4
tm3	X		0.11	18.28	8.35
Atv		X			X
Bloomberg TV		X		4.1	11.02
CNN Germany		X		7.5	
Eurosport[2]		X		——— 28.33 ———	
H.O.T.		X	7.7	9.65	
MTV		X		——— 17.72 ———	
NBC Europe[2]		X		X	X
n-tv		X	0.17	17.47	11.16
ONYX		X		9.6	10
QVC		X		6.5	8.5
VH-1		X		8.7	0.18
VIVA		X		19.28	4.8
VIVA Zwei		X		13.76	4.8

[1] Frequency allotment or distribution in at least one federal state
[2] No detailed information on technical distribution

Source: Concentration report KEK 2000.

EXHIBIT 2 Overview of Pay-TV Channels in Germany

Program	Description
Premiere	Analog movie channel
Premiere World	Digital Pay-TV-platform with own category channels: Star Kino, Cine Action, Cine Comedy, SCI Fantasy, Romantic Movies, Sport World, Krimi & Co, Heimatkanal, Filmpalast, Sunset
13th Street, Studio Universal	Movie channel of Universal Studios. Distributed through Premiere World
CLASSICA	24-hour classical music channel. Distributed through Premiere World
Discovery Channel	24-hour category channel with focus on nature, adventure, history and technology. Distributed through Premiere World
Disney Channel	24-hour category channel for families with children. Distributed through Premiere World
GoldStar TV	24-hour music channel. Distributed through Premiere World
K-toon, Junior	Junior and K-Toon constitute a 24-hour program of movies for children and teenagers. The channels are distributed through Premiere World (Junior is distributed during the day, K-toon in the evening and during the night)
MultiThématiques	Consists of the channels Planet, Seasons, CineClassics, Jimmy, CyberTV. Thereof, Planet and Seasons are distributed through Premiere World
Blue Channel	Near-video-on-demand
Cinedom	Near-video-on-demand

Source: Concentration report KEK 2000.

The development of the private TV market was accompanied by the creation of several additional public TV stations like the documentary and political channel Phoenix (1997) and the children's station Kinderkanal (1997). These public channels had to be carried in all cable networks by law, so that the capacity for private channels was limited. As a consequence, in 1988 only 15 out of 30 available program slots were available for private broadcasting companies in the German cable network.

Germany was home to some of the world's largest press and broadcasting conglomerates. The two dominating players in 2001 were the Bertelsmann/CLT-Ufa group, consisting of RTL, RTL2, Super RTL, and Vox, and the Kirch group, in which Rupert Murdoch had minority shareholdings, owning Sat 1, PRO 7, Kabel 1, and DSF. Although these two industry giants were fiercely competing against each other in the private-channel market, the two groups jointly operated the German pay-TV channel Premiere (Exhibit 3 gives a summary of the audience rating of the different programs). Moreover, they pressed ahead with the

development of digital radio and TV, as the German government was convinced that the analogue transmitters could be replaced by digital ones by the year of 2010 and eventually switched off.

INTERACTIVE MEDIA CONCEPTS

Germany

The German market for purely interactive television virtually did not exist at the time tm3 was planning the 9Live project. However, traditional TV stations were utilizing the basic concepts of interactivity to increase the attractiveness of traditional television concepts.

The so-called TED surveys (Tele-dialogue) were first introduced in 1979 and extensively used in the "ZDF-Hitparade" (voting for the winning song), and "Wetten dass. . .?" (voting for the best bet), which at the time were the most successful show concepts in German television. Unlike radio show concepts where call-in formats were frequently used to enrich the listening experience, they remained subdued in

EXHIBIT 3

Audience Ratings: German TV Channels

Program	Begin of distribution	West Germany[1]							Germany[1]								
		1985	1986	1987	1988	1989	1990	1991	1992	1993	1994	1995	1996	1997	1998	1999	2000
ARD	Nov-54	43,4	44,9	42,2	37,9	31,7	30,8	27,5	22,0	17,0	16,3	14,6	14,8	14,7	15,4	14,2	14,3
ZDF	Apr-63	42,6	40,2	40,7	36,2	32,4	28,8	25,6	22,0	18,0	17,0	14,7	14,4	13,6	13,2	13,3	
ARD (Dritte)	80s and 1992	10,2	10,1	10,5	10,7	10,4	9,0	8,8	8,3	7,9	8,9	9,7	10,1	11,6	12,3	12,5	12,7
RTL	Jan-84	0,4	0,7	1,2	4,1	10,0	11,5	14,4	16,7	18,9	17,5	17,6	17,0	16,1	15,1	14,8	14,3
SAT.1	Jan-84	-	-	1,5	5,8	8,5	9,0	10,6	13,1	14,4	14,9	14,7	13,2	12,8	11,8	10,8	10,2
3 sat	Dez-84	-	-	-	-	-	-	-	0,8	1,0	0,9	0,9	0,9	0,9	0,9	0,9	
Tele 5 / DSF	Jan-88, since Jan-93 DSF					-	0,6	1,9	3,0	1,3	1,2	1,3	1,1	1,2	1,1	1,3	1,2
ProSieben	Jan-89					-	1,3	3,8	6,5	9,2	9,4	9,9	9,5	9,4	8,7	8,4	8,2
Eurosport	Feb-89								-	1,2	1,2	1,2	1,1	1,1	1,1	1,1	1,0
Premiere / old [2]	Feb-91 - Sep-99								-	1,6	-	0,7	0,7	0,7	0,5	NA	
Kabel 1	Feb-92								-	0,1	2,0	3,0	3,0	3,8	4,4	5,4	5,5
Arte	Mai-92								-	-	0,2	0,2	0,3	0,3	0,3	0,3	0,3
n-tv	Nov-92								-	1,3	0,3	0,3	0,3	0,5	0,6	0,7	0,7
VOX	Jan-93								-	2,6	2,0	2,6	3,0	3,0	2,8	2,8	2,8
RTL II	Mrz-93									-	3,8	4,6	4,5	4,0	3,8	4,0	4,8
Super RTL	Apr-95										-	2,1	2,3	2,9	2,8	2,8	2,8
tm3	Aug-95										-	-	0,3	0,6	1,0	1,0	1,0
DF1 [2]	Jul-96 - Sep-99											-	-	0,2	0,6	1,0	NA
Kinderkanal	Jan-97													0,6	0,9	1,3	1,2
Phoenix	Apr-97													-	0,3	0,4	0,4
Premiere World [2]	Oct-1999 (Relaunch)															0,3	1,1
N24	Jan-00																NA

[1] The overview shows the GfK market shares.

[2] On October 1, 1999, the channels DF1 and Premiere, as well as their subscribers, were combined into the new Premiere World channel.

Source: Commission on Concentration in the Media

---

television concepts. Action on the screen, increased market share, and ultimately advertisement revenue were the objectives of the programming, whereas call-in shows such as "Hugo" (an arcade game per phone line) were merely used to fill program gaps rather than being telecast at prime time.

In the 1990s, though, an increasing trend towards home shopping television was observed with H.O.T. and QVC launching in 1995 and 1996 respectively. Viewers started to regard television not only as a one-way medium but as a transaction medium. These trends, among others, had already been successfully established in international markets.

United Kingdom

After BSkyB, Rupert Murdoch's rivalry with BBC in establishing the first satellite network, which went into operation in 1998, the British Digital Television Platform was the first to get established in the European countries.

Independent polls revealed a strong interest of English viewers for all kinds of interactive formats such as gaming and betting via the digital television platform. One of the most popular formats is "Two Way TV," which was established in 1996 and was broadcast to the BSkyB subscriber base of 5 million users in 2000. With moderate costs of 60 pence, more than 25 percent of these households had been attracted to play at least once, and 70,000 to play every day. Betting services on BSkyB, which faced legal restrictions in Germany, generated revenues of €53 million in the second half of 2000 with less than 20,000 customers.

The arcade gaming channel PlayJam, with a reach of about 9 million viewers, was launched in December 2000, and emerged as the second most popular channel on the Sky Digital platform, well ahead of the Paramount movie channel, MTV, and the Disney channel by early summer in 2001.

France

TPS started in the late 1990s as the second French digital satellite broadcasting station. Of the 1 million subscribers more than 90 percent had used one of the interactive services at least once. Betting and Meteo Express (an interactive weather channel) were the most popular formats and strong revenue drivers for TPS.

The more Christiane zu Salm thought about the 9Live project, the more she realized that 9Live shared the basic concept of interactivity with their UK and French peers, but none of them was based on the initial reaction of viewers to live produced content. 9Live would be the spearhead of the development of innovative interactive content. With the affirmative studies of the success and potential of interactive television formats in the UK and France, however, Christiane zu Salm felt confident that the German viewers could become as excited as the British and French viewers if the content and the concepts were right. Independent studies showed strong revenue potential for interactive television and call media formats. Being the first to dare tapping this very special market, she felt confident that 9Live could pre-empt any competition and secure a leading position in this new market segment.

THE NEW CONCEPT—INTERACTIVE TELEVISION

Basic Concept

Developments had not been too good at tm3. Desperately the little TV station needed a safe niche, staying clear of all the huge conglomerates battling over blockbuster movies, latest sports shows, and news coverage. The idea was to venture an interactive concept where viewers would actively participate in the shows, win prizes, and contribute to the channel's finances with their calling fees. The reason for this focus on interactivity was also founded in the belief that the advertising market was about to decline drastically after steeply growing for the past five years (Exhibit 4).

The plan was indeed not so complicated. Put on a show where a charismatic host played all kinds of little quizzes, puzzles, or asked not-too-hard common-knowledge questions. He or she would have to animate the viewers to start calling in order to win prizes, typically cash between €100 and €10,000 (approximately $100–$10,000). For each call, one had to pay an amount of money in order to enter the competition. Computer software would then randomly pick a caller, who then had a chance to answer the question. If he did so correctly, he would win the money, and the next game would start, with new people calling in. There would be slightly different shows on through the day, but essentially they all shared the same underlying concept. Maybe one would ask questions about history, one would play games in the format of a wheel of fortune, and another one would give little mathematical

riddles. Just nothing too complicated, as they wanted as many people to call as possible. In all this, the essential part was that there would be enough callers. In theory, if there would be only one caller for each game, all they would earn was the comparatively low calling fee, while losing all of the prize money. So there had to be at least more revenues from the callers than the prize value. And in the designed concept, they would do much more. Ideally, tm3 would earn money from this as more and more people started calling in to their shows. Their revenues would start coming more from this source than from the main source of all the other channels, namely TV commercials. Moreover, they would not have pressure anymore to buy expensive movie rights or sports shows. Also they didn't have to maintain a big editorial office, journalists, and correspondents as there was no need to broadcast any news show or documentaries.

Customers

Perhaps the most critical issue in the whole idea was the level of willingness of the viewers to call in to the shows and the ability of the show masters to motivate them to do so. They needed at least enough participants in their shows to earn the prizes they distributed, and cover parts of their costs. One of the few demands of Ms. zu Salm's superiors, i.e. the shareholders, had been to be less reliant on commercials and advertisement revenues, and this looked like the way to comply. In the context of participants, Ms. zu Salm had several concerns:

First, she was unsure about the general market environment. Were there enough people in the German

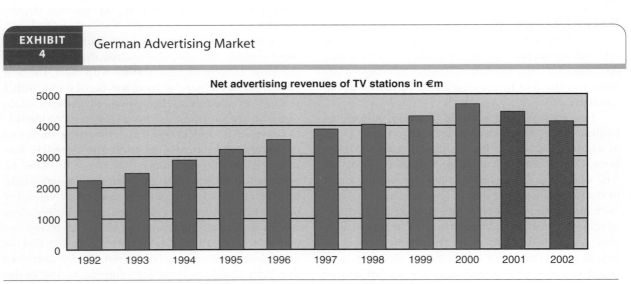

EXHIBIT 4 German Advertising Market

Net advertising revenues of TV stations in €m

Source: Central Committee of German Advertising Commerce, www.interverband.com/zaw, forecast for 2001 and 2002 figures.

market ready to call in to their shows in which they could perhaps win some prize money? And how could this be determined? Ms. zu Salm knew there were lots of ways Germans were similar to their French or British counterparts. But all too often, they were very different as well. Both in France and in the United Kingdom, interactive concepts had performed quite well, although nothing as daring as their planned business concept had been tried in these markets. Viewers used their TV sets to access interactive content but there was no show format solely relying on live produced shows to stimulate this interaction. In contrast to the UK and France, Ms. zu Salm sought a concept of mass interactivity, conveyed with the classic medium of television. Furthermore, Ms. zu Salm had with great interest realized how big the German market for all kinds of lotteries, competitions, riddle magazines, etc. was. It seemed that at every corner store there were heaps of weekly magazines consisting merely of crossword puzzles or riddles, where people could win prizes if the correct solution was sent in. Every supermarket had, often also as a marketing tool, some competition giving away cars, bicycles, trips, or money when people solved some participation game or riddle. Basically, she asked herself, were they following exactly the same pattern? It seemed obvious that there was a market that could well be served by the 9Live concept. But then again, crossword puzzles, for example, were mostly done by her grandmother's generation, Ms. zu Salm thought. Would these people be watching her shows, and more importantly calling in to her shows? Also the success of the home shopping channels made Ms. zu Salm optimistic. If 40,000 people were willing to call H.O.T. each day to order rose crystal fountains, Japanese knives, wine openers, or car wax, how many would start calling if they could win money?

This led her to the second issue: Which set of viewers comprised their main target group? Which group should they concentrate their attention on? Was it old people, young people, male or female, from rural or metropolitan areas? How could this be determined? In the case of the most popular TV show, "Wetten dass. . .?," for example, everybody watched it, and it was mostly advertised as a family happening, where everybody in the house would gather around the TV and enjoy a nice Saturday night together. This was probably not a viable option for tm3. They needed constant viewers, from morning to evening, who would constantly call in on their game shows. Also, their shows would have to focus much less on entertainment and more on motivating people to call, play, and win. Or should they concentrate on a certain time of the day? But then, Ms. zu Salm really thought that if

they launched the interactive program, it should be the whole day. Only if the channel had a distinct character, with a similar program whenever the viewer would zap in, could they be successful.

The third puzzle the team at tm3 was trying to solve was the right marketing solution. Once they could figure out who their potential customers—that is, the callers—were, they would have to get them to watch their program, fast. At the moment tm3 was not in best financial health. And with the new concept, the problem would be the money in the early months. Because not only did they have to build up the whole program from scratch, but also they had to give away considerable amounts of cash in prizes. So if they could not get a fair amount of people calling on their shows, there was a big danger of running out of cash early on. But what could they really do in terms of marketing? At the moment, the few people watching their program were a very diverse group due to the drastic changes in program focus in recent years. Many of them were women, mostly watching old soap operas, movies, or evergreen series. Probably commercials on their own program would not attract much attention. Going on other channels with TV spots might be an option, but unfortunately a very costly one. Then they could do poster advertisements in cities, radio spots, or newspaper ads. But would that be worth the money spent? Maybe they should just invest it in better shows, or higher prize money? The pricing of calls was also an issue here: How much should one call cost? And how much should people be able to win? How much difference would it actually make for the number of people calling if they could win €10,000 instead of €10?

Revenue

At the moment tm3 employed almost 100 employees, and had a cost structure roughly similar to ProSieben-Sat.1 Media AG (Exhibit 5). Most of these were employed in producing the content (editors, program producers, announcers, studio and technical staff). Christiane zu Salm thought that it should be possible to implement the interactive channel design with roughly the same amount of people because they could compensate for the increased show production demand for manpower by freeing most resources in the editorial departments. They would have to start producing the shows, hiring show masters, and install the IT system which was required for receiving the calls, randomly choose callers, and handle billing and settlement. This would primarily be done with the help of a telecommunication service provider, who would take a fixed percentage of each calling fee (about one third of calling revenues), and process the incoming calls. On

| EXHIBIT 5 | Overview of Pro7Sat1 Group 2000 |

Channel	Revenue (in Euro)	Employees	Advertisement Income	Licensing, Transmission fees	Wages
Sat1	971,000,000	552	-	-	-
Pro7	866,000,000	264	-	-	-
kabel 1	220,000,000	42	-	-	-
N 24	38,000,000	127	-	-	-
Total	2,095,000,000	3183*	2,083,000,000	118,669,000	191,723,000

*Most of the personnel were employed in services or multimedia; only 1,894 in television.

Source: Pro7 Annual Report 2000, www.pro7sat1.de, accessed November 29, 2004.

the whole, it seemed like the human resource factor and the technology of producing the actual shows would be manageable problems compared to the key question of whether viewers would actually call in. Another major cost block to cover was the distribution fee to be paid to the cable network and satellite operators, which would not shrink with different content. At the moment Christiane zu Salm was sitting in front of the half-finished financial plan for the next 12 months. About 28 million households were receiving their program. In the first quarter of 2001, tm3 had a market share of roughly 0.7 percent. But probably they would not be able to take these viewers with them into the interactive program. Overall industry earnings in commercials had been about €4.7 billion in 2000. Their share had been part of this, and with viewers continuing to stop watching their programs, it was bound to drop further and further, until they would get into serious financial conditions. And with the costs of the interactive concept getting even more expensive due to the new technology, and with the new challenge of producing live shows, they would have to get cash quickly.

Ethics/Legal Concerns

Another issue with the interactive channel was the fact that it would very likely attract some controversies in Germany. As people were supposed to spend money just for the chance of winning some prize, it was also subject to some regulatory restrictions. Firstly, tm3 felt that all callers should be older than 18 years of age, and were therefore sufficiently mature to decide to call or not.

The new project could still be based on the television license granted to tm3. Furthermore, in order not to be subject to gambling law, they would have to price the calls below 50 eurocents. This was approximately the same amount as the price to send a domestic postcard in Germany, as it was used in countless little competitions and open contests arranged by supermarkets, television stations or magazines. But there was also an intangible component: If people were actually calling every day, they could create an even larger amount in calling fees. But could tm3 also be held responsible if callers developed addictions to gaming and playing on the channel? The core and clear-cut goal was to offer entertainment for grown-up television viewers, and leave the decision whether or not to take part to the individual viewers. With a transparent caller selection mechanism on a purely random basis, every participant was treated equally, and with moderate participation fees, the risk of coming into an illegitimate position with these practices in place was not great.

Outlook

So many challenges were lying ahead of project 9Live. Most importantly, an audience had to be found and targeted the right way in order to become profitable as soon as possible. But even before that, TV hosts had to be hired and shows had to be invented and produced. This was not trivial as the shows were supposed to be live, and the TV hosts had to be charismatic enough to capture the viewers, attract them to watch other viewers playing games in the shows, and ultimately call themselves. Also very important for the whole concept to work were good producers. It was not very easy to find them, but tm3 was looking everywhere for new and open-minded talents. The issue here was that since there were not similar concepts around, they would have to train people for what they needed. This was another challenge on the way to 9Live. There was even the possibility to sell produced shows, if they were received well from the audience, and therefore produce programs for third-party providers. But there were more urgent challenges to master in the next couple of months.

The team of tm3 had already started to hire some hosts, but then it had not yet been decided how many they would actually need, and when, as it still had to be decided how the execution of project 9Live and thereby the whole TV channel was going to happen. Should it be a radical change or should they first start with a few game shows, and then, depending on the viewers' sentiment, gradually increase the amount of game shows until the point that it would be a sole game show channel? But could that work? A channel that consisted only of game shows, and profited only from the calling fees of their audience. Home shopping concepts had been successful, but this was something different, right?

Nonetheless, the team of tm3 had to make a change as even as its sixth-year profits were yet to materialize. The project 9Live was in fact more than just an attempt. Thus they needed a good action plan. Implementation of change was always difficult, and therefore it required everyone's absolute focus and dedication. One important guideline was to avoid any legal issues to gain credibility, and not lose potential callers. Moreover the show production process had to be engaged, and new talent had to be hired.

One other big topic that had been discussed by many employees of tm3 over the last month was whether it would be reasonable to rename the channel in order to complete the change into a new TV channel era. A completely new channel with a new name would certainly visualize the new start they were about to undertake, but should they give up the brand awareness of the name "tm3"? Not only was the problem of finding a name a challenge but it could also involve significant marketing expenses to be invested to make the TV channel known with its new name among all potential customers.

Christiane zu Salm read the different articles, reports, and business plans on her desk. Was 9Live really worth the risks they had to take? Tomorrow morning she had to present her ideas and give clear marching directions to all her employees. From that point on, there was no turning back. What was left was work to minimize the risks they had to take: Understand the new concept and its consequences, find a bullet-proof financing plan, motivate employees, and put the concept into an action plan everybody could follow.

MapQuest

Kevin K. Boeh
Paul W. Beamish

Richard Ivey School of Business, The University of Western Ontario

On October 1, 1999, Chief Executive Officer (CEO) Mike Mulligan's team at MapQuest closed the third quarter books. Revenue was strong and the company's cash position was good. During the past year, Mulligan had led the firm through a successful initial public offering (IPO) and record growth. However, Mulligan questioned being able to sustain the growth rate and the market value of the firm, which many called irrational. He wondered how he could take advantage of the stock price and continue to sustain growth (see Exhibits 1 and 2) and value going forward. Mulligan planned to lay out a course of action for the board later that month.

INDUSTRY BACKGROUND

Growth of the Internet

The Internet had become an increasingly significant global medium for distributing and collecting information, conducting commerce, and communicating. Internet growth was being fueled by increased use of personal computers, improvements in network infrastructure, more readily available and lower cost Internet access, an increased acceptance of conducting transactions online, and the proliferation of compelling available content.

MapQuest and many of its competitors had been in the mapping, printing, and location information businesses for years and were now faced with the prospects of this dynamic digital business environment. Many of the existing offline companies and many start-ups that were focused on the space, some very well funded with growth capital, saw the opportunity to leverage their offline assets online.

Convergence of Traditional and Digital Mapping

Geospatial information had traditionally been provided through reference materials including atlases, maps, travel guides, telephone directories, and textbooks. According to the International Map Trade Association, the annual market for such publications in the United States alone would exceed $1.6 billion. Advances in technology allowed companies to put their geospatial information into computer applications and to place their databases onto CD-ROMs and the Internet. MapQuest had followed just such a path and was using its extensive databases of geographically relevant information to provide online services.

Online Destination Information for Business and Consumers

Businesses had traditionally communicated their existence and location to customers using print media, including newspapers and the Yellow Pages, which

EXHIBIT
1

MapQuest—Income Statement and Projections

(all amounts in millions, except per share amounts)

	1996	1997	1998	1999e	2000e	2001e	2002e
Revenue							
Internet Business	$7.0	$4.8	$6.5	$12.8	$20.6	$42.6	$63.3
Internet Customer	0.1	1.3	1.4	6.4	13.9	26.4	44.4
Traditional DMS	12.4	15.4	16.8	14.7	20.0	24.0	28.0
TOTAL	**19.6**	**21.4**	**24.7**	**33.9**	**54.5**	**93.0**	**135.7**
Cost of Revenue							
Internet	4.3	4.5	4.8	9.7	13.2	18.5	24.4
Traditional DMS	8.0	10.8	12.8	11.4	14.7	17.6	21.0
TOTAL	**12.3**	**15.3**	**17.6**	**21.1**	**27.9**	**36.1**	**45.4**
Gross Profit	7.3	6.1	7.1	12.8	26.6	56.9	90.3
Sales & Marketing	4.5	7.3	5.2	19.0	25.1	30.0	40.0
General & Admin	1.9	1.8	2.3	4.8	6.4	8.0	11.5
Product Development	2.6	5.0	3.0	5.6	7.5	11.0	15.0
TOTAL OPEX	**9.0**	**14.1**	**10.5**	**29.4**	**39.0**	**49.0**	**66.5**
Operating Income	**(1.7)**	**(8.0)**	**(3.5)**	**(16.6)**	**(12.4)**	**7.9**	**23.8**
Interest Income (Expense)	0.2	0.1	0.1	1.6	1.0	–	–
Other Income (Expense)	0.2	0.3	0.2	0.3	0.4	–	–
Pretax Income	**(1.3)**	**(7.6)**	**(3.2)**	**(14.7)**	**(11.1)**	**7.9**	**23.8**
Tax Expense	0.0	0.0	0.0	0.0	0.0	0.0	0.0
EPS			$(0.12)	$ (0.47)	$ (0.33)	$ 0.21	$ 0.66
Total Shares Outstanding			27.6	31.4	33.8	36.9	36.2

Note: e = estimates

EXHIBIT
2

MapQuest—Balance Sheet

(all amounts in thousands, except share counts)

Assets	Dec. 31, 1998	Sep. 31, 1999
Current assets		
Cash and cash equivalents	$ 564	$ 29,685
Short term investments	–	17,940
Accounts receivable, net of allowances	6,647	9,840
Accounts receivable - affiliates	128	707
Inventories	1,365	1,126
Contracts works in progress	147	231
Prepaid expenses and other current assets	482	1,684
Total current assets	9,333	61,213
Property and equipment, net of accumulated depreciation (1998 - $3,433; 1999 - $4,455)	1,844	4,488
Goodwill, net	178	155
Other assets	95	825
Total assets	**$11,450**	**$66,681**

EXHIBIT 2 (Cont'd)

Liabilities and stockholders' equity (deficit)
Current liabilities

Accounts payable	$ 1,715	$ 2,719
Current portion of note payable	48	5
Accrued personnel costs	562	1,231
Advance billings on contracts	498	686
Deferred revenue	1,208	2,434
Other accrued liabilities	1,001	2,411
Total current liabilities	5,032	9,486
Stockholders' equity (deficit)		
Convertible Preferred Stock, Ser. A, B and C	26,477	–
Notes receivable from issuance of preferred stock	(291)	–
Preferred stock, $01 par; 5 million authorized	–	–
Common stock, $ 001 par; 100 million authorized; 336, 038 o/s in 1998; 33,572 562 o/s in 1999		
Notes receivable for common stock	–	–
Additional paid in capital	140	88,246
Retained deficit	(19,908)	(30,861)
Total stockholders' equity (deficit)	(19,768)	(57,195)
Total liabilities and SE (deficit)	**$11,450**	**$66,681**

targeted only a narrow geographic audience and had limited ability to provide updated information. MapQuest gave businesses the opportunity to provide customized driving directions and real-time physical location information. As well, MapQuest provided businesses with an additional set of information and tools that online sites used to enrich and differentiate their own offerings. Very few of these companies had the personnel or technical resources to cost effectively develop the services in-house that MapQuest provided to them.

Consumers and travelers had traditionally located businesses and other points of interest using maps and telephone inquiries, among other methods. As the Internet was growing, consumers were increasingly turning to the Internet for such information.

Geographically Targeted Online Advertising

Forrester Research estimated that online advertising of approximately $1.0 billion in 1998 would grow to over $8.1 billion over the next four years. While online advertising was growing, it was primarily national or international advertising. That is, the products and services offered were not location-specific, yet most actual consumer expenditure was indeed local. While figures varied, it was estimated that as much as 80 percent of

a consumer's expenditures, net of housing, occurred within five miles of the primary residence. As well, of the offline advertising market, nearly 80 percent of total expenditures was for local businesses, using location-specific advertising media. The opportunity to allow online advertising to be location-specific had yet to be realized.

COMPANY BACKGROUND

History and Transformation

RR Donnelley & Sons, a media and printing company, founded MapQuest, originally called GeoSystems Global Corporation, in Lancaster, Pennsylvania, in the late 1960s as a cartographic services division responsible for creating free road maps for gas station customers. In the 1970s, MapQuest became a leading supplier of custom maps to reference, travel, textbook, and directory publishers. The company grew in the mapping industry as a high-quality custom mapmaker and expanded its client base to include American Express, Bertelsmann, Langenscheidt, Reader's Digest, Houghton Mifflin, Reed Elsevier, The National Geographic Society, and World Book.

In 1991, RR Donnelley combined its mapping expertise with technology to pioneer electronic publishing software for interactive mapping applications. MapQuest developed electronic applications for call centers, kiosks, client-server environments, and wireless devices, as well as packaged software applications for travel, directory, reference, and street mapping. In 1994, MapQuest created travel titles for the first handheld devices brought to market by Apple Computer. MapQuest produced travel titles that allowed Fodor's, TimeOut, and Michelin to bring top international city guides, tour information, and directory mapping to consumers. In this same year, MapQuest was split into a separate entity from its corporate parent, RR Donnelley & Sons, to management and certain investors, including RR Donnelley.

In 1996, MapQuest launched the first consumer-focused interactive mapping site on the Web. The company began to offer business solutions to map-enable other Web sites. This innovative business model captured the attention of the Internet consumer and the business market.

In April 1997, The National Geographic Society entered into a cartographic product development, publishing, marketing, and distribution agreement with the firm. The agreement was for five years, ending in May 2002. National Geographic took a seat on the board and received warrants to purchase 954,147 shares at $1.04 per share.

In July of 1997, outside venture investors, including Highland Capital, Weston Presidio Capital, and Trident Capital, invested in the firm, taking 3.4 million shares for $12 million. In November of that year, insiders including the chief financial officer and senior vice-president also purchased stock, largely funded using interest-bearing notes from the firm.

In May 1998, RR Donnelley & Sons and 77 Capital Corporation, two of the original investors from the spin-off, sold their equity positions to Highland Capital, Weston Presidio Capital, and Trident Capital for an additional $7 million. In June of this same year, CEO Barry Glick took a voluntary termination of employment, whereby MapQuest agreed to pay Glick $43,000 representing separation and salary. In August, Michael Mulligan was hired from American Express Travel as CEO and chairman of the board. At American Express, Mulligan had been responsible for Corporate Services Interactive, an American Express Travel offering. Prior to American Express, Mulligan was the chief operating officer (COO) of OAG, the Official Airlines Guide, and was thus a very fitting candidate to lead the company.

The Initial Public Offering

In late 1998, the board of directors selected underwriters to lead an initial public offering. The company officially changed its name to MapQuest.com and established its corporate headquarters in New York City, along with its development facilities in Mountville, Pennsylvania, and Denver, Colorado. The investment banks drafted the IPO prospectus in January 1999, and filed an initial registration statement (S-1) on February 19 to sell up to $50 million of stock. On April 12, an amended S-1 was refiled with an offer to sell 4.6 million shares in the range of $10 to $12 per share with an over-allotment option to the underwriters to increase the number of shares by up to 15 percent (see Exhibit 3).

The IPO roadshow was held during the last two weeks of April, continuing into the first few days of May. On May 3, 1999, the pricing range was increased to $12 to $14 per share to allow flexibility of pricing to meet the hot market demand. The shares were priced after the close of Nasdaq trading on May 3 at $15 per share, and began trading on Tuesday, May 4. Shares debuted late in the morning at $28 per share, an 87 percent gain from the pricing to IPO buyers. The stock price made the market capitalization of the firm approach $1 billion in its first day of trading.

EXHIBIT 3	MapQuest.com Closing Stock Prices—Weekly	
Date	**Nasdaq Index**	**MQST**
7-May-99	$2,503.62	$22.19
14-May-99	2,527.86	21.38
21-May-99	2,520.14	17.56
28-May-99	2,470.52	16.75
4-Jun-99	2,478.34	16.38
11-Jun-99	2,447.88	15.69
18-Jun-99	2,563.44	15.00
25-Jun-99	2,552.65	15.69
2-Jul-99	2,741.02	18.13
9-Jul-99	2,793.07	19.63
16-Jul-99	2,864.48	20.13
23-Jul-99	2,692.40	17.00
30-Jul-99	2,638.49	14.94
6-Aug-99	2,547.97	10.13
13-Aug-99	2,637.81	10.31
20-Aug-99	2,648.33	13.94
27-Aug-99	2,758.90	12.38
3-Sep-99	2,843.11	12.00
10-Sep-99	2,887.06	12.88
17-Sep-99	2,869.62	13.50
24-Sep-99	2,740.41	12.50
30-Sep-99	2,746.16	11.88

MapQuest—The Business

The Solution

MapQuest was a leading online provider of mapping and destination information for businesses and consumers. MapQuest's online products and services enabled businesses to

- Provide customized maps, destination information, and driving directions to potential customers;
- Expand the service offerings of their Web sites to attract and retain users;
- Use outside sources to meet their map-generating and destination information needs, thereby avoiding a significant portion of the expenses normally associated with establishing and maintaining a map-generating personnel and technology organization; and
- Provide potential customers with information regarding which of a business's multiple locations was closest to the potential customer.

MapQuest's online products and services enabled consumers to

- Receive maps and destination information on a real-time basis based on specific location parameters provided by the customer;
- Generate detailed, door-to-door driving directions at any time; and
- Create and retrieve customized maps based on the consumer's preferences.

MapQuest was also a leading provider of traditional and digital mapping products and services to the educational, reference, directory, travel, and governmental markets in the United States. In addition, companies that incorporated call centers, CD-ROMs, or driving direction kiosks into their information delivery strategy required non-Internet customized mapping solutions. MapQuest had adapted its map-generating software to promote the rapid development of mapping applications in these environments.

MapQuest Strategy

MapQuest's objective was to be the leading online provider of destination solutions for businesses and consumers. Key elements of MapQuest's strategy, as put forth in the IPO prospectus, included their intention to

- *Build Brand Awareness:* In addition to branding on its Web site, MapQuest co-branded its products and services on each of its business customer's Web sites. MapQuest intended to expand its use of

advertising, public relations, and other marketing programs designed to promote its global brand and build loyalty among its customers. In the future, MapQuest planned to expand both its online and offline marketing programs.

- *Expand and Enhance the MapQuest Service:* The company planned to continue to broaden and deepen its services by providing comprehensive, cost-effective, accurate, and easily accessible information and value-added tools and features. The company was developing product and service enhancements aimed at its business customers, including enhancing their opportunity to offer geographically targeted advertising programs on their Web sites. MapQuest's planned enhancements to its consumer service included introducing greater personalization features to mapquest.com.

- *Grow Sales Channels Aggressively:* The company hoped to build its sales capabilities in order to broaden penetration of its products and services and increase revenue. The company planned to build its direct field sales force to target United States and international markets, and it sought to develop strategic relationships in the value-added-reseller channels. The company also intended to build its own advertising sales force in order to augment the current third-party representative sales force it had engaged to sell advertisements on mapquest.com.

- *Develop Additional Advertising Opportunities:* The company intended to increase and expand its advertising revenue opportunities by offering new methods of targeted advertising based on a consumer's geographic information. The company planned to use consumer-provided information to provide advertisers the ability to base their advertising and promotions on a consumer's geographic information.

- *Use Existing Integrated Geographic Data as a Platform:* The company wanted to develop new products and services by effectively employing the comprehensive integrated geographic databases it had been developing since 1967. The company had utilized proprietary editing software tools to create its geographic data from multiple content providers in a variety of data formats.

- *Pursue International Opportunities:* The company believed that significant opportunities existed to expand MapQuest's products and services internationally. As of December 1998, approximately 10.8 percent of the maps that MapQuest generated from its own Web site represented international locations. The company intended to expand its international marketing efforts to gain access to additional business customers seeking to improve

C

the service offerings of their Web sites and consumers seeking online map-related information.

MapQuest Products and Services— Internet and Traditional

Internet—Business Products/Services

Connect	Enabled businesses to display requested maps based on any combination of city, state, street address, and ZIP code.
InterConnect	Enhanced MapQuest Connect. Enabled consumers who visited a business's Web site to find the location closest to the user.
Locator	Enhanced MapQuest InterConnect. Enabled more advanced searching by integrating MapQuest with specific geographic search parameters contained in its business customer's database, such as "find closest gas station with a car wash."
TripConnect	Enabled businesses to provide consumers with door-to-door driving instructions, including a route-highlighted map, trip mileage, and estimated driving time.
Enterprise Service	Provided mapping and routing capability designed primarily for high-volume Web sites. Enabled business customers to integrate generated map pages into their Web sites.
Enterprise Server	Non-hosted. Provided mapping and routing capability designed primarily for high-volume Web sites. Enabled business customers to integrate generated map pages into their Web sites.
Server for NT	Non-hosted. Provided mapping and routing capability designed primarily for low-volume Web sites. Enabled business customers to customize their own mapping solutions.

Internet—Consumer Products/Services

The mapquest.com Web site offered several menu options for consumers:

- Maps—enabled map generation either based on detailed supplied information or a more general location request;
- Driving Directions—provided the most direct route from a point of origin to a destination using a variety of options and formats, including door-to-door, city-to-city, overview map with text, text only, or turn-by-turn;
- Travel Guide—provided access to lodging, dining, city, and weather information for most consumer-

requested destinations, all of which could be tailored by the consumer to fit his or her particular information needs;

- Buy A Map—provided access to the MapStore to buy U.S. and international maps, road atlases, travel guides, and other map and travel-related products; and
- Membership—by becoming a member, the consumer could save generated maps, place personalized icons on generated maps that could be stored for future use, receive advance notice of new MapQuest features and enhancements, and become eligible for promotional offers.

Digital Mapping (Traditional) Products/Services (DMS)

MapQuest published or provided the relevant geographic data for printed road maps, atlases, travel guides, hotel and telephone directories, maps used in textbooks and reference books, and CD-ROMs. In addition, MapQuest's products and services included software applications incorporating customized mapping solutions for publishers and producers of CD-ROMs. MapQuest also provided extensive cartography, geographic database development, comprehensive map data maintenance, advanced mapping technology, and consultation services to a wide variety of customers on a fee-for-service basis. MapQuest's traditional and digital mapping customers included National Geographic, Galileo International, Ryder, Exxon, Best Western, and the Alamo and National (Republic) car rental agencies.

Future Product and Service Directions

The technology team had integrated MapQuest services, including driving directions, into the Palm Pilot 7, the first full-time Internet-connected handheld, using an advertising-based business model. The firm planned and budgeted for a nationwide rollout later in the year. The firm also considered opportunities for products and services to be supplied and bundled with competing Internet appliances, including the latest cell phones with LCD screens. Finally, the team foresaw the integration of its products and services into the digital mapping capabilities and GPS in autos and other forms of transportation.

Sales and Marketing

MapQuest sold its Internet business products and services in the United States through a sales organization of 17 employees on January 31, 1999. This sales organization consisted of 12 direct field salespeople based throughout the United States and five telemarketers located at MapQuest's Denver office. In addition, MapQuest sold its Internet products and services through indirect sales channels, including value-added resellers such as Moore Data and SABRE BTS.

Sales of advertisements on mapquest.com were generated by third-party advertising sales representatives and, to a lesser extent, by MapQuest's internal advertising sales force, which consisted of two people on January 31, 1999.

MapQuest sold its traditional and digital mapping products through a direct sales force of 11 field salespeople and telemarketers. MapQuest marketed its products and services online by placing advertisements on third-party Web sites. In addition, MapQuest advertised through traditional offline media and utilized public relations campaigns, trade shows, and ongoing customer communications programs.

MapQuest Customers

MapQuest had licensed its products and services to over 380 business customers. No one customer accounted for over 10 percent of MapQuest's overall revenues (see Exhibit 4).

MapQuest Suppliers—Geographic Data

MapQuest licensed a significant portion of its primary geographic data from a limited number of sources through non-exclusive, short-term contractual arrangements. MapQuest relied on U.S. street-level data drawn

from the U.S. government and through agreements with NavTech and Geographic Data Technologies (GDT). Data covering Canada were supplied by Desktop Mapping Technologies Inc. MapQuest obtained Western European street and major road data from TeleAtlas, NavTech, and AND Mapping NV. Major road data for the rest of the world was obtained from AND Mapping NV. MapQuest relied on these sources of third-party data, and if any were to change, MapQuest would have needed to substitute alternative sources of data or attempt to develop substitute sources of data internally.

MapQuest's own proprietary data assets also supported its online and traditional and digital mapping products and services. MapQuest had spent approximately six years developing a U.S. major road database. MapQuest also maintained a graphical image database that contained over 190,000 archived files to serve as an internal reference library. In addition, MapQuest had developed a suite of international city map data that included over 300 metropolitan maps and over 500 downtown maps of most major international tourist and business destinations.

THE CAPITAL MARKETS

The capital markets for Internet and technology companies were doing well (see Exhibit 5), and had experienced one of the greatest run-ups in history (see Exhibit 6).

EXHIBIT 4	MapQuest Customers

Content Providers
Excite
Infoseek
Lycos
Ticketmaster Citysearch
Yahoo!

Media
LA Times
National Geographic

Real Estate
Cendant
Moore Data

Other
Citgo
Exxon

Telecoms/Directories
Ameritech
APIL (Don Tech)
GTE
Pacific Bell
Southwestern Bell
US West

Publishers/Ad Agencies
Classical Atla
DDB Needham
Harte-Hanks
McGraw-Hill
Modem Media-Poppe Tyson
RR Donnelley

Travel/Entertainment
American Auto Assoc.
American Express
Avis
Best Western
Budget
Galileo International
Hertz
Republic Industries
Ryder
Sabre Group (Travelocity)

Retail/Services
Blockbuster
Borders
Home Depot
Kinko's
Sears

EXHIBIT 5	Market Valuations and Statistics

Company	Ticker	Stock Price (Sep 3, 1999)	Shares O/S	Market Cap (M)	Trailing Quarter Rev (M)	Enterprise Value (EV)(M)	Unique Visitors Jul-99
About	BOUT	$ 39.50	12.1	$ 478	$ 3.7	$ 416.5	8.3
America Online	AOL	97.06	1,207.0	117,151	1,377.0	113,927.4	42.2
Ask Jeeves	ASKJ	33.75	24.9	840	2.7	777.1	4.2
CNET	CNET	41.50	80.1	3,324	25.6	3,083.0	8.2
EarthWeb	EWBX	35.88	9.1	327	7.2	293.9	0.6
Excite@Home	ATHM	40.94	361.0	14,779	100.4	14,654.0	16.4
Go2Net	GNET	66.81	41.1	2,746	5.7	2,475.1	11.2
GoTo	GOTO	37.56	35.8	1,345	3.6	1,217.8	7.3
Infoseek	SEEK	31.00	62.0	1,922	36.1	1,838.6	21.1
LookSmart	LOOK	27.50	84.1	2,313	10.5	2,214.4	10.1
Lycos	LCOS	44.75	89.4	4,001	45.1	3,850.2	30.2
MapQuest	**MQST**	**12.00**	**33.0**	**396**	**7.4**	**366.3**	**5.4**
The Globe	TGLO	10.63	24.4	259	4.1	187.1	3.7
Ticketmaster Citysearch	TMCS	25.63	72.9	1,868	25.5	1,779.6	4.0
Verticalnet	VERT	33.94	16.8	570	3.6	540.2	n/a
Xoom	XMCX	37.63	16.8	632	6.5	421.4	8.7
Yahoo!	YHOO	155.00	300.0	46,500	128.6	45,707.0	38.9
ZDNet	ZDZ	15.69	80.9	1,269	22.9	1,268.9	8.0

EXHIBIT 6	Geospatial Data and Mapping—Industry Structure

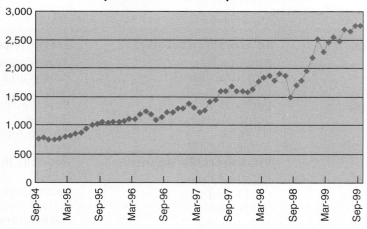

NASDAQ INDEX
September 1994 to September 1999

Initial Public Offerings and Venture Capital

The number of venture-backed companies was increasing as well, which made Mulligan feel that more potential customers would get funded, but might also allow more competitors to emerge (see Exhibit 7).

As more and more companies were funded in the private markets and had the capital to fuel growth,

EXHIBIT 7	Venture Capital Funding—United States	
Year	**Deals**	**US$ Total (Millions)**
1994	1,207	$ 4,143.9
1995	1,870	7,630.8
1996	2,609	11,506.8
1997	3,181	12,772.3
1998	3,691	21,244.3

Source: NVCA.

EXHIBIT 8	Initial Public Offering Market—United States		
Period	**Number of IPOs**	**Avg. Offer Amount US$ (Million)**	**Avg. Valuation US$ (Million)**
YTD 1999	180	$72.4	$435.6
1998	78	49.2	229.1
1997	138	35.9	164.3
1996	280	43.6	209.3
1995	204	$40.6	$163.0

Source: NVCA, as of October 1, 1999.

more companies drove quickly to the public markets and created a heated market for initial public offerings (see Exhibit 8).

Mergers and Acquisitions

The mergers and acquisitions market had picked up tremendously as new capital flowed into the hands of IPO- and venture-backed companies. Inflated stock valuations were driving many companies to use their own stock as acquisition consideration. These factors helped

drive the market for the acquisition of venture-backed companies (see Exhibit 9). However, there was fear that the Financial Accounting Standards Board (FASB) in the United States would rule to make the use of pooling of interests more difficult in a merger, if not impossible altogether. Such a move would require acquirers to use the purchase accounting method, likely slowing acquisition activity, since acquirers would have to immediately take a full write-off of goodwill rather than write it off over an extended period.

THE COMPETITIVE LANDSCAPE

The market itself was still shaping, and new players, new technologies, and new offerings were rapidly emerging. Stock analysts and venture capitalists frequently spoke of "eyeballs" (Internet traffic), stickiness (how long users used a site), and wallet-share (how much of a consumer's total expenditure could be influenced) when touting the merits of a particular business model or offering (see Exhibits 10 and 11).

Data and Map Data Vendors

There were two sources of data used in the industry. First, there were numerous data vendors that sold demographic and business information such as white pages listings, business listings, demographic, and address data. Players included:

- InfoSpace—(Nasdaq: INSP) A data and content provider to sites and online information providers, the company was also very focused on its consumer site. InfoSpace relied heavily on InfoUSA as a data source.
- InfoUSA—(Nasdaq: IUSA) A long-time data directory and demographic information provider, InfoUSA was a source of primary data to most white pages and directory publishers in the United States. The company's online site offering such information had little traffic.

EXHIBIT 9	Mergers of Venture-Backed Companies—United States		
Period	**Total # of Companies**	**Total US$ (Billions)**	**Avg. Price US$ (Millions)**
1999 (1st half)	91	$7.2	$119.9
1998	195	8.4	72.8
1997	161	7.6	66.4
1996	103	5.4	82.4
1995	99	3.7	65.6
1994	104	$3.2	$ 49.5

EXHIBIT
10
Internet Traffic Statistics—September 1999

Company	Reach % (Home & Work)	Avg. Daily Unique Pages Per Visitor (Home & Work) (millions)	Unique Visitors (Home & Work) (millions)	Home/ Work	Home	Work
Citysearch-Ticketmaster Online	7.8	12.5	3,112	9.7	9.1	9.9
MapQuest	**4.8**	**8.9**	**3,062**	**10.9**	**9.2**	**10.1**
Expedia	1.9	9.8	4,140	11.0	10.1	9.9
Travelocity	5.5	16.5	3,498	16.2	14.2	15.2
CheapTickets.com	1.6	7.3	1,002	9.5	9.6	8.7
Delta-Air.com	1.9	6.3	1,219	9.7	8.1	10.4
Lowestfare.com	2.2	4.7	1,382	3.6	3.2	3.6
Mapblast.com	1.1	10.9	707	n/a	n/a	n/a
MapsOnUs.com	1.3	2.0	831	0.9	0.9	0.8
Preview Travel	4.5	11.4	2,826	11.7	10.5	10.3
Ticketmaster	4.0	13.1	2,514	9.1	9.2	8.0
Trip.com	1.6	5.5	1,015	9.9	7.4	10.3
USAirways	1.5	7.4	961	7.1	6.1	6.4
OneTravel.com	0.7	8.5	287	8.2	7.2	9.7
AA.com	2.3	6.7	1,442	11.6	8.5	12.6
Travelscape	1.0	6.7	481	7.2	8.0	4.4
Tickets.com	0.5	7.5	311	6.7	6.9	n/a
UAL.com	2.1	5.6	1,317	11.5	9.7	9.9
NWA.com	1.9	7.0	1,175	6.2	5.8	5.3
Domain Category						
Travel/Tourism	31.3	21.2	19,857	22.7	17.2	22.5
Airline Sites	9.7	12.8	6,170	16.2	12.7	15.2
Shopping	66.1	72.2	41,869	70.2	55.7	56.5

EXHIBIT
11
MapQuest—Recent News

- Mapquest.com Licenses Routing Software to OnStar Communications
- NEW YORK, N.Y. (Dow Jones)—Sept 22, 1999—MapQuest formed an alliance with OnStar Communications, an in-vehicle safety, security and information service used in GM vehicles
- Nokia Selects MapQuest.com to Provide Driving Directions to Nokia's New Media Phones; MapQuest.com Expands Its Wireless Reach With Addition
- NEW YORK—(BUSINESS WIRE)—Sept. 22, 1999—MapQuest announced an agreement with Nokia (NYSE:NOK) to provide MapQuest.com driving directions and travel information
- AOL's Digital City, Inc. Expands Relationship With OnHealth Network Company
- SEATTLE, Sept. 21 /PRNewswire/—OnHealth Network Company (Nasdaq: ONHN), a leading online health and wellness destination, today announced the expansion of its strategic relationship with AOL's Digital City, Inc.
- Getting Local Online: Knight Ridder draws from its newspapers to build a national network of local portal sites
- Network World Fusion, 20 September 1999, From job portals to music portals to personal portals, it's hard to keep track. Here's another growing category to add to the list: local portals
- infoUSA.com Announces 5 New Partners for Free Internet White and Yellow Page Services.
- SILICON VALLEY—(BUSINESS WIRE)—Sept. 20, 1999—The leading provider of proprietary business and consumer databases and Internet white and yellow page directory services. . . .

EXHIBIT
11
(Cont'd)

- MapQuest.com Teams With AdAce to Provide Small Businesses With Geographically Targeted Advertising
- NEW YORK—(BUSINESS WIRE)—Sept. 14, 1999—MapQuest strengthens position as leader in Geo-targeted Web advertising by announcing a partnership with AdAce, a nationwide ad firm
- MapQuest Selects SpeechWorks Tech For Phone Svc < MQST
- NEW YORK (Dow Jones)—Sept 13, 1999—MapQuest selected SpeechWorks International Inc., to develop speech recognition technology for a MapQuest service that will provide driving directions over the telephone
- SPRINT PCS, MAPQUEST PARTNER ON DRIVING DIRECTIONS
- NEW YORK—Sept 13, 1999—MapQuest announced a new partnership with Sprint PCS to provide driving directions to Sprint PCS Wireless Web phone users
- Mapquest.com Seeks Agency Partner
- NEW YORK—Aug 30, 1999—MapQuest is looking for a medium to large-size agency to handle its estimated $10 million to $15 million account
- MapQuest.com Selected to Provide Enhanced Mapping Technology for Sabre Inc., Including the Travelocity.com Web Site
- NEW YORK—(BUSINESS WIRE)—August 23, 1999—Sabre Inc., Including Travelocity.com, Upgrades Agreement With MapQuest
- MapQuest.com Partners With Metro Networks, Adding Real-Time Traffic to MapQuest.com and Its Partner Sites
- NEW YORK—(BUSINESS WIRE)—August 18, 1999 MapQuest.com Now Offers Exclusive Package of State-of-the-Art Digital Traffic Information, Maps and Driving Directions

A second group of data providers included mapping-specialized data vendors. These vendors collected and created specific mapping information from primary sources, including governments and survey data, as well as from secondary sources. While there was some competition, these companies tended to offer coverage of specific locations or types of data. Major players included

- Nav-Tech—(Private) Founded in 1985, based in Chicago, the company offered digital mapping data and technologies, including GPS systems.
- GDT—(Private) Founded in 1980, the company was a major supplier of data to both Vicinity and MapQuest, the first use of its data on the Web.
- TeleAtlas—(Private) Founded in 1984, the company had broad data coverage of Europe.

See Exhibit 12.

Map Enablers

These companies offered products and services that enabled businesses and portals to offer richer, better content and services on their own sites. Since growth capital was plentiful among their customers (e.g., the portals), revenue growth was rapid. Key players included

- Zip2—(Owned by Alta Vista, owned by CMGI, Nasdaq: CMGI) A pioneer in local content and city

guides, the firm sold in February 1999 for $347 million to Alta Vista.

- MapInfo—(Nasdaq: MAPS) A software provider focused on location-enabling services for businesses.
- Vicinity—(Private, owned partly by CMGI, Nasdaq: CMGI) An information services provider to businesses, it also owned Mapblast, the consumer-focused mapping site. CMGI, the part-owner, was a holding company that invested in pre-IPO companies.
- Etak—(Owned by Sony) Sony had purchased Etak from NewsCorp. Etak was a provider of mapping software and technologies.
- ESRI—(Private) Primarily a software provider for GIS applications for locating telecom and pipeline infrastructure, as well as consumer application software.

"Local" Portals

The Internet mega-portals had realized the "local" opportunity and had each begun to offer localized content. These large players had abundant capital and were eagerly spending to gain market share. Major local offerings included

- AOL Digital Cities—(NYSE: AOL) AOL was the world's largest Internet service provider with a portal specifically for its subscribers.

EXHIBIT 12   Geospatial Data and Mapping—Industry Structure

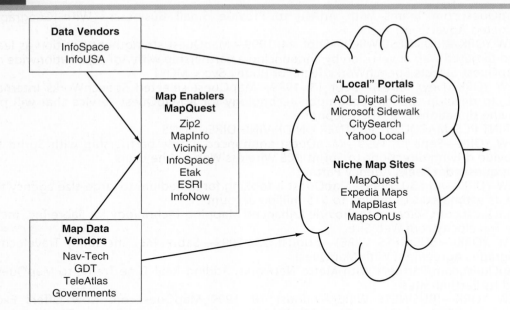

- Microsoft Sidewalk—(Nasdaq: MSFT) Microsoft offered a competing set of local sites. In July of 1999, it sold its Sidewalk business to Ticketmaster Citysearch in a deal that included providing local information and content back to Microsoft under the Sidewalk brand.
- Citysearch (Ticketmaster)—(Nasdaq: TMCS) A comprehensive set of city/local guides and information, including local event ticket sales, from the world's largest event ticketing company.
- Yahoo Local—(Nasdaq: YHOO) A set of localized subsites tailored to specific cities.
- AltaVista—(owned by CMGI, Nasdaq: CMGI) Purchased in August 1999 from Compaq, the firm announced its plans for an IPO. AltaVista owned Zip2.

Competition—MapQuest Business Offering

Of the approximately 764 Web sites that were currently map-enabled, MapQuest had roughly a 50 percent market share (see Exhibit 13). The largest historical competitors were Zip2 and Vicinity, but MapQuest was taking share and was by far the largest provider in the market. MapQuest also faced potential competition from "one-stop shop" content suppliers such as InfoSpace, which offered a wide range of services and had broad distribution for many of its products, but

EXHIBIT 13	Market Share of 764 Map-Enabled Web sites	
MapQuest		49%
Zip2		21%
Vicinity		11%
ESRI		10%
InfoNow		4%
MapInfo		3%
Etak		1%
InfoSpace		1%

Source: MediaMetrix.

no current focus on a competing product or service offering.

Competition—MapQuest Consumer Offering

MapQuest was the leading travel/mapping site on the Internet (see Exhibit 14). Traffic data showed MapQuest gaining share against competitors even while little was spent on marketing and promotion. After the IPO, the launch of a $2 million promotional campaign accelerated share gains.

EXHIBIT 14

Market Share of Site Page Traffic	
MapQuest	64%
Expedia Maps	18%
Mapblast	12%
MapsOnUs	3%
All others	3%

Source: MediaMetrix.

Competition—MapQuest Digital Mapping (Traditional)

The company faced a wide range of competitors including Rand McNally, Langenscheidt (American Map), Universal, Magellan, ESRI, and DeLorme. However, MapQuest management had planned to shift focus away from the DMS business to the high growth, higher margin Internet mapping opportunity.

THE MEETING OF THE BOARD

Mulligan and his executive team planned to present strategic alternatives to the board of directors. Recently, MapQuest stock traded around $12 per share. This price was below the IPO price of $15, while the Nasdaq index was up about 10 percent during the same period. Still, the $12 price made the firm worth around $400 million in market cap. However, other "pure-play" software and content providers were trading at higher multiples. Mulligan wondered whether the traditional DMS business was anchoring the firm value. Investors were hungry for Internet businesses. Or, given that the market valued revenue, how could he grow the revenue streams? If nothing else, Mulligan wondered whether to believe pundits in the market who were suggesting an overall market bubble. If this *was* a bubble, Mulligan wondered what he could do to take advantage of it.

Humana Inc.: Turnaround of a Health Insurer

Shalini
Sumit Kumar Chaudhuri

ICFAI University Press, Business School Case Development Centre

We turned our financial performance in 2000–2001, and then started to grow our commercial business.[1]

Today, we are one of the leaders in the area of consumer engagement, bringing a whole new idea around how benefits ought to work to the employer space through focusing on a consumer-centric value proposition. We're separating ourselves from the competition through technology and consumer engagement.[2]

— Michael B. McCallister, CEO and President of Humana Inc.

In 1999, Louisville, Kentucky–based health insurance company Humana Inc. was going through a tough time due to rising healthcare costs in the United States and class-action lawsuits against it. Humana reported a net loss of $382.42 million[3] for the fiscal year ending December 31, 1999. In February 2000, Michael B. McCallister was appointed as the new CEO of Humana. Realizing the growth potential in the healthcare business in the United States (Appendix 1), McCallister felt that Humana needed a consumer-centric approach along with a strong development in IT infrastructure to regain profitability and growth in its commercial and government business segments (Appendix 2). With innovative products and cost cutting strategies adopted since then, Humana earned a net income of $228.93 million in the fiscal year 2003. By 2004, Humana was serving 6.4 million medical members[4] in 18 states in the United States and Puerto Rico. Despite the increased income in the first quarter of 2004, Humana's stock prices declined as the company announced that it was expecting lower than expected profits in its commercial business for the second quarter. This was in anticipation of the aggressive lowering of prices by its competitors. However, McCallister has refused to be a part of aggressive pricing strategy and he aims to build sustainable competitive advantage through product innovations and enhanced technology. In the second quarter of 2004, Humana reported increased earnings due to strong growth in its government business. The company's net income increased to $80.8 million for the quarter ending June 30, 2004, from $69.3 million[5] in the corresponding period of the previous year. McCallister said, "We continue to expect 2004 revenue, earnings and cash flows to be the highest in Humana's history as a health benefits company."[6]

ABOUT HUMANA

Humana was started as a nursing home in 1961 by David A. Jones and Windell Cherry along with two contractors and two real estate agents. Each of them invested $1000 to start the nursing home, which was initially named Heritage Home. To fund further expansion, the company went public in 1968 under the name Extendicare. By then, Extendicare was operating seven nursing homes. But with the nursing home market getting saturated, David Jones started looking for new business segments. Jones had realized that there was potential in other business segments back in 1966 when a flu epidemic had erupted in Connecticut. He said, "The hospitals filled up and they began to send their older patients directly to us. In terms of medical patients and surgical patients, we did a pretty good job.

This case was written by Shalini, under the direction of Sumit Kumar Chaudhuri. © ICFAI University Press & ICFAI Business School Case Development Centre, 2004. Reprinted with permission. www.icfaipress.org; www.icfaipress.org/books.

| EXHIBIT 1 | Health Maintenance Organizations (HMO) in the United States |

The phrase originated in the United States to define any system by which one could obtain control over the delivery of health services. A health maintenance organization is a prepaid organized delivery system (a fixed amount of money is available to cover the health needs of members). The organization therefore assumes financial risk and may transfer some of that risk to doctors or other providers. Individuals enroll with a health premium.

Individuals who join an HMO are considered members. Typically HMOs provide members with comprehensive health care. When someone joins an HMO, they select a primary care physician from the list provided by the HMO. That primary care physician coordinates all of that member's medical care. If care by a specialist is needed, the primary care physician will refer the member to a specialist who is usually also in the HMO network. In an HMO, physicians may be employees of the HMO or the HMO may contract with independent physicians to provide care. Members who go outside of the network to receive care (unless given prior approval) will probably pay all or most of the cost of that care out of their own pockets.

A number of different models of HMOs have surfaced:

- **Staff model:** The practitioners are employed by the HMO and are paid on a salary basis plus bonuses. It is a "one stop shop" model—all medical practitioners are housed in one building and provide a comprehensive range of medical services. They charge a fixed fee per month.
- **Group model:** The HMO contracts with multispecialty practitioner groups. Practitioners are paid on a monthly salary basis. They are not all situated in one building. A hospital can treat private patients as well as HMO group.
- **Network model:** HMO would contract between group models. Practitioners are paid on a monthly salary basis and they are able to treat patients other than those in the HMO group.
- **IPA (Independent Practitioners Assoc.) model:** HMO contracts with an association of practitioners. The HMO collects a capitation fee from its members and pays the doctors on a fee-for-service basis. Doctors submit their accounts to the HMO directly and not patients.
- **Direct contract model:** HMO contracts directly with practitioners. This model operates on the same basis as the IPA model and doctors are paid on a fee-for-service basis.

Source: "Health Maintenance Organisation (HMO)," http://healthcare.oldmutual.co.za, http://bmj.bmjjournals.com, and Gail Carlson, "What Is a Health Maintenance Organization?" http://missourifamilies.org.

But the hospital was getting paid 10 times as much as we were, and so the light went off over my head and I said, 'Let's try hospitals.' So we began to design hospitals, but at the same time, we began to buy hospitals."[7] The late 1960s and the early 1970s marked a shift in the company's business from owning nursing homes to acquiring hospitals (Appendix 3). By 1972, Extendicare had divested all its nursing homes and was focusing on its hospital business. To reflect this shift in business focus, Extendicare was renamed Humana in 1974.

The merger with American Medicorp[8] in 1978 added 39 hospitals[9] to Humana. By the early 1980s, Humana was the largest hospital company[10] in the world with more than eighty hospitals across the globe. In 1982, Humana started its "Centers of Excellence" programs.[11] The program was started in hospitals that were using leading-edge technologies to provide the best specialty care. In 1984, Humana entered the health insurance business with the introduction of its flexible health insurance products called the Humana Health Care Plans. It also marked Humana's debut in developing the Health Maintenance Organization (Exhibit 1) industry in the United States (Appendix 4).

With the rapid evolution in both the hospital and the health insurance sectors, Humana decided to separate the two divisions into two independent publicly held companies. On March 1, 1993, Humana spun off its hospital division into a new company called Galen Health Care, which was eventually merged with Columbia Health Care Corporation in September 1993. The health insurance business continued under the name of Humana.

Humana increased its insurance business in the 1990s mainly through acquisitions. On October 11, 1995,

Humana acquired Emphesys Financial Group Inc. by paying $650 million. Emphesys had a strong position in sales, marketing, and customer service and was then the tenth largest health insurer[12] in the United States. Emphesys started operating as Humana's subsidiary under the name Employers Health Insurance Co. and offered products like group medical, group life, dental, and disability income insurance, mainly to small businesses. On November 30, 1995, Humana also purchased some primary care centers of Coastal Physician Group Inc. for $50 million[13] in South Florida and Tampa.

In 1996, a wholly owned subsidiary of Humana, Humana Military Healthcare Services, started its TRICARE[14] program. In 1997, Humana acquired Health Direct, Inc., a for-profit insurance subsidiary of

Advocate Health Care, for $23 million,[15] thereby expanding its market in Chicago and adding 50,000 members. The company also acquired Miami-based Physician Corporation of America (PCA), the largest health plan in the city, [16] for $411 million that included the absorption of PCA's debt of $121 million. During the acquisition, PCA was providing healthcare services through its HMOs in Florida, Texas, and Puerto Rico to 1.1 million medical members.[17] Humana acquired ChoiceCare[18] on October 17, 1997, for $250 million. This enabled Humana to expand into the Greater Cincinnati and the Ohio regions, where ChoiceCare already had its customer base. Until 1997, Humana experienced robust growth when it recorded net earnings of $173 million (Exhibit 2). However, in 1998, Humana recorded a reduced net income of $129 mil-

EXHIBIT 2	Financials of Humana Inc.

(Dollars in millions, except per share results)

For the years ended December 31	1999(a)	1998(b)	1997(c)	1996(d)	1995(c)
Summary of Operations					
Premiums	$ 9,959	$9,597	$7,880	$6,677	$4,605
Interest and other income	154	184	156	111	97
Total revenues	10,113	9,781	8,036	6,788	4,702
(Loss) income before income taxes	(404)	203	270	18	288
Net (loss) income	(382)	129	173	12	190
(Loss) earnings per common share	(2.28)	0.77	1.06	0.07	1.17
(Loss) earnings per common share —assuming dilution	(2.28)	0.77	1.05	0.07	1.16
Net cash provided by operations	217	55	279	341	150
Financial Position					
Cash and investments	$2,738	$2,812	$2,798	$1,880	$1,696
Total assets	4,900	5,496	5,600	3,306	3,056
Medical and other expenses payable	1,756	1,908	2,075	1,099	866
Debt and other long-term obligations	830	977	1,057	361	399
Stockholders' equity	1,268	1,688	1,501	1,292	1,287
Operating Data					
Medical expense ratio	85.7%	83.8%	82.8%	84.3%	81.7%
Administrative expense ratio	15.0%	15.2%	15.5%	15.5%	13.9%
Medical membership by segment:					
Health Plan:					
Large group commercial	1,420,500	1,559,700	1,661,900	1,435,000	1,502,500
Medicare HMO	488,500	502,000	480,800	364,500	310,400
Medicaid and other	661,100	700,400	704,000	152,900	164,000
TRICARE	1,058,000	1,085,700	1,112,200	1,103,000	
Administrative services	648,000	646,200	651,200	471,000	495,100
Total Health Plan	4,276,100	4,494,000	4,610,100	3,526,400	2,472,000

EXHIBIT 2 *(Cont'd)*

	1999(a)	1998(b)	1997(c)	1996(d)	1995(c)
Operating Data					
Small Group:					
Small group commercial	1,663,100	1,701,800	1,596,700	1,324,600	1,332,400
Total medical membership	5,939,200	6,195,800	6,206,800	4,851,000	3,804,400
Specialty membership:					
Dental	1,628,200	1,375,500	936,400	844,800	797,000
Other	1,333,100	1,257,800	1,504,200	1,039,400	1,063,000
Total specialty membership	2,961,300	2,633,300	2,440,600	1,884,200	1,860,000

(a) Includes expenses of $585 million pretax ($499 million after tax, or $2.97 per diluted share) primarily related to goodwill write-down, losses on non-core asset sales, professional liability, reserve strengthening, premium deficiency and medical reserve strengthening.

(b) Includes expenses of $132 million pretax ($84 million after tax, or $0.50 per diluted share) primarily related to the costs of certain market exits and product discontinuances, asset write-offs, premium deficiency and a one-time non-officer employee incentive.

(c) Includes the operations of Health Direct, Inc., Physician Corporation of America, Choice-Care Corporation and EMPHESYS Financial Group, Inc. since their dates of acquisition: February 28, 1997, September 8, 1997, October 17, 1997, and October 11, 1995, respectively.

(d) Includes expenses of $215 million pretax ($140 million after tax, or $0.85 per diluted share) primarily related to the closing of the Washington, D.C. and certain other markets, severance and facility costs for workforce reductions, product discontinuance costs, premium deficiency, litigation and other costs.

	2003(a)	2002(b)(c)	2001	2000	1999(d)
	(in thousands, except per share results, membership and ratios)				
Summary of Operations					
Revenues:					
Premiums	$11,825,283	$10,930,397	$ 9,938,961	$10,394,631	$ 9,958,582
Administrative services fees	271,676	244,396	137,090	86,298	97,940
Investment and other income	129,352	86,388	118,835	115,021	155,013
Total revenues	12,226,311	11,261,181	10,194,886	10,595,950	10,211,535
Operating expenses:					
Medical	9,879,421	9,138,196	8,279,844	8,781,998	8,533,090
Selling, general and administrative	1,858,028	1,775,069	1,545,129	1,524,799	1,466,181
Depreciation and amortization	126,779	120,730	161,531	146,548	123,858
Goodwill impairment and other expenses	—	—	—	—	459,852
Total operating expenses	11,864,228	11,033,995	9,986,504	10,453,345	10,582,981
Income (loss) from operations	362,083	227,186	208,382	142,605	(371,446)
Interest expense	17,367	17,252	25,302	28,615	33,393
Income (loss) before income taxes	344,716	209,934	183,080	113,990	(404,839)
Provision (benefit) for income taxes	115,782	67,179	65,909	23,938	(22,419)
Net income (loss)	$ 228,934	$ 142,755	$ 117,171	$ 90,052	$ (382,420)
Basic earnings (loss) per common share	$1.44	$0.87	$0.71	$0.54	$(2.28)
Diluted earnings (loss) per common share	$1.41	$0.85	$0.70	$0.54	$(2.28)
Financial Position					
Cash and investments	$ 2,927,213	$ 2,415,914	$2,327,139	$ 2,312,399	$2,785,702
Total assets	5,293,323	4,879,937	4,681,693	4,597,533	4,951,578
(in thousands, except per share results, membership and ratios)					

EXHIBIT
2

(Cont'd)

	2003(a)	2002(b)(c)	2001	2000	1999(d)
Financial Position					
Medical and other expenses payable	1,272,156	1,142,131	1,086,386	1,181,027	1,756,227
Debt	642,638	604,913	578,489	599,952	686,213
Stockholders' equity	1,835,949	1,606,474	1,507,949	1,360,421	1,268,009
Key Financial Indicators					
Medical expense ratio	83.5%	83.6%	83.3%	84.5%	85.7%
SG&A expense ratio	15.4%	15.9%	15.3%	14.5%	14.6%
Medical Membership by Segment					
Commercial:					
Fully insured	2,352,800	2,340,300	2,301,300	2,545,800	3,083,600
Administrative services only	712,400	652,200	592,500	612,800	648,000
Medicare supplement	—	—	—	—	44,500
Total Commercial	3,065,200	2,992,500	2,893,800	3,158,600	3,776,100
Government:					
Medicare+Choice	328,600	344,100	393,900	494,200	488,500
Medicaid	468,900	506,000	490,800	575,600	616,600
TRICARE	1,849,700	1,755,800	1,714,600	1,070,300	1,058,000
TRICARE ASO	1,057,200	1,048,700	942,700	—	—
Total Government	3,704,400	3,654,600	3,542,000	2,140,100	2,163,100
Total Medical Membership	6,769,600	6,647,100	6,435,800	5,298,700	5,939,200
Commercial Specialty Membership					
Dental	1,147,400	1,094,600	1,123,300	1,148,100	1,146,000
Other	520,700	545,400	571,300	678,900	1,333,100
Total specialty membership	1,668,100	1,640,000	1,694,600	1,827,000	2,479,100

(a) Includes expenses of $30.8 million pretax ($18.8 million after tax, or $0.12 per diluted share) for the writedown of building and equipment and software abandonment expenses. These expenses were partially offset by a gain of $15.2 million pretax ($10.1 million after tax, or $0.06 per diluted share) for the sale of a venture capital investment. The net impact of these items reduced pretax income by $15.6 million ($8.7 million after tax, or $0.05 per diluted share).

(b) Includes expenses of $85.6 million pretax ($58.2 million after tax, or $0.35 per diluted share) for severance and facility costs related to reducing our administrative cost structure with the elimination of three customer service centers and an enterprise-wide workforce reduction, reserves for liabilities related to a previous acquisition and the impairment in the fair value of certain private debt and equity investments.

(c) As described in Note 2 to our consolidated financial statements included herein, we adopted Statement of Financial Accounting Standard No. 142, Goodwill and Other Intangible Assets, as of January 1, 2002. We ceased amortizing goodwill upon adopting Statement 142 on January 1, 2002. Note 5 identifies goodwill amortized in 2001 and the estimated impact on our reported net income and earnings per common share had amortization been excluded from 2001 results.

(d) Includes expenses of $584.8 million pretax ($499.3 million after tax, or $2.97 per diluted share) primarily related to goodwill impairment, losses on non-core asset sales, professional liability reserve strengthening, premium deficiency and medical reserve strengthening.

Source: "Annual Report 1999" and "Annual Report 2003," www.humana.com.

lion. It was due to the severance and lease termination costs incurred due to Humana's exit from five market areas[19] and disposal of non-strategic products and assets.

THE INSURER GETS SICK

Troubles started in early 1999 when Humana faced various class-action lawsuits filed against it in Florida and Nevada. The Nevada lawsuit charged that Humana did not pass the special discounts that it received from certain hospitals on to its customers. In April 1999, Humana announced that it was expecting a reduced EPS of $0.20 to $0.24 per share against the estimated calculation of $0.34 per share[20] due to increased medical costs for the first quarter of fiscal year 1999. The company also announced an additional $90 million expenses during the first quarter. It included $50 million related to renegotiation of its contract with Columbia Healthcare Corporation that had ended on January 1, 1999, $35 million for strengthening its medical claim reserve, and $5 million to settle the outstanding issues with Columbia in the previous contract. The renewal of the contract enabled Humana's members in Florida to continue receiving hospital services from Columbia hospitals in the state. The then Humana's president and CEO, Gregory H. Wolf, said, "Although its immediate financial impact is adverse, the contract represents a new cost factor which we can address in our upcoming premium pricing actions. Most importantly, we believe that we made the right decision for our 1.3 million Florida members who would have been greatly inconvenienced by a termination of service with Columbia and the possible disruption of their health care."[21] Humana reported a net loss of $16 million in the first quarter of 1999. Further, as Humana had made efforts to increase its revenues for the quarter by increasing the premium charged to its members in its commercial business, this led to a decrease in the membership in its commercial business. The membership in commercial business further declined by 2.8 percent on June 30, 1999, as compared to the corresponding period in the previous year. Medical costs continued to increase and the EPS further decreased to 17 cents per share.[22] In July 1999, a class-action complaint was filed against Humana by Wolf Haldenstein Adler Freeman & Herz LLP[23] in the United States District Court for the Western District of Kentucky that caused unspecified financial loss to the company. It was alleged that Humana had misrepresented its operational and financial condition in its press releases, which had inflated its stock prices. The lawsuit was filed on behalf of investors who had purchased Humana's shares at higher prices during February 9, 1999, and April 8, 1999. When Humana announced additional $90 million charges in April, the share price decreased to $12.1875 per share as against the Class Period,[24] when the shares traded as high as $19.375 per share.[25] Gregory Wolf resigned as CEO and president in August 1999. David Jones, the founder and former CEO, was brought in as the interim CEO.

During the third quarter of 1999, David Jones worked closely with Michael McCallister, and five key initiatives were developed to mitigate the difficult situation faced by the company. These involved setting premiums above the rising medical costs, establishing large group commercial infrastructure, renegotiation of contracts with physicians and hospitals, better cost management, and rationalizing markets, products, and platforms. In September 1999, Employee Health Insurance Company (EHI), a subsidiary of Humana, acquired the operational control of Private Healthcare Systems (PHCS) of Waltham, Massachusetts, which controlled the network relationships for Humana's products on behalf of EHI. PHCS was renamed ChoiceCare network. With 330,000 physicians and 2,500 hospitals, the ChoiceCare network became the second-largest medical network in the United States[26] and was expected to provide cost efficiencies and sales leverage to Humana.

But, on October 4, 1999, a lengthy lawsuit (Appendix 5) was filed against Humana in the United States District Court for the Southern District of Florida (Miami Division). It charged that Humana "systematic[ally] and intentional[ly] conceal[ed] from members of its health plans . . . accurate information about when health care will be provided, when claims will be approved or disapproved, and what criteria and procedures are actually used to determine the extent and type of their coverage."[27]

The lawsuits and rising medical costs resulted in a net loss of $382.42 million for Humana in the fiscal year 1999. David Jones decided to refocus the company's business with significant investments in technology. In February 2000, Jones appointed Mike McCallister, who had been associated with Humana since 1974 and was serving as the company's vice president, as the new CEO of the company. Commenting on his decision, David Jones said, "Mike is well-known to our organization and was clearly a leading candidate to replace Greg Wolf as chief executive officer last August. Since then, he has distinguished himself in working alongside me, the other members of the office of the chairman—Ken Fasola and Jim Murray—and Humana's board of directors, in addressing the issues facing our company and in setting our plans for a return to sustained growth in profitability."[28]

BOUNCING BACK TO LIFE

McCallister said, "We intend to continue to focus on our core health insurance businesses. We will also continue to sell non-core assets and use the proceeds to pay down debt and invest in our industry-leading Internet initiatives."[29]

To come out of its financial challenges, Humana, in 2000, implemented its cost-cutting strategy by closing down offices that had less than 10 customers. Humana spokeswoman Pam Gadinsky said, "Managing our members' health care dollars responsibly is a part of what we do. When you look at offices with no members, there are administrative costs with having those offices in the network."[30] Humana also exited from some of its Medicare and Medicaid markets and also reduced the number of primary doctors in its offices in South Florida by 191. Humana sold its PCA Property & Casualty Insurance Company to New York–based FolksAmerica Holding Company Inc. for $125 million.[31] The move was taken to reduce debt and refocus the company's initiatives on its core business of health insurance. Humana also sold its non-profitable Medicaid business in North Florida, Texas, and Wisconsin in early 2000. The same year, Humana increased the number of actuaries and underwriters for its commercial business, and employed Rx3[32] to reduce its pharmacy cost. The company also developed a standard PPO product and eliminated 1,200 commercial products that were complex and involved higher costs. Humana started shifting towards a consumer-centric business approach to improve the healthcare experience for patients and physicians. The company reduced administrative difficulties for its consumers by increasing automatic approvals to hospital admissions to 71 percent in 2000 from 14 percent in 1999. It also reduced the need for prior authorization of the company for reviews on prescription drugs by 55 percent. In 2000, Humana started providing information to its customers about benefit and claims, identification cards, referrals, detailed pharmacy information, and personal health risk assessments. Other technological initiatives included the Web-based health plan humanacc.com[33] and PlanWizard.[34] The year 2000 also marked the introduction of new-generation products like Emphesys (Appendix 6). The turnaround efforts led to a net income of $90 million[35] in 2000.

By 2001, Humana had exited from 45 states where the cost of providing Medicare coverage was much higher than the federal government's reimbursement rates. In March 2001, Humana entered into a joint venture agreement with Navigy Inc., a wholly owned subsidiary of Blue Cross and Blue Shield of Florida,[36]

to provide a single Internet portal to the physicians and other health care providers in Florida to enable quick, accurate, and efficient claims processing of large number of customers. Humana's new product launches for the year included Humana Rx4, MyHumana, and Personal Nurse Service program (Appendix 6). To reduce the increasing medical costs, Humana developed consumer-centric and technology-enabled health care products like SmartSuite in 2001. SmartSuite was designed to provide enough choices to the customers to select a suitable plan for themselves. SmartSuite offers four options to the employers and each option has six health plans. Employers have to select an option and then employees are given the freedom to choose any of the six plans in that option as per their requirements. After the introduction of SmartSuite, Humana experienced only a 4.9 percent increase in medical claims cost as against the estimated 19.2 percent. SmartSuite enabled employees in many organizations to make their own health plan decisions, which were earlier made by the employers. Membership for the TRICARE and Administrative Services Only program increased significantly, and Humana net income increased to $117.2 million in 2001.

The SmartSuite plan enabled Humana to cut its own employees' health costs and save more than $2 million[37] in the twelve months ending June 2002. McCallister said, "I'm a big believer that the most powerful player in understanding and managing costs is going to be the individual consumer. When people are spending their own money, given good and actionable information, they're going to be much better than the current model at controlling costs."[38] Humana introduced a new health plan called HumanaOne that was designed for individuals and families who were not insured by employers, e.g., students, self-employed entrepreneurs, and retirees. The company's market leader for individual products of Medical Mutual[39] of Ohio, Kevin Lauterjung, said, "It's not a significant percentage of our business in terms of enrollment, but it is a significant part of our corporate strategic plan in terms of growth."[40] Humana also introduced a new health plan in September 2002 called HumanaCoverage-First PPO. Under this plan, customers are offered reduced premiums as Humana provides a benefit allowance of $500 to the customers for availing certain health services before they start paying any amount towards their deductible.[41] The vice president of Humana's small group division, Tod Zacharias, said, "According to Humana's own data, more than 60 percent of covered individuals incur less than $500 in claims each year. The Coverage-First plan gives these relatively healthy individuals some value for the premiums they pay. This may give healthier individuals a reason to keep, and not forgo, health coverage. That means a greater number of healthy individuals to balance the financial risk of illness, which can help keep the cost of health coverage down for everyone."[42] With these new products, Humana increased the membership in its commercial business by 3.4 percent in 2002 and Humana's net income increased by 22 percent to 142.8 million.

Humana also decided to reduce 17 percent of its workforce[43] by the end of 2003 as a cost reduction measure. One third of the job cuts were in customer service that answered customer queries over the phone, as Humana started providing health-plan information through the Internet or through Interactive Voice Responses. In February 2003, Humana started a new advertisement campaign to highlight the company's new approach to health benefits and the future measures of Humana to curb the rising medical cost in the United States through its Smart products. The theme of the campaign, "guidance when you need it most,"[44] was launched in five cities[45] in the United States and was aimed to run throughout the year representing customers who had gained significant cost benefits while using the company's SmartSuite health plans. Humana's vice president of marketing, Eileen Hutchison, said, "Humana has taken a critical look at how we're perceived by our customers. Though we're a well-established, 42-year-old company, what we realized was that key audiences are not aware of the company Humana is today and our success in addressing the health care cost crisis. . . . We want to reintroduce potential customers to our company."[46] The efforts resulted in increased growth in each business segment of the company. Humana's net income increased from $142.8 million in 2002 to $228.9 million[47] in fiscal year 2003 (Exhibit 2).

AN INSURED FUTURE?

Humana reported net earnings of $67.8 million in the quarter ending March 31, 2004, as compared to $31.2 million[48] during the corresponding period last year. The improvement was due to increased membership in its TRICARE and MedicareAdvantage insurance products and increase in government business. In spite of the significant rise in earnings, the share price decreased by $1.30 to $17.71. Analysts opined that the decline reflected Humana's susceptibility to aggressive pricing by its competitors (Exhibit 3). Unmoved, McCallister said, "In our opinion, there are some competitors who are clearly pricing for market share. We will not play the marketshare game and will continue to price our business for bottomline profitability."[49] He

added, "Short-term, it's not difficult to take a pricing strategy for share; long-term, however, it's a losing proposition. We're all about the underlying problem. We provide a value proposition that is different."[50]

In April 2004, Humana went in for a strategic acquisition of Ochsner Health Plan, the third-largest health benefit plan in Louisiana with 152,000 commercial medical members and 31,000 members in the MedicareAdvantage program.[51] The acquisition allowed Humana to increase its presence in the southern United States and expand into the New Orleans region. McCallister said, "We are excited to be able to combine Ochsner's reputation with Humana's consumer-centric philosophy, and anticipate our innovative products, supported by industry leading tools and technology, to complement the provider experience Ochsner's customers value today."[52] By June 2004, Smart products were sold to 145 employer groups. McCallister, who considered consumer products an effective tool to manage health costs, said, "The future is going to be different. Employees will have a lot more choices in choosing benefits, and technology will help. People are good at deciding what's good for them, but the program has to be managed very carefully. As a consequence of informed decision-making, members find ways to drive waste out of the health care system, creating room for saving money without old-style cost shifting."[53]

McCallister wants to gain competitive advantage through intelligent products and technologies rather than adopting a lower pricing strategy. To combat the double-digit growth in health costs, Humana introduced SmartAssurance in June 2004. It is "a program that caps any rate increase at 9.9 percent in the second year for customers in one of its plans called SmartSuite."[54] SmartAssurance is a consumer-driven plan aimed at moderating the rising health costs in the United States. Commenting on SmartAssurance, Hewitt Associates consultant Ken Sperling said, "The program differentiates Humana at a time when the insurance business is getting more competitive. This way they don't have to compete on price."[55] With Hewitt's prediction of health maintenance rates at 13.7 percent in 2005, McCallister is optimistic about SmartAssurance as he said, "It's going to grow membership because it's such a compelling offering for employers. And as we grow membership, we grow earnings."[56] With these products, Humana is shifting the focus of health care industry from doctors and physicians to customers.

Being regarded as a cutting edge product, SmartAssurance is expected to mitigate the employers' concerns on rising costs. It is designed for companies with at least 500 workers. Still, Humana is facing stiff competition from Aetna Inc. and Lumenos, who are also providing

C

| EXHIBIT 3 | A Competitive Landscape of the U.S. HMO Market |

HMO	Total Ending Enrollment	Total Market Share	Group Ending Enrollment	Group Market Share
HMO Blue Texas	396,464	13.8%	284,285	15.9%
Aetna Health Inc.	354,820	12.3%	354,820	19.8%
Amerigroup Texas, Inc.[1]	304,388	10.6%	48,602	2.7%
Humana Health Plan of Texas, Inc.	231,186	8.0%	186,692	10.4%
CIGNA Health Plan of Texas, Inc.	183,007	6.4%	182,932	10.2%
PacifiCare of Texas[2]	169,307	5.9%	63,797	3.6%
Scott and White Health Plan	167,879	5.8%	134,948	7.5%
UnitedHealthCare	155,551	5.4%	155,267	8.7%
Superior Healthplan, Inc.[1]	122,732	4.3%	23,170	1.3%
Parkland Community Health Plan, Inc.[1]	106,186	3.7%	—	—
Texas Children's Health Plan, Inc.[1]	106,168	3.7%	67,886	3.8%
Community First Health Plans, Inc.[1]	97,161	3.4%	59,622	3.3%
FIRSTCARE	92,083	3.2%	65,245	3.6%
UTMB Health Plans, Inc.[1]	45,999	1.6%	—	—
Cook Children's Health Plan[1]	40,728	1.4%	40,728	2.3%
Unicare Health Plans	40,120	1.4%	40,120	2.2%
Community Health Choice, Inc.[1]	36,824	1.3%	—	—
Seton Health Plan[1]	34,925	1.2%	10,755	0.6%
El Paso First Health Plans, Inc.[1]	34,016	1.2%	—	—
Evercare of Texas, LLC[2]	29,699	1.0%	—	—
Amil International (Texas), Inc.	23,738	0.8%	23,738	1.3%
Driscoll Children's Health Plan[1]	19,210	0.7%	—	—
One Health Plan of Texas	17,413	0.6%	17,413	1.0%
Mercy Health Plans[1]	17,346	0.6%	17,101	1.0%
SelectCare of Texas, LLC[2]	15,652	0.5%	—	—
Texas Healthspring, Inc.[2]	13,495	0.5%	—	—
Valley Baptist Health Plan	11,474	0.4%	11,474	0.6%
MetroWest Health Plan, Inc.[1]	7,905	0.3%	—	—
HealthPlan of Texas, Inc.	2,236	0.1%	2,236	0.1%
Total Basic Service	2,877,712		1,790,831	

[1] Enrollment is predominantly Medicaid or Children's Health Insurance Program (CHIP).
[2] Enrollment is predominantly Medicare.

Source: "HMO Market Share," www.opic.state.tx.us.

consumer-driven health plans. However, Humana is distinguishing its SmartSuite products as full replacement products. McCallister believes that offering SmartSuite as a full replacement product to the employers so as to manage the entire employee population will result in lowering the healthcare cost. But a Boston-based principal with human resources consulting firm Towers Perrin, Michael Taylor, said, "I think that's more of a strategy for the middle market. It's a risky strategy in the big accounts because they're not likely to give all their business to one [insurer]."[57]

The strong performance of TRICARE and Medicare continued to provide high earnings to Humana in the second quarter of 2004. The net income for the second quarter ending June 30, 2004, increased to $80.753 million from $69.276 million in the previous year (Exhibit 4). McCallister said, "The continued success we are experiencing with our traditional commercial and government products, combined with favorable results from and growing acceptance of our cutting-edge consumer strategy, are leading to record earnings for 2004."[58]

To control cost and cash in on new business opportunities, Humana is designing advanced analytical models. The Center for Health Metrics in Humana's Innovation Center has developed four predictive and

EXHIBIT
4

Consolidated Statements of Income

(Dollars in thousands, except per share results)

	Three months ended June 30		Six months ended June 30	
	2004	**2003**	**2004**	**2003**
Revenues:				
Premiums	$3,303,712	$2,913,405	$6,482,893	$5,756,354
Administrative services fees	81,346	71,668	159,583	132,804
Investment income	43,863	43,228	71,317	69,045
Other income	2,557	1,657	4,634	3,471
Total revenues	3,431,478	3,029,958	6,718,427	5,961,674
Operating expenses:				
Medical	2,789,740	2,444,977	5,473,256	4,816,411
Selling, general and administrative	486,895	448,537	956,524	912,815
Depreciation	24,272	25,550	48,195	66,286
Other intangible amortization	2,893	2,903	5,282	6,834
Total operating expenses	3,303,800	2,921,967	6,483,257	5,802,346
Income from operations	127,678	107,991	235,170	159,328
Interest expense	5,325	3,801	10,044	7,736
Income before income taxes	122,353	104,190	225,126	151,592
Provision for income taxes	41,600	34,914	76,543	51,086
Net income	$ 80,753	$ 69,276	$ 148,583	$ 100,506

Source: "Humana Inc. Reports Financial Results for Second Quarter and First Half of 2004," http://biz.yahoo.com, July 26, 2004.

analytical tools that the company calls "insight engines" and is developing a new model called SimHealth (Appendix 7). According to Senior Vice President and Chief Service and Information Officer Bruce J. Goodman, "IT is well aligned with the business. We anticipated what we had to do to make the data accessible . . . to enable the business to really take advantage of the technology and move forward."[59] McCallister said, "Through our increasingly successful turnaround strategy, and with the enthusiastic support of our talented employees, we will continue to make progress toward becoming the nation's leading Internet-enabled, customer-focused health services company."[60]

NOTES

1. "E-volutionizing Health Insurance," www.humana.com, January 2004.
2. "Humana 1 Wall Street Reporter . . .," www.wallstreetreporter.com, June 7, 2004.
3. "Annual Report 1999," www.humana.com.
4. www.humana.com.
5. "Humana Reports Sharply Higher 2Q Earnings," www.forbes.com, July 26, 2004.
6. Schreiner, Bruce, "Pricing Pressure Worries Weigh on Humana Stock," www.kentucky.com, April 26, 2004.
7. Tompkins, Wayne, "Nursing Home Helped Launch New Industry," www.courier-journal.com, December 31, 1999.
8. American Medicorp was a for-profit hospital company founded by Wharton alumnus Robert Goldsamt. It had 56 hospitals by 1978.
9. Stoesz, David and Karger, Jacob, "The Corporatization of the U.S. Welfare State," www.uh.edu.
10. www.humana.com.
11. The program combined research and education with state-of-the-art treatment and led to epochal artificial-heart research at Humana Hospital-Audubon in Louisville.
12. "Humana Assures Brokers It's Working on Responsiveness," www.bizjournals.com, September 20, 1996.
13. "Humana 1997 Annual Report: Notes to Consolidated Financial Statements," www.humana.com.
14. TRICARE provides health insurance coverage to the dependents of active duty military personnel and to retired military personnel and their dependents.
15. Ibid.
16. "More Than the Names Have Changed," www.bizjournals.com.
17. "Humana 1997 Annual Report: Management Discussion and Analysis . . .," www.humana.com.

18. By then, ChoiceCare provides health services products to approximately 250,000 medical members in Greater Cincinnati and Ohio.
19. Sarasota and Treasure Coast, Florida; Springfield and Jefferson City, Missouri; and Puerto Rico.
20. "Humana Earnings to Miss Expectations," www.bizjournals.com, April 8, 1999.
21. "Humana Reports Impact of Medical Cost Trends and Columbia/HCA Contract," www.prnewswire.com, April 8, 1999.
22. "Nasdaq Hopes for Rebound," http://money.cnn.com, August 4, 1999.
23. Wolf Haldenstein Alder Freeman & Herz LLP has a full-service commercial practice and the firm's litigation department has been recognized by courts throughout the country as highly experienced and skilled in complex litigation, particularly with respect to federal securities laws, class actions, and shareholder litigation.
24. The period between February 9, 1999, and April 8, 1999.
25. "Humana [NYSE:HUM]," www.whafh.com.
26. "Why Humana?," http://ir.thomsonfn.com, 1999.
27. "Managed Care Challenged in Class Action Lawsuit," http://library.lp.findlaw.com.
28. "Humana Names Michael B. McCallister President and Chief Executive Officer," www.prnewswire.com, February 3, 2000.
29. "Humana Names Michael B. McCallister President and Chief Executive Officer," op. cit.
30. Jackson, Cheryl, "Humana Restructures in South Florida, Drops Physicians," www.ama-assn.org, October 9, 2000.
31. "Humana to Sell Workers' Compensation Business," www.systoc.com, January 3, 2000.
32. Rx3 is a three-tiered copayment design for prescription drug coverage that provides the members more value in their pharmacy benefits and helps its clients reduce overall increases in premium. It is a prescription drug plan with three levels of benefit. Level One includes generic drugs on the Drug List. Level Two includes brand-name drugs on the Drug List. Level Three includes both generic and brand name drugs not on the Drug List.
33. Humanacc.com is a comprehensive health plan management tool that allows physicians to access a member's health plan information to determine a co-pay amount or a claim status, and provides Humana health guidelines, treatment protocols, patient authorizations, and approvals for treatment and access to global patterns of care.
34. PlanWizard helps people choose the plan that's right for them through a series of interactive questions and answers that takes just seconds to complete online.
35. "Annual Report 2000," www.humana.com.
36. Blue Cross and Blue Shield of Florida is the state's largest and oldest health insurance provider to more than six million members in Florida. The company's health insurance products include HMO, PPO, traditional indemnity, and supplemental Medicare. Blue Cross and Blue Shield of Florida also provides accident & dismemberment, dental, disability, and workers compensation insurance.
37. Rambo, Larry, "'Consumerizing' Health Care Is Best Hope," http://milwaukee.bizjournals.com, April 4, 2003.
38. "The New Face of Health Plans," www.healthleaders.com, January 1, 2003.
39. Medical Mutual has been a trusted health insurance provider in Ohio since 1934 when it pioneered the concept of prepaid health insurance.
40. Dubose, Jane, and DeWitt, Paula, "Individual Health Plans: Not Cinderella, But Not The Ugly Stepsister," www.healthleaders.com, October 8, 2003.
41. A clause in an insurance policy that relieves the insurer of responsibility to pay the initial loss up to a stated amount.
42. "Humana Debuts Consumer-Focused Health Plan for Small Groups," www.humana.com, September 20, 2002.
43. Carrns, Ann, "Humana to Cut 17% of Staff," http://tricare.osd.mil, December 5, 2002.
44. "Humana Launches Innovative Communications and Advertising Campaign to Support New Consumer-Driven Health Benefits Solutions," www.humana.com, February 26, 2003.
45. Chicago, Phoenix, Houston, Cincinnati, and Dayton, Ohio.
46. "Humana Launches Ad Campaigns in Five Cities," www.bizjournals.com, February 26, 2003.
47. Barrouquere, Brett, "Commercial Business Boosts Humana Profit," www.softcom.net, February 2, 2004.
48. Schreiner, Bruce, "Pricing Pressure Worries Weigh on Humana Stock," op. cit.
49. Ward, Karla, "Humana Earnings More Than Double," www.kentucky.com, April 27, 2004.
50. DeWitt, Paula, "Mike McCallister: Not Playing Games," www.healthleaders.com, July 23, 2004.
51. "Humana Completes Acquisition of Ochsner Health Plan of Louisiana," www.humana.com, April 1, 2004.
52. "Humana Inc. to Acquire Ochsner Health Plan of Louisiana," www.ochsner.org, December 19, 2003.
53. "In Depth: Health Care Report," http://houston.bizjournals.com, July 9, 2004.
54. Schreiner, Bruce, "Humana Introduces Health Offering That Caps Premium Increases," www.myrtlebeachonline.com, June 9, 2004.
55. Schreiner, Bruce, "Humana Health Plan Caps Premium Increases," www.softcom.net, June 11, 2004.
56. Ibid.
57. DeWitt, Paula, "Mike McCallister: Not Playing Games," op. cit.
58. "Humana Posts Increases in Revenue, Profit," www.bizjournals.com, July 26, 2004.
59. Anthes, Gary H., "Refocusing the Future," http://computerworld.com.my, July 7, 2004.
60. Ibid.

C

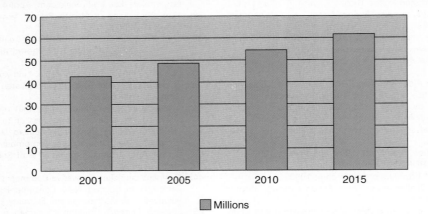

By the year 2010, the U.S. Census Bureau estimates the growth rate of the 60+ age group population will be 3.5 times as high as that of the total population, increasing the need for health care services to meet the needs of an aging population.

Source: "Humana, Inc.," www.mcareol.com, February 2001.

APPENDIX 2
Humana's Products in Commercial and Government Business Segment

Products Marketed to Commercial Segment Employers and Members

HMO

The health maintenance organization, or HMO, products provide prepaid health insurance coverage to the customers through a network of independent primary care physicians, specialty physicians, and other health care providers who contract with the HMO to furnish such services. Primary care physicians generally include internists, family practitioners, and pediatricians. An HMO member, typically through the member's employer, pays a monthly fee, which generally covers, with some copayments, health care services received from or approved by the member's primary care physician.

PPO

The preferred provider organization, or PPO, products, which are marketed primarily to commercial groups and individuals, include some elements of managed health care. However, they typically include more cost sharing with the customer, through co-payments and annual deductibles. PPOs also are similar to traditional health insurance because they provide a customer with more freedom to choose a physician or other health care provider.

Administrative Services Only

Humana offers an administrative services only, or ASO, product to those who self-insure their employee health plans. The company receives fees to provide administrative services which generally include the processing of claims, offering access to our provider networks and clinical programs, and responding to customer service inquiries from employees of self-funded employers.

Specialty Products

Humana offers various specialty products including dental, group life, and short-term disability.

Products Marketed to Government Segment Members and Beneficiaries

Medicare+Choice Product

Medicare is a federal program that provides persons age of 65 and over and some disabled persons certain hospital and medical insurance benefits, which include hospitalization benefits for up to 90 days per incident of illness plus a lifetime reserve aggregating 60 days. Each Medicare-eligible individual is entitled to receive inpatient hospital care, known as Part A care, without the payment of any premium, but is required to pay a premium to the federal government, which is adjusted annually, to be eligible for physician care and other services, known as Part B care.

Medicaid Product

Medicaid is a federal program that is state-operated to facilitate the delivery of health care services to low income residents. Each electing state develops, through a state specific regulatory agency, a Medicaid managed care initiative that must be approved by CMS. CMS requires that Medicaid managed care plans meet federal standards and cost no more than the amount that would have been spent on a comparable fee-for-service basis.

TRICARE

TRICARE provides health insurance coverage to the dependents of active duty military personnel and to retired military personnel and their dependents. In November 1995, the United States Department of Defense awarded Humana its first TRICARE contract for Regions 3 and 4 covering approximately 1.1 million eligible beneficiaries in Florida, Georgia, South Carolina, Mississippi, Alabama, Tennessee and Eastern Louisiana. On July 1, 1996, Humana began providing health insurance coverage to these approximately 1.1 million eligible beneficiaries.

Source: Compiled by IBS CDC from "Annual Report 2002," www.humana.com.

APPENDIX
3

Difference between Nursing Homes and Hospitals

America's health care system relies on nursing homes to fill a special niche in the Continuum of Care—the provision of skilled care and custodial care to elder Americans who do not need the intensive, acute care of a hospital but for whom remaining at home is no longer appropriate. Nursing homes are capable of caring for individuals with a wide range of medical conditions.

The number of beds in a particular nursing home can range from approximately 25 to 500; the average number of beds per facility across America is about 102. Nursing homes may be called:

- health centers
- havens
- manors
- homes for the aged
- nursing centers
- nursing homes
- care centers
- continuing care centers
- living centers
- or convalescent centers.

The goals of the nursing home are to:

- Rehabilitate the resident to maximum potential and enable him or her to return to independent living arrangements if possible;

- Maintain that maximum rehabilitation as long as possible within the realities of age and disease;
- Delay deterioration in physical and emotional well-being; and
- Support the resident and family, physically and emotionally, when health declines to the point of death.

"Hospital" means any institution, place, building or agency, public or private, whether organized for profit or not, devoted primarily to the maintenance and operation of facilities for the diagnosis, treatment or care of patients admitted for overnight stay or longer in order to obtain medical care, surgical care, obstetrical care, or nursing care for illness, disease, injury, infirmity, or deformity. Places where pregnant women are admitted and receive care incident to pregnancy, abortion or delivery shall be considered to be a "hospital," regardless of the number of patients received or the duration of their stay. The term "hospital" includes general and specialized hospitals, tuberculosis sanitoria, maternity homes, lying-in homes, and homes for unwed mothers in which care is given during delivery.

"General hospital" means a hospital maintained for the purpose of providing hospital care in a broad category of illness and injury.

"Specialized hospital" means a hospital maintained for the purpose of providing hospital care in a certain category, or categories, of illness and injury.

"Related institution" means an institution, or an industrial or other type of infirmary, providing limited medical or surgical care to ill or injured persons on a temporary basis, or a birthing center.

Sources: "Nursing Homes," www.carescout.com; "Myths & Realities of Living in a Nursing Home," http://seniors-site.com; and "Hospital, Definition," www.cfharchitects.com.

**APPENDIX
4**

Growth in the HMO Industry in the United States: Proportion of Overall Total HMO Enrollment in the Ten Largest National Managed Care Firms, 1987–January 1998.

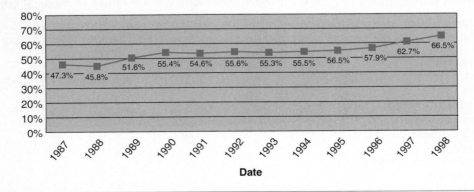

Source: "A Financial Overview of the Managed Care Industry," www.kff.org, March 1999.

Lawsuit Allegation against Humana

The lawsuit's core allegation is that Humana falsely represented to its enrollees that all coverage and treatment decisions would be made on the basis of "medical necessity" when, in fact:

- Humana bases its coverage and review decisions "on a variety of concealed cost-based criteria that were unconcerned with, and sometimes inimical to, the medical needs" of enrollees.
- Humana "concealed" from enrollees "that it has established a set of financial incentives for claims reviewers—including direct cash bonus payments—designed to encourage denial of claims without regard to [the] medical needs" of enrollees.
- Humana "concealed" from enrollees that it "subcontracts the claims review process—and with it, the authority to decide the scope of [enrollees'] medical coverage—to third parties" who (1) hired "persons without appropriate medical training and specialization to make claims review determinations" and (2) use "criteria different from and more restrictive than" Humana's medical necessity criteria.
- Humana "concealed" from enrollees that Humana "provides direct financial incentives to treating physicians and other health care professionals to deny coverage" to enrollees, "even where the proposed treatment satisfies" Humana's "[m]edical [n]ecessity definition."

Source: "Managed Care Challenged in Class Action Lawsuit," http://library.lp.findlaw.com.

Prescription Drug Benefits

Humana's innovative prescription drug benefits include Rx4, Rx4 + Deductible, and RxImpact. With all three benefit designs, covered prescription drugs are grouped into four levels.

- **Rx4:** The lower the drug's coverage level (One, Two, Three or Four), the less the member pays.
- **Rx4 + Deductible:** The member pays an annual deductible for those in Levels Two, Three and Four combined (but no deductible for Level One drugs). After meeting the deductible, the member pays a fixed copayment or percentage for each prescription; the plan pays the rest.
- **RxImpact:** Drugs are grouped into the four coverage groups according to evidence-based information about the drugs' efficiency. Humana pays a fixed allowance toward the cost of drugs in each group; the member pays the difference between the allowance and Humana's discounted price at participating pharmacies.

MyHumana: Taking advantage of the Internet's unique ability to customize information one person at a time, *My*Humana allows members to design a "personal home page" on www.humana.com based on their individual preferences. Members may choose health topics to quickly review current information about them. They may also review recent claims, learn about prescription and alternative drug options, access provider information including consumer assessments of doctors and hospitals, utilize decision-support tools and condition workbooks, access more than 24,000 pages of health content, take a health risk assessment and read personal messages from Humana in a secured message center.

Emphesys: With this new, online, fully interactive health plan, Humana delivers unmatched customer service, via user-friendly technology developed "from the ground up" exclusively for the Internet. Nearly all plan transactions are available on the Web. For example, members can enroll, add or delete dependents, and access information about claims and prescription drugs, all online. Employers have convenient Web-based enrollment and other self-service options to more easily administer their health benefits. These simplified processes save time, reduce the chance of error and decrease the need for paper forms, files and records.

C

SmartSuite^SM: SmartSuite is the first of two innovative consumer-choice products from Humana. Employees use online tools to compare benefits and costs, then select the plan that works for their health care needs and budget.

- Available to self-funded groups of 300+ and fully-insured groups of 100+ in single or multiple locations
- Employer offers a "bundle" of health plans from which the employee chooses a plan
- Plan options may include HMOs, PPOs, and the CoverageFirst PPO

SmartSelect^SM: SmartSelect is Humana's second generation of consumer-choice plans. Using the online Wizard, employees compare costs and benefits, estimate their health care spending, and customize their plan.

- Available to self-funded groups of 300+ in single or multiple locations
- Employer chooses from a variety of PPO plans, some of which include a Personal Care Account (PCA) funding option.
- Employees select varying levels of copayments, coinsurance and premium costs, as well as prescription benefit options that fit their cost and coverage preferences.

CoverageFirst PPO: CoverageFirst is a PPO plan for people who want just basic coverage plus the security of a "safety net" for a major unexpected illness or injury. CoverageFirst has a unique four-phase design:

- Annual allowance of $500 per person to be used for the following eligible in-network expenses:
  - Physicians' services like office visits
  - Routine outpatient laboratory tests and X-rays
  - Hospital services, including semiprivate room and board, emergency room services, and outpatient surgery
  - Preventive care, including annual exams
  - Other care services, including home health care; physical, speech and hearing therapy; and hospice care
  - Care for psychiatric disorders, alcoholism and drug dependency
- Annual individual deductible—applies when any covered member spends the entire $500 allowance
- Coinsurance—covers most additional eligible medical expenses until the member satisfies the annual out-of-pocket maximum amount
- Safety net—ensures 100% coverage of expenses, except copayments, for the rest of the plan year

Personal Care Account (PCA) Funding Option: A Personal Care Account, or PCA, is an employer-funded medical expense account built into some of Humana's PPO plans.

- The PCA amount may vary by plan
- Once the PCA is depleted, the employee is covered by the PPO plan
- Employee can use PCA funds for a wide range of medical expenses, which may include:
  - Prescription copayments
  - Vision care
  - Dental services
  - Other items and services the employer chooses from the IRS-approved list of eligible expenses
- Employees can spend PCA funds easily at many pharmacies and other providers using their Humana Access Card

Source: "Annual Report 2001," www.humana.com.

SmartStart Plus

Goal: Predict the consumer's choice of benefit plan; explore benefit/contribution strategies.

Approach: Models consumers as "rational agents" that evaluate plans and trade off costs, benefits and risks to pick the best plan.

Predictive Modeling

Goal: Predict future high-cost (illness-prone) members; improve customer relations.

Approach: Combines medical knowledge, engineering methods (asynchronous signal processing, nonlinear dynamic time series) and computer science (learning algorithms, advanced visualization).

Impact Tool

Goal: Evaluate effectiveness of programs; analyze consumer behavior.

Approach: Creates control and test groups on the fly for dynamic analysis of clinical and financial results.

Insight Tool

Goal: Enhance pricing and underwriting competitiveness; early detection of trends.

Approach: Uses historical data and predictions of individuals' future health to identify patterns and drivers of health care costs, including early trend and anomaly detection at the employer, market and provider levels.

SimHealth

Goal: Simulate consumer choice and behavior via self-evolving models.

Approach: In development now, SimHealth uses "rules of the game" (weighted consumer objectives) to evaluate different benefits-plan/consumer scenarios. Evolves using the results of other models, genetic algorithms and agent-based modeling.

Source: Anthes, Gary H. "Sidebar: Analytic Engines Deliver Insights," www.computerworld.com, March 8, 2004.

Marks and Spencer: The Downfall and Leadership Vacuum

G. Saradhi Kumar
Sumit Kumar Chaudhuri

ICFAI University Press, Business School Case Development Centre

Marks's problem is that it is a very old-fashioned sort of company, which found a winning formula decades ago and failed to see the world changing round about it.[1]

We lost touch with our customers and forgot about the competition. Those are quite fundamental for a retailer.[2]

— Peter Salsbury, Former Chief Executive, Marks and Spencer

Marks & Spencer failed to anticipate trends and became too quantity-driven, rather than quality-driven.[3]

— Edward Whitefield, Chairman of Management Horizons Europe[4]

Started in 1884, Marks and Spencer (M&S) grew as the iconic British retailer within a century. By 2004, M&S, with more than 365 stores across Britain (Appendix 1), was serving 14 million customers per week. In spite of a strong brand image and a huge customer base, since the late 1990s, profits have come down and share prices have tumbled, making the retail giant vulnerable to takeover. On June 3, 2004, Philip Green, a retail tycoon of Britain, made a £9 billion ($16.5 billion)[5] bid for M&S. It was his second attempt, after a failed attempt in 1999. Even as late as 1998, M&S was competing with Wal-Mart for the title of the most profitable retail chain worldwide, when for the financial year 1997–1998, M&S, with Sir Richard Greenbury as its chairman and chief executive, earned a profit of £1.16 billion ($1.9 billion).[6] However, in 1998–1999, the company announced a 42 percent[7] decline in its pre-tax profits, which further decreased to £418 million[8] in 1999–2000 (see Exhibit 1).

In February 1999, a decision was made to split the posts of chairman and chief executive. Sir Richard Greenbury quit the post of chief executive and continued as chairman until June 1999. Since then, the two key positions in the company have been rarely occupied. This leadership crisis, coupled with the traditional inward-looking culture of the company, invited a hostile takeover bid. Thus, the company, with its rich history (Appendix 2) and emotional attachment with the average Briton, struggled for survival.

M&S: FROM A STALL TO INTERNATIONAL RETAILING

In 1884, Michael Marks, a Russian-born Polish refugee, opened a stall in Leeds. In 1893, he moved the business to Manchester, where a year later he entered into a partnership with Tom Spencer, who worked at IJ Dewhirst, a wholesale company. In 1904, they acquired premises for a shop in Leeds. This marked the transition from a market stall to a covered arcade. In the 1920s, the retail chain introduced a revolutionary method of purchasing its supplies directly from the manufacturers, thereby avoiding the intermediaries. In 1928, the St. Michael brand of clothing was introduced, which "grew from a mere shop label into the nation's most trusted brand."[9]

In the 1930s, Café Bars were introduced in many M&S stores. These provided cheap, hygienic, and

EXHIBIT
1

Earnings and Share Price of M&S

Poor Marks

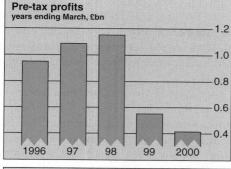

Pre-tax profits
years ending March, £bn

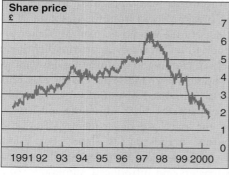

Share price
£

Source: "Does M&S Have a Future?" www.economist.com, October 26, 2000.

nutritious food to the general public, making an efficient use of food that had become scarce due to the Great Depression and World War II. Further strengthening its position in food retailing, M&S introduced a food department selling fresh and canned food. In 1934, a scientific research lab was established to develop new fabrics. This was the first research lab of its kind established by any British retailer. In 1948, M&S introduced the concept of self-service in its stores in London. It was an instant success. In 1974, expanding its offerings in the food division, the retailer introduced Indian and Chinese dishes. In 1975, it entered continental Europe by opening its stores in Boulevard Haussman, Paris, and in Brussels, Belgium. In 1984, Lord Derek Rayner took over as chairman and expanded into the U.S. market. The company acquired Brooks Brothers, an American clothing company, and Kings Super Markets, a U.S. food chain, in 1988. The same year, the first M&S stores were opened in Hong Kong. In 1991, Sir Richard Greenbury became chairman and led the company till the late 1990s when M&S encountered trouble. Sir Richard's resignation left a vacuum at the top of the company. As The Econ-

omist pointed out, "When nemesis arrived, the company was largely unprepared, run 'by people who had known nothing but success.'"[10]

DAUNTING TASKS

The sudden dip in the company's profits in the late 1990s reflected the weaknesses of the company—its reluctance to adjust with the changing times, its complacency about the growing competition, and its failure to prepare an able leader. The company faced challenges in its apparels division, which contributed about 60 percent to its sales. Traditionally, M&S used only British suppliers for most apparels, the cost of which was high, while the other apparel retailers imported to save costs. British suppliers accounted for more than 50 percent of M&S supplies, which was much higher than the industry average of 30 percent. The company not only bore higher costs for sticking to the British suppliers, it also lost on the latest fashion trends. The British suppliers were not able to provide new designs for the M&S stores, forcing the stores to rely on outdated designs, which did not lure younger buyers. By 2001, due to all these factors, the company was losing 10 percent[11] per year in clothing sales. For almost two decades, the retail chain was reluctant to accept any major credit cards but they had released their own cards. The sales were largely cash sales.

M&S, over the years, had been ignoring the growing competition in clothing and food businesses. Foreign apparel stores like the United States' Gap, Sweden's Hennes & Mauritz, and Spain's Zara were expanding out of their saturated home markets. Leveraging on their economies of scale and just-in-time manufacturing, the competitors were eating into the market share of M&S with a wide range of international trendy designs and high-quality products at comparatively lower prices. Domestic suppliers of M&S failed to match their foreign counterparts. In its food business, which for decades accounted for 40 percent of the revenue, the riders were the British supermarket biggies like Tesco and Sainsbury, which consistently kept increasing their market shares in the ready-made food segment.

Another major problem with M&S was its poor management of floor space and employee time. M&S followed "nonvalue-adding"[12] practices like cash counting in the tills and checking stock, which consumed a major portion of the floor space and employee workday that could have been utilized in selling goods. Thereby, the company could have saved £40 million[13] a year. Further, as M&S lacked an efficient system of evaluating the performance of its individual stores, it had to carry on with the stores whose performances were lower than average. Verdict, a British retail consultant, disclosed that the top 100 retail locations of Britain accounted for 60 percent sales of all the retailers, while they occupied only 40 percent of the floor space.

The inward-looking management failed to look beyond their stores. Employees joined M&S upon graduation from college and worked their way up the ranks. Few senior appointments were made from outside the company. As a result, the company lacked new ideas and innovative techniques. This was worsened by the centralized decision-making process that bred the rigid top-down culture of "head office knows best."[14] "This was fine so long as customers kept coming and the competition lagged behind, but it also made it difficult to question the M&S way of doing things."[15] All this contributed to the downslide of M&S by the end of the 20th century, the problems being further compounded by the resignation of Sir Richard without proper succession. As The Economist put it, "Without either a chairman or an independent-minded board to harry him, Sir Richard has mismanaged what is probably any boss's most important task—to provide for his own succession."[16]

BOARD ROOM BATTLES AND LACK OF COMMON VISION

In February 1999, Sir Richard stepped down as the chief executive and continued as chairman until July. He left M&S because of "irreconcilable differences"[17] with Peter Salsbury, who was then the chief executive. "He sent it into free fall with a series of restructurings that rooted out some of the company's smugness but at the cost of destroying its soul."[18] Salsbury appointed twelve teams of management consultants that included one team to advise the company how to use the services of the other teams. The teams initiated a reorganizing across the board. Most of the top managers in the purchasing department were fired. Many of the staff were asked to re-apply for their jobs, which demoralized them. The supply-chain reorganization was not successful. M&S initiated a global supply chain with manufacturing hubs in Portugal, Morocco, and Sri Lanka, and the number of direct suppliers was reduced to half. Many suppliers became upset, controlling imports from far-off places proved to be a difficult task, and quality of the apparels was reduced. The reorganization also increased distribution costs. The management and the consultants developed new brands and brought in new designers. In spite of launching the first advertising campaign in the history of the company, with the fashion magazines giving adequate publicity, it failed to attract the regular customers.

The food department was also reorganized to introduce in-house bakeries, delicatessens,[19] and meat counters. This increased the requirements of floor space and workforce, thus increasing operating costs. As a result, operating profits from food fell from £247 million in 1997 to £137 million[20] in 1999. Another decision that boomeranged was accepting credit cards. In 2000, M&S started accepting credit cards by paying the credit card companies three percent on credit card transactions.

In early 2000, M&S appointed Luc Vandevelde, the chairman of Promodès, a French chain of supermarkets and hypermarkets, as its chairman. For the first time in the history of the company the position of marketing director was created and Alan McWalter from Woolworth was appointed as the marketing director, breaking away from the tradition of promoting insiders to the top posts. Alan McWalter provided a new look to the stores by improving lighting, reducing stocks of clothing in uniform designs and fashions, and grouping merchandise to enable easy shopping. He also decentralized operations, giving local buyers and store managers more autonomy and less domination by the purchase department. M&S introduced other firms' brands in its shops. For example, it offered products like Orange mobile phones and Philips toasters and introduced Autograph (co-labeled Marks & Spencer), a high-fashion label created by prominent British designers. Autograph clothing had limited ranges that changed every few weeks and were sold in a separate area of the M&S stores. However, sales did not improve and in October 2000, Luc Vandevelde fired Salsbury and appointed Roger Holmes as the chief executive.

Luc Vandevelde went on to close the French operations along with a total of 38 non-performing stores across Europe. He also spun off the U.S. subsidiaries Brooks Brothers and Kings Super Markets Inc. He replaced all M&S senior managers as well as board members with a younger management team and laid off as many as 4,000 employees. Luc Vandevelde invested $115 million[21] in 2001 to modernize one-third of M&S stores in Britain. He hired top talent to change the chain's frumpy image. Notable among them were George Davies, who created the successful George line of clothing at ASDA Group Ltd, a British subsidiary of Wal-Mart, and Vittorio Radice, who had revived Selfridges, a department store in Britain. Still, the M&S market share kept falling. M&S had a 15 percent share in 1998, which fell to 12 percent[22] by 2002 and further slid to 11.1 percent[23] by 2003. Under such circumstances, shares of the company fell to 274.75 pence, valuing the firm at around £6.5 billion[24] by

C

May 2004. This was followed by the offer of Philip Green to buy M&S. The board rejected the offer and also appointed a non-executive director, Paul Myners, as the interim chairman to lead the company through the troubled times. The board also appointed Stuart Rose, a former employee of M&S, who had a long 17-year stint in M&S from 1972 before leaving the company. He replaced Roger Holmes as the chief executive. Stuart Rose quickly installed his own management team, replacing some of the M&S advisers. Commenting on the appointment of Stuart Rose, *The Economist* wrote, "He has returned to M&S, he says, in order to rebuild the business to its 'former glory,' not simply to sell it to someone else."[25] However, analysts were skeptical. "There's no guarantee that an offer will go ahead, but equally it could open up the field to other potential bidders,"[26] said Richard Ratner, retail analyst at Seymour Pierce.[27]

NOTES

1. "Iconoclasm," www.economist.com, May 20, 1999.
2. "Food for Thought," www.economist.com, July 8, 1999.
3. Cohn, Laura, "Shopping for Marks & Sparks," www.businessweek.com, June 14, 2004.
4. A London-based retail consultancy.
5. "Buying the Store," www.economist.com, June 3, 2004.
6. "Marks's Failed Revolution," www.economist.com, April 12, 2001.
7. Op. cit., "Food for Thought."
8. "Does M&S Have a Future?," www.economist.com, October 26, 2000.
9. "Shelving the Saint," www.economist.com, March 16, 2000.
10. "Marksism Today," October 18, 2001.
11. "High Street Woes," www.economist.com, July 26, 2001.
12. "Black Marks," www.economist.com, November 4, 1999.
13. Ibid.
14. Op. cit., "Black Marks."
15. Op. cit., "Does M&S Have a Future?"
16. "Poor Marks," www.economist.com, November 19, 1998.
17. "Clarification," www.economist.com, November 16, 2000.
18. Op. cit., "Marksism Today."
19. A store specializing in imported or unusual foods and ingredients, for example, cooked meats, cheeses, and pickles.
20. Op. cit., "Does M&S Have a Future?"
21. Capell, Kerry, "A Sigh of Relief at Marks & Sparks," www.businessweek.com, January 21, 2002.
22. Ibid.
23. Murden, Terry, "Marks Attack," business.scotsman.com, May 30, 2004.
24. Dowsett, Sonya, "Marks & Spencer to Replace Chairman," www.uk.news.yahoo.com, May 10, 2004.
25. "Buying the Store," June 3, 2004.
26. Op. cit., "Marks Attack."
27. A London-based group, which provides brokerage and corporate finance services primarily to small-cap businesses of the UK.

MARKS & SPENCER

	Number of Stores
United Kingdom	365
M&S Direct	1
Republic of Ireland	7
Hong Kong	10
TOTAL	**383**

UK Regional Stores

England	*320*
Northern Ireland	*7*
Scotland	*26*
Wales	*13*
Outlets	*16*
Simply Food	*49*

MARKS & SPENCER FRANCHISES

	Number of Outlets
Bahrain	1
Bermuda	1
Canary Islands	4
Gran Canaria 3	
Tenerife 1	
Channel Islands	3
Guernsey 1	
Jersey 2	
Croatia	1
Cyprus	9
Czech Republic	3
Gibraltar	1
Greece	30
Hungary	4
India	4
Indonesia	9
Kuwait	1
Malaysia	2
Malta	3
Oman	1
Philippines	11
Poland	2
Qatar	1
Romania	2
Singapore	7
Saudi Arabia	7
South Korea	12
Thailand	11
Turkey	17
UAE	3
UK Simply Food	12
TOTAL	**162**

KING SUPERMARKETS

USA	27

GROUP WORLDWIDE LOCATIONS

TOTAL	572

Source: www2.marksandspencer.com.

1884–1907

1884:   Michael Marks, a Russian-born Polish refugee, opened a stall at Leeds Kirkgate Market.

1893:   Michael moved to 20 Cheetham Hill Road, Manchester. In the following year, he opened a shop in the lower part of the same building.

1894:   Michael formed a partnership with Tom Spencer, a former cashier from the wholesale company IJ Dewhirst.

1901:   A new warehouse and head office opened at Derby Street, Manchester. It was the first property that was built to the business' specifications.

1904:   The business acquired premises for a shop at the recently opened Cross Arcade in Leeds. This was a prestigious site and marked the transition from market stall to a covered arcade.

1905:   Tom Spencer died on 25 July.

1907:   Michael Marks died on 31 December. It was now time for a new generation to advance the success of the two founders.

Michael Marks

Tom Spencer

1908–1931

1920s: The business adopted a revolutionary policy, at that time, of buying directly from manufacturers.

1926:   Marks & Spencer Limited became a public company.

1928:   The St. Michael trademark was registered.

1930:   The flagship store was opened at Marble Arch, London.

1931:   A food department was introduced, selling produce and canned goods.

St. Michael trademark

1932–1955

1930s: Café Bars were introduced in many stores. These provided cheap, hygienic, and nutritious mass catering. This was a valuable resource during the war, making efficient use of scarce food.

1933:   Simon Marks commissioned Flora Solomon to set up a staff welfare service that provided pensions, subsidized staff canteens, health and dental service, hairdressing, rest rooms, and camping holidays.

1934:   A scientific research lab was established, headed by Dr. Eric Kann. This was the first research lab of any British retailer, allowing the company to pioneer new fabrics.

1939–
1945:   The advent of the Utility Clothing Scheme in wartime meant that there were strict specifications on the use of materials and trimmings for all clothing. One of Marks and Spencer's scientists was seconded to help develop the scheme to produce a range of quality garments throughout the period of restriction.

1941:   Marks & Spencer staff raised funds to present a Spitfire, *The Marksman*, to the country, to aid the war effort.

Flagship store, Marble Arch

Café Bar

Scientific research lab

1932–1955

1948:   Marks & Spencer held their first self-service trial at their store in Wood Green, London. It was a great success.

1956–1979

1959:   The company introduced no-smoking rules in their stores.

1961:   Dogs, with the exception of guide dogs, were banned from stores to ensure hygiene at the food counters.

1964:   Simon Marks died after 56 years of service to the company, and Israel Sieff took over as chairman.

1973:   The company sold wine for the first time.

1974:   Indian and Chinese food was introduced; dishes included chicken korma and lamb rogan josh.

1975:   Marks & Spencer's first stores in Continental Europe opened in Boulevard Haussman, Paris, and Brussels, Belgium.

1980–2001

1985:   The Marks & Spencer charge card was launched nationally.

1986:   Marks & Spencer opened its first edge of town store at the Metro Centre in Gateshead. The introduction of furniture was supported by the launch of the home furnishing catalogue.

1988:   The company acquired Brooks Brothers, an American clothing company, and Kings Super Markets, a U.S. food chain. The first Marks & Spencer stores were opened in Hong Kong.

1999:   The company published its own code of practice with global sourcing principles as a minimum standard for all suppliers in an effort to improve conditions for workers overseas.

1999:   Online shopping was launched on the Marks & Spencer Web site.

2000:   Twelve items were awarded Millennium Product status, the highest number of awards made to any single company. These included Body Sensor Hosiery, Machine Washable Wool Tailoring, Non-Iron Cotton Clothing, Non-Polish Shoes, Imagemaster, Gas Powered Lorries, In-Store Bakery Oven, Thermotext Security Thread in Gift Vouchers, Advanced Design Refrigerator Display Case, Ultimate Body Bra, Sensitive Skin Clothing for Children, and Secret Support Clothing.

2000:   The Count on Us range of food products was launched.

2000:   £15 million was raised via the Marks & Spencer Children's Promise Millennium appeal.

2001:   Machine washable suits for men and the Bioform bra were launched.

2001:   The Portrait of the Nation—commissioned on behalf of Marks & Spencer as sponsors of the self portrait zone at the Millennium Dome—began a tour of the country. The 15 panels displaying 250,000 photographs were created by artist David Mach R.A.

Source: www.examstutor.com

Israel Sieff

Marks & Spencer wine

Edge of Town store

Marks & Spencer Web site

Machine washable

Wal-Mart Stores Inc.: Dominating Global Retailing

Kannan Ramaswamy

Thunderbird, The Garvin School of International Management

Mr. Lee Scott could afford the look of confidence. He had just spoken to investment analysts about the phenomenal results from the second quarter of 2003. Despite the general weakness in the world economy and the uncertain environment that prevailed, Wal-Mart had reported sales growth of 11 percent, amounting to $6.4 billion. The company's associates were indeed doing the Wal-Mart cheer in faraway places like Germany, South Korea, China, and the United Kingdom. In three decades, it had grown from its rural Arkansas roots to become the world's largest company, and quite possibly the most powerful retailer.

The meteoric growth did bring with it a fair share of problems. At a macro level, there had always been questions about the ability of Wal-Mart to sustain the pace of growth it had demonstrated in recent years. Once the company vaulted over the $200 billion level in annual sales, it was clear that incremental growth would be challenging. There was a nationwide backlash against big-box retailers, and Wal-Mart was front and center in that controversy. Some of the upstart chains such as Dollar General were gearing up to nip at the heels of Wal-Mart. They claimed that customers felt lost inside the cavernous stores of Wal-Mart and that they would gladly shop at Dollar General stores, which, although much smaller, offered comparable low prices.

The emerging markets that held a lot of promise were being bitterly contested by other major players such as Carrefour, Metro, Auchan, Ahold, and Tesco. Since many of these competitors had moved into the international marketplace long before Wal-Mart, there was an experience curve handicap that Wal-Mart had to contend with.

From an operational viewpoint, the suppliers were in for a rocky ride, since the nature of their relationship with Wal-Mart had begun to change radically. Given its huge base of power, the company was able to extract significant price concessions from its suppliers. It had recently intensified promotion of its own labels and store brands that competed directly against the likes of Procter & Gamble (P&G) and Kraft. The suppliers felt that their long years of belt-tightening were not being rewarded by Wal-Mart and that they were increasingly asked to do more for less. Some had been reduced to contract manufacturers, churning products that would be sold under one of Wal-Mart's many labels.

All was not well within the Wal-Mart family either. Some employees had filed suit against Wal-Mart, alleging that the company forced them to work overtime without any pay. This suit, some believed, had the makings of a large class-action suit, probably amongst the biggest in the realm of employment law in recent years. A similar case in Oregon was decided in favor of the employees. There was yet another pending lawsuit that charged that the company routinely discriminated against women in job promotions, especially at the supervisory and managerial levels. It was reported that although roughly 90 percent of Wal-Mart associates were women, they represented only 15 percent of the positions in top management, a disparity that was at the heart of the gender discrimination suit. To complicate matters further, in late October 2003, Wal-Mart was the target of raids by the Immigration and Naturalization Service of the U.S. Government. The agency reported that it was examining whether Wal-Mart was hiring illegal immigrants in contravention of the law.

THUNDERBIRD
THE GARVIN SCHOOL OF
INTERNATIONAL MANAGEMENT

The challenges were indeed formidable, despite the legendary strengths that the company had built upon in the past. Even Mr. Lee Scott acknowledged the uphill climb when he observed, "We'd be silly to sit here and tell you it's not a challenge."[1] Although Wal-Mart had systematically decimated the negative projections of analysts in the past, it was once again the subject of doubt and naysaying. Mr. Scott had to prove himself all over again.

THE WORLD OF DISCOUNT RETAILING

Discount retailing had evolved into a global industry within a fairly short span of time. Pushed in large part by Wal-Mart in the U.S. and counterparts such as Carrefour, Ahold, Metro, Tesco, and others worldwide, global discount chains had cornered a significant chunk of the global retail business (see Exhibit 1). The fundamentals of the business models that had evolved in various parts of the world seemed to coalesce around the principles that had been perfected by Wal-Mart. All the chains leveraged global economies of scale in purchasing, and negotiated favorable volume-based contracts with manufacturers, many of whom were themselves global. Coupled with sophisticated information systems that optimized supply chain planning and execution, the retailers were able to cut a lot of excess cost from the system and pass on some of the savings to the end customer. The competitive battle was, therefore, fought largely in terms of their ability to lure shoppers on the basis of their merchandise mix, price offers, and convenience. International expansion outside their own regions of familiarity became the norm rather than the exception. Carrefour, for example, operated in 32 countries; many of them, such as Taiwan and Brazil, were distinctly different from France, the company's home base. The global expansion was based on the simple premise that customers everywhere, irrespective of nationality, would be attracted to the value of the offer that the global retail chains made—a selection of merchandise that was unrivalled at prices that were unequalled.

The evolution of the discount concept had come full circle, and the major players were locked in competitive battles that transcended mere national boundaries. They catered to a global customer base that was very much multicultural. They carefully orchestrated strategies in each country setting so that they could dominate both at the local and global levels, often using mergers and acquisitions to gain market share quickly. As a result of this growth trajectory, many of the large markets were contested by more than one global retailer. Competitive advantage in this elite group seemed to turn on deep pockets, innovative strategic thinking, and faultless execution. Contemporaneous with the jockeying for position in the developed country markets, the major chains were locked in battles for supremacy in the emerging markets as well. Many of the emerging markets had begun a wave of deregulation and allowed even *de novo* entry of established global players. Markets such as Argentina, Brazil, Hungary, Turkey, and India were within sight of the global discount retailing revolution (see Exhibit 2). Given the significantly higher growth rates that these markets promised, the early entrants were sure to profit.

CREATING THE WAL-MART EMPIRE

Mr. Sam Walton founded the first Wal-Mart in 1962, originally christened as Wal-Mart Discount City. The store was located in Rogers, Arkansas, a rural town of budget-conscious shoppers. The Wal-Mart concept had evolved from a chain of Ben Franklin stores that Mr. Walton and his brother operated in Arkansas and Missouri as franchisees. When Sam took his discount retailing concept to Ben Franklin's management, they did not seem interested in it. He decided to set off on his own—and the rest, as they say, is history.

EXHIBIT 1	The World's Five Leading Global Retailers (2002)				
Rank	**Retailer**	**Sales ($bn)**	**Earnings ($mil)**	**Stores (#)**	**Nationality**
1	Wal-Mart	244.5	8,039	4,688	US
2	Carrefour	86.3	1,440	9,725	French
3	Ahold	81.7	n/a	8,800	Dutch
4	Metro	57.9	464	2,310	German
5	Tesco	45.8	1,178	2,291	British

Source: *DSN Retailing Today*, July 7, 2003, and *MMR*, May 26, 2003.

EXHIBIT 2

Global Market Penetration by International Retailers (2004)

Country	Global Retailers (no.)
France	14
Poland	13
Spain	12
Germany	11
USA	11
Belgium	11
UK	10
Thailand	10
Taiwan	10
China	10
Portugal	10
Czech Republic	10
Denmark	8
Netherlands	7
Italy	7

Source: Data from www.planetretail.net 2004.

Mr. Walton was an astute entrepreneur beyond compare. He quickly realized that volume and inventory-turn velocity were the defining elements of competitive advantage in the discount retail business. He was convinced that the concept would work in small towns with populations of 5,000 to 25,000 people, locations that often lacked viable retail alternatives. Armed with the conviction of a true entrepreneur, Mr. Walton and his brother had opened 18 Wal-Mart stores by 1969 when the company was incorporated formally. In a little over the three decades that followed, the company had 4,750 stores in a variety of formats across the globe, and sales had grown to roughly $245 billion. The company was widely seen as the beacon of shareholder value, the darling of investors, and the customer's champion.

Wal-Mart capitalized on its rural locations to establish important competitive advantages during its infancy. Many rural markets were characterized by populations that were scratching a subsistence level of living with very few employment alternatives. Mr. Walton saw this as a captive market that was tailor-made for a successful rollout of the discount retail model. It also proved to be a recruiter's paradise where a steady job at a decent wage was all that was needed to attract employees to staff its stores. Retail competition was minimal, and this allowed some flexibility in pricing merchandise, since price wars were unlikely. Local labor and real estate costs were also much lower compared to competitors who were focused on the larger cities. The

stores were decidedly austere in appearance. They were essentially big boxes illuminated brightly with fluorescent lighting, stocked with shelves that carried a wide range of merchandise. All of these advantages translated into a superior operating cost structure and a veritable fortress of profitability for Wal-Mart that its city rivals found impossible to duplicate.

The company was able to quickly expand its range of merchandise in becoming a convenient one-stop shop for a large rural base. However, the rural market strategy did come with its own challenges.

Wal-Mart initially found it difficult to persuade its suppliers to serve the remote stores that formed its network. This meant that inventories were replenished more slowly, leaving empty shelves and lost sales. Because inventory velocity was such an important part of Mr. Walton's original concept, the company was forced into building large warehouses to fill its own needs. This subsequently led to establishing its own logistics operations, complete with a fleet of trucks, and a private satellite system as well. All of this saved money and helped the company deliver on its promise to offer some of the lowest prices to its customers.

In becoming the largest company in the world, Wal-Mart spawned a wide range of best practices across all managerial functions. The wheel had turned full circle from the days when Mr. Walton would scour discount chain competitors for best practices, to a time when Wal-Mart was being constantly studied for new wisdom on management and strategy. Contemporary thinking on retail operations, location, and supply chain management was being shaped by Wal-Mart's success.

THE WAY THINGS WORKED

By 2003, Wal-Mart stores were located very close to major cities, mostly along the outer edges in the suburbs. The rural network was still intact and the company had stores in all 50 states in the United States. All stores were quite uniform, both in their external and internal appearance. A substantial part of the real estate was leased and custom-built by the property owners. Given the fact that many of the smaller communities had been blanketed with stores, the company started driving into suburbs. It was, however, not met with quite the same enthusiasm that it received in the rural settings. Local community activists in various parts of the country were banding together to use zoning laws to keep the big-box retailer out of their backyard. It was against this backdrop that Wal-Mart started conceptualizing new store formats that would have a small enough footprint to remain unobtrusive.

Irrespective of the store format, some of the fundamentals remained the same. Every prospective Wal-Mart shopper was greeted at the door by a cheerful greeter. Most of the greeters were senior citizens from the local communities. The company found that the greeters had the desirable effect of reducing pilferage as well, and the cheerful welcome did help the courteous image. The shelves were fully stocked with a wide range of products—over 120,000 in standardized layouts. The stores did not carry any backroom inventory, and this helped maximize retail selling space. Each store was broken down into smaller departments such as housewares, pharmaceuticals, and horticulture—each with a department manager in control. A substantial portion of employee bonuses was linked to departmental level performance, thus motivating employees to do their best within their assigned departments. Although centrally orchestrated, managers did have some leeway in adjusting prices to factor in local realities. Wal-Mart did not necessarily price its products below the lowest competitor price; instead, it aimed to set prices as low as possible. This meant that the prices did vary from store to store to reflect the level of competition that prevailed. The company did very little direct advertising. In contrast to competitors such as Target, who regularly featured glossy advertisements, Wal-Mart limited its advertising to 12 or 13 circulars a year. The circulars reflected the same bare-bones approach that the stores had adopted. There were no expensive models or glossy spreads. The company used its own associates as models for the circulars, and even used it as a motivational tool by choosing associates based on their performance.

Selling to Wal-Mart

The second worst thing a manufacturer can do is sign a contract with Wal-Mart. The worst? Not sign one.

— Anonymous Consultant[2]

Wal-Mart managed all its purchasing functions from its offices in Bentonville, Arkansas. It deployed a fairly small group of buyers who were charged with managing the entire buying function for the giant retailer. Manufacturers were not permitted to use middlemen or agents to mediate the relationship with the buyers. All negotiations were carried out in small, windowless offices with a décor that could be described as Spartan at best—"one fluorescent light, one table, one photo of Mr. Sam."[3] The buyers were tough negotiators and demanded a wide array of price and service concessions. For example, Mr. Katzenberg, CEO of Dream-Works, one of the world's leading movie companies, was requested by Wal-Mart to produce a customized video of *Shrek*, a mega-hit cartoon character, doing the Wal-Mart cheer, as a motivating tool for Wal-Mart associates. DreamWorks produced a suitable video in keeping with Wal-Mart's wishes. Despite the bare-knuckles negotiating environment, Mr. Katzenberg observed, "I've been there three times in the last 45 days. I cannot tell you how much I respect and love the bare-essentials efficiency . . . I'm flattered by the opportunity they've offered."[4] Indeed, Wal-Mart was the largest single revenue generator for Hollywood. The same was true of several other industries as well. For example, Wal-Mart in the U.S. was individually responsible for selling 35 percent of all pet food, 24 percent of all toothpaste,[5] the largest volume of jewelry, groceries, DVDs, CDs, toys, guns, diapers, sporting goods, bedding, and much, much more. Needless to say, this retail channel power was instrumental in helping establish a very favorable negotiating position for the company. Its purchasing volumes were gargantuan and the company had the power to bestow its riches on any supplier it chose. It was clear that the legion of over 30,000 suppliers needed Wal-Mart much more than Wal-Mart needed them, and they would do all they could to make sure that the retail giant was appeased and happy (see Exhibit 3).

Right from its inception, the company had employed a "national brand" strategy in its merchandising. By carrying all the well-known brands at relatively lower prices, it was able to demonstrate the superior value it brought to its customers. The national brands were also important from an advertising point of view. Because the manufacturers either ran large campaigns themselves or shared campaign expenses with retailers, Wal-Mart was able to proportionately reduce its advertising budgets. The national brand approach was also central to Wal-Mart's approach of capturing market share from its competitors. For example, in September 2003, well ahead of the peak of the toy season, Wal-Mart began discounting the price of a dancing toy, a sure winner from Fisher Price, a unit of Mattel, the leader in toys. It was priced at an amazing 22 percent below what Toys 'R' Us was charging. Wal-Mart believed that its discounting approach would help customers clearly see where the bargains were and help pull market share from its toy store rivals. After all, national brands were quite visible and sought after. Mattel, however, was quite concerned that its brand might be tarnished as a result of such discounting practices.

Once the stores had gained some recognition of their own, Mr. Walton launched the idea for in-store brands, starting with a dog food named Ol' Roy after his pet golden retriever. Since then, the company

| EXHIBIT 3 | Wal-Mart's Influence Over Its Suppliers |

Supplier Company	Main Products	% of Sales from Wal-Mart
Dial Corporation	Toilet soaps	28
Clorox Corporation	Liquid bleach	23
Mattel Corporation	Toys	23
Revlon	Perfumes/cosmetics	22.5
Procter & Gamble Co.	Toilet soaps, detergents	17
Energizer Holdings Inc.	Batteries	16.3
Kraft Foods	Packaged foods	12.2
Gillette Co.	Shavers, batteries	12
Kellogg Co.	Breakfast cereals	12

Source: Company annual reports.

leveraged its scale and shelf space to pit its own brands against those that are nationally established. The bad news for its suppliers was that Wal-Mart was winning big with its in-store brands. Ol' Roy, for example, was the world's biggest selling dog food, outstripping such established giants as Ralston Purina and Nestle. Nationally, the trend toward store brands was gathering momentum. According to a study by A. C. Nielsen, national brands grew by 1.5 percent in 2001 and 2002, but store brands grew by 8.6 percent. The loss of share for the national manufacturers had been so steep that many of them had shifted their manufacturing capacity to produce store brands for the leading retailers such as Wal-Mart.[6] One analyst estimated that about 40 percent of Wal-Mart revenues were attributable to its in-store brands, which ran the gamut from batteries to ibuprofen, from tuna to dog food, and most other items in between.[7]

Getting Wal-Mart supplier credentials was a laborious and taxing process. The company articulated very stringent requirements ranging from product quality, shipping, stocking, and in-store displays. It required all its suppliers to transact business using Retail Link, a proprietary electronic data interchange (EDI), an information processing system that allowed the electronic tracking of purchase orders, invoices, payments, and inventories. The company had moved to require some of its suppliers to incorporate RFID (Remote Frequency Identification Devices) technology in all their packaging. These RFID chips were small, unobtrusive chips that would form part of individual packages of goods that the suppliers sold through Wal-Mart. This technology would offer the company significantly enhanced capabilities in tracking sales of individual items within the stores, a potential gold mine of inventory and customer preference data. Although many suppliers had to scale a steep learning curve and make significant resource commitments to make their operations compatible with Wal-Mart's automated technology demands, there were tangible payoffs. Given the close linkage with Wal-Mart, the system allowed suppliers to monitor inventory levels and stock movements in each store. This was valuable in understanding customer preferences and also in predictive modeling to plan for inventory several months ahead of time. The company was a willing teacher, often educating its suppliers on the finer points of cost control and efficiency. It routinely dispensed advice to its suppliers on how they could redesign their product, packaging, or process to reduce costs. When Wal-Mart taught, the suppliers were willing pupils. Jack Welch, the former CEO of General Electric, once observed that he learned more about the customers who bought GE light bulbs from Wal-Mart's supplier reports than he did from his own marketing department. After all, the relationship between the manufacturer and the end user was no longer a direct one. It increasingly went through Wal-Mart.

Raising prices was unheard of. Suppliers who sent in invoices at higher prices compared to the past continued to be compensated at old rates. Wal-Mart simply ignored price increases. As a matter of management practice, it had even begun billing its suppliers for missed or delayed deliveries. It was experimenting with a new system called *Scan 'n Pay* under which suppliers would be paid for an item after it had been scanned out upon sale to a customer. Thus, the supplier was actually going to bear much of the risk associated with the goods that it had offered for sale at Wal-Mart. Suppliers had to participate in *Roll Back* campaigns which were essentially funded by selling at extremely low margins, often much lower than the already low margins that Wal-Mart negotiated. The roll back price offerings were meant to attract store traffic.

Rubbermaid's brush with Wal-Mart was a textbook example of the company's approach to supplier management. When resin prices rose by 80 percent, Rubbermaid was forced to increase its prices for plastics products that were bestsellers at Wal-Mart stores. Wal-Mart believed that Rubbermaid ought to absorb much of the price increases instead of passing it along to buyers. When Rubbermaid seemed disinclined to listen, Wal-Mart cut the shelf space it had allocated for Rubbermaid products and promoted competitors who were more willing to listen. Rubbermaid was soon forced into a merger with Newell as a consequence.

On-time delivery was not just a goal that suppliers aspired to reach—it was demanded as a prerequisite for a continued working relationship with Wal-Mart. On-time delivery meant that the products were expected to show up just as they were needed—not earlier, and certainly not later. There was an opportunity cost associated with empty shelf space, and the supplier who caused the stockout was held responsible for compensating the company. These penalties were typically deducted before Wal-Mart settled its payments with the supplier in question. The company used a supplier scorecard to keep track of the performance metrics of each of its suppliers. Much of this data was also accessible to the suppliers in the spirit of full transparency. In addition to superior supply-chain performance, suppliers were required to uphold quite stringent standards of employment and fair labor practices at all their manufacturing facilities worldwide. Wal-Mart deputed audit teams to ensure compliance at manufacturer locations. The range of standards included issues such as compensation and overtime pay, working conditions and environment, and discrimination. All suppliers were required to prominently display the Wal-Mart code of standards at their facilities. Although this had the desirable effect of emphasizing an image of honesty and fairness, critics often viewed these measures with suspicion, seeing them as public relations ploys.

In building its *Modular Category Assortment Planning System* (MCAP), Wal-Mart designated *category captains* in each product category. The category captain had to pull together a variety of such packages integrating its own products with those of other competitors. These packages had to take into account local demand patterns and preferences, store traffic flows, and mix of price points to fit with market needs. Some of the category captains designed over a thousand such integrated packages each year for Wal-Mart.

Suppliers employed a wide variety of strategies to sell to Wal-Mart. These options ranged from passive submission to the dictates of the giant retailer, to active engagement in maximizing their own piece of the Wal-Mart pie. Newell-Rubbermaid exemplified a creeping shelf-capture approach. It offered a wide range of largely nonseasonal, low-technology, high-volume essentials that were relatively low priced. It positioned itself as a single source for a large range of products that included a diverse portfolio spanning paint brushes, blinds, storage containers, plastic furniture, writing instruments, household tools, and cookware. Although seemingly diverse, the company used its portfolio to acquire more and more shelf space at the mass-market retailers. Wal-Mart accounted for 16 percent of Newell's sales in 2003. The company had positioned itself as a very responsive, highly flexible supplier, often taking the lead in proposing new ways to improve retailer efficiency. Newell was the originator of the legendary supplier scorecard that Wal-Mart used to rate all its suppliers. Its inventory management skills were admired at Wal-Mart to such an extent that Wal-Mart began using Newell as the benchmark for supplier performance. Newell had even invested a sizable sum in building a scaled version of a Wal-Mart store at its Bentonville office. It experimented with various in-store displays and storage optimization techniques, using its scale model of the store, before recommending alternatives to the giant retailer. It adopted a good, better, best approach to managing its product lines. Each line had options across the three price points. This provided the important benefit of capturing shelf space because the mass market retailer did not have to shop with multiple suppliers to fill out its offerings across a range of price points. Newell had multiple sales teams that specialized in each product line. Initially, this had the additional advantage of having different personnel negotiate with Wal-Mart buyers for distinct pieces for Newell's business. However, all its dealings with Wal-Mart were internally coordinated through a separate office dedicated to Wal-Mart and managed by a presidential level executive. It continuously sought to acquire new product lines by taking over poorly managed manufacturing operations. Every single acquisition had to meet the basic requirement of using the mass retailer as its primary sales channel. These acquisitions benefited from the pre-existing relationship with retailers such as Wal-Mart who were willing to give the new lines a shot in the marketplace. The company was very forthcoming in sharing its insights about its customers and product

C

ideas with Newell, all in the name of making Wal-Mart a more comprehensive shopping experience. After all, distribution channel access was half the battle.

Rayovac, the battery manufacturer, chose a different path in entrenching itself at Wal-Mart. To begin with, it offered prices that were about 20 percent lower than Duracell and Energizer, the competing battery brands. In some cases, it was able to offer 50 percent more product at the same price points as its competitors. This was an important encouragement to Wal-Mart, which proceeded to designate more shelf space for Rayovac products. Seeing the rise of Rayovac's market share, Wal-Mart declared that it would enter the battery business with its own private label. Although Rayovac shares dropped dramatically in response to the announcement, the company was able to work out a private label manufacturing arrangement with Wal-Mart, restricting the entry to alkaline batteries. The belief was that Rayovac's superior branding and dominant market share (>80 percent) in its high margin products, batteries for hearing aids, would be protected from the Wal-Mart juggernaut. This strategy had the twin benefits of giving Wal-Mart what it wanted and at the same time ensuring that Duracell and Energizer were held at bay. Rayovac had, in essence, used Wal-Mart to outrun its competitors. By 2003, Wal-Mart accounted for 26 percent of Rayovac revenues in a relationship that was very much similar to that between a vassal and the king. Rayovac even acquired Varta, a large battery manufacturer in Germany, to keep pace with Wal-Mart's globalization effort.

Leveraging Technology and Logistics

Wal-Mart was a leader in the use of technology to maximize operational efficiency. Very early on, the company realized the value of proactive investments in technology and deployed a private satellite network. The satellite network worked in conjunction with the EDI system and a point-of-sales system to capture store sales data in real time. Every time a customer made a purchase, the point-of-sales system transmitted the details of the transaction through the satellite network to the warehouses which were the staging grounds for inventory management. Wal-Mart had progressively moved from simple inventory management to data mining, an approach that offered the company rich insights into customer buying patterns. This allowed the company to better customize some of its offerings on a regional basis along with its usual traiting approaches which factored in local consumer tastes and preferences. These insights helped manufacturers understand regional differences much better and design their products accordingly.

The company managed much of its own logistics through a central hub-and-spoke system of warehouses and distribution centers. It was estimated that the corporate logistics department handled over a million loads each year. These central hubs were located in such a way as to cater to Wal-Mart stores within a 250-mile radius. All of them had easy access from interstates and were conveniently located in less-populated rural areas that were within driving distance from store concentrations. The warehouses were quite massive structures with loading and unloading bays on either side of the building. There was very little inventory storage in these centers. Instead, the company designed them to use cross-docking, a practice that allowed the transshipment of inventory from an inbound truck to an outbound truck that was loading to carry merchandise to the stores. The whole process was orchestrated through a system of conveyors within the warehouse to route the correct merchandise to each truck. Much of the seasonal merchandise was unloaded from trucks coming in from manufacturers to trucks that were outbound to stores in a matter of ten minutes. Distribution orders were generated based on previous-day sales, with allowances for weather patterns and seasonality. This resulted in a replenishment cycle that was only 48 hours long at most.

During the return leg of the trip to deliver merchandise, the trucks stopped off at manufacturer locations to haul inventory to the warehouses. This process, known as backhauling, minimized the need for contracted shipping services, and saved shipping costs. Instead, the suppliers had to pay a fee for using the Wal-Mart system for distribution. It was believed that most of the suppliers willingly did so because they were unable to match the efficiency levels that Wal-Mart's distribution setup offered. All suppliers were required to use the Retail Link system to keep the logistics planners in Bentonville informed about the availability of cargo for shipping to warehouses, thus enabling backhauling. It was a veritable logistics company with a level of efficiency that rivaled even dedicated trucking fleets. Appendix 1 provides indicators of comparative efficiency for major U.S. retailers.

Different Stores for Different Folks

By early 2004, Wal-Mart had come a long way from its big-box rural beginnings. It now operated four different store formats: Wal-Mart discount stores, Supercenters, Neighborhood Markets, and Sam's Clubs, in addition to its walmart.com online store (see Exhibit 4). Within the United States, the first three formats were referred to as *Domestic One* formats.

EXHIBIT 4   Store Formats, Target Markets, and Unique Features

Format	Size	Unique features
Discount Stores	40,000–120,000 sq. ft. 80,000 SKUs 1,600 in operation	• The original format for Wal-Mart in rural locations • Brightly lit atmosphere • Wide product selection ranging from apparel to lawn and garden items • Offered the initial learning for the firm in inventory management
Supercenters	110,000–220,000 sq. ft. 100,000 SKUs, of which 30,000 are grocery items 1,300 in operation	• Combines fresh vegetables, dairy products, and other groceries with nonfood items • Open 24 hours a day • Includes additional features such as a tire and lube outlet, restaurant, portrait studio, film processing, hair salon, bank, and gas station • Ideal vehicle to leverage the frequency of grocery purchase to increase spillover nonfood revenues
Neighborhood Markets	42,000–55,000 sq. ft. 24,000 SKUs	• Targeted toward the urbane city markets • Styled as a more modern retail format with contemporary fittings and fixtures • Carries an extensive range of fresh vegetables, fruits, dairy products, and other groceries • More accessible in-city locations • Offers a drive-through pharmacy, bakery, and an in-store coffee bar • Typically located in markets where Supercenters are located so that distribution synergies can be leveraged while reaching a distinctly different market audience
Sam's Clubs	110,000–130,000 sq. ft. 4,000 SKUs	• Geared toward the small businesses that buy in bulk and large families that might be attracted to buying in larger quantities to take advantage of price discounts • Warehouse format with little customer service • Requires an annual membership ($35 for individuals and $30 for small businesses) to shop at these stores

Appendix 2 provides comparative financial and operating statistics for major U.S.-based retailers that compete against Wal-Mart.

Culture, People, and Processes

By 2004, Wal-Mart was the largest employer in private industry worldwide. It counted over 1.3 million associates amongst its ranks. Mr. Walton had imparted a very strong sense of identity among his employees, which was largely rural at the time. The company employed a flat organizational structure with the store managers playing pivotal roles in linking management personnel in Bentonville with field operations.

Frugality was a central tenet at the company, and every associate was expected to fully adopt this value in all its manifestations. This meant that, as a matter of policy, all company travel was limited to economy class, although Wal-Mart had a fleet of 20 aircraft that ferried executives to various parts of its empire. Associates who traveled on buying trips to manufacturer locations were expected to stay in a budget motel. Even executives stayed two to a room and eschewed taxis to the extent possible. Wal-Mart's buyers sometimes called suppliers collect. New supplier proposals that lacked detail were returned at the expense of the suppliers. The company's headquarters were also reflective of the tightfistedness. They were housed in warehouse style buildings with a minimalist décor. Visitors had to pay for a cup of coffee or a soda even at headquarters.

The customer centric dictum permeated everything that Wal-Mart did. Mr. Walton had set out the basic tenets of the company upon its founding. These tenets included a "10-foot rule," which required every employee to greet a customer who came within ten feet of the employee. Mr. Walton exhorted all his associates to practice "aggressive hospitality," to exude caring, warmth, and hospitality towards every single customer who walked into the store. Given the rural roots of the company, these basic values of customer service became an integral part of the way in which Wal-Mart did business.

The company prided itself on the deep connections that it had with its associates. It offered a range of development opportunities spanning scholarships to college-bound associates, business skill acquisition programs, and a systematic mentoring program that paired successful managers with junior associates, to name a few. Almost all senior positions within the company were filled through promotions from within. Many amongst the upper echelon had started on the shop floor or in the warehouses and had moved their way up the ladder. Roughly 65 percent of Wal-Mart's management associates started out as hourly associates.

It hired locally for most of its foreign operations, supplementing the local workforce with a handpicked team of managers who had to go through a grueling program in the United States before they took charge of overseas operations. Employees who worked at the foreign stores had an equal chance at being promoted into management ranks and moved to headquarters. The company launched a new *Accelerated International Management Program* for a select group of associates who were identified for assuming leadership roles in international operations. This premier program was run collectively by the senior leadership of the company and focused on cross-border learning, knowledge

management, and international best practices. The company was quite receptive to the idea of job enrichment and job rotation as a means of developing its human resources. Many of these lateral and vertical moves resulted from an elaborate performance appraisal system that the company had developed. The appraisal included elements of the 360° feedback approach under which the associates were evaluated by their peers, superiors, and subordinates.

Harnessing a veritable army of associates did indeed pose important challenges. The company was accused of paying very low wages—about $8.23 an hour in the case of sales clerks, according to *Business Week*.[8] This amounted to $13,861 per year, below the federal poverty line of $14,630 for a family of three. Its record in terms of employee diversity also came under increasing fire. Some critics noted that although women comprised 90 percent of the customer service managers, they accounted for only 15 percent of store manager positions. This alleged unfair labor practice was the subject of a lawsuit in California. This lawsuit had the potential of ballooning into a major issue for the company since the judge was considering class action status so that a large number of plaintiffs might join the class action against the company. Wal-Mart associates nationwide filed 40 cases against the company, alleging that it sought to keep labor costs low by leveraging its clout to force employees to work overtime without offering overtime pay.[9] These transgressions were closely watched by the unions who had always wanted to bring Wal-Mart employees under their fold. The nonunion moniker was being chipped away. The first salvo had been launched by the meat-cutters in a store in Jacksonville, Texas, who won the right to unionize in early 2003. They would have been the first group in 41 years to bargain collectively with Wal-Mart but for an operational change that was instituted by the company. Wal-Mart announced that it would sell only pre-cut meat in its stores, with immediate effect.

IT'S A SMALL WORLD AFTER ALL

Wal-Mart first set foot outside the United States in 1991 when it acquired a minority interest in a joint venture with a Mexican company, Cifra, a retailer of repute. In a short span of time, the company set up operations in nine countries with over 1,300 stores system-wide. By 2003, international operations accounted for close to 17 percent of total revenues. It had started in textbook fashion, sticking close to home with forays into countries of geographic proximity such as Mexico, Puerto Rico, and Canada. After penetrating promising regions of South America, the company had ventured into Europe.

Wal-Mart evaluated market potential based on economic and political risk, growth potential, and availability of real estate for development. In countries where the market had become saturated, Wal-Mart used acquisitions to gain a toehold. In markets where land was easily available, it pursued organic growth. The acquisition strategy paid off in locations such as Puerto Rico and the United Kingdom, where the target firms were already adopting many of the core Wal-Mart practices, but in countries like Germany, there were big questions that remained.

The Americas

Wal-Mart launched its globalization efforts with an initial foray into Mexico with a local partner, Cifra. Boosted by the tremendous success of the Mexican operations, Wal-Mart increased its ownership position over time, and controlled 62 percent of Walmex, the joint venture, by 2004. The Mexican strategy was a blend of elements culled from the successful approach that the company had adopted in the United States, along with significant local twists. The partner, Cifra, brought along a range of store formats and retail outlets including restaurants, apparel stores, a chain of Bodega Aurrera stores targeted at the lowest income strata, and Superama stores which were geared to mid-dle- and high-income customers. The company managed to rationalize these different store formats, focusing on the Bodega stores as the primary vehicle for expansion along with Sam's Club and Supercenter concepts imported from the United States. After some initial hiccups, the Mexican operations became an important shot in the arm for Wal-Mart, contributing 26 percent of all international revenues. The company leveraged important location specific advantages in Mexico to grow a supplier base at relatively low cost and augment needs in other parts of the world. It held major buyer-seller meets and was able to groom close to 300 reliable suppliers with enough muscle to export to the United States and also pursue additional opportunities in other markets in the Wal-Mart empire (see Exhibit 5). The Mexican retail experience served as a good template for stores in Brazil and Puerto Rico as well. In Brazil, for example, Wal-Mart duplicated many of the defining features of its Bodega stores from Mexico in its Todo Dia stores that were geared toward the low income customer segment. The company also pursued opportunistic product expansion in Mexico to enter segments that were outside the scope of traditional retail operations. For example, it offered a money transfer service between the United States and Mexico that targeted the immigrant community. This

EXHIBIT 5	Wal-Mart's Global Empire		
Country	**Mode of Entry**	**Store Population**	**Associates**
Argentina	Greenfield	11 Supercenters, 1 Distribution Center	4,000
Brazil	Greenfield	13 Supercenters, 9 Sam's Clubs, and 2 Todo Dia stores	6,000
Canada	Acquisition	213 Discount Stores	52,000
China	Joint venture	21 Supercenters, 5 Sam's Clubs, and 2 Neighborhood Stores	15,000
Germany	Acquisition	92 Supercenters	15,500
Japan	Joint venture	400 Supermarkets	30,500
Korea	Acquisition	15 Supercenters	3,000
Mexico	Joint venture	124 Bodega Stores, 51 Sam's Clubs, 78 Supercenters, and 457 other stores	96,000
Puerto Rico	Greenfield; acquired local chains after entry	9 Discount Stores, 9 Sam's Clubs, 2 Supercenters, and 33 other stores	11,000
United Kingdom	Acquisition	247 Discount Stores, 21 Distribution Centers	125,000
United States		1,494 Discount Stores, 1,386 Supercenters, 56 Neighborhood Markets, and 532 Sam's Clubs	More than 1 million

C

service was so popular that the industry leader, Western Union, witnessed steep declines in its market share.

The company's fortunes outside Mexico were quite mixed. Brazil and Argentina had been quite unstable given the fluctuating fortunes of their respective economies. In Brazil, the company was a victim of intense price wars and strategic maneuvering by its rival, Carrefour, which adopted aggressive tactics. Wal-Mart accused its rivals of leaning on suppliers to choke its supply lines. Carrefour demonstrated a new variation of the "Everyday Low Price" strategy when its employees began distributing fliers in Wal-Mart parking lots showing price comparisons between the two stores on an almost real-time basis. Wal-Mart had also taken longer to climb the experience curve in these markets since its merchandising approach had to be rethought several times before it captured the attention of the local customers. Rivals such as Carrefour were much ahead in the merchandising game and were able to leverage their longer experience in South America to their advantage.

Europe

Breaking into Europe was quite difficult and expensive. Wal-Mart first set foot in Europe when it acquired Wertkauf, a German retailer that had fallen on bad times in 1997. It subsequently bought another chain, Interspar, to gain more reach and size in the country. It proceeded to import its own management team from the U.S. to convert these chains into Wal-Mart stores. Wal-Mart's rural culture did not blend well with German sensibilities, and integration soon became a flashpoint. The peculiarities of German law that prohibited some of the staple discounting approaches of the company, combined with the language differences and distinctive market preferences, further accentuated the problems. Local competition was quite strong, and the reigning leader, Metro, A.G., proved to be a formidable competitor. The home-grown management talent was surprisingly unable to implement the Wal-Mart way at the new acquisitions. As one analyst observed, "One of the surprises about Wal-Mart is how weak in conventional managers they are. They are very good at what they do in the Wal-Mart way. But you wouldn't put them in the same roles in other groups."[10]

Beleaguered by troubles in Germany, Wal-Mart decided to search for a better foothold in Europe and was attracted to Asda, a Wal-Mart look-alike that had a sizable footprint in the United Kingdom. Asda had imbibed some of the very same practices in inventory control, merchandising, and pricing that Wal-Mart had pioneered, right down to its own morning cheer. The acquisition proved to be phenomenally successful even at the steep price of £6.7 billion in 1999. Since Asda was a successful venture even at the time of the acquisition, and perhaps reeling from the bad experience at *Wal-Martization* in Germany, the company did not send in the troops of managers from Bentonville to oversee the Asda integration. Local managers were given much more leeway in decision-making. Asda managers actually helped Wal-Mart resuscitate its failing German business. They also developed new techniques in merchandising. John Menzer, the chief of Wal-Mart's International division, observed, "What we learnt from Asda is now incorporated in our systems in Korea, the U.S., South America, and everywhere."[11] One example was the adoption of the *George* line of fashion clothing that was developed by Asda. This line had proven to be such a powerful draw among the fashion-conscious buyers that Wal-Mart decided to bring the line to its operations in the U.S. as well. It was part of Wal-Mart's desire to expand its appeal to the up-market clientele that was the exclusive domain of Target, its competitor in the U.S. "As we grow around the world, it is important to our success that we exchange best practices among all the countries where we operate," observed Mr. Craig Herkert, Executive Vice President and COO of Wal-Mart International.

Although Asda had proven to be a remarkable success, the rivalry for supremacy in Europe was far from settled. Carrefour, Tesco, Ahold, and Metro were all fighting for the crown. Carrefour had a much wider reach and a portfolio of different store formats that seemed to give it an advantage in the marketplace where property was expensive. Tesco also proved to be a worthy rival since it, too, had originated with a "pile 'em high and sell 'em cheap" philosophy. It had expanded rapidly from its fresh-food origins as a grocer into non-foods and hard goods. It had also built a network of stores across significant markets in Europe, especially in developing countries and emerging markets of the old Communist world. These were regions where price was a key competitive weapon and being first counted a lot.

Asia

Wal-Mart's Asia strategy began to unfold in 1996 with the opening of a Supercenter and a Sam's Club in the economically rich region of Shenzhen in China. The company later established operations in Korea through an acquisition of four stores from Makro. Given the relatively high real estate costs in Seoul, Wal-Mart adopted a multistory format, with stores often encompassing six to eight stories. Japan was the third component of the Asia strategy. Wal-Mart built on its Mexican experience with joint ventures and initially entered

Japan through a minority joint venture with Seiyu, a well-established local retail chain. In two years, the company was quite happy with the results of the joint venture, and hence exercised its option to increase its holdings and become a majority partner. While China and Japan proved to be relatively successful entries, the performance in Korea was disappointing. Chains owned by the Korean *chaebols* had forged better supplier links than Wal-Mart could, and in a tradition-bound society, those ties were vital. These chains also had better access to real estate and, consequently, proved to be tenacious competitors.

China was especially promising since the company had been able to roll out many of its core strategies successfully. It bought 95 percent of its products locally, and even leveraged its Chinese supply network to export products worth $12 billion[12] to its U.S. operations and close to $20 billion by mid 2003. The company was China's eighth largest trading partner, ahead of Russia and the U.K. After entering Shenzhen, the company moved into Beijing through a separate joint-venture arrangement and also expanded to the rural heartland of the country. Asia was indeed a very promising market, but one fraught with challenges like the Korean experience had shown. It was clear that the company had a long way to go before it dominated these regional markets.

The value of the global network that Wal-Mart was building could be gleaned from a comment made by Mr. John Menzer, the Chief of International Operations at Wal-Mart. In describing the key elements of Wal-Mart's strategy for its apparel lines, Mr. Menzer observed, "Fashion starts in Europe. Next stop is now South America, because they are half a season behind. We're able to forecast U.S. buying patterns by what happens in South America. That is globalization."[13]

BEING BIG ISN'T SO EASY

As Wal-Mart moved forward to assert its dominance as the world's largest retailer, the road was not very clear. The company was increasingly coming under fire on a variety of fronts, ranging from employee compensation to supplier control and de facto censorship. On the competitive front, although there was no obvious threat that was readily visible, it was believed that the emergence of Dollar General and similar firms in the United States was serious enough to warrant a close watch. The mixed results of international expansion were yet another aspect that required long-term thinking.

Given the large size and reach that the company had built, many feared that it had grown to become too

powerful. For example, some recording artists contended that Wal-Mart filtered the music that it sold in its stores, thus acting as a self-appointed censor. Music that was believed to carry a message that did not blend with Wal-Mart's values was not sold in its stores. This, some said, had a chilling effect on creativity and was working toward homogenizing the marketplace by letting smaller towns dictate popular culture. The same filtering effect was noticed in magazines and books. Publications such as *Maxim* and *Stuff* were summarily banned from stores. The covers of magazines such as *Cosmopolitan, Glamour, Redbook,* and *Marie Claire* were routinely obscured with opaque binders. The enforcement appeared selective in the eyes of some. Wal-Mart claimed that it was just responding to the concerns expressed by the local community. The censorship even spread to drugs and medications. Wal-Mart was the only large pharmacy chain to refuse to stock *Preven*, a morning-after contraceptive manufactured by Gynetics that was legally approved for sale in the U.S. by the Food and Drug Administration. Gynetics' salespeople were apparently told that Wal-Mart did not want its pharmacists grappling with the moral dilemma of abortion. The drug, however, prevented pregnancies and did not cause abortions, according to the manufacturer. Mr. Roderick McKenzie, the founder of Gynetics, observed, "When you speak to God in Bentonville, you speak in hushed tones,"[14] although it did not seem to help Gynetics. Was Wal-Mart deciding what was good for the world?

Dollar Stores was a phenomenon that had the makings of a niche-based challenger. This company was catering to the low-income strata, "the salt of the earth" as it characterized it. The market was indeed sizable since 37 percent of all U.S. households earned less than $25,000 per year. Interestingly, this was also one of the fastest growing segments of the population. The Dollar General store was about 6,800 square feet—roughly 1/6 the size of the smallest Wal-Mart store. It kept its inventory low by trimming the variety of products it offered. It carried about 3,500 items on average, leaning more heavily on hard goods and non-perishables. It used an innovative pricing approach that comprised only 20 price points, ranging from $1 to $35. The simplicity of this system was an important factor in attracting a customer's attention to potential bargains. The stores did not offer special sales, nor did they use advertising to attract customers. They relied on word-of-mouth instead. Although it was a tough negotiator when it came to suppliers, the suppliers were indeed happy to do business with Dollar General. After all, they were assured that they would not be competing against the top brand in their category. Dollar General largely relied on a #2 brand approach, stocking a selection of five or six brands at most, a mix that typically excluded the top industry brand. The company had over 6,000 stores in the U.S., most of them in communities of less than 25,000 or in low-income urban neighborhoods. The company relished its locations that were close to the big-box retailers. Mr. Cal Turner, Jr., remarked, "We love to be next to them. We are in a different niche. We're a convenience bargain store, and our prices are excellent, relative to theirs. They run their promotions . . . we inherit the traffic."[15] The company had almost doubled its sales revenue in the five-year period from 1999 to 2003. Although with over $6 billion in sales (it was still not anywhere comparable in size to Wal-Mart), it did seem to have the ingredients of a disruptive innovator in the retailing world.

NOTES

1. Neil Buckley, "As annual sales reach $240bn, can Wal-Mart conquer markets outside the U.S.?" *Financial Times*, January 8, 2003.
2. "Is Wal-Mart too powerful?" *Business Week*, October 6, 2003.
3. J. Useem, "One Nation under Wal-Mart," *Fortune*, March, 3, 2003.
4. Ibid.
5. O. Thomas, "Lord of Things," *Business* 2.0, March 2002.
6. M. Boyle, "Brand killers," *Fortune*, August 11, 2003.
7. Ibid.
8. A. Bianco, and W. Zellner, "Is Wal-Mart too powerful?" *Business Week*, October 6, 2003.
9. M. Freedman, "Wal-Mart's Women Trouble," www.forbes.com, July 22, 2003.
10. N. Buckley, "As annual sales reach $240 bn, can Wal-Mart conquer markets outside the U.S.?" *Financial Times*, January 8, 2003.
11. Ibid.
12. For the year 2002.
13. N. Buckley, "As annual sales reach $240 bn, can Wal-Mart conquer markets outside the U.S.?" *Financial Times*, January 8, 2003.
14. A. Bianco and W. Zellner, "Is Wal-Mart too powerful?" *Business Week, October 6, 2003.*
15. W. Joyce, N. Nohria, and B. Roberson, *What Really Works.* New York: HarperCollins. 2003.

| APPENDIX 1 | Comparative Efficiencies of Leading U.S. Retailers |

Merchandiser	SPF 2000	SPF 2001	SPF 2002	Sq. ft. Basis	Avg. sq. ft. per Store	Sales per Store	Total Stores	Total sales ($000)
Costco	$763	$757	$771	gross	137,000	105,683,152	374	37,993,093
Sam's Club	$469	$491	$497	gross	124,462	61,857,561	525	31,702,000
Wal-Mart	$387	$406	$422	gross	135,195	55,924,898	2,875	244,524,000
Target	$268	$274	$278	selling	122,28	32,942,045	1,147	36,236,250
Kmart	$236	$235	$212	selling	73,601	15,603,348	1,829	30,762,000
Dollar Tree Stores	$238	$217	$199	selling	5,442	1,083,000	2,263	2,329,188
Dollar General		$142	$148	gross	6739		6113	
Home Depot	$415	$388	$370	gross	108,000	40,144,000	1,532	58,247,000

SPF = sales per foot

Source: www.bizstats.com/spf1.htm.

APPENDIX 2

Comparative Statistics for Large U.S.-Based Discount Retailers

Indicator	Wal-Mart 2001	Wal-Mart 2002	Wal-Mart 2003	Costco 2000	Costco 2001	Costco 2002	Dollar General 2001	Dollar General 2002	Dollar General 2003	Target 2001	Target 2002	Target 2003
Sales	193,116	219,672	244,524	31,621	34,137	37,993	4,550	5,322	6,100	36,851	39,826	43,917
Cost of sales	150,255	171,562	191,838	28,322	30,598	33,983	3,300	3,813	4,376	25,214	27,143	29,260
Operating expenses	31,550	36,173	41,043	2,805	3,207	3,648	935	1,136	1,297	8,218	8,924	10,181
Advertising expenses	574	618	676							824	924	962
Operating profit	11,311	11,937	13,644	1,037	992	1,131	1,250	1,509	1,724	3,419	3,759	4,476
Net income	6,295	6,671	8,039	631	602	700	71	208	265	1,264	1,368	1,654
Net income per share	1.4	1.49	1.81	1.35	1.29	1.48	0.21	0.62	0.79	1.4	1.52	1.82
Inventories	21,644	22,614	24,891	2,490	2,739	3,127	896	1,131	1,123	4,248	4,760	4,449
Long-term debt	12,501	15,687	16,607	790	859	1,211	720	339	330	5,634	8,088	10,186
Shareholder equity	31,343	35,102	39,337	4,240	4,883	5,694	862	1,041	1,288	6,519	7,860	9,443
Total stores	4,188	4,414	4,688	313	345	374	5,000	5,540	6,113	1,307	1,381	1,475
Total assets		83,527	94,685	8,634	10,090	11,620		2,552	2,333		24,154	28,603
International sales												
International assets												
Operating profit (Intl)												
ROS (Intl)												
ROA (Intl)												
Cost of sales/sales	0.78	0.78	0.78	0.90	0.90	0.89	0.73	0.72	0.72	0.68	0.68	0.67
Operating margin%	5.86	5.43	5.58	3.28	2.91	2.98	27.47	28.35	28.26	9.28	9.44	10.19
Net margin %	3.26%	3.04%	3.29%	2.00%	1.76%	1.84%	1.56%	3.91%	4.34%	3.43%	3.43%	3.77%
Inventory /sales	0.11	0.10	0.10	0.08	0.08	0.08	0.20	0.21	0.18	0.12	0.12	0.10
Inventory turns	6.94	7.75	8.08	11.37	11.70	11.59	3.68	3.76	3.88	5.94	6.03	6.35
Operating exp./sales	0.16	0.16	0.17	0.09	0.09	0.10	0.21	0.21	0.21	0.22	0.22	0.23
Adv. exp/sales	0.30%	0.28%	0.28%							2.24%	2.32%	2.19%
Sales/assets		2.63	2.58	3.66	3.38	3.27		2.09	2.61		1.65	1.54
Return on assets		7.99%	8.49%	7.31%	5.97%	6.02%		8.15%	11.36%		5.66%	5.78%
Return on equity		19.00%	20.44%	14.88%	12.33%	12.29%	8.24%	19.98%	20.57%	19.39%	17.40%	17.52%
Return on sales	3.26%	3.04%	3.29%	2.00%	1.76%	1.84%	1.56%	3.91%	4.34%	3.43%	3.43%	3.77%

Dell in China: The Strategic Rethinking

R. Muthukumar
Srinath Manda

ICFAI University Press, Business School Case Development Centre

Dell is changing the way computers are being sold in Asia.[1]

— Archana Gidwani, Analyst, Gartner Group

We worry more about ourselves than the competition. The thing that can trip us up is our own execution.[2]

— Michael Dell, Chairman, Dell Inc.

Dell, the world's largest computer vendor (Exhibit 1), offers network servers, workstations, storage systems, and ethernet switches for enterprising customers in addition to desktops and notebook PCs for individual consumers. The company also sells handheld computers and markets third-party software and peripherals (Appendix 1). Dell, with revenues of $41 billion in fiscal year 2004 (Exhibit 2), generates about 80 percent of its sales from desktop and notebook PCs[3] (Exhibit 3). Dell operates in 13 Asia Pacific markets, with plants in China and Malaysia, and had sales of $4,346 million in that region in fiscal year 2004 (Appendix 2). The company started focusing on China in 1998. With a population of 1.3 billion, the number of PCs sold in China in 2003 reached 22 million (second after the United States).[4] About 40 percent of the world's computers were made in China.[5] Dell's share of the PC market in China rose from less than 1 percent in 1998 to 7.4 percent in 2004.[6] But the local PC vendors like Legend and Founder in China began to give stiff competition to Dell in pricing. Due to this, Dell decided to change its strategy by withdrawing from the consumer market and to focus on servers and other high-end products.

EVOLUTION OF DELL IN CHINA

Michael Dell started selling personal computers directly to customers in Texas, bypassing intermediary retailers and distributors, in 1984. The company was named Dell Computer and international sales offices were established in 1987. In 1988 the company started selling to larger customers, including government agencies, and became a publicly traded company. Dell opened subsidiaries in Japan and Australia in 1993. It abandoned retail stores in 1994 to focus on its mail-order origins. In 1996 the company started selling PCs through its Web site.

Dell entered China in 1995. In 1998 the company started a production and customer facility in China. Dell advertised aggressively on billboards.[7] Its "just-in-time" model helped Dell to keep its inventory levels low at about six days' worth of supply, compared with 40 days of Chinese PC leader Legend. Dell's "built-to-order" strategy helped to maintain lower inventories, lower costs, and higher profit margins. Dell saved time and money that would otherwise be wasted on warehousing. Due to these strategies, in 1998 Dell's market share in China increased to 1.2 percent from less than one percent, while Compaq's, with the largest market share in the world at that time, fell from 3.5 percent to 2.7 percent.[8]

IBM, Compaq, and Hewlett-Packard, which entered the Chinese market in the early 1990s, gradually lost market shares when local companies such as Legend, Founder, and Tongfang began expanding. By 1999, Dell became the country's eighth-largest PC maker, with a 3.8 percent market share (Exhibit 4).[9]

Dell in China: The Strategic Rethinking by R. Muthukumar, under the direction of Srinath Manda. © ICFAI University Press & ICFAI Business School Case Development Centre, 2004. Reprinted with permission. www.icfaipress.org; www.icfaipress.org/books.

| Case 13 / Dell in China: The Strategic Rethinking

142

C

EXHIBIT 1 — Worldwide PC Shipments (2003–2004, 3Q)

Rank	Vendor	3rd Quarter 2004 (units in millions)	Market Share (%)	3rd Quarter 2003 (units in millions)	Market Share (%)	Unit growth (%)
1	**Dell**	**8.05**	**18.2**	**6.67**	**16.9**	**20.7**
2	HP	7.15	16.2	6.56	16.6	9.1
3	IBM	2.64	6	2.27	5.8	16.4
4	Fujitsu	1.73	3.9	1.56	4	10.7
5	Toshiba	1.6	3.6	1.38	3.5	16.5
6	Others	23.01	52.1	21.05	53.3	9.3

Source: www.itfacts.biz

EXHIBIT 2 — Dell (Global): Sales and Income (1997–2004)

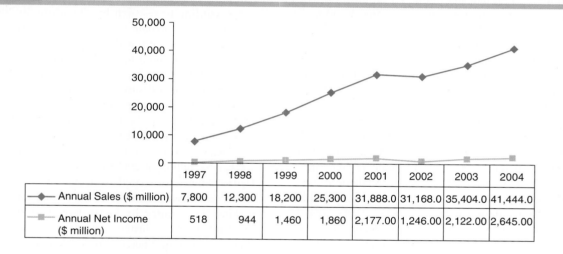

	1997	1998	1999	2000	2001	2002	2003	2004
Annual Sales ($ million)	7,800	12,300	18,200	25,300	31,888.0	31,168.0	35,404.0	41,444.0
Annual Net Income ($ million)	518	944	1,460	1,860	2,177.00	1,246.00	2,122.00	2,645.00

EXHIBIT 3 — Dell: Sales by Product (2004)

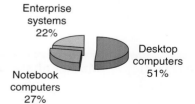

Enterprise systems 22%

Notebook computers 27%

Desktop computers 51%

	$ million	% of total
Desktop computers	21,026	51
Notebook computers	11,380	27
Enterprise systems	9,038	22
Total	41,444	100

EXHIBIT 4 — Top 10 PC Vendors in China (1999)

1. Legend
2. IBM
3. Hewlett-Packard
4. Founder
5. Compaq
6. Great Wall
7. Toshiba
8. Dell
9. NEC Japan
10. Acer

Source: Chowdhury, Neel, "Dell Cracks China," *Fortune*, Vol. 139, Issue 12, p. 120, June 21, 1999.

State-owned companies, MNCs, and government and educational institutions accounted for most of the PC sales in China. China was the fifth-largest PC market in 1999, behind the United States, Japan, Germany, and Britain. IBM, Hewlett-Packard, and other PC makers were focusing more on big nationwide technology projects.[10] Dell focused at the low-priced end of the PC market with direct sales. Internet users in China were relatively uncommon, so Dell made only 5 percent of its direct sales in China via the Internet, compared with 25 percent globally.[11] Dell maintained 110 toll-free numbers across China in 2000, to offer customers sales and technical support, and its sales personnel went around cities to enlist new customers. Dell concentrated on large enterprises, particularly state-owned companies of China, and gained two-thirds of its sales from them. In the Large Corporate Account (LCA) segment, which included firms with 1,500 or more employees, Dell had substantial repeat business. Within the LCA segment, five main industries accounted for 50 percent of Dell's business: government, education, telecoms, power, and finance.[12]

In order to give its customers better products and services, Dell introduced many models at lower prices. In addition to its previous products like Optiplex desktop PCs, Latitude notebooks, and PowerEdge servers for large businesses, it launched Dimension PCs to attract small and medium businesses. Dell offered a dramatic price drop in its 4500S Dimension PC model in 2000 to attract individual customers through its Web site at a relatively low price of $966. In retaliation, Legend reduced the price of a comparable PC, the Tianlin, by 14 percent, offering it for only $967. Dell's advantage was that through its direct sales model consumers could order computers online and over phone instead of through traditional stores.[13] In November 2000 Dell increased its capacity to 1.5 times more computer servers and twice as many desktops and laptops.[14]

In 2001, Dell moved its desktop production activities for the Japanese market from Malaysia to China since operating costs were cheaper there.[15] Dell introduced its SmartPC model in 2001, which targeted the low-end market, focusing on three different functions—Internet connectivity, entertainment, and educational programs for kids. A SmartPC was sold for about $600, while on an average a computer of other international brands required an investment of more than $1,000. Tongxi, the lowest-priced model offered by Legend, was sold for about $628.[16] The SmartPC helped Dell to become the top foreign supplier in China.

Chinese customers preferred to have a trial use of computers before buying them. Most of the suppliers believed that the best way to reach them was through vast retailing. Dell set up kiosks to demonstrate its SmartPC and other products[17] by which consumers could see and touch Dell's computers and other products instead of buying without seeing. Dell representatives explained technology, applications, system set-up options, and current purchasing programs to consumers.

According to research by ChinaInfo, in 2002 only 2.5 percent of urban Chinese households owned a computer, compared with 55 percent in the United States. China decided to withdraw tariffs on information technology products such as computers, telecom equipment, and software and the non-tariff trade barriers, such as quotas, licensing, and permits, by 2005.[18] In 2002, Dell set up its first research and development center outside the United States, in Shanghai, China.[19]

Dell's revenue in the Chinese computer market reached $8 billion in 2003, almost double that of 2002. Dell's China sales soared from 45 percent in 2002 to about 60 percent of its total Asia-Pacific sales in 2003, making the country its fourth-largest market, behind the United States, Britain, and Japan.[20] Dell's market share increased to 7 percent in the Chinese market while Legend's share decreased to 27 percent (Exhibit 5). China's Internet population grew by 28 percent in one year, to 87 million in 2003. The number of Internet users per computer in China was growing more rapidly than in the rest of the world (Exhibit 6). The computers

EXHIBIT 5	Top PC Vendors in China (2002–2003)			
	Company	**PC Shipments**	**Market Share (2003)**	**Market Share (2002)**
1	Legend	3,545,000	27%	30%
2	Founder	1,314,000	10%	10%
3	Tongfang	995,000	8%	6%
4	**Dell**	**860,000**	**7%**	**5%**
5	IBM	642,000	5%	4%
6	HP	442,000	3%	3%

Source: www.siliconstrategies.com

EXHIBIT 6	Growth of Internet Usage in China (2000–2004)

Year	Users	% of total
2000	22,500,000	1.70%
2001	33,700,000	2.60%
2002	59,100,000	4.60%
2003	69,000,000	5.40%
2004	87,000,000	6.80%

Internet Users—Top 10 Countries (2004)

	Country	Internet Users	Population	Internet Penetration	% World Users
1	United States	202,452,190	293,271,500	69.00%	25.30%
2	China	87,000,000	1,288,307,100	6.80%	10.90%
3	Japan	66,548,060	127,853,600	52.10%	8.30%
4	Germany	47,182,668	82,633,200	57.10%	5.90%
5	United Kingdom	34,874,492	59,595,900	58.50%	4.40%
6	South Korea	30,670,000	49,131,700	62.40%	3.80%
7	Italy	28,610,000	57,987,100	49.30%	3.60%
8	France	23,216,191	60,011,200	38.70%	2.90%
9	Canada	20,450,000	31,846,900	64.20%	2.60%
10	Brazil	19,311,854	179,383,500	10.80%	2.40%

Source: www.internetworldstats.com, September 30, 2004.

and high-speed Internet access cost less than in the United States or Europe. In November 2003, Dell set up a hardware support facility called an Enterprise Command Center (ECC) in Texas and opened another one in Xiamen, China, in 2004, to offer service to users. Dell planned to use the ECCs to continuously monitor, track, and manage service jobs from beginning to end.[21]

Growing Challenges

Despite these measures, Dell had been facing continuous pressure from the local PC manufacturers in China. According to Gartner, a research and analysis provider about the IT industry, prices and profit margins had been decreasing dramatically, and PC vendors aiming for increased market share were not making much profit. To survive in these market conditions, Dell had to either lower its quality and service levels, which would result in customer dissatisfaction, or maintain its quality and service levels and accept a decline in profits. So, Dell decided to change its existing focus from low-end consumer segment to high-end segment. This decision was made not only due to pricing pressure but was also a result of Dell's direct-sales model. Dell handled these functions from major cities, which led to complaints about slow delivery and poor service and support. The PC vendors started focusing on consumers in smaller cities and towns and

in rural areas. In 2004, Dell left the low-end consumer sector in China and cut its overall growth target due to stiff competition. The move came amid price wars at the low end of the consumer segment in China. The local competitors cut prices to as low as $360 per unit. Legend offered its PC model priced at $362. Langchao introduced a PC at $241. Dell's PCs aimed at this market, priced at $483, had been selling poorly. Dell decided to move into the high-end segment and focus on servers, printers, and data storage gear.[22] Apart from that, Dell raised its prices as much as 13 percent on several products.[23] Dell focused mostly on the corporate market. Despite this, Dell was China's third largest PC seller, with about 7.4 percent market share.

As a strategic move to benefit from the growing popularity of Linux (Appendix 3), an open source, stable, and cheaper operating system, Dell tied up with Oracle in China to offer Linux-based Oracle Software on its products.[24] The move was also influenced by the Chinese government's push for a national standard on open source software to counter the reign of Windows.

Dell captured a share of 24.1 percent in server shipments in 2004, while its PC shipments held third place, capturing a 7.3 percent share of the China market. Dell received the 2003 "Best Overseas PC Corporation" award from the China Centre of Information Industry Development (CCIID) at the 2004 China IT

Annual Conference[25] for its products' performance. But Legend and Founder Electronics both ranked ahead of Dell with market shares of 25.7 percent and 11.3 percent, respectively. Since 2002, the popularity of Legend, Dell's main competitor in China, had been declining. It had entered too many fields, and had lost focus on its core business of computers. This brought benefits to Dell to make sales inroads into Chinese government ministries and agencies, which had formerly been loyal Legend buyers. Legend (which changed its name to Lenovo as part of its rebranding campaign in 2004) started following Dell's direct sales model in China to grab the market share. Legend entered into an agreement to supply computer technology equipment for the 2006 Turin Winter Olympics and the 2008 Beijing Summer Olympics, which would help improve its brand recognition and create a global image. IBM and Legend planned to establish a joint venture in the PC business to tap the Chinese market.[26] China's PC market was estimated to grow by about 19 percent in 2004–05. Dell planned to make its PC plant in China into its primary production facility for all of north Asia, including Japan, Korea, and Taiwan. For both end-user and enterprising customers, Dell planned to provide high-quality products, support, and service—elevating the Dell customer experience in China to the highest possible level.[27]

Observers believe that the change in its strategy shows that Dell is confident about its market position and brand recognition in China, and does not feel the need to compete with other Chinese companies in the entry-level market. And there is the possibility that Dell will re-enter the market as some companies pull out of the market. According to Dell the move would mean that growth would slow from the current 300 percent unit sales growth to 200 percent.[28] Bill Amelio, president of Dell's Asia Pacific region, told *Reuters* in a telephone interview that the company could drop from third position to fourth position when IDC releases its data, due to a push by Tongfang Co. Ltd. in the educational sector. Other major foreign sellers in the market include Hewlett-Packard Co., which has been aggressive in China's consumer market, and IBM at the higher end of the market. Dell has focused most of its China PC efforts to date on the corporate market, where profit margins are typically higher.[29]

Kevin Rollins, Dell CEO, had slammed news reports that the PC leader had exited the low-end consumer market in China as a "misrepresentation" of the company's strategy. Reiterating that the company remains committed to both the consumer and business markets in China, he clarified, "What we will do from time to time is, we will emphasize or de-emphasize certain products and certain customer segments." He said that Dell constantly evaluates the relative strengths of its various markets. "What we might do from time to time, in Germany, in the U.S., in China, anywhere, is push ahead or pull back, based on the profitability characteristics. And if you look around the globe, and you look at the least profitable customer segments, it's in the consumer world. All the others are better. Dell never exits; we just emphasize or de-emphasize."[30]

NOTES

1. Chowdhury, Neel, "Dell Cracks China," *Fortune*, Vol. 139, Issue 12, p. 120, June 21, 1999.
2. Barker, Colin, "Dell is gathering speed in storage, printers and China—talks with Michael Dell about his confident push into new markets and his plans for globalisation," www.computing.co.uk, September 23, 2003.
3. Lower, Josh, "Dell Inc.—Company Fact sheet," www.hoovers.com.
4. "China Market Report—China Internet Market Brief," www.internetworldstats.com, October 27, 2004.
5. Lengel, Jim, "Teaching with technology—Technology in China," www.powertolearn.com, April 13, 2004.
6. Hamm, Steve; Kripalani, Manjeet; Einhorn, Bruce; and Reinhardt, Andy, "Tech's Future," www.businessweek.com, September 27, 2004.
7. "Dell Cracks China," op.cit.
8. Ibid.
9. "Dell puts classic strategy on back burner," Country Monitor, Vol. 8 Issue 3, p. 7, January 26, 2000.
10. "Dell Cracks China," op.cit.
11. "Dell puts classic strategy on back burner," op.cit.
12. Ibid.
13. Tanase, Corey, "Dell Computers in the China PC Market," www.babsonfreepress.com, October 10, 2002.
14. "Dell Upbeat on Chinese Market," www.china.org.cn, March 23, 2001.
15. Tham, Irene, "Dell transfers desktop production to China," www.zdnet.com, September 21, 2001.
16. "Dell entices China with cheap computers," www.news.com, November 29, 2001.
17. "Tech's Future," op.cit.
18. Xu, Shidong, "The China Syndrome," www.cio.com, September 1, 2002.
19. "PC Giant Dell Sets up R&D Center in Shanghai," www.china.org.cn, July 6, 2002.
20. "Dell-Oracle China tie-up may squeeze Microsoft," www.obsidian.co.za, March 3, 2004.
21. Perez, Juan Carlos, "Dell hopes support hubs will improve service delivery," www.computerworld.com, September 13, 2004.
22. "Dell gets out of China's low-end PC market," www.silicon.com, August 16, 2004.
23. Park, Andrew, and Young, Lauren, "Dell Outfoxes Its Rivals," www.businessweek.com, September 6, 2004.
24. "Dell-Oracle China tie-up may squeeze Microsoft," op.cit.
25. "Dell Leads China Server Market," www.dell.com, March 2, 2004.
26. "Lenovo, IBM to set up JV," www.chinadaily.com.cn, November 10, 2004.
27. www.dell.com
28. Denlinger, Paul, "China Business Strategy: Dell China Heads For Mid-Market," www.china-ready.com, August 16, 2004.
29. Young, Doug, "Dell exits low-end China consumer PC market," www.isyourjobgoingoffshore.com, August 16, 2004.
30. "Dell CEO slams China exit report," Business Times, www.it.asia1.com, October 12, 2004.

APPENDIX 1 — Dell: Products and Services

Products	Description
PowerEdge Servers	Servers used by businesses for carrying out complex applications
PowerConnect Switches	Used to connect computers with servers
Storage Products	Database storage systems with flexible scalability
Optiplex Desktops	Computers for corporate and institutional customers
Dimension Desktops	For small businesses and home users
Latitude Notebooks	Portable systems for corporate customers
Inspiron Notebooks	Portable systems for small businesses
Precision Workstations	Systems with computer-aided design, digital content creation, financial and economic modeling
Monitors	Square and flat panel monitors
Printers	Value imaging products
Handheld Computers	Systems with built-in features, color screens, extension slots to add memory
Peripherals	Offered in-house as well as third party peripherals like cameras, monitors, projectors, etc.
Services	Offered deployment and professional services and training and certification to business groups.

Source: www.dell.com

APPENDIX 2 — Dell: Sales by Region (2004)

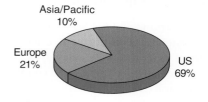

Asia/Pacific 10%
Europe 21%
US 69%

	$ million	% of total
US	28,603	69
Europe	8,495	21
Asia/Pacific	4,346	10
Total	41,444	100

APPENDIX 3 — Worldwide Server Customer Revenues by Operating System (in $U.S. billion), 2002 and 2007

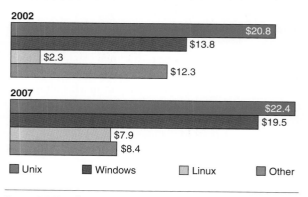

2002
- Unix: $20.8
- Windows: $13.8
- Linux: $2.3
- Other: $12.3

2007
- Unix: $22.4
- Windows: $19.5
- Linux: $7.9
- Other: $8.4

■ Unix ■ Windows □ Linux ■ Other

Source: Is It Time for Linux? www.emarketer.com, October 26, 2004.

Lucchetti

David Wylie
Srinivasa Rangan
Ed Cale

Babson College

In the spring of 2004, Andrónico Luksic was preparing to climb Mount Everest, the highest peak in the world. He believed that an accomplishment such as this one required both a clear vision and the support of the very best people, an underlying strategy that had served him well in his business ventures and that had earned him the reputation of having something of a Midas touch. So on this adventure he had hired the leader of a recent Chilean Everest expedition who had also been part of the team that had first conquered the perilous ascent of K2.

While this strategy had proved to be successful in many of his business dealings, it had not worked in his recent venture in Peru, and the experience still nagged at him. Lucchetti, his pasta company, had grown to the point where there was no room to expand in the Chilean market. The Peruvian market, however, looked extremely promising. Thus, in 1996 Lucchetti Peru was born.

By late 2003, however, the new state-of-the-art pasta plant was being liquidated. Luksic was considering whether he should leave the Peruvian market altogether and absorb a $150 million write-off or, alternatively, to continue and build a new plant to take advantage of what was left of the Lucchetti market share, even though it would require a considerable additional investment.

While Luksic's vast business empire, largely concentrated in Chile and operated under the Quiñenco masthead, was not in jeopardy, he liked to learn from every experience. Had this been a case of a good strategy plagued by Murphy's Law "everything that can go wrong will go wrong"? Was there something he should have known or was there a point where he or his trusted team members had made the wrong decision? The lesson to be gleaned from this failed Peruvian venture remained unclear and Luksic wanted to apply those lessons as he charted the course for future domestic and international expansion in this and other ventures.

THE LUKSIC GROUP AND QUIÑENCO

Founded by Andrónico Luksic Sr. in the early 1950s in the city of Antofagasta in northern Chile, the Luksic Group's initial activities were related to the mining industry, principally copper, the country's most important natural resource. By the early 1960s, the Luksic Group had expanded its interests to several other industries, thereby taking advantage of growth opportunities in key sectors of the Chilean economy such as metal processing, electric power distribution, general manufacturing, shipping, agriculture, fishing, food processing, and forestry.

David Wylie, Director of Babson College Case Publishing, prepared this case under direction of Professor Srinivasa Rangan and with the support of Professor Ed Cale and the Institute of Latin American Business of Babson College, as a basis for class discussion rather than to illustrate either effective or ineffective handling of an administration situation. Reprinted by permission.

EXHIBIT
1

Organizational Structure of Quiñenco (as of March 31, 2003)

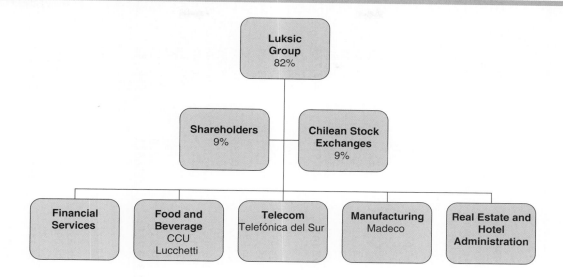

Between 1970 and 1973, when the activities of the private sector in Chile were restricted, the Luksic Group expanded into Argentina, Colombia, and Brazil, moving into sectors such as metal manufacturing, agriculture, and vehicle distribution. Nonetheless, when restrictions eased in Chile in 1974, the Luksic Group renewed its interest in Chile, most notably in the mining sector. Subsequent expansion led to diversification in telecommunications, banking, food and beverages, hotels and railways.

Quiñenco, formerly named Forestal Quiñenco S.A., was established in 1957 and was originally engaged in logging and supplying wood to the Chilean coal mining industry, principally for use in the fabrication of supports for underground tunnels. In the mid-1960s, Andrónico Luksic Sr. acquired a majority interest in the company.

In 1996, the Luksic Group ownership structure was reorganized. All financial and industrial investments were placed under the control of Quiñenco, while mining and railway investments remained part of Antofagasta plc. This new structure simplified control within the Luksic Group and opened the doors to the capital markets for Quiñenco. By 1996, the Luksic Group beneficially owned approximately 82.4 percent of the shares of Quiñenco. (See Exhibits 1 and 2.)

In June 1997, Quiñenco succeeded in raising US$280 million on the New York and Chilean stock exchanges. At roughly the same time, the Luksic Group pushed ahead with the Los Pelambres mining project,

which by 2003 had become one of the world's largest copper mines.

Quiñenco's Strategy

Following the 1996 reorganization, Quiñenco formalized its hitherto informally understood strategy: "to maintain its position as Chile's leading diversified company in the industrial and service sectors, to strengthen the value creation potential of its existing businesses, and to continue expanding into the Southern Cone region and Brazil while seeking opportunities for entry into new and complementary products or industry sectors." Key elements of this strategy included the following excerpts from some of the firm's publications:

Strengthen Value Creation in Core Businesses

Strengthen the ability of each of our businesses to generate value for our shareholders. For certain businesses, this may be through a strategy of growth and market leadership. For other businesses, we may seek to increase productivity and efficiencies, in some cases through restructuring. In each of its existing businesses, we will promote the adoption of "best practices" from leading competitors and industry peers, the identification of synergies across business units, and the attraction and retention of high-quality personnel.

In the consumer product packaging sector (including Lucchetti), we expect long-term value creation to come from increases in productivity and

EXHIBIT 2

Quiñenco Financial Statements

Balance Sheet
Millions of Chilean Pesos

	1995	1996	1997	1998	1999	2000	2001	2002
	As of Dec. 31, 1995	As of Dec. 31, 1996	As of Dec. 31, 1997	As of Dec. 31, 1998 Restated as of Dec. 31, 1999	As of Dec. 31, 1999 Restated as of Dec. 31, 2000	As of Dec. 31, 2000 Restated as of Dec. 31, 2001	As of Dec. 31, 2001 Restated as of Jun. 30, 2003	As of Dec. 31, 2002
Assets								
Cash	5,814	13,793	6,023	3,353	5,623	5,002	4,324	5,038
Time Deposits	33,792	426	53,535	36,938	137,027	15,016	17,832	6,730
Marketable Secs.	151,275	36,383	4,554	7,980	6,237	4,397	1,454	2,222
Accounts Rcvbl.	172,450	94,935	136,252	126,149	97,834	108,617	94,492	71,601
Other Rcvbls.	18,622	15,141	21,413	27,454	4,021	6,053	9,418	3,314
Inventories	76,936	71,389	76,761	85,122	84,648	86,799	81,033	63,417
Other Assets	44,188	31,117	46,101	119,732	66,759	158,035	65,171	106,269
Total Current Assets	**503,077**	**263,184**	**344,639**	**406,728**	**402,149**	**383,919**	**273,724**	**258,591**
Building/Install	79,017	74,859	102,560	117,829	142,686	204,300	199,868	188,838
Land	13,075	13,121	21,697	24,457	24,452	24,550	25,024	23,589
Machinery/Equip.	187,012	210,433	259,889	312,906	335,150	341,982	383,284	403,405
Telephone Plant	99,485	123,703	146,006	138,175	65,094	NA	NA	NA
Other/Constr.	74,729	87,279	97,652	105,806	82,857	60,236	73,653	55,137
Revaluation	NA	NA	NA	NA	NA	26,820	25,399	25,978
Depreciation	(118,259)	(128,825)	(172,570)	(201,981)	(209,306)	(235,765)	(276,910)	(304,481)
Goodwill	60,114	67,508	71,395	81,491	109,352	140,437	356,848	341,554
Investments	191,685	222,324	272,524	301,790	359,966	407,643	489,598	493,161
LT Notes Rcvbl.	NA	NA	NA	176	38	39	40	4,739
Other Assets	8,567	27,236	214,678	27,461	46,833	52,310	57,552	32,726
Total Assets	**1,098,502**	**960,824**	**1,358,480**	**1,314,838**	**1,359,271**	**1,406,471**	**1,608,080**	**1,523,237**
Liabilities								
Accounts Payable	63,293	52,829	69,463	49,142	64,517	71,827	47,887	36,881
Related Acct Pay	24,830	18,217	4,206	22,764	377	472	434	322
Accrued/Other	21,377	19,411	54,086	31,791	86,859	30,488	28,678	23,362
ST Bank Loans	162,040	116,485	89,132	91,537	94,096	160,013	125,464	107,329
Cur.Port.LT Debt	46,794	40,759	64,567	62,342	62,396	75,330	61,181	135,928
Total Current Liabilities	**318,334**	**247,702**	**281,454**	**257,576**	**308,245**	**338,130**	**263,644**	**303,822**
Long Term Debt	220,400	185,582	271,567	300,463	213,824	225,343	324,317	302,490
Bonds/Notes Pay.	28,094	45,937	32,957	32,124	29,844	68,119	215,574	199,736
Total Long Term Debt	**248,494**	**231,519**	**304,524**	**332,587**	**243,668**	**293,462**	**539,891**	**502,226**

	1995	1996	1997	1998	1999	2000	2001	2002
Minority Int.	168,096	187,116	279,916	211,829	104,130	105,499	92,566	79,314
Accrued/Other	5,792	5,142	7,177	5,861	10,783	12,618	14,280	7,363
Total Liabilities	**740,716**	**671,479**	**873,071**	**807,853**	**666,826**	**749,709**	**910,381**	**892,725**
Shareholder Equity								
Common Stock	84,181	254,942	382,202	409,001	428,224	441,499	454,744	454,744
Reserves	157,099	7,862	11,543	12,602	15,683	17,286	25,357	41,418
Retained Earning	116,508	26,541	91,667	85,380	248,538	197,978	217,601	134,353
Total Equity	**357,788**	**289,345**	**485,412**	**506,983**	**692,445**	**656,763**	**697,702**	**630,515**
Total Liabilities & Shareholders' Equity	**1,098,504**	**960,824**	**1,358,483**	**1,314,836**	**1,359,271**	**1,406,472**	**1,608,083**	**1,523,240**
S/O-Common Stock	925	1,024	1,080	1,080	1,080	1,080	1,080	1,080
Total Common Shares Outstanding	NA	1,024	1,080	1,080	1,080	1,080	1,080	1,080

Income Statement
Millions of Chilean Pesos[6]

	1995 12 Months Dec. 31, 1995	1996 12 Months Dec. 31, 1996	1997 12 Months Dec. 31, 1997 Restated as of Dec. 31, 1999	1998 12 Months Dec. 31, 1998 Restated as of Dec. 31, 2000	1999 12 Months Dec. 31, 1999 Restated as of Dec. 31, 2001	2000 12 Months Dec. 31, 2000 Restated as of Dec. 31, 2002	2001 12 Months Dec. 31, 2001 Restated as of Dec. 31, 2002	2002 12 Months Dec. 31, 2002
Net Sales	413,869	411,413	566,712	578,978	438,987	479,744	488,258	396,299
Total Revenue	**413,869**	**411,413**	**566,712**	**578,978**	**438,987**	**479,744**	**488,258**	**396,299**
Cost of Sales	302,000	299,259	409,451	417,209	357,164	383,003	387,902	315,941
Sell./Gen./Admin.	79,732	75,703	112,048	113,397	103,495	80,095	82,315	70,080
Total Operating Expense	**381,732**	**374,962**	**521,499**	**530,606**	**460,659**	**463,098**	**470,217**	**386,021**

continues

C

EXHIBIT 2 *(Cont'd)*

	1995	1996	1997	1998	1999	2000	2001	2002
Interest Expense	(35,851)	(36,291)	(42,856)	(49,272)	(43,136)	(39,242)	(60,780)	(50,727)
Interest Income	NA	NA	10,129	20,197	20,971	9,041	8,177	5,348
Non-Operating Inc.	NA	NA	199,286	50,048	285,818	35,325	106,024	33,542
Non-Operating Exp.	NA	NA	(22,733)	(14,059)	(54,912)	(36,139)	(71,878)	(85,688)
Price-level Restate.	NA	NA	(7,931)	(7,854)	13,581	(6,343)	(10,951)	(8,896)
Other, Net	99,182	39,189	NA	NA	NA	NA	NA	NA
Net Income Before Taxes	**95,468**	**39,349**	**181,108**	**47,432**	**200,650**	**(20,712)**	**(11,367)**	**(96,143)**
Provision for income Taxes	8,595	4,804	28,747	7,199	23,098	(7,541)	(4,893)	(141)
Net Income After Taxes	**86,873**	**34,545**	**152,361**	**40,233**	**177,552**	**(13,171)**	**(6,474)**	**(96,002)**
Minority Interest	8,244	(5,498)	(66,641)	(11,939)	(4,504)	7,174	22,448	20,522
U.S. GAAP Adjustment	(2,634)	25,285	(11,074)	(23,718)	10,843	(14,496)	(4,733)	(4,008)
Net Income Before Extra Items	**92,483**	**54,332**	**74,646**	**4,576**	**183,891**	**(20,493)**	**11,241**	**(79,488)**
Accounting Change	NA	NA	NA	NA	NA	0	2	5,909
Net Income	**92,483**	**54,332**	**74,646**	**4,576**	**183,891**	**(20,493)**	**11,243**	**(73,579)**

Ratios	1995	1996	1997	1998	1999	2000	2001	2002
Return on Equity	26%	19%	15%	1%	27%	–3%	2%	–12%
Return on Sales	22%	13%	13%	1%	42%	–4%	2%	–19%
Asset Turnover	0.38	0.43	0.42	0.44	0.32	0.34	0.30	0.26
Debt to Equity	207%	232%	180%	159%	96%	114%	130%	142%

6 Chilean Pesos per US$ as of January 1 of each year.

1995	1996	1997	1998	1999	2000	2001	2002	2003
400.8	406.5	424.5	438	471.66	529.15	573.9	679.11	696.5

efficiency, the restructuring of certain operations, as well as long-term growth in Chile, Peru, Argentina and Brazil.

In the pasta sector, we will seek to improve production and enhance distribution efficiencies, volume growth in Chile in line with increasing consumption, and volume growth outside of Chile through overall market growth and increases in market shares.

Continue Managed Expansion in the Southern Cone Region and Brazil

We believe that our management experience, the location of our facilities and the strength of our products, services and distribution networks position us to take advantage of growth opportunities elsewhere in South America, with a particular emphasis on the neighboring countries of Argentina, Peru, and Brazil.

Our approach to international expansion is managed and gradual. As it has done in the past . . . we may first choose to develop an export-based presence and, once a customer base, distribution network and critical mass are established, to construct manufacturing facilities in the foreign markets.

Alternatively, as it has done in the past with CCU[1] in Argentina and Madeco in Argentina and Brazil, we may choose to establish an immediate foreign presence via acquisitions of existing local firms. Given the leading market shares that our Chilean businesses already enjoy, we believe that growth in neighboring countries will be a key component of our long-term development. By participating in an expanded four-country market, we seek to participate not only in the growth of these economies, but also to make significant gains in market share, as it has already done in the beer business in Argentina and the pasta and metals manufacturing businesses in Argentina, Brazil and Peru.

Form Strategic Alliances

We intend to continue, where advantageous, to form strategic alliances in Chile and abroad and to capitalize on the benefits provided by these strategic relationships.

Acquire and Divest Businesses to Create Value

Quiñenco's strategy is to create value for shareholders through the acquisition and active management of a diversified group of complementary businesses through long-term controlling stakes or strategic alliances. In pursuing this strategy, the Company considers and will consider from time to time

acquiring control of, or making substantial new investments in, other companies engaged in the industrial, services, and financial sectors, with a geographic focus on the Southern Cone region and Brazil. We intend to focus on products and services where its existing strengths—such as its management expertise, strategic partners or distribution networks—offer competitive advantages. In addition, we have divested several businesses and will evaluate future divestitures, particularly when we believe that the opportunity to divest creates more value for shareholders than retaining the business.

LUCCHETTI

Lucchetti Empresas S.A. was founded in the early 1900s and was purchased by the Luksic group in 1965. With the reorganization in 1996, it became a 93.7 percent consolidated subsidiary of Quiñenco. Its pasta, edible oils, soups, and broths were known for quality, nutritional value, and competitive prices. Lucchetti was continuously launching new products under its household brand names such as Lucchetti, Napoli, Talliani, Romano, Miraflores, Oro Vegetal, El Dorado, Doña Sofia, and Naturezza.

Lucchetti's strategy revolved around making the most of its brand names with the idea of holding and building the strong market share it had earned over the years. By 1996, Lucchetti reached 38 percent of the Chilean pasta market. Carozzi, its main competitor in Chile, had a 39 percent market share. The balance was spread among a number of smaller manufacturers and pasta importers such as Molinas Rio de la Plata from Argentina and Alicorp from Peru. Lucchetti's profit margins were relatively high since a number of its products were placed in the higher end of the price and quality spectrum. (See Exhibit 3).

With powerful competition and sales growth slowing, in 1994 Lucchetti management realized that future expansion in Chile would stem from growth of the overall market rather than from gains in market share. The challenge was to find new growth opportunities. With prior success in distributing and marketing pasta products in Argentina but with little presence in Peru, expansion in these two markets appeared most promising. Furthermore, with a rise in sales volume, the company ultimately considered the construction of production facilities in Argentina.

The consideration of entering Peru was buoyed by the success of Madeco, another Luksic holding that had successfully entered the Peruvian market in 1993 by acquiring a controlling interest in Indeco S.A., the largest Peruvian manufacturer of copper cable.

EXHIBIT 3

Lucchetti Peru SA Financial Statements

Balance Sheet
Thousands of US$, December 31 of each year

	1995	1996	1997	1998	1999	2000	2001	2002
ASSETS								
Current Assets								
Cash	$ 23	$ 52	$ 3,526	$ 1,253	$ 686	$ 1,008	$ 2,665	$ 1,705
Term Deposits	$ –	$ –	$ –	$ –	$ –	$ –	$ 559	$ 466
Accounts Receivable	$ 903	$ 2,032	$ 7,339	$ 4,815	$ 7,555	$ 9,690	$ 6,666	$ 4,407
Accounts Receivable from Personnel	$ –	$ –	$ 21	$ 18	$ 7	$ 725	$ 6	$ 10
Accounts Receivable from Shareholders	$ –	$ –	$ 23	$ –	$ –	$ –	$ –	$ –
Other Receivables	$ 10	$ 95	$ –	$ 213	$ 214	$ 45	$ 68	$ 45
Inventory	$ 461	$ 1,128	$ 4,177	$ 879	$ 918	$ 746	$ 772	$ 384
Finished Goods	$ –	$ –	$ –	$ 4,167	$ 1,685	$ 1,504	$ 1,210	$ 1,523
Goods in Process	$ –	$ –	$ –	$ 31	$ 14	$ 4	$ 7	$ 1
Raw Materials	$ –	$ –	$ –	$ 2,250	$ 304	$ 942	$ 532	$ 485
Packaging and Shipping Materials	$ –	$ –	$ –	$ 247	$ 271	$ 242	$ 229	$ 179
Other Supplies	$ –	$ –	$ –	$ 45	$ 219	$ 214	$ 215	$ 227
Prepayments for Inventory	$ 1	$ 15	$ 8,517	$ 4,721	$ 6,199	$ 3,051	$ 667	$ 1,959
Deferred Expenses	$ 679	$ 434	$ 2,272	$ 1,830	$ 1,248	$ 1,238	$ 885	$ 412
Prepaid Charges	$ 23	$ 255	$ 9	$ 583	$ 655	$ 678	$ 390	$ 349
Fiscal Credit of IGV	$ 266	$ 904	$ 7,716	$ 11,197	$ 10,484	$ 6,945	$ 1,085	$ 1,017
Advances Granted	$ 45	$ 2,268	$ 313	$ 365	$ 1,140	$ 83	$ 192	$ 268
Accounts Receivable from Affiliates	$ –	$ –	$ –	$ –	$ –	$ 261	$ –	$ –
	$ 2,412	$ 7,182	$ 33,913	$ 32,615	$ 31,602	$ 27,376	$ 16,148	$ 13,169
Factory, Machinery, and Equipment								
Land	$ –	$ 1,798	$ 1,798	$ 1,798	$ 1,798	$ 1,798	$ 1,798	$ 1,798
Cost	$ 35	$ 590	$ 28,051	$ 44,196	$ 52,957	$ 53,073	$ 51,357	$ 51,337
Depreciation	$ (2)	$ (12)	$ 21	$ (91)	$ (1,913)	$ (3,055)	$ (3,814)	$ (5,157)
Machinery in Transit	$ –	$ –	$ 2,030	$ 105	$ 101	$ 103	$ –	$ –
	$ 33	$ 2,376	$ 31,858	$ 46,008	$ 52,943	$ 51,919	$ 49,342	$ 47,978
Fiscal Credit	$ –	$ –	$ –	$ –	$ –	$ –	$ 5,383	$ 5,278

continues

Other Fixed Assets								
Securities	$ —	$ —	$ 10	$ —	$ —	$ —	$ 170	$ 170
Intangible Assets	$ —	$ —	$ —	$ 6,898	$ 6,456	$ 6,719	$ 1,874	$ 1,874
Amortization	$ —	$ —	$ —	$ —	$ (1,086)	$ (2,299)	$ (633)	$ (908)
Total Other Fixed Assets	$ —	$ —	$ 10	$ 6,898	$ 5,370	$ 4,420	$ 1,411	$ 1,136
Total Assets	$ 2,445	$ 9,557	$ 65,782	$ 85,521	$ 89,915	$ 83,715	$ 72,284	$ 67,560
LIABILITIES and EQUITY								
Current Liabilities								
Bank Line of Credit	$ —	$ 131	$ 5	$ 139	$ 9	$ 39	$ 361	$ —
Taxes Payable	$ 12	$ 65	$ 790	$ 134	$ 160	$ 380	$ 222	$ —
Compensation Payable	$ —	$ 26	$ 82	$ 153	$ 226	$ 331	$ 215	$ 158
Vacation Accruals	$ 3	$ —	$ —	$ —	$ —	$ —	$ —	$ 259
Domestic Accounts Payable	$ 69	$ 802	$ 6,848	$ 2,665	$ 4,066	$ 2,788	$ 1,270	$ 1,783
Foreign Accounts Payable	$ 1,488	$ 1321	$ 68	$ —	$ —	$ —	$ —	$ —
Other Payables	$ 714	$ —	$ —	$ 2	$ 116	$ 1,274	$ 1,273	$ 1,380
Other Accounts Payable	$ 3	$ 14	$ 624	$ 678	$ 852	$ 1,360	$ 472	$ 516
Payables to Affiliates	$ —	$ —	$ —	$ 3,922	$ 867	$ 721	$ 100	$ 32
Loans from Affiliates	$ —	$ 1,103	$ 10,128	$ 26,096	$ 28,959	$ 14,417	$ 5,912	$ 2,643
Loans from Banks	$ —	$ —	$ 734	$ 27,836	$ —	$ 1,246	$ 2,448	$ 2,295
Leases Payables	$ —	$ —	$ 21,522	$ —	$ —	$ —	$ —	$ —
Total Current Liabilities	$ 2,289	$ 4,098	$ 40,801	$ 61,625	$ 35,255	$ 22,556	$ 12,272	$ 9,065
Long Term Liabilities								
Taxes Payable—REFT	$ —	$ —	$ —	$ —	$ —	$ —	$ 91	$ 7
Loans from Affiliates	$ —	$ —	$ —	$ —	$ 6,221	$ —	$ 4,367	$ 5,040
Loans from Foreign Banks	$ —	$ —	$ 26,000	$ 26,000	$ 12,600	$ 18,350	$ —	$ 4,400
Leases Payables	$ —	$ —	$ —	$ —	$ —	$ 12,177	$ 9,818	$ 8,072
Total Long Term Liabilities	$ —	$ —	$ 26,000	$ 26,000	$ 18,821	$ 30,527	$ 14,276	$ 17,520
Social Benefits	$ 3	$ 6	$ 24	$ 27	$ 29	$ 36	$ 25	$ 21
Equity								
Capital	$ 1,420	$ 10,205	$ 16,728	$ 30,035	$ 83,291	$ 84,179	$ 110,644	$ 110,644
Accumulated Profits/(Losses)	$ —	$ (1,315)	$ (4,754)	$ (17,777)	$ (32,167)	$ (47,489)	$ (57,615)	$ (64,934)
Profit (Losses) for Period	$ (1,218)	$ (3,437)	$ (13,017)	$ (14,390)	$ (15,323)	$ (6,093)	$ (7,319)	$ (4,756)
Exchange Rate Adjustment	$ (49)	$ —	$ —	$ —	$ —	$ —	$ —	$ —
Total Equity	$ 153	$ 5,453	$ (1,043)	$ (2,131)	$ 35,802	$ 30,596	$ 45,710	$ 40,954
Total Equity and Liabilities	$ 2,445	$ 9,557	$ 65,782	$ 85,521	$ 89,915	$ 83,715	$ 72,284	$ 67,560
Sales	$ 1,525	$ 11,998	$ 30,625	$ 32,433	$ 36,203	$ 44,906	$ 33,921	$ 25,590
Cost of Sales	$ 1,522	$ 12,271	$ 32,828	$ 32,738	$ 33,537	$ 36,398	$ 27,323	$ 20,652
Gross Margin	$ 3	$ (273)	$ (2,202)	$ (305)	$ 2,666	$ 8,508	$ 6,598	$ 4,938

EXHIBIT 3 *(Cont'd)*

	1995	1996	1997	1998	1999	2000	2001	2002
Cost of Operations								
Administration	$ 180	$ 604	$ 1,006	$ 1,474	2,628	2,295	2,242	1,212
Marketing	$ 1,038	$ 2,132	$ 3,307	$ 2,412	1,614	977	1,211	1,103
Selling Expenses			$ 4,521	$ 5,983	4,366	4,330	4,640	3,612
Other Operating Expenses					1,020	231	273	264
	$ 1,218	$ 2,736	$ 8,834	$ 9,599	$ 9,628	$ 7,833	$ 8,366	$ 6,191
Gain (Loss) from Operations	$(1,215)	$(3,010)	$(11,045)	$(9,904)	$ (6,962)	$ 675	$ (1,768)	$ (1,255)
Other Income and Expenses	$ 2	$ 427	$ 1,972	$ 4,486	$ 8,361	$ 6,768	$ 5,551	$ 3,501
Net Income (loss)	$(1,217)	$(3,437)	$(13,017)	$(14,390)	$ (15,323)	$ (6,093)	$ (7,319)	$ (4,756)
Cumulative Net Losses	$(1,217)	$(4,645)	$(17,671)	$(32,061)	$(47,384)	$(53,477)	$(60,796)	$(65,552)
Cumulative Operating Losses	$(1,215)	$(4,255)	$(15,270)	$(25,174)	$ (32,136)	$(31,461)	$(33,229)	$(34,484)
Sales	100%	100%	100%	100%	100%	100%	100%	100%
Cost of Sales	100%	102%	107%	101%	93%	81%	81%	81%
Gross Margin	0%	–2%	–7%	–1%	7%	19%	19%	19%
Cost of Operations								
Administration	12%	5%	3%	5%	7%	5%	7%	5%
Marketing	68%	18%	11%	7%	4%	2%	4%	4%
Selling Expenses	0%	0%	15%	18%	12%	10%	14%	14%
Other Operating Expenses	0%	0%	0%	0%	3%	1%	1%	1%
	80%	23%	29%	30%	27%	17%	25%	24%
Gain (Loss) from Operations	(80%)	(25%)	(36%)	(31%)	(19%)	(2%)	(5%)	(5%)
Other Income and Expenses	0%	4%	6%	14%	23%	15%	16%	14%
Net Income (Loss)	(80%)	(29%)	(43%)	(44%)	(42%)	(14%)	(22%)	(19%)
Ratios								
Return on Equity	–795%	–63%	1248%	675%	–43%	–20%	–16%	–12%
Return on Sales	–80%	–29%	–43%	–44%	–42%	–14%	–22%	–19%
Asset Turnover	0.62	1.26	0.47	0.38	0.40	0.54	0.47	0.38
Debt to Equity	1,498%	75%	–3,914%	–2,893%	99%	74%	27%	22%

THE MARKET OPPORTUNITY IN PERU

The Peruvian pasta market appeared to be ripe for harvesting. Consumption rates of 8 to 9 kilos per capita per year were virtually identical to those of Chile, but the competition was only beginning to offer packaged pasta. Indeed, packaged pasta had historically accounted for a relatively small proportion of total Peruvian pasta consumption, with pasta sold in bulk accounting for approximately 95 percent of all Peruvian pasta sales prior to 1993. Packaging remained rudimentary by Chilean standards.

The main players in the market were still offering lower quality pasta that was produced in older production facilities. Peruvian pasta was generally made of flour rather than from the higher-quality semolina. Prices for pasta were nearly US$900 per ton compared to about US$1,000 per ton in the Chilean market or US$1,200 per ton in Argentina. Clearly there was an opportunity for Lucchetti to enter the market as it had in Argentina by selling pasta imported from Chile and, once sufficient volumes had been achieved, to build a plant in Peru. In addition, Lucchetti managers believed that there were opportunities to gain better margins by offering pastas marketed at the higher ranges of the price spectrum as Peruvian consumers gained greater spending power and learned to appreciate higher-quality pasta products.

Competition in Peru

At the end of 1994, Lucchetti learned that one of the largest companies in the food industry, La Fabril, a holding of the Bunge & Born Group, was for sale at auction. Lucchetti bid US$98 million but lost to its rival, the Romero Group, which acquired La Fabril for US$214 million. Romero merged La Fabril with its subsidiary Peru-Pacifico, the second largest edible oils producer in Peru. Two years later, Romero further consolidated these companies with its traditional flour and producer subsidiary, Nicolinni Hermanos S.A., to create Alicorp S.A. This became the 3,000-pound gorilla of the Peruvian pasta market. Alicorp was one of the largest private economic groups in Peru with interests in banking, port handling, and consumer products distribution. Its holdings represented the fourth largest company in Peru accounting for over 2 percent of the Peruvian GDP and was the dominant market leader in wheat flour, cookies and crackers, pasta, edible oils, and margarines and shortening. Its massive distribution network reached 90 percent of all points of sale, carrying 400,000 tons of goods per year. Industry analysts considered this to be a key advantage, since in Peru only 10 percent of food was sold in supermarkets, compared with 60 percent in most other Latin American countries. The majority of food sales were through 35,000 small neighborhood mom-and-pop stores.

The Romeros had been one of Peru's largest farmers of cotton, but the military government had nationalized all landholdings in 1969, including the family's farms. It was not until 1990 with the Fujimori reforms that they reentered the cotton business and quickly took control of 30 percent of the market.

Carrozzi, Lucchetti's main competitor in Chile, had also decided to enter Peru. Instead of choosing to begin with exporting, however, it purchased the Peruvian company Molitalia (which had 18 percent of the Peruvian market). However, Carrozzi never changed the name or built a new facility, so that Peruvian consumers still generally considered Molitalia to be a domestic company. Indeed, Lucchetti had considered the possibility of buying Molitalia, but rejected the idea since it lacked the production facilities or the reputation of offering the high-quality pastas that formed the basis for Lucchetti's market positioning. Molitalia was, however, upgrading some of its plants in order to raise quality and lower costs, using much of the same equipment and technology that Lucchetti had incorporated into its award winning plant in Santiago.

Luksic and Lucchetti management therefore thought that, in spite of the strength of the competition, Peru represented a great opportunity. The Peruvian government had attempted to make foreign investment attractive by allowing foreign investment returns to be taxed at the same rate that was effective when the investment was initially made. It allowed foreign investors to repatriate profits without restriction, and there was no discrimination between local and foreign investors. Peru had a basically sound and growing economy, prices would go up, and the demand for higher-quality pasta could be exploited. While some members of the Lucchetti board privately expressed concerns about this tactic, they consented in the face of such strong enthusiasm from Andrónico Luksic. The Peruvian pasta seemed ripe for conquest. Lucchetti management was confident in its ability to venture forth without any partners since it already had the internal capabilities for such expansion.

Politics in Peru

Alberto Fujimori, originally elected president of the republic of Peru in 1990, was overwhelmingly re-elected in 1995 to an additional five-year term. Fujimori had proven to be a man of strong will and many surprises. Soon after first taking office he implemented an economic shock program, quickly dubbed "Fujishock." He launched an anti-corruption campaign that resulted in many firings and prosecutions and aggressively attacked guerrilla insurgents. Encountering congressional opposition, Fujimori and the armed forces overthrew his own government. In the 1992 "autogolpe" (or "Fujigolpe"), Congress was dissolved, many judges were fired, and secret military courts were established for terrorism trials. Later that year the anti-terror campaign had decisive successes against Sendero Luminoso when its leader and most members of its central committee were captured. Both Alan García Pérez and Mario Vargas Llosa went into voluntary exile.

A new constitution promulgated in 1993 provided for presidential re-election to a second consecutive term. By 1995, Fujimori was overwhelmingly popular. Although there was great concern with human rights violations in the war against terror, including death squad activities and village massacres as well as secret trials, the level of violence had fallen and the guerrilla organizations were weakened. The Fujishock had made life difficult for domestic manufacturers, workers, and the poor, but on the other hand, the economy was growing and inflation was low. Relations with international lenders were good and foreign investment was flowing in. Fujimori easily won re-election over former UN Secretary General Javier Pérez de Cuéllar, becoming the first Peruvian president ever elected to two consecutive terms. Fujimori thus appeared to have a strong grasp on the political machinery so that any political risk of a foray into Peru seemed minimal.

1995 AND THE BEGINNINGS OF PERUVIAN OPERATIONS

The decision was made to begin the Peruvian operation in stages. Lucchetti would start by building up market share and volume with pasta imported from Chile until a volume was attained that would support building a separate production facility in Peru. The Chilean plant had some extra capacity, but not enough to support the anticipated demand in Peru.

While 90 percent of the distribution channel was represented by small neighborhood mom-and-pop stores, Lucchetti thought that development of its own distribution capabilities for pasta and other related products such as edible oil, milk, soups, creams and bouillons, dehydrated milk, and packaged rice would be an important strategic aspect of the Peruvian venture. Lucchetti initially decided to form a partnership with a local distributor, Richard O. Custer y Compania, for direct sales and distribution. Custer would receive

between 16 percent and 18 percent of net sales. Meanwhile, Lucchetti would retain control of the brand management, advertising, and importing. Lucchetti was positioned as a premium brand—"Quality at an affordable price."

Lucchetti thought that pasta might be a loss leader but by creating a distribution network it might use for other food products it could become a very important component of a larger business. Lucchetti believed a strong distribution network would be its primary source of competitive advantage in what was a fragmented market.

On June 13, 1995, Lucchetti Peru SA (LP) was incorporated as a subsidiary of Empresas Lucchetti S.A. de Chile, which retained 98 percent of the ownership. In August, the first shipments arrived from Chile.

Early results were promising and confirmed, at least in part, the projection that quality pasta would be in demand in Peru. In the first six months of operations, LP spent just over US$1 million in advertising and generated US$1.5 million in sales. At first, prices were set at close to parity with competing brands to generate exposure and volume, but LP executives expected to be able to raise prices to levels comparable to those in Chile. In 1995, pasta prices were somewhat lower in Peru than elsewhere, but a premium product such as that offered by Lucchetti, they surmised, should be able to justify a premium price.

Because the cost of importing pasta was so high compared to the introductory or launching prices, the cost of goods sold was virtually equal to sales. Gross margins, therefore, were only US$3,000 in 1995. (See Exhibit 2, Lucchetti Income Statement.)

1996

Sales continued to grow in 1996 and as capacity to produce in the Chilean plant outstripped the demand in the Peruvian market, LP started to import pasta from Italy at $760 per ton. Aggressive competitive pricing in Peru, however, and the continuing high costs of importing pastas, prompted Pacheco and his colleagues to consider accelerating the construction of a plant in Lima. The alternatives under consideration were either to build the plant to supply the Peruvian market by the second half of 1997 or to wait to build until ItalPasta, from whom LP was importing from Italy, was no longer capable of supplying the market. Estimates were that this milestone would be reached in 2000.

LP management, in a report assessing the merits of building the plant, recommended, "We should tackle this manufacturing project as soon as possible to fully exploit favorable market trends by ensuring

TABLE 1	Market Share in Lima		
	1994	**1995**	**March 1996**
Nicolini*	23.7	19.3	16.7
Don Vittorio*	30.0	33.4	28.7
Moliatia	18.1	23.6	22.5
Lavaggi*	5.8	6.1	5.1
Cogorno	6.0	7.3	7.9
Others	16.4	10.3	7.8
Lucchetti	0	0	11.3
*Alicorp Brands	66.5	58.8	50.5

Note: Alicorp S.A. was formed from the merger of Consorcio de Alimentos Fabril-Pacífico S.A. and Nicolini S.A. in October 1996.

the quality of our product and taking advantage of the weak position of the competition" (Proyecto Peru, "Factibilidad Planta Industrial," March 1996). (See Table 1, Market Share in Lima.) In assessing the projected return on investment for this plant, Lucchetti typically used the hurdle rate of 12 percent for foreign investments. In order to remain conservative in its projections, it assigned no terminal value to the project. Overall, Quiñenco's weighted average cost of capital was 9.5 percent in 1996.

This same assessment made a number of assumptions: 30 percent market share would be attained by 2003, the pasta market would grow at a rate of 1.5 percent per year, and prices, after emerging from the current doldrums, would start to rise at an annual rate of 4 percent by 1997 and would stabilize in 2000 at a level where gross margins would be 50 percent before distribution costs. Distribution costs were estimated to drop from 17 percent to 13.5 percent of sales by 2000. Supply of grain would be totally sourced from Canada for Peruvian production at US$230 per ton. Marketing costs, after an initial burst of US$2 to US$3 million, would level off at 6 percent of sales by 2002. (See Exhibit 4).

In late March of 1996, the final decision was made to move ahead with construction (see Table 2).

Several months after the decision was made, apparently in an effort to support established Peruvian pasta makers who were losing market share, the Peruvian government increased the import duty tariff from 15 percent to 20 percent, and imposed a 5 percent additional duty on wheat derivative products, exacerbating the need to build domestic production. Among the beneficiaries of this tariff was Alicorp, from whom LP had already captured over 11 percent of the market share.

By July, plans were finalized for a plant very similar to that in Chile, a state-of-the-art facility that had won an international award for best industrial design in 1992. Pacheco estimated that the new plant, with the capacity to produce 35,000 metric tons, would save LP about $153 per metric ton. This would represent a savings of about $5.4 million on estimated 1997 sales of 35,000 metric tons. Production from any excess capacity could be exported.

In September, LP purchased a 60,000 square meter property for US$1.8 million in the township of Chorillos on the southern outskirts of Lima, bordering the Pantanos de Villa wetlands. This location offered good access from the highway and ready access to a nearby port facility, promising to offer substantial savings on transportation of all the grain they would need to import once the plant neared capacity. Until the plant reached the capacity to merit improving the port facility to specifications, LP personnel decided to bring the grain through a facility just north of Lima.

The central government had nothing to do with awarding the required permits to build there, but Pablo Gutierrez, the mayor of Chorillos, thought that the plant would add significant employment to the area. In late July, therefore, LP applied for an authorization to build and a certificate of compatibility from both the district of Chorillos and the city of Lima.[2] While the usual practice in Peru was to build first and seek building and operating permits once the facility was complete, Pacheco wanted to do everything above board and according to regulations.

The plant was designed to reflect LP's concern for the sensitive environment of the neighboring wetlands. Water would be taken from sources that did not draw on the swamp's aquifer, special noise abatement treatments were included that would reduce the total noise to below the level of the traffic on the adjacent highway, and efforts were made to protect the wildlife from reflection, noise, and light. In October, an environmental impact statement prepared by the environmental consulting firm Ecofish S.A. was submitted to INRENA, the institute for natural resources in Peru in charge of improving environment. It was not accepted, however, for administrative reasons.

On December 5 the mayor of Chorillos, Pablo Gutierrez, granted LP a construction license to install a fence around the property.

Meanwhile sales continued to grow in 1996 to US$12 million. Another US$2 million had been devoted to advertising. Net operating losses for the year were US$3 million.

EXHIBIT 4 · 1996 Pro Forma Income Statement and Statement of Cash Flow

PRO FORMA INCOME STATEMENT

	1996	1997	1998	1999	2000	2001	2002	2003	2004	2005	2006	2007
Sales	$ 12,296	$ 23,950	$ 31,318	$ 35,363	$ 42,981	$ 49,646	$ 56,524	$ 63,972	$ 64,707	$ 65,650	$ 66,445	$ 67,414
Cost of Sales	$ 9,233	$ 15,416	$ 15,137	$ 16,802	$ 20,800	$ 24,025	$ 27,350	$ 30,955	$ 31,306	$ 31,762	$ 32,144	$ 32,612
Gross Margin	$ 3,063	$ 8,534	$ 16,181	$ 18,561	$ 22,181	$ 25,621	$ 29,174	$ 33,017	$ 33,401	$ 33,888	$ 34,301	$ 34,802
Cost of Operations												
Administration	$ 735	$ 1,483	$ 2,801	$ 2,861	$ 3,023	$ 3,023	$ 3,083	$ 3,190	$ 3,190	$ 3,190	$ 3,190	$ 3,190
Marketing	$ 2,190	$ 3,250	$ 2,505	$ 2,517	$ 2,794	$ 2,979	$ 3,391	$ 3,838	$ 3,882	$ 3,939	$ 3,987	$ 4,045
Distribution Expenses	$ 2,090	$ 4,071	$ 4,854	$ 5,574	$ 5,802	$ 6,702	$ 7,631	$ 8,636	$ 8,735	$ 8,863	$ 8,970	$ 9,101
Depreciation	$ —	$ 617	$ 1,852	$ 2,184	$ 2,551	$ 2,906	$ 3,204	$ 3,260	$ 3,319	$ 3,379	$ 3,483	$ 3,440
Gain (Loss) from Operations	$ (1,952)	$ (887)	$ 4,169	$ 5,425	$ 8,012	$ 10,012	$ 11,865	$ 14,094	$ 14,274	$ 14,518	$ 14,717	$ 15,027
Financing Costs	$ —	$ 320	$ 742	$ 907	$ 1,074	$ 1,269	$ 1,457	$ 1,655	$ 1,769	$ 1,793	$ 1,817	$ 1,843
Net Income (loss)	$ (1,952)	$ (1,207)	$ 3,191	$ 3,927	$ 6,185	$ 6,885	$ 7,626	$ 8,011	$ 7,789	$ 7,633	$ 7,458	$ 7,403

PRO FORMA STATEMENT OF CASH FLOW

	1996	1997	1998	1999	2000	2001	2002	2003	2004	2005	2006	2007
Net Income (Loss)	$ (1,952)	$ (1,207)	$ 3,191	$ 3,927	$ 6,185	$ 6,885	$ 7,626	$ 8,011	$ 7,789	$ 7,633	$ 7,458	$ 7,403
Plus Depreciation	$ —	$ 617	$ 1,852	$ 2,184	$ 2,551	$ 2,906	$ 3,204	$ 3,260	$ 3,319	$ 3,379	$ 3,483	$ 3,440
Cash from Operations	$ (1,952)	$ (590)	$ 5,043	$ 6,111	$ 8,736	$ 9,791	$ 10,830	$ 11,271	$ 11,108	$ 11,012	$ 10,941	$ 10,843
Plus Financing Costs	$ —	$ 320	$ 742	$ 907	$ 1,074	$ 1,269	$ 1,457	$ 1,655	$ 1,769	$ 1,793	$ 1,817	$ 1,843
Changes in Sales Taxes Due	$ (1,091)	$ (654)	$ 2,011	$ —	$ —	$ —	$ —	$ —	$ —	$ —	$ —	$ —
Changes in Working Capital	$ 39	$ (4,520)	$ (3,191)	$ (1,150)	$ (1,876)	$ (1,676)	$ (1,739)	$ (1,869)	$ (198)	$ (238)	$ (211)	$ (244)
Import Rights	$ (92)	$ (367)	$ (610)	$ (1,160)	$ (1,164)	$ (871)	$ (180)	$ —	$ —	$ —	$ —	$ —
Capital Investment	$ (11,386)	$ (19,449)	$ (4,386)	$ (4,853)	$ (4,694)	$ (3,942)	$ (737)	$ (712)	$ (712)	$ (712)	$ (712)	$ (712)
Gross Cash Flow	$ (14,482)	$ (25,260)	$ (391)	$ (145)	$ 2,076	$ 4,571	$ 9,631	$ 10,345	$ 11,967	$ 11,855	$ 11,835	$ 11,730
Interest Payments	$ —	$ (320)	$ (742)	$ (907)	$ (1,074)	$ (1,269)	$ (1,457)	$ (1,655)	$ (1,769)	$ (1,793)	$ (1,817)	$ (1,843)
Amortization of Short Term Debt	$ —	$ 5,811	$ 1,860	$ 1,150	$ 1,876	$ 1,676	$ 1,739	$ 1,869	$ 198	$ 238	$ 211	$ 244
Net Cash Flow	$ (14,482)	$ (19,769)	$ 727	$ 98	$ 2,878	$ 4,978	$ 9,913	$ 10,559	$ 10,396	$ 10,300	$ 10,229	$ 10,131

Project IRR 1996–2007 10.480%

TABLE 2

Projected Investment Requirements for New Plant (US$ millions)

1996	1997	1998	1999	2000	2001	2002	2003	Total
16.2	14.6	4.4	0.7	8.5	4.4	0.7	0	49.5

Alicorp was active during 1996 as well, consummating the acquisition of Consorcio de Alimentos Fabril-Pacífico S.A. and Nicolini S.A. in October.

1997

Planning and permitting efforts continued into 1997, while sales continued to boom. LP's market share grew to 20 percent mostly at the expense of the giant Alicorp.

Alicorp was meanwhile in the process of building a new pasta plant using the most advanced technology to attain a production capacity of 220,000 tons. It was also beginning construction of a mill, located near the pasta plant, to allow flour production for both its pasta and cookie production.

On April 11, Lima's Comisión de Habilitación Urbana de la Municipalidad de Lima (Urban Habilitation Commission), acting on a LP request for partial approval, approved a preliminary urban plan, and on May 23, the Municipality of Chorillos granted LP a provisional construction permit. The mayor of Chorillos declared that a "simultaneous administrative process" was possible, allowing for permissions procedures to take place while the factory was being built. The municipal director of urban development, however, added that such authorization was possible only if it was approved by the municipality of Lima and a definite approval was expected.

Construction proceeded full steam ahead, led by a Peruvian contractor, JJ Camet Contratistas Generales, a firm owned by the sons of then Peruvian minister of economics Jorge Camet (minister between March 1993 and May 1998). Still outstanding were the environmental impact approval and a definitive study on the impact on the urban environment.

At that point, in an effort to address any future environmental concerns, LP added Carlos Aramburu to the staff as head of quality control and environmental compliance. His responsibilities included supervising all construction to meet building codes and environmental restrictions. Aramburu, with the blessing of senior Lucchetti executives, decided to meet both ISO 9002 and 14001 standards. These were even more than Peruvian regulators had asked for, but the objective was to exceed all regulatory requirements. Indeed, this was the first use of ISO 14001 for a pasta plant in Peru, and LP was the first to receive both ISO designations in Peru.

With construction in full swing, at first everything looked promising and it seemed as though many of the early obstacles had been surmounted. In late May, however, the press started to express concerns about the factory's larger-than-expected size. As it turned out, just on the other side of the swamp was a resort area used by a number of prominent politicians and business people and several golf clubs, one of which was owned by the Romero family, the primary owner of Alicorp. The mayor of Lima, Alberto Manuel Andrade, weighed in against the LP plant as well, citing his concerns about the environmental impact the plant might have on the neighboring wildlife preserve. The son of an old military family and indoctrinated in long-standing rivalries between Chile and Peru, Andrade held the powerful position of mayor of Lima, which many thought was the most powerful political office next to the president of Peru. Indeed, he led the opposition party to Peruvian president Fujimori.

Pacheco dismissed this turmoil, thinking that it represented only an expected reaction to the construction of any large project. He suspected, however, that it might be the result of the political influence of the Romero group during a reelection period of Alberto Andrade for mayor.

Other industrial neighbors to the LP plant appeared to escape the same level of criticism that LP was facing. Somehow, Pacheco surmised, the rules were different for them. U.S.-owned Kimberly-Clark operated a factory next door to the LP facility that used cut fiber cellulose as a raw material and had been penalized on two occasions by the Environmental Police because of a leakage of liquid residues into the swamp. Another U.S.-owned company, 3M, had a distribution and fractioning facility less than a kilometer south whose drainage went right into the swamp. Vegallona, the CEO of the anti-drug government office, owned Globe International, a dye and flavoring plant on the other side of the swamp that also drained its waste directly into the wetlands. There had never been any suggestion that any of these facilities should comply with ISO 9002 or 14001.

In July, the Direccion de Desarrollo Urbano de la Municipalidad de Lima approved the preliminary studies concerning the industrial use of the LP property. The Direccion General de Obras de la Municipalidad de Lima, however, added that district authorities such as the municipality of Chorillos could not grant provisional construction permits when no study on the urban impact had been submitted. The mayor of Lima announced that he would seek a zoning change for the area around the Pantanos de Villa to protect the wildlife in the swamp because the presence of industrial plants seemed to be irreversible. Meanwhile the government of Chorillos, pursuant to an order of the municipality of Lima, issued an order to stop construction. The same month, the Pantonas de Villa was declared a protected natural wildlife preserve.

In early August, LP requested that its construction plans be approved, but the government of Chorillos repeated its order to suspend construction under pressure from the municipality of Lima that permits should not be issued without the completion of all necessary procedures. LP responded that for technical reasons, construction could not be completely stopped. It meanwhile requested an approval of urban fit and submitted a new environmental impact statement. The Direccion General de Obras de la Municipalidad de Lima decreed that construction could continue. INRENA declared the environmental impact statement to be sufficient with only a few minor changes that were immediately incorporated into the plans. Interestingly, INRENA had suggested the ISO 14001 as a voluntary criterion for acceptance, but ultimately it would adopt it as mandatory. As required, LP had an outside environmental engineering firm submit an Environmental Impact Study to INRENA.

August brought another set of problems. Alicorp accused Lucchetti of economic dumping and filed suit. While this suit was later to be dismissed, another bombshell came several days later when the Lima city council, under the guidance of Andrade, held that Lucchetti could not operate in an environmentally protected area and ordered all work in the area to stop even though by that time the factory was almost completely built. Purportedly on the same day that the Lima city council revoked the operation permit, the city received a large donation from Alicorp.

Andrade also began a new strategy to secure the plant's removal by calling for Peruvians to boycott all Lucchetti products. Meanwhile, a number of local organizations were encouraged to picket in front of the new factory.

In September, Andrade formed a commission to investigate the factory and said that the city of Lima had been misled by LP and that new permits would be required. He noted that the original applications had been for an I-2 industrial use permit,[3] but he said that LP was an I-3, a more stringent designation generally reserved for mining and petroleum operations. Alicorp's pasta plant, in contrast, was designated only as an I-1.

Andrade also hired the International Union for the Conservation of Nature (IUCN), an international organization dedicated to environmental conservation. It turned out to be a thorough investigation, studying the impact of all the facilities bordering on the swamp. The only suggestion it made, however, was to close an abattoir next to the LP plant. There were no recommendations that significantly impacted LP's plans.

Andrade also accused LP and Luksic himself of collusion with Camet, whose sons' construction firm was building the LP factory. Apparently, there was no love lost between Camet and Andrade. One reason for this was that when Andrade needed to raise money for the city of Lima, the banks wanted federal guarantees that were ultimately denied by Camet in his role as minister of economics.

On October 23, the municipality of Lima again ordered all construction to stop. After LP applied for reconsideration, on December 16 the municipality of Lima approved the continuation of construction. Three days later Mayor Andrade presented legislation to reconsider the approval, which had the potential to win with just the votes of the members of his group, and referred the LP file to a technical commission. By this time, most of the investment had been made in the plant. Thinking that Andrade was simply posturing to show his strength, the LP management renewed its commitment to pursue its objectives.

In an advertisement that ran in the local newspapers, Lucchetti maintained that it was in compliance with the environmental standards set out by the city of Lima. The city of Lima was, however, quoted in the same papers as saying that the concerns over the Los Pantanos de Villa nature preserve prevented it from giving the plant its stamp of approval. Several other NGOs also protested the plant's construction.[4]

"Lucchetti is still importing pasta, so they can just continue to do that," said Bromwin Griffith, a sector analyst with ING Barings in Lima. "This slows things down for them, but it won't be enough that Alicorp or another competitor will be able to step in and take advantage unless it lasts a very long time."[5]

Meanwhile, LP continued to gain ground in the Peruvian pasta market. Market share had grown during 1997 to 25 percent in Peru and 30 percent in Lima, all from pasta imported from Chile and Italy.

Having reached the level of sales where doing its own distribution made sense, and having added a number of related products to the offering, LP created its own distribution capabilities. Some products and markets were still served by Custer, but the compensation rate was negotiated down to 12 percent.

LP was faced, however, with strong competitive pressures and a virtual price war had erupted. Wholesale prices for pasta dropped from $900 per ton to $650. The cost of imported Italian pasta was $680 per ton, while domestic production was $430 per ton. Chilean imports were still subject to tariffs. By meeting market prices, LP's cost of goods per ton sold grew to 107 percent of sales. The management did not believe, however, that the competitive pricing strategies were sustainable in the long run and would recover enough to allow for profitable production. By the end of the year, 80 percent of construction had already been completed on the new production facility.

On the positive side, Alicorp's charges of dumping had been dropped by the courts. Andrade called for another meeting and reconciliation was proposed, but ultimately construction was stopped again.

1998

The new year started out badly. On January 2, 1998, while the technical commission to which Andrade had referred the matter only found some minor administrative problems but no problems with the factory itself, the city of Lima declared all permits null and void and nullified all municipal licenses obtained by Lucchetti.

Lucchetti immediately responded by suing the city of Lima for restitution of permits, saying that it had a right to build and produce. On January 8, at the request of President Fujimori, Gonzalo Menendez, the general manager of Lucchetti, met with the very influential Vladimir Montesinos, main presidential advisor and chief of Peruvian national intelligence, to warn the central government about the risk to foreign investors implied by Major Andrade.

On January 17, a group of Chilean ecologists invited to Lima by Mayor Andrade announced its support for Andrade's argument and declared that even if the plant of Lucchetti S.A. qualified as "light industry," if it began operations it would damage the fragile ecosystem of the Villa wetlands. In their opinion, the ecosystem was primarily affected by the Huaylas speedway and the operation of the other factories that had been located in the surround of Villa's wetlands. Manuel Baquedano, president of the Instituto Ecología y Política de Chile, offered the support of Chilean ecologists to defend the wetlands.

On February 11, the Chilean magazine *Que Pasa* suggested that Andrade was favoring the local group, Grupo Romero, which owned Alicorp.

At the beginning of March, just before the notification of the ruling regarding the claim by Lucchetti Peru against Lima, Montesinos requested to meet with Andrónico Luksic in person. He expressed the president's concern with respect to Lucchetti's problems, even though the court had apparently already made its decision. This conversation was secretly taped by Montesinos.

With the suit resolved, construction was started again. Lucchetti's head of operations, Salvador Calvo-Perez, calculated that the stoppage cost LP US$3.5 million, which represented an increase in the forecasted investment.

By August, the factory was completed, and all that remained before it could go into production was to ramp systems up to speed, test all the processes, hire and train staff, and fine tune other supply and support systems. Production was scheduled to begin by the end of 1998.

Molitalia meanwhile offered to buy Lucchetti's Peruvian operation, but because LP was on the verge of becoming profitable, the board declined to pursue this possibility. Molitalia, owned by Chilean Carozzi, had caused major pollution in a residential area of Lima in 1998, but was never reprimanded.

November brought another reason to accelerate bringing the plant on line. Duties were increased on all imported wheat products from 18 percent to 25 percent. Meanwhile the price war continued and the price per ton fell to $630 per ton. Estimates for local production costs grew to slightly more than $460 per ton while distribution costs were pegged at 12 percent of sales.

By this time, a total of $67 million had been invested in LP. Finally, on the last day of his tenure the mayor of Chorillos, Pablo Gutierrez, approved the Lucchetti plant and gave it the license to operate.

As of December 1998, Lucchetti's pasta products ranked second in terms of net sales by volume in Peru, with a market share of approximately 23 percent. Pacheco believed that on a brand-by-brand basis, its Lucchetti brand pasta was the leading brand in sales volume in Peru during 1998.

Lucchetti's principal customers and distribution channels were very different in Chile, Peru, and Argentina (see Table 3). Lucchetti executives, however, expected the channel structure in Peru to change over time, becoming more like those of Chile and Argentina, and believed that, as a major producer in Peru, it would benefit from such a shift.

| TABLE 3 | Lucchetti Channels of Distribution and Customers |

	Chile	Peru	Argentina
Channels of Distribution	65% supermarkets	65% wholesalers 23% small wholesalers 2% supermarkets	65% supermarkets
Customers			
Supermarkets	60%	2%	67%
Distributors	31%	73%	
Mini-markets			20%

By the end of 1998, Lucchetti Argentina was also proving to be successful. Its products ranked third in net sales by volume there, with a market share of approximately 10 percent, compared to a market share of approximately 19 percent for Argentina's largest domestic pasta producer. Lucchetti's Argentine pasta business generated sales representing 14.8 percent of Lucchetti's total net sales. The Argentine pasta manufacturing operations, however, had not reached the point of operating profit breakeven. In management's opinion, the inability to reach this desirable performance outcome was at least partly due to under-utilization of production capacity and to high costs of distribution through third parties (compared to competitors with broader product lines and in-house distribution).

In December, the new LP plant began production.

1999–2000

With the new plant on line, continued advertising, and its own distribution network, 1999 sales at LP grew to US$36 million and gross margins were for the first time positive. Net losses for the year, however, exceeded US$15 million, reflecting an increase in net operating expenses. This was the result of financial cost and extraordinary amortization of expenses incurred during the trial period.

The year 2000 heralded a political upheaval in Peru, which ultimately would prove to have a direct impact on LP. In October, one of the videotapes that Montesinos made of his dealings with a number of politicians and businesspeople surfaced showing him bribing an opposition congressman elect in an effort to persuade him to switch to President Fujimori's party. Montesinos fled to Venezuela, while Fujimori fled to Japan.

2001

It was not until June of 2001 that Montesinos was captured in Venezuela and arrested on charges of murder, corruption, and influence peddling to keep Fujimori in power.

After his extradition to Peru, investigators released the videos that Montesinos had secretly taped, including the one of his meeting in January 1998 with Menendez, the general manager of Lucchetti. Montesinos would later say that he had had an influence on the judicial results in favor of Lucchetti. People connected to Montesinos stated that Luksic donated US$2 million to Montesinos at the end of 1999 in order to help reelect Fujimori. Montesinos publicly admitted this once, but not in court, and he later made contradictory statements on the matter.

It seemed, however, that this scandal had opened old wounds and the new government was eager to distance itself from the corruption that was so pervasive in the Fujimori government. In August, Andrade and the city council of Lima cited environmental violations and voted 26 to 4 to issue an order to close the LP plant by August 23, revoking the operating license and giving it one year to move the plant. Prior to soliciting arbitration under the auspices of ICSID as defined in the Reciprocal Investment Promotion and Protection accord signed by Chile and Peru in February 2000, Lucchetti requested the new president, Alejandro Toledo, to initiate a six-month conversation period during which time a friendly resolution to the problem would be sought.

In October, Judge Jorge Barreto was suspended from his position after having issued a ruling clearing Luksic, Montesinos, and Pacheco from the offense of influence peddling.

By the end of 2001, LP's sales dropped from US$45 million to US$34 million, mainly due to

TABLE 4

Market Share in Peru

	1995	1996	1997	1998	1999	2000	2001	2002
Alicorp		61%	36%	35%				40%
Lucchetti		6%	28%					15%
Molitalia		20%	18%	14%				16%
Cogorno		11%	13%					

adverse publicity from the municipality and the central government. In spite of this, local production allowed the company to obtain a gross margin of US$6 million. Accumulated losses from operations now exceeded US$33 million and net losses approached US$61 million.

2002

In June, the ongoing criminal investigation in Peru resulted in the exoneration of Luksic, Menendez, and Pacheco regarding corruption. Nevertheless, the accusation of influence peddling because of the meetings held with Montesinos still persisted. Luksic traveled to Lima to declare, regarding the influence peddling accusation, "I have come to comply with my duties and I trust Peruvian justice." Influence-peddling charges were dropped against the people related to Lucchetti by a lower court, a decision that was revoked by a Superior Court and was still pending resolution at the Supreme Court in Peru.

In November, Andrade was defeated by Luis Castaneda Lossio in the Lima mayoral election. He would take over at the beginning of 2003. Andrade was meanwhile quoted in newspapers that he would make sure that the city council passed a final and irrevocable resolution to the Lucchetti issue before his tenure ended at the end of the year.

In keeping with Andrade's promise, on December 16 the city council of Lima voted 24 to 11 that the plant should be shut down because it was causing environmental damage to the nature preserve, in spite of the fact that Lucchetti had renewed both its ISO 14001 certificate in September and its INRENA approval certificate. The council revoked Lucchetti's operating license, rejecting the company's request dated August 23 for a six-month extension period.

Lucchetti immediately filed a complaint with the World Bank's International Center for Settlement of Investment Disputes (ICSID) and published a full-page advertisement in the Lima newspaper saying that the company had been a victim of discrimination and arbitrary decisions.

Rafael Helser, chief of systems at the plant, told reporters on behalf of the 400 employees at the plant, "We are going to fight to keep our jobs until the end of the day!" adding that the workers would seek a legal injunction against the closure order, invoking the right to work.

Peruvian president Alejandro Toledo suggested that the plant be turned into an ecological museum.

LP sales plummeted to only US$25 million in 2002 with net losses of almost US$5 million. Cumulative losses from operations had mounted to $34.5 million and net losses over US$65 million. See Table 4 for market share statistics.

2003

On January 6, Mayor Augusto Miyashiro of the Chorillos district gave Lucchetti seven days to shut down the plant, executing the order of the provincial municipality of Lima. Lucchetti's board decided to close immediately, and ordered the managers to act in accordance with the district's order.

In the ensuing months, several local mayors in other parts of Lima offered to allow Lucchetti to relocate to their districts at preferential prices with favorable tax terms. These offers created several options for Luksic to consider. He could seek to rebuild and try to take advantage of the Lucchetti market share or he could absorb a US$150 million write-off and leave the country altogether. In the latter case, he could apply the loss to his overall Quiñenco operations and achieve substantial tax benefits.

This was not the best of timing for this to all fall apart. The Quiñenco ADR that fueled part of the foreign expansion had fallen from a market value of US$19.38 in 1997 to a low of US$3.30 in 2002.

In 2001, Lucchetti sold its interests in Argentina, absorbing a loss of Ch$7,543 million. In the 2002 20K report, Lucchetti management noted that this move was undertaken "in order to concentrate its efforts mainly in Chile where it has strong brand recognition, significant market share, access to a critical mass of consumers which facilitates new product launches, and in-house distribution capabilities." In its 2002 annual report, Quiñenco stated that Lucchetti's "strategy will

be based in Chile, where it will focus on three strategic pillars: growth, profitability, and sustainability." Overall, Quiñenco said that the "group's business strategy is fundamentally based on the strengthening and consolidation of each of the companies in which it participates."

NOTES

1. Quiñenco's beer, wine, and beverage company.
2. The municipality of Lima was divided into 42 districts, one of which was Chorillos, where the Pantanos de Villa wildlife reserve was located. According to laws instituted in July of 1997, Lima exercised judicial power over the district for issuance of construction licenses, the location and size of naturally protected areas, and the constitution of parks and green zones. Both the municipality and the districts had their own mayors, elected every five years by their electoral districts.
3. Industrial use permits ranged from I-1, the least stringent classification, to I-3, the most stringent.
4. Dow Jones Emerging Markets Reports, June 6, 1997.
5. Ibid.

Whole Foods Market, 2005: Will There Be Enough Organic Food to Satisfy the Growing Demand?

C-15

Patricia Harasta
Alan N. Hoffman

Bentley College

Reflecting about his three decades of experience in the grocery business, John Mackey smiled to himself over his previous successes. His entrepreneurial history began with a single store which he has now grown to become the nation's leading natural food chain. While proud of the past, John had concerns about the future direction in which the Whole Foods Market chain should head. Whole Foods Market was an early entrant into the organic food market and it has used its early mover advantage to solidify its position and continue its steady growth.

With the changing economy and a more competitive industry landscape, John Mackey is uncertain about how to meet the company's aggressive growth targets. Whole Foods Markets' objective is to reach $10 billion in revenue with 300-plus stores by 2010 without sacrificing quality and its current reputation. This is not an easy task and John is unsure of the best way to proceed.

COMPANY BACKGROUND

Whole Foods carries both natural and organic food offering customers a wide variety of products. "Natural" refers to food that is free of growth hormones or antibiotics, and "certificated organic" food conforms to the standards as defined by the U.S. Department of Agriculture in October 2002.[1] Whole Foods Market is the world's leading retailer of natural and organic foods, with 172 stores in North America and the United Kingdom. John Mackey, cofounder and current president of Whole Foods, opened Safer Way natural grocery store in 1978. The store had limited success as it was a small

location allowing only for a limited selection, focusing entirely on vegetarian foods.[2] John joined forces with Craig Weller and Mark Skiles, founders of Clarksville Natural Grocery (founded in 1979), to create Whole Foods Market.[3] This joint venture took place in Austin, Texas, in 1980 resulting in a new company, a single natural food market with a staff of 19.

In addition to the supermarkets, Whole Foods owns and operates several subsidiaries. Allegro Coffee Company was formed in 1977 and purchased by Whole Foods Market in 1997; it now acts as Whole Foods' coffee roasting and distribution center. Pigeon Cove is Whole Foods' seafood-processing facility, which was founded in 1985 and known as M & S Seafood until 1990. Whole Foods purchased Pigeon Cove, located in Gloucester, Massachusetts, in 1996. The company is now the only supermarket to own and operate a waterfront seafood facility.[4] The last two subsidiaries are Produce Field Inspection Office and Select Fish, which is Whole Foods' West Coast seafood-processing facility, acquired in 2003.[5] In addition to the above, the company has eight distribution centers, seven regional bake houses, and four commissaries.[6]

"Whole Foods Market remains uniquely mission driven: The Company is highly selective about what they sell, dedicated to stringent quality standards, and committed to sustainable agriculture. They believe in a virtuous circle entwining the food chain, human beings and Mother Earth: each is reliant upon the others through a beautiful and delicate symbiosis."[7] The message of preservation and sustainability are followed while providing high-quality goods to customers and high profits to investors.

Whole Foods Market, 2005: Will There Be Enough Organic Food to Satisfy the Growing Demand? by Patricia Harasta and Alan N. Hoffman. The authors would like to thank Ann Hoffman, Christopher Ferrari, Robert Marshall, Julie Giles, Jennifer Powers, and Gretchen Alper for their research and contributions to this case. Please address all correspondence to Dr. Alan N. Hoffman, AGC 320, Department of Management, Bentley College, 175 Forest Street, Waltham, MA 02452-4705, voice (781) 891-2287, ahoffman@bentley.edu, fax (781) 459-0335. Printed by permission of Dr. Alan N. Hoffman, Bentley College.

Whole Foods has grown over the years through mergers, acquisitions, and several new store openings.[8] Today, Whole Foods Market is the largest natural food supermarket in the United States.[9] The company employs over 32,000 people who are operating 172 stores in the United States, Canada, and the United Kingdom with an average store size of 32,000 square feet.[10] While the majority of Whole Foods locations are in the United States, the company has made acquisitions expanding its presence in the United Kingdom. European expansion provides enormous potential growth because of the large population, and it holds "a more sophisticated organic-foods market . . . in terms of suppliers and acceptance by the public."[11] Whole Foods targets its locations specifically by an area's demographics. The company targets locations where 40 percent or more of the residents have a college degree, as they are more likely to be aware and supportive of nutritional issues.[12]

WHOLE FOODS MARKET'S PHILOSOPHY

The company's corporate Web site defines the company philosophy as follows:

> Whole Foods Market's vision of a sustainable future means our children and grandchildren will be living in a world that values human creativity, diversity, and individual choice. Businesses will harness human and material resources without devaluing the integrity of the individual or the planet's ecosystems. Companies, governments, and institutions will be held accountable for their actions. People will better understand that all actions have repercussions and that planning and foresight coupled with hard work and flexibility can overcome almost any problem encountered. It will be a world that values education and a free exchange of ideas by an informed citizenry; where people are encouraged to discover, nurture, and share their life's passions.[13]

While Whole Foods recognizes it is only a supermarket, it is working toward fulfilling its vision within the context of its industry. In addition to leading by example, it strives to conduct business in a manner consistent with its mission and vision. By offering minimally processed, high quality food, engaging in ethical business practices and providing a motivational, respectful work environment, the company believes it is on the path to a sustainable future.[14]

Whole Foods incorporates the best practices of each location back into the chain.[15] This can be seen in the company's store product expansion from dry goods to perishable produce, including meats, fish, and prepared foods. The lessons learned at one location are absorbed by all, enabling the chain to maximize effectiveness and efficiency while offering a product line that serves its customers' needs. Whole Foods carries only natural and organic products. The company believes that the best tasting and most nutritious food available is found in its purest state—unadulterated by artificial additives, sweeteners, colorings, and preservatives.[16]

Whole Foods continually improves customer offerings, catering to its specific locations. Unlike business models for traditional grocery stores, Whole Foods products differ by geographic regions and local farm specialties.

EMPLOYEE & CUSTOMER RELATIONS

Whole Foods encourages a team-based environment, allowing each store to make independent decisions regarding its operations. Teams consist of up to eleven employees and a team leader. Each store employs anywhere from 72 to 391 team members.[17] The manager is referred to as the "store team leader." The store team leader is compensated by an Economic Value Added (EVA) bonus and is also eligible to receive stock options.[18]

Whole Foods tries to instill a sense of purpose among its employees and for six years, it was named one of the "100 Best Companies to work for in America" by *Fortune* magazine. In employee surveys, 90 percent of its team members stated that they always or frequently enjoy their job.[19]

The company strives to take care of its customers, realizing they are the "lifeblood of our business," and the two are "interdependent on each other."[20] Whole Foods' primary objective goes beyond 100 percent customer satisfaction with the goal to "delight" customers in every interaction.

COMPETITIVE ENVIRONMENT

At the time of Whole Foods' inception, there was almost no competition, with less than six other natural food stores in the United States. Today, the organic foods industry is growing and Whole Foods finds itself competing hard to maintain its elite presence. As the population has become increasingly concerned about its eating habits, natural foods stores such as Whole Foods are flourishing. Other successful natural food grocery chains today include Trader Joe's Co. and Wild Oats Market.[21] (see Exhibit 1).

Trader Joe's, originally known as Pronto Markets, was founded in 1958 in Los Angeles by Joe Coulombe. By expanding its presence and product offerings while maintaining high quality at low prices, Trader Joe's has found its competitive niche.[22] The company has 215

NATURAL PRODUCTS SALES TOP $45 BILLION IN 2004

American shoppers spent nearly $45.8 billion on natural and organic products in 2004, according to research published in the "24th Annual Market Overview" in the June issue of *The Natural Foods Merchandiser*. In 2004, natural products sales increased 6.9 percent across all sales channels, including supermarkets, mass marketers, direct marketers, and the Internet. Sales of organic products rose 14.6 percent in natural products stores. As interest in low-carb diets waned, sales of organic baked goods rose 35 percent. Other fast-growing organic categories included meat, poultry, and seafood, up 120 percent; coffee and cocoa, up 64 percent; and cookies, up 63 percent.

EXHIBIT 1	Sales ($ millions)						
Company	2000	2001	% Growth	2002	% Growth	2003	% Growth
Whole Foods Market[a]	$1,838.60	$2,272.20	23.60%	$2,690.50	18.40%	$3,148.60	17.00%
Trader Joe's Company[b]	$1,670.00	$1,900.00	13.80%	$2,200.00	15.80%	$2,500.00	13.60%
Wild Oats Market[c]	$838.10	$893.20	6.60%	$919.10	2.90%	$969.20	5.50%

[a] Hoovers Online: http://www.hoovers.com/whole-foods/-ID_10952-/free-co-factsheet.xhtml, December 1, 2004.

[b] Hoovers Online: lhttp://www.hoovers.com/trader-joe's-co/-ID-47619-/free-co-factsheet.xhtm, December 1, 2004.

[c] Hoovers Online: http://www.hoovers.com/wild-oats-markets/-ID_41717-/free-co-factsheet.xhtml, December 1, 2004.

stores, primarily on the west and east coasts of the United States. The company "offers upscale grocery fare such as health foods, prepared meals, organic produce and nutritional supplements."[23] A low cost structure allows Trader Joe's to offer competitive prices while still maintaining its margins. Trader Joe's stores have no service department and average just 10,000 square feet in store size. A privately held company, Trader Joe's enjoyed sales of $2.5 million in 2003, a 13.6 percent increase from 2002.[24]

Wild Oats was founded in 1987, in Boulder, Colorado. Its founders had no experience in the natural foods market, relying heavily on their employees to learn the industry. Acknowledging the increased competition within the industry, Wild Oats is committed to strengthening and streamlining its operations in an effort to continue to build the company.[25] Its product offerings range from organic foods to traditional grocery merchandise. Wild Oats, a publicly owned company on Nasdaq, is traded under the ticker symbol of OATS and "is the third largest natural foods supermarket chain in the United States in terms of sales." Although it falls behind Whole Foods and Trader Joe's, the company enjoyed $1,048,164 in sales in 2004, a 7.5 percent increase over 2003. Wild Oats operates 100 full-service stores in 24 states and Canada.[26]

Additional competition has arisen from grocery stores, such as Stop 'N Shop and Shaw's, which now incorporate natural foods sections in their conventional stores, placing them in direct competition with Whole Foods. Because larger grocery chains have more flexibility in their product offerings, they are more likely to promote products through sales, a strategy Whole Foods rarely practices.

Despite being in a highly competitive industry, Whole Foods maintains its reputation as "the world's #1 natural foods chain."[27] As the demand for natural and organic food continues to grow, pressures on suppliers will rise. Only 3 percent of U.S. farmland is organic, so there is limited output.[28] The increased demand for these products may further elevate prices or result in goods being out of stock, with possible price wars looming.

THE CHANGING GROCERY INDUSTRY

Before the emergence of the supermarket, the public was largely dependent upon specialty shops or street vendors for dairy products, meats, produce, and other household items. In the 1920s, chain stores began to threaten independent retailers by offering convenience and lower prices by procuring larger quantities of products. Appel explains that the emergence of the supermarkets in the 1930s was a result of three major changes in society:

1. The shift in population from rural to urban areas.
2. An increase in disposable income.
3. Increased mobility through ownership of automobiles.[29]

Perhaps the earliest example of the supermarket as we know it today is King Kullen, "America's first supermarket," which was founded by Michael Cullen in 1930. "The essential key to his plan was volume, and he attained this through heavy advertising of low prices on nationally advertised merchandise." As the success of Cullen's strategy became evident, others such as Safeway, A&P, and Kroger adopted it as well. By the time the United States entered World War II, 9,000 supermarkets accounted for 25 percent of industry sales.[30]

Low prices and convenience continue to be the dominant factors driving consumers to supermarkets today. The industry is characterized by low margins and continuous downward pressure on prices made evident by coupons, weekly specials, and rewards cards. Over the years firms have introduced subtle changes to the business model by providing additional conveniences, such as the inclusion of bakeries, banks, pharmacies, and even coffee houses co-located within the supermarket. Throughout their existence, supermarkets have also tried to cater to the changing tastes and preferences of society such as healthier diets, the Atkins diet, and low carbohydrate foods. The moderate changes to strategy within supermarkets have been imitated by competitors, which are returning the industry to a state of price competition. Supermarkets themselves now face additional competition from wholesalers such as Costco, BJ's, and Sam's Club.

A DIFFERENT SHOPPING EXPERIENCE

The setup of the organic grocery store is a key component to Whole Foods' success. The store's setup and its products are carefully researched to ensure that it is meeting the demands of the local community. Locations are primarily in cities and are chosen for their large space and heavy foot traffic. According to Whole Foods' 10K, "approximately 88 percent of our existing stores are located in the top 50 statistical metropolitan areas."[31] The company uses a specific formula to choose its store sites that is based upon several metrics, which include but are not limited to income levels, education, and population density.

Upon entering a Whole Foods supermarket, it becomes clear that the company attempts to sell the consumer on the entire experience. Team members (employees) are well trained and the stores themselves are immaculate. There are in-store chefs to help with recipes, wine tastings, and food sampling. There are "Take Action food centers"[32] where customers can access information on the issues that affect their food such as legislation and environmental factors. Some stores offer extra services such as home delivery,

cooking classes, massages, and valet parking.[33] Whole Foods goes out of its way to appeal to the above-average-income earner.

Whole Foods uses price as a marketing tool in a few select areas, as demonstrated by the 365 Whole Foods brand name products, priced less than similar organic products that are carried within the store. However, the company does not use price to differentiate itself from competitors.[34] Rather, Whole Foods focuses on quality and service as the competitive dimensions on which it is differentiated from competitors.

Whole Foods spent only 0.5 percent[35] of total sales from fiscal year 2004 on advertising; the company relies on other means to promote its stores. The company relies heavily on word-of-mouth advertising from its customers to help market itself in the local community. Whole Foods is also promoted in several health-conscious magazines, and each store budgets for in-store advertising each fiscal year.

Whole Foods also gains recognition via its charitable contributions and the awareness that it brings to the treatment of animals. The company donates 5 percent of after-tax profits to not-for-profit charities.[36] The company is also very active in establishing systems to make sure that the animals used in its products are treated humanly.

THE AGING BABY BOOMERS

The aging of the Baby Boomer generation will expand the senior demographic over the next decade as their children grow up and leave the nest. Urban singles are another group with extra disposable income, due to their lack of dependents. These two groups present an opportunity for growth for Whole Foods. Americans spent 7.2 percent of their total expenditures on food in 2001, making it the seventh-highest category on which consumers spend their money.[37] Additionally, U.S. households with income of more than $100,000 per annum represent 22 percent of aggregate income today compared with 18 percent a decade ago.[38]

This shift in demographics has created an expansion in the gourmet store group, while slowing growth in the discount retail market.[39] To that end, there is a gap in supermarket retailing between consumers who can afford to shop only at low cost providers, like Wal-Mart, and the population of consumers who prefer gourmet food and are willing to pay a premium for perceived higher quality.[40] " 'The Baby Boomers are driving demand for organic food in general because they're health-conscious and can afford to pay higher prices,' says Professor Steven G. Sapp, a sociologist at Iowa State University who studies consumer food behavior."[41]

The perception that imported, delicatessen, exotic, and organic foods are of higher quality, therefore commanding higher prices, continues to bode well for Whole Foods Market. As John Mackey explains, "We're changing the [grocery-shopping] experience so that people enjoy it. . . . It's a richer, [more fun], more enjoyable experience. People don't shop our stores because we have low prices."[42] The consumer focus on a healthy diet is not limited to food. More new diet plans emerged in America in the last half of the 20th century than in any other country. This trend has also increased the demand for nutritional supplements and vitamins.[43]

In recent years, consumers have made a gradual move toward the use of fresher, healthier foods in their everyday diets. Consumption of fresh fruits and vegetables and pasta and other grain-based products has increased.[44] This is evidenced by the aggressive expansion by consumer products companies into healthy food and natural and organic products.[45] "Natural and organic products have crossed the chasm to mainstream America."[46] The growing market can be attributed to the acceptance and widespread expansion of organic product offerings, beyond milk and dairy.[47] Mainstream acceptance of the Whole Foods offering can be attributed to this shift in consumer food preferences as consumers continue to identify taste as the number one motivator for purchasing organic foods.[48]

With a growing percentage of women working outside of the home, the traditional role of home-cooked meals, prepared from scratch, has waned. As fewer women have the time to devote to cooking, consumers are giving way to the trend of convenience through prepared foods. Sales of ready-to-eat meals have grown significantly. "The result is that grocers are starting to specialize in quasi-restaurant food."[49] Just as women entering the work force has propelled the sale of prepared foods, it has also increased consumer awareness of the need for the one-stop shopping experience. Hypermarkets such as Wal-Mart that offer non-food items and more mainstream product lines allow consumers to conduct more shopping in one place rather than moving from store to store.

The growth in sales of natural foods is expected to continue at the rate of 8-10 percent annually, according to the National Nutritional Food Association. The sale of organic food has largely outpaced traditional grocery products because of the consumer perception that organic food is healthier.[50] The purchase of organic food is perceived to be beneficial to consumer health by 61 percent of consumers, according to a Food Marketing Institute/Prevention magazine study. Americans believe organic food can help improve fitness and increase the longevity of life.[51] Much of this perception has grown out of fear of how non-organic foods are treated with pesticides for growth and then preserved for sale. Therefore, an opportunity exists for Whole Foods to contribute to consumer awareness by funding non-profit organizations that focus on educating the public on the benefits of organic lifestyles.

OPERATIONS

Whole Foods purchases most of its products from regional and national suppliers. This allows the company to leverage its size in order to receive deep discounts and favorable terms with its vendors. The company still permits stores to purchase from local producers to keep the stores aligned with local food trends and is seen as supporting the community. The company owns two procurement centers and handles the majority of procurement and distribution itself. Whole Foods also owns several regional bake houses, which distribute products to its stores. The largest independent vendor is United Natural Foods, which accounted for 20 percent of Whole Foods total purchases for fiscal year 2004.[52] Product categories at Whole Foods include but are not limited to:

- Produce
- Seafood
- Grocery
- Meat and Poultry
- Bakery
- Prepared Foods and Catering
- Specialty (Beer, Wine, and Cheese)
- Whole body (nutritional supplements, vitamins, body care, and educational products such as books)
- Floral
- Pet Products
- Household Products.[53]

While Whole Foods carries all the items that one would expect to find in a grocery store (and plenty that one would not), its "heavy emphasis on perishable foods is designed to appeal to both natural foods and gourmet shoppers."[54] Perishable foods accounted for 67 percent of its retail sales in 2004 and are the core of Whole Foods' success.[55] This is demonstrated by the company's own statement: "We believe it is our strength of execution in perishables that has attracted many of our most loyal shoppers."[56]

Whole Foods also provides fully cooked frozen-meal options through its private label Whole Kitchen, to satisfy the demands of working families. For example, the Whole Foods Market located in Woodland Hills, California, has redesigned its prepared foods section more than three times in response to a 40 percent growth in prepared foods sales.[57]

Whole Foods doesn't take just any product and put it on the shelves. In order to make it into the Whole Foods grocery store, products have to undergo a strict test to determine if they are "Whole Foods material." The quality standards that all potential Whole foods products must meet include:

- Foods that are free of preservatives and other additives
- Foods that are fresh, wholesome and safe to eat
- Promote organically grown foods
- Foods and products that promote a healthy life.[58]

Meat and poultry products must adhere to a higher standard:

- No antibiotics or added growth hormones
- An affidavit from each producer that outlines the whole process of production and how the animals are treated
- An annual inspection of all producers by Whole Foods Market
- Successful completion of a third party audit to attest to these findings.[59]

Also, because of the lack of available nutritional brands with a national identity, Whole Foods decided to enter into the private label product business. The company currently has three private label products with a fourth program called Authentic Food Artisan, which promotes distinctive products that are certified organic. The three private label products: (1) 365 Everyday Value: A well-recognized and trusted brand that meets the standards of Whole Foods and is less expensive then the regular product lines; (2) Whole Kids Organic: Healthy items that are directed at children; and (3) 365 Organic Everyday Value: All the benefits of organic food at reduced prices.[60]

When opening a new store, Whole Foods stocks it with almost $700,000 worth of initial inventory, which its vendors partially finance.[61] As with most conventional grocery stores, the majority of Whole Foods' inventory is turned over fairly quickly; this is especially true of produce. Fresh organic produce is central to Whole Foods existence and turns over on a faster basis than other products.

FINANCIAL OPERATIONS

Whole Foods Market focuses on earning a profit while providing job security to its workforce to lay the foundation for future growth. Interested in serving the needs of all stakeholders, the company is determined not to let profits deter the company from providing excellent service to its customers and quality work environment for its staff. Its mission statement defines its recipe for financial success.

"Whole Foods, Whole People, Whole Planet— emphasizes that our vision reaches far beyond just being a food retailer. Our success in fulfilling our vision is measured by customer satisfaction, Team Member excellence and happiness, return on capital investment, improvement in the state of the environment, and local and larger community support."[62]

Whole Foods also caps the salary of its executives at no more than fourteen times that of the average annual salary of a Whole Foods worker; this includes wages and incentive bonuses as well. The company also donates 5 percent of its after-tax profits to non-profit organizations.[63]

Over a five-year period from 2000 through 2004, the company experienced an 87 percent growth in sales, with sales reaching $3.86 billion in 2004. Annual sales increases during that period were equally dramatic: 24 percent in 2001, 18 percent in 2002, 17 percent in 2003, and 22 percent in 2004.[64] (see Exhibit 2) This growth is perhaps more impressive, given the relatively negative economic environment and recession in the United States.

Whole Foods' acquisition strategy as a means of expanding has fueled growth in net income since the company's inception. This is particularly evident when looking at the net income growth in 2002 (24.47 percent), 2003 (22.72 percent), and 2004 (27.94 percent).[65]

The ticker for Whole Foods, Inc. is WFMI. A review of the performance history of Whole Foods stock since its IPO reveals a mostly upward trend. The 10-year price trend shows the company increasing from under $10 per share to a high of over $100 per share, reflecting

EXHIBIT 2	Whole Foods Annual Sales (thousands)			
	2001	**2002**	**2003**	**2004**
Sales	2,272,231.00	2,690,475.00	3,148,593.00	3,864,950.00
%	23.58%	18.04%	17.03%	22.75%
Net Income	67,880	84,491	103,687	132,657
%		24.47%	22.72%	27.94%
Increase from 2000 to 2003 = 87%				

an increase of over 1,000 percent.[66] For the past year, the stock has been somewhat volatile, but with a mostly upward trend. The current price of $136 with 65.3 million shares outstanding gives the company a market valuation of $8.8 billion (as of August 2005).[67] Details about Whole Foods' financial performance are shown in Appendices 1, 2, and 3.

THE CODE OF CONDUCT

From its inception, the company has sought to be different from conventional grocery stores, with a heavy focus on ethics. Besides an emphasis on organic foods, the company has also established a contract of animal rights, which states the company will only do business with companies that treat their animals humanely. While Whole Foods realizes that animal products are vital to its business, it opposes animal cruelty.[68]

The company has a unique fourteen-page Code of Conduct document that addresses the expected and desired behavior for its employees. The code is broken down into the following four sections:

- Potential conflicts of interest
- Transactions or situations that should never occur
- Situations where you may need the authorization of the ethics committee before proceeding
- Times when certain actions must be taken by executives of the company or team leaders of individual stores.[69]

This Code of Conduct covers, in detail, the most likely scenarios a manager of a store might encounter. It includes several checklists that are to be filled out on a regular, or at least an annual, basis by team leaders and store managers. After completion, the checklists must be signed and submitted to corporate headquarters and copies retained on file in the store.[70] They ensure that the intended ethical practices that are part of Whole Foods are being followed by everyone. The ethical efforts of Whole Foods do not go unrecognized; the company recently was ranked number 70 out of the "100 Best Corporate Citizens."[71]

POSSIBLE SCARCE RESOURCES: PRIME LOCATIONS AND THE SUPPLY OF ORGANIC FOODS

Prime store locations and the supply of organic foods are potential scarce resources and could be problematic for Whole Foods Market in the future.

Whole Foods likes to establish a presence in highly affluent cities, where its target market resides. The majority of Whole Foods customers are well-educated, thereby yielding high salaries enabling them to afford the company's higher prices. Whole Foods is particular when deciding on new locations, as location is extremely important for top and bottom line growth. However, there are a limited number of communities where 40 percent of the residents have college degrees.

Organic food is another possible scarce resource. Organic crops yield a lower quantity of output and are rarer, accounting for only 3 percent of U.S. farmland usage.[72] Strict government requirements must be satisfied; these are incredibly time consuming, more effort intensive, and more costly to adhere to. With increased demands from mainstream supermarkets also carrying organics, the demand for such products could exceed the limited supply. The market for organic foods grew from $2.9 billion in 2001 to $5.3 billion in 2004, an 80.5 percent increase in the three-year period.[73]

Whole Foods recognizes that the increased demand for organic foods may adversely affect its earnings and informs its investors as such. "Changes in the availability of quality natural and organic products could impact our business. There is no assurance that quality natural and organic products will be available to meet our future needs. If conventional supermarkets increase their natural and organic product offerings or if new laws require the reformulation of certain products to meet tougher standards, the supply of these products may be constrained. Any significant disruption in the supply of quality natural and organic products could have a material impact on our overall sales and cost of goods."[74]

NOTES

1. www.organicconsumers.org/organic/most071904.cfm.
2. Julia Boorstin, "No Preservatives, no unions, lots of dough," *Fortune*, September 15, 2003, Volume 148, Issue 5, page 127.
3. Whole Foods, www.wholefoods.com/company/timeline.html, November 4, 2004.
4. Julia Boorstin, "No Preservatives, no unions, lots of dough," *Fortune*, September 15, 2003, Volume 148, Issue 5, page 127.
5. Whole Foods, www.wholefoods.com/company/facts.html, November 5, 2004.
6. Whole Foods, www.wholefoods.com/issues/org_comments-standards0498.html, November 5, 2004.
7. Whole Foods, www.wholefoods.com/company/index.html, November 5, 2004.
8. Ibid.
9. "The Natural: Whole Foods founder John Mackey builds an empire on organic eating," *Time*, 2002.
10. Whole Foods www.wholefoods.com/company/facts.html, November 11, 2004.

| Case 15 / Whole Foods Market, 2005: Will There Be Enough Oraganic Food to Satisfy the Growing Demand?

174

C

11. Robert Elder Jr., "Whole Foods buying chain of stores based in London: $38 million deal marks U.S. health-food retailer's initial thrust into overseas market," January 17, 2004.

12. Jeanne Lang Jones, "Whole Foods is bagging locations," *Puget Sound Business Journal*, August 13, 2004, Volume 25, issue 15, page 1.

13. Whole Foods, www.wholefoodsmarket.com/company/sustainablefuture.html, November 5, 2004.

14. Ibid.

15. Julia Boorstin, "No Preservatives, no unions, lots of dough," *Fortune*, September 15, 2003, Volume 148, Issue 5, page 127.

16. www.wholefoodsmarket.com/products/index.html, July 25, 2005.

17. Whole Foods 10K-Q 2003 (page 7) November 11, 2004, www.wholefoodsmarket.com/investor/10K-Q/2003_10K.pdf.

18. Ibid.

19. Whole Foods 10K-Q 2004 (page 10) August 15, 2005, www.wholefoodsmarket.com/investor/10K-Q/2004_10KA.pdf.

20. www.wholefoodsmarket.com/company/declaration.html. July 29, 2005.

21. Hoovers Online, www.hoovers.com/whole-foods/-ID_10952-/free-co-factsheet.xhtml, November 8, 2004.

22. Trader Joe's Company, www.traderjoes.com, November 8, 2004.

23. Hoovers Online, www.hoovers.com/trader-joe's-co/-ID-47619-/free-co-factsheet.xhtm, November 8, 2004.

24. Ibid.

25. Wild Oats Market, www.wildoats.com, November 8, 2004.

26. Hoovers Online, www.hoovers.com/wild-oats-markets/-ID_41717-/free-co-factsheet.xhtml, November 8, 2004.

27. Hoovers Online, www.hoovers.com/whole-foods/-ID_10952-/free-co-factsheet.xhtml, November 8, 2004.

28. Paul Grimaldi, "Providence, RI, grocery targets new approach to pricing," *Knight Ridder Tribune Business News*, September 28, 2004.

29. David Appel, "The Supermarket: Early Development of an Institutional Innovation," *Journal of Retailing*, Volume 48, Number 1, Spring 1972, p. 40.

30. Ibid.

31. Whole Foods 10K-Q for 2003 (page 8) November 11, 2004 www.wholefoodsmarket.com/investor/10K-Q/2003_10K.pdf.

32. Ibid.

33. Ibid.

34. Whole Foods www.wholefoodsmarket.com/investor/10K-Q/2003_10K.pdf (page 10) November 12, 2004.

35. Whole Foods 10K-Q 2004 (page 10) August 15, 2005. www.wholefoodsmarket.com/investor/10K-Q/2004_10KA.pdf.

36. Whole Foods 10K-Q 2003 (page 9) November 11, 2004 www.wholefoodsmarket.com/investor/10K-Q/2003_10K.pdf.

37. Consumer Lifestyles in The United States (May 2003) 12.2 Expenditure on Food. *Euromonitor*. Solomon Smith Baker Library, Bentley College, Waltham, MA. November 1, 2004.

38. John Gapper, "Organic food stores are on a natural high," *The Financial Times*, September 2004.

39. Ibid.

40. Ibid.

41. Richard Murphy McGill, "Truth or Scare," *American Demographics*, March 2004, Vol. 26, Issue 2, p. 26.

42. Bob Sechler, "Whole Foods picks up the pace of its expansion," *Wall Street Journal* (eastern edition), September 29, 2004, p. 1.

43. "Consumer Lifestyles in the United States (May 2003) 12.7 What Americans Eat," *Euromonitor*. Solomon Smith Baker Library, Bentley College, Waltham, MA. November 1, 2004.

44. "Consumer Lifestyles in the United States (May 2003) 12.4 Popular Foods," *Euromonitor*. Solomon Smith Baker Library, Bentley College, Waltham, MA. November 1, 2004.

45. "Profile in B2B Strategy: Supermarket news sidles into natural, organic trend with new quarterly," *Business Customer Wire*. Regional Business News. October 25, 2004.

46. Ibid.

47. "The World Market for Dairy Products (January 2004). 4.5 Organic Foods. 4.5.1 Global Market Trends in Organic Foods," *Euromonitor*. Solomon Smith Baker Library, Bentley College, Waltham, MA. November 1, 2004.

48. Ibid.

49. "Supermarkets' prepared meals save families time," *KRTBN Knight-Ridder Tribune Business*, September 13, 2004.

50. "Packaged Food in the United States (January 2004) 3.4 Organic Food," *Euromonitor*. Solomon Smith Baker Library, Bentley College, Waltham, MA. November 1, 2004.

51. Ibid.

52. Found on 10K-Q for 2004 (page 10) August 15, 2005. www.wholefoodsmarket.com/investor/10K-Q/2004_10KA.pdf Found on 10K-Q for 2003 (page 8) November 11, 2004.

53. Whole Foods 10K-Q for 2003 (page 6) November 13, 2004.

54. Whole Foods 10K-Q 2003 (page 5) Whole Foods www.wholefoodsmarket.com/investor/10K-Q/2003_10K.pdf, November 13, 2004.

55. Whole Foods 10K Q 2004 (page 14) August 15, 2005, www.wholefoodsmarket.com/investor/10K-Q/2004_10KA.pdf.

56. Whole Foods 10K-Q 2003 (page 6) www.wholefoodsmarket.com/investor/10K-Q/2003_10K.pdf November 13, 2004.

57. "Supermarkets' prepared meals save families time," *KRTBN Knight-Ridder Tribune Business*, September 13, 2004.

58. Whole Foods 10K-Q 2003 (page 5) www.wholefoodsmarket.com/investor/10K-Q/2003_10K.pdf November 13, 2004.

59. Whole Foods 10K-Q 2003 (page 6) www.wholefoodsmarket.com/investor/10K-Q/2003_10K.pdf November 13, 2004.

60. www.wholefoodsmarket.com/investor/10K-Q/2003_10K.pdf. Found on 10K-Q for 2003 (page 7) (On November 11, 2004),

61. Whole Foods 10K-Q for 2003 www.wholefoodsmarket.com/investor/10K-Q/2003_10K.pdf (Page 8), November 7, 2004.

62. Whole Foods www.WholeFoodsmarket.com/company/declaration.html, November 7, 2004.

63. Ibid.

64. Whole Foods 10K-Q for 2003 www.WholeFoodsmarket.com/investor/10k-Q/2003_10k.pdf November 7, 2004.

65. Ibid.

66. Nasdaq.com Market Symbol for Whole Foods is WFMI; quotes.nasdaq.com/quote.dll?page=charting&mode=basics&intraday=off&timeframe=10y&charttype=ohlc&splits=off&earnings=off&movingaverage=None&lowerstudy=volume&comparison=off&index=&drilldown=off&symbol=WFMI&selected=WFM, November 11, 2004.

67. quotes.nasdaq.com/Quote.dll?mode=stock&symbol=wfmi&symbol=&symbol=&symbol=&symbol=&symbol=&symbol=&symbol=&symbol=&multi.x=31&multi.y=6, November 11, 2004.

68. Whole Foods www.wholefoodsmarket.com/investor/10K-Q/2003_10K.pdf, Page 6, November 11, 2004.

69. Whole Foods Code of Conduct found at company Web site, www.wholefoodsmarket.com/investor/codeofconduct.pdf, November 11, 2004.

70. Whole Foods Code of Conduct found at company Web site, www.wholefoodsmarket.com/investor/codeofconduct.pdf (page 11).

71. Business Ethics 100 best companies to work for, www.business-ethics.com/100best.htm, November 12, 2004.

72. Paul Grimaldi, "Providence, RI, grocery targets new approach to pricing," *Knight Ridder Tribune Business News*, September 28, 2004, p. 1.

73. www.preparedfoods.com/PF/FILES/HTML/Mintel_Reports/Mintel_PDF/Summaries/sum-OrganicFoodBeverages-Aug2004.pdf.

74. Whole Foods 10K (page 14) www.wholefoodsmarket.com/investor/10K-Q/2004_10KA.pdf.

75. finance.yahoo.com/q/bs?s=WFMI&annual May 26, 2005.

76. finance.yahoo.com/q/is?s=WFMI&annual, July 27, 2005.

Case 15 / Whole Foods Market, 2005: Will There Be Enough Oraganic Food to Satisfy the Growing Demand?

175

C

Unaudited consolidated statements of operations information for the fiscal year ended September 26, 2004

	First Quarter	Second Quarter	Third Quarter	Fourth Quarter
First Year 2004				
Sales	$1,118,148	$902,141	$917,355	$927,306
Cost of goods sold and occupancy costs	733,721	582,597	600,961	606,537
Gross profit	384,427	319,544	316,394	320,769
Direct store expenses	282,596	229,995	232,649	240,800
General and administrative expenses	35,869	28,783	27,551	27,597
Pre-opening and relocation costs	4,073	4,040	4,966	5,569
Operating income	61,889	56,726	51,228	46,803
Other income (expense)				
Interest expense	(2,478)	(1,859)	(1,319)	(1,593)
Investment and other income	1,464	1,503	1,782	1,707
Income before income taxes	60,875	59,370	51,691	46,917
Provision for income taxes	24,350	22,548	20,676	18,767
Net income	$ 36,525	$ 33,822	$ 31,015	$ 28,150
Basic earnings per share	$ 0.61	$ 0.55	$ 0.50	$ 0.45
Diluted earnings per share	$ 0.57	$ 0.52	$ 0.47	$ 0.43
Dividends per share	$ 0.15	$ 0.15	$ 0.15	$ 0.15

Whole Foods Market Balance Sheet for Fiscal Year Ending September 26, 2004[75]

Period Ending	September 26, 2004	September 28, 2003	September 29, 2002
Assets			
Current Assets			
Cash and Cash Equivalents	221,537	165,779	12,646
Short-Term Investments	—	—	—
Net Receivables	94,421	61,554	42,356
Inventory	152,912	123,904	108,189
Other Current Assets	16,702	12,447	8,950
Total Current Assets	**485,572**	**363,684**	**172,141**
Long Term Investments	—	2,206	4,426
Property Plant and Equipment	904,825	718,240	644,688
Goodwill	112,186	80,548	80,548
Intangible Assets	24,831	26,569	22,889
Accumulated Amortization	—	—	—
Other Assets	20,302	5,573	11,159
Deferred Long-Term Asset Charges	—	—	7,350
Total Assets	**1,547,716**	**1,196,820**	**943,201**
Liabilities			
Current Liabilities			
Accounts Payable	328,977	233,778	170,509
Short-/Current Long-Term Debt	5,973	5,806	5,789
Other Current Liabilities	—	—	—
Total Current Liabilities	**334,950**	**239,584**	**176,298**
Long-Term Debt	164,770	162,909	161,952
Other Liabilities	1,581	2,301	3,774
Deferred Long-Term Liability Charges	77,760	15,850	12,091
Minority Interest	—	—	—

| Case 15 / Whole Foods Market, 2005: Will There Be Enough Oraganic Food to Satisfy the Growing Demand?

176

C

Period Ending	September 26, 2004	September 28, 2003	September 29, 2002
Negative Goodwill	—	—	—
Total Liabilities	**579,061**	**420,644**	**354,115**
Stockholders' Equity			
Misc. Stocks Options Warrants	—	—	—
Redeemable Preferred Stock	—	—	—
Preferred Stock	—	—	—
Common Stock	535,107	423,297	341,940
Retained Earnings	431,495	351,255	247,568
Treasury Stock	—	—	—
Capital Surplus	—	—	—
Other Stockholder Equity	2,053	1,624	-422
Total Stockholder Equity	**968,655**	**776,176**	**589,086**
Net Tangible Assets	**$ 831,638**	**$ 669,059**	**$ 485,649**

Whole Foods Market Income Statement for Fiscal Year ending September 26, 2004[76]

Period Ending	September 26, 2004	September 28, 2003	September 29, 2002
Total Revenue	**$3,864,950**	**$3,148,593**	**$2,690,475**
Cost of Revenue	2,523,816	2,067,939	1,757,213
Gross Profit	**1,341,134**	**1,080,654**	**933,262**
Operating Expenses			
Research Development	—	—	—
Selling General and Administrative	1,107,797	893,229	771,631
Non Recurring	11,449	12,091	12,485
Others	—	—	—
Total Operating Expenses	1,119,246	905,320	784,116
Operating Income or Loss	**221,888**	**175,334**	**149,146**
Income from Continuing Operations			
Total Other Income/Expenses Net	6,456	5,593	2,056
Earnings Before Interest And Taxes	228,344	180,927	151,202
Interest Expense	7,249	8,114	10,384
Income Before Tax	221,095	172,813	140,818
Income Tax Expense	88,438	69,126	56,327
Minority Interest	—	—	—
Net Income from Continuing Ops	132,657	103,687	84,491
Nonrecurring Events			
Discontinued Operations	—	—	—
Extraordinary Items	—	—	—
Effect of Accounting Changes	—	—	—
Other Items	—	—	—
Net Income	**132,657**	**103,687**	**84,491**
Preferred Stock and Other Adjustments	—	—	—
Net Income Applicable to Common Shares	**$ 132,657**	**$ 103,687**	**$ 84,491**

L'Oréal's Business Strategy

Neeraj Kumar Singh
Srikanth G

*ICFAI University Press, Business School Case
Development Centre*

The success of new products, the international breakthroughs made by our brands and our spectacular progress in the emerging markets have enabled L'Oréal to achieve another year of strong sales growth. This momentum, combined with the tight control of costs, led to an important improvement in profitability, despite an exceptionally unfavourable economic and monetary environment.[1]

— Lindsay Owen-Jones, Chairman and Chief Executive Officer of L'Oréal Group

INTRODUCTION

Founded in 1909, L'Oréal had become the world leader in the cosmetics market by 2003. Providing a variety of beauty products, it has transformed from a French company in the early 1900s to a global titan in the 2000s. Its product range included makeup, perfume, and hair and skin care products, which were tailored according to the consumer needs. The company believed in the strategy of innovation and diversification. L'Oréal's growth depended on the global brand, which helped in sustaining the mature consumer-products market even in times when global markets themselves were shaky. High profile, celebrity-driven marketing campaigns and Web-enabled information and customization sites as well as aggressive expansion and acquisition enhanced its global brand image. The cosmetic market as a whole had been slightly on the decline since the late 1990s. But the L'Oréal products were becoming popular due to their uniqueness and catering to the beauty needs of different ethnic groups

and gender. In 2003, the group was number one in the U.S. cosmetic market, but it faced tough competition from Estée Lauder and Procter & Gamble. This made the group refocus its business strategies.

BACKGROUND

L'Oréal, the world's largest cosmetic company, was established in 1909 by a French chemist, Eugene Schueller. After manufacturing and selling the cosmetic products in Paris for a few years, Schueller started exporting to other European countries like Holland, Austria, and Italy. Gradually the L'Oréal products were distributed to the United States, South America, Russia, and the Far East. By 2003, the L'Oréal group had entered 130 countries, through its 290 subsidiaries and around a hundred agents. More than 80 percent of group sales were generated outside France, with operations in every major territory.

In the 1970s, it acquired Laboratories Garnier of Paris, and this group became one of L'Oréal's largest divisions. The heart of L'Oréal's strategy was the cosmetic and dermatological research department. The group earmarked 3 percent of its turnover (sales) to the research and development work. Since the 1980s, the group had particularly focused its attention on North America with a series of smart launches, clever acquisitions, and dynamic marketing causing problems for domestic rivals.

Since its establishment, the L'Oréal group had marketed over 500 brands, consisting of more than 2,000 products. It provided products for all sectors of

| Case 16 / L'Oréal's Business Strategy

178

C

L'Oréal's Business Strategy by Neeraj Kumar Singh, under the direction of Sritkanth G. © ICFAI University Press & ICFAI Business School Case Development Centre, 2004. Reprinted with permission. www.icfaipress.org; www.icfaipress.org/books.

beauty business, such as hair color, permanents, styling aid, body care and skincare, cleansers, and fragrances.[2] Its general cosmetics portfolio contained many of the world's biggest beauty products. It owned numerous brands, including Kerastase, Garnier, Maybelline, Helena Rubenstein, Giorgio Armani, Vichy, and La Roche Posay.

The company believed that diversification and innovation were its critical success factors. L'Oréal's concern for offering products that were adaptable to the demands of its clients showed its passion for innovations. Thus, it invested heavily in research and development and recovered its investment by globally launching its new products. All research was centered in France. As finished products were developed, they were offered to subsidiaries across the world. Because brand life cycles for cosmetics could be very short, L'Oréal tried to introduce one or two new products every year in each of its worldwide markets. L'Oréal marketed products under its own name as well as under a number of other individual and family brand names. For example, it marketed Anaïs Anaïs perfume, the high-end Lancôme line of cosmetics, and L'Oréal brand haircare products.

L'Oréal's strategy was to trickle down technology over time from high-end outlets like department stores to mass markets, such as drugstores. The mass-market brand Plenitude had become the market leader in France, but sales in the United States had not been promising. With innovations and diversifying strategies L'Oréal overcame all these hurdles to an extent. In 2001, the Group, headed by CEO Lindsay Owen-Jones, had a turnover (sales) of €13.7 billion. In 2003, L'Oréal was the world's largest skincare company, with revenues of US$17 billion, and employed 50,000 people.[3]

PRODUCT CATEGORIES

Since its beginning, the L'Oréal Group had developed products in the field of cosmetics. It had four product categories: consumer, luxury, professional, and active (Exhibit 1). These products catered to the needs of hair, skin, makeup, and so on. The consumer products encompassed all the brands distributed through mass-market channels, ensuring that L'Oréal quality was available to the maximum number of consumers. The consumer division accounted for more than half of the sales in 2003. The luxury division offered a range of prestigious international brands selectively distributed through perfumeries, department stores, and duty-free shops. The professional division, the market leader in its sector, offered specific hair care products for use by professional hairdressers and products sold exclusively through hair salons. The active division created and marketed brands of cosmetics and dermatological products for selective distribution through pharmacies and specialty health and beauty outlets. The major brands in these divisions were L'Oréal Paris, Biotherm, Giorgio Armani, Lancôme, Shu Uemura, Polo Ralph Lauren Blue, and L'Oréal Professional.

Innovations from the research laboratories and a large number of initiatives ensured growth for the

| EXHIBIT 1 | Breakdown of 2003 Consolidated Cosmetics Sales by Division |

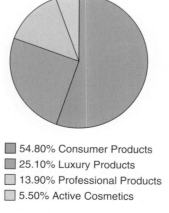

■ 54.80% Consumer Products
■ 25.10% Luxury Products
□ 13.90% Professional Products
■ 5.50% Active Cosmetics

Source: www.loreal.com.

group's core brands. The company achieved major market share in all of its product divisions. The Professional Products Division achieved 8.8 percent growth in the first half of 2003. The division took new initiatives in all business segments, particularly in colorants with the launch of Luo (a new translucid colorant) and Equa (a formula developed specifically for the needs of the Japanese market). The Consumer Products Division achieved 9.3 percent growth for the first half of 2003 over that of the previous year, which was well ahead of the growth rate for mass-market products. This growth could be attributed in particular to the launch of innovative products such as Couleur Experte colorants and Double Extension mascara. The Luxury Products Division, operating in markets that were more sensitive to the economic slowdown and the reduction in air travel, managed to maintain growth of 0.2 percent. This performance came from the success of new products such as the Résolution facial skincare from Lancôme, a brand that at the end of 2002 became the world's number one in the selective retailing channel. In perfumes, the successful European launch of Polo Blue by Ralph Lauren confirmed the excellent results achieved in the United States. The Active Cosmetics Department continued its international rollout, while improving its market shares in Europe. It thus achieved a growth rate of 10.9 percent, in line with the figure for the first half of 2002. This was boosted especially by the successful Myokine facial skincare from Vichy and the skin redensifier Innéov Fermeté, launched in five European countries, heralding the group's first move into the cosmetic nutritional

supplement market. Dermatology achieved sales of €139 million, representing like-for-like growth of 7 percent. Galderma performed well on the acne and rosacea markets. In geographic terms, Galderma continued to achieve sustained growth in North America and made strong advances in Latin America (growth in Brazil was 8 percent and in Mexico 22 percent) and Asia (growth in South Korea was 23 percent).

NEW WORLDWIDE MARKETS

L'Oréal was surging in markets from China to Mexico (Exhibit 2). Its secret was conveying the allure of different cultures through its products. Whether it was selling Italian elegance, New York street smarts, or French beauty through its brands, L'Oréal was reaching out to more people across a bigger range of incomes and cultures than just about any other beauty-products company in the world.[4]

The success of L'Oréal cosmetics had been built on the promotion of different brands in different nations, the choice of which was based on views of the local culture. For people interested in finding the most American product possible, the French company used the name Maybelline. Those preferring the most French were given the L'Oréal brand. All the different lines were sold in all of the markets, but only one was excessively promoted, depending on the market.

L'Oréal was number one in the cosmetic industry but competition in the U.S. market as well as international markets such as Japan, China, etc., was growing. In the United States, L'Oréal and Estée Lauder were

EXHIBIT 2	Breakdown of 2003 Consolidated Cosmetics Sales by Geographic Zone

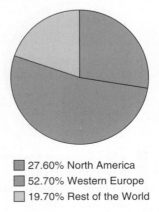

- 27.60% North America
- 52.70% Western Europe
- 19.70% Rest of the World

Source: www.loreal.com.

head to head and Procter & Gamble was slightly behind them. Internationally L'Oréal was facing competition from global as well as local players. Germany's Beiersdorf had stolen a march on L'Oréal by beating it to the market with its Nivea Kao brand of strips used to clean pores. Worldwide, Nivea ranked number one in mass-market face cream, with 11 percent share, slightly ahead of L'Oréal's Plenitude. Procter and Gamble's Oil of Olay skin cream was on par with L'Oréal's Plenitude around the globe.

By tailoring its products to the demands of a specific marketing group with the backing of the international brand name, L'Oréal achieved profitable results for the year 2000, in countries such as Japan (up 46 percent), Korea (70 percent), Brazil (44 percent) and Russia (47 percent) to name but a few. The growth continued in 2003 also. It was very strong in Central and Eastern Europe (up 26.2 percent), particularly in the Russian Federation, where sales advanced once more (up 38.8 percent) after three years of extremely fast growth.

The group made important breakthroughs in the newer markets in 2003. It ventured into the Chinese market, which was crowded with 3,000 domestic cosmetic manufacturers. More than 450 foreign companies had invested in excess of US$300 million in China over the last decade, further stimulating the rapid growth of this sector. L'Oréal, Procter & Gamble, Unilever, and Shiseido ranked among notable international competitors in China. Total sales of cosmetic products in 2000 exceeded RMB30 billion (US$3.66 billion). Since economic reform started 20 years ago, China's cosmetics market had grown an average of 23.8 percent a year from 1982 to 1998. Although this growth slowed down to about 12.9 percent a year after 1998, cosmetic sales in China were expected to reach RMB80 billion (US$9.76 billion) by 2010.[5] L'Oréal wanted to cash in on this opportunity.

Achieving success in the Asian market was a goal for L'Oréal in 2000, an aim the company saw as "internationalization" as opposed to "globalization." Beatrice Dautresme, vice-president in charge of strategic business development, commented, "L'Oréal sees the world as a mosaic of different cultures."[6] In China, where the group's core brands are now fully installed, the growth rate was 69.3 percent, largely thanks to the emblematic success of Maybelline, the country's number one makeup brand. Alongside L'Oréal Paris, which reinforced its luxury brand image, Garnier successfully extended its product offering, particularly in the skincare market. Vichy strengthened its number one position in the 2,500 pharmacies that sold the brand's products across the Russian Federation. In Japan the growth was maintained due to the acquisition of Shu Uemura, cosmetics giant in Japan, and the launch of L'Oréal Paris skincare and makeup lines in Japan, which marked a major advance in establishing the brand in the Japanese market. In India too, growth was extremely rapid at 33.4 percent. This strong performance reflected the breakthroughs achieved by the Garnier brand, which had managed to launch modern colorants that met women's needs at affordable prices. To help fulfill the growth potential in India, the group had started a new factory near the city of Pune (in Western India), which benefited from the most advanced production quality standards.

CHANGING STRATEGY

L'Oréal was gradually turning marketing efforts to the ethnic beauty industry, and reaping profits. L'Oréal was working hard to grab a portion of the estimated $14 billion[7] (by 2008) ethnic beauty industry by focusing product lines and marketing on African-American and Asian-American communities. Since 1998, L'Oréal had purchased Soft Sheen and Carson, two black-centered beauty companies, and rolled them into one mega-company. The company had also been busy in acquiring Asian-centered companies, such as Mininurse of China and Shu Uemura of Japan.

L'Oréal had also tuned its research work for developing products specific for the ethnic groups. L'Oréal opened a new research center in Chicago in 2003, to research and study the skin and hair of different ethnic groups. The Institute's first major project was centered on characterizing the chemical and physical properties of African hair. The goal of this research was to better classify hair according to fiber structure so that the performance of hair relaxers currently in the market could be improved. Other projects would investigate skincare problems such as pigment and scarring disorders. Chicago was chosen for a number of reasons. Soft Sheen had long been headquartered in the city; Chicago had historically been a center of black American culture and learning; and there were a number of renowned universities in the area that provided opportunities for synergy with L'Oréal's new research institute. The needs and requirements of consumers of different ethnic origins were different. They had specific skin and haircare needs that required products especially formulated for them. L'Oréal's acquisition of the Soft Sheen–Carson brand, a world leader in skin and haircare for black women, had greatly expanded the Group's activities in this market sector. Jean-Paul Agon, president and CEO of L'Oréal USA, says about the new research center, "The knowledge and insights that we gain through research conducted at the Institute will ultimately allow us to develop innovative new products that better serve the beauty care needs of the global ethnic market."[8]

As the cosmetic market for women was becoming somewhat saturated, the cosmetic companies shifted their target. The male cosmetic market, a slow burner in beauty, was predicted to take off in the future. The overall market for men's cosmetics grew by 9 percent in 1999, according to NPD Beauty Trends (source: Euro RSCG report).[9] Research showed that men were far more brand loyal in this market than women, mainly because they disliked shopping around.[10] An industry insider commented, "The global male cosmetics market is growing 30 percent annually."[11] L'Oréal had some of the most popular male cosmetics brands in Europe and the United States—including Biotherm Homme, a high-end brand with more than 50 percent market share in Europe. The company began introducing its Biotherm Homme skincare products in China in 2002. The firm had targeted young and fashionable male customers. L'Oréal saw the potential of the cosmetics market for men, although cosmetics for men in 2003 accounted for a very small portion of L'Oréal's sales in China.

In 2003, for the 19th consecutive year, the L'Oréal group showed a double-digit profit growth rate. The net operational profit rose by 13.5 percent to €1.65 billion ($2.1 billion) (Exhibit 3). But its consolidated sales (Exhibit 4) had fallen by 9 percent, mainly due to currency fluctuations. In 2003, L'Oréal battled economic slowdown and adverse currency moves, while war in Iraq forced it to cram product launches into the first and fourth quarters of the year. In 2003, L'Oréal was number one in the United States with a market share of 21.2 percent. Comparatively, its competitors Estée Lauder and Procter & Gamble held market share of 19.6 percent and 13 percent respectively.

In 2004, L'Oréal climbed 10 places to the 20th position in the annual *Financial Times* survey of the "World's Most Respected Companies," compared to the 30th position it held in 2003's ranking. L'Oréal Group CEO Lindsay Owen-Jones also made a very strong impression for his leadership qualities; he was ranked number 16 on the list of the "World's Most Respected Business Leaders," climbing 14 positions in only three years. In the sector rankings, L'Oréal was placed fourth on the list of some of the world's largest consumer goods manufacturers.[12]

EXHIBIT 3

Ten Years of Consolidated Financial Data of L'Oréal Group

(€ millions)	2004	2003	2002	2001	2000 (2)	1999 (1) (2)	1998 (1)	1998	1997	1996	1995	1994
RESULTS OF OPERATIONS												
Consolidated sales	14,534	14,029	14,288	13,740	12,671	10,751	9,588	11,498	10,537	9,200	8,136	7,260
Pre-tax profit of consolidated companies	2,063	1,870	1,698	1,502	1,322	1,125	979	1,339	1,183	1,011	897	816
As a percentage of consolidated sales	*14.2*	*13.3*	*11.9*	*10.9*	*10.4*	*10.5*	*10.2*	*11.6*	*11.2*	*11.0*	*11.0*	*11.2*
Income tax	696	629	580	536	488	429	375	488	422	328	285	256
Net operational profit	1,659	1,661	1,464	1,236	1,033	833	722	807	722	644	579	529
As a percentage of consolidated sales	*11.4*	*11.8*	*10.2*	*9.0*	*8.2*	*7.7*	*7.5*	*7.0*	*6.9*	*7.0*	*7.1*	*7.3*
Net operational profit after minority interests	1,656	1,653	1,456	1,229	1,028	827	719	719	641	568	515	476
Total dividend	554	494	433	365	297	230	191	191	165	144	125	114
BALANCE SHEET												
Fixed assets	11,534	8,136	8,130	8,140	7,605	5,918	5,299	5,590	5,346	4,687	3,550	3,366
Current assets	6,645	6,876	6,843	6,724	6,256	5,139	4,229	4,937	4,512	4,048	3,617	3,182
Of which cash and marketable securities	*1,981*	*2,303*	*2,216*	*1,954*	*1,588*	*1,080*	*762*	*903*	*825*	*810*	*685*	*844*
Shareholders' equity (3)	10,564	8,136	7,434	7,210	6,179	5,470	5,123	5,428	5,015	4,429	3,938	3,642
Borrowings and debts	2,175	1,941	2,646	2,939	3,424	1,914	1,718	1,748	1,767	1,598	848	979
PER SHARE DATA (notes 4 to 6)												
Net operational profit after minority interests per share (7) (8) (9)	2.46	2.45	2.15	1.82	1.52	1.22	1.06	1.06	0.95	0.84	0.76	0.70
Net dividend per share (10) (11)	0.82	0.73	0.64	0.54	0.44	0.34	0.28	0.28	0.24	0.21	0.18	0.17
Tax credit	—	0.37	0.32	0.27	0.22	0.17	0.14	0.14	0.12	0.11	0.09	0.09
Share price as of December 31 (10)	55.85	65.00	72.55	80.90	91.30	79.65	61.59	61.59	35.90	29.79	18.17	15.09
Weighted average number of shares outstanding	673,547,541	676,021,722	675,990,516	676,062,160	676,062,160	676,062,160	676,062,160	676,062,160	676,062,160	676,062,160	614,601,970	614,601,970

Continues

EXHIBIT 3 *(Cont'd)*

(1) For purposes of comparability, the figures include:
- in 1998, the pro forma impact of the change in the consolidation method for Synthélabo, following its merger with Sanofi in May 1999,
- the impact in 1998 and 1999 of the application of CRC Regulation no. 99-02 from January 1, 2000 onwards.

This involves the inclusion of all deferred tax liabilities, evaluated using the balance sheet approach and the extended concept, the activation of financial leasing contracts considered to be material, and the reclassification of profit sharing under "Personal costs"

(2) The figures for 1999 and 2000 also include the impact on the balance sheet of adopting the preferential method for the recording of employee retirement obligation and related benefits from January 1st 2001 onwards. However, the new method had no material impact on the profit and loss account of the years concerned.

(3) Plus minority interests.

(4) Including investment certificates issued in 1986 and bonus share issues. Public Exchange Offers were made for investment certificates and voting right certificates on the date of the Annual General Meeting on May 25, 1993 (see Commission des Opérations de Bourse information note of June 3, 1993).

The certificates were reconstituted as shares following the Special General Meeting on March 29, 1999 and the Extraordinary General Meeting on June 1, 1999.

(5) Figures restated to reflect the one-for-ten bonus share allocation decided by the Board of Directors as of May 23, 1996.

(6) Ten-for-one share split (Annual General Meeting of May 30, 2000).

(7) Net earnings per share are based on the weighted average number of shares outstanding in accordance with the accounting standards in force.

(8) In order to provide data that are genuinely recurrent, L'Oréal calculates and publishes net earnings per share based on net operational profit after minority interests, before allowing for the provision for depreciation of treasury shares, capital gains and losses on fixed assets, restructuring costs, and the amortization of goodwill.

(9) At December 31, 2004, 8.5 million subscription options have been allocated to group executives, and could lead to the issue of the same number of shares.

(10) The L'Oréal share has been listed in euros on the Paris Bourse since January 4, 1999, where it was listed in 1963. The share capital was fixed at €135,212,432 at the Annual General Meeting of June 1, 1999: the par value of one share is now €0.2.

(11) The dividend is fixed in euros since the annual General Meeting of May 30, 2000.

Source: www.loreal-finance.com.

EXHIBIT
4
Consolidated Sales of L'Oréal Group in 2003

1) Breakdown of consolidated sales by branch

	2003		Growth (as %)		2002		2001	
	€ millions	% of total	Published figures	Excluding exchange effect	€ millions	% of total	€ millions	% of total
Cosmetics	13,704.3	97.7	−1.8	7.1	13,951.8	97.6	13,394.2	97.5
Dermatology	306.5	2.2	−4.5	10.5	321.1	2.3	292.2	2.1
Other	18.3	0.1	21.2	21.2	15.1	0.1	54.0	0.4
Group	**14,029.1**	**100.0**	**−1.8**	**7.2**	**14,288.0**	**100.0**	**13,740.4**	**100.0**

Group Share, i.e. 50%

2) Breakdown of consolidated sales by geographic zone

	2003		Growth (as %)		2002		2001	
	€ millions	% of total	Published figures	Excluding exchange effect	€ millions	% of total	€ millions	% of total
Western Europe	7,309.7	52.1	3.8	5.0	7,044.6	49.3	6,667.2	48.5
North America	3,981.4	28.4	−10.3	6.8	4,438.7	31.1	4,450.5	32.4
Rest of the World	2,738.0	19.5	−2.4	14.3	2,804.7	19.6	2,622.7	19.1
Group	**14,029.1**	**100.0**	**−1.8**	**7.2**	**14,288.0**	**100.0**	**13,740.4**	**100.0**

3) Breakdown of cosmetics sales by geographic zone

	2003		Growth (as %)		2002		2001	
	€ millions	% of total	Published figures	Excluding exchange effect	€ millions	% of total	€ millions	% of total
Western Europe	7,221.7	52.7	3.7	4.9	6,962.8	49.9	6,580.6	49.1
North America	3,783.7	27.6	−10.4	6.6	4,224.8	30.3	4,256.9	31.8
Rest of the World	2,698.9	19.7	−2.4	14.3	2,764.2	19.8	2,556.7	19.1
Cosmetics branch	**13,704.3**	**100.0**	**−1.8**	**7.1**	**13,951.8**	**100.0**	**13,394.2**	**100.0**

Source: www.loreal-finance.com.

NOTES

1. "Strong increase in 2003 net operational profit*: +13.5 percent," www.loreal.com, February 20, 2004.
2. "Brands," www.chamberoman.com, 2002.
3. "L'Oréal—World's Largest Skin Care Company—Licenses Tissue-informatics Automated Pathology Slide Screening Software," www.tissueinformatics.com, November 12, 2003.
4. Edmondson, Gail, and Ellen Neuborne, "L'Oréal: The Beauty of Global Branding (int'l edition)," www.businessweek.com, June 28, 1999.
5. "China's Booming Cosmetic Market," www.prorenata.com, February 14, 2002.
6. O'Reilly, Deirdre, "L'Oréal Conquers Asia with Tailored Products," www.archives.tcm.ie, April 22, 2001.
7. "L'Oréal Turns to Black and Asian Communities," www.racerelations.about.com, January 25, 2004.
8. L'Oréal Press, "The Diversity of Beauty," www.loreal.com, August 19, 2003.
9. Lyons, Kate, "Beauty make over," www.bandt.com.au, August 23, 2001.
10. Ibid.
11. Jingjing, Jiang, "Male Cosmetics Consumers Smell Trend's Scent," www.chinadaily.com.cn, March 2, 2004.
12. "L'Oréal Moves Up among World's Most Respected Companies," www.financialtimes.com, January 27, 2004.

CQUAY Technologies Corp.

Kevin K. Boeh
Paul W. Beamish

Richard Ivey School of Business, The University of Western Ontario

It was April 2004, and Calvin McElroy had just closed the CQUAY ("seek way") financials for the quarter. A year earlier, the board had asked McElroy to shape the company into an acquisition target over the next 18 to 24 months. There were no imminent acquisition discussions, and recent customer traction and the sales pipeline seemed to merit raising growth capital instead of following the acquisition-focused plan. McElroy wanted to keep his stockholders and board happy by executing the plan they had given him, but he did not want to jeopardize possible customer growth. If he refocused the plan, McElroy feared it might change acquisition opportunities. Without further contracts, the existing cash would sustain the company for only another six to eight months. McElroy thought the most likely outcome was to sell the company, but he needed to make the company more attractive. He planned to present options and a recommendation to the board of directors later that month.

THE COMPANY

CQUAY Technologies Corporation ("CQUAY") was a privately held Canadian company with offices in Toronto, Calgary, and Washington, D.C. CQUAY marketed a patented location intelligence engine called Common Ground®[1] to enterprise customers, software developers and systems integrators. The company's technology was designed for an emerging, multibillion-dollar segment of the spatial information management (SIM) market, as defined by International Data Corporation (IDC).

CQUAY History and Board of Directors

CQUAY's predecessor company was founded in 1995 as a data management consultancy with customers in the telecom, utility, and oil and gas industries. The projects undertaken by the company evolved into complex Web-enabled databases and applications. Management identified an opportunity, in 1998, to jointly develop a technology platform to manage address and mapping information with a major Canadian telecommunications company. An initial Cdn$1.2 million was secured for the initial technology research and application prototype. This funding was provided by this telecommunications customer, as well as profits from the company's consulting business and certain private investors close to the company. In 2001, the company raised Cdn$5.6 million in an external venture capital round of financing. In January 2002, the company entered into a marketing and implementation agreement with Telus Corporation, the second largest Canadian telecommunications company. In March 2002, the company

Richard Ivey School of Business
The University of Western Ontario **IVEY**

Kevin K. Boeh prepared this case under the supervision of Paul W. Beamish solely to provide material for class discussion. The authors do not intend to illustrate either effective or ineffective handling of a managerial situation. The authors may have disguised certain names and other identifying information to protect confidentiality.

Ivey Management Services prohibits any form of reproduction, storage or transmittal without its written permission. This material is not covered under authorization from CanCopy or any reproduction rights organization. To order copies or request permission to reproduce materials, contact Ivey Publishing, Ivey Management Services, c/o Richard Ivey School of Business, The University of Western Ontario, London, Ontario, Canada, N6A 3K7; phone (519) 661-3208; fax (519) 661-3882; e-mail cases@ivey.uwo.ca.

Copyright © 2004, Ivey Management Services

achieved a significant milestone by demonstrating its Common Ground location services platform using an open location services (OpenLS) compliant interface. The company was the first in the world to demonstrate an online geo-coding and map portrayal service based on this important new specification. In 2002, this predecessor company became illiquid and was unable to raise additional growth capital in the depressed capital markets environment.

Founded in 2002, CQUAY secured its technology, patent interests, trademarks and team from the predecessor company and thereafter offered commercial products and services in Canada and the United States.

A year before, in early 2003, McElroy and his board of directors had decided to pursue a strategy that would prepare the company for its eventual sale. It was agreed that then-current market and economic conditions constrained the possible valuation and likelihood of a near-term acquisition outcome, and, as such, the company should instead lay the groundwork for its sale in 18 to 24 months. The tactics laid out for the company included:

1. Keeping operational costs minimal;
2. Minimizing future-focused research and development expenditure;
3. Securing three to five lead customers;
4. Creating a recurring revenue stream;
5. Validating the pricing models; and
6. Keeping the company structure flexible, if not virtual, so as to facilitate a merger or acquisition.

Industry—The Business Problem

Business and government organizations had created a massive and rapidly growing amount of information in databases, Web pages and files. Inaccurate or outdated information was negatively affecting operational efficiency, customer satisfaction and business decision-making. In areas of public safety and national security, these costs were substantially higher and could include non-financial costs. For many, data quality had become a cornerstone of organizational efficiency.

> By 2005, Fortune 1000 enterprises will lose more money in operational inefficiency due to data quality issues than they will spend on data warehouse and CRM initiatives combined.
>
> — The Gartner Group

One of the most pervasive data quality problems related to address information. An "address" was commonly attached as an "attribute" to computerized records about people, places, and things. An estimated 80 percent of all databases and 15–20 percent of all Web pages in the world contained address data. Address errors and discrepancies were common due to:

- The lack of a standard format for storing address data;
- Duplication of address data in a myriad of systems, in varied, incompatible formats;
- "Free form" data entry fields in applications and databases, with little or no validation;
- Spelling and transposition errors made and liberties taken during data entry (e.g. "West Pender Street" versus "Pender St. W"); and
- Constantly changing "real world" data due to new building construction, building subdivision, boundary changes and street name changes.

Address problems were universal and a major issue for most organizations. Technologies and tools that improved address data quality were in high demand.

> Address data errors alone cost U.S. businesses US$611 billion a year in postage, printing and staff costs related to re-work.
>
> — The Data Warehousing Institute

In addition to data quality issues, information technology (IT) organizations were faced with a major challenge in linking and integrating disparate data sources to support many business processes. The integration of two or more databases required a "common key" to join records. This key could be a customer name, customer identification (ID) number, or asset ID number as long as the reference was unique and consistent. An address match was seemingly another obvious key. Unfortunately, due to errors, discrepancies and the lack of a standard format, address fields were not reliable as a unique key for data integration.

The Location Dimension

Location is an abstract concept associated with:

1. Places and things (e.g. buildings, oil wells, cellular towers, street intersections and other physical structures);
2. Geographic areas with boundaries (e.g. cities, countries, postal codes, sales territories or census tracts); or
3. Positions (e.g. the latitude and longitude coordinates for a mobile device or vehicle).

Most things have a location. A location is simply the point or extent of space that is occupied by a person, place or thing. As such, a location always has geographic context and dimensions. Location intelligence is about understanding where locations are in the real world and knowing how one location relates to another in a geographic sense.

An address record contained numbers or words that identified a place and referred to its associated boundaries (e.g. building numbers as well as street, city, postal, state or province, and country names or codes). However, these were simply location references and did not encode, enable or provide location intelligence.

Understanding the geographic relationship between places and boundaries was important. Those relationships were hard-coded in databases by replicating location references within address records. This approach was inefficient and caused data quality problems whenever a boundary changed. McElroy's idea was that humans have spatial intelligence and enough geographic knowledge to look at an address record and understand location context. Even if not familiar with the street-level address, the reference to "Canada," "USA," or "Europe" enabled a rudimentary level of location intelligence. In comparison, the average computer did not understand that White Plains, New York, was in the United States, and that the state of New York was adjacent to Canada.

An address referred to a unique location. Therefore, address data quality and location intelligence were interrelated. These relationships between addresses and locations were important to certain industries and to organizations with geographically dispersed operations. For example:

- Telecom: determining available network capabilities for a particular service address;
- Wireless telecom carriers: determining tax zones and tariffs for telephone calls and services;
- Utilities: ensuring valid addresses and postal service formats on bills;
- Call centres: entering valid addresses on orders or trouble tickets;
- Oil and gas: retrieving public and private data regarding a geographic area of interest;
- Retailers: associating customer locations to stores and service centres;
- Public safety: identifying geographic patterns associated with emergencies and events;
- Marketing: linking demographic, census and lifestyle data to customer sales records;
- Technical services: tracking staff, equipment and parts in regard to field service calls;
- Financial services: using address as a key to create a single view of a customer; and
- Real estate: buying, selling and renting based on location.

Virtually all information technology (IT) systems contained location references but lacked location intelligence. Computer system users had access to computerized address records but had to use manual methods to determine location.

Until the advent of CQUAY's Common Ground product, the only way to organize, search for and analyse business information based on location context was to extract data from operational systems and upload them into a mapping system. This approach was costly, technically complicated and raised many concerns about data security and integrity. As such, less than 5 percent of knowledge workers used a location-enabled application or analysis tool that was dynamically linked to proprietary business data sources.

The real value of location technology lies in better customer relationships and improved business processes.

— IDC

One of the three or four big trends in software is location-enabled applications.

— Bill Gates, Microsoft

The CQUAY Common Ground Solution

Over US$5 million had been invested in developing this innovative system that solved the address data quality problem while at the same time enabling IT staff to simply "plug in" location intelligence to existing applications or system. Common Ground was based on the notion that a unique "key" in databases, application systems, files and Internet content could be used to encode location context. The goal was that such a key could uniquely identify a place along with its location in the world.

Research into this idea led to a breakthrough concept called a "location object." In Common Ground, locations were modeled as intelligent "objects." The location objects incorporated a robust addressing model supporting 11 different methods (e.g. civic (street) address, aliases (Empire State Building), municipal survey (lot/block/plan), section/township/range). The object model also incorporated location context. As such, each place could "respond" to a range of address queries, "know" where it was in the world and "understand" its geographic relationships with other location objects.

Common Ground could be used as a master repository to store and maintain the valid locations that mattered to an organization. Customers could register the locations of buildings, assets (e.g. oil wells, cell towers), or boundaries (e.g. geopolitical, taxation, sales territory or serving area boundaries) in the Common Ground Location Registry.

The platform also incorporated a patented index method, where every registered location was assigned a unique key called a Universal Spatial Locator™ (USL). The USL provided the link between an external data source or application and the location intelligence contained in Common Ground. Common Ground, along with the Location Registry and USLs, served as a location intelligence engine that understood location context and the relationships among any registered locations.

A location intelligence engine was similar to a search engine like Google™. A search engine registered and cross-referenced key words, in Web pages, to an associated URL or Internet address. Common Ground registered and cross-referenced "location references" in database records, Web pages and files to the associated USL. The platform provided a secure, centralized, location-smart index to widely distributed data sources (see Exhibit 1).

The Common Ground platform came bundled with a subscription to high-quality mapping and address data for the customer's geographic area of interest. This simplified deployment as well as ongoing updates and maintenance. The engine and its location data were licensed to enterprise customers or online application service providers. The platform was based on highly scalable Web services architecture and used standard XML-based interfaces (compatible with IBM, SUN Microsystems and Microsoft) to link securely, through firewalls, to other applications and systems.

A Java-based Web Services Kit (WSK) enabled easy and rapid integration with existing customer relationship management (CRM), enterprise resource planning (ERP), asset or inventory management (AM/IM), workforce management (WFM) systems, or custom developed Web applications, in order to:

- Match, cleanse and reconcile address data discrepancies within existing systems;
- Provide dynamic address validation and address standardization (e.g. U.S. Postal Service and Canada Post standards) to external applications (e.g. Siebel CRM);
- Tag enterprise databases, Web pages and files with USLs;
- Pass a USL from one system to another as an address proxy to avoid propagating address errors through mechanized interfaces;
- Register the places, things and boundaries used by the enterprise within the Location Registry;

| EXHIBIT 1 | Location-Centric Data Integration |

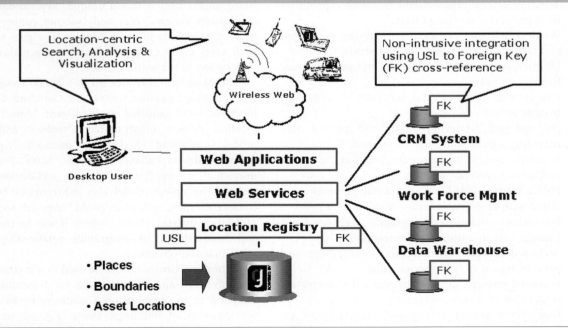

Source: CQUAY Business Plan—March 2004.

- Index, integrate, correlate, search, analyse and visualize widely distributed data sources based on location-centric or geographic criteria (e.g. within a boundary, nearest, within five miles, adjacent); and
- Dynamically associate the real-time position of wireless devices and fleet vehicles to places, things and boundaries registered with Common Ground, thereby linking mobile resources to back office enterprise applications.

CQUAY generated revenue in four ways:

1. Software license fees for the Common Ground platform;
2. Recurring annual software maintenance and support fees;
3. Recurring annual location data subscription services; and
4. Professional services to assist customers in implementing the platform.

CQUAY was the first company to integrate tools for address data management and quality assurance with location intelligence capabilities in a single platform.

The CQUAY Value Proposition

McElroy felt the potential for Common Ground was enormous. It cut across virtually all industries, business functions, processes and application systems. An estimated 80 percent of all databases in the world contained either address or some other location reference. These estimates did not include Web content and the billions of electronic documents that had been created by organizations. The problems and costs associated with address data quality were well understood by most organizations and were a cause of great concern. Common Ground could help customers:

- Reduce operational costs through reducing address data errors;
- Increase revenue through cross-selling, based on better customer information and knowledge;
- Improve customer satisfaction through reduced errors on orders and invoices, more predictable and reliable delivery and installation timeframes and faster responses to inquiries with more accurate information;
- Achieve strategic advantage through insights provided by the "lens" of location intelligence;
- Improve business decision-making through access to more accurate information; and
- Optimize the management of mobile assets, equipment and staff resources by rationalizing workload and task assignments based on location context.

Client Case Studies

Bell West Inc., a division of Bell Canada, was experiencing a 30 percent customer cancellation rate on new service orders caused by address data errors and an inability to accurately associate a customer location to network boundaries and associated telecom facilities. The company implemented Common Ground and integrated the engine with Bell West's existing Siebel CRM, Metasolv (equipment inventory and provisioning planning) and data warehouse systems. The project was completed in six months and dramatically reduced order cancellation rates and operating costs, with a return on investment of just over eight months.

The U.S. National Sheriff's Association was implementing a secure, national messaging and information sharing network. Over 500 disparate databases in 220 different organizations were indexed and cross-referenced using Common Ground and USLs. In a subsequent phase, location intelligence was planned to be used to navigate a massive multi-agency and multi-jurisdictional resource directory and to generate alerts and notification lists based on location context (e.g. all agencies within 500 miles of an emergency or incident).

The Market and Competition

Systems with location intelligence were not new. According to Daratech, the global Geographic Information Systems (GIS) market size was approximately US$7 billion, including software, map data, related hardware and consulting services. However, 75 percent of this revenue was attributed to back-office engineering systems in telecom and government organizations. IDC had identified a US$1.5 billion spatial information management (SIM) market (software only) that was very fragmented and had three segments:

- Traditional GIS and mapping software: Focused on engineering users, characterized as mature, saturated and dominated by established vendors, such as Intergraph, ESRI and Autodesk with growth rates of 2–5 percent per year;
- Web mapping services: Currently less than 5 percent of total SIM revenue, viewed as a nascent but potentially large market that had consolidated into a battle between Microsoft's MapPoint and AOL's MapQuest services; and
- Spatially enabled business support systems (BSS): An emerging high-growth segment, projecting 30–60 percent annualized growth to US$1.2 billion in software by 2006, without a dominant player. This market extended to support mobile applications as well.

According to IDC and other industry experts, traditional GIS and mapping software vendors had been unsuccessful at moving into the Web mapping and emerging location-enabled BSS segments. The high-growth BSS segment was projected to overtake the traditional GIS market within three years. CQUAY was exclusively focused on this SIM market segment and its extension into "mobilized" applications. Common Ground, as a master repository and Web services platform, provided a complementary capability to data quality tools from companies like First Logic, Group 1, Trillium, QAS and Ascential, as well as integration technologies from companies like WebMethods, BEA, Vitria and TIBCO. There were perhaps 5,000 to 7,000 companies or government agencies in North America that had licensed software products from these companies that could also benefit from location technology. An average licence price of US$250,000 per customer supported the projected US$1.2 billion market identified by IDC.

Data quality tool vendors were starting to augment address data with latitude/longitude coordinates through a technique called "geo-coding" but did not offer an engine for location-centric data indexing, integration and search. Online mapping services could resolve a building number on a street to a valid "address range" only and could show the place on a map but had limited knowledge of "real world" places, things, or boundaries (e.g. customer or facilities data). See Exhibit 2 for a summary of market competition.

CQUAY Intellectual Capital

In August of 2003, CQUAY was granted a broad patent by the United States Patent and Trademark Office (Number 6,611,751) for the USL concept. The Location Object model and technology platform had required US$5 million to develop the proprietary technology. The robust address model (not duplicated by any of the traditional mapping or GIS vendors, nor by Oracle or IBM) included substantial intellectual property created in a joint venture research project with TELUS Communications.

CQUAY Marketing Strategy

Virtually any application, database, Web site or document with location references could be parsed and tagged with USLs and enhanced with Common Ground Web services. However, CQUAY planned to focus on the telecom and utility markets, specifically on supporting business areas and applications:

- Applications: CRM, WFM, and AM/IM were large and growing enterprise application segments. Users recognized address data problems as well as the lack of location intelligence in current solutions. These areas also represented cross-industry market extension potential;
- Industry: Telecom and utility companies had been early adopters of CRM, WFM, and AM/IM applications and, as users of traditional GIS systems, also recognized the value of location intelligence. Wireless carriers were starting to leverage the power of location-based services; and
- Relationships: The CQUAY principals, board of directors and advisors had extensive experience and relationships within the telecom and utility marketplaces.

EXHIBIT 2	Competitive Landscape in Location Technology

	CQUAY	Intergraph ESRI MapInfo	Group 1 1st Logic Ascential	MapPoint MapQuest	IBM Oracle
Robust address model	✓		✓		
OGC geometry model	✓	✓			✓
Location index (e.g. USL)	✓				
Web services API	✓	Map	Address	Map	
Enterprise scalability	✓			✓	✓
Location object database	✓				
Address geo-coding	✓	✓	✓	✓	
Bundled address & map data subscription	✓	Map	Address	Map	
Address validation & standardization	✓		✓		

Source: CQUAY Business Plan—March 2004.

CQUAY's market entry and development strategy involved three key elements:

- Direct sales to enterprise customers: Direct sales, supported by consulting and systems integration (SI) partners, were used to sell and implement Common Ground for enterprise customers. A potential customer's current investment in systems encouraged relationships with certain independent software vendors (ISVs) and SI firms. The direct sales program was supported by seminar and trade show marketing as well as by analyst and media tours;
- Leverage ISV alliances: CQUAY used its enterprise customer success stories to build support from ISVs for collaborative development and co-marketing agreements. Through these partnerships CQUAY leveraged the ISV direct sales forces as a channel; and
- Enterprise application SI channel: CQUAY planned to recruit the implementation partners of ISVs to extend the reach of its direct marketing efforts.

McElroy thought that success in the CRM/WFM/AM in the telecom and utility spaces would lead to a horizontal extension into other verticals, by leveraging the same ISV and channel partnerships. The successful integration of Common Ground with a CRM, WFM, or AM solution would lead to projects involving other applications such as data warehouse, ERP, supply chain management, workflow, document management, or wireless applications.

A secondary but high-profile market opportunity existed in public safety under the auspices of Homeland Security in the United States. CQUAY had secured a significant contract as part of a consortium bid in the United States. CQUAY planned to leverage this in direct sales and marketing, as well as SI partnerships within the state and federal government markets, with an emphasis on Homeland Security and public safety.

CQUAY had also established collaborative marketing relationships with a number of related companies, including:

- Viewpoint Support—A Canadian systems integrator in the telecom and utility markets. Also, the prime contractor on Bell West;
- eLabs—Canadian Billing/CRM software platform vendor, partner on National Sheriff's Association;
- Coronado Group—U.S. federal government-focused systems integrator, with a joint proposal to a major U.S. federal agency;
- Visionquest—Atlanta-based vendor of project information management, with joint proposals to several telecom prospects; and

- UMA Group—A Canadian consulting engineering firm with a joint proposal under development to a large municipal government prospect.

The company was also in early stages of partnering discussions with several other technology and systems integration partners.

The Team

The CQUAY management and technical team had extensive experience in the SIM industry and within the initial target vertical markets. The company's chief executive officer and chairman, Calvin McElroy, had more than 24 years of successful sales, operational and executive management experience with companies, including Oracle and Intergraph. Both Oracle and Intergraph were successful marketing traditional SIM technologies in telecom, utility, emergency 911, and public safety markets. Vice-President and Chief Operating Officer Peter Lee had over 19 years of experience with Intergraph and Enghouse Systems, both companies in the SIM market. The team also included Vice-President of Research and Development and Chief Technical Office David Warren, who had 25 years of experience in similar roles with Intergraph, Encor and Texaco. The executives had worked together with McElroy for several years. All company employees were located in Calgary and Toronto, with a sales office in Washington, D.C. The three key executives plus the technology development team were dedicated staff, but other workers were hired as independent contractors as needed to fulfil customer integration requirements.

Capitalization

CQUAY Technologies Corporation was incorporated in March 2002 and raised US$150,000 in seed capital from management and other founding stockholders. With this seed funding, the company secured the Common Ground technology, patent interests and trademarks in a liquidation sale by the predecessor company. CQUAY had subsequently generated over US$350,000 in positive cash flow from two commercial contracts. In the fiscal year ending March 31, 2004, the company had generated US$1 million in revenue and was slightly profitable (see Exhibit 3). As of December 31, 2003, CQUAY had a total of 78.8 million common shares outstanding and had neither issued nor granted any preferred shares, warrants or options and had no debt.

THE FUTURE OF CQUAY

Over the past year, McElroy had been able to secure two major customer implementations with a handful more in various stages of discussion. While each new

EXHIBIT 3

CQUAY, Inc. Financial Projections (in US$)

Fiscal Year End March 31	2004	2005e	2006e	2007e	2008e
Revenue					
Software licence	$ 312,000	$ 350,000	$2,050,000	$6,150,000	$14,350,000
Professional services	586,139	500,000	615,000	1,537,500	2,870,000
Data subscription	62,563	110,000	520,000	1,750,000	4,620,000
Maintenance	48,263	95,000	402,500	1,325,000	3,477,500
	1,008,964	1,055,000	3,587,500	10,762,500	25,317,500
Cost of Revenue					
Cost of services	618,837	610,000	1,013,500	2,612,500	5,687,500
Data royalties	11,700	55,000	260,000	875,000	2,310,000
	630,537	665,000	1,273,500	3,487,500	7,997,500
Operating Margin	$ 378,427	$ 390,000	$2,314,000	$7,275,000	$17,320,000
Operating Expenses					
General and administration	203,697	205,000	538,125	968,625	1,519,050
Sales and marketing	17,625	165,000	1,363,250	3,121,125	6,329,375
Research and development	108,987	175,000	538,125	968,625	1,519,050
	330,309	545,000	2,439,500	5,058,375	9,367,475
EBITDA	48,118	(155,000)	(125,500)	2,216,625	7,952,525
Interest, depreciation and taxes	4,358	(2,000)	5,000	789,088	3,192,138
Net Income	$ 43,760	$(153,000)	$ (130,500)	$1,427,537	$ 4,760,387

e = estimates

Summary Balance Sheet
FY March 31, 2004

Cash	$ 158,188
Accounts receivable	76,861
Other	10,000
Net capital assets	29,942
Total Assets	**$274,991**
Accounts payable	88,112
Other	22,799
Debt	–
Total Liabilities	**$110,910**
Share capital	204,874
Retained earnings	(40,794)
Stockholders' Equity	**$164,080**
Total Liabilities and Stockholders' Equity	**$274,991**

contract generated positive cash flow, he knew that aggressive growth would require additional capital. The predecessor company had intended to grow using private capital until it was large enough to undertake an initial public offering; unfortunately the capital markets were depressed at the time. McElroy and the board that had been newly formed with the refounding of CQUAY decided that the company should instead focus on being bought, since the ability to raise capital was unpredictable. Without further contracts, the existing cash would sustain the company for only another 9–12 months. McElroy thought the most likely outcome would be to sell the company, but he wanted to ensure he maximized its valuation in the current market environment (see Exhibit 4). McElroy had to decide what to recommend to the board.

EXHIBIT
4

Selected Comparable Market Data (as of March 31, 2004; in US$ millions)

	Ticker	Market Cap	Price	Shares O/S (M)	Cash	Debt	Sales (ttm)	EBITDA (ttm)
Traditional GIS and Mapping Software								
Intergraph	INGR	$ 886	$24.26	37	$ 251	$ –	$ 540	$ 46
ESRI	Private							
Map Info	MAPS	259	12.81	20	36	18	118	13
Business Support Systems (BBS) Providers								
Group 1	GSOF	249	16.36	15	60	1	119	25
First Logic	Private							
Ascential	ASCL	1,294	21.82	59	510	–	212	10
QAS	Private						71	
BSS Integration Technologies								
Webmethods	WEBM	495	9.36	53	120	1	195	(20)
BEA	BEAS	5,180	12.72	407	1,560	766	1,040	228
Vitria	VITR	194	5.88	33	91	–	72	(14)
Tibco	TIBX	1,621	8.17	198	379	53	295	42
Database Vendors								
IBM	IBM	155,210	91.84	1,690	8,500	23,670	91,320	15,190
Oracle	ORCL	$ 62,040	$12.00	5,170	$8,590	$ 172	$10,160	$ 4,100
Web Mapping Services								
MapPoint	Owned by Microsoft							
MapQuest	Owned by Time Warner Inc (America Online)							

ttm = trailing twelve months.

NOTE

1. Common Ground is a registered trademark of CQUAY Technologies Corp.

News Corp. in 2005: Consolidating the DirecTV Acquisition

C-18

Ravi S. Madapati

ICFAI University Press, Business School Case Development Centre

DirecTV is important to News Corp. because it provides the missing link in News Corp.'s network of satellite TV platforms around the world.

— Rupert Murdoch[1]

INTRODUCTION

Rupert Murdoch, News Corp.'s chairman, seemed to be on top of the world in early 2005. (DirecTV's stock price between 2004 and 2005 is shown in Exhibit 1.) With the successful acquisition of DirecTV, Murdoch's dreams of building a content and distribution empire were coming true. With savvy investments in Internet technologies, quality content, and a strong hold on distribution, News Corp. looked like an invincible media powerhouse at the end of 2004. This optimism was reflected in Murdoch's own words:[2]

> Our satellite platforms now span four continents, and we have more than 26 million subscribers. What that network of platforms gives us is, I believe, the perfect balance of assets for any media company: We have a great mix of subscription and advertising revenue, as well as a great mix of content and distribution businesses—[and] we're spread geographically in a way no other media company in the world can match.

BACKGROUND NOTE

The DirecTV acquisition seemed to mark a turning point for Murdoch. DirecTV's roots went back to 1932, when Hughes Aircraft was set up to build exper-

imental airplanes for Howard Hughes. During World War II, the company began building a mammoth flying boat to serve as a troop carrier. After the war, the company entered the growing defense electronics field. In 1953, it underwent a major shake-up when about 80 of its top engineers walked out, dissatisfied with Hughes, who was becoming distant and difficult to deal with. The U.S. Air Force also threatened to cancel the company's contracts because of Hughes's erratic behavior.

Hughes transferred the company's assets to the Howard Hughes Medical Institute (with himself as its sole trustee) and hired former Bendix Aviation executive Lawrence Hyland to run the company. The institute produced the first beam of coherent laser light in 1960 and placed the first communications satellite into geosynchronous orbit in 1963. The Hughes-built Surveyor landed on the moon in 1966.

In 1984, the Department of Defense canceled several missile contracts and the institute found it difficult to fund research and development. The next year the institute sold Hughes Aircraft to General Motors (GM) for $5.2 billion. GM combined its Delco Electronics auto parts unit with Hughes to form GM Hughes Electronics (GMHE). GMHE acquired General Dynamics' missile business in 1992.

In 1995, GMHE became Hughes Electronics and launched its DirecTV satellite service. The same year, the company strengthened its defense business by acquiring CAE-Link (training and technical services) and Magnavox Electronic Systems (warfare and communications systems). Hughes bought a majority stake in satellite communications provider PanAmSat in 1996.

Case 18 / News Corp. in 2005: Consolidating the DirecTV Acquisition

News Corp in 2005: Consolidating the DirecTV Acquisition. Reprinted by permission of Ravi S. Madapati, ICFAI Knowledge Center, ICFAI University, Hyderabad, India.

In 1998, the company boosted its stake in PanAmSat to 81 percent.[3] The investment and sluggish sales led to a drop in profits for 1998. Hughes also took a public relations hit in 1998, when several of its satellites failed and temporarily halted most U.S. pager activity.

To gain customers and expand its broadcast channel offerings, Hughes bought United States Satellite Broadcasting and the satellite business of rival Primestar and folded the businesses into DirecTV in 1999.

In early 2000, Hughes sold its satellite manufacturing business to Boeing in an effort to focus on its faster growing communications services businesses. GM also issued a tracking stock for Hughes but retained ownership of all the company's assets. Also that year, GM announced that it would try to sell Hughes.

Hughes bought Telocity (later renamed DirecTV Broadband), an Internet service provider that used DSL (digital subscriber line) technology, for about $177 million in 2001. As negotiations to sell Hughes to Rupert Murdoch's News Corp. continued in 2001, EchoStar made an unsolicited bid to buy Hughes for $30.4 billion in stock and $1.9 billion in assumed debt. Soon News Corp. dropped out of the bidding and GM reached a $25.8 billion deal with EchoStar. Even as the Justice Department and the FCC looked likely to block the company's sale to EchoStar, Hughes announced that it was confident the deal would win regulatory approval by the end of the year. However, the companies abruptly called off the merger in December 2002.

In a sudden turn of events, GM sold its 19.8 percent interest in Hughes Electronics to News Corp. in 2003. News Corp. acquired another 14.2 percent from common stockholders, amounting to a 34 percent stake in Hughes Electronics, which it quickly transferred to its 82 percent-owned Fox Entertainment Group. In 2004, Hughes Electronics changed its name to The DirecTV Group, declaring its focus and commitment to the DirecTV brand.

DirecTV's Business

DirecTV, the first entertainment service in the United States to deliver all digital-quality, multichannel TV programming to an 18-inch satellite dish, provided people across the United States with a much-needed alternative to cable. For the first time, rural consumers who were not being served by cable had access to programming like their urban and suburban counterparts. DirecTV's business included:

- DirecTV US, which was the largest provider of direct broadcast satellite (DBS) television services and the second largest MVPD[4] provider in the United States behind Comcast. DirecTV provided its customers with access to hundreds of channels of digital-quality video and audio programming that was transmitted directly to its customers' homes or businesses via high-powered geosynchronous satellites. As of December 31, 2003, DirecTV had about 12.2 million subscribers, of whom about 10.7 million were DirecTV's subscribers (see Exhibit 2). The remaining subscribers received DirecTV service from members and affiliates of the National Rural Telecommunications Cooperative. DirecTV also provided premium professional and collegiate sports programming such as the NFL[5] Sunday Ticket package, which allowed subscribers to view as many as 14 NFL games played each Sunday during the regular season.

- PanAmSat, which owned and operated 25 satellites that were capable of transmitting signals to geographic areas covering over 98 percent of the world's population. PanAmSat provided satellite capacity for the transmission of cable and broadcast television programming from the content source to the cable operator or to the consumer's home. PanAmSat's satellites were able to reach nearly 100 percent of all cable subscribers in the United States. In addition, PanAmSat provided satellite services to telecommunications carriers, government agencies, corporations, and Internet service providers.

- Hughes Network Systems provided broadband satellite networks and services to both consumers and enterprises. Hughes Network Systems (HNS) constituted the DirecTV Network Systems segment. HNS was a leader in the global market for VSAT private business networks with more than 500,000 terminals shipped or ordered. Spaceway, a more advanced satellite broadband communications platform under development, would provide customers with high-speed, two-way data communications on a more cost-efficient basis than systems that were currently available. The first Spaceway satellite service was expected to be introduced in 2005.

The DirecTV Deal

Don't worry. We don't want to take over the world. We just want a piece of it.

— Murdoch[6]

Television programs were delivered by cable or through satellite. Satellite had broader reach than cable. Cable operators beamed programming content through cables to the subscribers' homes. In the case of satellite television, satellites orbiting in the sky did the job, without the need for any cable connection.

Murdoch had been excited about satellite communications right from his childhood. In the mid-1980s, Murdoch paid £10 million for a controlling interest in Sky Television (Sky), a pan-European channel that aired common programs to several European countries. By 1987, Murdoch had spent £40 million on Sky, which reached nearly 12 million homes in 20 European countries. In 1990, after prolonged negotiations, BSB, a television channel, merged with Sky into a single company, British Sky Broadcasting (BSkyB). Between 1989 and 1992, the combined entity reported losses of about $1.2 billion. As BSkyB introduced better programs and aired soccer matches exclusively, it achieved a turnaround by the end of 1992 and revenues rose to £385 million.

By 1993, BSkyB reached financial stability. Over the next four years, the company developed new content and innovative programs. By 1997, 25 percent of British homes were subscribers to the channel. By 2001, Sky had 5 million customers and had become the first digital television channel in the world by moving its operations from analog to digital. By June 2002, BSkyB had 6.1 million subscribers and a 20 percent increase in revenues over 2001.

Meanwhile, DirecTV had made significant progress with its direct broadcast satellite services. Attractive sports content, aggressive marketing, and free installation resulted in rapid penetration of DirecTV. By 2000, DirecTV had enrolled more than 9.5 million subscribers to become the largest satellite-based provider of television content in the United States. DirecTV offered more than 225 programming channels to 60 million homes in about 40 cities in the United States.

Murdoch realized DirecTV would add the strategic U.S. market to his worldwide network of satellite distribution that included BSkyB in Britain, Star TV in Asia, Foxtel in Australia, SkyTel in Latin America, and Stream in Italy. DirecTV would eliminate dependence on cable distribution in the U.S. market and fortify News Corp.'s fast-growing cable networks, which included Fox News, Fox Sports, National Geographic, and Speed Channel, which carried motor sports. DirecTV gave Murdoch the missing link in News Corp.'s worldwide satellite-distribution system. As press reports put it, the DirecTV acquisition made Murdoch "a general in both the content and distribution camps."[7]

In September 2000, Murdoch offered $22 billion for a 35 percent stake in DirecTV. But negotiations between News Corp. and DirecTV proceeded slowly. A 25 percent decline in the stock of Hughes Electronics in February 2001 slowed down the talks further. In April 2001, Murdoch reduced his bid for a 30 percent stake and got Microsoft to commit $3 billion in cash for the deal. In August 2001, EchoStar surprised everyone by announcing an unsolicited $32.3 billion bid for DirecTV. EchoStar and DirecTV together controlled about 92 percent of the U.S. satellite pay-TV market. Murdoch lobbied intensely and succeeded in getting the merger blocked on antitrust grounds. Finally in April 2003, News Corp. acquired GM's 19.9 percent stake in Hughes and a further 14.1 percent from public shareholders and GM's pension and other benefit plans.

Following the completion of the acquisition, Murdoch became chairman of Hughes, while News Corp.'s former co-chief operating officer, Chase Carey, became the president and chief executive officer. The public shareholders as well as GM's pension and other benefit plans owned all of GM's common stock, which represented 80.1 percent of interest in Hughes Electronics. GM retained a 19.9 percent stake in Hughes.

DirecTV gave News Corp. considerable bargaining power. News Corp. had plans to add one million subscribers a year, using DirecTV. Fox TV stations were expected to let DirecTV viewers choose their angle on their television sets at sports events or create their own video newsmagazines.[8] At any given time, as many as one in five U.S. households would be watching News Corp.'s shows. DirecTV was also expected to fortify News Corp.'s own channels against competition from Comcast and Time Warner. News Corp. looked well placed to drive down the prices of entertainment and sports programming. With so many viewers hooked up to DirecTV, no programmer would risk not being in News Corp.'s system. At the same time, Murdoch, known for his aggressive marketing tactics, would have the leverage to force his cable and satellite rivals to carry his programs at premium prices.

It was widely reported that Murdoch might distribute set-top boxes at a very low price to attract subscribers to DirecTV. Meanwhile, rivals such as Comcast and Time Warner Cable were attempting to expand their own distribution networks. Comcast acquired AT&T Broadband in 2003 for $54 billion. AT&T Broadband owned regional sports rights, telephony, and two-way Internet interactivity over cable lines. Comcast was also seeking to enhance its partnership with programmers such as Viacom.

In many ways, Comcast, the Number 1 cable system in the United States, looked to be the only rival that could remotely match the power of News Corp. After closing the AT&T Broadband deal, Comcast had pursued various deals to strengthen its distribution network. Comcast had even made a hostile bid to take over Walt Disney in February 2004 for $56 billion before backing out. Comcast had held firm on fees for pricey cable channels, won favorable deals for equipment, and put pressure on Hollywood to change its long-standing movie-release tradition so that it could get movies ahead of video stores and sell them over cable.

Comcast had launched various initiatives to strengthen its content. It had partnered with Radio One to launch a new channel targeting African Americans. Comcast had also acquired TechTV to cater to video gamers. In December 2003, Comcast struck a deal with Chicago's major sports teams—the Chicago Bulls, Cubs, White Sox, and Blackhawks—to create a new sports channel, leaving Murdoch's Fox Sports Chicago with no big draws. Comcast had also struck a deal with Viacom channels, such as MTV and Nickelodeon, to supply content to Comcast's 21 million subscribers for as long as five years.

Cable had an important advantage over satellite. Cable offered high-speed, two-way Internet access, including phone capability. Satellite was still mostly a one-way service. But cable still needed millions of dollars of investments to upgrade to digital technology. About 40 million cable subscribers in 2005 did not have digital technology. Satellite, by default, was digital. This meant that cable companies such as Comcast could offer digital technology features such as electronic program guides and video-on-demand only if they upgraded. By the end of 2004, both systems (satellite and cable) were engaged in intense competition to be big players in new consumer technologies such as the digital video recorder (DVR), high-definition TV, and a host of other products that were reshaping home entertainment.

AFTER THE ACQUISITION

Murdoch's BSkyB had already redefined the way people watched television programs in the UK, where the company controlled about 70 percent of the pay-TV market. It had launched many innovative programs for the UK consumer, such as alternating camera angles to stay focused and switching off the sound and listening to a different channel broadcast, among others. With the help of DirecTV, Murdoch planned to introduce these features in the much bigger U.S. market.

After acquiring DirecTV, News Corp. immediately restructured DirecTV and settled labor disputes. News Corp. dismantled everything at DirecTV that did not have anything to do with satellite broadcasting. Half of the employees were retrenched. Then, Murdoch sold DirecTV's 80 percent stake in satellite-launch service business PanAmSat to leverage buyout firm KKR for $2.5 billion. DirecTV's set-top-box manufacturing business was sold to Thomson. The company's holdings in XM Satellite Radio were sold for a pretax profit of $387 million. Murdoch then spent about $1.4 billion to buy Pegasus Communications and the National Rural Telecommunications Cooperative, both rural satellite companies with about 1.4 million subscribers combined.

DirecTV launched new satellites. Modeling itself on the success of BSkyB, DirecTV announced it would introduce interactive television features to the American audience. From a technology-driven company, DirecTV was becoming more like a content-house, like the rest of News Corp. Carey commented, "At the end of the day, people buy DirecTV because they care about great television."[9]

DirecTV was betting heavily on the popularity of football. Just as it did in the UK, DirecTV finalized a five-year $3.5 billion deal with NFL Football Games for broadcasting rights. This was a critical deal for DirecTV to keep cable operators such as Comcast and Time Warner Cable out of the reach of football, a popular game in the United States. A DirecTV employee commented, "People have been fooling around with interactive TV for four to five years. Finally, this marriage of interactive TV and the NFL may be the thing that breaks the dam wide open."[10]

The company sent two-minute clips of every NFL game every Sunday evening to subscribers who had DVRs.

DirecTV was also meeting real-time statistics requests during football games. Viewers could also receive information from DirecTV about a particular team or a particular player. DirecTV was also revamping its movie programs based on the popular video-on-demand programs of cable companies. While DirecTV could not beam video-on-demand due to technical reasons, it was compiling requests from subscribers and getting ready to start video-on-demand.

In 2004, News Corp. launched various aggressive promotion campaigns. In an effort to increase its reach, DirecTV dropped the price of its DVR. It also launched a promotion that would give new customers a DirecTV set-top box for free. According to analysts, DirecTV spent about $670 to acquire and keep a new subscriber in 2002, while it spent about $758 in 2003 and $894 in 2004. Operating profits fell from about $459 million in 2003 to about $54 million in 2004. Meanwhile, the churn rate (the rate at which customers leave each month) was increasing. Compared to the monthly average of 1.5 percent in 2003, the rate climbed to 1.7 percent in 2004 (see Exhibits 3 and 4 for more information about DirecTV).

Murdoch and Carey remained upbeat about DirecTV even as competition from cable companies increased. Carey commented, "We've been helped by the fact that we are very focused on the television experience. The cable companies are fighting the broadband battle and are much more commoditized than television."[11]

But News Corp.'s position had been weakened by some compromises made while closing the DirecTV deal. The FCC had already banned large cable operators from discriminating against rival programmers. So News Corp. could not use to its advantage the muscle power of DirecTV. News Corp. also had to submit to arbitration, if cable operators accused it of using its most popular channels as bargaining tools. But these restrictions were temporary as they expired in six years. By then News Corp. would have about six million more subscribers according to company projections. There was also nothing in law that could stop DirecTV from collaborating with Fox Sports, another News Corp. subsidiary, for content.

THE ROAD AHEAD

We want DirecTV to be the best television experience in the world and The DirecTV Group to realize its value potential for our shareholders. We plan to reinvent DirecTV into an entrepreneurial, efficient and agile business. Our management team will establish DirecTV as the leader in exciting, rewarding and compelling television and we are determined to grow our business while maximizing profitability.

— Murdoch[12]

With DirecTV, Murdoch had gained access to 12 million subscribers in the United States. In early 2004, Murdoch's media empire consisted of businesses that generated $30 billion a year and reached out to just about every corner of the world. No other media company controlled such a mix of programming and the means to deliver it to households as News Corp. did.

For the nine months ended 2004, revenues at DirecTV rose 21 percent to $8 billion. Net loss from continuing operations and before changes in account-

ing standards from Australian to U.S. GAAP rose from $68 million to $768 million. These results reflected a larger subscriber base and gains on the sale of XM Satellite stock, offset by asset impairment charges.

Meanwhile, in early January 2005, DirecTV announced plans to make its own DVR by the middle of 2005. DirecTV outsourced its DVR requirements to TiVo, the industry leader. According to DirecTV, the new device would be a step-up from the current TiVo offering with a 90-minute live TV buffer, a built in TV "bookmarking" system, and other interface refinements.

DirecTV did face a few concerns at the end of 2004. DirecTV Latin America had filed for Chapter 11 bankruptcy in early 2003, and withdrawn from the market in 2004. Later in the year, DirecTV announced plans to reorganize its Latin American operations.

In January 2005, DirecTV reported that the Securities and Exchange Commission (SEC) was seeking further accounting details on deals done with Pegasus Communications, the National Rural Telecommunications Cooperative, and Thomson, all done in the second quarter of 2004. The SEC had also launched an investigation on the $1.47 billion write-down of its Spaceway satellites in the third quarter 2004. DirecTV reported that it might be required to change how it accounted for those transactions, which might increase its depreciation and amortization expenses.

A DirecTV spokesman commented, "We're providing them with the information they requested. This is not an investigation, it's a routine inquiry."[13]

Meanwhile, Moody's, the credit rating agency, had raised its bond ratings on DirecTV, citing improving operating performance and a focus on its satellite pay-TV business. Moody's raised the company's rating to "Ba2," which was two steps below investment grade, from "Ba3." Analysts saw this as a positive reinforcement on how DirecTV was managed.

News Corp. moved fast to acquire complete control in Fox Entertainment Group, which in turn held a controlling interest in DirecTV. In an effort to simplify News Corp.'s corporate structure, Murdoch offered to buy the remaining publicly held shares of Fox Entertainment Group in a $6 billion stock deal in January 2005. News Corp. owned about 82 percent of the equity and 97 percent of the voting power of Fox Entertainment.

NOTES

1. Murdoch, Rupert, "News Corp.," www.hollywoodreporter.com, 22 June 2004.
2. Ibid.
3. Which it later sold to the buyout firm Kolhberg, Kravis & Roberts (KKR) in 2004.
4. Multichannel Video Programming Distributors such as cable companies like Comcast. DirecTV is the second largest MVPD,

exceeded only by Comcast. AOL Time Warner is third followed by EchoStar, which is the fourth largest player.
5. National Football League.
6. Ronald Grover and Tom Lowry, "Rupert's World," Cover Story, *BusinessWeek*, 26 January 2004.
7. Ibid.
8. Ibid.

9. Lashinsky, Adam, "Murdoch's Air War," *Fortune,* 13 December 2004, p. 60, Vol. 150, Issue 11, pp. 55–61.
10. Bruce Mohl, "A Marriage of Convenience," *Boston Globe,* 9 January 2005.
11. Lashinsky, Adam. "Murdoch's Air War," *Fortune,* 13 December 2004, p. 60, Vol. 150, Issue 11, pp. 55–61.
12. A Message to Shareholders, DirecTV Annual Report, 2003.
13. "SEC Asks DirecTV to Explain Transactions," www.washington post.com, 23 January 2005.

BIBLIOGRAPHY

William Shawcross, "Murdoch, the Making of a Media Empire," Simon & Schuster, 1992.

Carla Rapoport, "Linking the World with TV," *Fortune,* Autumn/Winter 1993.

"Comrade Murdoch," *The Economist,* June 17, 1995.

"The Gambler's Last Throw," *The Economist,* September 9, 1996.

"Crossed Wires," *The Economist,* December 12, 1996.

"Star Woes," *The Economist,* November 4, 1998.

Marc Günter, "The Rules According to Rupert," *Fortune,* October 26, 1998.

"Rupert's Misses," *The Economist,* March 7, 1999.

"Rupert Laid Bare," *The Economist,* March 20, 1999.

"Baker Russ, Murdoch's Mean Machine," *Columbia Business Review,* June 1999.

Bill Hagerty, "Interview with Rupert Murdoch," *British Journalism Review,* Volume 10, No. 4, 1999.

Stuart Crainer, "Business the Rupert Murdoch Way," Capstone Publishing, 1999.

Bharat Anand, Kate Attea, "News Corporation," *Harvard Business School Case,* June 19, 2002.

Jeff Randall, "The Fallout from ITV Digital Collapse," BBC, May 2002.

"Rupert the Invincible," *The Economist,* August 17, 2002.

Arlyn Tobias Gajilan, "They Coulda Been Contenders," *Fortune Small Business,* September 9, 2002.

"Still Rocking," *The Economist,* November 23, 2002.

Neil Chenoweth, "The Untold Story of the World's Greatest Wizard," www.randomhouse.com, November 2002.

Neil Chenoweth, "Rupert Murdoch: The Untold Story of the World's Greatest Media Wizard," Crown Publications, November 2002.

John Cassy, "Untouchable BBC Angers Murdoch," *The Guardian,* November 2002.

Jamie Doward, "Sun King Rising in the East," *The Observer,* January 2003.

Roy Greenslade, "Their Master's Voice," *The Guardian,* February 2003.

Mark Günter, "Murdoch's Prime Time," *Fortune,* February 17, 2003.

Marc Günter, "A Rival for Rupert," *Fortune (Asia),* March 3, 2003.

John Helyar, "Media Strike Out," *Fortune,* March 17, 2003.

Raymond Snoddy, "News Corp. Bid for DirecTV Expected Today," *Time Online,* April 2003.

Ronald Grover and Tom Lowry, "Rupert's World," *BusinessWeek,* January 26, 2004.

Rupert Murdoch, "News Corp.," www.hollywoodreporter.com, 22 June 2004.

Adam Lashinsky, "Murdoch's Air War," *Fortune,* December 13, 2004, Vol. 150, Issue 11, pp. 55–61.

Bruce Mohl, "A Marriage of Convenience," *Boston Globe,* January 9, 2005.

"SEC Asks DirecTV to Explain Transactions," www.washingtonpost com, January 23, 2005.

http://finance.yahoo.com/

EXHIBIT 1	DirecTV Stock Price (January 2004–January 2005)

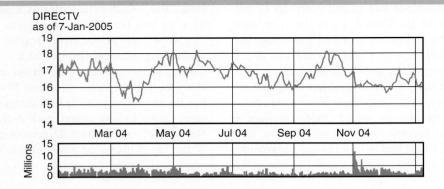

DIRECTV
as of 7-Jan-2005

Source: http://finance.yahoo.com/

EXHIBIT
2

DirecTV: Important Numbers

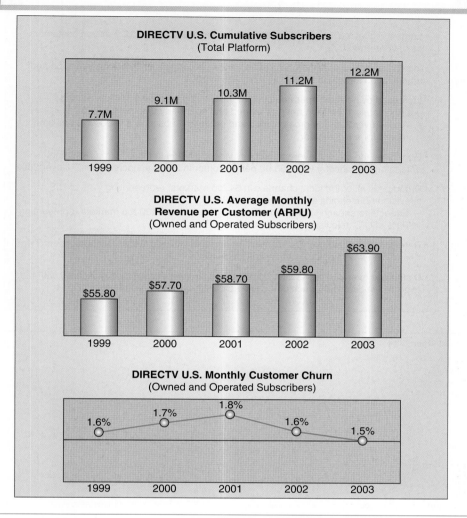

DIRECTV U.S. Cumulative Subscribers
(Total Platform)

7.7M 1999
9.1M 2000
10.3M 2001
11.2M 2002
12.2M 2003

DIRECTV U.S. Average Monthly
Revenue per Customer (ARPU)
(Owned and Operated Subscribers)

$55.80 1999
$57.70 2000
$58.70 2001
$59.80 2002
$63.90 2003

DIRECTV U.S. Monthly Customer Churn
(Owned and Operated Subscribers)

1.6% 1999
1.7% 2000
1.8% 2001
1.6% 2002
1.5% 2003

Source: DirecTV Annual Report, 2004.

EXHIBIT 3   DirecTV: Highlights

- Largest digital multi-channel service provider in the U.S. with 12.2 million customers as of year-end 2003

- Increased revenues 19% to $7.7 billion and operating profit before depreciation and amortization improved 59% to $970 million in 2003

- Increased owned and operated customer base approximately 13% by adding approximately 1.2 million net new owned and operated customers in 2003
  - Added over 3 million gross owned and operated subscribers in 2003, an all-time record for a single year

- Generates the highest average monthly video revenue in the U.S. multi-channel entertainment industry with $63.90 per customer in 2003, an increase of 7% over 2002

- Broadcasts all of the local channels in 64 top markets, representing 72% of U.S. television households as of year-end 2003
  - Expects to expand local channel coverage to at least 130 top markets representing 92% of U.S. television households during 2004

- Ranked "#1 in Customer Satisfaction Among Satellite and Cable TV Subscribers Two Years in a Row" by J.D. Power and Associates

- Distributes over 850 digital video and audio channels, expanding significantly with the expected successful launch of the DIRECTV 7S satellite in 2004

Source: DirecTV Annual Report, 2004.

EXHIBIT 4   DirecTV: Important Financials

Valuation Measures

Market Cap (intraday)	22.48B
Enterprise Value (10 Jan 05)	21.60B
Trailing P/E (ttm, intraday)	N/A
Forward P/E (fye 31-Dec-05)	70.52
PEG Ratio (5 yr expected)	N/A
Price/Sales (ttm)	2.12
Price/Book (mrq)	2.86
Enterprise Value/Revenue (ttm)	2.06
Enterprise Value/EBITDA (ttm)	N/A

Financial Highlights

Fiscal Year

Fiscal Year Ends	31 Dec
Most Recent Quarter (mrq)	30 Sep 04

Profitability

Profit Margin (ttm)	−5.70%
Operating Margin (ttm)	−16.03%

Management Effectiveness

Return on Assets (ttm)	−3.51%
Return on Equity (ttm)	−6.79%

Income Statement

Revenue (ttm)	10.49B
Revenue Per Share (ttm)	7.578
Revenue Growth (lfy)	N/A
Gross Profit (ttm)	4.49B
EBITDA (ttm)	−939.80M
Net Income Avl to Common (ttm)	−592.80M
Diluted EPS (ttm)	−0.427
Earnings Growth (lfy)	N/A

Balance Sheet

Total Cash (mrq)	3.31B
Total Cash Per Share (mrq)	2.39
Total Debt (mrq)	2.43B
Total Debt/Equity (mrq)	0.313
Current Ratio (mrq)	1.975
Book Value Per Share (mrq)	5.608

Source: Reuters, Yahoo Finance.

China on the I-Way

P. Venkatesh
Sumit Kumar Chaudhuri

ICFAI University Press, Business School Case Development Centre

The Internet had its beginning in China in 1987, when the first computer network, the China Academic Network (CANET), was set up. The Internet was used primarily for academic purposes until 1995, when the Ministry of Post and Telecommunications (MPT) of China set up the first commercial network, ChinaNET(C), in May 1995. Since then, the Chinese Internet bandwidth[1] and the number of Internet users had been on the rise (Appendix 1). The Internet penetration in China grew in leaps and bounds and despite stricter control measures imposed by the Chinese government on the Internet, the number of users had risen from around 1.175 million[2] in 1998 to nearly 79.5 million[3] by the end of 2003.

EMERGENCE OF THE INTERNET IN CHINA

The CANET was established with the main purpose of facilitating academic research in computer science. It provided e-mail services through the World Wide Web via a gateway at Karlsruhe University in Germany. Subsequently, the Institute of High Energy Physics (IHEP) in China developed its local network in 1988, which was followed by a similar facility at the National Computer Networking Facilities of China (NCFC) in 1989. NCFC was developed jointly by the Chinese Academy of Sciences, Tsinghua University of Beijing, and the Beijing University and funded by the State Planning Commission and the World Bank. The NCFC was also called the ChinaNet and it was used for academic purposes. In 1990, China registered its domain name of "cn" with the U.S. Network Information Center.[4]

The early Chinese networks lacked direct international Internet connections. The first official international Internet link to the Chinese Internet was established in 1993. This link was a 64[5] kilobits per second (kbps) leased line from AT&T that allowed the IHEP connectivity with Stanford Linear Accelerator Center (U.S.) for international collaboration in high energy physics and to provide e-mail accounts to many top scientists in China. The following years saw more networks being connected directly to the Internet like the one operated by the Beijing University of Chemical Technology (BUCT) and the China Education and Research Network (CERNET). Further, in order to develop the information infrastructure in China, "Golden Projects" (Exhibit 1), a series of high priority proposals, was announced by the then Vice Premier of China, Zhu Rongji, in 1993. The primary focus of these projects was the nationwide penetration of the Internet in China.

In 1995, China's first commercial network, ChinaNet(C), started operating in Beijing and Shanghai selling Internet accounts directly to the Chinese people. During the first month of its operation, 800[6] subscribers signed up for ChinaNet(C).

With the commercialization of the Internet and the Golden Projects initiative, Chinese Internet embarked on a fast track growth. By mid-1998, there were four primary state-run Internet Service Providers (ISPs) in China: CSTNet (China Academy of Sciences), CERNet (China State Education Commission), ChinaNet (China Telecom), and JiTong Communications, servicing over 1.175 million[7] Internet users. By 1999, the number of Internet users increased to almost four million[8] of which 400,000 used the Internet through leased line connections, 2,560,000 through dial-up connections and 680,000 through both.[9] China also witnessed the emergence of Internet cafés in its capital

This case was prepared by P. Venkatesh, under the direction of Sumit Kumar Chaudhuri. © ICFAI University Press & ICFAI Business School Case Development Centre, 2004. Reprinted with permission. www.icfaipress.org; www.icfaipress.org/books.

city, Beijing. Apart from the increase in the number of Internet users, the nature of Internet usage also underwent radical changes. The late 1990s witnessed the advent of online advertising and e-commerce in China. Xinhua Bookstore[10] was the first to commence e-tailing (e-retailing or electronic retailing) in China. By 2000, the total number of Internet users in China had increased to 16,900,000.[11] With China signing its accession to WTO in late 2001, the Chinese government allowed foreign participation in the Internet sector to the extent of 49 percent foreign ownership in the first year of accession and 50 percent from the second year onward.[12]

SCENARIO IN THE NEW MILLENNIUM

By 2001, the number of Internet users in China had grown by almost 50 percent[13] over the previous year to 33.7 million[14] with the majority of users in the age group of 18 to 24 (Exhibit 2). Apart from the usual leased line and dial-up connections, 1.2 million[15] users had mobile terminals or other Internet appliances to go online. Online stock trading was worth $43.23 billion[16] and accounted for 4.38 percent[17] of total stock trading in China in 2001.

By the turn of the 21st century, the primary reason for accessing the Internet in China remained

---

EXHIBIT 1	Golden Projects

In the early 1990s, the Chinese government embarked on an agenda of several "Golden Projects" that aimed to modernize the country's information technology infrastructure by establishing a data communications network.

Golden Bridge

First announced in March 1993, the Golden Bridge Project was China's version of the information superhighway. According to the Chinese Ministry of Electronics Industry, the network was to be constructed across China and was to ultimately incorporate all of China's information systems efforts. The backbone of Golden Bridge was an interconnected space satellite and ground fiber optic networks linked to a domestic private network. Apart from providing Internet access, the system was also supposed to allow e-mail, electronic data interchange, database online services, information sources, and applications service systems.

Major vendors involved:* Bell South, Cisco, Hughes, IBM, Scientific Atlanta, Intel, and Sun Microsystems.

Golden Customs

Initiated in June 1993, this initiative was to connect foreign trade companies with banks and China's customs and tax offices. The project aimed to create paperless trading by automating customs checks and eliminate cash transactions for international trade. It was to feature e-mail, electronic data interchange (EDI), and an electronic post office.

Golden Card

This project began in 1995 to create a nationwide banking and credit card system in China. Its goal was to use telecom networks to replace cash transactions with electronic systems for savings, withdrawals, and payments. The plan was estimated to deliver 300 million credit/cash cards to 300 million people in 400 urban areas by 2005.

Major vendors involved:* IBM, Ameritech, General Electric, and Tandem.

Golden Tax

Launched in 1995, this initiative, co-sponsored by the Ministry of Finance and the People's Bank of China, planned to spend more than $1.2 billion to computerize the tax collection system. The system was expected to be expanded to include 400 cities in 4,000 districts and counties.

Major vendors involved:* AST Research, Compaq, Hewlett-Packard, and IBM.

---

* For company information, refer to Appendix 2.

Source: Compiled by IBS-CDC from Black, Jane, "Golden projects," http://news.com.com, June 27, 1997.

| EXHIBIT 2 | Age Profile of Chinese Internet Users |

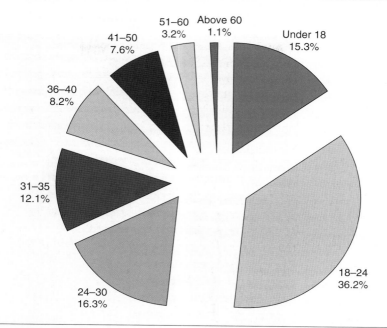

51–60
3.2%

Above 60
1.1%

41–50
7.6%

Under 18
15.3%

36–40
8.2%

31–35
12.1%

24–30
16.3%

18–24
36.2%

Source: "Internet in China Report 2002," www.ahk-china.org.

information collection. With the passage of time, Internet users started accessing some sensitive information that had been kept secret by the state. It resulted in online debates on state policies and practices based on such information. The Chinese government tried to control the flow of such information by blocking certain Web sites that "jeopardized state security, disrupted social stability, contravened laws and spread superstition and obscenity"[18] (Exhibit 3). When the Internet cafés did not comply with government rules and regulations regarding the banned Web sites, the government closed down 17,000 such cafés[19] in late 2001. Another matter of concern was the proliferation of unlicensed Internet cafés that came to light in mid-2002, when a fire broke out in one of the unlicensed Internet cafés in Beijing's Haidian district, killing 25 people.[20] The café was set ablaze by two youngsters who had been denied entry into the café. Subsequently, the Chinese government started to focus on streamlining Internet café operations through the formulation of "Regulations on the Administration of Business Sites of Internet Access Services" in November 2002. According to the regulation, Internet cafés were not permitted within a radius of 200 meters[21] around schools; minors under the age of 18 were prohibited from entering cafés; gambling was prohibited,

and the cafés had to be closed between midnight and 8 A.M. The drastic step taken by the Chinese government reduced the number of Internet cafés from 200,000 to 110,000 in 2003.[22] The government, in late 2003, had further planned to consolidate all Internet cafés under the management of larger, state-owned companies by 2006. These state-owned companies included telecom providers such as China Unicom, Great Wall Broadband Network, and China Netcom.

A blessing in disguise for the Chinese Internet was the SARS[23] epidemic that struck China in 2003. As the government closed public places of entertainment to contain the contagious disease, Chinese people went online to seek entertainment within the confinement of their homes. Online shopping, short messages services (SMS), and online games became the most sought-after applications of the Internet. According to Beijing Netcom (a subsidiary of China Netcom), Internet usage increased by 40 percent[24] in mid-2003. Even online banking experienced a surge in transaction volumes from a monthly average of RMB[25] 786 billion[26] in the first quarter of 2003 to RMB 1.29 trillion[27] in April 2003. Online games also flourished as many youngsters found it a principal reason to access the Internet. The number of people playing online games in China increased by 63.8 percent[28] in 2003 with

EXHIBIT
3

Blocked Sites in China

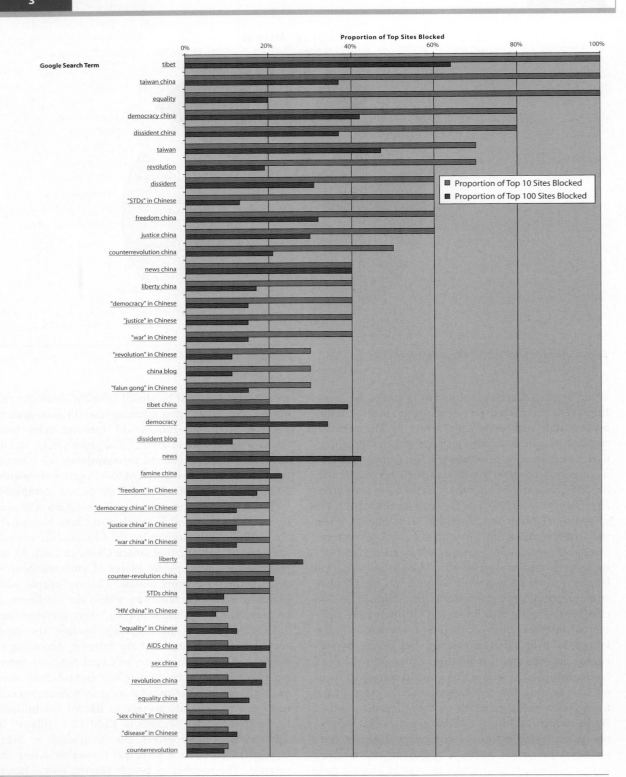

Proportion of Top Sites Blocked

Google Search Term

- Proportion of Top 10 Sites Blocked
- Proportion of Top 100 Sites Blocked

tibet
taiwan china
equality
democracy china
dissident china
taiwan
revolution
dissident
"STDs" in Chinese
freedom china
justice china
counterrevolution china
news china
liberty china
"democracy" in Chinese
"justice" in Chinese
"war" in Chinese
"revolution" in Chinese
china blog
"falun gong" in Chinese
tibet china
democracy
dissident blog
news
famine china
"freedom" in Chinese
"democracy china" in Chinese
"justice china" in Chinese
"war china" in Chinese
liberty
counter-revolution china
STDs china
"HIV china" in Chinese
"equality" in Chinese
AIDS china
sex china
revolution china
equality china
"sex china" in Chinese
"disease" in Chinese
counterrevolution

Source: "Chart—Proportion of Sites Blocked by Google Search Term," http://cyber.law.harvard.edu.

sales worth $157 million.[29] By the end of 2003, the total number of Internet users in China had increased to 79.5 million.[30]

BRASS TACKS

Though 79.5 million Internet users in China was a huge number, it was just 6 percent of China's total population of 1.28 billion.[31] On the other hand, Internet users in the United States constituted 57 percent of the total population of 290.34 million.[32] Thus there was still a huge growth potential in China's Internet market. However, with the rise in the number of Internet users, the government increased its control measures to curb misuse of the Internet. Amnesty International, a worldwide voluntary human rights movement, said, "As the Internet industry continues to expand in China, the government continues to tighten controls on on-line information. These have included the filtering or blocking of some foreign Web sites, the creation of special Internet police, the blocking of search engines and actions to shut down Web sites which post information on corruption or articles critical of government."[33]

The new millennium witnessed a surge in the number of Internet users being detained or imprisoned by the Chinese government. From November 2002, this number grew by 60 percent to 54 users[34] in January 2004. The Chinese Premier (2004), Wen Jiabao, said, "Rapid growth of the globalized economy and information technology has a great and profound impact on the world cultural development. It requires, more than ever before, close inter-governmental and non-governmental cooperation to promote the fine culture of every nation and defuse moral crises in the world."[35]

NOTES

1. The bandwidth determines the rate at which information can be sent through a channel. The greater the bandwidth, the more information that can be sent in a given amount of time. It is usually measured in bits per second.
2. Cullen, Richard, and Choy, Pinky D. W., "The Internet in China," http://austlii.edu.au, 1999.
3. "New Standard: Imprisonment on the Rise in China for Internet-Related Activities," http://faluninfo.net, February 6, 2004.
4. Operated by VeriSign Global Registry Services (U.S.), a leading provider of digital trust services that enables everyone, everywhere to engage in commerce and communications with confidence. VeriSign's digital trust services creates a trusted environment through three core offerings—Web identity, authentication, and payment services—powered by a global infrastructure that manages more than five billion network connections and transactions a day.
5. "The Internet in China," op. cit.
6. Ibid.
7. Ibid.
8. "Semi-Annual Survey Report on Internet Development in China," www.cnnic.com.cn, 1999.
9. Ibid.
10. A state-run bookstore in China.
11. "Semi-Annual Survey Report on Internet Development in China," op. cit.
12. Yu, Peter K., "Barriers to Foreign Investment in the Chinese Internet Industry," www.gigalaw.com, March 2001.
13. "Internet in China Report 2002," www.ahk-china.org.
14. Ibid.
15. Ibid.
16. Ibid.
17. Ibid.
18. "China: Internet Users at Risk of Arbitrary Detention, Torture and Even Execution," www.hrea.org, November 26, 2002.
19. "China 'Shuts Down 17,000 Internet Bars,'" www.ananova.com, November 21, 2001.
20. Murray, Brendan, "Internet Café Regulation in China: A Policy Review," www.mfcinsight.com, May 2003.
21. Ibid.
22. "Most Internet cafés in China to Be Chains in Three Years," www1.chinadaily.com.cn, October 27, 2003.
23. Severe Acute Respiratory Syndrome: symptoms being fever and coughing or difficulty in breathing or hypoxia. First appeared in China in November 2002. Since then, the disease had spread worldwide. By July 2003, SARS had infected thousands of people and resulted in more than 850 deaths.
24. Dean, Ted, "SARS Drives Internet Boom," www.bdaconnect.com, May 15, 2003.
25. Renminbi (Chinese currency).
26. "SARS Drives Internet Boom," op. cit.
27. Ibid.
28. "China's Online Games Sales Double," http://news.bbc.co.uk, January 16, 2004.
29. Ibid.
30. Wagner, Jim, "China's Internet Use Surges: Report," www.internetnews.com, January 15, 2004.
31. "China's Internet Use Surges: Report," op. cit.
32. Ibid.
33. "China: Internet Users at Risk of Arbitrary Detention, Torture and Even Execution," op. cit.
34. "New Standard: Imprisonment on the Rise in China for Internet-Related Activities," op. cit.
35. Ibid.

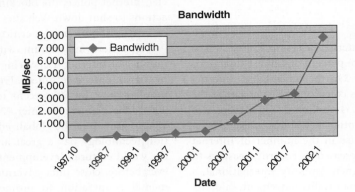

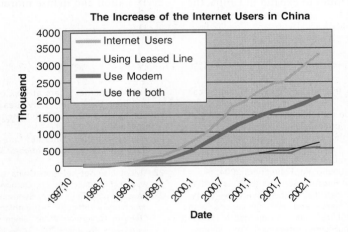

Source: "Internet in China Report 2002," www.ahk-china.org.

APPENDIX 2 — Company Overview

BellSouth Corporation—a Fortune 100 communications services company headquartered in Atlanta, U.S.A., serving more than 44 million customers in the United States and 14 other countries.

Cisco Systems, Inc. (CA)—the worldwide leader in networking for the Internet.

Hughes Network Systems, Inc. (HNS)—a wholly owned subsidiary of Hughes Electronic Corporation. It is the world's leading provider of broadband satellite network solutions for businesses and consumers.

Scientific-Atlanta—a leading global manufacturer and supplier of products, systems, and services that help operators connect consumers with a world of integrated, interactive video, data, and voice services.

International Business Machines (IBM)—the world's top provider of computer hardware. The company makes desktop and notebook PCs, mainframes and servers, storage systems, and peripherals.

Intel Corporation—designs, develops, manufactures, and markets microcomputer components of desktop and server systems.

Sun Microsystems—a leading maker of UNIX-based servers that are used to power corporate computer networks and Web sites. It also makes workstation computers and a wide range of disk- and tape-based storage systems.

Ameritech—develops and deploys emerging technologies in broadband delivery systems, information technology, voice technology, video, data, and wireless networks.

General Electric Corporation (Connecticut)—produces aircraft, locomotives, and other transportation equipment, lighting, electric distribution and control equipment, generators and turbines, nuclear reactors, medical imaging equipment, and plastics.

Tandem Computers Incorporated—designs and delivers technology solutions that companies rely on in a business world that runs 24 hours a day. A $2.0 billion company headquartered in Cupertino, California, Tandem has offices, strategic partners, and providers in more than 50 countries around the world.

AST Research—a company formed sometime before 1980 that was a leading personal computer manufacturer. AST developed desktop, mobile, and server PCs that were sold in more than 100 countries worldwide.

Hewlett-Packard—a technology solutions provider to consumers, businesses, and institutions globally. The company's offerings span IT infrastructure, personal computing and access devices, global services, and imaging and printing for consumers, enterprises, and small and medium businesses.

Compaq Computer Corporation—a leading global provider of information technology products, services, and solutions for enterprise customers. Compaq designs, develops, manufactures, and markets information technology equipment, software, services, and solutions, including industry-leading enterprise storage and computing solutions, fault-tolerant business-critical solutions, communication products, personal desktop and notebook computers, and personal entertainment and Internet access devices that are sold in more than 200 countries directly and through a network of authorized Compaq marketing partners.

Source: Compiled by IBS-CDC.

Succession Battles at Viacom

Daksha Bhat
Nagendra V. Chowdary

ICFAI University Press, Business School Case Development Centre

Viacom, News Corp., and Disney are among the largest and most influential companies in the world—with more presence in our daily lives and more power over the direction of the real desires and beliefs of the nation than any other force, including government—but they have no future. They'll be traded, broken up, merged, picked apart without Redstone, Murdoch, and Eisner.

— Michael Wolff[1]

Viacom is a $27 billion a year media conglomerate with operations in cable networks, television, radio, outdoor, entertainment, and video. It is the parent company behind some of the most recognized brands in television, film, and publishing, including the CBS Television Network, United Paramount Network (UPN), MTV Networks, Black Entertainment Television, Paramount Home Entertainment, and Simon & Schuster publishing group. It also owns Infinity Broadcasting (Exhibit 1).

Viacom has a major presence in most of the industries it is in, and was the third largest media group in the United States in 2003.[2] Sumner Redstone, chairman and president, has built Viacom through years of acquisitions and divestments (Exhibit 2). In 1999 when Viacom purchased CBS for $40 billion, the transaction was thought to be one through which major synergies would be created between the two highly complementary media companies, with Viacom's content pairing up with CBS's distribution. The combination of Sumner Redstone and Mel Karmazin, CEO of CBS, was referred to as "one that's worth banking on"[3] and the company was dubbed the "ultimate media battleship,

a magnificent warship fueled by advertising."[4] Karmazin was touted to be the ideal successor to run Viacom after Redstone retired.

On June 1, 2004, in an unexpected turn of events, Viacom announced that Karmazin had resigned and his place was to be filled by two executives, Leslie Moonves, chairman of CBS, and Tom Freston, chairman of MTV, who would be the leading candidates for the CEO post. The announced plan clarified that Redstone would step down in three years if there was an agreement regarding his successor.[5] Until he left the top post, Redstone would "continue to work with the board to identify his successor and to designate candidates for other senior positions in the company."[6] Commenting on these events, Merrill Lynch said the departure of an extremely talented operating executive such as Karmazin was a very significant loss for Viacom. But an analyst at Sanford Bernstein said the news was positive, "They have put in two of the strongest executives in the company. They both have been managing organizations that have been gaining share. Now we have a date when Sumner will step down."[7]

SUMNER REDSTONE

80-year-old Sumner Redstone has been ranked 35th in Forbes' list of billionaires, with a net worth of $8.9 billion.[8] His father opened one of the first drive-in movie operations in the United States after starting out selling newspapers and linoleum. He graduated first in his class from the very demanding Boston

Succession Battles at Viacom by Daksha Bhat under the direction of Nagendra V. Chowdary. ©ICFAI University Press & ICFAI Business School Case Development Centre, 2004. Reprinted with permission. www.icfaipress.org; www.icfaipress.org/books.

EXHIBIT
1

Viacom Business Segments

Cable Networks (21%, 19%, and 19% of the company's consolidated revenues in 2003, 2002, and 2001, respectively)
The company owns and operates advertiser-supported basic cable television program services through MTV Networks ('MTVN') and BET: Black Entertainment Television ('BET') and premium subscription television program services through Showtime Networks Inc. ('SNI') in the United States and internationally.

Television (29%, 30%, and 31% of the company's consolidated revenues in 2003, 2002, and 2001, respectively)
The television segment consists of the CBS and UPN television networks, the company's owned broadcast television stations, and its television production and syndication businesses.

Radio (8%, 9%, and 9% of the company's consolidated revenues in 2003, 2002, and 2001, respectively)
The company's radio broadcasting business operates through Infinity Radio, which owns and operates 185 radio stations serving 41 markets. It is one of the largest operators of radio stations in the United States.

Outdoor (7%, 7%, and 7% of the company's consolidated revenue in 2003, 2002, and 2001, respectively)
The company sells, through Viacom Outdoor, advertising space on various media, including billboards, transit shelters, buses, rail systems (in-car, station platform and terminal), mall kiosks, and stadium signage.

Entertainment (15%, 15%, and 16% of the company's consolidated revenues in 2003, 2002, and 2001, respectively)
The entertainment segment's principal businesses are Paramount Pictures, which produces and distributes theatrical motion pictures; Simon & Schuster, which publishes and distributes consumer books; Paramount Parks, which is principally engaged in the ownership and operation of five regional theme parks and a themed attraction in the United States and Canada; Famous Players, which operates movie theaters in Canada; and Famous Music.

Video (22%, 23%, and 22% of the company's consolidated revenues in 2003, 2002, and 2001, respectively)
The company operates in the retail home video business, which includes both the rental and sale of movies on DVD and VHS as well as the rental and sale of video games, through its approximately 81.5% equity interest in Blockbuster Inc.

Source: www.viacom.com.

Latin School and went to Harvard at age 17. When he graduated in 1944, he was fluent in Japanese and served in an elite army code cracking unit for three years, after which he received a commendation and graduated from Harvard Law School in 1947. Redstone practiced law for some time before joining the family business, National Amusements Inc. (NAI) in 1954. In 1967, he became the CEO of NAI, eventually becoming the chairman in 1986.[9] His daughter Shari Redstone is now president of NAI, which owns and operates over 1,425 motion picture screens across the United States, Europe, and Latin America.[10]

In 1979, Redstone sustained severe burns in a hotel fire. Doctors did not expect him to live, and later told him he would never walk. Redstone gradually started using a treadmill and later played tennis regularly. While recuperating, he used his knowledge of the movie business to trade stocks of Hollywood studios, making millions of dollars. Viacom, then a small television company owning MTV, Showtime, Nickelodeon, and cable networks, with revenues of $900 million[11] was at first just one of his stock market investments. Redstone realized that it needed new management and in 1987 he decided to take over operations. At the age of 63, Redstone entered a highly leveraged and controversial $3.4 billion takeover of Viacom. The executives at Viacom tried to raise funds and prevent the takeover, resulting in a six-month battle in which Redstone was forced to raise his offer three times.[12]

| EXHIBIT 2 | An Indicative Chronology |

1908	Paramount studios formed
1924	Simon & Schuster founded
1927	Columbia Broadcasting System (CBS) formed
1938	CBS buys Columbia Records (formed in 1889)
1949	US Department of Justice forces Paramount and other studios to spin off their cinema operations. United Paramount Theatres is established.
1954	Sumner Redstone gains control of National Amusements Inc (NAI), builds multinational cinema group
1971	Viacom formed when FCC rules force CBS to spin off some cable TV and program-syndication operations
1985	Blockbuster video rental chain founded
1987	NAI buys majority interest in Viacom
1993	Blockbuster invests US$600 million in Viacom
1993	Paramount and Chris-Craft Industries announce plans to launch new broadcast network
1994	Blockbuster invests US$1.25 billion in Viacom, which then buys Blockbuster for US$8.4 billion
1994	Viacom and Paramount announce US$8.4 billion merger after Viacom wins bidding war with USA Networks/QVC
1994	Viacom sells its 33% of Lifetime Television to Hearst Corporation and Capital Cities/ABC
1994	Sells Madison Square Garden for US$1.075 billion
1994	Sells KRRT-TV San Antonio, WLFL-TV Raleigh/Durham and WTXF-TV Philadelphia; buys WGBS-TV Philadelphia, WBFS-TV Miami and WSBK-TV Boston
1995	Launches Sams.net
1995	Buys Atlanta station WVEU-TV, sells KSLA-TV in Shreveport
1995	Acquires controlling interest in Grupo Mexicano de Video, which operates 100 video stores
1995	Spins off its cable systems to Tele-Communications (TCI)
1995	Launches the MTV Radio Network
1995	Westinghouse Electric buys CBS
1996	Viacom announces it will exercise its option for 50% ownership interest in UPN
1996	CBS buys Infinity radio broadcasting and outdoor advertising group for US$4.7 billion
1997	Westinghouse Electric changes name to CBS and sells off traditional power-generation business.
1997	Viacom's equity in Spelling increased to 80%
1997	Paramount sells ten-station Radio Group to Chancellor Media
1997	Paramount Stations Group increases to 17 stations, making it the sixth-largest broadcasting group in United States
1997	CBS buys American Radio Systems chain for US$2.6 billion, increasing its radio stations to 175
1997	Viacom sells interest in USA Networks to Seagram
1998	Las Vegas Star Trek theme park opens
1997	Sale of educational, professional and reference publishing businesses to Pearson for US$4.6 billion, with Viacom retaining the consumer operations (including the Simon & Schuster name)
1998	CBS sells 17% of Infinity Broadcasting for US$2.9 billion
1999	CBS buys King World Productions, leading television program syndicator, for US$2.5 billion
1999	Viacom buys CBS

There was criticism that Redstone paid too much for Viacom, and the lending banks wanted him to sell the programming properties, Showtime and MTV, which were regarded as a fad. Redstone called in Frank Biondi, who had previously worked for HBO as president and CEO, to be president and CEO of Viacom. Biondi later said, "Sumner's a lot of things. One of them is that he's stubborn and tenacious. He wasn't going to sell. He just knew in his bones—and I certainly agreed with him—that those were going to be very, very valuable assets."[13]

As cable television, program syndication, broadcasting, and entertainment programming evolved into one of the fastest-growing and most exportable parts of America's economy, Viacom expanded. Under Redstone, Viacom went through a series of acquisitions and divestments. In 1993, Viacom bought video rental empire Blockbuster Video for $8.4 billion and entered a $10 billion merger with Paramount Pictures Corporation in a hard-fought legal and bidding battle. Paramount added a Hollywood studio and a film distributor to Viacom's repertoire, and also included publisher Simon & Schuster and 50 percent of the television broadcast company United Paramount Networks (UPN). In 1995, Viacom spun off its cable systems and launched the MTV Radio Network.

In January 1996, Biondi was out after a showdown and Redstone took over as CEO of Viacom. According to Biondi, Redstone came to his office and said, "I want to make a change. I always wanted to run my own company. It's been great. I'll be great."[14] Redstone said they had differed on really critical matters, citing an incident when he had been pushing to make a presentation in Europe. Biondi had not been interested and Redstone went alone and made a successful deal.[15] An insider commented that Redstone wanted to run the company, and he did not want anyone in his way.[16]

In 1996, Viacom purchased the Chris Craft Industries' 50 percent share in the UPN network. Simon & Schuster's educational, professional, and reference publishing businesses were sold to Pearson in 1997 for $4.6 billion, with Viacom retaining the consumer operations and the name.[17] In 2004, Redstone purchased a majority holding in Midway games[18] through NIA, raising his holdings to 74 percent of Midway's stock. He also initiated the launch of the first cable network catering to gay and lesbian viewers by MTV.

Redstone is known to favor gambles and big acquisitions,[19] has a reputation for using litigation to get his own way, and is known for his tough deal making. He has been called "unpredictable, irascible and used to getting his way,"[20] and also referred to as "a strictly 'Jump!'—'How high?' kind of executive."[21] In his book, *A Passion to Win*, published by Simon and Schuster in 2001, he wrote, "Viacom is my life." Reviews of the book say that Redstone seems to feel he has not received enough credit for his accomplishments.[22] *Forbes* said in 2002 that despite pushing 80, he is still looking for a way to overtake AOL Time-Warner to become the world's biggest media mogul.[23]

MEL KARMAZIN

Karmazin's roots are in operating radio and TV stations and analysts consider him as the ultimate ad salesman.[24] Karmazin spent several years at an ad agency, and three years selling radio spots for WCBS-AM in New York when Infinity Broadcasting, a small radio group, hired him as chief executive. He built Infinity Broadcasting from a small group of three radio stations into a national powerhouse and added the Howard Stern Show.[25] In 1981, he became the president and CEO of Infinity. He acquired a reputation for releasing managers who did not meet budget goals and had a sign in his office that was a variation of the "No Smoking" sign with a line drawn through the word "Excuses." Infinity's stock price increased nearly 60 percent in each of the four years between the company's going public in 1992, and its sale to CBS.[26]

In 1996 when FCC[27] rules changed and limits on radio-station ownership were relaxed, Karmazin approached CBS chairman Michael Jordan with an offer to buy out CBS's lagging radio stations. In June 1996, CBS bought the Infinity radio broadcasting and outdoor advertising group for $4.7 billion and Karmazin was appointed the chairman and CEO of CBS Radio. Karmazin was also the largest individual shareholder of CBS, which now had 79 stations with 64 of those stations located in the top-ten markets.[28]

After a year, Karmazin was appointed as the CEO and president of the CBS Television Network amid reports that president Peter Lund resigned following a stormy meeting at which Karmazin complained about the poor performance of the 14 CBS-owned TV stations.[29] Karmazin laid off salespeople at the TV stations and took the staff off salary, putting them on 100 percent commissions-based compensation.[30] Revenues and profits at the TV stations improved. In two years, Karmazin had nudged aside Jordan at CBS.

Karmazin is said to have a relentless focus on the practical. Radio host Jonathan Schwartz said about him, "It mattered not what a station proffered, only how it profited."[31] In 1998, CBS added to its broadcasting empire by paying about $2.6 billion to acquire American Radio Systems Corporation, increasing the number of

C

radio stations to 175. In 1999, Infinity bought Outdoor Systems Inc., a leader in outdoor advertising, for $8.7 billion, extending CBS's advertising reach to media besides radio and TV, which enabled it to sell advertising packages and reach all possible customers. A year later, CBS paid $2.5 billion to acquire King World Productions, a television syndication company whose programs include *The Oprah Winfrey Show* and *Wheel of Fortune*. Donna Halper, programming consultant and media historian, said, "CBS Radio was at the bottom of the barrel, Mel gave that company credibility again."

Karmazin has been called a very private person with few social engagements. "This is relaxing," he said of work in the office, where days may begin at 6 a.m. His conversation style is to the point, without much attention to subtle manners of exchange and very little patience.[32]

VIACOM UNDER KARMAZIN

In 1999, the FCC proposed relaxing the rules on media concentration in local television markets that prevented a company from owning two stations in one market. Viacom bought out CBS after Karmazin approached Redstone with an offer to buy Viacom and its holdings, claiming a better track record with programming. CBS's broadcast outlets complemented Viacom's Paramount movie studio and cable channels such as MTV, creating a company powerful in both production and distribution. The merger was announced by the two CEOs at a news conference, where the 76-year-old Redstone appeared in monotone light-brown hair, and the 56-year-old Karmazin in contrasting untouched gray. Redstone was chairman and CEO, and Karmazin was designated president and chief operating officer. Redstone's chief deputies at Viacom, Philippe Dauman (deputy chairman and executive vice president) and Tom Dooley (deputy chairman) left the company with severance pay amounting to $150 million each, clearing Karmazin's way to the top post.[33]

Viacom became financially healthier. Karmazin cut costs and steered clear of the Internet deal-making that afflicted other media giants.[34] Viacom was sticking to its knitting, selling advertising against good content delivered via cable and broadcast. In the downturn after September 11, the ad recession brought about a new level of uncertainty in the business and Viacom's radio stations and billboards performed only about half as well as cable-networks and television divisions.[35] When asked if Viacom would get into businesses that were less ad-sensitive, Karmazin insisted that ad-supported content is a "pretty good business."[36]

There was considerable friction between Karmazin and Redstone and at times they hardly spoke to each other. Karmazin is said to have clashed with Redstone over the years over various issues, including Viacom's acquisition strategy, the sluggish performance of its radio business, Karmazin's sale of stock in the past, and advertising sales strategy.[37] Karmazin refused to allow Viacom investment in Midway, and put plans for a gay channel on the back burner because it would cost $30 million.[38] He also opposed plans to increase budgets for films at Paramount.[39]

Their disagreements were mostly about control and personality. Redstone felt that Karmazin's cost-consciousness was not always in the interests of a creative company. When Karmazin was opposed to a corporate Christmas party at Sotheby's, Redstone paid for it himself. In 2003, Redstone wanted the company to pay a dividend, but Karmazin argued that the capital should be used internally. Redstone tried to foster a collegial environment at Viacom, dining out with company executives, saying, "It builds bonds of friendship, bonds of trust, bonds of loyalty." He viewed himself as a father figure in the company. Karmazin cultivated a reputation for being a tough boss and said, "My image is very important to me. The words 'nice guy' and 'Mel Karmazin' better not be written in the same sentence."[40] Redstone also felt Karmazin did not show enough deference and did not attempt to build a friendship.[41]

The constant tension between the two gave rise to speculation whether Karmazin's contract would be renewed in 2003. At the height of the controversy, Redstone stated that he could run the company for another 15 years, attributing his longevity to a high-protein diet, and there were comments that shareholders were stuck with him for as long as he wanted to hold on.[42] In March 2003, when a three-year contract was signed that left Karmazin's titles in place but gave Redstone the last word on corporate decisions, many believed it to be a sign that the two executives had put aside their differences,[43] and Viacom's share price jumped 5 percent.[44]

In 2003, Viacom's earnings growth did not keep pace with its peers. The company projected 19 percent growth in earnings per share for 2004, while average earnings for 30 other media companies were projected to jump 76 percent.[45] Infinity's profit from operations fell by 3 percent in 2003 from the previous year, though in the first quarter of 2004 operating income rose by 5 percent.[46] There were rumors that Redstone wanted one last big media deal, believed to have been TimeWarner, but Karmazin wanted to extract profit from the existing business and bolster the falling share price.[47]

Karmazin's decision to resign came after published reports stated that Redstone's daughter, Shari Redstone, would be expanding her role at the company and would probably inherit her father's control of the voting stock. Karmazin said Shari Redstone's higher profile was not a factor in his decision to step down.[48] He did not inform Redstone directly of his resignation; instead he had a fellow executive deliver the message.[49] Karmazin left with a severance package that included $31 million in cash, options on Viacom shares, and without a non-compete clause, leaving him free to work for anyone.[50]

Karmazin said it was not succession but the never-ending media stories about their frayed relationship that ultimately led to his resignation.[51] He claimed Viacom did not have a succession plan until he informed board members on May 19 that he planned to resign. Karmazin said it had become increasingly obvious to him that Redstone, who controlled 71 percent of Viacom's voting stock, would never fully relinquish control of the company.[52] People close to the board said perhaps he had resigned after learning that he was not on the short list of likely candidates for the post of CEO after Redstone stepped down.[53]

Redstone told investors that neither he nor any other executive had asked Karmazin to leave and that his relationship with Karmazin was at an all-time high. He attributed Karmazin's departure to frustration over the company's relatively low share price and the financial outlook for the radio business.[54] Redstone also said Karmazin had been a candidate in the succession plan until he took himself out of the running with his resignation. Commenting on the company's future without Karmazin, Redstone said he had been very effective when the economic environment was poor and the company agenda was to cut costs and control expenses, but in an escalating economy the name of the game was creativity and content.[55]

"Ending an internal feud could be viewed as a positive not a negative," Fulcrum Global Partners' Rich Greenfield said, pointing out that Karmazin's credibility had waned significantly in recent months due to weakness in the company's Infinity radio unit.

A CHANGE OF GUARD

There were reports that Redstone's original succession plan called for Freston as his sole deputy, and he eventually named Freston and Moonves co-presidents after Moonves protested, saying he did not want to report to Freston and he would leave the company if he was not given an equal rank.[56]

Tom Freston, 58, has been chairman and CEO of the MTV Networks unit since 1987. In 1980 he joined Warner Amex Satellite Entertainment (WASEC), which was the predecessor to MTV Networks, and was a member of the team that launched MTV. He oversaw the breakthrough "I want my MTV" campaign, which helped the channel immensely.[57] Known for a management style that is easygoing and accessible, Freston in his new assignment would have additional responsibility for the operations of Showtime, Simon & Schuster, and the motion picture divisions of Paramount.

Leslie Moonves, 54, chairman and CEO of CBS since 2003, worked for five years at Warner Bros., and joined CBS in 1995 as president of its entertainment operation. Moonves embarked on a major reconstruction project—time slot by time slot, executive by executive—that finally fell into place in 2000, when *Survivor* and *CSI: Crime Scene Investigation* became hits and *Everybody Loves Raymond* gained popularity.

Moonves, who has been given responsibility for Paramount TV, Infinity Broadcasting, and Viacom Outdoor, stated that Freston was his best choice as a corporate partner, citing a shared vision of the company and the fact that both of them came from the creative side. He said, "Even though we have separate areas of responsibility, we'll both be involved in running all the businesses."[58] Insiders said they were both good at handling Redstone's whims and making him feel important, in contrast with Karmazin who had little patience for corporate diplomacy.[59]

Redstone has denied that his daughter, Shari Redstone (age 50), a corporate lawyer, is being positioned for the top slot at Viacom. Shari is a director at Viacom and will be the main stockholder after she inherits her father's share. She has said she can "play a key role" at Viacom as a member of the board and plans to work more closely with Freston and Moonves.[60]

"Mel stepped down, but Viacom's headaches are still there," said Oppenheimer media analyst Peter Mirsky.[61] In the past one and a half years, Viacom's share price has fallen 16 percent (Exhibit 3) while the Bloomberg Media Index comprising of 33 companies rose 11 percent.[62] Redstone told reporters that they would take a hard look at all assets, including radio,[63] saying there were no plans to sell Infinity, which he said had high margins and "an enormous part of our free cash flow.[64] See Appendices 1 and 2 for additional information about Viacom's financial performance and condition.

A commentator said that though entertainment enterprises are often run by two individuals because of the need for both creative and financial expertise, Redstone could be sowing the seeds of dissension.[65] John Challenger, CEO of outplacement firm Challenger, Gray & Christmas, commented that Viacom suffered from a split culture during the Karmazin era and that by appointing two co-presidents the company was prolonging the split culture. He predicted that Karmazin supporters would not remain at the company for long.[66] With Freston and Moonves taking on new responsibilities, their former posts would have to be filled. Reports in the media indicate that the succession battle may not yet be over, as "Redstone has a knack for outlasting people seen as successors."[67]

EXHIBIT 3

Viacom's Stock Price

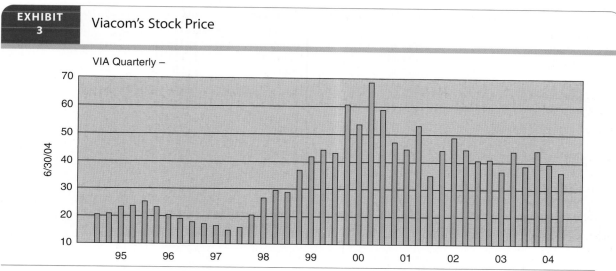

VIA Quarterly –

Source: www.fool.com.

Annual Financials for Viacom Inc. ($millions)

	Revenues	Operating income	Net earnings (loss)	Total assets
1994	4,485.60	354.40	89.60	28,273.70
1995	8,700.10	1,247.20	222.50	28,991.00
1996	9,683.90	1,197.20	1247.90	28,834.00
1997	10,684.90	685.40	793.60	28,288.70
1998	12,096.10	751.60	(122.40)	23,613.10
1999	12,858.80	1,247.30	334.00	24,486.40
2000	20,043.70	1,320.90	(816.10)	82,646.10
2001	23,222.80	1,460.20	(223.50)	90,809.90
2002	24,605.70	4,596.70	725.70	90,043.20
2003	26,585.30	3,625.80	1,416.90	89,848.50

Source: Viacom Annual Reports.

Revenues:	2003	2002	2001	Revenues:	2000	1999	1998
Cable Networks	5,645.50	4,726.70	4,297.60	Cable Networks	3,895.00	3,045.50	2,607.90
Television	7,761.00	7,456.80	7,218.70	Television	5,381.70	2,352.00	2,271.40
Radio	2,097.60	2,121.60	2,014.80	Infinity	2,764.70	—	—
Outdoor	1,748.30	1,633.50	1,656.60				
Entertainment	4,101.30	3,680.10	3,626.80	Entertainment	2,758.30	2,665.90	2,914.30
Video	5,911.70	5,565.90	5,156.70	Video	4,960.10	4,463.50	3,893.40
				Publishing[1]	596.00	610.70	564.60
				Online[2]	100.70	29.80	13.70
Eliminations	(680.10)	(578.90)	(748.40)	Intercompany eliminations[3]	(412.80)	(308.60)	(169.20)
Total Revenues	26,585.30	24,605.70	23,222.80	Total Revenues	20,043.70	12,858.80	12,096.10
Operating Income (Loss):				Operating Income (Loss):			
Cable Networks	2,172.30	1,772.20	1,234.90	Cable Networks	1,250.00	932.40	744.30
Television	1,238.10	1,177.60	385.80	Television	431.20	143.40	262.40
Radio	975.00	1,007.60	382.40	Infinity	589.40	—	—
Outdoor	207.90	218.00	(90.60)				
Entertainment	271.40	358.30	215.30	Entertainment	209.70	231.10	235.50
Video	(847.80)	355.80	(219.60)	Video	75.70	127.90	(342.20)
				Publishing	49.60	54.30	53.20
				Online	(256.70)	(64.50)	(7.50)
				Segment Total	2,348.90	1,424.60	945.70
Corporate Expenses	(187.90)	(159.00)	(169.10)	Corporate expenses/ eliminations	(950.50)	(177.30)	(194.10)
Elimination	(56.70)	(66.00)	(191.70)				
Residual Cost	(146.50)	(67.80)	(87.20)	Residual	(77.50)	—	—
Total Operating Income	**3,625.80**	**4,596.70**	**1,460.20**	**Total Operating Income**	**1,320.90**	**1,247.30**	**751.60**

(1) The company later operated its online businesses under the Cable Networks and Television segments.
(2) Publishing business was later moved to the Entertainment segment.
(3) Indicates sales between group entities.

Source: Viacom Annual Reports.

NOTES

1. Wolff, Michael, "Sumner Squall," www.newyorkmetro.com, February 18, 2002.
2. "Top 25 Media Groups," www.broadcastingcable.com, May 12, 2003.
3. Mallas, Steven, "Viacom Rakes in Ad Sales," www.fool.com, April 23, 2004.
4. Cramer, James, "Viacom SOS," www.newyorkmetro.com, June 21, 2004.
5. Stern, Christopher, "Viacom President Resigns," www.washingtonpost.com, June 2, 2004.
6. Viacom Press Release, www.viacom.com, June 1, 2004.
7. Atkinson, Claire, "Viacom Chief Details Succession Plan," www.adage.com, June 1, 2004.
8. www.forbes.com.
9. www.museum.tv.
10. NAI press release, www.showcasecinemas.com, May 6, 2004.
11. "Frank J. Biondi, Jr.," www.cablecenter.org, October 3, 2000.
12. "Redstone Sumner," www.museum.tv.
13. "Frank J. Biondi, Jr.," op. cit.
14. "Frank J. Biondi, Jr.," op. cit.
15. Rich, Laura, "A Succession Plan: Well Almost,"www.newscoast.com, June 20, 2004.
16. Battelle, John, "Biondi and Redstone" www.wired.com, May 1996.
17. Media Profiles, www.ketupa.net.
18. Midway's business is the development and marketing of interactive entertainment software. It develops and publishes games for all new generation home video game consoles and handheld game platforms.
19. Gross, Daniel, "Exit the Antimogul," www.slate.msn.com, June 3, 2004.
20. Fitzgerald, Toni, "Moonves' Task: Fending off Sumner," www.medialifemagazine.com, June 2, 2004.
21. Wolff, Michael, "Sell High," www. newyorkmetro.com, September 20, 1999.
22. Editorial Review, www.amazon.com.
23. World's Richest People 2002, www.forbes.com.
24. Isidore, Chris, "Mel May Have a Tough Job Hunt," www.money.cnn.com, June 1, 2004.
25. The Howard Stern show is known for its explicit banter about sex and the virtues of slavery. Karmazin hired Howard Stern after he was fired by WNBC in 1985 and helped turn him into a national celebrity. In 1985 Infinity stood by Stern and paid a $1.7 million settlement over FCC indecency rulings.
26. Auletta, Ken, "The Invisible Manager," www.kenauletta.com, July 27, 1998.
27. The Federal Communications Commission regulates interstate and international communications by radio, television, wire, satellite and cable in the United States.
28. "The Invisible Manager" op. cit.

29. "Mel's In, Peter's Out," www.west.net, May 23, 1997.
30. Wilkerson, David, "Karmazin's Radio Legacy: Aggressive and Also Loyal," www.investors.com, June 1, 2004.
31. "Exit the Antimogul," op. cit.
32. "The Invisible Manager," op cit.
33. McLaughlin, Martin, "CBS-Viacom Merger: Monopolies Tighten Their Grip on the Media," www.wsws.org, September 11, 1999.
34. Lowry, Tom, & Ronald Grover, "Can Redstone Boost Growth?" www.businessweek.com, June 14, 2004.
35. Morgan, Richard, "Viacom May Shed Assets," www.thedailydeal.com, June 2, 2004.
36. Lowry, Tom, & Grover, Ronald, "Viacom: Too Addicted to Ads?" www.businessweek.com, April 19, 2004.
37. "Viacom's Mel Karmazin Resigns," www.msnbc.msn.com, June 1, 2004.
38. "A Succession Plan: Well Almost,"op. cit.
39. Grover, Ronald, & Tom Lowry, "Karmazin's Exit: Old Plot, Same Ending," www.businessweek.com, June 2, 2004.
40. Gunther, Marc, "The Kid Stays in the Picture," www.fortune.com, April 14, 2003.
41. Fabrikant, Geraldine, "Viacom's No. 2 Executive Karmazin Abruptly Resigns,"www.jsonline.com, June 2, 2004.
42. "Sumner Squall," op. cit.
43. "Viacom President Resigns," op. cit.
44. Larsen, Peter, & Holly Yeager, "Change of the Guard at Viacom," www.news.ft.com, June 1, 2004.
45. "Can Redstone Boost Growth?" op. cit.
46. "Karmazin's Radio Legacy: Aggressive and Also Loyal," op. cit.
47. Doran, James, "Viacom President Quits with $30m," www.timesonline.co.uk, June 2, 2004.
48. "Viacom President Resigns," op. cit.
49. "Viacom May Shed Assets," op. cit.
50. "Viacom President Quits with $30m," op. cit.
51. "Viacom's No. 2 Executive Karmazin Abruptly Resigns," op. cit.
52. "Viacom President Resigns," op. cit.
53. "Viacom's No. 2 Executive Karmazin Abruptly Resigns," op. cit.
54. "Viacom: Farewell, Mel," www.money.cnn.com, June 1, 2004.
55. "A Succession Plan. Well, Almost," op. cit.
56. Arango, Tim, "Tom's the Favorite," www.nypost.com, June 9, 2004.
57. "Tom Freston," www.akamai.com.
58. Wallenstein, Andrew, & Cynthia Littleton, "Dynamic TV Duo on Top of Viacom," www.hollywoodreporter.com, June 2, 2004.
59. "Change of the Guard at Viacom," op. cit.
60. Gatlin, Greg, "Daughter Sizing up Redstone's Shoes?" www.bostonherald.com, June 3, 2004.
61. Furman, Phyllis, "Sumner Shoulders Viacom Headaches," www.nydailynews.com, June 3, 2004.
62. "Can Redstone Boost Growth?" op. cit.
63. "Viacom May Shed Assets," op. cit.
64. "Viacom President Resigns," op. cit.
65. Wallenstein, Andrew, "Split Decision for TV Biz on Top Executive Duos," www.reuters.com, June 28, 2004.
66. Millard, Elizabeth, "Viacom's Boardroom Shakeup," www.ecommercetimes.com, June 2, 2004.
67. "Change of the Guard at Viacom," op. cit.

Name Index

Company Index

Subject Index

Horizontal acquisitions, 193–194
Horizontal complementary strategic alliances, 267–268
Horizontal organizational structures, 403
Hospitals, integration in, 202
Hostile takeovers, 207, 310–312
Household average income, 43
Human resources
  for competitive advantage, 70
  in cost leadership strategies, 111
  developing, 376–377
  in differentiation strategies, 117
  in internal environment, 76, 78–80
  in international strategies, 235
  management skills for, 364, 374
  in value chain analysis, 87–88
Hybrid structures, 348
Hypercompetition, 7

I

I/O model of above-average return, 15–17
IM (instant-messaging) services, 269
Imitation, 395
Implementation of above-average return models
  I/O, 16
  resource, 18
Inbound logistics, 86, 88
Incentives
  compensation as, 291–292
  first-mover, 141–143
  for value-neutral diversification, 175–178
Income distribution, 43
Income taxes in diversification, 176
Incremental innovation, 399–400
Independence in multidivisional competitive structure, 343
India, intellectual property enforcement in, 247–248
Indirect acquisition costs, 204
Individualism in entrepreneurship, 397
Induced strategic behavior, 401
Industrial market segmentation, 104
Industrial organization (I/O) model of above-average return, 15–17
Industries
  analysis of, 35–37, 49–51
  buyer bargaining power, 55

interpreting, 59
  new entrants, 51–55
  rivalries, 56–59
  substitute products, 55–56
  supplier bargaining power, 54–55
  in I/O model, 16
  market commonality in, 135–136
  in resource model, 18
Inefficiencies from acquisitions, 206
Information age, 11, 13
Information networks, 123
Information technology industry
  innovation in, 278
  strategic alliances in, 259, 265
Infrastructure
  in cost leadership strategies, 111
  in value chain analysis, 87–88
Innovation
  and acquisitions, 205, 207, 407
  for competitive advantage, 69–70
  in differentiation strategies, 335
  in entrepreneurial mind-set, 378
  in fast-cycle markets, 151–152
  internal. See Internal innovation
  international strategies for, 224, 244–245
  licensing, 238
  network alliances for, 277–278
  perpetual, 10–11
  resources for, 76
  in standard-cycle markets, 153
  in strategic entrepreneurship, 394–395
  from technical excellence, 391
  through cooperative strategies, 405–407
  by top management teams, 367
Insiders on boards of directors, 303–304
Instant-messaging (IM) services, 269
Institutional factors
  in global markets, 48
  in international strategies, 249
Institutional owners, 301–302
Intangible resources, 76–79
Integrated activities, 107

Integrated cost leadership/differentiation strategies, 121–122, 336–337
  competitive risks in, 123–124
  flexible manufacturing systems in, 122–123
  information networks in, 123
  total quality management systems in, 123
Integration
  in acquisitions, 201–202
  in internal innovation, 403–404
Intellectual property rights
  in international strategies, 247–248
  managing, 375
Intelligence, competitor, 61, 63
Internal business processes perspective in balanced scorecards, 383
Internal capital market allocation, 173–174
Internal competition, 343
Internal corporate venturing, 400
Internal environment, 68–71
  analysis of
    challenges, 73–75
    context, 71
  capabilities in, 79–80
  core competencies in, 80–81, 91–92
  for sustainable competitive advantage, 81–85
  value chain analysis in, 85–88
  outsourcing in, 88–91
  resources in, 75–79
  strengths and weaknesses in, 91–92
  summary, 92
  value creation in, 71–73
Internal innovation, 397, 399
  autonomous strategic behavior in, 400–401
  cross-functional product development teams for, 403
  implementing, 402–403
  incremental and radical, 399–400
  induced strategic behavior in, 401
  integration in, 403–404
  success through, 398
  value from, 404
Internal managerial labor markets, 369–370
International corporate governance, 312–313
  in Germany, 313–314
  global, 315
  in Japan, 314–315

International entrepreneurship, 396–397
International strategies, 220–223, 232–233
  business-level, 228–230
  cooperative, 275–276, 353–354
  corporate-level, 230–233
  diversification and returns in, 243–245
  entry modes in, 237
    acquisitions, 240–241
    dynamics of, 242
    exporting, 237–238
    licensing, 238–239
    strategic alliances, 239–240
    wholly owned subsidiaries, 241–242
  environmental trends in, 233–237
  franchising in, 273
  incentives for, 224–225
    economies, 226–227
    location advantages, 227
    market size, 225–226
    return on investment, 226
  innovation in, 224, 244–245
  intellectual property in, 247–248
  limits to, 248–249
  outcomes, 243–245
  risk in, 245–249
  worldwide structure matches with, 344–350
Internet
  acceptance of, 10
  bubble burst, 204, 206
  in customer relations, 102–103
  as disruptive technology, 11
  in international strategies, 227, 233, 235
  product substitutes on, 56–57
  for scanning, 38
  shopping on, 13, 55, 105
  and slow-cycle markets, 264
  in technological segment, 46–47
  in value chain, 86–88
Intraorganizational conflicts, 73
Invention vs. innovation, 394–395
Investment bankers for due diligence, 202
Investments in cooperative strategies, 280
iPods, 11
IPOs, 300–301
Iraq war, economic risks in, 43

J

Japan, corporate governance in, 314–315
Jia meng, 273